A History of Civilization

NINTH EDITION

A HISTORY OF CIVILIZATION

VOLUME II: 1648 TO THE PRESENT

ROBIN W. WINKS

CRANE BRINTON

JOHN B. CHRISTOPHER

ROBERT LEE WOLFF

Prentice Hall, Upper Saddle River, New Jersey 07458

Library of Congress Cataloging-in-Publication Data

A history of civilization : prehistory to the present / Robin W. Winks
. . . [et al.]. — 9th ed.
    p. cm.
  Includes bibliographical references and index.
  ISBN 0-13-228339-5 (case)
  1. Civilization—History. I. Winks, Robin W.
CB69.H58 1995
909—dc20

              95-33646
              CIP

ACQUISITIONS EDITOR: *Sally Constable*
DEVELOPMENT EDITOR: *Carolyn Smith*
EDITORIAL/PRODUCTION SUPERVISION: *Virginia M. Livsey*
INTERIOR DESIGN: *Christine Gehring Wolf*
COVER DESIGN: *Thomas Nery*
PHOTO EDITOR: *Lorinda Morris-Nantz*
PHOTO RESEARCHER: *Carolyn Gault*
COVER PHOTO: *La Gare Saint Lazare (oil on canvas) 1877.*
   Musee d'Orsay, Paris, France. ERICH LESSING/ART RESOURCE.
PAGE LAYOUT: *Job Lisa*
BUYER: *Nick Sklitsis*
LINE ART COORDINATOR: *Michele Giusti*
SUPPLEMENTS EDITORS: *Virginia M. Livsey/Elizabeth M. Best*
ART DIRECTOR: *Anne Bonanno Nieglos*
CREATIVE DESIGN DIRECTOR: *Leslie Osher*
MARKETING MANAGER: *Alison Pendergast*
EDITOR IN CHIEF/EDITORIAL DIRECTOR: *Charlyce Jones Owen*

 © 1996, 1992, 1988, 1984, 1976, 1971,
1967, 1960, 1955 by Prentice-Hall, Inc.
Simon & Schuster / A Viacom Company
Upper Saddle River, New Jersey 07458

Printed in the United States of America

10 9 8 7 6 5 4 3 2 1

ISBN 0-13-228321-2

Prentice-Hall International (UK) Limited, **London**
Prentice-Hall of Australia Pty. Limited, **Sydney**
Prentice-Hall Canada Inc., **Toronto**
Prentice-Hall Hispanoamericana, S.A., **Mexico**
Prentice-Hall of India Private Limited, **New Delhi**
Prentice-Hall of Japan, Inc., **Tokyo**
Simon & Schuster Asia Pte. Ltd., **Singapore**
Editora Prentice-Hall do Brasil, Ltda., **Rio de Janeiro**

Dedicated to historians
and those who enjoy history everywhere

BRIEF CONTENTS

The Second World War and Its Aftermath—Twentieth-Century Thought and Letters—Our Times:
Arriving at the Present

CONTENTS

THE PROBLEM OF DIVINE–RIGHT MONARCHY—THE OLD REGIMES—THE ENLIGHTENMENT—
THE FRENCH REVOLUTION AND NAPOLEON

CHAPTER 15

THE PROBLEM OF DIVINE-RIGHT MONARCHY   306

CHAPTER **18**

*T*HE FRENCH REVOLUTION AND NAPOLEON   378

ROMANTICISM, REACTION, AND REVOLUTION—INDUSTRIAL SOCIETY—THE MODERNIZATION
OF NATIONS—MODERN EMPIRES AND IMPERIALISM

CHAPTER 21

*T*HE MODERNIZATION OF NATIONS 457

CHAPTER 22

MODERN EMPIRES AND IMPERIALISM   495

GREAT WAR, GREAT REVOLUTION—BETWEEN THE WARS: A TWENTY-YEAR CRISIS—
THE DEMOCRACIES AND THE NON-WESTERN WORLD

CHAPTER 23

GREAT WAR, GREAT REVOLUTION   528

THE SECOND WORLD WAR AND ITS AFTERMATH—TWENTIETH-CENTURY THOUGHT AND LETTERS—
OUR TIMES: ARRIVING AT THE PRESENT

CHAPTER 26

THE SECOND WORLD WAR AND ITS AFTERMATH 606

CHAPTER 27

TWENTIETH-CENTURY THOUGHT AND LETTERS   643

CHAPTER 28

OUR TIMES: ARRIVING AT THE PRESENT   661

Boxes

The Written Record

A Closer Look

Doing History

MAPS

Each generation will write its own history and will find that the present is best decoded by different approaches to the past. By the end of World War II Americans found that they were expected to be the leaders of "the West"— which was generally taken to mean Western civilization— and they extended their study of history to include non-Western societies in Africa and Asia, both because these societies deserved to be studied for their own sake, and also as a simple matter of prudence. Diplomatic history moved into the space often reserved for political or administrative history, and intellectual history (most especially the history of art and of thought) also became both important and popular—which are not the same thing. As a result, a textbook used by thousands of readers in hundreds of schools, colleges, and universities, known familiarly as "Brinton, Christopher, Wolff," went through periodic revision to keep pace with changing expectations.

The 1970s through the 1990s saw the most exceptional array of changes in the discipline of history since the nineteenth century—changes both in the way people think about history and in our knowledge of its content. Economic and intellectual history have been transformed, and social history has altered our entire way of looking at ourselves and at our past. Historical scholarship must now embrace statistics, psychohistory, geography, and the arguments usually reserved to political science, environmental studies, sociology, and anthropology. Yet the historian and the student must not forget that the purpose of history is to explain how we came to be as we are: why we find ourselves in our present predicaments, how we achieved our present triumphs, how we have developed across centuries through a *process* to a specific point in time—*our* specific point in time—when a savage light known as the present beats down upon us.

History cannot be told simply in chronological form, for it is necessary at times to carry a particular story forward for purposes of continuity, and then to double back, returning to an earlier time to pick up a different thread. This means that there are occasions, though not many, when a reader may meet a figure briefly in one context, only to encounter that figure again in greater depth later. The timelines and the index, in particular the boldface entries in it, have been developed so that the student can quickly find other strands of the same story as needed.

History is a narrative, a story; history is concerned foremost with major themes, even as it recognizes the significance of many fascinating digressions. Because history is largely about how and why people behave as they do, it is also about patterns of thought and belief. Ultimately, history is about what people believe to be true. To this extent, virtually all history is intellectual history, for the perceived meaning of a specific treaty, social treaty, or scientific discovery lies in what those involved in it and those who came after thought was most significant about it. History makes it clear that we may die, as we may live, as a result of what someone believed to be true in the relatively remote past.

A History of Civilization is about how we, as readers studying the past through the traditions and events of the West, have come to think about civilization. Neither the title nor the content is meant to imply that there are not equally complex, challenging, and productive civilizations elsewhere. But we must recognize, even as more material relating to the Far East, South Asia, Africa, or Latin America is incorporated into the present edition, that we read history to understand our own ancient beginnings or our own modern heritage. Though this is our primary reason for studying Western civilization, we must also recognize that it is impossible to do justice to all civilizations in a single text. If this enables us to understand history as a process, and if it illustrates the methodology of history, then it will surely lead us to appreciate other civilizations as well. The text is, therefore, implicitly and on occasion explicitly comparative. Western civilization may not be typical. Nor need we conclude that our ways are either "right" or "wrong" simply because they are ours and are known to us. They are the views by which we perceive our world; they are the windows on the world that our own historical experience has opened for us. Since Western societies have had so great an impact on the non-Western world in recent centuries, there is a sense in which world history is also quite legitimately viewed through the windows of Western history.

We cannot each be our own historian. In everyday life we may reconstruct our personal past, acting as detectives for our motivations and attitudes. But formal history is a much more rigorous study. History may give us some very small capacity to predict the future. More certainly, it should help us arrange the causes for given events into meaningful patterns. History also should help us sort out the important from the less important, the relevant from the irrelevant, so that we do not fall prey to those who propose simple-minded solutions to vastly complex human problems. We must not yield to the temptation to blame one group or individual for our problems, and yet we must not fail to defend our convictions with vigor.

To recognize, indeed to celebrate, the equality of all civilizations is essential to the civilized life itself. To understand that we see all civilizations through the prism of our specific historical past is simply to recognize that we too are the products of history. That is why we must study history and ask our own questions in our own way. For if we ask no questions of our past, there may be no questions to ask of our future.

Robin W. Winks
For the Ninth Edition

Goals of the Text

- To present a body of information, argument, and interpretation that is meant to help the reader understand humanity's long search for security, for meaning, for purpose in life.

- To represent a book by which students may locate themselves in time, decoding in their own way the relevance of the past for the present and which demonstrates the state of historical learning at the level of broad generalization and for the broadest general need in the mid 1990s.

- To preserve the great strengths in the breadth, depth, and grasp of the original editions of Brinton, Christopher, and Wolff, retaining for these distinguished authors their many loyal readers, while also incorporating the new trends in the study of history.

New in the Ninth Edition

Substantially Shorter Text.   The book has been rewritten, streamlined, and given a new design, making it more accessible for students. This text is approximately 20% shorter than the previous edition.

- *NEW Timelines.* Provide a simplified overview of a particular historical terrain before elaborating on its detail.

- *NEW Boxed Sections.* The Written Record (selections from original sources), Doing History (how historians approach their work), and A Closer Look (expanded treatment of topics discussed in the text).

- *NEW All-New Chapter Introductions.*

- *NEW All-New Chapter Summaries.* Designed to recapitulate major ideas and events.

- *NEW Review Questions.* At the end of each chapter, helping students review the material and may be used in class discussions.

- *NEW Map Program.* All maps have been updated and revised to facilitate learning and understanding of the material.

- *NEW Suggested Readings.* This section now includes 100 entries on books published since 1990.

- *NEW More coverage of Women's History*

- *NEW Recent Historical Events of the 1990s* have been added.

Ancillary Package

Instructor's Manual and **Test Item File** prepared by Gordon Mork of Purdue University. Includes a section on goals and objectives for each chapter, discussion questions, multiple-choice, true/false, and essay questions.

Computerized Test Bank for IBM 3.5 compatible and Macintosh systems, consisting of multiple-choice and essay questions from the Test Item File.

Map Transparencies in full color of all maps in the text.

Blank Maps which are provided for map testing or various class exercises.

Study Guide prepared by Beverly Blois of Northern Virginia Community College. For each chapter there's an overview, key terms for discussion, multiple-choice and fill-in questions, and documents section.

Computerized Study Guide in an IBM 3.5 format, consisting of the multiple-choice and fill-in questions with answers that are cross-referenced to the text.

Hammond Historical Atlas of the World, available packaged with the text.

Much appreciated criticism and guidance was provided by the following reviewers: Robert Lerner, Northwestern University; Joachim Baer, The University of North Carolina at Greensboro; Arthur Auten, University of Hartford; Thomas Schilz, San Diego Miramar College; Larry Quinn, College of Southern Idaho; Paul Enea, Delaware County Community College; and Arnold Sherman, Champlain College.

THE NEW YORK TIMES and PRENTICE HALL are sponsoring A CONTEMPO-RARY VIEW: a program designed to enhance student access to current information of relevance in the classroom.

Through this program, the core subject matter provided in the text is supplemented by a collection of time-sensitive articles from one of the world's most distinguished newspapers, THE NEW YORK TIMES. These articles demonstrate the vital, ongoing connection between what is learned in the classroom and what is happening in the world around us.

To enjoy the wealth of information of THE NEW YORK TIMES daily, a reduced sub-scription rate is available in deliverable areas. For information, call toll-free: 1-800-631-1222.

PRENTICE HALL and THE NEW YORK TIMES are proud to co-sponsor A CON-TEMPORARY VIEW. We hope it will make the reading of both textbooks and newspapers a more dynamic, involving process.

THE VALUE OF HISTORY

History is a series of arguments to be debated, not a body of data to be recorded or a set of facts to be memorized. Thus controversy in historical interpretation—over what an event actually means, over what really happened at an occurrence called "an event," over how best to generalize about the event—is at the heart of its value. Of course history teaches us about ourselves. Of course it teaches us to understand and to entertain a proper respect for our collective past. Of course it transmits to us specific skills—how to ask questions, how to seek out answers, how to think logically, cogently, lucidly, purposefully. Of course it is, or ought to be, a pleasure. But we also discover something fundamental about a people in what they choose to argue over in their past. When a society suppresses portions of its past record, as the Soviet Union did until recently, that society (or its leadership) tells us something about itself. When a society seeks to alter how the record is presented, well-proven facts notwithstanding, we learn how history can be distorted to political ends.

Who controls history, and how it is written, controls the past, and who controls the past controls the present. Those who would close off historical controversy with the argument either that we know all that we need to know about a subject, or that what we know is so irrefutably correct that anyone who attacks the conventional wisdom about the subject must have destructive purposes in mind, is in the end intent upon destroying the very value of history itself—that value being that history teaches us to argue productively with each other.

Obviously, then, history is a social necessity. It gives us our identity. It helps us to find our bearings in an ever more complex present, providing us with a navigator's chart by which we may to some degree orient ourselves. When we ask who we are, and how is it that we are so, we learn skepticism and acquire the beginnings of critical judgment. Along with a sense of narrative, history also provides us with tools for explanation and analysis. It helps us to find the particular example, to see the uniqueness in a past age or past event, while also helping us to see how the particular and the unique contribute to the general. History thus shows us humanity at work and play, in society, changing through time. By letting us experience other lifestyles, history shows us the values of both subjectivity and objectivity—those twin conditions of our individual view of the world in which we live, conditions between which we constantly, and usually almost without knowing it, move. Thus, history is both a form of truth and a matter of opinion, and the close study of history should help us to distinguish between the two. It is important to make such distinctions, for as Sir Walter Raleigh wrote, "It is not truth but opinion that can travel the world without a passport." Far too often what we read and believe to be truth—in our newspapers, on our television sets, from our friends—is opinion, not fact.

History is an activity. That activity asks specific questions as a means of arriving at general questions. A textbook such as this is concerned overwhelmingly with general questions, even though at times it must ask specific questions or present specific facts as a means of stalking the general. The great philosopher Karl Jaspers once remarked, "Who I am and where I belong, I first learned to know from the mirror of history." It is this mirror which any honest textbook must reflect.

To speak of "civilization" (of which this book is a history) is at once to plunge into controversy, so that our very first words illustrate why some people are so fearful of the study of history. To speak of "Western civilization" is even more restrictive, too limited in the eyes of some historians. Yet if we are to understand history as a process, we must approach it through a sense of place: our continuity, our standards, our process. Still, we must recognize an inherent bias in such a term as "Western civilization," indeed two inherent biases: first, that we know what it means to be "civilized" and have attained that stature; and second, that the West as a whole is a single unitary civilization. This second bias is made plain when we recognize that most scholars and virtually all college courses refer not to "Eastern civilization" but to "the civilizations of the East"—a terminology that suggests that while the West is a unity, the East is not. These are conventional phrases, buried in our Western perception of reality, just as our common geographical references show a Western bias. The Near East or the Far East are, after all, "near" or "far" only in reference to a geographical location focused on western Europe. The Japanese do not refer to London as being in the far West, or Los Angeles as being in the far East, though both references would be correct, if they saw the world as though they stood at its center. Though this text will accept these conventional phrases, precisely because they are traditionally embedded in our Western languages, one of the uses of history—and of the study of a book such as this one—is to alert us to the biases buried in our language, even when necessity requires that we continue to use its conventional forms of shorthand.

But if we are to speak of civilization, we must have, at the outset, some definition of what we mean by "being civilized." Hundreds of books have been written on this subject. The average person often means only that others, the "noncivilized," speak a different language and practice alien customs. The Chinese customarily referred to all foreigners as barbarians, and the ancient Greeks spoke of those who could not communicate in Greek as *bar-bar*—those who do not speak our tongue. Yet today the ability to communicate in more than one language is one hallmark of a "civilized" person. Thus definitions of civilization, at least as used by those who think little about the meaning of their words, obviously change.

For our purposes, however, we must have a somewhat more exacting definition of the term, since it guides and shapes any textbook that attempts to cover the entire sweep of Western history. Anthropologists, sociologists, historians, and others may reasonably differ about the essential ingredients of a civilization. They may also differ as to whether, for example, there is a separate American civilization that stands apart from, say a British or Italian civilization, or whether these civilizations are simply particular variants on one larger entity, with only that larger entity—the West—entitled to be called "a civilization." Such an argument is of no major importance here, although it is instructive that it should occur. Rather, what is needed is a definition sufficiently clear to be used throughout the narrative and analysis to follow. This working definition, therefore, will hold that "civilization" involves the presence of several (though not necessarily all) of the following conditions within a society or group of interdependent societies:

1. There will be some form of government by which people administer to their political needs and responsibilities.

2. There will be some development of urban society, that is, of city life, so that the culture is not nomadic, dispersed, and thus unable to leave significant and surviving physical remnants of its presence.

3. Human beings will have become toolmakers, able through the use of metals to transform, however modestly, their physical environment, and thus their social and economic environment as well.

4. Some degree of specialization of *function* will have begun, usually at the work place, so that pride, place, and purpose work together as cohesive elements in the society.

5. Social classes will have emerged, whether antagonistic to or sustaining of one another.

6. A form of literacy will have developed, so that group may communicate with group, and more important, generation with generation in writing.

7. There will be a concept of leisure time—that life is not solely for the work place, or for the assigned class function or specialization—so that, for example, art may develop beyond (though not excluding) mere decoration and sports beyond mere competition.

8. There will be a concept of a higher being, though not necessarily through organized religion, by which a people may take themselves outside themselves to explain events and find purpose.

9. There will be a concept of time, by which the society links itself to a past and to the presumption of a future.

10. There will have developed a faculty for criticism. This faculty need not be the rationalism of the West, or intuition, or any specific religious or political mechanism, but it must exist, so that the society may contemplate change from within, rather than awaiting attack (and possible destruction) from without.

A common Western bias is to measure "progress" through technological change and to suggest that societies that show (at least until quite recently in historical time)

little dramatic technological change are not civilized. In truth, neither a written record nor dramatic technological changes are essential to being civilized, though both are no doubt present in societies we would call civilized. Perhaps, as we study history, we ought to remember all *three* of the elements inherent in historical action as recorded by the English critic John Ruskin: "Great nations write their autobiographies in three manuscripts, the book of their deeds, the book of their words, and the book of their art."

The issue here is not whether we "learn from the past." Most often we do not, at least at the simple-minded level; we do not, as a nation, decide upon a course of action in diplomacy, for example, simply because a somewhat similar course in the past worked. We are wise enough to know that circumstances alter cases and that new knowledge brings new duties. Of course individuals "learn from the past"; the victim of a purse snatching takes precautions in the future. To dignify such an experience as "a lesson of history," however, is to turn mere individual growth from child into adult into history when, at most, such growth is a personal experience in biography.

We also sometimes learn the "wrong lessons" from history. Virtually anyone who wishes to argue passionately for a specific course of future action can find a lesson from the past that will convince the gullible that history repeats itself and therefore that the past is a map to the future. No serious historian argues this, however. General patterns may, and sometimes do, repeat themselves, but specific chains of events do not. Unlike those subjects that operate at the very highest level of generalization (political science, theology, science), history simply does not believe in ironclad laws. But history is not solely a series of unrelated events. There are general patterns, clusters of causes, intermediate levels of generalization that prove true. Thus, history works at a level uncomfortable to many: above the specific, below the absolute.

If complex problems never present themselves twice in the same or even in recognizably similar form—if, to borrow a frequent image from the military world, generals always prepare for the last war instead of the next one—then does the study of history offer society any help in solving its problems? The answer surely is yes—but only in a limited way. History offers a rich collection of clinical reports on human behavior in various situations—individual and collective, political, economic, military, social, cultural—that tell us in detail how the human race has conducted its affairs and that suggest ways of handling similar problems in the present. President Harry S Truman's secretary of state, a former chief of staff, General George Marshall, once remarked that nobody could think about the problems of the 1950s who had not reflected upon the fall of Athens in the fifth century B.C.. He was referring to the extraordinary history of the war between Athens and Sparta written just after it was over by Thucydides, an Athenian who fought in the war. There were no nuclear weapons, no telecommunications, no guns or gunpowder in the fifth century B.C..; the logistics of the war were altogether primitive, yet twenty-three hundred years later one of the most distinguished leaders of American military and political affairs found Thucydides indispensable to his thinking.

History, then, can only approximate the range of human behavior, with some indication of its extremes and averages. It can, though not perfectly, show how and within what limits human behavior changes. This last point is especially important for the social scientist, the economist, the sociologist, the executive, the journalist, or the diplomat. History provides materials that even an inspiring leader—a prophet, a reformer, a politician—would do well to master before seeking to lead us into new ways. For it can tell us something about what human material can and cannot stand, just as science and technology can tell engineers what stresses metals can tolerate. History can provide an awareness of the depth of time and space that should check the optimism and the overconfidence of the reformer. For example, we may wish to protect the environment in which we live—to eliminate acid rain, to cleanse our rivers, to protect our wildlife, to preserve our majestic natural scenery. History may show us that most peoples have failed to do so, and may provide us with some guidance on how to avoid the mistakes of the past. But history will also show that there are substantial differences of public and private opinion over how best to protect our environment; or that there are many people who do not believe such protection is necessary; or that there are people who accept the need for protection but are equally convinced that lower levels of protection must be traded off for higher levels of productivity from our natural resources. History can provide the setting by which we may understand differing opinions, but recourse to history will not get the legislation passed, make the angry happy, make the future clean and safe. History will not define river pollution, though it can provide us with statistics from the past for comparative measurement. The definition will arise from the politics of today and our judgments about tomorrow. History is for the long and at times for the intermediate run, but seldom for the short run.

So, if we are willing to accept a "relevance" that is more difficult to see at first than the immediate applicability of science and more remote than direct action, we will have to admit that history is "relevant." It may not actually build the highway or clear the slum, but it can give enormous help to those who wish to do so. And failure to take it into account may lead to failure in the sphere of action.

But history is also fun, at least for those who enjoy giving their curiosity free rein. Whether it is historical gossip we prefer (How many lovers did Catherine the Great of Russia actually take in a given year, and how much political influence did their activity in the imperial bedroom give them?), or the details of historical investigation (How does it happen that the actual treasures found in a buried Viking ship correspond to those described in an Anglo-Saxon poetic account of a ship-burial?), or more complex questions of cause and effect (How influential have the writings of revolutionary intellectuals been upon the course of actual revolutions?), or the relationships between politics and economics (How far does the rise and decline of Spanish power in modern times depend upon the supply of gold from the New World colonies?), or cultural problems (Why did western Europe choose to revive classical Greek and Roman art and literature instead of turning to some other culture or to some altogether new experiment?), those who enjoy history will read almost greedily to discover what they want to know. Having discovered it, they may want to know how we know what we have learned, and may want to turn to those sources closest in time to the persons and questions concerned—to the original words of the participants. To read about Socrates, Columbus, or Churchill is fun; to read their *own* words, to visit with them as it were, is even more so. To see them in context is important; to see how we have taken their thoughts and woven them to purposes of our own is at least equally important. Readers will find the path across the mine-studded fields of history helped just a little by extracts from these voices—voices of the past but also of the present. They can also be helped by outlines, summaries, bibliographies, pictures, maps—devices through which historians share their sense of fun and immediacy with a reader.

In the end, to know the past *is to know ourselves*—not entirely, not enough, but a little better. History can help us to achieve some grace and elegance of action, some cogency and completion of thought, some harmony and tolerance in human relationships. Most of all, history can give us a sense of excitement, a personal zest for watching and perhaps participating in the events around us which will, one day, be history too.

DATES	POLITICAL	THOUGHT AND ARTS	ECONOMY AND SOCIETY
1580 A.D.			1580–1650 Witchcraft trials commonplace
	1585–1642 Cardinal Richelieu		c. 1590–1650 The Little Ice Age
1600	17th century Age of France	17th century The Baroque Era	17th century Beginning of the Modern Age
			17th century Property rights of women increase
	1601 Elizabethan Poor Law		
	1602–1661 Cardinal Mazarin	1606–1669 Rembrandt Van Rijn	
	r. 1610–1643 Louis XII of France	1611 *King James Bible* completed	
	1621 Great Protestation of the House of Commons	1622–1673 Jean-Baptiste Moliére	1624–1691 George Fox
	r. 1629–1640 Personal rule of Charles I of England	1631–1700 John Dryden	
		1635 Peter Paul Rubens, *Massacre of the Innocents*	
		1639–1699 Jean Racine	
	r. 1640–1688 Frederick William, the Great Elector, of Prussia		
	1642–1649 The English Civil War		
	r. 1643–1714 Louis XIV of France	1644 John Milton, *Areopagitica*	
	1648–1652 The *Fronde*		
	1649–1660 The Interregnum		
1650	1651 Navigation Act	1651 Thomas Hobbes, *Leviathan*	
	1653–1743 Cardinal Fleury	1660s Frans Hals, *The Women Regents of the Haarlam Hospital*	
	r. 1660–1685 Charles II of England		1665 London Plague kills 100,000
	1661–1714 Personal rule of Louis XIV of France	1667 John Milton, *Paradise Lost*	
	1668–1711 Construction of Palace of Versailles	1673–1710 St. Paul's Cathedral built	
		1674–1741 Jethro Tull	
	r. 1682–1725 Peter the Great of Russia	1685–1759 George Frederick Handel	1685 Revocation of the Edict of Nantes
		1685–1750 Johann Sebastian Bach	
	1688–1697 War of the League of Augsburg		
	1688–1689 Glorious Revolution		
	1689 Bill of Rights	1690 John Locke, *Second Treatise of Government*	
	r. 1697–1718 Charles XII of Sweden		
	1699 Treaty of Karlovitz		
1700	18th century Century of the Balance of Power	18th century Age of Enlightenment	18th century Agricultural Revolution
			18th century Beginning of the Industrial Revolution
			18th century Popular literacy becomes widespread
	r. 1700–1721 Great Northern War		
	1701–1714 War of the Spanish Succession		1703–1791 John Wesley
	1701 Act of Settlement		
	r. 1711–1740 Charles VI of Austrian Habsburgs	1711–1776 David Hume	
	r. 1713–1740 Frederick William I of Prussia		
	1713 Treaties of Utrecht		
	r. 1714–1727 George I		
	r. 1715–1774 Louis XV of France		
	1720 Mississippi and South Sea Bubbles burst		
	1721–1745 Administration of Robert Walpole		
	1723 Waltham Black Act	1724–1804 Immanuel Kant	
		1725 Giovanni Vico, *Scienza Nuova*	
		1726 Jonathan Swift, *Gulliver's Travels*	
	r. 1727–1760 George II of Britain		
	1730–1762 Russian nobles gain increased authority		
	1732–1799 George Washington		

DATES	POLITICAL	THOUGHT AND ARTS	ECONOMY AND SOCIETY
1737 A.D.		1737–1788 Thomas Gainsborough	
	1739–1815 Second Hundred Years' War		
	1739–1748 War of the Austrian Succession		
	r. 1740–1786 Frederick the Great of Prussia		
	r. 1740–1780 Maria Theresa of Austrian Habsburgs	1743–1779 Antoine Lavoisier	
	1746 Battle of Culloden		
		1747 Julien Offroy de la Mettrie, *Man and Machine*	
		1748 Baron Montesquieu, *Spirit of the Laws*	
		1749 Henry Fielding, *Tom Jones*	
1750		**mid-18th century** German *Sturm und Drang* movement	**mid-18th century** Construction of turnpikes begins in Britain
		1751 Denis Diderot, ed., *Encyclopédie*, founded	
		1751 Samuel Johnson, *Dictionary*	
	1756–1763 Seven Years' War	1756–1791 Wolfgang Amadeus Mozart	
	1758–1794 Maximilien Robespierre		
	1759–1806 William Pitt the Younger	1759 Voltaire, *Candide*	1759–1761 First canal built in Britain
	r. 1760–1820 George III of Britain		1760s James Watt introduces steam engine
	late 18th century Era of the Enlightened Despots		
	r. 1762–1796 Catherine II the Great of Russia	1762 Jean-Jacques Rousseau, *Emile* and *Social Contract*	
	r. 1764–1795 Stanislas II of Poland	1765 William Blackstone, *Commentaries on the Laws of England*	
	1769–1821 Napolean Bonaparte		
	1773–1775 Pugachev Rebellion	1774 Johann Wolfgang von Goethe, *Sorrows of Young Werther*	1773 Pope Clement XIV dissolves Jesuit Order
	r. 1774–1792 Louis XVI of France		
	1775–1783 American War of Independence	1776 Adam Smith, *Wealth of Nations*	**late 18th–early 19th centuries** English enclosure movement at its height
	July 4, 1776 American Declaration of Independence		
	1787 American Constitutional Convention		
		1788 Edward Gibbon, *Decline and Fall of the Roman Empire*	
	1789 Louis XVI summons Estates General		
	July 14, 1789 Fall of the Bastille		
	1789 Declaration of the Rights of Man		
	1791 U.S. Bill of Rights		
	1792 First Coalition against France formed		
	1793–1794 The Reign of Terror		
		1794 Condorcet, *The Progress of the Human Mind*	
	1795 Third Partition of Poland		
	1795 Thermidorean Constitution		
	1799 Coup d'état of Brumaire		
	1799 The Second Coalition		
1800	r. 1801–1825 Alexander I of Russia		
	1803 The Louisiana Purchase		
	1804 Napolean crowns himself Emperor		
	1805 Battle of Trafalgar		
	1805–1807 The Third Coalition		
	1805 Battle of Austerlitz		
	1807 Serfdom abolished in Prussia	1807–1808 J. G. Fichte, *Addresses to the German People*	
	1808–1813 Peninsular War		
	1812–1813 The Russian Campaign		
	1815 Battle of Waterloo		
		late 1830s Alexis de Tocqueville, *Democracy in America*	

The Problem of Divine-Right Monarchy

*T*HE PEACE OF WESTPHALIA IN 1648 ended the Thirty Years' War but also marked the end of an epoch in European history. It ended the Age of the Reformation and Counter-Reformation, when wars were both religious and dynastic in motivation, and the chief threats to a stable international balance came from the Catholic Habsburgs and from the militant Protestants of Germany, the Netherlands, and Scandinavia. After 1648 religion, though continuing to be a major source of friction in France and the British Isles, ceased to be a significant international issue elsewhere. The main force jeopardizing the European balance thereafter was the entirely secular ambition of Bourbon France on the Continent and abroad. For seventy-two years (1643–1714) France was under a single monarch, Louis XIV, who inherited the throne when only four.

Louis was the embodiment of the early modern form of royal absolutism—monarchy by divine right—and he was the personification of royal pride, elegance, and luxury. To the French, Louis XIV was *le grand monarque*. His long reign brought to an end *le grand siècle*, that great century (begun under Cardinal Richelieu in the twenty years before Louis's accession) that was marked by the international triumph of French arms and French diplomacy and, still more, of French ways of writing, building, dressing, eating—the whole style of life of the upper classes in France, which called itself *la grande nation*.

While French culture went from triumph to triumph, Louis XIV's bid for political hegemony was ultimately checked. His most resolute opponent was England, still in the throes of the greatest political upheaval in its history, an upheaval that resulted from the collision between the forces of the Stuart monarchy and High Church Anglicanism, on the one hand, and those of Parliament and the Puritans, on the other. The final settlement, after decades of violence and change, was a compromise weighted in favor of the parliamentary side, with one English king executed and another forced into exile. While France appeared stable, England was racked by revolution and insecurity.

The seventeenth century, during which the struggle for stability could be seen in most societies of early modern Europe, was an age of crisis. In England the aristocracy faced unique challenges; a steady decline in population in war-ravaged Germany and in Spain changed society drastically; and the years after 1648 were marked throughout most of Europe by a severe depression, by social upheavals, and by a struggle between the capitalism espoused by the rising middle class and the agrarian traditions of the landed classes, who feared displacement. Revolution—successful, abortive, plotted, rumored—seemed almost commonplace in England, France, Portugal, Spain, and elsewhere. Still, since the province or an even smaller local unit generally remained relatively self-sufficient economically, these broad generalizations about trends are open to many exceptions. And as always, amid change there was continuity.

It was also a century of intellectual ferment, as writers, philosophers, theologians, and painters sought to justify monarchy by divine right or revolution by various groups that saw themselves as "the people," and as the basic intellectual underpinnings of society were changed. The seventeenth century is often called the "century of genius," for so many innovative ideas sprang forth during it: from explorers and conquerors, from simple sailors and soldiers, from figures like Bacon, Descartes, Pascal, Newton, or Locke, as well as from inventors who drew upon the theories of Galileo and others. According to different historians, "modern history" began with a different event or development, but nearly all agree that it was with the 1600s that Western civilization passed into what is known as the Modern Age.

The intimations of popular revolution in the seventeenth century, the impact of new ideas on a broader public, and the slow but certain change of even traditional peasant culture, which was becoming more articulate, more observable through the printed record, were yet other dividing lines between the Middle Ages and the modern period. Before 1700 most people apparently were basically illiterate; a century later, literacy was apparently far more widespread.

*B*OURBON FRANCE

In 1610 the capable and popular Henry IV was assassinated in the prime of his career by a madman who was believed at the time to be working for the Jesuits—a charge for which there is no proof. The new king, Louis XIII (r. 1610–1643), was nine years old; the queen mother, Marie de Medici, served as regent but showed little political skill. Her Italian favorites and French nobles, Catholic and Huguenot alike, carried on a hectic competition that threatened to undo all that Henry IV had accomplished. During these troubles the French representative body, the Estates General, met in 1614 for what was destined to be its last session until 1789. Significantly, the meeting was paralyzed by tensions between the noble deputies of the second estate and the bourgeois of the third. Meanwhile, Louis XIII, though barely into his teens, tried to assert his personal authority and reduce the role of his mother. Poorly educated, sickly, masochistic, and subject to depression, Louis needed expert help.

Louis XIII and Richelieu, 1610-1643

Louis was fortunate in securing the assistance of the remarkably talented duc de Richelieu (1585–1642), who was an efficient administrator as bishop of the remote diocese of Autun. Tiring of provincial life, Richelieu moved to Paris and showed unscrupulous skill in political maneuvering during the confused days of the regency. He emerged as the conciliator between the king and his mother and was rewarded, first, by being made a cardinal and then, in 1624, with selection by Louis as his chief minister. While the king maintained a lively interest in affairs of state, Richelieu was the virtual ruler of France for the next eighteen years. He proved to be a good Machiavellian, subordinating religion and every other consideration to *raison d'état* (reason of state)—a phrase that he may have coined himself.

Richelieu had four goals for the France of Louis XIII: to eliminate the Huguenots as an effective political force; to remind the nobles that they were subordinate to the king; to make all of France conscious of a sense of national greatness; and, through these measures, to make the monarchy truly rather than only theoretically absolute. *Raison d'état* made the ruin of the Huguenots the first priority, for the political privileges they had received by the Edict of Nantes made them a major obstacle to the creation of a centralized state. The hundred fortified towns they governed, chiefly in the southwest, were a state within the state, a hundred centers of potential rebellion. Alarmed, the Huguenots rebelled. The fall of La Rochelle, their chief stronghold, in 1628 and Richelieu's unexpectedly humane approach—by which the political and military clauses of the Edict of Nantes were revoked while partial religious toleration continued—helped Richelieu neutralize the Huguenots.

The siege of La Rochelle was prolonged because France had no navy worthy of the name. Over the next ten years Richelieu created a fleet of warships for the Atlantic and a squadron of galleys manned by European slaves for the Mediterranean. Meanwhile, he guided France expertly through the Thirty Years' War, committing French resources only when concrete gains seemed possible and ensuring favorable publicity by supplying exaggerated accounts of French victories to the *Gazette de France*.

Next Richelieu tried to humble the nobles, with only partial success, by ordering the destruction of some of their fortresses and forbidding private duels. More effective was his transfer of supervision of local administration from the

This illustration from Abraham Bosse's "Le Palais Royal" (1640) provides a good picture of French fashions and tastes. Bosse (1602–1676) took a particular interest in etchings that showed how the upper middle class dressed. Furniture also evolved in new styles to accommodate the new clothing.

New York Public Library Picture Collection

nobles and officeholders of doubtful loyalty who had purchased their posts to more reliable royal officials called *intendants*. These officials had existed earlier but had performed only minor functions; now they were given greatly increased powers over justice, the police, and taxation.

Richelieu made possible *la grande nation* of Louis XIV by building an efficient, centralized state. But in a sense he built too well, making the French government so centralized, so professionally bureaucratic, that it became too inflexible for the give and take of politics. Moreover, Richelieu did little to remedy the chronic fiscal weakness of the government, particularly the corruption in tax collection and the recurrent deficits. His concentration on *raison d'état* led him to take a callous view of the subjects on whose loyal performance of their duties the strength of the state depended. He believed that the masses were best kept docile through hard work, that

leisure led to mischief, and that the common people ought to take pride in the splendors of the monarchy, in the accomplishments of French literary culture, and in victories over the monarch's enemies. Individual hardship, especially among the lower classes, was to be accepted in the interests of national glory. Such acceptance is a common ingredient of nationalism.

Mazarin

The deaths of Richelieu in 1642 and Louis XIII in 1643, the accession of another child king, and the regency of the hated queen mother, Anne of Austria (actually a Habsburg from Spain, where the dynasty was called the house of Austria), all seemed to threaten a repetition of the crisis that had followed the death of Henry IV. The new crisis was dealt with by the new chief minister, Jules

Few official portraits from this period have survived. The only ones fully authenticated are those of Louis XIII and Richelieu. Philippe de Champaigne (1602–1674) often depicted Richelieu, and in this triple portrait he sought to emphasize the rationalism of the age. The painting is now in the National Gallery, London.

The National Gallery, London

Mazarin (1602–1661), a Sicilian who had been picked and schooled by Richelieu himself and was exceptionally close to Anne. Mazarin, too, was a cardinal (though not a priest, as Richelieu had been) and a supreme exponent of *raison d'état*. Mazarin also was careless about the finances of France, but, unlike Richelieu, he amassed an immense personal fortune during his career. He antagonized both branches of the French aristocracy: the nobles of the sword, descendants of feudal magnates, and the nobles of the robe (the reference is to the gowns worn by judges and other officials), descendants of commoners who had bought their way into government office. The former resented being excluded from the regency by a foreigner; the latter, who had invested heavily in government securities, particularly disliked Mazarin's casual way of borrowing money to meet war expenses and then neglecting to pay the interest on the loans.

In 1648 discontent boiled over in the *Fronde* (named for the slingshot used by Parisian children to hurl pellets at the rich in their carriages), one of several mid-century uprisings in Europe. Some of the rioting involved the rural peasantry and the common people of Paris, impoverished by the economic depression accompanying the final campaigns of the Thirty Years' War and deeply affected by the peak famine years of 1648–1651. But the Fronde was essentially a revolt of the nobles, led first by the judges of the Parlement of Paris, a stronghold of the nobles of the robe, and then, after the Peace of Westphalia, by aristocratic officers returned from the Thirty Years' War. Various "princes of the blood" (relatives of the royal family) confusingly intervened with private armies. Though Mazarin twice had to flee France and go into exile, and though the royal troops had to lay siege to Paris, and despite concessions Mazarin felt forced to make, the end result of what was in reality two revolts in one—of the Parlement and of the nobles—was to weaken both. The Fronde prepared the way for the personal rule of Louis XIV, with the mass of ordinary citizens in Paris supporting the queen and her son when they returned in triumph in October of 1652. Essentially, the Fronde

failed because it had no real roots in the countryside, not even in the rising middle classes of the provincial cities. Rather, it was essentially a struggle for power, pitting Mazarin and his new bureaucracy against the two privileged groups of nobles, each of which distrusted the other. All Mazarin had to do was to apply the old Roman maxim, "Divide and rule."

Louis XIV, 1643–1714

When Mazarin died in 1661, Louis XIV began his personal rule. He had been badly frightened during the Fronde when rioters had broken into his bedroom, and he was determined to suppress any challenge to his authority, by persuasion and guile if possible, and by force if necessary. In 1660 he married a Spanish princess for political reasons; after a succession of mistresses, he married again, in 1685. Madame de Maintenon, a devout former Huguenot, was the governess of his illegitimate children; she did much to assure dignified piety at court for the rest of his reign.

Louis XIV, the Sun King, succeeded as *le grand monarque* because by education, temperament, and physique he was ideally suited to the role. He had admirable self-discipline, patience, and staying power. He never lost his temper in public and went through long daily council meetings and elaborate ceremonials with unwearied attention and even enjoyment, to which his conspicuous lack of a sense of humor may have contributed. He had an iron physical constitution, which enabled him to withstand a rigorous schedule, made him indifferent to heat and to cold, and allowed him to survive both a lifetime of gross overeating and the crude medical treatment of the day.

He was five feet five inches tall (a fairly impressive height for that day) and added to his stature by shoes with high red heels. To provide a suitable setting for the Sun King, to neutralize the high nobility politically by isolating it in the ceaseless ceremonies and petty intrigues of court life, and also to prevent a repetition of the rioters'

THE WRITTEN RECORD

Le Grand Monarque

At age twenty-two Louis XIV already displayed an impressive royal presence, as reported by Madame de Motteville (d. 1689), an experienced observer of the French court:

As the single desire for glory and to fulfill all the duties of a great king occupied his whole heart, by applying himself to toil he began to like it; and the eagerness he had to learn all the things that were necessary to him soon made him full of that knowledge. His great good sense and his good intentions now made visible in him the rudiments of general knowledge which had been hidden from all who did not see him in private. . . . He was agreeable personally, civil and easy of access to every one; but with a lofty and serious air which impressed the public with respect and awe . . . , though he was familiar and gay with ladies.

_____

Madame de Motteville, *Memoirs of Madame [Françoise Bertaut] de Motteville on Anne of Austria and Her Court,* trans. Katherine Prescott Wormeley (Boston: Hardy Pratt, 1902), III, 243.

As she noted, the young king never laughed in games or at play, and he said of himself that he must be "perfect in all things" and never be found "to fail in anything."

---

intrusion into his bedroom in Paris, he moved the capital from Paris to Versailles, a dozen miles away. There, between 1668 and 1711, he built a vast palace more than a third of a mile long, set in an immense formal garden with fourteen hundred fountains supplied by water which had to be pumped up from the River Seine at great expense. Versailles housed, mainly in cramped, uncomfortable quarters, a court of ten thousand, including dependents and servants of all sorts. This was self-conscious government by spectacle, and it would be copied by every monarch who could afford it—and some who could not.

Divine-Right Monarchy

The much admired and imitated French state, of which Versailles was the symbol and Louis XIV the embodiment, is also the best historical example of divine-right monarchy. Perhaps Louis never actually said, "L'état c'est moi" (I am the state), but the phrase clearly summarizes his convictions about his role. In theory, Louis was the representative of God on earth—or at least in France. He was not elected by the French, nor did he acquire his throne by force of arms; rather, he was born to a position God had planned for the legitimate male heir of Hugh Capet, who had been king of France in the tenth century. As God's agent his word was final, for to challenge it would be to challenge the structure of God's universe; disobedience was a religious as well as a political offense. Thus the origins of divine right were a logical extension of Gallicanism.

In some ways the theory that justified divine-right monarchy looked back to the Middle Ages, to the view that right decisions in government are not arrived at by experiment and discussion but by "finding" the authoritative answer provided for in God's scheme of things. In other ways the theory was "modern" or forward looking, in that it derived from expectations about national loyalties and the growth of a sense of nationalism. Henry IV, Richelieu, and Louis XIV sought to fuse the 16 million inhabitants of France into a single national unit. The problem was to make these millions think of themselves as French and not as Normans, Bretons, Flemings, Alsatians, Burgundians, Gascons, Basques, and Provençaux. The makers of the Bourbon monarchy could not rely on a common language, for only a minority spoke the standardized French that the French Academy tried to foster. Nor could they rely on a common education, a common national press, or a common participation in political life. They could, and did, attempt to set the king up as the symbol of common Frenchness. The king collected taxes, raised armies, and touched the lives of his subjects in a hundred ways. The French had to believe that the king had a right to do all this, and that he was doing it for them rather than to them.

Divine-right monarchy, with its corollary of unquestioning obedience on the part of subjects, was thus one ingredient in the growth of the modern centralized nation-state. It was an institution that appealed to old theological ideas, such as the biblical admonition to obey the powers that be, for "the powers that be are ordained of God." But it was also inspired by the newer ideas of binding people together in a productive, efficient, and secure state. Naturally, in practice the institution did not wholly correspond to theories about it. Louis XIV was not the French state, and his rule was not absolute in any true sense of that word. He simply did not have the physical means to control in detail everything his subjects

The Palace of Versailles, outside Paris, grew to immense proportions. Built for Louis XIV, the Sun King, construction took forty-three years, from 1668 to 1711. The central portion was the work of Louis Le Vau (1612–1670). This early picture from the museum at Versailles shows the original chateau in its more modest 1668 dimensions. The painting is by Pierre Patel (1648–1707).

did; but his policies could touch their daily lives by bringing relative prosperity or hardship, peace or war. And Louis XIV could endeavor, in the majesty of his person, to act out the theories of those, like Bishop Jacques Bossuet (1627–1704), who provided the intellectual foundations for a universal history that justified divine-right arguments.

Increasingly, the chief opposition to such ideas came not from the various faiths but from the feudal nobles, so that in both France and England the seventeenth century brought a crisis to the aristocracy. The degree to which the nobility was integrated into the new state machinery was of crucial importance in the development of modern Europe. In Habsburg Spain and in the Habsburg lands of central Europe the old nobility generally accepted the new strength of the Crown but maintained many of their privileges and all of their old pride of status. In Prussia they were more successfully integrated into the new order, becoming servants of the Crown, yet with a social status that set them well above bourgeois bureaucrats. In England the nobility achieved a unique compromise with the Crown. In France the nobles of the sword were deprived of most major political functions, but they were allowed to retain social and economic privileges and important roles as officers in the king's army.

The process of reducing the old French nobility to relative powerlessness in national political life had begun as early as the twelfth century and had been much hastened by the religious and civil wars of the sixteenth century. An important part of the nobility, perhaps nearly

half, had become Protestant, in large part from sheer opposition to the Crown. The victory of Henry IV, purchased by his conversion to Catholicism, was a defeat for the nobility. Under Richelieu and Louis XIV the process was completed by the increasing use of commoners to run the government, from the great ministers of state, through the intendants, down to local administrators and judges. These commoners were usually elevated to the nobility of the robe, which did not at first have the social prestige of the nobility of the sword. But the Fronde had shown that these new nobles could not be counted upon as loyal supporters of the Crown, and among the old nobles they aroused contemptuous envy. Though at times the nobles were able to work together, they posed no long-term threat to the Crown.

Nor did the church. Under Louis XIV the French clergy continued to possess important privileges; they were not subject to royal taxation; they contributed a voluntary grant of money that they voted in their own assembly. Carefully the Crown fostered the evolution of a national Gallican church, firmly Catholic though controlled by the monarchy. The Gallican union of throne and altar reached a high point in 1682, when an assembly of French clerics drew up the Declaration of Gallican Liberties, asserting in effect that the "rules and customs admitted by France and the Gallican church" were just as important as the traditional authority of the papacy. Louis XIV thereupon took as the goal of his religious policy the application of a French motto—*un roi, une loi, une foi* (one king, one law, one faith).

Louis XIV was sixty-three and at the height of his power when Hyacinthe Rigaud (1659–1743) painted this strikingly posed portrait. In the background Rigaud has invoked memories of another great empire, Rome, while showing Louis's strength and sense of elegance in the flowing robe, the great ceremonial sword of office, and the coiffed wig. This portrait hangs in the Louvre in Paris.

Scala/Art Resource

Where Richelieu had attacked only the political privileges of the Huguenots, Louis attacked their fundamental right of toleration and finally revoked the Edict of Nantes in 1685. Fifty thousand Huguenot families fled abroad, notably to Prussia, Holland, the Dutch colony in southern Africa, England, and British North America. The practical skills and the intellectual abilities of the refugees strengthened the lands that received them, and the departure of industrious workers and thousands of veteran sailors, soldiers, and officers weakened France. Some Huguenots remained in France, worshiping secretly despite persecution.

Within the Catholic church itself, Louis had to contend with two important elements that refused to accept Gallicanism. Both groups saw themselves as countering the Counter-Reformation while remaining within the Catholic church. The Quietists, a group of religious enthusiasts led by Madame Jeanne Marie Guyon (1648–1717), sought a more mystical and emotional faith and believed in direct inspiration from God and perfect union

with him, so that a priesthood was not needed; but their tendency to exhibitionism and self-righteousness, and their zeal for publicity, belied their name and offended the king's sense of propriety. The Jansenists, sometimes called the Puritans of the Catholic church, were a high-minded group whose most distinguished spokesman was the scientist and philosopher Blaise Pascal (1622–1662). Named for Cornelius Jansen (1585–1638), bishop of Ypres, the Jansenists took an almost Calvinistic stand on predestination. They stressed the need to obey God rather than man, no matter how exalted the position of the particular man might be. They therefore questioned the authority of both king and pope, and attacked the pope's agents, the Jesuits. On the surface, Louis repressed both Quietists and Jansenists, but the latter survived two papal bulls of condemnation (1705, 1713) to trouble his successors in the eighteenth century.

The Royal Administration

Of course, in a land as large and complex as France, even the tireless Louis could do no more than exercise general supervision. At Versailles he had three long conferences weekly with his ministers, who headed departments of war, finance, foreign affairs, and the interior. The king kept this top administrative level on an intimate scale; he usually had only four ministers at one time and gave them virtually permanent tenure. Jean Colbert (1619–1683) served as controller general for eighteen years; Michel Le Tellier (1603–1685) was secretary of state for the army for thirty-four years, a post later entrusted to his son, who had been ennobled as the marquis de Louvois (1639–1691). All told, only sixteen ministers held office during the fifty-four years of Louis's personal reign. Yet in practice the royal administration was full of difficulties and contradictions. There were many conflicting jurisdictions, survivals of feudalism; the officials of Louis XIV, being nobles of the robe, had a privileged status they could hand down to their heirs. The thirty key provincial administrators, the intendants, were agents of the Crown, but many of them exercised considerable initiative on their own, despite being moved about from one administrative unit to another.

A particularly important potential for trouble existed in the parlements, the supreme courts of appeal in the various provinces. The Parlement of Paris enjoyed special prestige and power from its place in the capital and from the size of its territorial jurisdiction—almost half of France. The judges who staffed these courts headed the nobility of the robe, owned their offices, and could not be removed by the king. Besides the usual work of a court of appeals, the parlements also had to register royal edicts before they went into force. They thus claimed the right to refuse an edict if they thought it not in accord with the higher law of the land. Although this claim negated theoretical royal absolutism, Louis got around it in his own lifetime by using another old institution, the *lit de justice* (literally, "bed of justice"), in which he summoned the Parlement of Paris before him in a formal session and ordered the justices to register a royal edict. In this way, for instance, he enforced measures against Jansenism, which was strong among the judges. But the parlements were also to continue to plague his eighteenth-century successors.

Mercantilism and Colbert.   Divine-right monarchy was not peculiarly French, of course, nor was the mercantilism practiced by the France of Louis XIV. But like divine-right rule, mercantilism flourished most characteristically under the Sun King. Mercantilism was central to the early modern effort to construct strong, efficient political units. The mercantilists aimed to make their nation as self-sustaining as possible, as independent as possible of the need to import goods from other nations, which were its rivals and potential enemies. The mercantilists held that production within a nation should provide all the necessities of life for a hard-working population and also provide the power needed to fight and win wars. They believed that these goals required planning and control from above. They wished to sweep away such medieval remnants as the manor and the guild, which, they felt, reduced the energies and abilities needed in an expanding economy. But they did not believe, as free-trade economists would later argue, that people should be free to do whatever they thought would enrich themselves. Instead, the mercantilists would channel the national economic effort by protective tariffs, by government subsidies, by grants of monopolies, by industries run directly by the government, and by scientific and applied research.

The mercantilists viewed overseas possessions as a particularly important part of France, which should be run from the homeland by a strong government. Many foodstuffs and raw materials were more easily available overseas than in Europe. Colonies therefore should be encouraged to provide necessities, so that the mother country need not import them from competitors. In return, the mother country would supply industrial goods to the colonies and have a monopoly over colonial trade. This mercantilistic approach to colonies was followed not only by France and Spain but by the less absolutist governments of England and Holland.

The great French practitioner of mercantilism was Colbert, who had served his apprenticeship under Mazarin and advanced rapidly to become controller general early in the personal reign of Louis. He never quite attained the supremacy reached by Richelieu and Mazarin; he was the collaborator, never the master, of Louis XIV, since other great ministers, especially Louvois for military affairs, stood in the way of his supremacy. Yet Colbert was influential in all matters affecting the French economy, most interested in foreign trade and in the colonies and therefore in the merchant marine and in the navy. His hand was in everything: in invention, in technological education, in designing and building ships, in attracting foreign experts to settle in France.

Among the industries Colbert fostered were the processing of sugar, chocolate, and tobacco from the colonies;

the production of military goods by iron foundries and textile mills; and the manufacture of the luxuries for which the French soon became famous. The fifteenth-century Gobelins tapestry enterprise in Paris was taken over by the state and its output expanded to include elegant furniture, for which the king was a major customer. Glassblowers and lace makers were lured away from Venice, despite strenuous efforts by the Venetian republic to keep their valuable techniques secret. In a blow against French competitors, Colbert imposed heavy tariffs on some Dutch and English products. To promote trade with the colonies and also with the Baltic and the Mediterranean, he financed trading companies, of which only the French India Company eventually succeeded.

At home, Colbert encouraged reforestation, so that iron foundries could have abundant supplies of charcoal (then essential for smelting); he also promoted the planting of mulberry trees to nourish the silkworms vital to textile output. He even attempted—vainly, as it turned out—to control quality by ordering that defective goods be prominently exhibited in public, along with the name of the offending producer, and that the culprit be exhibited for a third offense. He also endeavored, again for the most part in vain, to break down the barriers to internal free trade, such as provincial and municipal tariffs or local restrictions on the shipment of grain to other parts of France. He did, however, successfully sponsor the construction of important roads and canals—the Canal du Midi, linking the Atlantic port of Bordeaux with the Mediterranean port of Narbonne, reduced transport charges between the two seas by three-fourths and was described as the greatest engineering feat since Roman days.

Whether the great prosperity France achieved in the first thirty years of Louis's reign came about because of, or despite, the mercantilist policies of Colbert is difficult to decide. Under the mercantilist regime France did attain undoubted leadership in European industry and commerce. That lead was lost in part because the last two wars of Louis XIV were ruinously expensive, in part because in the eighteenth century France's rival, England, introduced new methods of power machinery and concentrated on large-scale production of inexpensive goods, while France clung to the policies set by Colbert, favoring relatively small-scale production of luxuries and other consumer goods. But the difference between French and English industry was also a difference in the focus of national energies; while for the time, England focused inwards, France, like Spain before it, spent an exceptional proportion of its national product in an unfruitful effort to dominate through the force of arms both Europe and the known overseas world.

French Expansion

France was the real victor in the Thirty Years' War, acquiring lands on its northeastern frontier. In a postscript to the main conflict, it continued fighting with Spain until the Treaty of the Pyrenees in 1659, securing additional territories. Prospering economically, France was ready for further expansion when the young and ambitious Louis XIV began his personal rule in 1661. Louis hoped to complete the gains of 1648 and 1659 and secure France's "natural frontiers" along the Rhine and the Alps. As his sense of confidence grew, he waged a mercantilist war against France's major economic competitors, Holland and England. At the height of his prestige, Louis probably wanted to revive the multinational empire that Charlemagne had ruled nine hundred years earlier. He was also keenly aware of cultural imperialism, and he wanted the French language, French taste in the arts, and French customs to spread their influence over Europe.

Louis XIV and his talented experts fashioned splendid instruments to support this aggressive foreign policy. In 1661 half a dozen men made up the whole ministry of foreign affairs; half a century later it had a large staff of clerks, archivists, coders (and decoders) of secret messages, secret agents, and great lords and prelates who lent their dignity to important embassies. The growth of the French army was still more impressive, from a peacetime force of twenty thousand to a wartime one almost twenty times larger. Louis and his lieutenants almost revolutionized the character of France's fighting forces. At the ministry of war the father and son team of Le Tellier and Louvois grouped regiments in brigades under a general to bring them under closer control. They also introduced two new ranks of officer, major and lieutenant colonel, to give more opportunity to talented commoners; these new commissions were awarded only for merit and were not available for purchase, like the ranks of colonel or captain. Supplies were more abundant, pay was more regular, and an effort was made to weed out the lazy. The inspector general of infantry, Jean Martinet (d. 1672), was so rigorous in drilling and discipline that his name added a word to the modern vocabulary. The armies showed particular strength in artillery, engineering, and siege techniques, all important in the days when armies moved ponderously and did much fighting in the waterlogged Low Countries. The French boasted an engineer of genius, Marshal de Vauban (1633–1707), of whom it was said that a town he besieged was indefensible and a town he defended was impregnable. And though military medical services remained crude and sketchy, a large veterans' hospital, the Hôtel des Invalides, was built in Paris.

The First Two Wars of Louis XIV.

The main thrust of this vast effort was northeast, toward the Low Countries and Germany. Louis XIV sought also to secure Spain as a French satellite with a French ruler. Finally, French commitments overseas in North America and in India drove him to attempt, against English and Dutch rivals, to establish a great French empire outside Europe.

The first war of Louis XIV was a minor one, with Spain, and it ended quickly with the peace of Aix-la-Chapelle in 1668. Furious at the Dutch because of their economic ascendancy, their Calvinism, and their republicanism, Louis resolved to teach them a lesson for entering into an alliance with England and Sweden against him. He bought off Sweden and England, and in 1672 French forces invaded Holland. The terrified Dutch turned to the youthful William III of Orange (1650–1702), great-grandson of the martyred hero of Dutch independence, William the Silent. But the French advance was halted only by the extreme measure of opening the dikes.

Thereupon, Spain, the Holy Roman Empire, and Brandenburg-Prussia joined against France and her allies. French diplomacy separated this ineffective coalition at the six treaties of Nijmegen (Nimwegen) in 1678–1679. Holland was left intact at the cost of promising to remain neutral, and the French gave up Colbert's tariff on Dutch goods; Spain ceded to France the Franche Comté (Free Country of Burgundy), part of the Habsburgs' Burgundian inheritance, plus some towns in Belgium; Prussia, which had defeated Louis's ally, Sweden, at Fehrbellin (1675), was nonetheless obliged by French pressure to return Swedish lands in Germany. The power and prestige of France were now at their peak, as rulers all over Europe, and in particular the host of minor German princes, tried to copy the standards of Versailles.

The Last Two Wars.

But in the last three decades of Louis's reign most of his assets were consumed. Not content with the prestige he had won in his first two wars, Louis took on most of the Western world in what looked like an effort to destroy the independence of Holland and most of western Germany and to bring the Iberian peninsula under a French ruler. As a prelude to new military aggression special courts, "chambers of reunion," were set up by the French in the early 1680s to tidy up the loose ends of the peace settlements of the past generation. And there were loose ends aplenty on the northern and eastern frontiers of France, a zone of political fragmentation and confused feudal remnants, many of which were technically within the Holy Roman Empire. After examining the documents in disputed cases, the chambers of reunion "reunited" many strategic bits of land to territories controlled by France. In this way the former free city of Strasbourg, the chief town of Alsace, passed under French control.

Continued French nibbling at western Germany and Louis's assertion of a dynastic claim to most of the lands of the German elector Palatine set off the third of his wars, the War of the League of Augsburg, 1688–1697. This league against Louis was put together by his old foe, William of Orange, who after 1688 shared the throne of England with his wife Mary, daughter of James II. Thereafter England was thoroughly against Louis. The League also included Spain, the Holy Roman Empire, and Savoy, which was threatened by Louis's tactics of "reunion." The English won a great naval victory at Cape La Hogue in 1692, but William was repeatedly defeated on land in the Low Countries, though never decisively crushed. In Ireland, French (and thus Catholic) attempts to restore the deposed English king, James II, were foiled at the battle of the Boyne in 1690. France and England also exchanged blows in India, the West Indies, and North America, where the colonists called the conflict King William's War. The Treaty of Ryswick ended the war in a peace without victory, an agreement to hold to the status quo.

In 1701 Louis XIV took a step that led to his last and greatest conflict, the War of the Spanish Succession (1701–1714). Charles II, the Habsburg king of Spain and Louis's brother-in-law, had died in 1700 without a direct heir. For years diplomats had been striving to arrange a succession that would avoid putting on the throne either a French Bourbon or an Austrian Habsburg. Although they had agreed on a Bavarian prince, he had died in 1699, and plans were made to partition the Spanish inheritance between Habsburgs and Bourbons. Charles II left his lands intact to Philip of Anjou, grandson of Louis XIV. Louis accepted on behalf of Philip, even though he had signed the treaty of partition. This threat to the balance of power was neatly summarized in the remark a gloating Frenchman is supposed to have made, "There are no longer any Pyrenees." England, Holland, Savoy, the Holy Roman Empire, and many German states formed the Grand Alliance to preserve a separate Spain.

In the bloody war that followed, the French were gradually worn down. In North America they lost Nova Scotia to the English, and in Europe they were beaten by the allies in four major battles, beginning with Blenheim in 1704 and concluding with Malplaquet in 1709. The allied armies were commanded by two great generals, the French-born Prince Eugene of Savoy (1663–1736) and the English John Churchill (1650–1722), first duke of Marlborough. But the French were not annihilated, and Malplaquet cost the allies twenty thousand casualties, at least as many as the French suffered. By scraping the bottom of the barrel for men and money, the French still managed to keep armies in the field.

Moreover, the Grand Alliance was weakening. The English, following their policy of keeping any single Continental power from attaining too strong a position, were almost as anxious to prevent the union of Austria and Spain under a Habsburg as to prevent the union of France and Spain under a Bourbon. At home they faced a possible disputed succession to the throne, and the mercantile classes were sick of a war that was injuring trade and seemed unlikely to bring any compensating gains. In 1710 the pro-peace party won a parliamentary majority and began negotiations that culminated in a series of treaties at Utrecht in 1713.

Utrecht was a typical balance-of-power peace, which contained France without humiliating it. France lost Newfoundland, Nova Scotia, and the Hudson Bay territories to England, while preserving Quebec, Louisiana, and its Caribbean islands. In a sense Louis gained what he had gone to war over, for Philip of Anjou was formally recognized as King Philip V of Spain and secured the Spanish lands overseas. However, the French and Spanish crowns were not ever to be held by the same person, so the allies, too, had won their point. Furthermore, England took from Spain the Mediterranean island of Minorca and the great Rock of Gibraltar guarding the Atlantic entrance

to the Mediterranean. The English also gained the *asiento*, the right to supply slaves to the Spanish colonies—a right that also gave them opportunities for smuggling. The Austrian Habsburgs were compensated with Belgium and the former Spanish possessions of Milan and Naples. In Belgium—now the Austrian Netherlands—the Dutch were granted the right to garrison certain fortified towns, "barrier fortresses," for better defense against possible French aggression. For faithfulness to the Grand Alliance, the duke of Savoy was eventually rewarded with Sardinia and the title of king. The elector of Brandenburg was also rewarded with a royal title, king *in* (not *of*) Prussia, which lay outside the Holy Roman Empire.

Yet the rivalry between France and England for empire overseas was undiminished. After Utrecht, in India, as in North America, each nation would continue to try to oust the other from land and trade. In Europe the Dutch did not feel secure against the French, and the Austrian Habsburg emperor, Charles VI (1711–1740), never gave up hope of becoming "Charles III" of Spain. The distribution of Italian lands satisfied no one, Italian or outsider, and the next two decades were filled with acrimonious negotiations over Italy. In short, the peace was fatally flawed.

French Aggression in Review

Proponents of the view that Europe underwent a severe crisis during the seventeenth century can find much evidence in the horrors resulting from Louis XIV's aggressions. The total cost of his wars in human lives and economic resources was very great, especially in the deliberate French devastation of the German Palatinate during the War of the League of Augsburg. The battle of Malplaquet, which left forty thousand men wounded, dying, or dead in an area of ten square miles, was not surpassed in bloodshed until Napoleon's Russian campaign a century later. There was also much suffering behind the lines, notably in the great famine that struck France in 1693–1694. And the year of Malplaquet, 1709, was one of the grimmest in modern French history, as bitter cold, crop failures, famine, skyrocketing prices, and relentless government efforts to stave off bankruptcy by collecting more taxes caused almost universal misery. The Parisians complained bitterly in a mock paternoster: "Our Father which art at Versailles, thy name is hallowed no more, thy kingdom is great no more, thy will is no longer done on earth or on the waters. Give us this day thy bread which on all sides we lack."*

Louis set himself up as a champion of Catholicism, especially after the revocation of the Edict of Nantes in 1685, and William of Orange was hailed as a Protestant champion. Yet Louis, unlike his predecessor in aggression, Philip II of Spain, had no real hope of stamping out Protestantism among the Dutch. William's victory at the Boyne brought new hardship to Irish Catholics, and in

*Quoted in G. R. R. Treasure, *Seventeenth Century France*, 2nd ed. (London: John Murray, 1981), p. 441.

England and New England the French were hated because they were Catholics. In the end, however, the Grand Alliance against Louis was a complex mixture of Catholic and Protestant in which religion played a comparatively minor role. Louis XIV had achieved no permanent stability for Europe or France, and his authority would die with him; his funeral procession was mocked as it passed through the streets of Paris, though he remained a figure of veneration to the rural masses who made up the majority of France.

$\mathcal{S}$TUART ENGLAND

To the extent that English government utilized the new methods of professional administration developed in the fifteenth and sixteenth centuries, it was potentially as absolute as any divine-right monarchy. But the slow growth of representative government checked this potential, generating a set of rules not to be altered easily by the ordinary processes of government. These rules might be written down, but they might also be unwritten, being a consensus about certain traditions. These rules came to be regarded as limiting the authority not only of the king but even of a government elected by a majority of the people—a guarantee to individuals that they had "civil rights" and might carry out certain acts even though those in authority disapproved. Without such rules and habits of constitutionalism, and without the powerful and widespread human determination to back them up, the machinery of English parliamentary government could have been as ruthlessly absolute as any other government.

French kings and ministers could govern without the Estates General. In England, however, King Charles I, who had governed for eleven years without calling Parliament, felt obliged in 1640 to summon it and, though he dismissed it at once when it refused to do his bidding, he had to call another in the same year. This was the Long Parliament, which sat—with changes of personnel and with interruptions—for twenty years and which made the revolution that ended the threat of absolute divine-right monarchy in England.

Charles was ultimately obliged to call Parliament for two basic reasons that go back to medieval history. First, in the English Parliament the House of Commons represented two different social groups not brought together in one house elsewhere: the aristocratic knights of the shire and the burgesses of the towns and cities. The strength of the Commons lay in the practical working together of both groups, which intermarried quite freely and, despite economic and social tensions, tended to form a single ruling class, with membership open to talent and energy from the lower classes. Second, local government continued to be run by magistrates who were not directly dependent on the Crown. True,

England had its bureaucrats, its clerks and officials in the royal pay, but where in France and in other Continental countries the new bureaucracy tended to take over almost all governmental business, especially financial and judicial affairs, in England the gentry and the higher nobility continued to do important local work. The Elizabethan Poor Law of 1601 put the care of the needy not under any national ministry but squarely on the smallest local units, the parishes, where decisions lay ultimately with the amateur, unpaid justices of the peace, recruited from the local gentry. In short, the privileged classes were not, as in France, thrust aside by paid agents of the central government; nor did they, as in Prussia, become agents of the Crown. Instead, they preserved secure bases in local government and in the House of Commons. When Charles I tried to govern without the consent of these privileged classes, when he tried to raise money from them and their dependents to run a bureaucratic government, they had a solid institutional and traditional basis from which to resist his unusual demands.

Because Elizabeth I was childless, she was succeeded by the son of her old rival and cousin, Mary Queen of Scots, in 1603. James Stuart, already king of Scotland as James VI, became James I of England (1603–1625), thus bringing the two countries, still legally separate, under the same personal rule. James was a well-educated pedant, sure of himself, and above all certain that he ruled by divine right. As a Scottish foreigner, he was an object of distrust to his English subjects. He totally lacked the Tudor heartiness and tact, the gift of winning people to him. His son Charles I (1625–1649), under whom the divine-right experiment came to an end, had many more of the social graces of a monarch than his father, but he was still no man to continue the work of the Tudors. Although he was quite as sure as his father had been that God had called him to rule England, he could neither make the compromises the Tudors made nor revive their broad popular appeal. Thus an accident of personality was also important in shaping the outcome of divine-right theories in England.

The business of state was also gradually growing in scope and therefore in cost. The money required by the Stuarts—and indeed by the Bourbons, Habsburgs, and all monarchs—did not go only for high living by royalty and to support hangers-on; it also went to run a government that was beginning to assume many new functions. Foreign relations, for example, were beginning to take on modern forms, with a central foreign office, ambassadors, clerks, travel allowances, and the like, all requiring more money and personnel. James I and Charles I failed to get the money they needed because those from whom they sought it, the ruling classes, had succeeded in placing the raising and spending of it in their own hands through parliamentary supremacy. The Parliament that won that supremacy was a kind of committee of the ruling classes; it was not a democratic legislature, since only a small fraction of the population could vote for members of the Commons.

In this struggle between Crown and Parliament, religion helped weld both sides into cohesive fighting groups. The struggle for power was in part a struggle to impose a uniform worship on England. The royalist cause was identified with High Church Anglicanism, that is, with bishops and a liturgy and theology that made it a sacramental religion relatively free from left-wing Protestant austerities. The parliamentary cause, at first supported by many moderate Low Church Anglicans, also attracted strong Puritan or Calvinist elements; later it came under the control of Presbyterians and then of extreme Puritans, the Independents of Congregationalists. The term *Puritanism* in seventeenth-century England is confusing because it covered a wide range of religious groups, from moderate evangelical Anglicans all the way to radical splinter sects. But the core of Puritanism went back to Zwingli and Calvin, to the repudiation of Catholic sacramental religion and the rejection of most music and the adornment of churches; it emphasized sermons, simplicity in church and out, and "purifying" the tie between the worshiper and God.

James I, 1603-1625

In the troubled reign of James I there were three major points of contention—money, foreign policy, and religion. In all three issues the Crown and its opposition each tried to direct constitutional development in its own favor. In raising money James sought to make the most of revenues that did not require a parliamentary grant; Parliament sought to make the most of its own control over the purse strings by insisting on the principle that it had to approve any new revenues. When James levied an import duty without a parliamentary grant, an importer of dried currants refused to pay; the case was decided in favor of the Crown by the Court of Exchequer, and the decision attracted much attention because the judges held the king's powers in general to be absolute. Then a royal appeal for a general "benevolence"—a euphemism for a contribution exacted from an individual—was resisted with the support of the chief justice, Sir Edward Coke (1552– 1634). James summarily dismissed Coke from office for asserting the independence of the judiciary and thereby drew attention once again to his broad use of the royal prerogative.

The Tudors had regarded foreign affairs as entirely a matter for the Crown. The delicate problem of a marriage for Elizabeth I, for instance, had concerned her parliaments and the public; but Parliament made no attempt to dictate a marriage, and Elizabeth was careful not to offend her subjects in her own tentative negotiations. On the other hand, when James I openly sought a princess of hated Spain as a wife for his son Charles, the Commons in 1621 petitioned publicly against the Spanish marriage. When James rebuked them for meddling, they drew up the Great Protestation, the

first of the major documents of the English Revolution, in which they used what they claimed were the historic privileges of Parliament to assert what was in fact a new claim for parliamentary control of foreign affairs. James responded by dissolving Parliament and imprisoning four of its leaders. The Spanish marriage fell through, but the betrothal of Charles in 1624 to the French princess Henrietta Maria, sister of Louis XIII, who was also Catholic, was hardly more popular with the English people.

Though refusing to permit public services by Catholics and Puritans, Elizabeth had allowed much variety of practice within the Anglican church. James summed up his policy in the phrase "no bishop, no king"—by which he meant that the enforcement of the bishops' authority in religion was essential to the maintenance of royal power. James at once took steps against what he held to be Puritan nonconformity. He called a conference of Anglican bishops and leading Puritans at Hampton Court in 1604, at which he presided in person and used the full force of his scholarship against the Puritans. After the conference dissolved with no real meeting of minds, royal policy continued to favor the High Church, anti-Puritan party.

Despite James's failure to achieve anything like religious agreement among his subjects, his reign is a landmark in the history of Christianity among English-speaking peoples, for in 1611, after seven years' labor, a committee of forty-seven ministers authorized by him completed the English translation of the Bible that is still the most widely used. The King James version was a masterpiece of Elizabethan prose, perhaps the most remarkable literary achievement a committee has ever made.

Charles I, 1625-1642

Under his son, Charles I, all James's difficulties came to a head very quickly. England was involved in a minor war against Spain, and though the members of Parliament hated Spain, they were most reluctant to grant Charles funds to support the English forces. Meanwhile, despite his French queen, Charles became involved in a war against France, which he financed in part by a forced loan from his wealthier subjects and by quartering troops in private houses at the householders' expense. His financial position was tenuous; as a French observer remarked, "They wish for war against heaven and earth, but lack the means to make it against anyone." The military preparations were the greatest since 1588, when there had been a visible enemy; in 1626–1628 Charles's subjects were less certain of the need for extraordinary measures. Consequently, in 1628 Parliament passed the Petition of Right—"the Stuart Magna Carta"—which for the first time explicitly stated some of the most basic rules of modern constitutional government: no taxation without the consent of Parliament; no billeting of soldiers in private houses; no martial law in time of peace; no imprisonment except on a specific charge and subject to the protection of regular legal procedures. All of these were limitations on the Crown.

Charles consented to the Petition of Right to secure new grants of money from Parliament. But he also collected duties not sanctioned by Parliament, which thereupon protested not only against his unauthorized taxes but also against his High Church policy. The king now switched from conciliation to firmness. In 1629 he had Sir John Eliot (1592–1632), mover of the resolutions, arrested, together with eight other members. He then dissolved Parliament, in part for refusing to vote supplies to the king, in part because he felt Parliament was meddling in matters of religion beyond its authority, and in part because Eliot intended to appeal over the king's head to the country. Eliot died a prisoner in the Tower of London, the first martyr in the parliamentary cause, having in effect driven Charles I to take a calculated risk.

For the next eleven years, 1629–1640, Charles governed without a Parliament. He squeezed every penny he could get out of royal revenues that did not require parliamentary authorization, never quite breaking with precedent by imposing a wholly new tax but stretching precedent beyond what his opponents thought reasonable. For example, ship money had been levied by the Crown before, but only on coastal towns for naval expenditures in wartime; Charles now imposed ship money on inland areas and in peacetime. John Hampden (1594–1643), a rich member of Parliament from inland Buckinghamshire, refused to pay it. He lost his case in court (1637) but gained wide public support for challenging the king's fiscal expedients.

In religious matters Charles was guided by a very High Church archbishop of Canterbury, William Laud (1573–1645), who systematically enforced Anglican conformity and deprived even moderate Puritan clergymen of their pulpits. Puritans were sometimes brought before the Star Chamber, an administrative court that denied the accused the safeguards of the common law. In civil matters Charles relied on an opportunist conservative, Thomas Wentworth, first earl of Strafford (1593–1641), who had deserted the parliamentary side and went on to become lord lieutenant of Ireland, a country that was a source of continued conflict and expense.

England was seething with repressed political and religious passions underneath the outward calm of these years of personal rule. Yet to judge from the imperfect statistics available, the relative weight of the taxation that offended so many Englishmen was less than on the Continent, and far less than taxation in any modern Western state. The members of Parliament who resisted the Crown by taking arms against it were not downtrodden, poverty-stricken people revolting out of despair, but self-assertive people defending their concept of civil rights and their own forms of worship, as well as seeking power and wealth.

Why, then, was there a revolution? Historians are not agreed, especially about the economic motivations of the English revolutionaries. There is evidence that the more capitalistic gentleman farmers—rural bourgeoisie—supported the Puritans; but other scholars argue that the elements from the gentry who supported the Puritans were those who saw themselves sinking on the economic scale, because of inflation, because of the enclosure of once common lands for sheep farming, and because of competition by the new secular owners of the old monastic lands. This debate about the nature and role of the gentry illustrates two problems faced by the historian: first, that of definitions, since the debate turns in part on how social classes are defined, or defined themselves in the past; second, that of interpretation, since two historians examining the same evidence, or different evidence that overlaps at certain points, may arrive at quite different conclusions about the meaning of that evidence. Was the English Revolution caused by despair—a declining gentry seeking to turn the clock back, so that the revolution was actually conservative in its goals—or was it caused by the perception of the need to modernize, to change the institutions of government to more rational, efficient purposes—that is, the final stage of the long movement away from feudalism?

The English Revolution did not, in fact, greatly alter the face of England. The laboring poor played almost no role in the Revolution. Nonetheless, a precedent of great significance was established, for a king was brought to trial and executed and his office abolished; an established church was disestablished and its property taken; less emphasis was placed on deference. All this would later be undone, the monarchy and the established church restored. Yet in the process, many would perceive that human beings could alter their world if they chose, and many would see the importance of the political process. And they would see that the Crown was neither rational nor truly responsible in various aspects of finance; in government credit, in the use of improper taxes for purposes considered immoral, and in placing the government's financial interest before its social responsibilities. Thus religion, economics, and politics would prove inseparable, a linked chain of causation.

Charles I could perhaps have weathered his financial difficulties if he had not had to contend with the Scots. Laud's attempt to enforce the English High Church ritual and organization came up against the three-generations-old Scottish Presbyterian *kirk* (church). In 1638 a Solemn League and Convenant bound the members of the kirk to resist Charles by force if need be. Charles marched north against the Scots and worked out a compromise with them in 1639. But even this mild campaign was too much for the treasury, and in 1640 Charles had to call Parliament back into session. This Short Parliament denied him any money unless the piled-up grievances against Charles and his father were settled; it was dissolved almost at once. Then the Scots went to war again, and Charles, defeated in a skirmish, bought them off by promising the Scottish army £850 a day until peace was made. Since he could not raise the money, he had to call another Parliament, which became the Long Parliament of the revolution.

Since the Scottish army would not disband until it was paid off, the Long Parliament held it as a club over Charles's head and put through a series of reforms striking at the heart of the royal power. It abolished ship money and other disputed taxes and disbanded the unpopular royal administrative courts, such as the Star Chamber, which had become symbols of Stuart absolutism. Up to now Parliament had been called and dismissed at the pleasure of the Crown; the Triennial Act of 1640 required that Parliament be summoned every three years, even if the Crown did not wish to do so. Parliament also attacked the royal favorites, whom Charles reluctantly abandoned; Archbishop Laud was removed, and Strafford was declared guilty of treason and executed in May 1641.

Meanwhile, Strafford's harsh policy toward the Irish had led to a rebellion that amounted to an abortive war for national independence by Irish Catholics and caused the massacre of thirty thousand Protestants in the northern Irish region of Ulster. Parliament, unwilling to trust Charles with an army to put down this rebellion, drew up in 1641 a Grand Remonstrance summarizing all its complaints. Charles now made a final attempt to repeat the tactics that had worked in 1629. Early in 1642 he ordered the arrest of five of his leading opponents in the House of Commons, including Hampden of the ship money case. The five took refuge in the privileged political sanctuary of the City of London, where the king could not reach them. Charles left for the north and in the summer of 1642 rallied an army at Nottingham. Parliament simply took over the central government, and the Civil War had begun.

During these years of political jockeying, signs were already evident that strong groups in England and in Parliament wanted something more than a return to the Tudor balance between Crown and Parliament, between religious conservatives and religious radicals. In politics the Nineteen Propositions that Parliament submitted to the king in June 1642 would have established parliamentary supremacy over the army, the royal administration, the church, and even the rearing of the royal children. Charles turned down the propositions, and they became the parliamentary positions in the war that followed. In religion a Root and Branch Bill, introduced in 1641 but not enacted into law, would have radically reformed the Church of England, destroying "root and branch" the bishops and much of what had already become traditional in Anglican religious practices. In the midst of such extreme contentiousness, a middle path seemed impossible to find.

The Civil War, 1642-1649

England was split along lines that were partly territorial, partly social and economic, and partly religious. Royalist strength lay largely in the north and west, relatively less urban and less prosperous than other parts, and largely

Sir Anthony Van Dyck (1599–1641) painted King Charles I hunting. Probably completed in 1638 and now in the Louvre, this portrait shows the king informally dressed, having dismounted from his horse. The arrogant pose, with hand on hip and cane, was used from medieval times to represent nobility. Contrast the dress and compare the pose with Rigaud's portrait of Louis XIV (p. 312) and with Charles V (p. 241).

Réunion des Musées Nationaux

controlled by gentry who were loyal to throne and altar. Parliamentary strength lay largely in the south and east, especially in London and in East Anglia, where Puritanism commanded wide support. The Scots were a danger to either side, distrustful of an English Parliament but equally distrustful of a king who had sought to put bishops over their kirk.

In the field, the struggle was at first indecisive. The royalists, or Cavaliers, recruited from a class used to riding, had the initial advantage of superior cavalry. What swung the balance to the side of Parliament was the development of a special force recruited from ardent Puritans in the eastern counties and gradually forged under strict discipline into the Ironsides. Their leader was a Puritan, Oliver Cromwell (1599–1658), who won a crucial battle at Marston Moor in 1644. The parliamentary army, reorganized into the New Model Army and staffed by radicals in religion and politics, stood as Roundheads (from their short-cropped hair) against the Cavaliers. At the battle of Naseby in 1645, the New

Model Army was completely victorious, and Charles in desperation took refuge with the Scottish army, who turned him over to the English Parliament in return for their £400,000 back pay.

A situation now arose that was to be repeated, with variations based on time and place, in the French Revolution in 1792 and the Russian Revolution in 1917. The moderates who had begun the revolution and who controlled the Long Parliament were confronted by a much more radical group who controlled the New Model Army. In religion the moderates, seeking to retain some ecclesiastical discipline and formality, were Presbyterians or Low Church Anglicans; in politics they were constitutional monarchists. The radicals, who were opposed to churches disciplined from a central organization, were Independents or Congregationalists, and they already so distrusted Charles that they were thinking about a republican England. The situation was further complicated by the Presbyterian Scots, who regarded the Roundheads as religious anarchists.

The years after 1645 were filled with difficult negotiations, during which Charles stalled for time to gain Scottish help. In 1648 Cromwell beat the invading Scots at Preston, and his army seized the king. Parlia-

ment, with the moderates still in control, now refused to do what the army wanted—to dethrone Charles. The Roundhead leaders then ordered Colonel Thomas Pride (d. 1658) to exclude by force from the Commons ninety-six Presbyterian members. This the colonel did in December 1648, with no pretense of legality. After "Pride's Purge" only some sixty radicals remained of the more than five hundred original members of the Long Parliament; this remnant was known thereafter as the Rump Parliament. The Rump brought Charles to trial before a special high court of radicals, fifty-nine of whom condemned him to death. On January 30, 1649, Charles I was beheaded. To the end he insisted that a king could not be tried by any superior jurisdiction on earth, that his cause was the cause of the people of England, and that if he could be silenced, so might all others. The monarchs of Europe now had their own martyr, and Parliament was, in the eyes of many in England, stained by a clearly illegal act.

Cromwell and the Interregnum, 1649-1660

The next eleven years are known as the Interregnum, the interval between two monarchical reigns. England was now a republic under a government known as the Commonwealth. Since the radicals did not dare to call a free election, which would almost certainly have gone against them, the Rump Parliament continued to sit. Thus, from the start, the Commonwealth was a dictatorship of a radical minority come to power through the tight organization of the New Model Army. From the start, too, Cromwell dominated the new government. In religion an earnest and sincere Independent, a patriotic Englishman, strong-minded, stubborn, if now power-mad, still by no means unwilling to compromise, Cromwell was nevertheless a prisoner of his position.

Cromwell faced a divided England, where the majority was royalist at heart and certainly sick of the fighting, the confiscations, the endless confusing changes of the last decade. He faced a hostile Scotland and an even more hostile Ireland, where the disorders in England had encouraged the Catholic Irish to rebel once more in 1649. In 1650 Charles II, eldest son of the martyred Charles I, landed in Scotland, accepted the Covenant (thereby guaranteeing the Presbyterian faith as the established Scottish kirk), and led a Scottish army against the English. Once more the English army proved unbeatable, and young Charles took refuge on the Continent after a romantic escape in disguise. Cromwell then faced a war with Holland (1652–1654) brought on by the Navigation Act of 1651, which forbade the importation of goods into England and the colonies except in English ships or in ships of the country producing the imported goods, thus striking at the Dutch carrying trade.

In time Cromwell mastered nearly all his foes. He himself went to Ireland and suppressed the rebellion with

Oliver Cromwell is invariably depicted as stern and dedicated, staring into the future. This painting by Samuel Cooper (1609–672), who specialized in miniature portraits of figures from the Commonwealth and Restoration, emphasizes Cromwell's sense of force by focusing solely on the head, devoid of background or distracting detail.

By kind permission of the Master, Fellows and Scholars of the College of the Lady Frances Sidney Sussex in the University

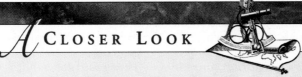

A CLOSER LOOK

Oliver Cromwell

Even today the character of Oliver Cromwell is the subject of much debate. Judgments on the English Civil War are shaped in some measure by opinions about Cromwell's motives, actions, and policies. His supporters and detractors are no less firmly committed today than in Cromwell's time, especially in Britain, where the role of the monarchy continues to be debated even now. Some commentators feel that Cromwell, as Lord Protector, simply replaced the king; others argue that he fundamentally transformed England, despite the eventual restoration of the monarchy. One of the most interesting commentaries is by Cromwell's contemporary, the poet (and official in Cromwell's government) John Milton. In 1654 Milton wrote, in his *Second Defense of the People of England*, one of the most interesting defenses of Cromwell, entitled "To You Our Country Owes Its Liberties":

The whole surface of the British empire has been the scene of [Cromwell's] exploits, and the theatre of his triumphs. . . . He collected an army as numerous and as well equipped as any one ever did in so short a time; which was uniformly obedient to his orders, and dear to the affections of the citizens; which was formidable to the enemy in the field, but never cruel to those who laid down their arms; which committed no lawless ravages on the persons or the property of the inhabitants; who, when they compared their conduct with the turbulence, the intemperance, the impiety and the debauchery of the royalists, were wont to salute them as friends and to consider them as guests. They were a stay to the good, a terror to the evil, and the warmest advocates for every exertion of piety and virtue.

But when you saw that the business [of governing the realm] was artfully procrastinated, that every one was more intent on his own selfish interest than on the public good, that the people complained of the disappointments which they had experienced, and the fallacious promises by which they had been gulled, that they were the dupes of a few overbearing individuals, you put an end to their domination.

In this state of desolation which we were reduced to, you, O Cromwell! alone remained to conduct the government and to save the country. We all willingly yield the palm of sovereignty to your unrivalled ability and virtue,

except the few among us who, either ambitious of honors which they have not the capacity to sustain, or who envy those which are conferred on one more worthy than themselves, or else who do not know that nothing in the world is more pleasing to God, more agreeable to reason, more politically just, or more generally useful, than that the supreme power should be vested in the best and the wisest of men. Such, O Cromwell, all acknowledge you to be. . . .

But if you, who have hitherto been the patron and tutelary genius of liberty, if you, who are exceeded by no one in justice, in piety and goodness, should hereafter invade that liberty which you have defended, your conduct must be fatally operative, not only against the cause of liberty, but the general interests of piety and virtue. Your integrity and virtue will appear to have evaporated, your faith in religion to have been small; your character with posterity will dwindle into insignificance, by which a most destructive blow will be leveled against the happiness of mankind.*

---

*As reprinted in Perry M. Rogers, ed., *Aspects of Western Civilization: Problems and Sources in History*, 2nd ed. (Englewood Cliffs, N.J.: Prentice Hall, 1992), II, pp. 32–33.

extreme bloodshed. In the so-called Cromwellian Settlement of 1652–1654, he dispossessed rebel Irish landholders in favor of Protestants, achieving order in Ireland but not peace. He brought the naval war with the Dutch to a victorious close in 1654. Later Cromwell also waged an aggressive war against the Spanish (1656–1658), from whom the English acquired the rich Caribbean sugar island of Jamaica. Even in time of troubles, the British Empire kept growing.

Cromwell, however, could not master the Rump Parliament, which brushed aside his suggestions for an increase in its membership and a reform of its procedures. In April 1653 he forced its dissolution by appearing in Parliament with a body of soldiers. In December he took the decisive step of inaugurating the regime called the

Protectorate, with himself as lord protector of England, Scotland, and Ireland, and with a written constitution, the only one Britain has ever had: the Instrument of Government. It provided for a Parliament with a single house of 460 members, who were chosen solely by Puritan sympathizers since no royalist dared vote. Even so, the lord protector had constant troubles with his parliaments, and in 1657 he yielded to pressure and modified the Instrument to provide for a second parliamentary house and to put limits on the lord protector's power. Meanwhile, to maintain order, Cromwell had divided the country into twelve military districts, each commanded by a major general.

Oliver Cromwell died in 1658 and was succeeded as lord protector by his son Richard, who was a nonentity. The army soon seized control, and some of its leaders regarded the restoration of the Stuarts as the best way to end the chronic political turbulence. To ensure the legality of the move, General George Monck (1608-1670), commander of the Protectorate's forces in Scotland, summoned back the Rump and readmitted the surviving members excluded by Pride's Purge. This partially reconstituted Long Parliament enacted the formalities of restoration, and in 1660 Charles Stuart accepted an invitation to return from exile and reign as Charles II.

The Revolution in Review

At the height of their rule in the early 1650s some Puritans had attempted to enforce on the whole population the austere life of the Puritan ideal. This enforcement took the form of "blue laws": prohibitions on horse racing, gambling, cock fighting, bear baiting, dancing on the greens, fancy dress, the theater, and a host of ordinary pleasures of daily living. Yet this attempt to legislate morality, coming too early for modern techniques of propaganda and regimentation, was not entirely effective. Many an Anglican clergyman, though officially "plundered"—that is, deprived of his living—continued worship in private houses, and many a cock fight went on in secluded spots. Nevertheless, the strict code was there, with earnest persons to try to enforce it and with implacable enemies to oppose it. The remark of the great Victorian historian T. B. Macaulay (1800-1859)—that the Puritans prohibited bear baiting not because it gave pain to the bear but because it gave pleasure to the spectators—showed the deep hostility that survived in England toward the reign of the Puritan "saints" two centuries later.

Despite this negative judgment, the events of 1640–1660 are of major importance in the history of the West. For the first time a monarch was challenged in a major revolt by politically active private citizens. Though the Stuarts were ultimately restored, no English king could ever hope to rule again without a Parliament, or revive the court of Star Chamber, or take ship money, benevolences, and other controversial taxes. Parliament thereafter retained that critical weapon of the legislative body in a limited monarchy, control of the public purse by periodic grants of taxes.

Another basic freedom owes much to this English experience. Freedom of speech was a fundamental tenet of the Puritans, even though at the height of their power they did not observe it themselves. It received its classic expression in 1644 by the poet John Milton (1608–1674), in his *Areopagitica*. While Milton defended free speech principally for an intellectual and moral elite, one of his arguments was characteristically pragmatic and English, namely, that attempts to curb free expression just would not work.

The voluminous pamphlet literature of the early years of the great turmoil was a lively manifestation of free speech in action. The extraordinary rise of radical minorities foreshadowed modern political and social thought. One such group, the Levelers, found many sympathizers in the revolutionary army and advanced a program later carried by emigrants to the American colonies. They called for political democracy, universal suffrage, regularly summoned parliaments, progressive taxation, separation of church and state, and the protection of the individual against arbitrary arrest. There were even hints of economic equality, a goal then closely tied to biblical ideas. The Diggers, for example, were a small sect that preached the sharing of earthly goods in a kind of communism. They advocated plowing up common and waste land throughout England, regardless of ownership, in the interests of social reform. The Ranters attacked "respectable" beliefs, arguing that sin hardly existed, that a reformation in behavior would free the oppressed from the nobility and gentry. Fifth Monarchy advocates, Millenarians, and a dozen other radical sects preached the Second Coming of Christ and the achievement of a utopia on earth.

Still more important, there emerged from the English Revolution, even more clearly than from the religious wars on the Continent, the concept of religious toleration. The Independents, while they were in opposition, stood firmly for the right of religious groups to worship God as they wished. Though in their brief tenure of power they showed a readiness to persecute, they were never firmly enough in the saddle to make England into a seventeenth-century version of Calvin's Geneva. At least one sect, the Quakers, led by George Fox (1624–1691), held to the idea and practice of religious toleration as a positive good. The Quakers denounced all worldly show, finding even buttons ostentatious. They found the names of the days and months indecently pagan, the polite form "you" in the singular a piece of social hypocrisy, and the taking of legal oaths impious. Hence they met for worship on what they called the First Day rather than the day of the sun god; they addressed each other as "thee" or "thou"; and they took so seriously the Protestant doctrine of the priesthood of the believer that they eliminated any formal ministry. In the Religious Society of Friends, as they were properly known, any worshiper who felt the spirit move might testify—give what other sects would call a sermon. The Friends felt too deeply the impossibility of forcing anyone to see the "inner light" for them to force people to accept their faith. They would abstain entirely from force, particularly from war, and would go their own way in Christian peace.

Among the Quakers the religious rights of women reached new heights. Any Friend could speak and prophesy; Fox declared that the subjection of women, which had been decreed at the fall of man in the garden of Eden, was ended through the sacrifice made by the Redeemer. Women were priests, and Christ was both male and female. Thus women played a major role in Quakerism and, from 1671, held women's meetings, which gave them a share in church government. The Civil War sects also gave women important, if not equal, roles

THE WRITTEN RECORD

Blackstone on the Law

By the eighteenth century the English recognized that a unique constitution had evolved from the period of their Civil War. Basically unwritten, rooted in the common law, this constitution would contribute to a remarkable period of political stability. In 1765 an English jurist, William Blackstone (1723–1780), would prepare a lengthy set of commentaries on the laws of England in which the process dramatically accelerated by the English Revolution was described:

And herein indeed consists the true excellence of the English government, that all the parts of it form a mutual check upon each other. In the legislature, the people are a check upon the nobility, and the nobility a check upon the people; by the mutual privilege of rejecting what the other has resolved: while the king is a check upon both, which preserves the executive power from encroachments. And this very executive power is again checked and kept within due bounds by the two houses, through the privilege they have of inquiring into, impeaching and punishing the conduct (not indeed of the king which would destroy his constitutional independence; but, which is more beneficial to the public,) of his evil and pernicious counsellors. Thus every branch of our civil polity supports and is supported, regulates and is regulated, by the rest. . . . Like three distinct powers in mechanics, they jointly impel the machine of government in a direction different from what either, acting by itself, would have done . . . a direction which constitutes the true line of the liberty and happiness of the community.

William Blackstone, *Commentaries on the Laws of England*, 15th ed. (London: A. Stralan, 1809), I, 153.

By 1651 the House of Commons was depicted on the Great Seal of England as used by the Commonwealth—testimony to the symbolic significance that Cromwell attached to the House. This scene is a Dutch rendition of Cromwell's dissolution of Parliament in 1653. The owl and small lion made to look like a dog are intended as a satirical commentary on the debate and the dissolution.

New York Public Library Picture Collection

to play, challenging orthodox arguments for the exclusion of women from church office. The sects focused often on the family and its ethical and moral role; combined with the spread of religious toleration, this led to some weakening of the idea of paternal authority, with spheres being defined in which maternal authority was to govern.

The Restoration, 1660-1688

The Restoration of 1660 left Parliament essentially supreme but attempted to undo some of the work of the Revolution. Anglicanism was restored in England and Ireland, though not as a state church in Scotland. Protestants who would not accept the Church of England were termed dissenters. Although they suffered many legal disabilities, dissenters remained numerous, especially among artisans and middle-class merchants. As time went on they grew powerful, so that the noncomformist conscience became a major factor in English public life. Indeed, the three-century progression of names by which these non-Anglican Protestants were called shows their rise in status: the hostile term "dissenter" became "nonconformist" in the nineteenth century, and "free churchman" in the twentieth.

The Restoration was also a revulsion against Puritan ways. The reign of Charles II (r. 1660–1685) was a period of moral looseness, of lively court life, of Restoration drama with its ribald wit, and of the public pursuit of pleasure, at least among the upper classes.

But the new Stuarts were not as adept at public relations as the Tudors had been. Charles II dissipated some of the fund of goodwill with which he started by following a foreign policy that seemed to patriotic Englishmen too subservient to Louis XIV. Yet Charles's alliance with Louis in 1670 did result in the extinction of any Dutch threat to English sea power, and it confirmed an important English acquisition, that of New Amsterdam, now New York, first taken in the Anglo-Dutch War of 1664–1667.

What really undid the later Stuarts and revealed their political ineptitude was the Catholic problem. Charles II had come under Catholic influence through his French mother and probably became a Catholic before he died in 1685. Since he left no legitimate children, the crown passed to his brother, James II (1685–1688), who was already an open Catholic. To enlist the support of the dissenters for the toleration of Catholics, James II issued in 1687 a Declaration of Indulgence, granting freedom of worship to all denominations in England and Scotland. While this was, in the abstract, an admirable step toward full religious liberty, to the majority in England Catholicism still seemed a great menace, and it was always possible to stir them to an irrational pitch by an appeal to their fear of "popery." Actually, by the end of the seventeenth century the few remaining Catholics in England were glad to accept the status of the dissenters and were no real danger to an overwhelmingly Protestant country. In Ireland, however,

the Catholics remained an unappeasable majority, and Ireland posed a genuine threat.

The political situation was much like that under Charles I: the Crown had one goal, Parliament another. Although James II made no attempt to dissolve Parliament or to arrest its members, he went over Parliament's head by issuing decrees based on what he called the "power of dispensation." Early in his reign he had used a minor rebellion by the duke of Monmouth, a bastard son of Charles II, as the excuse for two ominous policies. First, his judges punished suspected rebel sympathizers with a severity that seemed out of all proportion to the extent of the rebellion. Second, he created a standing army of thirty thousand men, part of which he stationed near London in what appeared as an attempt to intimidate the capital. To contemporaries it looked as though James were plotting to force both Catholicism and divine-right monarchy on an unwilling England.

The Glorious Revolution and Its Aftermath, 1688-1714

The result was the Glorious Revolution, a coup d'état engineered at first by a group of James's parliamentary opponents who were called Whigs, in contrast to the Tories who tended to support at least some of the policies of the later Stuarts. The Whigs were the heirs of the moderates of the Long Parliament, and they represented an alliance of the great lords and the prosperous London merchants.

James II married twice. By his first marriage he had two daughters, both Protestant—Mary, who had married William of Orange, the Dutch opponent of Louis XIV, and Anne. Then in 1688 a son was born to James and his Catholic second wife, thus apparently making the passage of the crown to a Catholic heir inevitable. The Whig leaders responded with propaganda, including rumors that the queen had never been pregnant, that a baby had been smuggled into her chamber in a warming pan so that there might be a Catholic heir. Then the Whigs and some Tories negotiated with William of Orange, who could hardly turn down a proposition that would give him the solid assets of English power in his struggle with Louis XIV. He accepted the invitation to take the English crown, which he was to share with his wife, the couple reigning as William III (r. 1689–1702) and Mary II (r. 1689–1694). On November 5, 1688, William landed at Torbay on the Devon coast with some fourteen thousand soldiers. When James heard the news he tried to rally support in the West Country, but everywhere the great lords and even the normally conservative gentry were on the side of a Protestant succession. James fled from London to France in December 1688, giving William an almost bloodless victory.

Early in 1689 Parliament (technically a convention, since there was no monarch to summon it) formally offered the crown to William. Enactment of a Bill of

Rights followed. This document, summing up the constitutional practices that Parliament had been seeking since the Petition of Right in 1628, was, in fact, almost a short written constitution. It laid down the essential principles of parliamentary supremacy: control of the purse, prohibition of the royal power of dispensation, and frequent meetings of Parliament.

Three major steps were necessary after 1689 to convert Britain into a parliamentary democracy with the Crown as the purely symbolic focus of patriotic loyalty. These, were, first, the concentration of executive direction in a committee of the majority party in the Parliament, that is, a cabinet headed by a prime minister, achieved in the eighteenth and early nineteenth centuries; second, the establishment of universal suffrage and payment to members of the Commons, achieved in the nineteenth and twentieth centuries; and third, the abolition of the power of the House of Lords to veto legislation passed by the Commons, achieved in the early twentieth century. Thus democracy was still a long way off in 1689, and William and Mary were real rulers with power over policy.

Childless, they were succeeded by Mary's younger sister Anne (r. 1702–1714), all of whose many children were stillborn or died in childhood. The exiled Catholic Stuarts, however, did better; the little boy born to James II in 1688 and brought up near Paris grew up to be known as the "Old Pretender." Then in 1701 Parliament passed an Act of Settlement that settled the crown—in default of heirs to Anne, then heir presumptive to the sick William III—not on the Catholic pretender, but on the Protestant Sophia of Hanover or her issue. Sophia was a granddaughter of James I and the daughter of Frederick of the Palatinate, the "Winter King" of Bohemia in the Thirty Years' War. On Anne's death in 1714, the crown passed to Sophia's son George, first king of the house of Hanover. This settlement made it clear that Parliament, and not the divinely ordained succession of the eldest male in direct descent, made the kings of England.

To ensure the Hanoverian succession in both Stuart kingdoms, Scotland as well as England, the formal union of the two was completed in 1707 as the United Kingdom of Great Britain. Scotland gave up its own parliament and sent representatives to the parliament of the United Kingdom at Westminster. Although the union met with some opposition from both English and Scots, on the whole it went through with ease, so great was Protestant fear of a possible return of the Catholic Stuarts.

The Glorious Revolution did not, however, settle the other chronic problem—Ireland. The Catholic Irish rose in support of the exiled James II and were put down at the battle of the Boyne in 1690. William then attempted to apply moderation in his dealings with Ireland, but the Protestants there soon forced him to return to the Cromwellian policy. Although Catholic worship was not actually forbidden, many galling restrictions were imposed on the Catholic Irish, including the

prohibition of Catholic schools. Moreover, economic persecution was added to religious, as Irish trade came under stringent mercantilist regulation. This was the Ireland whose deep misery inspired the writer Jonathan Swift (1667–1745) in 1729 to make his satirical "modest proposal," that the impoverished Irish sell their babies as articles of food.

Absolutism was thus almost universal in Europe. On the Continent enlightened despots ruled with an often intelligent but determined hand. In the British Isles a tenuous balance had been struck, though for those outside the United Kingdom the rule of the monarch was no less absolute and perhaps less enlightened. While writers of genius might criticize governments, everyman still had no way of doing so, save through peasant revolts.

CENTURY OF GENIUS/ CENTURY OF EVERYMAN

In the seventeenth century the cultural, as well as the political, hegemony of Europe passed from Italy and Spain to Holland, France, and England. Especially in literature, the France of *le grand siècle* set the imprint of its classical style on the West through the writings of Corneille, Racine, Molière, Bossuet, and a host of others. Yet those writers who exerted the greatest influence on modern culture were not exclusively French and were philosophers and scientists (see Chapter 13). Their arguments were expressed in political and economic constructs that justified or attacked the conventional wisdom of the age. In all fields of intellectual endeavor the seventeenth century saw such a remarkable flowering that historians have called it "the century of genius."

Progress and Pessimism

Scientists and rationalists helped greatly to establish in the minds of the educated throughout the West two complementary concepts that were to serve as the foundations of the Enlightenment of the eighteenth century: first, the concept of a "natural" order underlying the disorder and confusion of the universe as it appears to unreflecting people in their daily life; and, second, the concept of a human faculty, best called reason, which is obscured in most of humanity but can be brought into effective play by good—that is, rational—perception. Both of these concepts can be found in some form in the Western tradition at least as far back as the ancient Greeks. What gave them novelty and force at the end of the seventeenth century was their being welded into the doctrine of progress—the belief that all human beings can attain here on earth a state of happiness, of perfection, hitherto in the West generally thought to be

This is the illustration from the title page of Hobbe's *Leviathan*. While it shows the ruler in absolute control over the land, his body symbolically consists of all those individuals whose self-interest is served by their consent to accept the collective rule of the state for the general welfare. All look to him, and each loses individuality; but the mass is, nonetheless, composed of individual figures. This title page is considered to be a masterpiece, summarizing a philosopher's view in a single illustration. The Latin quotation from the book of *Job* translates, "Upon the earth there is not his like."

Hobbes's Leviathan, title page illustration

possible only in a state of grace, and then only in a heaven after death.

Not all the great minds of the seventeenth century shared this optimistic belief in progress and in the infallibility of reason. The many-sided legacy of this century of genius is evident, for example, in the contrast between two of the most important political writings issuing from the English Revolution: Thomas Hobbes's *Leviathan* and John Locke's *Second Treatise of Government*. Published in 1651 and much influenced by the disorders of the English Civil War, *Leviathan* was steeped in Machiavellian pessimism about the inherent sinfulness of human beings. The state of nature, when people live without government, is a state of war, Hobbes argued, where people prey upon each other and human life is

"solitary, poor, nasty, brutish, short." The only recourse is for people to agree among themselves to submit absolutely to the Leviathan—an all-powerful state that will force peace upon humankind.

Hobbes (1588–1679) turned the contract theory of government upside down by having people consent to give up all their liberties; Locke (1632–1704) put the contract right side up again. Locke was a close associate of the Whig leaders who engineered the Glorious Revolution. In his *Second Treatise of Government*, published in 1690 as a defense of their actions, Locke painted a generally hopeful picture of the state of nature, which suffers only from the "inconvenience" of lacking an impartial judicial authority. To secure such an authority, people contract among themselves to

THE WRITTEN RECORD

Curiosity and Change

In his *Pensées* (Thoughts), Blaise Pascal (1623-1662) remarked upon the transitions in history:

Rivers are roads which move, and which carry us whither we desire to go.

When we do not know the truth of a thing, it is of advantage that there should exist a common error which determines the mind of man, as, for example, the moon, to which is attributed the change of seasons, the progress of diseases, etc. For the chief malady of man is restless curiosity about things which he cannot understand; and it is not so bad for him to be in error as to be curious to no purpose.

───────

Blaise Pascal, *Thoughts, Letters, and Opuscules,* trans. O. W. Wight (New York: Hurt and Houghton, 1869), p. 211.

accept a government—not an omnipotent Leviathan—that respects a person's life, liberty, and property; should a king seize property by imposing unauthorized taxes, then his subjects are justified in overthrowing their monarch. Locke's relative optimism and his enthusiasm for constitutional government nourished the major current of political thought in the next century, culminating in the American and French revolutions. But events after 1789 brought Hobbesian despair and authoritarianism to the surface once more.

Meantime, exponents of the older Christian tradition continued to flourish on the Continent. One example is Blaise Pascal, a one-man personification of the complexities of the century of genius. He won an important place in the history of mathematics and physics by his work with air pressure and vacuums and, at the practical level, by his invention of the calculating machine and his establishment of the first horse-drawn bus line in Paris. Yet he was also profoundly otherworldly and became a spokesman for the high-minded, puritanical Jansenists, whose doctrines he defended with skill and fervor. He dismissed as unworthy the concepts of God as mere master geometer or engineer and sought instead for the Lord of Abraham and the Old Testament prophets. He advocated acts of charity, especially by those with wealth and status, for God's incomprehensible love had placed on them the obligation to look after the weak and poor. One night in November 1654, he underwent a great mystical experience in which he felt with absolute certainty the presence of God and of Christ. He spent his final years in religious meditation.

Another example is Baruch Spinoza (1632–1677), the century's most controversial thinker, who was the son of a Jewish merchant in Amsterdam. Spinoza tried to reconcile the God of Science and the God of Scripture. He constructed a system of ethical axioms as rigorously Cartesian and logical as a series of mathematical propositions. He also tried to reunite the Cartesian opposites—matter with mind, body with soul—by asserting that God was present everywhere and in everything. His pantheism led to his ostracism in Holland by his fellow Jews and also by the Christians, who considered him an atheist; his rejection of rationalism and materialism offended intellectuals. Spinoza found few admirers until the romantic revolt against the abstractions and oversimplifications of the Enlightenment over a century later.

Literature

Just as Henry IV, Richelieu, and Louis XIV brought greater order to French politics after the civil and religious upheavals of the sixteenth century, so the writers of the seventeenth century brought greater discipline to French writing after the Renaissance extravagance of a genius like Rabelais. It was the age of classicism, which insisted on the observance of elaborate rules, on the authority of models from classical antiquity, and on the employment of a more polite, stylized vocabulary. In the early 1600s the example of greater refinement in manners and speech was set by the circle who met in the Paris *salon* (reception room) of an aristocratic hostess, the marquise de Rambouillet (1588–1665). Later, proper behavior was standardized by the court ceremonial at Versailles, and proper vocabulary by the famous dictionary of the French language that the experts of the academy founded by Richelieu finished compiling in the 1690s, after more than half a century of labor. Nicholas Boileau (1636–1711), the chief literary critic of the day, set the rules for writing poetry with his Cartesian pronouncement, "Think well, if you wish to write well." Exaggerated notions of propriety outlawed from polite usage the French counterparts of such terms as *spit* and *vomit* and obliged writers to seek euphemisms for dozens of commonplace activities. Indeed, many of our notions of which words are vulgar or obscene derive from this time, though they were later reinforced by Victorian prudery and class concern for "nicety" in the nineteenth century. Already there were indications of the social divisions that would produce the Revolution of 1789 in the enormous gap between the classical French speech of the court and the plainer, coarser language of the average French person.

On the other hand, the linguistic standards of the seventeenth-century court also brought substantial benefits to literature. Without its discipline, French would not have won its unique reputation for clarity and elegance. The leading tragic dramatists of *le grand siècle* made observance of all the classical dos and don'ts not an end in itself but a means to probe deeply into the endless variety of human personalities. Pierre Corneille (1606–1684) and Jean Racine (1639–1699) created moving portraits of people upholding exalted ideals of honor or crushed by overwhelming emotion. The French tragedies of the seventeenth century were worthy successors to the Greek dramas of the fifth century B.C., not merely because of their classical form but also because of their powerful rhetoric, complex structure, psychological insight, and clarity of expression.

As a writer of comedies, Jean Baptiste Molière (1622–1673), the other great French dramatist of the age, was less constrained to employ a dignified vocabulary and to heed the other rules of classicism. The main characters of his satirical comedies were not only sharply etched personalities but social types as well—the overrefined pedantic ladies of the salons, the hypocrite in *Tartuffe* (1664), the ignorant and self-important newly rich in *Le Bourgeois Gentilhomme* (1670). In Molière, as in all good satire, there is more than a touch of moralizing. Didactic overtones are also present in two other characteristic works of the Great Century: the *Fables* of Jean de La Fontaine (1621–1695) reworked in lively fashion tales borrowed from antiquity; the *Maxims* of the duc de la Rochefoucauld (1613-1680) were even more disenchanted in their estimates of human nature. "Judged by most of its reactions, love is closer to hatred than to friendship." "Men would not get on for long in society if they did not fool one another." "In general, we give praise only that we may get it." But la Rochefoucauld could also write, "Perfect courage means doing unwitnessed what we would be capable of with the world looking on," and "The fame of great men should always be judged by the methods they employed to achieve it."*

Seventeenth-century English literature also had its cynics, notably William Wycherley (c. 1640–1716), William Congreve (1670–1729), and other playwrights who wrote witty, bawdy, and disillusioned Restoration comedies. Under Charles II and his successors the pendulum of public taste and morality made a particularly violent swing as a reaction to the midcentury Puritans, who had closed down the theaters as dens of sinfulness. One of those Puritans, John Milton, secretary of the council of state produced his major work of literature, *Paradise Lost* (1667), the only English epic in the grand

manner that still attracts many readers, after going blind. Though Milton was a classical scholar of great learning, his often complex style and his profound belief in Christian humanism really made him a belated representative of an earlier literary age, the last great writer of the English Renaissance.

What was needed to prepare for the classical age of English letters was the modernization of the English language by pruning the elaborate flourishes, standardizing the chaotic spelling, and eliminating the long flights of rhetoric characteristic of Elizabethan and early seventeenth-century prose. Under the influence of John Dryden (1631–1700), English began to model itself on French, adopting a straightforward word order, comparatively brief sentences, and the polish, neatness, and clarity of the French school. English letters were entering the Augustan Age, which lasted through the first half of the eighteenth century.

The Baroque Era

Baroque, the label usually applied to the arts of the seventeenth century, probably comes from the Portuguese *barroco*, "an irregular or misshapen pearl." Some critics have seized upon the suggestion of deformity to criticize the impurity of seventeenth-century art in contrast with the purity of the Renaissance. Especially among Protestants, the reputation of baroque suffered because it was identified with the Counter-Reformation and many of its leading artists appeared to be propagandists for Rome. Many viewers were also repelled by the flamboyance of baroque works.

Baroque art was closely associated with the Jesuits, with the successors of Philip II in Spain, and above all with Rome during the century following the Council of Trent. Catholic reformers enlisted the arts in propagating the faith and endowing it with greater emotional intensity. But not all the baroque masters were Catholic—Rembrandt, for instance, was a Mennonite, and Sir Christopher Wren an Anglican—nor were all their patrons Catholic prelates or grandees. Portraits of the Protestant Charles I of England brought Van Dyck fame and wealth; and in the Dutch republic, where the Calvinist churches frowned on all ornamentation, painters won support from the business community and sometimes became prosperous businessmen themselves.

The unprecedented financial success of some artists is one of the distinguishing characteristics of the baroque period. Rubens, Van Dyck, and Wren lived like lords, in contrast to the relatively austere existence of such Renaissance masters as Leonardo and Michelangelo. A second characteristic is the baroque stress on sheer size, as exemplified by the vast canvases of Rubens, the immense palace of Versailles, and Bernini's decorative canopy over the high altar in St. Peter's in Rome. A third characteristic is theatricality, as painters intensified the illusion of brilliant lighting and placed figures in the immediate foreground of a canvas to draw the spectator into the scene. A final characteristic is the realistic depiction of a wide range of humanity—clowns, beggars,

---

* *The Maxims of La Rochefoucauld*, trans. Louis Kronenberger (New York: Random House, 1959), maxims 72, 87, 146, 216, 157.

gypsies, cardsharps, cripples, and dwarfs, as well as ordinary people, praying, laughing, or eating. In France, for example, Georges de La Tour (1593–1652) took everyday subjects and people—a woman retrieving a flea as she undresses, a hurdy-gurdy player, and, at the height of the seventeenth century devotional cult of Mary Magdalen, a painting of her pensively contemplating a candle—and executed them in a nighttime setting that permitted dramatic contrasts of light and shadow.

Painting. The most restrained baroque painter was probably Diego Velásquez (1599–1660), who spent thirty-four years at the court of Philip IV of Spain. Velásquez needed all his skill to soften the receding chins and large mouths of the Habsburgs and still make his portraits of Philip IV and the royal family instantly recognizable. His greatest feat of technical wizardry is *The Maids of Honor.* A little princess, having her portrait painted, is surrounded by a pet dog, dwarfs, and other attendants; it is the moment when the royal parents are looking in on the scene, but only their reflections are seen in a mirror at the rear of the room. As Velásquez turns to greet them and looks at the viewer, the latter realizes he is standing where the royal couple must have stood. With its adroit use of mirrors, *The Maids of Honor* is a splendid example of baroque attempts to make the spectator an active participant.

Unlike the aristocratic Velásquez, the Flemish Peter Paul Rubens (1577–1640) was the baroque counterpart of the Renaissance universal man. A diplomat, a linguist, and a student of antiquity and archaeology, he amassed a fortune from his painting and collected such impressive honors as being knighted by Charles I of England and elevated to the nobility by the king of Spain. Rubens made his studio, with its two hundred students, a factory of art. He himself is estimated to have contributed to over two thousand pictures, whose subjects ranged from simple portraits to ambitious political themes. He was commissioned by Marie de' Medici, widow of Henry IV of France, to execute a series of canvases glorifying Henry and herself. As monarchs by divine right, Henry and Marie were portrayed more as mythological figures than as mere mortals.

One of Ruben's pupils was a fellow Fleming, Anthony Van Dyck (1599–1641), whose portraits of Charles I captured the casual elegance and confident authority of the Stuart monarch. Although courtly style was not highly valued by the Flemings' northern neighbors in the Netherlands, the officers of Dutch civic guards, the governing boards of guilds, and other important organizations of Dutch merchants liked to be portrayed for posterity. Dutch middle-class families favored small, cheerful pictures, preferably showing the leisure activities cherished by these hard-working people. The consequence was a veritable explosion of artistic output that coincided with the heyday of Dutch prosperity during the first two-thirds of the century. With the French invasion of the 1670s, both the economic and artistic hegemony of the Dutch began to fade.

Seventeenth-century Dutch painters were admired both for their subtle depiction of light and color in landscapes and for their realistic representations of the interiors of Dutch houses, with their highly polished or well-scrubbed floors and their strong contrasts of light and shade. The best-known baroque painters in the Netherlands were Frans Hals (c. 1580–1666) and Rembrandt Van Rijn (1606–1669). Hals used bold

Diego Velásquez painted many portraits of Spain's King Philip IV, but perhaps his most famous royal painting is *The Maids of Honour.* Here is Princess Margarita, only four years old, dressed as the times and her station required. With her are two young noblewomen, the court jester, a female dwarf, and others. The child is receiving cold, perfumed water to drink.

Museo del Prado, Madrid/Scala/Art Resource

Peter Paul Rubens (1577–1640) painted his *Massacre of the Innocents* about 1635. The painting
shows King Herod's decree that all children under age two should be killed—to eliminate the
newborn Christ—being carried out with ruthless bloodshed. But Rubens was also recording current
events, for in 1635 France prolonged the Thirty Years' War by its entry. Thus, a historical and
biblical scene, a contemporary scene, and an allegory were all represented in a single painting, for
in the background Rubens showed angels with flowers, to suggest that a heavenly hand still guided
earthly events.

Bayerischen Staats-gemäldesammlungen/München, Alte Pinakothek

strokes to paint cheerful contingents of civic guards, laughing musicians, and tavern drunks. As he aged, he himself became a chronic drinker; yet in his eighties, a penniless inmate in a poorhouse, he painted the most remarkable group portrait in baroque art—*The Women Regents of the Haarlem Hospital*, dour, formidable, and aging matrons in all their Calvinist severity.

Rembrandt, too, attained fame early, then slipped into obscurity and poverty; he documented his troubles in a series of moving self-portraits. He also executed famous group portraits—*The Night Watch* and *The Syndics of the Drapers' Guild*. Rembrandt painted an exceptional scientific subject, *The Anatomy Lesson of Dr. Tulp*, in which a physician is explaining the structure of blood vessels and tendons in the arm of an executed criminal, the only kind of cadaver available to anatomists.

Architecture and the Art of Living.   Baroque architecture and urban planning were at their most flamboyant in Rome, where Urban VIII (1623–1644) and other popes sponsored churches, palaces, gardens, fountains, avenues, and piazzas in their determination to make their capital once again the most spectacular city in Europe. St. Peter's Church, apart from Michelangelo's dome, is a legacy of the baroque rather than the Renaissance.

In the last third of the century the France of Louis XIV set the trends in architecture, landscape gardening, town planning, and furniture—especially at Versailles and in Paris. Vienna, Munich, Madrid, Warsaw, and Prague also became major baroque cities, though their styles tended to be imitative of the Italian or French. Great architectural feats sometimes took two generations or more, and the post-1630 period (known as high baroque) was marked by constant building, even in lesser cities like Würzburg or Dresden.

In England baroque building was much diluted by classicism. Under Charles II the chief architect was Sir Christopher Wren (1632–1723), a talented engineer and astronomer who was deluged with commissions after a great fire destroyed much of London in 1666. St. Paul's and the orchestra. The star system reached its height at Naples, where conservatories (originally institutions for "conserving" talented orphans) specialized in voice training. Many Neapolitan operas were loose collections of songs designed to show off the talents of the individual stars. The effect of unreality was heightened by the custom of having male roles sung by women and some female roles sung by *castrati*, male sopranos who had been castrated as young boys to prevent the onset of puberty and the deepening of their voices.

In England, Henry Purcell (c. 1659–1695), the organist of Westminster Abbey, produced a masterpiece for the

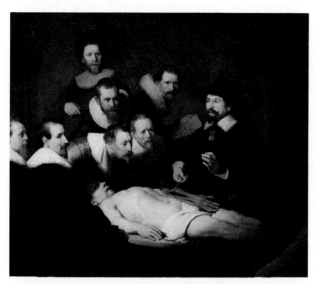

Rembrandt used light and facial expression as well as the position of the figures in his paintings to capture a sense of psychological truth. Here, in *The Anatomy Lesson of Dr. Tulp*, the first commission he completed after moving from Leiden to Amsterdam, he showed a demonstration given by the leading professor of anatomy of the time. Those around him are members of the surgeon's guild. Each figure is individually realized, as Rembrandt draws attention to the developing science of pathology.

The Mauritshuis, The Hague

In the famous St. Peter's Church at Rome, the proportions of Michelangelo's Greek-cross design were altered when a greatly lengthened nave was constructed in the early 1600s. With the vast space of the nave leading into the space beneath the dome, it was imperative to find a way of filling the latter. Urban VIII entrusted the commission to a young architect, Gian Lorenzo Bernini (1598–1680), who hit upon the ingenious solution of the *baldachin* (tabernacle), an enormously magnified and strengthened version of the canopy used to cover the sacrament. This 85-foot structure made elaborate use of the Barberini family symbols and was supposedly modeled on Solomon's Temple. To obtain bronze for the columns and canopy, Urban VIII had the bronze roof of the Pantheon—the best preserved of Rome's ancient monuments—melted down.

Saskia/Art Resource

Cathedral, in particular, drew upon Wren's capacity to fuse varying styles into a harmonious whole.

The arts of good living made substantial progress in the seventeenth century, despite the ravages of disease and famine that reduced the European population by at least 15 percent between 1648 and 1713. The expansion of Europe overseas made available the new beverages of coffee, tea, and cocoa, the new cotton fabrics, and luxuries like Chinese porcelain and lacquer ware. Exotic tropical woods were used to inlay and veneer furniture. On the whole, furniture was becoming more specialized: dining chairs replaced dining benches; chairs were made both with arms and, to accommodate hoop skirts, without. Table napkins came into use; individual plates and glasses replaced communal bowls and goblets. Families of moderate means could afford these innovations, as well as a teapot, a pitcher, and a few items of plain silver, and thus shared in what amounted to a revolution in domestic arrangements.

Music.   Baroque composers, especially in Italy, moved further along the paths laid out by their Renaissance predecessors. In Venice, Claudio Monteverdi (1567–1643) wrote the first important operas. The opera, a characteristically baroque mix of music and drama, proved so popular that Venice soon had sixteen opera houses, which focused on the fame of their chief singers rather than on the overall quality of the supporting cast

The great Piazza Obliqua was added to St. Peter's by Bernini in 1657–1666, completing a masterpiece of the baroque. This was the first large open space within a city, in contrast to the enclosed squares typical of the Renaissance, the great colonnades providing a massive space that focuses on St. Peter's itself.

New York Public Library Picture Collection

graduation exercises of a girls' school, the beautiful and moving *Dido and Aeneas*. Louis XIV, appreciating the obvious value of opera in enhancing the resplendence of his court, imported from Italy the talented Jean-Baptiste Lully (1632–1687). In his operas Lully united French and Italian musical, dance, and literary traditions, and took over the artificiality, gaiety, and weight of court ballet. No artist of the time was more representative, and none was more distant from the concerns of the people who, though they might admire the majesty of the court from a distance, could know no part in it—the common people, who saw little if any of the art and architecture, read none of the literature, and heard none of the music of baroque high society.

Social Trends

Throughout the seventeenth century the laborer, whether rural or urban, faced repeated crises of subsistence, with a general downturn beginning in 1619 and a widespread decline after 1680. Almost no region escaped plague, famine, war, depression, or even all four. Northern Europe and England suffered from a general economic depression in the 1620s; Mediterranean France and northern Italy were struck by plague in the 1630s; and a recurrent plague killed 100,000 in London in 1665.

The "little ice age"—a gradual onset of acute cold too severe for most crops—began in the late sixteenth century and made harvests unpredictable until 1650, and for a decade there was a perceptible advance of glacial ice. Population increase slowed dramatically, and general stagnation was the norm, despite important regional exceptions. Given the emphasis on high fashion at the French court, the gap between the rich and the poor was perceived as growing.

In France and Russia the sixteenth century was marked by peasant revolts. In France the revolts were directed against the tax collectors, who raised revenues "for the needs of the state"—needs that were felt to be a pretext for enriching a few private persons. The peasants especially resented the tax-farmer, who was a vigorously efficient tax collector because he kept part of what he raised. They also resented the tendency toward centralization that the new taxes, and most especially the *gabelle*, a tax on salt, represented. Peasant revolts in 1636, 1637, 1639, and 1675 underscored the general discontent.

Discontent and fear also help explain the renewal of the search for witches. Witches had once been part of the general belief in magic and religion. In the fifteenth century a substantial handbook on the detection

St. Paul's Cathedral in London, built between 1673 and 1710, became the architectural model for much public architecture well into the nineteenth century.

Joyce Photographics, Photo Researchers, Inc.

except to say that where popular magic was commonplace, so was the fear of witches. Trials also usually followed a period of fear about the future and concern over apparent changes in ordered and stable conditions. Nor were the educated spared—indeed, they were often in the lead when a community sought out a witch.

In 1691, in Massachusetts, the strange behavior of two small girls led the community of Salem into a mass witchhunt that did not stop until twenty persons had been executed. Some historians believe the hallucinations of the children thought to be under the influence of witches were induced by ergot poisoning from a fungus that grows on barley in a moist season. Elsewhere fertility cults were accused of performing black magic. In southern France witchcraft may simply have been a form of rural social revolt in which the Mass could be mocked and the church hierarchy challenged.

The clergy did not have all the needed answers for the peasant, and were often challenged by astrologers, village wizards, "cunning folk." Popular magic often seemed to provide a more ready remedy for illness, theft, unhappy personal relationships, or a world in which meanings were shifting. In the seventeenth century magic declined in relation to religion; increased popular literacy, improved communications, the slow recognition that diseases such as epilepsy were open to human investigation instead of partaking of the supernatural, the failures of divination, and perhaps reaction against the horrors of the witchcraft craze, all contributed to the turn toward rationalism that occurred first in the cities.

Still, there was continuity amid change. The old traditional rhythms continued in marriage, childrearing, death, and burial. As feast and famine alternated, people continued to try to explain insecurity, sought for stability, and realized that their lives were racked by events not only beyond their control but beyond their understanding. These fears were also true of the upper classes. Indeed, in some matters the lower classes had more control over their lives. The children of those who owned no property were freer to choose a spouse, since their parents had little economic leverage over them, having nothing to bequeath to them, than were the children of the aristocracy, who had to make carefully calculated marriage alliances to hold on to or increase family property.

By the seventeenth century the position of women with respect to property was improving. On the Continent perhaps 20 percent of families had daughters and no sons; when women inherited land, the social implications were far reaching, since ownership might pass to a different family at every generation. By the eighteenth century the "female presence" in landholding had become very important in England, finally matching the position women had held in ancient Sparta and Crete. Marriages were thereby encouraged between persons of similar status and wealth, hardening class lines. The marriage of a widow had become of great importance to her adult children, since it would influence the estate.

and interrogation of witches had been widely read, and by 1669 it was in its twenty-ninth edition. Witchcraft combined sorcery and heresy; the first was to be feared and the second condemned. Though skeptics and rationalists doubted the existence of witches or the Devil, theologians and the great mass of people did not. Moreover, both law and medicine accepted the existence of witchcraft.

Between 1580 and 1650 witchcraft trials were commonplace; there probably were nearly 100,000 such trials, amounting to epidemics of mass hysteria. Even in England, where the common law prohibited torture to extract confessions, there were over a thousand trials. The great majority of the prosecutions were of women at a time of growing sexual tension. Although concern about witches was almost universal, the greatest number of executions took place in Calvinist areas. Historians are not agreed on why an outbreak of witch persecutions would occur in one place rather than another—in Scotland and New England, in Switzerland and France—

THE WRITTEN RECORD

Who Built the Towers of Thebes?

In the seventeenth century the underclasses, that unspoken for and, for the historian who relies solely on written records, unspeaking mass of humankind, began to speak and to answer the questions posed in the twentieth century by a radical German dramatist and poet, Bertolt Brecht (1898-1956):

Who built Thebes of the seven gates?
In the books you will find the names of kings.
Did the kings haul up the lumps of rock?
And Babylon, many times demolished
Who raised it up so many times? In what houses
Of gold-glittering Lima did the builders live?
Where, the evening that the Wall of China was
finished
Did the masons go? Great Rome
Is full of triumphal arches. Who erected them?
Over whom
Did the Caesars triumph? Had Byzantium, much
praised in song
Only palaces for its inhabitants? Even in fabled
Atlantis
The night the ocean engulfed it
The drowning still bawled for their slaves.
The young Alexander conquered India.

Was he alone?
Caesar beat the Gauls.
Did he not have even a cook with him?
Philip of Spain wept when his armada
Went down. Was he the only one to weep?
Frederick the Second won the Seven Years' War.
Who Else won It?
Every page a victory.
Who cooked the feast for the victors?
Every ten years a great man.
Who paid the bill?
So many reports.
So many questions.

Bertolt Brecht, "Questions from a Worker Who Reads," trans. Michael Hamburgh, in *Bertolt Brecht Poems,* ed. John Willett and Ralph Manheim (London: Eyre Methuen, 1976), pp. 252–53.

When they were excluded from the land, younger children had to be given an equivalent share in some other way. Thus the custom grew of a younger son's buying a commission in the army, or entering the church, or joining the faculty of a university, or being given a stake in business. However, since the family name remained attached to the land, the aristocracy remained one of land rather than of wealth or of intelligence, so that being a "counter jumper" (a merchant, or "in trade") might lead to far more income but much less prestige. Since common people were unlikely to be able to break into the aristocracy of prestige, successful commoners cast their lot with the merchant class and with capitalism, which was increasingly open to talent rather than to inherited wealth.

Increasingly, the law was used to hold society in balance: to keep people in their place, to assure that the poor did not poach upon the land of the rich, to define acts of social unrest as crimes. The growth in individualism—whether among contributors to the "century of genius" or among those who emerged from "Everyman"—led to greater variation in human behavior. As a result, there was a perceived need to use laws to define appropriate behavior, with greater interference by the state (as well as the church) in matters relating to sexuality, bastardy, and marriage. Mere nakedness was not yet considered indecent, nor was drunkenness thought to be a public vice. Destruction of the family unit, however, by failing to observe the laws of inheritance was a clear offense against continuity and propriety. It remained one small area of stability that rich and poor could, to some extent, control.

Perhaps we speak today of the seventeenth century as the "century of genius" because so much that is still central to our thought—in politics, economics, literature, art, and science—can be traced most immediately to the great thinkers of that century. But the seventeenth century was also the century of the inarticulate, of the far-less-than-great, of common people who labored for themselves, their families, their church, and, often and increasingly, for their nation. The Fronde was not a popular uprising, but there were many peasant revolts in the seventeenth century and thereafter. The English Civil War was not a "war of people," but the people were intimately touched by its events.

"The past is a foreign country: they do things differently there."* The past summarized so scantily in this volume is indeed, to the twentieth century, a vast foreign land—more different by virtue of the distance of time than modern countries may be from one another despite the distances imposed by language and technology. In 1513 Niccolò Machiavelli had written in *The*

---

* From the twentieth-century English novelist L. P. Hartley *The Go-Between* (London: Harnish Hamilton, 1953), p. 9.

Prince, "There is nothing more difficult to take in hand, more perilous to conduct, or more uncertain in its success, than to take the lead in the introduction of a new order of things." Soon the introduction of new orders of things would become frequent, even seem commonplace, as the pace of known history—of recorded events that bear directly upon our understanding of the present—speeded up dramatically. To tread on the dust of the past, as the early nineteenth-century English poet Lord Byron wrote, is to feel the earthquake waiting below.

SUMMARY

The seventeenth century was dominated by France. During the reign of Louis XIII, Cardinal Richelieu created an efficient centralized state. He eliminated the Huguenots as a political force, made nobles subordinate to the king, and made the monarchy absolute. Louis XIV built on these achievements during his long reign. Louis XIV moved his capital from the turbulence of Paris to Versailles, where he built a vast palace and established elaborate court rituals that further limited the power of the nobles.

From Versailles, the Sun King demanded unquestioning obedience from his subjects, seeing himself as the representative of God on earth and ruling by divine right. In religion, Louis XIV encouraged the evolution of the Gallican church. In 1685, he revoked the Edict of Nantes, ending toleration of Huguenots. Mercantilism, practiced by Colbert, was central to French economic policy. Colbert's policies promoted foreign trade and the expansion of industry.

Hoping to expand France to its "natural frontiers," Louis XIV pursued an aggressive foreign policy that embroiled the nation in numerous wars. In the War of the Spanish Succession (1701–1714), England, Holland, the Holy Roman Empire, and German states joined forces to prevent a union of Spain and France. The treaties of Utrecht (1713) preserved the balance of power in Europe but left many unresolved issues.

In England, the Stuart monarchs James I and Charles I violated traditions limiting royal authority and protecting individual rights. Their attempts to rule without Parliament brought matters to violent conflict between the Crown and the members of Parliament. During the Civil War (1640–1649), England was split between royalists and parliamentarians. Under Puritan leader Oliver Cromwell, the New Model Army decisively defeated the king. Radicals in the Rump Parliament tried and condemned the king to death in 1649.

During the Interregnum, England was a republic dominated by Oliver Cromwell and the Puritans. They faced opposition at home and abroad. In 1660, the monarchy was restored. But the Interregnum marked the first successful challenge to a monarch by a politically active citizenry. Moreover, the events of the Civil War affirmed the existence of an unwritten constitution rooted in English common law. Belief in freedom of speech and religious toleration also emerged in this period.

During the Restoration, Parliament was supreme. The Catholic sympathies of James II so alienated his subjects that he was toppled by the Glorious Revolution of 1688, which put William of Orange and Mary on the throne. Parliament then enacted the Bill of Rights of 1689, which embodied the principles of parliamentary supremacy. In the next two hundred years, England would become a parliamentary democracy.

The seventeenth century was an age of intellectual ferment dominated by France, Holland, and England. Two concepts underlay thought: the idea of a natural order and the importance of reason. In England, Thomas Hobbes in *Leviathan* (1651) and John Locke in his *Second Treatise of Government* (1690) set out ideas on government and human nature that would greatly influence political thought. On the Continent, Pascal and Spinoza made equally significant contributions to Western thought.

During the Age of Classicism, French dramatists such as Corneille, Molière, and Racine dominated literature just as the court of Louis XIV influenced all of Europe. In *Paradise Lost*, John Milton combined classical scholarship and profound Christian faith.

Baroque masters produced flamboyant works of art that emphasized size and theatricality. Flemish and Dutch painters including Rubens, Rembrandt, and Van Dyck won widespread acclaim.

In the seventeenth century, laborers faced hardships of plague, famine, and warfare. An epidemic of witch-hunts and witch trials reflected a pervasive fear. Yet belief in popular magic declined as literacy spread. The property rights of women were recognized, thereby helping to improve their position. Despite gradual change, traditional patterns of life continued, and law was used to affirm social rights and traditions.

CRITICAL THINKING

1. What is meant by "divine-right monarchy" and what were the principal challenges to it?

2. What problems are posed for a society when someone claims to be in a position of authority by divine right? What are the strengths and weaknesses of social or political governance by divine right?

3. Discuss the importance of Richelieu and Mazarin to the development of the theory of royal absolutism.

4. How did the policies of Louis XIII and Louis XIV compare?

5. What was mercantilism and how did it influence state formation, royal absolutism, and the economy?

6. What distinguished Stuart England from Tudor England?

7. What were the causes and consequences of the English Civil War?

8. Why was the "Glorious Revolution" called "glorious"?

9. What sets Baroque art, architecture, and music apart from other expressions of art, architecture, and music at other times?

10. Account for the apparent contradiction in referring to the seventeenth century as both a "century of genius" and a "century of everyman"?

The Old Regimes

HE TERM *OLD REGIME* IS used to describe the institutions prevailing in Europe, and especially in France, before 1789. This was the "Old Regime" of the eighteenth century, in contrast to the "New Regime" that was to issue from the French Revolution. On the surface, the Old Regime followed the pattern of the Middle Ages, though the forces that were to transform the economy, society, and politics of modern Europe were already at work. To be sure, the economy was still largely agrarian, for most Europeans lived in farming villages and retained the localized outlook of the peasant.

The social foundations of the Old Regime rested on the medieval division of society into the first estate of the clergy, the second estate of the nobility, and the third estate of the commoners, which included the urban bourgeoisie and working people as well as the peasantry. Within the third estate, only those at the top exerted much political influence—well-to-do business leaders in England and Holland, French lawyers or merchants wealthy enough to purchase government office, women who had married well or who had the ear of the influential people who attended their salons. Every government in Europe tended to represent the interests of the few rather than the many. In this respect, it made little difference whether it was an absolute monarchy like France or Prussia, a developing constitutional monarchy like Britain, or a republic like the Dutch United Provinces.

As the eighteenth century advanced, the political and social status quo came under increasing attack from the leaders of the intellectual movement known as the Enlightenment (see Chapter 17). The economic foundations of the Old Regime were eroding under the pressure of revolutionary change, and the balance of power achieved by the Utrecht settlement was undermined. The defeat and death of Louis XIV did not end the worldwide rivalry of England and France. Meanwhile, further shifts in the international balance resulted from the appearance of two important newcomers: Russia and the German state of Brandenburg-Prussia.

A CLOSER LOOK

The Coffeehouse

The thriving maritime trade changed public taste, as it brought a variety of new produce into the British and Continental markets. Dramatic examples are the rise of the coffeehouse and the drinking of tea at home. In the seventeenth and early eighteenth centuries the coffeehouse was referred to as the "penny university," for the price of entry, which was a penny (and two pennies extra for the coffee itself), admitted one to a room where the daily newspaper could be found and where animated political discussion was taking place. The Turks had called coffeehouses "schools of the wise," and the tendency for them to become centers for subversion led the Russians to attempt to suppress them.

In 1675 England's Charles II tried to close coffeehouses, acting upon the pretext that coffee was injurious to health, as a pamphlet, *The Women's Petition against Coffee, representing to public consideration the grand inconveniences accruing to their sex from the excessive use of the drying and enfeebling liquor*, had argued. In truth, as his proclamation showed, Charles was more concerned that "in such Houses . . . divers False, Malitious and Scandalous Reports are devised and spread abroad, to the Defamation of his Majestie's Government, and to the Disturbance of the Peace and Quiet of the Realm." Eleven days later the king withdrew the edict of prohibition on the grounds of "royal compassion." Until the end of the reigns of the early Georges, the coffeehouse, at least in London, remained a male social center; in Queen Anne's time there were five hundred such houses.

In Ned Ward's *Wealthy Shopkeeper*, published in 1706, a typical day of a well-to-do Londoner was laid out:

Rise at 5; counting-house till 8; then breakfast on toast and Cheshire cheese; in his shop for two hours then a neighbouring coffee house for news; shop again, till dinner at home (over the shop) at 12 on a "thundering joint"; 1 o'clock on Change; 3, Lloyd's Coffee House for business; shop again for an hour; then another coffee house (not Lloyd's) for recreation, followed by "sack shop" to drink with acquaintances, till home for a "light supper" and so to bed, "before Bow Bell rings nine."

G. M. Trevelyan, *Illustrated English Social History*, Vol. III: *Eighteenth Century* (London: Longmans, Green, 1951), p. 30.

THE ECONOMIC "REVOLUTIONS"

The changes that undermined the Old Regime were most evident in western Europe. They were in some respects economic revolutions. In the eighteenth century the pace of economic change was slower than it would be in the nineteenth or twentieth, and it provided less drama than such political upheavals as the American and French revolutions. Yet in the long run the consequences of the economic "revolutions" were fully as revolutionary as were the political and social ones of 1776 and 1789.

Commerce and Finance, 1713–1745

Many of the basic institutions of European business life had developed before 1715—banks and insurance firms in the Renaissance, for example, and chartered trading companies in the sixteenth century. Mercantilism had matured in the Spain of Philip II, in the France of Louis XIV and Colbert, and in Britain between 1651 and the early eighteenth century. The steady growth of seaborne trade, stimulated by an increasing population and a rising demand for food and goods, was a main force in quickening the pace of commerce.

The growing maritime trade increased the demand for insurance of ships and cargoes. In London early in the century marine insurance brokers gathered at Edward Lloyd's coffeehouse in Lombard Street to discuss business, news, and politics. Thus was born Lloyd's of London, a firm that developed the standard form of policy for marine insurance and published the first detailed and accurate shipping newspaper. Another great London institution to emerge from the informal atmosphere of the coffeehouse was the stock exchange.

Marine insurance prospered in part because improved charts and the installation of lighthouses and buoys made navigation safer. Captains could determine their geographical position at sea by using two new instruments, the sextant and the chronometer. The sextant, an

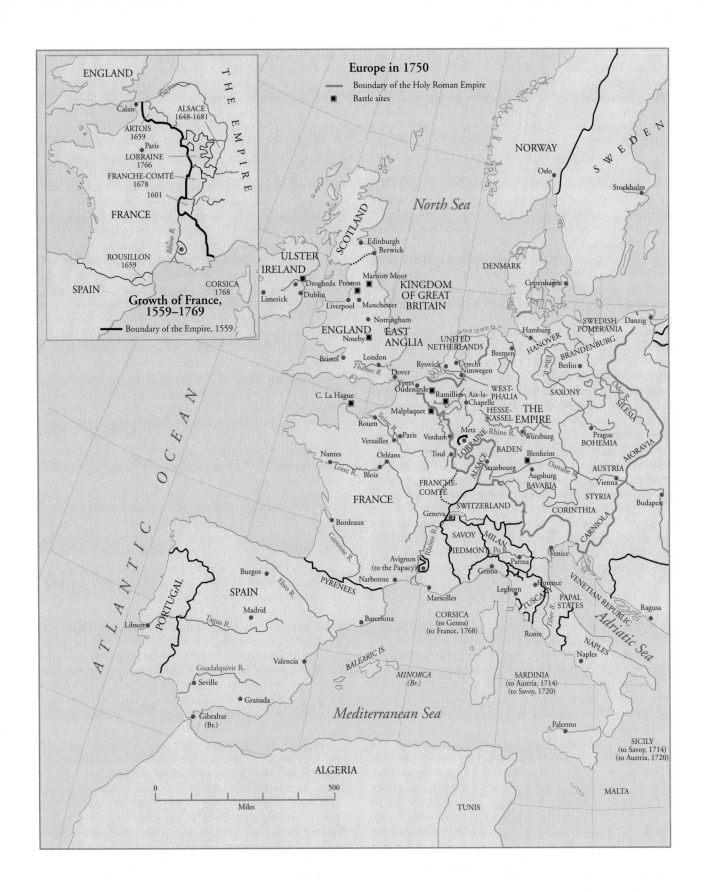

Europe in 1750

— Boundary of the Holy Roman Empire

■ Battle sites

Growth of France, 1559–1769

— Boundary of the Empire, 1559

ENGLAND

THE EMPIRE

Calais

ALSACE 1648–1681

ARTOIS 1659

Paris

LORRAINE 1766

FRANCHE-COMTÉ 1678

1601

FRANCE

Rhône R.

ROUSILLON 1659

SPAIN

CORSICA 1768

NORWAY

Oslo

SWEDEN

Stockholm

North Sea

DENMARK

Copenhagen

SCOTLAND

Edinburgh

Berwick

ULSTER

IRELAND

Drogheda

Dublin

Limerick

Preston

Marston Moor

Liverpool

Manchester

KINGDOM OF GREAT BRITAIN

Nottingham

ENGLAND

Naseby

EAST ANGLIA

Bristol

London

Thames R.

Dover

Hamburg

Bremen

SWEDISH POMERANIA

Danzig

HANOVER

BRANDENBURG

Berlin

Elbe R.

Oder R.

SILESIA

UNITED NETHERLANDS

Ryswick

Utrecht

Nimwegen

WEST-PHALIA

SAXONY

MORAVIA

C. La Hague

Ypres

Oudenarde

Ramillies

Aix-la-Chapelle

HESSE-KASSEL

THE EMPIRE

Würzburg

Prague

BOHEMIA

Malplaquet

Rouen

Seine R.

Paris

Verdun

Metz

Rhine R.

Versailles

LORRAINE

Toul

ALSACE

BADEN

Blenheim

Danube R.

AUSTRIA

Vienna

Nantes

Orléans

Strasbourg

Augsburg

BAVARIA

STYRIA

ATLANTIC OCEAN

FRANCE

Loire R.

Blois

FRANCHE-COMTÉ

Geneva

SWITZERLAND

CORINTHIA

CARNIOLA

Budapest

Bordeaux

Garonne R.

Rhône R.

SAVOY

MILAN

PIEDMONT

Po R.

Parma

Venice

VENETIAN REPUBLIC

Adriatic Sea

Avignon (to the Papacy)

Genoa

Burgos

Ebro R.

PYRENEES

Narbonne

Leghorn

Florence

TUSCANY

Ragusa

PORTUGAL

SPAIN

Madrid

Marseilles

CORSICA (to Genoa) (to France, 1768)

PAPAL STATES

Tiber R.

Lisbon

Tagus R.

Rome

NAPLES

Naples

Valencia

BALEARIC IS.

MINORCA (Br.)

Guadalquivir R.

Seville

Granada

SARDINIA (to Austria, 1714) (to Savoy, 1720)

Gibraltar (Br.)

Barcelona

Mediterranean Sea

Palermo

ALGERIA

SICILY (to Savoy, 1714) (to Austria, 1720)

0   500

Miles

MALTA

TUNIS

elaboration of the telescope, showed the altitude of the sun at noon and thus indicated the ship's latitude. The chronometer, a clock unaffected by the motion of the ship, was kept on Greenwich mean time (the time at the meridian running through Greenwich, near London). The two new instruments also made it possible to calculate the ship's longitude.

On land, improvements in communication and transport came much more slowly. Except for the relatively good highways of France, European roads were scarcely more than wide paths. The shipments of goods overland remained slow, unsafe, and expensive until after 1750, when the construction of turnpikes and canals gradually improved the situation.

Business people faced the handicaps imposed by restrictive guild regulations, by the many different coins, weights, and measures, and by the numerous local tolls. Sweden, for example, minted only copper money, including a coin weighing 43 pounds. Baden, one of the smaller German states, had 112 separate measures for length, 65 for dry goods, 123 for liquids, and 163 for cereals, not to mention 80 different pound weights. Even in France, a relative model for uniformity and centralization, all sorts of local taxes and other obstacles to internal trade persisted.

The survival of local vested interests showed the limitations of the power of the mercantilist state. Although mercantilism required the regulation of trade on a national basis, no eighteenth-century government had the staff needed to make national regulation effective. Austria, Prussia, and some other German states endeavored to assimilate mercantilism into a more systematized policy called *cameralism* (from *camera*, the council or chamber dealing with expenditures and income). Their main effort was directed toward planning state budgets, especially the increase of revenues. Other states often relied heavily on private companies and individuals to execute economic policies.

Thus the English and Dutch East India companies exercised not only a trading monopoly in their colonial preserves but also virtual sovereign powers, including the right to maintain soldiers and conduct diplomacy. Inventors worked on their own, not in government facilities. On the whole, private initiative accomplished more than governments did, though it could also get out of control, as demonstrated by two speculative booms early in the century—the Mississippi Bubble in France and the South Sea Bubble in England.

In 1715 hardly a state in Europe could manage the large debts that had piled up during the recent wars. Yet all of them had to find some way of meeting at least part of the large annual interest on bonds and other obligations or else go bankrupt. The governments of France and England transferred the management of state debts to joint-stock companies, which they rewarded for their risk taking with trading concessions. The commerce of the companies, it was hoped, would prove so lucrative that their profits would cover the interest charges on government bonds.

John Law (1671–1729), a Scottish mathematical wizard and financier, presided over the experiment in France. Law asserted that the limited supply of silver and gold made it difficult to increase the amount of *specie* (coined money) circulating in any country, and therefore made it difficult to promote business. Paper money, Law concluded, was the solution—paper money backed by a nation's wealth in land and trade.

The death of Louis XIV gave Law his opportunity. The regent for Louis XV, the duke of Orléans, permitted Law to set up a central bank in Paris. Whereas the value of French money had been sinking as the government progressively debased the coinage, Law's bank issued paper notes of stable value. Business activity at once increased. Next, Law set up the Compagnie des Indies, commonly called the Mississippi Company, which received a monopoly of commerce to and from the Louisiana colony.

Law's system reached to almost every corner of the French economy. Merging with the royal bank, his company took over the government debt and agreed to accept government bonds in partial payment for shares of Mississippi stock. Many bondholders responded enthusiastically to Law's offer. Law, however, had to sell additional shares of Mississippi stock to obtain sufficient working capital for his company. To attract cash purchasers, he promoted a boom in Mississippi stock. Investors caught the fever of speculation, and by the close of 1719 Mississippi stock was selling at forty times its par value.

The Mississippi Bubble soon burst. As the price of Mississippi shares rose higher and higher, cautious investors decided to cash in. They sold their shares, received payment in banknotes, then took the notes to Law's bank and demanded their redemption in specie. The bank exhausted its reserves of gold and silver and suspended specie payments in February 1720. Law was forced to resign in May 1720; he fled France shortly thereafter.

Within a few weeks of Law's resignation the South Sea Bubble burst in London. Management of the English government's debt had been assigned to the Bank of England. Founded in 1694 as a private institution, the bank issued notes and performed other services for the government during the last wars against Louis XIV; but in negotiations for the privilege of managing the debt, the bank was outbid by the new South Sea Company, which paid the government an exorbitant sum. The resources of the company were slim, consisting largely of the right to exploit the trading concessions that Britain obtained at the end of the War of the Spanish Succession. These privileges were limited to furnishing Spain's American colonies with forty-eight hundred slaves annually and sending one ship a year to Panama for general trade.

The South Sea Company invited government creditors to transfer their bonds into company stock. The directors of the company bought and sold shares in secret to create a more lively market, encouraged purchases of stock with a down payment of only 10 percent in cash, and spread reports of forthcoming sailings by the company's ships on voyages that did not take place. The gullibility of the investing public, though remarkable, was not inexhaustible. South Sea shares fell; Parliament ordered an investigation and, to protect the company's creditors, seized the estates of its directors, who had in the meantime destroyed the company's books and fled the country.

The bubbles were an extreme instance of the economic growing pains suffered as Europe groped for solutions to new and baffling financial problems. Law's system released French business from the depression induced by the defeats of Louis XIV. It also stimulated settlement in Louisiana. The Mississippi Company, reorganized after 1720, consistently made a large profit. In England the strongest institutions rode out the bursting of the South Sea Bubble; the East India Company continued to pay an annual dividend of 5 to 10 percent, and the Bank of England again became the financial mainstay of the realm.

In the political shakeup following the collapse of the Bubble, the Whig statesman Robert Walpole (1676–1745) came to power with a program of honoring the debt as a *national* debt. This was a novel concept in an age when most states treated their debts as the monarch's personal obligation. No subsequent stock crisis assumed the proportions of that of 1720, and thereafter British banking grew rapidly and on a stable foundation.

Agricultural Improvements

The agricultural revolution—the second force transforming the modern economy—centered on improvements that enabled fewer farmers to produce more crops. The Netherlands were the leaders, producing the highest yields per acre while also pioneering in the culture of new crops like the potato, the turnip, and clover. Turnips furnished feed for livestock until the spring pasturing season began, thus eliminating the necessity for massive slaughtering of stock at the onset of winter. Clover, by fixing nitrogen in the soil, increased the fertility of the land and ended the need to have fields lie fallow every third year. Livestock breeding was also improved.

In England the new crops were taken up by Lord ("Turnip") Townshend (1674–1738), whose plan for a four-year rotation—planting a field in turnips, barley, clover, and wheat in successive years—became standard on many English estates. Jethro Tull (1674–1741) adapted French methods to the grain fields of England. In place of the inefficient custom of scattering seed broadcast, he planted it deep in regular rows with a horse-drawn hoe. The improvements of Tull and Townshend won enthusiastic praise from Arthur Young (1741–1820), who published lengthy reports on his frequent trips through the farming districts of Britain and the Continent. Young won an international following that included George III, George Washington, the marquis de Lafayette, and Catherine the Great.

The agricultural revolution of the eighteenth century came close to ending wholesale famines in Europe, even if it did not prevent recurring food shortages. It also marked an important stage in the gradual shift from the largely self-sufficient manor of the Middle Ages to the capitalist farm producing specialized crops. The "improving landlords" needed large amounts of capital and large plots of land that were not subdivided or otherwise used

in common by many farmers. There was a mounting demand that common fields be fenced off as the private lands of single landlords. Enclosures, which in Tudor England were introduced to extend sheep pastures, were now sought to increase cropland.

Enclosure created large farms well suited to drill-planting, horse-hoeing, and crop rotation, but it also created widespread social misery. The development of large estates ruined many small farmers, or yeomen, who could not survive without the right to use common lands, and who could not afford to buy tools and install fences. Many of them became hired hands on big farms or sought work in the expanding towns. Some became poachers, illegally taking game from the great estates. In 1723 Parliament passed the Waltham Black Act, which was aimed at controlling new crimes that were, in effect, socially defined, such as being armed with weapons and appearing in forests or enclosed lands with faces blackened, which was taken as evidence of the intention to steal or kill animals, to take crops or wood, or to set fire to the property of the owners.

The Beginnings of the Industrial Revolution, to 1789

By increasing productivity and at the same time releasing part of the farm labor force for other work, the revolution in agriculture contributed to that in industry. Industry also required raw materials, markets, and capital to finance the building and equipping of factories. Thus the prosperity of commerce also nourished the growth of industry.

The first major changes were in textile manufacture, where the making of yarn and cloth had long been organized under the *domestic system*, in which spinners and weavers worked at home with wheels and looms. Often they did not buy their own raw materials or market their finished products, but worked as wage-laborers for someone who furnished the raw materials and sold the finished products. In other industries, however, production was sometimes organized in simple factories, which brought together many laborers in a large workshop. These factories were particularly common in enterprises requiring close supervision for reasons of state, like cannon foundries, or because they used expensive materials, like gold or silver threads for luxury cloth.

The industrial revolution made the domestic system obsolete and transformed the early factory system. Machines superseded the spinning wheel, hand loom, and other hand tools, and water or steam replaced human muscle and animal energy as the chief source of power. Because power-driven machines were often cumbersome and complicated, larger factories were needed to house them.

Coal mining was becoming a big business, largely because of increased demand for coke by iron smelters, which had previously used charcoal to make ore into iron. Ordinary coal could not replace charcoal as smelter fuel because the chemicals in coal made the iron too brittle.

James Hargreave's spinning jenny revolutionized the textile industry. Put into use about 1764, it rapidly increased the production of thread. It also assured women a place in the work force, a boon at first to hard-pressed families.

Culver Pictures, Inc.

The Darby family of Shropshire discovered how to remove the chemical impurities from coal by an oven process that converted it into coke. The Darbys and other private firms were the pioneers in metallurgy.

The revolution in textiles focused on the cheaper production of cotton cloth. The flying shuttle, a technical device first applied to the hand loom in England (1733), enabled a single weaver to do the work that had previously required the services of two. Looms equipped with the flying shuttle used up the supply of hand-spun thread so rapidly that a private organization, the London Society for the Encouragement of Arts, Manufacturers and Commerce, offered a prize for improving the spinning process. James Hargreaves (d. 1778) won the prize in 1764 with his spinning jenny, a series of wheels geared together to make eight threads simultaneously. Soon the jenny was adapted to water power, and its output was increased to more than a hundred threads at once. The eventual emancipation of industry from dependence on unreliable water power was foreshadowed in the 1760s when the Scotsman James Watt (1736–1819) introduced the steam engine.

Although Britain had nearly 150 cotton mills in 1789, woolens and dozens of other basic commodities were still made by hand. Full industrial development would not occur until the canals and railroads permitted cheap transport of heavy freight and until shortages of capital and skilled labor were overcome. The difficulty of making precisely machined parts for Watt's engine delayed its production in large quantities. Although the eighteenth century had taken many of the initial steps in the industrial revolution, it remained for the next century to apply them on a truly revolutionary scale.

THE ESTABLISHED POWERS

Britain and France were the dominant European powers of the eighteenth century. At the beginning of the century Spain was still powerful, though it would decline throughout the century. The Dutch remained prosperous, while the once-powerful Swedes declined even further. Economic change was the touchstone.

Britain, 1714–1760

In the eighteenth century British merchants outdistanced their old trading rivals, the Dutch, and gradually took the lead over their new competitors, the French. Judged by the touchstones of mercantilism—commerce, colonies, and sea power—Britain was the strongest state in Europe. The British colonial empire, however, was not a mercantilist undertaking in the fullest sense. Supervision of the colonies rested with the Board of Trade, which followed a policy of "salutary neglect." In the long run, salutary neglect did not satisfy the colonists, who found British policy neither salutary nor neglectful, but in the short run it promoted the colonists' prosperity and self-reliance.

The Royal Navy enjoyed the assets of a disciplined officer corps and more ships than any other power possessed. Future captains went to sea at the age of sixteen or even younger and passed through long practical training before receiving commissions. Britain had a two-to-one advantage over France in number of warships, a six-to-one lead in merchant ships, and a ten-to-one lead in total number of experienced seamen, merchant and naval. In wartime the fleet could draw on the merchant marine for additional sailors and auxiliary vessels.

The British army, by contrast, was neither large nor impressive. Its officers were reputed to be the worst in Europe, and many of its soldiers were mercenaries from the German state of Hesse-Cassel, or Hessians. Neglect of the army was a deliberate decision. The British Isles were relatively safe from invasion; moreover, the English people feared a standing army as an instrument of potential absolutism.

The Glorious Revolution, which had done much to confirm distrust of the army, had also confirmed the supremacy of Parliament. Parliament had approved the accession of William and Mary in place of James II. When Anne, Mary's sister and the last Stuart monarch, died in 1714, Parliament had already arranged for the succession of the house of Hanover.

Under the first kings of the new house—George I (r. 1714–1727) and George II (r. 1727–1760)—the cabinet was only starting to gain authority. George I and George II by no means abdicated all the old royal prerogatives. They often intervened in the conduct of war and diplomacy. They chose their cabinet ministers from the Whig party, then in control of the Commons. They did so, however, not because they were required to, but because it suited their convenience and because they distrusted the Tories, some of whom were involved in Jacobite plots to restore to the throne the descendants of James II (Jacobite from *Jacobus*, Latin for "James").

From 1721 to 1742 Robert Walpole, who led the Whigs in the Commons, headed the cabinet; he was in fact prime (or first) minister, although the title was still unofficial. Walpole was a master politician who maintained his majority in the Commons by skillful manipulation. The task was not easy, for party discipline did not yet exist. The terms *Whig* and *Tory* referred to shifting interest groups, not to parties in a formal sense.

Under the first two Georges the Whigs were a coalition of landed and "funded" gentry—that is, of nobles and squires from the country and of business and professional men from London and provincial towns. The Whigs thus renewed a political alliance that had first appeared in the later Middle Ages when the knights of the shire had joined the burgesses to form the Commons. Family ties, common political aims, and common respect for property bound together the rural and urban Whigs.

What did terms like *gentry* and *squire* connote about social class in the eighteenth century? Historians generally agree that they referred to a class just below the titled nobility. The ranks of the gentry included the younger sons of nobles, technically not nobles themselves since a seat in the House of Lords passed only to the eldest son. They also included other owners of landed estates, all of whom were addressed verbally as "sir" and in writing as "Esquire." Historically, the gentry lived off the revenues of landed property, but by the eighteenth century many of them also had a stake in commerce. Successful businessmen sometimes bought country estates, set themselves up as gentlemen, and were often accepted as such by the local gentry. This intermingling of country gentlemen with men of business and the intermarriage of the two classes demonstrated that Britain was experiencing greater social mobility than were the states of the Old Regime on the Continent.

In its social and political structure the Britain of Walpole was not democratic. Only gentlemen could hope to rise in the professions, to become army and navy officers, lawyers, clergymen, and physicians. In local affairs the landed gentry alone supplied the justices of the peace, who presided over courts, fixed wage scales, superintended the relief of the poor, maintained bridges and highways, and defended the propertied classes. Until the 1740s only gentlemen had the right to vote for members of Parliament. The small number of voters in many constituencies encouraged corruption, particularly in the "rotten" or "pocket" boroughs, which had such a tiny electorate that control of their vote reposed in the "pocket" of some wealthy lord.

Thus the ruling classes governed the generally voteless masses. London was already big enough to have slums, crimes of violence, and traffic jams—accompanied by an almost complete lack of police and fire protection. Children generally began to work when they were eight years old. Yet the British ruling classes, selfish and narrow though they often were, had at their best a sense of public spirit and civic-mindedness toward the less fortunate. Furthermore, the memory of Cromwell's rebellion and the recurrent food riots because of the effects of the enclosure movement also provided sharp incentives for the nobility to maintain political control.

France, 1715–1774

Where Britain was strong, France was weak. Barriers to social mobility were more difficult to surmount, though commoners who were rich or aggressive enough did overcome them. France suffered particularly from the rigidity of its colonial system, the inferiority of its navy refused to allow the colonies administrative control of their own affairs. The numerous controls stifled the initiative of the colonists. The mother country, however, prospered, as commercial activity doubled in the ports and refineries were set up to process the raw sugar imported from the plantations of Guadeloupe and Martinique.

The French navy needed greater resources and better leadership. Since Dutch and British vessels carried much of French commerce, the merchant marine was small. French naval officers, rigorously trained in the classroom, lacked the practical experience gained by captains with a lifetime at sea.

French rulers neglected the navy in favor of the army, since France was, above all, a land power, and its vulnerable northeastern frontier invited invasion. However, the troops were poorly trained, and the organization was top-heavy; there was one officer to fifteen men, compared with one to thirty-five in the more efficient Prussian army. Many aristocratic officers regarded a commission as simply a convenient way of increasing their personal wealth.

Both the navy and the army were reformed after the defeats suffered by France in the Seven Years' War (1756–1763). The number of warships was increased, the army officer corps was cleared of much deadwood, and more aggressive military tactics were introduced. These improvements accounted in part for the excellent showing made by France in the American Revolutionary War and in the military campaigns resulting from its own revolution. They came too late, however, to save the vanishing prestige of the Old Regime.

The Old Regime was weakest in the monarchy itself. The duke of Orléans, regent from 1715 to 1723, gambled with the nation's treasury. He tried to get the nobility to play an active role in government, but the nobles, who had been reduced by Louis XIV to ceremonial roles, lacked the knowledge and ability to apply themselves to the daily routine of government. The French second estate had, it seemed, outlived its usefulness.

William Hogarth was especially known for his satirical view of the political and social customs of the English. He intended to be a silversmith but became an engraver of satirical prints for publishers instead; he then extended his work to moral commentaries on everyday life. His Election series shows both fine draftsmanship and skill as a caricaturist. Here he shows a campaign in progress, in *Canvassing for Votes.*

Memorial Art Gallery of the University of Rochester, gift of Mr. and Mrs. Herman Cohn

The remaining stronghold of the nobles of the robe were the important courts (known as *parlements*) in Paris and in some provincial capitals. The parlements took advantage of the regency to extend their claim to register government edicts before they were published and enforced. A papal bull condemned the doctrines of the influential French Catholic minority of Jansenists, who had family ties with the judges of the parlements; when the Parlement of Paris refused to register the bull, Orléans held a special royal session obliging the Parlement to follow the royal command. The judges of the parlements in Paris and elsewhere retaliated by going on strike, refusing to carry on their normal court business. There followed a crippling feud between the king and the judges.

In 1726 power passed to Cardinal Fleury (1653–1743), who remained chief minister until his death. Fleury brought together the most able team of ministers in eighteenth-century France and set out to put royal finances in order by avoiding foreign wars. He stabilized the coinage, restricted tax farmers to a comparatively modest profit, made loans more readily available by establishing state pawnshops in the chief cities of France, encouraged new industries with subsidies and other privileges, embarked on a new program for building roads and bridges, and restored relative peace and prosperity to the countryside.

Louis XV began his personal rule in 1743. Intelligent but timid, lazy, and pleasure loving, he did not have the interest or patience to supervise the details of

Beautiful, intelligent, and ambitious, Madame de Pompadour was Louis XV's most powerful mistress. This portrait, by Francois Boucher (1703–1770), a master of the rococo style, provides the historian with valuable details concerning clothing, hair styles, decorations, and furniture.

government. He appointed and dismissed ministers on personal whim or at the bidding of his mistresses and court favorites. In thirty years he had eighteen different foreign secretaries and fourteen chief fiscal officers. Each change in personnel meant a shift in policy, and Louis aggravated the instability by conspiring against his own appointees. France sometimes had two conflicting foreign policies: that of the diplomatic corps, and that of the king, secretly conducted by royal agents who operated at cross-purposes with the regular diplomats.

Nevertheless, France remained a great power. Still the most populous country in Europe, France possessed great reserves of strength; its army, though enfeebled, was the largest in the world, and its navy was the second largest. France led the world in overseas trade until Britain forged ahead in the last quarter of the eighteenth century.

Other States of Western Europe

Spain was the only other state in western Europe with a claim to great power status. Sweden and the Dutch republic could no longer sustain the major international roles they had undertaken during the seventeenth century. The Great Northern War had withered Sweden's Baltic empire. The Dutch, exhausted by their wars against Louis XIV, could not afford a large navy or an energetic foreign policy. Still, Dutch seaborne trade remained substantial, and the republic settled down to a life of relative prosperity and decreased international significance.

Spain suffered comparatively little damage from the War of the Spanish Succession of the early 1700s. The loss of Belgium and parts of Italy in the Utrecht settlement of 1713 reduced the unwieldy Spanish domains to more manageable size, and Philip V (r. 1700–1746), the first Bourbon monarch, infused fresh life into the country's traditional institutions. Philip and his advisers cut down the excessive formalities and long delays of Spanish administration, reasserted the authority of the monarchy over the nobility and clergy, improved the tax system, encouraged industry, built up the navy, and fortified strategic points of the Spanish Empire in America.

This new administration, however, did not strike at the root causes of Spanish decline. The greed of governors and the restrictions of mercantilism still checked the growth of the colonies. The mother country remained impoverished, burdened with noble and clerical castes, and hampered by inadequate resources. Philip V himself was neurotic and was dominated by his strong-willed second wife, Elizabeth Farnese. Since Philip's son by his first marriage would inherit Spain, Elizabeth was determined to find thrones for her own two sons, and her persistent attempts to secure Italian states for them repeatedly threatened the peace of Europe.

During this time Spain was also preoccupied with events in Italy. By 1715 the Italian states had lost much of the political and economic power they had enjoyed during the Renaissance. The opening of new lands overseas and the rise of the Atlantic powers had diminished the importance of the Mediterranean. In the Mediterranean itself, the Ottoman Turks and their satellites in North Africa had long menaced Italian shipping and trade. Moreover, from the time of the French invasion of 1494 the Italian states had lived in fear of conquest by one or another of the new national monarchies.

It was the Spanish Habsburgs who had made that conquest. For almost two centuries they ruled Milan, Naples, and Sicily directly and dominated the rest of the peninsula. By 1720 Austria was firmly established in Lombardy, flanked by the decaying commercial republics of Venice and Genoa. In the mountainous northwest was the small but rising state of Piedmont-Savoy (technically the kingdom of Sardinia after its acquisition of that island in 1720). Farther down the peninsula were the grand duchy of Tuscany (formerly the republic of Florence), the Papal States, and the kingdom of Naples and Sicily. None of these states was more than a minor power.

Yet Italy could not be written off as a negligible quantity in the eighteenth century. Rome remained the capital of Catholicism, Venice still produced fine painters, and Naples remained the school for European musicians. Lombardy, Tuscany, and Naples all contributed to the economic and intellectual advances of the century.

THE WRITTEN RECORD

An Age of Manners

In 1729 a French guide to behavior for the "civilized Christian" covered such subjects as speech, table manners, bodily functions, spitting, nose blowing and behavior in the bedroom. This guide to good manners was reissued with increasingly complex advice through 1774, though with significantly changing emphases, as certain behavior (blowing one's nose into a kerchief no longer worn about the neck but now carried in the hand, hence *handkerchief*) became acceptable, and other behavior more closely regulated. These guides emphasized class differences, pointing out that behavior that was acceptable in the presence of one's social inferiors was to be avoided in the presence of one's equals or social superiors.

It is a part of decency and modesty to cover all parts of the body except the head and hands. You should take care . . . not to touch with your bare hand any part of the body that is normally uncovered. . . . You should get used to suffering small discomforts without twisting, rubbing, or scratching. . . . It is far more contrary to decency and propriety to touch or see in another person, particularly of the other sex, that which Heaven forbids you to look at yourself. When you need to pass water, you should always withdraw to some unfrequented place. And it is proper (even for children) to perform other natural functions where you cannot be seen. It is very impolite to emit wind from your body when in company, either from above or from below, even if it is done without noise. . . . It is never proper to

speak of the parts of the body that should be hidden, nor of certain bodily necessities to which Nature has subjected us, nor even to mention them. . . . You should avoid making a noise when blowing your nose. . . . Before blowing it, it is impolite to spend a long time taking out your handkerchief. It shows a lack of respect toward the people you are with to unfold it in different places to see where you are to use it.

Sieur La Salle, *Les Règles de la bienséance et de la civilité Chrétienne* (Rouen, 1729), quoted in Norbert Elias, *The History of Manners*, vol. I: *The Civilizing Process*, trans. Edmund Jephcott (New York: Pantheon, 1982), pp. 132, 156.

In the 1730s a series of exchanges gave Naples and Sicily to Elizabeth's older son, while the Austrians gained the right to succeed the last Medici grand duke of Tuscany. In 1768 Genoa sold the island of Corsica to France. Italy was, in an old phrase, merely "a geographical expression"—not a single political entity but a series of parts manipulated by ambitious dynasts and empire builders from outside the peninsula.

In some respects Germany deserved even more to be called a geographical expression, for it was divided into three hundred states. The Peace of Westphalia in 1648 had enhanced the sovereign rights of the particular German states and virtually extinguished the authority of their nominal overlord, the Holy Roman emperor. Unlike Italy, however, Germany did include two considerable powers—one long established (Austria) and one recently arrived (Prussia).

The Habsburg rulers of Austria won a series of military and diplomatic victories in the two decades before 1715. In 1699, by the Treaty of Karlovitz, they had recovered Hungary from the Ottoman Turks. In 1713, though they failed to keep the old Habsburg crown of Spain from going to the Bourbon Philip V, they were compensated with Spain's Belgian and Italian territories.

Charles VI (r. 1711–1740) spent much of his reign persuading his own noble subjects to ratify the Pragmatic Sanction, the constitutional agreement that established the

principle of linking together the scattered family territories, whereby, in the absence of sons, Charles's daughter Maria Theresa (1717–1780) would succeed him in all his lands. Much, however, remained to be done to consolidate Habsburg rule over an assemblage of lands that represented many different nations and would never be forged into a single national monarchy. In three key national areas—German Austria, Czech Bohemia, and Magyar Hungary—the nobles still kept most of their medieval prerogatives and, by controlling local estates and diets, controlled grants of taxes and the appointment of officials. The financial and military weakness of the Habsburg regime was underlined by the fact that when Charles VI died in 1740, the treasury was nearly empty and the pay of both army and civil service was more than two years overdue.

THE NEWCOMERS

Significant new players were emerging onto the international stage throughout the first half of the eighteenth century. The most important of these would be Prussia and Russia. Two once-powerful states would suffer as a result: Poland and the Ottoman Turks. The result would be a series of diplomatic and far-reaching political changes and growing international instability.

Prussia and the Hohenzollerns, 1715–1740

Prussia's territories were scattered across north Germany from the Rhine on the west to Poland on the east. Consisting in good part of sand and swamp, these lands had meager natural resources and supported relatively little trade. With fewer than 3 million inhabitants in 1715, Prussia ranked twelfth among the European states in population. Its capital city, Berlin, had few of the obvious geographical advantages enjoyed by Constantinople, Paris, London, and other great capitals. The Hohenzollerns had been established since the fifteenth century as electors of Brandenburg, which lay between the Elbe and Oder rivers. In 1618, when East Prussia fell to the Hohenzollerns, it was separated from Brandenburg by Polish West Prussia and was still nominally a fief held from the Polish king. In western Germany in the meantime the Hohenzollerns had acquired (1614) Cleves, Mark, and some other parcels in the lower Rhine valley and Westphalia. Thus, when Frederick William, the Great Elector (r. 1640–1688), succeeded to the Hohenzollern inheritance, his lands consisted of a nucleus in Brandenburg with separate outlying regions to the east and west. With extraordinary persistence, the rulers of Brandenburg-Prussia for the next two hundred years devoted themselves to the task of making a solid block of territory out of these bits and pieces.

The Great Elector won recognition from Poland as the full sovereign of Prussia. He also tried, with less success, to dislodge the Swedes from the Pomeranian territories between Brandenburg and the Baltic that they had acquired in 1648. In domestic policy his accomplishments were more substantial. He had found his domains largely ruined by war, the farms wasted, the population cut in half, the army reduced to a disorderly rabble of a few thousand men. The Great Elector repaired the damage thoroughly. To augment the population, he encouraged the immigration of Polish Jews and other refugees from religious persecution. He built a small, efficient standing army. In peacetime he assigned the soldiers to the construction of public works, including a canal between the Elbe and the Oder.

The Great Elector initiated the Hohenzollern pattern of militarized absolutism. On his accession he found that in all three territories—Prussia, Brandenburg, and Cleves-Mark—the authority of the ruler was limited by the estates, medieval assemblies representing the landed nobles and the townspeople. He battled the estates for supremacy and won, thereby delaying for two centuries the introduction of representative government into the Hohenzollern realm. He gradually gathered into his own hands the crucial power of levying taxes.

Like Louis XIV, the Great Elector reduced the independence of the aristocracy; unlike Louis, however, he relied not on bourgeois officials but on a working alliance with the landed gentry, particularly the Junkers of East Prussia. He confirmed the Junkers' absolute authority over the serfs on their estates and their ascendancy over the towns, and he encouraged them to serve the state, especially as army officers. In contrast with other monarchies, the absolutism of the Hohenzollerns rested on the cooperation of the sovereign and the aristocracy, not on their mutual antagonism.

The Great Elector's son, Frederick I (r. 1688–1713), assumed the title "King of Prussia" and insisted on international recognition of his new status as the price for his entry into the War of the Spanish Succession. The next king, Frederick William I (r. 1713–1740), devoted himself entirely to economy, absolutism, and the army. His frugality enabled him to undertake occasional projects that he thought worthwhile, such as financing the immigration of twelve thousand south German Protestants to open up new farmlands in eastern Prussia.

To strengthen royal control over the apparatus of state, Frederick William I instituted a small board of experts charged both to administer departments of the central government and to supervise provinces. The arrangement detached provincial administration from local interest and brought it under closer royal control.

Frederick William I doubled the size of the standing army and established state factories to provide guns and uniforms. To conserve the strength of the laboring force in his underpopulated state, he furloughed troops to work on the farms nine months a year. He was too cautious to undertake an adventurous foreign policy; his only significant military campaign was against Sweden in the last phase of the Great Northern War, whereby Prussia obtained in 1720 part of Swedish Pomerania and also the important Baltic port of Stettin at the mouth of the Oder River.

Eighteenth-century observers rightly called the Prussia of Frederick William an armed camp. The king neglected the education of his subjects, showed little concern for the arts, and carried miserliness to the extreme of refusing pensions to soldiers' widows. Yet in terms of power, his regime worked extremely well. The Junkers were intensely loyal to the Hohenzollerns and made excellent officers. The army, though smaller than those of France, Russia, or Austria, was the best drilled and disciplined in Europe.

Russia and Peter the Great, 1682–1725

Even more spectacular than the rise of Prussia was the emergence of Russia as a major power during the era of Peter the Great (r. 1682–1725). In 1682, at the death of Czar Fëdor Romanov, Russia was still a backward country, with few diplomatic links with the West and very little knowledge of the outside world. Contemporaries, Russians as well as foreigners, noted the brutality, drunkenness, illiteracy, and filth prevalent among all classes of society. Even most of the clergy could not read.

Czar Fëdor died childless in 1682, leaving a retarded brother, Ivan, and a capable sister, Sophia, both

This contemporary caricature shows Peter the Great clipping the beard of a Boyar as part of his campaign to modernize Russia.

New York Public Library Picture Collection

children of Czar Alexis (r. 1645–1676) by his first wife. The ten-year-old Peter was the half-brother of Ivan and Sophia, the son of Alexis by his second wife. A major court feud developed between the partisans of the family of Alexis's first wife and those of the family of the second. At first the old Russian representative assembly, the Zemski Sobor, elected Peter czar. But Sophia, as leader of the opposing faction, won the support of the *streltsi*, or "musketeers," a special branch of the military. Undisciplined and angry with their officers, the streltsi were a menace to orderly government. Sophia encouraged the streltsi to attack the Kremlin, and the youthful Peter saw the infuriated troops murder some of his mother's family. For good measure, they killed many nobles living in Moscow and pillaged the archives where the records of serfdom were kept. Sophia now served as regent for both Ivan and Peter, who were hailed as joint czars. In the end, however, the streltsi deserted Sophia, who was shut up in a convent in 1689; from then until Ivan's death in 1696 Peter and his half-brother technically ruled together.

The young Peter was almost seven feet tall and extremely energetic. Fascinated by war and military games, he had set up a play regiment as a child, staffed it with full-grown men, enlisted as a common soldier in its ranks (promoting himself from time to time), ordered equipment for it from the Moscow arsenals, and

drilled it with unflagging vigor. When he discovered a derelict boat in a barn, he unraveled the mysteries of rigging and sail with the help of Dutch sailors living in Moscow. Maneuvers, sailing, and relaxing with his cronies kept him from spending time with his wife, whom Peter had married at sixteen and eventually sent to a convent. He smoked, drank, caroused, and seemed almost without focus; at various times he took up carpentry, shoemaking, cooking, clock making, ivory carving, etching, and dentistry. Peter was a shock to Muscovites, and not in keeping with their idea of a proper czar. Society was further scandalized when Peter took as his mistress a girl who had already been mistress to many others; after she gave birth to two of his children, he finally married her in 1712. This was the empress Catherine (c. 1684–1727), a hearty and affectionate woman who was able to control her difficult husband as no one else could.

Meanwhile, Peter led a campaign against the Turks around the Black Sea. With the help of Dutch experts, he sailed a fleet of river boats down the Don and defeated the Turks at Azov in 1696. The project of forming an anti-Turkish league with the states of western Europe now gave Peter a pretext for the first trip outside Russia taken by a Russian sovereign since the Kievan period. What fascinated him was Western technology, especially in naval matters, and he planned to go to Holland, England, and Venice. He hired several hundred technicians to work in Russia, raised money by selling the monopoly of tobacco sales in Russia to an English peer, and on his journey visited every sort of factory, museum, or printing press he could find.

Before Peter reached Venice, his trip was interrupted by news that the streltsi had revolted again (1698); Peter rushed home and personally participated in their punishment. Though many innocent men suffered torture and death, Peter broke the streltsi as a power in Russian life. He was more determined than ever to modernize his country, and on the day of his return summoned the court jester to assist him as they went about clipping off courtiers' beards. This was an act full of symbolism, for the tradition of the Orthodox church held that God was bearded; if man was made in the image of God, man must also have a beard; and if he was deprived of it, he became a candidate for damnation. Peter now decreed that Russian nobles must shave or else pay a substantial tax for the privilege of wearing their beards. Peter also commanded that all *boyars* (members of the gentry class) and the city population in general must abandon long robes with flowing sleeves and tall bonnets, and adopt Western-style costume. The manufacture of traditional clothes was made illegal, and Peter took up his shears again and cut off the sleeves of people wearing them.

Peter's policies at home can be understood only in light of his ever-mounting need to support virtually incessant warfare, together with his intense desire to modernize Russia. His plan for an international crusade against the Turks collapsed when the Austrians and the Ottoman Empire agreed to the Treaty of Karlovitz in

THE WRITTEN RECORD

Peter the Great

Interpretations of Peter the Great vary enormously. Voltaire considered him to be the model of the "enlightened despot." Nicolai M. Karamzin (1766–1826), who was Russia's first widely read novelist, attacked the Petrine myth and argued that Peter was subverting traditional Russian values:

At this point Peter appeared. In his childhood, the license of the lords, the impudence of the *Streltsy*, and the ambition of Sophia had reminded Russia of the unhappy times of boyar troubles. But deep inside of him the youth already had the makings of a great man, and he seized hold of the helm of state with a mighty hand. He strove toward his destination through storms and billows. He reached it—and everything changed!

His goal was not only to bring new greatness to Russia, but also to accomplish the *complete* assimilation of European customs. . . . Posterity has praised passionately this immortal sovereign for his personal merits as well as for his glorious achievements. He was magnanimous and perspicacious, he had an unshakable will, vigor, and a virtually inexhaustible supply of energy. He reorganized and increased the army, he achieved a brilliant victory over a skillful and courageous enemy, he conquered Livonia, he founded the fleet, built ports, promulgated many wise laws, improved commerce and mining, established factories, schools, the academy, and, finally, he won for Russia a position of eminence in the political system of Europe. And speaking of his magnificent gifts, shall we forget the gift which is perhaps the most important of all in an autocrat: that of knowing how to use people according to their ability? Generals, ministers, or legislators are not accidentally born into such and such a reign—they are chosen. . . . To choose good men one must have insight; only great men have insight into men. Peter's servants rendered him remarkable assistance on the field of battle, in the Senate, and in the Cabinet. But shall we Russians, keeping in

mind our history, agree with ignorant foreigners who claim that Peter was the founder of our political greatness? . . . Shall we forget the princes of Moscow, Ivan I, Ivan III, who may be said to have built a powerful state out of nothing, and—what is of equal importance—to have established in it firm monarchical authority? Peter found the means to achieve greatness—the foundation for it had been laid by the Moscow princes. And, while extolling the glory of this monarch, shall we overlook the pernicious side of his brilliant reign?

Let us not go into his personal vices. But his passion for foreign customs surely exceeded the bounds of reason. Peter was unable to realize that the national spirit constitutes the moral strength of states, which is as indispensable to their stability as is physical might. This national spirit, together with the faith, had saved Russia in the days of the Pretenders. It is nothing else than respect for our national dignity. By uprooting ancient customs, by exposing them to ridicule, by causing them to appear stupid, by praising and introducing foreign elements, the sovereign of the Russians humbled Russian hearts. Does humiliation predispose a man and a citizen to great deeds? The love of the fatherland is bolstered by those national peculiarities which the cosmopolite considers harmless, and thoughtful statesmen beneficial.

Karamzin's Memoir on Ancient and Modern Russia, trans. Richard Pipes (Cambridge, Mass.: Harvard University Press, 1959), pp. 120–22. Copyright © 1959 by the President and Fellows of Harvard College. Reprinted by permission.

1699. Feeling that Austria had betrayed Russia, Peter made a separate peace with the Turks in 1700. By then he was already planning to attack Sweden. Peter's allies in the enterprise were Denmark and Poland.

Led by Charles XII (r. 1697–1718), Sweden won the opening campaigns of the Great Northern War (1700–1721). Charles knocked Denmark out of the fighting, frustrated Poland's attempt to take the Baltic port of Riga, and completely defeated a larger but ill-prepared Russian force at Narva (1700). Instead of marching into Russia, however, Charles detoured into Poland, where he spent seven years pursuing the king, who finally had to abandon both the Russian alliance and the Polish crown. Charles thereupon secured the election of one of his protégés as king of Poland.

In the interim, Peter rebuilt his armies and took from the Swedes the Baltic provinces nearest to Russia—Ingria and Livonia. In the former, he founded in 1703

the city of St. Petersburg, to which he eventually moved the court from Moscow. In 1708 Charles swept far to the south and east into the Ukraine in an effort to join forces with the Cossacks. Exhausted by the severe winter, the Swedish forces were defeated by the Russians in the decisive battle of Poltava (1709). Peter now reinstated his king of Poland, but he was not able to force the Turks to surrender Charles, who had taken refuge with them.

To avenge his defeat Charles engineered a war between Turkey and Russia (1710–1711), during which the Russians made their first appeal to the Balkan Christian subjects of the Turks on the basis of their common faith. Bearing banners modeled on those of Constantine, first emperor of Byzantium, Russian forces crossed into the Ottoman province of Moldavia. Here the Ottoman armies trapped Peter in 1711 and forced him to surrender; the Turks proved unexpectedly lenient, requiring only the surrender of the port of Azov and the creation

Russian Expansion in Europe, 1689-1796

Acquired by Peter the Great, 1689-1725
Acquired 1730-1740
Acquired by Elizabeth, 1741-1762
Acquired by Catherine, 1762-1796
■ Battle sites

he eventually decreed "civil death," which removed them from the protection of the law and made them subject to attack with impunity. State service became compulsory for life; at the age of fifteen every male child of the service nobility was assigned to his future post in the army, in the civil service, or at court. When a member of this class died, he was required to leave his estate intact to one of his sons, not necessarily the eldest, so that it would not be divided anew in every generation. Thus the service nobility was brought into complete dependence upon the czar. The system opened the possibility of a splendid career to men with talent, for a person without property or rank who reached a certain level in any branch of the service was automatically ennobled and received lands.

To raise cash, Peter debased the currency, taxed virtually everything—sales, rents, real estate, tanneries, baths, and beehives—and appointed special revenue finders to think of new levies. The government held a monopoly over a variety of products, including salt, oil, coffins, and caviar. However, the basic tax on each household was not producing enough revenue, partly because the number of households had declined as a result of war and misery, and partly because households were combining to evade payment. Peter's government therefore substituted a head tax on every male. This innovation required a new census, which produced a most important, and unintended, social result. The census-takers classified as serfs many who were between freedom and serfdom; these people thus found themselves and their children labeled as unfree, to be transferred from owner to owner.

In administration, new ministries (*prikazy*) were first set up to centralize the handling of funds received from various sources. A system of army districts adopted for reasons of military efficiency led to the creation of provinces. Each province had its own governor, and many of the functions previously carried on inefficiently by the central government were thus decentralized.

Ultimately, Peter copied the Swedish system of central ministries to supersede the old prikazy and created nine "colleges"—for foreign affairs, the army, justice, expenditure, and the like—each administered by an eleven-man collegium. This arrangement discouraged corruption by making any member of a collegium subject to checking by his colleagues; but it caused delays in final decisions, which could only be reached after lengthy deliberations.

To educate future officers and also many civil servants, Peter established naval, military, and artillery academies. Because of the inadequacy of Russian primary education, which was still controlled by the church, foreigners had to be summoned to provide Russia with scholars. At a lower level, Peter continued the practice of importing technicians and artisans to teach their skills to Russians. The czar offered the inducements of protective tariffs and freedom from taxation to encourage manufacturing. Though sometimes employing many laborers, industrial enterprises remained inefficient. Factory owners could buy and sell serfs if the serfs were bought or sold as a body together with the factory itself.

of an unfortified no man's land between Russian and Ottoman territory.

On the diplomatic front Russia made a series of alliances with petty German courts. The death of Charles XII in 1718 cleared the way for peace negotiations, though it took a Russian landing in Sweden proper to force a decision. At Nystadt (1721) Russia handed back Finland and agreed to pay a substantial sum for the former Swedish possessions along the eastern shore of the Baltic. The opening of this "window on the West" meant that seaborne traffic no longer had to sail around the northern edge of Europe to reach Russia.

Constant warfare requires constant supplies of men and money. Peter's government developed a form of conscription according to which a given number of households had to supply a given number of recruits. Although more of these men died of disease, hunger, and cold than at the hands of the enemy, the very length of the Great Northern War meant that survivors served as a tough nucleus for a regular army. Peter also built a Baltic fleet at the first opportunity, but a Russian naval tradition never took hold. From eight hundred ships (mostly very small) in 1725, the fleet declined to fewer than twenty a decade later; there was no merchant marine at all.

To staff the military forces and the administration, Peter rigorously enforced the rule by which all landowners owed service to the state. For those who failed to register

This "possessional" industrial serfdom did not provide much incentive for good work.

Peter also brought the church under the collegiate system. Knowing how the clergy loathed his new regime, he began by failing to appoint a successor when the patriarch of Moscow died in 1700. In 1721 he placed the church under an agency called at first the spiritual college and then the Holy Directing Synod, headed by a layman. Churchmen of the conservative school were more and more convinced that Peter was the Antichrist himself.

The records of Peter's secret police are full of the complaints his agents heard as they moved about listening for subversive remarks. Peasant husbands and fathers were snatched away to fight on distant battlefields or to labor in the swamps building a city that only Peter appeared to want. The number of serfs increased. Service men found themselves condemned to work for the czar during the whole of their lives and were seldom able to visit their estates.

Among the lower orders of society resistance took the form of peasant uprisings, which were punished with extreme brutality. The usual allies of the peasant rebels, the Cossacks, suffered mass executions, and sharp curtailment of their traditional independence. The leaders of the noble and clerical opposition focused their hopes on Peter's son Alexis. Alexis fanned their hopes by indicating that he shared their views. Eventually, he fled abroad and sought asylum with his brother-in-law, the Austrian emperor Charles VI. Promising him forgiveness, Peter lured Alexis back to Russia and had him tortured to death in his presence.

In many respects Peter simply fortified already existing Russian institutions and characteristics. He made a strong autocracy even stronger, a universal service law for service men even more stringent, a serf more of a serf. His trips abroad, his fondness for foreign ways, his regard for advanced technology, his mercantilism, his wars, all had their precedents in Russian history before his reign. Before he attacked it, the church had already been weakened by the schism of the Old Believers. Perhaps Peter's true radicalism was in the field of everyday manners and behaviors. His attacks on beards, dress, the calendar (he adopted the Western method of dating from the birth of Christ), his hatred of ceremony and fondness for manual labor—these were indeed new; so, too, were the exceptional vigor and passion with which he acted. They were decisive in winning Peter his reputation as a revolutionary—Peter the Great.

In foreign affairs Russia found itself persistently blocked, even by its allies; whenever Russia tried to move into central or western Europe, Prussia or Austria would desert any alliance with the Russians. As a result, Russian rulers distrusted European diplomacy and followed an essentially defensive policy. The Russians had become a formidable military power capable of doubling their artillery in a single year, with perhaps the best infantry and most able gunnery in Europe by the mid-eighteenth century. A lack of heavy horses held back the cavalry, as did the undisciplined nature of Cossack warfare. But by the time the Russians occupied East Prussia (from 1758–1761), the Cossacks, too, were noted for their discipline, and European monarchs, fearful of Russian influence, increasingly used propaganda against the czars, even when allied to them.

The Polish and Ottoman Victims

By the early eighteenth century, Poland and the Ottoman Empire still bulked large on the map, but both states suffered from incompetent government, a backward economy, and the presence of large national and religious minorities. The Orthodox Christians in Catholic Poland and Muslim Turkey were beginning to look to Russia for protection. Moreover, the evident decay of both states stimulated the aggressive appetites of their stronger neighbors. Poland would disappear as an independent power before the end of the century, partitioned by Russia, Austria, and Prussia. Turkey would hold on, but was already beginning to acquire its reputation as "the Sick Man of Europe."

The Polish government was a political curiosity. The monarchy was elective: Each time the throne fell vacant, the Diet chose a successor, usually the candidate who had offered the largest bribes, and sometimes even a foreigner. Once elected, the king was nearly powerless. The Diet was dominated by the nobility and since the 1650s had practiced the *liberum veto*, whereby any one of its members could block any proposal by shouting "I do not wish it!" The Diet was not a parliament but as assembly of aristocrats, each of whom acted as a power unto himself; unanimity was therefore almost impossible. This loosely knit state had no regular army, no diplomatic corps, no central bureaucracy.

The Ottoman Empire was still a functioning state, yet it was falling further and further behind the major European powers, particularly in fiscal stability and technology. Not until the nineteenth century did it produce a sultan who would attempt the kind of massive assault on tradition that Peter the Great had mounted. In the eighteenth century, with rare exceptions, the sultans were captives of harem intrigue and could do little to discipline such powerful groups as the *janissaries*—members of the elite military caste—who exploited their privileges and neglected their soldierly duties. This backward government did at least govern, however, and it showed considerable staying power in war. The so-called Polish and Turkish questions would dominate international politics for the next half-century.

War and Diplomacy, 1713–1763

In the early eighteenth century the international balance was precarious. Should the strong states decide to prey upon the weak, the balance was certain to be upset. One such upset resulted from the Great Northern War, which enabled Russia to replace Sweden as the dominant power in the Baltic. The expansion of Russia continued to threaten the balance during most of the eighteenth century, and the chief victims were Poland and Turkey. A second major threat to the balance came from the expansion of Prussia at the expense of Austria, Poland, and Sweden. A third arose out of the colonial and commercial rivalry between Britain and the French and Spanish Bourbons.

These were not the only international issues of the day. The old competition between Austria and France remained lively. It was complicated by the ambitions of Elizabeth Farnese, second wife of Philip V of Spain, who won the support of France and threatened Austrian power in Italy. The Austrian Habsburgs were vigorous expansionists, aiming to drive the Turks from the Danube and extend their own domains southeast to the Black Sea.

Although the interplay of all these rivalries led to frequent shifts in power, an international balance was generally maintained. The limited financial resources of the governments of the Old Regime generally permitted only limited warfare. On the battlefield, generals were reluctant to risk losing soldiers who represented a costly investment in training; they favored sieges executed according to conventions well understood by all belligerents. At the peace table, diplomats were reluctant to destroy an opponent; they generally sought to award a bit of territory or a minor throne as compensation for a greater loss. The handling of the Polish and the Turkish questions afforded clear examples of conventional international politics in operation.

The Turkish and Polish Questions, 1716–1739

In 1716 the Ottoman Empire became embroiled in a war with Austria that resulted in the Treaty of Passarowitz (1718), by which Charles VI recovered the portion of Hungary still under Turkish rule, plus some other Ottoman lands in the Danube valley. Another Austro-Turkish war (1735–1739) modified the Passarowitz settlement. In this war Austria was allied with Russia, but they fell to quarreling over division of the prospective spoils. In the end there was little to divide, and Charles VI had to hand back to Turkey the Danubian lands annexed in 1718. During the negotiations leading to the Austro-Turkish settlement of 1739, France gave the Ottoman Empire powerful support. In the early 1730s Bourbons and Habsburgs also chose opposing sides in a crisis over the kingship of Poland. The stage was set for the War of the Polish Succession (1733–1735), pitting a Polish contender, Stanislas Leszcynski, protégé of Charles XII, plus France and Spain, against Augustus III, a protégé of Peter the Great, who also had Austrian support.

The diplomats quickly worked out a compromise settlement. Much to the satisfaction of Austria and Russia, Augustus III secured the Polish throne. Yet from the French standpoint, Stanislas Leszcynski was well compensated for his loss. He acquired the duchy of Lorraine on the northeastern border of France, with the provision that when he died Lorraine would go to his daughter Marie, wife of Louis XV of France, and thence to the French Crown. The incumbent duke of Lorraine, Francis, future husband of the Habsburg heiress Maria Theresa, was awarded the grand duchy of Tuscany. Finally, as a by-product of the settlement, Elizabeth Farnese of Spain capped twenty years of perseverance by procuring the kingdom of Naples for her elder son.

The War of the Polish Succession may seem like much ado about a kingship possessing no real power; and the postwar settlement, which affected chiefly Italy and Lorraine, may appear to be a striking case of diplomatic irrelevance. Yet the whole Polish crisis neatly illustrates the workings of dynastic politics and the balance of power. Statesmen regarded thrones as diplomatic prizes, to be assigned without reference to the wishes of the populations involved. The complicated arrangements of the 1730s preserved the balance of power by giving something to almost everyone. Although the diplomats had not prevented a little war over Poland, they did keep it from becoming a big one.

The Austrian Succession, 1739–1748

Britain and France collaborated in the 1720s and 1730s because both Walpole and Fleury sought stability abroad to promote economic recovery at home. The partnership, however, collapsed over the competition between the two Atlantic powers for commerce and empire. Neither Walpole nor Fleury could prevent the worldwide war between Britain and the Bourbon monarchies that broke out in 1739 and that lasted, with intervals of peace, until the final defeat of Napoleon in 1815. This "Second Hundred Years' War" had, in fact, already begun half a century earlier, in the days of Louis XIV. The Utrecht settlement of 1713 had not fully settled the rivalry between Britain and France (and France's Bourbon partner, Spain). Thus the war of 1739 was as much the renewal of an old struggle as the onset of a new one.

The specific issue behind the crisis of 1739 was the comparatively minor question of British disappointment over the results of the Asiento privilege. As the South Sea Company discovered, the Asiento gave Britain only a token share in the trade of the Spanish American colonies. What British captains could not get legitimately they got by smuggling, and Spain retaliated with a coast guard patrol in American waters to ward off smugglers. British merchants complained of the rough treatment handed out by the Spanish guards, and in 1736 they exhibited to Parliament a Captain Robert Jenkins (fl. 1731–1738), who claimed that Spanish brutality had cost him an ear, which he duly produced, preserved in salt and cotton batting. Asked to state his reaction on losing the ear, he replied, "I commended my soul to God and my cause to my country." In October, to the joyful pealing of church bells, Britain began the War of Jenkins's Ear against Spain. The British fleet lost the opening campaign in the Caribbean, and France showed every sign of coming to Spain's assistance.

In 1740 a chain of events linked the colonial war to the great European conflict over the Austrian succession. On the death of Charles VI in 1740, the Habsburg dominions passed to his twenty-three-year-old daughter, Maria Theresa (r. 1740–1780). The German princes ignored the Pragmatic Sanction guaranteeing her succession and looked forward to partitioning the Habsburg inheritance. The elector of Bavaria, a cousin of the Habsburgs, also hoped to be elected Holy Roman emperor. The first of the German princes to strike, however, was Frederick the Great (r. 1740–1786), who had just inherited the Prussian throne. In December 1740 Frederick suddenly invaded the Habsburg province of Silesia.

In the ensuing War of the Austrian Succession, England and Austria were ranged against France, Spain, Prussia, and Bavaria. The Prussian army astounded Europe by its long night marches, sudden flank attacks, and other surprise tactics quite different from the usual deliberate warfare of sieges. Frederick, however, antagonized his allies by repeatedly deserting them to make secret peace arrangements with Austria. And he did little to support the imperial aspirations of the Bavarian elector, who enjoyed only a brief tenure as Emperor Charles VII.

The Anglo-Austrian alliance worked no better than the Franco-Prussian one. Many of the English felt that George II was betraying their interests by entangling them in the Austrian succession and other German problems. Nevertheless, British preference for the Hanoverians over the Stuarts was evident when Bonnie Prince Charles, grandson of the deposed James II, secured French backing and landed in Britain in 1745. He won significant recruits only among the Highlanders of Scotland, where he was thoroughly defeated at Culloden in 1746.

In central Europe, the war was a decisive step in the rise of Prussia to the first rank of powers. The new province of Silesia brought not only a large increase in the Prussian population but also an important textile industry and large deposits of coal and iron. Maria Theresa got scant compensation for the loss of Silesia; although her husband, Francis, won recognition as Holy Roman emperor, she had to surrender Parma and some other territorial crumbs in northern Italy to Philip, the second son of Elizabeth Farnese.

The peace made in 1748 at Aix-la-Chapelle lasted only eight years. Then the Seven Years' War of 1756–1763 broke out, caused partly by old issues left unsettled at Aix-la-Chapelle and partly by new grievances arising from the War of the Austrian Succession. In southern India the English and French East India companies fought each other by taking sides in the rivalries of native princes. By 1751 the energetic French administrator Joseph Dupleix (1697–1763) had won the initial round in the battle for supremacy in the Indian subcontinent.

Then the English, led by the equally energetic Robert Clive (1725–1774), seized the initiative. In 1754 Dupleix was called home by the directors of the French company, who were unwilling to commit costly resources to his aggressive policy.

In North America English colonists from the Atlantic seaboard had already staked out claims to the rich wilderness between the Appalachians and the Mississippi. But the French, equally intent on mastering the area, moved first and established a string of forts in western Pennsylvania from Presque Isle (later Erie) south to Fort Duquesne (later Pittsburgh). In 1754 a force of Virginians under a youthful George Washington (1732–1799) tried unsuccessfully to dislodge the French from Fort Duquesne, initiating a war that would end in a British victory.

The Diplomatic Revolution and the Seven Years' War, 1756–1763

In Europe the dramatic shift of alliances called the Diplomatic Revolution immediately preceded the formal outbreak of the Seven Years' War, which had already begun in the colonies. Britain, which had joined Austria against Prussia in the 1740s, now paired off with Frederick the Great. And in the most dramatic move of the Diplomatic Revolution, France, joined with its hereditary enemy, Habsburg Austria.

In 1755, the British touched off this Diplomatic Revolution. To enlist a second power in the task of defending Hanover, they concluded a treaty with Russia, which had taken a minor part in the War of the Austrian Succession as an ally of England. The Anglo-Russian treaty alarmed Frederick the Great. In January 1756 the Prussian king concluded an alliance with Britain that detached it from Russia. The alliance between England and Prussia isolated France and gave the Austrian chancellor the opportunity he had been waiting for. What Austria needed to avenge itself on Frederick and regain Silesia was an ally with a large army; this required an alliance with France, not Britain. The last act of the Diplomatic Revolution occurred when Russia joined the Franco-Austrian alliance.

The new war, like its predecessor, was really two separate wars—one Continental, the other naval and colonial. In the European campaigns of the Seven Years' War, Frederick the Great confronted the forces of Austria, France, and Russia, whose combined population was more than fifteen times larger than Prussia's. Frederick had almost no allies except Britain, which supplied financial subsidies but little actual military assistance. To fill up the depleted ranks of his army, he violated international law by impressing soldiers from Prussia's smaller neighbors, Mecklenburg and Saxony. Since British subsidies covered only a fraction of his war expenses, he seized Saxon, Polish, and Russian coins and melted them down for Prussian use.

A final factor in saving Prussia was the shakiness of the coalition arrayed against it. Russia's generals

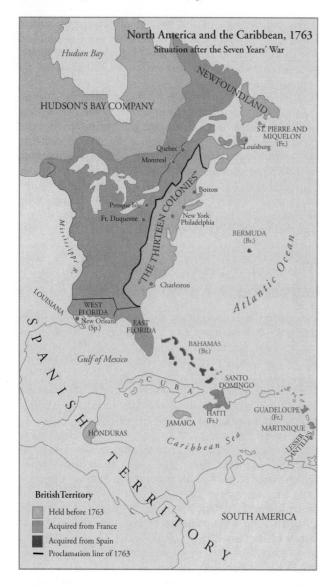

North America and the Caribbean, 1763
Situation after the Seven Years' War

Hudson Bay

NEWFOUNDLAND

HUDSON'S BAY COMPANY

ST. PIERRE AND
MIQUELON
(Fr.)

Quebec

Louisburg

Montreal

Boston

Presque Isle

Ft. Duquesne

New York
Philadelphia

BERMUDA
(Br.)

Mississippi R.

Charleston

Atlantic Ocean

LOUISIANA

WEST
FLORIDA

New Orleans
(Sp.)

EAST
FLORIDA

BAHAMAS
(Br.)

Gulf of Mexico

CUBA

SANTO
DOMINGO

HAITI
(Fr.)

GUADELOUPE
(Fr.)

HONDURAS

JAMAICA

MARTINIQUE

Caribbean Sea

LESSER ANTILLES

SOUTH AMERICA

British Territory

Held before 1763

Acquired from France

Acquired from Spain

Proclamation line of 1763

sea they lost the important Mediterranean base of Minorca in the Balearic Islands. In North America the British lost time and again, but the most dramatic of Britain's misfortunes occurred in India. In June 1756, the nawab of Bengal, an ally of the French, crowded 146 British prisoners at Calcutta into a small room with only two windows. The resulting incident, as described by an officer of the English East India Company, came to be known as the Black Hole:

> It was the hottest season of the year, and the night uncommonly sultry. . . . The excessive pressure of their bodies against one another, and the intolerable heat which prevailed as soon as the door was shut, convinced the prisoners that it was impossible to live through the night in this horrible confinement; and violent attempts were immediately made to force the door, but without effect for it opened inward. At two o'clock not more than fifty remained alive. But even this number were too many to partake of the saving air, the contest for which and for life continued until the morn. . . .
>
> An officer . . . came with an order to open the prison. The dead were so thronged, and the survivors had so little strength remaining, that they were employed near half an hour in removing the bodies which lay against the door before they could clear a passage to go out one at a time; when of one hundred and forty-six who went in no more than twenty-three came out alive.*

It was William Pitt (1708–1778) who turned the tide in favor of Britain. He strengthened the Anglo-Prussian alliance by sending Frederick substantial subsidies and placing English forces in Hanover under an able Prussian commander. He replaced blundering generals and admirals and took energetic measures that transformed the naval and colonial campaigns.

After the Royal Navy defeated both the French Atlantic and Mediterranean squadrons (1759), Britain commanded the seas. Britain could thus continue trading abroad at a prosperous pace, while French overseas trade rapidly sank to one sixth of the prewar rate. Cut off from supplies and reinforcements from home and faced by generally superior British forces, the French colonies fell in quick succession. In Africa, Britain's capture of the chief French slaving stations ruined the slavers of Nantes; in India Clive and others avenged the Black Hole by punishing the nawab of Bengal and capturing the key French posts near Calcutta and Madras; in the West Indies the French lost all their sugar islands except for Santo Domingo. In North America the sixty-five thousand French, poorly supplied and poorly led, were helpless against the million British colonists, fully supported by their mother country. Fort Duquesne was taken at last and was renamed after Pitt, and the British went on to other triumphs in the war that the English colonists called the French and Indian War. In Canada the English general James Wolfe (1727–1759) took Louisburg (1758); in

were unexpectedly timid, and those of France and Austria proved incompetent. Moreover, the French, the strongest of the allies, had to fight a two-front war, in Europe and overseas, without the financial resources to do both.

The grand alliance created by the Austrian chancellor, Prince von Kaunitz (1711–1794), suffered to an unusual extent from the frictions, mistrust, and cross-purposes typical of wartime coalitions. In fact, the coalition did not last out the war. When Elizabeth of Russia (r. 1741–1762) died in January 1762, she was succeeded by Czar Peter III, a passionate admirer of Frederick the Great, who at once placed Russia's forces at Frederick's disposal. Although he occupied the Russian throne only until July, Peter's reign marked a decisive turning in the Seven Years' War. In 1763 Prussia won its war.

Meanwhile, Frederick's British partner was losing abroad. During the first year and a half of the fighting the British suffered setbacks on almost every front. At

---

* Robert Orme, *A History of the Transactions of the British Nation in Indostan* (London: J. Nourse, 1778), pp. 74, 76.

the next year he lost his life but won immortal fame in a great victory on the Plains of Abraham above Quebec. When the remaining French stronghold, Montreal, fell in 1760, France's American empire was over.

Though Pitt had won the war, he did not make the peace; George III (r. 1760–1820) dismissed him in 1761. In the Peace of Paris (1763) the French recovered their islands in the West Indies, highly valued as a major source of sugar. While British planters in the Caribbean were much relieved, since their markets had been flooded by sugar from captured French islands during the war, it seemed to outraged patriots as though Britain had let a grand prize slip through its fingers.

France, however, lost all its possessions on the mainland of North America. Britain secured both Canada and the disputed territories between the Appalachians and the Mississippi. Moreover, Spain, which had joined France in 1762 when the war was already hopeless, ceded to Britain the peninsula called East Florida and the coast of the Gulf of Mexico as far as the Mississippi called West Florida. In compensation, France gave Spain the city of New Orleans and the vast Louisiana territories west of the Mississippi. In India, France recovered its possessions on condition that it would not fortify them. For Britain the Seven Years' War marked the beginning of virtually complete ascendancy in India; for France it marked the virtual end of its "old Empire."

The International Balance in Review

The peace settlements of Hubertusburg and Paris ended the greatest international crisis that was to occur between the death of Louis XIV and the outbreak of the French Revolution. New crises were to arise, but they did not fundamentally alter the international balance; they accentuated the shifts that had long been underway. And although American independence cost Britain thirteen of its colonies, the maritime and imperial supremacy it had gained in 1763 was not otherwise seriously affected.

Thus the international balance established in 1763 remained largely unchanged until 1789. In the incessant struggle for power during the eighteenth century, the victorious states were Britain, Prussia, and Russia. France, Spain, Austria, Turkey survived, though they suffered serious losses. As a Spanish diplomat observed early in the century, the weakest units, Poland and Italy, were being "pared and sliced up like so many Dutch cheeses."

The world struggle between Britain and the Bourbon empire did much to justify the mercantilist view that conceived of international relations in terms of incessant competition and strife. According to the mercantilist doctrine of the fixed amount of trade, a state could enlarge its share of the existing supply only if it reduced the shares held by rival states, either through war or through smuggling and retaliatory legislation. All this was borne out by British success (and French failure) in maintaining overseas trade during the Seven Years' War.

Economics did not wholly explain the changes in the international balance during the century. For example, increasingly efficient utilization of Prussian resources played its part in the victories of Frederick the Great. But his success depended still more on his own leadership and the discipline of the society that he headed. Britain seemingly offers evidence for the supreme power of commerce, as Pitt turned the country's formidable financial and commercial assets to practical advantage. Yet Pitt himself cannot be explained solely in economic terms, for his accession as prime minister was made possible by a political system, social concepts, and a pragmatic approach to leadership that enabled the right man to come forward at the right time.

The eighteenth century, despite its wars, was an interlude of comparative calm between the period of religious strife that had preceded it and the storms of liberalism and nationalism that would be loosed by the French Revolution. The Seven Years' War, for example, did not begin to equal in destructive force the Thirty Years' War, in more ways than just the relative shortness of the war: Few of the combatants had the feeling of fighting for a great cause, like Catholicism or Protestantism or national independence; the fighting itself was conducted in a more orderly fashion than it had been a hundred years before; soldiers were better disciplined and armies were better supplied; troops lived off the land less often and no longer constituted such a menace to the lives and property of civilians. Even warfare reflected the order and reason characteristic of the Age of Enlightenment.

And yet below the reality of this relative sense of order—of reason and compromise, of enlightened despots and rational, even cynical, diplomacy—the great mass of the population continued to live with debt, disease, deprivation, and destitution. The competitive state system, increasingly efficient at the top, seemed increasingly makeshift at the bottom.

ʃUMMARY

The Old Regime, the institutions that existed in France and Europe before 1789, exhibited features of both the medieval and early modern worlds. The economy was largely agrarian, but in western Europe serfdom had disappeared. The social foundations of the Old Regime were based on three estates. Increasingly, the economic, social,

and political order of the Old Regime came under attack in the eighteenth century.

The economic foundations of the Old Regime were challenged in part by the quickening pace of commerce. European states were hard pressed to service debts accumulated in the wars of the seventeenth century. In France,

John Law attempted to restore monetary stability by issuing paper money backed by the nation's wealth. Both in France and England, attempts to manage the national debt caused chaos when these experiments resulted in huge speculative bubbles that burst. The failure of the South Sea Company rocked England, but forced the government to establish a more secure banking system.

Another economic revolution occurred in agriculture. Improvements in farming techniques and the use of new crops such as turnips enabled farmers to produce more food. Increased production ended widespread famines in Europe. In England, enclosures caused widespread social dislocations but created a new labor pool.

A third economic revolution was the beginning of the Industrial Revolution, notably in the textile industry. New machines enabled rapid production and led to the organization of simple factories. New techniques in metallurgy helped make coal mining into a big business.

Britain took the lead in these economic revolutions, becoming the wealthiest nation in the world. Under the first two Hanoverian kings, Parliament was supreme, and the cabinet system took shape under Walpole. Yet Britain was not democratic because only "gentlemen" had the right to vote. For the masses, especially in the growing urban slums of London, life was extremely harsh, but the ruling class was responsive to the need for change.

In the eighteenth century France suffered from mediocre leadership. Cardinal Fleury was the exception. He pursued economic policies designed to stabilize coinage and encourage industry. Despite the failure of Louis XV to institute needed reform, France remained a great power, and French culture dominated Europe.

By the eighteenth century Spain was no longer dominant in the European balance of power. Spanish rulers were preoccupied with Italy, where their claims clashed with those of the Austrian Habsburgs.

Since the mid-seventeenth century, the Hohenzollern rulers of Prussia had worked hard to increase their territories and gain international recognition. Their efforts centered on the economy, absolutism, and the army. The miserly Frederick William I built the Prussian army into the finest force in Europe.

Under Peter the Great, Russia emerged as a great power. Fascinated by Western technology, Peter brought foreign experts to teach Russians modern skills. In foreign policy, Peter expanded Russia by engaging in constant warfare. As a result of the Great Northern War against Sweden (1700–1721), Peter gained his "window on the West." His economic and social policies fortified the autocracy.

The expansion of Russia and Prussia, rivalry between Britain and France, and competition between Austria and France frequently threatened the balance of power in the eighteenth century. In the early 1700s Britain and France cooperated diplomatically to maintain the balance. By 1740, however, colonial and commercial rivalry set the two powers at odds. Thus, in the War of the Austrian Succession (1739–1748), Britain and Austria were allied against France, Prussia, Spain, and Bavaria.

A diplomatic revolution occurred on the eve of the Seven Years' War (1756–1763), when Britain and Prussia paired off against France and Austria, traditional enemies. In the power struggles of the eighteenth century, Britain, Prussia, and Russia were the winners. France, Spain, Austria, and Turkey suffered losses.

CRITICAL THINKING

1. What is meant by the "commercial revolution"?
2. Compare and contrast the "agricultural revolution" with the early "industrial revolution." Why do we call these developments "revolutions"?
3. Summarize developments in Britain and France during the eighteenth century. How would you contrast these developments between the two nations and elsewhere in western Europe?
4. Account for the growing power of Prussia during this time.
5. What were Peter the Great's contributions to the development of Russia?
6. Discuss the essential points at issue in the Turkish and Polish "questions." Why did western Europeans use the term *questions* for these issues?
7. What is a "diplomatic revolution"? How did such a revolution occur between 1739 and 1763?
8. What is the practice of "balance of power" diplomacy and how was it applied in the eighteenth century?
9. For the first time events in North America began to play a role in international affairs. Describe these events and weigh their general significance for Europe.
10. Why did war continue to be used so often to resolve international disputes?

C H A P T E R   1 7

The Enlightenment

looked back to (handwritten)

Century of Genius (handwritten)
1600 – 1700 (handwritten)
Newton, Locke Descartes (handwritten)

Philosophes (handwritten)
1700 – 1800 (handwritten)

- **The Philosophes and their Program of Reform, 1690–1776**

  French Leadership
  Laissez-Faire Economics
  Justice and Education
  The Attack on Religion
  Political Thought

- **Enlightened Despots**

  Frederick the Great, r. 1740–1786
  Maria Theresa, Joseph II, Leopold II, 1740–1792
  Charles III, Pombal, Gustavus III, 1759–1792
  The Limitations of Enlightened Despotism

- **Russia, 1725–1825**

  Nobles and Serfs, 1730–1762
  Catherine the Great, r. 1762–1796
  Paul, 1796–1801, and Alexander I, r. 1801–1825
  Foreign Policy, 1725–1796

- **George III and American Independence**

  Background of the American Revolt, 1760–1776
  Implications of the Revolution

- **Challenges to the Enlightenment**

  Pietists and Methodists
  Literature and the Arts

REASON, NATURAL LAW, PROGRESS—these were key words by the eighteenth century. It was the Age of Enlightenment, when it was widely assumed that human reason could cure past ills and help achieve utopian government, perpetual peace, and a perfect society. Reason would enable humanity to discover the natural laws regulating existence and thereby assure progress.

The intellectuals who professed this creed were known by the French name of *philosophes*. They included critics, publicists, economists, political scientists, and social reformers. The most famous philosophe, Voltaire, in his most famous tale, *Candide*, ridiculed optimists who thought that all was for the best in the best of all possible worlds. Many intellectuals followed Voltaire in stressing the unreasonable aspects of human behavior and the unnatural character of human institutions. On the whole the Enlightenment was based on the belief that people could correct the errors of their ways, once those errors had been pointed out to them.

The philosophes derived their basic principles from the writers of the preceding "century of genius." Their faith in natural law came from Isaac Newton, and their confidence in the powers of human reason in part from René Descartes. But it was John Locke (1632–1704) to whom the rationalists particularly turned. In the *Second Treatise of Government* (1690), Locke contended that people are "by nature all free, equal, and independent," and that they submit to government because they find it convenient to do so, not because they acknowledge any divine right on the part of the monarchy.

The new psychology that Locke advanced in his *Essay Concerning Human Understanding* (1690) also strengthened his argument against absolute monarchy. Defenders of political and religious absolutism had contended that the inclination to submit to authority was present in the human mind from birth; Locke's *Essay* denied the existence of such innate ideas. He called the newborn mind a *tabula rasa*, a "blank slate" upon which experience would write. The two "fountains of knowledge" were environment, rather than heredity, and reason,

Voltaire was among the intellectual giants of the age. His contemplative, bemused skepticism is captured here in a remarkable statue by Jean Antoine Houdon (1741–1828). Houdon traveled widely, and in 1785 he went to America to create one of the most famous busts of George Washington.

Giraudon/Art Resource. LAC 61.271. J.A. Houdon, Voltaire, *Versailles, Musee Lambinet.*

rather than faith. Locke's empiricism (that is, reliance on experience) places him among the rationalists. He believed that human reason, though unable to account for everything in the universe, could explain all that one needs to know.

Locke also pointed the way to a critical examination of the Old Regime. The philosophes submitted existing social and economic institutions to the judgment of common sense and discovered many to be unreasonable and unnecessarily complex. Locke's psychology suggested to them that teachers might improve human institutions by improving the thinking of the rising generation. The philosophes sought, in effect, the right kind of chalk to use on the blank slates of young minds.

The Enlightenment seized on Newton's discoveries as revelations of ultimate truth. Newton had disclosed the natural force—gravitation—that held the universe together; in so doing, he made the universe make sense. The philosophes believed that comparable laws could be found governing and explaining all human activity. They saw themselves as the Newtons of statecraft, justice, and economics, who would reduce the most intricate institutions to formulas of almost mathematical exactness.

The world, they argued, resembled a giant machine whose functioning had hitherto been impeded because the machinery was not properly understood; once the basic laws that governed it were grasped, the world-machine would operate as it should.

The optimistic implications of the belief were expressed most completely in *The Progress of the Human Mind* (1794) by the marquis de Condorcet (1743–1794), written when he was in hiding from political persecution during the French revolutionary Reign of Terror. "Nature has placed no bounds on the perfecting of the human faculties," Condorcet concluded, "and the progress of this perfectibility is limited only by the duration of the globe on which nature has placed us." He foresaw a society that would enjoy a much higher standard of living, more leisure, and more equality among people in general and between the sexes in particular. War would be given up as irrational, and disease would be so effectively conquered by medicine that the average life span would be greatly lengthened.

A shortcut to utopia was proposed by the advocates of enlightened despotism, who believed that rulers should act as benevolent reformers. Like a new Solon, the enlightened despot should clear away the accumulation of artificial law that was choking progress and permit natural laws decreed by God to be applied freely. Many monarchs, among them Frederick the Great of Prussia, Catherine II of Russia, and Joseph II of Austria, adopted the notion of enlightened despotism because it gave them the opportunity to act as the champions of reason and progress while making royal authority more absolute.

THE PHILOSOPHES AND THEIR PROGRAM OF REFORM, 1690–1776

The philosophes hailed improvements in industry and agriculture and the continued advance of science. A Swedish botanist and physician, Carolus Linnaeus (Carl von Linné, 1707–1778), proposed a system for classifying plants and animals by genus and species, which biologists still follow today. Modern chemical analysis started with Joseph Black (1728–1799), a Scottish professor who exploded the old theory that air was composed of a single element by proving the existence of several discrete gases. Black's French contemporary, Antoine Lavoisier (1743–1794), continued the study of gases and demonstrated that water is made up of hydrogen and oxygen. Lavoisier asserted that all substances were composed of a relatively few basic chemical elements, of which he identified twenty-three.

In the eighteenth century astronomy and physics consolidated the advances they had made in the seventeenth. The marquis de Laplace (1749–1827) rounded out Newton's investigation of celestial mechanics and

THE WRITTEN RECORD

Locke's Theory of Knowledge

In the age-old debate as to the most formative influences on an individual's life—heredity or environment—and the most significant tool for comprehending either—faith or reason—John Locke came down squarely in favor of environment and reason.

Let us then suppose the mind to be . . . white paper, void of all characters, without any ideas. How comes it to be furnished? Whence comes it by that vast store, which the busy and boundless fancy of man has painted on it with an almost endless variety? Whence has it all the materials of reason and knowledge? To this I answer, in one word, from experience. . . . Our observation, employed either about external sensible objects, or about the internal operations of our minds, perceived and reflected on by

ourselves, is that which supplies our understandings with all the materials of thinking. These two are the fountains of knowledge, from whence all the ideas we have, or can naturally have, do spring.

John Locke, *Essay Concerning Human Understanding*, in *The English Philosophers from Bacon to Mill*, ed. Edwin A. Burtt (New York: Modern Library, 1939), p. 248.

explained the movements of the solar system in a series of mathematical formulas and theorems. In the American colonies Benjamin Franklin (1706–1790) showed that electricity and lightning are really the same. He obtained an electrical charge in a key attached to the string of a kite flown during a thunderstorm in Philadelphia.

Almost every state in Europe had its philosophes and its royal or learned society to promote the progress of knowledge. Intellectual life was by no means limited to the capitals and big cities; by the middle of the eighteenth century, for example, many provincial towns in France had academies with reading rooms and lending libraries. Intellectuals paid scant attention to national frontiers and, even in wartime, continued to visit enemy countries and correspond with their citizens.

French Leadership

The cosmopolitan qualities of the century were expressed in the Enlightenment. Yet the Age of Reason also marked the high point of French cultural leadership, when, as Thomas Jefferson put it, every man had two homelands, his own and France. By the eighteenth century French was the accepted international language. Louis XIV had made it supreme in diplomacy; the writers of his age, like Boileau, La Rochefoucaud, Racine, and Molière, had made it preeminent in literature. There was much justice in the claim that "a dangerous work written in French is a declaration of war on the whole of Europe."

The great organ of the philosophes was the *Encyclopédie*, begun in 1751 and completed a generation later. Its contributors included Voltaire, Montesquieu, Rousseau, Condorcet, Quesnay, and Turgot. Its editor-in-chief, Denis Diderot (1713–1784), did not intend to compile an objective compendium of information; rather, he and his encyclopedists sought to assemble

knowledge and experience "in order that the labors of past centuries should not prove useless for succeeding centuries; that our descendants, by becoming better informed, will at the same time become happier and more virtuous."

The purposes of the *Enclyclopédie* were didactic, the effect subversive: to expose and thereby ultimately to destroy what its contributors saw as the superstition, the intolerance, and the gross political and religious inequalities of the Old Regime and to instruct the public in the virtues of natural law and the wonders of science. It accomplished its purposes, antagonizing many defenders of the Old Regime while gaining enough subscribers to prove a profitable business venture. Louis XV tried to prevent its being printed or circulated, the church condemned it for its materialism and skepticism, and even the publishers, without consulting Diderot, ordered the printers to cut out passages likely to cause offense—to no avail. The *Encyclopédie* reached a substantial reading public.

Laissez-Faire Economics

The economic program of the philosophes was introduced in articles written for the *Encyclopédie* by the versatile François Quesnay (1694–1774), biologist, surgeon, and personal physician to the French court. Quesnay headed a group of publicists who adopted the name Physiocrats—believers in the rule of nature. The Physiocrats expected that they would, as Quesnay claimed, discover natural economic laws "susceptible of a demonstration as severe and incontestable as those of geometry and algebra."

This new Physiocratic concept of natural wealth clashed with the mercantilist doctrine of equating money (or bullion) and wealth. "The riches which men need for their livelihood do not consist of money," Quesnay argued; "they are rather the goods necessary both for life

The Parisian salons of this period taught writers precision and brought them together for elegant, stylized conversation. The salon was most often the reception room of a large, private home, where guests assembled under the guidance of a hostess, a wealthy woman from the nobility or the upper bourgeoisie. In the salon good conversation could flourish, and new ideas were encouraged. Pressure from the salons helped determine who was elected to the French Academy, which passed under the control of the philosophes in the 1760s, and thus the women who presided over the salons often became the arbiters of good taste. The salon shown here is from the time of Louis XVI.

BBC Hulton Picture Library

and for the annual production of these goods." In his judgment, the emphasis placed by mercantilist states on the accumulation of wealth was therefore excessive. They made goods more expensive by levying tariffs and other indirect taxes, whereas they should have collected only a single, direct tax on the net income from land. "*Laissez faire, laissez passer,*" the Physiocrats urged—"Live and let live; let nature take its course."

The classic formulation of laissez-faire economics was made by the Scotsman Adam Smith (1727–1790) in his *Inquiry into the Nature and Cause of the Wealth of Nations*, published in 1776. Smith leveled a vigorous attack on mercantilism, maintaining that it was wrong to restrict imports by tariffs intended to protect home industries. Like the Physiocrats, Smith attributed the wealth of nations to the production of goods; but for him production depended less on the soil (the Physiocratic view) than on the labor of farmers, artisans, and mill hands. He minimized the role of the state, claiming that

people who were freely competing for their own wealth would be led to enrich their whole society, as if they were guided by "an invisible hand"—that is, by nature.

The mercantilists had raised the state over the individual and had declared a ceaseless trade warfare among nations. Adam Smith and the Physiocrats, reversing the emphasis, proclaimed both economic liberty for the individual and free trade among nations to be natural laws. The laissez-faire program of the Enlightenment marked a revolutionary change in economic thought. It did not, however, revolutionize the economic policies of the great powers, who remained stubbornly mercantilist.

Justice and Education

The disposition to let nature take its course also characterized the outlook of the philosophes on questions of justice. They believed that legislation created by humans prevented the application of the natural laws of justice.

THE WRITTEN RECORD

Adam Smith on Free Trade

Adam Smith extended the theory of natural liberty to the realm of economics, formulating the classic statement in favor of free trade.

It is the maxim of every prudent master of a family, never to attempt to make at home what it will cost him more to make than to buy. The taylor does not attempt to make his own shoes, but buys them of the shoemaker. The shoemaker does not attempt to make his own clothes, but employs a taylor. . . . What is prudence in the conduct of every private family, can scarce by folly in that of a great kingdom. If a foreign country can supply us with a commodity cheaper than we ourselves can make it, better buy it of them with some part of the produce of our industry.

According to the system of natural liberty, the sovereign has only three duties to attend to: . . . first, the duty of protecting the society from the violence and invasion of other independent societies: secondly, the duty of protecting, as far as possible, every member of the society from the injustice and oppression of every other member of it, or the duty of establishing an exact administration of justice; and, thirdly, the duty of erecting and maintaining certain public works and certain public institutions, which it can never be for the interest of any individual, or small number of individuals, to erect and maintain.

Adam Smith, *The Wealth of Nations*, 1776 (New York: Modern Library, 1937), pp. 424, 651.

They were horrified by the cumbersome judicial procedures of the Old Regime and by its antiquated statutes. New lawgivers were needed to simplify legal codes, and a new science was needed to make the punishment of crime both humane and effective. The new science, which laid the foundations of modern sociology, was promoted by Cesare Beccaria (1738–1794), an Italian philosophe and the author of *Essay on Crimes and Punishments* (1764). Beccaria formulated three natural laws of justice. First, punishments should aim to

> prevent the criminal from doing further injury to society, and to prevent others from committing the like offense. Such punishments, therefore . . . ought to be chosen, as will make the strongest and most lasting impressions on the minds of others, with the least torment to the body of the criminal.

Second, justice should act speedily

> because the smaller the interval of time between the punishment and the crime, the stronger and more lasting will be the association of the two ideas of Crime and Punishment.

And last:

> Crimes are more effectively prevented by the certainty than by the severity of the punishment. . . . The certainty of a small punishment will make a stronger impression than the fear of one more severe.*

Beccaria attacked both torture and capital punishment because they deviated from these natural laws. The use of torture falsely assumed that "pain should be the test of truth, as if truth resided in the muscles and fibres of a wretch in torture." Jail sentences, not execution, should be imposed as punishments.

In education too the Old Regime failed to pass the philosophes' tests of reason and natural law. They deplored the almost universal church control of teaching and demanded that more stress be placed on science and less on theology; more on modern languages and less on Greek and Latin; more on modern and less on ancient history.

In primary education the most sweeping revisions were proposed by the nonconformist Jean-Jacques Rousseau (1712–1778). Rousseau rebelled against the strict and disciplined society of his birthplace, Geneva. He rebelled against the intensive bookish studies he had been forced to pursue as a young boy and against the polite conventions he later encountered in the Paris salons. The result was his book *Emile* (1762), half treatise and half romance, a fervent plea for progressive education. *Emile* had two heroes—Emile, the student, and Rousseau, the teacher. The training that Rousseau prescribed for his pupil departed in every particular from eighteenth-century practice: "Life is the trade I would teach him. When he leaves me, I grant you, he will be neither a magistrate, a soldier, nor a priest; he will be a man."* Rousseau followed a laissez-faire policy toward his pupil. He did not argue with Emile, or discipline him, or force him to read at an early age. Emile observed the world of nature firsthand, not in books. He learned geography by finding his own way in the woods (with his tutor's help), and agriculture by working in the fields.

Rousseau's educational program had many faults. It was impractical, for it assumed that every child could

---

* Cesare Beccaria, *Essay on Crimes and Punishments,* 1764 (Stanford, Calif.: Stanford University Press, 1953), pp. 47, 75, 93.

* Jean-Jacques Rousseau, *Emile,* 1762 (New York: Everyman, 1911), p. 9.

have the undivided attention of a tutor, and it fostered the permanent dependence of pupil upon teacher. Yet *Emile* was a most important book, because Rousseau returned to the Renaissance concept of the universal man and to the ancient Greek ideal of the sound mind in the sound body.

The Attack on Religion

Attacks on clerical teaching formed part of a vigorous body of criticism of the role of the clergy in the Old Regime. In denouncing fanaticism and superstition, the philosophes singled out the Society of Jesus. Pressure for the dissolution of the Jesuits gained the support of Catholic rulers, who had long been annoyed by Jesuit intervention in politics, and in the 1760s the Jesuits were expelled from several leading Catholic countries, including Portugal, France, and Spain. Pope Clement XIV (1769–1774) dissolved the Jesuit order in 1773; it would not be revived until forty years later, when the political and intellectual climate had become less hostile.

As champions of tolerance, the philosophes showed a particular affinity for the religious attitude called deism (from the Latin *deus,* "god"). Deist doctrines arose in seventeenth-century England, where the deists hoped to settle religious strife by reason rather than by arms. All persons, they asserted, could agree on a few broad religious principles. Since the Newtonian world-machine implied the existence of a master mechanic, the deists accepted God as the creator of the universe. But they limited his role to the distant past and the remote future, and they doubted that he had any concern with day-to-day human activities. The deists particularly denounced beliefs and practices arising from mysteries and miracles, such as the Trinity, the Virgin Birth, and the Eucharist.

The chief exponent of deism in France was François-Marie Arouet, who took the pen name of Voltaire (1694–1778). He poured forth letters, plays, epics, histories, and essays. Clear, witty, and often bitingly satirical, his writings were enormously popular, and they were viewed by the authorities as so subversive that they were often printed under an assumed name or outside France to evade censorship. It was Voltaire who broadened the writing of history to include economics and culture as well as war and politics.

Voltaire had experienced political intolerance first-hand. As a young man he had spent a year as a prisoner in Paris and three years of exile in England because he had criticized the French government. The religious and political freedom of Britain made an immense impression on the refugee. Back home, Voltaire carried on a lifelong crusade for tolerance. In 1762 a Protestant merchant of Toulouse, Jean Calas, was accused of having murdered his son to prevent his conversion to Catholicism and was executed by being broken on the wheel. Voltaire discovered that the accusation was based almost wholly on rumor, and he believed that the court had acted out of anti-Protestant hysteria. Voltaire campaigned for three years until the original verdict was reversed and the name of Calas was cleared.

The existence of evil confronted the Age of Reason with a major problem. Few of the philosophes accepted the traditional Christian teaching that evil arose from original sin. If God were purely benevolent, they asked, why then had he created a world in which evil so often prevailed? Could a perfect God produce an imperfect creation? Voltaire took his stand in his most famous work, *Candide* (1759), which showed the disasters abounding in the best of all possible worlds.

Deism enabled Voltaire to effect a reconciliation between a perfect God and an imperfect world. Voltaire believed that God was indeed the Creator but that there was no way to determine whether God would attempt to perfect his creation. Even so, Voltaire had no doubts about the usefulness of religion for the masses. "Man," he stated, "has always needed a brake.... If God did not exist, He would have to be invented."

It was another French philosopher, the baron d'Holbach (1723–1789), who pressed the antireligion argument furthest, however. Mankind, Holbach wrote, was innately moral and was perverted by education and the church. God need not be invented, Holbach thought, for all that was needed ethically came from an individual's pursuit of pleasure.

Political Thought

In *The Spirit of the Laws* (1748), the baron de la Brède et de Montesquieu (1689–1755), an aristocratic French lawyer and philosophe, laid down the premise that no one system of government suited all countries. Laws, he wrote,

> should be in relation to the climate of each country, to the quality of its soil, to its situation and extent, to the principal occupation of the natives, whether husbandmen, huntsmen, or shepherds; they should have relation to the degree of liberty which the constitution will bear; to the religion of the inhabitants, to their inclinations, riches, numbers, commerce, manners, and customs.*

In spelling out the influence of tradition and environment upon forms of government, Montesquieu concluded that republics were best suited to small and barren countries, limited monarchies to the middle-sized and more prosperous, and despotisms to vast empires. Britain, being middle-sized and prosperous, was quite properly a monarchy limited by aristocracy. A hereditary nobility sat in the House of Lords; a nobility of talent, the elected representatives, sat in the Commons. All this was admirable in Montesquieu's view, for he pronounced the mass of people "extremely unfit" for government. If only the French monarchy had let the aristocracy retain its old political functions, he intimated, France would never have sunk to its low state.

Montesquieu found another key to the political superiority of Britain in the concept of checks and balances. In Parliament the Lords and Commons checked each other; in the government as a whole, the balance was

---

* Montesquieu, *The Spirit of the Laws,* 1748, trans. Thomas Nugent (New York: Everyman, 1949), book 1, chap. 3.

DOING HISTORY

The Beginning of "Modern History"

Identifying when modern history began is really only a matter of convenience. *Modern history* relates to the presence of activities and customs that seem less strange to us today than do certain very ancient customs. Consider the range of such changes. In the Renaissance astrology was an accepted branch of learning; religious objections to it, largely because its concept of human actions as being governed by the heavenly bodies threatened the doctrine of free will, lessened its significance, until Pope Sixtus V condemned it in 1586. The plague, which brought vast changes to the pattern of population, sets two major periods off from each other: the Black Death in 1347–1348 and the great Venetian outbreak of 1575–1577.

Social historians find significance in the changing nature of slavery. Until about 1450 slaves were commonly used as domestic servants and might be of any race. After the Ottoman advance cut off the usual sources of non-European slaves, and the plantation economy of the New World gave rise to the need for large-scale slave labor, slavery began to change and was generally limited to only one race by the seventeenth century.

Historians of climate point to the crucial changes between 1500 and 1800 and to the environmental crisis in Scandinavia caused by overexploitation of forest and agricultural land. Still other historians note the growing emphasis during the Renaissance on individualism, while others find no less individualism in the Middle Ages, whether in William the Conqueror or Peter Abelard. Nor does a general theory of individuality necessarily apply to an entire society; an elite group may emphasize individualism for itself while representing it among the lower classes.

A shift in the meaning of "glory" also helps set the periods apart, though there can be no agreement on when this occurred. In the Middle Ages, glory was attached to the afterlife; modernity argues for the significance of having one's deeds recognized during one's lifetime and also commemorated posthumously—a shift reflected in literature, portraits, political rhetoric, and tombstones. Clearly changes in banking, business methods, taxation, industry, and the economy generally also set the periods apart, though these changes were gradual. Depending upon one's perspective, the primary determining date for modern history may turn on attitudes toward the environment, the status of women, or a scientific discovery that takes on new significance when reinterpreted by a future generation.

maintained by means of the separation of powers. Here Montesquieu failed to take into account a development that was not yet obvious in the mid-eighteenth century: the British constitution was moving toward a concentration of powers in the House of Commons rather than their greater separation.

Yet it was Jean-Jacques Rousseau who inspired the radicals of the French Revolution. Rousseau's ideas proceeded from a sweeping generalization: Whereas nature dignifies people, he contended, civilization corrupts them; people would be corrupted less if civilized institutions followed nature more closely. Rousseau's major political work, *The Social Contract* (1762), attempted to reconcile the liberty of the individual and the institution of government through a new version of the contract theory of government. Earlier theories of contract, from the Middle Ages to Hobbes and Locke, had hinged on the agreement between the people to be governed, on the one hand, and a single governor or small group of governors, on the other. Earlier theories postulated a political contract;

Rousseau's contract was social in that a whole society agreed to be ruled by its general will. If a person insists on putting self-interest above community interest, that person must be forced to observe the general will. Thus, the general will was moral as well as political in nature, for it represented what was best for the whole community, what the community ought to do.

Formulating this general will, Rousseau believed, was the business of the whole people. The power of legislation, he argued, could never be properly transferred to an elected body. Executing the general will, however, could legitimately be the business of a smaller group. Like Montesquieu, Rousseau believed that the number of governors should vary inversely with the size and resources of the state—monarchy was for the wealthy state, aristocracy for the state of middling size and wealth, and democracy for the small and poor.

Almost every radical political doctrine in the past two centuries has owed something to Rousseau. Socialists justified collectivism on the basis of his insistence that

Rousseau and Voltaire were very different in temperament, though they shared the Enlightenment ideal of reshaping the environment so that human beings might not be corrupted. This contemporary print shows them in sharp argument, each in defense of his own writing.

The Granger Collection

"the fruits of the earth belong to us all." Patriots and nationalists hailed him as an early prophet of the creed that nations do—and should—differ. Throughout his writings, he referred to "the dear love of country." Indeed, *The Social Contract* concluded with a plea for the establishment of a "civil religion," which would displace the traditional faith. The moral code of early Christianity might be retained, Rousseau thought, but the state should no longer have to compete with the church for the allegiance of citizens.

A political prescription more practical than *The Social Contract* and clearly more in keeping with existing monarchical institutions was enlightened despotism. The Physiocrats, chief theorists of enlightened despotism, did not share the concern of Montesquieu and Rousseau for the status of the legislative power. In the Physiocratic view, God was the legislator, nature preserved the divine legislation, and the sole duty of government was to administer these natural laws. Democracy and autocracy alike had the fatal weakness of delegating administrative authority to individuals whose short-term selfish aims

clashed with the permanent welfare of the nation. By contrast, the Physiocrats explained, the personal interests of a hereditary monarch coincided with the national interests through "co-ownership" of the territories the monarch ruled. This amounted to saying that, since the whole kingdom was in a sense the king's property, whatever he did would be right, so long as it was both reasonable and natural. This came close to being a secular restatement of divine-right theory, and it is not surprising that many eighteenth-century monarchs proclaimed themselves to be enlightened despots.

ENLIGHTENED DESPOTS

The concept of an enlightened despot has proved attractive in many cultures. Those rulers who were versed in the thought of the Enlightenment, may have realized that great social and economic changes were at hand, but some were more adept than others in their understanding of these changes and of how best to prepare their states for the future. Of course, a bookish knowledge of Enlightenment thinkers was not always translated into enlightened actions.

Frederick the Great, r. 1740–1786

Prussia

Of all the eighteenth-century rulers, Frederick II, the Great, king of Prussia from 1740 to 1786, appeared best attuned to the Enlightenment. As a youth he had rebelled against the drill-sergeant methods of his father, Frederick William I. An attentive reader of the philosophes, he exchanged letters with them and brought Voltaire to live for a time as his pensioner in his palace at Potsdam, near Berlin.

Frederick conducted foreign and military affairs with cunning and guile. "The principle of aggrandizement is the fundamental law of every government,"* he wrote. Viewed as a general, diplomat, and the master mechanic of Prussian administration, Frederick the Great was efficient and successful, but, if enlightened, he was also quite clearly a despot.

No Physiocrat could have done more than Frederick to improve Prussian agriculture. From western Europe he imported clover, potatoes, crop rotation, and the iron plow. He drained the swamps of the lower Oder valley, opened up farms in Silesia and elsewhere, and brought in 300,000 immigrants, mainly from other areas of Germany, to settle the new lands. After the ravages of the Seven Years' War, Frederick gave the peasants tools, stock, and seed to repair their ruined farms. Frederick, however, was hostile to the doctrine of laissez faire. His mercantilism stimulated the growth of Prussian industry, particularly the textiles and metals needed by the army,

---

* Quoted in G. Ritter, *Frederick the Great: A Historical Profile* (Berkeley: University of California Press, 1968), p. 7.

but it also placed a staggering burden of taxation on his subjects.

The religious and social policies of Frederick the Great combined the Age of Reason at its most reasonable with the Old Regime at its least enlightened. A deist, Frederick prided himself on religious tolerance. When the Jesuits were expelled from Catholic states, he invited them to seek refuge in predominantly Lutheran Prussia. He boasted that he would build a mosque in his capital if Muslims wanted to settle there. Yet Frederick alleged that Jews were "useless to the state"; he levied special taxes on the Jewish subjects and tried to exclude them from the professions and from the civil service.

Frederick rendered Prussians a great service by his judicial reforms, which freed the courts from political pressures. He put an end to the unusual custom of turning over appeals from the ordinary courts to university faculties, setting up a regular system of appellate courts instead. He mitigated the practice of bribing judges by insisting that gratuities received from litigants be placed in a common pool, from which each judge should draw only his fair share as a supplement to his meager salary.

Yet the same Frederick took a medieval view of the merits of social caste. Although he abolished serfdom on the royal domains, he did little to loosen the bonds of serfdom generally, except to forbid the sale of landless serfs in East Prussia in 1773. When he gave the peasants material assistance and urged them to become literate, his aims were utilitarian. Peasants were to learn nothing beyond the rudiments of reading and writing; otherwise, they might become discontented. He regarded the middle class, too, with disdain. At the close of the Seven Years' War he forced all bourgeois officers in the army to resign their commissions; business and professional men were to be exempt from military service but subject to heavy taxation. Even the favored Junkers did not escape Frederick's bureaucratic absolutism. Although he appointed only Junkers as army officers, he discouraged their marrying, so as to reduce the number of potential widows to whom the state would owe a pension.

Many historians pronounce Frederick's supposed enlightenment a mere propaganda device, an attempt to clothe the nakedness of his absolutism with the intellectual garments of the age. It is fairer to recognize that Frederick espoused two often-conflicting philosophies—the Spartan traditions of the Hohenzollerns and the humane principles of the Enlightenment. The grim overtones of the former kept him from sharing the latter's optimistic estimate of human nature and potentiality. Frederick was an enlightened despot in his general religious toleration and his reform of court procedure and criminal law, but he was also bent on centralization that enhanced the Prussian kingship.

Maria Theresa, Joseph II, Leopold II, 1740–1792

Frederick's decisive victory in the War of the Austrian Succession had laid bare the basic weaknesses of the Habsburgs' dynastic empire. The empress Maria Theresa (r. 1740–1780) believed in the need for reform and often took as her model the institutions of her hated but successful rival, Frederick II of Prussia. The empress increased taxes, especially on the nobility, and strengthened the central government at the expense of local aristocratic assemblies, building up departments for central administration. She also took the first steps toward the eventual abolition of serfdom by placing a ceiling on the amount of taxes and of labor service that the peasants could be compelled to render. While personally devout, she subjected the church to heavier taxation, confiscated monastic property, and expelled the Jesuits. But she banned the works of Rousseau and Voltaire from her realm and even forbade the circulation of the Catholic Index. It was her eldest son, Joseph II, who instituted the major reforms associated with the enlightened despots.

Joseph (r. 1765–1790), who became emperor in 1765, ruled jointly with his mother until her death in 1780. Thwarted and restrained by Maria Theresa in her lifetime, the impatient emperor plunged into activity after his mother died. During his ten years as sole ruler (1780–1790), eleven thousand laws and six thousand decrees issued from Vienna.

For the first time, Calvinists, Lutherans, and Orthodox Christians gained full toleration. The emperor took measures to end the ghetto existence of the Jews, exempting them from the special taxes applied to them and lifting the requirement of wearing a yellow patch as a badge of inferiority. On the other hand, Joseph continued his mother's moves to increase state control over the church. He encouraged what he considered socially useful in Catholicism and dealt ruthlessly with what he judged superfluous or harmful. Thus he established hundreds of new churches while reducing the number of religious holidays. Calling monks "the most dangerous and useless subjects in every state," he suppressed seven hundred monasteries and nunneries. The government sold or leased the lands of the suppressed establishments, applying the revenue to the support of hospitals.

Unlike Frederick the Great, Joseph believed in popular education and social equality. His government provided teachers and textbooks for primary schools. More than a quarter of the school-age children in Austria actually attended school. Everyone in Vienna, high and low, was invited to visit the Prater, the great public park of the capital. The new Austrian legal code followed the recommendations of Beccaria in abolishing capital punishment and most tortures and in prescribing equality before the law. Aristocratic offenders, like commoners, were sentenced to stand in the pillory and, later, to sweep the streets of Vienna.

Joseph's policy toward the peasants marked the climax of his equalitarianism. He freed the serfs, abolished most of their obligations to manorial lords, and deprived the lords of their traditional right of administering justice to the peasantry. He also experimented with a single tax on land—a revolutionary innovation because the estates of the aristocracy were to be taxed on the same basis as the farms of the peasantry.

Joseph's economic and political policies, however, often followed the paths of absolutism. In economics he practiced mercantilism, notably in the erection of high protective tariffs and in the government's close supervision of economic life. In politics he appointed commoners to high governmental posts. He also attempted to terminate the autonomous rights of his non-German possessions, notably Belgium, Bohemia, and Hungary.

stupid vicious thugs

Joseph's measures aroused mounting opposition. Devout peasants, almost oblivious to his attempts to improve their social and economic status, resented his meddling with old religious customs. The nobility clamored against his equalitarian legislation; their opposition to the single-tax experiment was so violent that he had to revoke the decree a month after it was issued. Hungary and Belgium rose in open rebellion against his centralizing efforts and forced him to confirm their autonomous liberties.

In foreign policy, too, his ambitious projects miscarried. By supporting Russian plans for the dismemberment of Turkey, Austria gained only a narrow strip of Balkan territory. Joseph also attempted to annex lands belonging to the neighboring south German state of Bavaria, where the death of the ruler opened another succession quarrel. But Frederick the Great was determined to check any advance of Habsburg power in Germany. In the halfhearted "Potato War" of the late 1770s, Austrian and Prussian troops spent most of their time foraging for food, and Joseph secured only a tiny fragment of the Bavarian inheritance.

Joseph died convinced that he had pursued the proper course, yet believing that he had accomplished nothing. In fact, his course was too insensitive to the feelings of others; but he attempted more in ten years than Frederick attempted in almost half a century, and not all of Joseph's attempts failed. Though some of his major reforms, such as the abolition of serfdom, were repealed soon after his death, others survived.

The reforms that survived profited from the conciliatory policies of Joseph's successor, his younger brother Leopold II (r. 1790–1792), who was an enlightened despot in his own right. As grand duke of Tuscany (1765–1790), he had improved the administration of his Italian duchy. He also introduced economic and judicial reforms. Unlike his brother, Leopold actively enlisted the participation of his subjects in affairs of state.

Charles III, Pombal, Gustavus III, 1759–1792

As king of Spain (r. 1759–1788), Charles III energetically advanced the progressive policies begun under his father, Philip V. Though a pious Catholic, Charles forced the Jesuits out of Spain. He reduced the authority of the aristocracy, extended that of the Crown, and made Spain more nearly a centralized national state. He curbed the privileges of the great sheep ranchers. To give new life to the economy, he undertook irrigation projects, reclaimed waste lands, and established new roads, canals, textile

Francisco Goya (1746–1828) shows Charles III of Spain (1716–1788) in hunting costume. Goya sought to analyze character as shown by social position, and he became increasingly less subtle in intimating human capacity for evil through his canvases. Living at the royal court, he became disillusioned by the later corruption of Charles IV, and his work took a savage turn. Compare this hunting portrait with Van Dyck on Charles I of England (p. 319).

Scala/Art Resource

mills, and banks. Spain's foreign commerce increased fivefold during the reign of Charles III. His successor, however, abandoned many of his policies.

In Portugal, the marques de Pombal, the first minister of King Joseph I (r. 1750–1777), secured his reputation by the speed and good taste with which he rebuilt Lisbon after the earthquake of 1755. The Portuguese economy depended heavily on income from the colonies, especially Brazil, and on the sale of port wine to and the purchase of manufactured goods from Britain. Pombal tried to enlarge the economic base by fostering local industries and encouraging the growth of grain production. In an attempt to weaken the grip of clericalism, he ousted the Jesuits and advanced religious toleration. To weaken the nobles, he attacked their rights of inheritance.

But Pombal's methods were high-handed, and when he fell from power in 1777 the prisons released thousands of men whom he had confined years earlier for their alleged involvement in aristocratic plots.

Equally high-handed in the long run was Sweden's benevolent despot, Gustavus III (r. 1771–1792), a nephew of Frederick the Great. He resolved not to be cramped by the noble factions that had run the country since the death of Charles XII. While he distracted Swedish party leaders at the opera one evening, his soldiers staged a coup that enabled him to revive royal authority and to dissolve the factions. In economics and religion his enlightenment outdistanced that of his uncle in Prussia, for he removed obstacles to both domestic and foreign trade and extended toleration to both Jews and non-Lutheran Christians. Success, however, went to his head. As the king became more and more arbitrary, the nobles determined to recover their old power; in 1792 Gustavus was assassinated.

The Limitations of Enlightened Despotism

Enlightened despotism was impaired by the problem of succession. So long as monarchs came to the throne by the accident of birth, there was nothing to prevent the unenlightened or incapable from succeeding the enlightened and able. Even the least of the enlightened despots deserves credit for having reformed some of the bad features of the Old Regime; but not even the best of them could strike a happy balance between enlightenment and despotism. Joseph II was too doctrinaire, too inflexible in his determination to apply the full reform program of the Age of Reason. Pombal and Gustavus III were too arbitrary. Frederick the Great, obsessed with strengthening the Crown, entrenched the power of the Junkers, who were hostile to the Enlightenment. And in Russia events after the death of Peter the Great furnished another lesson in the difficulty of applying rational principles to political realities.

*R*USSIA, 1725–1825

Russia had two sovereigns who could be numbered among the enlightened despots: Catherine II, the Great (r. 1762–1796) and her grandson Alexander I (r. 1801–1825). For the thirty-seven years between the death of Peter the Great and the accession of Catherine the autocracy was without an effective leader as the throne changed hands seven times. More important than the individuals who governed during these years were the social groups contending for power and the social processes at work in Russia. The guards regiments founded by Peter came to exercise a decisive influence in the series of palace overturns, and the service nobility, no longer restrained by the czar, became dominant.

Nobles and Serfs, 1730–1762

In 1730 the gentry set out to emancipate themselves from the servitude placed upon them by Peter. By 1762 the nobles no longer needed to serve at all unless they wished to do so; simultaneously, the authority of noble proprietors over their serfs was increased. The former became the government's agents for collecting the poll tax; the latter could no longer obtain their freedom by enlisting in the army and could not engage in trade or purchase land without written permission from their masters.

To understand the revolutionary nature of the liberation of the nobles from the duty to give military service, one must remember that they had historically obtained their lands and serfs only on condition that they would serve. Now they could keep their lands and serfs with no obligations. Yet the service that had been hated when it was compulsory became fashionable when it was optional. There was really little else for a Russian noble to do except serve the state and to tighten controls over the serfs.

In these middle decades of the eighteenth century, successive waves of foreign influence affected the Russian nobility. German influence gave way to French, and with the French language came French literature. French styles of dress were copied by both men and women, and some gentlemen claimed that it would be impossible to fall in love with a woman who did not speak French. Quite literally, nobles and peasants no longer spoke the same language.

Catherine the Great, 1762–1796

Brought up in a petty German court, Catherine found herself transplanted to St. Petersburg as a young girl, living with a husband she detested, and forced to pick her way through the intrigues that flourished in the Russian capital. Catherine was particularly concerned that Western leaders think well of her and of the condition of Russia under her rule. When Diderot visited Russia in 1773, he reported that Catherine had the soul of Brutus and the charms of Cleopatra. Voltaire stayed out of Russia but accepted Catherine's bounty, in return for which he called her "the north star" and "the benefactress of Europe."

Catherine would perhaps have liked to reform conditions in Russia, but as a woman, a foreigner, and a usurper (she owed her throne to a conspiracy that deposed and murdered her husband, Peter III), she could not act upon her inclinations. Depending as she did upon the goodwill of the nobility, she could not interfere with serfdom. She had to reward her supporters with vast grants of state land, inhabited by hundreds of thousands of state peasants, who now became privately owned serfs who could be sold.

Once firmly established on the throne, however, Catherine decided to convoke a commission to codify the laws of Russia, for the first time since 1649. With the help of advisers, Catherine herself spent three years composing the *Instruction* to the delegates, full of abstract argument drawn from Montesquieu's *Spirit of the Laws* and Beccaria's *Crimes and Punishments*. The 564 delegates to the commission were elected by organs of the central government and by every social class in Russia except the serfs. Each delegate was charged to bring with him a collection of written documents from his neighbors presenting their grievances and demands for change.

Each class of representatives was eager to extend the rights of that class: The free peasants wanted to own serfs; the townspeople wanted to own serfs and be the only class allowed to engage in trade; the nobles wanted to engage in trade and have their exclusive right to own serfs confirmed. After 203 sessions of inconclusive debate, lasting over a year and a half, Catherine ended the labors of the commission in 1768. The commission was the last effort by czardom to consult the Russian people as a whole until the early twentieth century.

In 1773 Yemelyan Pugachev (d. 1775) roused the Cossacks to revolt against Catherine's cancellation of their special privileges. Pretending to be her murdered husband, Czar Peter III, and promising liberty and land to the serfs who joined his forces, Pugachev swept over a wide area of southeastern Russia and marched toward Moscow. Like the disturbances of the seventeenth century, Pugachev's revolt revealed the existence of bitter discontent in Russia.

Catherine took action. Her reorganization of local government (1775) created fifty provinces where there had been twenty before. She thus replaced a small number of unwieldly units with a larger number of small provinces, each containing roughly 300,000–400,000 inhabitants. While the reform of 1775 gave the nobles the lion's share of provincial offices, it also subjected them to the close direction of the central government. The revolt was brutally crushed.

In a charter of 1785 the nobles again received exemption from military service and taxation and secured absolute mastery over the fate of their serfs and their estates. A charter to the towns in the same year disclosed Catherine's sympathy with the tiny but growing urban middle class and established the principle of municipal self-government, although it remained a dead letter because of the rigorous class distinctions maintained in the urban centers of Russia. For the serfs, however, there was no charter.

Paul, r. 1796–1801, and Alexander I, r. 1801–1825

Catherine's son Paul succeeded her in 1796 at age forty-two. He appeared to be motivated chiefly by a wish to undo his mother's work. He exiled some of her favorites and released many of her prisoners. Paul's behavior, however, was unpredictable. On the one hand, he imposed a strict curfew on St. Petersburg and forbade the importation of sheet music. On the other hand, in a decree in 1797 he prohibited the requirement of labor on Sunday.

What was probably fatal to Paul was his policy of toughness toward the nobility. He restored compulsory service from the nobles and curtailed their powers in the provinces. Nobles were forced to meet the bills for public buildings and to pay new taxes on their lands; they were also subjected to corporal punishment for crimes. Paul wanted to develop in the army's officers a sense of responsibility for their men. The guards regiments detested his programs, and a conspiracy of guardsmen resulted in the murder of Paul and the succession of Alexander in 1801.

Educated by a liberal Swiss tutor, Alexander I (r. 1801–1825) had absorbed much of the new eighteenth-century teachings. Yet the application of liberal principles in Russia would directly challenge the most powerful forces in society and would also require the czar to relinquish some of his own power. Alexander compromised and in the end accomplished very little. He did sponsor a law creating a new category of free farmers—serfs who had been freed by their masters—and prescribing that if a proprietor freed an entire village of serfs, he must also confer their lands upon them. This mild initiative depended on the voluntary cooperation of the proprietors, however, and it resulted in the freeing of fewer than forty thousand of the many millions of serfs.

Alexander had as his chief mentor Michael Speransky (1772–1839), son of a Russian priest, intelligent, well educated, and conscientious. Speransky drafted a constitution that would have made Russia a limited monarchy. A series of locally elected assemblies would culminate in a national assembly, the Duma, which would have to approve any law proposed by the czar and would act as a Russian parliament. Because it would have enormously favored the nobility and excluded the serfs, Alexander balked at implementing the project he had commissioned. A council of state was created to advise the czar, but since he appointed and dismissed its members and was not obliged to take its advice, the effect was simply to increase imperial efficiency, not to limit imperial authority. Further efficiency was achieved through the reorganization of the ministries, whose duties were set out clearly for the first time, eliminating overlapping.

During the last decade of Alexander's reign, 1815–1825, the most important figure at court was Count Alexsey Arakcheev (1769–1834), an efficient and brutal officer who reformed the army and organized a hated system of "military colonies," drafting the population of whole districts to serve in the regiments quartered there. When not drilling or fighting, these soldiers were to work their farms, and their entire lives often were subject to the whims of their officers. By the end of Alexander's reign, almost 400,000 soldiers were living in these harsh military camps.

Though Alexander gave Russia no important reforms, he did act as the "liberal czar" in his dominions outside Russia proper. Made king of a partially restored Poland in 1815, he gave the Poles an advanced constitution, with their own army and officials and the free use of their own language. After the annexation of Finland from Sweden in 1809, he allowed the Finns to preserve their own law codes and the system of local government introduced during the long period of Swedish rule.

Foreign Policy, 1725–1796

Between the death of Peter the Great and that of Catherine, Russian foreign policy still pursued the traditional goals of expansion against Sweden, Poland, and Turkey. But Russia found that these goals increasingly involved it with the states of central and western Europe. In the War of the Polish Succession (1733–1735) Russian forces were allied with those of Austria. The Russians and Austrians then became allies in a new war against the Turks from 1735 to 1739. Though the Russians invaded the Crimea successfully, their territorial gains were limited to Azov. The Austrians failed to cooperate in an invasion of the Danubian principalities and made it clear that they did not relish a Russian advance toward the Habsburg frontiers. Prussian influence, which was anti-Austrian, manifested itself with the designation of the German grandson of Peter the Great (the future Peter III) as heir and with the selection of the German Catherine, whose father was a Prussian general.

The Russians remained loyal to Austria and fought the Prussians in the Seven Years' War. Russian forces invaded East Prussia and in 1760 entered Berlin; the accession of the pro-Prussian Peter III early in 1762 led the Russians to change sides and join the Prussians briefly against the Austrians and the French. When Catherine, on her accession, withdrew Russian forces, Russia was excluded from the peace conferences of 1763.

In foreign policy Catherine the Great was vigorous and unscrupulous in pursuing Russia's traditional goals. When the throne of Poland fell vacant, Catherine secured the election of her former lover, Stanislas Poniatowski, who became Stanislas II (r. 1764–1795). Frederick the Great then joined with Catherine in a campaign to win rights for the Lutheran and Orthodox minorities in Catholic Poland. One party of Polish nobles, offended at foreign intervention, secured the aid of France and Austria, which adopted the stratagem of pressing Turkey into war with Russia to distract Catherine from Poland.

In the Russo-Turkish War (1768–1774) the Russian Baltic fleet sailed into the Mediterranean and destroyed the Turkish fleet in the Aegean (1770). While Russians and Turks were discussing peace terms, Frederick the Great concluded that Russia's success with the Turks might lead it to seize most of Poland unless he acted quickly; he therefore arranged the first partition of Poland (1772), which lost to Russia, Prussia, and Austria almost one third of its territory and one half of its population. Russia received a substantial area of what became Belorussia, or White Russia. Two years later, in the treaty of Kutchuk Kainardji, Catherine annexed much of the formerly Turkish stretch of the Black Sea coast; the Crimea was separated from the Ottoman Empire and annexed by Russia in 1783. She also obtained something the Russians had long coveted—freedom of navigation on the Black Sea and the right of passage through the Bosporus and the Dardanelles.

Now Catherine began to dream of expelling the Turks from Europe and reviving the Byzantine Empire under Russian protection. She had her younger grandson

Alexander I of Russia was interested in the thought of the philosophes and began his reign expecting to carry out liberal reforms. He soon found that traditional autocracy served his interests best, however, and he became increasingly reactionary. Vain, he often had his portrait painted in full regalia. This portrait was by the French artist François Gérard (1770–1837).
New York Public Library Picture Collection

christened Constantine and imported Greek-speaking nurses to train him in the language. She also proposed to set up a kingdom of Dacia (the Roman name for "Romania"). By way of preparation, in 1783 Catherine built a naval base at Sebastopol in the newly annexed Crimea. To achieve these grandiose designs, Catherine sought the consent of Austria and took Joseph II on a boat tour of the recently acquired territories of the Russian southwest. However, in a Second Russo-Turkish War (1787–1791) Catherine's Austrian allies again provided feeble assistance and soon became embroiled in a conflict of interest with Russia over the European lands of the sultan. In the end Catherine contented herself with acquiring the remaining Turkish lands along the northern coast of the Black Sea.

Before her death Catherine participated in two more partitions of Poland. The second partition came as the result of a Polish constitutional movement, supported by the Prussians in opposition to Russian interests. Catherine intervened on the pretext of defending the established order in Poland and fighting revolution. In 1793 both the Russians and Prussians took large slices of Polish territory. An attempted Polish revolution was followed by the third partition, in 1795, by which Poland disappeared from the map. This time Austria joined the other two powers and obtained Krakow; Prussia got Warsaw, and Russia got Lithuania and other Baltic and east Polish lands.

The spectacular successes of Catherine meant the transfer to Russia of millions of people—Poles, Lithuanians, Belorussians, Tatars—who hated the Russians, and it left a legacy of instability and insecurity. It also meant that Russia had destroyed the useful buffers of the Polish and Tatar states, and now had common frontiers with its potential enemies, Prussia and Austria.

$\mathscr{G}$EORGE III AND AMERICAN INDEPENDENCE

Though Catherine the Great failed to apply the ideas of the Age of Reason, her name often appears on lists of enlightened despots. Another name is at times added to the list—George III, king of Great Britain (r. 1760–1820). George III tried to wrest control of the House of Commons from the long-dominant Whig oligarchy and retain it through patronage and bribery. Virtuous as a person and devoted to his family, George as a monarch was stubborn, shortsighted, and in the long run unsuccessful. It was easy for him at first to exploit the factional strife among the Whigs, maneuver William Pitt out of office in 1761, and make his tutor Lord Bute (1713–1792) head of the cabinet. Bute and the king, however, found it hard to justify their failure to deprive France of its sugar-rich West Indian islands in the Peace of Paris, which concluded the Seven Years' War. The Commons approved the treaty, but George dismissed Bute.

The harshest criticism came from John Wilkes (1727–1797), a member of Commons. Wilkes' attack on the treaty in his paper the *North Briton* infuriated the king; bowing to royal anger, the Commons ordered the offending issue of the paper burned. Later, Wilkes ran for Parliament three times, and each time the Commons, under royal pressure, threw out his election. When Wilkes finally took his seat again in 1774, he was a popular hero.

A wiser king would have reconsidered his course, but George III did not relax his determination to manage both Parliament and cabinet. After seven years of short-lived, unstable ministries (1763–1770), George finally found a man to fill Bute's old role and do the king's bidding—Lord North, who headed the cabinet until 1782. Under North royal intervention in domestic politics at first stiffened, then wavered, and at length collapsed in the face of a revolt.

Background of the American Revolt, 1760–1776

The breach between the colonies and Britain first became serious after the Seven Years' War, when Britain began to interfere more directly and frequently in colonial matters.

By 1763 the colonies had become accustomed to regulating their own affairs, though the acts of their assemblies remained subject to the veto of royally appointed governors or of the king himself. The vast territories acquired in 1763 in Canada and west of the Allegheny Mountains brought Britain added opportunities for profitable exploitation and added responsibilities for government and defense. When an uprising of Indians under Pontiac (c. 1720–1769) threatened frontier posts in the area of the Ohio Valley and the Great Lakes, colonial militias failed to take effective action, and British regulars were brought in. The continuing threat prompted the royal proclamation of October 1763 forbidding "all our loving subjects" to settle west of a line running along the summit of the Alleghenies. To His Majesty's "loving subjects" in the seaboard colonies, however, the proclamation seemed deliberately designed to exclude them from the riches of the West.

The colonies resented still more keenly the attempt by Parliament to raise revenue in North America. The British government had very strong arguments for increasing colonial taxes: The national debt had almost doubled during the Seven Years' War; the colonies' reluctance to recruit soldiers and raise taxes themselves had increased the cost of the war to British taxpayers; now the mother country faced continued expense in protecting the frontier. Surely the Americans would admit the reasonableness of the case for higher taxes, the members of Parliament thought.

That, however, was precisely what the Americans did not admit. The first of the new revenue measures, the Sugar Act of 1764, alarmed the merchants of the eastern seaboard because the customs officers actually undertook to collect duties on molasses, sugar, and other imports. Here was a threat to the colonial economy, for the import duties had to be paid out of the colonies' meager supply of coins. The second revenue measure, the Stamp Act of 1765, imposed levies on a wide variety of items, including legal and commercial papers, liquor licenses, playing cards, dice, newspapers, calendars, and academic degrees. These duties further drained the supply of coins.

The revenue measures touched off a major controversy. Indignant merchants in the New World boycotted all imports rather than pay the duties, and in October 1765 delegates from nine of the colonies met in New York City as the Stamp Act Congress. The Congress, complaining that the new duties had "a manifest tendency to subvert the rights and liberties of the colonists," proclaimed the principle that there was to be no taxation without representation. Britain surrendered on the practical issue, but did not yield on the principle. The appeals of London merchants, nearly ruined by the American boycott against British goods, brought about the repeal of the Stamp Act in 1765. In 1766, however, Parliament passed a Declaratory Act asserting that the king and Parliament could indeed make such laws affecting the colonies.

For the next decade Britain adhered firmly to the principles of the Declaratory Act, and colonial radicals just as firmly repeated their opposition to taxation

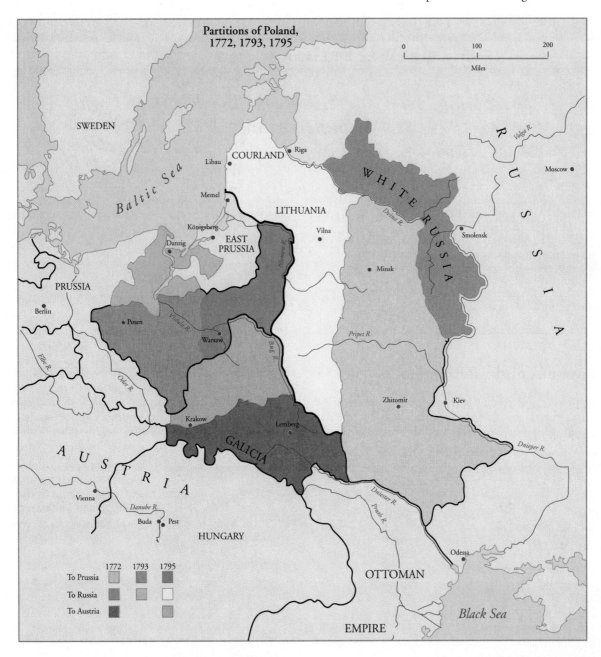

Partitions of Poland, 1772, 1793, 1795

0   100   200
Miles

SWEDEN

COURLAND

Riga

Libau

Memel

LITHUANIA

Vilna

WHITE RUSSIA

Moscow

Smolensk

Königsberg

EAST PRUSSIA

Danzig

PRUSSIA

Minsk

Berlin

Posen

Warsaw

Zhitomir

Kiev

Krakow

Lemberg

GALICIA

AUSTRIA

Vienna

Danube R.

Buda Pest

HUNGARY

OTTOMAN

Odessa

EMPIRE

Black Sea

Volga R.

Dvina R.

Pripet R.

Dnieper R.

Dniester R.

Prut R.

Bug R.

Niemen R.

Vistula R.

Oder R.

Elbe R.

Baltic Sea

RUSSIA

	1772	1793	1795
To Prussia			
To Russia			
To Austria			

without representation. Parliament again tried to raise revenue, this time by the Townshend duties (1767) on colonial imports of tea, paper, paint, and lead. Again the merchants of Philadelphia, New York, and Boston organized boycotts. In 1770 Lord North's cabinet withdrew the Townshend duties except for a three-penny tariff on a pound of tea. Three years later the English East India Company attempted to sell surplus tea in North America, hoping to overcome American opposition to the hated duty by making the retail price of East India tea, duty included, far cheaper than that of Dutch tea smuggled by the colonists. The result was the Boston Tea Party. On December 16, 1773, to the cheers of spectators lining the waterfront, a group of Bostonians who had a large financial stake in smuggled tea disguised themselves as Native Americans, boarded three East India ships, and

dumped chests of tea worth thousands of pounds into the harbor.

Britain answered defiance with force and the colonists met force with resistance. The Quebec Act (1774), incorporating the lands beyond the Alleghenies into Canada, bolted the door to the westward expansion of colonial frontiers. The Intolerable Acts (1774)—so called because taken together the colonists found them intolerable—closed the port of Boston to trade and suspended elections in Massachusetts. At Lexington and Concord in April 1775 the farmers of Massachusetts fired the opening shots of what became the War of Independence. At Philadelphia on July 4, 1776, delegates to a Continental Congress formally declared thirteen of the American mainland colonies independent of Great Britain.

THE WRITTEN RECORD

The Stamp Act Congress Asserts the Right of Local Representation

The Stamp Act Congress met in New York City in October 1765 and declared:

That His Majesty's liege subjects in these colonies are entitled to all the inherent rights and liberties of his natural born subjects within the kingdom of Great Britain.

That it is inseparably essential to the freedom of a people, and the undoubted right of Englishmen, that no taxes be imposed on them but with their own consent, given personally or by their own representatives.

That the people of these colonies are not, and from their local circumstances cannot be, represented in the House of Commons in Great Britain.

That the only representatives of these colonies are persons chosen therein by themselves, and that no taxes ever have been, or can be constitutionally imposed on them, but by their respective legislatures.

From *Documents of American History*, 9th ed. ed. Henry S. Commager (Englewood Cliffs, N.J.: Prentice Hall, Inc., 1973), p. 58.

Implications of the Revolution

For the mother country the American Revolution implied more than the secession of thirteen colonies. It involved Britain in a minor world war that jeopardized its dominance abroad and weakened the power and prestige of King George III at home. The most crucial battle in North America came early in the war—the surrender at Saratoga in 1777 of the British forces under General John Burgoyne (1722–1792). Burgoyne's surrender convinced

Paul Revere's drawing of "the bloody Massacre" in Boston, which now hangs in the Metropolitan Museum of Art.

The Metropolitan Museum of Art

the French that support of the American colonists would give them an excellent chance to avenge the humiliation of 1763. Entering the war in 1778, France soon gained the alliance of Spain and eventually secured the help or friendly neutrality of most other European states.

French intervention prepared the way for eventual victory. In the peace signed at Paris in 1783, Britain recognized the independence of the former colonies. To Spain it handed back Florida, which it had taken in 1763, and the strategic Mediterranean island of Minorca. But it kept Gibraltar, which the Spanish had also hoped to recover, and it ceded only minor territories to France.

During the early years of the war, the British public was intensely anti-American; but the temper of opinion changed as the strength of American resistance became evident. Instances of British mismanagement piled up, while most of Europe rallied to the rebellious colonies. By 1780 George III and his policies were so unpopular that the House of Commons passed a resolution declaring that "the influence of the Crown has increased, is increasing, and ought to be diminished." In 1782 Lord North stepped down. In the next year the post of prime minister fell to William Pitt the Younger (1759–1806), son of the heroic Pitt of the Seven Years' War. With the advent of Pitt, control of British politics shifted away from the king and back to professional politicians.

Support of the revolution in the colonies was by no means unanimous. Many well-to-do colonists, including southern planters and Pennsylvania Quakers, either backed the mother country or took a neutral position in the struggle; New York supplied more recruits to George III than to George Washington. However, revolutionary sentiment ran particularly high in Virginia and New England and among social groups who had the habit of questioning established authority—many merchants, pioneers living on the frontier, and the numerous religious groups who had come to the New World in protest against the Old.

At the heart of the draft composed by the delegates to the Constitutional Convention at Philadelphia in 1787 was the separation of the executive, legislative, and judicial arms of government. Each of the branches of government had the power to check the other two. The Founding Fathers of the American republic sought guidance not only from Montesquieu's *The Spirit of the Laws* but also from the constitutions of the thirteen original states and from English precedents. The first ten amendments to the United States constitution (1791), guaranteeing freedom of religion, freedom of the press, and other basic liberties, were taken mainly from the English Bill of Rights of 1689.

CHALLENGES TO THE ENLIGHTENMENT

The philosophes expected people to see reason when it was pointed out, to give up the habits of centuries, and to revise their behavior in accordance with natural law.

But the rationalism of the Enlightenment tended to omit from its calculations the unpredictable complexities of human nature. A minor philosophe, the abbé de Mably, got at this central problem when he asked: "Is society, then a branch of physics?" Most of the philosophes and their followers believed that it was, and they applied to unpredictable people the mathematical methods used in the physical sciences. The Physiocrats, for example, tried to reduce the complexities of human economic activities to a few simple agricultural laws.

A few outspoken critics, however, disagreed. The Italian philosopher Giovanni Vico (1668–1744) published in 1725 *Scienza Nuova* (New Science), which looked at the state not as a piece of machinery subject to natural laws but as an organism with a pattern of growth, maturity, and decay imposed by its own nature. A Scottish philosopher, David Hume (1711–1776), dramatized his opposition to mercantilism and his advocacy of free international trade by avowing that he prayed for the prosperity of other nations. Yet his profound skepticism and his corrosive common sense caused him to make short work of the philosophes' appeals to nature and reason. To Hume the laws of justice, for instance, were not unalterable but varied with circumstances and, in an emergency, might yield entirely to "stronger motives of necessity and self-preservation. Is it any crime, after a shipwreck, to seize whatever means or instrument of safety one can lay hold of, without regard to former limitations of property?"*

Immanuel Kant (1724–1804), who taught philosophy at the University of Königsberg in East Prussia, raised the debate to the level of metaphysics. While advocating many of the doctrines of the Enlightenment, Kant also believed in a higher reality reaching ultimately to God. He called the eternal verities of the higher world *noumena* (from a Greek word meaning "things thought"), in contrast to the *phenomena* of the material world that are experienced through the senses. Knowledge of the noumenal realm, Kant believed, reached us through reason—reason, however, not as the Enlightenment used the term, not as common sense, but as intuition. The highest expression of the Kantian reason was the "categorical imperative." This was the moral law within the conscience implanted by God. Kant's redefinition of reason and his rehabilitation of conscience exemplified the growing philosophical reaction against the dominant rationalism of the Enlightenment.

Pietists and Methodists

The popular reaction, on the other hand, was an evangelical revival that began with the German Pietists. The Pietists asserted that religion came from the heart, not the head, and that God was far more than a watchmaker, more than the remote creator of the world-machine. One of the chief leaders of Pietism was Count Nikolaus Zinzendorf (1700–1760), founder of the Moravian

---

* David Hume, *Enquiries Concerning the Human Understanding and Concerning the Principles of Morals*, 1751, ed. L.A. Selby-Bigge, 3rd ed. (Oxford: Clarendon Press, 1975), p. 186.

Brethren, who set up a model community based on Christian principles. Moravian emigrants to America established a colony at Bethlehem, Pennsylvania, helping to create the reputation for thrift, hard work, and strict living enjoyed by the Pennsylvania Dutch ("Dutch" meaning *Deutsch*, German).

In England John Wesley (1703–1791), ordained in the Church of England, at first stressed the ritualistic aspects of religion but then felt his own faith evaporating. Pietism converted Wesley to the belief that he would find faith through inner conviction. For more than fifty years Wesley labored to share his discovery, preaching throughout the British Isles in churches, in the fields, at the pitheads of coal mines, and in jails. When Wesley died, his movement had already attracted more than 100,000 adherents, called "Methodists" because of their methodical devotion to piety and to plain dress and plain living. Though Wesley always considered himself an Anglican, the Methodists eventually set up a separate organization. The new sect won its following almost entirely among the lower and middle classes, among people who sought the religious excitement and consolation they did not find in deism or in the Church of England.

Although their beliefs diverged entirely from those of the Enlightenment, the Methodists, too, worked to improve the condition of society. Where the philosophes advocated public reform, the Methodists favored private charity; where the philosophes attacked the causes of evils, the Methodists accepted these evils as part of God's plan and sought to mitigate their symptoms. They began agitation against drunkenness, the trade in slaves, and the barbarous treatment of prisoners, the insane, and the sick. Wesley established schools for coal miners' children and opened dispensaries for the poor. The Methodists' success derived in part from their social programs and in part from the magnetism of Wesley and his talented associates. In America, Methodist missionaries flourished under the dynamic leadership of Francis Asbury (1745–1816). The number of colleges called Wesleyan and the number of churches and streets called Asbury testify to the significance of Methodism in North American social history.

Literature and the Arts

The literary landmarks of the century included both the classical writings of the French philosophes and the English Augustans, and new experiments in the depiction of realism and "sensibility," that is, the life of the emotions. In England the Augustan Age of letters took its name from the claim that it boasted a group of talents comparable to those of Vergil, Horace, and Ovid, who had flourished under the emperor Augustus in Rome.

The greatest of the Augustans was Jonathan Swift (1667–1745), a pessimistic and sometimes despondent genius. In his great work *Gulliver's Travels* (1726), the broad and savage satirization of scientific endeavors and the startling contrast between the noble and reasonable horses, the Houyhnhnms, and the brutish and revolting human Yahoos were intended as attacks on easy assumptions of rational human behavior.

Much closer to the classical temper were Edward Gibbon's *History of the Decline and Fall of the Roman Empire* (1788) and Dr. Johnson's *Dictionary*. Gibbon (1737–1794) made history the excuse for a sustained attack on Christian fanaticism. The lexicographer Samuel Johnson (1709–1784) expressed another concern of the age in the preface to his *Dictionary*:

> When I took the first survey of my undertaking, I found our speech copious without order and energetic without rules; wherever I turned my view, there was perplexity to be disentangled and confusion to be regulated; choice was to be made out of a boundless variety, without any established principle of selection; adulterations were to be detected, without a settled test of purity; and modes of expression to be rejected or received, without the suffrages of any writers of classical reputation or acknowledged authority.*

Meantime, the rapid development of the novel greatly increased the popularity of more down-to-earth and emotional reading. Two of the earliest examples of the new type of fiction were by Daniel Defoe—*Robinson Crusoe* (1719) and *Moll Flanders* (1722). Both were far removed from the refinements and elevated feelings of classicism. Realism was also evident in two celebrated midcentury novels: In *Roderick Random* (1748), Tobias Smollett (1721–1771) drew an authentic picture of life in the British navy, with its cruelty and hardship; *Tom Jones*, by Henry Fielding (1707–1754), published in 1749, was the first truly great social novel, with convincing portraits of the toughs of London slums and the hard-riding, hard-drinking country squires.

Fielding also delighted in parodying the sentimental fiction of Samuel Richardson (1689–1761), who created three giant novels cast in the form of letters by the hero or heroine. An example was *Clarissa Harlowe* (1748), which described in 2400 pages the misfortunes of Clarissa, whose lover was a scoundrel and whose greedy relatives were scheming to secure her property. With all Richardson's excessive emotionalism and preachiness, his descriptions of passion and conscience carried such conviction to a growing reading public that his novels did much to establish the tradition of moral earnestness in English fiction and public discussion.

In France the novel of sensibility came into its own with the very popular *Manon Lescaut* (1731) of Antoine François Prévost, which related the adventures of a young woman sent to the colony of Louisiana. Much closer to Richardson in style and tone was Rousseau's long novel about the conflict of love and duty, *La Nouvelle Héloïse* (1761). Increasingly readers were turning to such fiction, rather than to the church, for guidance on moral and especially sexual questions.

In Germany the most important literary works were the dramas of Lessing and the outpourings of writers associated with the *Sturm und Drang* (storm and stress) movement. Lessing (1729–1781) combined the sensibility of Richardson and the tearful sentimentality of French

---

* Samuel Johnson, *A Dictionary of the English Language* (London: William Stralan, 1755), p. 4.

Public excitement over adventure or exploration led to the popularity of tales of discovery and, in particular, of human ingenuity when confronting utterly new environments. An especially popular theme was the desert island story in which an intrepid European was put to the test of survival by being marooned without hope of rescue. Here the twentieth-century American artist N. C. Wyeth (1882–1945) captures the romanticism of *Robinson Crusoe,* Daniel Defoe's 1719 tale.

The Granger Collection

comedies with an enlightened devotion to common sense and toleration. In *Nathan the Wise* (1779) he dramatized the deistic belief that Judaism, Christianity, and Islam are all manifestations of a universal religion.

Yearning, frustration, and despair characterized the most successful work of the Sturm and Drang period, *The Sorrows of Young Werther* (1774), a short novel that made the youthful Johann Wolfgang von Goethe (1749–1832) famous overnight. Napoleon claimed to have read it seven times, weeping copiously at each reading when the hero shoots himself because the woman he loves is already married. The themes of self-pity and self-destruction were to be prominent in the romantic movement that swept over Europe at the close of the eighteenth century.

The classicism of the century more strongly affected its art. Gibbon's history, the research of scholars and archaeologists, and the discovery in 1748 of the ruins of Roman Pompeii, well preserved under lava from Vesuvius, raised interest in antiquity to a high pitch. For

the scholars of the Enlightenment, the balance and symmetry of Greek and Roman temples represented, in effect, the natural laws of building. Architects adapted classical models with great artistry and variety.

In painting, neoclassicism had an eminent spokesman in Sir Joshua Reynolds (1723–1792), president of the Royal Academy. Beauty, Sir Joshua told the academy, rested "on the uniform, eternal, and immutable laws of nature," which could be "investigated by reason, and known by study." This was the golden age of English portraiture, the age of Reynolds, Thomas Gainsborough (1737–1788), George Romney (1734–1802), and Sir Thomas Lawrence (1769–1830). But it was also the age of William Hogarth (1697–1764), who created a mass market for the engravings that he turned out in thousands of copies, graphic sermons on the vices of London—*Marriage à la Mode, The Rake's Progress, The Harlot's Progress,* and *Gin Lane.*

In France the decorative style called *rococo* prevailed during the reign of Louis XV. It was even more fantastic than the baroque, but lighter, airier, more delicate and graceful, addicted to the use of motifs from bizarre rock formations and from shells. The style captured the social graces of the period, for it was elegant while superficial, elaborate while stereotyped, and, at its best, cheerfully playful while, at its worst, florid and self-conscious.

Meanwhile, three artistic fashions that were to figure significantly in the age of romanticism were already catching on—the taste for the oriental, for the natural, and for the Gothic. Rococo interest in the exotic created a vogue for things Chinese—Chinese wallpaper, the "Chinese" furniture of Thomas Chippendale (c. 1718–1779), and the delicate work in porcelain or on painted scrolls that is called *chinoiserie.* Eighteenth-century gardens were bestrewn with pagodas and minarets.

But music was the queen of the arts in the eighteenth century. A German choirmaster, Johann Sebastian Bach (1685–1750), mastered the difficult art of the fugue, an intricate version of the round in which each voice begins the theme in turn while other voices repeat it and elaborate upon it. Bach composed fugues and a wealth of other material for the organ; for small orchestras he created numerous works, including the Brandenburg Concertos, in which successive instruments are given a chance to show off their potential. His sacred works included many cantatas, the Mass in B minor, and two gigantic choral settings of the Passion of Christ.

Bach's quiet provincial life contrasted sharply with the stormy international career of his countryman George Frederick Handel (1685–1759). Handel spent most of his adult years in London trying to run an opera company. He wrote more than forty operas and used themes from the Bible for *The Messiah* and other vigorous oratorios arranged for large choruses and directed at a mass audience.

Although Bach and Handel composed many instrumental suites and concertos, it was not until the second half of the century that orchestral music really came to the fore. New instruments were invented, notably the piano, which greatly extended the limited range of the harpsichord. New forms of instrumental music—the sonata and the symphony—were also developed, largely by an Austrian, Franz Joseph Haydn (1732–1809). Haydn wrote more than fifty piano pieces in the sonata form, in which two contrasting themes are started in turn, developed, interwoven, repeated, and finally resolved in a *coda* (Italian for "tail"). Haydn also arranged the sonata for the orchestra, grafting it onto the Italian operatic overture to create the first movement of the symphony.

The operatic landmark of the early century was John Gay's (1685–1732) *Beggar's Opera* (1728), a tuneful work caricaturing the London underworld. Later, the German Christoph Gluck (1714–1787) made opera a well-constructed musical drama, not just a vehicle for the display of vocal skill. He kept to the old custom of taking heroes and heroines from classical mythology, but he tried to invest these figures with new vitality.

Opera, symphony, concerto, and chamber music all reached a climax in the works of another Austrian, Wolfgang Amadeus Mozart (1756–1791). As a boy Mozart was exploited by his father, who carted him all over Europe to show off his virtuosity on the harpsichord and his amazing talent for composition. Overworked throughout his life, and in his later years burdened with

debts, he died a pauper at the age of thirty-five. Yet his youthful precocity ripened steadily into mature genius, and his facility and versatility grew ever more prodigious.

The Enlightenment also saw a flowering of women as writers, especially on social issues. They were leaders in the movement to abolish slavery, played significant roles as hostesses of salons where writers met to debate the issues of the day, and founded new religious movements. The concept of romantic love and of marriage as not only a contract but also companionship for life, changed attitudes toward the family. One early feminist writer stood above all others, however: Mary Wollstonecraft (1759–1797). A rebel against society's conventions in dress and behavior, she wore trousers, championed the poor, and left home at an early age. An essayist and novelist, she called for sexual liberation, openly spoke of woman's sexual passion, and compared women to slaves. Her *A Vindication of the Rights of Woman* (1792) is now used to date the beginning of the modern women's rights movement. Her work would be forgotten, however, because she seemed too radical and shocking: She had a child out of wedlock, lived openly with a leading anarchist, William Godwin (1756–1836), and scandalized British society. She was not rediscovered until the end of the nineteenth century.

⨍UMMARY

French cultural leadership in the eighteenth century was preeminent. The key concepts of the eighteenth-century philosophes, or intellectuals, were reason, natural law, and progress. Philosophes, who expressed optimism in human abilities to apply reason, owed a debt to John Locke for their ideas on government and human psychology. Under the direction of Diderot, philosophes produced the thirty-three-volume *Encyclopédie*, advancing views of progress and reason, exposing superstition and ignorance, and denouncing inequality in the light of natural law and science.

François Quesnay and Adam Smith summed up the economic principles of those philosophes known as Physiocrats. The Physiocrat's program of laissez faire, or "let nature take its course," clashed with traditional mercantilist doctrines.

In justice and education, philosophes sought reforms based on reason and natural law. They championed tolerance and attacked superstition. The well-known philosophe Voltaire professed belief in God but rejected intolerance and furthered deist doctrine.

Like many other philosophes, Montesquieu in *The Spirit of the Laws* (1748) expressed admiration for British ideas on government. In *The Social Contract* (1762), Jean-Jacques Rousseau set out his theory of the general will to reconcile the needs of the individual and the institution of government. Rousseau's ideas have formed the basis of radical political doctrines ever since.

Enlightened despots of the period displayed a mix of Enlightenment ideas and absolute monarchy. Frederick

the Great read the works of philosophes and promoted Physiocratic ideas in agriculture. But he rejected laissez-faire ideas. In religion and social policy, he inaugurated a measure of tolerance and supported judicial reforms but did not move to reduce social inequality.

Joseph II of Austria, Charles III of Spain, as well as rulers in Portugal and Sweden instituted enlightened reforms. However, the successors of these enlightened rulers did not continue their programs.

In Russia, Catherine was an absolute autocrat who liked the idea of reform. She tried to codify laws based on enlightened ideas, reorganized local government, and introduced some municipal reform. But under Catherine, serfdom grew as the nobility gained increased authority over their serfs.

Czar Alexander I had absorbed enlightened ideas but was hesitant and accomplished little despite good intentions. Russia continued its expansionist foreign policy. Catherine annexed the Crimea and participated in the partitions of Poland.

In Britain, George III, stubborn and shortsighted, tried to reassert royal prerogative. After the Seven Years' War, a breach divided Britain and its North American colonies. Colonists' resistance to Britain's attempt to raise revenue in North America resulted in the issuing of the Declaration of Independence on July 4, 1776.

With French help, the colonists won their independence, which was recognized in 1783 at the Peace of Paris. The successful revolt of the American colonists weakened the power and prestige of George III. The Declaration of Independence appealed to the laws of nature described by Locke, while the new Constitution of the United States reflected Montesquieu's ideas on the separation of powers.

Philosophes failed to take into account the complexities of human nature. Their appeals to the laws of nature and reason did not reform states. David Hume and Immanuel Kant reflected the philosophic reaction to rationalism. Popular reaction to the Enlightenment was expressed in German Pietism and the Methodist movement in England.

A new type of fiction appeared in the works of Daniel Defoe and the social novels of Henry Fielding. In Germany, Goethe's *Sorrows of Young Werther* embodied the frustration of the Sturm and Drang movement. Neoclassicism influenced the arts, but the age of romanticism was foreshadowed in the growing taste for the oriental, natural, and Gothic.

CRITICAL THINKING

1. What was "the Enlightenment"? What did the *philosophes* contribute to it?

2. Why did the French take the lead in the development of Enlightenment thought?

3. What elements of this thought remain predominant today?

4. What is meant by "laissez-fiare economics" and how did this concept differ from mercantilism? What is its relationship to capitalism?

5. Why were certain despots labeled "enlightened"? What did they actually do to deserve this label?

6. Discuss the development of Russia from 1725 to 1825. What do you consider to be the most important change in Russia during this hundred-year span? Where do you place responsibility for these developments?

7. What were the basic causes of the revolution in Britain's North American colonies?

8. Looking forward, what do you see as the long-range significance of the American Revolution?

9. Who opposed Enlightenment thought and policies and why? What did they do in opposition?

10. Compare English, French, and German literature during this time. Do you see similar comparisons valid for art and music?

CHAPTER 18

The French Revolution and Napoleon

N FRANCE, AS IN BRITAIN'S North American colonies, a financial crisis preceded a revolution. There was not only a parallel but also a direct connection between the revolution of 1776 and that of 1789. French participation in the American War of Independence enormously increased an already excessive governmental debt. Furthermore, the example of America fired the imagination of those French who were discontented. To them Benjamin Franklin, the immensely popular American envoy to France, was the very embodiment of the Enlightenment. Yet it would be going too far to claim that the American Revolution actually caused the French Revolution; rather, it speeded up developments in France that had long been underway. And, just as the reasons for revolution were more deeply rooted and more complicated in France than in America, so the revolution itself was to be more violent and more sweeping.

The immediate cause of the Revolution was financial. King Louis XVI tried one expedient after another to avert bankruptcy and at last summoned the Estates General, the representative assembly that had not met for 175 years. Once assembled, the Estates initiated reforms that were to destroy the Old Regime in France. The more deep-rooted causes of the Revolution, however, reached into France's society and economy and into its political and intellectual history. Behind the financial crisis of the 1780s lay many decades of fiscal mismanagement. The nobles and clergy refused to pay the necessary share of the taxes. Resentment against inequitable taxation and inefficient government built steadily among the unprivileged peasantry, the workers, and above all, the bourgeoisie. What translated bourgeois resentment into the potential for revolution was the program of change put forward by the philosophes.

THE CAUSES OF REVOLUTION

Honest, earnest, and pious, but also clumsy, irresolute, and stubborn, Louis XVI (r. 1774–1792) was most at home hunting, eating, or tinkering with locks. He also

Marie Antoinette's sense of regal isolation from the larger problems of the French nation is unintentionally illustrated by this flattering portrait of her and her children at Versailles. The artist, Elisabeth Vigée-Lebrun (1755–1842), was a leading court painter who emphasized the sense of grace so important to royalty at the time. After the Revolution she emigrated to Italy and then to Russia. The painting hangs today in the Musée de Versailles.

Réunion des Musées Nationaux Giraudon/Art Resource

labored under the handicap of a politically unfortunate marriage to a Habsburg. Marie Antoinette (1755–1793), the youngest of the empress Maria Theresa's sixteen children, was badly educated, extravagant, and completely isolated in the artificial social world of Versailles. To French patriots she was a constant reminder of the ill-fated alliance with Austria during the Seven Years' War.

For want of a good administrator, the machinery of centralized royal absolutism was gradually falling apart. That it functioned at all could be credited to a few capable administrators, notably the intendants who ran so much of provincial France. The most efficient of the intendants provided a sense of direction, but most could do little to slow the disintegration of the central government.

The whole legal and judicial system required reform. The law needed to be codified to eliminate obsolete medieval survivals and to end the overlapping of the two legal systems—Roman and feudal—that prevailed in France. The courts needed a thorough overhaul to make them swift, fair, and inexpensive. Many judges and lawyers purchased or inherited their government positions and regarded them as a means to private enrichment and elevation to the nobility of the robe. Louis XV had permitted his ministers to attack the strongholds of these vested interests, the parlements. One of the last acts of his reign had been their replacement by high courts of royal appointees. One of the first moves taken by Louis XVI was to restore the parlements, a popular measure because many viewed the parlements as a check on absolute monarchy. They often failed to see that the parlements were also an obstacle to social and economic reform.

The Clergy and the Nobility

The first estate, the clergy, occupied a position of conspicuous importance in France. Though only .5 percent of the population, the clergy controlled about 15 percent of French lands. They performed many essential public functions—running schools, keeping records of vital statistics, and dispensing relief to the poor. The French church, however, was a house divided. The lower clergy came almost entirely from the third estate; humble, poorly paid, and generally hardworking, the priests resented the wealth and arrogance of their ecclesiastical superiors. The bishops and abbots held to the outlook of the noble class into which they had been born; although some of them took their duties seriously, others regarded clerical office simply as a way of securing a large private income. Dozens of prelates turned the administration of their bishoprics or monasteries over to subordinates, kept most of the revenue themselves, and lived in Paris or Versailles.

bandits or robbery

Taxpayers hated the tithe levied by the church, even though the full 10 percent implied by the word *tithe* was seldom demanded. They also complained about the church's exemption from taxation. While the peasants remained moderately faithful Catholics and regarded the village priest, if not the bishop, with esteem and affection, the bourgeoisie increasingly accepted the anticlerical views of the philosophes.

Like the higher clergy, the wealthy nobles of the Old Regime, the second estate, were increasingly unpopular. Although less than 2 percent of the population, they held about 20 percent of the land. They had virtual exemption from taxation and monopolized army commissions and appointments to high ecclesiastical office. The French aristocracy, however, was not a single social unit but a series of differing groups. At the top were the hereditary nobles—a few descended from royalty or from feudal lords of the Middle Ages but more from families ennobled within the past two or three centuries. These "nobles of the sword" tended to view most of their countrymen, including the lesser nobility, as vulgar upstarts.

Below the nobility of the sword came the "nobility of the robe," including the justices of the parlements and other courts and a host of other officials. The nobles of the robe, or their ancestors, had originally become nobles by buying their offices. But since these offices were then handed down from father to son, the mercenary origins of their status had become somewhat obscured over time. By the late eighteenth century there was often little practical distinction between the nobility of the robe and of the sword; marriages between members of the two groups were common. On the whole, the nobles of the robe were, in fact, richer than the nobles of the sword, and their firm hold on key governmental positions gave them more power and influence.

Many noblemen, however, had little wealth, power, or glamor. They belonged to the lowest level of French aristocracy—the *hobereaux*, the "little falcons." In an effort to conserve at least part of their traditional status, almost all of the hobereaux insisted on the meticulous collection of the surviving feudal and manorial dues from the peasantry. Their search through old documents to justify levies sometimes long forgotten earned them the abiding hatred of the peasants and prepared the way for the document burning that occurred during the Revolution.

The Third Estate

The first two estates included only a small fraction of the French nation; over 97 percent of the population fell within the third estate. Most of these commoners were peasants, whose status was in some respects more favorable in France than anywhere else in Europe. Serfdom, still prevalent in central and eastern Europe, had disappeared almost entirely. While enclosures were gradually pushing small farmers off the land in England, small peasant holdings existed by the millions in France.

Nevertheless, rural misery was widespread. The peasants did not understand the many wars in which France had been engaged, which had led to heavier taxation, but they could see how the nobility and clergy lived lavishly while they themselves existed at the subsistence level. This was especially so when, faced by rapid population growth, the peasantry had little or no surplus agricultural produce to sell. Although the degree of agrarian distress varied greatly from province to province, the overall picture was bleak. Part of the trouble lay with such economic fundamentals as backward methods of farming, the shortage of land, and overpopulation. Vast areas were not cultivated at all or lay fallow every second or third year in accordance with medieval practice. Landless peasants drifted to the cities or turned to brigandage, and the constantly increasing rural population simply could not find steady employment or a decent livelihood.

Financially the peasants saw themselves as in decline. Inflation hurt them; most farmers found that the prices of the products they sold rose less swiftly than those of the goods they had to buy. Moreover, the peasants owed a heavy burden of taxes and other obligations—the tithe to the church, feudal and manorial dues to the nobility, and to the state a land tax, an income tax, a poll tax, and other duties, of which the most widely detested was the *gabelle*, the obligatory payment of a salt tax to financiers who acted as government agents and usually overcharged. Unemployment and poverty had created a revolutionary temper among the peasants. But they did not demand a change in the form of government. They most emphatically wanted more land, if need be at the expense of the clergy and the nobility; they wanted an end to obsolete manorial dues; and they wanted relief from a system of taxation that bore hardest upon those who could least afford to pay.

The other members of the third estate—the urban workers and the bourgeoisie—were also increasingly alienated. Nearly every major city was faced with discontented wage earners and apprentices who were seriously disadvantaged by the pinch of rising prices. This was especially true of day laborers, who were not allowed to organize unions and who turned to badly led strikes. Apprentices and journeymen found their way blocked along the normal if slow path to master carpenter, bookbinder, or ribbon weaver, and these groups as well as stocking-frame weavers, journeymen hatters, dyers, and workers in the building trades resorted to strikes. The working classes, who had seen themselves as divided into distinct groups, were now beginning to think of their problems in common despite their specialized trades or the gap between semiskilled, manual, and technically trained workers. In time this group, known as the *sans-culottes* (those without knee breeches), were united by a common fear that they could not buy bread and would starve.

However, it was the bourgeoisie that focused these discontents and ultimately provided the leadership. The bourgeoisie included people of varied resources and interests—rich merchants and bankers in the cities, storekeepers and lawyers in country towns and villages, doctors and other professionals, and thousands upon thousands of crafts workers running their own little businesses. The bourgeoisie suffered fewer hardships than the peasants and workers did, but they resented the abuses of the Old

Regime perhaps even more keenly. Though they paid a smaller proportion of their incomes in taxes, they violently denounced the inequality of tax assessments. They found it galling to be snubbed by the nobility, treated as second-class subjects by the monarchy, and excluded from posts of power in government, church, and army. Wealthier, better-educated, and more articulate than the peasants and wage earners, the middle class at first took the lead in formulating the grievances of the entire third estate. These grievances were compiled in statements called *cahiers* and were submitted to the Estates General in 1789.

The Financial Emergency, 1774–1788

The chronic financial difficulties of the French monarchy strengthened the hand of the middle-class reformers. The government debt, already large at the accession of Louis XVI, tripled between 1774 and 1789. The budget for 1788 had to commit half the total estimated revenues to interest payments on debts already contracted; it also showed an alarming deficit in the face of continued high expenditures to support the court. In 1786 the bankers, disturbed by the movement of prices and convinced of governmental mismanagement, refused to make new advances to the French government, which was caught between the third estate's demands for tax relief and the other estates' refusal to yield their fiscal exemptions. The monarchy had temporized and borrowed until it could afford neither fresh delays nor new loans. In the hope of persuading the first two estates to consent to heavier taxation, the Assembly of Notables was convened in 1787. But the Notables declined to be persuaded, whereupon the king dissolved them.

Serious trouble arose in 1788 when the king tried to levy a uniform tax on all landed property without regard to the social status of the holder. The Parlement of Paris declared the new tax law illegal and asserted that only the nation as a whole assembled in the Estates General could make so sweeping a change. The king next resorted to Louis XV's expedient of shifting judicial authority from the parlements to new royal appellate courts. Again, however, there was a storm of disapproval and an outbreak of rioting, led by both aristocrats and bourgeois in several provincial cities. The king retreated and announced that the Estates General would be summoned for the spring of 1789.

The Estates General, 1789

In summoning the Estates General Louis XVI revived a half-forgotten institution that he thought was unlikely to initiate drastic social and economic reforms. The three estates, despite their immense variation in size, had customarily received equal representation and equal voting power, so that the two privileged orders could be expected to outvote the commoners.

The Estates General of 1789, however, met under unique circumstances. Its election and subsequent meetings took place during an economic crisis marked by a continued influx of unemployed peasants into the cities, especially Paris, and by continued inflation, with prices rising at twice the rate of wages. There was also severe unemployment in some textile centers as a result of the treaty of 1786 with England, which increased British imports of French wines and brandies in return for eliminating French barriers to importing cheaper English textiles and hats.

A final difficulty was the weather. Hail and drought had reduced the wheat harvest in 1788, and the winter of 1788–1789 was so bitter that the Seine froze over at Paris, blocking arrivals of grain and flour by barge, the usual way of shipping bulky goods. Half-starved and half-frozen, Parisians huddled around bonfires provided by the municipal government. By the spring of 1789 the price of bread had almost doubled—a very serious matter, for bread was the mainstay of the diet, and workers normally spent almost half their wages on bread for their families. Now they faced the prospect of having to lay out almost all their wages for bread alone.

France had survived bad weather and poor harvests many times in the past without experiencing revolution; this time, however, the economic hardships were the last straw. Starving peasants begged, borrowed, and stole, poaching on the hunting preserves of the great lords and attacking their game wardens. The concern over meat and bread in Paris erupted in a riot in April 1789 at the establishment of Réveillon, a wealthy wallpaper manufacturer.

The method of electing the deputies aided the champions of reform. In each district of France the third estate made its choice directly, at the public meeting, by choosing electors who later selected a deputy. Since this procedure greatly favored the articulate, middle-class lawyers and government administrators won control of the commoners' deputation. The reforming deputies of the third estate found some sympathizers in the second estate and many more in the first, where the discontented poorer priests had a large delegation. Moreover, in a departure from precedent, the king agreed with his advisers' plan to "double the third," giving it as many deputies as the other two estates combined to forestall dominance by the aristocracy. Altogether, a majority of the deputies stood prepared to demand drastic changes in the practices of the Old Regime.

In all past meetings of the Estates General, each estate (or order) had deliberated separately, with the consent of two estates and of the Crown required to pass a measure. In 1789 the king and privileged orders favored retaining this "vote by order," but the third estate demanded "vote by head," with the deputies from all the orders deliberating together, each deputy having a single vote, at least on tax questions.

The question of procedure became crucial after the Estates General convened on May 5, 1789, at Versailles. Emmanuel Siéyès, (1748–1836), a priest, and Count Honoré Mirabeau (1749–1791), a renegade nobleman, both deputies of the third estate, led the campaign for counting votes by head. On June 17 the assemblage cut through the procedural impasse by accepting Siéyès's invitation to proclaim itself a National Assembly. The third estate invited the deputies of the other two estates to join its sessions; a majority of the clerical deputies, mainly parish priests, accepted, but the nobility, leaders of the early phases of the reform movement, refused. When the king barred the commoners from their usual meeting place, the deputies of the third estate and their clerical sympathizers assembled at an indoor tennis court nearby. There, on June 20, they swore never to disband until they had given France a constitution. Louis replied to the Tennis Court Oath by commanding each estate to resume its separate deliberations. The third estate and some deputies of the first disobeyed. Louis, vacillating as ever, gave in to the reformers, especially when he realized that the royal troops were unreliable. On June 27 he directed the noble and clerical deputies to join the new National Assembly. The nation, through its representatives, had successfully challenged the king and the vested interests. The Estates General was dead, and in its place sat the National Assembly, pledged to reform French society and give the nation a constitution. The Revolution had begun.

THE DISSOLUTION OF THE MONARCHY

The National Assembly had barely settled down to work when a new wave of rioting swept over France, further undermining the position of the king. Economic difficulties grew more severe in the summer of 1789. Unemployment increased, and bread seemed likely to remain scarce and expensive, at least until after the harvest. Meanwhile, the commoners feared that the king and the privileged orders might attempt a counterrevolution. Large concentrations of troops appeared in the Paris area early in July—to preserve order and protect the National Assembly, the king asserted. But the Parisians suspected that Louis was planning the forcible dissolution of the Assembly. Suspicion deepened into conviction after Louis dismissed Jacques Necker (1732–1804), a popular Swiss banker who had been serving as the chief royal adviser.

Popular Uprisings, July–October 1789

Reaction to Necker's dismissal was immediate. On July 12 and 13 the Parisian electors formed a new municipal government and a new militia, the National Guard, both loyal to the National Assembly. Paris was forging the weapons that made it the leader of the Revolution. Crowds were roaming the streets, demanding cheaper bread and parading busts of Necker draped in black. On July 14 they broke into government buildings in search of arms. They found one arsenal in the Invalides, the great military hospital, and they hoped to find another in the Bastille, a fortress-prison in the eastern part of the city.

An armed group several hundred strong stormed the Bastille, killing part of the garrison and suffering many casualties themselves. The legend, cherished by defenders of the Old Regime, that participants in the assault were simply "rabble" or a "mob" is untrue. An official list of participants compiled some time after the event showed that most were neighborhood merchants and artisans, especially woodworkers. The fall of the Bastille was of enormous symbolic significance. Though there were only seven prisoners to be released, all of whom deserved to be in prison, an aroused people had demonstrated what it could accomplish. The capture and subsequent demolition of the Bastille did much to ensure the destruction of the Old Regime, as rioting spread throughout France in July 1789. Thus the Fourteenth of July became the great French national holiday, the counterpart of the American Fourth of July.

Parts of the countryside, meantime, were experiencing the Great Fear, an extraordinary attack of mass delusion. From village to village word spread that "brigands" were coming, aristocratic hirelings who would destroy the now ripe crops and force the National

This contemporary work shows the march of the fishwives and other women to Versailles in October of 1789.

Bibliothèque Nationale, Paris

Assembly to preserve the status quo. There were in fact no bands of brigands, only an occasional starving farm-hand and, on some occasions, foraging national guards-men trying to steal food. But the peasants in several districts went berserk, grabbing hoes and pitchforks, anything resembling a weapon, and driving many of the nobility to flight and ultimately to emigration. They attacked châteaux and broke into other buildings that might house a hoard of grain or the hated documents justifying collection of manorial dues. Some nobles voluntarily gave the peasants what they wanted; others saw their barns and archives burnt; a few were lynched.

The October Days, the last crisis of a tumultuous year, again demonstrated the impotence of Louis XVI and the power of his aroused subjects. The harvest of 1789 had been good, but a drought crippled the operation of watermills for grinding flour from the wheat. Thus, as autumn drew on, Parisians still lined up for bread and still looked suspiciously at the royal troops stationed near their city. Rumors of the queen's behavior at Versailles further incensed them: Marie Antoinette made a dramatic appearance at a banquet of royal officers, clutching the heir to the throne in her arms, striking the pose that her mother, Maria Theresa, had employed to win the support of the Hungarians in the 1740s. And on hearing that the people had no bread, she was reported to have remarked callously, "Let them eat cake." This story was false, but it was repeated in the lively new Paris papers that delighted in denouncing the queen.

The climax came on October 5, when an array of determined marketwomen and fishwives, neatly dressed milliners, and even middle-class "ladies with hats" marched from Paris to Versailles in the rain to demand bread. They disrupted the National Assembly and penetrated the palace, where they might have lynched Marie Antoinette if she had not taken refuge with the king. The next day the women marched back to Paris, escorting the royal family, who took up residence in the Tuileries Palace. More important, the National Assembly also moved to Paris.

Forging a New Regime

The outlines of the new regime were already starting to take shape before the October Days. The Great Fear prompted the National Assembly to abolish in law what the peasants were destroying in fact. On the evening of August 4, 1789, the deputies voted that taxation would be paid by all inhabitants of the kingdom in proportion to their revenues, and that public expenses would be borne equally by all. The clergy also gave up tithes, and the liberal minority of the second estate surrendered the nobility's game preserves and manorial dues and courts. The Assembly abolished the remnants of serfdom, forbade the sale of justice or of judicial office, and decreed that "all citizens, without distinction of birth, can be admitted to all ecclesiastical, civil, and military posts and dignities." The Old Regime was dead.

Three weeks later, on August 26, the National Assembly formulated the Declaration of the Rights of Man. "Men are born and remain free and equal in rights," it asserted. "These rights are liberty, property, security, and resistance to oppression." It called property "an inviolable and sacred right," and liberty "the exercise of the natural rights of each man" within the limits "determined by law." "Law," the Declaration stated, "is the expression of the general will. All citizens have the right to take part, in person or by their representatives, in its formation." Further, "Any society in which the guarantee of rights is not assured or the separation of powers not determined has no constitution."*

The Declaration of the Rights of Man mirrored the economic and political attitudes of the middle class, though it was also attractive to many aristocrats. It insisted on the sanctity of property, and it proclaimed that "social distinctions may be based only on usefulness," thus implying that some social distinctions were to be expected. It incorporated the key phrases of the philosophes: natural rights, general will, and separation of powers. The National Assembly made a resounding statement of the ideals of the Enlightenment; yet, as the subsequent history of the Revolution demonstrated, it found no formula by which to translate these ideals into practice.

The economic legislation of the National Assembly provided a case in point. Belief in the theory of equal taxation did not solve urgent financial problems, for the new and just land tax imposed by the deputies could not be collected. Tax collectors had vanished in the general liquidation of the Old Regime, and peasants now assumed that they owed the government nothing. Once again, the French state borrowed until its credit was exhausted, and then, in desperation, the National Assembly ordered the confiscation of church lands (November 1789).

The government thus acquired assets worth at least 2 billion livres. On the basis of this collateral it issued *assignats*, paper notes used to pay the government's debts, which temporarily eased the financial crisis. Unfortunately, the Revolution repeated the mistake of John Law at the time of the Mississippi Bubble: It did not know when to stop. As the state sold parcels of confiscated land—that is, as it reduced the collateral securing its paper money—it was expected to destroy the same amount of assignats. But the temptation not to reduce the number of assignats proved too great to resist, and inflation resulted. The assignats, progressively losing their solid backing, depreciated until in 1795 they were worth less than 5 percent of their face value.

The state sold at auction the property seized from the church and from aristocratic *émigrés* (those who had left the country). Some peasants profited by the opportunity to enlarge their holdings, and many bourgeois also bought up land, sometimes as a short-term speculation. The poor and landless, however, gained nothing, since they could not afford to buy, and the National Assembly made no move to help them. Following laissez-faire doctrines, the Assembly abolished the guilds

---

* Quoted in Georges Lefèbvre, *The Coming of the French Revolution*, trans. R. R. Palmer (Princeton, N.J.: Princeton University Press, 1976), pp. 221–23.

$\mathcal{A}$ CLOSER LOOK

Women's Rights in the French Revolution

Olympe de Gouges (b. 1748) was a leading female revolutionary. A butcher's daughter, she believed that women had the same rights as men, though these rights had to be spelled out in terms of gender. In 1791 she wrote her *Declaration of the Rights of Women* and for the next two years demanded that the revolutionary government act upon it. In November 1793, the National Convention, worried that her demands would threaten the revolution by losing supporters for it, charged her with treason. Found guilty, she was sent to the guillotine.

Following are some of the basic rights set forth in the Declaration:

1. Woman is born free and remains equal to man in rights. Social distinctions can be founded only on general utility.
2. The goal of all political association is the preservation of the natural and imprescriptible rights of Woman and Man: These rights are liberty, property, security, and above all resistance to oppression.
3. The source of all sovereignty resides in the nation, which is nothing but the union of Woman and Man: No body, no individual, may exercise any authority not emanating expressly therefrom.
4. Liberty and justice consist of returning all that belongs to another; thus, the only limits on the exercise of woman's natural rights are the perpetual tyranny wielded by men; these limits must be reformed by the law of nature and the law of reason.
5. The laws of nature and of reason prohibit all actions harmful to society: Anything not forbidden by these wise and divine laws, cannot be forbidden, and no one can be forced to do that which the law does not require.
6. The law should be the expression of the general will; all female and male citizens should concur either personally or by their representatives in its formulation; it should be the same for all: All female and male cit-

izens are equal in its eyes, and equally entitled to all honors, places and public employments according to their abilities without any other distinction than that of their virtues and their talents.
7. No woman is an exception; she is accused, arrested, and detained in cases determined by law. Women, like men, obey this rigorous law.
8. The law should only impose those penalties which are strictly and absolutely necessary, and one may be punished only by a law that has been established and promulgated prior to the offense and legally applied to women.
9. Once a woman has been declared guilty, the law should be applied rigorously.
10. No one is to be harassed for their fundamental beliefs; a woman has the right to mount the scaffold; she also has the right to mount the rostrum, providing that her actions do not threaten lawful public order.*

---

* Olympe de Gouges, *La Nation à la Reine: Les Droits de la Femme* (Paris: Momoro, [1791], as translated by and quoted in *The Global Experience: Readings in World History since 1500* 2nd ed. eds. Philip F. Riley et al. (Englewood Cliffs, N.J.: Prentice Hall, 1992), pp. 94–95.

---

and the tariffs and tolls on trade within France. And deeming the few simple organizations of labor unnatural restrictions on economic freedom, it abolished them, too. In June 1791, after an outbreak of strikes, it passed the Loi de Chapelier, banning strikes, labor unions, and many guilds.

Reforming the Church

Since the suppression of tithes and the seizure of ecclesiastical property deprived the church of its revenue, the National Assembly agreed to finance ecclesiastical salaries. The new arrangement made the French church subject to constant government regulation. Few difficulties arose from the Assembly's prohibition of monastic vows or from the liquidation of some monasteries and convents, since many of these establishments were already far gone in

decay, but an uproar arose over legislation altering the status of the secular clergy.

The Civil Constitution of the Clergy (June 1790) redrew the ecclesiastical map of France. It reduced the number of bishoprics by more than a third, making the remaining dioceses correspond to new civil administrative units. It transformed bishops and priests into civil officials, paid by the state and elected by the population of the diocese or parish. A new bishop was required to take an oath of loyalty to the state.

These provisions ran counter to the tradition of the Roman church as an independent ecclesiastical monarchy. Naturally the pope denounced the Civil Constitution. When the National Assembly then required that every member of the French clergy take a special oath supporting the Civil Constitution, only a few bishops and fewer than half the priests complied. Thus a breach was opened between the leaders of the Revolution and a large segment of the population. From Louis XVI down to humble peasants, Catholics rallied to the nonjuring clergy, as those who refused the special oath were termed. The Civil Constitution of the Clergy was thus the first great blunder of the Revolution.

The Constitution of 1791

The major undertaking of the National Assembly was the Constitution of 1791. To replace the bewildering complex of provincial units that had existed under the Old Regime, the Assembly divided the territory of France into eighty-three departments of approximately equal size; the departments were subdivided into *arrondissements*, or "districts," and the districts into communes—that is, municipalities. In the communes and departments, elected councils and officials enjoyed considerable self-government.

The Constitution established an independent, elected judiciary to replace the parlements and other courts of the Old Regime. It vested legislative authority in a single elected chamber. Although the king still headed the executive branch, his actions now required the approval of his ministers. The ministers, in turn, were responsible only to the king and not to the legislature, as they generally are in a parliamentary or cabinet government. Although the king received the power of veto, it was only a suspensive veto that could block legislation for a maximum of four years. The new constitution undertook to give France a uniform code of law, declared marriage a civil contract rather than a religious sacrament, and promised free public education.

While the constitution of 1791 went a long way toward popular government, implementing slogans of popular sovereignty and social equality, it stopped well short of full democracy. It created two classes of citizens—active and passive—and limited the right of voting to those citizens who annually paid in taxes an amount equal to at least three days' wages for unskilled labor in their locality. The passive citizens, numbering about a third of the male population, enjoyed the full protection of the law but did not receive the vote. Moreover, the new legislature was chosen by indirect election. Active citizens voted for electors, who were required to be men of substantial wealth and who ultimately elected the deputies.

But the majority in the National Assembly suffered a fate often experienced by political moderates in a revolution: They were squeezed out by extremists. Despite moderate intentions, the majority were driven to enact some drastic legislation, notably the Civil Constitution of the Clergy, which weakened their own position. And they failed to develop an effective party organization in the face of the radical minority, called *Jacobins*. The Jacobins wanted to abolish the monarchy and to set up a republic based on universal suffrage. Their network of political clubs, which extended throughout the provinces, was the only nationwide party organization in France. Almost everywhere, Jacobins captured control of the new department and commune councils.

The defenders of the Old Regime unwittingly helped the Jacobins. After the summer of 1789, alarmed prelates and nobles fled France, leaving behind more rich estates to be confiscated. Many émigrés gathered in the German Rhineland to intrigue for Austrian and Russian support of a counterrevolution. The king's misgivings about the Civil Constitution of the Clergy prompted his disastrous attempt to join the émigrés on the Franco-German frontier. In June 1791, three months before the completion of the new constitution, Louis and Marie Antoinette left the Tuileries disguised as a valet and governess. But a local official along the route recognized Louis; the alarm was sent ahead, and a detachment of troops forced the royal party to make a hot, dusty, dispirited journey back to Paris. After the abortive flight, the revolutionaries viewed Louis XVI as a potential traitor and kept him closely guarded in the Tuileries.

The Legislative Assembly

On October 1 the first and only Legislative Assembly elected under the new constitution began deliberations. No one faction commanded a majority in the new Assembly, though the Center had the most seats.* Since they occupied the lowest seats in the assembly hall, the deputies of the center received the derogatory nickname of the Plain or Marsh. The capable politicians of the left soon captured the votes of the Plain, following the leadership of a loose grouping of Jacobins known in time as *Girondins*. Their chief spokesman was Jacques Brissot (1754–1793), an ambitious lawyer, journalist, and champion of reform causes. The Girondins were held together by their patriotic alarm over France's situation at home and abroad.

Accordingly, the Girondins specialized in fervent nationalist oratory. They pictured revolutionary France as the intended victim of a reactionary conspiracy—a conspiracy engineered by the émigrés, aided at home by the nonjuring clergy and the royal family, and abetted abroad by a league of monarchs under Leopold II, the Austrian emperor and brother of Marie Antoinette. The sudden death of Leopold in March 1792 and the accession of his inexperienced and less cautious son, Francis II (r. 1792–1835), increased the Austrian threat. On April 20 the Legislative Assembly declared war on Austria; the war was to continue, with a few brief intervals of peace, for the next twenty-three years.

The war went badly for France at the outset. Prussia soon joined Austria, and morale sagged on the home front when Louis dismissed the Girondin ministers because they had proposed to banish nonjuring priests and appointed more conservative replacements. Spirits began to rise in July, especially with a great celebration of the third anniversary of the assault on the Bastille. Paris was thronged with national guardsmen from the provinces on the way to the

---

* In the practice followed by most Continental European assemblies, the right sat to the right of the presiding officer as he faced the assembly, the left to his left, and the center in between; thus the common usage of *left* for radical and *right* for conservative parties.

front, and the contingent from Marseilles introduced to the capital a patriotic hymn which became the national anthem of republican France.

Through the early summer of 1792 the Jacobins of Paris had been plotting an insurrection. They won the support of a formidable following—army recruits, national guardsmen, and the rank-and-file Parisians who were angered by the depreciation of assignats and by the high price and short supply of food and other necessities. One by one the forty-eight wards into which the city was divided came under the control of Jacobins. The climax came on the night of August 9–10, when the regular municipal authorities were ousted from the Paris city hall and the Jacobins installed a new and illegal commune.

The municipal revolution had immediate and momentous results. On the morning of August 10 the forces of the new commune, joined by national guardsmen, attacked the Tuileries and massacred the king's Swiss guards, while the royal family took refuge with the Legislative Assembly. With most of the deputies of the Right and the Plain absent, the Assembly voted to suspend the king from office, to imprison the royal family, and to order the election of a constitutional convention. Until this new body should meet, the government was to be run by an interim ministry staffed largely by Girondins, but in which the strong-man was Georges Danton (1759–1794), a radical and an exceptional orator.

THE FIRST REPUBLIC

The weeks between August 10 and the meeting of the Convention on September 21 were a time of extreme tension. The value of the assignats depreciated by 40 percent during August alone. Jacobin propagandists, led by Jean Paul Marat (1743–1793), an embittered Swiss physician turned journalist, continually excited the people of Paris. Excitement mounted still higher when the news arrived that Prussian troops had invaded northeastern France. In the emergency, Danton, the minister of justice, won immortality by urging patriots to employ "boldness, more boldness, always boldness."

In Paris, boldness took the form of the September Massacres, mass killings of supposed traitors and enemy agents made possible by the collapse of normal police authority. For five days, beginning on September 2, mobs moved from prison to prison; at each stop they held impromptu courts and summary executions. Neither the new Paris commune nor the national ministry could check the hysterical wave of killings. The number of victims exceeded a thousand and included ordinary criminals and prostitutes as well as aristocrats and nonjuring priests, who were often innocent of the treason they were charged with. The September Massacres foreshadowed the terror to come.

On September 20 a rather minor French victory, grandly styled "the miracle of Valmy," turned the enemy

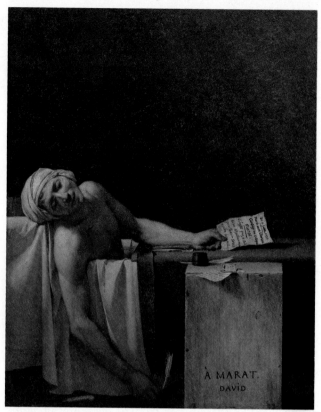

Jacques Louis David's dramatic and symbolic painting, *The Death of Marat* (1793) hangs in The Royal Museum of Fine Arts in Brussels. David drew upon the conventions of classical art while imposing a sense of dramatic realism on his work. The details of the composition provide narrative drive to the scene. Marat, David's friend, is seen as a betrayed hero. He lies in his bath, stabbed to death by a political enemy, Charlotte Corday (1769–1793), who was admitted to Marat's bath chamber on the basis of the letter he still holds.

Musées Royaux des Beaux-Arts de Belgique

forces back from the road to Paris; more solid French successes in Belgium, Savoy, and the Rhineland followed in late 1792. Then the tide turned again, washing away the conquests of the autumn. By the summer of 1793 a half-defeated France faced a hostile coalition including almost every major power in Europe. An atmosphere of perpetual emergency surrounded the Convention.

Gironde and Mountain, 1792–1793

In theory the election of deputies to the National Convention in 1792 marked the beginning of political democracy in France. Virtually all male citizens were invited to the polls. Yet only 10 percent of the potential electorate of 7 million actually voted; the rest abstained or were turned away from the polls by the watchdogs of the Jacobin clubs, ever on the alert against "counterrevolutionaries." The Convention was numerically dominated by the Center, or the Plain, but again, as in the Legislative Assembly, the Plain was politically irresolute, though now sympathetic to a republic. Many ties existed between the Gironde on the right and the Mountain (so named because its deputies sat high up in the meeting hall), who made up the left.

Gironde and Mountain united to declare France a republic on September 21, 1792. The Girondins wanted a breathing spell in revolutionary legislation; they also defended provincial interests against possible encroachments by Paris. The Gironde, therefore, favored a large measure of federalism—which in the revolutionary vocabulary meant decentralization and a national government limited by many checks and balances. The details were set forth in a draft constitution completed early in 1793 by the marquis de Condorcet: The executive and the legislature would be independent of each other and separately elected; the results of elections would be adjusted according to proportional representation; laws would be submitted to a popular referendum; and voters could recall unworthy officials. But the leaders of the Mountain denounced federalism and advocated an all-powerful central government.

The chief spokesman for the Mountain was Maximilien Robespierre (1758–1794). This earnest young lawyer did not look like a revolutionary. He powdered his hair neatly and wore the knee breeches of the Old Regime. Yet Robespierre was a political extremist whose speeches were lay sermons couched in the language of a new faith. Apparently Robespierre was sure that he knew the general will, and that it demanded a Republic of Virtue. If the French would not act in a free and virtuous fashion voluntarily, then, as Rousseau had recommended, they should be "forced to be free."

Robespierre and the Republic of Virtue triumphed. The Mountain won out over the Gironde in the Convention. The first step came when, after one hundred hours of continuous voting, the Convention declared the king, "Citizen Louis Capet," guilty of treason, and by a narrow margin sentenced him to the guillotine without delay. Louis XVI died bravely on January 21, 1793.

In February the Convention rejected Condorcet's draft constitution and declared war on Britain, Spain, and the Netherlands. France now faced a formidable coalition of opponents, including Austria and Prussia. In March the French army suffered a series of defeats in the Low Countries, and in April its Girondin commander deserted to the enemy. Marat now loudly denounced many Girondists as traitors; the Girondin deputies countered by calling for the impeachment of Marat, who was brought before a special tribunal and triumphantly acquitted. In July, Marat was assassinated in his bath by Charlotte Corday, a young woman wielding a butcher's knife who was convinced that she was a new Joan of Arc called to deliver France from Jacobin radicalism.

By then, however, the Girondins had been completely vanquished. In the face of unemployment, high prices, and shortages of food, soap, and other necessities, they had little to prescribe except more laissez faire. The sections, or wards, of Paris demanded price controls and food requisitioning; they also pressed for the expulsion of Girondins from the Jacobin clubs and the Convention. Finally, on June 2, 1793, a vast crowd of armed sansculottes from the sections, following the precedent of August 1792, invaded the hall and forced the arrest of twenty-nine Girondin deputies. Backed by these armed Parisians, the Mountain intimidated the Plain, and the Convention consigned the arrested Girondins to the guillotine. The Reign of Terror had begun.

The Reign of Terror, 1793–1794

How was it that the advocates of democracy now imposed a dictatorship on France? Let Robespierre explain:

> To establish and consolidate democracy, to achieve the peaceful rule of constitutional laws, we must first finish the war of liberty against tyranny. . . . We must annihilate the enemies of the republic at home and abroad, or else we shall perish.
>
> If virtue is the mainstay of a democratic government in time of peace, then in time of revolution a democratic government must rely on virtue and terror. . . . Terror is nothing but justice, swift, severe, and inflexible; it is an emanation of virtue. . . . It has been said that terror is the mainstay of a despotic government. . . . The government of the revolution is the despotism of liberty against tyranny.*

The Convention duly voted a democratic constitution, drawn up by the Mountain, granting universal manhood suffrage and giving supreme power, unhampered by Girondin checks and balances, to a single legislative chamber. The constitution of 1793 was approved by a large majority, but its operation was deferred, and it never came into force.

The actual government of the Terror centered on a twelve-man Committee of Public Safety, composed of Robespierre and other stalwarts largely from the Mountain. Though nominally responsible to the Convention, the Committee of Public Safety acted as a kind of war cabinet. Never under the dominance of a single member, it really functioned as a committee—"The Twelve Who Ruled." A second committee, that of General Security, supervised police activities and turned suspected enemies of the republic over to the new Revolutionary Tribunal.

The Mountain scrapped much of the local self-government inaugurated under the constitution of 1791. It also whittled away steadily at the prerogatives assumed by the Paris sections. Local Jacobin clubs purged department and commune administrations of members considered politically unreliable. Special local courts supplemented the grim labors of the Revolutionary Tribunal. To make provincial France toe the line, the Mountain sent out trusted "deputies on mission."

The "swift, severe, and inflexible justice" described by Robespierre took the lives of nearly twenty thousand French men and women. Although the Terror claimed such social outcasts as criminals and prostitutes, its main purpose was to clear France of suspected traitors, including Marie Antoinette (executed in Paris on October 16,

---

* *Le Moniteur Universel*, February 7, 1794. Our translation.

1793), and to purge the Jacobins of dissidents. It fell with the greatest severity on the clergy, the aristocracy, and the Girondins. Many of its victims came from the Vendée, a strongly Catholic and royalist area in western France that had risen in revolt. Prisoners from the Vendée were among the two thousand victims of drownings at Nantes, where the accused were manacled and set adrift on the River Loire in leaky barges.

The wartime hysteria that helped to account for the excesses of the Terror also inspired a very practical patriotism. The army drafted all bachelors and widowers between the ages of eighteen and twenty-five. Hundreds of open-air forges were installed in Paris to manufacture weapons. By the close of 1793 the forces of the republic had driven foreign troops from French soil.

Credit for this new shift in the tide of battle did not rest solely with the Jacobins. The military successes of the republic reflected in part the improvements made in the army during the dying years of the Old Regime; they resulted still more from the weaknesses of the coalition aligned against France. Yet they could scarcely have been achieved without the new democratic spirit that allowed men of the third estate to become officers.

Total mobilization demanded equality of economic sacrifice. To combat inflation and scarcity, the Terror issued "maximum" legislation, placing ceilings on prices and wages. In theory, wages were held at a maximum 50 percent above the wage rate of 1790, and prices were halted at 33 percent above the price level of 1790. The government rationed meat and bread, forbade the use of the more expensive white flour, and directed all patriots to eat *pain d'égalité* (equality bread), a loaf utilizing almost the whole of the wheat. Finally, early in 1794 the Convention passed the Laws of Ventôse, named for the third winter month in the new revolutionary calendar. These laws authorized seizure of the remaining properties of the émigrés and other opponents of the republic and recommended their distribution to landless French citizens.

Attempts by the government to enforce wage ceilings enraged Parisian workers. And though the "maximum" on prices temporarily checked the depreciation of the assignats, many price-controlled articles were available only on the black market, which even the government had to patronize. Moreover, the redistribution of property permitted by the Laws of Ventôse was never implemented.

The guillotine was the symbol of the Reign of Terror. As crowds watched, prisoners were decapitated and their heads held up for display. Popular engravings were sold to townspeople unable to witness the executions so that they could be reminded of them. In this illustration Marie Antoinette is executed, her head ceremonially held out to the assembled revolutionary army.

New York Public Library Picture Collection

THE WRITTEN RECORD

The Death of a King

There were many eyewitnesses to the events of the French Revolution. The English, of course, followed its destructive path with fascination. The following is an account (no doubt biased) by one such eyewitness, Henry Essex Edgeworth, a Catholic who went to Paris to be spiritual director to the Irish who lived in the capital.

The carriage proceeded thus in silence to the Place de Louis XV,* and stopped in the middle of a large space that had been left round the scaffold: this space was surrounded with cannon, and beyond, an armed multitude extended as far as the eye could reach. . . . As soon as the King had left the carriage, three guards surrounded him, and would have taken off his clothes, but he repulsed them with haughtiness: he undressed himself, untied his neckcloth, opened his shirt, and arranged it himself. The guards, whom the determined countenance of the King had for a moment disconcerted, seemed to recover their audacity. They surrounded him again, and would have seized his hands. "What are you attempting?" said the King, drawing back his hands. "To bind you," answered the wretches. "To bind *me*," said the King with an indignant air. "No! I shall never consent to that: do what you have been ordered, but you shall never bind me. . . ."

Many voices were at the same time heard encouraging the executioners. They seemed reanimated themselves, in seizing with violence the most virtuous of Kings, they dragged him under the axe of the guillotine, which with one stroke severed his head from his body. All this passed in a moment. The youngest of the guards, who seemed about eighteen, immediately seized the head, and shewed it to the people as he walked round the scaffold; he accompanied this monstrous ceremony with the most atrocious and indecent gestures. At first an awful silence prevailed; at length some cries of "Vive la République!" were heard. By degrees the voices multiplied, and in less than ten minutes this cry, a thousand times repeated, became the universal shout of the multitude, and every hat was in the air.

* Now the Place de la Concorde.

From *English Witnesses of the French Revolution*, ed. J. M. Thompson (Oxford: Basil Blackwell, 1938), pp. 230–31.

The Terror presented its most revolutionary aspect in its drastic social and cultural reforms. The Convention abolished slavery in the colonies (though it was to be reintroduced by Napoleon a decade later). At home, clothing, the arts, amusements, the calendar, religion, all were changed, for the Republic of Virtue could tolerate nothing that smelled of the Old Regime. Even the traditional forms of address, "Monsieur" and "Madame," gave way to "Citizen" and "Citizeness." The Convention also introduced the metric system as more in keeping with the Age of Reason; a special committee, devised new weights and measures based on the decimal system rather than on the haphazard accumulations of custom.

Sometimes the forces of tradition resisted the Terror, which tried to destroy the old religion but never succeeded in legislating a new faith. Many churches were closed and turned into barracks or administrative offices. Some of the Jacobins launched a "de-Christianization" campaign to make Catholics into philosophes and their churches into "Temples of Reason." Robespierre, however, disliked the cult of Reason; the Republic of Virtue, he believed, should acknowledge an ultimate author of morality. The Convention therefore decreed in May 1794 that "the French people recognize the existence of the Supreme Being and the immortality of the soul."

The France of Robespierre demanded superhuman devotion to duty and inhuman indifference to hardship and bloodshed. During the first half of 1794 Robespierre pressed the Terror so relentlessly that even the members of the Committees of Public Safety and General Security began to fear that they would be the next victims. The Law of the 22 Prairial, Year II (that is, June 10, 1794) enormously expanded the definition of "enemies of the people" who were subject to punishment by the Revolutionary Tribunal so as to include the following: "Those who have sought to disparage the National Convention . . . to have sought to impede the provisioning of Paris . . . to inspire discouragement . . . to mislead opinion, to deprave morals," and "those who, charged with public office, take advantage of it in order to serve the enemies of the Revolution, to harass patriots, or to oppress the people."*

Thus Robespierre began to lose his following both in the Convention and in the two powerful committees. More and more of his former supporters favored moderation and argued that the growing French success in the war called for less, not more, terror. The crucial day was the Ninth of Thermidor (the month of Heat, or July 27, 1794), when shouts of "Down with the tyrant!" and the refusal of the presiding officer to give Robespierre the

* From *A Documentary Survey of the French Revolution*, ed. J. H. Stewart (New York: Macmillan, 1951), pp. 528–29.

floor blocked his efforts to address the Convention. The Convention ordered his arrest, and on the next day he went to the guillotine.

Why had Robespierre fallen so quickly? He lost control because of the very situation he had created. An idealist who believed that a political society must guarantee the natural rights of humanity, he also believed that a Supreme Being protects the oppressed and punishes their oppressors. He had concluded that it was temporarily necessary to suspend the institutions in which he believed in order to break the chains imposed by tradition, to return in time to a life based on the principles he espoused. He sought, therefore, to destroy each faction systematically as it arose against him. But the charges he brought against others who could be considered as idealistic as he, and the summary justice meted out by his followers angered and frightened opposition groups in his own party. They united to fight back, both to protect the principles they felt he had abandoned and to protect their own lives.

The Thermidorean Reaction and the Directory, 1794–1799

The leaders of the Thermidorean Reaction, or the move toward moderation, many of them former Jacobins, now dismantled the machinery of the Terror. They disbanded the Revolutionary Tribunal, recalled the deputies on mission, and deprived the Committees of Public Safety and General Security of their independent authority. They closed the Paris Jacobin club and invited the surviving Girondin deputies to resume their old seats in the Convention. They took the first step toward restoring Catholicism by permitting priests to celebrate Mass, though under state supervision and without state financial support.

But instability, personal insecurity, and class and caste hatred were by now rife. In Paris long-haired young bourgeois calling themselves the *jeunesse dorée* (gilded youth) went about dressed like dandies and carrying long sticks, which they used to attack suspected Jacobins. They organized the destruction of busts of Marat and forced the removal of his remains from their burial place. The leaders of Thermidor caused an acute inflation by canceling the economic legislation of the Terror; no longer checked by the "maximum," the prices of some foods rose to a hundred times the level of 1790, and the assignats sank so low in value that businesses refused to accept them. Popular suffering became more intense than it had ever been under the Terror. Desperate, half-starving Parisians staged several demonstrations against the Thermidoreans during 1795, clamoring for bread and lower prices.

The Thermidorean Reaction concluded with the passage of the constitution of 1795, the last major act of the Convention. The Thermidoreans wanted both to retain the republic and to assure the dominance of the propertied classes. The new constitution therefore denied the vote to the poorest quarter of the nation and required that candidates for public office possess considerable property. It established two legislative councils, the Five Hundred and the Elders. The Council of Five Hundred nominated and the Elders chose five persons who headed the executive Directory, which otherwise was almost totally independent of the legislative councils.

The constitution of 1795 demonstrated that the most radical phase of the Revolution had passed. But three weeks before it was to go into operation, more trouble broke out in Paris. The counterrevolutionary insurgents were put down in the massacre of Vendémiaire (October 5, 1795), dispersed in part by the young Napoleon Bonaparte, who commanded troops loyal to the Thermidorean Convention. The first winter of the Directory (1795–1796) brought France the most intense popular suffering of the revolutionary period as a consequence of inflation, chronic shortage of food, and extreme cold. Thereafter, the situation steadily improved, thanks to good harvests and the Directory's vigorous attack on economic problems.

The new regime levied high protective tariffs, both as a war measure against England and as a concession to French business. Again responding to business pressure, it destroyed the plates used to print the assignats and in 1797 withdrew paper money from circulation. The return to hard money required stringent government economies, which the Directory instituted. Tax collection was made more efficient, and France enjoyed considerable loot from victorious wars. The Directory eased the crushing burden of the national debt by repudiating two thirds of it and gave the old unit of currency, the livre, a new and lasting name, the franc.

The Directory easily suppressed the amateurish Conspiracy of the Equals (1796–1797), sponsored by François Gracchus Babeuf (1760–1797), who has come down in socialist teachings as the first modern communist. The Directory experienced much greater difficulty, however, in steering a cautious middle course between the two extremes of restoring the monarchy and reverting to Jacobin terrorism. The constitution of 1795 was repeatedly violated, as the directors and the legislative councils clashed, each seeking to shift the political balance in its own favor. The councils fired directors before their terms were finished, and directors refused to allow duly elected council members to take their seats. Disgruntled politicians and apprehensive moderates, fearing the collapse of the regime, began to maneuver for the help of the increasingly successful army. The result was the coup d'état of Brumaire (that is, October) in 1799 and the dictatorship of Napoleon.

NAPOLEON AND FRANCE

As late as 1792 Catherine the Great predicted that ten thousand soldiers would suffice to douse the "abominable bonfire" in France. The war that broke out in the spring of 1792 soon destroyed such illusions. Almost all the European powers eventually participated, and the fighting

THE WRITTEN RECORD

Napoleon Rallies His Troops

In the Italian campaign Major General Bonaparte, still only in his twenties, cleared the Austrians out of their strongholds in one year and made them sue for peace. He showed a remarkable ability to strike quickly and to surprise his opponents before they could consolidate their defenses. He also showed a gift for propaganda and public relations, as this proclamation from the early phases of the campaign illustrates:

Soldiers! In two weeks you have won six victories; you have made fifteen-thousand prisoners; you have killed or wounded more than ten-thousand men.

Deprived of everything, you have accomplished everything. You have won battles without cannon, negotiated rivers without bridges, made forced marches without shoes, encamped without brandy, and often without bread. Only the phalanxes of the Republic, only the soldiers of Liberty, would have been capable of suffering the things that you have suffered.

You all burn to carry the glory of the French people; to humiliate the proud kings who dared to contemplate shackling us; to go back to your villages, to say proudly: "I was of the conquering army of Italy!"

Friends, I promise you that conquest; but there is a condition you must swear to fulfill: to respect the people whom you are delivering; to repress horrible pillaging.

Peoples of Italy, the French army comes to break your chains; greet it with confidence; your property, religion and customs will be respected.

Abridged from *Le Moniteur Universel*, May 17, 1796. Our translation.

---

ranged far beyond Europe. By the time the war was a year old, Austria and Prussia had been joined by Holland, Spain, and Great Britain. By 1794 the French had definitely gained the advantage, and in 1795 French troops occupied Belgium, Holland, and the Rhineland.

One reason for French success was the Convention's energetic mobilization of national resources, which enabled France to have the unprecedented total of a million men under arms by the spring of 1794. Another reason lay in the weakness of the first coalition, which lacked a first-rate commander. Moreover, the partitions of Poland in 1793 and 1795 greatly assisted the French because they kept Russia out of the war and greatly distracted Austria and Prussia. By 1795 mutual mistrust had reached the point where the Prussians dared not attack the French for fear of being attacked themselves by their nominal allies, the Austrians.

Prussia was the first member of the coalition to make peace. In the Treaty of Basel (1795), Prussia yielded to France the scattered Hohenzollern holdings west of the Rhine. Spain, which ceded to France the western part of the island of Santo Domingo (today the Dominican Republic), soon deserted the coalition, as did the Netherlands. Besides Belgium and the Rhineland, France had also annexed Savoy and Nice, thereby extending its southeastern border to the crest of the Alps. These conquests, however, belied the ideals of the Revolution. In declaring war on Austria in 1792, France had sworn to uphold a promise of the constitution of 1791: never to undertake a war of conquest. This was to be "not a war of nation against nation, but the righteous defense of a free people against the unjust aggression of a king."

But the conquering armies of the First Republic brought closer the day when nation would fight nation—when the other European nations would invoke "the righteous defense of a free people against the unjust aggression," not of a king, but of revolutionary France.

Bonaparte's Rise

By the close of 1795 only Britain and Austria remained officially at war with France. To lead the attack against Habsburg forces in northern Italy, the French Directory picked a youthful general who was something of a philosophe and revolutionary, as well as a ruthless, ambitious adventurer. He was born Napoleone Buonaparte on Corsica in 1769, soon after the French acquisition of that Mediterranean island from Genoa, and he retained throughout his life an intense family loyalty and a view of public affairs that was essentially anti-French.

As a boy of nine Napoleon began to attend military school in France and, though he now spelled his name in the French style, was snubbed as a foreigner by some of his fellow cadets. He immersed himself in reading Rousseau and dreamed of the day when he might liberate Corsica from French control.

When the Revolution broke out, the young artillery officer helped to overthrow the Old Regime in Corsica and then returned to France to resume his military career. He commanded the artillery in December 1793, when the forces of the Convention recaptured the Mediterranean port of Toulon, which had fallen to the British earlier in the year. After Thermidor he fell under a cloud as a suspected "terrorist" and settled for a desk job in Paris. He was available to rescue the Thermidorean Convention in Vendémiaire. He married Josephine de Beauharnais, a widow who was an intimate of the ruling clique of the Directory. The combination of Josephine's connections and Napoleon's talent gained him the Italian command in 1796.

In the Treaty of Campo Formio (1797), ending the Italian campaign, Austria acknowledged the loss of Belgium and recognized two puppet states that Napoleon set up in northwestern Italy: the Ligurian Republic (Genoa) and the Cisalpine Republic (the former Austrian possession of Lombardy). In return, the Habsburgs received the Italian territories of the Venetian Republic.

Only Britain remained at war with France. Napoleon decided to attack it indirectly through Malta and Egypt, the latter a semi-independent vassal of the Ottoman Empire. He invited more than a hundred archaeologists, geographers, and other scholars to accompany his army and thereby helped to found the study of Egyptology. Napoleon's experts established in Egypt an outpost of French culture that lasted into the twentieth century. From the military standpoint, however, the campaign failed. Having eluded the British Mediterranean fleet commanded by Horatio Nelson (1758–1805), Napoleon landed in Egypt in July 1798 and routed the Mamluks, the ruling oligarchy. Then disaster struck. On August 1, 1798, Nelson discovered the French fleet moored at Abukir Bay along the Egyptian coast and destroyed it before its captains could weigh anchor. Nelson's victory deprived the French of both supplies and reinforcements. After a year of futile campaigning in the Near East, Napoleon suddenly left Egypt in August 1799 and returned to France.

Napoleon found the situation in France ripe for a decisive political move, for the Directory was shaken by a strong revival of Jacobinism. Several hundred deputies in the legislative councils belonged to the Society of the Friends of Liberty and Equality, essentially the old Jacobin club. Under their influence, the councils in 1799 decreed a forced loan from the rich and passed a Law of Hostages, designed to make the émigrés stop plotting against the Directory by threatening their relatives in France with reprisals.

Abroad, the Directory had established four new satellite republics with classical names: the Batavian (Holland), the Helvetian (Switzerland), the Roman, and the Parthenopean (Naples). But this new success of French imperialism provoked the formation of the second coalition, headed by Britain, Austria, and Russia. Czar Paul I (r. 1796–1801) was head of the Knights of Malta, which Napoleon had expelled from its headquarters on the island of Malta. In the campaign of 1799 Russian troops fought in Italy and Switzerland, and the Russian general Alexander Suvorov (1729–1800), who defeated the French repeatedly, became the hero of western Europe. By August 1799 the French had been expelled from Italy.

In these circumstances, Napoleon was given a rousing reception on his return from Egypt. Soon he was plotting to overthrow the Directory, with the complicity of two of the five directors. On November 9 and 10, 1799 (18 and 19 Brumaire by the revolutionary calendar), the plot was executed. The three directors not in the plot resigned, and the two legislative councils named Napoleon military commander of Paris. He then barely persuaded the councils to entrust to the two remaining directors and himself the task of drafting a new constitution, and a detachment of troops loyal to Napoleon expelled the hostile deputies.

Consulate and Empire

The constitution of the Year VIII was the fourth attempt by revolutionary France to provide a written instrument of government, its predecessors being the constitutions of 1791, 1793, and 1795. The new document erected a very strong executive, the Consulate. Although three consuls shared the executive, Napoleon as first consul left the other two only nominal power. Four separate bodies had a hand in legislation: The Council of State proposed laws; the Tribunate debated them but did not vote; the Legislative Corps voted them but did not debate; the Senate had the right to veto legislation. The members of all four bodies were either appointed by the first consul or elected indirectly by a process so complex that Bonaparte had ample opportunity to manipulate candidates. The core of this system was the Council of State, staffed by Bonaparte's hand-picked choices, which served both as a cabinet and as the highest administrative court. The three remaining bodies were intended merely to go through the motions of enacting whatever the first consul decreed. Even so, they were sometimes unruly, and the Tribunate so annoyed Napoleon that he finally abolished it in 1807.

Meantime, step by step, Napoleon increased his own authority. In 1802 he persuaded the legislators to make him first consul for life, with the power to designate his successor and to amend the constitution at will. France was now a monarchy again in all but name. In 1804 Napoleon prompted the Senate to declare that "the government of the republic is entrusted to an emperor." A magnificent coronation took place at Notre Dame in Paris on December 2. The pope consecrated the emperor, but, following Charlemagne's example, Napoleon placed the crown on his own head.

Each time Napoleon revised the constitution in a nonrepublican direction, he made the republican gesture of submitting the change to the electorate. Each time the results were overwhelmingly favorable: In 1799–1800 the vote was 3,011,107 for Napoleon and the constitution of the Year VIII, and 1,562 against; in 1803 it was 3,568,885 for Napoleon and the life consulate, and 8,374 against; in 1804 it was 3,572,329 for Napoleon and the empire, and 2,579 against. Although the voters were exposed to considerable official pressure and the announced results were perhaps rigged a little, the majority in France undoubtedly supported Napoleon. His military triumphs appealed to their growing nationalism, and his policy of stability at home ensured them against further revolutionary crises and changes.

Men of every political background now staffed the highly centralized imperial administration. Napoleon cared little whether his subordinates were returned émigrés or ex-Jacobins, so long as they had ability. Besides, their varied antecedents reinforced the impression that narrow factionalism was dead and that the empire rested on a broad political base. Napoleon paid officials well and offered the additional inducement of high titles. With the establishment of the empire he created dukes by the dozen and counts and barons by the hundred. He rewarded outstanding generals with the rank of marshal and other officers with admission to the Legion of Honor, which also paid its members an annual pension. "Aristocracy always exists," Napoleon remarked. "Destroy it in the nobility, it removes itself to the rich and powerful houses of the middle class."

Law and Justice

Napoleon revived some of the glamor of the Old Regime but not its glaring inequalities. His series of law codes, the Code Napoléon (1804–1810), declared all men equal before the law without regard to rank and wealth. It extended to all the right to follow the occupation and embrace the religion of their own choosing. It gave France the single coherent system of law that the philosophes had demanded and that the revolutionary governments had been unable to formulate.

The Code Napoléon did not, however, embody the full judicial reform program of the Enlightenment. It favored the interests of the state over the rights of the individual, and it permitted some use of torture in trial procedure. Judges were appointed by the emperor; jurors were selected by his prefects. Though Napoleon confirmed the revolutionary legislation permitting divorce by mutual consent, the code canceled other revolutionary laws protecting wives, minors, and illegitimate children, and restored the man of the family to his former legal superiority. It also restored slavery in French colonies.

Ambiguity also clouded Napoleon's attitude toward civil liberties. Although he prided himself on welcoming former political heretics into his administration, his generosity always stemmed from expediency, never from fundamental belief in liberty. If he failed to get his way by conciliation, he used force. In the western departments, where royalist uprisings had become chronic, he massacred rebels who declined his offer of amnesty in 1800. In 1804 he kidnapped a Bourbon prince from the neutral German state of Baden because the prince was believed to be the choice of monarchist conspirators for the throne of France. Though Napoleon immediately discovered the prince's innocence, he had him executed nonetheless.

Religion and Education

Political considerations generally colored Napoleon's decisions on religion. Since French Catholics loathed the anticlericalism of the Revolution, Napoleon sought to appease them by working out a reconciliation with Rome. The Concordat (a treaty with the Vatican) negotiated with Pope Pius VII (r. 1800–1823) in 1802 accomplished this reconciliation. While it canceled only the most obnoxious features of the Civil Constitution of the Clergy, the French state agreed to end the popular election of bishops and priests. The bishops were to be nominated by the government and then consecrated by the pope; the priests were to be appointed by the bishops. But by declaring that Catholicism was the faith of the "great majority of Frenchmen," rather than the state religion, the Concordat implicitly admitted the toleration of Protestants and Jews, both of whom were expected to accept state supervision of their governing councils.

Finally, the Concordat made the activities of the church in France subject to the "police regulations" of the state. The French government was to supervise the publication of papal bulls, the establishment of seminaries, the content of catechisms, and a host of other details. Despite all this, the anticlericals opposed the Concordat, and it took all Napoleon's influence to obtain its ratification by the legislative bodies of the Consulate.

The Concordat, then, made the church a ward of the French state. Though it antagonized anticlericals, it conciliated many Catholics, and it remained in force until 1905. The Concordat, however, did not bring complete peace between France and the Vatican. When Pius VII objected to Napoleon's making a French satellite of the Papal States, the "new Caesar" lectured him on the proper division of authority between the spiritual and temporal powers. Pius passed the last years of the Napoleonic regime as a prisoner, in northern Italy and then in France.

The Revolution and Napoleon also cost the church its monopoly over education. The constitution of 1791 had promised France a system of state schools. The Thermidorean Convention established a "central school" in each department of France to provide secondary education of good quality at relatively low cost to students. Napoleon abolished these central schools in 1802 and replaced them with a smaller number of central lycées open only to the relatively few pupils who could afford the tuition or who received state scholarships. The students wore uniforms and marched to military drums, and the curriculum, too, served the ends of patriotic indoctrination. Napoleon neglected primary schooling almost completely, yet he did advance the construction of secular schools. The way was open for bitter educational competition between church and state in nineteenth-century France.

Economics

Political aims also governed the economic program of an emperor determined to promote national unity. French peasants wanted to be left alone to enjoy the new freedom acquired in 1789. Napoleon did little to disrupt them, except to raise army recruits. He continued the hard money policy of the Directory and, unlike the Directory, balanced the budget, thanks in part to the plunder that he gained in war. He greatly improved the efficiency and honesty of tax collectors and established the semiofficial

This romantic portrait of Napoleon, also by Jacques Louis David, shows him pausing after working early into the morning (note the clock behind him) on his famous Code Napoléon. He appears to be exceeding even his own demand for "two-o'clock-in-the-morning courage." He wears the insignia of the Legion of Honor (which he created) and the epaulettes of a general. Upon seeing this flattering portrait, Napoleon said to David, "You have understood me. By night I work for the welfare of my subjects and by day for their glory." The painting is in the National Gallery in Washington.

National Gallery of Art, Washington, Samuel H. Kress Collection

Bank of France (1800) to act as the government's financial agent. He strengthened the curbs placed on strikes and labor unions and obliged every worker to carry a *livret* (booklet), in effect an identity card recording the worker's jobs and general reputation. Though seaports suffered from the decline of overseas trade, rich war contracts and subsidies kept employment and profits generally high. As the war went on and on, however, Napoleon found it increasingly difficult to keep the peasantry and the bourgeoisie contented, and the seaport populations suffered grievously. Despite the levies on conquered countries, he had to draft more soldiers from the peasantry and increase the already unpopular taxes on salt, liquor, and tobacco.

In summary, Napoleon paid lip service to the republic while subverting republican institutions; he used prefects to impose centralized authority, and he scorned free speech. Yet Napoleon was an enlightened despot. His law code and some of his educational reforms would have delighted the philosophes. He ended civil strife without sacrificing the redistribution of land and the equality before the law gained in 1789 and the years following. Abandoning some revolutionary policies, modifying others, and completing still others, Napoleon regimented the Revolution without wholly destroying it.

NAPOLEON AND EUROPE

To many in France, Napoleon was and remains the most brilliant ruler in French history. To many Europeans, on the other hand, Napoleon was a foreigner who imposed French control and French reforms. Napoleonic France succeeded in building up a vast and generally stable empire, but only at the cost of arousing the enmity of other European nations.

The War, 1800–1807

Napoleon had barely launched the Consulate when he took to the field again. The second coalition was falling to pieces. Czar Paul of Russia alarmed Britain and Austria by his interest in Italy, and Britain offended him by retaining Malta, the headquarters of his Knights. Accordingly, the czar formed a Baltic League of Armed Neutrality linking Prussia, Sweden, and Denmark with Russia against Britain. He even contemplated joining with France to drive the British out of India; this scheme collapsed when he was murdered in 1801 and succeeded by his son, Alexander I. The Baltic League disintegrated in the same year after Nelson violated Denmark's neutrality to bombard its fleet in port at Copenhagen. Napoleon defeated the Austrians in Italy and negotiated the Treaty of Lunéville (1801), whereby Austria recognized the reconstituted French satellites in Italy and agreed that France should have a hand in redrawing the map of Germany.

After Lunéville, Britain again remained alone at war with France. British taxpayers, however, wanted relief from their heavy burden; British merchants longed to resume trading with the Continental markets partially closed to them since 1793. Though Britain had been unable to check Napoleon's expansion in Europe, it had very nearly won the colonial and naval war by 1801. The British had captured former Dutch and Spanish colonies, and Nelson's fleet had expelled the French from Egypt and Malta. The British cabinet was confident that it held a strong bargaining position and could obtain favorable terms from Napoleon. Yet in the Peace of Amiens (1802) the British promised to surrender part of their colonial conquests and got nothing in return. The French failed either to reopen the Continent to British exports or to relinquish Belgium.

The one-sided Peace of Amiens provided only a year's truce in the worldwide struggle of France and Britain. Napoleon soon aroused British exporters by a more stringent tariff law and jeopardized British interests in the Caribbean by a grandiose project for a colonial empire based on Haiti and on the vast Louisiana territory ceded back to France in 1800 by Spain. In Haiti, the blacks revolted against the efforts of the Consulate to reimpose slavery. Stubborn black resistance under Francois Toussaint L'Ouverture (c. 1744–1803) and Jean Jacques Dessalines (c. 1758–1806), ex-slaves, and an outbreak of yellow fever took a fearful toll of French troops and forced Napoleon to abandon the American project. In 1803 he sold to the United States for 80 million francs (about $16 million) all of the Louisiana territory.

When the Louisiana Purchase was completed, France and Britain were again at war. From 1803 through 1805 Napoleon actively prepared to invade England. He assembled more than 100,000 troops and a thousand landing barges on the French side of the Straits of Dover. In 1805 he sent Admiral Pierre de Villeneuve (1763–1806) and the French fleet to the West Indies to lure the British fleet away from Europe. Villeneuve was to slip back to Europe to escort the French invasion force across the Channel while Nelson was still combing the Caribbean in search of the French fleet.

Villeneuve failed to give Nelson the slip; back in European waters, he put in at a friendly Spanish port instead of heading directly for the Channel, as Napoleon had ordered. Nelson engaged the combined French and Spanish fleets off Cape Trafalgar at the southwest corner of Spain (October 1805). He lost his own life, but not before he had destroyed half of his adversaries' ships without sacrificing one of his own. The battle of Trafalgar gave the British undisputed control of the seas and blasted French hopes of a cross-Channel invasion.

By the time of Trafalgar, Austria and Russia had joined with Britain in a third coalition. Austria in particular had been alarmed by Napoleon's efforts to promote a major revision of the political map of Germany by abolishing more than a hundred German city-states and small ecclesiastical principalities. The chief beneficiaries of this readjustment were south German states that Napoleon clearly intended to form into a bloc dominated by France, as opposed to Austria and Prussia.

Napoleon routed the Continental members of the coalition in the most dazzling campaign of his career. At Ulm, on the upper Danube (October 1805), he captured thirty thousand Austrians who had moved westward without waiting for their Russian allies. He met the main Russian force and the balance of the Austrian army near the village of Austerlitz. The ensuing battle (December 2, 1805) fittingly celebrated the first anniversary of Napoleon's coronation as emperor. Bringing up reinforcements secretly and with great speed, Napoleon completely surprised his opponents; their casualties were three times greater than his own. Within the month he forced the Habsburg emperor, Francis II, to sign the humiliating Treaty of Pressburg, giving the Austrian Tyrol to Bavaria, and Venetia to the Napoleonic puppet kingdom of Italy.

A still harsher fate awaited the Prussians, brought back into the war for the first time since 1795 by Napoleon's repeated interventions in German affairs. In October 1806 the French smashed the main Prussian contingents in the twin battles of Jena and Auerstädt and occupied Berlin. But Napoleon postponed a final settlement with Prussia until he had beaten his only remaining Continental opponent, Russia, at Friedland in June of 1807.

Even though Napoleon's great string of victories against the third coalition resulted partly from the blunders of his enemies, the French army was now the most seasoned and feared force in Europe. New recruits were furnished by conscription, which raised an average of eighty-five thousand men a year under Napoleon, and they were quickly toughened by being assigned in small batches to veteran units. French officers were promoted on the basis of ability rather than seniority or influence, and they were, on the whole, more concerned with maintaining the morale of their men than with imposing strict discipline. Napoleon seldom risked an engagement unless his forces were the numerical equal of the enemy's; then he staked everything on a dramatic surprise. Yet even his seemingly invincible French army had defects. The medical services were poor, so that most deaths on campaigns were from disease or improperly treated wounds. Pay was low and irregular, and supplies were also irregular, since it was French policy to have men and horses live off the land as much as they could.

Napoleon reached the pinnacle of his career when he met Czar Alexander I on the "neutral ground" of a raft anchored in the Niemen River at Tilsit, on the frontier between East Prussia and Russia. There, in July 1807, the two emperors drew up a treaty dividing Europe between them. Alexander acknowledged France's hegemony over central and western Europe and secured in return the recognition of eastern Europe as the Russian sphere. Napoleon pledged Russia a share in the spoils of the Ottoman Empire if it were dismembered. He demanded no territory from the defeated czar, only a commitment to cease trade with Britain and to join the war against it.

While the two emperors negotiated on the raft, Frederick William III (r. 1797–1840), the Prussian king, nervously paced the banks of the Nieman. He had good cause to be nervous, for Tilsit cost him almost half his territory. Prussia's Polish provinces formed a new puppet state, the grand duchy of Warsaw. Prussian territory west of the Elbe River went to Napoleon to dispose of as he wished.

Thus all Europe was divided into three parts: first came the French Empire, including France proper and the territories annexed since 1789; second were the satellites, ruled in many cases by relatives of Napoleon; and third came Austria, Prussia, and Russia, forced by defeat to become allies of France. The only powers remaining outside the Napoleonic system were Britain, Turkey, and Sweden.

In central Europe Napoleon decreed a further reduction in the number of German states, and in 1806 he aided the formal dissolution of the Holy Roman Empire. Francis II, the reigning Habsburg, now called himself emperor of Austria. To replace the vanished empire, Napoleon created the Confederation of the Rhine, which included almost every German state except Austria and Prussia. At the heart of this confederation Napoleon carved out for his brother Jerome the kingdom of Westphalia, which incorporated the Prussian holdings west of the Elbe seized at Tilsit.

Napoleon longed to give dignity and permanence to his creations. It was not enough that his brothers and his in-laws should sit on thrones; he himself must found a dynasty, must have the heir so far denied him in fifteen years of childless marriage. He divorced Josephine, therefore, and in 1810 married Marie-Louise, the daughter of the Habsburg Francis II. In due time Marie-Louise bore a son, called "the king of Rome" but destined never to rule in Rome or anywhere else.

The Continental System

Nowhere was Napoleon's imperialism more evident than in the Continental System. This was an attempt to regulate the economy of the whole Continent. It had a double aim: to build up the export trade of France and to cripple that of Britain. The Berlin Decree, issued by Napoleon in November 1806, forbade all trade with the British Isles and all commerce in British merchandise. It ordered the arrest of all Britons on the Continent and the confiscation of their property. Britain replied by requiring that neutral vessels wishing to trade with France put in first at a British port and pay duties. Napoleon retaliated with the Milan Decree (December 1807), ordering the seizure of all neutral ships that complied with the new British policy. The neutrals, as neutrals often are, were caught in the middle; the two decrees effectively instituted a Continental blockade.

Napoleon's vassals and allies had to support the Continental System or suffer the consequences. Of all the "un-French" activities countenanced in Holland, the worst, in Napoleon's view, was toleration of Dutch smuggling of English contraband. The emperor also expected the satellites to feed French industrial prosperity.

The Continental System failed almost totally. Only a few French industries benefited; the cessation of sugar imports from the West Indies, for example, promoted the cultivation of native sugar beets. But the decline of overseas trade depressed Bordeaux and other French Atlantic ports, and the increasing difficulty of obtaining such raw materials as cotton caused widespread unemployment and produced a rash of bankruptcies. Since the new French markets on the Continent did not compensate for the loss of older markets overseas, the value of French exports declined by more than a third between 1805 and 1813.

The Continental System did not ruin Britain, although it did confront the British with a severe economic crisis. Markets abroad for British exports were uncertain; food imports were reduced; while prices rose sharply, wages lagged behind; and because of hoarding, coins were in such short supply that not enough could be minted to keep pace with the demand. Both farm and factory workers suffered acutely. Yet Britain rode out the storm. More land was brought under the plow. Factory owners improvised substitute payments for their workers when coins were unavailable. Exporters not only developed lucrative new markets in the Americas, the Ottoman Empire, and Asia but also smuggled goods to old customers on the Continent. Napoleon lacked the naval force to seize smugglers at sea, and he lacked a staff of incorruptible customs inspectors to control contraband in the ports.

The Continental System antagonized both the neutral powers and Napoleon's allies. French seizure of United States merchant vessels in European ports under the terms of the Milan Decree put a dangerous strain on Franco-American relations. But British restrictions also weighed heavily on the Americans. British impressment of American seamen on the pretext that they were deserters from the Royal Navy, together with the designs on Canada of expansionists in the United States, produced an indecisive and minor Anglo-American war in 1812–1814.

The Peninsular War, 1808–1813

In Europe the political and military consequences of the Continental System formed a decisive and disastrous chapter in Napoleonic history, a chapter that opened in 1807 when the emperor decided to impose the system on Britain's traditional ally, Portugal. The Portuguese expedition furnished Napoleon with an excuse for the military occupation of neighboring Spain. In 1808 he overthrew the Spanish royal family and made his brother Joseph his puppet king of Spain. But every measure taken by Napoleon—the installation of a foreign monarch, the attempted enforcement of the Continental System, the suppression of the Inquisition, and the curtailment of noble and clerical privileges—violated Spanish customs and offended Spanish pride. The population of Madrid rose in revolt on May 2, 1808.

Although the uprising in Madrid was brutally repressed, the Peninsular War (named after the Iberian peninsula) rapidly grew. The Spaniards employed ambushes and poisoned wells and used other guerrilla devices. The expedition that Britain sent to assist the Spaniards was ably commanded and generously supplied. Napoleon poured more than 300,000 troops into the campaign, but his opponents gained the upper hand in 1812, when he detached part of his forces for an invasion of Russia.

German National Awakening

German intellectuals launched a campaign to check the great influence that the French language and French culture had gained over their divided lands. Jacob Grimm (1785–1863) and his brother Wilhelm (1786–1859) contributed not only their very popular *Fairy Tales* (published 1812–1815) but also research designed to prove the superiority of the German language. The philosopher J. G. Fichte (1762–1814) delivered at Berlin the highly

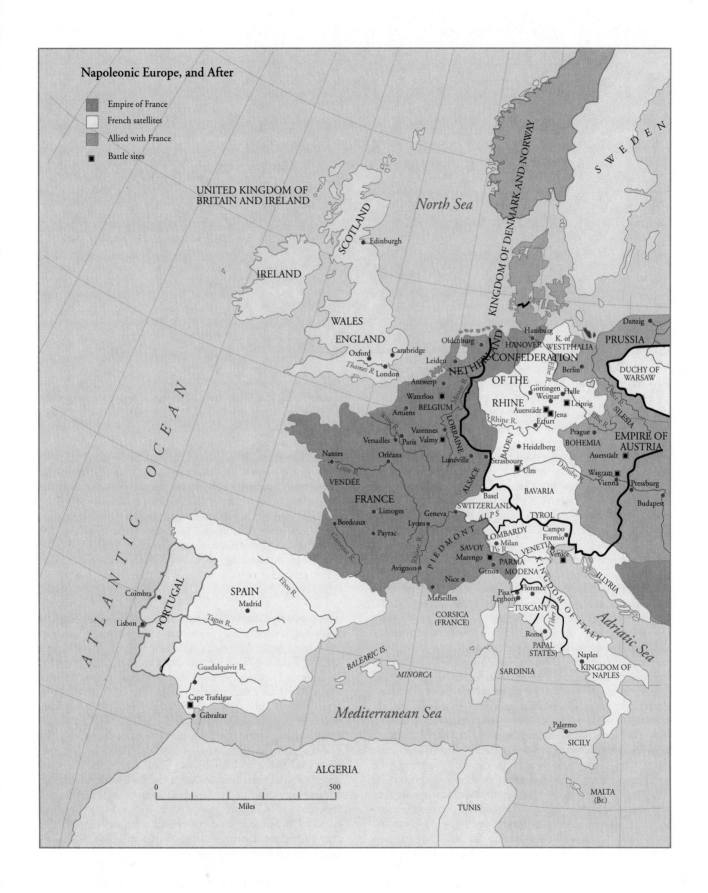

Napoleonic Europe, and After

- Empire of France
- French satellites
- Allied with France
- ■ Battle sites

ATLANTIC OCEAN

North Sea

UNITED KINGDOM OF BRITAIN AND IRELAND

SCOTLAND

Edinburgh

IRELAND

WALES

ENGLAND

Oxford

Cambridge

Thames R. London

SWEDEN

KINGDOM OF DENMARK AND NORWAY

Hamburg

Oldenburg

HANOVER

K. of WESTPHALIA

PRUSSIA

Danzig

DUCHY OF WARSAW

NETHERLAND

CONFEDERATION

Berlin

Leiden

Antwerp

BELGIUM

Waterloo

Amiens

LORRAINE

OF THE

RHINE

Göttingen

Weimar

Halle

Auerstädt

Jena

Erfurt

Leipzig

Oder R.

SILESIA

Elbe R.

Prague

BOHEMIA

EMPIRE OF AUSTRIA

Seine R.

Versailles

Paris

Varennes

Valmy

Nantes

Orléans

Lunéville

Auerstädt

Loire R.

VENDÉE

FRANCE

Limoges

Bordeaux

Payrac

Garonne R.

Rhône R.

Geneva

Lyons

Avignon

ALSACE

Basel

Strasbourg

Ulm

Heidelberg

BADEN

SWITZERLAND

ALPS

PIEDMONT

Savoy

Nice

Marseilles

CORSICA (FRANCE)

Rhine R.

BAVARIA

Danube R.

Wagram

Vienna

Pressburg

Budapest

TYROL

LOMBARDY

Milan

Campo

Formio

VENETIA

Venice

Marengo

Genoa

PARMA

MODENA

ILLYRIA

Adriatic Sea

Pisa

Leghorn

Florence

TUSCANY

KINGDOM OF ITALY

Tiber R.

Rome

PAPAL STATES

Naples

KINGDOM OF NAPLES

PORTUGAL

Coimbra

Lisbon

SPAIN

Madrid

Ebro R.

Tagus R.

Guadalquivir R.

Cape Trafalgar

Gibraltar

BALEARIC IS.

MINORCA

SARDINIA

SICILY

Palermo

Mediterranean Sea

ALGERIA

TUNIS

MALTA (Br.)

0   500

Miles

The Spanish artist Francisco de Goya (1746–1828) had the deepest sympathy for the victims of war and none at all for royalty—including Spain's. It was said that he made his initial sketches in the blood of executed Spanish patriots. Here he shows the point-blank executions of Spaniards by the French in Madrid on May 3, 1808. The painting hangs in the Prado in Madrid; Goya painted it in 1814, in continued protest against war.

Museo del Prado, Madrid

patriotic *Addresses to the German People* (1807–1808), claiming that German was the *Ursprache*—the fountainhead of language. The Germans themselves, Fichte continued, were the *Urvolk*—the oldest and most ethical of nations.

The new German consciousness was evident even when Austria had reentered the war against France in 1809. While the new spirit enabled the Austrians to make a better showing, they were narrowly defeated at Wagram (1809) and for the fourth time in a dozen years submitted to a peace dictated by Napoleon. The Treaty of Schönbrunn (1809) stripped them of their coastline on the Adriatic and assigned their Polish territory of Galicia to the grand duchy of Warsaw. Francis II gave his daughter to Napoleon in marriage, and his defeated land became the unwilling ally of France. Leadership in the German revival passed to Prussia.

The shocks of Jena and Tilsit jarred Prussia out of the administrative lethargy that had overtaken it since the death of Frederick the Great in 1786. The University of Berlin attracted Fichte and other prophets of German nationalism, and there they began to lay down the theories of a new German national state. Able generals and statesmen, most of them non-Prussian, came to power. General Gerhard von Scharnhorst (1755–1813) headed a group of officers who reorganized the army on more democratic principles and improved its efficiency. The ceiling of forty-two thousand soldiers imposed by Napoleon was evaded by the simple device of assigning recruits to the reserve after a fairly brief period of intensive training and then inducting another group of recruits. By 1813 Prussia had more than 150,000 trained men available for combat duty.

The social and administrative reorganization of the Prussian state was inspired by the energetic Baron Karl von und zum Stein (1757–1831), an enlightened aristocrat from the Rhineland. Stein conciliated the middle class by granting towns and cities some self-government. He granted some civil rights to Jews. To improve the status of the peasantry, he sponsored an edict of October 1807 abolishing serfdom in Prussia. The edict, however, did not break up the large Junker estates or provide land for the liberated serfs, many of whom thereafter led a difficult existence as day laborers. Nor did it terminate the feudal rights of justice the Junkers exercised over their peasants. Stein and others eliminated only the worst abuses of the Old Regime and left authority where it had traditionally rested—with the king, the army, and the Junkers.

Prussian Landed Aristocracy

The Russian Campaign, 1812–1813

The event that defeated Napoleon's great designs was the French debacle in Russia. French actions after 1807 soon convinced Czar Alexander that Napoleon was not keeping the Tilsit bargain and was intruding on Russia's sphere in eastern Europe. When Alexander and Napoleon met again at the German town of Erfurt in 1808, they could reach no agreement. For Alexander, French acquisitions from Austria in 1809 raised the unpleasant prospect of French domination over the Balkans, and the transfer of Galicia from Austria to the grand duchy of Warsaw suggested that this Napoleonic vassal might next seek to absorb Russia's acquisitions from the partitions of Poland. Meanwhile, Napoleon's insistent efforts to make Russia enforce the Continental System increasingly angered Alexander. These grievances caused a break between the czar and the emperor and led to the invasion of Russia by the French in 1812.

For the invasion Napoleon assembled nearly 700,000 men, most of whom were unwilling conscripts. The supply system for so distant a campaign broke down almost immediately, and the Russian scorched-earth policy made it hard for soldiers to live off the land and impossible for horses to get fodder, so that many of them had to be destroyed. As the army marched eastward, one of Napoleon's aides reported:

> There were no inhabitants to be found, no prisoners to be taken, not a single straggler to be picked up. We were in the heart of inhabited Russia and yet we were like a vessel without a compass in the midst of a vast ocean, knowing nothing of what was happening around us.*

Napoleon had hoped to strike a quick knockout blow, but the battle of Borodino was indecisive. Napoleon entered Moscow and remained in the burning city for five weeks (September–October 1812) in the vain hope of bringing Czar Alexander to terms. But Russian stubbornness, typhus, and the shortage of supplies forced Napoleon to begin a nightmare retreat. Ill-fed, inadequately clothed and sheltered, without medical help, the retreating soldiers suffered horribly. Less than a quarter of the army survived the retreat from Moscow; the rest had been taken prisoner or had died of wounds, starvation, disease, or had frozen to death.

Napoleon's Fall, 1813–1815

The British had been the first to resist Napoleon successfully, at Trafalgar and on the economic battlefields of the Continental System. Then had come Spanish resistance, followed by Russian. Now in 1813 almost every nation in Europe joined the final coalition against the French. Napoleon raised a new army, but he could not so readily replace the equipment lost in Russia. In October 1813 he lost the "Battle of the Nations," fought at Leipzig in Germany, necessitating his retreat into France. The German troops in his army were deserting, the Confederation of the Rhine collapsed, Italian support was increasingly unreliable, and the mystique of Napoleon was blighted. By April 1814 the well-organized forces of the coalition occupied Paris. Faced also with mounting unrest and conspiracy at home, the emperor abdicated when his marshals refused to continue the war. Napoleon was sent into exile as ruler of the island of Elba, off the western coast of Italy.

The statesmen of the victorious coalition gathered in the Congress of Vienna to draw up the terms of peace. The Bourbons returned to France in the person of Louis XVIII, a younger brother of Louis XVI. Realizing that he could not revive the Old Regime intact, the new king issued the Charter of 1814 establishing a constitutional monarchy. Then, on March 1, 1815, Napoleon pulled his last surprise: He landed on the Mediterranean coast of France.

For a hundred days, from March 20, when Napoleon reentered Paris, the French empire was reborn. Once again the emperor rallied the French people, this time by promising a truly liberal regime with a real parliament and genuine elections. He never had time, however, to show whether his promise was sincere, for on June 18 the British under Sir Arthur Wellesley (1769–1852), the duke of Wellington, and the Prussians under General Gebhard von Blücher (1742–1819) delivered the final blow at Waterloo, near Brussels. Again Napoleon was sent into exile, this time to the remote British island of St. Helena in the South Atlantic. There in 1821 he died, perhaps from arsenic poisoning. Bonapartism, however, did not die with him. A Napoleonic legend arose, glossing over the faults and failures of the emperor, depicting him as a champion of liberalism and patriotism, and paving the way for the advent of another Napoleon in 1848.

THE LEGACY OF THE REVOLUTION

The French Revolution was the most fundamental event of the nineteenth century, and its meaning, its causes, and its impact continue to be debated. One debate is whether there was an autonomous peasant revolution directed against feudalism imbedded within the larger revolution, with the peasants seeking their own road to capitalism. Clearly hostility to harvest dues and other seigneurial burdens had unified many rural communities to the point that protests continued well after the National Assembly had declared feudalism abolished. But peasants did not generally take a stand for or against the republic, and while administrative changes had a deep effect on rural society, peasants continued to favor collective use of the land. On the whole the rhetoric of revolutionaries in Paris had little influence on seigneurial obligations, especially when fiscal problems forced the revolutionaries to abandon efforts to privatize common lands. While peasants near Paris did demand individual allotments from the commons, such changes do not appear to have been widespread. Nonetheless, for the peasantry the Revolution brought significant changes, especially in southern France, by abolishing the seigneurial system, encouraging birth control, creating formal municipal institutions, reforming the judicial system, and reducing fiscal inequities.

Another debate is over the role of women in the revolution. Working through a variety of power brokers, many women sought to achieve greater equality, to break from the church, and to play political roles, if largely behind the scenes. Ultimately the Revolution deeply disappointed them, and the most articulate of the women made it clear that they considered their hopes had been betrayed, that "prosperity" for some was not prosperity for them.

Perhaps the most overriding debate is between the Marxists and non-Marxists, and within each school, between early analysts and revisionists. Often these debates turn upon preconceptions of the nature of human motivation, sometimes on the nature of language and the

---

* Armand Augustin Louis, Marquis de Caulaincourt, *With Napoleon in Russia: The Memoirs of General de Caulaincourt, Duke of Vicenza* (New York: Morrow, 1935), p. 62.

intent, as opposed to the performance, of specific individuals and groups. Often the debate is over the relative significance of cultural and political factors as opposed to social and economic, or over the extent to which even this most revolutionary of revolutions was evolutionary. As study of the French Revolution has broadened and deepened, especially during the observation of the Revolution's bicentennial in the 1980s, historians have come to realize how difficult generalization can be: what was true for Paris was not true for Bordeaux; the revolt of 1793 in Lyons arose from causes in some significant measure different from events in Marseilles. Thus the French Revolution continues to be eternally fascinating, eternally studied, and eternally debatable.

The Napoleonic legend, with its hero worship and belligerent nationalism, was one element in the legacy bequeathed by revolutionary and Napoleonic France. A second and much more powerful element was the great revolutionary motto—*Liberté, Egalité, Fraternité*—which inspired later generations in France and elsewhere. Behind the motto was the fact that the French, though not yet enjoying the full democracy of the twentieth century, enjoyed greater liberty, equality, and fraternity in 1815 than they had ever known before 1789. Although French institutions in 1815 did not measure up to the ideals of

liberty expressed in the Declaration of the Rights of Man, the ideals had been stated.

The revolutionary and Napoleonic regimes established the principle of equal liability to taxation. They provided more economic opportunity for the third estate by removing obstacles to the activity of business people and by breaking up the large estates of the clergy and nobility; these lands passed mainly to the urban bourgeois and the well-to-do peasants. The only gesture toward full equality of property was the Laws of Ventôse of 1794, and they were never implemented. The Revolution was an important step in the ascendancy of middle-class capitalism, both urban and rural. In this sense the work of the Revolution was not truly democratic, since the sans-culottes had apparently gained so little. Yet the Code Napoléon did bury beyond all hope of return the worst legal and social inequalities of the Old Regime.

The Revolution and Napoleon promoted fraternity in the legal sense by making all French men equal in the eyes of the law. In a broader sense they advanced fraternity by encouraging nationalism, the feeling of belonging to a great corporate body, France, that was superior to all other nations. The Napoleonic empire then showed how easily nationalism on an unprecedented scale could lead to imperialism of unprecedented magnitude.

SUMMARY

Years of fiscal mismanagement contributed to the severe financial crisis that precipitated the French Revolution. Louis XVI, irresolute and stubborn, was unable to meet the overwhelming need for reform. The third estate, which constituted over 97 percent of the population, held some land, but rural poverty was widespread. Moreover, this estate bore the heavy burden of taxation. Discontent was rife among urban workers. The bourgeoisie helped focus this discontent against the privileged estates and called for an end to the abuses of the Old Regime, especially the inequalities of tax assessments.

The financial emergency of the heavily indebted monarchy forced the king to summon the Estates General. Bad weather and poor harvests in the winter of 1788–1789 led to demands for drastic change. When the Estates General met, the third estate successfully challenged the king over procedure, transforming the Estates General into a National Assembly charged with writing a constitution.

Popular uprisings pushed the Revolution along at an increasing pace. The National Assembly abolished the abuses of the Old Regime and in August 1789 issued the Declaration of the Rights of Man, embodying the ideals of the Enlightenment.

By 1791 the National Assembly had completed its task and established a government based on a separation of powers. The activities of French émigrés and of Louis XVI and the outbreak of war in 1792 opened a gulf

between moderates and extremists. In Paris the Jacobins led a municipal revolution that resulted in the abolition of the monarchy.

In 1793 Robespierre, an advocate of democracy, imposed a dictatorship on France. During the Reign of Terror twenty thousand were killed. Calling for total mobilization and economic sacrifice, Robespierre and the Committee of Public Safety organized a drive to push foreign invaders from France.

The excesses of the Terror created the conditions for Robespierre's downfall in July 1794. A new Constitution of 1795 established the Directory, which assured the dominance of the propertied classes.

In 1799 Napoleon engineered a coup d'état ending the Directory and establishing the Consulate. Napoleon became first consul for life in 1802 and emperor in 1804. He moved quickly to centralize imperial administration and appointed talented ministers to office.

The Code Napoléon embodied some ideas of the Old Regime as well as revolutionary principles such as the equality of all citizens before the law.

In religion, Napoleon made peace with the church in the Concordat of 1802. Education was subservient to the state, with lycées established to train administrators. Napoleon established the Bank of France and improved tax collection.

In Europe, Napoleon built a vast empire. He forced Prussia, Russia, and Austria to accept peace terms, leaving only Britain in the war against France. The French Empire was divided into three parts: France and the territories it annexed; French satellite states; and Austria, Prussia, and Russia. In Germany, Napoleon formally dissolved the Holy Roman Empire and created the Confederation of the Rhine.

Napoleon's effort to wage economic warfare against Britain backfired, hurting France and antagonizing neutral powers. Nationalist movements in Spain and Prussia threatened the French Empire after 1808.

When Napoleon's Russian campaign of 1812 ended in disaster for his Grand Army, the nations of Europe formed a new coalition that presided over Napoleon's downfall. In 1814 the Bourbons were restored to power. The Napoleonic legend, however, would haunt France, as would the revolutionary goals of liberty, equality, and fraternity.

CRITICAL THINKING

1. The French Revolution often is singled out as the most important, and most enduring, of all political revolutions. Do you agree? Why or why not?

2. Few revolutions have been as complex as the French Revolution. Still, the most basic causes are apparent. What were they?

3. Outline the various phases through which the French Revolution passed between 1789 and 1799.

4. Why did the French Revolution go far beyond the intent of the first revolutionaries? Is this a characteristic of revolutionary change?

5. What were the basic characteristics and achievements of the First Republic in France?

6. What accounts for the rise of Napoleon Bonaparte?

7. Describe Napoleon's policies for France.

8. How and why did France go to war? What were the major developments during the Napoleonic wars?

9. How did the Napoleonic wars contribute to both German and Russian national identities? What was the impact of the war on the Iberian Peninsula?

10. Evaluate the overall legacy of the French Revolution. What remains that we would regard as good? What resulted that we would think of as harmful?

ROMANTICISM, REACTION, AND REVOLUTION – The Industrial Society – The Modernization of Nations – Modern Empires and Imperialism

Timeline Covers: 1745–1911

DATES	POLITICAL	THOUGHT AND ARTS	ECONOMY AND SOCIETY
1746 A.D.		1746–1828 Francisco de Goya 1748–1832 Jeremy Bentham	
1750	1754–1823 Charles Maurice de Talleyrand	1759–1805 J. C. F. Schiller	1751–1900 British population increases from 7.5 million to 32.5 million 1760s Industrialization begins in Britain 1771–1858 Robert Owen
		1770–1827 Ludwig van Beethoven 1775–1851 J. M. W. Turner 1780–1830 The romantic period	c. 1780 Rise of Nationalism
	1784–1865 Lord Palmerston	1790 Edmund Burke, *Reflections on the Revolution in France* 1798 William Wordsworth and Samuel Coleridge, *Lyrical Ballads* 1798 Thomas Malthus, *Essay on Population* 1798–1857 Auguste Comte	1792–1871 Charles Babbage 1793 Eli Whitney invents the cotton gin
1800			19th century Rise of industrial and scientific society 19th century The Imperial Revolution 1805–1881 Auguste Blanqui
	1801 Union of Great Britain and Ireland 1808–1873 Louis Napoleon Bonaparte (Napoleon III) 1809–1898 William Ewart Gladstone 1809–1865 Abraham Lincoln 1809–1848 Klemens von Metternich serves as Austrian foreign minister 1810–1861 Count Camillo Cavour		
	1814–1815 Congress of Vienna r. 1814–1824 Louis XVIII of France 1815 Quadruple and Holy Alliances founded 1818 Foundation of the *Zollverein*	1812–1870 Charles Dickens	1814–1876 Mikhail Bakunin
	1820–1823 Spanish, Portuguese, and Neopolitian uprisings 1820 Brazil declares its independence 1821 Beginning of the Greek Rebellion 1823 Monroe Doctrine 1825 Decembrist Revolt in Russia r. 1825–1855 Czar Nicholas I 1829 Catholic Emancipation 1830–1833 Revolutions of 1830 r. 1830–1848 Louis Philippe of France 1832 First Reform Act 1833 Slavery abolished in the British Empire 1834 New Poor Law r. 1837–1901 Queen Victoria of Britain 1839 Lord Durham, *Report on the Affairs of British North America* 1839–1848 The Chartist Movement	1819–1880 George Eliot 1820–1903 Herbert Spencer 1830 Victor Hugo, *Hernani* 1834–1896 Heinrich von Treitschke	1820s–1890s Spread of industrialization 1820s Living standards begin to rise and cities to grow 1830s First European railroads open
	1846 Repeal of the Corn Laws 1846–1848 Mexican War 1848 Revolutions of 1848 r. 1848–1916 Francis Joseph of Austria	c. 1840–c. 1990 Era of the Novel and of Realism 1840–1902 Emile Zola 1840–1917 Auguste Rodin 1840 Louis Blanc, *The Organization of Labor* 1844–1900 Friedrich Engles, *The Communist Manifesto*	1840 First regular Atlantic steamer service 1844 First message sent by telegraph of Samuel Morse 1845–1846 Irish potato blight and European harvest failure 1846 Introduction of ether anesthesia

DATES	POLITICAL	THOUGHT AND ARTS	ECONOMY AND SOCIETY
1850 A.D.	1850–1937 Thomas Masaryk 1851 Coup of Louis Napoleon 1854–1856 Crimean War 1854 Japan opened by Matthew Perry 1857 Sepoy Rebellion 1861–1865 American Civil War 1861 Proclamation of the Kingdom of Italy 1861 Serfdom abolished in Russia 1863 Slavery abolished in United States 1866 Austro-Prussian War 1867 Canada granted dominion status 1867 Creation of dual monarchy of Austria-Hungary **late 19th century** Labor unions gain legal recognition 1870 Franco-Prussian War 1870 Married Women's Property Act 1871 German Empire established 1871–1890 Otto von Bismarck serves as Chancellor of Germany 1874–1880 Administration of Benjamin Disraeli 1878 Congress of Berlin 1878 German Anti-Socialist Law passed 1880s–1910s Rise of Anglo-Germany antagonism 1880s British preeminence begins to fade **r.** 1888–1918 William II of Germany 1890 Battle of Wounded Knee 1892 Kier Hardie elected to House of Commons **r.** 1894–1917 Nicholas of Russia 1894–1906 Dreyfus Affair 1896 Battle of Adowa 1898 First German Naval Law 1898 Fashoda Crisis 1898 Spanish-American War 1898 Russian Soical Democratic Party formed 1899–1902 Boer War 1903 Joesph Chamberlain proposes tariff reform 1904 Anglo-French Entente 1904–1905 Russo-Japanese War 1905 Russian Revolution of 1905 1908 Turkish Revolution 1911 Parliament Act	1853 Joseph de Gobineau, *Essay on the Inequality of the Human Races*, part I 1856–1936 Rudyard Kipling 1858–1943 Beatrice Webb 1859 J. S. Mill, *On Liberty* 1859 Charles Darwin, *On the Origin of Species* 1862 Ivan Turgenev, *Fathers and Sons* 1863–1890 Vincent Van Gogh 1865–1869 Leo Tolstoy, *War and Peace* 1867 Karl Marx, *Das Kapital*, volume one 1869 J. S. Mill, *The Subjection of Women* 1880 Feodor Dostoevsky, *The Brothers Karamazov* 1890 Alfred T. Mahan, *The Influence of Sea Power upon History* 1902 Sigmund Freud, *The Intrepretation of Dreams* 1902 John A. Hobson, *Imperialism: A Study* 1908 Georges Sorel, *Reflections on Violence*	1850–1900 23 million emigrate from Britain 1859–1869 Construction of the Suez Canal 1864 Pope Pius IX, *Syllabus of Errors* 1865–1880 World steel production increases tenfold 1870s European birth and death rates begin to decline 1873–1896 The "Great Depression" 1870s Rise of European anti-Semitism 1870s Rise of the New Imperialism 1876 First telephone 1880s First skyscrapers erected in Chicago 1880s The scramble for Africa 1891 Pope Leo XIII, *Rerum novarum*
1900			

CHAPTER 19

Romanticism, Reaction, and Revolution

reaction against the Enlightenment

HE ORIGINS OF THE MODERN West lay in the French Revolution, and the rising nationalism stimulated by it and by the conquests of Napoleon. They lay also in the developments of the short, intense period between the Congress of Vienna and the wave of revolutions that moved across Europe in 1848. During this time and into the 1880s, the industrial revolution was also transforming Western societies, especially Britain, Germany, and the United States. At the same time new developments in scientific thought, especially those associated with the work of Charles Darwin, led to yet another series of dramatic changes in how philosophers, politicians, and scientists perceived the world. Romanticism, idealism, and materialism well described the various conflicting, overlapping, and prevailing strands of thought by which people tried to account to themselves for their actions, to provide continuity, security, and stability amid rapid change.

The labels *reaction* and *counterrevolution* are often applied to the events of 1815–1830. By 1815 Europe was reacting strongly against the French Revolution, which had made Napoleon possible, and against the Enlightenment, which was believed to have made the Revolution possible. The reaction against the Enlightenment took the form of the romantic movement. Romantic writers and artists protested against the rationalism and classicism of the eighteenth century and championed faith, emotion, tradition, and other values associated with the more distant past. The political counterrevolution came of age at the Congress of Vienna in 1814–1815, where the leaders of the last coalition against Napoleon reestablished the European balance of power and repudiated revolutionary principles.

Yet despite the ascendancy of counterrevolutionary forces, the spirit of 1789 did not die in 1815. It inspired new and progressively more intense outbreaks of revolution in the 1820s, in 1830, and in 1848. The revolutions of 1848, though put down, marked a critical turning point in the development of the liberalism and nationalism bequeathed by the great French Revolution.

THE ROMANTIC PROTEST

1780 — 1830

The romantic period (usually dated 1780 to 1830) was one in which political and cultural thought showed such a varied concern for tradition that many historians dispute that there was sufficient unity of thought to refer to a "movement" at all. Moreover, writers of "the romantic school" in Germany were quite different from writers in England or France at the same time; the various romantic thinkers tended to be united by what they disliked more than by what they liked.

There was a general revolt against what many viewed as the "narrowness" of the eighteenth century—the emphasis on the purely logical, on the tightly ordered rules of poetry and prose, on what was felt to be an unimaginative approach to history, science, and politics. The romanticists accused their Enlightenment predecessors of being unduly optimistic about the perfectibility of human nature and argued that pleasure can also be taken from the grotesque, the disorganized, and the irrational. The English romantic artist William Blake (1757–1827) subtly attacked the veneration of Sir Isaac Newton, seeing him less as a scientific genius and more as a materialist without emotional inspiration. God existed and was to be found in Nature, the romantics argued, not in Science.

Paradoxically, the revolutionary qualities of the romantics were always evident in literature and the arts, where they rebelled against Jacobin and Napoleonic France's devotion to the cult of classical antiquity. Revolutionary France was attached not only to Roman names, furniture, and fashions but also to neoclassical painting and architecture. The romantics were most revolutionary in their disdain for the literary and artistic standards of neoclassicism and their attraction to the medieval and the Gothic, to the colorful and the exotic, to the visually undisciplined and the emotional.

If the protest against reason reached full force during the first third of the nineteenth century, it had been building up for a long time in contemporary challenges to the Enlightenment. Before 1750 Wesley in England and the Pietists in Germany were protesting against the deism of the philosophes and preaching a religion of the heart, not the head. Rousseau proclaimed conscience, not reason, as the "true guide of man." The protest against oversimplification of the individual and society, and the insistence on the intricacy and complexity of humanity, formed the common denominators of romanticism.

An Age of Feeling and Poetry, 1790–1830

Romanticism is best revealed through literature. Literary romanticism may be traced back to the mid-eighteenth century—to novels of "sensibility" like Rousseau's *La Nouvelle Héloïse* and to the sentimental "tearful comedies" of the French stage. In the 1770s and 1780s a new intensity appeared in the very popular works of the German Sturm und Drang, for example, Goethe's morbidly sensitive *Sorrows of Young Werther*, and *The Robbers*, a drama of social protest by J. C. F. von Schiller (1759–1805).

Goethe (1749–1832) was a good eighteenth-century exponent of reason, yet romantic values lie at the heart of his most famous writings—his short lyrics and, above all, *Faust*. Begun when Goethe was in his twenties and finished only when he was eighty, this long poetic drama was a philosophical commentary on the main currents of European thought. According to the traditional legend, the aged Faust, weary of book learning and pining for eternal youth, sold his soul to the Devil, receiving back the enjoyment of his youth for an allotted time, and then, terror-stricken, going to the everlasting fires. Goethe partially transformed this legend: Faust makes his same infernal compact with Mephistopheles, who points out how disillusioning intellectual pursuits are, but Faust is ultimately saved through his realization that he must sacrifice selfish concerns to the welfare of others. A drama of sinning, striving, and redemption, Goethe's *Faust* reaffirmed the Christian values that the Enlightenment had belittled.

The Enlightenment had also belittled any poetry except that following very strict forms, like the heroic couplets of Racine and Pope. The romantics decried this neoclassicism as artificial and praised the vigor, color, and freedom of the Bible, Homer, and Shakespeare. The result was a great renaissance of poetry all over Europe, especially in England, which produced a galaxy of great poets: Lord Bryon (1788–1824), Percy Bysshe Shelley (1792–1822), John Keats (1795–1821), William Wordsworth (1770–1850), Samuel Taylor Coleridge (1772–1834), and others.

Of them all, Wordsworth and Coleridge pressed furthest in their reaction against classicism and rationalism. In 1798 the two men published *Lyrical Ballads*, to which Coleridge contributed the "Rime of the Ancient Mariner," a supernatural tale of the curse afflicting a sailor who slays an albatross. Later he created "Kubla Khan," which has a surrealistic quality and probably was induced by taking drugs. In place of a mathematically ordered world-machine, Coleridge's "Kubla Khan" has its Xanadu:

Where Alph, the sacred river, ran
Through caverns measureless to man
Down to a sunless sea.

Wordsworth, who had lived in France during the early years of the Revolution and had been disillusioned by the failure of rational reform, abandoned the philosophes' confidence in human perfectibility through reason to put his faith in the "immortal spirit" of the individual. In place of the light shed by Newton's laws, he found "a dark inscrutable workmanship." God was to be found in all things.

THE WRITTEN RECORD

Shelley on the Decay of Kings

In 1817 the English poet Percy Bysshe Shelley captured the romantic sense of despair in his poem "Ozymandias," which stated anew the biblical warning that the overweening aspirations of arrogant humanity would be as dust to dust.

I met a traveler from an antique land
Who said: "Two vast and trunkless legs of stone
Stand in the desert. Near them, on the sand,
Half sunk, a shattered visage lies, whose frown,
And wrinkled lip, and sneer of cold command,
Tell that its sculptor well those passions read
Which yet survive, stamped on these lifeless things,
The hand that mocked them, and the heart that fed;
And on the pedestal these words appear:
"My name is Ozymandias, King of Kings:

Look on my works, ye Mighty, and despair!'
Nothing beside remains. Round the decay
Of that colossal wreck, boundless and bare,
The lone and level sands stretch far away."

Percy Bysshe Shelley, "Ozymandias," in *The Complete Works of Percy Bysshe Shelley:*, ed. Neville Rogers, I, 1814–1817 (Oxford: Clarendon Press, 1975), pp. 319–20.

The Return to the Past

The romantics' enthusiasm for the Middle Ages in general and for the earlier history of their own nations in particular linked the universal (nature) to the particular (the nation-state). Nationalism was an emotional, almost mystical force. The romantic return to the national past, though intensified by French expansionism, had begun before 1789 as part of the repudiation of the Enlightenment. The pioneers of romanticism tended to cherish what the philosophes detested, notably the Middle Ages and the medieval preoccupation with religion.

The German writer Johann Gottfried von Herder (1744–1803) provided intellectual justification for medieval studies with his theory of cultural nationalism. Each separate nation, he argued, had its own distinct personality, its *Volksgeist*, or "folk spirit," and its own pattern of growth. The surest measure of a nation's progress was its literature—poetry in youth, prose in maturity. Stimulated by Herder, students of medieval German literature collected popular ballads and folk tales. In 1782 the first complete text of the *Nibelungenlied* (Song of the Nibelungs) was published, a heroic saga of the nation's youth that had been forgotten since the later Middle Ages. By putting a new value on the German literature of the past, Herder helped to free the German literature of his own day from its bondage to French culture. He was no narrow nationalist, however, and he asserted that the cultivated person should also study other cultures. So Herder also helped to loose a flood of translations that poured over Germany beginning about 1800: of Shakespeare, of *Don Quixote*, of Spanish and Portuguese poetry, and of works in Sanskrit.

Other nations also demonstrated that the return to the past meant veneration of the Middle Ages rather than of classical antiquity. In Britain Sir Walter Scott (1771–1832) collected medieval folk ballads and wrote more than thirty historical novels, of which *Ivanhoe*, set in the days of Richard the Lionhearted and the Crusades, is the best known. In Russia the poet Alexander Pushkin (1799–1837) deserted the Slavonic language of the Orthodox church to write the first major Russian literary works in the vernacular: *Boris Godunov* (published in 1831) and *Eugene Onegin* (1832).

In France, the romantic reaction gathered slowly, beginning in the first years of the new century with the vicomte de Chateaubriand (1768–1848) in *The Genius of Christianity* (1802). In 1811 Madame Germaine de Staël (1766–1817), who was the daughter of the banker Necker, published *De l'Allemagne* (Concerning Germany), a plea for the French to remember that they were the descendants not only of ancient Romans but also of Teutonic Franks. The most direct blow against classicism came early in 1830, however, at the first night of the play *Hernani* by Victor Hugo (1802–1885), who flouted the classical rules of dramatic verse. When one of the characters uttered a line ending in the middle of a word, traditionalists in the audience set off a riot, and the issues were fought and refought at the theater and in the press for weeks. In the next year Hugo published his great historical novel, *Notre Dame de Paris*, set in the France of Louis XI.

Music

Romantic musicians, like romantic poets, sought out the popular ballads and tales of the national past; they also sought to free their compositions from classical rules. Composers of opera and song turned to literature: Shakespeare's plays, Scott's novels, Byron's poetry, and the poems and tales of Goethe and Pushkin. Yet, although literature and music often took similar paths during the romantic era, there were significant differences. Romantic musicians did not revolt against the great eighteenth-century composers as Wordsworth and Coleridge revolted against their predecessors. Rather, romantic music evolved out of the older classical school.

The composer who played the commanding role in this evolution was Ludwig van Beethoven (1770– 1827), who lived most of his life in Vienna. Where earlier composers had indicated tempo with a simple "fast" or "slow," Beethoven added such designations as *appassionate* and

"Strife between Head and Heart." Part of the color and passion of Beethoven's works derived from his skill in exploiting the resources of the piano, an instrument that was perfected during his lifetime, and his use of more instruments—especially winds, percussion, and double basses—than was traditional. In his Ninth (and final) Symphony, Beethoven introduced a chorus in the last movement to sing his setting of Schiller's "Ode to Joy."

After Beethoven, orchestral works took on increasingly heroic dimensions. The French composer Hector Berlioz (1803–1869) projected an orchestra of 465 pieces, including 120 violins, 37 double basses, and 30 each of

This cartoon of Hector Berlioz shows his dramatic use of percussion, string, and wind instruments to drive out classical modes of art in favor of "radical romanticism." Berlioz was also the founder of modern orchestral conducting, bringing his own dramatic personality onto the podium.

New York Public Library Picture Collection

pianos and harps. The *Symphonie Fantastique*, which he supposedly based on Goethe's *Werther*, was completed in 1830. Berlioz's *Requiem* called for a full orchestra, a great pipe organ, four brass choirs, and a chorus of two hundred. The romantic propensity for bigness also affected the presentation of Bach's choral works, like *The Passion According to St. Matthew*, originally composed for relatively few performers but revived with a full orchestra and a large chorus in a precedent-setting performance directed by Felix Mendelssohn (1809–1849) in 1829.

Music for the human voice reflected both the increased enthusiasm for instruments, particularly the piano, and the general romantic nostalgia for the past. In composing songs and arias, romantic musicians devoted as much skill to the accompaniment as to the voice part itself. Franz Schubert (1797–1828), Beethoven's Viennese contemporary, made a fine art of blending voice and piano in more than six hundred sensitive *lieder* (songs), seventy of them musical settings of poems by Goethe. Meantime, Carl Maria von Weber (1786–1826) was striving to create a fully German opera, taking an old legend as the libretto for *Der Freischütz* (The Freeshooter, 1821). Its plot ran the romantic gamut of an enchanted forest, a magic bullet, and an innocent maiden outwitting the Devil, and its choruses and marches employed folklike melodies. In Russia, Mikhail Glinka (1804–1857) cast aside the Italian influences that had dominated the secular music of his country, to base his opera *Russlan and Ludmilla* (1842) on a poem by Pushkin, embellishing it with dances and choruses derived from Russian Asia.

Perhaps most romantic of all was the Polish composer Frédéric Chopin (1810–1849). Writing almost exclusively for the piano, drawing heavily on the melodic forms of Polish popular music, Chopin best combined romantic music with national idioms, especially in his polonaises, which were written to accompany traditional Polish dances. His work was passionate and stirring, and he made the piano the most popular instrument of the century.

The Arts

The virtual dictator of European painting during the first two decades of the nineteenth century was the French neoclassicist Jacques Louis David (1748–1825). David became a baron and court painter under Napoleon, then was exiled by the restored Bourbons. No matter how revolutionary the subject, David employed traditional neoclassical techniques, stressing form, line, and perspective.

The works of the Spaniard Francisco de Goya (1746–1828) were much closer to the romantic temper, with their warmth, passion, and sense of outrage. No one could have any illusions about Spanish royalty after looking at Goya's revealing portraits of Charles III and his successors.

Romantic painting did not acquire formal recognition until an official Paris exhibition in 1824. Although many of the pictures shown there came from the school of David, two leaders of romantic painting were also represented—the Englishman John Constable (1776–1837) and the Frenchman Eugène Delacroix (1798–1863). Constable took painting out of the studio, studied nature afresh, and produced landscapes that stressed light and color more than classical purity of line, thus paving the way for the impressionists of the later nineteenth century. Even more influential was J. M. W. Turner (1775–1851), precursor of the impressionists, who developed British landscape painting to the heights of the sublime and romantic. Delacroix, too, championed color and light and urged young painters to study the flamboyant canvases of Rubens, whom David had banished from the ranks of acceptable artists. The purpose of art, Delacroix claimed, was "not to imitate nature but to strike the imagination." By the 1830s French painters were divided into opposing schools: the still-influential disciples of David and the romantic followers of Delacroix.

In architecture also two schools flourished during the first half of the nineteenth century: the neoclassical, looking to Greek and Roman antiquity, and the neo-Gothic or Gothic revival, looking to the Middle Ages. Many architects of the early 1800s mastered both styles, not so much copying ancient or medieval structures as adapting them to the needs and tastes of the day. Generally, basic design was classical in its proportions, while decoration was medieval. The Houses of Parliament in London were Gothic in their spires and towers, but they also embodied classical principles of balance and symmetry.

At the beginning of the nineteenth century the Roman vogue, firmly set by the French Revolution, reached its peak in Napoleonic Paris with triumphal arches, columns, and churches patterned after Roman forms. In America Thomas Jefferson, who was a gifted designer, provided the University of Virginia with distinguished academic buildings focused on a circular library derived from the Roman Pantheon (the perfect example of "spherical" architecture). Yet by the second quarter of the nineteenth century neo-Roman was yielding to Greek revival, stirred in part by a wave of enthusiasm for the Greek independence movement.

Religion and Philosophy

The romantic religious revival was marked at the institutional level by the pope's reestablishment in 1814 of the Jesuit order, whose suppression in 1773 had been viewed as one of the great victories of the Enlightenment. Catholicism gained many converts among romantic writers, particularly in Germany, and the Protestants also made gains. Pietism found new strength in Germany and Russia. In England Coleridge vigorously defended the established church, while also introducing the new German idealist philosophy. Chief among these romantic German philosophers was G. W. F. Hegel (1770–1831). Like Kant, Hegel attacked the tendency of the Enlightenment to see in human nature and history only what met the eye. Human history, properly understood, was the history of efforts to attain the good, and this in turn was the unfolding of God's plan for the world. For Hegel, history was a *dialectical* process—that is, a series of conflicts; the two contending elements in the conflict

Thomas Jefferson greatly admired Roman architecture and especially a Roman temple in southern France known as the Maison Carrée, or square house, and he adapted this style to secular purposes for the capitol building of Virginia. He then used the Pantheon as the model for this circular library, at the University of Virginia in Charlottesville. It approximated a Roman villa, with rows of smaller structures on both sides.

Alderman Library, University of Virginia

were the *thesis*, the established order of life, and the *antithesis*, a challenge to the old order. Out of the struggle of thesis and antithesis emerged a *synthesis*, no mere compromise between the two but a new and better way—a combination that was another step in humanity's slow progress toward the best of all possible worlds. In turn, the synthesis broke down by becoming conventional and unproductive; it became locked in conflict with a new antithesis, and the dialectic produced another synthesis— and so on and on.

The dialectical philosophy of history was the most original and influential element in Hegel's thought; it would help to shape the dialectical materialism of Karl Marx. Still, Hegel was once even more famous as a liberal idealist. His emphasis on duty, his choice of Alexander the Great, Caesar, and Napoleon as "world-historical" heroes, his assertion that the state "existed for its own sake"—all suggest a link with authoritarianism. Yet Hegel foresaw the final synthesis of the dialectic not as a brutal police state but as a liberalized version of the Prussian monarchy.

The Romantic Style

The style of romanticism was not totally at variance with that of the Enlightenment; not only a modified doctrine of progress but also the cosmopolitanism of the eighteenth century lived on into the nineteenth. Homer, Cervantes, Shakespeare, and Scott had appreciative readers in many countries; giants of the age such as Beethoven and Goethe were not merely Austrian or German citizens but citizens of the world.

Yet despite these similarities and continuities, romanticism did have a decided style of its own—imaginative, emotional, and haunted by the supernatural, by the terrific (in the sense of inspiring awe and even terror), and by history. History was an organic process of growth and development, which was indebted to the Middle Ages for magnificent Gothic buildings, religious enthusiasm, folk ballads, and heroic epics.

Just as the romantics rejected the Enlightenment's view of the past, so they found the Newtonian world-machine an entirely inadequate interpretation of the universe. It was too static, too drab and materialistic. In its place they put a neo-Gothic world of religious mystery, the Hegelian mechanics of dialectic, the poetic and artistic vision of feeling, color, and impulses in nature. The romantics wanted to recreate a sense of wonder, to inspire a belief in the essential unity of God, man, and nature, to show that humanity lived in a world of endless "becoming."

Romanticism pervaded all forms of thought. As in the early Middle Ages, once again Europeans were fascinated with death, and especially with dying heroically. Two immensely popular paintings of the time captured the *frisson*, the chill of pleasure down the spine, that merged romanticism and a form of social realism. One, by a German romantic landscape painter, Caspar David Friedrich (1774–1840), depicted the wreck of the *Hope*, a vessel trapped in ice, never to escape from its destiny. Another, earlier work, by the French artist Théordore Géricault (1791–1824), showed the fate of passengers from the frigate *Medusa*, which had foundered on the way to Senegal. The passengers, 149 in all, were put onto an open raft and cut adrift at sea; a handful lived to tell the tale, and Géricault devoted himself to studying corpses in a morgue so that he might capture this horrific moment of both realistic and romantic revelation.

THE RECONSTITUTION OF A EUROPEAN ORDER

The romantic movement was too intellectually scattered to provide a blueprint for the reconstruction of Europe after the defeat of Napoleon. The general guidelines for reconstruction were to be found in the writings of the

English orator Edmund Burke (1729–1797), who set the tone for counterrevolutionary conservatism. Burke strongly believed that some form of divine intent ruled society and that through individual conscience a chain was forged between rights and duties; there were no rights for those who did not do their duty. He was convinced that civilized society required orders and classes, though movement should be possible between these groups. Because people were governed more by emotion than by reason (as the romantics also argued), some control must be put on the free exercise of the will.

Burke felt affection for the variety and mystery of tradition; reform, while at times desirable, should be approached with caution to preserve what was valuable from the past. He therefore welcomed American independence, which he viewed more as a reaffirmation of the glorious English tradition of 1688 than as a revolution. The same reasoning drove him to violently condemn the French Revolution, which destroyed everything, good, bad, and indifferent. Rage and frenzy, he observed, "pull down more in half an hour, than prudence, deliberation and foresight can build up in a hundred years."*

Burke's doctrines were especially welcomed by the émigrés. Among them was Joseph de Maistre (c. 1753–1821), a diplomat in the service of the king of Sardinia who had been forced into exile when the French overran Savoy and Piedmont. De Maistre combined Burke's conservatism with a belief in the viciousness of the state of nature and a traditional Catholic view of human depravity and the need for discipline. The French Revolution, he believed, had been God's punishment for the philosophes' arrogance in believing that society could be remade without divine assistance. The postrevolutionary world needed firm control by an absolute monarch and inspired guidance from the church.

The force of tradition bore heavily upon the politics of post-Napoleonic Europe. Yet it was not so much ideological conviction as political realism that accounted for the conservatism of the man who presided over the actual reconstruction of Europe. That man was Prince Klemens von Metternich (1773–1859), Austrian foreign minister from 1809 to 1848. Handsome, dashing, aristocratic, Metternich retained some of the eighteenth century's belief in reform through enlightened despotism; but he also believed that reform should proceed with caution. Moreover, Metternich served a state that was particularly threatened by the liberal and nationalist energies released by the Revolution. Conservatism, he knew, was the cement that held together the very different parts of the multilingual, potentially multinational realm of the Austrian Habsburgs.

The Congress of Vienna, 1814–1815

In 1814 and 1815 Metternich was host to the Congress of Vienna, which approached its task of rebuilding Europe with conservative deliberateness. For the larger part of a

year, the diplomats indulged in balls and banquets, concerts and hunting parties. "The Congress dances," quipped an observer, "but it does not march." Actually, the brilliant social life distracted hangers-on while the important diplomats settled matters in private.

Four men made most of the major decisions at Vienna: Metternich; Czar Alexander I; Viscount Castlereagh (1769–1822), the British foreign secretary; and Charles Maurice de Talleyrand (1754–1838), the French foreign minister. Castlereagh was at Vienna, he said, "not to collect trophies, but to bring the world back to peaceful habits." The best way to do this, he believed, was to restore the balance of power and keep the major states, including France, from becoming either too strong or too weak.

At Vienna, Talleyrand scored the greatest success of his long career. Originally a worldly bishop of the Old Regime, he had in succession rallied to the Revolution in 1789, become one of the very few bishops to support the Civil Constitution of the Clergy, served as Napoleon's foreign minister, and then, while still holding office, intrigued against him after 1807. This adaptable diplomat soon maneuvered himself into the inner circle at Vienna. He was particularly adept in exploiting the differences that divided the victors.

To these differences Alexander I contributed greatly. Alexander's Polish policy nearly disrupted the Congress. He proposed a partial restoration of eighteenth-century Poland, with himself as its monarch; Austria and Prussia would lose their Polish lands. Alexander won the support of Prussia by backing its demands for the annexation of Saxony. Metternich, however, did not want Prussia to make such a substantial gain. Moreover, both Metternich and Castlereagh disliked the prospect of a large, Russian-dominated Poland.

Talleyrand joined Metternich and Castlereagh in threatening both Prussia and Russia with war unless they moderated their demands. The threat produced an immediate settlement. Alexander obtained Poland but agreed to reduce its size and to allow Prussia and Austria to keep part of their gains from the partitions. Prussia took about half of Saxony, while the king of Saxony was allowed to keep the rest.

Once the Saxon-Polish question was out of the way, the Congress was able to turn to other important dynastic and territorial questions. According to what Talleyrand christened "the sacred principle of legitimacy," thrones and frontiers were to be reestablished as they had existed in 1789. In practice, however, legitimacy was ignored almost as often as it was applied, since the diplomats realized that they could not undo all the changes brought about by the Revolution and Napoleon. Although they sanctioned the return of the Bourbons to the thrones of France, Spain, and Naples in the name of legitimacy, they did not attempt to resurrect the republic of Venice or to revive all the hundreds of German states that had vanished since 1789. In Germany the Congress provided for thirty-nine states grouped in a weak confederation. The Diet, chief organ of the German Confederation, was to be a council of diplomats from sovereign states rather than a representative national assembly. Its most important

---

* Edmund, Burke, *Reflections on the Revolution in France*, 1790 (New York: Everyman, 1910), p. 164.

members were to be Prussia and Austria, for the German-speaking provinces of the Habsburg realm were considered part of Germany.

The land exchanges were complex and often cynical, with little or no regard for the wishes of the people. Prussia, besides annexing part of Saxony, added the Napoleonic kingdom of Westphalia to its scattered lands in western Germany, creating the imposing Rhine Province. Austria lost Belgium, which was incorporated into the kingdom of the Netherlands to strengthen the northern buffer against France. But Austria recovered the eastern Adriatic shore and the old Habsburg possession of Lombardy, to which Venetia was now joined. The Congress of Vienna restored the Bourbon kingdom of Naples, the States of the Church, and, on their northern flank, the grand duchy of Tuscany. The kingdom of Piedmont-Sardinia acquired Genoa as a buttress against France. Another buttress was established in the republic of Switzerland, now independent again and slightly enlarged. The Congress confirmed the earlier transfer of Finland from Sweden to Russia and compensated Sweden by the transfer of Norway from the rule of Denmark to that of Sweden. Finally, Great Britain received the strategic Mediterranean islands of Malta and the Ionians at the mouth of the Adriatic Sea and, outside Europe, the former Dutch colonies of Ceylon and the Cape of Good Hope, plus some minor French outposts.

France at first was given its boundaries of 1792, which included minor territorial acquisitions made during the early days of the Revolution. Then came Napoleon's escape from Elba and the Hundred Days. The final settlement reached after Waterloo assigned France the frontiers of 1790, substantially those of the Old Regime plus Avignon.

To quarantine any possible new French aggression, Castlereagh conceived the policy of strengthening France's neighbors. Thus, to the north the French faced the Belgians and the Dutch combined in the single kingdom of the Netherlands; on the northeast they faced the Rhine Province of Prussia; and on the east, the expanded states of Switzerland and Piedmont. In the Quadruple Alliance, signed in November 1815, the four allies—Britain, Prussia, Austria, and Russia—agreed to use force, if necessary, to preserve the Vienna settlement.

The Holy Alliance, signed in September 1815, was dedicated to the proposition that "the policy of the powers . . . ought to be guided by the sublime truths taught by the eternal religion of God our Savior." However, neither the Holy Alliance nor the Quadruple Alliance fulfilled the expectations of their architects. At the first meeting of the Quadruple Alliance, in 1818, the allies agreed to withdraw their occupation forces from France, which had paid its indemnity. At the next meeting of the allies, two years later, Metternich and Castlereagh would find themselves ranged on opposite sides on the issue of putting down revolutions under international auspices.

For these revolutions of 1820–1821 the Congress of Vienna was itself partly to blame, through its attempt to suppress liberal and nationalist aspirations. Yet as major international settlements go, that of Vienna was a sound one. There was to be no war involving several powers until the Crimean conflict of the 1850s, and no major war embroiling the whole of Europe until 1914. Seldom have victors treated a defeated aggressor with the wisdom and generosity displayed in 1815. Most of the leading diplomats at Vienna could have said with Castlereagh that they acted "to bring the world back to peaceful habits."

The Persistence of Revolution, 1820–1823

The revolutionary leaders of the post-Napoleonic generation remained firm for liberty, equality, and fraternity. The first two words of the great revolutionary motto continued to signify the abolition of noble and clerical privileges in society and, with few exceptions, laissez-faire economics. They also involved broadening civil rights, instituting representative assemblies, and

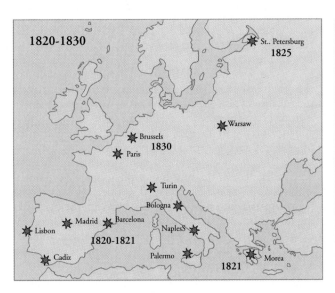

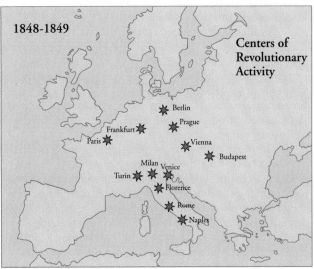

granting constitutions, which would bring limited monarchy or possibly even a republic.

Fraternity, intensified by the romantic cult of the nation, continued to evolve into the formidable doctrine of nationalism. The nationalists of the post-1815 generation dreamed of a world in which each nation would be free of domination by any other, and all nations would live together harmoniously. In practical terms, this signified movements toward national unity and national independence. It meant growing pressure for the unification of Germany and Italy. And it inspired demands for freedom by peoples living under the control of a foreign power—by Belgians against their Dutch rulers, by Poles against Russians, by Greeks and Serbs against Turks, and by Italians, Hungarians, and Czechs against the Habsburgs.

The first revolutionary outbreaks after 1815 took place in Spain, Portugal, and the Kingdom of the Two Sicilies. The trouble began in Spain. During the war against Napoleon, representatives from the liberal middle class of Cadiz and other commercial towns had framed the Constitution of 1812. Based on the French constitution of 1791, this document greatly limited the power of the monarchy, gave wide authority to a Cortes elected by a broad suffrage, and deprived the Spanish church of some of its lands and privileges. The Bourbon Ferdinand VII (r. 1814–1833) suspended the constitution, restored the social inequalities of the Old Regime, and reestablished the Jesuits and the Inquisition.

It was Ferdinand's attempt to subdue the rebellious colonies that triggered revolution at home. The independence movement in Spanish America had been the outcome of the refusal of the colonial populations to accept either Napoleon's brother Joseph as their king or the closer ties between colonies and mother country implicit in the constitution of 1812. Behind the movement lay several other factors: the powerful examples of the American and French revolutions, the sympathetic interest of Great Britain, and the accumulated resentment of colonial peoples at centuries of indifferent rule by Spanish governors. The colonial rebels had won their initial success at Buenos Aires in 1810, and their movement spread rapidly to Spain's other American possessions.

Ferdinand determined to crush the rebels by force. To transport troops he bought three leaky hulks from Russia. At the end of 1819 this motley new armada, carrying twenty thousand men, was about to sail from Cadiz. It never sailed, for on January 1, 1820, a mutiny broke out at Cadiz. Uprisings soon followed in Madrid, Barcelona, and other Spanish cities. Ferdinand, virtually a prisoner, surrendered.

Napoleon's attempt to place his brother on the Spanish throne gave the many people in South America who were chafing under so-called tax reform, disastrous market manipulation, and heavy-handed administration their opportunity. The Creoles—people of Spanish descent who were born in America—led the way, for they once had held many important positions from which a nervous Spain had been removing them for years. With

the loss of their king, they argued that sovereignty had moved from the monarchy to the people, by which they meant themselves. They intended no reconstruction of society, for they controlled wealth and education and considered themselves superior to the indigenous peoples and those of mixed race, and they wished to govern the Spanish colonies without interference.

Thus there arose Simón Bolívar (1783–1830), "the Liberator," who led Latin American armies to victory over the royalists. In 1819 he became president of Greater Colombia, and in 1826 he called for a conference of South American republics to meet in Panama. He organized the government of Bolivia, was head of state in Peru, and inspired followers throughout Latin America. Competing interest groups, regional differences, and unstable economies split Greater Colombia, however, and Bolívar went into exile, declaring America to be ungovernable. Nonetheless, by 1825 all of Latin America had broken away from Spain.

The liberal minorities in Portugal and Naples followed the Spanish lead. An army faction seized control of the Portuguese government in 1820, abolished the Inquisition, and set up a constitution. Brazil declared its independence, with a prince of the Portuguese royal house as its emperor. In Naples the revolution was the work of the *Carbonari* (Charcoal Burners). This secret society, with a membership exceeding fifty thousand, had been opposed to the French and their reforms in the days of Napoleon, but it now sponsored a vaguely liberal program inspired by the French Revolution and the Spanish constitution of 1812. King Ferdinand I of the Two Sicilies (1759–1825) gave in at the first sign of opposition in 1820 and accepted a constitution.

However, the strength of the revolutionary movement of 1820 ebbed as quickly as it had risen. The reforms introduced hastily by the inexperienced liberal leaders in Spain and Naples alienated the bulk of the population at home and so alarmed the conservative leaders of the great powers that they sponsored counterrevolutions. The Spanish revolutionaries were further weakened by a split between *moderados*, who wanted to keep the constitution of 1812, and *exaltados*, who wanted to set up a violently anticlerical republic. Only in Portugal did the revolutionary regime survive, and only because it had British protection.

The revolutions of 1820 tested both the stability of the Vienna settlement and the solidarity of the Quadruple Alliance of Britain, Prussia, Austria, and Russia. Though legitimacy was restored in Spain and Italy, the Quadruple Alliance was split in two. While the Continental allies increasingly favored armed intervention to suppress revolution, Britain inclined toward nonintervention. The split became evident at the meeting of the Quadruple Alliance at Troppau in Silesia late in 1820. Castlereagh was willing to see Austria intervene in Naples, but without the backing of the Alliance. The Alliance, Castlereagh declared, was never designed "for the superintendence of the internal affairs of other states," and Britain refused to participate formally in the Troppau meeting. Metternich, supported

THE WRITTEN RECORD

1823 [handwritten]

The Monroe Doctrine

useless till backed up by Brit. navy [handwritten]

In foreign relations, the United States sought to isolate itself as best it could from the contamination of European wars. Clearly those wars would spread to the New World if the European powers acquired new colonies in the Western Hemisphere. President James Monroe addressed this point in 1823 in what came to be known as the Monroe Doctrine.

In the wars of the European powers in matters relating to themselves we have never taken any part, nor does it comport with our policy so to do. It is only when our rights are invaded or seriously menaced that we resent injuries or make preparation for our defence. With the movements in this hemisphere we are of necessity more immediately connected, and by causes which must be obvious to all enlightened and impartial observers. The political system of the allied powers is essentially different in this respect from that of America. . . . We owe it, therefore, to candor and to the amicable relations existing between the United States and those powers to declare that we should consider any attempt on their part to extend their system to any portion of this hemisphere as dangerous to our peace and safety. With the existing colonies or dependencies of any European power we have not interfered and shall not interfere. But with the governments who have declared their independence and maintained it, and whose independence we have, on great consideration and on just principles, acknowledged, we could not view any interposition for the purpose of oppressing them, or controlling in any other manner their destiny, by any European power in any other light than as the manifestation of an unfriendly disposition toward the United States.

James Monroe, Message to Congress, December 2, 1823, in *Compilation of the Messages and Papers of the Presidents, 1789–1897*, ed. James D. Richardson (Washington, D.C.: U.S. Government Printing Office, 1969), II, pp. 207–209.

---

by Alexander, pressed for a blanket commitment from the Alliance, and the result was the Troppau Protocol, signed by Austria, Prussia, and Russia. It declared war on all revolutionary governments that threatened European stability. Under the terms of the Troppau Protocol, an Austrian army toppled the revolutionary government of Naples in 1821. In 1823 a French army restored the absolute authority of Ferdinand VII.

French intervention in Spain provoked the strong opposition of Great Britain and ended the Quadruple Alliance. George Canning (1770–1827), who became British foreign minister in 1822, suspected that the Continental powers might now help Spain recover its former American colonies; so did the United States, which had recognized the independence of the new Latin American republics. But America also feared a possible Russian move southward from its outpost in Alaska along the Pacific coast or an attempt by Britain to extend its possessions in the Caribbean. Therefore, when Canning proposed a joint Anglo-American statement to ward off European interference in Latin America, the government of President James Monroe (1758–1831) refused the invitation. However, in a message to the American Congress in December 1823, the president included a statement that later became known as the Monroe Doctrine. Although this document marked an important assertion of policy by the youthful American republic in opposing European intervention in the Americas, it had little immediate international significance. The European

powers were not fully committed to restoring Spain's American empire in any event.

↑ by russians [handwritten]

Serbian and Greek Independence, 1804–1829

↳ Brits, French & russians all wanted mediterranean lands [handwritten]

The Greek revolt was part of the general movement of the Balkan nations for emancipation from their Turkish overlords. During the last quarter of the eighteenth century many peoples of the Balkan peninsula were awakening to a sense of national identity under the impact of French revolutionary and romantic ideas. They examined their national past with new interest and put particular stress on their native languages and on their Christian religion, which separated them from the Islamic Turks.

The first outbreak against the Turkish authorities came in 1804 among the Serbs, now one of the peoples of Yugoslavia. Ably led by Karadjordje Petrovic (c. 1752–1817), these early Serbian nationalists knew they would need outside help to win their independence. Some turned to Austria, which was nearby and ruled over their fellow Yugoslavs, the Croats and Slovenes; others looked to distant Russia, which attracted them because it was both Slavic in language and Orthodox in religion, for the Serbs were Orthodox, unlike the other Yugoslavs, who were Roman Catholic. Thus was established a pattern of conflicting Austrian and Russian interests that ultimately erupted in World War I. Abandoned by the Russians in

1812, Karadjordje fled to Austria, and leadership of Serb nationalism passed to his rival, Milosh Obrenovich (1780–1860), who won Russian support and succeeded by 1830 in becoming prince of an autonomous Serbia. Although Milosh still paid tribute to the Ottoman emperor and a Turkish garrison remained in the Serb capital of Belgrade, a major step toward independence had been completed.

Meantime, the Greeks had launched a revolution. Leadership came from two groups—the Phanariot Greeks, named for the quarter where they lived in Istanbul, and the Island Greeks, merchants from the ports and islands of the Aegean. The Phanariots had long held positions of power and responsibility in governing the Orthodox subjects of the Ottoman Empire. Greek nationalists sponsored a campaign to purge the modern Greek language of its Turkish and Slavic words and to return it to the classical tongue of the Age of Pericles. A revolutionary secret society was formed in the Russian port of Odessa, patterned after the Carbonari of Italy and headed by Alexander Ypsilanti (1792–1828), a Phanariot who was an officer in the Russian army.

In 1821 Ypsilanti led an expedition into the Danubian provinces of the Ottoman Empire; it failed to stir up a major revolt. The conspirators were more successful in the Morea (the ancient Peloponnesus), where they launched a peasant uprising. The ensuing war for independence was a ferocious conflict. The Morean peasants slaughtered every Turk they could find; the Ottoman government retaliated by killing or selling into slavery thirty thousand Greeks from the prosperous Aegean island of Chios. To help with the repression, the Ottoman sultan called in the forces of his vassals, especially the governor of Egypt. By 1827 when it appeared likely that the Egyptian expedition would recapture the last rebel strongholds, Britain, France, and Russia intervened to save the Greek independence movement at its darkest hour.

The three-power action resulted from the combined pressures of public opinion and strategic interests. In Britain, France, Germany, and the United States, the Philhellenic (pro-Greek) movement had won many supporters. Philhellenic committees sent supplies and money and demanded that their governments intervene directly. But intervention hinged on Russia, for Greek patriots had formed their secret society on Russian soil and with Russian backing. Ultimately, Russia's desire to dominate the Balkans won out over its concern for preserving the status quo, and it rallied openly to the Greek cause. Britain and France now felt obliged to take action because of Philhellenic pressure and, still more, because they feared to let Russia gain mastery over the Near East. A three-power intervention seemed the only course that would both rescue the Greeks and check the Russians.

Neither aim was fully achieved. In October 1827 Russian, British, and French squadrons sank the Turkish and Egyptian fleet. The subsequent Treaty of Adrianople (1829), while allowing Russia to annex outright only a little Turkish territory, arranged that the provinces of Moldavia and Wallachia should become a virtual Russian protectorate. After considerable wrangling, the European powers accorded formal recognition to a small independent Greek kingdom, which left most Greeks still within the Ottoman Empire.

The Decembrist Revolt in Russia, 1825

Russia, which did so much to determine the outcome of revolutions elsewhere, itself felt the revolutionary wave, but with diminished force. Liberal ideas continued to penetrate the country, spread by the secret societies that flourished in Russia after 1815. The introduction of Freemasonry during the eighteenth century had enabled nobles to meet on equal terms with men from other ranks of society. Moreover, the contrast between the relatively enlightened West and backward Russia made a deep impression on officers who had served in the campaigns against Napoleon. High-ranking officers at St. Petersburg secretly formed the Northern Society, which aimed to make Russia a limited, decentralized monarchy, with the various provinces enjoying rights somewhat like those of American states. The serfs would receive their freedom but no land. These reforms would be achieved by peaceful means. A second secret organization, the Southern Society, with headquarters at Kiev, included many relatively impoverished officers among its members. It advocated a highly centralized republic, the granting of land to liberated serfs, and the assassination of the czar to gain its ends.

Both societies tried to profit by the political confusion following the sudden death of Alexander I in December of 1825. Since Alexander left no son, the crown would normally have passed to his younger brother, Constantine. Constantine, however, had relinquished his rights to a still younger brother, Nicholas, but in a document so secret that Nicholas never saw it. On the death of Alexander, Constantine declared that Nicholas was the legal czar, and Nicholas declared that Constantine was. While the two brothers were clarifying their status, the Northern Society summoned the St. Petersburg garrison to revolt against Nicholas. Throughout the day of December 26, 1825, the rebels stood their ground in Russia's capital city until Nicholas subdued them.

The Decembrist revolt thoroughly alarmed Czar Nicholas I (r. 1825–1855), who resolved to follow a severely autocratic policy. Nicholas had five Decembrists executed and exiled more than a hundred others to Siberia, where many of them contributed to the advance of local government and education. The Decembrists were the first in a long line of modern Russian political martyrs.

THE REVOLUTIONS OF 1830

The next revolutionary wave, that of 1830, swept first over France. King Louis XVIII (r. 1814–1824) would have preferred to be an absolute ruler, but he knew that returning to the Old Regime was impractical, especially since he was declining in health and suffered from the additional political handicap of having been imposed on the French by their enemies.

Success in France

The ambiguities of Louis XVIII's policies were most evident in the constitutional charter that he issued in 1814. Some sections sounded like the absolute monarchy of Louis XIV; for example, the preamble asserted the royal prerogative: "The authority in France resides in the person of the king." But the charter also granted a measure of constitutional monarchy. There was a legislature, composed of a Chamber of Peers, appointed by the king, and a Chamber of Deputies, elected on a very restricted suffrage that allowed fewer than 100,000 of France's 30 million the right to vote. The charter stated, and the Chambers had no formal right to confirm the king's choices as ministers. Yet since Louis tended to select ministers acceptable to majority opinion in the legislature, this was a kind of functional compromise with parliamentary government. Furthermore, the charter guaranteed religious toleration, a measure of freedom for the press, equality before the law, and equal eligibility to civil and military office. It also accepted the Code Napoléon and, still more important, the revolutionary property settlement.

The charter, however, greatly irritated the ultra royalists or "Ultras," the noble and clerical émigrés who had returned to France after their revolutionary exile. They were determined to recover both the privileges and the property they had lost during the Revolution. When the election of 1815 gave the Ultras control of the Chamber of Deputies, they proposed to set up special courts to deal with suspected revolutionaries. At the insistence of the allies, Louis XVIII dismissed the Chamber and held a new election, which returned a more moderate majority.

Events, however, soon strengthened the Ultras' hand. Antirevolutionary fears swept France after the Spanish uprising of 1820. The Ultras won control of the Chamber of Deputies, reimposed censorship of the press, and put through a law giving extra weight to the votes of the wealthiest 25 percent of the already very restricted electorate. In 1821 French education was placed under the direction of the Roman Catholic bishops.

The tempo of the reaction quickened when Louis died, and his brother, the Ultra leader, became King Charles X (r. 1824–1830). Charles greatly extended the influence of the church by encouraging the activities of the Jesuits, who were still legally banned from France; and he sponsored a law compensating the émigrés for their confiscated property. The measure could be defended as a sensible political move, but it was widely, if inaccurately, believed that a concurrent reduction of the annual interest on government obligations from 5 to 3 percent was intended to defray the cost of the annuities. Many influential Parisian bondholders were infuriated by the move.

After a brief attempt to conciliate the liberals, Charles X appointed as his chief minister the ultra royalist prince de Polignac. Polignac hoped to bolster Charles's waning prestige by scoring a resounding naval victory.

He attacked the Bey of Algiers, a largely independent vassal of the Ottoman emperor, who was notorious for his collusion with the Barbary pirates; the capture of Algiers (July 5, 1830) laid the foundation of the French empire in North Africa. On July 25, 1830, without securing the legislature's approval, Charles and Polignac issued the Four Ordinances, muzzling the press, dissolving the newly elected Chamber, ordering a new election, and introducing new voting qualifications that would have disenfranchised the bourgeois who were the mainstay of the opposition. The king and his chief minister believed that public opinion, mollified by the recent victory at Algiers, would accept these measures calmly. They miscalculated utterly.

Aroused by the protests of liberal journalists, encouraged by the hot summer weather, and impatient from a three-year economic recession, the Parisians initiated a riot that became a revolution. During *les trois glorieuses* (the three glorious days of July 27, 28, and 29) they threw up barricades, captured the Paris city hall, and hoisted the tricolor atop Notre Dame cathedral. Charles X abdicated in favor of his grandson and sailed to exile in England.

The revolutionary rank and file in 1830 came mainly from the lower bourgeoisie and the skilled workers. Their leadership came from the parliamentary opponents of Charles X and from cautious young liberals like Adolphe Thiers (1797–1877) and François Guizot (1787–1874). Thiers edited the opposition paper *Le National*; he had also written a history of the great revolution to show that it had not been all bloodshed but had also had a peaceful and constructive side. Guizot, too, had written history, a survey of civilization focused on the rise of the bourgeoisie.

The revolutionaries of 1830, like those of 1789, were not agreed on the kind of regime they wanted. A minority would have liked a democratic republic with universal suffrage. But many others, who identified a republic with the Terror, wanted a constitutional monarchy with a suffrage restricted to the wealthy. The moderate leaders were ready with a candidate for the throne—Louis Philippe, the duke of Orléans.

Louis Philippe (r. 1830–1848) had fought in the revolutionary army, then had emigrated in 1793 before the worst of the Terror. He claimed to have little use for the pomp of royalty, and he dressed and acted like a sober and well-to-do businessman. However, he accepted the crown at the invitation of the Chamber.

The Chamber revised the Charter of 1814 and called Louis Philippe, not "King of the France" but "King of the French." It also substituted the red, white, and blue revolutionary tricolor for the white flag of the Bourbons. The July Monarchy, as the new regime was termed, left France far short of realizing the democratic potential of liberty, equality, and fraternity.

Success in Belgium

The union of Belgium and the Netherlands, decreed by the peacemakers of 1815, worked well only in economics. The commerce and colonies of Holland supplied raw materials and markets for the textile, glass, and other manufactures of Belgium. In language, politics, and religion, however, King William I of Holland exerted power arbitrarily. He made Dutch the official language throughout his realm, including the French-speaking Walloon provinces. He denied the pleas of Belgians to rectify the "Dutch arithmetic" that gave the Dutch provinces, with 2 million inhabitants, and the Belgian, with 3.5 million, equal seats in the States-General. He refused to grant special status to the Catholic church in Belgium, and particularly offended the faithful by insisting that the education of priests be subject to state supervision. All these grievances tended to create a Belgian nationalism and to forge common bonds between the Catholic Dutch-speaking Flemings of the provinces north of Brussels and the Catholic French-speaking Walloons of the highly industrialized southern provinces.

The revolution broke out in Brussels on August 25, 1830. Headed by students inspired by the example of Paris, the riots were directed against Dutch rule. The insurgents recruited their fighters chiefly from the industrial workers, many of whom complained of low pay and frequent unemployment. However, the better-organized middle-class leadership soon controlled the revolutionary movement and predominated in the Belgian national congress that convened in November 1830.

This congress proclaimed Belgium an independent constitutional monarchy. The new constitution granted religious toleration, provided for wide local self-government, and put rigorous limits on the king's authority. Although it did not establish universal suffrage, the financial qualifications for voting were lower in Belgium than they were in Britain or France. When the congress chose as king a son of Louis Philippe, the British foreign minister protested vehemently. The congress then picked Leopold of Saxe-Coburg (r. 1831–1865). Leopold had already shown his political shrewdness by refusing the shaky new throne of Greece; he now repeated it by marrying a daughter of Louis Philippe.

King William stubbornly tried to reconquer Belgium in 1831–1832. A French army and a British fleet successfully defended the secessionists, however, and prolonged negotiations resulted in Dutch recognition of Belgium's new status in 1839. In 1839 also, representatives of Britain, France, Prussia, Austria, and Russia guaranteed both the independence and the neutrality of Belgium.

Failure in Poland, Italy, and Germany

The course of revolution in Poland contrasted tragically with that in Belgium. In 1815 the kingdom of Poland had the most liberal constitution on the Continent; twenty years later it had become a dependency of the Russian Empire. The constitution given to the Poles by Czar Alexander I preserved the Code Napoléon and endowed the Diet with limited legislative power. A hundred thousand Poles received the franchise. In practice, however, difficulties arose. Many of the men chosen for

official posts in Poland were not acceptable to the Poles; indeed, probably no government imposed by Russia would have satisfied them. Censorship, unrest, and police intervention marked the last years of Alexander I.

The advent of Nicholas I in 1825 increased political friction, although the new czar at first abided by the Polish constitution. Meantime, romantic nationalism made many converts at the universities of Warsaw and Vilna (in Lithuania). Polish nationalists demanded the transfer from Russia to Poland of Lithuania, White Russia, and the Ukraine. Secret societies on the Carbonari model arose in these provinces and in the kingdom of Poland.

A secret society of army cadets in Warsaw launched a revolution in November 1830. Leadership of the movement was soon assumed by Polish nobles, but they were at best reluctant revolutionaries who had no intention of emancipating the Polish peasants. This was a revolution for national independence, not for righting the wrongs of the Old Regime. Radicals in Warsaw and other cities disrupted the revolutionary government, which collapsed in September 1831. Once the Russians were in control again, Nicholas I scrapped the Polish constitution, imposed martial law, and closed the universities.

In Italy and Germany news of the July Revolution in Paris stimulated abortive, revolutionary efforts. In 1831 Carbonari insurgents briefly controlled the little duchies of Parma and Modena and a sizable part of the Papal States. The revolutionaries counted on French assistance, but the July Monarchy had no intention of risking war with Austria. Again, as in 1821, Metternich sent troops to restore legitimacy in Italy.

In Prussia King Frederick William III (r. 1797–1840) had never fulfilled his promise to grant a constitution, though he did set up provincial diets. After 1815 German university students formed the *Burschenschaft* (Students' Union), and in October 1817 students of the University of Jena held a rally. During the rally the Burschenschaft burned books by reactionary writers. In March 1819 one of these writers, August von Kotzebue, who was also a Russian agent, was assassinated by a student. Metternich used the incident to suppress student clubs, getting the Diet of the German Confederation to approve the Carlsbad Decrees (September 1819), which stiffened press censorship, dissolved the Burschenschaft, and curtailed academic freedom.

Despite the Carlsbad Decrees, mild political ferment continued in Germany, and the Burschenschaft reorganized underground. In 1830 and the years following, a few rulers in northern Germany, notably in Saxony and Hanover, were forced to grant constitutions. Excited by these minor successes and by the appearance of Polish refugees, thirty thousand revolutionary sympathizers, including many students from Heidelberg and other universities in the region, gathered at Hambach in the Palatinate in May 1832. There they demanded the union of the German states under a democratic republic. Effective action toward unification was another matter. In 1833 some fifty instructors and students tried to seize

The French artist Eugéne Delacroix, in *Liberty at the Barricades* (the reference is to the events of July 28, 1830), shows Liberty as a woman moving the flag of liberation forward over the bodies of both the troops and the people. The towers of Notre Dame rise through the smoke as a symbol of the traditions of France. Liberty is joined in revolution by representative Parisian types: a member of the proletariat with cutlass, an intellectual with sawed-off musket, and a street boy with pistols.

Réunion des Musées Nationaux, Paris

Frankfurt, the capital of the German Confederation and seat of its Diet. The insurgents, together with hundreds of other students accused of Burschenschaft activities, were given harsh sentences by courts in Prussia and other German states.

The Lessons of 1830

The revolutionary wave of the 1830s confirmed two major political developments. First, it widened the split between the West and the East already evident after the revolutions of 1820. Britain and France were committed to support cautiously liberal constitutional monarchies both at home and in Belgium. On the other hand, Russia, Austria, and Prussia were more firmly committed than ever to counterrevolution. In 1833 Czar Nicholas I, Metternich, and King Frederick William III formally pledged their joint assistance to any sovereign threatened by revolution.

Second, revolution succeeded in 1830 only where it enlisted the support of a large part of the population. It failed in every country where the revolutionaries represented only a fraction of the people. In Poland the social policies of aristocratic nationalist leaders alienated them from the peasants. Italian revolutionaries still relied on their romantic Carbonari tradition and on unrealistic hopes of foreign aid. In Germany revolution was a matter of student outbursts and other gestures by a small minority. Conspirators and intellectuals needed to make their doctrines penetrate to the grass roots of society; they needed to develop able political leaders and to mature well-laid plans for political reform. These tasks they undertook after 1830; their success was to be tested in the revolutions of 1848.

THE REVOLUTIONS OF 1848

Nationalism was a common denominator of several revolutions in 1848. It prompted the disunited Germans and Italians to attempt political unification, and it inspired the subject peoples of the Habsburg Empire to seek political and cultural autonomy. The new nationalism tended to focus on language. The Czech language, for example, was almost extinct in the late eighteenth century. By 1848, however, a Czech linguistic and literary revival was in full swing. Patriotic histories and collections of Czech folk poetry kindled a lively interest in the national past and fostered dreams of a Pan-Slavic awakening.

Liberalism, the second common denominator of the revolutions, encompassed a wide range of programs. In central and western Europe, liberals demanded constitutions to limit absolute monarchy and to liquidate feudal rights and manorial dues. In France, many liberals sought to replace the July Monarchy with a democratic republic. But what did they mean by "democratic"? For some, democracy meant that every man (not yet every woman) should have not only the right to vote but also the "right to work"—a phrase that implied the need for governments to take measures against unemployment and other social ills aggravated by the alternating prosperity and depression associated with industrial growth.

An economic crisis helped to catalyze discontent into revolution. A blight ruined the Irish potato crop in 1845 and soon spread to the Continent; the grain harvest of 1846 also failed in western Europe. The consequences were a sharp rise in the price of bread and bread riots; mass starvation occurred in Ireland, and widespread misery affected France, Germany, and Austria. The food crisis was compounded by an industrial depression. The number of unemployed mounted just as food prices were rising, thus intensifying popular suffering.

Scholars generally agree that these revolutions did not arise from conspiracies of Masons, Jews, or radicals, though many observers at the time blamed such scapegoats. While the fermentation of ideas had prepared the soil, and while social problems had created worried, angry populations, the long-term cause was a growing conjunction between political and economic crises. Demographic shifts, attacks on traditional social practices, and the effects of industrialism gave ideas of nationalism and liberalism a force they had not had since 1789.

France

The economic crisis hit France with particular severity. Railroad construction almost ceased, throwing more than half a million out of work; coal mines and iron foundries, in turn, laid off workers. Unemployment increased the discontent of French workers already embittered by their low wages and by the still lower esteem in which they were held by the government of Louis Philippe. Under the July Monarchy, French agriculture experienced a golden age at the same time that industrialization was beginning to develop. The government, however, appeared to be indifferent to the social misery that accompanied the new prosperity.

The main beneficiaries of the July Monarchy were the social and economic elite who had the right to vote. The government banned labor organizations and harshly repressed the workers of Paris and Lyons who demonstrated in the early 1830s to demand a republic and higher wages.

Opposition to the July Monarchy grew during the next decade. Heading what might be termed the official opposition was Adolphe Thiers, who continued to support the principle of constitutional monarchy. The republicans formed a second opposition group, which increased in numbers with the growing political awareness and literacy of the working classes. The third, and smallest, group took in the exponents of various doctrines of socialism, who gained recruits from the economic depression of the late 1840s. Potentially more formidable than any of these, but as yet representing only a vague, unorganized sentiment, were the Bonapartists. The return of the emperor's remains from St. Helena to Paris in 1840 revived the legend of a glorious and warlike Napoleon, so different from the uninspiring Louis Philippe.

In the summer of 1847 constitutional monarchists of the Thiers faction joined with republicans to stage a series of political banquets throughout France calling for an extension of the suffrage and the resignation of chief minister Guizot. This campaign appeared harmless until a huge banquet was announced for February 22, 1848, to be held in Paris. When the Guizot ministry forbade the banquet, the Parisians substituted a large demonstration. On February 23, Louis Philippe dismissed Guizot and prepared to summon Thiers to the ministry. But his concessions came too late. Supported by workers, students, and the more radical republican leaders, the demonstration of February 22 turned into a riot on February 23, in which more than fifty of the rioters were killed or wounded. The number of casualties intensified the revolutionary atmosphere.

On February 24, Louis Philippe abdicated, and the Chamber set up a provisional government headed by an eloquent, cautious advocate of a republic, the romantic poet Alphonse de Lamartine (1790–1869). Popular unrest, mounting along with unemployment, obliged the provisional government to take in a few socialists. Notable among these was Louis Blanc (1811–1882), an advocate of social workshops which the workers themselves would own and run with the financial assistance of the state. As a gesture toward the "right to work," and also as a measure to restore calm in Paris, the provisional government authorized the establishment of national workshops in the capital. These national workshops, however, were not a genuine attempt to implement the blueprint of Louis Blanc but a relief project organized along semimilitary lines and enrolling more than 100,000 unemployed persons from Paris and the provinces.

The future shape of France now hinged on the outcome of the elections of April 23, 1848, when all adult males would be qualified to vote for the National Assembly, which would draw up a constitution for the Second Republic. (The first Republic had lasted officially from September 1792 until Napoleon's coronation in 1804.) In this election 8 million, 84 percent of the potential electorate, went to the polls. The conservative peasants, who still made up the bulk of the population, approved the fall of the July Monarchy but dreaded anything resembling an attack by the socialists on the private property they had recently acquired. Of the almost nine hundred deputies elected, therefore, most were either monarchists or conservative republicans.

The Paris radicals refused to accept the results. Demonstrators invaded the National Assembly and proposed the formation of a new provisional government; alarmed moderates arrested the radical leaders and decided that the national workshops threatened law and order. The Assembly decreed the orderly closing of the workshops; their workers could either enlist in the army or accept work in the provinces. The poorer districts of the capital responded by revolting from June 23 to June 26, 1848, when they were subdued by the troops brought in from the conservative rural areas by General Louis Eugène Cavaignac (1802–1857), the energetic minister of war.

These June Days were a landmark in modern history, the first large-scale outbreak with clear overtones of class warfare. Most of the insurgents seem to have come from the unemployed who had tried vainly to enroll in the workshops and were now desperate. Among them were workers of the new industrial age—mechanics, railroad men, dockworkers—as well as winesellers, masons, locksmiths, cabinetmakers, and other artisans of the type who had been prominent in the capture of the Bastille in 1789. The prospect of a social revolution terrified the propertied classes; peasants, shopkeepers, landowners, and nobles were all poured into Paris on the new railroads to quell the uprising. About ten thousand were killed or wounded, and about the same number were subsequently deported, chiefly to Algeria. All socialist clubs and newspapers were padlocked, and Louis Blanc fled to England. France became a virtual military dictatorship under General Cavaignac.

The fears of the middle-class moderates were evident in the constitution of the Second Republic, which the National Assembly completed in November 1848. The Assembly declared property inviolable and refused to include the right to work among the fundamental rights of French citizens. The president was to be chosen by popular election every four years, and the single-chamber legislature was to be elected every three years.

Circumstances did not favor the success of the Second Republic. In the presidential election of December 1848 the presidency of the republic went to Louis Napoleon Bonaparte (1808–1873). This nephew of the great Napoleon was not an impressive figure. Yet he bore the magical name of Bonaparte and could tap the glamor of the Napoleonic legend. In 1848 he staged a clever campaign to identify himself with the cause of order, stability,

and democracy. In domestic politics he would subvert the constitution of the Second Republic in a coup d'état late in 1851 and proclaim himself Emperor Napoleon III a year later. The French Revolution of 1848, like that of 1789, had established a republic that ended in a Napoleonic empire.

Italy

In Italy new reform movements supplanted the discredited Carbonari. By the 1840s three movements were competing for the leadership of Italian nationalism. Two were moderate. One of these groups, based in the north, favored the domination of Piedmont; its leader, Count Camillo Cavour (1810–1861), was an admirer of British and French liberalism. Cavour was the editor of an influential Turin newspaper, *Il Risorgimento* (resurgence, regeneration), which gave its name to the movement for unification. The other moderate group called themselves Neo-Guelfs because, like the Guelf political faction of the Middle Ages, they hoped to engage the pope in the task of freeing Italy from the control of a German emperor. The Neo-Guelf leader, the priest Vincenzo Gioberti (1801–1852), declared that the future depended on "the union of Rome and Turin." The pope would head, and the army of Piedmont would defend, a federation of Italian states, each with its own monarch and constitution.

The third group of liberals, Young Italy—so named because only those under the age of forty could join—asserted that Italy should be unified as a democratic republic. Its founder, Giuseppe Mazzini (1805–1872), hoped to create an organization more effective than the Carbonari, but was frustrated by prolonged exile and the ineptitude of his lieutenants. Nevertheless, Mazzini did win an enduring reputation as the great democratic idealist of modern Italian politics.

The prospects for reform in Italy brightened in 1846, when a new pope, Pio Nono (Pius IX, 1846–1878), was elected. His initial progressive actions, such as the release of political prisoners and steps to modernize the administration of the Papal States, aroused hopes for a liberalized papal government.

In January 1848 an uprising in Sicily, at first aimed at independence from Naples, forced King Ferdinand II to grant a constitution on the pattern of the French Charter of 1814 (as revised by the July Monarchy); in mid-February the grand duke of Tuscany was forced to follow suit. News of the rising in Paris quickened the pace of the Italian revolutions, as King Charles Albert of Piedmont (1798–1849) and Pius IX agreed to become constitutional rulers like Louis Philippe. Next came Lombardy and Venetia, where the ideas of Young Italy had inspired revolutionary movements. Ever since January 1 citizens of Milan, the capital of Lombardy, had been boycotting cigars as a protest against the Austrian tax on tobacco. Severe rioting resulted. News of revolution in Vienna touched off five days of heavy fighting in Milan, which forced the Austrians to withdraw their forces. At the same time, Venice, the capital of Austria's other Italian province, proclaimed itself the independent Republic of St. Mark.

This rapid collapse of Habsburg rule in Lombardy-Venetia inspired a national crusade against the Austrians. Charles Albert of Piedmont assumed command of the Italian forces, and refused an offer of help from the provisional government of the French republic. As town and country had opposing views and the Austrians exploited these divisions well, the decision to "go it alone" proved unwise. Piedmont moved too far too fast, annexing Lombardy and the two small north Italian duchies of Parma and Modena. The other Italian states began to fear the imperialism of Piedmont more than they desired the unification of Italy. On April 29, Pius IX announced that his "equal affection" for all peoples obliged him to adopt a neutral position in the war with Austria and to recall his soldiers. The pope could not act both as an Italian patriot and as an international spiritual leader. The Neo-Guelf cause thus received a fatal blow. In the Two Sicilies, the king scrapped the constitution and followed the papal example in withdrawing his troops from the war. The Austrians, taking the offensive, reconquered Lombardy and crushed the forces of Charles Albert at Custozza in July.

In Rome adherents of Young Italy rose up in November 1848. After Pius IX fled to Neapolitan territory, they transformed the Papal States into a democratic Roman Republic headed by Mazzini. In March 1849 radicals in Piedmont forced the reluctant Charles Albert to renew the war with Austria, but within the month Austria prevailed. In August 1849 the Austrians put an end to the Republic of St. Mark after a prolonged siege and bombardment of Venice. Meanwhile, Mazzini's Roman Republic had surrendered to French troops sent by President Bonaparte in a bid for Catholic gratitude. Both the Neo-Guelfs and Young Italy were discredited.

Piedmont, however, had emerged as the leader of Italian nationalism and liberalism. It had defied the hated Austrians, and was also the only Italian state to retain the constitution granted in 1848. When Charles Albert abdicated, the crown passed to Victor Emmanuel II (1820–1878), who was to become the first king of modern Italy.

Germany

Now the German revolutions in 1848 roughly paralleled those in Italy. In Germany, too, liberalism and nationalism won initial victories and then collapsed before internal dissension and Austrian resistance. The failure in Germany was the more surprising since the revolutionary movement had begun to recruit support among industrial workers, artisans fearing industrial competition, and peasants seeking to abolish the relics of manorialism that had already been swept away in France. Liberal and nationalist agitation, however, was centered in the well-to-do business and professional classes. Most German liberals wanted constitutional monarchies in the various German states, a stronger German Confederation, and an end to the repressive hegemony of Metternich.

The hero of German liberals was King Frederick William IV of Prussia (r. 1840–1861). Attractive and cultivated, Frederick William promised to carry out his father's unhonored pledge to give Prussia a constitution and an elected assembly. However, the meeting of representatives from the provincial diets that he finally convoked in 1847 did little.

It was, in fact, the *Zollverein* (Customs Union) which constituted Prussia's most solid contribution to German unification before 1848. In 1818 Prussia had abolished internal tariffs within its scattered territories and applied a uniform tax on imports. Membership in the Zollverein proved so profitable that by 1844 almost all the German states except Austria had joined. The Zollverein liberated Germany from an oppressive burden of local tolls and taxes and cleared the way for its phenomenal economic development later in the century. The success of the Zollverein suggested that Prussia might naturally take the initiative in political unification.

Stimulated by the example of Paris, the revolutionaries of 1848 scored their first successes in the western German states early in March; from there the demands for constitutions and civil liberties fanned out rapidly. By mid-March most of the rulers of the smaller German states had yielded to the pressure, and in Berlin demonstrators were erecting barricades. Frederick William accepted some of the liberals' demands and appealed for calm, but before his appeal could be publicized, rioting broke out with redoubled violence. More than two hundred rioters, chiefly workers, were killed. The mob broke into the royal palace and forced the king to accept the demands of liberals and nationalists. He summoned an assembly to draw up a constitution, declared Prussia "merged in Germany," and proclaimed himself "king of the free, regenerated German nation."

Drastic reform of the German Confederation now began. In May 1848 a constitutional convention met at Frankfurt, the capital of the Confederation. Its 830 members were elected throughout Germany, but often by electoral colleges and with suffrage restrictions that made the results less than a true popular mandate. The assembly lacked a broad popular base. Moreover, its members lacked political experience and talent for practical statesmanship when they had to decide the geographical limits of Germany. The Confederation included Austria proper but excluded most of the non-German Habsburg territories; nor did it include the eastern provinces of Prussia, notably those acquired in the partitions of Poland. The Austrian issue divided the assembly into two camps: the "Big Germans," who favored the inclusion of Austria and of Bohemia, with its large Czech population, in the projected German state; and the "Little Germans," who opposed the idea. Austrian objections to a "Big Germany" ensured the assembly's adoption of the "Little Germany" proposal, while nationalism overcame liberalism on the question of Prussian Poland. By a large majority the assembly voted to include Prussian areas in which the Poles formed most of the population.

In contrast, in March 1849 the Frankfurt Assembly adopted a liberal national constitution based on the American federal system and British parliamentary practice. The individual states were to surrender many of their powers to the German federal government. The federal legislature would consist of a lower house, elected by universal male suffrage, and an upper house, chosen by the state governments and the legislatures. Ministers responsible to the legislature would form the federal executive. Over all would preside a constitutional monarch, the German emperor.

But the Frankfurt constitution died at birth. The assembly elected the king of Prussia to be emperor, but Frederick William rejected the offer, and the assembly soon disbanded. It had never secured recognition from foreign governments, had never raised a penny in taxes, and had never ruled over Germany.

The Habsburg Domains

The fate of German and Italian nationalism in 1848 hinged partly on the outcome of the revolutions in the Habsburg Empire. If these revolutions had immobilized the Habsburg government for a long period, the Italian and German unification might have been realized. But Austria rode out the storm. The success of the counterrevolution in the Habsburg Empire also assured its victory in Italy and Germany.

The nature and the outcome of the Habsburg revolutions depended in turn on the complex structure of nationalities with the Austrian Empire. There were several nationalities under Habsburg rule in 1848:

Nationality (by language spoken)	Percentage of Total Population
German	23
Czech and Slovak	19
Magyar (Hungarian)	14
South (Yugo-) Slav	
Slovene	4
Croat	4
Serb	5
Ruthenian (Little Russian)	8
Romanian	8
Italian	8
Polish	7

These national groups were not always separated geographically. For instance, in the Hungarian part of the empire—which had large minorities of Slovaks, Romanians, Serbs, Croats, and Germans—the dominant Magyars fell just short of a majority. Throughout the empire, moreover, the German element, chiefly bureaucrats and merchants, predominated in most of the towns and cities.

Among the peoples of the Habsburg realm in 1848, nationalism ran strongest among the Italians of Lombardy-Venetia, the Czechs of Bohemia, and the Magyars and Croats of Hungary. Language was an important issue among Magyars, as it was with Czechs; the replacement of Latin by Hungarian as the official language of the eastern part of the empire in 1844

marked a victory for Magyar nationalism. The spellbinding orator Lajos Kossuth (1802–1894), an ardent nationalist, regarded the linguistic reform of 1844 as but the first in a series of revolutionary projects cutting all ties with Vienna. But Magyar nationalists bitterly opposed the national aspirations of their own Slavic subjects. The most discontented were the Croats, whose national awakening had begun when their homeland was absorbed into Napoleon's empire.

The antagonism between Croats and Magyars revealed an all-important fact about the nationalistic movements within the Habsburg Empire. Some groups—Italians, Magyars, Czechs, Poles—resented the German-dominated government in Vienna. Others, notably the Croats and Romanians, were less anti-German than anti-Magyar. Here was a situation where the central government in Vienna might apply a policy of divide and conquer, pitting anti-Magyar elements against anti-German Maygars, and subduing both. This was substantially what happened in 1848. A similar policy had already been used in 1846 to suppress a revolt in Austrian Poland. When the Polish landlords had revolted, their exploited Ruthenian peasants had risen against them and received the backing of Vienna.

From 1815 to 1848 the Habsburg government virtually ignored the grumblings and protests that arose in almost every quarter of the empire. Metternich probably wanted to make some concessions to liberal and nationalist aspirations, but he was blocked by the emperors—the bureaucratic Francis I (r. 1792–1835) and the weak Ferdinand I (r. 1835–1848)—and by the vested interests of the aristocracy.

The news of the February revolution in Paris shook the empire to its foundations. Four separate revolutions broke out almost simultaneously in March 1848: in Milan and Venice, in Hungary, in Vienna itself, and in Bohemia. In Hungary, Kossuth and his Magyar supporters forced Emperor Ferdinand to give Hungary political autonomy, institute parliamentary government, and substitute an elected legislature for the feudal Hungarian diet. New laws abolished serfdom and ended the immunity of nobles and gentry from taxation.

Aroused by the Hungarian revolt, university students and unemployed workers rose in Vienna on March 12. On the next day Metternich resigned and fled to Britain. Although the imperial government repeatedly promised reforms, the constitution it granted seemed woefully inadequate to the Viennese insurgents. By May the political atmosphere was so charged that Emperor Ferdinand and his family left the capital for the Tyrol. Pending a meeting of a constituent assembly in July, a revolutionary council ran affairs in Vienna. In the meantime, Austrian forces were at war in Piedmont. In September a constituent assembly, meeting in Vienna and representing all the Habsburg provinces except the Italian and the Hungarian, emancipated the peasants from their obligation to work for the landlords.

Meanwhile, in Prague, Czech nationalists were demanding rights similar to those granted the Magyars. In June 1848 the Czechs organized a Pan-Slav Congress

DOING HISTORY

Literature and Historical Analysis

Some of the most acute observers of social conditions are writers of fiction, and the historian often turns to literature in historical analysis. The subject matter chosen by a contemporary writer tells the historian much about the concerns of the literature section of society. The writer's approach to subject matter—reportorial, magical, realistic, satirical, and so on—reveals even more to the historian of culture. Often the fullest description of a place, a scene, even an event, especially in the time before the camera was invented, comes from the pages of fiction. To be sure, fiction takes liberties with scenes, accents, even sequences of time, and the historian must use fiction, even "historical fiction"— that body of writing in which the novelist attempts, through research, a reasonably exact depiction of time and place—with caution. A good example comes from the writings of the great English satirist and social critic Charles Dickens (1812–1870), who was very popular in his day and who continues to be drawn upon by historians as much as any writer in the century. His book *Hard Times* is one historians use most. In it he describes a society devoted to alleged self-improvements, to the power of facts, statistics, and surveys, and to the notion that the "lower orders" could not help themselves and were not to be trusted:

It contained several large streets all very like one another, and many small streets still more like one another, inhabited by people equally like one another, who all went in and out at the same hours, with the same sound upon the same pavements, to do the same work, and to whom every day was the same as yesterday and tomorrow, and every year the counterpart of the last and the next....

You saw nothing in Coketown but what was severely workful. If the members of a religious persuasion built a chapel there—as the members of eighteen religious persuasions had done—they made it a pious warehouse of red brick. ... All the public inscriptions in the town were painted alike, in severe characters of black and white. The jail might have been the infirmary, the infirmary might have been the jail, the town-hall might have been either, or both, or anything else, for anything that appeared to the contrary in the graces of their construction. Fact, fact, fact, everywhere in the material aspect of the town; fact, fact, fact everywhere in the immaterial. The M'Choakumchild school was all fact, and the relations between master and man were all fact, and everything was fact between the lying-in hospital and the cemetery, and what you couldn't state in figures, or show to the purchaseable in the cheapest market and saleable in the dearest, was not, and never should be, world without end, Amen. ...

Coketown did not come out of its own furnaces, in all respects like gold that had stood the fire. First, the perplexing mystery of the place was, Who belonged to the eighteen denominations? Because, whoever did, the labouring people did not. It was very strange to walk through the streets on a Sunday morning, and note how few of *them* the barbarous jangling of bells that was driving the sick and nervous mad, called away from their own quarter, from their own close rooms, from the corners of their own streets, where they lounged listlessly, gazing at all the church and chapel going, as at a thing with which they had no manner of concern. Nor was it merely the stranger who noticed this, because there was a native organization in

Coketown itself, whose members were to be heard of in the House of Commons every session, indignantly petitioning for acts of parliament that should make these people religious by main force. Then, came the Teetotal Society, who complained that these same people *would* get drunk, and showed in tabular statements that they did get drunk, and proved at tea parties that no inducement, human or Divine (except a medal), would induce them to forego their custom of getting drunk. Then, came the chemist and druggist, with other tabular statements, showing that when they didn't get drunk, they took opium. Then, came the experienced chaplain of the jail, with more tabular statements, outdoing all the previous tabular statements, and showing that the same people *would* resort to low haunts, hidden from the public eye, where they heard low singing and saw low dancing, and mayhap joined in it; and where A. B., aged twenty-four next birthday, and committed for eighteen months' solitary, had himself said (not that he had ever shown himself particularly worthy of belief) his ruin began, as he was perfectly sure and confident that otherwise he would have been a tip-top moral specimen. Then, came Mr Gradgrind and Mr Bounderby, the two gentlemen at this present moment walking through Coketown, and both eminently practical, who could, on occasion, furnish more tabular statements derived from their own personal experience, and illustrated by cases they had known and seen, from which it clearly appeared—in short it was the only clear thing in the case—that these same people were a bad lot altogether, gentlemen; that do what you would for them they were never thankful for it, gentlemen; that they were restless, gentlemen; that they never knew what they wanted; that they lived upon the best, and bought fresh butter, and insisted on Mocha coffee, and rejected all but prime parts of meat, and yet were eternally dissatisfied and unmanageable.

Charles Dickens, *Hard Times*, 1854 (New York: Penguin, 1978), pp. 65–67.

to promote the solidarity of Slavic peoples against "Big German" encroachments. The Pan-Slav Congress set off demonstrations, during which the wife of the commander of the Austrian garrison in Prague was accidentally killed. Five days later the commander, after bombarding Prague, dispersed the Czech revolutionaries and established a military regime in Bohemia. The counterrevolution had begun. The imperial government authorized the governor of Croatia to invade central Hungary to put down revolt there. While the Magyars held off the imperial forces, the radicals of Vienna revolted again, proclaiming their support of the Magyars and declaring Austria a democratic republic. But the Habsburg armies crushed the Vienna revolution (October 31, 1848) and executed the radical leaders.

In November 1848 the energetic and unscrupulous Prince Felix Schwarzenberg (1800–1852) became the Austrian prime minister. Schwarzenberg arranged the abdication of Ferdinand I and the accession of Ferdinand's nephew, Francis Joseph (r. 1848–1916). He then declared that the promises made by the old emperor could not legally bind his successor and shelved the projects of the constituent assembly, though he honored the emancipation of the peasantry. The Magyars fought on. In April 1849 the parliament of Hungary declared the country an independent republic and named Kossuth its chief executive. Russia now offered Austria military assistance. In August 1849 Russian troops helped to subjugate the Hungarian republic.

"The narrow spirit of nationalism" was to grow ever more intense after 1848. It was eventually to destroy the Habsburg Empire. The failure of the liberals to unify Italy and Germany in 1848 transferred the leadership of the nationalist movements from the amateur revolutionaries to the professional politicians of Piedmont and Prussia. Piedmont, alone among the Italian states, retained the moderate constitution it had secured in 1848; in Germany the antiliberal Count Otto von Bismarck was to achieve through "blood and iron" what the Frankfurt Assembly had not accomplished peacefully.

Equally dramatic was the role of the working class, particularly in France, and of the peasantry, which arose in violent revolt in 1851, only to be crushed. Europe was experiencing the challenge of the forces released by the industrial revolution, and new demands for drastic social and economic changes were arising alongside the older demands for political liberties, constitutions, and the end of peasant servitude. The year 1848 was not only the year of abortive revolution but also the year in which Karl Marx and Friedrich Engels published their guidelines for future revolutions in *The Communist Manifesto.*

$\mathcal{S}$UMMARY

Romanticism, materialism, and idealism overlapped as strands of thought in a period of rapid change. Romantics rejected the narrow optimism and mechanistic world of Enlightenment rationalists. The style of the romantics was imaginative, emotional, and haunted by the supernatural and by history. They stressed the individual and emotional ties to the past.

In literature and music, romanticism triumphed. In Germany, the Sturm und Drang movement and in England the poetry of Byron, Shelley, Keats, and others symbolized the romantic protest. Romantic musicians renounced classical rules and sought out popular ballads and tales of the past.

In the fine arts, romantics shared the stage with neoclassicists. In architecture, neoclassical styles gave way to the Gothic revival. In philosophy, Hegel proposed a theory of history as a dialectical process, an organic process of growth and development.

Politically, reactionaries were in power after 1815. The writings of Burke formed the foundation for the reconstruction of Europe. Conservatives believed society required orders and classes. The forces of tradition and political realism were epitomized by Metternich, Austrian foreign minister from 1809 to 1848.

At the Congress of Vienna, European leaders met to rebuild Europe with conservative underpinnings. Metternich, Alexander I, Castlereagh, and Talleyrand sought to restore the balance of power. Dynastic and territorial questions were settled on the principle of legitimacy. The Quadruple Alliance was formed to hold periodic meetings to maintain the peace of Europe.

The spirit of 1789 persisted, however. In 1820–1823, revolutions broke out in Spain, Portugal, and Naples. Revolutionaries fought to abolish the privileges of the nobility and clergy, establish representative assemblies, and write constitutions.

Nationalist aspirations led to independence movements in Serbia and Greece. With the aid of Britain, France, and Russia, Greek nationalists eventually prevailed.

Revolutions erupted again in 1830. In France, riots in Paris against the reactionary forces of Charles X led to a revolution in which the French opted for a constitutional monarchy under Louis Philippe. A nationalist revolt in Belgium succeeded in establishing a separate, independent nation whose neutrality was guaranteed in 1839. Revolts in Poland, Italy, and Germany failed, thereby widening the split between the more liberal governments of western Europe and the repressive regimes in eastern Europe.

In 1848 revolutions inspired by nationalist and liberal agitation again rocked Europe. An economic crisis was the catalyst for revolution in France. During the June Days, Paris was the scene of the first large-scale outbreak of class warfare. Using the magical name of his famous uncle, Louis Napoleon was elected president of the Second Republic.

In Italy and Germany, nationalist movements seeking unification failed. However, Piedmont emerged as the leader of Italian nationalist liberal forces.

In the Habsburg domain, revolts at first immobilized the government, but the Habsburgs soon reasserted their control. Moreover, the government played on the mutual distrust among the many nationalities to divide and conquer the rebel forces. Although the revolutions of 1848 failed, they left a legacy to be fulfilled later in Italy and Germany.

CRITICAL THINKING

1. Many people feel that "the modern age" was ushered in by the Napoleonic wars and their aftermath. Yet many others argue that both earlier or later periods first denote "modernity." What is the case for and against choosing a date between 1790 and 1830 as the beginning of the modern age?

2. What were the elements of the "romantic protest"? What was being protested? What was romantic about this protest? Did the romantic protest have a style of its own and if so, how would you describe it?

3. What is the significance of the Congress of Vienna? In terms of diplomatic relations among nation-states, the Congress often is taken as the beginning date for modern relations. Why?

4. Discuss the emergence of independent states in the Balkans.

5. What was the nature of the revolutions of the 1820s? Which succeeded, which failed, and why?

What do we mean by "success" and "failure" when discussing a revolution?

6. How did the revolutions of the 1830s differ from those that went before, and how were they similar? Again, what was success and what was failure in these revolutions?

7. Describe the third wave of revolutions in Europe, those of 1848. Why were there so many at roughly the same time? How did each differ from the other?

8. What is meant by the forces of reaction? How does *reactionary* differ from terms like *Tory, anti-revolutionary* or *conservative*? Do reform and revolution represent similar goals? If not, how do they differ?

9. Relate the romantic protest to this period of revolution from 1820 to 1848.

10. What do you see as the main heritage of this period for twentieth-century concerns?

C H A P T E R   2 0

The Industrial Society

WHEN THE LIVERPOOL AND
MANCHESTER Railway line opened
in September of 1830, the railway
train—drawn by the Rocket, then
the fastest and strongest of the locomotives—ran down and killed William
Huskisson, a leading British politician
and an ardent advocate of improving transport and communication, who had underestimated its speed. This, the first railway accident
in history, was symbolic of the new age to come,
which benefited many, brought destruction to some,
and transformed society far more rapidly than anyone
had predicted.*

The industrial revolution proceeded in stages, the
speed and sometimes sequence of which differed in different nations. Along with an economic revolution in Britain,
a political revolution continued in France, which deeply
influenced industrial development. This dual revolution led
to patterns of cause and effect that are so complex that
philosophers, economists, and political scientists continue
to argue about their meanings today. These arguments—
in defense of capitalism, in support of socialism, in advocacy of communism—produced ideologies so powerful that
their exponents often dominated the intellectual history
of their time.

Frequently necessity did prove to be the mother of
invention. As each new machine, each new adjustment
in manufacturing technique produced the need for yet
another new machine or another adjustment in the laboring force, inventors, entrepeneurs, and managers showed
remarkable innovative capacity. Urbanization accelerated
because industry worked best on the basis of concentrated
centers of production. Concentrated in these specific centers of production and often working at the same job,
laborers developed a sense of class consciousness. Periodic
dislocations in the market, overproduction, or perhaps
the failure to procure a needed supply of raw materials

---

* In the United States the railroads promoted the idea of time zones,
reflecting more closely the realities of the position of the sun in relation
to the speed of travel, so that California is reckoned to be three hours
"earlier" than New York.

The Crystal Palace Exposition was one of the first world's fairs in which industrial societies displayed their triumphs. Officially called the Great Exhibition of the Works of Industry of All Nations and opened in 1851, the fair housed a variety of technological marvels within another such marvel—a "Crystal Palace" of iron and glass. Six million people visited the Great Exhibition. Queen Victoria is shown at left making a royal procession through the Foreign Nave, where the largest collection of foreign goods ever shown in England was on display.

New York Public Library Picture Collection

sometimes led to unemployment. The cities thus became centers for both the laboring classes and "the dangerous classes"—those who through discontent, anger, despair, or the inability to find a role to play in an increasingly complex, specialized working class, turned to lives of crime. Simultaneously, a transportation revolution—the railroad on land and the steamship by sea—brought the problems and the successes of one area ever more quickly to another.

The industrial revolution was truly a revolution in both senses of the word. It transformed the lives of millions of people, and it proceeded to "revolve," to unfold at greater speed, to influence those who thought of themselves as distant from the centers of production or unconcerned with the changes brought to society. Just as mechanization of one stage of textile manufacturing virtually demanded mechanization of the next stage, so did changes in the relationships between stages of production lead to changes in the nature of labor, of the family, of nutrition, and of disease. By the 1890s the industrial revolution had produced an industrial society.

The industrial society developed new tastes in art, literature, and music. Interest in science became increasingly utilitarian. The revolutionary theory of evolution—applied originally to biology but quickly adapted to economics, society, and even politics—reinforced an emphasis on competition, on survival by contest. The search for knowledge became less intuitive, less romantic, and more capable of being quantified, more open to statistics, research, and the "objective" gathering of data.

Competition between nations, between businesses, even between individuals and teams through organized athletics, would mark the industrial society.

STAGES OF INDUSTRIAL GROWTH

Economic change generally takes place gradually, and therefore some historians feel it is misleading to speak of an industrial *revolution*, since the process was clearly evolutionary, rather than revolutionary. However, growth did not proceed at an even pace, and developments in one country or one sector of industry often altered circumstances so rapidly as virtually to transform styles of life and modes of work within a generation or less. Generally, the growth of industry was identified with the introduction of machine production, making mass markets possible and the factory system essential.

Historians once believed that production expanded most rapidly at moments of economic "take-off," when various factors that had blocked sustained growth were removed by the forces of capitalism. Among the factors often credited with the economic take-off that ushered in the nineteenth century were the rise of a merchant class during the Renaissance, colonialism and mercantilism, the American and French revolutions, the rise of the competitive state system, the Protestant emphasis on hard work and material progress as signs of salvation, the rise of modern science, and the social theories of the philosophes. Obviously these all played a role, though historians no longer generally agree that a sharp line separated the industrial revolution from the years that preceded it. They do, however, generally agree that between the 1820s and the 1890s industrialization spread from England across Europe and eventually to Russia in four stages. Initially there was a transition from agricultural to industrial priorities for society. Industrial expansion then accelerated as capital was mobilized, raw materials were secured through treaty or annexation, managerial skills were developed, and unified national states turned to the business of competition for markets, influence, and prestige.

The first developments were in textiles, in which Britain led. The second stage was in metallurgy, in which Belgium joined Britain in leadership until Germany overtook both around 1900 (and the United States, in turn, overtook them). In the third stage the chemical industry developed from improvements in mining techniques. By the 1850s new methods for recovering minerals from the earth meant that potassium, phosphate, sulfur, and rock salt were the center of attention; these, in turn, made the development of new fertilizers possible, vastly increasing the productivity of the soil. The fourth stage came after the 1890s, first in Britain and Germany, when electricity marked the move to a new form of industry based on more specialized skills. By 1914 Germany led the world in the production of lights, cables, generators, transformers, ultimately changing both public and private life dramatically by bringing appliances within reach of thousands of purchasers. The age of the consumer had begun.

British Leadership, 1760–1850

The process of industrialization began in Britain. After the 1760s England enjoyed a long period of relative economic prosperity. Starting in the sixteenth century, a new group of landed proprietors—squires and townspeople—saw land as an investment; thus they were concerned with improved production and profit. The enclosure movement had, in effect, transformed estates into compact farms, set off from others by fences or hedgerows. Marginal cottagers and garden farmers were eliminated, landowners were freed from manorial restrictions on farming practices, and the division of markets and of labor stimulated individual and geographically localized productivity.

A sharp rise in the price of grain, caused by wars and by industrialization in local centers such as Manchester, meant that more land was put into crops, leading to a greater demand for labor. Waste lands were put into production for vegetable crops to feed to animals, and eastern England in particular became a center of experimentation with new fertilizers, crops, and methods of crop rotation. Wealthy, aristocratic proprietors adopted the new methods and also financed canals, roads, mines, and eventually railroads to carry their produce to market. Increased productivity led to a rapid growth in population in

England and Wales—from 7.5 million in 1751 to 21 million in 1851—creating a large pool of workers for the new industries.

England's good fortune was enhanced not only by ample supplies of capital from foreign and colonial trade but also by the possession of large deposits of coal and iron. The geographical compactness of the British Isles made shipments from mine to smelter and from mill to seaport short, fast, and cheap. The marginal farmers, and also the Irish, driven from their overpopulated and famine-ridden island, formed a large reservoir of eager labor. The Napoleonic wars further stimulated the demand for metal goods and the invention of new machines.

Thus the twin needs of economic activity—labor and capital—were met. The rising population became a market for simple manufactured goods while also supplying labor. Women and children were employed, especially in the textile industries, because they could be paid less and were suited to jobs requiring dexterity of hand and eye rather than a strong back. The large landowners had capital to spare, and from their ranks, and even more from the ranks of the middle class, came the entrepreneurs. The middle class enjoyed a secure social status, partly as a result of the law of primogeniture by which land passed undivided to the eldest son. Since second sons, gentlemen in birth and education, could not inherit the estate, they could enter trade, the military, the church, and the colonial service without serious social stigma.

Textiles, Coal, and Iron

The textile industry was the first to exploit the potentialities of power-driven machinery. Beginning with the spinning jenny in the 1760s, the use of machinery gradually spread to other processes. In 1793 an American, Eli Whitney (1765–1825), devised the cotton gin, an engine that separated the fibers of raw cotton from the seeds and enabled a single slave to do what had previously required the hand labor of fifty slaves. Meanwhile, British inventors perfected a power-driven loom for weaving cotton thread into cloth. By 1830 Britain operated more than fifty thousand power looms, and cotton goods accounted for half of its exports.

Advances in mechanical engineering made this rapid expansion possible. Earlier, for instance, the difficulty of procuring exactly fitting parts had restricted the output of Watt's steam engine. Then British engineers, by studying the precision techniques of watchmakers, devised a lathe that turned screws of almost perfect regularity. They also developed machines for sawing, boring, and turning the pulley blocks used by British ships in the Napoleonic wars. Meantime, Eli Whitney undertook important experiments at his arms factory in Connecticut, using the concept of standardized and interchangeable parts, one of the basic principles of mass production.

New processes in industry were not uniformly adopted, of course. The survival of handicraft techniques and the workers' fear that they would be displaced by machines also slowed down the process of mechanization. Even in the cotton industry, weaving on the hand loom

This rural vista of London in 1816, by George Samuel (1785–1823), shows the intrusion of factory smoke over an industrializing city. The nostalgic view is from Greenwich Park.

Yale University Art Gallery, John Hill Morgan Fund

continued in areas with an especially large reservoir of cheap labor, like Ireland and central Europe, where peasants could produce cloth in their cottages and be paid by the piece. In the woolen and clothing industries, mechanization did not come until the 1850s, when Britain produced a machine for combing wool, and an American, Isaac Singer (1811–1875), popularized the sewing machine.

Coal ranked with cotton as an industry that pioneered in the solution of technical problems. Steam engines were used to pump water from the mines; ventilating shafts and power fans supplied them with fresh air; and safety lamps gave miners some protection against dangerous underground gases. The coal output of Britain, the world's leading producer, rose steadily from about 16 million tons in 1816 to 65 million in 1856. The consumption of coal mounted because of its increased use as a household fuel in wood-short Britain, its importance in producing steam power, and its vital contribution to the expanding iron industry, which required large quantities of coal to make the coke used in smelting.

The efficiency of smelting advanced rapidly after the development of the blast furnace (1828), in which fans provided a blast of hot air to intensify the action of the hot coke on the iron. Thanks to the blast furnace, Britain produced iron strong enough for use in bridges and in factory buildings. Yet the best grade of iron lacked the tremendous strength of steel, which is iron purified of all but a minute fraction of carbon by a process of prolonged, intense heating. Steel for industrial purposes could be made in the early 1800s, but only by ruinously expensive methods. Then in 1856 the Englishman Henry Bessemer (1813–1898) invented the converter, which accelerated the removal of impurities by shooting jets of compressed air into the molten metal. A decade later William Siemens (1823–1883), a German living in England, devised the open-hearth process, which utilized scrap as well as new iron, and which handled larger amounts of metal than the converter could. The inventions of Bessemer and Siemens lowered the cost of making steel so substantially that the world output increased tenfold between 1865 and 1880.

Transport and Communication

Steam, coal, and iron brought the railway age. Coal powered the railways and the railways carried coal. Though railways based on wooden rails were known from the sixteenth century, iron and steel rails made it possible to carry huge weights and mount giant locomotives to pull long trains.

Canals and hard-surfaced roads had preceded railroads in Europe and North America. A Scot, John McAdam (1756–1836), had devised a means of surfacing (called "macadamizing") roads so that they could be traveled in all weather, but extra-heavy shipments nonetheless broke the road's surface. The railway was the answer, once cast-iron rails were developed. By the 1820s only mechanization remained to be accomplished. George Stephenson (1781–1848) and others put the steam engine on wheels and created the modern locomotive. The railroad-building boom was soon in full swing: Britain had 500 miles of track in 1838, 6,600 miles in 1850, and 15,500 in 1870.

Steam also affected water transport, though at a less revolutionary pace. Robert Fulton's (1765–1815) steamboat, the *Clermont*, made a successful trip on the Hudson River in 1807, and soon paddle-wheel steamers plied the inland waterways of the United States and Europe. However, when the Scot Samuel Cunard inaugurated the first regular transatlantic steamer service (between Liverpool and Boston in 1840), the coal required for the voyage took up almost half the space on his vessels. Consequently, only passengers and mail went by steamship, most freight being handled by sailing ships. Finally, in the 1860s, the development of improved marine engines and the substitution of the screw propeller for the paddle wheel forecast the doom of the commercial sailing vessel.

Communications also experienced radical improvement. In 1840 Great Britain inaugurated the penny post; a letter could go from London to Edinburgh, for instance, at the cost of one penny, less than a tenth of the old

rate. More dramatic was the utilization of electricity for instantaneous communication, beginning with the first telegraph message from Baltimore to Washington in 1844. Then came the first submarine cable (under the English Channel) in 1851, the first transatlantic cable in 1866, and the first telephone in 1876.

This communications revolution was not limited to Britain. Belgium also used the turnpike principle, establishing all-weather roads financed by tolls, so that by 1850 most major centers were reachable even in the worst weather. The Ruhr River, made navigable by 1780, was tied in by roads and canals to the rest of Germany, France, and the Low Countries. But canals were frequently built too soon, before there was enough traffic to pay for them. It was the railways, which could transport goods, passengers, and armies, that truly transformed the Continent as they had Britain.

The first British railroad opened in 1830; the rest of Europe was not far behind. By 1870, 897,000 miles of rails had been laid in western Europe, the United States had its own transcontinental line, and railroads were flourishing in Canada and in faraway Australia. The lines differed in one important respect. In Britain traffic for the lines existed before they were built, and railway companies could easily find private capital for finances. In western Europe and in much of the United States, however, lines were built as traffic grew to require them, and private capital needed a government guarantee or subsidy, since the profit margin was precarious. In eastern Europe lines were built well before there was enough traffic to make them profitable, and state financing was necessary. Thus a varying pattern of private capital, state-aided capital, foreign capital, and state-controlled capital developed. In Britain the railways boosted an industrial revolution already in progress; in western Europe the railways often created the revolution; in eastern Europe, to which the iron, rails, locomotives, engineers, and capital all had to be imported, the railway boom led countries into debt and threatened ruin.

Here workers are engaged in spinning in a Lancashire mill in 1834.

The Granger Collection

Money, Banking, and Limited Liability

The exploitation of these new developments required a constant flow of fresh capital. From the first, the older commercial community supported the young industrial community. Bankers played such an important role that the Barings of London and the international house of Rothschild were among the great powers of Europe. In the early nineteenth century each of five Rothschild brothers, sons of a German Jewish banker, established himself in an important economic center—London, Paris, Frankfurt, Naples, and Vienna. The Rothschilds prospered because, in an age of frequent speculation, they avoided unduly risky undertakings, and because they facilitated investment by residents of one state in the projects of other states.

Banks further assisted economic expansion by promoting the use of checks and bank notes in place of coins. During the Napoleonic wars, when the shortage of coins forced some British millowners to pay their workers in goods, the British government empowered local banks to issue paper notes supplementing the meager supply of coins. But whenever financial crises occurred—and they came frequently before 1850—dozens of local banks failed, and their notes became valueless. Parliament therefore encouraged the absorption of shaky banks by the more solid institutions, and in 1844 it gave the Bank of England a virtual monopoly on issuing bank notes, thus providing a reliable paper currency. It also applied, the principle of limited liability (indicated by "Ltd." after the name of British firms). Earlier, the shareholders in most British companies were subject to unlimited liability, and they might find their personal fortunes seized to satisfy the creditors of an unsuccessful company. The practice of limiting each shareholder's liability to the face value of that person's shares encouraged investment by diminishing its risks.

By the mid-nineteenth century, the tangible signs of Britain's economic predominance were evident on every hand—in the teeming docks and thriving financial houses of London; in the mushrooming factory and mining towns of the Midlands, the north of England, and Scotland; and in other quarters of the globe as well. Yet Britain, even in the heyday of its leadership, had no monopoly on inventive skill. The French, for example, devised the chlorine process of bleaching cloth and the Jacquard loom for weaving intricate patterns. German technicians led the world in agricultural chemistry and in the utilization of the valuable by-products of coal. And from the United States came Eli Whitney and the cotton gin, Samuel F. B. Morse (1791–1872) and the telegraph, Singer and the sewing machine, and the young Cyrus McCormick (1809–1884), whose reaper was the first of many agricultural machines developed for the vast agricultural expanse of America.

British Decline

After 1850 Britain began to lose its advantage. Politically its leaders had positioned it well to the forefront. The Reform Act of 1832 had put Parliament into the hands of the propertied classes, which proceeded to pass legisla-tion favorable to industry. In 1846 Parliament had repealed the Corn Laws, which had limited the import of grain, and the nation began eighty-five years of nearly tariff-free trade. But the food supply was no longer keeping up, and while the growing empire—the sheep stations of Australia and New Zealand, the vast stretches of prairie in Canada—might meet the need, supplies from nearby Denmark or Holland were obviously cheaper. With the abolition of the Corn Laws, Britain accepted the principle of heavy specialization, of full commitment to private initiative, private property, and the mechanism of the marketplace. But this also made Britain increasingly dependent on others for certain necessities, so that it had to be able to assure itself of a supply of those necessities by colonial or foreign policy.

As the middle class became more comfortable and the working class more demanding, the possibilities for peaceful innovation free of clashes between management and labor decreased. A period of prolonged inflation, from 1848 to 1873, and another of depression, from 1873 to 1896, intensified the perception of inequalities of wealth between classes and genders and between cities and the countryside. After 1873 British agriculture could no longer compete with that of the Continent or the United States; agriculture began to stagnate, and the overall rate of British growth decreased.

In the new phase of the industrial revolution in Britain, the initial advantage was slowly lost—to Germany, to Belgium, and to the United States. The lead in developing new techniques passed in agricultural machinery to the Americans, in chemical and steel production to the Germans, in electricity to both. England, and particularly London, remained the undoubted financial center of the world, but by 1890 industrial leadership had passed elsewhere.

Industrial and agricultural changes are often mutually dependent. For sustained growth, industry relies on an efficient agriculture for its raw materials and for additions to its labor force, recruited from surplus workers no longer needed on mechanized farms. Agriculture depends on industry for the tools and fertilizers that enable fewer workers to produce more and transform farms into agrarian factories. In the nineteenth century factory-made implements like the steel plow and the reaper improved the cultivation of old farmlands. The mechanical cream separator raised the dairy industry to a big business, and railroads and steamers sped the transport of produce from farm to market. The processes of canning, refrigeration, and freezing—all industrial in origin and all first applied on a wide scale during the last third of the century—permitted the preservation of many perishable commodities and their shipment halfway around the world.

Farmers found steadily expanding markets both in the industrial demand for raw materials and in the food required by mining and factory towns. International trade in farm products increased rapidly during the second half of the nineteenth century. The annual export of wheat from the United States and Canada rose from 2.2 million bushels in the 1850s to 15 million in 1880. Imported flour accounted for a quarter of the bread consumed in Britain during the 1850s and for half by the 1870s. Denmark and

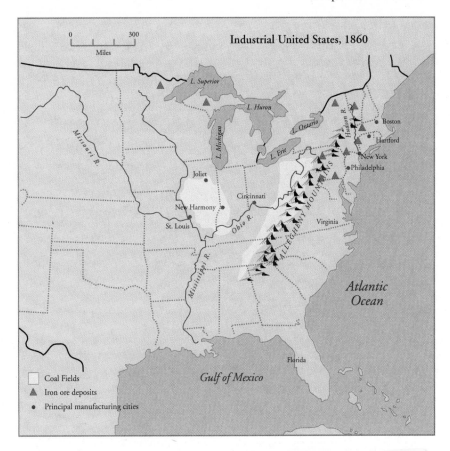

the Netherlands increasingly furnished the British table with bacon, butter, eggs, and cheese; Australia supplied its mutton, and Argentina its beef.

Germany now partly assumed Britain's old role as the pioneer of scientific agriculture. Shortly after 1800 German experimenters had extracted sugar from beets in commercially important quantities, thus ending Europe's dependence on the cane sugar of the West Indies. In the 1840s the German chemist Justus Liebig (1803–1873) published a series of influential works on the agricultural applications of organic chemistry. These promoted even wider use of fertilizers: guano from the nesting islands of sea birds off the west coast of South America, nitrate from Chile, and potash from European mines.

The agricultural revolution exacted a price. Faced with the competition of beet sugar, the sugar cane islands of the West Indies went into a depression from which they did not recover. In the highly industrialized countries the social and political importance of agriculture began to decline. The urban merchants and manufacturers demonstrated their dominance in British politics when they won their campaign to abolish the tariffs on grain, which, they said, kept the price of food high. Decisive in the abolition of the Corn Laws in 1846 was an attack of black rot that devastated the Irish potato crop for two years and made it essential to bring in cheap substitute foods.

Meanwhile, across the Channel, France was industrializing far more slowly. Public finance continued to be unstable, capital formation was far more difficult, and France remained wed to tariff protection, which retarded change. Railways were built hesitantly, and the revolution of 1848, caused by an economic crisis, made French financiers even more hesitant. Agriculture remained especially important, and both farm and city workers in France were reluctant to innovate. An "aristocracy of labor" set crafts workers apart from manual laborers, and some of the working class successfully resisted mechanization. To the inhibitions of small farms and inadequate capital was added the effect of equal inheritance laws, which led to the division of land into tiny parcels so that the peasant could not accumulate capital to take risks on new crops. Businesses were owned by single families, who could not be protected by limited liability laws or easily recruit new managers. Since bankruptcy had to be avoided above all else, owners could not afford to take risks with new products or new methods. Economic and social conservatism thus limited efforts to create large-scale production or a high degree of specialization.

ECONOMIC AND SOCIAL CHANGE

With industrialization there came a population explosion, a dramatic rise in the standard of living for many (and harsh, but different, conditions for others), and a desire to have greater control over birth and death rates. This

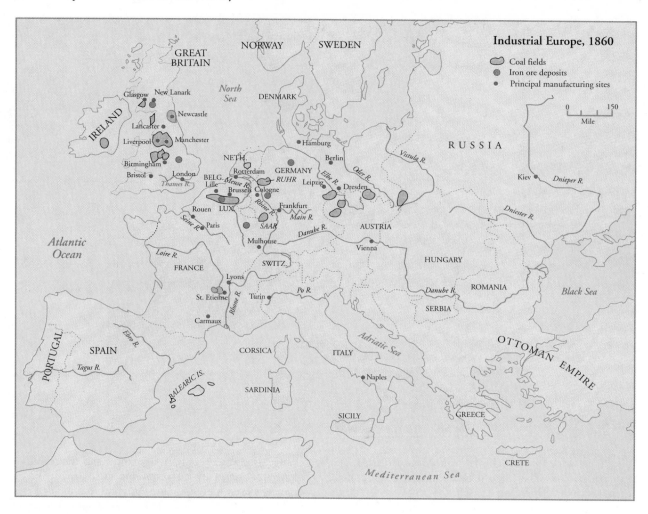

desire expressed itself through the state and also in a social demand for improved working conditions.

The Population Explosion and the Standard of Living

When Britain abandoned any pretense of raising all the basic foods its people needed, its population was growing so rapidly that self-sufficiency was no longer possible. The number of inhabitants in England and Wales more than tripled during the nineteenth century, from about 9 million in 1800 to 32.5 million in 1900. Some demographers have attributed this population explosion not to a higher birth rate but to the lowered death rate resulting from the improved food and sanitation—especially cheap, washable cotton materials—brought by industrialism. Others claim that the population increase in the first half of the century may be attributed to the rural areas and not to the cities, which had a much higher death rate.

A similar controversy is focused on the extent to which the industrial revolution improved the standard of living not just of the new capitalist and managerial classes but of the workers themselves. After about 1820 the purchasing power of the workers seems to have grown very

gradually, as more and cheaper goods became available. Opportunities for steady, regular employment also grew, as did chances for laborers to climb up the economic ladder by mastering a skill and getting a better-paying job. But all these factors varied in their effect from industry to industry and from one locality to another; they also fluctuated with the ups and downs of the economic cycle. Many people, consequently, appear to have found that their standard of living was declining.

There is little debate about the truly revolutionary changes industrialism caused in the structure and distribution of the population. Wherever mines and factories were opened, towns and cities appeared. The growth of an urban population increased the numbers and influence of business people and workers. Industrialists, bankers, investors, managers, and promoters of every sort joined the already established capitalists to form the modern middle class, or bourgeoisie. Mill hands, railway workers, miners, some artisans, clerks, and a host of other recruits swelled the ranks of wage-earning workers.

The impact of capital and labor upon the life of industrial nations was becoming increasingly evident by the middle of the nineteenth century. Some of the signs pointed to steady material progress—better food and the conquest of distance by the railroad, the steamship, and the telegraph. Other signs, however, foretold serious dislocation

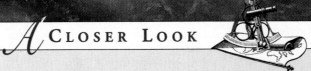

A CLOSER LOOK

The Experience of Immigration

The movement of people from one land to another, from one continent to another, has marked history since antiquity, and today is one of the most notable realities of a world in a steady state of enormous change. Entire societies have moved from one place to another; millions of individuals change the place where they live, the environment in which they work and learn, even the language they speak, every year. The age of empire and colonialism spurred two enormously important movements, one of Africans as slaves to the New World, the other of south Asians throughout Southeast Asia, East Africa, the West Indies, and into the Pacific; and by the twentieth century both groups were entering western Europe and North America. No one can know how many people have immigrated, for only in relatively recent times have there been governmental bureaucracies to keep reasonably accurate records; further, such records tell us only of legal, not of unrecorded or illegal, immigration.

Still, we have some figures that are revealing. Between 1815 and 1932 some 60 million people left Europe, largely to new areas of settlement in the Americas, the southwest Pacific, and Siberia. As Europeans had a higher birth rate in the nineteenth century, Europeans and people who had originated in Europe grew from 22 percent of the world's population to 38 percent by 1914. The United States received just under half the European immigrants, but Europeans accounted for a much higher proportion of the populations of Canada, Argentina, and Brazil by 1914. Some were migrants—that is, they returned home after living elsewhere—but Irish, Italian (to Argentina and the United States), Jewish, and later Asian immigrants remained. Most immigrants found themselves forced into the least well-paid jobs, the poorest housing; as each succeeding wave achieved some measure of success, they moved into better jobs and housing, and the next ethnic community to arrive would begin anew at the bottom. Thus suspicion and hostility between groups became commonplace, and immigrant communities chose either to live compactly and to retain their customs and language, in part as protection against others, or took the opposite path, as in the United States, and until the 1950s abandoned their original languages and many of their customs.

To leave one's home for a foreign land, where one has neither friend nor, as yet, job, and whose language one cannot speak, requires enormous courage. The thousands upon thousands of people, largely from Europe (after 1870 increasingly from southern and eastern Europe), who journeyed to the United States and Canada, were not received with open arms. The attitudes shown in the following letter, written by the medical superintendent of a receiving station for immigrants, were representative:

Out of the 4,000 or 5,000 emigrants that have left this island since Sunday, at least 2,000 will fall sick somewhere before three weeks are over. They ought to have accommodation for 2,000 sick at least at Montreal and Quebec, as all the Cork and Liverpool passengers are half dead from starvation and want before embarking; and the least bowel complaint, which is sure to come with change of food, finishes them without a struggle. I never saw people so indifferent to life; they would continue in the same berth with a dead person until the seamen or captain dragged out the corpse with boathooks. Good God! what evils will befall the cities wherever they alight. Hot weather will increase the evil.

Quoted in Terry Coleman, *Going to America* (Garden City, N.Y.: Anchor Books, 1973), p. 147.

and violent change. The repeal of the Corn Laws buried an old agrarian way of life in Britain, and the collapse of the French railroad boom in the late 1840s suggested that economic slumps in an industrial society might have alarming consequences, for the hundreds of thousands thrown out of work aggravated the political unrest that culminated in the June Days of 1848 in Paris (see Chapter 19).

The remarkable rise of population tested the earth's resources and environment even before people thought in these terms. Perhaps ten thousand years ago the total population of the globe was under 10 million. By 1750, when the modern rise was beginning, the figure was 750 million. By 1930 it was 2 billion, and only forty-five years later, in 1975, it was double that. Thus, human

By the mid-nineteenth century boxing had become a popular sport, especially in England. Here, in 1860, John C. Heenan and Tom Sayers square off in a championship bout that, after forty-two rounds, was ended by the spectators rushing in to put a stop to it.

New York Public Library Picture Collection

population expanded to reach its first thousand million over hundreds of thousands of years; the second thousand million was added in a single century; the third in only thirty years, and the fourth in only fifteen. This uncontrollable explosion in population, with its untold impact on the planet's resources, was made evident in the nineteenth century as people flocked to the cities, which grew far more rapidly than sanitation, police, or education could provide for, creating teeming slums that bred disease, crime, and discontent. Population growth in England and Wales was even more striking than the above figures indicate, as England, and later Belgium, became the most crowded nations in the West; indeed, as early as 1600 England had reached a population density that the United States would not reach until 1961. In the midst of the industrial revolution, however, fewer people worried about overpopulation than rejoiced in the growth of the labor force and the increase in potential consumers.

While population increased in many societies, the growing acceptance of contraceptive methods in post-revolutionary France and a rise in abortions, despite church opposition to both practices, contributed to a decline in the French birth rate. The death rate had declined in France from about 1800; after 1870 both the death and birth rates declined in England and Wales. Birth rates were related in part to marriage rates, which were related to economic circumstances; as real wages increased, so did marriage rates. In Ireland postponement of marriage was increasingly common, reducing the total number of children a woman might bear in her lifetime.

By modern standards the mortality rate remained very high in the first half of the century, largely owing to infectious disease. While families grew larger in Victorian times because the comfortable middle class could afford to clothe, house, and educate larger families, mortality also increased with increasing family size. Many wives died in childbirth, and men frequently had a succession of children by two or three wives.

Overall mortality rates declined throughout Europe, especially after 1850. This was due in good measure to a decline in certain communicable diseases, as scientific research found both causes and cures. Murder, infanticide, and death in war remained commonplace, but starvation was slowly reduced as a cause of death, as greater agricultural productivity, better nutrition, and more rapid movement of foodstuffs from area of production to area of need reduced it to a local phenomenon in the West. Certain airborne diseases increased—bronchitis, pneumonia, influenza—as people lived and worked closer together, and by 1901 the death rate was higher than in 1854. Some diseases were reduced marginally, despite crowded conditions, as medicine developed means of combating them; measles, whooping cough, and scarlet fever remained common occurrences in childhood but did not normally lead to death, as they once had done. The death rate from tuberculosis, diphtheria, and small pox was cut drastically. Thus an English death rate in 1700 of thirty persons per thousand was reduced most dramatically by bringing infectious diseases under control. Deaths from industrial accidents, war, localized famine, and physical attack remained relatively high, however.

The expectation of the enjoyment of good health, also increased in the industrial society. Purification of water and efficient disposal of sewage (both requiring public measures, usually by municipalities) helped reduce the incidence of typhus. So did better hygiene—for example, in the introduction of the water closet, or flush toilet; more frequent bathing as water became more readily available; and cleaner bedding. The condition of food improved, though milk—important to childhood diets—remained unpasteurized until after 1900. Because surgery was increasingly performed in well-equipped hospitals with antiseptics and effective anesthesia, especially after the introduction of ether in 1846, certain medical problems no longer led to death—except on the battlefield, where far more soldiers died of disease and infection after surgery than from their wounds.

From the time of Hippocrates to the nineteenth century, few significant new drugs had been developed, and often treatment for a specific disease was totally wrong according to present-day medical knowledge. For example, sufferers from malaria were subjected to leeching (the drawing of blood from the body by bloodsucking leeches), which caused dehydration at a time when their bodies needed all their strength and an increase in liquids. But the kind of research on a mass basis that it is possible to conduct only on the battlefield or in a hospital led first to the isolation of infectious patients in separate hospital wards after 1875, and then to specific studies of specific diseases. While some diseases increased, notably cancer, the chances of surviving to die of old age were materially greater at the end of the century than at the beginning. However, since access to such improvements in health often depended upon the ability to pay, death rates varied substantially according to class.

Class Grievances and Aspirations

In the Britain of the 1820s, the new industrialists had small opportunity to mold national policy. Booming industrial cities like Manchester and Birmingham sent not a single representative to the House of Commons. A high proportion of business leaders belonged not to the Church of England but were nonconformists who still suffered discrimination when it came to holding public office or sending their sons (not to speak of their daughters) to Oxford or Cambridge. Even in France, despite the gains made since 1789, the bourgeoisie often enjoyed only second-class status.

In western Europe the middle classes very soon won the place they felt they deserved; in Britain a gradual process of reform gave them substantially all they wanted. The high spot was the Reform Bill of 1832, which extended the suffrage to the middle class. In 1830 the French bourgeoisie got their citizen-king. In Piedmont the middle class secured at least a narrowly liberal constitution in 1848. In southern and central Europe, by contrast, the waves of revolution that crested in 1848 left the bourgeoisie frustrated and angry.

The grievances of workers were more numerous than those of their masters, and they seemed harder to satisfy. The difficulties may be illustrated by the protracted struggle of laborers to secure the vote and to obtain the right to

The industrial revolution introduced women into the work force outside the home in a massive way. This nineteenth-century print shows women at work on the assembly line of a pen-grinding factory. The introduction of uniform cheap postage created a heavy demand for pens, and the flow of mail soared to unexpected heights.

The Illustrated London News Picture Library

THE WRITTEN RECORD

A Day at the Mills

Frequently, entire families had to work as a matter of sheer economic necessity. A factory worker testified before a British parliamentary committee in 1831–1832:

At what time in the morning, in the brisk time, did those girls go to the mills? *In the brisk time, for about six weeks, they have gone at 3 o'clock in the morning, and ended at 10, or nearly half-past, at night.*

What intervals were allowed for rest or refreshment during those nineteen hours of labour? *Breakfast a quarter of an hour, and dinner half an hour, and drinking of ale a quarter of an hour.*

Was any of that time taken up in cleaning the machinery? *They generally had to do what they call dry down; sometimes this took the whole of the time at breakfast or drinking, and they were to get their dinner or breakfast as they could; if not, it was brought home.*

Had you not great difficulty in awakening your children to this excessive labour? *Yes, in the early time we had them to take up asleep and shake them when we got them on the floor to dress them, before we could get them off to their work; but not so in the common hours.*

What was the length of time they could be in bed during those long hours? *It was near 11 o'clock before we could get them into bed after getting a little victuals, and then*

at morning my mistress used to stop all night, for fear that we could not get them ready for the time. . . .

So that they had not above four hours' sleep at this time? *No, they had not. . . .*

Were the children excessively fatigued by this labour? *Many times, we have cried often when we have given them the little victualling we had to give them; we had to shake them, and they have fallen to sleep with the victuals in their mouths many a time.*

Did this excessive term of labour occasion much cruelty also? *Yes, being so very much fatigued the strap was very frequently used.*

What was the wages in the short hours? *Three shillings a week each.*

When they wrought those very long hours what did they get? *Three shillings and sevenpence halfpenny.*

From *English Economic History: Select Documents* ed. A. Bland, P. Brown, and R. H. Tawney (London: Clarendon, 1915), pp. 510–13.

---

organize and to carry on union activities. In Britain substantial numbers of workers first won the vote in 1867, a generation after the middle class did. In France universal male suffrage began in 1848. The unified German Empire had a democratic suffrage from its inception in 1871, but without some other institutions of democracy. Elsewhere, universal manhood suffrage came slowly—not until 1893 in Belgium, and not until the twentieth century in Italy, Austria, Russia, Sweden, Denmark, the Netherlands, and (because of restrictions on black voters) the United States.

During most of the nineteenth century, labor unions and strikes were regarded by employers as improper restraints on the free operation of natural economic laws; accordingly, a specific ban on such *combinations,* as they were termed, had been imposed by the British Combination Acts at the close of the eighteenth century. Parliament moderated the effect of these acts in the 1820s but did not repeal them until 1876. Continental governments imposed similar restrictions. France's Loi de Chapelier was relaxed only in the 1860s and repealed in 1884. Everywhere labor slowly achieved full legal recognition of the legitimacy of union activities: in 1867 in Austria, in 1872 in the Netherlands, and in 1890 in Germany.

Labor's drive for political and legal rights, however, was only a side issue during the early industrial revolution. Many workers faced the more pressing problems of finding jobs and making ends meet on wages that ran

behind prices. The Western world had long experienced the business cycle, with its alternation of full employment and drastic layoffs; the industrial revolution intensified the cycle, making boom periods more hectic and depressions more severe. At first factories made little attempt to provide a fairly steady level of employment. When a batch of orders came in, machines and workers were pushed to capacity until the orders were filled; then the factory simply shut down to await the next orders.

Excessively long hours, low pay, rigorous discipline, and dehumanizing working conditions were the most common grievances of early industrial workers. Many plants neglected hazardous conditions, and few had safety devices to guard dangerous machinery. Cotton mills maintained the heat and the humidity at an uncomfortable level because threads broke less often in a hot, damp atmosphere. Many workers could not afford decent housing, and if they could afford it, they could not find it. Some few of the new factory towns were well planned, with wide streets and space for lawns and parks. Some had an adequate supply of good water and arrangements for disposing of sewage, but many had none of these necessities.

The industrial nations also threatened to remain nations of semiliterates; until they made provision for free public schools during the last third of the nineteenth century, education facilities were grossly inadequate. In England, as often as not, only the Sunday school gave the mill hand's child a chance to learn the ABCs. A worker with great ambition and fortitude might attend an adult school known as a "mechanics' institute." In the 1840s a third of the men and half of the women married in England could not sign their names on the marriage register and simply made their mark.

Laborers did attempt to join the ranks of the middle class by adhering to the precepts of thrift, hard work, and self-help. Samuel Smiles (1812–1904) pointed the way in a number of books with didactic titles such as *Character, Thrift,* and *Duty,* which preached a doctrine of self-salvation. Through joining a temperance society and by regular attendance at a worker's institute, a laborer might rise to become a master cotton spinner, a head mechanic, even a clergyman, shopkeeper, or schoolmaster. For some, the demands of hard work, self-reliance, and adherence to duty paid off in upward social mobility; for others, life was a round of exploitation, poverty, and demoralization. For many, alcohol was a way of forgetting the demands of the day, prostitution a means of income, religion a path to peace of mind.

Preceding the revolutions of 1848, Europeans discussed at length the "social question," or, as it was called in Britain, "the condition-of-England question"; these terms were code language for pauperism and the evident decline of the lower classes. Pauperism was most visible in the cities, though conditions of poverty may in fact have been harsher in the countryside. Many social observers, while welcoming the clear benefits arising from industrialization, predicted that social calamity lay ahead. Some thought overpopulation was the main problem and suggested that "redundant populations" be sent overseas to colonies; others thought the problem lay in the decline of agriculture, forcing mechanically unskilled workers to migrate to the cities; yet others thought the oppressive conditions were limited to specific trades and locations. None could agree whether the overall standard of living was increasing for the majority, if at the cost of the minority—nor can historians agree today.

Historians generally do agree on some conclusions, however. There was an aggregate rise in real wages, which went largely, however, to the skilled worker, so that the working class was really two or more classes. Prices for the most basic foodstuffs declined, so that starvation was less likely. Conditions of housing worsened, however, and the urgency of work increased. Workers in traditional handicrafts requiring specialized skills might now have meat on their table three times a week, but workers displaced by a new machine might not have meat at all. Fear of unemployment was commonplace. A mill hand could barely earn enough to feed a family of three children if fully employed; economic necessity compelled him to limit the size of his family, and he had to remain docile at work to assure that he would remain employed. Dependence on public charity, with its eroding effects on self-confidence, was necessary during periods of layoffs in the factory. Women and children were drawn increasingly into the labor force, since they would work at half a man's wage or less, and this led to tension between the sexes, since men saw their jobs being taken by women. In Britain, France, Belgium, and Germany half the mill employees were boys and girls under eighteen.

Work began at dawn and ended at dusk; there was no time for leisure, and often the only solace was in sex, increasing the size of the family and adding to the economic burdens of the parents. Food was dreary and often unhealthy: bread, potatoes, some dubious milk, turnips, cabbage, on occasion bacon. Meat was a luxury; in the sixteenth century the average German was estimated to consume two hundred pounds of meat in a year: in the nineteenth century, forty pounds. The workingman and workingwoman, as well as the working child, lived at the margin of existence. Yet they did live, as their predecessors might not have done. There was a "hierarchy of wretchedness" that was relative rather than absolute, but now was felt all the more acutely.

THE RESPONSES OF LIBERALISM

Faced with the widening cleavage, both real and psychological, between rich and poor, nineteenth-century liberals at first held to the doctrine of laissez faire:

> *Suffering and evil are nature's admonitions; they cannot be got rid of; and the impatient attempts of benevolence to banish them from the world by legislation . . . have always been productive of more evil than good.* *

The thinkers who held to these ideas in the early nineteenth century were the classical economists, the architects of "the dismal science"—so called because of its pessimistic determinism. The most famous were two Englishmen: Thomas Malthus (1766–1834) and David Ricardo (1772–1823).

The Classical Economists

Educated for the ministry, Malthus became perhaps the first professional economist in history; he was hired by the East India Company to teach its employees at a training school in England. In 1798 he published his *Essay on Population,* a dramatic warning that the human species would breed itself into starvation. In the *Essay,* Malthus formulated a series of natural laws:

> *The power of population is indefinitely greater than the power in earth to produce subsistence for man.*
>
> *Population, when unchecked, increases in a geometrical ratio. Subsistence only increases in an arithmetical ratio.* **

Misery and vice would spread, Malthus believed, because the unchecked increase in human numbers would

---

* *The Economist,* May 13, 1848.

** Thomas Malthus, *First Essay on Population,* 1798 (Chicago: Henry Regnery, 1965), pp. 13–15.

lower the demand for labor and therefore lower the wages of labor. The reduction of the human birth rate was the only hope held out to suffering humanity. It was to be achieved by "moral restraint," that is, by late marriage and by "chastity till that period arrives."

Ricardo, too, was a prophet of gloom. He attributed economic activity to three main forces: rent, paid to the owners of great natural resources like farmland and mines; profit, accruing to enterprising individuals who exploited these resources; and wages, paid to the workers who performed the actual labor. Of the three, rent was the most important in the long run. Farms and mines would become depleted and exhausted, but their yield would continue in great demand. Rent, accordingly, would consume an ever-larger share of the "economic pie," leaving smaller and smaller portions for profit and wages.

Ricardo did not believe that the size of the economic pie was necessarily fixed, and thus did not subscribe entirely to the mercantilist idea that the total wealth of humanity was severely limited, so that more for one person meant less for another. And yet he did predict eventual stagnation. Whereas Adam Smith had cheerfully predicted an increasing division of labor accompanied by steadily rising wages, Ricardo brought labor and wages under the Malthusian formula. Ricardo's disciples hardened this principle into the Iron Law of Wages, which bound workers to an unending cycle of high wages and large families, followed by an increase in the labor supply, a corresponding increase in competition for jobs, and an inevitable slump in wages. The slump would lead workers to have fewer children, followed by a resulting shortage of labor and rising wages; then the whole cycle would begin again. Ricardo himself, however, regarded the cycle not as an Iron Law but simply as a probability. Unforeseen factors in the future might modify its course and might even permit a gradual improvement of the worker's lot.

The classical economists were proved wrong. The size of the economic pie expanded far beyond the expectations of Ricardo, as did the portions allotted to rent, to profit, and to wages. Malthus did not foresee that scientific advances would make the output of agriculture expand at a nearly geometrical ratio. He did not foresee that the perils of increasing birth rates would sometimes be averted by contraception or by emigration. Many millions of people moved from crowded Europe to lightly populated North America and Australia during the nineteenth century. The exodus from overcrowded Ireland, in particular, continued so briskly after the famine of the 1840s that by 1900 the Irish population was little more than half what it had been fifty years earlier.

Although the classical economists did not take sufficient account of the immense changes being worked by the agricultural and industrial revolutions, their laissez-faire liberalism won particular favor with the new industrial magnates. The captains of industry were perhaps disturbed by Ricardo's prediction that profits would inevitably shrink; but they could take comfort from the theory that suffering and evil were "nature's admonitions." It was consoling to the rich to be told, in effect, that the poor deserved to be poor because they had indulged their appetites to excess. The poor did not like to hear that they deserved to be poor. Working-class leaders attacked supporters of the classical economic doctrines for acting without heart and without conscience and for advancing economic theories that were only rationalizations of their own economic interests.

The Utilitarians

One path of retreat from stark laissez-faire doctrines originated with Jeremy Bentham (1748–1832), an eccentric philosopher. Bentham founded his social teachings on the concept of utility: that the goal of action should be to achieve the greatest good for the greatest number. Ordinarily, he believed, governments could best safeguard the well-being of the community by governing as little as possible. In social and economic matters, they should act as "passive policemen" and give private initiative a generally free hand. Yet Bentham realized that the state might become a more active policeman when the pursuit of self-interest by some individuals worked against the best interests of other individuals, since the goal was the greatest good for the greatest number. If the pains endured by the many exceeded the pleasures enjoyed by the few, then the state should step in.

Twentieth-century doctrines of the welfare state owe a considerable debt to the utilitarianism of analysts like Bentham, and James Mill (1773–1836) and his son the young John Stuart Mill (1806–1873). By the time of his death, Bentham was already gaining an international reputation. He had advised reformers in Portugal, Russia, Greece, and Egypt, and his writings were to exert a broad influence. His most important English disciples, the Philosophic Radicals, pressed for reform of court procedures, local government, and poor relief so as to free humanity from the artificial constraints of the environment. The argument over whether nature (genetic inheritance) or environment (education, family, and state) most determined one's fate was now fully joined (see pp. 446–450).

Humanitarian Liberalism

John Stuart Mill grew up in an atmosphere dense with the teachings of utilitarianism and classical economics. From his father, he received an education almost without parallel for intensity and speed. He began the study of Greek at three, was writing history at twelve, and at sixteen organized an active Utilitarian Society. At the age of twenty the overworked youth suffered a breakdown. He turned for renewal to music and to the poetry of Wordsworth and Coleridge; presently he fell in love with Mrs. Harriet Taylor, to whom he assigned the major credit for his later writings. They remained friends for twenty years, until the death of Mr. Taylor at length enabled them to marry. The intellectual partnership was important to them both, and they endowed the liberal creed with the warmth and humanity it had lacked.

Mill's humane liberalism was expressed most clearly in his *On Liberty* (1859), *Utilitarianism* (1863),

This 1872 engraving after Gustave Doré (1832–1883), *Over London by Rail,* shows how the city was transformed by the industrial revolution. Crowded living conditions, air pollution, and tiny back gardens for breathing space were the most the working class could hope for. The illustration incidentally shows why economists sometimes measured the health of the economy in terms of construction—specifically in terms of the number of bricks manufactured.

New York Public Library Picture Collection

The Subjection of Women (1869), and his posthumous *Autobiography* (1873). But it is evident, too, in his more technical works, notably *Principles of Political Economy.* He first published this enormously successful textbook in 1848 and later revised it several times, each revision departing more and more from the "dismal science" of Ricardo and Malthus.

Mill outlined the schemes for curbing overpopulation by promoting emigration to the colonies and "elevating the habits of the labouring people through education." This one example is typical of the way in which Mill's quest for positive remedies led him to modify the laissez-faire attitude so long associated with liberalism. He asserted that workers should be allowed to organize trade unions, form cooperatives, and receive a share of profits. However, these changes could best be secured within the framework of private enterprise, and not by public intervention. But he also believed that there were some matters so pressing that the state would have to step in—to protect laboring women and children and to improve intolerable living and working conditions.

Mill made universal suffrage and universal education immediate objectives. All men should have the right to vote; all should be prepared for it by receiving a basic minimum of schooling, if need be at state expense; women should have the same rights. He proposed the introduction of proportional representation in the House of Commons so that political minorities might be assured of a voice. Protection of the rights of the individual became the basis of his essay *On Liberty.*

Liberalism, as it is understood today, is the legacy not of the "dismal scientists" but of Mill and other political thinkers and politicians who have shaped modern Western democracies. What, in fact, was *liberalism*?

Those who thought of themselves as liberals were somewhat less unified than those who referred to themselves as conservatives, though they had certain characteristics in common. They began with the assumption that people ought to enjoy as much freedom as possible, in keeping with an orderly society. And they believed that law was the root cause of that orderliness, and that laws ought to grow from the participation of the governed. They saw humanity essentially in social terms and believed that social organization preceded political organization. They sought to educate the individual, so that in the pursuit of personal ambitions and in the service of personal ideals, a person would also contribute to the general welfare.

Although the liberals spoke of "self-realization" (developing the inner being), "self-improvement" (individualism), and "moral autonomy" (the right to private moral commitments), they saw these individualistic needs of humanity as contributing to a collective sense of community. They believed, therefore, in self-criticism, in free speech, in freedom of worship, and in restraining the state. They recognized the delicate balance needed to protect the coherence of a nation while still preserving the rights of the minority. Depending upon the particular liberal democracy, this balance would fall at different points on a scale. In time—especially within the liberal democratic states—they tended to engage in "social engineering" to better the standard of living through improved communications, sanitation, and education. Thus, though they professed to believe in the autonomy of differing systems of ethics for different societies, they could not resist the temptation to apply their system of government, their system of education, or their system of commerce to their colonial dependencies.

SOCIALIST RESPONSES: TOWARD MARXISM

In his later years, Mill referred to himself as a socialist; by his standard, however, most voters today are socialists. Universal suffrage for men and for women, universal free education, the curbing of laissez faire in the interests of the general welfare, the use of the taxing power to limit the unbridled accumulation of private property—all these major changes foreseen by Mill are now widely accepted. But the modern socialist does not stop, as Mill did, with changes in the distribution of wealth but goes on to propose changes in arrangements for the production of goods. The means of production are to be transferred from the control of individuals to the control of the community as a whole.

Historically, *socialism* denotes any philosophy that advocates the vesting of production in the hands of society and not in those of private individuals. In practice it usually means that the state, acting as the theoretical trustee of the community, owns at least the major industries, such as coal, railroads, and steel. Socialism in its most complete form involves public ownership of almost all the instruments of production, including the land itself, virtually eliminating private property. To varying degrees in the late twentieth century, most states control some industries and the means of public transportation; Canada, Australia, and Sweden are examples of what are referred to as "mixed enterprise economies."

Today the complete form of socialism is often called *communism*; in the mid-nineteenth century, however, the terms *socialism* and *communism* were used almost interchangeably. Over a hundred years of history have gone into making the distinction now drawn between the two. Especially since the Bolshevik revolution in Russia in 1917, a *communist* has come to mean someone who believes that the collectivization of property must be accomplished swiftly and violently, by revolution and direct seizure, often at bloody cost to those defeated in class warfare. A *socialist* has come to mean someone who believes that collectivization should be accomplished gradually and peacefully through democratic political procedures and with compensation to private owners. Though the ends may be similar, the means are worlds apart. This highly significant difference started to become apparent long before 1917, with the development of two divergent schools of socialist thought in the mid-nineteenth century, often called the Utopian and the Marxian.

The Utopians

Utopian socialists derived their inspiration from the Enlightenment. If only people would apply reason to solving the problems of an industrial economy, if only they would wipe out artificial inequalities by letting the great natural law of brotherhood operate freely—then utopia would be within their grasp, and social and economic progress would come about almost automatically. This was the common belief linking together the four chief Utopians of the early nineteenth century: Saint-Simon, Charles Fourier, Robert Owen, and Louis Blanc.

Claude-Henri de Saint-Simon (1760–1825) belonged to a family so old and aristocratic that it claimed direct descent from Charlemagne. Educated by philosophes, Saint-Simon fought with the French army in the American War of Independence. During the French Revolution he made and lost a large fortune, but despite his own reverses he never lost his enthusiasm for the enormous potential of the industrial age. He admonished the members of the new elite: "Christianity commands you to use all your powers to increase as rapidly as possible the social welfare of the poor!"* Reform should come peacefully, through "persuasion and demonstration." Combining the Enlightenment's respect for science with romanticism's zeal for the community, Saint-Simon proclaimed the one science transcending all others to be the application of the Golden Rule.

"Organization," "harmony," and "industry" were three of Saint-Simon's catchwords; when all three elements were coordinated, humanity would achieve some of the major improvements he proposed, among them great networks of highways and waterways, and would become a single, rational society. After Saint-Simon's death, his followers focused on the strain of social Christianity in his teaching. Prosper Enfantin (1796–1864) combined local railroads into a Paris-Lyon-Mediterranean trunk line, and another Saint-Simonian, Ferdinand de Lesseps (1805–1894), promoted the building of a Suez Canal and made an abortive start at digging across the Isthmus of Panama.

The vagueness of Saint-Simon's concepts permitted almost every kind of social thinker—from laissez-faire liberal to communist—to cite him with approval. Among his disciples were Giuseppe Mazzini and Louis Blanc, the Russian revolutionary pioneer Alexander Herzen, and the French positivist philosopher Auguste Comte. What was socialistic about Saint-Simon was his goal of reorganizing and harmonizing society as a whole, rather than merely improving the well-being of some of its individual members.

Saint-Simon's compatriot and contemporary, Charles Fourier (1772–1837), also extolled harmony and drew up an elaborate blueprint for achieving it. At the French textile center of Lyons, Fourier was shocked by the contrast between the wealth of the silk manufacturers and the misery of their workers. In Paris he was shocked when he found that a single apple cost a sum that would have bought a hundred apples in the countryside. Clearly, he concluded, something was amiss in a society and economy that permitted such divergences.

Just as Newton had found the force holding the heavenly bodies in a state of mutual attraction, so Fourier

---

* Claude-Henri de Saint-Simon, *Selected Writings*, ed. F. M. H. Markham (New York: Harper and Row, 1952), p. 116.

claimed to have discovered the force holding the individuals of human society in a state of mutual attraction. This force was *l'attraction passionnelle*; that is, human beings were drawn to one another by their passions. Fourier drew up a list of passions—sex, companionship, food, luxury, variety, and so on, to a total of 810. Since existing society thwarted their satisfaction, Fourier proposed it be remodeled into units that he called *phalanges* (phalanxes), each containing 400 acres of land and accommodating 500 to 2,000 (though ideally 1,620) persons. Volunteers would form a phalanx by setting up a community company and agreeing to split its profits three ways—five twelfths to those who did the work, four twelfths to those who undertook the management, and three twelfths to those who supplied the capital.

Fourier's phalanx, with its relatively generous rewards to managers and capitalists, fell short of complete equality. Yet it did assign to labor the largest share of the profits, and it foreshadowed many other features of socialist planning. Each phalanx would be nearly self-sufficient, producing in its own orchards, fields, and workshops most of the things required by its inhabitants. Adult workers who performed the most dangerous or unpleasant tasks would receive the highest remuneration. Members of the phalanx would change their jobs eight times a day because "enthusiasm cannot be sustained for more than an hour and a half or two hours in the performance of one particular operation." They would work from four to five in the morning to eight or nine at night, enjoying five meals. They would need only five hours of sleep, since the variety of work would not tire them. All would become so healthy that physicians would be superfluous, and everyone would live to age 140.

Both to eliminate the evil of prostitution and to allow human association the fullest possible scope, Fourier advocated complete sexual freedom in the phalanx; he recommended marriage only for the elderly, whose passions had begun to cool. While colonies sprang up in which Fourierism was tried, especially in the New World, public opinion, including working-class opinion, remained hostile to surrendering the privacy of the family.

Underneath the perhaps foolish details lay significant contributions to socialist theory and social psychology. Some of Fourier's recommendations, like higher pay for dangerous jobs and devices for relieving the tedium of work, have become common practice in modern business. In the short run, however, Utopian socialism came to be identified with free love and therefore, in the popular mind, with the grossest immorality.

Another Utopian was a self-made British businessman, Robert Owen (1771–1858). In 1800 Owen took over the large cotton mills at New Lanark in Scotland and found conditions that shocked him. A large part of the working force in the mills consisted of children who had been recruited from orphanages in Edinburgh when they were between six and eight years old. Although the youngsters did get a little schooling after hours, Owen found many of them "dwarfs in body and mind." Adult laborers at New Lanark fared little better.

Remaking New Lanark into a model industrial village, Owen set out to show that he could increase profits and the welfare of his laborers at the same time. For the adults he provided better working conditions, a ten-and-one-half-hour day, higher pay, and improved housing. He raised the minimum age for employment to ten, hoping ultimately to put it at twelve, and he gave his child laborers time off for schooling. A properly educated nation, Owen believed, would refute the gloomy predictions of Malthus, who "has not told us how much more food an intelligent and industrious people will create from the same soil, than will be produced by one ignorant and ill-governed."*

In the 1820s Owen visited America to finance an abortive effort to set up a colony at New Harmony, Indiana. Undaunted by this failure, he spent the rest of his career publishing and supporting projects for social reform. He advocated the association of all labor in one big union—an experiment that failed, though the call was taken up later in the United States; and he sought to reduce the workers' expenditures by promoting the formation of consumers' cooperatives—an experiment that succeeded. He, too, offended many of his contemporaries by his advocacy of sexual freedom, by his attacks on established religion, and by his enthusiasm for spiritualism.

Both Owen and Fourier relied on private initiative to build their model communities. In contrast, Louis Blanc (1811–1882) developed Saint-Simon's vaguely formulated principle of "organization" into a doctrine of state intervention to achieve Utopian ends. Blanc outlined his scheme for social workshops in a pamphlet, *The Organization of Labor* (1840), which began with the statement, "The other day a child was frozen to death behind a sentry-box in the heart of Paris, and nobody was shocked or surprised at the event."

"What proletarians need," Blanc wrote, "is the instruments of labor; it is the function of government to supply these. If we were to define our conception of the state, our answer would be that the state is the banker of the poor."** The government would finance and supervise the purchase of productive equipment and the formation of social workshops; it would withdraw its support and supervision once the workshops were on their feet. As the workshops gradually spread throughout France, socialistic enterprise would replace private enterprise, private profits would vanish, and labor would emerge as the only class left in society, thereby achieving a classless society.

Much of Louis Blanc's socialism was characteristically Utopian, particularly in his reliance on workers to make their own arrangements for communal living. The real novelty of his plan lay in the role he assigned to the state and in the fact that he began to move socialism from philanthropy to politics. Ironically, politics was to prove his undoing. Alarmed conservatives identified the national

---

* Robert Owen, *A New View of Society*, 1812–1813 (New York: Penguin, 1969), p. 192.

** Louis Blanc, *L'Organisation du Travail*, 1840, in *The French Revolution of 1848*, ed. J. A. R. Marriott (Oxford: Oxford University Press, 1913), I, p. 14. Our translation.

workshops of 1848 as an effort to implement his social ideas, and he was forced into exile.

Marx

With Karl Marx (1818–1883) socialism moved to a far more intense form—revolutionary communism. Whereas the early socialists had anticipated a gradual and peaceful evolution toward Utopia, Marx forecast a sudden and violent proletarian uprising by which the workers would capture governments and make them the instruments for securing proletarian welfare. From Blanc he derived the summary of socialist goals: "From each according to his abilities, to each according to his needs."

Marx found three laws in the pattern of history. First, *economic determinism*: He believed that economic conditions largely determined the character of all other human institutions—society and government, religion and art. Second, *the class struggle*: he believed that history was a dialectical process, a series of conflicts between antagonistic economic groups, ideas, and practices. In his own day the antagonists were the "haves" and the "have-nots"—the bourgeois against the proletarians. Third, the *inevitability of communism*: He believed that the class struggle was bound to produce one final upheaval that would raise the victorious proletariat over the prostrate bourgeoisie. As he wrote to a friend in 1852, "What I did that was new was to prove (1) that the *existence of classes* is only bound up with *particular historical phases in the development of production*, (2) that the class struggle necessarily leads to the *dictatorship of the proletariat*, (3) that this dictatorship itself only constitutes the transition to *abolition of all* classes and to a *classless society*."*

Although Marx was born and died in the nineteenth century, he belonged in spirit partly to the eighteenth. Marx early acquired a faith in natural law, fortified by the materialistic teachings of the German philosopher Ludwig Feuerbach (1804–1872), who proclaimed that *Man ist was er esst* (One is what one eats). From all this followed the boast made by Marx and his disciples that their socialism alone was "scientific," as opposed to the romantic doctrines of the Utopians.

The romantic philosophy of Hegel, however, provided the intellectual scaffolding of Marxism. Although Hegel had died in 1831, his influence permeated the University of Berlin during Marx's student days there (1836–1841). Marx translated the Hegelian dialectic of thesis/antithesis/synthesis into the language of economic determinism and the class struggle. He believed that capitalistic production and the bourgeoisie comprised the thesis; the antithesis was the proletariat; and the synthesis, issuing from the communist revolution, would be true socialism.

By age thirty Marx had completed the outlines of his theory of scientific, revolutionary socialism. He had also become a permanent exile from his native Germany.

---

* From *Karl Marx*, ed. Tom Bottomore (Englewood Cliffs, N.J.: Spectrum Books, 1973), p. 144.

Though the ideas of Karl Marx were under constant revision by socialists, especially in the Soviet Union, his basic arguments triumphed over other socialist views. As modified by later theorists, he would become the father of twentieth century communism.

The Bettmann Archive

On leaving the University of Berlin, he worked for a newspaper at Cologne in the Prussian Rhineland, then moved to Paris in 1843 after his espousal of atheism had aroused the authorities against him. Exiled again because the government of Louis Philippe feared his antibourgeois propaganda, he went to Brussels in 1845.

From Adam Smith's labor theory of value Marx concluded that only the worker should receive the profits from the sale of a commodity, since the value of the commodity should be determined by the labor of the person who produced it. The Iron Law of Wages, however, confirmed Marx's belief that capitalism would never permit the worker to receive this just reward. And from observing the depression of the late 1840s, he concluded that economic crises were bound to occur again and again under a system by which capital produced too much and labor consumed too little. Essentially a scholar and a philosopher, Marx had initially expected that people would see the wisdom behind his ideas; that violence should be committed in his name was not his original intention.

Engels and *The Communist Manifesto*

Meanwhile, Marx began his friendship and collaboration with Friedrich Engels (1820–1895). In many ways, the two men made a striking contrast. Marx was poor and quarrelsome, a man of few friends; except for his devotion to his wife and children, he was utterly preoccupied with his economic studies. Engels, on the other hand, was the son of a well-to-do German manufacturer and represented the family textile business in Liverpool and Manchester. He loved sports and high living, but he also hated the evils of industrialism. When he met Marx, he had already written a bitter study, *The Condition of the Working Class in England*, based on his firsthand knowledge of the situation in Manchester.

Both Engels and Marx took an interest in the Communist League, a small, secret international organization of radical workers. In 1847 the London office of the Communist League requested them to draw up a program. Engels wrote the first draft, which Marx revised; the result, *The Communist Manifesto*, remains the classic statement of Marxian socialism.

The *Manifesto* opened with the dramatic announcement that "A spectre is haunting Europe—the spectre of Communism." It closed with a stirring and confident appeal:

> Let the ruling classes tremble at a Communistic revolution. The proletarians have nothing to lose but their chains. They have a world to win.
>
> Working men of all countries, unite!*

In between it traced a communist view of history: "The history of all hitherto existing society is the history of class struggle." Changing economic conditions determined that the struggle should develop successively between "freeman and slave, patrician and plebeian, lord and serf, guildmaster and journeyman." The guild system gave way first to manufacture by large numbers of small capitalists and then to "the giant, modern industry." Modern industry would inevitably destroy bourgeois society. It creates mounting economic pressures by producing more goods than it can sell; it creates mounting social pressures by depriving more and more people of their property and forcing them down to the proletariat. These pressures would increase to the point where a revolutionary explosion would occur. Landed property would be abolished outright; other forms of property would be liquidated more gradually through the imposition of crushing income taxes and the abolition of inherited wealth.

Eventually, social classes and tensions would vanish, and "we shall have an association in which the free development of each is the condition for the free development of all." The *Manifesto* provided only this vague description of the situation that would exist after the revolution. Since Marx defined political authority as "the organized power of one class for oppressing another," he apparently expected that "the state would wither away" once it had created a classless regime. He also apparently assumed that the great dialectical process of history, having achieved its final synthesis, would then cease to operate in its traditional form.

Marx oversimplified human nature by trying to force it into the rigid mold of economic determinism and ignoring nonmaterial motives and interests. Neither proletarians nor bourgeois have proved to be the simple economic stereotypes Marx supposed them to be: Labor has often assumed a markedly bourgeois outlook and mentality; capital has eliminated the worst injustices of the factory system. No more than Malthus did Marx foresee the notable rise in the general standard of living that began in the mid-nineteenth century and continued well into the twentieth.

Since Marx also failed to take into account the growing strength of nationalism, the *Manifesto* confidently expected the class struggle to transcend national boundaries. In social and economic warfare, nation would not be pitted against nation; the proletariat everywhere would join to fight the bourgeoisie. In Marx's own lifetime, however, national differences and antagonisms were, in fact, increasing rapidly from day to day.

The Communist Manifesto anticipated the strengths as well as the weaknesses of the communist movement. First, it foreshadowed the important role to be played by propaganda. Second, it anticipated the emphasis to be placed on the role of the party in forging the proletarian revolution. The communists, Marx declared, were "the most advanced section of the working-class parties of every country." In matters of theory, they had the advantage over the great mass of the proletariat of "clearly understanding the line of march, the conditions, and the ultimate general results of the proletarian movement." Third, the *Manifesto* assigned the state a great role in the revolution. Among the policies recommended by Marx were "centralization of credit in the hands of the state" and "extension of factories and instruments of production owned by the state." And, finally, the *Manifesto* clearly established the line dividing communism from the other forms of socialism. Marx's dogmatism, his philosophy of history, and his belief in the necessity of a "total" revolution made his brand of socialism a doctrine apart.

Marxism after 1848

From 1849 until his death in 1883, Marx lived in London, where, partly because of his own financial mismanagement, his family experienced the misery of a proletarian existence in the slums of Soho. After poverty and near-starvation had caused the death of three of his children, he eventually obtained a modest income through the generosity of Engels and from his own writings. Throughout this time he revised his writings, setting out his main principles in the *Grundrisse* and then departing from the outline thus completed in 1858 to write the first volume of *Das Kapital* in 1867. Two further volumes of *Das Kapital*, pieced together from his notes, were published after his death.

In *Das Kapital* Marx spelled out the labor theory of value according to which the workers created the total value of the commodity that they produced, yet received in the form of wages only a small part of the price for the item. The difference between the sale price and the workers' wages constituted *surplus value*, something actually created by labor but appropriated by capital as profit. It was the nature of capitalism, Marx argued, to diminish

---

* Karl Marx and Friedrich Engels, *The Communist Manifesto*, 1848 (New York: Monthly Review Press, 1964), trans. Paul M. Sweezy, p. 62.

its own profits by replacing human labor with machines and thus gradually choke off the source of surplus value. Thus would arise a mounting crisis of overproduction and underconsumption.

In 1864, three years before the first volume of *Das Kapital* was published, Marx joined in the formation of the First International Workingmen's Association. This was an ambitious attempt to organize workers of every country and variety of radical belief. A loose federation rather than a coherent political party, the First International soon began to disintegrate; it expired in 1876. Increasing persecution by hostile governments helped to bring on its end, but so, too, did the factional quarrels that repeatedly engaged its members.

In 1889 a Second International was organized; it lasted until World War I and the Bolshevik revolution in Russia. The Second International represented the Marxian Socialist or Social Democratic parties, which were becoming important forces in the major countries of Continental Europe. Among its leaders were men and women more politically adept than Marx. Yet factionalism continued to weaken the International. Some of its leaders tenaciously defended the precepts of the master and forbade any cooperation between socialists and the bourgeois political parties; these were the orthodox Marxists. Other leaders of the Second International revised his doctrines in the direction of moderation and of harmonization with the views of the Utopians. These "revisionists" believed in cooperation between classes rather than in a struggle to the death, and they hoped that human decency and intelligence, working through the machinery of democratic government, could avert outright class war.

Both orthodox and heretical Marxists have persisted to the present day, with the orthodox view itself fragmenting, and the heretical views proliferating, as theoreticians and political leaders in Asia, Africa, and Latin America attempted, especially after World War II, to adapt Marxian analysis to the perceived realities of their situations. Marx's views would be significantly added to by V. I. Lenin, so that scholars prefer to speak of Marxism-Leninism when referring to the practices of the principal modern advocate of orthodoxy, the former Soviet Union (see Chapter 23).

*A*POSTLES OF VIOLENCE AND NONVIOLENCE

The various forms of liberalism and socialism did not exhaust the range of responses to the economic and social problems created in industrial societies. Nationalists reinvigorated old mercantilist ideas, not only advocating tariffs to protect agriculture and industry but also demanding empires abroad to provide new markets for surplus products, new fields for the investment of surplus capital, and new settlements for surplus citizens. Others advocated anarchy and violence, while nonviolent preachers of

mutualism, goodwill, and good work sought to return to primitive Christianity.

Tradition assigns the honor of being the first modern socialists to Gracchus Babeuf and his fellow conspirators under the French Directory in 1796–1797. The equalitarianism of Babeuf was too loosely formulated to be called truly socialist, however; the only direct link between him and later socialist doctrines derives from his followers' belief that human nature could change only through immediate violent action in the manner of the Reign of Terror. The leader of these new terrorists was Auguste Blanqui (1805–1881), a professional revolutionary who participated in the Paris revolts of 1830, 1848, and 1870–1871 (after France's defeat in the Franco-Prussian War). Blanqui believed that the imposition of a dictatorial regime by an elite vanguard of conspirators would be the only way to deal with a bourgeois capitalist society. An inveterate plotter of violence, he spent forty of his seventy-six years in prison. When his movement died out in the 1870s, his followers tended to join the Marxian Socialists.

Anarchists

Other apostles of violence called themselves anarchists, believing that the best government was no government at all. For them it was not enough that the state should wither at some distant time, however; such an instrument of oppression should be annihilated at once. The weapon of the anarchist terrorists was the assassination of heads of state, and by the turn of the century they had killed the French president Carnot in 1894, King Humbert of Italy in 1900, and the American president William McKinley in 1901.

The anarchist ideal exerted an important influence on the proletarian movement. The Russian scientist and thinker Prince Peter Kropotkin (1842–1921) made the most complete statement of its theory in his book *Mutual Aid: A Factor in Evolution* (1902). Kropotkin foresaw a revolution that would abolish the state as well as private property, and that would lead to a new society of cooperating autonomous groups wherein workers would achieve greater fulfillment and would need to labor only four to five hours a day. Kropotkin's countryman and fellow anarchist Mikhail Bakunin (1814–1876) helped to shape the Russian revolutionary movement and won the attention of workers from many countries by his participation in the First International.

Bakunin contributed to the formation of the program known as anarcho-syndicalism (from the French word *syndicat*, which means an economic grouping, particularly a trade union). The anarcho-syndicalists scorned political parties, even Marxist ones; they believed in direct action by the workers culminating in a spontaneous general strike that would free labor from the capitalistic yoke. Meantime, workers could rehearse for the great day by engaging in acts of anticapitalist sabotage. In 1908 these theories received their most forceful expression in *Reflections on Violence* by a French engineer and anarcho-syndicalist, Georges Sorel (1847–1922), who declared that belief in the general strike constituted a kind of false

THE WRITTEN RECORD

Pope Leo XIII Attacks Socialism

Pope Leo XIII was concerned with issues of liberty and political power. He was sympathetic to the plight of the workers and felt that the Church should recognize their concerns, though he did not believe in the inevitable clash of labor and capital. Thus in *Rerum novarum* he wrote that it was a "great mistake" to believe

that class is naturally hostile to class, and that the wealthy and the workingmen are intended by nature to live in mutual conflict. . . . Each needs the other: Capital cannot do without Labor, nor Labor without Capital. . . .

Religion teaches the laboring man . . . to carry out honestly and fairly all equitable agreements freely entered into; never to injure the property, nor to outrage the person, of an employer; never to resort to violence. . . ; and to have nothing to do with men of evil principles, who work upon the people with artful promises, and excite foolish hopes which usually end in useless regrets, followed by insolvency. Religion teaches the wealthy owner and the employer that their workpeople are not to be accounted

their bondsmen; that in every man they must respect his dignity and worth as a man and as a Christian; that labor is not a thing to be ashamed of, if we lend ear to right reason and to Christian philosophy, but is an honorable calling, enabling a man to sustain his life in a way upright and creditable; and that it is shameful and inhuman to treat men like chattels to make money by, or to look upon them merely as so much muscle or physical power.

Pope Leo XIII, *Rerun novarum*, 1891, in *The Great Encyclical Letters of Pope Leo XIII* (New York: Benziger Bros., 1903), pp. 218, 219.

hope that would convert all workers into saboteurs. But the writer most frequently cited by the anarcho-syndicalists was the French publicist Pierre Joseph Proudhon (1809–1865). "What is property?" Proudhon asked in a pamphlet in 1840. "Property is theft," he answered.

Christian Socialists and Christian Democrats

Still other efforts to mitigate class antagonisms came from the Anglican and Catholic churches. In England the Christian Socialists urged the Church of England to put aside theological disputes and direct its efforts toward ending social abuses. The Christian Socialists attacked materialism and championed brotherly love against unbrotherly strife, association and cooperation against exploitation and competition. They relied far more on private philanthropy than on state intervention, however, as did their Catholic counterparts on the Continent, who advocated what they called Christian democracy or social Christianity.

By the second half of the nineteenth century an atmosphere of crisis was enveloping the Roman church. A thousand years of papal rule in central Italy ended when the city of Rome passed to the newly unified kingdom of Italy in 1870; anticlerical legislation threatened traditional Catholic bulwarks in Italy, France, and Germany; and the materialism of the industrial revolution and the new ideologies of science, nationalism, and socialism were all competing for the allegiance of Catholics. The church initially responded to these problems by seeking refuge in

the past. Pope Pius IX (r. 1846–1878) issued the *Syllabus of Errors* in 1864, condemning many social theories and institutions not consecrated by tradition. While Pius also condemned the materialism implicit in laissez faire, socially minded Catholics were disturbed by his apparent hostility to trade unions and democracy.

His successor, Leo XIII (r. 1878–1903), recognized that the church could not continue to turn its back on modernity without suffering serious losses. He knew that Catholicism was flourishing in the supposedly hostile climate of the democratic and largely Protestant United States. Moreover, his study of St. Thomas Aquinas convinced him that the church had much to gain by following the middle-of-the-road social and economic policies recommended by that medieval Schoolman. Accordingly, Leo XIII issued a series of modernizing documents, notably the encyclical *Rerum novarum* (Concerning New Things, 1891).

In *Rerum novarum* Pope Leo wrote of the defects of capitalism as vigorously as any socialist, and then attacked with equal vigor the socialist view of property and the doctrine of class war. Leo believed that the workers must help themselves, and *Rerum novarum* concluded with a fervent appeal for the formation of Catholic trade unions.

These Catholic unions exist today, but they are only a minority in the realm of organized labor. Neither the Christian democracy of Leo XIII nor the Christian socialism of the Anglican reformers has achieved all that their founders hoped. Yet the Christian democrats eventually came to play a central part in the politics of Germany, Italy, and other European states. And in Britain at the beginning of the twentieth century, both Marxism and the Christian socialist tradition helped to attract workers and middle-class intellectuals to the developing Labour party. It was not, in any case, socialism that had proved to be the major threat to traditional religion, nor the most significant product of the industrial society. The new science, which challenged biblical views of creation and other essentially materialist philosophies, had ushered in an age of materialism.

A New Age of Science

The telegraph, the submarine cable, the telephone, the massive railroad bridges and tunnels, and the high-speed printing press not only improved communications but also demonstrated the practical utility of science. Chemistry and physics were especially important. The study of thermodynamics was fostered by the steam engine, which used heat to create power and led physicists to study the conservation of energy. The second law of thermodynamics held that all energy was ultimately dissipated; though the total amount of energy in the universe remained constant, the amount useful to human beings was capable of being steadily degraded. This in turn led to an interest in the conservation of the resources on which energy was based. Scientists who studied electricity and magnetism developed a new body of study, electromagnetism. They maintained that light was a series of waves. Since light waves must move through some medium, not empty space, it was hypothesized that space was filled with a conductor, a substance called ether. Many scientists abandoned the Newtonian concept of light as made up of minute particles.

To other physicists, and also chemists, biologists, and physicians, humanity continued to live in a world of particles—a world of atoms. Atoms of one chemical element combined with those of another to form molecules of some familiar substance, such as hydrogen, oxygen, and water. But the process of combination raised some important questions. For example, the volume of hydrogen in water was twice that of oxygen, as indicated by the familiar formula H_2O; but experiments showed that the weight of the oxygen was eight times that of the hydrogen. It seemed evident, therefore, that an atom of oxygen must weigh sixteen times more than an atom of hydrogen. To establish a standard table of atomic weights, an international congress of experts met in 1860 in Germany. To understand the interactions of atomic weights, scientists felt, was to approach an understanding of the nature of energy in the universe.

The biological counterpart of the atomic theory was the cell theory: All plant and animal structures are composed of living units known as cells. The medical counterpart was the theory of germs—a great advance over the older belief that disease was in effect a phenomenon of spontaneous corruption. Biology, like all other sciences, was international: A German microbiologist discovered

This painting (1885) shows Louis Pasteur in his laboratory examining the spinal marrow of a rabbit that died of hydrophobia. Such scientific exploration brought medicine, surgery, and public health to a point of impressive growth by 1900.
Giraudon/Art Resource

the organisms causing tuberculosis and cholera; an American doctor found that the virus responsible for yellow fever was transmitted by a mosquito; in Britain a Quaker physician demonstrated that germs were responsible for the infection of wounds; in France the chemist Louis Pasteur (1822–1895) became popular when he was credited with the development of a vaccine for inoculating victims of rabies and by devising a process for sterilizing milk. By the twentieth century the average life expectancy in North America and many European countries was to increase by twenty to thirty years.

Darwinism, 1859–1871

It was a revolutionary new theory in biology that most transformed thought, and thus action. In 1859 there was published in London Charles Darwin's *On the Origin of Species by Means of Natural Selection*. It rested in the study of natural history, the long record of the hundreds of thousands of years of organic life on earth. Already well established by geologists and paleontologists, this record told of the rise, the development, and sometimes the disappearance of thousands of different forms of plant and animal organisms, or species. The record appeared to contradict the biblical book of Genesis, which described all forms of life as having been made by a Creator in the space of a single week about six thousand years ago.

Darwin (1809–1882) found one clue to the past in Malthus's *Essay on Population*, which maintained that organisms tended to multiply to a point where there was not sufficient food for them all. In the intense competition for food, some of these organisms did not get enough and died. This was the *struggle for existence*. Darwin next asked himself what determined that certain individuals would survive and that others would die. Obviously, the surviving ones got more food, better shelter, better living conditions of all sorts. If they were all identical organisms, then the only explanation would have to be some accidental variation in the environment. But it was clear from observation that individual organisms of a given species are not identical. Variations appear even at birth. Thus in a single litter of pigs there may be sturdy, aggressive piglets and also a runt, who is likely to get shoved aside in suckling and starve. In the struggle for existence, the runt is proved "unfit."

This was the second of Darwin's key phrases—the *survival of the fittest.* The organism best endowed to get food and shelter lives to procreate young that will tend to inherit these favorable variations. The variations may be slight indeed, but over generations they are cumulative; finally an organism is produced that is so different from the long-distant ancestor that it can be considered to be a new species. This new species has *evolved* by the working of *natural selection*. Plant and animal breeders had long made use of this process and had even directed it by breeding only the most desirable strains.

Darwin held that the variations in individuals of the same species at birth are accidental and that they are generally transmitted through inheritance. Darwin's theory was later modified as scientists concluded that the important variations in the evolutionary process were not so much the numerous tiny ones Darwin emphasized but rather bigger and much rarer ones known as *mutations*. The actual mechanism of heredity we know much better than Darwin did, thanks to the Austrian priest Gregor Mendel (1822–1884), whose experiments with crossbreeding garden peas laid the scientific basis of modern genetics and its study of genes and chromosomes.

The Origin of Species became a best seller, reviewed all over the world. The major reason for this attention was almost certainly the challenge that orthodox Christians felt they found in the book. Darwin received such wide attention because he seemed to provide for the secularist a process (evolution) and a causal agent (natural selection), where before there had been only vague "materialistic" notions that emphasized accident rather than order. He also seemed to have struck a final blow against the argument, still very popular in Victorian times, that the organic world was full of evidence of God, the great designer. Finally, Darwin gained notoriety because of the frequent, though quite wrong, accusation that he made the monkey the brother of man. Later, in *The Descent of Man* (1871), Darwin carefully argued that *Homo sapiens* was descended not from any existing ape or monkey but from a very remote common primate ancestor.

Charles Darwin, the theorist of evolution, is shown here in a caricature, or cartoon, by Spy.
The Bettmann Archive

The Origin of Species stirred up a most heated theological controversy. Fundamentalists, both Protestant and Catholic, damned Darwin and much of science itself. But the Catholic church and many Protestant bodies eventually viewed Darwinism as a scientific biological hypothesis, neither necessarily correct nor necessarily incorrect. Most Christians tacitly accepted sufficient modification of Genesis to accommodate the scientist's time scale, and they adjusted the classic theological arguments to propose a God who worked through organic evolution. Moreover, it was quite clear to reflective individuals that nothing any scientist could produce could give the ultimate answers to the kind of problems set by the existence of God; it was quite clear to them that just as God's eye is on the sparrow, it must once have also been on the dinosaur.

Social Darwinism

This theological conflict had pretty well run its course by the beginning of the twentieth century. More important in the long run was the use made of some of Darwin's basic concepts in debates on matters moral, economic, and political. The blanket term *Social Darwinism* covers these transfers of ideas from biology to the social sciences and human relations. The central idea that social and political thinkers took over from Darwin was that of competition among individuals and groups. Most of these late-nineteenth-century thinkers interpreted the human struggle as a battle for the means of livelihood in which the variations that counted were those that brought success in economic, political, and cultural competition—variations that produced inventors, business moguls, and statesmen. Darwin's work in natural history confirmed the economists' doctrine of laissez faire and the liberals' doctrine of individual freedom.

Here was scientific validation of the middle-class conviction that the universe was designed to reward hard work, attention to duty, thrift, intelligence, and self-help, and to punish laziness, waste, stupidity, sexual promiscuity, and reliance on charity. Above all, Darwin seemed to vindicate the notions that the poor were poor because they were unfit, badly prepared by nature for living a competitive life, and that efforts by private charity or by state action to take from the well-to-do and give to the poor were useless attempts to reverse the course of evolution. Herbert Spencer (1820–1903) summed up this view:

> Of man, as of all inferior creatures, the law by conformity to which the species is preserved, is that among adults the individuals best adapted to the conditions of their existence shall prosper most, and that individuals least adapted to the conditions of their existence shall prosper least. . . . The ultimate result of shielding men from folly is to fill the world with fools.*

Spencer later decided that the emotions promoted by religion—kindness, compassion, love—were also in accord with the intentions of the laws of the universe as summed up in evolution. Mutual extermination might be the law for tigers, but not for human beings. Indeed, Spencer and many other Social Darwinists held that the altruistic moral sentiments that impel one toward acts of charity were the highest achievement of the evolutionary process.

The Social Darwinists were, then, faced with this primary difficulty: Darwin seemed to have shown that the struggle for life within a given species and among rival species was the law of the universe; but human history and human feelings showed that humanity could not look on suffering with indifference. One way out of this dilemma was to humanize and ease the struggle, so that

---

* Herbert Spencer, *Principles of Ethics* (1879) (New York: D. Appleton, 1900), II, p. 17; Spencer, *Social Statics* (London: Williams and Norgate, 1851), pp. 149, 174; Spencer, *Autobiography* (London: Williams and Norgate, 1904), II, p. 100.

the incompetent were shelved but not destroyed. Many who held this view turned to eugenics, or selective breeding. Since, according to strict Darwinian theory, acquired characteristics were not transmitted by heredity, no amount of manipulation of the social environment, no amount of wise planning of institutions, would alter human beings. Therefore, the only way to secure permanent improvement of the race was by deliberate mating of the fit with the fit.

The eugenicists, however, immediately ran up against the fact that in choosing a mate the individual human being is influenced by many motives, and no master breeder can decide who shall mate with whom. Eugenicists have urged that the feebleminded, the insane, the pathologically criminal be prevented from having children. Only a tiny handful of human beings have undergone such treatment, and then usually in dictatorships where the safeguards of democracy did not apply. A greater effect might possibly result from testing human fetuses in the early stages of pregnancy and aborting those destined to have serious birth defects. However, such attempts run directly counter to deeply held religious convictions about the sanctity of life from the moment of conception. The clash between the ethics of science and the ethics of religion continues in complex ways to the present day.

Racism

By far the commonest way out of the dilemma facing the Social Darwinists lay in the notion that the struggle for existence really goes on among human beings organized in groups—as tribes, races, or national states. The struggle for existence was thus lifted from the biology of the individual to the politics of the group. Accordingly, a group that defeated another group in war had thereby shown itself to be fitter than the beaten group; it had a right—indeed, in evolutionary terms, a duty—to eliminate the beaten group, seize its lands, and people them with its own fitter human beings. The English imperialist Cecil Rhodes (1853–1902) once held that a world wholly and exclusively peopled with Anglo-Saxons would be the best possible world. Thus racism held that inherent differences among the various races determined cultural and individual achievement, so that one race might be considered superior to another in a given context.

Racists like Rhodes believed that *Homo sapiens* had already evolved into what were really separate species. A black skin, for instance, was for them a sign of innate inferiority; and blacks would have to go the way of the dinosaurs. Intermarriage between the races was forbidden by custom or by law as contrary to God's intention and because it would degrade the "higher race." As yet few dared to preach genocide, the wholesale murder of those held to be of inferior race; most racists wished to see the "inferiors" duly subjected to their "superiors," or "kept in their own place," or "among their own kind."

Other Social Darwinists applied their theories to a new form of caste organization that came to be known as *elitism*. The fit were not limited to any one race, but they were the master group, the elite, the "supermen," and they should band together against the dull, average people. The German philosopher Friedrich Nietzsche (1844–1900), who gave currency to the term *superman*, was a subtle and difficult thinker, neither racist nor Social Darwinist. But like Darwin he was easily misunderstood by the half-educated who used distortions of his arguments to further racist and elitist causes. Scientific "objectivity" came for a time to mean measurement of cranial capacities in order to judge the intelligence of entire races.

Though Darwinism and its offshoots could be misread as the basis for a new doctrine of progress, and though it supported the industrial societies in their expectation of unlimited growth, essentially Darwinism and much of racism were intensely pessimistic. Darwin had emphasized accident, not order, as the nature of causation. Many commentators believed that the "lower races" would eventually triumph, for brute strength would overtake sensitivity. In 1853 the French count Joseph Arthur de Gobineau (1816–1882) published the first part of his *Essay on the Inequality of the Human Races*. Civilizations fell, Gobineau argued, because of racial mixing; he and many others considered the ultimate degradation of civilization to be inevitable. The "lower races" were breeding faster and less selectively, democratic egalitarianism was leveling down the best while encouraging the worst; consequently, evolution was sliding downward rather than heading upward.

A wide variety of forms of historical determinism accompanied the industrial process. To the pessimistic Social Darwinists, the racists, and the exponents of the "dismal science" were added determinists who were convinced that they knew where history was leading and that they felt they had a duty to lead it there more rapidly, at the cost of massive violence over the short run in order to benefit civilization in the long run. The extraordinary acceleration of technological improvements, of scientific research, and of more broadly based education that had produced the industrial revolution and the industrial societies lent strength to the view that moral and political improvements could also be speeded up by a drastic redirection of public energies. The doctrine of evolution added to tensions in society by reinforcing the popular conviction that evolution need not be slow, that one could increase the speed of change.

In the age of science and industry many believed that politics was no longer, if it ever had been, an art. They now spoke of "political science." Just as Darwinism had a massive public impact in a vulgarized form, so did the most sweeping effort to work out a comprehensive philosphical program for the improvement of humanity—positivism, a school of thought that sought to apply evolutionary theory to human governance.

Comte and Positivism

It was Auguste Comte (1798–1857) who coined the term *positivism*. His recommendations for bettering the human conditions retained some of the utopian and messianic qualities of Saint-Simonian teachings. Comte applied the term *positivist* to the third stage of humanity's attitude toward the world. First, in the infant period of history, humanity was in the theological age, standing in awe and fear of nature and seeking to placate the gods that controlled it. Second, in the adolescence of human history, metaphysical concepts replaced divinities as the perceived controlling forces of the world. Finally, science would enable people to understand nature without recourse to theological or metaphysical intermediaries, so that they might take positive action to manipulate the world to their advantage.

In many ways Comte was simply restating the Enlightenment's optimistic faith in the miracle-working potential of science. Yet he also realized that the French revolutionary attempt to build a new society from the blueprints of eighteenth-century intellectuals had ended in terror and dictatorship. Accordingly, Comte concluded, utopia must be achieved peacefully through dedicated teaching, so that the masses could free themselves from their old dependence on theology and metaphysics. Comte envisaged these liberators as preachers of a new "religion of humanity," but his critics argued that they were propagandists of a new positivist dogma that might be more intolerant than old religious dogmas.

The attraction of Comte's positivism lay in assembling diverse beliefs and arranging them with new emphases. The social problem was growing more urgent every day, he felt, and humanity required a sweeping intellectual system if it was to resolve its problems before destroying itself. Comte scorned metaphysical philosophy in favor of systematized common sense, as he called his views. In so calling them, he hoped to appeal to women, to the working class, and to those who were generally thought (wrongly) to be unable to deal with abstract reasoning.

Positivism found clear expression in public issues. In Britain, Comte's arguments were used to formulate debate on "the condition-of-England question" and also on whether the British ought to intervene directly in their nonwhite colonies in order to effect social change. In France those who rejected both the Revolution and the restoration of the monarchy found in positivism a way to enjoy bourgeois comforts while rejecting bourgeois values. The movement was solidly middle class, generally professional and academic. In an age acutely aware of history, the positivists believed that they could bring to history and society the predictive abilities of science. This was a comforting doctrine that formed an ethical bridge between science and religion.

Idealism and Realism

The American philosopher William James (1842–1910) summed up the antithesis of idealism and realism by arguing that people are either "tender-minded" or "tough-minded." The tough-minded are convinced that the world of sense experience is the real world; the tender-minded are convinced that the world of sense experience is somehow an illusion, or at any rate a flawed copy of the real world, which exists perfectly only in God's mind. This abstract argument was a modern formulation of the ancient debate between the Platonists and the Aristotelians.

Another distinct note in the thought and language of the period was an emphasis on will. The word appeared everywhere, even as a title—in Nietzsche's *Will to Power*, in William James's *Will to Believe*. The pragmatism of William James was a philosophy of the will. To James reality was not absolute, as in the idealist tradition; indeed, reality was not fixed and certain. Reality was what "works" for human beings, truth was what humanity wanted to, had to, believe. To many of his critics, James had by no means saved himself from subjectivism. Pragmatism remained, for these critics, a doctrine dangerously erosive of traditional values.

The cult of the will intensified the revolt against reason. The basic position of antirationalism was a rejection of the Enlightenment's belief that the typical human being is naturally reasonable. Antirationalism also had its positive side—the belief that if people can accept their true nature as human beings, they can lead richer lives than any rationalist ever planned for them. To use a metaphor from John Locke, moderate antirationalists regarded human reason as a flickering candle, not as a great white universal light. They wanted to keep it alive, to nurse it along to greater brightness. In keeping with the views of the evolutionists, they regarded this process as long and slow. By contrast, extreme antirationalists would put out the candle of human reason, which they regarded as not only feeble but downright bad. For them, reason was, so to speak, a mistake evolution had made—a wrong turn from which the human race must somehow retrace its steps to a sounder life of instinct, emotion, and faith.

Many of the extreme antirationalists turned violently against democracy, which seemed to them to rest on an altogether false evaluation of what human beings were really like. Because antirationalists hold that most people are by nature incapable of fair, dispassionate thinking and discussion, they favored leadership and rule by an elite.

Elitism

The German philosopher Nietzsche was representative of the elitist view. The central line of his thinking led to the concept of a new aristocracy—the "higher man" or *Übermensch*. Nietzsche's followers insisted that he meant a *spiritual* aristocracy; the superman would be above the petty materialism and national patriotism of the middle classes. Nietzsche's opponents held that he was a preacher of Nordic superiority. Whichever, Nietzsche was clearly an enemy of democracy, which he held to be second only to its child, socialism, as a system in which the weak unjustly and unnaturally ruled the strong.

By 1914 the broad lines of the social attitudes of the present time were laid out. One line of argument favored some kind of revolutionary elitism, the seizure of power by a minority that believes itself to have the formula whereby the gifted few can bring order to a society threatened with chaos. As Lenin developed Marxian

Friedrich Nietzsche, German philosopher.
New York Public Library Picture Collection

socialism (see p. 443–441), its elitist implications came out clearly. The enlightened minority would seize power and rule dictatorially in the name of, and in the true interest of, the masses. Others dreamed of a new elite, such as Nietzsche's superman, to be created by a kind of new religion. Still others looked to eugenics to make possible the breeding of the new elite.

A second line of argument favored a more flexible form of elitism, one that tried to conserve democratic values. The leaders of such movements believed in gradualness. But all of them had doubts about the political capacity of the average man and woman. They hoped they could persuade the millions to listen to the wise planners, who had studied the social sciences and could devise the new institutions that would make human life better.

A third line sought to preserve and protect an existing elite from democratic drives toward equality, especially in the form of state intervention in economic and social life to promote security for all. Followers of this line believed in progress, and most of them prized material plenty, peace, the industrial society. They feared planners and planning, at least in political positions. They distrusted the state, for they believed that the evolutionary process depended on the struggle for life among competing individuals, fettered as little as possible by government attempts to influence the struggle.

The Song of the Shirt

"The Song of the Shirt," by the minor English poet Thomas Hood (1799–1845), was prompted by a London news report about the arrest of a seamstress for pawning articles belonging to her employer. Paid by the piece, she could earn at the maximum seven shillings a week, on which she was expected to support herself and two young children.

Work—work—work
Till the brain begins to swim;
Work—work—work
Till the eyes are heavy and dim!
Seam, and gusset, and band,
Band, and gusset, and seam,
Till over the buttons I fall asleep
And sew them on in a dream!

O! Men, with Sisters dear!
O! Men! with Mothers and Wives!

It is not linen you're wearing out,
But human creatures' lives!
Stitch—stitch—stitch
In poverty, hunger, and dirt,
Sewing at once, with a double thread
A Shroud as well as a Shirt.

Thomas Hood, "The Song of the Shirt," in *British Poetry and Prose*, ed. Paul Robert Lieder, Robert Morss Lovett, and Robert Kilburn Root (Boston: Houghton-Mifflin, 1936), II, p. 171.

ℒITERATURE AND THE ARTS IN INDUSTRIAL SOCIETIES

The scientific and industrial revolutions and the debate over idealism and realism helped to stimulate an explosion of creativity and artistic experimentation that transformed the novel, drama, and the fine arts. The gap between "genteel" writing and the cruder and more vigorous forms was widening because so much important work was produced and encouraged by men and women in conscious revolt against the tastes of the politically and economically dominant class of their time—that is, the middle class.

Literature

In literature the last two thirds of the nineteenth century proved to be a great period for the novel of realism that depicted the problems and triumphs of the industrial society, drawing upon the stylistic canons of the romantics while pursuing starkly realistic themes. The English novelists Charles Dickens (1812–1870) and William Makepeace Thackeray (1811–1863), the French Honoré de Balzac (1799–1850), and the Russian Feodor Dostoevsky (1821–1881) all poured out undisciplined torrents of words, often taking little time to revise or polish. Yet they were thoroughly immersed in the world of their time and were in many ways realists. Thackeray's *Vanity Fair* was a condemnation of the false values of a money-mad, power-hungry society. The

novels that constituted what Balzac called "the human comedy"—*Pére Goriot, Eugénie Grandet, Cousine Bette*, and many others—were a savage exposé of the crassness and corruption of bourgeois society under the July Monarchy. The leading French realist of the next generation, Gustave Flaubert (1821–1880), hated the bourgeois world he wrote about in his masterpiece, *Madame Bovary*.

By the end of the century, these realists were confronted by writers who sought an almost scientific accuracy of observation in their novels, giving attention (and a sense of power) to minutely observed physical details and social nuances. The Russian Ivan Turgenev (1818–1883), the English George Eliot (1819–1880), and above all, the French Emile Zola (1840–1902) showed clearly the influence of the scientific revolution inspired by Darwin. Zola sought to arrive at laws of human development, much as the biologist seeks laws of organic development. He called his twenty volumes about a family the "natural history" of a family. Each novel focused on some problem: *La Terre* (The Earth) on the land and peasantry; *L'Assommoir* (The Killer) on alcoholism; *La Débâcle* on the trauma of the war of 1870. Literature was exhibiting a pessimistic strain that has continued ever since.

The pessimists reacted against the eighteenth-century doctrine of the natural goodness of humanity. By the close of the Victorian era, nature apparently had made most people greedy, selfish, combative, and addicted to sexual irregularities. Some writers, like the English novelist Thomas Hardy (1840–1928), built this pessimism from a series of incidents in private lives into a grand, cosmic irony. Hardy's characters were often the victims of coincidence, accident, and other unforeseen circumstances; they could hardly be held responsible for their own misfortunes.

Anton Chekhov (1860–1904) in Russia used the prose drama and the short story to show how life harasses everyone. Henrik Ibsen (1828–1906) in Norway and George Bernard Shaw (1856–1950) in England helped to develop that characteristically late-nineteenth-century form of the drama, the problem play. The problem was sometimes one of wide moral and political concern, as in Ibsen's *Enemy of the People* or Shaw's *Man and Superman*, but it was very often concerned mainly with the stupid tangles of private lives. Ibsen shocked his contemporaries in *A Doll's House* by having the play begin at the point where the usual nineteenth-century drama ended and by permitting his heroine to rebel against the doll-house atmosphere her husband had created for her.

Most of this realistic or naturalistic writing, even when not Marxist inspired, was hostile to the middle class. The bourgeois was the rapacious titan of industry, the authoritarian browbeater of children, the hypocritical practitioner of a double standard of sexual morality. Shaw found a simple phrase to sum up what was wrong—"middle-class morality."

The American poet Walt Whitman (1819–1892) exalted democracy and the common man, employing free verse (which has no regular patterns of rhyme and meter). Whitman was no radical innovator, however, and the common man he celebrated had no trouble understanding his poems. He sang, he said, "of the body electric," and one of his most famous poems was to a locomotive, comparing it to a horse at rest, filled with the energy of the new industrial society.

Painting

In the nineteenth century the painter faced a formidable competitor in depicting the physical realities of nature and life—the photographer. After Louis J. M. Daguerre (1789–1851) made the daguerreotype commercially possible, the science and art of photography developed until, through the work of the American George Eastman (1854–1932), roll film made it feasible for each person to be an artist. Thus painting moved in two directions, either toward the meticulously exact and technically skillful reproduction of scenes in direct competition with the photograph, or toward impressionism as an expression of the artist's inward feelings about the subject.

The rebellion against academic painting, begun by Delacroix, continued in the mid-nineteenth century with the French artists Honoré Daumier (1808–1879) and Gustave Courbet (1819–1877), who also protested

Among the paintings of the *Refusés* was *Le Dejeuner sur l'Herbe* (Picnic Lunch) by Edouard Manet (1832–1883), depicting two fully dressed young men with a nude female companion. The way in which Manet saw reality shocked contemporary opinion because it did not correspond to what the camera saw.

against the values of laissez-faire capitalism and the social mores of the middle class. Daumier exploited to the full the new technological developments that made it possible to mass produce inexpensive copies of his lithographs. With moral indignation and savage bite, Daumier exposed the evils of French society. Courbet upset the academic painters by taking commonplace subjects—wrestlers, stonecutters, nudes who bore no resemblance to classical nymphs—and portraying them without attempting to prettify them. The hostility of the academics reached a peak in 1863, when canvases by followers of Courbet were refused a showing in the annual Paris Salon. The rejected artists countered by organizing their own *Salon des Réfusés*, which gained the backing of Emperor Napoleon III.

That science might encourage as well as impede artistic revolution was evident in the case of the impressionists, whose name was invented by hostile critics after viewing a painting entitled *Impression: Sunrise* by Claude Monet (1840–1926), the leader of the school. The impressionists learned from physics that color was a complex phenomenon put together by the human eye from the prismatic reflections of nature. They proposed to break both light and shadow into their component colors and then allow the viewer's eye to reassemble them. They painted landscapes and seascapes for the most part, using thousands of little dabs of color; the result, when seen from up close, is hardly more than a formless mesh of color, but, when viewed from the proper distance, it is magically transformed into a recognizable scene flooded with light.

Two other qualities augmented the revolutionary impact of impressionist painting. One was the abandonment of traditional conventions of symmetry in favor of an arrangement that put the principal figure well to one side. This technique was employed with telling effect by the Frenchman Edgar Degas (1834–1917) and the American James McNeill Whistler (1834–1903). The other departure was a return to subjects evoking everyday life. Milliners, prostitutes, card players or solitary drinkers in a café, cabaret and circus performers, and ballerinas in rehearsal populate the canvases of Degas, Henri de Toulouse-Lautrec (1864–1901), Auguste Renoir (1841–1919), Vincent Van Gogh (1863–1890), and other masters. Most of these artists are postimpressionists, in that they went beyond impressionism to further experiments. Paul Cézanne (1839–1906) in particular thought impressionism too obsessed with light at the expense of the geometrical and architectural qualities also to be found in nature, and he proposed to restore these qualities with blocks or chunks of color. His was perhaps the single greatest influence in modern painting.

The Other Arts

An age that had mastered the industrial arts so well produced monumental statues, of which the most famous was *Liberty* in New York harbor, the work of the French

Auguste Rodin's *The Thinker*.
The Metropolitan Museum of Art; gift of Thomas F. Ryan, 1910

sculptor Frédéric Bartholdi (1834–1904), a gift from the Third French Republic to the American republic. But the statues of statesmen and warriors that came to adorn public places everywhere in the West were conventionally realistic, designed for formal display to honor the subject rather than the artist. Toward the end of the century the French sculptor Auguste Rodin (1840–1917) began to simplify, strengthen, and, to a degree, exaggerate the contours of men and women, treating subjects with less academic convention and more power. Inexpensive, small-scale copies of the great sculpture of antiquity and of the Renaissance also became common. Museums could all afford large plaster casts of classical works, so some exposure to the great artistic achievements of the past was now possible for a very wide general public. In particular, the middle class saw the museum and art gallery as educational institutions.

In architecture, as in painting and sculpture, true innovation began toward the end of the century. Structural steel freed construction from the limitations that had so taxed the Gothic builders; structures could now go almost as high as architects pleased. Thus the first "skyscrapers" were put up in Chicago in the 1880s. The general tendency imposed by the materials was toward simplicity of line. This taste for simplicity began to spread, and by the twentieth century the way was open for modern "functional" architecture. Often the architect was also an engineer, and perhaps the finest and most

Parisians felt that their city offered the world's most advanced feat of engineering when the massive, soaring tower constructed by Gustave Eiffel opened in 1889. Emphasizing the upward thrust and verticality so characteristic of the Gothic cathedral, this gigantic structure was seen as a symbol of the triumph of science over religion—a secular cathedral by which the eye and spirit of the beholder could ascend to heaven.

Robin W. Winks

aesthetic structures of the industrial societies were the great railway bridges, the complex Brooklyn Bridge begun in 1869 by John Roebling (1806–1869) and not completed until 1883, and the massive work of Gustave Eiffel (1832–1923) in France.

Perhaps the least immediate response to the interests and new technical capacities of the industrial society was to be found in music. Here, too, there was emphasis on monumentality and education—in the founding of many of the great modern symphony orchestras and opera companies, in the creation of touring groups that brought the oratorios of Handel and others to country towns, and in the presence of pianos in thousands of private homes. But in musical taste, most people remained firmly rooted in the era of the romantics.

The most ambitious composer of the age did attempt to break with tradition. Richard Wagner (1813–1883) He called opera "music drama" and set out to make it the supreme synthesis of the arts, with drama, music, costumes, and scenery all fused into one. His characteristic device was the *leitmotif*, a recurring melodic theme associated with a given character or symbolizing an element in the drama. Wagner chose subjects from the Arthurian legends or the heroic epics of medieval Germany. These subjects showed his awareness of the human need for archetypes and myths, the demigods and supermen of the past who still haunt the memory.

The Frenchman Claude Debussy (1862–1918) holds the now-conventional title of founder of modern music. Debussy developed new rhythms, harmonies, and dissonances that were a radical change from conventional composition. In reaction against Wagnerian gigantism, he attempted to convey the subtle, sensuous moods of *The Afternoon of a Faun* or the sounds of the sea (*La Mer*). Debussy's style is often called impressionistic, for he sought to convey the sounds and emotions of a transitory moment, much as the impressionist painters sought to capture its light and color.

This sense of life as transitory, like the colors observed and recorded by the artists, pervaded thought in all its forms by the end of the century. The *fin de siècle*, the last years of the nineteenth century, was marked by materialism and pessimism. Somehow the new and better world promised by the revolutions of 1776 and

1789 and by the remarkable industrial explosion prior to 1850 had not arrived. Even religion, that anchor against a transitory world, was under attack and being replaced by secular messiahs. As the American writer Henry David Thoreau (1817–1862) remarked, people everywhere led lives of quiet desperation. Mental illness and crime seemed on the increase, war was ever more destructive, and the earth's resources were being used too rapidly for replenishment. Fear of environmental catastrophes, while essentially limited to some intellectuals, was already a worm in the bud of late Victorian optimism.

The nineteenth century had been called the "century of hope," for most people throughout the West continued to believe in progress. They continued to believe that what the individual wrote, said, and did would bring positive results, that despite all the pleas of the pessimists for elites, for limiting the expansion of democracy, for inhibiting self-expression in art, literature, or politics, or even for restricting the growth of the industrial society, the future was even yet "big with blessings." In the search for security and stability, humanity had again reminded itself of nature and its own ambivalence.

$\int$ UMMARY

The industrial revolution transformed people's lives in western Europe, the United States, and elsewhere. Most historians agree that from the 1820s to the 1890s industrialization proceeded in four stages mechanization of the textile industry, metals, chemicals, and finally electricity. Each stage led to the next.

Britain held the lead in the early industrial revolution from the 1760s to the 1850s. It had developed an efficient agriculture system, accumulated capital from foreign and colonial trade, had extensive iron and coal deposits, and was favored by geographic compactness.

A series of inventions in the textile industry made rapid expansion possible. Coal benefited from new inventions, while transportation and communications were revolutionized by new devices. Banks assisted economic expansion by issuing bank notes in place of coins. Companies limited shareholders' liability, reducing the risk of investment.

After 1850 Britain began to lose its advantages. Its rate of growth decreased, and the lead passed to the United States and Germany by the end of the century.

A major feature of the nineteenth century was rapid population expansion. Controversy surrounds the theories that have been advanced to explain this rapid expansion. Another controversy concerns improvement in the standard of living. That towns and cities grew, however, is true. Moreover, mortality rates in Europe declined after 1850.

During the nineteenth century the middle class in western Europe won political power. Workers struggled for the right to vote and the right to organize and strike. Economic cycles during the industrial revolution caused hardships for workers. Gradually real wages, especially for skilled workers, rose; however, the threat of unemployment remained. Women and children were drawn into the work force. Basic food prices declined, but work places were dangerous, unhealthy places.

In response to the social and economic problems caused by the industrial revolution, classical economists formulated natural laws based on laissez-faire doctrines. Malthus warned of the dangers of overpopulation.

Ricardo and his disciples formulated the Iron Law of Wages that condemned workers to cycles of high wages and large families followed by lower wages and decreasing birth rate.

The utilitarian Jeremy Bentham supported laissez faire but saw some instances where the state might step in to ensure the greatest good for the greatest number. The human liberalism of John Stuart Mill led him to modify his laissez-faire belief and demand that the state protect workers and improve working conditions.

Socialists advocated that the means of production be in the hands of society rather than in those of private individuals. Inspired by Enlightenment ideas, Utopian socialists applied reason to the problems of industrial society and thought that utopia was within reach.

Marx transformed socialism into revolutionary communism, forecasting a violent uprising of the proletariat. In January 1848 Marx and Engels published *The Communist Manifesto*, the classical statement of Marxian socialism that presented the communist view of history. Others responded to the new industrial society by advocating mercantilist ideas, anarchy and violence, or a return to primitive Christianity.

A new age of science produced revolutionary theories in physics and biology. In 1859 publication of Darwin's *The Origin of Species* touched off controversy because his theories challenged orthodox Christian teachings based on the Bible. Social Darwinists transferred ideas of biology to society and human relations. Social Darwinism was used to justify the nationalism and racism of the late nineteenth century.

The late nineteenth century was the age of the novel in literature. Writers depicted the problems and triumphs of the industrial society. Photography and lithography made mass-produced works of art widely available. Painters turned to realism, portraying what they saw. Led by Claude Monet, impressionists developed new techniques that allowed viewers to reassemble light and color. The major innovation in architecture was the use of steel in the building of skyscrapers.

CRITICAL THINKING

1. Why was Great Britain the first society to experience the industrial revolution?

2. Describe the basic stages of industrial growth.

3. How did the industrial revolution influence population and the standard of living?

4. What are the basic tenets of the concept of class warfare? Who espoused this argument and developed it into an economic and political doctrine? How?

5. How did the classical economists, utilitarians, and humanitarian liberals respond to such arguments?

6. What was the link between the Utopians and the development of Marxism?

7. How did the anarchists justify a turn toward violence to achieve social change? What counterarguments were offered to the anarchist call for violence?

8. What is racism and how did it express itself in social, economic, or political policy?

9. What is the difference between Darwinism and Social Darwinism? What arguments can be offered against either? What was the relationship between Darwinism and positivism?

10. How did the industrial revolution influence literature and the arts?

CHAPTER 21

The Modernization of Nations

I

N RECENT YEARS HISTORIANS HAVE often asked whether the best unit for study is a society or a nation, since many questions relating broadly to demography and society cannot be properly addressed within a single nation's borders. But because nationalism was triumphant in western Europe between 1848 and 1914, the nation as a unit of study appears to make particular sense for this period. As humanity sought to define a sense of security, as it identified that security with a particular nation, church, ideology, economic doctrine, or tribe, both *cooperation*—that is, a bringing together of once-diverse groups into ever larger and self-consciously identified groups—and *competition* among these groups became more intense.

Meliorism, the term for the belief that the world could be improved by human effort, gave a special dynamism to nationalism, imperialism, socialism, communism, and democracy. At the same time, movements and dangers (such as famine) that once affected only a relatively specific place became generalized, in the sense that falling cash crop prices in West Africa, depletion of oil production in the Middle East, or major technological innovations in Japan could have rapid repercussions in Europe and North America. Technology in the nineteenth and twentieth centuries would alter the world radically, so that within a decade a person might experience more change than an earlier civilization had seen in a century.

Perhaps the most symbolically significant nineteenth-century scientist was Charles Babbage (1792–1871), an English mathematician and inventor. Babbage invented the digital computer, which in the twentieth century made it possible for human beings to travel in outer space, for governments to amass vast statistics for new social purposes, and for armies to destroy each other though separated by thousands of miles. Often the most significant events are not obvious at the time they occur, and the most telling generalizations must often wait a century or more to become evident. In the nineteenth century societies often measured their sense of progress by the growth of literacy; in the latter part of the twentieth century the parallel of the literate reader is the numerate reader who can understand the "language" of computers.

France: A Second Empire, A Third Republic

Sometime between 1850 and the outbreak of World War I in 1914, rural France joined urban France in expressing a common sense of identity—nationhood. By the end of the century popular and elite cultures were united in their sense of *patrie* (fatherland), of nationality, even when they continued to disagree over the nation's goals. The modernization of France at times set one French group against another; equally often, as external forces appeared to threaten France, it strengthened the sense of common identity and community.

The basic argument of Karl Marx, that class is best understood in terms of its relation to the mode of production, was increasingly accepted by various economic theorists; however, those who looked first to social or political realities found that class was better understood in the context of its historical time and its social friction with other contemporary classes. According to Marxism, the middle class was not just middle in the economic spectrum, but middle in sequence—arising out of feudalism and followed by industrial working-class triumphs. Others saw the middle class as the principal impetus for historical change. French culture had been a peasant culture overlaid by a Parisian veneer of great urbanity and sophistication; by 1914 the peasant was on the verge of what the historian would call modernity. This modernization changed the forms of collective action—and thus of collective violence—that had marked the French Revolution.

France's democratic revolution, so optimistically begun in 1848, had by 1852 brought still another Bonaparte to the throne: Napoleon III (1808–1873), nephew of the first Napoleon. As president of the Second Republic, "Prince" Louis Napoleon soon quarreled with the National Assembly elected in 1849, in which monarchist sentiment greatly outweighed Bonapartism. The Assembly refused to amend the constitution of 1848 to allow him a second four-year term. Fearful of radicals and socialists, the Assembly also compromised the universal male suffrage of 1848, depriving about 3 million French men of the vote—an act that enabled the prince-president to denounce the move and act as the champion of democracy.

A Second Empire, 1851–1870

The coup d'état of December 2, 1851, was skillfully timed to coincide with the anniversaries of the coronation of Napoleon I and the greatest Napoleonic victory, Austerlitz. In control of the army and the police, Louis Napoleon and his supporters arrested seventy-eight noted anti-Bonapartists. Street fighting in Paris ended with hundreds of casualties, mainly bystanders fired upon by panicky soldiers. It gave Louis Napoleon the chance to act as the champion of order against armed insurrection. He strengthened his position by massive arrests, which ultimately sent twenty thousand to prison or into exile.

Napoleon restored universal male suffrage for a plebiscite; by 7.5 million votes to 640,000 it gave him the right to draw up a new constitution. The plebiscite was accompanied by skillful propaganda. Many opponents of Napoleon simply did not vote, and a substantial majority of French men over twenty-one were apparently willing to accept authoritarian rule rather than face renewed upheaval. For nearly three decades the full force of fashionable French literature had been at work embellishing the Napoleonic legend and identifying the name of Napoleon with an elite French patriotism. Many voted yes, not to Louis Napoleon, nor to any approval of dictatorship in the abstract, but to the music of the "Marseillaise," the cannon of Austerlitz, the growing cult of Joan of Arc—to all the intangible glories of France.

In 1852 another plebiscite authorized Louis Napoleon to assume the title of emperor and to inaugurate the Second Empire, which he did on December 2. The new constitution sponsored by the two plebiscites set up a lightly veiled dictatorship very much like that of Napoleon I. The emperor, who was responsible only to "the nation," governed through ministers, judges, and bureaucrats—whom he appointed. The popularly elected assembly, the Corps Législatif, was filled with candidates whose success at the polls was assured by the pressure of the emperor's loyal prefects. The Assembly had little power to initiate or amend legislation.

Urban France still bears the stamp of the Second Empire, especially in Paris, where the emperor's prefect, Georges-Eugène Haussmann (1809–1891) cut broad straight avenues with splendid vistas through the medieval maze of streets. The Second Empire also helped with housing and encouraged workers' mutual aid societies. Still, the legal protection of labor in the France of 1860 was less generous than that of Britain, and the standard of living of the working class in French cities remained below that in Britain, Germany, and the smaller European democracies. Although French labor benefited from the general prosperity of the 1850s, the gains in wages were partly offset by rising prices, and by 1868 demonstrations and strikes, once again legal, were commonplace.

The bourgeoisie may have gained the most from the Second Empire, assisted as it was by capital supplied through the government-sponsored Crédit Foncier and Crédit Mobilier. Napoleon's government also encouraged improvements in banking facilities, helped the rapid extension of French railways by state guaranties, and in general furthered the rise of industry. Yet many of the French remained loyal to older methods of doing business, to small firms under family control, to luxury trades in which handicraft skills remained important despite the machine. The industrial growth of France in most heavy industries was somewhat slower than that of the leading economic powers; in the 1860s France was losing its

In 1887 a French civil engineer proposed the first Paris underground railway, or Métro, to carry traffic beneath the clogged streets. After a proposed elevated line, as in New York City, was rejected as unaesthetic, the builders of the Métro had to solve the complex problems of underground ventilation and illumination. In 1892 the Paris Municipal Council approved their scheme. Rejecting the London system in which tubes were run far below the surface, the Paris Métro authority built close to ground level. Construction began in October 1898, and two thousand workers labored day and night to have the system ready for the Paris Exposition of 1900.

Archives Editions. Robert Laffont, Paris

Continental leadership in iron and steel production to Germany and ultimately was far outdistanced by the burgeoning economy of the new United States.

The French rate of population growth also lagged between 1840 and the 1880s, and an exodus to the cities from impoverished rural departments accelerated under the Second Empire. At the end of the nineteenth century France was not much more than 50 percent more populous than at the beginning, in great part because of a steep decline in birth rate. Britain, despite considerable outward migration to its empire, had about tripled its population, and Germany, too, was growing rapidly. Though the reasons for French demographic changes are imperfectly understood, one major factor in a country of many small proprietors appears to have been the determination to avoid the division of already modest inheritances among many heirs. This meant that methods of birth control spread quickly. Late marriage, the practice of birth control by *coitus interruptus*, and continuing high levels of infant mortality, were also features of the French demographic pattern until the 1890s.

Despite demographic weakness, the France of the Second Empire was still a great power. Although the French gained little from the Crimean War, they had the satisfaction of playing host to the postwar congress at Paris in 1856. And the Paris Exposition of 1855 was an international success that showed Napoleon III at the height of his diplomatic powers. In 1859 he joined Piedmont in a war against Austria for the liberation of Italy. French armies won victories at Magenta and Solferino, but the defeated Austrians refused to yield. Fearful that Prussia might come to Austria's assistance, Napoleon III suddenly made a

separate peace with Austria, which agreed to relinquish Lombardy, but not Venetia, to Piedmont.

In 1860 the Italians set about organizing most of the peninsula, including papal Rome, into a single kingdom. Napoleon depended too much on Catholic support at home to permit the extinction of papal territorial power; he therefore permitted the union of most of Italy under the house of Savoy, but he protected the pope's temporal power with a French garrison in Rome and left Venetia in Austrian hands. In 1860 he received from Piedmont the French-speaking part of Alpine Savoy plus the Mediterranean city of Nice and its hinterland. In the end Napoleon III had offended most Italians, Austria and Prussia, liberals everywhere, and most of his Catholic supporters at home.

To make matters worse, in 1861 Napoleon used the Mexican government's default on payments of its foreign debt as the pretext for what proved to be a foolish imperialist venture. A French expedition installed the Austrian archduke Maximilian as emperor of Mexico, and French arms and men continued to assist him. The Europeanized Mexican upper classes were in part willing to support this venture, but from the start most other Mexicans resented foreign intruders, and Maximilian had to rely heavily on French support to reach Mexico City, where he was formally proclaimed emperor in June 1863. The United States, preoccupied by a crippling civil war, could do nothing at the time against what Americans regarded as an infraction of the Monroe Doctrine. But after peace had been restored in the United States, the American government protested strongly. The able Mexican republican leader Benito Juárez (1806–1872) had no difficulty in prevailing, especially after American pressure forced Napoleon to abandon Maximilian and his Mexican supporters. Maximilian fell before a firing squad in 1867.

By this time Napoleon realized that he could not function as a dictator-emperor in France. He could not be a republican. Nor could he act as a legitimized monarchist, for much of conservative France was loyal to the Bourbons or to the house of Orléans. He could only head an "official" party, relying on the manipulative skills of his bureaucrats to work the cumbersome machinery of a parliamentary system originally designed as a disguise for authoritarian rule.

Napoleon slowly abandoned the repressive measures with which he had begun. An act of 1860 gave the assembly power to discuss freely a reply to an address from the throne, and from 1867 to 1870 these powers were extended. Gradually, political life in France began to assume the pattern of a parliamentary or deliberative government, with parties of the right, center, and left. After the general election of 1869, the government faced a strong legal opposition, many of whom declared themselves to be republicans. On July 12 Napoleon granted the assembly the right to propose laws and to criticize and vote on the budget. A plebiscite in May 1870 overwhelmingly ratified these changes.

The Third Republic, 1870–1914

The Second Empire might have converted into a constitutional monarchy with full parliamentary government. Yet the changes had been wrung from an ailing and vacillating emperor by frequent popular agitation. It is also possible that a radical republican groundswell would have submerged the empire in any case. But a Franco-Prussian War put an abrupt end to the experiments of the Liberal Empire. Sluggish mobilization and French overconfidence, together with Prussian superiority in arms, gave the Prussians a decisive head start. Within only six weeks Napoleon III and a large French army capitulated humiliatingly at Sedan. Two days later rioting Parisians forced the remnant of the assembly to decree the end of the empire, and a Third Republic was proclaimed. Napoleon III went into captivity in Germany and then into exile in England, where he died in 1873.

The new republic tried to continue the war with Prussia, but within a month a second large French force surrendered at Metz. Meanwhile Paris, besieged by the German forces, had resisted desperately, the citizens killing even the zoo animals for food, until starvation brought surrender in January. Even under pressure of the siege, Paris radicals tried to seize power and revive the old Paris Commune, or city government, of 1792. These radicals could not accept the capitulation for which the rest of the country seemed to be preparing. In the elections to the National Assembly their stubbornness helped to turn provincial voters toward more conservative candidates who were pledged not only to make peace but to restore the old monarchy.

In February 1871 an exhausted nation elected a National Assembly that met at Bourdeaux and sued for peace. On March 1, the new Assembly voted to accept a peace ceding Alsace and part of Lorraine to Germany and paying an indemnity of 5 billion francs. The Paris National Guard thereupon went over to the radicals because the National Assembly had suspended its pay. The Assembly and the provisional government it had set up under Adolphe Thiers sent troops into Paris in a vain attempt to seize National Guard artillery. Thiers and the Assembly established themselves in Versailles, while in Paris the Commune took over the functions of government.

Most of the communards were Jacobins who wanted a democratic society of small independent shopkeepers and artisans, not the abolition of private property. Although some communards were affiliated with the First International, most of these were followers of Proudhon rather than of Marx. Other communards were followers of Auguste Blanqui, the aged champion of revolutionary violence who was arrested in the provinces before he could reach Paris.

In the Bloody Week of May 21–28 troops of the National Assembly advanced through the barricades to clear the city; twenty thousand died in the fighting. The Third Republic, born in the trauma of defeat and civil war, at once came into a heritage of strife. From 1871 to 1879 French politics seesawed between the left and right. Most members of the new National Assembly were monarchists. About half the monarchist deputies were pledged to the elder legitimate Bourbon line represented by the count of Chambord, who was childless. The other half supported the younger Orléanist line, represented by the count of Paris, grandson of Louis Philippe. Although Chambord agreed to designate the count of Paris as the eventual heir to the throne, he stubbornly refused to accept the revolutionary blue, white, and red tricolor flag that Louis Philippe had himself accepted as the flag of France, demanding instead the white flag and gold lilies of Bourbon, which for millions meant complete repudiation of all that had happened since 1789.

Political stalemate followed the emotional debates over the symbols of legitimacy, monarchy, and France; in the resulting impasse the republican minority was able to gather strength. Thiers, recognized as "President of the Republic," carried through the final settlement with Germany. In 1873, however, he lost a vote of confidence in the Assembly and was succeeded by Marshal MacMahon (1808–1893), a soldier and a monarchist who was chosen to hold the government together until the monarchist majority of the Assembly could work out a compromise between its wings. The compromise was never achieved, as Chambord continued to insist on the white flag. Ultimately, Thiers's strategy worked, and in 1875 enough Orléanists joined with the republicans for the Assembly to pass a series of constitutional measures formally establishing the Third Republic, with MacMahon as president.

These laws, known collectively as the constitution of 1875, provided for a president elected by an absolute majority of Senate and Chamber of Deputies sitting together as a National Assembly. The Chamber of Deputies was elected by universal male suffrage; the Senate was

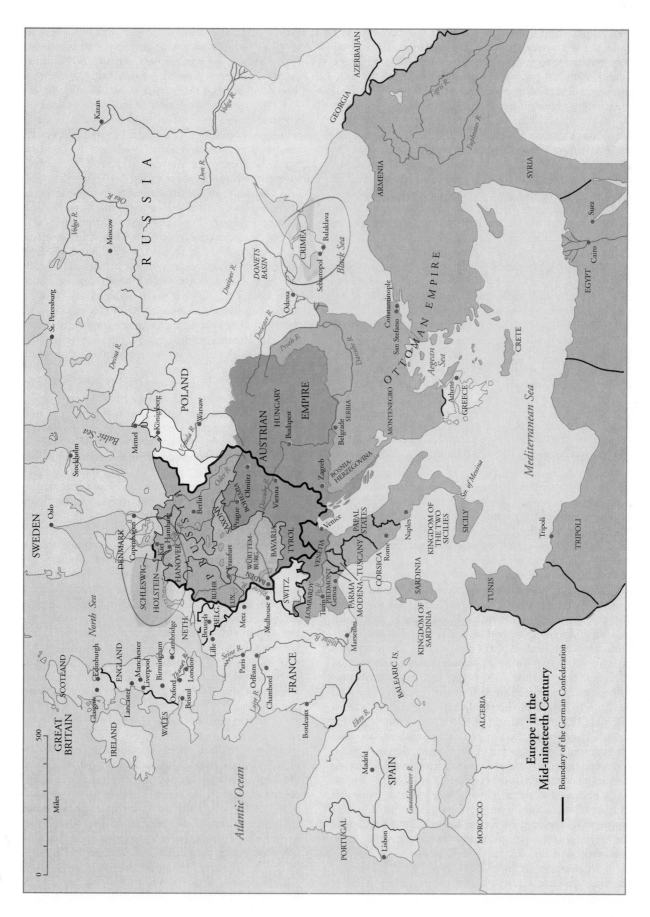

Europe in the Mid-nineteenth Century

— Boundary of the German Confederation

chosen, one third at any given time, by elected members of local governmental bodies. All legislation had to pass both houses, though only the lower could initiate finance bills. The critical point was the responsibility of the ministers, which was not spelled out in the laws of 1875. Had the president been able to dismiss them, a new Napoleon III might easily have arisen to destroy the republic. MacMahon attempted to exercise this power on May 16, 1877, when he dismissed an anticlerical premier. But the Chamber was now antimonarchist and voted no confidence in MacMahon's new premier; MacMahon then dissolved the Chamber and called for a new national election. In the election the republicans retained a majority in the Chamber and could have forced the president to name a republican premier. Disgruntled, MacMahon resigned in 1879 and was succeeded by a conservative republican, and the presidency became a largely ceremonial office.

The Third Republic was a republican constitutional monarchy, with an ornamental president instead of an ornamental king. The real executive was the ministry, which was in effect a committee responsible to the Chamber of Deputies. The latter soon became the focus of political action, leaving the Senate little real power. The Chamber was composed of a dozen or more parties, so that any ministry had to be supported by a coalition subject to constant shifting of personalities and principles.

The day-to-day task of governing was carried on by a civil service. This permanent bureaucracy, subject only to broad policy control from above, preserved the basic continuity in French political action. Functionally, the system was highly democratic, for it could work only through constant and subtle compromise arrived at by the several parties in open debate and voting in the legislature *after* an election.

Bitter antagonisms continued to threaten the Third Republic between 1879 and 1914, but they did not destroy it. On the right, many in the church, the army, and among the wealthy still hoped for government by a single strong man, but they remained divided over the extent of their monarchism. The political left was also divided, between pro- and anti-Marxist socialists, anarchists, and syndicalists. After the accession of Pope Leo XIII in 1878 the Catholics were gradually encouraged to accept the freedom of worship that the constitution of the republic offered them. But many Catholics feared the anticlericalism of the republicans, particularly after a law of 1882 made education free and compulsory for French children to the age of thirteen and forbade religious instruction in public schools. Party fragmentation remained intense, and sodalities, religious associations, semisecret lodges, and other forms of voluntary associations became the focus of both political and social life outside of Paris. Slowly but decisively, communal groups began to be replaced by formal organizations that spoke for special-interest groups, especially for segments of the industrial working class.

In the late 1880s those who feared this shifting, growing fragmentation turned to General George Boulanger (1837–1891) in the hope that he might unite France under authoritarian leadership. Boulanger was an ambitious soldier who had, as minister of war, catered to French desires for revenge on Germany. But as it became clear that if given power he might rush the country into war, his following threatened to desert him. In January 1889 he swept a by-election in Paris, but instead of seizing power by force of arms, he waited to see if his followers would act. The Chamber of Deputies threatened to try him for treason; Boulanger fled to Brussels, where he committed suicide in 1891. The republic had surmounted its first great crisis.

But three major scandals next confronted the republic. The president's son-in-law was implicated in the selling of posts in the Legion of Honor. More fuel was added to the fire in the early 1890s with the Panama scandal, brought on by the failure of Ferdinand de Lesseps's attempt to duplicate in Panama his success in building the Suez Canal. Ministers and deputies had accepted bribes for backing the shaky Panama company. Anti-Semitic propagandists were able to make much of the fact that several Jewish financiers were implicated. Bad as it was, the Panama scandal was to pale before the Dreyfus affair, in which the force of modern anti-Semitism first attained worldwide attention.

Captain Alfred Dreyfus (1859–1935), a Jew from a wealthy family that had fled to France when Alsace was lost to Germany, was the almost accidental victim of an espionage intrigue and of the anti-Semitism then prevalent in France. Accused of selling military secrets to the Germans, he was railroaded to trial as a scapegoat because he was the first Jew to serve on the French general staff. He was convicted of treason in 1894 and sentenced to life imprisonment on Devil's Island. In 1896 Colonel Georges Picquart (1854–1914), an intelligence officer, became convinced that the document on which Dreyfus had been convicted was a forgery and that the real traitor was a disreputable adventurer, Major Ferdinand Esterhazy (1849–1923). Picquart was quietly shipped off to Africa by his superiors, but the Dreyfus family, by independent investigation, arrived at the conclusion that Esterhazy was the traitor and sought to reopen the case. Esterhazy was tried and acquitted, but the affair was now too public for such silencing. In 1898 the famous novelist Emile Zola brought matters to a crisis by publishing his open letter *J'Accuse*. Zola accused the military leaders, one by one, of deliberately sacrificing an innocent man to save the reputation of the army.

France was now divided into Dreyfusards and anti-Dreyfusards. Dreyfus was retried in the midst of a frenzied campaign in the press. The military court, faced with new evidence brought out by the suicide of the forger of the most incriminating of the original documents used to convict Dreyfus, nonetheless again found Dreyfus guilty of treason. However, Dreyfus was then pardoned by the president of the republic, and in 1906, after the tensions had abated, he was acquitted by a civilian court and restored to the army with the rank of major.

The Dreyfus affair divided France as the Paris Commune had done in 1871. But the years of debate brought radicals, socialists, liberals, republicans, anticlericals, and intellectuals—all who were suspicious of the army, of the church, and of anti-Semitism—into a loose alliance. Many on both sides of the question worked themselves into a mass hysteria in which the question of Dreyfus's guilt was wholly submerged in the confrontation between the "two Frances"—the France of the republic, heir to the great revolution and the principles of 1789, and the France of the monarchy, of throne and altar, and of the army, which had never reconciled itself to the great revolution.

With the victory of the Dreyfusards, the republic punished the church for supporting the army and the anti-Dreyfusards. In a series of measures between 1901 and 1905 the triumphant republicans destroyed the Concordat of 1801 between Napoleon I and the pope that had established the Roman Catholic church in a privileged position in the French state. Catholic teaching orders were forced to dissolve, and some twelve thousand Catholic schools were closed. The state would no longer pay the clergy, and private corporations organized by the faithful would take over the expenses of worship and the ownership and maintenance of the churches. But Catholicism was not outlawed. Catholic education, while severely handicapped, was not formally persecuted. Indeed, the separation did not radically alter the fundamental social position of the church in France: The upper classes and the peasantry of the north, northeast, and west remained for the most part loyal Catholics; many of the urban middle and working classes and many peasants in parts of the south, southwest, and center remained indifferent Catholics or determined secularists.

The Third Republic had become more republican without moving noticeably toward the welfare state. This was hardly surprising in a country that remained essentially a land of small farm-owning peasants, conservative in their agricultural methods, and of relatively small family-controlled industries, conservative in their business methods. French business owners preferred internal financing because they wished to maintain their independence, either because the firm was part of family property or because they preferred substantial emergency reserves to meet sudden drops in the market or unexpected technological changes, mostly from outside France.

For many in France, life improved during the second half of the nineteenth century, though at the cost of vast dislocation for others. In the growing cities a wandering population, sometimes turning to crime or to organized violence, contended with the migration of the law-abiding poor, who sought greater security in areas of new industrial growth or in the new labor organizations. The transportation system could not always cope with these shifts in population, so that resources were scarce in various regions at different times, enhancing a common sense of social identity among the activist and the angry. Increasingly, women became part of the working class, sharing its grievances and its growth, though the only jobs open to them were those that demanded the least skills and were therefore the lowest paid. By the second half of the century women would be found in metal foundries, bleaching mills, potteries, and brickyards, and at the mouths of coal pits and stone

quaries. However, most women working outside of agriculture were in the textile industry, the garment industry, or domestic service.

The upper and middle classes ate and lived well, though the petty bourgeois found that inflation often forced economies on them, and wives became increasingly expert at specialized shopping and cooking. "Secondhand" foods became commonplace—foods that had been prepared and served to one family, with the remainder, often decayed, sold to a poorer family. There was an especially brisk trade in Paris in such leftovers, as population growth moved too rapidly for economic adjustments to provide, or transport to supply, sufficient staples. Historians have estimated that of the 1.2 million Parisians in the Second Empire, perhaps 400,000 ate sufficient and healthy food, while the rest ate poorly, or consumed decaying and rotten food, adding to the growing problems of public health. Throughout the nineteenth century the policing of food and water supplies was a subject of middle-class concern. The women working in a textile factory—exposed to dangerous machinery, laboring for fifteen to eighteen hours without sanitary facilities (there were no public or workplace toilets), subjected to chemicals and fibers that brought on brown lung and early death—could hope for little more than food that was, at the least, "ripe." And yet French men and women were devoted to the fatherland, *la patrie*. Their growing sense of nationalism led to an increasing assumption that public authorities must deal with such matters as health, transport, and safety.

ITALY AND UNION, 1849–1914

Italian national unity seemed remote after Piedmont's two decisive defeats by Austria in 1848 and 1849, yet it was accomplished by 1870. The three leaders of the Risorgimento in its years of triumph were the romantic nationalist adventurer Giuseppe Garibaldi (1807–1882); Victor Emmanuel II of the house of Savoy (1849–1878), king of Piedmont-Sardinia (and later of a united Italy); and, above all, Victor Emmanuel's chief minister, Count Camillo Cavour (1810–1861). Though of aristocratic origin and trained for the army, Cavour enthusiastically supported the economic revolutions and the aspirations of the business classes. He applied the newest agricultural methods to his family estates and promoted the introduction of steamboats, railroads, industries, and banks to prepare Piedmont for leadership in a unified Italy.

Cavour and Garibaldi

Cavour was a superlatively adept practitioner of the brand of diplomacy often called *Realpolitik*, or the politics of realism and power. As chief minister of Piedmont, he cultivated French and English support, bringing Piedmont

THE WRITTEN RECORD

Eating Well in the Nineteenth Century

In June 1867, the Dinner of the Three Emperors brought together Alexander II, czar of Russia, the czarevich (the future Alexander III), and the future emperor William I (then king of Prussia) at the Café Anglais in Paris to dine most royally, as the menu indicates. Guests had a choice of soups and could substitute fritters of beef brain steeped in Seville orange juice for one of the main courses. Otherwise all foods and wines were served to everyone.

Soups

Impératrice   Fontanges

Intermediate Course

Soufflé à la Reine   Collops of turbot au gratin
Fillet of sole Venetian   Saddle of mutton with purée bretonne

Main Course

Chicken à la portugaise   Lobster à la parisienne
Hot quail paté   Champagne sherbets

Roast Course

Duckling á la rouennaise   Canapés of bunting [a small bird]

Final Course

Aubergines á l'espagnole   Cassolettes princesse
Asparagus   Cheese
Iced bombe   Fruit

Wines

Madeira 1846   Château-Margaux 1847
Sherry 1821   Château-Latour 1847
Château-Yquem 1847   Château-Lafite 1848
Chambertin 1846

Adapted from Prosper Montagne, *Larousse Gastronomique* (New York: Crown Publishers, 1961), p. 619. Copyright © 1961 Crown Publishers, Inc; © Librairie Larousse Paris; English text © The Hamlyn Publishing Group Limited. Reprinted by permission of The Hamlyn Publishing Group Limited and Crown Publishers, Inc.

into the Crimean War on their side against Russia. He received no immediate reward, but he finally persuaded Napolean III that the Austrian hold in northern Italy was a denial of the principle of nationality. Thus in 1859 France and Piedmont went to war with Austria. Meantime, sympathetic nationalistic uprisings in Tuscany and the Papal States seemed likely to bring about their merger into an expanding Piedmont. Dismayed by this prospect and by possible Prussian intervention on Austria's behalf, Napoleon III backed out of the war. At a conference with

Francis Joseph, the Austrian emperor, at Villafranca in July 1859, Napoleon arranged his compromise whereby Lombardy was to go to Piedmont, Venetia was to remain Austrian, and the old arrangements were to be restored in the other states. Cavour resigned in bitter protest.

He had, however, already won. The wave of popular agitation rose higher in northern and central Italy; in Parma, Modena, Tuscany, and the Romagna (the most northerly province of the Papal States) bloodless revolutions and plebiscites demanded annexation to Piedmont.

Giuseppe Garibaldi was frequently shown on horseback or in a horse-drawn carriage, leading the "war for Italian independence" to the applause of the multitudes. Here he is seen triumphantly entering Naples on September 7, 1860.

Scala/Art Resource

Early in 1860 Cavour returned to office to manage the annexations and also to pay off Napoleon III by ceding Savoy and Nice to France. He turned next to the rapidly developing situation in the Papal States and the south. In May an expedition outfitted in Piedmontese ports, but not formally acknowledged by Cavour's government, set out for Naples and Sicily under Garibaldi.

A republican as well as a nationalist agitator, Garibaldi had defended Mazzini's Roman Republic against a French siege. Cavour deeply distrusted Garibaldi, who he feared might make Italy a republic and so alarm the powers that they would intervene to undo Cavour's own achievements. Cavour therefore sought to control Garibaldi's expedition and exploit its success in the interests of his own policy.

Garibaldi and his thousand Red Shirts had relatively little trouble in overcoming the feeble opposition of the Bourbon king in Sicily. Recruits swarmed to his flag. Garibaldi, who had announced his loyalty to Victor Emmanuel, crossed the Straits of Messina to continue his victorious march on the mainland territories of Naples. He had the support of the British prime minister, with the implication that British naval forces might act to block outside intervention against his movement. Cavour, alarmed lest Garibaldi bring on a new crisis by marching north to take Rome from the pope and offend France and other Catholic powers, sent Piedmontese troops to occupy all the remaining papal territories except Rome and its environs. King Victor Emmanuel soon joined forces with Garibaldi near Naples and assured the triumph of Cavour's policy. In the autumn of 1860 Sicily, Naples, and the papal domains of Umbria and the Marches voted for union with Piedmont.

The result was the proclamation in March 1861 of the kingdom of Italy—essentially a much enlarged Piedmont-Sardinia, but with Florence as its capital and Victor Emmanuel as its monarch. Territorially, the work of the Risorgimento was almost complete. Only two more major areas were needed—Austrian Venetia and Papal Rome. Venetia came as a reward for Italy's siding with Prussia in the brief war of 1866 in which Prussia defeated Austria; Rome came when the Franco-Prussian War forced Napoleon III to withdraw from papal territory. On October 2, 1870, Rome was annexed to the kingdom of Italy and became its capital.

Assets and Liabilities of a United Italy

The new kingdom started out with the asset of favorable public opinion. Italian national unity seemed natural and desirable, and it had been achieved with little bloodshed through a mixture of Garibaldian romance and Cavourian realism. The enthusiasm that had brought the Risorgimento to fruition was now in the service of a united Italy.

Yet striking liabilities also impeded the new Italy. The Italians, like the French, were divided between Catholics and anticlericals. Ardent Catholics were deeply embittered by the annexation of the Papal States without papal consent. Italy lacked coal and iron; in terms of modern economic competition, Italy was a "have-not" country. Much of mountainous central Italy and all southern Italy were marginally productive, with a poverty-stricken, illiterate peasantry and a small but tenacious feudal aristocracy. Neapolitans and Sicilians resented the new political preponderance of northern Italians in the unified kingdom. At least half of Italy lacked experience in self-government. It was also a land of deep-seated class antagonisms, profound mistrust of governments, and fervent localism.

Consequently, united Italy moved very cautiously toward greater democracy. Its constitution remained that granted to Piedmont in 1848 by Charles Albert; it put effective checks on the power of the king by making the ministers responsible to the Chamber of Deputies, but it also put severe limitations on the suffrage. After 1881 the property qualification was lowered to the payment of a relatively modest direct tax, but it was not until 1912 that something close to universal male suffrage was introduced.

1870

The pope, who refused to accept the legality of the new kingdom, stayed in the Vatican palace as a "prisoner." The Vatican remained the center of the worldwide organization of the Roman Catholic church, and in no important sense was the pope impeded in the exercise of his powers over the faithful throughout the world. Within Italy, the church forbade Catholics to participate in politics and urged a Catholic boycott of the new state. Gradually, Catholics did take an increasing part in politics, but the "Roman question" remained unsettled until 1929, when Benito Mussolini and Pope Pius XI agreed to set up Vatican City as a tiny sovereign state of 108 acres.

The new kingdom did make appreciable economic progress, however. Railroads built and managed by the state pushed rapidly into the backward south. A new merchant marine and an army and navy gave Italy some standing as a power. Even the national finances seemed for a time to be sound. In politics the 1880s saw the growth of parliamentary corruption and the beginning of a long era of unashamed political opportunism. Meantime, the industrial proletariat was small, labor poorly organized, and the socialists both too few and too divided to be an effective instrument of opposition and reform. Moreover, the economic progress of the north, achieved in part at the expense of a south both exploited and neglected, increased regional differentiation.

Finally, in the 1880s and 1890s, Italy developed imperial aspirations. Since France and Britain had empires, and since a great power had to have "a place in the sun," some way of territorial expansion had to be found if Italy was to be taken seriously as a "great power." Economic explanations of this imperialist drive make little sense. True, Italy had a rapidly expanding population that found relatively few economic opportunities at home, especially in the south. But since other countries had a head start in empire building, very little was left for the Italians. Nonetheless, Italy acquired two of the poorer parts of Africa in the late nineteenth century: Eritrea on the Red Sea, and Somaliland on the "horn" of Africa where the Red Sea meets the Indian Ocean.

Next Italy attempted to conquer the independent highland empire of Ethiopia (then known as Abyssinia). The Abyssinian War drained the resources of the Italian government and was abruptly ended by the disastrous defeat of the Italian expedition by a larger Ethiopian army at Adowa in 1896. The disaster at Adowa cast a shadow over Italy that has been compared to that cast over France by the Dreyfus case. The shadow was deepened by a bank scandal and by the general depression of the 1890s. Severe bread riots broke out in Milan in May 1898. In 1900 King Humbert I, who had succeeded Victor Emmanuel II in 1878, was assassinated by an anarchist. The accession of a new king, Victor Emmanuel III (r. 1900–1946), who was believed to have liberal leanings, gave heart to many, and the years just before World War I were years of comparative quiet, prosperity, and partial reconciliation with the church. And in 1890–1914 a vast emigration to North and South America almost canceled out the serious economic difficulties attendant on a high birth rate and the lack of new industrial employment.

Yet frustrated Italian imperialism was still seeking an outlet. Denied Tunisia by French occupation in 1881 and then forced out of Ethiopia, Italy finally got from the great powers a free hand in poverty-stricken and parched Tripoli, a fragment of the old Ottoman Empire in North Africa, later to be known as Libya. In 1911 Italy went to war with Turkey for Libya.

The industrial growth of Europe, which had begun in Britain, spread to the Continent after 1880, but Italy presented a pattern of substantial industrialization in some areas and continued sluggishness in others. Italy remained on the margin of the industrializing process that was so rapidly transforming Germany, partly for economic reasons but partly because of a growing preoccupation with winning an overseas empire. The gap widened between the northern industrial triangle of Genoa, Milan, and Turin and the south. By 1900 the south (which constituted 41 percent of Italian land) had only 17 percent of the industrial workers; it had 26 percent of the population and only 12 percent of the taxable property. The south was unable to supply a market for northern Italian goods, while the north could not find work for all its surplus labor. The result was a widespread emigration exceeded in Europe only by that of the Irish.

Demographic and economic factors left Italy divided internally along geographic and class lines. The political left advocated further social reforms to achieve social justice and political equality, but accomplished relatively little because of internal dissension. The remnants of the left wing of the Risorgimento split into largely non-Marxist factions, and no successful reform party emerged from the middle class. Italian parliamentary government remained weak, Italian class structure militated against the development of effective multiple parties, and political debate increasingly appeared to be shaped by intellectuals who purported to speak either for a ruling elite or the Italian masses.

GERMANY, THE NATION-STATE

The creation of a united imperial Germany was above all the work of Prince Otto von Bismarck (1815–1898). Brilliant, unscrupulous, ruthless, a genius at maneuvering and at concealing his real intentions, Bismarck sometimes pursued two apparently contradictory policies at the same time, until the moment came when he had to make a final decision on which policy to follow. His loyalty to the Prussian Crown, even when he manipulated it to his own purposes, did not falter during his long years in office. Influential before 1862, he towered over Prussia

Prince Otto von Bismarck, the pragmatic German chancellor.

New York Public Library Picture Collection

from 1862 to 1871, and over the German Empire thereafter until 1890. Yet his efforts could not have succeeded had they not met with general approval from the German people, who had long hungered for unity.

Prussia and the German Confederation, 1848–1862

The first major question facing the leaders of central Europe after the revolutions of 1848 was whether Prussia or Austria would dominate the German Confederation. The "Big German" solution called for federation with Austria; the "Little German" solution called for separation from Austria or even from south Germany. The "Little German" program also meant Prussian domination of the non-Austrian states, and therefore became Bismarck's goal.

Prussia was aided and Austria was hindered by the rising sense of nationalism. Austria contained many language groups, each of which hoped for a national destiny of its own, while Prussia became increasingly centralized. In the 1850s Prussia moved steadily forward in administrative efficiency, well-planned industrialization, financial prudence, and military strength. Furthermore, despite the constitution of 1850, which technically provided for universal male suffrage, the electorate was divided into three classes on the basis of taxes paid, so that the wealthier voters could continue to control the less well-to-do in the lower house, or *Landtag*.

The Frankfurt Diet had long since lost the support of artisans and industrial workers, as it espoused increasingly conservative policies. From 1851 to 1859 the Prussian minister to the Frankfurt Diet had been Bismarck. At the Diet, Bismarck took every occasion to thwart Austrian designs. He favored Prussian neutrality in the Crimean War (1854–1856), in which Britain and France fought (with Turkey) against Russia, while Austria harassed rather than helped the Russians. Realizing that Austrian behavior was alienating Russia, and that Russian friendship

would be valuable later when Prussia came to grips with Austria, Bismarck frustrated those Prussians who hoped that Prussia would enter the war against Russia and thus line up with the West. Counting on a military showdown with Austria, Bismarck also wooed the French emperor Napoleon III.

These diplomatic and military concerns led directly to the beginning of Bismarck's undisputed domination of Prussian policies. King William I was above all a soldier. His minister of war, a friend of Bismarck's, easily persuaded the king that an army reorganization was necessary. He wanted to increase the number of conscripts drafted each year from 40,000 to 63,000, and to lengthen the term of their service from two to three years. A conscript army took time to mobilize, but a professional army (like Britain's) did not. A liberal majority in the Landtag opposed funds for the increase in troops, and a prolonged political crisis over the budget threatened to block other legislation as well. At the height of the crisis, the king, convinced that Bismarck could outwit the parliament, called him back from Paris, where he was serving as ambassador, and appointed him to the key posts of prime minister of Prussia and minister of foreign affairs.

On the grounds that the constitution permitted the government to use taxes collected for other purposes even when the budget had not been approved by parliament, Bismarck carried out the army reforms. Again and again he dissolved parliament, called new elections, faced another hostile house, and then repeated the process. He suppressed opposition newspapers in defiance of a constitutional provision that the press should be free. Yet despite four years of this illegal behavior (1862–1866), Bismarck got away with everything in the end because of the glittering successes he scored by his unorthodox and daring foreign policy. In 1866 an admiring parliament voted retroactive approval of his unauthorized expenditures, rendering them legal.

Since Bismarck probably intended to overthrow the German Confederation as it was then constituted, he opposed Austrian efforts to reform it. Austria wished to create an assembly of delegates chosen by the parliaments of the member states, in addition to those delegates named by the princes, all to be responsible to a directorate of six monarchs. In 1862 Bismarck prevented William I from attending a congress of princes called by Austria to discuss these proposals, and thus wrecked the congress. In 1863 he kept Austria out of the *Zollverein*, the German Customs Union. He also consolidated his good relations with Russia during a Polish revolt by an agreement that allowed the Russians to pursue fleeing Poles onto Prussian territory.

War and the Strengthening of German Nationhood, 1863–1871

When the king of Denmark died in late 1863, a controversy over Schleswig-Holstein gave Bismarck further opportunities. In brief, the duchies of Schleswig and Holstein at the southern base of the Danish peninsula had been ruled by the king of Denmark, but not as part of Denmark. A fifteenth-century guarantee assured the duchies that they could never be separated from one another. Yet Holstein to the south was a member of the German Confederation; Schleswig to the north was not. Holstein was mostly German in population; Schleswig was mixed German and Danish. In 1852 Prussia joined the other powers in the Protocol of London, agreeing on an heir who would succeed both to the Danish throne and to the duchies, and recommending that Denmark and the duchies be united by a constitution. But when the constitutional union of Denmark and the duchies was attempted, the duchies resisted, and the Danes tried to incorporate Schleswig alone. German patriots there and elsewhere objected. The Prussians and Austrians wanted the duchies to have special representation in the Danish parliament and insisted that Schleswig not be incorporated into Denmark; nonetheless, the king of Denmark had supported annexation.

In 1863 Bismarck moved to win the duchies for Prussia. First, he maneuvered Prussia and Austria together into a victorious war against Denmark (1864). Then he quarreled with the Austrians over the administration of the duchies. At the Convention of Gastein in 1865 it was decided that Prussia was to administer Schleswig and that Austria was to administer Holstein.

Bismarck next tried to tempt France into an alliance. He failed, but he did succeed in signing a secret treaty with the Italians, who obliged themselves to go to war on the side of Prussia if Prussia fought Austria within three months, the stake being Venetia. This was contrary to the constitution of the German Confederation, which forbade members to ally themselves with a foreign power against other members. Finally, Bismarck suddenly proposed that the German Confederation be reformed, and that an all-German parliament be elected by universal suffrage, which everybody knew he actually opposed.

Bismarck probably advanced this proposal to make it appear that his quarrel with Austria involved more than the Schleswig-Holstein question. Yet the proposal may also have reflected his calculation that enfranchisement of all Germans would weaken the Progressive party and would produce many conservative and royalist votes from the peasantry. Historians continue to debate Bismarck's actual intentions, many of them contending that it is from his rise to power that the German states departed from the broad western European movement toward parliamentary democracy.

Austria now laid the Schleswig-Holstein question before the Diet of the Confederation. Bismarck ordered Prussian troops into Holstein and declared that Austrian motions in the Diet were unconstitutional, provoking war with Austria. The result was a German civil war, since Bavaria, Württemberg, Saxony, Hanover (the other four German kingdoms), and most of the lesser German states sided with Austria.

The war lasted only seven weeks and was decided in three. The Austrians, fighting on two fronts, had to commit a substantial part of their forces against Italy. Skillfully using their railway network, the telegraph, and

Napoleon III and Bismarck meet after the battle of Sedan.
The Bettmann Archive.

their superior armaments, the Prussians quickly overran the northern German states, invaded Bohemia and defeated the Austrians at Sadowa, defeated the Bavarians, and entered Frankfurt, seat of the German Confederation. Hanover, Hesse-Cassel, and Nassau were annexed to Prussia and their dynasties expelled, and Schleswig and the free city of Frankfurt were taken over by terms of the Peace of Prague in August. Except for the cession of Venetia to Italy in the Peace of Vienna in October, Austria suffered no territorial losses but did pay a small indemnity. Most important from Bismarck's point of view, Austria had to withdraw forever from the German Confederation, which now ceased to exist.

An assembly elected by universal manhood suffrage now adopted a constitution for the new North German Confederation, of which the Prussian king was president. The future parliament (*Reichstag*) was to have no power over the budget, and the ministers were not to be responsible to it. Instead, a Federal Council (*Bundesrat*) of delegates from the member states, who voted according to instructions from their sovereigns, would reach all key policy decisions in secret and would have veto power over any enactment of the Reichstag. A chancellor would preside over the Bundesrat, but would not have to defend its decisions before the Reichstag. Since Prussia now had not only its own votes in the Bundesrat but also those of the newly annexed states, Bismarck's plan in effect made it possible for the king of Prussia to run Germany.

As long as Bismarck needed the benevolent neutrality of Napoleon III, he had hinted that he might not object if Napoleon took Belgium. Now the gullible Napoleon found that Bismarck no longer remembered the matter. Hoping to be compensated for his assistance in making peace between Prussia and Austria, Napoleon III tried to acquire Luxembourg by purchase from the king of Holland. Again he was frustrated by Bismarck. Napoleon III tried to obtain an alliance with Austria and Italy to thwart further Prussian expansion, but the Austrians shied away from a commitment, and the Italians were unable to reach an agreement with the French because of the Roman question.

The Spaniards ousted their queen in 1868, and one of the candidates for the throne was a Hohenzollern prince, whom Bismarck secretly backed by discreetly bribing influential Spaniards. Because of family dynastic practice, it was necessary to secure the consent of King William I of Prussia, a consent Bismarck finally extracted without hinting that war with France might result. Napoleon III, also deep in Spanish intrigue, feared that a Hohenzollern on the Spanish throne would expose France to a two-front attack. French diplomatic pressure was exerted directly on King William, and the Hohenzollern candidate withdrew. At this moment, Bismarck seemed to be defeated.

But the French, made overconfident by their success, now demanded that William publicly endorse the withdrawal of the Hohenzollern candidacy and promise never to allow it to be renewed. William, who was at Ems, courteously refused and sent a telegram to Bismarck describing his interchange with the French ambassador. Bismarck then abridged the Ems telegram and released his doctored version to the press and all the European chanceries. He made it seem that the ambassador had provoked William, who in turn had snubbed the ambassador. Public opinion in Germany was now inflamed, and Bismarck set out to bait the French still further by encouraging a violent campaign against them in the German press. The French, led by a war party eager to stop German expansion, reacted as Bismarck had hoped; they declared war on July 19, 1870.

Within six weeks the Germans had advanced into France, bottled up one French army inside the fortress of Metz, defeated another at Sedan, and captured Napoleon III himself. The protracted siege of Paris followed, ending in surrender early in 1871. A new French government had to sign the treaty of Frankfurt. Bismarck forced the French to pay a massive indemnity, to cede Alsace and much of Lorraine, and to support German occupying forces until the indemnity had been paid.

Imperial Germany, 1871–1914

Even before this peace had been imposed, King William of Prussia was proclaimed emperor of Germany. When a constitution for the new empire was adopted, it was simply an extension of the constitution of the North German Confederation of 1867. As chancellor of the German Empire from 1871 to 1890, Bismarck became the leading statesman in Europe. As diplomat, he worked for the preservation of Germany's gains against threats from abroad, especially by any foreign coalition against Germany. As politician, he worked for the preservation of the Prussian system against all opposing currents.

A multitude of economic and legal questions arose as a result of the creation of the new empire. Working with the moderate Liberal party in the Reichstag, Bismarck put through a common coinage and a central bank, coordinated and further unified the railroads and postal systems, and regularized the legal and judicial systems. In 1874 Bismarck, by threatening to resign, forced the Reichstag to fix the size of the army at 401,000 men until 1881; in 1880 he forced an increase to 427,000 until 1888. The privileged position of the army made a military career ever more attractive and served as a constant spur to German militarism.

But the great drama of the 1870s in Germany was furnished by Bismarck's attack on the Roman Catholic church—the *Kulturkampf* (battle for civilization). A *Syllabus of Errors* published by the Vatican in 1864 had denounced toleration of other religions, secular education, and state participation in church affairs. Then in 1870 the Vatican Council adopted the dogma of papal infallibility. This dogma asserted that the judgments of the pope on questions of faith and morals were infallible. To many non-Catholics, this seemed to say that no state could count on the absolute loyalty of its Catholic citizens.

In Germany the Catholics were a large minority of the population. They had formed a political party, the Center, that quickly became the second strongest party in the Empire. The Center defended papal infallibility and wished to restore the pope's temporal power, which had been ended by the unification of Italy. Catholic peasants, workers, priests, and nobles opposed the largely Protestant urban middle class and the Prussian military predominance in the state. Bismarck identified his clerical opponents with nominally Catholic France and Austria, the two nations he had defeated in forging the new Germany. In collaboration with the Liberals, Bismarck put through laws expelling the Jesuits from Germany, forbidding the clergy to criticize the government, and closing the schools of religious orders. The pope declared these laws null and void and instructed Catholics to disobey them.

By declaring that he would not "go to Canossa," Bismarck summoned up for Protestant Germans the picture of the German emperor Henry IV humbling himself before the pope in 1077. But in the 1880s Bismarck had to repeal most of the anti-Catholic measures he had passed in the 1870s, for by then he needed the support of the Center party against his former allies, the Liberals, whose demands for power he found exorbitant, and against the growing attraction of the Social Democrats, who were moderate socialists.

In 1877 and 1878 Bismarck had begun a gradual shift in policy, dictated at first by the need for more revenue. The empire obtained its money in part from indirect taxes imposed by the Reichstag on tobacco, alcohol, sugar, and the like. The rest came from the individual states, which controlled all direct taxation and made contributions to the imperial budget. As military costs mounted, the government's income became insufficient, and Bismarck did not want to increase the empire's dependence on the states by repeatedly asking them to increase their contributions. He wanted the Reichstag to vote higher indirect taxes.

Up to this point German tariff policy had basically been one of free trade, with little protection for German goods. But after a financial panic in 1873, the iron and textile industries put pressure on Bismarck to shift to a policy of protection that would help them compete with England. Moreover, an agricultural crisis led conservatives to abandon their previous support of free trade and to demand protection against cheap grain coming in from eastern Europe. In 1879 Bismarck finally put through a general protective tariff on all imports. The Catholic Center favored his protectionist policy. Bismarck thus secured the support of both the Center and the conservatives and was able to avoid making concessions to the Reichstag.

While he was swinging toward protection in 1878–1879, Bismarck also began to move against the Social Democratic party. Two Marxists, Wilhelm Liebknecht (1826–1900) and August Bebel (1840–1913), had founded this small party in 1869; in 1875 they enlarged it, much to Marx's disgust, by accepting the followers of Lassalle, an apostle of nonviolence. The German Social Democrats were not nearly as revolutionary as their Marxist phraseology suggested. They were prepared to concentrate their efforts on improving working conditions rather than on revolution. But Bismarck needed an enemy against whom he could unify his supporters; besides, he had been deeply distressed by the Paris Commune of 1871 and feared that something similar might occur in Germany.

Using as a pretext two attempts by alleged Social Democrats to assassinate William I, Bismarck called a general election in 1878 and rammed through the Reichstag a bill making the Social Democratic party illegal, forbidding its meetings, and suppressing its newspapers. The Liberals supported this law, but they would not allow Bismarck to make it a permanent statute. He had to apply to the Reichstag for its renewal every two or three years; it was renewed each time, until just before Bismarck's downfall in 1890. Social Democrats were still allowed to run for the Reichstag as individuals, and their votes increased during the years when they were suffering legal restrictions.

But Bismarck felt that "a remedy cannot be sought merely in repression of Socialist excesses—there must be simultaneously a positive advancement of the welfare of the working classes." As a result, during the 1880s the government put forward bills in favor of the workers: compulsory insurance against illness in 1882, and against accidents in 1884. The sickness insurance funds were raised by contributions from both workers and employers; the accident insurance funds were contributed totally by the employers. In 1889 old-age and disability insurance followed, with employers and employees contributing equally, and with an additional subsidy from the state.

Bismarck also moved away from the Liberals because he blamed them for the market crash of 1873. The rage for speculation that had swept Germany, especially after currency reform in 1871, had moved through railways and into the construction industry. The entire nation seemed caught up in the search for pleasure. When the market collapsed in 1873, the Liberals were blamed. With confidence weakened, a wave of selling on the stock exchange led to a serious collapse, followed by a depression throughout central Europe. Bismarck used the changed economic climate to justify protectionism and to shift the balance of political forces away from liberalism.

Anti-Semitic attitudes, which had been dormant in Germany since the 1820s, were rekindled by those who identified Jews with the Liberal party, and with stock-market manipulation in general and unearned capital in particular. Thereafter, the myth of a Jewish conspiracy was a recurring theme of German politics, and neither Bismarck nor his successors did much to stop its growth. In 1880 Berlin had forty-five thousand Jewish residents (at a time when all of France had only fifty-one thousand). The most respected historian of the time, Heinrich von Treitschke (1834–1896), a father of modern German nationalism, declared in a much-quoted article late in 1879 that "the Jews are our national misfortune." Though Treitschke based his argument on religious and nationalistic grounds, others were prepared to move to "racial" and ethnic arguments, for he had made anti-Semitism respectable; thereafter, it was never far below the surface of modernizing Germany.

When William I died at the age of ninety in 1888, his son, Frederick III, already mortally ill, ruled for only three months. The next emperor was Frederick's son, William II (1859–1941), a young man of twenty-nine whose accession his grandfather had greatly feared because of his impulsiveness. William I had allowed Bismarck to act for him, but William II was determined to act for himself. This determination underlay the subsequent controversy between him and Bismarck.

Bismarck believed politics to be "the art of the possible." Since further conflict in the future was inevitable, wisdom dictated moderation toward defeated enemies, for they might be needed one day as allies. Since life threw into conflict a shifting kaleidoscope of social classes, political parties, special-interest groups, sectional loyalties, intemperate individuals who had attained positions of power, and entire nations and states, one could not expect to predict with accuracy a nation's future needs in terms of alliances. Therefore, a nation's leaders must always have an alternative course of action ready, a course not too brutally contradicted by any former alliance, so that the middle ground might be credibly taken. After Bismarck, Germany appeared to lose sight of these principles.

On his accession, William proclaimed his sympathy for the workers. When the antisocialist law came up for renewal, the emperor supported a modified version that would have taken away the power of the police to expel certain Social Democrats from their homes. Bismarck, while hoping that the Social Democrats would indulge in excesses that would give him the excuse to suppress them by armed force, opposed the measure. He lost, and as a result there was no antisocialist law after 1890. Other differences arose between the chancellor and the emperor over an international workers' conference, over relations with Russia, and over procedures in reaching policy decisions. Finally, in March 1890, William commanded Bismarck to resign.

Energetic but unsteady, pompous and menacing but without the intention or the courage to back up his threats, William was ill-suited to govern any country, much less the militaristic, highly industrialized imperial Germany, with its social tensions and its lack of political balance. Tendencies already present under Bismarck became more apparent. The Prussian army, and especially the reserve officers, came increasingly to exercise great influence on William II. Party structure reflected the strains in German society. The Liberals, a party of big business, usually had little strength in the Reichstag. The Liberals were also divided by local and regional rivalries. The great landowners banded together in protest against a reduction in agricultural duties. In 1894 they organized an Agrarian League, which spearheaded conservative measures. In 1902 they forced a return to protection.

The electoral strength of the Social Democrats increased during William II's reign. Freed from interference by the removal of the antisocialist law, they organized trade unions, circulated newspapers, and successfully pressured the regime for more social legislation. The party had no immediate plan for a revolution, although its radical wing expected, especially after a Russian revolution in 1905, that a German revolution would come. The "revisionist" wing, which expected no open conflict between capital and labor, hoped that, by allying themselves with the middle class to attain a majority in the Reichstag, the Social Democrats might eventually overturn the militarist government peacefully.

In Germany, unlike France and Britain, women were generally given little role to play in the reform movement. Denied the right to vote, they were usually barred from membership in political organizations and trade unions. Whereas in France women had traditionally been leaders in the arts, in Germany they were denied access to professional training, and there were no secondary schools for women comparable to the excellent and rigorous *Gymnasium* educational system established for males. Until the turn of the century, the only women admitted to German universities were foreigners, and until after World War I no women were permitted to work for higher degrees. The goal set for women was to provide their husbands with "a proper domestic atmosphere."

Those few women who were active politically usually joined socialist associations, since the socialists advocated equal pay for equal work. By 1900 there were over 850 associations working for women's rights in Germany, but during the empire few of their stated goals were achieved. Though the Progressive party endorsed the

principle of suffrage for women in 1912, it did nothing to achieve that end. Many women worked in the textile industry, and in 1878 women were admitted to the German civil service—a move prompted not so much by feminist efforts as by the need for people who could operate the telegraph, telephone, and typewriter. Women of the upper middle class were thus brought into the work force, though they were paid less than men.

Women were assigned, or accepted, roles in childhood nurturing which in time led to careers in teaching, especially in the kindergarten movement which had its origins in Germany. Though suppressed in Prussia, in part because kindergartens were viewed as too progressive, the movement took root elsewhere in western Europe and later in Germany once again. The feminist movement in Germany embraced child care as a profession, held that the sacred role of women was to be mothers of the nation, and argued that women must take the lead in agitating for legislation by which the state would recognize its obligation to care for women and children, protecting them against abusive husbands and fathers and from homelessness. Germany prepared a uniform civil code that, in 1896, permitted women to become guardians over children, and motherhood was seen as a career. Women also led the way in the campaign against infant mortality, initiated widespread debates about reproductive rights and the concept of population quality, and launched the new profession of social work. One leader, Frieda Duensing (1864–1933), studied law in Switzerland, entered the field of child welfare services, and helped to put female social workers at the heart of Germany's growing juvenile court system.

Meanwhile, issues of military, colonial, and foreign policy began to complicate the tense internal politics of Germany. After Admiral Alfred von Tirpitz (1849–1930) became minister of the navy in 1897, the emperor and Tirpitz planned a high-seas fleet to replace the naval forces that had originally been designed for coastal and commercial defense. But the army and navy were only the most obvious weapons of world power. The Colonial Society, founded to support the case for overseas expansion, grew rapidly in membership as Germany acquired territories in the Far East and in Africa, despite the drain on the budget (for the German colonies were never profitable). Pan-Germans planned a great Berlin-Baghdad railway to the Near East and cried for more adventure and more conquest.

However, William's naval and colonial policies embittered Germany's relations with Great Britain. So long as Bismarck was in control, the British hoped Germany would limit its goals to altering the existing order of power in Europe; after 1890 it seemed clear that Germany also intended to alter the world balance of power, and the British felt their interests directly threatened. Foreign policy in both nations was shaped by a complex mixture of social, economic, political, and ideological factors ranging from religious and cultural connections through the changing attitudes of parties, the press, pressure groups, and the bureaucracies. Leaders in business and politics in both countries worked for a

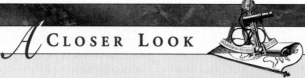

A CLOSER LOOK

The Growth of Bureaucracy

Bureaucracy is one of those words that has changed in connotation while also describing a major development that is part of "modernization." As nation-states became ever more centralized and powerful, they tended to take on more and more responsibilities with respect to their citizens. Agencies of government, that is *bureaus*, were created to administer the various aspects of government: foreign affairs, excise and taxation, the police, social welfare, national education, and so forth. Increasingly these bureaucracies took on a life of their own: Made up of employees—increasingly civil servants—hired by the state to administer policy, the agencies were regarded as expert in a given area of human activity. Often the employees were entrenched within their departments and at times forgot that they had been placed in positions of trust and authority in order to work to the ends of the state or on behalf of the people. In time the term *bureaucracy* became one of ill-repute describing a presumably inflated and at times less-than-competent or compassionate arm of government. There would be periodic populist revolts against enlarged bureaucracies in the twentieth century, and especially so in most countries in the West in the 1980s and 1990s. The phenomenon was first described in relation to the German army and navy by a German sociologist, Max Weber (1864–1920), who discussed the problem of group consciousness and the conservatism that often accompanies it as follows:

The decisive reason for the advance of bureaucratic organization has always been its purely *technical* superiority over any other form of organization. The fully developed bureaucratic apparatus compares with other organizations exactly as does the machine with the nonmechanical modes of production. Precision, speed, unambiguity, knowledge of the files, continuity, discretion, unity, strict subordination, reduction of friction and of material and personal costs—these are raised to the optimum point in the strictly bureaucratic administration, and especially in its monocratic form. As compared with all collegiate, honorific, and avocational forms of administration, trained bureaucracy is superior on all these points. And as far as complicated tasks are concerned, paid bureaucratic work is not only more precise but, in the last analysis, it is often cheaper than even formally unremunerated honorific service. . . .

Today, it is primarily the capitalist market economy which demands that the official business of public administration be discharged precisely, unambiguously, continuously, and with as much speed as possible. Normally, the very large modern capitalist enterprises are themselves unequalled models of strict bureaucratic organization. Business management throughout rests on increasing precision, steadiness, and, above all, speed of operations. This, in turn, is determined by the peculiar nature of the modern means of communication, including, among other things, the news service of the press. The extraordinary increase in the speed by which public announcements, as well as economic and political facts, are transmitted exerts a steady and sharp pressure in the direction of speeding up the

tempo of administrative reaction toward various situations. The optimum of such reaction time is normally attained only by a strictly bureaucratic organization. . . .

The more complicated and specialized modern culture becomes, the more its external supporting apparatus demands the personally detached and strictly objective *expert*, in lieu of the lord of older social structures who was moved by personal sympathy and favor, by grace and gratitude. Bureaucracy offers the attitudes demanded by the external apparatus of modern culture in the most favorable combination. In particular, only bureaucracy has established the foundation for the administration of a rational law conceptually systematized on the basis of "statutes," such as the later Roman Empire first created with a high degree of technical perfection. . . .

The bureaucratic structure is everywhere a late product of historical development. The further back we trace our steps, the more typical is the absence of bureaucracy and of officialdom in general. Since bureaucracy has a "rational" character, with rules, means-ends calculus, and matter-of-factness predominating, its rise and expansion has everywhere had "revolutionary" results . . . , as had the advance of *rationalism* in general. The march of bureaucracy accordingly destroyed structures of domination which were not rational in the sense of the term.

Max Weber, *Economy and Society: An Outline of Interpretive Sociology,* 1922, ed. Guenther Roth and Claus Wittich (Berkeley: University of California Press, 1978), II, pp. 973–75, 1002–1003.

harmonious relationship between the nations, but in the end they failed.

Britain had other than diplomatic and military reasons to be apprehensive of German power. By the turn of the century Germany had clearly overtaken Britain

industrially. This surging development of Germany made its militarism possible, while its militarism in turn fed industrialism. Beginning later and with fewer advantages than England, Germany recognized that it lagged behind commercially and made an early commitment to sophisticated technology. As in Britain, railroads provided the first surge of activity, followed by the opening of the Ruhr Valley. Germany soon forged ahead in steel, organic chemistry, and electricity.

Economic issues were always close to the surface in all German political debate. When the Ruhr proved to be rich in coal, and transportation costs were moderate, a mixture of private initiative and state assistance industrialized the region almost before political debate could take shape. Agriculture became more efficient. Assisted by an active cooperative movement and by state-supported agricultural schools and experimental stations, German grain growers exported food until 1873. Thereafter, as cheap grain from eastern Europe began to enter Germany, economic policy turned toward protectionism. National efficiency—whether in the growth of larger and larger factories, firms, and cartels, or in more productive agriculture—became a goal on which nearly all parties could agree. By 1914 Germany was largely self-sufficient in many significant areas of industry.

THE HABSBURG EMPIRE: DIVIDING HUMANITY INTO NATIONS

In a sense, nationalism was a doctrine invented in Europe in the nineteenth century to account for social, economic, and political changes that required a single descriptive term. The notion of nationhood easily led to the assumption that humanity was divided—by divine intent, nature, or the material force of history—into nations, and that therefore the course of history was toward the self-determination of those peoples. The American Declaration of Independence had asserted such a principle, and by the mid-nineteenth century most people in western Europe appear to have assumed that the only legitimate type of government was that which carried a society toward independence.

Most commentators on nationalism argue that certain common characteristics can be identified, so that a "nation" can be objectively defined. These characteristics include a shared language, a common object of love (usually called the homeland), a shared life in a common territory under similar influences of nature and common outside political pressures, and the creation of a state of mind that strives toward a sense of homogeneity within the group. This sense of common identity is fostered by holding to common symbols, rituals, and social conventions through a common language (or variant of it), religion, and sense of mutual interdependence. Usually the positive aspects of such a sense of group identity will be strengthened by a negative emphasis on those who lack such characteristics.

Nationalism may be fed by what some historians call "vital lies"—beliefs held to be so true and so central to a sense of identity that to question them at all is to be disloyal. Thus certain historical ideas may be untrue—even lies consciously fostered—but because of widespread belief in them, they have the vitality and thus the function of truth. Most modern societies think of their way of life as superior to others. Most peoples believe themselves chosen—whether by God or by history.

In the twentieth century such assumptions about national identity and the nation as the source of group and individual security and stability are commonplace. But what now seems natural was, in fact, unfamiliar or still emerging as part of the process of modernization in the nineteenth century. This was especially so among the many language groups of the Habsburg Empire. For the Habsburg Empire, "modernization" did not mean unification. It meant fragmentation and a trend toward representative government only in relation to divisive nationalisms, not toward new national unities.

For over sixty years, from 1848 to 1916, the German-speaking emperor Francis Joseph sat on the Habsburg throne. Immensely conscientious, he worked hard reading and signing state papers for hours every day. But he was without imagination, inflexibly old-fashioned and conservative. He was intensely pious, and his mere longevity inspired loyalty. His decisions usually came too late and conceded too little. His responsibility for the course of events is large.

Habsburg history between 1850 and 1914 divides naturally into equal portions at 1867, when the empire became the dual monarchy of Austria-Hungary. After the suppression of the revolution of 1848, there was a decade of repression usually called the Bach system, from the name of the minister of the interior, Alexander Bach (1813–1893), ending in 1859 with the war against Piedmont and France. Eight years of political experimentation followed, from 1859 to 1867, punctuated by the war of 1866 with Prussia.

In 1849 all parts of the empire were for the first time unified and directly ruled from Vienna by German-speaking officials. In 1855 the state signed a concordat with the Catholic church giving clerics a greater influence in education and other fields than they had enjoyed since the reforms of Joseph II. The repressive domestic policies of the Bach period required expensive armies and policemen. Instead of investing in railroads and industry, Austria went into debt to pursue centralization, an enlarged bureaucracy, and Germanization. These expenditures left it at a disadvantage compared with Prussia. Then during the Crimean War Francis Joseph failed to assist the Russians and kept them in fear of an attack by occupying the Danubian principalities (modern Romania). Defeat in 1859 at the hands of the French and Italians and the loss of Lombardy with its great city of Milan brought about the end of the Bach system.

War continued to threaten, and the nationalities inside the empire, especially the Magyars, could not be left in a state of perpetual discontent, which would render their troops unreliable. Several solutions were tried in an effort to create a structure that would withstand the domestic and foreign strains but that would not jeopardize the emperor's position. Francis Joseph listened first to the nobles, who favored loose federalism, and then to the bureaucrats, who favored tight centralism. In 1860 he set up a central legislature to deal with economic and military problems. To it the provincial assemblies (diets) throughout the empire would send delegates. All other problems were left to the provincial diets, elected by a system that worked to disfranchise the peasants. This solution, known as the October Diploma, did not satisfy the Magyar nobility of Hungary. Even so, Austrian liberals and bureaucrats felt that the October Diploma gave the Magyars too much. It seemed to them that the empire was being dismembered on behalf of the nobility, who dominated the provincial assemblies. Therefore, in 1861 the February Patent reinterpreted the Diploma, creating an even more centralized scheme. A bicameral imperial legislature took over most of the powers that the October Diploma had reserved for the provincial assemblies or diets.

Naturally, the Magyars objected to this second solution even more than to the first, and they flatly refused to participate. To the applause of the Germans in Vienna, including the liberals, Hungary returned to authoritarian rule. Czechs and Poles also eventually withdrew from the central parliaments and left only a German rump. Disturbed, the emperor suspended the February Patent and began to negotiate with the Magyars, who were represented by the intelligent and moderate Ferenc Deák (1803–1876). The negotiations were interrupted by the war with Prussia in 1866. The Austrian defeat at Sadowa, the expulsion of Austria from Germany, and the loss of Venetia threatened the entire Habsburg system. Clearly Austria could not risk war with any combination of Prussia, France, or Russia. Francis Joseph resumed negotiations with the Magyars. In 1867 a formula was found that was to govern and preserve the Habsburg domain down to the World War of 1914–1918.

The Dual Monarchy, 1867

This formula was the *Ausgleich*, or "compromise," which created the unique dual monarchy of Austria-Hungary. The Hungarian constitution of 1848 was restored, and the entire empire was reorganized as a strict partnership. Austria and Hungary were united in the person of the emperor, who was always to be a Catholic and a legitimate Habsburg, and who was to be crowned king of Hungary in Budapest. For foreign policy, military affairs, and finance, the two states had joint ministers appointed by the emperor. A customs union, subject to renewal every ten years, united them. Every ten years the quota of common expenditure to be borne by each partner was to be renegotiated. A unique body, the "delegations," made up of sixty members from the Austrian parliament and sixty members from the Hungarian parliament, meeting alternately in Vienna and in Budapest, was to decide on the common budget, which had to be ratified by the full parliaments of both countries. The delegations also had supervisory authority over the three joint ministers and might summon them to account for their activities.

In practice, however, the delegations seldom met and were almost never consulted on questions of policy. The system favored Hungary, which had 40 percent of the population but never paid more than a third of the expenses. Every ten years, therefore, when the quota of expenses and the customs union needed joint consideration, a new crisis arose.

One overwhelming problem remained common to both halves of the monarchy: that of the national minorities who had not received their autonomy. Some of these minorities (Czechs, Poles, Ruthenes) were largely in Austria; others (Slovaks, Romanians) were largely in Hungary; the rest (Croats, Serbs, Slovenes) were in both states. These nationalities were at different stages of national self-consciousness. Some were subject to pressures and manipulation from fellow nationals living outside the dual monarchy. All had some leaders who urged compromise and conciliation with the dominant Austrians and Magyars, as well as others who advocated resistance and even revolution. The result was a chronic and often unpredictable instability in the dual monarchy.

The Austrian constitution of 1867 provided that all nationalities should enjoy equal rights and guaranteed that each might use its own language in education, administration, and public life. And in 1868 the Hungarians passed a law that allowed the minorities to conduct local government in their own language, to hold the chief posts in the counties where they predominated, and to have their own schools. But in practice the minority nationalities suffered discrimination and persecution.

The Nationality Question in Austria

After 1867 many Czechs argued that the lands of the Crown of St. Wenceslaus, a martyred prince of Bohemia (d. 929), possessed rights comparable to those that the Magyars had successfully claimed for the lands of the Crown of St. Stephen (c. 975–1038), who had been crowned as first king of Hungary in 1001. But the Czechs never had the power or the opportunity that the Magyars had to bring pressure on the Austrians, although Czech deputies boycotted the Austrian parliament in the hope that Francis Joseph would consent to become king of Bohemia in Prague, as he had become king of Hungary in Budapest.

In 1871 the emperor did indeed offer to be crowned as king of Bohemia. The Bohemian Diet, from which all Germans had withdrawn, drew up proposals that would have produced a triple instead of a dual monarchy. The rage of Austrian and Bohemian Germans, the opposition of Magyar politicians, and a Slavic uprising in southern Austria forced Francis Joseph to change his mind. Deeply disappointed, the Czech nationalist leaders turned to passive resistance.

By 1879, when the Czech deputies finally returned to the Vienna parliament, they were divided into moderate "old Czechs" and radical "young Czechs." In the 1880s and 1890s each time the Czechs won cultural or political gains, the German extremists bitterly opposed them, strengthening the Czech extremists and weakening the moderates. A law requiring all judges in Czech lands to conduct trials in the language of the petitioner led to the development of an experienced body of Czech civil servants, since many Czechs knew German already, while Germans usually had to learn Czech. In 1890 the government and the old Czechs tentatively agreed on an administrative division of Bohemia between Germans and Czechs, but the young Czechs rioted in the Bohemian Diet, and Prague was put under martial law, which lasted until 1897. When a new law was passed requiring that all civil servants in the Czech lands be bilingual after 1901, the Germans in the Vienna parliament forced out the ministry, while Czech extremists began to talk ominously about a future Russian-led Slavic showdown with the Germans. No Austrian parliament could stay in session, and government had to be conducted by decree.

Under the stress of prolonged agitation and influenced by the apparent triumph of constitutionalism in Russia, Francis Joseph finally decided to reform the franchise. In 1907 all male citizens of the Austrian lands were enfranchised and could vote for deputies of their own nationality. Of the 516 deputies in the new parliament, 233 would be German and 107 Czech, a figure nearly proportional to the census figures, since Czechs constituted 23 percent of the Austrian population. Yet in 1913 the Bohemian Diet was dissolved, and in 1914 Czech deputies in the Austrian parliament refused to allow national business to proceed. Thus World War I began with both parliament and the Bohemian Diet dissolved and with the emperor and ministers ruling by themselves. Perhaps chief among the many causes for this general parliamentary breakdown was the failure to give the Czech provinces the full internal self-government they had vainly sought since 1867.

Czech nationalism was fostered by an active Czech-language press, by patriotic societies, by Czech schools, and by the *sokols* (hawks), a physical-training society with strong nationalist leanings. At the ancient Prague University, Czech scholars supported the idea of a separate national identity. Perhaps the most influential was Thomas Masaryk (1850–1937), professor of philosophy and student of Slavic culture, who deeply influenced generations of students and upheld democratic ideals in politics. He inspired poets and novelists to write of a glorified national past for a popular audience, and from 1907 he formally led the Czech independence party. In 1918 Masaryk would become president of the new nation.

Of all the minority nationalities in the dual monarchy, the Czechs were in the best position to exercise independence. Substantial in population, with a high percentage of artisans skilled in the porcelain, glassware, lace, Pilsen beer, and sugar beet industries, and with a thriving tourist trade that gave them access to the broader world, the Czechs also were at the center of growing heavy industry.

Of all the minorities in Austria, the Poles (18 percent of the population) were the least overtly discontented. Most of them lived in Galicia, where they formed the landlord class. Like the Czechs, the Galician Poles asked for provincial self-government on the Magyar model and were denied. But they had their own schools, and Polish was the language of administration and the courts. The Poles enjoyed favorable financial arrangements, and after 1871 there was a special ministry for Galicia in Vienna.

The contrast between this relatively nondiscriminatory treatment of Poles in Austria and the brutality suffered by Poles living in Prussian and Russian Poland led Poles everywhere to look to Austrian Galicia as the center of national life and culture. Polish refugees took refuge in the cities of Kracow and Lemberg (later, Lvov). Here were splendid Polish universities and opportunities to serve the Habsburg Crown in the provincial administration. The universities trained generations of Poles who would be available later for service in independent Poland. Polish literature and the study of Polish history flourished. Slowly, industrialization began, and a promising petroleum industry was launched. Only the Ruthenians (Ukrainians) and the Jews suffered systematic discrimination and hardship.

The other minorities in Austria were far less numerous: In 1910 less than 3 percent of the population was Italian; about 4.5 percent was Slovene; and less than 3 percent was Serb and Croat. The Italians of the south Tyrol and Istria were far more important than their numbers suggest, however. Of all the Austrian minorities, the Italians proved to be the most anxious to get out of the Habsburg monarchy altogether. Both Serbs and Croats in Austria were divided; some preferred autonomy within the empire, and others hoped one day to join a south Slav state.

Minorities in Hungary

In Hungary minority problems were more acute. The Slovaks, the Romanians, and the Serbs and Croats living in Hungary were the worst victims of a deliberate policy of Magyarization. The Magyar aim was to destroy the national identity of the minorities and to transform them into Magyars; the weapon used was language.

The Magyars, who made up only 55 percent of the population of their own country (exclusive of Croatia), had an intense devotion to their own language—an Asian tongue quite unrelated to the German, Slavic, or Romanian languages of the minorities. They tried to force it upon the subject peoples, particularly in education. All state-supported schools, from kindergartens to universities, wherever located, had to give instruction in Magyar, and the state postal, telegraph, and railroad services used only Magyar.

The Slovaks, numbering about 11 percent of the population of Hungary, were perhaps the most Magyarized. Poor peasants for the most part, the more ambitious of them often became Magyars simply by adopting the Magyar language as their own. As time passed, a few Slovaks came to feel a sense of unity with the closely related Czechs across the border in Austria. The pro-Czechs among the Slovaks were usually liberals and Protestants, while Catholic and conservative Slovaks advocated Slovak autonomy.

The Romanians, who lived in Transylvania, amounted in 1910 to about 17 percent of the population of Hungary and were a majority in Transylvania itself. For centuries they had fought constantly to achieve recognition of their Greek Orthodox religion. Despite laws designed to eliminate the use of the Romanian language, the Romanians fiercely resisted assimilation. Some hoped that Transylvania might again be made autonomous, as it had been in the past. Many pressed for the enforcement of the liberal Hungarian nationalities law of 1868. But when in 1892 they petitioned Vienna on these points, their petition was returned unopened and unread, and when they circulated the petition widely abroad, their leaders were tried and jailed.

Under Magyar rule, some Serbs and Croats lived in Hungary proper and others in Croatia; in 1910 those in Hungary totaled about 600,000, of whom two thirds were Serbs living in a compact mass in the southern and western frontier regions. They had been transferred to Magyar rule in 1869, and they disliked Hungarian administration, hoping to be united with the independent kingdom of Serbia to the south.

A greater menace to Hungarian unity was provided by the existence of Croatia itself. The Croats, though connected since the eleventh century with the Crown of Hungary, had become strongly nationalistic under the impact of the Napoleonic occupation and had fought on the side of the monarchy against the Magyar revolutionaries of 1848. Nonetheless, Francis Joseph, as part of the Ausgleich settlement, handed them back to the Magyars.

Croatian nationalists were deeply disappointed. Led by a Roman Catholic bishop, Josef Strossmayer (1815–1905), they had hoped for an autonomous Croatia and Dalmatia (the coastal strip along the Adriatic inhabited largely by Croats but governed by Vienna), which would serve as a nucleus to attract all southern Slavs. Instead, the Magyar moderates, led by Deák, worked out in 1868 an Ausgleich of their own between Hungary and Croatia. All military and economic affairs were to be handled in Budapest by a special cabinet minister for Croatian affairs. Representatives from the Croatian parliaments at the Croatian capital of Zagreb would sit in Budapest whenever Croatian affairs were under discussion. Croatian delegates would be part of the Hungarian "delegation" to the dual monarchy. The Croatian language would be spoken by Croat representatives at the sessions of any body they attended, and the language of command in the Croatian territorial army would be Croatian. The Croats would control their own educational system, their church, their courts, and police; however, taxes would be voted and collected by Budapest.

The Croat Party of the Right wanted a completely autonomous Croatia and scorned as inferior the Serbs and other non-Catholic south Slavs, whom Strossmayer had hoped to attract. Further problems were created in Catholic Croatia by the existence of a Serb Orthodox minority (more than a quarter of the population), which spoke the same language as the Croats. But the Serbs worshiped in different churches and were therefore subject to religious discrimination. The Hungarian-appointed governor received the support only of those Croats who had become Magyar speaking, usually great landowners or government officials.

In 1907 the hopes of moderate leaders on all sides were dashed by an unpopular Railway Servants Act, which forced all railroad workers to speak Magyar. Croats began to boycott Hungarian-made goods; the Croatian Diet refused to collaborate with the new governor, who in 1909 arrested fifty-odd Croats and Serbs and charged them with plotting to unite Croatia and Bosnia with Serbia. The evidence was inadequate, and the defendants, though condemned, obtained a reversal of the sentences on appeal to a higher court. But these Zagreb trials gave the Slavic press a splendid opportunity to denounce the policy of the dual monarchy. Nationalism soon found expression in terrorism, and in 1912, 1913, and again in 1914, Bosnian students tried to assassinate the Hungarian governor of Croatia.

The region of Bosnia-Herzegovina had a special status in the dual monarchy. By the 1870s these two provinces had been part of the Ottoman Empire for about four centuries. Although solidly south Slavic, the population in 1879 included about half a million Muslims, half a million members of the Orthodox church, and perhaps 150,000 Catholics. Most of the Orthodox Christians were peasants, working on the estates of Muslim landlords. In 1875 a Herzegovinian uprising against the Turks precipitated a general Balkan Slavic attack on the Turks. Russia, too, went to war against the Ottoman Empire. At the Congress of Berlin in 1878, the Habsburgs obtained the right to occupy the provinces, but not to annex them. Until 1908 the dual monarchy occupied both.

These provinces perpetually threatened to create an explosion. Many observers in Vienna pressed for some sort of all-south-Slav solution that would join Dalmatia, Croatia, and Bosnia-Herzegovina into one kingdom under Francis Joseph, with the same status as Hungary—a triple rather than a dual monarchy. However, the advocates of this solution, known as "Trialists," met with violent Magyar opposition.

Then in 1908 a revolution in Turkey led by young army officers gave the Austrian foreign minister a chance to act. Fortified by a prior secret agreement with Russia, he annexed the two provinces in October and announced that they would be given a diet of their own. This move precipitated a major European crisis, which threatened world war but which eventually subsided, leaving the Serbs bitterly resentful and the Balkan peoples in turmoil.

Society and Politics in Austria and Hungary, 1867–1914

Since Austria was 90 percent Catholic, it did not experience the strenuous Kulturkampf of Germany. However, liberals did fight clerical conservatives over religious issues and forced through bills legalizing civil marriages, quasi-secularized schools, and taxes on church property. Many liberals were discredited by the financial crash of 1873, during which it was revealed that some of them had accepted bribes, and, as in Germany, anti-Semitism grew as a political force. The working class turned toward socialism after the crash, while the Austrian nobles took little interest in the nation's problems. The large size of noble estates was a fundamental reason for the small size of the average peasant holding, and made it necessary even for landowning peasants to seek supplementary employment on a noble's property. The peasant's standard of living and level of literacy were extremely low, so that communication and organization for political unity were limited. Furthermore, the Austrian clergy remained loyal to the dynasty and worked on behalf of the nobles against possible peasant uprisings.

The middle class was small. Among the bourgeoisie were many Jews, who generally could not be nobles, bureaucrats, or army officers. Forced to enter trade, the professions, and the arts, where they prospered, the Jewish minority gave Viennese life much of its charm and gaiety, its music, its cafés, its image of "the good life" that was so attractive to western European visitors yet so offensive to peasant and noble in the provinces. Anti-Semitism grew rapidly among the lower middle classes, often unsuccessful competitors in the world of small shop-keeping. One response among the Jews was Zionism—sponsorship of a future Jewish state.

Zionism began as a Jewish minority movement. Many Jewish leaders were convinced that anti-Semitism was a passing phase, a throwback to earlier forms of discrimination and hostility that had largely been outlawed. But as attacks on Jews increased, and as popular stereotypes began to identify them with banking and finance, there was a growing cry for the establishment of a Jewish state. In 1896 Theodor Herzl (1860–1904), a Jew who had experienced anti-Semitism firsthand in France, published a pamphlet, *The Jewish State*, in which he argued that the "Jewish question" was essentially a national question; soon thereafter he began to organize the Zionist movement.

In the late nineteenth century the stresses and strains inherent in this social structure produced two important new political movements among the Germans of Austria: Pan-Germanism and Christian Socialism. In the early 1880s, moderate Austrian Germans had wanted to hand over the Slavic lands of Austria to the Hungarians to rule, and then to unite economically with Germany. The Pan-Germans were more radical. They demanded that Austria become Protestant, and agitated for political union with Germany. The Christian Socialists, however, became the most important Austrian political party. Strongly Catholic and loyal to the Habsburgs, they appealed to both the peasant and the small business owner by favoring social legislation and by opposing big business. The most famous Christian Socialist leader was the mayor of Vienna, Karl Lueger (1844–1910). For years he sponsored public ownership of city utilities, parks, playgrounds, free milk for schoolchildren, and other welfare services, while catering to his followers' hatred of Jews, Marxists, and Magyars.

To the Pan-Germans and the Christian Socialists, the Austrian Social Democrats, founded in 1888, responded with a Marxist program calling for government ownership of the means of production and for political action organized by class rather than by nationality. But the Austrian Social Democrats were not revolutionaries, and they set as their goals such political and social gains as universal suffrage, fully secular education, and the eight-hour working day. They were usually led by intellectuals, many of them Jewish, but they were followed by an ever-increasing number of workers. On the nationality question, Social Democratic leaders strongly urged democratic federalism. Each nationality should have control of its own affairs in its own territory; in mixed territories, minorities should be protected; and a central parliament should decide matters of common interest.

Through it all Emperor Francis Joseph thought of himself as the last "monarch of the old school." He faced bitter personal loss time and again. His son Rudolf committed suicide in a scandal in 1889; his wife Elisabeth was killed by an anarchist at Geneva in 1898; and his nephew's assassination at Sarajevo in 1914 would trigger a world war. Still, he reigned with determination far longer than any other European monarch, loyal to the Habsburg ideal to the end.

Despite imperial tragedy and divisive politics, Vienna was one of the great cities of Europe in the years between 1870 and 1914. Its cosmopolitan air, its rapid growth, its mixture of frivolity and high seriousness were remarkable. Here controversy over art, literature, dance, music, and sexual morality would explode into revolt against the old norms.

In Hungary the situation was rather different. The great landed nobility, owning half of Hungary in estates of hundreds of thousands of acres apiece and loyal to the dynasty, were a small class numerically. Hungary had a much larger class of country gentlemen whose holdings were far smaller and whose social position was lower, but whose political influence as a group was greater. After the emancipation of the serfs in 1848 many members of the gentry became civil servants or entered the professions. During the nineteenth century the towns became steadily more Magyar, as members of the gentry and peasantry moved into them. At the bottom of the social pyramid was a class of industrial workers in the cities, mostly in the textile and flour-milling industries.

The Jewish population grew rapidly, mostly by immigration. Many Jews were converted and assimilated and became strongly Magyar in sentiment; but, as in Austria, they were disliked, especially among the poorer city population and in the countryside, where they were associated with money lending and tavern keeping, two professions that kept the peasant in their debt. Nonetheless, though anti-Semitism existed in Hungary, it never became as important a political movement as in Austria.

The Catholic church was immensely powerful and rich, but it was the faith of only about 60 percent of the population. Some magnate families and many of the gentry had never returned to Catholicism after the Reformation, remaining Calvinists. Several hundred thousand Germans, chiefly in Transylvania, were Lutheran, and there also were Magyar Unitarians. Clericalism could

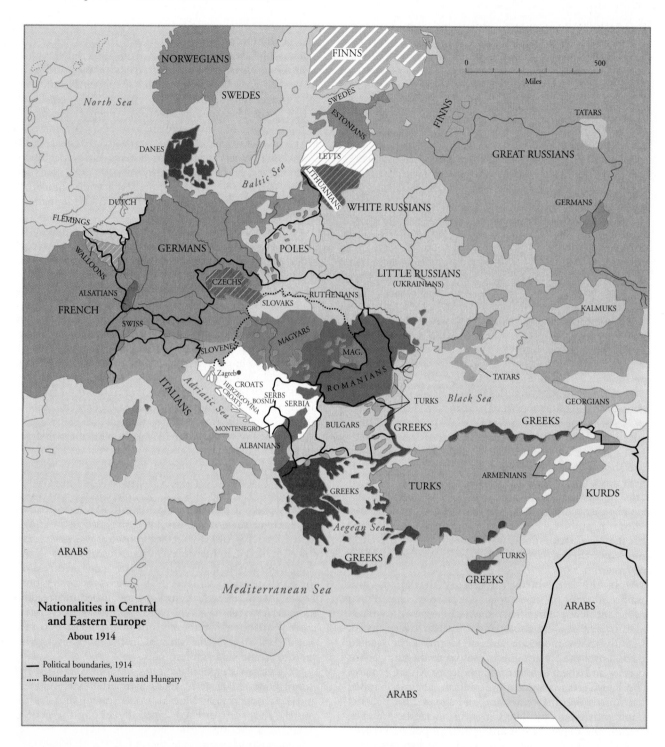

**Nationalities in Central
and Eastern Europe**
About 1914

—— Political boundaries, 1914
····· Boundary between Austria and Hungary

never become the dominant force in Hungary that it was in Austria.

Thus, because of its differing social and religious structure, Hungary did not produce strong parties like the Austrian Social Democrats and Christian Socialists. Hungary never effectively changed its law of 1874, by which only about 6 percent of the population could vote. The only real source of Magyar political differences was the question of Hungary's position in the dual monarchy.

Some, followers of Lajos Kossuth (1802–1894), favored complete independence; others, called the Tigers, wished to improve the position of Hungary within the monarchy by securing Hungarian control over its own army, diplomatic service, and finances, and by limiting the tie with Austria to the person of the monarch. While the Tigers were generally victorious, the Kossuthists were able to disrupt the government in 1902, and in 1905 they won a majority. When Francis Joseph refused to meet the demands of the new majority and appointed a loyal general as premier, the Kossuthists urged patriots not to pay taxes or perform military service, and until 1910 they kept parliament in convulsion. It was in this utterly unstable atmosphere that Hungary received the news on June 8, 1914, that Francis Ferdinand, heir to the throne of the dual monarchy, had been assassinated.

RUSSIA, 1825–1914

In Russia the process of modernization took far longer than in western Europe. There was no parliament in Russia until 1905. Serfdom was not abolished until 1861. Each time reform came—in the 1860s and in 1905 and 1906—it came as a result of military defeat abroad. The reforms of Alexander II (1855–1881) arose from Russia's defeat in the Crimean War (1854–1856); the Revolution of 1905 was made possible by Russia's failure in the Russo-Japanese War (1904–1905). During most of the nineteenth and early twentieth centuries, even after the reforms, the Russian czars claimed for themselves the autocratic rights that Peter the Great had exercised. Thus the Russian people experienced long periods of repression and reaction.

The failure to adjust to the currents of the times and the attempt to preserve autocratic rule produced unparalleled discontent in Russia. Disillusioned and angry intellectuals in the 1830s and 1840s gave way to proponents of social change in the 1850s and early 1860s, and these in turn yielded to determined revolutionaries and terrorists in the late 1860s and the years that followed. Although Marxist political groupings existed after 1896, the Marxists were neither numerous nor effective in the nineteenth century. Non-Marxist revolutionary parties performed the acts of violence that convulsed the regime and won the support of large groups of Russians. It was only V. I. Lenin's transformation and adaptation of Marxist doctrine specifically to Russia that enabled his Bolsheviks to emerge as an important threat. And it was only Lenin's supreme tactical skill and boldness that enabled him to bring the Bolsheviks, still a minority, to power during the Revolution of 1917.

Amid official attempts to preserve sixteenth-century patterns, Russia was experiencing the impact of nineteenth- and twentieth-century industrialization and modernization. New resources were developed, thousands of miles of railroads were built, and many factories were engaged in both heavy and light industry. A new laboring class thronged the cities. Most Russian revolutionaries looked to the peasants to provide them with their political and social base, and they therefore considered the peasants' problems paramount. The Marxists, on the other hand, recruited their following among the new urban proletariat and focused their attention on its problems; but they relied for their tightly organized leadership

almost exclusively on a small body of intellectuals and theorists. And despite censorship and repression, Russia experienced during the nineteenth century a substantial literary flowering, as poets, novelists, and playwrights produced works that rank with the greatest of all time.

Nicholas I, 1825–1855

Reactionary and autocratic, literal-minded and devoted to military engineering, Nicholas I worked hard at the business of the state. Although he despised all constitutions, he honored the liberal constitution that his elder brother Alexander had granted to the Poles until the Poles themselves revolted in 1831. He believed that his autocratic power had been ordained by God; he was prepared to make improvements but not to touch the fundamental institution of the autocracy. Though he was uneasy over the dangers inherent in serfdom, he was afraid to reform it in any significant way, because he feared that concessions would stimulate revolution among his peasants.

Nicholas's secretariat became the most important organ of Russian government. He enlarged it by creating several sections, often under close personal friends. This enormous expansion of the czar's secretariat did not result in the abolition of any of the older organs of government; consequently, bureaucratic confusion became great, paperwork was multiplied, and much injustice was done through sheer incompetence.

Nicholas was deeply worried about the possibility that subversive foreign ideas might penetrate into the universities. After the revolutions of 1848 in Europe, his reactionary minister of education abolished the study of philosophy at the University of St. Petersburg because, as he said, the usefulness of the subject had not been proved. Formulated under the three heads of Autocracy, Orthodoxy, and Nationality—unlimited power of the monarch, sanctity of the Russian church, and conformity with the "Russian national character"—Nicholas's policies resulted in a police state.

Like other Russian rulers before him, Nicholas confidently expected the collapse of the Ottoman Empire. Russia wished to protect the Orthodox subjects of the sultan and also had important economic interests at stake. The great wheat-producing areas in the south were being developed intensively, and Odessa on the Black Sea had become the major commercial port for the grain trade. Nicholas hoped to establish a Russian sphere of influence in the Balkans and even to take possession of Istanbul itself. Thus he intervened in the Greek War of the late 1820s, and when the governor of Egypt, Mehmet Ali, revolted against the Ottoman sultan in 1832 and threatened Istanbul, he landed a Russian army and got credit for saving the sultan's capital.

In 1833 the Turks paid the bill for these services. Instead of wishing to annex large sections of the Ottoman Empire, the czar, under the influence of a well-argued memorandum from his foreign minister, Count Karl Nesselrode (1780–1862), now preferred to maintain a weak and friendly Ottoman Empire that would serve as a buffer between Russia and the Habsburg Empire. In the Treaty of Unkiar Skelessi Nicholas took the Ottoman Empire under his protection, and the Turks agreed to close the Bosporus and Dardanelles to the warships of any nation.

Alarmed at the control the treaty gave to Russia in an area of the world vital to British imperial and commercial interests, British diplomacy was geared to undoing it. The next time Mehmet Ali revolted (in 1839), the British were able to put him down with their fleet before he came near a Russian land force. In 1841 all the other important powers joined Russia in guaranteeing the integrity of Turkey, thus ending the exclusive position obtained by Russia at Unkiar Skelessi.

For twelve years (1841–1853) Nicholas tried to reach an agreement with Britain on what should be done with Ottoman territory if Turkey collapsed. The British did not believe that such collapse was imminent, and they hoped to prevent Russia from doing anything to hasten it. By 1853 the czar mistakenly believed that Britain was not opposed to Russian domination of Turkey, and Britain mistakenly believed that the czar would not act in Turkey without consultation.

Russian relations with the Ottoman Turks were further complicated by religion. The Turks were Muslim; the czar saw himself as the protector of the Orthodox Christians; the Russian Empire in the Caucasus region was filled with diverse nationalities, several of them followers of Islam. While the Georgians and Armenians had been Christians for centuries, the Muslim subjects of the empire had been under pressure throughout the eighteenth century to accept conversion. The Tatars, centered in Kazan, had risen in the Pugachev rebellion in 1773–1775; Nicholas again focused attention on the Tatars when he broke up the University of Kazan, where Western and Eastern culture had met effectively in a center of high repute, and began urging conversions to Orthodoxy. The Tatars of the Crimea and the Turks of Azerbaijan, who viewed themselves as culturally different from the people of Kazan, were strongly influenced by developments in Turkey. Thus the czar had religious as well as political reasons to assert his authority over the sultan's Christian population.

A dispute arose over whether the Roman Catholics, backed by Napoleon III, or the Orthodox clergy, backed by the czar, should have the right to perform certain functions in the Christian Holy Places in Palestine, which was still part of the Ottoman dominions. This dispute was the immediate cause of the Crimean War, since the sultan ruled in favor of the Roman Catholics. But the underlying cause was the czar's wish to reestablish Russian dominance. Nicholas coupled his demand for Russia's exclusive position with the demand that the Turks settle the dispute over the Holy Places amicably, and he occupied the Danubian principalities to enforce his demands. Despite many months of elaborate diplomatic negotiations, Turkey declared war on Russia and lost its fleet. Britain, France, and eventually the Italian kingdom of Sardinia then fought the Russians, ostensibly to protect the Turks though in fact to preserve the balance of power.

Famous in myth and legend as the occasion of the charge of the Light Brigade and of pioneer efforts by Florence Nightingale (1820–1910) to save the lives of sick and wounded soldiers, the Crimean War consisted mostly of a joint French and British seige of the great Russian naval base at Sevastopol in the Crimea. Military operations on both sides were conducted inefficiently, but eventually the Russians were compelled to surrender. In the Treaty of Paris of 1856, Russia was forbidden to fortify the Black Sea coast or to maintain a fleet there. Because this made it impossible for the Russians to defend their own shores or to conduct their shipping in security, it became the paramount object of Russian foreign policy to alter the Black Sea clauses of the treaty.

Alexander II and Reform, 1855–1881

The economic developments of the early nineteenth century had rendered the system of serfdom less and less profitable. In the south, where land was fertile and crops were produced for sale as well as for use, the serf usually tilled his master's land three days a week, but sometimes more. In the north, where the land was less fertile and could not produce a surplus, the serfs often had a special arrangement with their masters called *quit-rent*. This meant that the serf paid the master annually in cash instead of in work, and usually had to labor at home as a craftsman or go to a nearby town and work as a factory hand or small shopkeeper to raise the money. As industries grew, it became clear to factory owners, who experimented with both serf and free labor, that serf labor was not as productive. Yet free labor was scarce, and the growing population needed to be fed.

Serfdom had become uneconomic. But this fact was not widely recognized among Russian landowners. The nobility wished to keep things as they were and did not as a class feel that emancipation was the answer. Yet the serfs showed increasing unrest. Alexander II, though personally almost as conservative as his father, determined to embark on reforms, preferring, as he put it, that the abolition of serfdom come from above rather than from below.

Through a cumbersome arrangement in which local commissions made studies and reported their findings to members of the government, an emancipation law was eventually proclaimed early in 1861. A general statute declared that the serfs were now free, laid down the principles of the new administrative organization of the peasantry, and set out the rules for the purchase of land. All peasants, crown and private, were freed, and each peasant household received its homestead and a certain amount of land, usually the amount the peasant family had cultivated for its own use in the past. The land usually became the property of the village commune, or *obshchina*, which had the power to redistribute it periodically among the households. The government bought the land from the proprietors, but the peasants had to redeem it by payments extending over a period of forty-nine years. The proprietor retained only the portion of his estate that had been farmed for his own purposes.

In 1855 the allied fleet gathered in Balaclava harbor in the Crimea. From the ordinance wharf there the siege of Sevastopol was supplied. Control of the Black Sea ports proved crucial to the allied victory.

BBC Hutton Picture Library

This statute, liberating more than 40 million human beings, has been called the greatest single legislative act in history. But there were grave difficulties inherent in so sweeping a change in the nature of society. The peasant had to accept the allotment, and since his household became collectively responsible for the taxes and redemption payments, his mobility was not greatly increased. The commune took the place of the proprietor. Moreover, most peasants felt that they got too little land and had to pay too much for it.

The end of the landlords' rights of control and police authority on their estates made it necessary to reform local administration. By statute in 1864, provincial and district assemblies, or *zemstvos*, were created. Chosen by an elaborate electoral system that divided the voters into categories by class, the assemblies gave substantial representation to the peasants. The zemstvos dealt with local finances, education, medical care, scientific agriculture, maintenance of the roads, and other economic and social questions. Starting from scratch in many cases, the zemstvos made great advances in primary education and in improving public health. They led tens of

thousands of Russians to hope that this progressive step would be crowned by the creation of a central parliament, or *duma*. But the duma was not granted, partly because, after an attempted assassination of the czar in 1866, the regime swung away from reform.

But before this happened, other advances had been made. The populations of the cities were given municipal assemblies, with duties much like those of the zemstvos in the countryside. The antique Russian judicial system and legal procedure were modernized. For the first time juries were introduced, cases were argued publicly and orally, and all classes were made equal before the law. Censorship was relaxed, and the often brutal system of military service was reformed and rendered less severe.

In foreign policy, Alexander II's record was uneven. The Russians successfully repressed the Polish uprising of 1863. They seized the opportunity provided by the Franco-Prussian War of 1870 and simply tore up the Black Sea provisions of the Treaty of Paris, declaring unilaterally that they would no longer be bound by them. In 1877 the Russians went to war against Turkey once again, now on behalf of the rebellious Balkan Christians of Bosnia, Herzegovina, and Bulgaria. By the Peace of San Stefano Russia obtained a large, independent Bulgarian state. But the powers—England, France, Germany, Austria, Italy, and Russia—at the Congress of Berlin later in the same year reversed the judgment of San Stefano. They permitted only about half of the planned Bulgaria to come into existence as an autonomous state, while another portion obtained autonomy separately as East Rumelia and the rest went back to Turkey.

Meanwhile, encroachments begun under Nicholas I against Chinese territory in the Amur River Valley remained undeflected by the Crimean War, and Russian gains were confirmed by the Treaty of Peking in 1860. Russian settlements in the "maritime province" on the Pacific Ocean continued to flourish, and Vladivostok was founded in 1858 and grew rapidly. In central Asia a series of campaigns conquered the Turkish khanates by 1896 and added much productive land to the Crown. Here, however, the advance toward the northwest frontier of India appeared to threaten British interests and aroused public opinion in Britain against Russia, and after a brutal conquest of the Turkomans in 1881, the Russian Empire was, for the time, complete.

The Idea of an Intelligentsia

Early in Nicholas's reign, Russian professors and students, influenced by German philosophers, were devoting themselves to discussions on art, philosophy, and religion. Russian universities were generally excellent and at the cutting edge of the great variety of modernizing ideas associated with the nineteenth century. Many intellectuals outside the universities followed suit. These were the first groups to be known as *intelligentsia*, originally a class limited to Russia, though the concept of the intelligentsia soon spread to the rest of the European Continent and drew upon themes from the Enlightenment. By the 1830s the intelligentsia was beginning to discuss Russia's place in the world, and especially its relationship to the West. Out of its debates arose two important opposing schools of thought: the Westerners and the Slavophiles.

The Westerners stated their case in a document called the *Philosophical Letter*, published in 1836 though written earlier. Its author, Peter Chaadaev (c. 1794–1856), lamented the damaging effect of Byzantine Christianity and Tatar invasion upon Russian development and declared that Russia had made no contribution of importance to the world. Nicholas I had Chaadaev certified as insane and commanded that he be put under house arrest, while the journal in which the letter appeared was banned and its editor sent into exile. Yet despite scorn and censorship, the Westerners continued to declare that Russia was a society fundamentally like the West, though far behind it, and that Russia should now catch up.

In contrast, the Slavophiles vigorously argued that Russia had its own national spirit. Russia was, they maintained, essentially different from the West. The orthodox religion of the Slavs was not legalistic, rationalistic, and particularistic, like that of the Roman Catholic states of the West, but emotional and organically unified. The Slavophiles attacked Peter the Great for embarking Russia on a false course. The West ought not be imitated, but opposed. The Russian upper classes should turn away from their Europeanized manners and look instead for inspiration to the Russian peasant, who lived in the truly Russian institution of the village commune. Western Europe was urban and bourgeois; Russia was rural and agrarian. Western Europe was materialistic; Russia was deeply spiritual.

This view also led to a demand for a thorough change in the country, however. The Slavophiles opposed the tyranny and the bureaucracy of Nicholas I as bitterly as did the Westerners, but they wanted a patriarchal, benevolent monarchy of the kind they argued had existed before Peter the Great, instead of a constitutional regime on the Western pattern. Instead of a central parliament, they looked back to the feudal Muscovite assembly, to the *zemski sobor*, and to other institutions of czardom before Peter.

Michael Bakunin (1814–1876) pushed these ideas to an extreme. He was a tactician of violence who advocated "anarchism, collectivism, and atheism." He looked forward to a great revolution spreading perhaps from Prague to Moscow and thence to the rest of Europe, followed by a tight dictatorship; beyond this he was entirely vague about the future. Atheism was a fundamental part of his program. In his long career, Bakunin was to exert from exile abroad a considerable influence on Russian radicals.

The Russian intelligentsia, like intellectuals elsewhere in Europe, reacted against the romanticism of their predecessors. They turned to a narrowly utilitarian view of art and society. All art must have a social purpose, and those bonds holding the individual tightly to the traditions of society must be smashed: parental authority, the marriage tie, the tyranny of custom. For these people, the name *nihilist* (a person who believes in nothing) quickly became fashionable.

In the 1860s many young Russian intellectuals went to Switzerland. Also present in Switzerland were two important Russian revolutionary thinkers, Peter Lavrov and Peter Tkachev. Lavrov (1823–1900) taught his followers that as intellectuals they owed a great debt to the Russian peasant, whose labor had enabled their ancestors to enjoy leisure and had made their own education possible. Lavrov advised the nihilist students to complete their education and then return to Russia and go among the peasants, educating them and spreading among them propaganda for an eventual, revolution of the masses. On the other hand, Tkachev (1844–1886) taught that revolution would have to come from a tightly controlled revolutionary elite, a little knot of conspirators who would seize power.

Under the influence of these teachers, especially Bakunin and Lavrov, Russian nihilists turned to a new kind of movement, called *populism*. Young men and women of education decided to return to Russia and live among the peasants. When a government decree in 1872 actually summoned them back, they found that a parallel

Shown here is an artist's reconstruction of the assassination of Czar Alexander II on March 13, 1881. A nihilist had thrown a bomb at Alexander's carriage, but the emperor was not harmed. He left the carriage to talk to the wounded Cossacks, and at that moment a second assassin threw a second bomb under Alexander's feet. Mutilated, Alexander said, "Home to the Palace, to die there," and did so ninety minutes later.

New York Public Library Picture Collection

movement had already begun at home. About three thousand young people now took posts as teachers, innkeepers, or store managers in the villages. Their romantic views of the peasantry were soon dispelled, however. Suspicious of their motives, the peasants often betrayed them. The populists became conspicuous and were easily traced by the police, who arrested them. Two mass trials were held in the 1870s. After the trials those populists who remained at large decided that they needed a determined revolutionary organization. With the formation of the Land and Freedom Society in 1876, the childhood of the Russian revolutionary movement was over.

The revolutionaries had been further stimulated by Alexander II's grant of reforms. So great had the discontent become that it is doubtful whether any Russian government could have proceeded fast enough to suit the radicals. Russian socialism was not yet greatly influenced by the gradualism of Marx. It was not urban but rural, not evolutionary but revolutionary, not a mass political party but a conspiracy. The movement became more and more radical, and in 1879 those who believed in the use of conspiracy and terror separated from the others and founded a group called the People's Will; the antiterrorists called themselves the Black Partition. The first deeply influenced Lenin's party; the second was an ideological ancestor of Bolshevism.

The members of the People's Will now systematically went on a hunt for Czar Alexander II himself. They shot at him and he crawled on the ground to safety. They mined the track on which his train was traveling, and blew up his baggage train instead. They put dynamite under the dining room of the palace and exploded it, but the czar was late for dinner that night, and eleven servants were killed instead. They rented a shop on one of the streets along which he drove and tunneled under it. Finally, in March of 1881, they killed him with a handmade grenade, which also blew up the assassin.

Not all Russian intellectual life was so directly concerned with the problem of revolution and social reform. Many intellectuals preferred to work within the creative arts. Here, too, artists tended to be taken up with the kinds of issues that divided the Westerners and the Slavophiles. For example, Nikolai Rimsky-Korsakov had used the sounds of folk music in his compositions, and in his operatic work Modest Moussorgsky had given Russians pride in their national past. Above all, Russian prose writers of the late nineteenth century towered above the cultural landscape. All of Europe read Alexander Pushkin, Ivan Turgenev, Anton Chekhov, Nikolai Gogol, or the poet Mikhail Lermontov (1814–1841). To non-Russian readers, two writers seemed to best express the romantic sense of despair to be found in the Russian revolutionaries. One, Feodor Dostoevsky, had died in 1881, but his brilliant, disturbed work seemed best to represent the trend of Russian thought: compassion for all humanity, an almost frenzied desire to remake society—a mixture of socialist commitment and religious conviction that was both understandable and exotic to the West. In *Crime and Punishment, The Possessed*, and *The Brothers Karamazov*, the last completed in 1880, he had shown himself to be a giant of modern literature.

The most influential voice of the time in circles outside Russia was that of Count Leo Tolstoy (1828–1910), who had participated in the Crimean War and, in *War and Peace* (1865–1869), had pungently revealed the failings of the Russian nobility during the Napoleonic wars. In 1876, while writing *Anna Karenina*, a masterpiece of moral tragedy, he underwent what he called a conversion to a belief in Christian love and nonresistance to evil. He shared the romantics' view that the Russian future lay with the peasants, for urban society became inevitably corrupt and violent. He thus became a spokesman for pastoral simplicity and Christian anarchism, and he was widely read in Russia and abroad.

The Years of Reaction, 1881–1904

The reign of Alexander III and the first decade of the reign of his son, Nicholas II, formed a quarter-century of consistent policies (1881–1904) of the kind Tolstoy attacked so eloquently. Both czars hated the earlier liberal reforms and were determined that there would be no more. Yet a peasant bank set up under Alexander III made redemption payments easier for the peasants, and a few pieces of labor legislation made working conditions somewhat more tolerable. Countering these measures were the establishment of a special bank that extended credit to the improverished nobility, the reinstitution of rigorous censorship, and the institution in the countryside of so-called rural leaders or land captains in place of the elected justices of the peace. Election procedure for the zemstvos and for the city assemblies was made far less democratic. There began a vigorous persecution of the minority nationalities and of Jews, a policy called Russification. In 1891 twenty thousand Jews were evicted from Moscow, and most were restricted to the Pale of Settlement, an area roughly identical to Byelorussia and the Ukraine. Official pogroms (organized massacres) were directed against them, especially in Kiev. A quota was applied to Jews, limiting their entry to high schools and universities. One result was massive emigration; over a million Jews, in a population of 5 million, left, many for America. Another result was that the intellectuals joined the various revolutionary movements.

Yet these years were also notable for steady growth. In 1892 Count Sergei Witte (1849–1915) came to the ministry of finance. Witte began the Trans-Siberian Railroad, put Russia on the gold standard, attracted much foreign capital (especially French) for investment, and balanced the budget, in part through a government monopoly of the sale of vodka. The state-owned railroad network doubled in length between 1894 and 1904, and the need for rails stimulated the steel industry. Correspondingly, the number of urban workers multiplied, and many strikes were called in protest against wretched working conditions. In 1897 the working day was fixed by the state at eleven hours for adults, and other provisions were adopted to improve and regularize conditions. These laws, however, proved difficult to enforce.

Under the circumstances, many of the young generation of revolutionaries now turned to Marxist "scientific" socialism, embracing the class struggle and predicting the inevitable downfall of capitalism. A small clandestine group of the intelligentsia, formed in 1894–1895 at St. Petersburg, proposed to overthrow the regime, working with all opponents of the class system. The members of the group included Lenin, a vigorous young intellectual of upper-middle-class origins. In 1898 this group and others formed the Social Democratic party, which in 1900 began to publish its own newspaper. Within party ranks, dissension soon arose over the question of organization. Should the party operate under a strongly centralized directorate, or should each local group of Social Democrats be free to agitate for its own ends? Lenin insisted on a small, tightly knit group of directors at the center. At the party congresses of Brussels and London in 1903, the majority voted with him. Lenin's faction thereafter was called by the name *Bolshevik*, meaning majority, as against the *Menshevik*, or minority group,

which favored a loose, democratic organization for the party. The Mensheviks held to the ideas of George Plekhanov (1857–1918), who felt that Russia would be ripe for socialism only after capitalism and industrialism had progressed sufficiently to fulfill the needs of a Marxist class structure. Both groups remained Social Democrats, or SDs as they were often called.

Meanwhile, in 1901 the non-Marxist revolutionaries also organized a political party, the Socialist Revolutionaries, or SRs. Whereas the SDs as Marxists were initially interested almost exclusively in the urban workers, the SRs as populists were chiefly interested in the peasantry. Their aim was to redistribute the land, and they continued in their terrorist ways. They assassinated several cabinet ministers between 1902 and 1907, using as their slogan the cry "We don't want reforms. We want reform!"

The moderates and liberals were a third political grouping—intellectuals indignant over government repression who favored nothing more radical than compulsory free private education and agrarian reform. The regime stubbornly made no distinction between them and the terrorists and Marxists. Thus the moderates also were forced to organize. In 1905 they took the name Constitutional Democratic party and were thereafter usually referred to as *Kadets*, from the Russian initials KD.

The Russo-Japanese War

Trans-Siberian railway construction made it desirable for the Russians to obtain a right-of-way across Chinese territory in Manchuria. The Russians took the initiative in preventing Japan from establishing itself on the Chinese mainland after Japan defeated China in 1895; in exchange, Russia then required the Chinese to allow the building of the new railroad. In 1897 Russia seized Port Arthur, the very port it had earlier kept out of Japanese hands. Further friction with the Japanese took place in Korea, in which both Japan and Russia were interested. Then, after the Boxer Rebellion of 1900 in China, the Russians kept their troops in Manchuria when the other nations withdrew theirs. Although the Russians promised to withdraw their forces by stages, they failed to do so. After it became apparent that the war party had won control in Russia, the Japanese, without warning, attacked units of the Russian fleet anchored at Port Arthur in February 1904. The Russo-Japanese War had begun.

The Russian fleet, which had steamed all the way around Europe and across the Indian Ocean into the Pacific, was decisively defeated by the Japanese in the battle of Tsushima Strait (May 27, 1904). To the Russian people, the war was a mysterious, distant political adventure of which they wanted no part and by which they were now humiliated. Many intellectuals opposed it, and the SRs and SDs openly hoped for a Russian defeat, which they expected would shake the government's position. Alarmed at the growing unrest at home, the Russian government was persuaded by the president of the

Russian realistic and commemorative art is used to depict events from Russian history. These two scenes by I. A. Vladimirov show the revolution of 1905: on the left, "Shooting of Workers at the Winter Palace in Petersburg" (on January 22, 1905), and on the right, "1905 Barricades," from the Museum of Revolution in Moscow.

Sovfoto

United States, Theodore Roosevelt, to accept his mediation, which the Japanese also actively wished.

Witte, who had opposed the war from the first, was sent to Portsmouth, New Hampshire, as Russian representative. Here he not only secured excellent terms for Russia but also won a favorable verdict from American public opinion, which had thought of Russians as either brutal aristocrats or bomb-throwing revolutionaries. By the Treaty of Portsmouth (1905), Russia recognized the Japanese protectorate over Korea, ceded Port Arthur and the southern half of Sakhalin Island, together with fishing rights in the North Pacific, and promised to evacuate Manchuria. Russian prestige as a Far Eastern power was not deeply wounded or permanently impaired by the defeat or by the treaty. Yet the effect of the defeat in Asia was to transfer Russian attention back to Europe, where a world crisis had already begun.

The Revolution of 1905

Immediately after the Russo-Japanese War the future Kadets held banquets throughout Russia to adopt a series of resolutions for presentation to a kind of national congress of zemstvo representatives. Although the congress was not allowed to meet publicly, its program—a constitution, basic civil liberties, class and minority equality, and extension of zemstvo responsibilities—became widely known and approved. The czar issued a statement so vague that all hope for change was dimmed, and took measures to limit free discussion.

Ironically, it was a police agent of the government who struck the fatal spark. He had been planted in the St. Petersburg iron works to combat SD efforts to organize the workers, and to substitute his own union. He organized a parade of workers to demonstrate peacefully and to petition the czar directly for an eight-hour day, a

national assembly, civil liberties, the right to strike, and other moderate demands. When the workers tried to deliver the petition, Nicholas left town. Troops fired on the peaceful demonstrators, some of whom were carrying portraits of the czar to demonstrate their loyalty. Hundreds of workers were killed on "Bloody Sunday" (January 22, 1905).* The massacre made revolutionaries of the urban workers, and the increasingly desperate moderate opposition joined with the radical opposition.

Amid mounting excitement, the government at first seemed to favor the calling of a zemski sobor—consultative not legislative, but still a national assembly of sorts. But while the czar hesitated, demonstrations occurred throughout the summer of 1905. In October the printers struck. No newspapers appeared, and the printers, with SD aid, formed the first *soviet*, or workers' council. When the railroad workers joined the strike, communications were cut off between Moscow and St. Petersburg. Soviets multiplied and relations between the czar and his subjects collapsed.

The Bolsheviks saw the soviet as an instrument for the establishment of a provisional government, for the proclamation of a democratic republic, and for the summoning of a constituent assembly. This program differed relatively little from the program of the moderate liberals, who originally had hoped to keep the monarchy and obtain their ends by pressure rather than by violence. At the time, the Bolsheviks, like other Marxists, accepted the view that it was necessary for Russia to pass through a stage of bourgeois democracy before the time for the proletarian revolution could come. They were therefore eager to help along the bourgeois revolution.

---

* All dates in this text use the Western, rather than the Russian, calendar.

Nicholas was faced, as Witte told him, with the alternatives of either imposing a military dictatorship or summoning a truly legislative assembly with veto power over the laws. The czar finally chose the latter course, and in October 1905 he issued a manifesto that promised full civil liberties at once, and a legislative assembly or duma to be elected by universal suffrage. In effect, this October Manifesto ended the autocracy, since the duma was to be superior to the czar in legislation.

Yet the October Manifesto did not meet with universal approval. On the right, a government-sponsored party called the Union of the Russian People demonstrated against the manifesto, proclaimed their undying loyalty to the autocrat, and organized their own storm troops, or Black Hundreds, which killed more than three thousand Jews in the first week after the issuance of the manifesto. The armies that had returned from the Far East remained loyal to the government. On the left, the Bolsheviks and SRs made several attempts to launch their violent revolution but failed, and the government was able to arrest their leaders and to put them down after several days of street fighting in Moscow in December 1905. In the center, one group of propertied liberals, pleased with the manifesto, urged that it be used as a rallying point for a moderate program; they were the Octobrists, so called after the month in which the manifesto had been issued. The other moderate group, the Kadets, wished to continue to agitate by legal means for further immediate reforms. But the fires of revolution burned out by early 1906 as Witte used the army to put down any new disturbances.

The Dumas, 1906–1914

Suffrage for the Duma was universal but indirect. Voters chose an electoral college, which then selected the 412 deputies. Although SRs and SDs boycotted the elections, many of them were elected. The Kadets were the strongest party. Contrary to the expectations of the government, the peasant vote was highly liberal. But even before the First Duma had met, Witte was able to reduce its powers. He secured a large French loan, which made the government financially independent of the Duma, and issued a set of "fundamental laws," which the Duma was not to alter. The Crown was to continue to control war making and foreign policy; the minister of finance was to control loans and currency. The czar's council of state was transformed by adding members from the clergy, nobility, the zemstvos, the universities, and chambers of commerce. It became a kind of upper house that had equal legislative rights with the Duma and could therefore submit a rival budget, which the government could then adopt in preference to that of the Duma. Finally, the czar could dissolve the Duma at will, provided he set a date for new elections; when it was not in session he could legislate by himself, although his enactments had later to be approved by the Duma.

The First Duma, the "Duma of Popular Indignation," met between May and July 1906. It addressed a list of grievances to the czar, asking for a radical land reform that would give the peasants all state and church land and part of the land still in private hands. The government flatly refused, and after some parliamentary skirmishing the Duma was dissolved. The Kadet membership, maintaining that the dissolution was unconstitutional, crossed the frontier into Finland, and there issued a manifesto urging the Russian people not to pay taxes or report for military service unless the Duma was recalled. Its authors were tried in absentia and declared ineligible for office. Future dumas were thus deprived of the services of these capable Kadet moderates.

With the dissolution of the First Duma, the highly intelligent and conservative Prince Peter Stolypin (1862–1911) came to power as minister of the interior. Stolypin put through a series of agricultural laws that enabled the peasants to free themselves from the commune. A peasant wishing to detach his property could demand that he be given a single unitary tract. His program accomplished much of what he hoped for; about a quarter of the peasant households of European Russia (almost 9 million) emancipated themselves from the communes between 1906 and 1917. Lenin and others who hoped for the revolution were deeply suspicious of Stolypin's agrarian reforms; they feared that the peasant grievances would be satisfied, and that no revolution in Russia could succeed without the peasants.

At the same time that his agrarian program was going into effect, Stolypin carried on unremitting war against terrorists and other revolutionaries. He did everything he could to interfere with elections to the Second Duma, but the SRs and SDs were well represented, so that the Duma (March–June 1907) would not work with the government. It was dissolved because it refused to suspend parliamentary immunity of the SD deputies, whom Stolypin wanted to arrest.

After the dissolution of the Second Duma, the government illegally altered the election laws, cutting the number of delegates from the peasants and national minorities, and increasing the number from the gentry. By this means the government won a majority, and the Third Duma (1907–1912) and the Fourth (1912–1917) lived out their constitutional terms of five years apiece. Though unrepresentative and limited in their powers, they were still national assemblies. The dumas improved the conditions of peasant and worker and helped strengthen national defense. Their commissions, working with individual ministers, proved extremely useful in increasing the efficiency of government departments. The period of the Third Duma, however, was also notable for the continuation of Russification.

Under the Fourth Duma, the government tended even more toward reaction. The leftists organized for another revolution, working in unions, cooperatives, evening classes for workers, and a network of other labor organizations. A vast web of police spies challenged them at every turn. Meanwhile, the imperial family drifted into a dangerous situation as the religious and autocratic empress fell under the spell of a half-mad and power-hungry monk from Siberia. This man, Gregory Rasputin (1872–1916), was said to have the mysterious ability, possibly hypnotic, to stop the bleeding of the young heir to the throne, who suffered from hemophilia. Since the empress had enormous influence on her beloved husband, Nicholas II, Rasputin was widely rumored to be the ruler of Russia, much to the horror of loyal supporters of the imperial house, and greatly to the benefit of those who knew how to manipulate rumor. When World War I began, Russia was in the throes of a major crisis precipitated by the government's reactionary policies, the scandal of Rasputin's influence, and the indignation of the loyal Duma.

Thus, by 1914 in Russia, the Habsburg Empire, and Germany, modern political parties had coalesced around principles. What each party stood for was determined largely by the peculiar circumstances of the country that gave it birth; the same was true in France and Italy. Yet certain parallels reached across national boundaries. Although no group in either Germany or Austria was comparable with the Russian populists (Social Revolutionaries), German Liberals, Austrian Liberals, and Russian Kadets or Octobrists had similar views. So had the Pan-Germans and the Pan-Slavs. The Social Democrats were Marxist in all three countries, but becoming less revolutionary in Germany and Austria-Hungary, and more so in Russia.

During this period all five countries experienced economic boom and occasional depression; the industrial revolution hit central and eastern Europe late, but with terrific impact. By the start of the twentieth century, Germany had made such advances that its steel production surpassed that of England and was second in the world only to that of the United States. Though far behind Germany both in resources and in technology, Austria-Hungary, too, was rapidly becoming industrialized. In Russia transport and industry boomed. Yet in these three countries, the landed nobility continued to exercise political influence quite out of proportion to their numbers. Everywhere the existence of a new and underprivileged class of urban workers stimulated intellectual leaders to form Marxist political groups, to preach the class struggle, and, except in Russia, to strive for immediate improvements in conditions rather than for the violent overthrow of the regime.

Russia emancipated its serfs in 1861; the most rapidly modernizing nation of the nineteenth century, the United States, freed its slaves two years later. The United States had stood aloof from the developments on the European continent, opening and exploiting its own vast frontier regions. But by the end of the century, it, too, was moving onto the world scene. Its modernization was extraordinarily rapid, and while its political system bore marked comparisons to that of Britain, and its industrialization to that of Germany, it demonstrated that its path to modernization was in many significant ways unique.

THE UNITED STATES: MODERNIZATION AT TOP SPEED

Two sets of statistics dramatically point up the speed of American growth. In 1790 the United States comprised 892,000 square miles, and in 1910, 3,754,000 square miles. Even more important, the population of the United States was 3,929,000 in 1790, and 91,972,000 in 1910—a total greater than that of either of the most powerful European states, Germany and Great Britain, and second only to that of Russia. And, still more important, the combined industrial and agricultural capacities of America by 1910 were greater than those of any other single country.

The Federal Union, 1787–1861

The land that became so powerful in little more than a century was, in the late 1700s, almost empty of cultivation beyond the Appalachians. Most observers expected the central parts of the North American continent to fill up eventually with settlers, but few realized how quickly this would occur. Moreover, most commentators felt that the developed and fully occupied continent could not possibly come under one political rule. Some unsympathetic observers did not believe that the thirteen Atlantic seaboard colonies that had gathered together to fight the British could possibly maintain their postwar union. Yet hold together they did. Though the union was often to be sorely tested, the process of unification produced a single nation.

Why the United States held together cannot be explained by any one factor. Geography was certainly kinder than in Latin America, for the Appalachians were no real barrier at all; the Rockies were not the barrier the Andes were; and the Mississippi valley, unlike that of the Amazon, helped rather than hindered settlement and communications. The railroad and the telegraph were developed in time to enable goods and ideas to move fast and far enough to hold Americans together. The communications and transportation network already developed by 1860 enabled the North to count on the West in the decisive struggle of the war between the Northern and Southern states. The sheer size of the new republic seemed compatible with a loosely held empire of many tongues and peoples, not with a unified nation-state. But modern technology reduced sheer size to manageable proportions.

Moreover, the resistance to Britain had helped forge a sense of national patriotism. The colonists all recognized one language and one law. Almost all the colonies had frontiers—freely accessible areas on their western edges where an expanding population was carving new

Abraham Lincoln, sixteenth president of the United States, painted by George Healy (1813–1894) from photographs.

The Bettmann Archive

lands from the wilderness. This frontier population was a powerful force for unity, for it had little attachment to the older colonial centers. The frontier settlers had great confidence in their own "manifest destiny" to keep pushing westward with the blessing and patronage of the new federal government, but with only remote control from that government.

Americans had gained their independence from Britain by a war and a revolution that were rather mild compared with the French Revolution. After the more committed Loyalists had left for Canada or Britain, Americans shared a growing sense of national unity, without any seriously alienated European minorities. At the Philadelphia convention of 1787 and in the campaign for adoption during the next two years, they put together a federal constitution that set up a central government with the ability to tax individuals (not just to ask for contributions from constituent states), to control armed forces, and to conduct all foreign relations. The new constitution, in short, set up a sovereign federal nation, not a mere league of sovereign states. On the whole, this result was achieved under conservative leaders, anxious

to preserve their economic and social privileges and afraid that democracy in separate, quasi-independent states might go too far.

Thus the new republic entered the world war of the Napoleonic period in 1812. Neither the French nor the British had been observing the freedom of commerce that the United States claimed as the right of a neutral, but the British seemed to the Americans to be infringing upon neutral rights more seriously than the French were. Moreover, American expansionists saw a possible prize in winning Canada from England, but no comparable prize to be won from France. An American attempt to invade Canada failed, but on the seas the United States won victories that made up for its failures on land and helped bolster national pride. On the whole, the war was a stalemate, and the United States experienced no important gains or losses.

A generation later, however, the United States acquired an enormous block of territory, from Texas to California, at the expense of Mexico. This came in part as a result of annexing the republic of Texas (1845), which had been settled by pioneers from the southern states and had broken away from Mexico in 1836. President James K. Polk (1795–1849) also resolved to acquire Mexican territories west of Texas by purchase and, when negotiations collapsed, launched the Mexican War of 1846–1848, which ended with Mexico's cession of New Mexico and California to the United States in the Treaty of Guadalupe Hidalgo.

Civil War and Reconstruction, 1861–1877

The greatest test of the Federal Union was the war that broke out in 1861 after long years of sectional strife within the union between North and South. The Civil War was really an abortive nationalist revolution, the attempt of the Confederate (Southern) states to set up a separate sovereignty, as the southern Democrats lost political control at the national level. The South was predominantly agricultural, with a society based largely on plantation slavery and on cotton and tobacco, much of which was exported abroad. The North was increasingly industrial, with a society based largely on free labor and independent farm owners. Northern business owners preferred protective tariffs, which hurt the South in its competition for markets.

To the conflict of economic interest was added a conflict of ideals, of ways of life. The fires of conflict were fanned by the question of slavery, which seemed immoral to many in the North, and which seemed the order of nature to many in the South. With the election of Abraham Lincoln (1809–1865) in 1860, the South anticipated an attack on the institution of slavery, which was increasingly defended on ideological grounds that made compromise difficult. Upon the secession of South Carolina and its sister states in the winter of 1860–1861, antagonism reached the point of open war.

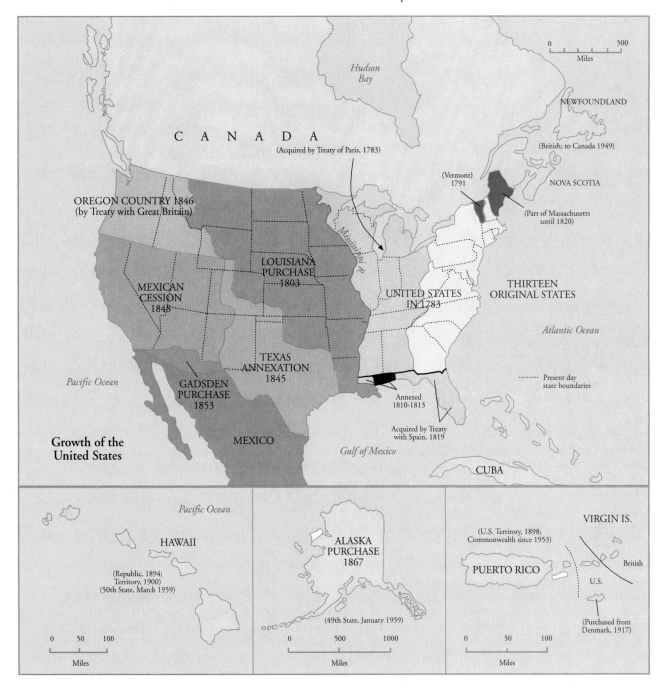

Growth of the United States

CANADA
(Acquired by Treaty of Paris, 1783)

Hudson Bay

0   500 Miles

NEWFOUNDLAND

(British; to Canada 1949)

(Vermont) 1791

NOVA SCOTIA

(Part of Massachusetts until 1820)

OREGON COUNTRY 1846
(by Treaty with Great Britain)

LOUISIANA PURCHASE 1803

Mississippi R.

UNITED STATES IN 1783

THIRTEEN ORIGINAL STATES

MEXICAN CESSION 1848

Atlantic Ocean

Pacific Ocean

GADSDEN PURCHASE 1853

TEXAS ANNEXATION 1845

Annexed 1810-1813

Acquired by Treaty with Spain, 1819

- - - - Present day state boundaries

MEXICO

Gulf of Mexico

CUBA

Pacific Ocean

HAWAII

(Republic, 1894;
Territory, 1900)
(50th State, March 1959)

0   50   100 Miles

ALASKA PURCHASE 1867

(49th State, January 1959)

0   500   1000 Miles

(U.S. Territory, 1898;
Commonwealth since 1953)

VIRGIN IS.

PUERTO RICO

British

U.S.

(Purchased from Denmark, 1917)

0   50   100 Miles

In retrospect, the victory of the North has an air of inevitability. The North was greatly superior in population—especially since the South did not dare use slaves as soldiers—and in industrial resources. Yet aided by an able corps of officers, by the advantages in morale that determined underdogs have, and by disastrous Northern overconfidence, the South won initial victories that gave its cause great momentum. But the North thwarted the efforts of Confederate diplomats to secure British intervention and was able to improvise a naval force that gradually established a blockade, shutting off the South from importation of necessary war materials. Northern determination, manpower, and materials wore

the Southern armies down by the spring of 1865, and the last Confederate forces capitulated in May. In the previous month, President Lincoln had been assassinated.

The road to reunion after 1865 was not easy, and in the first years of the Reconstruction period after the war it appeared to be almost impossible. The South was occupied by Northern soldiers, the former slaves were enfranchised, and a period of political instability followed. Yet the Civil War did not end as such wars have often ended, in wholesale reprisals, executions, and exile. There were very few political refugees of the kind that often emerge from defeated causes; the soldiers of the South returned to devastated homes and lost fortunes, but under

General Ulysses S. Grant (1822–1885) ultimately led the North to victory. Willing to accept appalling losses, Grant waged the "first modern war," defeating the Southern commander, Robert E. Lee (1807–1870). Both were graduates of West Point. Grant, born in Ohio, was moved from the Western front into direct confrontation with Lee after his victory at Vicksburg. Lee, born in Virginia, had fought for the United States in the war with Mexico. He was not sympathetic to the Southern secession movement. Offered a field command in the United States Army, Lee resigned his commission when he learned of Virginia's secession and was made commander of Virginia's forces three days later.

Library of Congress

amnesty. Gradually the crusading fervor of the North over matters of racial freedom subsided, as a generally conservative view prevailed in both major postwar political parties. Conservative, business-conscious Northerners were anxious to get back to normal conditions and quite prepared to compromise with like-minded Southerners at the expense of racial equality and other democratic ideals. By 1877 the Southerners had regained control over their states through a political bargain. Slavery was never restored, but blacks were in effect disfranchised, and "white supremacy" was restored. An era of growing racism followed.

The end of Reconstruction left the Democratic party in control of what came to be called the "solid South." This was a natural development, for the Republican party had guided the North during the war and had tried to carry through Reconstruction. This situation worked to strengthen the American two-party system, since with so secure a voting block for the Democrats, the Republicans were forced either to make compromises among themselves to preserve their own party unity or lose power; and the northern Democrats were forced to make compromises with their southern wing. Third-party movements, whether radical or reactionary, did not develop as in Europe. Politically minded groups that could

offer attractive programs soon found their ideas absorbed by the two main parties.

Free Enterprise and Government Regulation, 1865–1917

In 1865 the American economy was still in some respects "colonial"; that is, it produced mainly foods and other raw materials, to be exchanged abroad for manufactured goods. In financial terms, it was dependent on foreign money markets. But in the northern and midwestern states the industrial revolution had already accelerated, and by 1914 the United States was transformed into a great industrial nation. This transformation could not have taken place at the rate it did without the existence of an abundant work force, especially so after massive waves of new emigration, largely from eastern and southern Europe in the 1890s. Also, the traditions of individual initiative and freedom of enterprise were a basis for a national sense of aggressive and buoyant optimism as the indigenous population was systematically pushed aside in the name of progress.

This great expansion in national wealth was achieved in a climate of opinion that overwhelmingly supported

During the Civil War free black troops were brought into action by the North. The South, fearing a slave insurrection, would make little use of this substantial portion of the population. Shown here is the band of the 107th U.S. Colored Infantry at Arlington, Virginia, at the end of the war.

Library of Congress

the view that the federal government should not interfere directly with business enterprise beyond maintaining public order, enforcing contracts, exercising control over the coinage of money, and, for much of this time, maintaining a protective tariff. Nor were state and local governments supposed to go beyond such limits, though at times some did. This laissez-faire view was reinforced by the Fourteenth Amendment to the constitution, which contained a "due process" clause: "nor shall any state deprive any person of life, liberty, or property without due process of law." In the era of free enterprise that followed the Civil War, the Supreme Court of the United States interpreted the clause to mean that state governments should not deprive business owners of property by regulating wages, prices, conditions of labor, and the like.

Many of the same forces that produced reform in Britain gradually brought to the United States minimum wage acts, limitation of child labor and women's labor, sanitary regulation, control of hours of labor, and workmen's compensation. By the early twentieth century public opinion was ready for increased participation by the national government in the regulation of economic life.

During this time the women's movement took on increased dimensions. Women had played important roles in the abolitionist and anti-slavery movements before the Civil War. They now turned to property rights, suffrage, and temperance. Elizabeth Cady Stanton (1815–1902) and Lucretia C. Mott (1793–1880) had worked together to call the first women's rights convention at Seneca Falls, New York, in 1848. Stanton became president of the National Woman Suffrage Association in 1869. She and Susan B. Anthony (1820–1906) lectured widely on women's rights, which they felt had to precede any truly effective contribution to social reform more broadly. Anthony also supported black suffrage for male and female and the Women's Christian Temperance Union. It was not until 1920, however, that women won the right to vote.

Theodore Roosevelt (1858–1919), Republican president from 1901 and 1909, promised to give labor a "square deal" and to proceed vigorously with *trust-busting*—attacks on great trusts or combinations that had come to monopolize important sectors of the American economy. Although Roosevelt did not fulfill all his promises, his administration did attack the trusts in railroads and tobacco and did press regulation of great corporations by the federal government. Federal prosecution of John D. Rockefeller's (1839–1937) Standard Oil Company resulted in 1911 in a Supreme Court decision dissolving the great holding company. The work of the social legislators of the early 1900s and of the *muckrakers*—who wrote exposés of questionable business practices for popular magazines—was not in vain. American big business in the later twentieth century was bigger than it had been in the day of Theodore Roosevelt, but it was also more aware of the need to court public opinion.

During 1913–1917, in the first administration of Woodrow Wilson (1856–1929), a Democrat, the process of regulation gained momentum. The Federal Reserve Act

THE WRITTEN RECORD

The Influence of Sea Power

The new "navalism," which already had assertive advocates in Britain and Germany, derived many of its doctrines from the writings of an American officer, Captain Alfred T. Mahan (1840–1914). Mahan's book *The Influence of Sea Power upon History* (1890), and his later works assigned navies a place of preeminent importance in determining power status and found an influential audience at home and abroad, especially in Germany, Britain, and Japan.

It has been said that, in our present state of unpreparedness, a trans-isthmian canal will be a military disaster to the United States, and especially to the Pacific coast. When the canal is finished the Atlantic seaboard will be neither more nor less exposed than it now is; it will merely share with the country at large the increased danger of foreign complications with inadequate means to meet them. The danger of the Pacific coast will be greater by so much as the way between it and Europe is shortened through a passage which the stronger maritime power can control. The danger lies not merely in the greater facility for dispatching a hostile squadron from Europe, but also in the fact that a more powerful fleet than formerly can be maintained on that coast by a European power, because it can be so much more promptly called home in case of need. The greatest weakness of the Pacific ports, however, if wisely met by our government, will go far to insure our naval superiority there. The two chief centres, San Francisco and Puget Sound, owing to the width and the great depth of the entrances, cannot be effectively protected by torpedoes; and consequently, as fleets can always pass batteries through an unobstructed channel, they cannot obtain perfect security by means of fortifications only. Valuable as such works will be

to them, they must be further garrisoned by coast-defense ships, whose part in repelling an enemy will be coordinated with that of the batteries. The sphere of action of such ships should not be permitted to extend far beyond the port to which they are allotted, and on whose defense they form an essential part; but within that sweep they will always be a powerful reinforcement to the seagoing navy when the strategic conditions of a war cause hostilities to center around their port. By sacrificing power to go long distances, the coast-defense ship gains proportionate weight of armor and guns; that is, of defensive and offensive strength. It therefore adds an element of unique value to the fleet with which it for a time acts. No foreign states, except Great Britain, have ports so near our Pacific coast as to bring it within the radius of action of their coast-defense ships....

The military needs of the Pacific States, as well as their supreme importance to the whole country, are yet a matter of the future, but of a future so near that provision should immediately begin.

A. T. Mahan, "The Influences of Sea Power upon History," *Atlantic Monthly,* LXVI (December 1890), pp. 22–24.

of 1913, for example, gave federal officials more control over banking, credit, and currency. Meantime, the Sixteenth Amendment, legalizing a progressive income tax, and the Seventeenth, providing for direct election of senators rather than their appointment by state governments, made the federal republic more democratic in practice. Approval of such measures was not, of course, unanimous, since Americans differed loudly and widely about almost everything, from the use of the environment to organized sports. To outsiders, and to many native critics, American life in the decades between the Civil War and 1917 often seemed one great brawl, a Darwinian struggle for wealth and power. Yet this apparently chaotic society achieved extraordinary material growth and political stability that required the tacit assent of millions of men and women holding to a generally common goal of modernization.

Despite general public distrust, government in the United States came to play a larger and larger part in the lives of all. Although this was also true of local and state government, it was especially so for the federal

government. The gradually increasing importance of the federal government and the gradually decreasing initiative of state governments were as clear in the period 1789–1917 as was the material growth and increased nationalism of the United States.

The United States Becomes a World Power, 1898–1914

Quite as clear, though still the subject of complex debate among Americans, was the emergence of the United States as a great international power. From the very beginning it had a department of state and a traditional apparatus of ministers, consuls, and, later, ambassadors. By the Monroe Doctrine of the 1820s it took the firm position that European powers were not to extend further their existing territories in the Western hemisphere. This was an active expression of American claims to a far wider sphere of influence than the continental United States. Although Americans took no direct part in the nineteenth-century balance-of-power politics in Europe, they showed an increasing concern with a balance of power in the Far East, where they had long traded and wanted an "Open Door" to commerce. As a result of a brief war in 1898 with Spain that broke out in Cuba, the United States annexed the Philippine Islands and Puerto Rico from Spain. The newly "independent" Cuba became a veiled American protectorate, and in 1900 Hawaii became a territory of the United States (see Chapter 22). All this seemed to many to constitute an American empire.

Theodore Roosevelt, who owed his rapid political rise partly to his military exploits in the Spanish-American War, was a vigorous expansionist. He pressed the building of the Panama Canal, which opened in 1914, stretched the Monroe Doctrine to justify American military intervention in Latin American republics, upheld the Far Eastern interests of the United States, and advocated a larger navy.

Roosevelt wanted to see his country play an active part in world affairs, as exemplified by his arbitrating the peace settlement between Russia and Japan in 1905.

After over a century of expanding wealth and trade, the United States had come to take full part in international commercial relations. Except when the federal government was blockading the Confederacy, it had stood firmly for rights to trade. This fact alone might have brought the United States into the world war of 1914–1918, as it had brought it previously into the world war of 1792–1815. But in 1917 America was an active participant in the world state system, even though it had avoided any formal, permanent entangling alliances. The great themes of modern European history—industrialization, modernization, national unity and nationalism, imperialism, intellectual ferment—were all so evident that Americans could not question that they were part of the broad stream of history.

$\mathcal{S}$UMMARY

During the nineteenth century a sense of *patrie*, or commonality, brought the French together. A coup d'état engineered by Louis Napoleon in 1851 ended the Second Republic and gave birth to the Second Empire. Napoleon III promised to reform but did little to improve the standard of living of the working class. Population expansion and industrial growth were smaller in France than in many other western European nations. The Franco-Prussian War ended the Second Empire.

The Third Republic was born amid defeat and civil strife. Antagonism between republicans and monarchists, and scandals such as the Dreyfus affair, mirrored serious rifts in French society.

Garibaldi, Victor Emmanuel, and Cavour led Italy to union. By 1870, only Trent and Trieste remained as part of *Italia Irredenta*. Public opinion in Italy favored the new kingdom, but deep divisions between Catholics and anticlericals and between north and south would pose difficulties for the new government. In the late 1800s Italy industrialized, but industrialization was unevenly distributed. At the same time, efforts at imperialist expansion went badly.

Bismarck, architect of the German state, was a ruthless genius completely loyal to the Prussian Crown. He used unorthodox policies to secure his own ends. Between 1864 and 1870 Prussia acquired Schleswig-Holstein, defeated Austria in a brief war, and won a stunning victory over France in the Franco-Prussian War. As a result of this war, France was forced to cede Alsace-Lorraine and pay a massive indemnity.

As chancellor of the German Empire from 1871 to 1890, Bismarck created a uniform monetary, legal, and judicial system and helped strengthen German militarism. In the late 1880s he introduced accident, health, and later old-age insurance for workers. When William II succeeded to the throne in 1890, he forced Bismarck to resign. By the early 1900s Germany was a strong modern industrial nation with an efficient agricultural system.

The Habsburg Empire, ruled from 1848 to 1916 by Francis Joseph, consisted of many national minorities. The dual monarchy of Austria-Hungary was created in 1867 to appease nationalist aims of Magyars. However, the formula left the many other national minorities in the empire dissatisfied.

Between 1825 and 1914 modernization proceeded slowly in Russia. Under Nicholas I, Russia became involved in the Crimean War, a balance-of-power conflict over the weakening Ottoman Empire.

Czar Alexander II embarked on reforms, abolishing serfdom in 1861 and reforming the legal and judicial system. His assassination in 1881 led his successors to return to a policy of repression. Intellectual ferment grew into protest movements. Political activity heightened in the early 1900s when Lenin founded the Bolshevik party.

Defeat in the Russo-Japanese War in 1905 sparked an uprising that forced Nicholas II to summon a Duma, or legislative assembly. But the dumas that met between 1906 and 1914 had little power, although czarist ministers such as Stolypin did manage to introduce some reform.

In the nineteenth century the United States expanded, building communication and transportation networks across the continent. By 1914 the United States was an industrial nation with a large labor pool provided by immigrants from Europe. As a result of its war with Spain, the United States became a major world power with territories in the Caribbean and the Pacific.

CRITICAL THINKING

1. What is mean by modernization of nations? How does "modernization" differ from "development"?

2. What were the differences between the French Second Empire and Third Republic? How do empires and republics themselves differ, regardless of country?

3. Describe the steps taken on the Italian peninsula toward national unification.

4. How did war contribute to the sense of both a Prussian and a larger German nationhood? In what way is the title *imperial* properly applied to Germany from 1871?

5. Describe the "minorities question" in the Habsburg Empire. What role did competing national interests in Austria and Hungary play with respect to either resolving or contributing to this question?

6. What is an "intelligentsia"? What role did it play in Russia? Is this a legitimate term to use for other western European societies? If so, which ones, and in what way? Can a democracy have an intelligentsia?

7. Compare and contrast the expansion of Russia and of the United States.

8. Describe how a federal nation is organized. How is power distributed? Why did the United States choose this form of government?

9. While European nations were facing revolution, the United States faced civil war. How do revolutions and civil wars differ?

10. Americans often argue that "modern history" begins with the entry of their own country onto the world stage between 1898 and 1914. Is this a manifestation of nationalism? Is the judgment defensible? What was the American role in world affairs prior to World War I?

Modern Empires and Imperialism

*I*N THE NINETEENTH CENTURY ONE Western democracy led all others—Britain. At its height Britain possessed the greatest empire the world has ever seen. Nineteenth-century Britain grew into a Greater Britain, and its domestic history was inextricably bound up in imperial history, as foreign affairs were yoked to economic and industrial developments. In the age of nationalism and imperialism, it was Britain that most often laid the political foundations for the European balance of power—sometimes by war, sometimes by treaty, often by holding aloof from any commitment to either side in a threatened conflict. No one doubted this supremacy from 1815 to 1850; clearly, Britain had challengers in the last half of the century, and equally clearly, by 1914 Britain was no longer preeminent.

Both economic and political factors account for Britain's leadership in the nineteenth century. Britain had become the first industrial nation, the first to experience the industrial revolution, with its attendant changes in demography, society, and politics. Thus for a time Britain was in a position to control the spread of the industrial revolution. In turn, this meant that Britain was the financial capital of the world. In 1900 this first modernized state enjoyed a favorable balance of trade of £100 million. Such financial strength meant that Britain was in a better position to use free trade, fair trade (which generally meant free trade within the empire and protective tariffs, the last after 1880, as economic conditions appeared to demand them.

But British dominance was based on more than economic factors. The British parliamentary system became for a time the model for representative government, so that political maturity was taken to mean achieving independence or stability through parliamentary government on British lines. The growth of constitutional government in western Europe, in Canada, Australia, and New Zealand, and in some measure in Argentina and Brazil, owed a heavy debt to British political thought and practice.

Britain also enjoyed enormous prestige, not alone for its economic leadership and democratic attainments but also for its influence in statecraft. British diplomacy

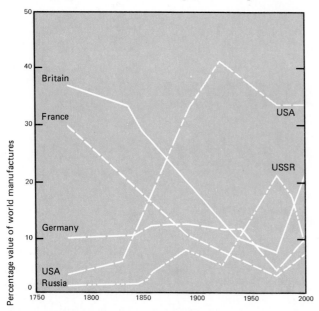

This chart shows the industrial output of five major powers, 1780–1958.

was the protector of European stability. Britain succeeded in forcing the other great powers into a position by which they could gain access to the world only by sea—a sea dominated by the British navy. Only Russia and the United States remained outside Britain's circle of maritime dominance. British statecraft was thus translated into real power and genuine influence that endured into the 1890s.

This influence was reinforced by a very real humanitarian impulse. At its best this impulse led to the abolition of the slave trade (1807), to the abolition of slavery throughout the British Empire (1833), to an extensive network of missionary activity abroad, and to the founding of the world's first systematic private philanthropic societies. At its worst this impulse led to direct intervention in the affairs of African and Asian states, allegedly for the good of their people, to bring them the fruits of modernization—improved transportation, communication, sanitation, and education. Such intervention, however, was often quite destructive and could easily serve the cynical manipulation of power. The idea that Britain knew best what "native" people needed, that Africans or Asians were civilized only if they dressed and spoke as the English did—such ideas fed on and would feed racism.

Important to the reforming impulse at home were various movements associated with women. As English society moved increasingly from an economic order based on land to one based on money, women became restive over their second-class status. The women's movement, which embraced many reforms, was essentially driven by the middle class. Beginning in evangelical sects, where women preachers were accepted, and moving on to the antislavery movement, woman played important roles in broad social change. However, as they became successful in these spheres, they found themselves increasingly

marginalized once again, being pressed into segregated ladies' associations, so that gains from the early nineteenth century seemed lost by the middle of the century.

In the last quarter century, however, in part because women realized that they would have to demand equality rather than achieve it more simply through doing good works, the "Woman Question" joined the "Irish Question" as a subject of intense public debate. Two organizations led the way for woman: the Ladies National Association, founded by Josephine Butler (1828–1906), and the British Women's Temperance Association. The latter showed how effectively women could organize, even when it was not in their economic interest (the majority of sellers of beer were women, and many were licensed as publicans). Thus women joined with many men to take on the "Drink Question" as well, arguing that alcohol was destroying the family and was a direct cause of the increase in crime. Between 1870 and 1890 women found their voice, speaking to often large audiences on a range of issues, establishing purely secular associations to achieve political change.

A crucial victory was won over the contagious diseases acts. On the continent many governments had passed laws recognizing and regulating prostitutes. Efforts to introduce regulation failed in Britain until military reform focused on the health of soldiers, who had suffered greatly from venereal diseases during the Crimean War. Soldiers were not permitted to marry, and they very often frequented prostitutes. An act passed in 1864 required the registration of prostitutes in military and port towns; any woman frequenting a public place alone was interpreted by local authorities as a prostitute. A second act gave the police the power to pick up any woman suspected of being a prostitute; a magistrate could order a medical examination and registration. A special police force was created to enforce the law, a clear invitation to abuse. No men were examined. Josephine Butler, the wife of an ordained Anglican minister, took the lead against the discriminatory acts in the 1870s. In 1886 the contagious disease acts were repealed.

The leaders of the movement to end the discriminatory acts went out into other reform movements. The first women's suffrage societies were formed in 1867. In 1888 they, with women from the United States, created the International Council of Women. The movement spread to New Zealand and throughout the empire. By the 1890s "Monster Public Meetings" focused on the franchise became commonplace. Women made it clear that the notion of British superiority must either include them or be seen as a discriminatory male preserve.

In part, British preeminence rested on the simple British conviction of their own superiority. It also rested on the presence of vast numbers of Britons around the world. The nineteenth century saw a mass movement of people from Europe, greater than the world had ever known. While much of this movement, especially after 1880, was from southern and eastern Europe, more of it was from the British Isles. Nearly 23 million emigrants left Europe between 1850 and 1900; 10 million of these were from Britain. Thus the English language and English,

Scots, Welsh, and Irish cultures were spread throughout the world in the nineteenth century, and entire new nations were founded on the basis of this great migration.

All these factors were reflected in, contributed to, and were supported by the British Empire. Emigrants went to it, founding new nations; the navy used its ports to dominate the seas; humanitarians sought to demonstrate within it the values of British, Christian society. Trade, finance, and technology migrated to an empire that was both formal and informal (informal, that is, in areas never annexed, though in fact dominated by the British economy, such as Argentina, Uruguay, parts of China, or the cattle kingdom of the United States). Each cause of preeminence fed another. As Britain transformed itself, it transformed other societies, until World War I—a war that it won, and in the winning, lost the world.

BRITAIN: TOWARD THE POSTMODERN, 1815–1914

In the years immediately after Waterloo, Britain went through an intense postwar economic crisis. Unsold goods accumulated, and the working classes experienced widespread unemployment and misery. Popular suffering increased as a result of the Corn Law of 1815, which forbade the importation of cheap foreign grain until the price of the home-grown commodity rose to a specified level. This assured the profits of the English grain farmer and probably raised the cost of bread for the average English family. Although trade unions were outlawed (see Chapter 20), workers nonetheless asserted themselves in strikes and in popular agitation that helped prepare for the parliamentary Reform Bill of 1832. By the 1820s economic conditions were improving, and Britain embarked on the process of reform that was to make it a modern democratic state.

Slow Democratization, to 1885

Britain emerged from the Napoleonic wars with an executive composed of a prime minister and his cabinet of ministers who were wholly under the control of Parliament. The Crown had become largely decorative. On that decorative post, held for much of the century (r. 1837–1901) by Queen Victoria, were centered the patriotic emotions of loyal British subjects. Victoria was the most popular British monarch since the days of the Tudors, and her name would be used to describe an entire era. Queen Victoria was also a dynastic focus, as her many children and grandchildren married into the royal families of the Continent.

Still, real power lay with Parliament, which in the early nineteenth century was very far from being a broadly representative body. The House of Lords, which

had equal power with the lower house except over money bills, was composed of the small privileged class of peers born to their seats, with the addition of a relatively few new peers created by the Crown from time to time. The House of Commons was recruited from the gentry, the professional classes, and very successful businessmen, with a sprinkling of sons of peers. It was chosen by less than one sixth of the adult male population, voting without a secret ballot. The working classes in both town and country and the run of moderately prosperous middle-class people were generally excluded from the franchise, although some few boroughs had a much broader electorate. None included women.

Proposals to modernize the structure of representation had come close to being adopted in the late eighteenth century, but the wars with revolutionary and Napoleonic France postponed reform. In wartime and in the immediate postwar years, even moderate reformers were denounced as Jacobins. Several disorders had frightened the upper classes, notably an attempt to arrest a speaker as he addressed a peaceful assemblage of nearly sixty thousand people, who carried banners advocating parliamentary reform, at St. Peter's Field near Manchester in August 1819. Eleven persons died and more than four hundred were wounded in what was called the Peterloo massacre. Entrenched positions hardened and class antagonisms became more evident. Postwar repression reached its height with Parliament's approval of six "gag acts," which curtailed freedom of speech, prohibited training in the use of firearms, and imposed a stamp tax on political literature.

The Whig party increasingly moved toward conciliation to avert the dangers of revolution. Many popular leaders talked as if the Reform Bill would bring immediate political democracy to England. Yet much of the preparation for reform was actually the work of conservatives. Guided by George Canning and Sir Robert Peel (1788–1850), the Tory governments of the 1820s lifted the restrictions on civil rights imposed during the long war with France and the postwar crisis. They permitted laborers to organize into unions, though not to strike; they reformed the antiquated criminal code, so that, for example, the theft of a sheep no longer carried with it a death penalty; and they began the reduction in protective tariffs (though not as yet affecting the Corn Laws) that was to lead to free trade. Civil restrictions for Roman Catholics now came under renewed fire, and the duke of Wellington, who in 1828 had reluctantly accepted the premiership, working with Robert Peel pressed legislation through Parliament in 1829 providing for Catholic emancipation. Now Catholics could enjoy all but the highest offices of state—which were still reserved to the established church.

The Reform Bill itself was enacted under the leadership of a Whig, the second Earl Grey (1764–1845). Tory opponents of parliamentary reform were won over—even the duke of Wellington was converted at the last moment—until only the Tory House of Lords blocked the measure. At this climax, Lord Grey, as prime minister, persuaded William IV (r. 1830–1837) to

This regal portrait of Queen Victoria presiding over the House of Lords was copied from the work of Benjamin Constant (1845–1902). It shows her in old age, caught in the radiance of majesty—the epitome of the mystique that was still attached to the monarchy.

The House of Lords, Westminster

threaten to create enough new Whig peers to put the reform through the Lords. This threat, combined with fears of a run on the Bank of England and of an outbreak of popular violence in Bristol, resulted in passage of the bill on June 4, 1832.

The First Reform Bill accomplished a potentially revolutionary change without revolutionary violence. It marked a distinct weakening of the established church and the Crown. It demonstrated that the working classes could be won to the cause of parliamentary reform, and that the masses need not be driven into the arms of the Jacobins.

Yet by no means did the Reform Bill bring political democracy to Britain. It did diminish the great irregularities of electoral districts, giving seats in the Commons to more than forty unrepresented industrial towns. The number of voters was increased by about 50 percent, so that virtually all the middle class got the vote, but the property qualifications for voting excluded the great mass of workers. As the bill extended the suffrage in the counties, which tended to vote conservative, its impact was not, in fact, as radical as its opponents had feared.

In the partly reformed Parliament, agitation went on for a wider suffrage. The more militant workers, not content to accept reform piecemeal, wanted immediate direct representation in Parliament to press for legislation that would mitigate the hardships brought on by the industrial revolution. These demands were formally drawn up in the People's Charter calling for universal manhood suffrage, the secret ballot, abolition of all property requirements for members of Parliament, payment of members, equal electoral districts, and annually elected Parliaments. The Chartists' strength lay in the urban industrial proletariat, particularly the unions, and was supported by many intellectuals of varied social and economic backgrounds. The movement presented to Parliament in 1839 a monster petition with several hundred thousand signatures, urging adoption of the People's Charter. Parliament never considered the petition, even after two additional Chartist initiatives in 1842 and 1848, but the Chartists' major demands were to become law in the next two generations.

By the 1860s the groundswell for more parliamentary reform was so powerful that Benjamin Disraeli (1804–1881), the leader of the Conservatives (as the former Tories were now officially designated), recognized that if his party did not put through the reform, the Liberals (former Whigs) almost certainly would, and that his party had best get the credit. Disraeli hoped that the newly enfranchised urban working class would vote for the Conservatives with the expectation that they would

Benjamin Disraeli, Lord Beaconsfield, was British prime minister in 1868 and again in 1874–1880. As a novelist Disraeli popularized the idea of Britain consisting of two nations—the rich and the poor. Through his policies he hoped to bring them closer together.

National Portrait Gallery, London

be responsible caretakers of the lower classes. But in 1868, in the first general election after the new reform, Disraeli (now prime minister) and the Conservatives were turned out. In the meantime, a potential embarrassment was removed. Though a Christian convert, Disraeli was of Jewish background, and Jews could not take seats in Parliament, since members were required to swear "on the true faith of a Christian." (In 1866 a new oath was at last drawn up removing the sectarian reference.)

Still, the Reform Bill of 1867 did not introduce full manhood suffrage. Like the first, it was a piecemeal change that brought the electoral districts into greater uniformity and equality, but it still left them divided into boroughs and shires, as in the Middle Ages. It about doubled the number of voters in Britain by giving the vote to householders—that is, settled men owning or paying rent on their dwellings—in the boroughs. But this Second Reform Bill did not give the vote in rural areas to men without the "stake in society" of property—that is, men who did not own a piece of real estate or a bank account, men who were therefore regarded by many upper-class Victorians as irresponsible, willing to vote away other people's property.

The next reforms were put through by the Liberal party under the leadership of William Ewart Gladstone (1809–1898). Bills of 1884 and 1885 again doubled the

size of the electorate, particularly by extending the franchise in rural areas. But migrant laborers, domestic servants, and bachelors living in parental households still did not have the vote. However, the medieval constituencies of borough and shire were finally modernized, and many smaller boroughs were lumped together with surrounding country areas to form single constituencies. The political map of Britain was beginning to be redrawn so that all districts would have roughly the same population. Some striking inequalities continued, however. Workers could scarcely hope to become members of Parliament, for MPs still served without pay; voters with business property in one district and a home in another could vote twice or more; and graduates of Oxford and Cambridge could vote a second time for special university members.

William Gladstone was Britain's pragmatic prime minister on four occasions—in 1868–1874, in 1880–1885, in 1886, and in 1892–1894. He and Disraeli were locked in a contest for political leadership until 1881. Queen Victoria, who greatly enjoyed Disraeli's company, complained that Gladstone was entirely too earnest and addressed her as though she were a public meeting.

The Granger Collection

Nor could women vote or, indeed, own property with any security, for the Married Women's Property Act of 1870, despite its title, only assured women of the right to keep money they personally earned, so that they were generally unable to acquire the theoretical "stake in society" on which the franchise had been based. Only by means of two acts, in 1882 and 1893, did women gain the right to separate ownership of property, the first act applying to married women, and the second to single women.

By 1885 Britain was, relative to other Western societies, a political democracy in which the majority of males were almost, if not quite, politically sovereign through their representatives in the House of Commons. The House of Lords retained the right to veto most legislative acts until 1911, when a Parliament Act ended the real power of the Lords, leaving them with no more than a delaying or suspensive veto. Other extensions of the logic inherent in the reforms were: the Local Government Act of 1894, in which urban and rural boards and local government parishes were granted wide public service powers, and women, whether married or single, were allowed both to vote in local elections and to stand as candidates; the institution of salaries for MPs in 1911; and a majority act in 1918 that nationally enfranchised all men over twenty-one, gave the vote to women over thirty, and limited plural voting to two votes—a property vote and a university vote.

Triumph of the Two-Party System

The Conservative and Liberal parties were very different from their ancestors, the oligarchical eighteenth-century factions of Tories and Whigs. The Conservatives kept their old electoral following among country gentlemen, army and navy officers, and Anglican clergymen, but they added many new supporters among agricultural laborers, tradespeople, and even some of the urban working and white-collar classes. The Liberals found many new supporters among businessmen, the nonconformists, white-collar radicals, and the more politically conscious workers. Both parties frankly appealed to the "people." The Conservatives, with their Primrose League in memory of Disraeli's favorite flower, their appeal to love of queen and country, their record of social legislation against the worst evils of the new factory system, did at least as good a job of building a party machine and getting out the vote as did the Liberals.

The two-party system was almost wholly confined to the English-speaking lands: Britain, the United States, and the British dominions. On the Continent, a multiparty or coalition system usually prevailed—not only in France, Italy, and Germany but also in the smaller democracies of Scandinavia, Switzerland, Holland, and Belgium, as well as in Spain, which had established a bicameral legislature in 1876. A two-party democracy had clear advantages in promoting continuity, clarity of debate and choice, and a sense of security. In the twentieth century neither two-party systems nor parliamentary governments proved ultimately to be the norm for newly independent and modernizing states, and even in the older democracies more and more voters saw themselves as "independents," casting their votes on issues rather than party loyalty. But in the nineteenth century the relative clarity of position, the stability of policy, and the possibilities for direct compromise that arose from two-party government made for relatively greater domestic peace. Yet it was also in some measure less democratic than a multiparty system, since it generally offered the voter relatively limited choices.

In terms of political psychology, a two-party system means that the millions of individual voters who make up each party must be in greater agreement than disagreement over what the party stands for—or at least when they vote they must feel that their candidate stands more for what they want than for what they are opposed to. Each voter makes some kind of compromise, takes something less in practice than is ideal, or else abstains. The reasons why the British made such compromises must be sought in history. One reason lies in the relative security of the British Isles from external foes. All the Continental states were repeatedly exposed to the dangers of war and the threat of invasion, but Britain was not seriously challenged internally or externally until the twentieth century.

Continental states in the nineteenth century were still torn by major antagonisms between the privileged nobles and the middle class. Another reason for Britain's relative stability at this time is the fact that the struggle against absolutism had occurred a century and a half earlier. It had left England with a moderate ruling class that was itself the product of a compromise between the old landed gentry and the new commercial classes. The deep abyss the French Revolution had dug on the Continent between royalists and republicans and between clericals and anticlericals did not exist in Britain, even though class bias was very real there.

Even more important than the individual readiness of Liberals and Conservatives to support their party's policies was the fact that both parties had a wide area of mutual agreement above and beyond party. There was not much ideological difference between the Conservatives and the Liberals. Her Majesty's Government and Her Majesty's Opposition, almost equally loyal to established ways, helped to develop in the British people practices of pragmatic compromise, of respect for law, and of remarkable political stability.

The Program of the Utilitarians

The Reform Bill of 1832 was soon followed by other reform measures. Part of the inspiration for these reforms came from a middle-class group of Utilitarians, the Philosophic Radicals, who believed that, if properly educated, people are impelled by rational self-interest and thus automatically do what is best for themselves and their fellows. Under their influence, local government and the legal system were made simpler and more efficient. Legal procedures were speeded up. The Municipal Corporations Act of 1835 vested basic authority in elected councilors who supervised professional civil servants, including the recently established professional police.

Middle-class radicals sought to expedite government rather than to add to its tasks. They believed in education, but not in compulsory public education. Large-scale government reform of British state-supported education had to wait until 1870, and then occurred only at the elementary level. Meanwhile, the private initiative preached by the Utilitarians led to mechanics' institutes and other adult and vocational education institutions. The upper-middle class also supported various private schools (which are called public schools in Britain). Many of these had grown from medieval religious foundations, and both discipline and education had fallen to low levels in most of them. Their reform began under Thomas Arnold (1795–1842), headmaster of Rugby from 1828 to 1842, who declared that henceforth the fee-supported schools were to teach religious and moral principles and gentlemanly conduct and to enhance intellectual ability. New schools founded under his influence restored the "public" schools' prestige, while the new railroads made it easier for parents to send their sons (and later their daughters) away to Marlborough, Wellington, Eton, Harrow, or Winchester. These schools fostered snobbery and class consciousness, but they also provided the first systematic instruction in the new sciences, introduced entrance by competitive exams, and became the chief nurseries of statesmen and officers. They introduced interschool athletic competition and improved the environment in which education takes place.

In the meantime, in London, Manchester, and other cities, new universities that resembled American urban universities in many ways were opened. These new "redbrick" institutions (so called in contrast to the medieval stones of Oxford and Cambridge) broke the centuries-old monopoly of "Oxbridge," though they did not have the same prestige.

The reform that stirred up public opinion most thoroughly was the New Poor Law of 1834. This bill made more coherent a system of public relief that had originated in the Elizabethan Poor Law of 1601 and in earlier Tudor legislation. But it also shifted the base of this relief. The old methods of "outdoor relief" had permitted supplementary payments from the parishes to able-bodied poor working on low wages, supplements for children, and "doles" direct to families living in their own homes. The New Poor Law united parishes for greater efficiency, permitted greater supervision by the central government in London, and supplied poorhouses in which able-bodied paupers were made as uncomfortable as the limits of decency would allow.

Poorhouses offended humanitarians in the upper classes, but to middle-class business interests, they had the merit of making poor relief more efficient—or so it was alleged. The ideology behind the law—that the Poor Law commissioners would teach discipline and restraint to the poor, including restraint in the size of families—was challenged by many, while the inefficiency of the operation of the law was challenged by even more. Clearly it did not work. In 1838 in England and Wales there were something over 80,000 workhouse inmates; by 1843 the figure was nearly 200,000.

The most successful of the Utilitarian reforms in its long-term consequences was the repeal of the Corn Laws in 1846, after a long campaign headed by the Anti-Corn Law League. This pressure group wanted Britain to adopt free trade so that it might use exports of manufactured goods to pay for imports of raw materials and food. In 1846 they persuaded Peel to abandon traditional Tory protectionism in the face of the tragic potato famine in Ireland and the urgent need for massive importation of cheap grain.

Still another series of reforms were the Factory Acts, begun very modestly in 1802 and 1819. The Act of 1819 applied only to the cotton industry, forbade night work for children and limited day work to twelve hours; it did not provide for effective inspection and was violated with impunity by many employers. The Act of 1833—forbidding child labor entirely below the age of nine and restricting it to nine hours for those below thirteen, and twelve hours for those below eighteen—marked an important stage mainly because it provided for salaried inspectors to enforce the law.

These and subsequent acts required the support of both political parties, as well as demands from below and paternalistic or self-interested concern from above. Given the prevailing laissez-faire economic philosophy and the Utilitarians' conviction that the state ought not to interfere with the natural order (by which the poor either bettered themselves through thrift, hard work, and a sense of duty, or else remained forever poor), and given the fact that labor was generally all that the working person had to sell, intervention by Parliament was slow and piecemeal. The single greatest intervention against the concept of personal property—the emancipation of slaves throughout the British Empire in 1833—had the united support of the humanitarians as well as the hard-headed calculations of many business and plantation owners that slavery was no longer economically sound.

To intervene in the free market in labor required a union of quasi-socialist and conservative paternalistic views. Such a political alliance ultimately led to a series of acts which established a basis on which later reformers could build. The major architects of this legislation were Richard Oastler (1789–1861), a Tory; Sir John Cam Hobhouse (1786–1869), a radical; Michael Sadler (1780–1835), the parliamentary leader behind the bill of 1833; and Lord Shaftesbury (1801–1885), a Liberal. Oastler led the Anti-Poor Law movement and together with Shaftesbury achieved the passage of the Ten Hours Act, which limited the normal workweek to ten hours a day, six days a week, in 1847. Shaftesbury himself sponsored legislation that took women and children out of coal mines and that provided for institutionalized care for the insane.

By the end of the nineteenth century, a complex code of labor legislation regulated the hours of labor for everyone, protected women and children, and made employers responsible for workers' compensation in industrial accidents. New unions in the 1880s and 1890s organized the dockworkers, gas workers, and other unskilled groups, and in 1892 Kier Hardie (1856–1915), a miner

Here J. G. Tissot (1836–1902) captured "a heavy swell"—an English gentleman—in 1870. This casual air of superiority was greatly admired and much imitated outside Britain as well.

National Portrait Gallery, London

who had turned to journalism, became the first independent worker to win election to Parliament. As the first leader of the new Labour party in Parliament (1906–1907), he broadened the base of the movement. Then in 1911 came the National Insurance Act, which inaugurated compulsory health and unemployment insurance through combined payments from the state, employers, and employees.

Two areas of entrenched privilege—the older universities and the army—were attacked successfully in the 1870s. The requirement that fellows and staff at Oxford and Cambridge take religious tests to confirm their Anglicanism was abolished by Gladstone with relative ease. And the sorry showing of the British army in the Crimean War (1854–1856) at last made it possible for reformers to change the military system.

Doctrines of economy and efficiency—so natural to the Utilitarians, to both political parties, and to the concept of the modern state—had clearly not been at work in the bungled Crimean War. Military reform was delayed, but in Gladstone's first ministry (1868–1874), his able secretary for war, Edward Cardwell (1813–1886), initiated a series of reforms that increased the efficiency and size of the British army while reducing its cost. In 1868 Cardwell abolished flogging during peacetime. The next year he began withdrawing troops from self-governing colonies while encouraging the colonies to raise their own militias. In 1870 he abolished bounty money for recruits. He then placed the commander in chief under the secretary for war and attacked the system by which commissions and promotions were obtained by purchase.

Almost all senior officers opposed this last change; in the House of Lords hostility to the bill was so intense that Gladstone asked the queen to abolish purchase by issuing a royal warrant. For the first time the Lords were revealed in complete opposition to the Commons on a class issue; they resorted to full-scale parliamentary obstruction. But demands for democratization of the military were joined by growing fears of Prussian professionalism. Some openly argued that an inefficient army was a protection against an authoritarian state. Gladstone and Cardwell carried the day, however, and the latter quickly began to modernize the army on the basis of the Regulation Bill of 1871.

In foreign relations, almost everyone agreed on Britain's fundamental position: maintain the European state system in balance, preferably by diplomatic rather than military action; police the seas with the British navy; open world markets to British goods; maintain and extend the vast network of the British Empire. The Liberals were more likely to side with the democratic and nationalist movements in Europe than the Conservatives were. In midcentury the Liberal Palmerston pursued an active policy of near-intervention on behalf of oppressed nationalities, and British "benevolent neutrality" was a factor in Italian unification. The Crimean War, the only European war in which Britain was directly involved between 1815 and 1914, was fought to maintain the balance of power; Britain had joined France to oppose what they judged to be a Russian threat to their Near Eastern interests. Although the war was mismanaged on both sides, it at least checked Russian advances for a time and made the ultimate disposition of the Balkan regions of the decaying Turkish empire a matter for joint action by all the great powers.

Issues and Parties in the Early Twentieth Century

By the 1880s the prosperity, sense of confidence, and general air of political and social innovation associated with early and mid-Victorian leaders were on the wane. There was an undeniable depression in arable farming, a drop in prices for commerce, and a slowing in the rate of industrial growth. A general decline in public and private morals and a move from duty toward frivolity seemed to mark the Edwardian period, named after the pleasure-loving though philanthropic King Edward VII (r. 1901–1910). Irish troubles, the war in South Africa (in which world opinion generally supported the Boers, not the British), the rising international tensions that were leading to World War I, and the difficulties of raising the additional government revenue to finance both the naval armament race with Germany and the measures inaugurating the welfare state—all confronted the British people at the same time.

Under such conditions, many Britishers came to doubt the wisdom of the free-trade policies that had prevailed in 1846. For the Germans and others were not only underselling the British abroad; they were invading the British home market! Why not protect that market by a tariff system? Few Britishers believed that the home islands, already too densely populated to constitute a self-sufficient economy, could surround themselves with a simple tariff wall. But the empire was worldwide, with abundant agricultural resources. Within it the classical mercantilist interchange of manufactures for raw materials could still (in theory) provide a balanced economic system.

A reform leader from Birmingham, Joseph Chamberlain (1836–1914), had become a leading protectionist, giving special importance to the establishment of a system of imperial preference through which the whole complex of lands under the Crown would work together in a tariff union. Many Conservatives, never wholly reconciled to free trade, welcomed the issue, and Chamberlain's new Unionist party had made protection a major plank in its program. Chamberlain organized a Tariff Reform League. In 1903 he made sweeping proposals that would have restored moderate duties on foodstuffs and raw materials and on foreign manufactured goods. But the new Conservative prime minister, Arthur Balfour (1848–1930), did not dare go so far, and Chamberlain resigned with his bill unpassed.

The Liberals were, however, increasingly committed to another policy. This was the welfare state—social security through compulsory insurance managed by the state and in part financed by the state; minimum wage laws; compulsory free public education; and a variety of public works and services. In 1909 the "People's Budget" was introduced by a relatively new figure on the political stage,

Under the youthful David Lloyd George, the Liberal party emerged as a major force in British politics.

National Portrait Gallery, London

David Lloyd George (1863–1945), the Liberal chancellor of the exchequer. This budget, which proposed making the rich finance the new welfare measures through progressive taxation on incomes and inheritances, was no ordinary tax measure. It was a means of altering the social and economic structure of Britain. The bill passed the Commons but was thrown out by the Lords. This rejection led to a general election, which the Liberals won. They then put through the Parliament Act of 1911, which took away from the Lords all power to alter a money bill and left them with no more than a delaying power of not more than two years over all other legislation. The Liberal program of social legislation was achieved after the new king, George V (r. 1910–1936), promised that, if necessary, he would create enough new peers to put the Parliament Act through the House of Lords. The threat was enough, and the peers yielded.

The dissenting Liberals who had followed Joseph Chamberlain out of the party in the 1880s did not think

THE WRITTEN RECORD

Beatrice Webb on "Why I Became a Socialist"

One of the leading intellectuals in the socialist movement in Britain was Beatrice Potter, who became the wife of the Fabian socialist and administrator Sidney Webb. In *My Apprenticeship* she addressed the question, "Why I Became a Socialist."

Can I describe in a few sentences the successive steps in my progress towards Socialism?

My studies in [London's] East End life had revealed the physical misery and moral debasement following in the track of the rack-renting landlord and capitalist profit-maker in the swarming populations of the great centres of nineteenth-century commerce and industry. It is true that some of these evils—for instance, the low wages, long hours and insanitary conditions of the sweated industries, and the chronic under-employment at the docks, could, I thought, be mitigated, perhaps altogether prevented by appropriate legislative enactment and Trade Union pressure. By these methods it might be possible to secure to the manual workers, so long as they were actually at work, what might be regarded from the physiological standpoint as a sufficient livelihood. Thus, the first stage in the journey—in itself a considerable departure from early Victorian individualism—was an all-pervading control, in the interest of the community, of the economic activities of the landlord and the capitalist.

But however ubiquitous and skillful this State regulation and Trade Union intervention might become, I could see no way out of the recurrent periods of inflation and depression—meaning, for the vast majority of the nation, alternate spells of overwork and unemployment—intensified, if not actually brought about by the speculative finance, manufacture and trading that was inspired by the mad rush to secure the maximum profit for the minority who owned the instruments of production. Moreover, "Man does not live by bread alone"; and without some "socialism"—for instance, public education and public health, public parks and public provision for the aged and infirm, open to all and paid for out of rates and taxes, with the addition of some form of "work or maintenance" for the involuntarily unemployed—even capitalist governments were reluctantly recognising, though hardly fast enough to prevent race-deterioration, and the régime of private property could not withstand revolution. This "national minimum" of civilised existence, to be legally ensured for every citizen, was the second stage in my progress toward socialism.

Beatrice Webb, *My Apprenticeship* (Hammondsworth: Penguin Books, 1938), II, pp. 439–40. Copyright by the London School of Economics and Political Science.

---

these measures were appropriate. In the generation after 1880 there was a major change in the political orientation of British parties. The Liberals, who had believed that that government governs best which governs least (and least expensively), had come to believe that the state must interfere in economic life to help the underdog and had adopted Lloyd George's plan for redistributing the national wealth by social insurance financed by taxation. And the Conservatives, who in the mid-nineteenth century had stood for factory acts and mild forms of the welfare state, were now in large part committed to a laissez-faire program against government "intervention"—a program much like that of the Liberals of 1850.

One factor in this reversal had been the growth of the political wing of the labor movement, which in 1906 won fifty-three seats in the Commons. Labourites wanted the welfare state, and many of them also wanted a socialist state in which at least the major industries would be nationalized. Labour had the backing of many upper- and middle-class people who sympathized with the quest for social justice. From their ranks came intellectuals like G. B. Shaw (1856–1950), H. G. Wells (1866–1946), G. D. H. Cole (1889–1959), and Sidney and Beatrice

Webb (1858–1947 and 1858–1943, respectively), who participated in the influential Fabian Society, formed in the 1880s. The Fabians preached the "inevitability of gradualness," the attainment of social democracy through the peaceful parliamentary strategy of advancing one step at a time, as was done by the Roman republican general Fabius to wear down the Carthaginians in the third century B.C.

By the early 1900s Fabianism seemed to be working, for the Liberals, who depended on Labour votes to maintain a majority, put through much important legislation in the interest of the worker: acceptance of peaceful picketing, sanctity of trade union funds, and employer's liability to compensate for accidents (all in 1906); modest state-financed old age pensions (1909); health and unemployment insurance (1911); and minimum wage regulations (1912). Part of the motivation for Liberal social legislation was a desire to forestall Labour initiatives. But over the long run the workers on the whole stuck by the Labour party. The Liberal party was beginning a long decline that would be hastened by the effects of World War I and would drive its right wing to Toryism and its left wing to Labour.

The imperialist wing of the Liberal party, led originally by Chamberlain, remained unreconciled to this trend, and in 1901 a union between the Fabians and disaffected Liberals began to hint that a new national party was needed to make national efficiency its goal. As the Liberal party fragmented, declined, and sought to hold on to its followers against the rise of Labour, it became more of a coalition than a functioning whole within a two-party system. On one subject it remained reasonably united, however—the significance of the British Empire. As one member of Parliament, Halford John Mackinder (1861–1947), the creator of geopolitics, noted after his election in 1910, free trade would protect imperialism. He maintained that Britain must become a nation of "organizers," of workers whose patriotism led them to realize that they existed primarily to serve the national ends of the state.

An Imperial Issue Close to Home: The Irish Question

As in eastern Europe, a nationality problem peculiar to Britain grew more acute near the end of the nineteenth century. This was "the Irish problem," as the English called it. The English, and the Scots who came to settle in the northern Irish province of Ulster in the sixteenth and seventeenth centuries, had remained as privileged Protestant landowners over a subject population of Catholic Irish peasants. Although there were also native Irish among the ruling classes, many of them had been Anglicized and had become Protestant.

For three centuries religious, political, and economic problems in Ireland had remained unsolved. Early in the nineteenth century the English attempted to solve the political problem by a formal union of the two kingdoms, with Irish members admitted to the British Parliament. On January 1, 1801, the United Kingdom of Great Britain and Ireland came into being. Beginning with the Catholic Emancipation Act of 1829, which allowed Irish voters to elect Catholics to office, most of the English reforms were extended to Ireland. The Irish, led by Daniel O'Connell (1775–1847), the Great Emancipator, organized politically to press for repeal of the union and in favor of home rule. They sought not only self-government but also land reform, to break the economic dominance of the Protestant minority, and disestablishment of the Anglican church in Ireland—that is, abolition of a state church supported by taxes levied both on its members and on the Irish majority, who were nonmembers.

Irish hatred for the English was fanned by the disastrous potato famine of the 1840s, when blight ruined a crop essential to the food supply. The British government did not provide prompt or efficient relief, and twenty-one thousand Irish deaths were attributed directly to starvation. At least a million more people, weakened by malnutrition, succumbed to disease. Many of these deaths occurred on ships, as up to a million Irish emigrated. Those who survived carried their hatred of the British with them.

Over the next decades British governments made piecemeal reforms. In 1869 they disestablished the Anglican church in Ireland, and in the next year the Irish Land Act began a series of agrarian measures that were designed to protect tenants from "rack renting" (rent gouging) by landlords. The reforms were neither far-reaching nor rapid, intensifying Irish awareness of cultural differences and nationality. Then in 1875 a brilliant Irish leader, Charles Parnell (1846–1891), was elected to the British Parliament. Under his leadership the Irish nationalists in the British Parliament were welded into a firm, well-disciplined party which could often swing the balance between Liberals and Conservatives.

The critical step came in 1885, when Gladstone was converted to the cause of Irish home rule. In the next year he introduced a bill providing for a separate Dublin-based Irish parliament under the Crown. Gladstone's decision split his own Liberal party, and a group led by Chamberlain seceded under the name of Liberal Unionists; in effect, they joined the Conservative party. Gladstone lost the election brought on by the split, and home rule was dropped for the moment.

Agitation continued in Ireland, however, becoming more and more bitter. In 1892, however, Gladstone won a close election on the Irish issue, obtaining enough English seats to get a second home rule bill through the Commons with the aid of eighty-one Irish nationalists. However, the bill was defeated in the House of Lords and was dropped once more. The Conservatives, when they came in for a ten-year reign in 1895, sought to "kill home rule by kindness," enacting several land reform bills that helped make Ireland a land of small peasant proprietors.

But Ireland was now beyond the reach of modest reforms. Irish nationalism was now in full flower, nourished by a remarkable literary revival in English and Gaelic by writers like the poet W. B. Yeats (1865–1939), the dramatist John Millington Synge (1871–1909), and Lady Augusta Gregory (1859–1932), cofounder of the Abbey Theatre, which staged plays with deeply Irish themes. Irish men and women everywhere—including Irish-Americans—would be satisfied with nothing less than an independent Irish state.

The Liberals, back in power after 1905, found that they needed the votes of the Irish nationalists to carry through their proposal for ending the veto power of the Lords. The Liberals struck a bargain: home rule in return for the Parliament Act of 1911. A home rule bill was placed on the books in 1912 but never went into force, for as home rule seemed about to become a fact, the predominantly Protestant north of Ireland, the province of Ulster, bitterly opposed to separation from Great Britain, threatened to resist by force of arms. The home rule bill as passed carried the rider that it was not to go into effect until the Ulster question was settled. The outbreak of the European war in 1914 put such a settlement out of the question, and the stage was set for the Irish Revolution of the 1920s and the long extension of the Time of Troubles, at least for Northern Ireland, into the present.

⊤HE GREAT MODERN EMPIRES AND THE QUESTION OF IMPERIALISM

The transition from modern to what some scholars refer to as postmodern history is marked by the rise and collapse of the great modern empires. The age of maritime exploration and early colonialism had knit the globe together into one intellectual construct; the age of imperialism would give political and economic reality to this set of mental maps. Imperialism, both as word and as deed, became part of the power struggle among the Western powers and, in the twentieth century, among non-Western nations as well.

Motives for Empire

Between 1800 and roughly 1870 European nations acquired new territories mainly from other European powers. Britain rested its continuing ascendancy upon sea power, and those colonies it kept after victories over Continental nations were retained largely for strategic reasons, such as the need to protect the sea route to India and the Far East. Thus Mauritius was taken from the French because it had the best harbor in the south Indian Ocean, Ceylon from the Dutch for its port of Trincomalee, and Malacca (by treaty in 1824, also from the Dutch) because it controlled the straits to China. Concern for trade routes led the British to found Singapore in 1819 and to retain Gibraltar, Malta, and the Ionian Islands in the Mediterranean.

The principles of free-trade imperialism were compromised toward the end of the century. On the whole, Britain professed to hold to a free-trade position from the abolition of the Corn Laws in 1846 until 1932. France moved toward protectionism. Germany and Belgium, despite moderate tariffs directed against Britain, generally held to free trade, and the Dutch belatedly went over to it in the 1870s. Yet, Britain was manipulating imperial preferences to its benefit while espousing the general principles of free-trade competition. Thus a modified form of mercantilistic thought came to be applied to the colonies. They would provide cheap raw materials for the industrial machine in Europe, since labor in the colonies cost a fraction of that at home; they would purchase finished products and provide strategic protection for the trade routes by which the bulk of these products moved to other nations; they would become centers for investment, absorbing surplus capital as well as produce; and, by helping to eliminate the surpluses that led to domestic cycles of unemployment, they would help to forestall the social revolution many feared.

The modern capitalist state would need new kinds of trading partners capable of sustaining a trend toward consolidation, large-scale marketing, and giant trading firms—a trend that made possible economies of scale that, in turn, either increased profits or lowered prices and broadened markets. Underconsumption at home was the primary cause of low wages, according to John A. Hobson (1858–1904), in his 1902 book *Imperialism: A Study*. Underconsumption prevented the profitable employment of capital at home and forced governments to seek out colonies as an outlet for their surpluses. Hobson saw this as a correctable problem, but another analyst, Lenin, saw it as the inevitable, irreversible, and destructive "highest stage of capitalism." This being so, he argued, colonies were adjuncts to capitalist balance-of-power politics, since colonies were needed as outlets for surplus capital.

The European state system had been remolded at the Congress of Vienna around the concept of a balance of power—a distribution of power among many states, so that no one state would be dominant. The purpose was to preserve independence of action and to protect national sovereignty. While this balance of power rested largely within Europe until the mid-nineteenth century, the growing importance of overseas trade appeared to shift the balance toward nations with colonial possessions after 1870.

To these economic and political motives for imperial expansion after the midcentury were added more emotional or psychological motivations, of which the desire for national and personal glory was the most evident. Imperialism was closely allied to nationalism. For a nation to be without a colony—an imperial "place in the sun"—was to confess to weakness. Colonies helped to assert the pride of the nation and to give it security. The quest for security on the ground that one's country is dearer than all others and must at all costs be made safe in a competitive world was basic to modern thought.

A related motive for the acquisition of territory was strategic. Islands, river mouths, or peninsulas that dominated trade routes and on which forts might be built were coveted because they could make economic and political goals more accessible. Often colonies were little more than adjuncts to some larger area of an empire; for example, after the completion of the Suez Canal in 1869 Britain took Perim, Aden, and Socotra solely to protect the new route to India and the East. Strategic considerations also altered with the new technologies—the telegraph, the steamship, and the airplane. Even so, an area was of strategic importance only in relation to the prevailing economic and political theories of the powers, and thus the strategic motive may largely be subsumed under the others. This was especially true in the acquisition of territories in East Africa after 1880 by Britain, France, Germany, and Italy. Britain wished to maintain control in Egypt, although without formal annexation; conquest of the Nile to its headwaters seemed a strategic necessity. To stabilize the Nile holdings, the highlands and parts of Kenya were therefore taken by Britain, while Germany acquired the vast land from Lake Tanganyika to the coast.

As strategic needs changed, the tenacity with which a nation held to an area might also have been expected to change, if imperialism were a wholly rational system of world organization. To some extent such changes did occur; yet for the most part empires continued to grow in defiance of economic wisdom and strategic planning. Nonrational impulses to empire were clearly at work.

Foremost among these was the humanitarian desire to reform, to help the native who was felt to need more efficient, liberal, or rational forms of government, economic organization, or worship. Christian missionaries desired to save souls. Evangelical Protestants in particular sent missionaries to China, Africa, and India to educate non-Christians. Some Christians saw the machine as an instrument of God, and many embraced the new imperialist trinity—railroads, sanitation, and good government—as the pathway to temporal elevation of humanity and ultimately to spiritual triumphs. From the time of John and Charles Wesley, who preached to the colonists in Georgia in the 1730s, independent Methodist churches had grown among the middle and lower class in Britain. The Wesleyan Methodists were competitive, especially where Anglican or Roman Catholic missions were present, as in Indo-China for example, where the latter were conscious instruments of the French expansion. Most of those missionaries who actively promoted imperialism, however, did so for their church, not their nation.

Humanitarianism also had its ethical, secular goals, as in the campaign to end slavery. Indigenous groups often practiced slavery or, as on the Malay peninsula, a form of debt bondage. A Western nation would be a powerful secular ally in the battle against cannibalism, *suttee* (the custom of burning a widow on the funeral pyre of her husband), child marriage, bride price, and nakedness. Frequently, the central authority of the imperial power was used to protect a local minority against exploitation by a local majority. Britain slowed the pace of self-government in Australia in the 1850s in order to speak out for the rights of the aboriginal population, accepted

a form of constitutional government for Canada in 1867 only after French-speaking rights were entrenched in the enabling acts, and refused independence to Rhodesia in the 1960s because the blacks there were not accorded a progressively equal political standing with whites in the colony's draft constitution. In the late nineteenth century the United States' federal government sought to slow the growth of statehood in certain western American territories because it feared that, once sovereign, they would create unrepresentative institutions.

In the final analysis, imperialism also rested upon humanity's acquisitive nature, the desire to influence, control, dominate, own, or crush another people. Racism fed upon such desires and also fed them, and racism usually was one facet of imperialism, in the sense that the imperialists held themselves to be superior to nonwhites. Some theorists of empire argued that racial differences were largely environmental; that is, that while the other races might appear inferior to the white, they were so only by virtue of historical circumstance and that sufficient exposure to more advanced customs and technologies would, in time, make the "lesser breeds" functionally equal within the law. This position helped justify taking and retaining land occupied by another race. Other theorists argued that some races were inherently inferior and would always need the protection of the stronger. The latter tended to think of the indigenous populations as useful labor forces, while the former thought of them as societies in need of transformation.

These motives were sustained by an infrastructure within most imperial nations that strengthened the ties between mother country and colony. The settlement colonies would absorb surplus population and often draw the military-minded to them. Civil servants and youthful adventurers, usually sons who could not expect to

President Theodore Roosevelt was one American leader who took up Rudyard Kipling's imperial command, and by the end of his presidency in 1909, the United States was a world power. Unhappy with the policies of his successor, William Howard Taft (1857-1930), Roosevelt ran on a third-party "Bull Moose" ticket in 1912, thus dividing the Republican vote and opening the door to Woodrow Wilson's victory.

The Granger Collection

THE WRITTEN RECORD

Kipling's View of Imperialism

Many were pleased to be called imperialists, determined to "take up the White Man's burden . . . To seek another's profit. And work another's gain." In the words of the poet laureate of empire, Rudyard Kipling (1865–1936), the United States too must

Take up the White Man's burden—
Send forth the best ye breed—
Go bind your sons to exile
To serve your captives' need;
To wait in heavy harness
On fluttered folk and wild—
Your new-caught, sullen peoples,
Half devil and half child.

. . .

Take up the White Man's burden—
The savage wars of peace—
Fill full the mouth of Famine
And bid the sickness cease;
And when your goal is nearest
The end for others sought,

Watch Sloth and heathen Folly
Bring all your hope to nought.

. . .

Take up the White Man's burden—
And reap his old reward:
The blame of those ye better,
The hate of those ye guard—
The cry of hosts ye humour
(Ah, slowly!) toward the light—
"Why brought ye us from bondage,
Our loved Egyptian might?"

From James Cochrane, ed., *Rudyard Kipling: Selected Verse* (New York: Penguin Books, 1977), pp. 128–29.

inherit their father's property, added to the spiral of imperial expansion.

But annexation was not necessary to imperial expansion. Not only was annexation expensive, it was also dangerous, perhaps bringing a reaction from another power; it produced shock waves within the interior of an area that might force further annexations to calm and control turbulent frontiers; it led local administrators to intervene in intertribal, interethnic, or interpolitical affairs that might draw a nation far more deeply into moral and political involvement than its population at home would accept. There were, therefore, other "empires," the so-called informal empires.

Informal empires were areas that were technically independent but whose economies, communication systems, and often politics and social life were inextricably bound up with an imperial power. The United States exercised such informal control over portions of Latin America and the Pacific. Russia came to hold influence over vast, contiguous territories, some of which were eventually absorbed into the Soviet Union. Germany and France sought to dominate much of the eastern end of the Mediterranean prior to World Wars I and II. In the nineteenth century Britain thought of Argentina as virtually another dominion, so closely connected were Argentine rails, beef prices, and minerals to the British Empire's needs.

Did formal colonies pay? In psychological terms, undoubtedly; in financial terms, generally no. Statistics are difficult to compare, given competing systems of trade,

inaccurate data, and the fact that different nations kept their statistics in different ways; nonetheless, for the neomercantilist period, certain conclusions can be drawn. Some historians have asserted, for example, that the profits from the slave trade paid for nearly 20 percent of Britain's industrial revolution. Others have argued that the midcentury industrial progress of Britain was financed largely from the cheap labor of India. Such judgments are at best guesses, although revenues from the colonies undoubtedly were drained to serve imperial interests. The Dutch drew 18 million guilders a year from the Dutch East Indies (Indonesia) from 1831 until 1877, at a time when the entire Dutch budget was only 60 million guilders. In 1890, 42 percent of Indian revenues went to finance the Indian Army, under British officers, which primarily served imperial purposes, when Britain's entire defense budget was 38 percent of its revenue.

Against such financial gains from empire must be set the heavy costs of the colonies, which ordinarily faced deficit budgets that had to be met by the imperial power, involved many small wars of great expense, and were also costly to administer in terms of health. French expenses in Morocco more than wiped out any profits from trade. Italy's colonies cost it 1,300 million lire, more than was produced by all Italian colonial trade between 1913 and 1932. Germany's external trade with its colonies was 972 million marks between 1894 and 1913, while the expenses of the colonies were 1,002 million marks. For Britain the colonies were more important, but there, too, the balance was generally unfavorable; in 1850 the empire took 28 percent of Britain's overseas trade and 40 percent in 1934. Of the 1934 figure, however, well over half was with the dominions, that is, Canada, Australia, New Zealand, Newfoundland, South Africa; 7 percent was with India; and only 9 percent was with the remainder of the empire. In short, for Britain the chief economic advantage lay in the former settlement colonies and in India, while the new African possessions were of little importance in economic terms.

Yet the nations of Europe, joined after 1808 by the United States, continued to acquire colonial possessions, until by 1930, 84 percent of the land surface of the globe was under control of the Western nations. Clearly there were powerful motivations toward empire, and clearly (in retrospect) they were not truly economic motivations. Yet we must remember that at the time many imperialists felt that the colonies could be made to pay eventually, and that the search for a balance of power lent special credence to those who wished to deny to another nation a new acquisition, initiating annexations intended only to deny land to a rival.

To these four causes of imperial expansion—the desire for economic gain, whether immediate or deferred; the need to dominate strategic passages; the emotional search for national prestige; the fervor to convert others to a more "civilized" religion or form of government—would be added a fifth, now referred to as the *collaborator model*. During the 1870s official British policy was outspokenly against the acquisition of further territory overseas; yet, that same decade saw the British Empire expand greatly. This *new imperialism*, as the post-1870 movement was called, arose in part because of growing British and French relations with indigenous leaders who cooperated with the imperialists and drew reluctant and penny-pinching administrators into costly new acts of expansion and annexation. "Native uprisings" and local conflicts with rival European powers or indigenous leaders were reported in the European press in increasingly emotional terms, and toward the end of the century the British, French and Germans were clamoring for imperial adventure.

The New Imperialism, 1870–1931

The industrial revolution had led to a demand for goods aimed at specific markets and appealing to national fashions. Higher-quality goods made for a critical market required European control over the processes of manufacture, over methods of planting and cultivation, over port facilities, storage depots, communications systems, and even local finance. Home industries often related to colonial markets and sources of materials in startling ways. The need for rubber, for instance, led the British to experiment with trees brought from Brazil to Kew Gardens, near London, and then to the introduction of rubber trees into Malay; the desire to control prime rubber-growing areas would lead in turn to further British expansion in southeast Asia. The need for skilled rubber tappers led

the British to introduce Indian and Ceylonese laborers into Malaya in the 1920s, creating an ethnic division that plagues Malaysia to this day.

European commerce required trained Europeans, who moved to the colonies in greater numbers each year. There they created their own housing compounds, offices, hotels, recreational facilities, schools, and resorts. Few among the local population could afford to use such facilities, even if granted access to them, so that whites came to be physically separated from native populations. Relations once relatively friendly became distant. The local inhabitants became employees of European companies that were in distant European capitals. The whites who supervised them were promoted within their companies largely on the basis of keeping costs low and production high, so that the welfare of local populations was not primary in their priorities. The labor situation was, by its nature, exploitative. Racial differences accelerated the obvious class problems.

Many areas in the tropics were thought to be unsuitable for whites to live in; therefore, Europeans preferred to work through friendly, stable, and powerful local rulers: the Egyptian khedives, the Indian maharajahs, or the shahs of Persia. Such rulers often became collaborators, their nations client states of the major powers. With massive investments at stake, European business people often sought to pressure their governments into direct intervention in the affairs of the client states if the pliant rulers appeared to be in danger of being overthrown. Often such intervention was entirely legal, under protective treaties signed by the local rulers who sought outside support for their regimes; where intervention was not legal, sheer force of arms made it possible nonetheless. Equally often, the threat of the use of force—"gunboat diplomacy"—was sufficient to secure concessions.

Gradually European governments were drawn deeper and deeper into the affairs of Africa and Asia. The Fiji Islands were ceded by King Thakambau to Britain in 1874; Britain left its island base in southeast Asia, which rested upon the Straits Settlements of Singapore, Malacca, Penang, and Labuan, to intervene directly in the Malayan mainland states of Perak and Selangor in 1875; and the British displaced the Dutch on the Gold Coast (now Ghana), in Africa, in 1872. In South Africa the British expanded north and east time and again, despite an expressed desire not to, because of incursions into white settlement areas by Bantu tribes, clandestine raids upon native areas by the Boers, and disruptions by successive Zulu chiefs. The British took such action because the mercantile community wanted peace, stability, and dependable communications with the interior, so that raw materials might flow freely into the ports that Europeans controlled.

The period from 1815 to 1870 saw a partial decline in imperialist fortunes, as most of Spain's American colonies gained their independence, as Brazil broke away from Portugal (1822), and as Britain took the first major steps leading to the independence of Canada. But other

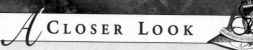

Technology and Empire

The industrial revolution in Europe had given the West an immense advantage throughout the world in weaponry, shipping, invention, and health. This advantage would last until air transport and the potential for atomic warfare again changed, by a quantum leap, the technological distance between societies, forcing a new formulation of the definitions of world power. Until that time, national pride was relatively simple in its expressions. Prince Bernhard von Bülow (1849–1929), chancellor of Germany from 1900 to 1909, whose aggressive policies over Morocco helped isolate his country and pave the way for World War I, remarked, "Where I have planted my foot, there shall no one else be permitted to place his." And a British writer, Hilaire Belloc (1870–1953), wrote satirically of how technology—in the form of the machine gun—gave the British led by a Colonel Blood, victory over the Boers in the South African war:

> I never shall forget the way
> That Blood upon this awful day
> Preserved us all from death.
> He stood upon a little mound,
> Cast his lethargic eyes around,
>
> And said beneath this breath:
> "Whatever happens we have got
> The Maxim gun,
> and they have not."*

Technological superiority was not, of course, to be measured only or even primarily in terms of instruments of war. Quinine, which helped to control malaria; the development of efficient steamships; the laying of submarine cables—the English Channel was first crossed by cable in 1850—and the explosion in information and communications; the building of railroads; these and many other technological developments gave Western nations more and more power. In 1837 Macgregor Laird (1808–1861), an explorer, early expert on steamboats, and co-owner of one of the most famous Scottish shipyards, wrote after going by steam vessel up the Niger River in West Africa:

We have the power in our hands, moral, physical, and mechanical; the first, based on the Bible; the second, upon the wonderful adaptation of the Anglo-Saxon race to all climates, situations, and circumstances, . . . the third, bequeathed to us by the immortal James Watt. By his invention every river is laid open to us, time and distance are shortened. If his spirit is allowed to witness the success of his invention here on earth, I can conceive no application of it that would meet his approbation more than seeing the mighty streams of the Mississippi and the Amazon, the Niger and the Nile, the Indus and the Ganges, stemmed by hundreds of steam-vessels, carrying the glad tidings of "peace and good will towards men" into the dark places of the earth which are now filled with cruelty.**

---

* Hilaire Belloc, "Colonel Blood," in *The Age of Imperialism,* ed. Robin W. Winks (Englewood Cliffs, N.J.: Prentice-Hall, Inc., 1969), p. 59. Reprinted by permission of Gerald Duckworth & Co., Ltd., and Random House, Inc.

** Macgregor Laird and R. A. K. Oldfield, *Narrative of an Expedition into the Interior of Africa, by the River Niger, in the Steam-Vessels Quorra and Alburkah, in 1832, 1833, and 1834* (London: Bentley, 1837), II, pp. 397–98.

---

nations surged forward: the French established themselves in Algeria in 1830; the Americans, through a society which sent free blacks to West Africa, established ties with Liberia in 1821; and the British annexed Lagos, the nucleus for Nigeria, in 1861. Russia parted with its vast but thinly inhabited possession in North America when the czarist government sold Alaska to the United States in 1867. But it began the effective settlement of the great areas east of the Urals and began to push into the borderlands of the Middle and Far East.

Throughout the century, the Americas and the old British settlement colonies were generally outside the scramble for empire. The Monroe Doctrine helped to keep both American continents free from further annexation by outside powers. So, too, did the British navy.

One major field of rivalry and penetration was the Near or Middle East. The whole "Eastern Question," as it was called, revolved around the problem of what was to be done with the Balkan and eastern Mediterranean territories, which were peopled principally by Muslims.

They were backward regions by nineteenth-century Western standards, their farmlands exhausted by centuries of simple agriculture and their ancient irrigation systems often in disrepair. They were poor also in natural resources, for their great wealth in petroleum would not be important until the twentieth century. England, France, Austria, and Russia were in active competition over the Near East early in the nineteenth century, and they were later joined by Italy and Germany.

Africa was the scene of the most spectacular imperial rivalry. In 1815 Africa was largely untenanted by Europeans and its interior almost unexplored. Islam had penetrated well below the Sahara, especially in the western Sudan, in Futa Jalon (northern Guinea), and in the empire of the Sokoto (roughly northern Nigeria), from which a flourishing trade had developed. Between 1840 and 1860 trade also developed substantially from the east African centers of Mombasa and Zanzibar, with Indians acting as moneylenders and Arabs leading the caravans that penetrated well into the interior. Traders brought out information about the interior, and the first missionaries, who established themselves in Mombasa after 1844, added to Western knowledge of African customs, geography, and resources. Soon exploration was well under way. In the latter half of the century the great powers blocked out territorial units over most of the continent. The only exceptions were the small Republic of Liberia and the mountainous inland state of Abyssinia (now Ethiopia).

The Far East was also a major scene of imperialist rivalries. European powers strengthened their hold on older colonies and acquired new ones in southeast Asia: the mainland areas of Burma, Indochina, and the Malay states, and the island groups of Melanesia and Polynesia. The ancient, thickly populated, highly complex Chinese Empire was never subjected to actual partition and direct annexation. However, China was not sufficiently united politically or advanced industrially to resist European penetration, and by the end of the century it was subjected to a de facto partitioning among Britain, France, Germany, and Russia. Each power operated from certain treaty ports and exercised some control over considerable areas—*spheres of influence*, as they were called. Often they conducted business through local go-betweens, or *compradors*. Rivalry among the European powers and the United States, which favored an Open Door policy of permitting as much free trade in China as was possible and of preserving Chinese sovereignty, served to counterbalance Chinese weakness and left China an independent nation.

Japan had isolated itself from the rest of the world from the mid-seventeenth to the mid-nineteenth centuries. This compact island empire was closed to foreigners during the period when European powers strengthened their small holds in China. Then in 1854 an American naval officer, Matthew C. Perry (1794–1858), persuaded Japan to open two ports to outside trade. By adopting some Western ways and by capitalizing on its own military tradition, Japan was able not merely to preserve real independence during the late nineteenth century but to begin its own imperial expansion on the mainland of Asia after winning a brief war with China in 1894–1895.

The British Empire

By 1815 the British recognized that colonies occupied largely by settlers from the British Isles would most likely move toward independence, and therefore they sought to control the pace and nature of this movement in order to assure continued loyalty to the concept of a Greater Britain. The colonies of settlement were originally rather thinly inhabited lands. The Europeans were not settling virgin land, however, and they had to displace a resident population. Though the settlers saw themselves as "civilized" and the indigenous population as "savages," these were relative terms. Scholars disagree over the size of the Native American population; earlier estimates that suggested 1 million have been scaled upward to 10 million to 12 million north of the Rio Grande and 80 million to 100 million south of that line. There is general agreement that the effects of "the Columbian exchange"—Europe's diseases, firearms, and disruptive practices in exchange for the New World's diseases, foods, and land—reduced the aboriginal population of the New World by 90 percent within a century of European contact.

In Tasmania, a large island to the south of the Australian mainland, the aborigines were totally wiped out. In Australia, the "blackfellows," as the settlers called them, came close to meeting the same fate. On the north island of New Zealand, the Maoris fought guerrilla wars in the 1840s and 1860s in a vain attempt to exclude white settlers from their lands; their numbers shrank from 250,000 to 40,000 during the nineteenth century.

Canada, the First Dominion, 1783–1931

Most of the precedents by which the British Empire evolved into a commonwealth of self-governing nations were first developed in Canada. Between 1783 and 1931 Canada became the first dominion, fully independent from at least 1931 and probably earlier, and essentially self-governing from 1867.

The defeat of the British in the American Revolution propelled thousands of loyal Tories northward to start life anew in Canada as United Empire Loyalists. These Loyalists wished protection from the French; they wished to secure their rights as Englishmen; and they wished to set themselves clearly apart from the new republic to the south. The result was a history of constitutional changes that provided the pattern for other colonies. Some of these changes arose from Loyalist demands, some from the need to achieve a balance between French-language

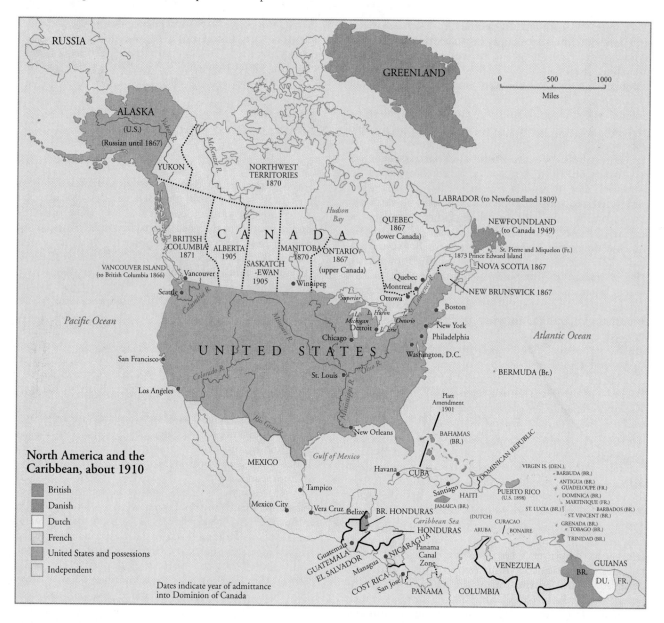

North America and the Caribbean, about 1910

British
Danish
Dutch
French
United States and possessions
Independent

Dates indicate year of admittance into Dominion of Canada

and English-language interests, and some from the need for protection against an expanding United States. First was the Constitutional Act of 1791, establishing elective assemblies in both Upper and Lower Canada, the first almost exclusively British and the second largely French. A constitutional struggle between the elective assemblies and the governors followed, with the central issues being the collecting of revenue, the granting of land for settlement, and the powers of the judiciary. Deadlock resulted by 1837.

Rebellion followed. In Upper Canada William Lyon Mackenzie (1795–1861), "the Firebrand," led a popular uprising. In Lower Canada Louis-Joseph Papineau (1786–1871) rallied the disgruntled in Montreal. When the mass of the population remained aloof, the two rebel leaders were easily defeated and fled to the United States. Relations with the U.S.—which had remained strained

since the War of 1812, during which American militia had burned York (present-day Toronto), the capital of Upper Canada—deteriorated further. Recognizing the dangers of continued discontent within its North American provinces, Britain sought pacification.

The solution was proposed in the Durham Report. Lord Durham (1792–1840), a Whig, was sent to Canada by the British to be governor-general with sweeping investigative powers. Concluding that two cultures were "warring within the bosom of a single state," Durham's massive 1839 *Report on the Affairs of British North America* proposed a union of the two Canadas, the British and the French, and the grant of full responsible government to the united colony. Britain would retain control over foreign relations, the regulation of trade, the disposal of public lands, and the nature of the constitution, surrendering all other aspects of administration to local

Chapter 22 • Modern Empires and Imperialism

authorities. The sense of the Durham Report was embodied in the Union Act of 1840 and in the governorship of Lord Elgin (1847–1854), who in 1849 refused to veto the Rebellion Losses Bill, intended to compensate those who had suffered losses in the uprisings of 1837.

The American Civil War sped the next phase of constitutional growth for the British North American provinces. As the conflict continued, many European and Canadian observers predicted that the North would lose the war and then invade Canada to compensate for the loss of the Southern states. To this fear were added two clear problems: No Canadian administration had been able to govern for long because the parties were so evenly matched that each election produced a near-deadlock; and Britain, hoping to avoid embroilment in colonial wars, threatened to withdraw the imperial troops. Britain counseled some form of regional union for the North American colonies.

In 1867 the united Canadas (now to be called Ontario and Quebec), Nova Scotia, and New Brunswick formed the Confederation of Canada, to be known as a *dominion*. Canada was not yet fully independent, but a giant stride toward this goal had been made.

The Canadian confederation added new provinces under the British North America Act of 1867. When British Columbia, which had recently united with Vancouver Island, joined the confederation in 1871, dominion from sea to sea was truly achieved. Thereafter, the interior was progressively settled and new provinces were carved out of the rich agricultural lands. Newfoundland had held aloof from unification, but it voted to join with Canada in 1949. Meanwhile, Canada had established other precedents by which complete independence from Britain was achieved: the negotiation of a treaty with the United States by which boundary disputes were settled (1871); the creation of its own Department for Foreign Affairs (1909); its assertion of an independent right to sign peace treaties at the end of World War I; its separate membership in the League of Nations (1919); and the removal of any remaining colonial subordination by the Statute of Westminster in 1931. Thus Canada contrasted with the United States, the other predominantly English-speaking North American frontier society, by achieving its independence through evolution rather than revolution.

Dominion status was applied to other colonies of white settlement. The six provinces of Australia had common British origins and relatively short lives as separate colonies, the oldest, New South Wales, dating from 1788. Nevertheless, they developed local differences. They gained the essentials of self-government in the Australian Colonies Government Act of 1850, but federal union and dominion status were not achieved until New South Wales, Queensland, Victoria, South Australia, Western Australia, and Tasmania were linked as the Commonwealth of Australia in 1901. The influence of the American example was clear in the constitution of Australia, which provided for a senate with equal membership for each of the six states, a house of representatives apportioned on the basis of population, and a supreme court with certain powers

of judicial review. But in Australia, as in the other British dominions, the parliamentary system of an executive (prime minister and cabinet) that could be dismissed by vote of the legislative body was retained. Long before it became a dominion, Australia pioneered in the secret printed ballot; New Zealand (in 1893) and South Australia (in 1894) extended universal suffrage to women well in advance of Britain and Canada (1918) or the United States (1920).

South Africa, 1815–1910

The legacy of empire was particularly complex in South Africa, where there were two, not one, white settlement groups. Britain acquired the Cape Colony from the Netherlands in 1815. Because the Cape was strategically important and the climate seemed suited to European settlement, Britishers arrived and soon began to compete for land with the older European colonists, the *Boers* (Dutch for "farmer"). The adoption of English as the sole official language, the abolition of slavery throughout the empire, and the attempts by London to protect the aboriginal population went against the grain of the patriarchal Boers, fundamentalist Christians who believed that the Bible told them that slavery was ordained of God. Between 1835 and 1837 some ten thousand Boers moved north into sparsely settled country in the Great Trek. Needing more land to support their custom that each farmhouse should be an hour's walk from any other house (making the average farm six thousand acres in size), and refusing to acknowledge any African rights to the land they were occupying, the Boers pressed against the Bantu and other groups. After some confused three-cornered fighting among Boers, British, and Zulus, the Boers established two virtually independent states—the Transvaal and the Orange Free State. The British settled another province to the east along the Indian Ocean, known as Natal. Cape Colony and Natal, which both had black populations heavily outnumbering the British and remaining Boer residents combined, acquired self-governing rights.

The British Empire at the southern end of the African continent grew slowly, caught up in contending policies between ambitious colonial politicians and imperial administrators on the one hand, and indigenous leaders on the other. In 1852, by the Sand River Convention, the British acknowledged the independence of the Transvaal; soon after they also acknowledged that of the Orange Free State. But in 1877 they reversed themselves and annexed the Transvaal as a step toward the federation of all South Africa under the British Crown. The Boers revolted in 1880, and the Liberal Gladstone lived up to his principles by making a treaty with the Boers at Pretoria in 1881 that reestablished the Transvaal as independent, though under the "suzerainty" of Great Britain.

The British were already filtering up through the arid country to the west of the Boer republics when the discovery of gold and the development of a diamond industry in these republics undid Gladstone's work. The Transvaal was no longer a poor and isolated grazing country; it offered a great source of wealth that tempted settlers

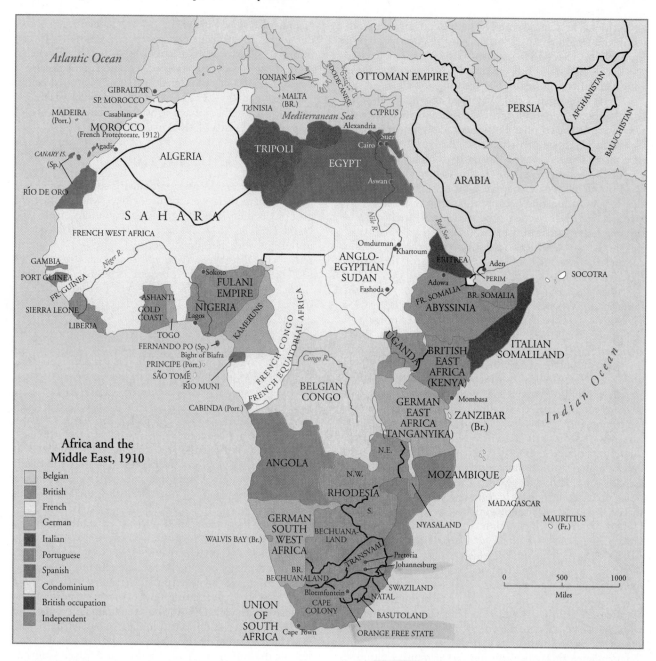

Africa and the Middle East, 1910

- Belgian
- British
- French
- German
- Italian
- Portuguese
- Spanish
- Condominium
- British occupation
- Independent

of a quite different kind. The region about Johannesburg, the Rand, filled up with adventurers and entrepreneurs of a dozen nations, all looking to Britain to protect them from the conservative Boers, to whom they were undesirable *Uitlanders* (outlanders).

The simmering conflict came to a head with the Jameson Raid of December 29, 1895.* The British in South Africa were now under the leadership of Cecil Rhodes, the prime minister of Cape Colony and a determined imperialist who had made a quick fortune consolidating the chaotic diamond industry. The raid itself,

under Dr. Leander Jameson (1853–1917), was an invasion of the Transvaal from British territory and was planned to coincide with an uprising of Uitlanders in Johannesburg. But the uprising did not take place, and the president of the Transvaal, Paul Kruger (1825–1904), had no trouble defeating Jameson's handful of invaders. Boer resistance to the Uitlanders hardened with alien expulsion and immigration restriction acts, and controls were placed over the right of assembly and freedom of the press. The two Boer republics renewed a defensive alliance and presented an ultimatum to the British government. The ultimatum was rejected, and the Boer War began on October 11, 1899.

The British did not have enough troops immediately available to put down determined Boer fighters, who were on their own ground and were accustomed to the rigors

---

* The seasons are, of course, reversed in the southern hemisphere from those of the northern hemisphere; hence, the December raid took place in midsummer.

Even as an undergraduate, Cecil Rhodes had in mind a grand plan for the British Empire in Africa. While at Oxford he wrote his "Confession of Faith," which asked, "Why should we not form a secret society with but one object, the furtherance of the British Empire and the bringing of the whole uncivilized world under British rule for the recovery of the United States, for the making the Anglo-Saxon race but one Empire? What a dream, but yet it is probable, it is possible."

The Granger Collection

of outdoor life. Western opinion generally sided with the underdog Boers, and even in Britain many Liberals and Labourites strongly opposed the war. But in the long run the overwhelming strength of British numbers and technology prevailed. By the middle of 1900 the British had won in the field, but it took another eighteen months to subdue the desperate guerrilla bands. In 1902, by the Treaty of Vereeniging, the Boers accepted British rule, with the promise of ultimate self-government. In 1910 the British created the Union of South Africa, linking Cape Colony, the Transvaal, the Orange Free State, and Natal.

Thus, on the eve of World War I South Africa was among the self-governing British dominions. Briton and Boer seemed to be ready to collaborate in developing an increasingly important outpost of the West. But there were ominous signs even then. The Boers resisted being Anglicized, and the foundations of an intensely divisive policy of racial segregation had been laid. Since racial barriers were applied to freedom of movement, the very notion of a "frontier" of opportunity failed to arise, and South Africa created for itself a major problem relating to migrant labor. The two European elements together

were in a minority of one to four compared with the non-Europeans: the Africans, the East Indians (who had immigrated in great numbers, especially to Natal), and the "coloured" peoples of mixed blood.

Egypt and Africa South of the Sahara, 1859–1914

In the late nineteenth century French prospects in Egypt seemed particularly bright. Between 1859 and 1869 the private French company headed by Ferdinand de Lesseps built the Suez Canal, which united the Mediterranean with the Red Sea and shortened the sea trip from Europe to India and the Far East by thousands of miles. The British had opposed the building of this canal under French patronage; but now that it was finished, the canal came to be considered an essential part of the lifeline of the British Empire.

The British secured a partial hold over this lifeline in 1875, when Disraeli arranged the purchase of 176,000 shares of stock in the canal company from the financially pressed *khedive* (prince) Ismail (r. 1863–1879). The shares gave Britain a 44 percent interest in the company. Despite the sale of the stock, Ismail's fiscal difficulties increased. The Egyptian national debt, which was perhaps £3.3 million at his accession, rose to £91 million by 1876. That year, the European powers (from whose private banks Ismail had borrowed large sums at high interest) obliged Egypt to accept the financial guidance of a debt commission that they set up.

Two years later Ismail had to sacrifice still more sovereignty when he was obliged to appoint an Englishman as his minister of finance and a Frenchman as his minister of public works to ensure that his foreign creditors had first claim to his government's revenues. In 1879, Ismail himself was deposed. Egyptian nationalists, led by army officers whose pay was drastically cut by the new khedive as an economy move, revolted against foreign control and against the government that had made this control possible. Using the slogan "Egypt for the Egyptians!" the officers established a military regime that the powers feared would repudiate Egyptian debts or seize the Suez Canal. In 1882 the British and French sent a naval squadron to Alexandria, ostensibly to protect their nationals. A riot there killed fifty Europeans. The Egyptian military commander began to strengthen the fortifications at Alexandria, but the British naval squadron destroyed the forts and landed British troops, declaring that they were present in the name of the khedive to put an end to the disorders. The khedive gave the British authority to occupy Port Said and points along the Suez Canal to ensure freedom of transit. Thus Britain acquired the upper hand in Egypt, taking the canal and occupying Cairo. Dual French-British control was over.

By the eve of World War I Britain exercised virtual sovereignty over Egypt. Legally, Egypt was still part of the Ottoman Empire, and the khedive's government remained; but a British resident adviser was always at hand to exercise control, and each ministry was guided by a British adviser. For a quarter of a century this British protectorate was in the hands of an imperial proconsul, Evelyn Baring, Lord Cromer (1841–1917), Resident in Cairo from 1883 to 1907. Under Cromer and his successors the enormous government debt was systematically paid off and a beginning made at Westernizing the economic base of Egypt. But nationalist critics complained that too little was being spent on education and public health, and that British policy was designed to keep Egypt in a perpetual colonial economic status, exporting long-staple cotton and procuring manufactured goods from Britain rather than establishing home industries.

Egyptian nationalists were also offended by British policy toward the Sudan. This vast region to the south of Egypt had been partially conquered by Muhammad Ali and Ismail, then lost in the 1880s as a result of a revolt by an Islamic leader, Muhammad Ahmad (c. 1844–1885), who called himself the *mahdi* (messiah). Fears that France or some other power might gain control over the Nile headwaters prompted Britain to reconquer the Sudan. The reconquest at first went very badly for the British. An

Egyptian army under British leadership was annihilated. The British press trumpeted for revenge, and General Charles George Gordon (1833–1885) was dispatched to Khartoum, the Sudanese capital. But Gordon was surrounded in Khartoum. A relief expedition to rescue Gordon left too late, and after passing most of 1884 under siege, Khartoum fell to the Mahdists on January 26, 1885, sixty hours before relieving steamers arrived. Gordon died in this final battle of the siege. Finding Khartoum occupied by the Mahdists, the expedition retired.

National pride required the avenging of Gordon and the reconquest of the Sudan. This was achieved by Lord Kitchener (1850–1916) in an overwhelming victory against the Mahdists at Omdurman in 1898. Between the defeat of Gordon and the battle of Omdurman the British had exploited their technological superiority. They had extended the rail line from Cairo into the heart of the Mahdists' land, and they had equipped their troops with new rifles, the Maxim machine gun, and field artillery. The Mahdists were armed with spears and muzzle-loading muskets. At Omdurman the Mahdists were destroyed and the superiority of European arms definitively established.

A week later news reached Kitchener that French troops were at Fashoda, within the Sudan and on the upper Nile, having crossed from the Atlantic coast. Fearing that the French intended to dam the Nile and block new irrigation for Egypt, Kitchener pressed on toward Fashoda. The French withdrew and renounced all claim to the Nile valley. The British made the Sudan an Anglo-Egyptian *condominium* (joint rule), of which they were the senior partner. This assured clear British dominance in Egypt, since they now controlled the source of the water supply, and it assuaged public opinion in Britain, which had clamored for war; but it aroused Egyptian nationalists, who feared Egypt had lost a province rightfully belonging to it alone.

The British steadily added to their African possessions throughout the century. At its end they had the lion's share of the continent. They had only 4 million square miles out of more than 11 million, but they controlled 61 million people out of some 100 million. The most significant areas were in West Africa. Sierra Leone had been founded after a British judge, Lord Mansfield (1772), had decided that slaves could not be held in England. Seeking some place for free blacks, the British established the "province of freedom" in 1787, adding to its population by bringing in slaves who had fled to freedom behind British lines during the American Revolution. More important in terms of resources and strategic location was the Gold Coast, acquired by the defeat of the Ashanti in 1874 and, more completely, in 1896 and 1900. The whole of Ashantiland was formally annexed in 1901.

The most important, however, was the colony and protectorate of Nigeria, to which one of Britain's ablest administrators, Sir Frederick (later Lord) Lugard (1858–1945), applied a method of colonial governance known as *indirect rule*. Centering on the great River Niger, Nigeria was formally put together from earlier West African colonies in 1914. Northern Nigeria was ruled by Muslim emirs of the Fulani people; southern Nigeria was

One of the richest men in India was the gaekwar of Baroda, whose opulent lifestyle quickly caught the imagination of the British. At that time court photographers were replacing court painters, and Raja Lala Deen Dayal, court photographer to the Nizam of Hyderabad, took this photograph of Fateh Singh Rao, the eldest son of the gaekwar, in 1891.

Pennwick Publishing, Inc. New York

inhabited by divided groups that had long been harassed by slave raids. The region over which the British asserted control comprised the lands of the Hausa, Yoruba, and Ibo peoples—the first Muslim, the others increasingly converted by Christian missionaries, and all three in conflict with each other.

In the Americas, Britain maintained its colonial dependencies in the Caribbean, in Bermuda and the Bahamas, and on the mainland in British Honduras (now Belize) and British Guiana (now Guyana). Tiny dependencies were held as well in the Atlantic, in particular the Falkland Islands, to which the independent nation of Argentina periodically asserted a claim. These were all tropical or semitropical lands, with a relatively small planter class, large black or "brown" lower classes, and often a substantial commercial class from South Asia. The West Indies suffered gradual impoverishment as a result of the competition offered to the local cane sugar crop by the growth in other countries of the beet sugar industry, together with an increase in population beyond the limited food resources of the region. By 1914 the once proud "cockpit of the British Empire" had become an impoverished "problem area."

As racism grew in most of the West toward the end of the century, the African and West Indian colonies tended to be lumped together in the official mind of

British imperialists. Racial disharmony became more common, but it did not reach its peak in the British Empire until the 1920s and early 1930s, when white settlers moved in substantial numbers into Kenya and the Rhodesian highlands. Nor would racist arguments be applied so stringently to the Asian areas of the empire, even though a sense of European superiority became ever more apparent.

India, the "Crown Jewel of Empire," 1815–1915

India was the richest of Britain's overseas possessions, the center and symbol of empire, as the imaginative Disraeli realized when in 1876 he had Queen Victoria proclaimed empress of India. It was over India that the British most often debated the merits of direct intervention versus indirect control, massive social reform imposed from without versus creation of a collaborating elite that would carry out the reforms from within, and whether nature (that is, race) or nurture (that is, environment) most determined a people's future.

In 1763 India was not a single nation but a vast collection of identities and religions. As the nineteenth century began, the two main methods of British control had already become clear. The richest and most densely populated regions, centering on the cities of Calcutta, Madras, and Bombay and on the Punjab, were maintained under direct British rule. The British government did not originally annex these lands; they were first administered by the English East India Company. The company in its heyday had taken on enormous territories and made treaties like a sovereign power. In 1857 the company's native army of Sepoys rebelled; the soldiers had come to fear that British ways were being imposed on them, to the destruction of their own ways. The Sepoy Rebellion was put down, but not before several massacres of Europeans had occurred and not without a serious military effort by the British, which ended in brutally harsh punishment and executions of some of the mutineers. The mutiny ended the English East India Company. In 1858 the British Crown took over the company's lands and obligations.

The rest of India came to be known as the "feudal" or "native" states. These were left nominally under the rule of their own princes, who might be fabulously rich sultans, as in Hyderabad, or merely local chieftains. The "native" states were governed through a system of British resident advisers, somewhat like the system later adapted to Nigeria. The India Office in London never hesitated to interfere when it was thought necessary. While it may not have been Britain's intention, the effect was to allow Britain to "divide and rule" the diverse continent.

Material growth under British rule in India is readily measurable. In 1864 the population of India was about 136 million; in 1904 it was close to 300 million. Although the latter figure includes additional territories in Burma and elsewhere, it is clear that nineteenth-century India experienced a significant increase in total population. In 1901 one male in ten could read and write—a high rate of literacy for the time in Asia; only one in 150 women could read and write. On the eve of World War I India had thousands of miles of railroads, telegraph lines, universities (where classes were conducted in English), hospitals, factories, and busy seaports. Statistics show a native ruling class sometimes fantastically rich, and an immense peasant class for the most part living as their ancestors had lived, at subsistence level. A middle class was just beginning to form, and it had proportionately far more aspirants to white-collar posts in law, medicine, and other liberal professions than to posts in international trade, engineering, and industry—fields badly needed by modernizing societies.

The total wealth of India increased under British rule and was spread more widely among the Indian populations in 1914 than it had been in 1763. Proportionately less and less wealth went directly from an "exploited" India to an "exploiting" Britain. Anglo-Indian economic relations typically took the form of trade between a developed industrial and financial society (Britain) and a society geared to the production of raw materials (India). Indians took an increasing part in this trade, and toward the end of the century local industries, notably textile manufacturing, began to arise in India.

Historians debate whether British rule in India brought social revolution or social stagnation. In some areas society seemed little touched by the transfer of power into British hands, yet in others the rate of colonial impact was startling. Historians do agree, however, that the union between British and Indian ideas and energies was unique: The humanitarians and evangelicals from Britain were matched by Indian leaders who added their own ethical standards to the desire for change; those British who saw themselves as trustees or guardians were met by Indians who considered themselves a chosen people and who espoused a caste system; and those who stressed duty and the close study of human institutions before attempting to alter them found many Indian thinkers already intent upon *dharma* (duty) and self-knowledge. While India had many leaders who drew upon both the British and the Indian ethical arguments, perhaps none blended the several points of view so well as did Mohandas K. Gandhi (1869–1948), who had been admitted to the British bar and had learned of racism firsthand while working for the rights of Indians in South Africa. In 1915 Gandhi returned to India to begin working for the independence of his people.

Throughout the nineteenth century many British "lived off India." Some of them were in private business, but most were military and civilian workers. Yet Indians were gradually working their way into positions of greater responsibility, into both private and public posts at the policy-making level. Both groups opposed the evolution toward independence for India, because their jobs and sometimes their fortunes depended upon continued colonial status. While the British acknowledged that one day India, and perhaps the great island off its southern tip, Ceylon, would be independent, they did not expect that day to come soon.

OTHER EMPIRES

Most industrial nations competed with the British for imperial riches, responsibilities, and "glory." France remained Britain's primary competitor, though Germany, Italy, Belgium, Portugal, the Netherlands, the United States, and Denmark had overseas empires or colonies by the end of the century. Japan, Russia, even remnants of the Spanish empire, remained players in "the great game."

The French

During the nineteenth century France acquired a colonial empire second in area only to that of the British. France, despite frequent revolutionary changes in government, maintained an imperialist policy that added some 50 million people and close to 3.5 million square miles to the lands under the French flag. This empire was concentrated in North, West, and Equatorial Africa, and in Indochina.

Little of this colonial empire was thought suitable for settlement by Europeans, especially since a third of it was taken up by the Sahara Desert. A major exception was French North Africa: Tunisia, Algeria, and Morocco. These lands, with a typically Mediterranean climate, were inhabited chiefly by Berber and Arab peoples of Muslim faith. Though the total indigenous population increased greatly under French rule, more than a million European colonists moved in. Mostly French, but including sizable groups of Italians and Spaniards, these *colons* took land from the native groups. Though they added to the total arable acreage by initiating irrigation projects and other improvements, they were hated by the native peoples.

The French spent forty years in "pacifying" the hinterland of Algiers in the face of stubborn local resistance. The French then added protectorates over Tunisia to the east (1881) and over Morocco to the west (1912). In 1904 Britain gave the French a free hand in Morocco as compensation for their exclusion from Egypt. In Algeria and Tunisia the French hoped to assimilate Africans into French civilization. They hoped to create an empire of "one hundred million Frenchmen," more than half of them overseas, and to draw on abundant local manpower to fill up the ranks of the republic's armies.

In the main, assimilation proved difficult and was only partly achieved. Militarily, the policy worked out pretty much as the French had hoped; black troops from Senegal and *goums* (Moroccan cavalry serving under French or Algerian Muslim officers) gained a reputation as tough fighters. The French, bequeathed their language and laws to part of the indigenous elite. Under the Third Republic they made Algeria politically a part of France itself, organizing it into three departments each with representatives to the Chamber of Deputies; the franchise was open to the relatively small group of Europeanized Algerians as well as to colons.

In Morocco the French took a somewhat different tack. They sought, in part successfully, to open the area to French business and to the international tourist trade. But even by World War I it was apparent that economies based in large measure on tourism were chronically dependent and unstable, so that a diversified economic base was badly needed. In 1912 the French colonial administrator Marshal Hubert Lyautey (1854–1934) began to apply a "splash of oil" policy—that is, he pacified certain key centers by establishing firm working relations with the local population, and then hoped to let pacification spread over the surface of Morocco like a splash of oil on water. The sultan and his feudal subordinates were maintained in Morocco by the French, left relatively free to carry on traditional functions but stripped of real power.

Tunisia, like Morocco, was formally a regency. Because Tunisia was small and easily pacified, assimilation was pursued more intensively there than in other French possessions.

By 1914 the French had been very successful in the partition of Africa. In 1914 France had nearly as many inhabitants in Africa as in the home territories (about 39 million). Yet outside of North Africa and certain coastal towns where their administration and business enterprises were concentrated, the French had not achieved much progress toward assimilating or Westernizing their vast districts.

In Asia, the French took over lands that came to be called French Indochina, which included two rich, rice-growing deltas around Hanoi in the north and Saigon in the south, inhabited by peoples culturally and ethnically related to the Chinese. They also included Cambodia, culturally related to Siam, and the remote mountain lands of Laos. In the process the French made many enemies: they fought the Vietnamese in 1883, forcing the status of a protectorate on the court at Hué in 1883; fought a war with China in 1884, since Peking claimed Vietnam as its own protectorate; assumed power in Cambodia in the face of a popular revolt; and claimed Laos by promoting a coup that threw off Siamese overlordship in 1893.

The French sought to assimilate the local elite class, and they turned Saigon into a French-style city of broad boulevards. They brought substantial material progress in medicine and hygiene, communications, roads, education, industry, and agriculture. They also applied to proud societies European notions of hierarchy. Nationalist movements, nourished by educated local leaders who held jobs of less dignity and authority than they believed should be theirs, rose in strength as the years went on.

Other Continental Powers

Italy got very little out of the partition of Africa. Tunis, which Italy coveted, went instead to France. Italy's major effort centered on the lands at the southern end of the Red Sea, but after the defeat by the Abyssinians in 1896, Italy had to be content with a few thousand square miles, most of it desert, in Eritrea and Somaliland. Italian efforts to add to this insignificant empire by taking Tripoli from its nominal Turkish ruler succeeded in 1912. The Italians also secured Rhodes and other islands off the southwestern corner of Anatolia, known collectively as the Dodecanese (the twelve). These acquisitions were the fruit of the Italo-Turkish War of 1911–1912.

Until the 1880s Bismarck had resisted calls for imperialism, for he felt that domestic unity and military strength on the European continent were paramount. In 1882 a German Colonial League was founded by north German merchants who feared that without overseas expansion Germany would not keep pace with Britain. Two years later Germany signed treaties creating a German protectorate in Southwest Africa, largely as a strategic challenge to Britain, and acquired Togoland and the Cameroons (Kamerun). In 1885 Germany declared an official protectorate over East Africa, but only Tanganyika and Zanzibar had any potential economic significance, and the latter was traded to Britain in 1890 for the tiny British-held island of Heligoland, in the North Sea. In the Pacific, the Germans picked up some small islands and a large territory on the island of New Guinea. Germany also took part in the attempted partition of China, taking a ninety-nine-year lease on Kiachow Bay, on the north China coast. The Portuguese had sought to extend their trading activities into the interior of both Angola and Mozambique, and they continued to control the strategic island of Sao Tomé in the Bight of Biafra. The Belgians helped to establish an International African Association 1876, with the purported goals of suppressing the illegal slave trade and gathering scientific information; the association sent Henry Morton Stanley (1841–1904) to open up the region of the Congo, at which he worked persistently until 1884.

The Germans and British feared this expansion, and they also feared that Belgian or French exploration would threaten the Portuguese territories, which controlled the approaches to the Congo River. Thus in 1884 an Anglo-Portuguese treaty guaranteed freedom of navigation on the Congo to all nations; however, British public opinion and the press opposed this support of Portugal. The treaty was shelved, and Bismarck summoned an international convention in Berlin to settle the Congo and Portuguese issues. The Congo basin was declared a free trade area by the conference in 1885; the independent state of the Congo—with King Leopold of Belgium as its sovereign—was recognized; and the Portuguese were left in possession of their territories, though frequently challenged by the British along the borders of Mozambique and by the Germans from south of Angola.

Thus Belgium, through the enterprise of its shrewd and ruthless king, Leopold II (r. 1865–1909), managed to acquire a large part of equatorial Africa. This project began as the Congo Free State; it ended up in 1908 simply as the Belgian Congo. The Belgians developed the Congo into one of the most profitable of colonies, thanks to its copper, rubber, and other riches, and Belgium made no move to prepare the Congolese for eventual self-government.

The Belgian Congo became one of the three foci of anti-imperial debate before World War I. The others were the rise of pro-Boer sentiment and opposition to the Boer War in Britain, and a sustained effort in the United States to prevent that country from acquiring an empire as the fruit of the Spanish-American War.

The United States

While the industrial powers of Europe were expanding overseas, the United States acquired by purchase and conquest the remainder of its Manifest Destiny—a dominion from sea to sea that was "to bring the blessings of liberty" to the entire continent. The United States believed it had a moral obligation to expand in order to extend the area of freedom against monarchical or dictatorial governments.

The first American empire was solely within the continent. By the end of the century the Native American had been swept aside into reservations and was a ward of the state. Once the Native Americans were "pacified"—the last major battle was fought at Wounded Knee in Dakota Territory, in December 1890—and the frontier was thought to be closed, the main thrust of the westward movement was over, and Americans would have to look elsewhere for new worlds to conquer. By the 1870s

In 1854 a Japanese artist portrayed Commodore Matthew Perry as shown here. The caption refers to Perry as "a high official of the North American Republic."

New York Public Library Picture Collection

a national consensus was emerging that the new frontiers should be sought overseas, particularly in the Caribbean and the Pacific. Control of the harbors of San Diego, San Francisco, and the Juan de Fuca Strait (near present-day Seattle) was a primary aim. Such needs strengthened the desire of American statesmen to find a peaceful solution to their controversy with the British over the Oregon Territory (1846); and the acquisition of California in 1848 was seen as essential to American advancement into the Pacific.

In 1854 Admiral Perry persuaded the Japanese to open two ports to American vessels by the Treaty of Kanagawa. But if the China trade and the expected Japan trade were to flourish, American vessels needed repair and refueling facilities elsewhere in the Pacific. The Hawaiian Islands now took on added significance, for, besides refuge, they also afforded supplies of sandalwood for the China trade. After the discovery of gold in California in 1848, the islands provided the mainland with badly needed sugar and foodstuffs. In 1875 the sugar growers in Hawaii, largely Americans, obtained a reciprocal trading agreement with the United States that stipulated that no part of Hawaii might be given by the Hawaiian Kingdom to any other country. Sugar exports to America increased, until the islands were utterly dependent upon the continental market, and in 1884, when the agreement was renewed, the United States was granted exclusive use of Pearl Harbor as a naval base. In the meantime, the indigenous population declined rapidly, and the planters, in need of labor, imported thousands of Chinese, Japanese, and Portuguese. Hawaii was annexed on July 7, 1898, the first land outside the North American continent to fly the American flag on a permanent basis.

As early as 1823 the Monroe Doctrine had made it clear that the United States saw itself as exerting a strong moral influence in Latin America. The Monroe Doctrine was given a corollary in 1895, when President Grover Cleveland (1837–1908) intervened in a boundary controversy between Venezuela and Britain, asserting that the United States had an obligation to the free nations of the entire Western Hemisphere to protect them from abuse by European powers. In the same year Cuba revolted against Spain. As the revolt spread, American sugar and tobacco growers and iron mine owners on the island complained of the destruction of their property. Outnumbered by the Spanish troops in Cuba, the revolutionaries turned to guerrilla warfare, hoping to draw the United States into intervening. A new governor, appointed in 1896, sought to limit the effects of guerrilla tactics by forcing large elements of the rural population into concentration camps. There thousands died. While American business opposed direct intervention in so unstable a situation, the "yellow" press printed atrocity stories that stirred up prorevolutionary sympathy. Then, on February 15, 1898, the U.S. battleship *Maine*, at anchor in Havana harbor, was destroyed by an explosion that killed 260 officers and men.

President William McKinley (1843–1901) sent an ultimatum to Spain demanding an armistice in the revolution and an end to the concentration camps. Spain revoked the camp policy at once, and instructions were sent to the governor ordering an armistice. But without waiting to learn the details of the Spanish armistice order, McKinley presented the Cuban crisis to Congress with the charge that Spain's response had been "disappointing." After lengthy debate, Congress voted recognition of Cuban independence on April 19, authorized the use of American troops to make recognition effective, and pledged "to leave the government and control of the Island to its people." McKinley signed the resolution, and the United States served an ultimatum upon Spain to grant Cuban independence. Spain broke diplomatic relations; the American navy blockaded Cuban ports; Spain declared war against the United States; and the United States countered with a declaration of war against Spain.

The Spanish-American War lasted 115 days, and the American forces swept all before them. The Spanish empire was broken, its army crushed, and virtually all of its battle fleet sunk or driven onto the beaches. Five days after war was declared, Admiral George Dewey (1837–1917), forewarned two months earlier by Theodore Roosevelt, then assistant secretary of the navy, to sail for Hong Kong, reached Manila Bay. There he methodically destroyed a larger Spanish fleet, and thirteen days later American troops, reinforced by Filipino guerrillas under General Emilio Aguinaldo (1869–1964), occupied Manila.

The Treaty of Paris, by which the Philippines were ceded to the United States, was signed on December 10. Spain surrendered all claim to Cuba, assumed the Cuban debt, ceded Puerto Rico and the Pacific island of Guam to the United States as indemnity, and received $20 million in payment for the Philippines. In one quick step the United States had become a maritime empire with interests in both the Caribbean and the Far East.

American troops remained in control of Cuba until 1902. In effect, Cuba became an American protectorate and the second largest recipient of American investments in the Western Hemisphere. Investment required stability, and from 1917 until 1934, the American government made it clear that it would recognize no hostile regime in Cuba.

The Pacific continued to be the testing ground for the growth of an American empire, however. To maintain control over Caribbean areas seemed natural, for Americans had long considered themselves to be the guardian of the New World. To attempt the same in the remote Pacific invited new dangers. The Filipinos felt betrayed by the continued presence of the American army, and when Aguinaldo learned that the Treaty of Paris had given the Philippines to the United States, he organized an armed revolt that continued as guerrilla warfare until mid-1902. A special commission established by President McKinley recommended ultimate independence for the islands, with American rule to continue indefinitely until the Filipinos proved themselves "ready for self-government." One condition of such proof was to terminate the rebellion and accept American rule. In 1916 partial home rule was granted to the Philippines; in 1935 the islands became a commonwealth; and in 1946 they were granted full independence.

On the whole, American imperialism in Asia was nonterritorial, since the British naval presence in the area made outright colonial expansion by the United States difficult and in most cases unnecessary. American policy was best symbolized by the Open Door concept. The Opium War of 1841 between Britain and China, the Sino-Japanese War (1894–1895), and the disintegration of the Manchu Empire in the 1890s had left the Chinese open to demands by European nations for political and economic concessions and the carving up of the China trade into spheres of influence. The British had taken Hong Kong, and the French, Germans, and Russians were on the move. The British suggested that the United States join in guaranteeing equality of commercial access to China for all Western nations. In a circular letter of September 6, 1899, Secretary of State John Hay (1838–1905) asked for assurances from Germany, Russia, and Britain (and later from France, Italy, and Japan as well) that none would interfere with any treaty ports in China and that none would discriminate in favor of their own subjects when collecting railroad charges and harbor dues. Although he received evasive replies, Hay announced in March 1900 that the principle of the Open Door was "final and definitive."

The Panama Canal Zone added a third and final chapter to the American attempt to compromise between

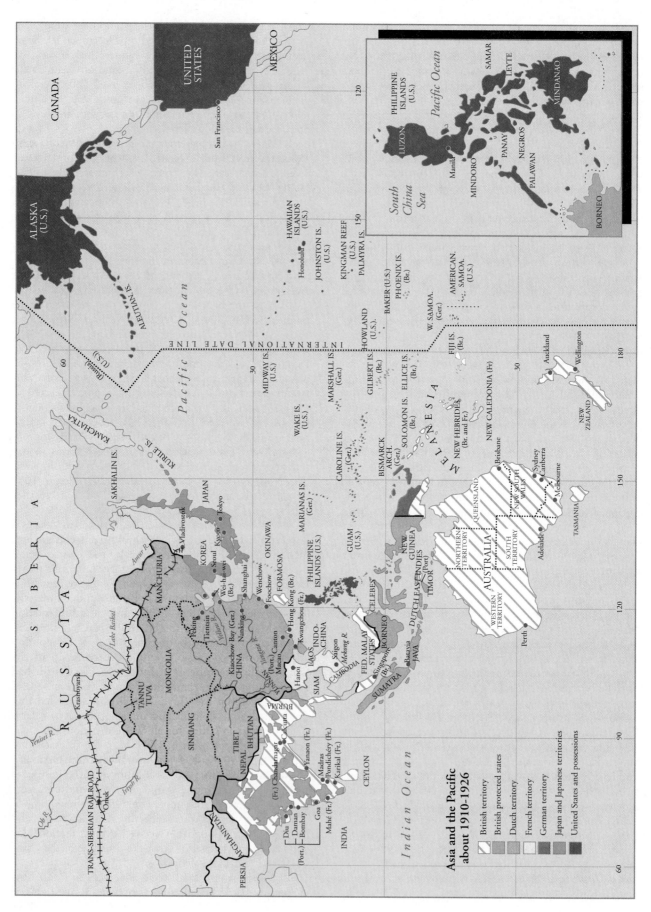

Asia and the Pacific about 1910–1926

British territory
British protected states
Dutch territory
French territory
German territory
Japan and Japanese territories
United States and possessions

CANADA

UNITED STATES

MEXICO

ALASKA (U.S.)

San Francisco

ALEUTIAN IS.

(U.S.)
(Russia)

Pacific Ocean

INTERNATIONAL DATE LINE

HAWAIIAN ISLANDS (U.S.)

Honolulu

JOHNSTON IS. (U.S.)

KINGMAN REEF (U.S.)

PALMYRA IS. (U.S.)

BAKER (U.S.)

PHOENIX IS. (Br.)

HOWLAND (U.S.)

AMERICAN. SAMOA. (U.S.)

W. SAMOA. (Ger.)

FIJI IS. (Br.)

MIDWAY IS. (U.S.)

MARSHALL IS. (Ger.)

GILBERT IS. (Br.)

SOLOMON IS. (Br.)

ELLICE IS. (Br.)

NEW HEBRIDES (Br. and Fr.)

NEW CALEDONIA (Fr)

Auckland

Wellington

NEW ZEALAND

WAKE IS. (U.S.)

CAROLINE IS. (Ger.)

BISMARCK ARCH. (Ger.)

M E L A N E S I A

MARIANAS IS. (Ger.)

GUAM (U.S.)

NEW GUINEA (Port)

DUTCH EAST INDIES

TIMOR (Port)

Brisbane

QUEENSLAND

NEW SOUTH WALES

Sydney
Canberra
Melbourne

TASMANIA

NORTHERN TERRITORY

SOUTH TERRITORY

A U S T R A L I A

WESTERN TERRITORY

Adelaide

Perth

S I B E R I A

KAMCHATKA

SAKHALIN IS.

KURILE IS.

JAPAN

Vladivostok

Tokyo

Kyoto

Seoul

KOREA

Wei-hai-wei (Br.)

Shanghai

Wenchow

Foochow

OKINAWA

FORMOSA

PHILIPPINE ISLANDS (U.S.)

CELEBES

BORNEO

JAVA

Batavia

SUMATRA

FED. MALAY STATES (Br.)

Singapore

INDO-CHINA

Saigon

CAMBODIA

Mekong R.

Hanoi

LAOS

SIAM

BURMA

Hong Kong (Br.)

Kwangchou (Fr.)

Macao (Port.)

Canton

Kiaochow Bay (Ger.)

Nanking

Yangtze R.

Peking

Tientsin

Yellow R.

C H I N A

MONGOLIA

TANNU TUVA

SINKIANG

TIBET

NEPAL

BHUTAN

MANCHURIA

Amur R.

Lake Baikal

R U S S I A

Krasnoyarsk

Omsk

Ob R.

Irtysh R.

Yenisei R.

TRANS-SIBERIAN RAILROAD

AFGHANISTAN

PERSIA

INDIA

CEYLON

Calcutta

Yanaon (Fr.)

Madras

Pondichéry (Fr.)

Karikal (Fr.)

Mahé (Fr.)

Goa (Port.)

Bombay

Daman

Diu (Port.)

Chandernagar (Fr.)

Indian Ocean

PHILIPPINE ISLANDS (U.S.)

Pacific Ocean

LUZON

Manila

MINDORO

SAMAR

LEYTE

PANAY

NEGROS

PALAWAN

MINDANAO

South China Sea

BORNEO

120

150

120

90

60

180

30

60

150

30

economic advantage and political interest. Concluding that intervention in the Caribbean and Central America would continue to be necessary to the United States, Theodore Roosevelt moved forward on two fronts. Roosevelt saw the election of 1900 as a mandate on imperialism. Desiring canal rights in Central America, he encouraged a Panamanian revolt against Colombia, immediately recognized the independence of Panama, and in November 1903, with the Hay-Bunau-Varilla Treaty, gained perpetual rights of use and control of a canal zone across the isthmus of Panama for the United States, in exchange for $10 million and an annual fee.

A year later "TR" added a further corollary to the Monroe Doctrine, fearing armed European intervention in Venezuela after that nation had defaulted on debts to Britain and Germany. Roosevelt stated that if Latin American nations could not administer their own financial affairs, and if they gave European nations cause for intervention, then the United States might be forced to "exercise . . . an international police power" in the Western Hemisphere. This was especially applicable to nations that could threaten access to the canal route, and when the Panama Canal was opened on August 15, 1914, the United States had further reason to protect its Caribbean approaches. Under Roosevelt's corollary, Santo Domingo became an American protectorate in 1907, as did Haiti in 1915. American marines were stationed in Nicaragua from 1912 until 1925; in 1916 the United States acquired the right to construct a canal across Nicaragua; and the Virgin Islands were purchased from Denmark in 1917. Even revolution in Mexico—which began in 1913 and led to American intervention at Vera Cruz in 1914 and along the northern border two years later—did not disturb the flow of commerce, investment, and shipping in the Caribbean, which had become "an American lake."

The Japanese Empire

One more empire was being formed during the decades before World War I, the only modern empire to be created by a non-European people. Even during their long, self-imposed isolation the Japanese had maintained an interest in Western developments. When Japan opened its ports in 1854, its basic political and economic structure had long been in need of overhauling. The ruling feudal oligarchy was ineffective and unpopular. Discontent was growing, especially among two important social classes. One was the urban middle class of merchants and artisans. Although the industrial revolution had not yet reached Japan, the country already had populous cities, notably Tokyo (then called Yedo or Edo). The urban middle class wanted political rights to match their increasing economic power. The other discontented class may be compared roughly with the poorer gentry and lesser nobility of Europe under the Old Regime. These were the *samurai*, or feudal retainers, a military caste threatened with impoverishment and political eclipse. The samurai dreaded the growth of cities and the subsequent threat to the traditional preponderance of agriculture and landlords. These social pressures, more than outside Western influences, forced the modernization of Japan.

Economically, the transformation proceeded rapidly. By 1914 much of Japan resembled a Western country, for it, too, had railroads, fleets of merchant vessels, a large textile industry, large cities, and big business firms. The industrialization of Japan was the more remarkable in view of its meager supplies of many essential raw materials. But it had many important assets. Japan's geographical position with respect to Asia was much like that of the British Isles with respect to Europe. Japan, too, found markets for exports on the continent nearby and used the income to pay for imports. The ambitious Japanese middle class, supplemented by recruits from the samurai, furnished aggressive and efficient business leadership. A great reservoir of cheap labor existed in the peasantry, who needed to find jobs away from the overcrowded farms and who were ready to work long and hard in factories for what seemed very low wages by Western standards.

Politically, Japan appeared to undergo a major revolution in the late nineteenth century and to remodel its government along Western lines. Actually, however, the change was by no means as great as it seemed. A revolution did indeed occur, beginning in 1868 when the old feudal oligarchy crumbled. In 1889 the *mikado* (emperor) bestowed a constitution on his subjects, with a bicameral Diet composed of a noble House of Peers and an elected House of Representatives. The architects of these changes were aristocrats and ambitious young samurai, supported by allies from the business world. The result was to substitute a new authoritarian oligarchy for the old. A small group of aristocrats dominated the emperor and the state. The constitution of 1889 provided only the outward appearance of full parliamentary government; the ministry was responsible not to the Diet but to the emperor, and hence to the dominant ruling class. The Diet itself was scarcely representative; the right to vote for members of its lower house was limited to a narrow male electorate, including the middle class but excluding the peasants and industrial workers.

Japan began its overseas expansion by annexing the island of Formosa from China after a short war in 1894–1895. China was also forced to recognize the independence of Korea, which Japan coveted. But Russia, too, had designs on Korea; the result of this rivalry was the Russo-Japanese War of 1904–1905. Japan secured unchallenged control in Korea (which was annexed in 1910), special concessions in the Chinese province of Manchuria, and the cession by Russia of the southern half of the island of Sakhalin, to the north of the main Japanese islands. Thus Japan had the beginnings of an empire.

Empire Challenged

By 1914 it was quite clear that many non-European peoples, including the colonies of exploitation, were beginning to reject claims of white supremacy. The concept of nationalism, new outside of Europe and the Americas, had continued to spread. In the early twentieth century it was most evident in Japan and, to some extent, China, Egypt, and India.

Egyptian, Indian, and Chinese patriots were primarily concerned with getting rid of their European imperial masters; their attitudes were those of oppressed nationalistic groups everywhere. In theory, nationality transcends the dividing lines of profession, social class, and even caste. The *fellah*, the Egyptian peasant whose ancestry reached back more than fifty centuries, could claim to be as good an Egyptian as the aristocratic *pasha*. People began to talk and write of "Arab" nationalism, of a spirit of *négritude* that might unite black Africa, of Irish nationalism, of a separate *canadienne* identity, of a separate Afrikaans language and faith. Imperialism, which had once looked as though it might unite peoples, had by 1914 become another cause of nationalism.

Imperialist rivalries, especially after 1870, exacerbated the normal rivalries among the European great powers and were thus a major factor in the complex of causes that brought on the war in 1914. This is particularly true of the Anglo-German rivalry, which was manifested everywhere by 1900—by commercial travelers of both nations trying to sell machinery in South America; by missionaries in Africa; by army and naval officers, editors, labor organizers, all seeking to make either German or British influence prevail.

Was imperialism harmful? All forms of imperialism—while often bringing stability, sanitation, education, and improved communications to an area—forced people to change at a pace set by someone else. All imperialisms, including those directed toward the ultimate independence of a colony, implied that only the superior power could name the stages through which the inferior must pass and the degree and speed of that passing. The most pervasive legacy of imperialism was the pernicious assumption that "superior" nations had the unquestionable right to judge the progress of "inferior" nations.

Imperialism was surely harmful in creating two special classes within colonial and postcolonial societies. The first were the products of racial intermixture—called half-breeds in the United States, *métis* in Canada, *lançados* in Portuguese colonies, *mestizos* in Spanish, and Eurasian throughout Asia. Such people often found that they were accepted by neither society from which they sprang. A second halfway group created by imperialism were those now referred to as *collaborators*—members of the indigenous culture who felt that the future lay with Europe and the colonial power. While some cooperated with the imperial powers for purely personal gain, others collaborated because they shared the European conviction that the values Europe brought to their society outweighed the disadvantages. Some saw the Europeans as peacemakers, since they often had the power to enforce peace where local chiefs could not; others chose to work with the conquerors because they were impressed by European forms of representative government.

Although Western influence was extensive at the surface, in many areas it did not touch the village level, and African, and Asian societies remained essentially unchanged at the bottom. But the intellectual and political elites were transmuted in fundamental ways, and even those who did not accept Western culture had to battle against it on Western terms. Military, technological, political, and intellectual patterns throughout the world were Westernized. Non-Western peoples faced crises of identity in Asia and Africa. That essentially European concept, the nation-state, and the rampant nationalism of the twentieth century became a basic heritage of the imperialism of the nineteenth. In this sense the Western impact on traditional societies was so great as to constitute an imperial revolution no less pervasive than the scientific, industrial, or commercial revolutions.

$\int$UMMARY

In the nineteenth century Britain emerged as a parliamentary democracy. The Reform Bills of 1832 and 1867 accomplished revolutionary changes without violence. The cabinet controlled Parliament; representation was increased through the extension of suffrage and the reform of electoral districts. In the stable political atmosphere of England, the two-party system grew. Disraeli and Gladstone, leaders of Conservatives and Liberals respectively, dominated politics in this age of reform.

By the late 1800s economic difficulties and challenges abroad led to calls for protectionism. Liberals gave up their classical laissez-faire doctrines in exchange for government interference. Conservatives became committed to laissez-faire. While the Liberal party fragmented and declined, the Labour party gained strength.

In Ireland, resistance to English dominance increased as a result of the potato famine. Piecemeal reforms did not satisfy Irish nationalists. The struggle for home rule

eventually produced a bill in 1912, but it never went into effect because of the outbreak of World War I.

Between 1800 and 1930, 84 percent of the world's land came under the control of Western nations. Economic, political, and psychological motives, including a desire for national glory, contributed to imperialism in the late nineteenth century. Strategic concerns also came into play as imperial powers sought to protect trade routes. A humanitarian impulse was evident in the desire to reform and Christianize other peoples.

Imperial powers acquired both formal and informal empires, exercising control over areas that were technically independent. The new imperialism after 1870 involved emotional and nationalist needs, but it was also tied to industrialization and cultural goals.

In the nineteenth century, the relationship that evolved between Canada and the British Parliament set the pattern for self-government in other white-settled colonies. These changes paved the way for independence without revolution. By 1914, Australia, New Zealand, and South Africa had also achieved self-government.

In Egypt, Britain gained the upper hand with control of the French-built Suez Canal, considered Britain's lifeline to India. Britain expanded into the Sudan and acquired colonies in East and West Africa as well as in the Caribbean and Central and South America.

After 1815 Britain dominated India, which became the symbol of empire when Disraeli had Queen Victoria proclaimed empress of India. The Sepoy Rebellion (1857) allowed the British government to take control of the lands formerly administered by the English East India Company. Other areas were ruled by local princes under the control of British administrators.

In the nineteenth century France acquired a colonial empire in North Africa and Indochina. After achieving national unity, Germany and Italy entered into the scramble for colonies. Italy acquired Tripoli and lands along the Adriatic. Germany acquired colonies in East Africa, southwest Africa, and among the Pacific islands.

Westward movement in the United States had characteristics similar to imperialist expansion elsewhere. The United States pushed through to new frontiers in the Pacific, acquiring Hawaii and the Philippines. In 1900 Americans supported the policy of an Open Door in China to guarantee equal commercial access to the disintegrating Manchu Empire.

After 1854 Japan experienced rapid modernization and industrialization, accompanied by imperial ambitions. In 1895 it annexed Formosa after a war with China, and in 1905 gained control of Korea after its defeat of Russia. Many non-Europeans rejected white supremacy, and many patriots worked against imperialist ambitions.

CRITICAL THINKING

1. How do you define *imperialism*?

2. Why was the British Empire both the first "modern empire" and the most powerful and extensive of modern empires?

3. What is the balance sheet of imperialism? Were there good effects as well as bad ones? What were they, and how do you weigh them against each other?

4. What is meant by "the new imperialism"? Was it in fact "new"?

5. Why do we call Canada "the First Dominion"? How did precedents set in Canada contribute to the evolution of constitutional government in other dependencies of the British Empire? How did Canada's development differ from that of the United States?

6. Justify calling India the "Crown Jewel of Empire." Compare British policy in India and southern Africa.

7. Looking back to earlier empires, compare the French, British, Dutch, Spanish, and Portuguese empires with respect to policies on trade, on slavery, and on race.

8. Were there any non-European empires? If so, where? How did they differ from European empires?

9. What does the concept of "postmodern" imply?

10. Can "imperialism" and the idea of "Western influence" be separated in describing relations between Western and non-Western peoples in the late nineteenth and early twentieth centuries?

Timeline Covers: 1847–1940

DATES	POLITICAL	THOUGHT AND ARTS	ECONOMY AND SOCIETY
1840 A.D.			
		1847 Charlotte Bronte, *Jane Eyre*	1847 Richard Hoe invents the rotary press
			1848–1849 California Gold Rush
1850		1849 Charles Dickens, *David Copperfield*	
			later 19th century Massive leap in sale of all reading materials
		1851 Herman Melville, *Moby Dick*	
		1852 Harriet Beecher Stowe, *Uncle Tom's Cabin*	
		1853 Giuseppi Verdi, "La Traviata"	
		1855–1927 Houston Stewart Chamberlain	
		1856 Gustave Flaubert, *Madame Bovary*	
	1859–1916 Yuan Shih-k'ai	1859 Charles Darwin *On the Origin of Species by Natural Selection*	1859 First oil well drilled (Titusville, PA.)
1860	1860–1934 Raymond Poincare	1860s Impressionist painting begins in France	1860 First recorded baseball game
			1862 R. J. Gatling invents the machine gun
	1863–1938 Gabriele d'Annunzio	1863 J. S. Mill, *Utilitarianism*	1863–1951 William Randolph Hearst
		1863 Edouard Manet, Dejeuner sur L'herbe	
	1864–1936 Eleutherios Venizelos	1864–1869 Leon Tolstoy, *War and Peace*	1864 Louis Pasteur develops pasteurization
		1864 Pope Pius IX issues the *Syllabus of Errors*	1864 Geneva Convention and the founding of the International Red Cross
		1865 Richard Wagner, "Tristan and Isolide"	1865 Joseph Lister initiates antiseptic surgery
	1866–1925 Sun Yat-sen	1866 Fyodor Dostoyevesky, *Crime and Punishment*	1869 Suez Canal opens
	1869–1935 Josef Pilsudski		
	1869–1948 Mohandas K. Gandhi	1870–1919 Rosa Luxemburg	
1870		1870 First Vatican Council proclaims papal infallibility	
	1871–1925 Friedrich Ebert	1872 James Whistler, The Artist's Mother	
	1872–1878 League of the Three Emperors	1874–1942 Alice Duer Miller	
			1877 Thomas Alva Edison invents the phonograph
			1877 First public telephone system (New Haven, CT.)
	1878–1929 Gustav Stresemann		
	1879–1953 Joseph Dzhugashvili (Stalin)		
	1879–1940 Lev Davidovich Bronstein (Leon Trotsky)		
	1879–1918 Dual Alliance		
1880	1880–1938 Mustafa Kamal		1880 Edison and Joseph Swan invent the electric light
	1881–1889 League of the Three Emperors		
	1882–1914 Triple Alliance		
	1882–1975 Eamon De Valera		1883–1889 Germany introduces the first social security laws
	1883–1945 Benito Mussolini		1883 First skyscraper, Chicago
	1883–1936 Gregory Zinoviev		1885 Pasteur's rabies vaccine
		1885 Vincent Van Gogh, The Potato Eaters	
	1887–1975 Chiang Kai-shek	1888–1938 Nikolai Bukharin	1888 Kodak camera invented
	1887–1890 Reinsurance Treaty	1889 The Eiffel Tower built in Paris	
	1889–1945 Adolf Hitler	1893–1918 Wilfred Owen	
1890	1892–1975 General Francisco Franco		1893 Karl Benz builds the first four-wheeled motor car
	1894–1917 Franco-Russian Alliance		1895 The Lumiere brothers invent the motion picture camera
		1896 Nobel Prizes established	1896 First modern Olympic Games held (Athens, Greece)
	1898 Fashoda Crisis		1898 Pierre and Marie Curie discover radium
	1899–1902 Boer War		
1900	1900 Boxer Rebellion	1900 Sigmund Freud, *The Interpretation of Dreams*	1900s Importance of Middle East oil grows
	r. 1900–1946 Victor Emmanuel III of Italy	1901 Ragtime Jazz develops in the U.S.	1901 Guglielmo Marconi sends the first radio message across the Atlantic
	1902 Anglo-Japanese Alliance	1902 V. I. Lenin, *What Is to Be Done?*	1903 Ford Motor Co. founded
			1903 Wright brothers invent the airplane
	1904 Anglo-French Entente		
	1905–1906 First Moroccan Crisis	1905 Claude Debussy, "La Mer"	1905 Albert Einstein, Theory of Relativity
	1905 Introduction of the Dreadnought class		
	1907 Anglo-Russian Entente		
	1908 Young Turk rebellion		1909 Robert E. Peary reaches the North Pole
1910			1910 The "weak end" becomes popular in the U.S. and Britain
	1911 Second Moroccan Crisis		

DATES	POLITICAL	THOUGHT AND ARTS	ECONOMY AND SOCIETY
1911 A.D.	1911–1912 Chinese Revolution 1912–1913 Balkan Wars 1914–1918 World War I 1914 Battle of the Marne 1914 Battles of Tannenberg and the Masurian Lakes 1914 First use of poison gas in war 1915 Sinking of the Lusitania 1915 Lloyd George becomes Prime Minister 1916 Easter Rebellion 1916 Battle of Jutland 1916 First use of the tank in war 1917 March Revolution in Russia 1917 United States joins the Allies 1917 Battle of Passchendaele 1917 Balfour Declaration 1917 November Revolution in Russia 1918–1921 Russian Civil War 1918 Treaty of Brest-Litovsk 1918 Woodrow Wilson issues the Fourteen Points 1918–1919 Spartacist uprisings in Germany 1918 Allies intervene in Russia 1919 Opening of the Versailles Peace Conference 1919–1922 Irish Revolution and Civil War 1919–1922 German Nazi Party organized 1919 Amritsar Massacre	1913 Igor Stravinsky, "The Rite of Spring" 1915 D. W. Griffith, "The Birth of a Nation" 	1911 Roald Amundsen reaches the South Pole 1912 S. S. Titanic sinks on its maiden voyage 1914 Panama Canal opens 1914 10.5 million European immigrants enter the U.S. 1918–1919 Influenza epidemic kills 20 million
1920	1920 Women in United States gain the vote 1920 U.S. Senate rejects Versailles Treaty 1920s–1930s Rise of Indian independence movement 1921–1927 Stalin and Trotsky struggle for power 1921–1928 The Soviet New Economic Policy 1922 Nine-Power Treaty 1922–1945 Mussolini rules Italy 1922–1923 German hyperinflation 1923–1925 French occupy the Ruhr 1924 Dawes Plan 1925 Locarno Treaties 1928 First Soviet five-year plan 1928 Kellogg-Briand Pact 1929–1939 Forced collectivization in Russia 1929 Lateran Treaty 1929–1934 The Great Depression	1920 Carl Jung, *Psychological Types* 1921–1923 Arnold Schoenberg develops 12-tone music 1922 James Joyce, *Ulysses* 1922 T. S. Eliot, *The Waste Land* 1923 Marcel Proust, *A Remembrance of Things Past* 1923 George Gershwin, "Rhapsody in Blue" 1924 Giacomo Matteotti, The Fascists Exposed 1925 Adolf Hitler, *Mein Kampf* 1927 Herman Hesse, *Steppenwolf* 1928 D. H. Lawrence, *Lady Chatterley's Lover* 1929 E. M. Remarque, *All Quiet on the Western Front* 1929 Virginia Woolf, *A Room of One's Own*	1923 First birth control clinic (New York) 1925 Werner Heisenberg and Max Born formulate quantum mechanics 1926–1940 Rapid urbanization of Soviet Union 1927 Charles Lindbergh flies non-stop from New York to Paris 1928 First television broadcasts 1928 Alexander Fleming discovers penicillin 1929 Collapse of the New York Stock Exchange
1930	1931 Statute of Westminister 1932 Britain enacts protective tariffs 1933–1945 Adolf Hitler rules Germany 1933–1945 Administration of Franklin Roosevelt 1933–1934 Gleichschaltung and the creation of the Nazi dictatorship 1934 Stavisky case 1934–1938 The Terror 1935 Nuremberg Laws 1935 Social Security Act 1936–1937 Premier Leon Blum leads French Popular Front 1936–1939 Spanish Civil War 1937 Japan invades China 1938–1940 King Carol II of Romania installs fascist dictatorship 1938 Germany occupies Austria	1931 Henri Matisse, The Dance 1936 J. M. Keynes, *General Theory of Employment, Interest, and Money* 1937 Pablo Picasso, Guernica	1930 Worldwide weekly movie attendance passes 250 million 1932 Great Depression: 30 million unemployed in Europe and the U.S. 1932–1933 Mass Famine in the U.S.S.R. 1937 Papal encyclical attacks National Socialism late 1930s Increasing veneration of the traditional in Soviet Union
1940	1940 Assassination of Leon Trotsky		

CHAPTER 23

Great War, Great Revolution

N June 28, 1914, the Habsburg archduke Francis Ferdinand, heir to the throne of Austria-Hungary, and his wife, Sophie Chotek, were assassinated in the streets of Sarajevo, capital of the province of Bosnia, which had been occupied by Austria-Hungary since 1878. The assassin, Gavrilo Princip (1895–1918), was a Serbian nationalist. The Austro-Hungarian government, alarmed by the ambitions of Serbian nationalists, took the occasion of the assassination to issue a severe ultimatum to Serbia. The Serbian government's refusal to accept the ultimatum in its entirety led to an Austrian declaration of war on Serbia on July 28. Within the week, the great states of Europe were engaged in a general war—the Central Powers (Austria-Hungary and Germany, joined by Turkey and, later, Bulgaria) against the Allies (Serbia, Russia, France, and Britain, eventually supported by eighteen other nations).

Princip's bullet would eventually cost 36 million casualties in killed, missing, and wounded. After the war, and particularly after the failure of the peace settlement and the widespread disillusionment with leaders who apparently had so naively fought a "war to end all wars," much public debate took place about where the greatest responsibility for the war lay. This debate over the *causes* of the war became confused with the moral issue of *responsibility* for the war.

CAUSES OF THE WAR

One factor that made war more likely was the unification of Germany and of Italy. The creation of these two new major states altered the balance of power in the European state system; the efforts of statesmen during the next forty years to adjust the system ultimately proved unsuccessful. The older established powers were unwilling to give up their own claims, and after 1850, with the principle series of alliances and agreements. By the early years of the twentieth century two increasingly armed camps existed: the Triple Alliance (Germany, Austria-Hungary, and Italy) and the Triple Entente (France, Britain, and Russia). After 1900 almost any crisis might lead to war.

Shifting National Self-Images

Nationalism and the accompanying shifts in the balance of power both influenced and were profoundly influenced by public opinion, often shaped by the public press. Throughout western Europe and in the United States a jingoistic press, often intent on increasing circulation, competed for "news," and not all papers were careful to separate the verifiable from the rumor, the emotional atrocity story (even when true) from the background account that would explain the context for the emotion.

Technology made printing far cheaper than it had ever been. In 1711 the highly influential English paper *The Spectator* sold two thousand copies a day, and there was only a handful of effective competitors; in 1916 a Paris-based newspaper sold over 2 million copies a day, and there were hundreds of other newspapers. This revolution in communicating the printed word had taken place in the nineteenth century. *The Times* of London began to use steam presses in 1814, producing copies four times as fast as before. In Britain and France and later in central Europe, the railway made a national press possible—the papers of Paris could be read anywhere in France the next day. After the 1840s the invention of the telegraph encouraged the creation of news services and the use of foreign correspondents, so that the same story might appear throughout the nation though in different papers.

When Richard Hoe (1812–1886), a New Yorker, invented a rotary press in 1847 that could produce twenty thousand sheets an hour, the modern newspaper was born. Linotype and, from the 1880s, monotype machines were also used to set books, and by 1914 there had been a massive leap in the sale of all reading matter. This in turn gave rise to greater censorship in some societies, and everywhere to an awareness that the printed word could be manipulated to political purposes.

The printed word was supplemented by illustrations. The battle map was introduced to the public in the American Civil War. After 1839 daguerreotypes began to replace painting as a means of conveying reality. In the 1880s, mass-produced cameras became available. A simple box camera, the Kodak, was invented in 1888, and with the concurrent commercialization of the halftone screen, newspaper pictures became commonplace.

Newspapers became more important in political life. In Britain Alfred Harmsworth (1865–1922), in France Charles Dupuy (1844–1919), and in the United States two competitors, Joseph Pulitzer (1847–1911) and William Randolph Hearst (1863–1951), brought all the elements together to create mass journalism. The two Americans worked to promote war with Spain in 1898,

On the morning of June 28, 1914, Archduke Francis Ferdinand and his wife set out on a round of ceremonial visits. There had been no signs of danger during the Bosnian tour, but in Sarajevo the archduke was greeted by a bomb attack, in which he was not injured. After completing his ceremonial functions, Ferdinand decided to visit the hospital where an officer wounded in the attack was being treated. The prearranged route for the motorcade was abandoned, and the archduke's car made a wrong turn. As the chauffeur applied the brakes preparatory to backing up the car, Gavrilo Princip, who apparently by chance was standing on the corner, stepped forward and fired point blank at the archduke and his wife.

The Bettmann Archive

of national sovereignty well established, smaller western European states were no longer open to annexation by the great powers. Thus there was little territory available in Europe for making adjustments. In the late nineteenth century only the Balkan lands of the weakening Turkish Empire remained as possible territorial pickings for ambitious powers. Even there, the growth of national feeling in Romania, Serbia, Bulgaria, and Greece made formal annexation difficult.

Meantime, influenced by their rivalries in Europe and abroad, the great powers were choosing sides in a

Some historians have argued that the four most important inventions of all time have been the wheel, the printing press, the steam engine, and the computer. Each grew from major societal needs, and each led to a major revolution that touched all spheres of human life. As shown here, crowds thronged to see the wonders that power-driven printing presses could produce: cheap newspapers in mass quantities that brought news, opinion, propaganda, and advertising onto the city streets, where news vendors sold the latest "scoop," and into thousands of libraries and millions of homes.

The Granger Collection

and all these papers supported the establishment and jingoist views.

The introduction of universal peacetime conscription by the Continental powers further stimulated the introduction of compulsory universal elementary education, and later of universal manhood suffrage. These led to a further growth in the number of readers, to greater political content in the press, and to the quest for technological innovation in rapid typesetting. One could, by 1900, genuinely speak of "public opinion" as a force in world affairs.

Thus the outbreak of war in 1914 saw in each belligerent nation broad public support of the government. Men marched off to war convinced that war was necessary. Even the socialists supported the war. Yet, public opinion might as easily have been led against war, had an increasingly complex alliance system not cut off national options and individual leaders not chosen the course they did. For example, in the hectic five weeks after the assassination at Sarajevo, the German kaiser, William II, belatedly tried to avoid a general war. But in the decisive years between 1888 and 1914 he had been an aggressive leader of patriotic expansion, encouraging German youth to believe that while their enemies were numerically superior, Germany's spiritual qualities would more than compensate for brute strength.

German ambitions and German fears had produced an intense hatred of Britain. At first few English returned this hate, but as the expensive race between Britain and Germany in naval armaments continued and as German wares progressively undersold British wares in Europe, in North and South America, and in Asia, the British began to worry about their prosperity and leadership. The British were worried about their obsolescent industrial plants and their apparent inability to produce goods as

efficiently as the Germans; they were critical of their commercial failures abroad and some feared their increasingly stodgy self-satisfaction. There was, in effect, a crisis of imperialism in British domestic politics.

In France prewar opinions on international politics ran the gamut. A large socialist left was committed to pacifism and to an international general strike of workers at the threat of actual war. However, an embittered group of patriots wanted *revanche* or revenge for the defeat of 1870. The revanchists organized patriotic societies and edited patriotic journals. The French, like the British, had supported movements for international peace—the Red Cross, conferences at the Hague in 1899 and 1907, and various abortive initiatives by the international labor movement. But French diplomats continued to preserve and strengthen the system of alliances against Germany, and in July 1914 it was clear that France was ready for war.

Triple Alliance and Triple Entente, 1879–1918

After 1871 Bismarck sought to isolate France diplomatically by building a series of alliances from which it was excluded. He sought to keep on good terms with both Austria and Russia, and, what was more difficult, to keep both these powers on good terms with each other. Since both wanted to dominate the Balkans, Bismarck's task was formidable.

Bismarck laid the cornerstone of his diplomatic system by a defensive alliance with Austria-Hungary in 1879, an alliance that held until 1918, and by the League of the Three Emperors (1872–1878, 1881–1889), which bound Germany, Russia, and Austria together. The three powers agreed to act in common when dealing with Turkey and to maintain friendly neutrality should any one of them be at war with a power other than Turkey. Next, Bismarck secured an alliance among Germany, Austria-Hungary, and Italy directed chiefly against France—the Triple Alliance of 1882, often renewed, which still existed on paper in 1914.

On this series of tightropes Bismarck maintained a precarious balance through the 1880s. Uppermost in his mind was the danger that the Russians, fearful of Austrian designs upon the Balkans, would desert him and ally themselves with France, always anxious to escape from the isolation that Bismarck had designed for it. In 1887 Russia did refuse to renew the League of the Three Emperors, but Bismarck was able to repair the breach by a secret Russo-German agreement known as the Reinsurance Treaty. The two promised each other neutrality in case either was involved in a war against a third power; but this neutrality was not to hold if Germany made an "aggressive" war against France, or if Russia made an "aggressive" war against Austria. Since Russian nationalist agitation continued against both Austria and Germany, Bismarck in 1888 made public the terms of the Austro-German alliance and allowed the main terms of the Triple Alliance to be known informally as a warning to Russia.

Then in 1890 William II dismissed Bismarck. The emperor's advisers persuaded him not to renew the Reinsurance Treaty with Russia, as it was incompatible with the Dual Alliance (the 1879 alliance with Austria-Hungary) and shortly afterward what Bismarck had worked so hard to prevent came about. After lengthy secret negotiations, Russia and France in 1894 made public an alliance that ended French isolation. It was a defensive agreement by which each was to come to the other's aid in the event that Germany or Austria made "aggressive" war against either ally.

Great Britain still remained technically uninvolved by a formal treaty with a European ally. The next development was to align Great Britain against the Triple Alliance by informal agreement. Britain sought first to come to an understanding with Germany; when rebuffed, the British then concluded a formal alliance with Japan (1902) and informal "understandings" (*ententes*) with France (1904) and Russia (1907). What chiefly drove Britain to these actions was the financially burdensome naval race with Germany and the rapid alienation of British public opinion. Fear of Russia rather than fear of Germany inspired Britain's alliance with Japan; in the Entente Cordiale France gave England a free hand in Egypt and England gave France a free hand in Morocco. More important, the base was laid for further collaboration, particularly in advance planning for military and naval cooperation in case of war.

The final stage in aligning the two camps came in 1907 when Russia came to an understanding with Great Britain. Both countries made concessions in regions where they had been imperialist rivals—Persia, Afghanistan, Tibet—and the British at last made some concessions to Russia's desire to open up the Bosporus and Dardanelles to its warships. The agreement was informal and left Britain less than fully committed to any binding Continental alliance system; nevertheless, it rounded out the Triple Entente against the Triple Alliance.

As the Entente took shape, a succession of military and diplomatic crises inflamed public opinion and further circumscribed the room to maneuver. First came a deliberately theatrical gesture by the kaiser, when in 1905 he made a ceremonial visit to Tangier in Morocco as a signal that the Germans would not recognize the Anglo-French assignment of Morocco to France. The British then indicated clearly to the French that they would not support them. Moreover, the British and the French now began informal military and naval conferences, which the French, at least, believed committed Britain to armed support if the Germans attacked.

At an international conference on the question of the independence and territorial integrity of Morocco, held at Algeciras in Spain (1906), Germany was outvoted, although it had called for the conference; France pursued plans for a protectorate in Morocco, dividing the country with Spain. The Algeciras conference also marked the beginnings of participation by the United States in the European system, though very tentatively. In 1904 a person thought to be a naturalized American citizen had been seized by a Moroccan chief, and Theodore Roosevelt had sent a truculent cable. Two years earlier, at the urging of Jewish citizens in the United States, the State Department had protested against Romanian persecution of Jews. Given this protest over a domestic Romanian matter, the State Department could not readily refrain from action where an American citizen was thought to be concerned. Roosevelt sent two representatives to Algeciras, who helped conciliate differences between the two camps.

A decisive turn came in 1908, when Austria formally proclaimed its annexation of the Turkish provinces of Bosnia-Herzegovina, already occupied for thirty years. Austria's actions infuriated the Serbs, who hoped to annex Bosnia. It also infuriated the Russians, who did not know that their foreign minister had informally agreed with his Austrian counterpart to permit the annexation in exchange for Austria's services in opening the Straits to the Russian fleet. But Russia gained nothing, for Britain would not permit the Straits to be opened.

What directly prompted the Austrian annexation of Bosnia-Herzegovina was the successful rising against the Ottoman sultan in the summer of 1908 by the Young Turks. A Pan-Turanian movement was instigated largely by Turks from central Asia (and named for their nomadic Turanian ancestors), whose independent principalities had been conquered by Russia during the reign of Alexander II and who were now undergoing forced Russification; they sought to group the Turkish peoples of central Asia with the Ottoman Turks and Magyars of Hungary. Austria was determined that Serbia and Croatia would remain under its rule.

A second Moroccan crisis in 1911 heightened tensions in western Europe. The kaiser sent a German gunboat, the *Panther*, to the Moroccan port of Agadir as a protest against French occupation of the old city of Fez.

In ensuing negotiations, well publicized in the press, the Germans agreed to give the French a free hand in Morocco, but only at a price the French considered blackmail: Part of the French Congo was ceded to Germany. French opposition to this bargain was so intense that the government fell, and thereafter no French ministry dared make concessions to the Germans.

Events followed with bewildering and interlocking impact. In 1911 Italy seized upon the Agadir crisis to demand Tripoli from Turkey. In the yearlong Turco-Italian war that followed, Italian nationalists, led by the writer Gabriele d'Annunzio (1863–1938), at last saw the chance for substantial imperial gains. Italy annexed Tripoli, bombarded the Syrian coast, and occupied Rhodes and the other Dodecanese islands. By the Treaty of Lausanne in October 1912, Italy confirmed its new possessions.

In the meantime, the war over Tripoli (Libya) had proved a prelude to the Balkan Wars of 1912–1913, as the Balkan states struck at a preoccupied Turkey. In the first of these wars, Montenegro declared war on Turkey, as did Bulgaria, Serbia, and Greece ten days later. The war went against the Turks, but Russia warned the advancing Bulgarians not to occupy Constantinople or the Russian fleet would be used against them. The Serbs reached the Adriatic by overrunning Albania; intent on preventing Serbian access to the sea, the Austrians declared for an independent Albania. Russia supported Serbia, and in November 1912 Austria and Russia began to mobilize. The Russians, belatedly realizing that they were not prepared for war, abandoned the Serbs, who, with Bulgaria, came to terms with Turkey. By a treaty of May 30, Turkey ceded substantial territory in Europe, abandoned its claims to Crete (which was annexed to Greece), and left the status of Albania and the Aegean islands to the powers.

One month later the second Balkan War erupted when the Bulgarian military commander attacked Serbia and Greece without informing his government. Both nations counterattacked, Romania and Turkey entered the war on their side, and in six weeks, by the Treaty of Bucharest, Bulgaria was stripped of much that it had gained. In a separate treaty with Turkey, Bulgaria was forced to give back Adrianople. During the negotiations Serbia invaded Albania and only withdrew in the face of an Austrian ultimatum.

During this time, the Anglo-German naval race had continued unabated. In February 1912 Lord Haldane (1856–1928), British secretary for war, went to Berlin to suggest that Britain would support German expansion in Africa in exchange for a freeze on the size of the German fleet. Germany refused.

Britain now faced a major dilemma. In 1897 its fleet had been the greatest in the world; with the introduction of its massive and expensive *Dreadnought* in 1905, a new standard in armor and armament had been attained. But the Germans had matched it, and escalation on both sides had continued. In 1911 Winston Churchill (1874–1965), who was committed to a fully modernized navy, became Britain's first lord of the admiralty. In 1912 a new naval law made it clear that Germany

intended to match the British. The British concluded that they could halt rising naval expenditures only through a naval agreement with France by which France would control the Mediterranean and Britain would focus on the North Sea, the Straits, and the Near East.

The Final Crisis, July–August 1914

The diplomats and statesmen were drawn into war because they believed that a diplomatic defeat or loss of face for their nation was worse than war. Austria-Hungary believed that the Serbian government had had some suspicion of Princip's assassination plot and should have given Austria warning. For this reason, Austria-Hungary decided to make stiff demands on Serbia after the assassination of Francis Ferdinand on June 28, 1914, which had involved agents of the Serbian terrorist organization, the Black Hand. Before doing so, however, Austria consulted Germany, which promised to support whatever policy Austria might adopt toward Serbia—the equivalent of a diplomatic "blank check."

Encouraged, the Austrian government on July 23 sent Serbia an ultimatum to be answered within forty-eight hours. The ultimatum may have been designed to be unacceptable. It required that publications hostile to Austria be suppressed, anti-Austrian patriotic organizations be dissolved, teachings that smacked of propaganda be barred from the schools, officials known for conducting anti-Austrian campaigns be dismissed, Serbian officials believed to be involved in the assassination plot be arrested, and a formal apology be made. These demands the Serbs might have accepted, but two others they could not: that Austrian officials work with the Serbians in investigating the plot, and that judicial action be taken against any found guilty by this joint investigation. While accepting most points, the Serbian reply was evasive on the most important ones, and the Serbs had begun mobilization before delivering it. Serbia apparently hoped this stratagem would allow time for further negotiations, but the Austrian minister immediately left Belgrade, and Austria began to call up its troops. Austria declared war on July 28.

Germany supported Austria in this decision, but the German diplomats still equivocated, putting pressure on Vienna to act against Serbia while trying to find out whether Britain would remain neutral in a general war—a constant German goal. If war were to come, the Germans wished to place the guilt on Russia. Since Russia was beginning the full mobilization of its armies, the kaiser, on July 29, told Czar Nicholas II in a personal telegram about German attempts to get the Austrians to compromise. Apparently this telegram caused full Russian mobilization to be modified into partial mobilization against Austria and caused the Austro-Russian talks to be resumed on July 30. If German Chancellor Theobald von Bethmann-Hollweg (1856–1921) could make it appear that a full-scale European war was the fault of the Russians, then he still had some hope of Britain's neutrality.

But mobilization was not easy in Russia, a country of vast distances and poor communications. The Russian

THE WRITTEN RECORD

The "Blank Check"

There is some debate among historians as to just how sweeping the "blank check" given to Austria by Germany actually was. A report by the Austrian ambassador on his meeting with the kaiser at Potsdam on July 5, 1914, indicates what the Austrian believed to be the case:

After lunch, when I again called attention to the seriousness of the situation, the Kaiser authorized me to inform our gracious Majesty that we might in this case, as in all others, rely on Germany's full support. He must . . . first hear what the Imperial Chancellor has to say, but he did not doubt in the least that Herr von Bethmann Hollweg would agree with him. Especially as far as our action against Serbia was concerned. . . . Russia's attitude will no doubt be hostile, but to this he had been for years prepared, and should a war between Austria-Hungary and Russia be unavoidable, we might be convinced that Germany, our old faithful ally, would stand at our side. Russia at the time was in no way prepared for war, and would think twice before it appealed to arms. But it will certainly set other powers on to the Triple Alliance and add fuel to the fire in the Balkans. He understands perfectly well that His Apostolic Majesty in his well-known love of peace would be reluctant to march into Serbia; but if we had really recognized the necessity of warlike action against Serbia, he would regret if we did not make use of the present moment, which is all in our favor.

From *Outbreak of the World War: German Documents Collected by Karl Kautsky*, ed. Max Montgelas and Walter Schücking (New York: Carnegie Endowment for International Peace, 1924), p. 76.

military feared that their enemies would get the lead on them, so the Russian government decided to renew general mobilization. Germany at once insisted that all Russian mobilization cease, and, when it continued, ordered its own at 4:00 P.M. on August 1. Germany declared war on Russia three hours later.

France, meantime, had determined to stand by its Russian ally and mobilized at 3:55 P.M. on August 1. Having failed to get Britain to guarantee French neutrality, and apparently convinced that France would come to Russia's support, Germany invaded Luxembourg on August 2 and demanded from Belgium permission to cross its territory, in exchange for Belgian neutrality. Belgium refused, and on August 3 Germany declared war on France and invaded Belgium to seize the ports on the English Channel and bear down upon Paris from the west.

Britain had been wavering. Although her entente with France did not legally bind the two nations together, it had led to close coordination of defense plans by the French and British military and naval staffs, and so perhaps Britain would have come into the war anyway. What made entry certain was German violation of the neutrality of Belgium. Sir Edward Grey seized firmly upon the German invasion of Belgium as grounds for taking action, which he supported for political reasons. On August 4 Britain declared war on Germany. Bethmann-Hollweg, informed of this action, let slip the phrase that Britain had gone to war just for a "scrap of paper"—the treaty of 1839 that established Belgian neutrality. This unhappy phrase not only solidified British opinion in favor of the war but was primarily responsible for the later charge of war guilt that was laid against Germany.

The Entry of Other Powers

By August 6, when Austria declared war on Russia, all the members of the Triple Alliance and the Triple Entente had entered the war, with the exception of Italy, which declared neutrality. The Central Powers of Germany and Austria-Hungary stood against the Allies—Russia, France, Britain, and Serbia. Japan came in on the side of the Allies late in August. Turkey joined the Austro-German side in November. After receiving competing territorial offers from both Allies and Central Powers, Italy joined the Allies in May 1915, and Portugal and Romania on the side of the Allies in 1916. In time much of the world joined in; there were fifty-six declarations of war before the end of 1918.

Americans had hoped to avoid entanglement in the European conflict, and for a time public opinion was deeply divided. While many Americans sided with Britain and France because they felt these two powers were fighting to assure that democratic government would survive in Europe, many others continued to think of Britain as the traditional enemy. Americans still thought of themselves as upholding a tradition of isolation from wars that originated in Europe. To a considerable extent this was true, for no overseas invader had set foot on American soil since 1815. The American government committed itself quickly to a policy of neutrality.

As the war raged in Europe, however, public sympathies increasingly turned against the Central Powers, and against Germany in particular. Americans read of the war through British dispatches, heard atrocity stories that were directed against the Germans, and viewed the Habsburgs as attempting to suppress legitimate aspirations

A famous American recruiting poster from World War I.

The Bettmann Archive

The United States protested in the strongest terms. Throughout 1915 German submarines complied, limiting their attacks to freighters. Nonetheless, further incidents followed, and in 1916 Germany formally agreed to abandon unlimited submarine warfare. Late that year Germany initiated peace efforts, but the Allies rebuffed these attempts. Early in 1917 German military leaders gained the upper hand, and on February 1 submarine attacks on all neutral and belligerent shipping became official policy. Three days later an American naval vessel was sunk after warning, and Wilson asked Congress to sever diplomatic relations with Germany. Six more ships were sunk in the next month. In the meantime, on March 12 a new democratic government was set up in Russia, effectively knocking Russia out of the war and potentially releasing German troops from the eastern front to the western. Wilson attacked the German submarine policy as "warfare against humanity," and on April 6 the United States declared war on Germany. Even so, Americans were careful to maintain their separate status, not joining the Allies formally.

German resumption of submarine warfare was the immediate cause of American entry into the war, but there were, of course, other causes. Though neutrality had paid well, interest groups in the United States assumed that war would bring even higher profits. So much had been lent to the Allied nations that American creditors could not afford to see them defeated. Public opinion was outraged by the German submarine policy. Many Americans feared that their nation's security would be hurt if Germany were victorious; at the least, the world order would be reorganized. Perhaps above all, more Americans simply felt emotionally closer to Britain than to the Germans, and they were unprepared to see Europe unified under German domination. Wilson no doubt did not believe that he was embarking on a war to "make the world safe for democracy," but he did believe that democracy would not be safe if the Central Powers were victorious.

Nationalism

Why did war begin precisely where and as it did? Need all the nations that were drawn into it have participated? Which nation was primarily responsible for causing the war? Within that nation, which groups, which leaders? Given war, need it have taken the form that it did? In part because the victor writes the history, the majority of historians have blamed Germany or the tottering Austro-Hungarian Empire for the war. However, most historians do agree on certain matters concerning the outbreak of the war.

Nationalism was the root cause of World War I. The heir to the Austro-Hungarian Empire was assassinated by a Serbian nationalist, and the empire determined to stamp out Serbian nationalism by extracting humiliating concessions from the Serbs. Since Russia was the defender of the Serbs and a supporter of Serbian nationalism, Russia was drawn into the circle of war; because Germany was the protector of Austria, it, too, saw no choice but

for the self-determination of peoples. Furthermore, the European war helped the United States economically, for Britain and France bought enormous quantities of goods from the United States. Within a year after the beginning of the war, the economies of the United States and the Allied powers were closely intertwined.

Still, the American business community had no reason to see the United States actively enter the war, for neutrality paid handsomely. President Woodrow Wilson (1856–1924) campaigned in 1916 on a pledge to keep the United States out of the conflict if possible. But he suspected that if German desperation over the flow of American foodstuffs to Britain were to continue, avoiding war would be very difficult. This proved to be so. American definitions of neutral shipping seemed to the Germans to openly favor the British. Germany felt obliged to use its most powerful maritime weapon, the submarine, and in 1915 it proclaimed the waters around the British Isles to be a war zone in which enemy merchant ships would be sunk on sight. Neutral vessels entering the zone did so at their own risk. Americans insisted on exercising their rights on the high seas, including traveling on passenger vessels of combatants. On May 7, 1915, the British transatlantic steamer *Lusitania* was sunk by a German submarine; 1,198 people died, including 124 Americans.

aggressive action. Because Russia was in alliance with France, that nation was drawn in. All sides used the rhetoric of defense, all took the actions of offense. No one could have guessed how destructive the war would be, or some nations might well have elected not to honor their treaty commitments. In a sense, the war was caused by a series of miscalculations as to the intentions of the enemy, the enemy's strengths, and where national self-interest lay.

Still, war between these nations alone need not have engulfed the world had other nations not feared one or more of the prospective combatants. Britain was convinced that the Germans were intent on asserting world power; the German invasion of Belgium appeared to confirm the German bid for, at the least, European dominance. The Ottoman Empire feared the Russians and distrusted French and British intentions in the Near and Middle East. Italy and Japan were determined not to be left out in any postwar realignment of power. The United States did not wish to see a German victory or the emergence on the European Continent of a military dictatorship that would threaten American growth and institutions. In the end the war became a world war because the belligerents either had or wished to have overseas colonies, so that their colonial dependencies, or the lands that they coveted, were swept into the conflict.

*T*HE COURSE OF THE WAR

World War I took the lives of 8 million soldiers, and caused far more deaths through malnutrition, war-spawned diseases, and birth deficits arising from economic dislocations and the loss of precisely the age-group most likely to beget children. The collapse of the Russian economy, followed by widespread famine and epidemic, meant that, despite staggering military losses, northwestern Europe emerged from the war in a dominant position once again.

Resources of the Belligerents

Even before the American entry, the Allies had an overwhelming superiority in total population and resources. The Central Powers had in their own Continental lands not more than 150 million people; Britain, France, Russia, and Italy in their own Continental lands had at least 125 million more people than their enemies. Moreover, in their overseas possessions, which included the 315 million people of India, the Allies had many millions more. As for material resources, the Central Powers had, especially in Germany, admirably organized industries and enough coal and iron to fight a long war, but here, too, the statistics were overwhelmingly in favor of the Allies. Moreover, though German submarines and surface raiders seriously interfered with Allied lines of communication, on the whole the Allies were still able to get food and other supplies from their overseas sources.

In the long run, the side with the most men and materials wore down its enemies and won the war, but it was by no means an uneven struggle. The Central Powers won many battles and seemed at critical moments close to final victory. Germany and Austria adjoined one another and had interior lines of communication, which enabled them to transfer troops rapidly from one threatened front to another, and had for years been firmly allied. Most important of all, Germany was ready for war, with an efficiently organized military machine and a good stock of munitions. The German people were united in support of the war, and they enjoyed the great psychological advantage of being on the offensive, of carrying the war to the enemy.

By contrast, geography and language separated the western Allies from Russia. German control of the Baltic and Turkish control of the Straits proved a serious obstacle to communication between Russia and its allies, which had to take roundabout and difficult routes. For the Allies, transfer of troops between eastern and western fronts was militarily almost impossible, even had it been politically possible.

Russia, Britain, and France had only recently come together, and then not as close allies. Each had many sources of conflict with the others. They had no experience of mutual cooperation, no common language. France and England were democracies, and though the peoples of both supported the war, Britain, in particular, was unused to centralized military and political control. Unified military planning and administration were never achieved between Russia and the western Allies. Even among Britain, France, and the United States on the western front, unification was not achieved until the French general Ferdinand Foch (1851–1929) was appointed commander in chief in 1918.

Finally, of the three great Allied powers in 1914, only France was ready, and France, with only 39 million people against Germany's 65 million, was the weakest of the Allies in manpower. Britain was well prepared on the sea, but the navy could not be of direct use against the German army. The situation in Ireland remained tense. Russia had universal military service and a huge army, but it had vast distances to overcome, an inadequate railway system, a less-developed heavy industry, and a military and political organization that was riddled with inefficiency and corruption.

Military Campaigns, 1914–1918

The Western Front. The German attack through Belgium was the first stage in the plan prepared by Alfred Graf von Schlieffen (1833–1913), chief of the general staff from 1891 to 1906. The strong right wing was to take Paris and fall on the rear of the French, who would be pinned down by the left wing. With France quickly eliminated, the Germans would then unite their forces and attack the Russians, who would still be in the throes of mobilization. Britain, an island nation, would be held off and attacked if necessary.

The German plan failed for two reasons. First, the German chief of staff, Helmuth von Moltke (1848–1916), who succeeded Schlieffen, had weakened the right wing to send divisions to the east. When the right wing neared Paris, it had too few divisions to take the capital and then turn on the French army as planned. Second, the French, though at first preparing an offensive eastward, shifted their armies northward and westward in time to meet the invading Germans. With the help of a small British force, the French exploited a gap that opened between the German armies, who lost their first great test, known as the battle of the Marne (September 5–12, 1914).

The opposing forces then engaged in what came to be called the "race for the Channel," with the Germans trying to outflank the Allies and reach the Channel ports first, thus shutting the short sea passage to future British reinforcements. But they failed here, too, and throughout the war the ports of Calais and Boulogne and the southwestern corner of Belgium were to remain in Allied hands.

By the autumn of 1914 this western front was stabilized. Between the Channel and the Swiss border of Alsace near Basel, hundreds of thousands of soldiers faced each other in a continuous line. Both sides dug in and made rough fortifications, the central feature of which was a series of parallel trenches deep enough to conceal a man standing upright. As time went on these trenches were supplied with parapets, machine-gun nests, and an elaborate network of approach trenches and strong points, until the entire front became one immense fortification. Thousands of local actions in the four years of trench warfare shifted the lines here and there, and a series of partial breakthroughs occurred on both sides. But on the whole the lines held, and the actual fighting in the West was confined to an extraordinarily narrow, though very long, field in which changing weaponry gave the defense increasing advantages over the offense.

The Eastern Front.   The eastern front, where the Russians faced both the Germans and the Austrians, was crucial to Allied tenacity in the West. Millions of men were involved on both sides, and had the Russians not held out until the end of 1917, the Allies in the West could hardly have withstood the reinforcements that the Germans and Austrians would have been able to send to France and Italy. Though the war in the East was more fluid than the war in the West, even in the East there were long periods of stalemate.

The Russians began well. They took the Galician capital of Lemberg, now Lvov, and by the end of September 1914 they had reached the northern ends of the passes leading into Hungary through the Carpathian Mountains. On August 19–20, 1914, the Russians won the battle of Gumbinnen. The alarmed Germans reorganized their eastern command. The brilliant general Erich Ludendorff (1865–1937), under the nominal command of Paul von Hindenburg (1847–1934) and aided by the exceptional staff officer Max von Hoffman (1869–1927), moved successfully against the two Russian armies. Late

in August at Tannenberg, the Germans decisively defeated a Russian army, taking 100,000 prisoners. Early in September the Germans again won decisively at the Masurian Lakes, taking another 125,000 prisoners.

The Germans' hard-pressed Austrian allies to the south were by now clamoring for help, and the western front was still demanding men. Hindenburg and his aides had to do their best with what they had. In a series of hard-fought battles in Poland, they relieved the pressure on the Austrians. The end of 1914 found the Austrians hanging on in Galicia and the Germans in a good position to push eastward from East Prussian and Polish bases. In two great joint offensives in May and July 1915 the Central Powers won substantial successes, inflicting on the underequipped Russians severe losses from which they never really recovered.

In 1916 the Russians, with a new commander, General Aleksei Brusilov (1853–1926), undertook a major new offensive against the Austrians in the south. The Brusilov offensive was begun without adequate preparation. It scored a striking success at first, in places driving the Austrians back some eighty miles, and taking 200,000 prisoners. Once more the Germans came to the rescue; with fresh troops transferred from the West, they halted Brusilov, costing him a million men and exhausting his supplies.

It was in the backlash of this defeat that the Russian Revolution, which began early in March 1917, was born. During the moderate early phase of that uprising, before the Bolshevik revolution of November 1917, Brusilov undertook one last desperate offensive. But he was soon checked, and the Russian army began to disintegrate; the way was open for the Bolsheviks to carry out their promise to make peace. By the end of 1917 Russia was out of the war. It was forced by the Central Powers to sign the punitive Peace of Brest-Litovsk (March 1918), by which Russia lost its Polish territories, its Baltic provinces, the entire Ukraine, Finland, and some lands in the Caucasus. The last went to Turkey; most of the others came under what proved to be the temporary domination of Austria and Germany.

The Italian Front.   In the meantime, in April 1915 Italy had concluded with Britain, France, and Russia the secret Treaty of London, which promised the Italians Trent and Trieste plus other lands at Austro-Hungarian and Turkish expense. In May the Italians formally declared war on Austria-Hungary, and a new front was added along the Austro-Italian frontier at the head of the Adriatic. Since much of this front was mountainous, action was largely confined to some sixty miles along the Isonzo River, where for two years there was a series of bloody but indecisive engagements that pinned down several hundred thousand Austrian troops. Then in the late autumn of 1917, with Russia already beaten, came a blow that very nearly knocked Italy out. The Germans and Austrians broke through at Caporetto and sent the Italians into retreat across the Venetian plains. French and British reinforcements were hastily rushed across the

Alps, but what did most to stop the Austro-Germans was the grave difficulty of supplying their armies in such a rapid advance. The Italians were finally able to hold along the line of the Piave River.

The Dardanelles and the Balkans.

Ultimately more significant was the Dardanelles campaign of 1915. With the entry of Turkey into the war on the side of the Central Powers in November 1914, and with the French able to hold the western front against the Germans, a group of British leaders decided that British strength should be put into amphibious operations in the Aegean area, where a strong drive could knock Turkey out of the war by the capture of Constantinople. The great exponent of this eastern plan was Winston Churchill, first lord of the admiralty. The point of attack chosen was the Dardanelles, the more southwesterly of the two straits that separate the Black Sea from the Aegean. The action is known as the Gallipoli campaign for the long, narrow peninsula on the European side of the Dardanelles that was a key to the action.

The British and French fleets tried to force the Straits in March 1915, but they abandoned the attempt when several ships struck mines. Later landings of British, Australian, New Zealand, and French troops at various points on both the Asian and European shores of the Dardanelles were poorly coordinated and badly backed up. They met fierce and effective resistance from the Turks, and in the end they had to withdraw without taking the Straits. The cost of this campaign was enormous: 500,000 casualties. The Anzac (Australian and New Zealand) troops felt they had been led into senseless slaughter by British officers, and a sense of a separate Australian nationalism was clearly expressed for the first time.

Serbia's part in the crisis that had produced the war meant that from the start there would be a Balkan front. In the end all Balkan states became involved. The Austrians failed here also, and although they managed to take the Serbian capital, Belgrade (December 1914), they were driven out again. Bulgaria, wooed by both sides, finally came in with the Central Powers in the autumn of 1915. The Germans sent troops and a general, August von Mackensen (1849–1938), under whom the Serbs were finally beaten.

To counter this blow in the Balkans, the British and French had already landed a few divisions in the Greek city of Salonika and had established a front in Macedonia. The Greeks themselves were divided into two groups. One was headed by King Constantine (1868–1923), who sympathized with the Central Powers but who for the moment was seeking only to maintain Greek neutrality. The other was a pro-Ally group headed by the able prime minister Eleutherios Venizelos (1864–1936), who had secretly agreed to the Allied landing at Salonika. Venizelos did not get firmly into the saddle until June 1917, when Allied pressure compelled King Constantine to abdicate in favor of his second son, Alexander (1893–1920). Greece then declared war on the Central Powers.

Meanwhile Romania, which the Russians had been trying to lure into the war, yielded to promises of great territorial gains at the expense of Austria-Hungary; Romania came in on the Allied side in August 1916. The Central Powers swept through Romania and by January 1917 held most of the country. When the Russians made the separate Peace of Brest-Litovsk with the Germans in March 1918, the Romanians were obliged to yield some territory to Bulgaria and to grant a lease of oil lands to Germany.

The Macedonian front remained in a stalemate until the summer of 1918. Then, with American troops pouring rapidly into France, the Allied military leaders decided they could afford to build up their forces in Salonika. The investment paid well, for under the leadership of the French general Franchet d'Esperey (1856–1942), the Allied armies on this front were the first to break the enemy completely. The French, British, Serbs, and Greeks began a great advance in September all along a line from the Adriatic to the Bulgarian frontier. They forced the Bulgarians to conclude an armistice on September 30, and by early November they had crossed the Danube in several places. The armistice in the West on November 11 found the tricolor of France, with the flags of many allies, well on its way to Vienna.

The Near East and the Colonies.

This truly worldwide war, fought in the Near East, Africa, and the Far East, as well as in every ocean, made it clear that non-Continental events were no longer mere sideshows. The war in the Near East, in particular, would unleash nationalisms that continue to the present day. The Turks, trained and officered by German experts, had often resisted effectively. In April 1916 they forced the surrender of the British forces at Kut in Mesopotamia, and marched up the Tigris-Euphrates Valley. The following year the British marched north again and took Baghdad, effectively ending Turkish authority in Mesopotamia.

In 1894 the Armenians had revolted and been brutally suppressed, leading Britain and France to pressure Turkey into promising reforms. The reforms were not put into operation, however, and the Armenian revolt continued. In 1895–1897 eight thousand Armenians were killed. The remaining Armenians in Turkey had bided their time; now they felt that the World War provided them with their opportunity. When the Russians launched an offensive near Lake Van, the Armenians nearby took over the Turkish fortress and turned it over to the Russians. Declaring that Armenians everywhere were helping the Russians, the Turkish government ordered the removal of all non-Muslims from military areas or lines of communication. In the forced removal thousands of Armenians died of exposure in the desert; Armenian men were massacred, the women raped, and survivors forcibly converted to Islam. The Armenians were reduced to a remnant at the end of the war, an estimated 1 million having died.

Elsewhere the British exploited Arab dislike for the Turks, with the particular assistance of the romantic

T. E. Lawrence worked among the Arabs, often in their own dress. Soon romantic legend gave him the title of Lawrence of Arabia.

Imperial War Museum, London

colonel T. E. Lawrence (1888–1935), who knew the Arabs intimately and helped coordinate an Arab revolt with a British expedition from Egypt under General Sir Edmund Allenby (1861–1936). By the end of 1917 the British held Jerusalem. In September 1918 a great British offensive in Syria was so successful that on October 30 the Turks concluded an armistice and left the war.

From these campaigns there later emerged not only the independent Arab states but also the Jewish national state of Israel. In November 1917, in the Balfour Declaration, the British promised "the establishment in Palestine of a national home for the Jewish people." This promise bore fruit in the mandate of 1922 from the League of Nations, by which such a home was set up under British protection.

In their overseas colonies the Germans, though cut off from the homeland by the British navy, fought with great skill. In East Africa they managed to hold out in a series of campaigns, so that they still had forces in the field on Armistice Day, November 11, 1918, and their commander did not surrender until November 23. But elsewhere the Germans fought from inadequate bases and with inadequate forces, so that by the end of 1914 the British, Australians, New Zealanders, South Africans,

French, and Japanese had pretty well taken over the German overseas possessions.

Allied Victory

The War at Sea. In the long run British sea power and American supplies proved decisive. The Allied command of the sea made it possible to draw on the resources of the rest of the world, and in particular to transfer large numbers of British and later American troops to the crucial western front. Sea power also enabled the Allies to shut Germany and its allies off from overseas resources. The Allied blockade slowly constricted Germany, limiting not merely military supplies for the armies but also food supplies for the civilian population. At the end of the war many Germans were suffering from malnutrition, and the death rate among children and old people was soaring, important factors in German surrender. Furthermore, it had been the doctrine of the freedom of the seas that had brought the United States into the war. In this sense Germany lost the war at sea doubly, because the submarine had made obsolete the traditional rules of war on blockade, stop-and-search before attack, and provision for the safety of passengers and crews. The United States had insisted on their observance, and yet they could not be observed if the submarine was to exploit its main strategy: remaining beneath the surface.

Nevertheless, when the Germans launched their unrestricted submarine warfare, they made serious inroads against the merchant ships that were essential to Britain. By the end of 1917 some 8 million tons of shipping had been sunk by the Germans, most of it by submarines. The submarine menace was only slowly overcome by extensive use of convoys, depth bombs, antisubmarine patrols, and the development of small, fast subchasers and destroyers.

The navy of surface vessels that the Germans had built up since the 1890s never played a decisive part in the war itself. German surface raiders caused severe damage in the first year, but in January 1915 British battle cruisers defeated the Germans in the battle of the Dogger Bank, and for the remainder of the year the Germans limited themselves to minelaying and to concentrating on their *Unterseeboot* (submarine) warfare. In 1916 a new commander sought to use the German high seas fleet more effectively; destroyer groups conducted raids, battle cruisers bombarded the English coast, and in May the Germans tried to trap part of the British grand fleet in harbor. Forewarned, British Admiral Sir John Jellicoe (1859–1935) put to sea, and in the running battle of Jutland, fought in the North Sea May 31–June 1, 1916, the British forced the Germans to run for port, although British losses were much heavier. The German surface navy never again seriously threatened Britain's command of the sea in European waters.

New Weapons. This war also saw the beginnings of air warfare. German dirigibles (known as *Zeppelins*) raided London many times in 1916 and 1917, and both sides made airplane bombing raids on nearby towns. But the total damage was relatively light and did not affect the final result. The airplane was more important for scouting. The fighter plane was greatly improved during the war, and a base was laid for the development of the modern air force.

Although the invention of the airplane did not alter traditional warfare, an intensified type of trench warfare was developed, especially on the western front. The machine gun, the repeating rifle, and fast-firing artillery, with the guidance of spotter planes, could pour in upon an attacking force such deadly fire that it was almost impossible for either side to break through the opposing trench systems on a wide front. Because of the new technology and trench warfare, both sides suffered losses of a magnitude never known before.

Two new weapons almost broke the deadlock. One was poison gas, first used by the Germans in shells in October 1914, with disappointing results. Then in April 1915 the Germans used chlorine gas discharged from cylinders. The overwhelmed French broke in a wave five miles wide, leaving the line completely undefended. But the Germans were not prepared to follow through, and the gap was closed once the gas had dispersed. Military technicians developed a simple countermeasure, the gas mask, which became part of the equipment of every soldier on both sides.

The second new weapon came much nearer to producing decisive success. This was the tank, a British invention. The tank acquired its name when early models were shipped under tarpaulins, which the curious were told covered water tanks. But the new weapon was used too soon, in inadequate numbers, and before sufficient mechanical tests had been made, in the British Somme offensive of 1916. With substantial modifications, tanks were used again at the battle of Cambrai late in 1917, when three hundred tanks broke through the German lines. Failure to follow up quickly gave the Germans a chance to drive the British back, but the battle had clearly shown what tanks could achieve when well used.

The Entry of the United States. Both sides knew that the entry of the United States, with its fresh forces and vast industrial capacity, would be telling, were the war to last another year. But the Central Powers anticipated victory before American forces could be in the field. The French were crumbling, the burden of fighting had fallen increasingly on the British during 1917, and the Allies attempted "the one big push" on the western front while they still could, in the spring of 1917. The British were successful at Arras, the Canadians at Vimy Ridge, but the French were denied the easy victory promised them by their generals in the ravines of the Aisne, and their exhausted troops mutinied. To contain the Germans, the British general, Sir Douglas Haig (1861–1928), threw his troops into nine successive attacks in waterlogged terrain at Ypres from July 31 to November 15. Except for the Canadian capture of Passchendaele, the British line gained only nine thousand yards at the cost of nearly half

a million casualties. Allied morale was low as the death rate soared and British military leadership proved inept. The establishment of a Supreme War Council in late November to unify Allied strategy did little to bring order to a chaotic and increasingly divisive situation.

Thus early in 1918 Germany decided to throw everything it had against the Allies on the western front before the American troops arrived in force. Germany now had troops released from the eastern front. General Ludendorff turned to massive application of the barrage, in which a long discharge of artillery would flatten out a section of enemy defenses and the no-man's land in front of the troops, forcing the enemy to retire to rear trenches. The initial barrage would include gas shells to knock out enemy observation posts and guns. A rolling barrage would ensue, advancing one kilometer an hour, with infantry following behind. Used on the Somme in combination with dense fog, this tactic had helped the Germans to pierce the British line along a 41-mile front, capture 80,000 prisoners, inflict 200,000 casualties, and approach Amiens, a major communications link. In the midst of this crisis General Foch, instructed to coordinate the Allied armies, became commander in chief.

Slowly the tide turned. The Germans sustained heavy losses as they advanced, and they lacked reserves. The French and British held the Germans after an advance on the Lys River. Ludendorff secretly shifted his troops and pressed on the Marne to within forty miles of Paris, where American and French troops held the south bank of the Marne at Chateau-Thierry on June 1–4. Ludendorff attacked along the Marne again in July, but by then he had lost 800,000 men, and British, French, and American troops drove the Germans back. On August 8 a surprise attack by the British, using 450 tanks, broke through the German lines near Amiens, and German units refused orders. Then, from September 26 to November 11, a Franco-British attack on the West and a Franco-American attack on the South nearly closed the Germans in a pincers in the Argonne forest and along the Meuse. Ludendorff's troops were in slow and generally orderly retreat, but suffering from low morale and without supplies, and he was determined that Germany itself should not be invaded. On September 29 he asked for an armistice; the German chancellor resigned the following day, and his successor appealed directly to President Wilson to call a peace conference on the basis of Wilson's Fourteen Points. The Allies were reluctant to accept these conditions, and Wilson hinted that the Americans would conclude a separate peace. On October 27 the Austro-Hungarian Empire, which was breaking up, also asked for an armistice. On November 3 mutiny in the German fleet at Kiel and in much of northwest Germany, and on November 7 revolution in Bavaria, made it impossible to continue. Ludendorff had been dismissed, and William II abdicated on November 9 and fled to Holland. Negotiations that had begun on November 8 were concluded at 5:00 A.M. on November 11, when the armistice was signed. All was, at last, quiet on the western front.

THE WRITTEN RECORD

War in the Trenches

The war in the trenches was unremitting tedium punctuated by moments of intense action. Long after the war a distinguished British historian, Charles Carrington (1897–1981), who was a young man on the Somme, wrote of his experience:

After a battle you buried your comrades and saw to it that their graves were marked with a wooden cross and a name. If you had time, and if it was not too dangerous, you did as much for other British dead. The enemy came last in priority, and more than once I have cleared a trench of its defunct tenants by throwing them over the parapet where someone might or might not find and bury them when the battle was over. There were so many live inhabitants in the landscape as I saw it at Contalmaison in November 1916 that corpses had been cleared off everyone's premises, unless you went up to the new front where it was too dangerous for burial-parties to work. But in rolling forward the armies left desert areas behind, where no one had either need or inclination to go, in winter dreary beyond description, inhabited only by giant rats, fattened on corpse-flesh, in summer strangely beautiful with carpets of wild flowers and loud with skylarks. Clumps of scarlet poppies sprang up wherever the chalky subsoil had been disturbed by digging or by shell-fire. Long afterwards you could find corpses in nooks and corners of this wilderness. . . .

The killed and wounded were all lost by harassing fire, mostly on their way up or down the line. Once in position at Le Sars you could not show a finger by daylight, and by night every path by which you might be supposed to move was raked by machine-guns which had been trained on it by day. The entrance to the village, that is the gap in the ruins where the Bapaume Road passed through, the only way, by which you must pass, was under continuous shell-fire. If you could reach your funk-hole, and crouch in it, there was a fair chance of your coming out of it alive next day to run the gauntlet of the Bapaume Road again. In your funk-hole, with no room to move, no hot food, and no chance of getting any, there was nothing worse to suffer than a steady drizzle of wintry rain and a temperature just above freezing-point. A little colder and the mud would have been more manageable. Life was entirely numbed; you could do nothing. There could be no fighting since the combatants could not get at one another, no improvement of the trenches since any new work would instantly be demolished by a storm of shell-fire.

THE HOME FRONTS

In World War I soldiers and sailors were, for the most part, civilians, unused to military ways. Behind the front—subject to rationing and regimentation in daily living—families, too, were part of this great "total war." They, too, bore up under it, though in France in 1917, after the bloody failure of the "one big push," civilian and military discontent almost broke French morale. And in Germany the armistice was the result, in part, of a psychological collapse under intolerable spiritual and material pressures.

The Germans were slow to organize for total war. They failed notably to ensure the proper and equitable distribution of food supplies, so that as 1918 wore on, whole sectors of the urban population began to suffer from malnutrition. Nor were their finances and war production managed as efficiently as industrial production before the war had led everyone to expect.

Sooner or later, all countries engaged in the war felt obliged to introduce drastic wartime economic planning.

In Britain the Defense of the Realm Act clamped down severely on the right to say and do what one liked. In the United States business executives who were working for the government flocked to Washington and helped build up an enormous new central government, which regulated the economy as it had never been regulated before. And of course all the belligerents engaged in a war of propaganda or, as it came to be called later, psychological warfare.

The Allies won the battle of the production lines, in which the United States played a major part. Allied production was slow in getting started and suffered from mistakes, bottlenecks, and hasty experiments. In the beginning the Allies were often at cross-purposes in production as well as in military strategy. Nevertheless, the Allies eventually fully exploited their potential superiority over the Central Powers in material resources.

The Allies also won the most critical phase of the war of propaganda. They sought to convince the neutral world, especially the United States, Latin America and the Swiss, Dutch, Scandinavians, and Spaniards, that the Allies were fighting for the right and the Central Powers for the wrong. Most of the neutral West was early convinced that the cause of the Allies was just, or would at

Women working in an American factory during World War I.
National Archives

least prove victorious—a conviction strengthened by the public perception of the traditional liberalism of France and Britain, in contrast with the traditional autocracy of the German and Austrian empires.

Allied propaganda was one-sided and unfair, notably in accusing the Germans of frightful atrocities in Belgium. The Germans imposed rigorous military controls on conquered populations, but their record was hardly worse than what was usual in warfare. Allied propaganda also simplified and falsified the complex causes of the war, making it appear that the Germans and Austrians were wholly responsible for its outbreak.

Except in Russia, the four years of war saw no major changes in political structure. The Central Powers retained their incompletely responsible parliamentary governments, and the parliaments on the whole were reasonably submissive. Despite the strengthening of the executive in wartime, France, Britain, and the United States carried on their democratic institutions. In Britain the skillful but indecisive Liberal leader Herbert Asquith (1852–1928) was succeeded in December 1915 by David Lloyd George, who had proved himself an admirable organizer of war production. Clemenceau—the Tiger, as he was known to his friends and enemies alike—came to power at the end of 1917, at a time when defeatism threatened both the military and the civilian strength of France. He took firm command of the war effort and disposed summarily of the disaffected politicians.

The war brought substantial changes to social life on the home front. An entire generation of young men, potential leaders in industry and politics, was destroyed in Britain and France. In both countries and in the United States women were employed in factories, on streetcars, at the lower levels of politics, and just behind the lines as nurses in military hospitals. At the end of the war, when demobilized men expected to return to their jobs, women who had acquired skills were thrown out of work, and many turned to socialism.

Moral codes concerning sexual propriety also changed, for the men felt they might never return from the front, and the old practices requiring a slow courtship were often cast aside. While the double standard in sexual conduct was intensified—soldiers could violate the conventions of marriage without blame, while women were expected to remain faithful to their departed men—there were many who began to question these conventions. Sexual promiscuity and "social diseases" became more prevalent, as all societies began to challenge the authority of the family, the church, or the school over moral conduct.

THE PEACE SETTLEMENTS

The warring powers met at Versailles to settle with the Germans and at other châteaux around Paris to settle with the rest. Peace congresses never meet in a world that is really at peace, for there is always an aftermath of local war, crises, and disturbances; in 1918–1919 these were so numerous and acute that they conditioned the work of the peace congresses. In addition, throughout 1918–1919 an influenza epidemic more devastating than any disease since the Black Death swept across the world, taking 20 million lives and disrupting families and work everywhere.

Postwar Instability

The most worrisome crises were in Russia. No sooner had the Germans been forced to withdraw from the regions they had gained at Brest-Litovsk than the Allies sent detachments to various points along the perimeter of Russia—on the Black Sea, on the White Sea in the far north, and on the Pacific. The Allies' dread of final Bolshevik success and of the possible spread of Bolshevism westward added to the tensions at Versailles.

Bolshevism was clearly spreading westward. While the German revolution of November 1918 had been carried out under socialist auspices, through the winter of 1918–1919 there were communist riots and uprisings, and in Bavaria in April a soviet republic was proclaimed. The new republican government of Germany put these communist movements down, but only by an appeal to the remnants of the old army and to officers thoroughly hostile to any type of republic. After the breakup of the Austro-Hungarian monarchy in the autumn of 1918, the successor states—Czechoslovakia, Austria, Hungary, Yugoslavia, Romania—were disturbed by deep social and economic upheaval. In Hungary Béla Kun (c. 1886–c. 1940), who had worked with Lenin in Moscow, won power through a socialist-communist coalition and then set up a Bolshevik dictatorship. In August 1919 a Romanian army forced Kun to flee. Finally, groups of German ex-soldiers—*Freikorps* (Free Corps) made up of embittered officers and recruits who could not adjust to civilian life, and joined by university students—were clamoring for the return of the monarchy and were attacking communists. Two major communist theoreticians, Karl Liebknecht (1871–1919), founder of the Spartacus party, which mounted the 1919 revolt, and Rosa Luxemburg (1870–1919), who had helped found the Communist party in Germany, were killed by soldiers while being taken to prison.

In the Near East the Allies had even greater instability to contend with. Greece was now up in arms against the Turks. Its nationalists had revived the hope of a restored Byzantine Empire. Greek armies landed at Smyrna in Asia Minor in the spring of 1919. The French and British, to whom control over different parts of the former Turkish Empire had been assigned, began at once having trouble with Arab leaders, while Jews were pressing for a national home in Palestine in accordance with the Balfour Declaration, to which the Arabs were bitterly opposed.

In India the aftermath of war was particularly disastrous as the epidemic of influenza swept the subcontinent. Indians had fought well as professional soldiers on the Allied side during the war; educated Indians thought their country was ripe for much more self-rule. Widespread disorders culminated in the Amritsar massacre in April 1919, in which a British general ordered his soldiers to fire on an unarmed crowd, killing or wounding some sixteen hundred people.

The situation in China was even less stable. There a revolution in 1911–1912 had ended the rule of the Manchu dynasty and inaugurated a precarious republic. The internal distractions of the Chinese and the weakening of Russia led the Japanese to renew their ambitious plans in north China. The presence of American troops in occupation of Archangel and Murmansk in north Russia, and within the port at Vladivostok, would color future relations with the Soviet Union.

The world was in turmoil when the Allies assembled to make peace. The problems that faced the peacemakers were worldwide, complex, and often insoluble, in the sense that no decision on a given problem could possibly satisfy all the groups concerned. Yet the world expected more from them than from any previous settlement. In the minds of many, this war had been a war to "make the world safe for democracy," a war to end war.

In 1918 many of these hopes were embodied in Woodrow Wilson's Fourteen Points. Wilson's primary concerns were to secure the freedom of the seas and to create a League of Nations to organize peace thereafter. He and his advisers had formulated the language of the Fourteen Points to make them useful in case of complete victory, a stalemate, or even defeat, for they were put forward as negotiating points. At the peace conference, however, they became rigid demands. These points were:

1. Open covenants of peace must be openly arrived at.
2. Absolute freedom of the seas must be guaranteed.
3. Economic barriers must be removed to establish equality of trade conditions among nations.
4. Guarantees must be given to reduce national armaments.
5. Colonial claims must be adjusted impartially, with the interests of the colonial populations given equal weight.
6. Russian territory must be evacuated.
7. Belgium must be restored.
8. All French territory should be freed, and Alsace-Lorraine restored to France.
9. The frontiers of Italy should be adjusted in accordance with "nationality."
10. The peoples of Austria-Hungary should be assured of autonomous development.
11. Romania, Serbia, and Montenegro should be evacuated and Serbia given access to the sea.
12. Turkey should be assured its sovereignty, but the nationalities under Turkish rule should be given an opportunity for autonomous development, and the Dardanelles should be opened to free passage.
13. An independent Polish state should be created with secure access to the sea.
14. A general association of nations must be formed to afford mutual guarantees "to great and small states alike."

Other hopes and promises that contradicted the Fourteen Points were not embodied in a single document. There were three categories: the previous diplomatic commitments made by the Allies; the widespread popular hopes fanned by Allied propaganda and promised at the end of the war by some Allied leaders; and the long-established habits and traditions that had become part of the dominant policies and trends of each nation.

In the first category, the most difficult of the diplomatic commitments was the contradictory set of promises made to Italy and Serbia by the original Entente, including Russia, about the disposal of Habsburg lands. In the second category were the promises, widely believed by the British and French peoples, that Germany would be made to pay the whole cost of the war in reparations, its war criminals would be punished, and it would be forever rendered incapable of aggression. In the third category were the deeply rooted drives of the various nations—French drives for revenge against Germany, for hegemony in Europe, and for security; British longing for Victorian serenity and economic leadership, safe from German commercial competition; and the nationalist aspirations of the new states of central Europe. Important, too, was the American desire to be free from European alliances and entanglements as soon as possible.

The question of German war guilt seemed to be confirmed by the peace settlements, but in the years to come the issue would be much debated, and by the 1930s, a resurgent German nationalism would have renounced both the guilt and the settlements. Historians have debated the question of war guilt, or primary responsibility for the war, or more simply the exact nature of the chain of cause and effect, and have arrived at often differing conclusions. Following a second World War, some German scholars in particular argued that blame for the first World War should not have been laid at Germany's door. Questions of war guilt are vexations, but it seems irreduceably true that Bosnia and Serbia bore much of the responsibility for putting a match to the powder keg. Yet, two small and undeveloped nations can hardly be held responsible for a war that engulfed the world, and specific decisions made by specific leaders in all the participating nations must also be taken into account. Still, when one asks which nation finally disturbed the status quo in Europe sufficiently to bring on the war, it is difficult to answer with any other name than Germany.

Peacemaking and Territorial Settlements, 1918–1923

The peace conference first met formally on January 18, 1919. Nearly thirty nations involved in the war against the Central Powers sent delegates. Russia was not represented. The defeated nations took no part in the deliberations; the Germans, in particular, were given little chance to comment on or criticize the terms offered them. German anger over this failure of the Allies to accept their new republic was to play a large part in the ultimate rise of Adolf Hitler.

The conference got off to a good start. Wilson's Fourteen Points already seemed to guarantee peace; it was believed that the proposed association of nations, working together in the freedom of parliamentary discussion, would eliminate the costly burdens of armament.

However, the conference took on a familiar pattern. The small nations were excluded from the real negotiations; the business of the conference was carried on in private among the political chiefs of the victorious great powers—the Big Four of Wilson, Lloyd George, Clemenceau, and Italian premier Vittorio Orlando (1860–1952). Decisions were made with only indirect consultation of public opinion and with all the pressures, intrigue, compromises, and bargaining common to earlier peace conferences.

The professional diplomats of the smaller states had probably never expected that they would be treated on equal terms, but the completeness of their exclusion from the work of the conference annoyed them and angered their peoples. More important, all the major powers had large staffs of experts—economists, political scientists, historians, specialists in many fields—who were confident that they would do the real work and make the real decisions. They drew up report after report, but they did not make policy. The most celebrated of these experts was an economist, John Maynard Keynes (1883–1946), who represented the British Treasury at Versailles until he quit in disgust and wrote a highly critical and influential analysis, *The Economic Consequences of the Peace*.

Keynes would become the most famous economist of the twentieth century. His work was both theoretical and practical. In *The Economic Consequences* he attacked the negotiators at Versailles, and especially Wilson, so skillfully, arguing that the treaty was unworkable as well as immoral and that it would lead to economic ruin throughout Europe, that the British were persuaded in the interwar years that so harsh a punishment of Germany required rectification. The reception of Keynes' work drove a wedge between the British, French, and Americans. In time Keynes would produce his *General Theory of Employment, Interest, and Money*, published in 1936, which would tackle the Great Depression that he had predicted, arguing that the usual government policy—cutting spending in the face of inflation—was wrong, and that governments should spend in order to pull the economy out of depression. This argument paved the way for deficit financing with its many short-range benefits and long-range problems.

Wilson and his experts were gradually persuaded to accept harsher peace terms. The reparations bill against Germany was lengthened; Poland, Italy, and Japan made claims to lands that could not be justified on the basis of self-determination by the peoples concerned. Wilson compromised on a dozen points, but he would not let the Italians have Fiume, though Italy might have neighboring Trieste and the coveted Trentino. Yet Fiume was Italian-speaking and historically was linked with Venice. The Italian delegation left the conference in anger, but Wilson was immovable.

The covenant of the League of Nations was an integral part of the Treaty of Versailles. The League was no supranational body but a kind of permanent consultative system initially composed of the victors and a few neutrals. The way was left open for the Germans and the Russians to join the League, as they later did. The League had an assembly in which each member state had one vote, and a council in which five great powers (Britain, France, Italy, the United States, and Japan) had permanent seats, and to which four other member states were chosen by the assembly for specific terms. A permanent secretariat, to be located at Geneva, was charged with administering the affairs of the League. The League never fulfilled the hopes it had aroused. It did not achieve disarmament, nor did its peacemaking machinery prevent aggression. The great powers simply went their usual ways, using the League only as their policy makers saw fit.

More relevant to the work in Paris was the problem of territorial changes. The peacemakers were confronted not merely with the claims of the victorious Allies but also with those of the new nations that had sprung up from the disintegrating Austrian, Russian, and Turkish empires. They had to try to satisfy diverse land hungers without too obviously violating the principle of "self-determination of peoples." This principle was hard to apply in much of central Europe, where peoples of different language and national consciousness were mixed together in a mosaic of minorities. The result was to multiply the number of sovereign nations.

France regained Alsace-Lorraine. The Saar Basin was to be separated from Germany for fifteen years as an international ward supervised by the League of Nations. During that period its coal output would go to France, and at its close a plebiscite would determine its political future. The Rhineland remained part of the German Republic, though it was to be demilitarized and occupied for a time by Allied soldiers. Belgium was given some small towns on the German border. After a plebiscite provided for in the Treaty of Versailles, Denmark recovered the northern part of Schleswig, which the Danish Crown had lost to Prussia in 1864. Poland, erased from the map as an independent state in 1795, was restored and given lands that it had possessed before the partitions of the eighteenth century but that contained large German and other minorities.

The old Habsburg Empire was completely dismembered. Charles I (1887–1922) had come to the Habsburg throne in 1916 and had sought separate peace negotiations. But the empire broke up under him as ice breaks in a spring river: on October 15, 1918, Poland declared its independence; on October 19, Serbs, Croats, and Slovenes at Zagreb declared the sovereignty of a south-Slav government; on November 1, Charles granted Hungary independence. When Austria-Hungary signed a separate armistice on November 3, it had virtually ceased to exist. The heart of its German-speaking area was constituted as the republic of Austria, which was forbidden to join itself to Germany, and the heart of its Magyar-speaking area became a diminished kingdom of Hungary. The Czech-inhabited lands of Bohemia and Moravia were joined with Slovakia, to which were added the Ruthenian lands of the Carpatho-Ukraine frontier further east to form the "successor state" of Czechoslovakia.

Another successor state was Yugoslavia, officially the kingdom of Serbs, Croats, and Slovenes, a union between prewar Serbia and the south-Slav territories of the Habsburgs. Romania, which received the former Hungarian province of Transylvania, was also rewarded with Bessarabia, a Russian province that the Bolsheviks could not defend. Greece received Thrace at the expense of Turkey and Bulgaria. Wilson's refusal to accept the partition of Albania among Yugoslavia, Italy, and Greece saved that country from destruction.

Out of the former czarist domains (other than Poland) held at the end of the war by the Germans, the Baltic republics of Estonia, Latvia, and Lithuania were created. In time plebiscites determined other territorial adjustments, notably whether parts of East Prussia and Silesia should go to Poland or remain German. The new Polish state was granted access to the Baltic Sea through the so-called Polish Corridor, a narrow strip of land that had once been Polish and that terminated in the almost wholly German port of Danzig. The Poles wanted Danzig, but the Allies compromised by making it a free city and by giving the Poles free trade with it. The Polish Corridor now separated East Prussia from the rest of Germany, and Germans had to cross it in sealed trains.

Outside Europe the Near East presented the most acute problems. By the Treaty of Sèvres of October 1920, the Turks were left with only Constantinople and a small area around it in Europe, and with Anatolia in Asia. Mesopotamia (contemporary Iraq) and Palestine were given as mandates to Britain, while Syria and Lebanon were granted as mandates to France. The Greeks were to hold Smyrna and nearby regions in Asia Minor for five years, after which the mixed Greek and Turkish population would be entitled to a plebiscite. But the Treaty of Sèvres never went into effect, though it was signed by the sultan. A group of army officers headed by Mustafa Kemal led a popular revolt in Anatolia against the government at Constantinople and galvanized the Turkish people into a renewed nationalism. In the Greco-Turkish War of 1921–1922, the Turks drove the Greek army into the sea and set up a republic with its capital at Ankara in the heart of Anatolia. The Allies were obliged to conclude the Treaty of Lausanne with this new government in 1923; the new treaty transferred the area of Izmir (Turkish for Smyrna) and eastern Thrace from Greek to Turkish control and was much more advantageous to the Turks than the Treaty of Sèvres had been.

The Lausanne settlement included a radical innovation: a formal transfer of populations, affecting 2 million people. Greeks in Turkey, except for Istanbul, were moved to Greece, and Turks in Greece, except for western Thrace, were moved to Turkey. Each government was to take care of the transferred populations, and though much hardship resulted, on the whole the plan worked. No such exchange occurred on Cyprus, the British-controlled island in the eastern Mediterranean, where Greeks outnumbered Turks four to one and where the two peoples were so thoroughly intermingled in the towns and villages that an exchange would have been extremely difficult. Nor were measures taken to satisfy the national aspirations of two other minorities—the Muslim Kurds of eastern Anatolia and the Christian Armenians, many now dispersed from northeastern Anatolia to northern Syria.

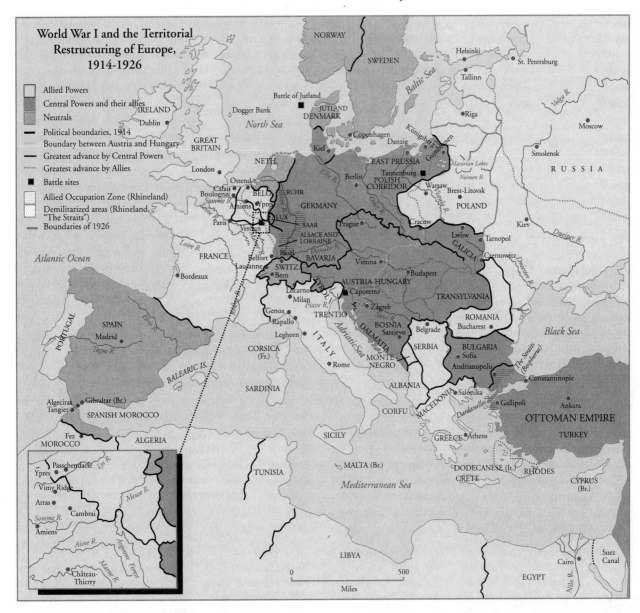

World War I and the Territorial Restructuring of Europe, 1914-1926

Legend:
- Allied Powers
- Central Powers and their allies
- Neutrals
- — Political boundaries, 1914
- ⋯ Boundary between Austria and Hungary
- — Greatest advance by Central Powers
- ⋯ Greatest advance by Allies
- ■ Battle sites
- Allied Occupation Zone (Rhineland)
- Demilitarized areas (Rhineland, "The Straits")
- — Boundaries of 1926

Under the mandate system, control over a conquered territory was assigned to a power by the League of Nations, which undertook to see that the terms of the mandate were fulfilled. This system was designed to prepare colonial peoples for eventual independence. Under it the former German overseas territories and the non-Turkish parts of the Ottoman Empire were distributed. Of Germany's African possessions, East Africa went to Britain; Southwest Africa went to the Union of South Africa; and both the Cameroons and Togoland were divided between Britain and France. In the Pacific the German portion of New Guinea went to Australia, western Samoa to New Zealand, and the Caroline, Marshall, and Mariana island groups to Japan. In the Near East France secured Syria and Lebanon, while Britain took Palestine, Transjordan, and Iraq (the new Arabic designation for Mesopotamia).

After land transfers, the most important business of the peace conferences was reparations, which were imposed on Austria, Hungary, Bulgaria, and Turkey, as well as on Germany. It was, however, the German reparations that so long disturbed the peace and the economy of the world. The Germans had to promise to pay for all the damage done to civilian property during the war, and to pay at the rate of $5 billion a year until 1921, when the final bill would be presented to them. They would then be given thirty years in which to pay the full amount. The amount was left indefinite at Versailles, for the Allies could not agree on a figure, but the totals suggested were astronomical.

The Versailles settlement also required Germany to hand over many merchant ships to the Allies and to make large deliveries of coal to France, Italy, and Belgium for ten years. The western frontier zone, extending to a line fifty kilometers east of the Rhine, was to be completely "demilitarized"—that is, to contain neither fortifications nor soldiers. In addition, the Allies could maintain armies of occupation on the left bank of the Rhine for fifteen years or longer. The treaty forbade Germany to have either submarines or military planes and severely limited the number and size of surface vessels in its navy. Finally, Article 231 of the Treaty of Versailles obliged Germany to admit that the Central Powers bore sole responsibility for starting the war in 1914.

The League of Nations was potentially a means by which a new generation of international administrators might mitigate the old rivalries. The reparations could be, and were, scaled down. The new successor states were based on a national consciousness that had been developing for at least a century. Though some might protest at the "Balkanization of Europe," it would have been impossible to deny national independence to the Czechs, the Poles, the Baltic peoples, and the south Slavs. Germany, though not treated generously, was not wiped off the map, as Poland had been in the eighteenth century. Versailles was simply a compromise peace.

It contained, however, too many compromises for the American people, who were not used to striking international bargains. The American refusal to ratify the Treaty of Versailles was the result of many forces. Domestic politics were an important part, for the Republicans had won control of Congress in the elections of November 1918. President Wilson, a Democrat, made no concessions to the Republicans, either by taking Republicans to Paris with him or by accepting modifications in the treaty that would have satisfied some of his Republican opponents. The Senate feared that the League would drag the United States into future wars. Wilson declared that Article X of the League Covenant had turned the Monroe Doctrine into a world doctrine, for it guaranteed "the territorial integrity and political independence" of all League members. But opponents argued that were the United States to sign the Covenant, the League could interfere with American tariffs and immigration laws. The Senate refused to ratify the treaty and ended the technical state of war with Germany by congressional resolution on July 2, 1921. Separate treaties were then signed with Germany, Austria, and Hungary, by which the United States gained all the rights stipulated for it by the Treaty of Versailles.

It is unlikely that even a more pliable and diplomatic president than Wilson could have won Senate ratification of a defensive alliance among France, Britain, and the United States. Without United States participation, Britain refused a mere dual alliance with France against a German attack. France, still seeking to bolster its security, thereupon patched up a series of alliances with the new nations to the east and south of Germany—Poland, and the Little Entente of Yugoslavia, Czechoslovakia, and Romania—a wholly unsatisfactory substitute for Britain and the United States as allies.

The peace left France with uneasy dominance of Europe, dependent on the continued disarmament and economic weakening of Germany, on the continued isolation of Russia, and on the uncertain support of unstable new allies. Moreover, France had been disastrously weakened by the human and material losses of the war. Germany was in fact still the strongest nation on the Continent. The Great War had checked, but not halted, its potential ability to dominate the Continent.

One most important matter was not directly touched upon by the Versailles settlement: Russia, or the Union of Soviet Socialist Republics (USSR), the formal name of the new communist state. Yet in many senses, the most important result of World War I was the emergence of this new state.

THE RUSSIAN REVOLUTION OF 1917

Though Russia was shaken by domestic crisis in 1914, the country greeted the outbreak of World War I with demonstrations of national patriotism. The Duma supported the war, while the left-wing parties abstained from voting for war loans but offered to assist the national defense. Yet it was the war and the regime's failure to deal with the crises it provoked that precipitated revolution.

The Immediate Background to Revolution, 1914–1917

Russia was geographically isolated from the munitions and supplies that would otherwise have come from the Allies. Despite Russia's great resources in agriculture and potential for industry, transportation was inadequate from the beginning, and when the trains were used to move troops, food shortages developed in the cities. Losses in battle were staggering from the first; the Russians suffered nearly 4 million casualties during the first year of war.

By mid-1915 the center and left groups in the Duma, known as the Progressive Bloc, were urging moderate reforms, such as the end of discrimination against minority nationalities and an increase in the powers of the zemstvos. In the autumn of 1915, in answer to a demand by the Progressive Bloc for a cabinet that would be responsible to it and not to the czar, Nicholas dismissed the Duma and took personal command of the armies in the field, leaving his wife in authority in St. Petersburg. She in turn left matters in the hands of her favorite, Rasputin.

With the empress and Rasputin in control, a gang of shady adventurers, blackmailers, and profiteers bought and sold offices, speculated in military supplies, put in their own puppets as ministers, and created a series of scandals. Confusion, strikes, and defeatism mounted at home during 1916, while the armies at the front, lacking transport, equipment, supplies, and medical care, slowly bled to death. The conservatives began to denounce Rasputin publicly, and in December 1916 he was murdered.

Despite repeated warnings from moderates in the Duma that the government itself was precipitating a revolution by its failure to create a responsible ministry, the czar remained apathetic. When news of Rasputin's death reached Berlin, the Germans saw a chance to knock Russia out of the war by promoting independence movements in the Ukraine, Poland, and Finland and by aiding Russian revolutionaries. Relatives of the imperial family and members of the Duma began to plot for Nicholas's abdication. In the early months of 1917 all conditions favored revolution, but the revolutionaries were not prepared.

The March Revolution.   By February only ten days' supply of flour was left in the capital, and the regional commander set up a rationing system. Long lines, closed shops, and the prospect of starvation led to disorder. In the Duma "unfit ministers" were attacked. The left-wing deputies turned to the secret organizations, which had already been working up public opinion against the government's dismissal of thousands of factory workers after a strike. The strikers demonstrated in the streets, and thousands of other workers, led by the wives of the workers, massed in a march that was broken up by mounted police. By the third day the Bolsheviks had taken charge of the continuing strikes and parades. The czar's secret police, the *Okhrana*, conducted mass arrests. But the soldiers were now refusing orders to stop the workers as they sought to march across the River Neva from the workers' quarter to the palaces, and on March 10 (February 27 in the old Russian calendar) many soldiers handed their weapons over to the crowd. The insurgents captured the arsenal with forty thousand rifles, and Petrograd (as St. Petersburg was now called) was in their hands.

The Revolution of February and March 1917, a product of despair and high emotion, remained virtually leaderless and without a program, since those who had been planning revolution were not yet fully prepared. The main Bolshevik leaders were still abroad or in exile, and the radical agrarian group (the Social Revolutionaries, SR) and the more philosophical Marxists (the Social Democrats, SD) were also caught by surprise. Nonetheless, by March the Romanov dynasty, which had ruled since 1613, was without hope.

A determining factor in the overthrow of the czar was the disintegrating loyalty of the garrison of Petrograd. When the czar ordered his troops to fire on the rioters, only a few obeyed, and in revulsion against the order, the troops joined the dissidents and began to hunt the police. On March 12 the Progressive Bloc in the Duma formed a provisional government to keep order until there could be a constituent assembly. By March 14, when the czar finally decided to appoint a responsible ministry, it was too late. On March 15 he abdicated in favor of his younger brother, Michael, and on March 16 Michael refused the throne.

Before that, on March 12, leftists, including many released from prison by the mobs, formed a Soviet of workers and soldiers, modeled on the 1905 Soviet. Its "Army Order No. 1," setting up a committee of soldiers within every unit of the army to control weapons, dealt a blow to military discipline and organization. The Soviet created a food-supply commission and published newspapers; its fifteen-man executive committee of SRs and Mensheviks became the policy makers of the revolution. The Soviet located its headquarters in the same building as the Duma and was soon in conflict with it. The Duma wanted to get its provisional government functioning quickly, to restore public order, and to carry on the war with efficiency for the honor of Russia. Some Duma members were monarchists; some wanted to continue the war and receive Constantinople as a reward; most felt the question of citizens' rights was secondary to these more pressing matters. The Soviet, on the other hand, knew that the great mass of Russian people did not care about Constantinople and wanted an immediate peace, as well as land and food.

The Marxists among the Soviet leaders—mainly Mensheviks—believed in the necessity of a preliminary bourgeois revolution, and they did not yet regard the Soviet itself as an organ of power. Therefore, though they would not participate in the provisional government, they offered it their limited support. Despite their widely differing political and economic aims, both the Duma and the Soviet agreed to grant political liberties immediately and to summon an assembly to establish the future form of government and give Russia a constitution. The provisional government was composed mainly of Kadets (Constitutional Democrats) and other moderates and was headed by the liberal prince Georgi Lvov (1861–1925). It also included one member of the Soviet, the moderate SR Alexander Kerensky (1881–1970), minister of justice, who was a member of the Duma.

The Provisional Government.   The provisional government—which held office between mid-March and early November 1917—was a total failure. Russian moderates had no experience of authority. They were separated by a great cultural gulf from the lower classes. Their opportunity to rule came amid a fearful war, which they felt they had to pursue while reconstructing and democratizing the enormous and unwieldy Russian Empire. Moreover, the Soviet held many of the instruments of power, yet refused to accept responsibility. Workers and soldiers in the capital supported the Soviet. In the provinces the new governors appointed by the provisional government had no weapon except persuasion to employ against the local peasant-elected soviets, which multiplied rapidly.

The two great issues facing the provisional government were agrarian discontent and the continuation of the war. The peasants wanted land, and they wanted it immediately. The provisional government, however, believed in acting with deliberation and according to law. It refused to sanction peasant seizures of land. Instead, it appointed a commission to collect material on which to base future agrarian legislation. As to the war, the provisional government still unrealistically hoped that Russia might win and thus gain the territories the Allies had promised. But the Soviet subverted discipline in the armies at the front by issuing a "declaration of the rights of soldiers," which virtually ended the authority of officers over enlisted men. Even the Bolshevik members of the Soviet, who now began to return from exile, demanded

DOING HISTORY

Simple Errors: The West and Russian History

The way in which certain simple matters of fact are sometimes dealt with in the West when the subject is Russia illustrates the problem of understanding the historical development of a relatively isolated nation. For example, for years some writers insisted that Lenin's first name was Nikolai or Nicholas because of his use of the initial N, not understanding Russian and communist customs concerning abbreviations and pseudonyms. This "discovery" was repeated in the American press as recently as 1983.

Many texts give different dates from those given here for certain events; virtually all disagree over the precise sequence of events and over the nature of leadership in the Duma and the first Soviet. Events that took place in March according to the Western calendar employed throughout this book are frequently referred to as taking place in February because of the different Russian calendar. The number of deaths in any specific demonstration, mutiny, or battle reveal dramatic discrepancies in different books. These inconsistencies in both Soviet and modern Western literature on the Russian Revolution are symptomatic of the degree to which Russia was cut off from the West at the time. Matters of straightforward chronology, of fact, even of names or birth and death dates were subjects of rumor or propaganda both inside and outside Russia. Later, when Soviet leadership ordered the rewriting of much of Russian history so that Russian citizens would not have access to other, and thus confusing, points of view, many aspects of Russian history fell under even greater suspicion.

Russian history clearly represents the problems of accurately recording and intelligently interpreting the past when a society has either been long ignored or cut off from alternative interpretations of its past. It also illustrates how a political leadership may attempt to make history as a discipline serve its own ends by rewriting the past to fit contemporary expectations.

---

only that Russia participate in general peace negotiations, which should begin at once.

Lenin

The most important of the returning Bolshevik exiles was Lenin. His real name was Vladimir Ilyich Ulianov (1870–1924), but in his writings he used the pen name Lenin, to which he sometimes prefixed the initial N, a Russian abbreviation for "nobody," to tell his readers that he was using a pseudonym. Son of a provincial official, Lenin became a revolutionary in the 1880s, and in the early years of the SDs he led the party's Bolshevik wing. He had returned to Russia from abroad for the Revolution of 1905, but he left Russia once more in 1908. From abroad he joined with a small group of socialists in opposing the war and urging that it be transformed into a class war. He considered the war to be the product of imperialism, itself produced by capitalism; thus, war, empires, and capitalism must all be destroyed if society was to be reformed.

Though he had for a time despaired of living to see a true socialist revolution, Lenin was anxious to get back to Russia. The German general staff thought his return would help disrupt the Russian war effort, so the German military transported Lenin and other Bolshevik leaders across Germany from Switzerland to the Baltic in a sealed railroad car. Lenin arrived at the Finland station in Petrograd on April 16, 1917, a little more than a month after the March revolution.

Most Russian Social Democrats had long regarded a bourgeois parliamentary republic as a necessary preliminary stage to an eventual socialist revolution. Therefore, they were prepared to help transform Russia into a capitalist society. They favored the creation of a democratic republic and believed that complete political freedom was absolutely essential for their own rise to power. Despite the Marxist emphasis upon the industrial laboring class as the only proper vehicle for revolution, Lenin early realized that in Russia, where the "proletariat" embraced only about 1 percent of the population, the SDs must seek other allies. During the Revolution of 1905 he had begun to preach the need for limited tactical alliances between the Bolsheviks and the SRs, who commanded the support of the peasantry; when that alliance had served its purpose, the SDs were to turn on their allies and destroy them. Then would come the socialist triumph. Lenin's view, however, was not adopted, even by most Bolsheviks. Together with the Mensheviks, they continued to urge that a bourgeois revolution and a parliamentary democracy were necessary first steps.

Because Lenin did not trust the masses to make a revolution (by themselves, he felt, they were capable only of trade-union consciousness), he favored a dictatorship of the Bolshevik party over the working class. Because he did not trust the rank and file of Bolshevik party workers, he favored a dictatorship of a small elite over the Bolshevik party. And in the end, because he did not trust anyone's views but his own, he favored, though never explicitly, his personal dictatorship over this elite. Another future Russian leader, the brilliant Lev Davidovich Bronstein, known as Leon Trotsky (1879–1940), early warned that Lenin's views implied one-man dictatorship.

Trotsky, for his part, argued that the Russian bourgeoisie was so weak that the working class could telescope the bourgeois and socialist revolutions into one continuous movement. After the proletariat had helped the bourgeoisie achieve its revolution, the workers could move immediately to power, and could nationalize industry and collectivize agriculture. Although foreign intervention and civil war were to be expected, the Russian proletariat would soon be joined by the proletariats of other countries, who would make their own revolutions. Except for this last point, Trotsky's analysis accurately forecast the course of events.

Lenin's greatest talent was as a skillful tactician. Even before he returned to Russia in 1917, he had assessed some of the difficulties facing the provisional government and decided that the masses could take over at once. Immediately upon his arrival, therefore, he hailed the worldwide revolution, proclaiming that the end of imperialism, the last stage of capitalism, was at hand and demanding that all power immediately be given to the soviets. These doctrines were known as the April Theses.

Almost no one save Lenin felt that the loosely organized soviets could govern the country or that the war would bring down the capitalist world in chaos. Still, Lenin called not only for the abandonment of the provisional government and the establishment of a republic of soviets but for the confiscation of estates, the nationalization of land, and the abolition of the army, government officials, and the police. He was offering land at once to the impatient peasants, peace at once to the war-weary populace. This program fitted the mood of the people far better than the cautious efforts of the provisional government to bring about reform by legal means. Dogmatic, furiously impatient of compromise, and entirely convinced that he alone had the courage to speak the truth, Lenin galvanized the Bolsheviks into a truly revolutionary group waiting only for the right moment to seize power.

The November Revolution

The provisional government faced a crisis. Kerensky, now war minister, emerged as the dominant leader. He failed to realize that it was no longer possible to restore the morale of the armies. A new offensive ordered on July 1 collapsed as soldiers refused to obey orders, deserted their

This "mug shot" of Leon Trotsky, taken after an arrest, was found by the victorious revolutionaries in the files of the czarist police.
New York Public Library Picture Collection

units, and hurried home to their villages, eager to seize the land. The soviets became gradually more and more Bolshevik in their views. Although the June congress of soviets in Petrograd was less than 10 percent Bolshevik, the Bolshevik slogans of peace, bread, and freedom won overwhelming support.

An armed outbreak by troops who had accepted the Bolshevik slogans found the Petrograd Soviet professing unwillingness to assume power. While crowds roared outside, the Soviet voted to discuss the matter two weeks later and meanwhile to keep the provisional government in power. The government declared that Lenin was a divisive agent of Germany, and Lenin went into hiding in Finland to avoid arrest.

Kerensky became premier. General Lavr Georgyevich Kornilov (1870–1918), chosen by Kerensky as the new commander in chief of the armies, quickly became the hope of all conservative groups. In August Kornilov plotted a coup, intending to disperse the Soviet. His attitude toward the provisional government was less clear, but had he succeeded he would probably have demanded a purge of its more radical elements. Tension between Kornilov and his superior, Kerensky, mounted. The Soviet backed Kerensky, fearing Kornilov's attack. When Kornilov refused to accept his dismissal as war minister and seemed about to march against Petrograd, the Bolsheviks threw themselves into preparations for defense. Kornilov's troop

THE WRITTEN RECORD

Lenin's Address at the Finland Station

On the day Lenin arrived at the Finland station in Petrograd, he declared that the World War must be transformed into a series of civil wars, the bourgeois revolution into a social revolution, so that a crisis of European capitalism might be precipitated. In a memorable confrontation, he instantly revealed that he would not accept the more moderate expectations of the Petrograd Soviet. The following account is drawn from the notebooks of a journalist who was on the spot:

The train was very late. . . . But at long last it arrived. A thunderous *Marseillaise* boomed forth on the platform, and shouts of welcome rang out. . . . Behind [the master of ceremonies] . . . Lenin came, or rather ran, into the room. He wore a round cap, his face looked frozen, and there was a magnificent bouquet in his hands. Running to the middle of the room, he stopped in front of [N. S.] Chkheidze [(1864–1926), the chairman of the Soviet] as though colliding with a completely unexpected obstacle. And Chkheidze, still glum, pronounced the following "speech of welcome" with not only the spirit and wording but also the tone of a sermon:

"Comrade Lenin . . . we welcome you to Russia. But—we think that the principal task of the revolutionary democracy is now the defence of the revolution from any encroachments either from within or from without. We consider that what this goal requires is not disunion, but the closing of the democratic ranks. We hope you will pursue these goals together with us." . . .

Lenin . . . stood there as though nothing taking place had the slightest connection with him . . . and then, turning away from the Ex[ecutive] Com[mittee] delegation altogether, he made this "reply":

"Dear Comrades, soldiers, sailors, and workers! I am happy to greet in your persons the victorious Russian revolution, and greet you as the vanguard of the worldwide

proletarian army. . . . The piratical imperialist war is the beginning of civil war throughout Europe. . . . The hour is not far distant when at the call of our comrade, Karl Liebknecht [who was still alive at the time], the peoples will turn their arms against their own capitalist exploiters. . . . The worldwide Socialist revolution has already dawned. . . . Any day now the whole of European capitalism may crash. The Russian revolution accomplished by you has prepared the way and opened a new epoch. Long live the worldwide Socialist revolution!" . . .

To another *Marseillaise,* and to the shouts of the throng of thousands, among the red-and-gold banners illuminated by the searchlight, Lenin went out by the main entrance and was about to get into a closed car, but the crowd absolutely refused to allow this. Lenin clambered on to the bonnet of the car and had to make a speech.

N. N. Sukhanov, *The Russian Revolution, 1917,* trans. Joel Carmichael (London: Oxford University Press, 1955), pp. 272–74, quoted in M. C. Morgan, *Lenin* (London: Edward Arnold, 1971), pp. 104–6. Sukhanov (1833?–1931?), while in favor of revolution, was anti-Bolshevik. Although Lenin criticized Sukhanov as a Social Democrat who did not understand the workers, he accepted his account of the revolution as factually accurate.

movements were sabotaged, however, and by September 14 he had been arrested.

The Kornilov affair turned the army mutiny into a widespread revolt. In the countryside farms were burned, manor houses destroyed, and large landowners killed. After the great estates were gone, the peasantry attacked the smaller properties, though they allowed owners in some districts to keep a portion of their former lands through redistribution.

Amid these disorders Lenin returned to Petrograd. Warning that Kerensky was planning to surrender Petrograd to the Germans, Trotsky gained control over a Military Revolutionary Committee to help defend the city and to transform the committee into a general staff for the revolution. Beginning on November 4, he addressed huge demonstrations and mass meetings, and on November 7 (October 25 on the old Russian calendar) the insurrection broke out as Trotsky intended. The February Revolution had failed, to be replaced by the October Revolution.

In Petrograd the revolution had been well prepared and proceeded with little bloodshed. Military groups loyal to the Bolsheviks took control of key points in the city. The Bolsheviks entered the Winter Palace, where the provisional government was meeting, and arrested the ministers. Kerensky escaped and the Military Revolutionary Committee took over. A long-awaited Congress of Soviets, representing less than half of the soviets in Russia, opened on November 8. Both Lenin and Trotsky appeared. When the Mensheviks and right-wing SRs walked out, Trotsky called them garbage that would be swept into the trash cans of history. Cooperating with the left-wing SRs and adopting their land program, Lenin abolished the property rights of the church, of landlords, and of the Crown. He transferred the land thus affected to local land committees and soviets of peasant deputies, transforming at a stroke the isolated Russian villages by "legalizing" a process already begun. He also urged an immediate peace without annexations or indemnities and appealed to the workers of Germany, France, and England to support him in this demand. Finally, a new cabinet, called a Council of People's Commissars, was chosen, with Lenin as president and Trotsky as foreign *commissar.*

The Bolsheviks installed as commissar of nationalities a younger man, a Georgian named Joseph Dzhugashvili (1879–1953), who had taken the name Stalin, suggesting a steel-like hardness. Under Lenin's coaching, Stalin had become the party authority on questions relating to the many minority nationalities and had published a pamphlet on the subject in 1913.

Outside Petrograd the revolution moved more slowly. In Moscow there was a week of street fighting between Bolshevik Reds and anti-Bolshevik Whites, as those opposed to the revolution were called. Elsewhere, in factory towns the Bolsheviks usually won speedily; in nonindustrial centers it took longer. A main reason for the rapid and smooth success of the Bolsheviks was that the provincial garrisons opposed the war and willingly allied themselves with the workers. Local military revolutionary committees were created in most places and held elections for new local soviets. Most of Siberia and central Asia came over, but Tiflis, the capital of Georgia, went Menshevik and passed resolutions calling for a constituent assembly and the continuation of the war. Gradually the

town of Rostov-on-Don, near the Sea of Azov, became the main center of White resistance, as Kornilov and other generals together with a number of the leading politicians of the Duma gathered there.

Late in November an agreement was reached with the left-wing SRs, three of whom entered the government, and peace negotiations were begun with the Germans. The revolution proper was over and Lenin was in power. The Russian state, however, was disintegrating and decomposing socially on all sides. On November 25 the Bolsheviks held elections for a constituent assembly, the first free election in Russian history. As was to be expected, the Bolshevik vote was heaviest in the cities, especially Moscow and Petrograd, while the SR vote was largely rural.

Disregarding the fact that 62 percent of the votes had been cast for his opponents, Lenin maintained that "the most advanced" elements had voted for him. The constituent assembly met only once, in January 1918. Lenin dissolved it the next day by decree and sent guards with rifles to prevent its meeting again. The anti-Bolshevik majority was deeply indignant at this unconstitutional act of force against the popular will, but there was no public outburst and the delegates disbanded. In part this was because the Bolsheviks had already taken action on

Demonstrators in the streets of Petrograd in July 1917 were fired upon by police and soldiers of the Kerensky government.

Sovfoto

A painting of Lenin by I. A. Serebryany, from the Central Lenin Museum in Leningrad, showing him speaking at the Second All-Russian Congress of Soviets.
Sovfoto

what interested the people most—peace, bread, and free-dom—and in part because the Russian masses lacked a democratic parliamentary tradition.

War Communism, 1917–1920

The first period of Soviet history, which runs from the end of 1917 to the end of 1920, is usually called the period of *war communism*, or military communism. The term implies that the main features of the period were deter-mined by military events; civil war raged, and foreign powers intervened on Russian soil. But the term is also somewhat misleading. This was a period of militant as well as military communism, symbolized early in 1918 by the change of the party's name from Bolshevik to the Russian Communist party. The capital was shifted from Petrograd, with its exposed location on the western fringe of Russia, to the greater security of Moscow. And a newspaper, *The Communist* began publication. The Bolsheviks firmly believed that world revolution was about to begin, prob-ably first in Germany, then spreading to Britain and ulti-mately to the United States. This view led the Bolsheviks to hasten the construction of a socialist state in Russia.

By 1920 the state had taken over all enterprises employing more than ten workers. Labor was compulsory and strikes were outlawed. The state organized a system of barter, which replaced the free market. Internal trade

was illegal; only the government food commissary could buy and sell. Money disappeared as the state took over distribution as well as production. It expropriated the banks and in effect wiped out savings. Church and state were separated by decree, and judges were removed from office and replaced by appointees of the local soviets. Nine opposition political parties were liquidated (among them the Kadets) or persecuted (the SRs and Mensheviks).

The government subjected the peasantry to ever more severe requisitioning. It mobilized the poorer peas-ants against those who were better off (called *kulaks*, from the word meaning "fist"). By calling for a union of the hungry against the better fed, the regime deliberately sowed class hatred in the villages and stimulated civil war in the countryside. A decree forming a secret police, the *Cheka* (from the initials of the words meaning "extraor-dinary commission"), was issued in December 1917, and terror became a weapon in the civil war.

Before the communist government could function at all, peace was necessary, as the army had virtually ceased to exist. Negotiations between the Russians and the Ger-mans and Austro-Hungarians at Brest-Litovsk dragged on into 1918. Finally, on March 3, 1918, the Russians signed the Peace of Brest-Litovsk, which deprived them of the entire Ukraine, the Baltic provinces, Finland, and some Caucasian lands, undoing three centuries of Russian territorial expansion. The treaty cost Russia a third of its population, 80 percent of its iron, and 90 percent of its coal. Many communists resigned rather than accept the peace, and the left SRs quit the government. The Germans overran the Ukraine and the Crimea and installed a highly authoritarian regime. The Whites, with German help, put down the Reds in Finland.

Civil War, 1918–1921

During the months following Brest-Litovsk, disorder in the countryside as a result of requisitioning and class warfare was swelled by the outbreak of open civil strife. During the war a legion of Czechs resident in the country and of deserters from the Habsburg armies had been formed inside Russia. When Russia withdrew from the war, the Czech nationalist leader, Thomas G. Masaryk (1850–1937), wanted to have the Czech corps sent to the French front. Czech, Soviet, and Allied representatives therefore decided to transport the Czech corps to Vladivostok, from which they could sail to France. As the Czechs gathered, the communists became suspicious of their intentions and ordered them to disarm. The Czechs then took control of the Siberian railroad. When the Soviet government tried to take reprisals against the Czechs, who numbered fewer than thirty-five thousand men, the Czechs seized several towns in western Siberia. The local soviets were unprepared, and the SRs were sympathetic to the Czechs. Local anti-Bolshevik armies quickly came into being. In July, in fear that the Whites would rescue the former czar and his family, in exile in Ekaterinburg in the Ural Mountains, the leader of the local soviet, encouraged by Lenin, executed Nicholas II, his wife, his son, his four daughters, his doctor, his servants, and his dog.

Shortly before the executions the Allies had decided to intervene in Russia on behalf of the opponents of Bolshevism. The withdrawal of Russia from the war had been a heavy blow to the Allies, and they now hoped to protect the vast amounts of war supplies still at Vladivostok and Archangel. They also wished to create a new second front against the Germans in the East.

The Czechs overthrew the local soviet in Vladivostok in June 1918, and by early August, British, French, Japanese and American forces had landed. The Americans occupied Vladivostok to safeguard railroad communications in the rear of the Czechs. Of the Allies, only the Japanese had long-range territorial ambitions in the area. In effect, the Bolshevik regime had now been displaced in Siberia. The SRs disbanded the soviets and reestablished the zemstvos. Soon there were three anti-Red governments in three different Siberian centers. In August 1918 a small British and American force landed at Archangel. Then on August 30 an SR assassin killed the chief of the Petrograd Cheka, and Lenin, who was in Moscow, was shot twice. The Bolshevik leadership feared a general counterrevolution in which any doctor might be involved, so the seriously wounded Lenin was taken directly to his apartment rather than to a hospital. The woman who allegedly had attempted to kill him was shot without a trial, and since responsibility for her

act was never proven, rumors multiplied. Blaming the bourgeoisie, the Moscow Cheka shot six hundred people. Cheka retaliation elsewhere was massive.

The regime now sped up its military preparations. As minister of war, Trotsky imposed conscription, and by a mixture of appeals to patriotism and threats of reprisals against their families secured the services of about fifty thousand czarist officers. The Red Army, which was Trotsky's creation, grew to more than 3 million strong by 1920. Its recapture of Kazan and Samara on the Volga in the autumn of 1918 temporarily turned the tide in the crisis that seemed about to engulf the Soviet state.

The German collapse on the western front in November 1918 permitted the Bolsheviks to repudiate the Treaty of Brest-Litovsk and move back into parts of the Ukraine, where they faced the opposition of local forces. Elsewhere, the opposition consisted of three main armies. An army of Whites moved from Rostov-on-Don south across the Caucasus and received French and British aid. Other forces in western Siberia overthrew the SR regime in Omsk, where their commander, Admiral Alexander Kolchak (1874–1920), became a virtual dictator. Yet another army, including many former members of the German forces, operated in the Baltic region and threatened Petrograd from the west.

In the spring of 1919 the Reds defeated Kolchak, and by winter took Omsk. Though the Reds also reconquered the Ukraine, mutinies in their own forces prevented them from consolidating their victories. In the summer of 1919 the White army took Kiev and struck north, advancing to within 250 miles of Moscow itself. A second army advanced to the suburbs of Petrograd, but by the end of 1919 the Reds were able to defeat the White threat, though one White general, Baron Peter Wrangel (1878–1928), retained an army in the Crimea in 1920. Trotsky now called for the militarization of labor to reconstruct the ravaged country.

After the defeat of the Whites, the Reds had to face a new war with the Poles in 1920, led by General Jòsef Pilsudski (1867–1935). Pilsudski wanted to reestablish the Polish frontier as it existed in 1772, the year of the first partition. His immediate objective in 1920 was to drive the Bolsheviks out of the Ukraine and associate the Ukraine with Poland in a common but federally organized state. Beyond that he intended to bring White Russia, Lithuania, and Latvia into the federation also. The effect on Soviet power in the loss of mineral resources and coastlines would have been substantial, which is why the Western powers now swung around in support of Pilsudski's enterprise.

Although after an initial retreat the Red Army nearly took Warsaw, it failed to do so. Eager to finish off the remnant of the Whites and persuaded that there was no hope for a communist regime in Poland, the Reds now concluded peace in October 1920. The Poles obtained much of White Russia and the western Ukraine. This area was not inhabited by Poles but had been controlled by Poland down to the eighteenth-century partitions. It lay far to the east of the "Curzon line," an ethnic frontier that had been proposed by the British foreign minister,

Stalin became so powerful, his figure looked down—in giant statues— upon the Soviet people in most large cities. This statue was duplicated hundreds of times. It was originally erected for the 1939 Al-Union Agricultural Exhibition in Moscow. This photograph is from 1941.
Sovfoto

Lord Curzon (1859–1925), during the Versailles negotiations and that Pilsudski had rejected. The final line, established at Riga in 1921, bisected Byelorussia and the Ukraine roughly where the Uniate (or church of Eastern rites that recognized papal authority) and Orthodox churches met. The size of the ethnic minorities transferred to Poland under this treaty, combined with their mistreatment by the government in Warsaw, was a principal factor making Poland ungovernable in the interwar years, except by military dictatorship.

The Reds now turned on Baron Wrangel, who had marched northward from the Crimea and had established a moderate regime in the territory he occupied. He was forced to evacuate, assisted by a French fleet, in November 1920. The White movement was virtually over. Many circumstances accounted for the Whites' failure and the Reds' victory. The Whites could not unite on any political program beyond the overthrow of the Reds, for they were deeply divided ideologically. Their numbers included everyone from czarists to SRs, and they disagreed so violently on the proper course for Russia to follow that they could agree only to postpone discussion of these critical problems. Their own regimes were often repressive, so that they did not build local

followings, and their troops were at times undisciplined. Moreover, although their movement was located on the geographical periphery of Russia—in Siberia, the Crimea, the Ukraine, the Caucasus, and the Baltic— the Whites never reached an understanding with the non-Russian minorities who lived in these regions.

Most important, the Whites could not command the support of the peasantry. Instead of guaranteeing the results of the land division already carried out with Bolshevik approval, the Whites often restored the landlords in areas they temporarily controlled. The peasantry grew sick of both sides. Food production was curtailed, and atrocities were frequent. Moreover, the Whites simply did not command as much military strength as did the Reds, who outnumbered them and who had inherited much of the equipment manufactured for the czarist armies. Holding the central position, the Reds had a unified and skillful command, which could use the railroad network to shift troops rapidly. The Whites, moving in from the periphery, were divided into at least four main groups and were denied effective use of the railroads. Finally, the intervention of the Allies on the side of the Whites was ineffectual and amateurish. It probably harmed the White cause, since the Reds could speak as the national defenders and could portray the Whites as the hirelings of foreigners. Without the "capitalist" and White threats on the periphery, the center might not have rallied behind Lenin.

The struggle for power in Russia in no sense ended with the civil war. Famine was raging, and class hatreds were exploited on an unparalleled scale. Industry was producing at only an eighth of its prewar output, agricultural output had fallen by 30 percent, and distribution was breaking down. The new regime was losing support. But by early 1921 all major nations in the West were undergoing intense political change as the postwar effort to absorb returning troops, to restore prewar conditions in the victorious nations, and to live with defeat in others created widespread instability.

In the nineteenth century the Russian population had grown nearly 200 percent, changing the Russian countryside from being underpopulated to being overpopulated. While emigration to Siberia had carried off 5 million people between 1870 and 1914 and another 3 million had gone to the New World, much of the surplus peasantry had been taken into the towns. Thus Russia had acquired that demographic group essential to the modern state and to its revolution: an urban proletariat. This group existed only in certain centers in Siberia or on the periphery, but it was powerful within the area where Lenin had built his authority. While the World War had cost Russia nearly 4 million, and 14 million more had died from disease and malnutrition during the revolution and the civil war, which produced a severe birth deficit in the 1920s, Russia continued to grow.

Having put down a serious rebellion of the naval forces at Kronstadt in March 1921, Lenin left a nation on its way toward unity, with a population that despite revolution, war, and famine had regained its prewar levels, and with the expectation of an international communist revolution. Ill from the end of 1921, the man who had reinterpreted Marx tried to prepare his successor. Lenin died in January 1924. By then much of the West was aware that the peacemaking at Versailles had not brought security to Europe, and that the Russian Revolution and its aftermath had assured continued instability for much of the world.

SUMMARY

The creation of a unified Italy and Germany altered the balance of power in Europe in the 1860s and 1870s. Nationalism, imperialism, great-power alliances, and public opinion—influenced by newspapers and photos—helped fuel tensions. By the early 1900s the Triple Alliance and the Triple Entente had taken shape. A naval arms race between Germany and Britain as well as diplomatic and military crises in Morocco, the Balkans, and elsewhere contributed to an uneasy peace.

The assassination of Habsburg archduke Francis Ferdinand, heir to the throne of Austria-Hungary, set off a crisis that led to war. Austria took a strong stand against Serbia, holding it responsible for the assassination. When Serbia rejected demands, Austria declared war. Germany, Russia, France, and Britain aided their respective allies. Italy declared its neutrality but later joined the Allies. Other European nations were drawn into the conflict. By 1917 repeated violations of neutral shipping brought the United States into the war.

The Schlieffen plan for German armies to eliminate France before turning to the Russian front did not succeed. German soldiers were pinned down on the western front, where a stalemate existed throughout much of the war. Millions more were tied down on the eastern front until 1917, when Russia withdrew from the war. The war was fought on other fronts in the Near East, East Africa, and the Far East, as well as on the oceans of the world. The last German offensive in the spring of 1918 could not be sustained, and by that summer the Allies were advancing on the western front. On November 11, 1918, a defeated Germany signed an armistice.

On the home fronts, wartime economic planning anticipated the regulated economies of the postwar era. Both sides waged virulent propaganda warfare. War contributed to changes in social life and in moral codes.

President Wilson's Fourteen Points embodied the hopes for peace. However, conflicting aims among the Allies over reparations, punishment of Germany, and territorial settlements soon dashed liberal hopes for peace. Russia and the Central Powers were not represented at Versailles as the Big Four—Wilson, Lloyd George, Clemenceau, and Orlando—bargained, compromised, and established new nations. An international organization, the League of Nations, was set up with a consultative assembly, but it did not fulfill the hopes of its early supporters.

In the end, the United States refused to ratify the treaty. France, weakened by the war, had its way with reparations, while Germany, still potentially the strongest nation in Europe, reluctantly accepted the treaty.

Strikes and shortages of bread as well as huge losses in the war prepared the way for revolution in Russia in 1917. From the outset, the provisional government and soviets were in conflict. When the moderate provisional government failed to meet crises at home and abroad, Lenin, who had returned to Russia from exile, called for a program that appealed to the Russian people.

In November 1917 the Bolsheviks seized power in Petrograd. The Bolshevik revolution brought great changes to Russia, although the new regime displayed much continuity with old Russia—an autocratic dictator, an elite of bureaucrats and managers, secret police, and Russian nationalism.

CRITICAL THINKING

1. Why is World War I referred to as the "Great War"? In what way was it "greater" than wars that occurred before or after it?

2. Outline the relations between the Triple Alliance and the Triple Entente. How did these relations contribute to the coming of war?

3. Describe the causes of World War I. Distinguish between the long-range causes and the more immediate causes.

4. Were you a neutral observer in 1914, how would you have assessed the relative strengths of the two opposing sides?

5. Describe the military campaigns of the war. At what point did the tide turn toward eventual victory by the Allied powers?

6. How did World War I change life on the home front? Which of these changes proved to be permanent? Which changes would you regard as beneficial to society and which were harmful over the long run?

7. What were the war aims of each belligerent? How did these aims change during the course of the war? Which aims were achieved? How did the peace settlements contribute to these achievements, and how did they hinder them?

8. What were the causes of the Russian Revolution of 1917?

9. Describe the arguments of Lenin and relate these to the ideology of communism. How did communism as first argued in Russia relate to communism as argued elsewhere? If there were differences, how do you account for them?

10. Describe the civil war in Russia. How did it differ from other civil wars, as in England in the seventeenth century or the United States in the nineteenth century?

Between the Wars: A Twenty-Year Crisis

THE YEARS BETWEEN WORLD WAR I and World War II were marked more by movements to the extreme right than by movements to the extreme left, despite the Western democracies' fear of Bolshevism. Beginning in the early 1920s a fascist regime took over in Italy and by the 1930s in Germany and Spain. Much of eastern and southeastern Europe were firmly fascist or quasi-fascist states by the late 1930s. Since these individual fascist states were the products of different societies, they came into power under different circumstances, commanded vastly different resources, and differed in other important respects. But they also had several characteristics in common. The fascist regimes in Italy and Germany in particular were products of disillusionment with the failure of democratic or even socialist policies to achieve stability and security. Economic depressions played a significant role in the rise of dictators almost everywhere. These dictators demonstrated a flair for the dramatic—war cries, special salutes, elaborate ceremonies, uniforms that set the faithful apart from the mass.

Europe's age of fascism, from roughly 1919–1945, did not envelop France, Scandinavia, Switzerland, Britain, or the United States, though they may have had vigorous fascist parties. Fascism everywhere was essentially a reaction against the devastating impact of the Great War on basically liberal nineteenth-century societies that found that victory had not brought harmony, as well as on fragmented and conservative societies that had been branded the aggressors in the war. Thus a sense of anger was basic to fascist states. Within each nation frightened peoples responded with a new nationalism in the face of an international challenge—communism—and an international disaster—universal war followed by universal depression after 1929.

In the phrase of many observers, the twentieth century became an "Age of Anxiety," especially as the European nations began to recognize that they were moving toward economic chaos and political collapse. The European nations had been bled far more deeply by World War I than they realized. Nations that were now powers of the second rank sought to continue to behave as though they were powers of the first rank, especially in aggressive foreign policies. Under such conditions renewed clashes, while not inevitable, were highly likely. Given the emotional base for most fascist movements, compromise was equally unlikely.

THE FIRST TRIUMPH OF FASCISM: ITALY

Although Italy was one of the victorious Allies, it finished World War I with a sense of defeat. Six hundred and fifty thousand Italians had been killed and a million wounded. Italian industry slumped immediately after the war, and within a few months 10 percent of the industrial workers were unemployed. Prices rose rapidly, and wages failed to keep up. The promised pensions for wounded veterans and families of those who had been killed were long delayed. Strikes and disorders became frequent. Many of the young men were released from the armies with no trade but war and no job to go to; they drifted restlessly, prey for leaders with glittering promises.

Perhaps most important, the Italian government began to spread propaganda among the Italian people to the effect that their wartime allies were robbing them of Dalmatia, which had been promised to Italy by the secret Treaty of London (1915) in exchange for Italy's entrance into the war. The United States had never agreed to this arrangement and now would not accept it. Although the Allied leaders at the Paris peace conference remained unaffected by the storms of protest arising from Italy, the Italian people came to believe that they had shed their blood in vain.

The Rise of Mussolini

Some Italians, supporting Gabriele d'Annunzio (1863–1938), seized the city of Fiume, which had not been awarded to Italy by the Treaty of London. D'Annunzio ran his own government in Fiume until the end of 1920. In November 1920, when the Italian government signed the Treaty of Rapallo with Yugoslavia by which Fiume was to become a free city, Italian forces drove d'Annunzio out. But d'Annunzio's techniques of force, haranguing of mobs from a balcony, straight-arm salute, black shirts, rhythmic cries, and plans for conquest inspired Benito Mussolini (1883–1945), founder of Italian fascism.

Between 1918 and 1922 Mussolini created and brought to power a new political force in Italy. In October 1922 he was summoned to office by King Victor Emmanuel III (r. 1900–1946) and gradually created a totalitarian state of which he was the undisputed ruler. Suppressing all opposition at home and threatening the peace abroad, fascist Italy served in some degree as a model for the Nazis in Germany, for the Falangists in Spain, and for totalitarian regimes in virtually all the European successor states of the Habsburg and Ottoman empires.

Mussolini was born in 1883; his father was a socialist who had begun his career as an anarchist under the influence of Bakunin. Trained as an elementary school teacher, Mussolini was a passionate socialist himself when young, and he was imprisoned for opposing the war against Turkey over Tripoli (1911). In 1912 he became editor of the most important Italian socialist newspaper, *Avanti* (Forward).

When World War I began, Mussolini opposed Italy's entry. He loathed militarism, was himself a draft dodger, and urged soldiers to desert the army. A vehement atheist, he also opposed nationalism and referred to the Italian flag as "a rag to be planted on a dunghill." But then, during 1914, Mussolini changed his mind, favoring "relative neutrality"—meaning that socialists should leave themselves free to support Italian entry if such a course seemed likely to prove favorable to them. When the Italian Socialist party refused to follow this idea, he resigned as editor of *Avanti* and founded his own newspaper, *Il Popolo d'Italia* (The People of Italy), in Milan and began to advocate an immediate Italian declaration of war on the side of the Allies. For this the Socialist party expelled him.

After his expulsion from the Socialist party, Mussolini agitated for war, speaking to groups of similarly minded young men called *fasci* (the image is of a bundle of rods, a symbol of office in the Roman Republic of antiquity). Soon after Italy entered the war in 1915, Mussolini was drafted and sent to the front. He was wounded in 1917; when out of the hospital, he again edited his newspaper. In 1919 Mussolini founded the first *fasci di combattimento* (groups for combat).

During 1920 and 1921 the industrialists and landowners, squeezed by taxation and inflation, became bitter. Shopkeepers and tradespeople wanted the street disorders to end and food prices to be regulated. Professionals and others with fixed incomes suffered, as prices and wages went up and salaries lagged behind. The police grew tired of suppressing local disorders; ex-servicemen, insulted by anarchists and communists for their war records, grew more patriotic.

All these groups identified those they did not like as Bolsheviks. After a series of fascist-socialist street fights and riots, these anti-Bolsheviks began to look to Mussolini's fascist bands to defend their interests. D'Annunzio's defeat left Mussolini as his natural heir. The leftist opposition to Mussolini was further weakened when the communists split off from the Socialist party in 1921. The fascists grew enormously, from 30,000 in May 1920, to 100,000 in February 1921, to more than 300,000 in October 1922. Liberal parliamentary leaders of Italy felt that the fascist bands were teaching the left a useful lesson, so they encouraged army officers to issue rifles, trucks, and gasoline to the fascists and assigned officers to command their operations. The police were encouraged to look the other way during disorders started by fascists, and local judges were urged to help by releasing arrested fascists. Mussolini's newspaper was circulated free to the soldiers in the army.

A campaign of terror now began against the socialists and Christian Democrats, as the fascist squadrons

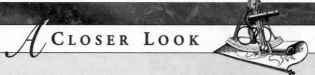

A CLOSER LOOK

Comparing Fascism and Communism

Speaking at Naples in October 1922, Mussolini recognized that at the heart of fascism, as at the heart of nationalism, lay a vital lie—a belief held so strongly that it had the force from truth. He referred to this belief as a myth that, if universally accepted, would become reality:

We have created our myth. The myth is a faith, it is passion. It is not necessary that it shall be a reality. It is a reality by the fact that it is a good, a hope, a faith, that it is courage. Our myth is the Nation, our myth is the greatness of the Nation! And to this myth, to this grandeur, that we wish to translate into a complete reality, we subordinate all the rest.*

This "vital lie" illustrates one of the differences between fascism and communism: The former places far greater emphasis on the nation. But there are many other differences as well. In a 1964 article in *World Politics*, Klaus Epstein, a professor of history at Brown University, explained the differences as follows:

It is a notorious fact that fascist regimes take on many of the features of the Communist enemy they combat (for example, the use of terror, concentration camps, single-party dictatorship and destruction of man's "private sphere"). Yet it is important to keep communism and fascism sharply distinct for analytical purposes. They differ in their avowed aim, ideological content, circumstances of achieving power, and the groups to which they appeal. Fascists seek the greatness of the nation (which need not exclude a racialist internationalism); Communists, the world triumph of the working class (which need not exclude a strong Russian nationalism). Fascists stand in avowed revolt against the ideas of 1789; Communists pose as the heirs and executors of those ideas. Fascism has a miscellaneous and heterogeneous ideological content; communism prides itself upon the all-embracing logic of its [world view]. Fascism glories in an irrational world of struggle; communism aims ultimately at a rational world of peace and harmony (which does not preclude some pride in the violent methods required prior to the final achievement of utopia). Fascism has triumphed in some highly developed communities through abuse of the electoral process (e.g., Germany); communism typically achieves power through military occupation or successful use of violence in backward communities demoralized by prolonged military strains (Russia, Yugoslavia, China). Fascism has special appeal to the lower middle class and sections of the frightened upper class; communism generally finds its greatest resonance in sections of the working class, peasantry, and intelligentsia. Fascism consists, finally, of a series of national movements lacking centralized overall direction, while communism is a centralized world movement in which each member party obeys the orders emanating from a single center.**

---

* Quoted in Herbert Finer, *Mussolini's Italy* (New York: Universal, 1935), p. 218.

** Klaus Epstein, "A New Study of Fascism," *World Politics,* XVI (1964), in *Reappraisals of Fascism,* ed. Henry A. Turner, Jr. (New York: Franklin Watts, 1975), p. 10.

---

cruised around Italy in trucks, burning down labor union offices, newspaper offices, and local Socialist party headquarters and attacking labor leaders and local antifascist politicians. An estimated two thousand people—antifascist and fascist, police and bystanders—died by violence between October 1920 and October 1922. Mussolini had demonstrated that control over sources of information, rapid mobility, and the use of terror and intimidation could effectively silence opposition in a divided and frightened society.

In the elections of May 1921 Mussolini and thirty-four other fascists were elected to the Chamber of Deputies (the lower house of the Italian parliament), along with ten Nationalists, their political allies. The momentum of the fascist movement was now too great to be slowed down. Fascism became a political party in November as a necessary step in the drive for power. Too late, the government became alarmed and tried to take measures against the fascists, but the squadrons were too strong, the police too accustomed to collaborating with them, and the liberal politicians themselves as yet unaware that a tightly directed armed mob could take over the state.

In the fall of 1922 it was clear that the army would not resist a fascist coup in Rome. When a decree of martial law was presented to the king, he refused to sign it, probably influenced by his knowledge that the army would not fight the fascists and that his cousin would gladly take his crown. The cabinet resigned, and on October 29 the king telegraphed Mussolini in Milan to come to Rome and form a cabinet. Mussolini arrived by sleeping car the next morning, just ahead of thousands of followers.

w/ Zukow Black Art

Mussolini was a dramatic public speaker who used theatrical gestures to reinforce his points. As this photograph shows, he made full use of the relatively new medium of radio to reach a mass audience.
UPI/Bettmann Newsphotos

Fascist Dictatorship and Corporative State

Mussolini gradually turned his premiership into a dictatorship. A month after coming to office he obtained dictatorial powers that were supposed to last only until the end of 1923. Although the constitution theoretically remained in force, Mussolini took over the administration. He created a fascist militia almost 200,000 strong, which owed complete allegiance to him. He enlarged the regular army and required its members to take an oath of personal loyalty to him. Before his dictatorial powers expired, he secured from parliament a new electoral law that provided that the political party that received the largest number of votes in a general election, if that amounted to at least one quarter of the vote, should automatically receive two thirds of the seats in parliament; the rest of the seats would be divided proportionately. In the election of April 1924 the fascists polled 65 percent of the votes cast; the first all-fascist cabinet was then appointed. Meanwhile, local administration was made secure by the appointment of fascist prefects and sub-prefects in the provinces.

Early in 1924 the leader of the opposition to Mussolini, the socialist Giacomo Matteotti (1885–1924), published *The Fascists Exposed*, in which he reviewed the outrages the fascists had committed on their way to power. It seemed probable that further revelations were in store, exposing some of Mussolini's cabinet members as corrupt. On June 10 Matteotti was murdered; the crime was traced to Mussolini's immediate circle. This scandal rocked Italy, and for a moment it seemed that

Mussolini would fall. But he dismissed from office those who were involved and pledged himself to restore law and order. In protest against the murder and the failure to vigorously prosecute those who had participated, opposition deputies walked out of the Chamber. Since they were then refused readmission, they thereby played into Mussolini's hand. In effect, the murder of Matteotti marked the beginning of Mussolini's true dictatorship.

Next, a series of new laws tightened control over the press, abolished secret societies like the Freemasons (whom Mussolini had loathed since his socialist youth), and replaced all elected local officials by men appointed from Rome. Opponents of the regime were arrested and exiled to islands off the Italian coast. Early in 1926 Mussolini was empowered to govern by decree. Three attempts on his life led to a new law providing the death penalty for action against the king, the queen, or Mussolini. All opposition political parties were abolished in that same year, and the Fascist party was left as the only legal political party in Italy.

The Italian state and the Fascist party were increasingly coordinated. Mussolini was both the *duce* (leader) of the fascists and the *capo di governo* (chief of state). At one time he held eight cabinet posts simultaneously. The members of the Fascist Grand Council, about twenty of the highest party functionaries, all appointed by Mussolini, held all the significant posts in the administration that were not held by Mussolini himself. In 1928 the Grand Council was given important constitutional duties: preparing the lists of candidates for election to the Chamber, advising Mussolini, and proposing changes in the constitution or in the succession to

THE WRITTEN RECORD

Ten Commandments for Fascists

By 1934 the fascists had pressed their campaign to the point where they could announce a set of ten "secular commandments" that emphasized their militarism, the idea of the garrison state, and the cult of the personality of *il Duce* (the Leader).

1. Know that the Fascist, and in particular the soldier, must not believe in perpetual peace.
2. Days of imprisonment are always deserved.
3. The nation serves even as sentinel over a can of petrol.
4. A companion must be a brother, first, because he lives with you, and secondly because he thinks like you.
5. The rifle and cartridge belt, and the rest, are confided to you not to rust in leisure, but to be preserved in war.
6. Do not ever say, "The Government will pay . . ." because it is *you* who pay; and the Government is that which you willed to have, and for which you put on a uniform.
7. Discipline is the soul of armies; without it there are no soldiers, only confusion and defeat.
8. Mussolini is always right.
9. For a volunteer there are no extenuating circumstances when he is disobedient.
10. One thing must be dear to you above all: the life of the Duce.

From *The Social and Political Doctrines of Contemporary Europe*, ed. Michael Oakeshott (Cambridge: Cambridge University Press, 1939). p. 180.

the throne. The Grand Council thus became a kind of third house, above the other two houses of parliament, the Senate and the Chamber.

Mussolini believed that the interests of labor and capital should be made to harmonize with the overriding interests of the state, and representation should be based on economic interests organized in "syndicates." Such an idea was not new. The French syndicalist Georges Sorel had already argued in this vein. But Sorel believed in syndicates of workers only. Mussolini believed in producers' syndicates as well as workers' syndicates.

In 1925 fascist labor unions were recognized by employers as having the sole right to negotiate labor contracts. In April 1926 the state officially recognized producers' and workers' syndicates in each of six areas—industry, agriculture, commerce, sea and air transport, land and inland waterway transport, and banking—plus a syndicate of intellectuals, making thirteen syndicates in all. Each syndicate could bargain and reach contracts and could assess dues upon everyone engaged in its economic field, irrespective of membership in the syndicate. Strikes and lockouts were forbidden.

In 1928 a new electoral law provided for a new Chamber of Deputies with 400 instead of 560 members. The national councils of the thirteen syndicates could nominate a total of 800 candidates. Each syndicate had a quota, half to be selected by the employers and half by the employees. Cultural and charitable foundations could nominate 200 more candidates. When the total list of 1,000 was completed, the Fascist Grand Council could either select 400 of them, or strike out names and add names of its own, or even substitute an entirely new list. The voters would then vote in answer to the question: "Do you approve of the list of deputies selected by the

Fascist Grand Council?" They could vote yes or no on the *entire* list, but they could not choose from among the candidates. If a majority voted yes, the list was elected; if not, the procedure was repeated. Universal suffrage was abolished, even for this very limited form of election. Payment of a minimum tax or dues to a syndicate was required of each voter; women could not vote.

In 1938 the impotent Chamber of Deputies replaced itself with the Chamber of Fasces and Corporations. Nothing remained of the old parliamentary constitution that had been set up by Cavour except the Senate, nominally appointed by the king but actually subservient to Mussolini. This new structure was the *corporative state* (so named because each of the seven syndicate areas had been declared a corporation). But despite much oratory by fascist sympathizers about the corporative state and its virtues, it appears that the new bodies never had much to do with running the economic or political life of Italy, which remained firmly under the direction of the fascist inner bureaucracy.

During the 1930s the fascist version of the planned economy made its appearance in Italy. A concerted effort was launched to make Italy more self-sufficient in agriculture. In 1932 official figures reported that domestic wheat production could supply 92 percent of the nation's normal needs, and the drive was enlarged to include other cereal products. The government subsidized steamship and air lines, encouraged the tourist trade, and protected Italian industries with high tariffs on foreign products. Marshes were drained and land was reclaimed. Enormous sums were spent on public works, and great strides were made in hydroelectric power. Public transportation became efficient.

The state also reached into the life of the individual at almost every point. Though Italy was overpopulated,

Mussolini made emigration a crime. Beginning in 1926 he pursued a vigorous probirth policy, encouraging people to marry and have the largest possible families by reducing their taxes, extending special loans, taxing bachelors, and extending legal equality to illegitimate children. He hoped in this way to swell the ranks of his armies and to strengthen his claim that Italy must expand abroad. Textbooks in the schools, books in the libraries, professors in the universities, plays on the stage, and movies on the screen became vehicles of fascist propaganda. The secret police endeavored to discover and suppress all opposition movements.

In 1929 Mussolini settled the Roman question—that of the annexation of the Papal States without the pope's consent—by entering into the Lateran Pact with the papacy. This treaty recognized the independence of Vatican City, over which the pope had temporal power. Mussolini also recognized Catholicism as the state religion. He gave up the power to tax contributions to the church or the salaries of the clergy, and paid $105 million to compensate the papacy for Italian confiscation of papal territories. On its part, the church agreed not to engage in politics in its publications.

Yet although many church officials viewed the fascist movement sympathetically, difficulties arose after these agreements had been concluded. In an encyclical, Pope Pius XI (r. 1922–1939) indicated his disapproval of Mussolini's economic policies and of the corporations as "serving special political aims rather than contributing to the initiation of a better social order." Mussolini now charged that the church's Catholic Action Clubs were engaged in politics and dissolved them. The pope denied the charges and denounced the Fascist party's practice of monopolizing the time and education of the young. In 1931, however, a further agreement was reached, and the clubs were reopened.

Mussolini's wish to re-create the glories of ancient Rome plus domestic population pressures impelled him to undertake a policy of adventure in the Mediterranean, which he called *Mare Nostrum* (Our Sea) as a sign that he was the heir to the Caesars. In time he would send settlers into Libya, which he called Italy's Fourth Shore. This policy of expansion began in 1923, after five Italians working for the League of Nations were assassinated as they marked out the new frontier between Albania and Greece. Mussolini thereupon bombarded and occupied the Greek island of Corfu, just off Albania, and refused to recognize the League's right to intervene until British pressure led to a settlement of the matter.

Most important, Mussolini alienated Italy from its earlier allies, France and Britain. His policy of adventure led him to military aggression in Ethiopia, in Spain, and in Albania. It drove him into an alliance—a Rome-Berlin axis—with another fascist, Adolf Hitler, and led him to voice loud claims against the French for Corsica, Tunisia, Nice, and Savoy. Mussolini's grandiose fascist ideology spurred Italy to win a larger degree of self-sufficiency, to rebuild its seaports, and to create a merchant fleet and navy.

The Italian alliance with Germany was also responsible for the official adoption of anti-Semitism in 1938.

With only seventy thousand Jews, most of whom had long been resident, Italy had no "Jewish problem" of the kind Hitler was alleging existed in Germany. Italian Jews were entirely Italian in their language and sentiments and were distinguished from other Italians only by their religion. Many of them were prominent fascists; many others were antifascist. There was no widespread sympathy in Italy for the government's adoption of Hitler's racial policies, yet Hitler's dominating influence led Mussolini to expel Jews from the Fascist party and to forbid them to teach or to attend school, to intermarry with non-Jews, or to obtain new licenses to conduct business.

Opportunistic, ruthless, quick-witted, Mussolini loved power, but he also genuinely cared about Italy. Although the lives of many improved under his regime, the lives of others were brutalized. Many commentators then and since would find him simple, a man floundering beyond his depth; other commentators would find him shrewd, careful, and well aware of how his unpredictable yet emotionally exciting personality could make him attractive to many and keep him firmly in power. The policies that carried him into war in alliance with Germany in 1940 would end in his death in 1945, hanging upside down on a communist gallows, his personality still an enigma.

THE WEIMAR REPUBLIC: GERMANY, 1918–1933

Two days before the armistice of November 11, 1918, the German Social Democrats proclaimed a republic. On July 31, 1919, this republic adopted a constitution drawn up by a national assembly at Weimar; it is therefore known as the Weimar Republic. The republic passed through three phases: a period of political threats from both left and right and of mounting economic chaos, from 1918 to the end of 1923; a period of political stability, fulfillment of the Versailles Treaty requirements, and relative economic prosperity, from 1924 to late 1929; and a period of economic depression and mounting right-wing power, from late 1929 to January 1933, when Hitler became chancellor.

Years of Instability, 1918–1923

Germans were shocked by their defeat in 1918. The military authorities who ran the German Empire during the last years of the war had not revealed to the public the extent of German reverses on the battlefield, and no fighting had taken place on German soil. Now the defeated and demoralized armies came home. Schooled in reverence for the military, the Germans could not grasp the fact that their armies had lost the war. Moreover, the Allies, under the leadership of Wilson, simply refused to deal with the supreme command of the German armies. Field Marshal von Hindenburg was never required to hand over his sword to Marshal Foch or to sign the armistice. Rather, it was the civilian politicians who had to bear the disgrace. Thus, the Allies unintentionally did the German military caste a great service.

The generals declared that the German armies had never really been defeated. A legend that Germany had been "stabbed in the back" by civilians—by liberals, socialists, communists, and Jews—took deep root. This legend was widely disseminated by politicians, especially those who had a stake in the old Prussian system—monarchists, large-scale agrarians, industrialists, militarists.

In retrospect, the Allies also blundered by including the "war-guilt" clause in the Treaty of Versailles. The German signatories were obliged to acknowledge what none of them believed (and what subsequent historians would disprove): that Germany alone had been responsible for the outbreak of the war. The clause made it harder for the German public to acknowledge defeat, to sweep away the militarists, and to create a republic. Instead, it led many Germans to devote their energies to denying war guilt, to attack the enemies who had saddled them with the charge, and to await a chance to show by force that the generals had been right—that Germany had been betrayed from within.

Threats to stability from the left strengthened the anti-republican forces of the right. Responsibility for launching the republic and for preventing disorder fell upon the "majority socialists," made up of Social Democrats and right-wing Independent Socialists, and led by a Social Democrat, Friedrich Ebert (1871–1925). A moderate group, the Social Democrats made no attack on agrarian property, and they allowed the Junkers to keep their estates and the social and political position that went with them. The Social Democrats concluded collective bargaining agreements with the industrialists that guaranteed an eight-hour day, rather than trying to nationalize German industry.

But the left wing of the Independent Socialists and the communist Spartacists agitated for proletarian revolution on the Russian pattern. Unable to operate effectively through soviets, the left tried to stage a revolution in the winter of 1918–1919, and Ebert called in the army to stop it. The generals used not only regular units but also the newly formed volunteer units, or Free Corps, made up mostly of former professionals who were embittered by Germany's recent military defeat and who were opposed to the new democracy. To protest the use of troops, the right wing of the Independent Socialists withdrew from the government, and as civil strife continued, the communists attempted a new coup, which the troops again put down.

The old parties of imperial Germany reappeared, often with new labels. The right wing of the old Liberals now emerged as the People's party, including the more moderate industrialists, with a platform of private property and opposition to socialism. Its leader was Gustav Stresemann (1878–1929). Former progressives and left-wing Liberals now formed the new Democratic party, a middle-class, republican, democratic group, including many of Germany's most distinguished intellectuals. The

Catholic Center party reemerged with its name and program unchanged. It accepted the republic, rejected socialism, and, under pressure from its trade union members, favored social legislation; but under pressure from its right wing of aristocrats and industrialists it opposed far-reaching reform. On the right, the former Conservatives reemerged as the National People's party, or Nationalists, dominated by the Junkers as before. The Nationalists had the support of some great industrialists, most of the bureaucrats, and a substantial section of the lower middle class who did not accept the republic.

When the Germans voted for a national constituent assembly in January 1919, the parties supporting the republic won more than 75 percent of the seats, with the Social Democrats alone obtaining nearly 40 percent. The assembly met in Weimar, elected Ebert president of Germany, and formed a government that reluctantly signed the Treaty of Versailles. The assembly also adopted the new constitution. The new Germany was still a federal state, but the central government had great authority to legislate for the entire country. The president might use armed force to coerce any of the states that failed to obey the constitution or national laws. The cabinet was responsible to the lower house, or Reichstag, which was to be chosen by universal suffrage of all citizens (including women) over twenty.

The president, who was to be elected every seven years, was given considerable authority. He was empowered to make treaties, appoint and remove the cabinet, command the armed forces, appoint or remove all officers, dissolve the Reichstag, and call new elections. Furthermore, he could take any measure he deemed necessary to restore order, and might temporarily suspend the civil liberties that the constitution granted. Yet the Reichstag could order such measures repealed. The chancellor was a prime minister, with responsibility for planning policy. The powers of the president made dictatorship a real possibility, while proportional representation required that votes be cast for entire party lists of candidates, thus preventing independent politicians from obtaining office and encouraging small splinter parties to multiply.

In March 1920 a right-wing *putsch*, or "coup," drove the government from Berlin for several days. The commander of the Berlin military district, supported by Ludendorff and Free Corps leaders, had hoped to bring to power an East Prussian reactionary. Ebert defeated the putsch by calling a general strike that paralyzed Germany. An immediate outgrowth of the strike was a communist revolt in the Ruhr. To suppress the communists, German troops entered the area, which had been demilitarized by the Versailles Treaty; this action led to French military intervention and a brief occupation of the Ruhr and Frankfurt.

In April 1921 the Allies presented their bill for reparations, which totaled 132 billion gold marks. The politicians of the right favored outright rejection, while the Weimar parties realistically decided that the threat of invasion made this course impossible. Again the moderates had to take responsibility for a decision that was certain to prove unpopular. The minister for reconstruction,

Walter Rathenau (1867–1922), a Democrat, hoped that a policy of "fulfillment" might convince the Allies that Germany was acting in good faith and might in the long run lead to concessions. An intensely patriotic German, Rathenau was also a Jew, and he attracted the particular venom of anti-Semitic nationalist orators.

Secret terrorist groups on the right now began a campaign of assassination. In August 1921 they murdered a Catholic Center politician who had signed the armistice, a leading moderate. The assassins escaped through Bavaria, and when one of them was caught, the courts acquitted him. When the League of Nations awarded to Poland a substantial area of the rich province of Upper Silesia containing many Germans, the right grew still angrier. Rathenau was killed in June 1922 by men who believed that by murdering a Jew they could avenge the "betrayal" of the German army. In the wake of this assassination, Stresemann's People's party moved away from the Nationalists, who were viewed as tainted with murder, and worked with the Center and Democrats.

The political maneuvers to meet the increasing threat from the right were largely nullified, however, by the economic problem posed by steadily growing inflation, which in 1922 and 1923 reached unprecedented extremes. Inflation is a complicated economic phenomenon still not well understood, but the single chief cause for the runaway inflation in Germany was probably the failure of the German government to levy taxes with which to pay the expenses of the war. The imperial regime had expected to win and to make the losers pay Germany's expenses by imposing huge indemnities. So it had paid for only about 4 percent of the war costs through taxation. As defeat neared, the government borrowed more and more money from the banks. When the loans came due, the government repaid them with paper money that was not backed by gold. Each time this happened, more paper money was put into circulation, and prices rose; each rise in prices led to a demand for a rise in wages, which were paid with more paper money. The inflationary spiral was underway. Instead of cutting purchasing power by imposing heavy taxes, the government permitted buyers to compete with each other for goods that were in short supply, thus causing prices to shoot up even further, and speeding up the whole process of inflation.

During these months the German government begged for a moratorium on reparations payments and for a foreign loan. But the French were unwilling. They had already spent billions to rebuild those parts of France that the Germans had devastated during the war, and they wanted the Germans to pay the bill. As a guarantee, the French demanded the vitally important German industrial region of the Ruhr. Despite British opposition, the French occupied the Ruhr in January 1923, after the Germans had defaulted on their reparations payments. The French declared their intention to run the mines and factories for their own benefit, and thus make up for the German failure to pay reparations.

The Germans could not resist with force, but they declared the occupation of the Ruhr illegal and ordered its inhabitants to embark on passive resistance—to refuse to work the mines and factories or to deliver goods to the French. This order the people of the Ruhr obeyed. Local tension in the occupied area became serious when the French took measures against German police and workers, and German Free Corps members undertook guerrilla operations against the French. But the most dramatic result of the French occupation of the Ruhr was its effect upon the already desperate German economy. Not only was the rest of Germany cut off from badly needed goods from the occupied area, but the Ruhr inhabitants were idle at the order of the German government and had to be supported at government expense. The printing presses ran off ever-increasing amounts of ever-more-worthless marks. The exchange rate went from thousands of marks to the dollar to millions, to billions, and by December 1923, well up into the trillions.

Such astronomical figures become meaningful only when we realize their personal and social consequences. A student who set off one afternoon for the university with a check for a year's tuition, room, board, and entertainment found, when he arrived the next morning, that the money would only pay for the journey. Lifetime savings were rendered valueless; people were seen trundling wheelbarrows full of marks through the street to buy a loaf of bread. Those who lived on fixed incomes were utterly ruined, and the investments of the middle classes were wiped out. Real estate took on fantastic value, speculation flourished, and some speculators made fortunes.

For the German worker, inflation did not mean the liquidation of savings, because the worker usually had none. But it did mean a great drop in the purchasing power of wages, so that the worker's family suffered from hunger and cold. Since the financial position of the labor unions was destroyed, they could no longer help the workers, who deserted the unions. The great industrialists, however, gained from the inflation, in part because it crippled the labor unions, but still more because it wiped out their own indebtedness and enabled them to absorb small competitors and build giant business combines.

Politically, therefore, inflation greatly strengthened the extremists of both right and left. The middle classes, although pushed down to the economic level of the proletariat, would not support the working-class parties of Social Democrats or Communists. Disillusioned, they would not support the moderate parties that bolstered the republic—the People's party, the Center, and the Democrats. So the Nationalists, and Hitler's Nazis above all, reaped a rich harvest of the frightened and the discontented. The hardships of the working class led many workers to turn from the Social Democrats to the Communists. But Soviet Russian constraints on the leaders of the German Communist party prevented any concerted revolutionary drive until the fall of 1923, by which time poor organization and strong governmental repression had doomed their efforts.

With the country seething in crisis, Stresemann became chancellor in the fall of 1923 and proclaimed that Germany could not keep up passive resistance in the Ruhr. He ordered work to be resumed and reparations

By the autumn of 1923 the German mark was virtually worthless. Here a German housewife lights her breakfast fire with several million marks, since kindling costs more than their total value.

UPI/Bettmann Newsphotos

to be paid once again. Political troubles multiplied when the right refused to accept the new policy. At the height of the agitation in Bavaria, Adolf Hitler broke into a right-wing political meeting in a Munich beer hall and announced that the "national revolution" had begun. At gunpoint he tried to get other local leaders to support him in a march on Berlin. Troops broke up the demonstration with only a few casualties. Hitler was allowed to use his trial as a propaganda platform for his ideas and was sentenced to the minimum term for high treason—five years. He spent only eight months in jail, during which time he wrote large portions of *Mein Kampf* (My Battle), soon to be the bible of the Nazis.

In 1921–1922 a new element had emerged among the welter of right-wing organizations in Bavaria. This was the National Socialist Party of the German Workers (called *Nazi* as an abbreviation of the word National) led by Hitler. Born in 1889, the son of an Austrian customs official, Hitler seems always to have felt bitter and frustrated. In 1907 he had been rejected by the Vienna Academy of Fine Arts, and he became an odd-job man, hovering on the edge of starvation. His hatred of the Jews began during these years. Because Karl Marx himself had been of Jewish origin and because many Viennese Jews were socialists, Hitler associated socialism

with the Jews and saw both as responsible for his personal troubles.

Hitler drew support for his anti-Semitism from several nineteenth-century theorists. The French count Joseph Arthur de Gobineau (1816–1882) had laid a pseudoscientific foundation for theories of "Nordic" and "Aryan" supremacy. One of Gobineau's most influential readers was the German composer Richard Wagner, whose son-in-law, the Englishman Houston Stewart Chamberlain (1855–1927), wrote *Foundations of the Nineteenth Century*, which glorified the Germans and assailed the Jews. Chamberlain opposed democratic government and capitalism. Thus he provided Hitler with a potent mixture of racism, nationalism, and radicalism.

Hitler moved to Munich in 1913. In 1914 he enlisted in the German army, fought through the war as a corporal, and then returned to Munich. While employed as a political education officer for the troops, Hitler discovered a small political group that called itself the German Workers' party, which espoused nationalism, militarism, and radicalism. Hitler joined the party in 1919 and soon proved himself to be far abler than any of his colleagues. He urged intensive propaganda to unite all Germans in a greater Germany, to eliminate Jews from political life, to guarantee full employment, to confiscate war profits, to nationalize trusts, to encourage small business, and to grant land to the peasants.

Hitler was a charismatic orator with almost hypnotic gifts in capturing a crowd. By 1921 he had made himself the absolute leader, the *Führer* (compare with *Duce*) of the Nazi party, and he had strengthened himself by founding the SA (originally meaning "Sports Division," but eventually *Sturmabteilung*, or "Storm Troops"), brown-shirted units copied from the black shirts of Italy and recruited largely from the Free Corps. These storm troopers wore armbands with a swastika emblem, patrolled mass party meetings, and performed other services for the leader. Hitler's closest collaborators included Hermann Göring (1893–1946), a wartime aviator who had shot down twenty Allied planes, who took on the job of giving the SA a military polish; Rudolf Hess (1894–1987), principal propagandist; and Alfred Rosenberg (1893–1946), a Baltic German distinguished for his fanatical hatred of Jews and Bolsheviks, the first editor of the party newspaper. They and others worked out the basic theories of Nazism, including several elements imitative of Marxism, of which the most important was the conviction that bourgeois politicians could not be expected to rescue the German people from their degradation because they could not unite mind and violence in one organization. This Hitler was determined to do, as he felt the Marxists had done, by uniting ideology and terror in one movement.

Economic Recovery, 1924–1929

Communist disorders and the Nazi beer hall putsch marked the last phase of the inflation period. Shortly before Hitler's move, Stresemann had given extraordinary financial powers to two tough-minded centrists, Hans Luther (1879–1962), minister of finance, and Hjalmar

Schacht (1877–1970), banker and fiscal expert. All printing of the old currency was stopped. A new bank was opened to issue new marks, which were assigned the value of the prewar mark. The new currency was backed not by gold but by an imaginary "mortgage" on all Germany's agricultural and industrial wealth. One trillion of the inflated marks equaled one of the new. Simultaneously, rigorous economies were put into effect in every branch of the government, and taxes were increased. The public protested loudly, but the measures remained in force until they had the intended effect. The cure for inflation produced serious hardships, too. Prices fell, and overexpanded businesses collapsed. Unemployment rose sharply, wages stayed low, and workers labored long hours.

During 1924 the Allies at last helped end the crisis in Germany by formulating the Dawes Plan, named for Charles G. Dawes (1865–1951), an American financier and vice-president under Calvin Coolidge (1872–1933). The plan recommended the evacuation of the Ruhr by the French, the establishment of a special bank to receive reparations payments, a gradual increase in annual payments for the first five years, and an international loan to finance the German deliveries in the first year. The Nationalists attacked these proposals as a scheme to enslave Germany to foreign masters, and in the Reichstag elections of May 1924 they scored impressive gains, as did the Nazis and the Communists, while moderate parties suffered. But a coalition managed to win acceptance of the Dawes Plan in August by promising the Nationalists seats in the cabinet. When new elections were held in December, the Nazis and Communists sustained losses and the Social Democrats and moderates gained. Early in 1925 a Center—People's party—Nationalist coalition took office. Though Germany had moved appreciably to the right, foreign policy remained in the conciliatory hands of Stresemann, who was foreign minister through all governments between November 1923 and his death in October 1929.

During these less-troubled years, economic recovery proceeded steadily, until in 1929 German industrial output exceeded that of 1913. First-rate German equipment, coupled with superb technical skill and systematic adoption of American methods of mass production, created a highly efficient industrial machine. This "rationalization" of industry increased production, but led to overborrowing and some unemployment. *Vertical trusts*—which brought together in one great corporation all the parts of an industrial process from coal- and iron-mining to the output of the finished product—and *cartels*—associations of independent enterprises that controlled sales and prices for their own benefit—became characteristic of the German system. Emphasis was always on heavy industry, which meant that a big armaments program might assure continued prosperity. Throughout, reparations were paid faithfully, with no damage to the German economy.

In 1925, after President Ebert died, a presidential election was held in which three candidates competed. The Catholic Center, the Democrats, and the Social Democrats all supported the Center candidate. The

Nationalists, People's party, and other right-wing groups supported Field Marshal von Hindenburg, then seventy-seven years old. The Communists ran their own candidate and thus contributed to the election of Hindenburg, who won by a small plurality. Until 1930 Hindenburg acted fully in accord with the constitution, to the distress of most of the nationalist groups. Though domestic issues of this period aroused great heat, they were settled by democratic process. In the elections of 1928 the Social Democrats were returned to power; prosperity had encouraged moderation and growing support for the republic.

In foreign affairs, this period saw a gradual increase in German participation in the system of collective security. In 1925 Germany signed the Locarno treaties, which took the French armies out of the Rhineland in return for a neutral zone and a frontier guaranteed by Britain and Italy, and set up machinery to arbitrate disputes between Germany and its neighbors. These treaties did not, however, guarantee Germany's frontiers with Poland and Czechoslovakia. In 1926 Germany was admitted to the League of Nations. In 1928 Germany accepted the Kellogg-Briand Pact, which outlawed aggressive war.

In 1929 a new reparations plan named after another American, Owen D. Young (1874–1962), chairman of the committee that drew it up, substantially reduced the total originally demanded by the Allies. The Young Plan also established lower rates of payments than those under the Dawes Plan and allowed the Germans a greater role in their collection. In June 1930 the Rhineland was evacuated by the Allies, four years ahead of the date set by the Treaty of Versailles.

Germany and World Depression, 1929–1933

But the economic depression had begun to knock the foundations out from under prosperity and moderation. An economic depression is a sharp and deep decline in trade and general prosperity. In the worldwide depression of 1873 to 1896, prices had fallen, agricultural distress had intensified—made worse in Europe by bad harvests followed by wet summers and by competition from Argentine and Australian meat and Canadian and American grain—and banks had collapsed, especially in Austria and France. While scholars do not agree on the long-range causes of the depression, it was apparent to all that the new "world slump" of 1929–1934, while short, was extremely intense and was particularly destructive of middle-class confidence in the United States, Germany, and Austria.

The depression had, in fact, already begun before the Wall Street stock market crash in October 1929, for agriculture had declined as overproduction and poor distribution brought prices down and as speculation on the stock market had led to general financial recklessness. American banks now withdrew their funds from Europe. The Austrian Kredit-Anstalt, the largest commercial bank in Austria, was made bankrupt in 1931 when the French, themselves in dire economic need, withdrew short-term credit. In Germany a shortage of capital and foreign credits quickly curtailed industrial production, leading to a decline in exports and a reduced need for transportation (especially shipping), which triggered further widespread unemployment.

The need for economic planning seemed evident, and since totalitarian movements of both left and right generally already had a commitment to such long-range planning, those most hurt by what quickly became known as the Great Depression turned increasingly toward these movements and away from a free-market economy. For capitalists, the Bolshevik solution was not acceptable; for nationalists, convinced that the depression had been caused by unsound economic practices in another country, one solution was tariffs. Since fascist movements advocated economic nationalism and centralized state planning for the economy, they quickly gained new adherents. In Germany unemployment insurance cushioned the first shock for the workers; the lower middle classes, painfully recovering from the period of inflation, had no such barrier between them and destitution. Their desperation helped Hitler, whose fortunes during the years of fulfillment had fallen low. Meanwhile, however, Hitler was preparing the instruments of force, especially by creating the *Schutzstaffel* (Defense Force, or SS), an elite, black-shirted guard of honor under the direction of Heinrich Himmler (1900–1945). The SS membership requirements emphasized "racial purity," and its members would become the nucleus for the *Gestapo*, or "secret police."

The government fell in 1930 over a disagreement on unemployment insurance benefits. Hindenburg appointed as chancellor Heinrich Brüning (1885–1970), a member of the Catholic Center party, and instructed him to shape an emergency cabinet not restricted by party allegiance. President Hindenburg, now eighty-two, had fallen under the influence of General Kurt von Schleicher (1882–1934), an ambitious and clever political soldier who had schemed his way into the president's favor. Hindenburg wanted to rule by decree, as the constitution authorized him to do in an emergency. By failing to pass Brüning's economic program, the Reichstag gave Hindenburg the opportunity he wanted.

A presidential decree proclaimed the new budget. When the Reichstag protested, Hindenburg dissolved it and called new elections for September 1930. Nazis and Communists fought in the streets and both gained greatly at the expense of the moderates. The Nazis' Reichstag representation rose from 12 to 107 and the Communists' from 54 to 77. Brüning had to carry on against the wishes of the electorate; supported only by Hindenburg, he, too, now turned authoritarian.

Political matters were now fueled almost exclusively by the deepening economic crisis. To avoid a new government in which Nazis would participate, the Social Democrats decided to support Brüning. When the Reichstag met, Nazis and Communists created disorder on the floor but voted together against government measures. These measures passed only because the Social Democrats voted for them. In 1931 Brüning tried to

arrange an Austro-German customs union to coordinate the tariff policies of the two countries and help them fight the depression without affecting their political sovereignty. Whether such an arrangement between two countries that were both suffering from unemployment would actually have succeeded cannot be surmised; the impulse for Germany and Austria to unite politically might not have proved overpowering. In any case, the project raised in the minds of the Allies, especially the French, the specter of a "greater Germany," and the scheme was vetoed by the World Court.

Nazis, Nationalists, the veterans' organization of the Steel Helmets (*Stahlhelm*), the Junkers' Agrarian League, industrialists, and representatives of the former princely houses now formed a coalition against Brüning. This coalition had great financial resources, mass support, and private armies in the SA, the Stahlhelm, and other semi-military organizations. Because the left was split, nothing stood between this new right-wing coalition and political victory except Hindenburg, who controlled the army. Early in 1932 Hitler was invited to address a meeting of coal and steel magnates, whose financial support he won. Though some of Hitler's followers were now impatient for a new putsch, he curbed them, believing that the Nazis could come to power legally.

In the presidential elections of March 1932, Hitler ran as the candidate of the Nazis, and Hindenburg as the candidate of the Center, Social Democrats, and other moderate parties. Hitler polled 11,338,571 votes, and Hindenburg polled 18,661,736, four tenths of a percent short of the required majority. In the runoff election, the Nationalists backed Hitler, whose total rose to 13,400,000, as against Hindenburg's 19,360,000. The eighty-four-year-old marshal reelected as the candidate of the moderates was, however, no longer a moderate himself, but the tool of the Junkers and the military.

Responding to pressure from the state governments, Brüning and Hindenburg tried to ban the SA and SS, while Schleicher orchestrated protests against such a ban. Feeling he had been ill advised, Hindenburg told his chancellor he would not sign any further emergency decrees, and Brüning resigned. Schleicher persuaded Hindenburg to appoint Franz von Papen (1879–1969), a rich Catholic nobleman and a member of the extreme right wing of the Center, and he installed a cabinet composed of other noblemen.

The Center, however, disavowed Papen, who had the support of no political party or group. The Nazis temporarily tolerated him because he agreed to lift the ban on the SA and SS. But in foreign policy, Papen succeeded where Brüning had failed, for the Allies scrapped the Young Plan and required Germany to pay only 3 billion gold marks into a fund earmarked for general European reconstruction.

On July 31, 1932, new elections for the Reichstag took place, called by Papen on the assumption that the Nazis had passed their peak, that their vote would decrease, and that they would then cooperate in the government. However, on July 20 Papen had dismissed the government of Prussia, where there had been over five hundred confrontations between storm troopers and those they saw as their enemies, on the grounds that it could not maintain public order. This played into the hands of the Nazis, who won 230 seats to become the biggest single party in the Reichstag; the Communists gained also, chiefly at the expense of the Social Democrats. The Democrats and the People's party almost disappeared.

Papen had failed. He now wanted to take some Nazis into the government, but the Nazis demanded the chancellorship, which Hindenburg was determined not to hand over to Hitler. Papen decided to dissolve the Reichstag and call new elections. By repeating this process, he hoped to wear down Hitler's strength each time, until he brought Hitler to support him and accept a subordinate place. Papen also put pressure on the industrialists who had been supporting Hitler, and Nazi funds began to dry up, leaving Hitler seriously embarrassed. The election of November 6, 1932, bore out Papen's expectations. The Nazis fell off from 230 seats to 196; and although the Communists gained substantially, Papen, too, won some support.

Thus emboldened, Papen designed a constitutional change that would have moved the Weimar Republic even closer to the policies of the corporative state: power was to be returned to the hands of the propertied elite. Schleicher persuaded Hindenburg that the plan was naive and tried desperately to form a new majority. Failing, he stepped down, leaving the way clear for Hitler as the only person with a program and public support. Hitler demanded the chancellorship for himself. Papen consented, provided Hitler undertook to govern in strict accord with parliamentary procedure. Papen was to be vice-chancellor, and still thought he could dominate the government, since only three of its eleven ministers would be Nazis. He therefore persuaded Hindenburg to accept Hitler as chancellor. But Papen underestimated Hitler. Though Hitler swore to Hindenburg that he would maintain the constitution, he did not keep his oath. The Weimar Republic was doomed from the moment Hitler became chancellor on January 30, 1933.

GERMANY UNDER HITLER, 1933–1939

Hitler's first weeks in power were devoted to transforming his chancellorship into a dictatorship. He dissolved the Reichstag and called for new elections. During the campaign, opponents of the Nazis were intimidated by violence and threats and were denied radio time and free use of the press. On the night of February 27, a fire mysteriously broke out in the Reichstag building. When he heard the news, Hitler exclaimed, "Now I have them," for he knew that the fire could be blamed on the communists. By the next morning, four thousand Communist party members were arrested, and by noon Hitler had persuaded Hindenburg to suspend the basic rights of the citizenry

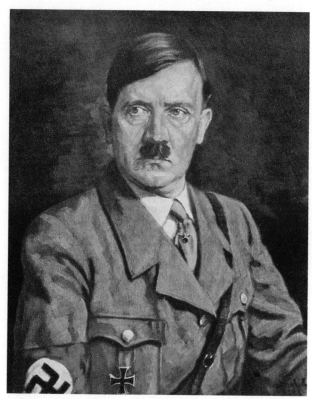

A portrait of Adolph Hitler in 1933.
The Bettmann Archive

during the emergency. Arrest, indefinite detention, and terror were now embraced by the state. Germany was, in effect, a dictatorship.

Nonetheless, in the election of March 5 the Nazis won only 44 percent of the votes, which gave them 288 seats in the Reichstag. Using the SA as a constant threat, Hitler bullied the Reichstag. Except for 94 Social Democrats (the Communists were denied their seats), all members voted for an Enabling Act on March 23, suspending the Weimar constitution.

Dictatorship

Now Hitler could act as he chose, unimpeded by the laws. He instituted a ministry of propaganda under Josef Goebbels (1897–1945). He stripped the state governments of their powers and appointed governors from Berlin who could override the state legislatures. When Hindenburg died in August 1934, Hitler became president as well as chancellor, but he preferred to use the title *Der Führer*. This new move was approved by a plebiscite in which Hitler obtained 88 percent of the votes.

Political parties that opposed Hitler were forced to dissolve. The government banned Communists and Socialists (May 1933); the Nationalists dissolved themselves (June 1933); the government put an end to the Catholic parties (July 1933) and all monarchist groups (February 1934). The Stahlhelm was incorporated into the Nazi party. In July 1933 the Nazis were declared to be the only legal political party in Germany.

The appeal of the Nazis to the German people lay partly in their denunciation of the "disorderly" parliamentary system; a strong man who got things done struck a responsive chord in the public. In the elections of November 1933, there were no opposition candidates, 92 percent of the electorate voting Nazi, and there were only two non-Nazi deputies in a chamber of 661. As in fascist Italy and communist Russia, youth groups fed the party, which soon had a powerful regional organization all over Germany and among Germans abroad.

Within the Nazi party itself, however, a difficult situation was created by those who had believed Hitler's more radical pronouncements on social and economic questions. Many of these Nazis were concentrated in the SA, whose members, most of them from the lower classes, were also distressed by how Hitler had treated their organization. The SA had made possible his rise to power, but it was now an embarrassment to Hitler, no longer quite respectable, and certainly not in favor, as were the SS and especially the army.

On June 30, 1934, Hitler ordered and personally participated in a "blood purge." Ernst Röhm (1887–1934), founder and leader of the SA, was shot, and so were as many as a thousand others, including the head of Catholic Action, and Schleicher and his wife. Hitler justified the murders, and house arrest for Papen, by declaring that the SA was planning a putsch and that the opposition and all who offended public morality (for Röhm was a homosexual) must be crushed. After June 1934 there was no effective opposition to Hitler left.

Racism and Political Theory in Practice

Soon after the passage of the enabling law, Hitler struck the first of his many blows against the Jews. In a country of approximately 60 million people, practicing Jews were less than 1 percent of the population. The Jews had become leading members of the professions and the arts and had made outstanding contributions to German culture. Since most Jews were patriotic Germans, many of them would probably have become Nazis if they had been permitted to. Instead, anti-Semitic doctrines required their ruthless elimination.

Racism now became part of state policy. The businesses and professions of the Jews were boycotted, and Jews were forbidden to hold office. In the "Nuremberg laws" of September 15, 1935, a Jew was defined as any person with one Jewish grandparent; all such persons were deprived of the rights of German citizenship. Intermarriage between Jews and non-Jews was forbidden as "racial pollution." Jews might not fly the national flag, write or publish, exhibit paintings or give concerts, act on stage or screen, teach in any educational institution, work in a bank or a hospital, enter any of the government's labor or professional bodies, or sell books or antiques. They were not eligible for unemployment insurance or charity. Many towns and villages refused to permit Jews to live inside their precincts.

Arms raised, faces white with fear, a group of Jews is led off by Nazi storm troopers during the destruction of Warsaw. This photograph, taken from an SS commander's report to his superior officer, was introduced at the Nuremberg trials as evidence of Nazi brutality.

UPI/Bettman Newsphotos

DEUTSCHE STUDENT

FÜR FÜHRUNG UND GEFOLGSCHAFT
IN DER MANNSCHAFT DES NSD-STUDENTENBUNDES

The Germans idealized the blond, blue-eyed "German student" as a physical and intellectual type. A handsome Nordic youth holds the flag while the poster urges Germans to join Hitler's National Student Organization for the glory of the Führer and the *volk*—the "pure strain" of German people.

Library of Congress

In November 1938 a Jewish boy of seventeen, driven to desperation by the persecution of his parents, shot and killed a secretary of the German embassy in Paris. Two days later organized German mobs looted and pillaged Jewish shops all over Germany, burned and dynamited synagogues, and invaded Jewish homes to batter the occupants and steal their possessions. Known as the *Kristallnacht*, this event made it quite clear even to foreign observers that Germany was officially pursuing anti-Semitism. The state then compelled the Jews to restore the damaged properties and pay a fine. Jews were forced to take special names, to wear yellow Stars of David, and to belong to a Reich "Union of Jews." Measures designed to drive the Jews into ghettos were but the prelude to their physical extermination in gas ovens during World War II.

Enthusiasm for "racial purity" led to the study of eugenics, to the promotion of widespread athleticism and the cult of physical health, and to the elevation of Hitler into a virtual messiah. Blond, blue-eyed, ideal "Nordic

types" were urged to mate with each other early and to have many children. By the time the average woman was twenty-four years old she was expected to be a mother. To keep the race pure, sterilization was introduced, supposedly to prevent inherited disease. Medical experimentation of horrifying cruelty and of no scientific value was practiced during the war on human beings of "inferior" races—Jews, Poles and other Slavs, and gypsies. These practices were the direct outcome of Nazi "eugenic" legislation.

In foreign affairs, German racism justified the conquest of all territory inhabited by Germans. In addition, the doctrine of *Lebensraum* ("living space" for the expanding "Nordic race") justified the incorporation of non-German areas. Hitler declared that what the Germans needed they were entitled to take, since they were a superior people.

Some German intellectuals had looked back with longing upon the Holy Roman Empire of the Middle Ages, the first Reich. Now that the war had ended the second Reich of William II, they hoped to create a third one, incorporating the old territories, no matter who now lived in them. This is the meaning of Hitler's use of the term "Third Reich" to describe the Nazi state, which he proclaimed would last a thousand years. A "scientific" basis for the Lebensraum theory was supplied by the teachers of "geopolitics," chief among whom was Karl Haushofer (1869–1946), who declared that Britain and France were decadent; that small powers must disappear; that Germany must expand ruthlessly, occupying the "heartland" of Eurasia, and dominate the world. Another school of thought argued that Germany's future lay in an alliance with the Soviet Union, in which its inexhaustible work force would be joined with Germany's industrial output and military techniques.

Hitler revamped the German judicial system, abandoning traditional legal principles and substituting "folk" justice, which, Hitler said, totally subordinated the individual to the people (*volk*). People's courts, to which Hitler appointed the judges, were established (May 1934) to try all cases of treason, a crime that was now logically extended to include many lesser offenses against "the people." Concentration camps were established for enemies of the state, who could be executed without appeal. The Gestapo (*Geheime Staatspolizei*, Secret State Police), formally established in April 1933 in Prussia, was extended to all of Germany in 1934, with a free hand in opening private correspondence, tapping wires, and spying on citizens.

All economic life was brought under the regime. In agriculture, the Nazis aimed at self-sufficiency and at control of the peasantry. The Junkers were protected, and no effort was made to divide their vast estates. In 1933 a special law protected smaller farms against forced sale and attachment for debt, an act that won the small farmer to Hitler. But the government determined the production required of farms, and fixed farm prices, wages, and fees for distributing farms products. Unused land was put under cultivation, and citizens had to grow vegetables in greenhouses in preparation for war.

In industry, Hitler proclaimed a four-year plan in 1933 and a second one in 1936. The first was aimed chiefly at economic recovery. Labor camps for men and women helped decrease unemployment, as did rearmament and public works. The second plan was designed to prepare for war. Output of raw materials was increased, and the materials were distributed first to armament and other war industries; labor was allocated in a similar way; prices and foreign exchange were controlled. The state also built strategic highways (*Autobahnen*), the first modern expressways, for the rapid movement of goods and troops.

The Nazis abolished all labor unions in 1933 and employers' associations in 1934. To replace them, a Labor Front was established to include all wage earners, salaried persons, professionals, and employers. Strikes and lockouts were forbidden. Workers were assured of jobs as long as they accepted the system. The Labor Front was also a spy organization, constantly on the alert for anti-Nazis in the factories; it could reduce their pay, fire them, or put them in jail.

As the second four-year plan went into effect, the workers became less mobile. They had work books detailing their past training and positions, and they could not get a new job unless the state decided it was more suitable. All graduates of secondary schools had to register with employment authorities, and men and women of working age could be conscripted for labor. Just before the outbreak of war, all agricultural and mining workers and certain industrial workers were frozen in their jobs. Meanwhile, the big cartel became the all-pervasive feature of German industrial organization—a system of profitable monopoly under state control. The minister of economics authorized controlled plant expansion, imports and exports, fixed prices and established costs, and allocated raw materials.

These processes of *Gleichschaltung* (coordination) were applied throughout German life, including education and the arts. Göring is said to have remarked, "When I hear anyone talk of culture, I reach for my revolver." Hitler's own artistic views were extremely simple: He denounced most modern art as non-Aryan. The school curriculum, especially history, had to be taught in accord with the Nazi doctrine of "blood and soil." Nazi racial doctrine, the great achievements of Germany's illustrious past, the military spirit, and physical fitness were the cornerstones of the new education.

The Christian churches, both Protestant and Catholic, were a problem for the Nazis. Extremists among Hitler's followers favored a return to a mystical paganism and the old German gods celebrated by Wagner's operas. Hitler himself, born a Catholic, had once declared that Germany was his only god. Yet power politics required him to come to terms with the churches, which still commanded the allegiance of most Germans. In the hope of avoiding state domination, the Lutheran ministry in 1933 organized a national synod, which the Nazis almost immediately took over by appointing their own bishop. The efforts of extremist Nazis to purge the Bible and to abandon the crucifix led to discontent.

In July 1933 Hitler and the Vatican reached a concordat guaranteeing freedom of worship and permitting

Powerful leaders have often exploited the human craving for the dramatic, and Hitler, above all others, was a master. "Vaults of light"—great beams that dazzled the eye and gave nighttime crowds a sense of unity and awe—were used skillfully by him to climax many Nazi mass meetings.

AP/Wide World Photos

religious instruction in the schools. Catholics were to be allowed to form youth groups and to appoint professors of theology. But the Nazis did not live up to these terms. On the other hand, the Catholic church found much to oppose in the teachings to which Catholic children were exposed in the Hitler youth groups; in 1937 a papal encyclical attacked National Socialism. Still, Catholics supported Hitler's territorial ambitions, and the church took an ambiguous position on his treatment of the Jews. In general, Hitler carefully avoided a direct clash with the churches, and they remained silent.

AUTHORITARIANISM IN IBERIA

In the troubled years between the wars, nondemocratic authoritarian governments emerged not only in Italy and Germany but also in Spain, in Portugal, in the successor states to the Habsburg Empire (except Czechoslovakia), and in the other states of eastern and southeastern Europe.

Spain

In 1918 Spain was still a nation in which local loyalties contested with national sentiment. Catalonians and Basques continued to work toward separate states, and though the Catholic religion had united Spaniards against Muslims in the Middle Ages and against Protestants in the sixteenth and seventeenth centuries, the church was no longer so strong a force for unity. While Spain at times approached self-sufficiency in agriculture and industrial raw materials, its soil was poor and its farming antiquated, and the rural areas were suffering from over-population. Poverty was commonplace, and the masses were increasingly discontented with their national leadership.

Spain had also suffered from a lowered sense of prestige. It had lost its empire to the United States in the short war of 1898, and in World War I it had remained neutral. The government had done little to improve agriculture, and farmers in Catalonia could not gain access to sufficient land to support themselves. There were many small landholdings and many large estates, but no middle ground for prosperous farmers. Spanish sheep, once prized, declined in competition against Australian and Argentine flocks, while Spanish grain from Castile cost more in Barcelona because of inadequate transport than did foreign grain from North America. By World War I Spain had no export market to itself in Europe except for cork, which was benefiting the area already best developed, intensifying the sense of disparity among the various regions.

Spanish industry was dominated by textiles. But production was largely confined to the home market, where the consumption of cotton was no higher than in eastern Europe. Though it was the most important part of Spain's industries, the cotton industry was unable to stimulate further stages of industrialization, as had occurred in France, Switzerland, and Belgium. Moreover, what small prosperity the textile industry brought to Spain was largely confined to Catalonia. Spain had little coal for heavier industry, and the iron industry in Bilbao used British coal until 1914. Spain also had to rely on British investments for its railroads, and both rails and rolling stock had been imported until the war curtailed them. In short, Spain had not achieved a breakthrough into modern industrialism, the level of agriculture remained low, the gap between the rich and the poor was very great, and there seemed little prospect of change.

When the Spaniards turned to revolutionary doctrine, it was chiefly to Bakunin's anarchist beliefs and later to Sorel's syndicalism. Anarchism (and anarcho-syndicalism) really took hold only in Spain. The industrial workers of Catalonia and the peasants of Andalusia who no longer attended Mass were anarchist; they wanted to destroy the state utterly rather than conquer and use it. Yet anarchism, which at its peak numbered a million to a million and a half adherents, could only harass governments, not overthrow them. The movement was deeply puritanical and anti-Catholic; its adherents burned churches and killed priests. A wave of assassinations put into office General Miguel Primo de Rivera (1870–1930), who proclaimed martial law, dissolved the Cortes (the Spanish parliament), imposed censorship, drove liberal critics into exile, and ruled from 1923 until 1930.

In the 1930s Spain also had a growing Marxist Socialist party with its own federation of trade unions. The socialists drew their first strength from the urban workers of Castile and from the mining and steel-producing centers of the north. When Spain became a republic in 1931, the socialists added many rural supporters, and the party numbered a million and a quarter in 1934. The socialists were moderates who had refused to adhere to the Comintern in 1920, but who had joined the revived Second International a few years later. Dissidents founded a small Communist party, and Catalonians had their own socialist organization.

On the extreme right was Carlism, founded in the nineteenth century as a movement supporting Don Carlos (1788–1855), a pretender to the throne. Carlism called for the restoration of the Inquisition, regarded the railroad and the telegraph as sources of evil, and rejected the Copernican theory of the universe. Carlism had its lower-class followers, too, especially among the rebellious farmers of Navarre in the north.

King Alfonso XIII (r. 1886–1931) ruled over Spain until 1931. Based on electoral corruption and intimidation, the "liberals" and "conservatives" in his governments took orderly turns at office, and the real power rested with the local political bosses. These alternating governments occupied the political center, which in fact was quite small. Once the prosperity brought by Spain's wartime neutrality was over, the clashes between the anarchists, the left, and the far right led many people to consider General Primo's rule necessary.

After Primo's resignation and death, King Alfonso restored the constitution. Municipal elections in April

Generalissimo Francisco Franco
UPI/Bettmann Newsphotos

lost the republicans many supporters, especially among the lower clergy.

The anarchists expressed their dissatisfaction by major uprisings (1933), which the government put down by force. The jails were full, and unemployment was as high as ever. Repression of the anarchists lost the republic much support on the left but failed to gain it support from the right, which came back strongly in the elections of November 1933 as the largest party in parliament. Now the government helplessly swung to the right, and much of its previous legislation, especially laws affecting the church and the working classes, remained unenforced.

The socialists now competed with the anarchists for the loyalty of Spanish workers. Strikes and disorders multiplied. In October 1934 the socialists called a general strike to protest the inclusion of fascists in the government. Catalonia, declaring itself an independent republic, was deprived of its autonomy. The coal miners of the Asturias region in the north staged a revolt, backed by both anarchists and socialists, which was put down with the loss of more than three thousand lives. Intense hatred was directed at the new minister of war, Francisco Franco (1892–1975).

Thus the right lost its public support; and now the left, under the impact of the Asturias uprising and influenced by the Comintern, united in a Popular Front for the elections of February 1936. For the first time anarcho-syndicalists went to the polls and voted for republicans, socialists, and communists. The left won a considerable victory, in part because it promised an amnesty for those involved in past outbreaks. Instead of entering the cabinet, Francisco Largo Caballero (1869–1946), leader of the left-wing socialists, now played at insurrection, acting as if he intended to seize power. Yet he had no forces of his own. The route to power for left-wing revolutionaries could open up only if the right attempted a military coup, if the government then armed the workers to fight it, and if the workers then won.

Simultaneously in 1936 the *Falange* (Phalanx) emerged on the right—a party founded in 1932 by the son of Primo de Rivera, José Antonia (1903–1936), a fascist who did not oppose agrarian reform or other socialist programs. The Falange used as its symbol a bunch of arrows and a yoke, and as its slogan *Arriba España* (Upward, Spain). Its program called for national expansion in Africa, the annexation of Portugal, and the building of an empire in South America. It established youth groups and a private army, as Hitler had done. Although the Falange polled relatively few votes in the election of 1936, it worked with army, monarchist, clerical, and Carlist groups for a counterrevolution. Everyone knew a military coup against the government was in the offing. In July it came, under the leadership of General Franco.

The Spanish Civil War (1936–1939) was the first act in the conflict that was to ripen into World War II. The right-wing rebels made Franco chief of staff in November 1936. Decisively aided by Germany and Italy, Franco's forces pushed on to eventual victory, capturing the republican strongholds of Madrid and Barcelona in 1939. During the war the functions of the weak republican

1931 were viewed as a plebiscite on the monarchy. They resulted in a victory for the republicans, representing the lower middle classes of the towns, small traders, intellectuals, teachers, and journalists. The king left the country without abdicating. Elections to a constituent assembly in June 1931 brought in a republican-socialist majority, and in November the assembly forbade the king's return and confiscated his property. Spain was now a republic.

The assembly adopted a new constitution in December. This provided for a responsible ministry, a single-chamber parliament, and a president to be chosen by an electoral college consisting of parliament and an equal number of electors chosen by popular vote. It was clear that the army would rise against the republic whenever the opportunity presented itself, and that the army would have the support of the church and the large landowners. Moreover, although the republic temporarily had socialist support, it did not have the support of the anarchists. Danger threatened from both the right and the left.

The first crisis arose over a new constitutional law defining the position of the church. The assembly rejected a moderate proposal that would have preserved the church as a special corporation with its own schools and might have proved acceptable to most Catholics. Instead, the assembly's law was more extreme; it closed church schools and ended state grants to the church after two years. This government were usurped by a series of workers' committees, and then a Popular Front regime under Largo Caballero came to office in September 1936. In government territory terror reigned, at first the work of anarchists, and after their suppression, of the communists, who—with the Soviet Union behind them—ruthlessly worked against their rival leftist parties in the regime.

For all its fascist trappings, the Franco regime still depended after the war upon the same classes that had supported the Spanish monarchy—the landowners, the army, and the church. The new regime was opposed by the poor in city and country, but the fear of a new civil war, which lay heavily on all classes, prevented open opposition. Franco ruled until his death in 1975.

Portugal

In the meantime, any Falangist designs on Portugal were blocked by the rise to power there of another dictator, Antonio de Oliveira Salazar (1889–1970). Portugal had participated in World War I, and the republican regime, which had driven King Manoel II (r. 1908–1910) from the country in 1910, governed until forced from office by a military coup in 1926. Two years later Salazar, a professor of economics at the University of Coimbra, became minister of finance on the condition that he be granted sweeping powers over the economy. Salazar's concern for sound finance during the world economic crisis won him many supporters, and in 1932 he became prime minister and progressively used his office to turn his party into the only legal option open to the Portuguese people. Salazar sought to remain neutral in the growing European conflict, and his authoritarian rule did not generate effective opposition from the political left. Not until 1968 did Salazar step down, Portugal's empire overseas still virtually intact but his dictatorship increasingly inert.

Successor States to the Habsburg Empire

The triumphs of the authoritarian right in eastern Europe are explained partly by the lack of a parliamentary tradition; partly by the failure to solve grievous economic problems; and partly by a popular fear of Bolshevism. Perhaps as important as all the other factors put together was the initial impression created by the successes of Mussolini and Hitler. The way to succeed, at least after 1935, seemed to be to put on a uniform, proclaim a doctrine of extreme nationalism, and launch a war of nerves against opponents and neighbors.

Austria

The Austria that was left at the end of World War I had a population of about 8 million, about 2 million of whom lived in Vienna. Long the market for an enormous

hinterland and the supplier of industrial finished goods to the agricultural provinces, Vienna was now cut off from its former territories by political boundaries and tariff walls. Between 1922 and 1925 Austrian finances were under direct League of Nations supervision. But one possible road to economic salvation—union of Austria with Germany—though voted by the assembly of the new Austrian republic in March 1919, was forbidden on political grounds by the Allies.

These two problems, economic survival and union with Germany, were complicated by the continuation of the political struggle between Social Democrats and Christian Socialists. The Social Democrats were a moderate Marxist party with strong urban support. The Christian Socialists were a conservative clerical party with a mass following in the countryside and among the urban lower middle classes and counted many priests among their leaders.

In the mid-twenties the two hostile parties organized private armies: the Christian Socialists, the *Heimwehr* (Home Guard), and the Social Democrats, the *Schutzbund* (Defense League). The Social Democrats governed Vienna, introducing measures for relief and for workers' housing, paid for by taxes on the rich. After 1930 Mussolini supported the Christian Socialists, who grew more fascistic in their outlook. The failure of Brüning's plan for a customs union with Germany and the related collapse of the Vienna Kredit-Anstalt bank increased tensions, and in September 1931 the Heimwehr tried its first coup, which failed. Efforts in 1932 to organize a Danubian economic cooperation scheme were rendered futile by Italian and German opposition. After Hitler came to power in early 1933, many Christian Socialists openly became Nazis.

The Christian Socialist chancellor, Engelbert Dollfuss (1892–1934), however, strove to curb the Nazis. To this end he suspended parliamentary government in March 1933. He forbade the wearing of uniforms by political groups and tried to expel Nazi agitators. In retaliation, Hitler made it prohibitively expensive for German tourists to visit Austria. In the face of Nazi-inspired disorder, Dollfuss banned the Nazi party. But he also attacked the Social Democrats, banning all parties except his own Fatherland Front, a union of all right-wing groups except the Nazis. A raid on Social Democratic headquarters precipitated a workers' riot. The government then bombarded the workers' new apartment houses in which the Social Democratic leaders had taken refuge breaking the Social Democratic party but alienating the workers and uniting them in opposition to the regime. Dollfuss had to depend on Italy to support him against the threat from Hitler.

Dollfuss's successor, Kurt von Schuschnigg (1897–1981), was committed to the same policies. But Mussolini now needed Hitler's support for Italian aggression in the Mediterranean. Schuschnigg tried to concentrate armed power in his own hands rather than those of the Heimwehr, and strove to come to an understanding with France and its allies to replace the tie with Italy. But he failed. To stave off violence he had to make concessions to Artur Seyss-Inquart (1892–1946), leader of the

Pablo Picasso's *Guernica* was an impassioned protest against the Spanish Civil War. Painted in 1937, it was kept from his native country by the artist and exhibited only in the United States until after the death of Franco, when it was finally returned to Spain as a gesture of healing between the opposing sides.

Austrian Nazis, and then humble himself by visiting Hitler at his Bavarian mountain retreat at Berchtesgaden. Hitler threatened full-scale invasion, and Schuschnigg agreed to bring the Nazi party into the Fatherland Front and to pursue the foreign policy goals dictated by Hitler. He also agreed to make Seyss-Inquart minister of the interior, the ideal position from which to direct a coup.

When Schuschnigg returned to Vienna, he realized that he had surrendered Austria, and he called for a sudden plebiscite, desperately hoping to win working-class support. This forced Hitler's hand. On March 2 he invaded Austria, even against the advice of Seyss-Inquart, and proclaimed his native land a province of Germany. In April a plebiscite on Austrian union with Germany—called *Anschluss*—resulted in a 99.75 percent yes vote.

Hungary

On October 31, 1918, eleven days before the armistice, Count Michael Károlyi (1895–1955) became prime minister of Hungary, after that country had severed its ties with Austria. One of the richest of the great landed nobles, Károlyi was also a democrat. He proved his sincerity as a social reformer by handing over the fifty thousand acres of his own estate to be divided among the peasants and by preparing a land-reform law. He made every effort to reach a compromise with the national minorities, but they were past the point where they would trust any Magyar. The French commander of the Allied armies demanded that the Hungarians withdraw from Slovakia. In March 1919 Károlyi resigned in protest over the loss of Transylvania.

Thwarted nationalism now combined with a growing radicalism. A left-wing government took over, dominated by Béla Kun, Lenin's agent. He put through revolutionary nationalization decrees and installed a soviet political system. The Allies could not tolerate a Bolshevik in Hungary. The Romanians invaded and drove Kun out; during 1919 and part of 1920 they occupied the country and stripped it of everything they could move. Meanwhile, under French protection, a counterrevolutionary government returned to Budapest, where Admiral Nicholas Horthy (1868–1957), a member of the gentry, became regent and chief of state in March 1920.

The Treaty of Trianon (June 1920) confirmed Hungary's losses: a small strip of land to Austria, Transylvania to Romania, Slovakia to Czechoslovakia, and Croatia and other Serb and Croat territories to Yugoslavia. Thereafter, the most important political issue for the ruling groups in Hungary was *revisionism*, the effort to revise the treaty and get these lands back.

Most Hungarians, however, cared relatively little about revisionism. Hungary had no land reform; the great estates remained intact; nobles and gentry remained dominant. Behind a screen of parliamentary government, an authoritarian dictatorship governed the country. It was helped by a swollen bureaucracy, and it became more and more fascist in character as the years went by. In 1927 a treaty with Italy began a close association between Hungary and Mussolini.

While the Italians supplied arms to the Hungarians, Hitler favored Hungarian revisionism along with his own. After Austria had fallen to Hitler, he had Hungary in his pocket, and when he broke up Czechoslovakia in March 1939, the Hungarians seized the extreme eastern portion, Ruthenia, and a small part of Slovakia. To pursue revisionism, the Hungarians had to follow Hitler, since he alone offered the opportunity to redraw the map as they felt it should be drawn; so before war broke out, they had withdrawn from the League of Nations and had enacted anti-Semitic laws in the Nazi pattern. But because Hitler needed Romania, too, he would not give the Magyars all of Transylvania. Thus Hungary remained dependent on German foreign policy.

Yugoslavia

In the new kingdom of the Serbs, Croats, and Slovenes, proclaimed in December 1918, there came together for the first time in one state the former south-Slav subjects of Austria and Hungary with those of the former kingdom of Serbia. This was in most respects a satisfactory state from the territorial point of view; revisionism therefore was not a major issue. But the new state had to create a governmental system that would satisfy the aspirations of each of its nationality groups. Over this problem democracy broke down and a dictatorship was established.

Serbian political ambitions had helped to start World War I. The Serbs were more numerous than Croats and Slovenes together, and many Serbs felt that the new kingdom should be the "greater Serbia" of which they had so long dreamed. Orthodox in religion, using the Cyrillic alphabet, and having experienced and overthrown Ottoman domination, Serbs tended to look down on the Croats. Roman Catholic in religion, using the Latin alphabet, and having opposed Germans and Magyars for centuries, Croats tended to feel that the Serbs were crude Easterners who ought to give them a full measure of autonomy within the new state. The battle lines were drawn: Serb-sponsored centralism against Croat-sponsored federalism.

The Croats, under their peasant leader Stephen Radić (1871–1928), boycotted the constituent assembly of 1920, and the Serbs put through a constitution providing for a strongly centralized state. Both sides refused to compromise, and when Radić was murdered on the floor of parliament in June 1928, a crisis arose that ended only when King Alexander II (r. 1921–1934) proclaimed a royal dictatorship in January 1929. Alexander tried to settle the problem by erasing old provincial loyalties. There would be no more Serbia or Croatia but new administrative units named after the chief rivers that ran through them. The whole country was renamed Yugoslavia, as a sign that there were to be no more Serbs and Croats. But it was still a Serbian government, and the Croats would not forget it. Elections were rigged by the government, and all political parties were dissolved.

One result was to strengthen Croat extremists who had wanted an independent Croatia in the days of the Habsburgs, and who now combined this demand with terrorism, supported by the enemies of Yugoslavia—Italy and Hungary. The Croat extremists were called *Ustashi* (Rebels), and they were assisted by Mussolini. The Ustashi were deeply involved in the assassination of Alexander during a state visit to France in October 1934. Under the regency of Alexander's cousin, the dictatorship continued. In the summer of 1939 an agreement was reached with the Croats that established an autonomous Croatia. But by then it was too late, for war soon engulfed the Balkans.

OTHER AUTHORITARIAN REGIMES IN EUROPE

In Poland Marshal Jósef Pilsudski led a military coup against the democratic government on May 11, 1926, and headed a military dictatorship that became ever more authoritarian. This coup was made possible largely because of the government's failure to grant concessions to national minorities and to deal with the economic problems left by the war and occupation. The violent hatreds that divided the political parties made Pilsudski's rule even easier. Once he had won power, he turned to the great landowners and big industrialists, building his government on their support and on that of his military clique.

In Romania entrenched corruption in political life coexisted with the parliamentary system. There was also widespread anti-Semitism, which was adopted as the chief program of the Iron Guard, a Romanian Nazi party. Green-shirted and wearing small bags of Romanian soil around their necks, the Guard began to assassinate moderate politicians early in the 1930s. Economic dislocation and peasant misery, brought about by the worldwide agricultural depression, strengthened the Guard and other fascist groups. To head off a Guardist coup, King Carol II installed his own fascist dictatorship in 1938. Although the Guardist leaders were "shot while trying to escape," Romania could not avoid German pressure. After Hitler had acceded to the Soviet seizure of Romanian Bessarabia and northern Bukovina and had given Hungary northern Transylvania (August 1940), Carol had to abdicate, and Hitler's man took over with Iron Guard support.

In Bulgaria the threat of communism was a serious problem. Moreover, Bulgaria, like Hungary, was revisionist because of its failure to gain the Macedonian territory given by the peace treaties to Yugoslavia and Greece. The issue was made more intense by the presence of thousands of Macedonian refugees, who tended to join revolutionary terrorist societies. Bulgaria, which had no serious minorities problem, no rich landowners, no aristocracy, and no great industries, nonetheless produced political hostilities even more violent than those in countries where economic inequality prevailed. In 1920–1923 a peasant politician, Alexander Stambolisky (1879–1923), gave the country a period of reasonably popular government. But even he curbed the press as he fought both Macedonian terrorists and communists. His imposition of high income taxes alienated the bourgeoisie. In 1923 right-wingers murdered him and installed a strongly authoritarian regime. From then on communist plots, bombings, and

Macedonian terrorist strife racked the country. After 1930 the Italian marriage of King Boris (r. 1918–1943) led to ties with Mussolini. In 1934 a military coup brought to power a group of army officers who installed a dictatorship of their own. But in 1936 King Boris imposed a royal dictatorship, which lasted until his death during World War II.

In Greece between the wars, the main issues were whether the country should be a monarchy or a republic and how to overcome the economic difficulties caused by the transfer of 1.25 million Greeks from Turkey. On the constitutional question, the Greeks wavered, voting for a monarchy in 1920, for a republic in 1924, and for a monarchy again in 1935. Economic dislocation strengthened communism among the refugees and in labor groups. Political instability was chronic, and the interwar period was punctuated by a series of coups, some by republican generals, some by monarchists, all more or less authoritarian. The last of these, General John Metaxas (1871–1941), was the most fascist. Metaxas, who became dictator in August 1936, abolished political parties, instituted censorship and political persecution of his opponents, and launched a program of public works.

None of these regimes in eastern Europe was fascist in the truest sense of the term. In Italy and Germany the regimes rested on considerable popular support, at least initially, even though that support was kept alive by propaganda. In eastern Europe, on the other hand, the dictatorships rested on the police, the bureaucracy, and the army, and not on the support of the masses. Most dictators (Franco was an exception) developed the cult of self. In most, but not all, Jews were systematically persecuted. While the various fascist states had much in common, they also differed, so that fascism never became the universalized international movement that communism explicitly aspired to become.

THE SOVIET UNION

During the twenty-year crisis between the wars, an already authoritarian government in the Soviet Union became a virtual dictatorship, though one of the left rather than the right. From 1914 Russia had been in turmoil. By 1921, with the end of civil war, industry and agriculture were crippled, distribution was near a breakdown, and the communist regime was perilously near the loss of public support. When a large-scale anarchist revolt broke out early in 1921 and could not be suppressed until mid-1922, Lenin remarked that he was, at last, deeply frightened for the future of his nation. The mutiny of sailors at the Kronstadt naval base near Petrograd in March 1921 triggered a change in policy. The mutineers called for "soviets without communists," to be chosen by universal suffrage and secret ballot, for free speech and assembly, for the liberation of political prisoners, and for the abolition of grain requisitioning. Trotsky now realized that the proletariat itself was opposing the dictatorship of the proletariat and needed educating. Furthermore, revolution was not going to sweep Europe; Russia would be, for a time, an island of revolutionary socialism in a sea of capitalism. Trotsky therefore used the Red Army to crush the rebellion while Lenin embarked upon economic reform.

The Kronstadt mutiny led directly to the adoption of the New Economic Policy (always referred to by its initials as the NEP). But the underlying reason for the shift was the need for reconstruction, which seemed attainable only if militant communism were at least temporarily abandoned. It was also necessary to appease the peasants and to avert any further major uprisings. Finally, since the expected world revolution had not taken place, the resources of capitalist states were badly needed to assist Russian reconstruction.

Under NEP the government stopped requisitioning the peasants' entire crop, taking instead only what was needed to meet the minimum requirements of the army, urban workers, and other nonfarm groups. The peasants still had to pay a very heavy tax in kind, but they were allowed to sell the remainder of their crop. Peasant agriculture became in essence capitalist once more, and the profit motive reappeared. The whole system tended to help the rich peasant grow richer and to transform the poor peasant into a hired, landless laborer.

Elsewhere in the economy, under NEP the state retained what Lenin called "the commanding heights"—heavy industry, banking, transportation, and foreign trade. In domestic trade and in light industry, however, private enterprise was once more permitted. This was the so-called private capital sector of the economy, in which workers could be paid according to their output and factory managers could swap some of their products for raw materials.

Lenin himself described NEP as a partial return to capitalism and urged the communists to become good at business. Yet NEP was never intended as more than a temporary expedient. Lenin believed that it would take a couple of decades before the Russian peasant could be convinced that cooperative agriculture would be the more efficient. He also argued that a temporary relaxation of government intervention would increase industrial production and give the Russians a useful lesson in managerial skills.

Economic recovery was indeed achieved. By 1928 industrial and agricultural production was back at prewar levels. But NEP was bitterly disliked by leading communists, who were shocked at the reversal of all the doctrines they believed in. Those who took advantage of the opportunities presented by the NEP were often persecuted in a petty way by hostile officials, who tried to limit their profits, tax them heavily, and drag them into court on charges of speculation. The kulak had essentially the same experience. Thus the government often seemed to be encouraging private enterprise for economic reasons and simultaneously discouraging it for political reasons.

The Struggle for Power:
Stalin against Trotsky, 1921–1927

Lenin died in January 1924. During the last two years of his life, he played an ever-lessening role. Involved in the controversy over NEP was also the question of succession to Lenin. Thus an answer to the questions of how to organize industry, what role to give organized labor, and what relations to maintain with the capitalist world depended not only upon an estimate of the actual situation but also upon a guess as to what answer was likely to be politically advantageous. From this maneuvering the secretary of the Communist party, Joseph Stalin, was to emerge victorious by 1928.

The years between 1921 and 1927, especially after Lenin's death, saw a desperate struggle for power between Stalin and Trotsky. Lenin foresaw this struggle with great anxiety. He considered Trotsky abler but feared that he was overconfident; he knew that Stalin had concentrated enormous power in his hands through his role as party secretary, and he feared that he did not know how to use it. When he learned that Stalin had disobeyed his orders in smashing the Menshevik Republic of Georgia instead of reaching an accommodation with its leaders, he wrote angrily that Stalin should be removed from his post as general secretary.

During these years Trotsky argued for a more highly trained managerial force in industry and for economic planning as an instrument that the state could use to control and direct social change. He favored the mechanization of agriculture and the weakening of peasant individualism by encouraging rural cooperatives. As Trotsky progressively lost power, he championed the right of individual communists to criticize the regime. He also concluded that only through the outbreak of revolutions in other countries could the Russian socialist revolution be carried to its proper conclusion. Only if the industrial output and technical skills of the advanced Western countries could be put at the disposal of communism could Russia hope to achieve its own socialist revolution; either world revolution must break out or Russian socialism was doomed to failure.

Trotsky's opponents found their chief spokesman in Nikolai Bukharin (1888–1938), the extremely influential editor of *Pravda*. A strong defender of NEP, Bukharin softened the rigorous Marxist doctrine of the class struggle by arguing that, since the proletarian state controlled the commanding heights of big capital, socialism was sure of success. This view was not unlike the gradualist position taken by western European Social Democrats. Bukharin did not believe in rapid industrialization; he favored cooperatives, but opposed collectives in which (in theory) groups of peasants owned everything collectively. In foreign affairs, he was eager to cooperate abroad with noncommunist groups who might be useful to Russia. Thus he sponsored Soviet collaboration with China and with the German Social Democrats.

In his rise to power Stalin used Bukharin's arguments to discredit Trotsky; then he adopted many of Trotsky's policies and eliminated Bukharin. He came to

favor rapid industrialization and to understand that this meant an unprecedentedly heavy capital investment. At the end of 1927 he shifted from his previous position on the peasantry and openly sponsored collectivization, since agricultural production was not keeping pace with industry. He declared that agriculture, like industry, must be transformed into a series of large-scale unified enterprises.

Against Trotsky's argument that socialism in one country was impossible, Stalin maintained that an independent socialist state could exist. This view did not imply abandoning the goal of world revolution, for Stalin maintained that the one socialist state (Russia) would inspire and assist communist movements everywhere. But, in his view, during the interim before the communists won elsewhere, Greater Russia could still exist and expand regionally as the only socialist state. In international relations, this doctrine allowed the Soviet Union to pursue a policy of "peaceful coexistence" with capitalist states when that seemed most useful or a policy of militant support of communist revolution when that seemed desirable. Stalin's doctrine reflected his own Russian nationalism, rather than the more cosmopolitan and more Western views of Trotsky.

At the end of the civil war, Stalin was commissar of nationalities. In this post he dealt with the affairs of 65 million of the 140 million inhabitants of the new Russian Soviet Republic. He took charge of creating the new Asian "republics," which enjoyed a degree of local self-government, programs of economic and educational improvement, and a chance to use their local languages and develop their own cultural affairs, so long as these were communist-managed. In 1922 Stalin proposed the new Union of Socialist Soviet Republics as a substitute for the existing federation of republics. In the USSR, Moscow would control war, foreign policy, trade, and transport and would coordinate finance, economy, food, and labor. In theory, the republic would manage home affairs, justice, education, and agriculture. A Council of Nationalities, with an equal number of delegates from each ethnic group, would join the Supreme Soviet as a second chamber, thus forming the Central Executive Committee, which would appoint the Council of People's Commissars—the government.

Stalin was also commissar of the Workers' and Peasants' Inspectorate. Here his duties were to eliminate inefficiency and corruption from every branch of the civil service and to train a new corps of civil servants. His teams moved freely through all the offices of the government, observing and recommending changes. Although the inspectorate did not do what it was established to do, it did give Stalin control over thousands of bureaucrats and thus over the machinery of government.

Stalin was also a member of the *Politburo*—the tight little group of party bosses elected by the Central Committee, which included only five men throughout the civil war. Here his job was day-to-day management of the party. He was the only permanent liaison officer between the Politburo and the *Orgburo*, which assigned party personnel to their various duties in factory, office, or army units. Besides these posts, Stalin became general

In the early years of the revolution, Russian adults were taught to read, write, and do arithmetic.
Sovfoto

secretary of the party's Central Committee in 1922. Here he prepared the agenda for Politburo meetings, supplied the documentation for points under debate, and passed the decisions down to the lower levels. He controlled all party appointments, promotions, and demotions. He saw to it that local trade unions, cooperatives, and army units were under communists responsible to him. He had files on the loyalty and achievements of all managers of industry and other party members. In 1921 a Central Control Commission, which could expel party members for unsatisfactory conduct, was created; Stalin, as liaison between this commission and the Central Committee, now virtually controlled the purges, which were designed to keep the party pure.

In a centralized one-party state, a man of Stalin's ambitions who held so many key positions had an enormous advantage in the struggle for power. Yet the state was so new, the positions so much less conspicuous than the ministry of war, held by Trotsky, and Stalin's manner so often conciliatory that the likelihood of Stalin's success did not become evident until it was too late to stop him. Inside the Politburo he formed a three-man team with two other prominent Bolshevik leaders: the demagogue Gregory Zinoviev (1883–1936) and the expert on doctrine Leo Kamenev (1883–1936). Zinoviev was chairman of the Petrograd Soviet and boss of the Communist International;

Kamenev was Lenin's deputy and president of the Moscow Soviet.

The combination of Stalin, Zinoviev, and Kamenev proved unbeatable. The three used the secret police to suppress all plots against them. They resisted Trotsky's demands for reform, which would have democratized the party to some degree and would have strengthened his position while weakening Stalin's. They initiated the cult of Lenin immediately before his death and kept it burning fiercely thereafter, so that any suggestion for change coming from Trotsky seemed an act of impiety. They dispersed Trotsky's followers by sending them to posts abroad.

Early in 1925 Stalin and his allies forced Trotsky to resign as minister of war. Soon thereafter the three-man team dissolved; Stalin allied himself with Bukharin and other right-wing members of the Politburo, to which he began to appoint his own followers. Using all his accumulated power, he beat his former allies on all questions of policy, and in 1926 they moved into a new but powerless alliance with Trotsky. Stalin now deposed Zinoviev from the Politburo, charging him with plotting in the army. Next, Trotsky was expelled from the Politburo, and Zinoviev was ousted as president of the Comintern. In December 1927 a Communist party congress expelled Trotsky from the party and exiled him. Stalin had won.

Mobilizing the Nation, 1928–1940

The Communist party congress also ended NEP and proclaimed that the new "socialist offensive" would begin in 1928. The twelve years between 1928 and 1940 were to see massive changes in Russian life—collectivized agriculture, rapid industrialization, forced labor, great purges, the extermination of all political opposition, the building of an authoritarian state apparatus, and a return of bourgeois standards in almost every aspect of social and intellectual life.

In 1928 the failure of the peasants to deliver as much grain to the cities as was required underlined the dangers inherent in the land divisions of 1917 and in the concessions of NEP. Farm productivity on the small individual holdings was not high enough to feed the city population. Food was expensive, yet the kulaks wanted more land. Grain was hoarded. The government economic plan issued during 1928 set a figure of 20 percent of Russian farms as the maximum to be collectivized by 1933. Yet during 1929 Stalin embarked on immediate full-scale collectivization.

The government did not have the money or the credit to import food and had no governmental machinery to force farmers to part with food that they were hoarding. Therefore, the government enlisted on its side the small peasants; in exchange for their assistance in locating and turning over the kulaks' crops, the peasants were promised a place on a collective farm to be made up of the kulaks' land and equipped with the kulaks' implements. The kulaks, Stalin declared in late 1929, were to be liquidated as a class. There were about 2 million households of them, perhaps as many as 10 million people in all. Their lands were now to be totally expropriated, and at the same time, they were to be barred from joining the new collectives. Since no provision was made for them, this move turned collectivization into an economic and social nightmare.

Peasants were machine-gunned into submission; kulaks were deported to forced labor camps or to desolate regions in Siberia. In desperate revolt the peasants burned crops, broke plows, killed and ate their cattle rather than turn them over to the state, and fled to the cities. More than half the horses in all the western Soviet Union, 45 percent of the cattle, and two thirds of the sheep and goats were slaughtered. Land lay uncultivated, and over the next few years millions died of famine. As early as March 1930 Stalin showed that he was aware of the incredible mistakes he had made, and he blamed local officials who, he said, had been too eager to rush through the program. Still, 50 percent of Russian farms had been hastily thrown together into collectives during that year. Only 10 percent more were added during the next three years, so that by 1933 a total of 60 percent had been collectivized. The number rose again, and by 1939 more than 96 percent of Russian farms had been collectivized.

Just as he stepped up the frantic pace of collectivizing agriculture, so at first gradually, then suddenly, Stalin shifted to forced draft in industry also. In 1928 the era of five-year plans began, each setting ambitious goals for production over the next five years. In 1929 and 1930 Stalin appropriated ever-higher sums for capital investment, and in June 1930 he declared that industrial production must rise by 50 percent in that year. Under the first five-year plan, adopted in 1928, annual pig-iron production was scheduled to rise from 3.5 million tons to 10 million tons by 1932, but in that year Stalin demanded 17 million tons instead. It was not produced, but Stalin's demand for it was symptomatic of the pace at which he was striving to transform Russia from an agricultural to an industrial country.

Part of the reason for this rapid pace lay in the collectivization drive itself. Large-scale farming must be mechanized farming. Yet there were only seven thousand tractors in all the western Soviet Union at the end of 1928. Stalin secured thirty thousand more during 1929, but industry had to produce millions of machines plus the gasoline to run them. Since the countryside had to be electrified, power stations were needed by the thousands. Millions of peasants had to be taught how to handle machinery. But there was no one to teach them and there were no factories to produce the machinery.

Another reason for the drive to industrialize lay in the tenets of Marxism itself. Russia had defied all Marx's predictions by staging a proletarian revolution in a country that lacked a proletariat. Yet despite the communists' initial political successes, Stalin felt that capitalism had a firmer basis than communism in the Soviet Union, so long as it remained a country of peasants. And so the communists were determined to create that massive urban proletariat which did not yet exist.

The goals of the first five-year plan were not attained, although fulfillment was announced anyway in 1932. Immediately, the second plan, prepared by the state planning commission, went into effect and ran until 1937; the third was interrupted by Hitler's invasion. Each plan emphasized the elements of heavy industry—steel, electric power, cement, coal, oil. Between 1928 and 1940 steel production was multiplied by four and one-half, electric power by eight, cement by more than two, coal by four, and oil by almost three. Similar developments took place in chemicals and in machine production. Railroad construction was greatly increased, and the volume of freight carried quadrupled with the production of the country's own rolling stock. By 1940 Soviet output was approaching that of Germany. What the rest of Europe had done in roughly seventy-five years, the Soviet Union had done in about twelve.

All this was achieved at the cost of dreadful hardship, yet eyewitnesses report that many workers were as enthusiastic as if they had been soldiers in battle. Valuable machinery was often damaged or destroyed by inexperienced workers. The problems of repair, of replacement, of achieving balance between the output and consumption of raw materials, of housing workers in the new centers were unending and cost untold numbers of lives.

Administratively, the Soviet economy was run by the state. The *Gosplan* (State Planning Commission) drew up the five-year plans and supervised their fulfillment at the management level. The *Gosbank* (State Bank) regulated the investment of capital. An economic council administered the work of various agencies; its major divisions were metallurgy and chemistry, defense, machinery, fuel and power, agriculture and procurements, and consumer goods. Production trusts controlled the mines, blast furnaces, and rolling mills; these were the so-called *combinats*, or "great production complexes." In each plant the manager was responsible for producing the quota set within the maximum cost allowed.

The social effects of this economic program were dramatic. Urban population rose from about 18 percent in 1926 to about 33 percent in 1940. The relative freedom to choose one's job that had marked the NEP disappeared. Individual industrial enterprises signed labor contracts with the collectives by which a given number of farm workers were obliged to go to the factories. Peasants who resisted collectivization were drafted into labor camps. In the factories the trade unions became an organ of the state. The chief role of the unions was to achieve maximum production and efficiency. Trade unions could not strike or quarrel with management, though they could administer the social insurance laws and negotiate to improve workers' living conditions.

Thus, Stalin set himself against the old Bolshevik principles of equality. The Marxist slogan, "From each according to his capacity, to each according to his needs" was shelved in favor of a new one: "From each according to his capacity, to each according to his work." Where Lenin had allowed none of the members of the government to earn more than a skilled laborer, Stalin set up a new system of incentives. A small minority of bureaucrats, skilled laborers, factory managers, and successful collective bosses earned vastly more than the unskilled laborers and peasants. Together with the writers, artists, musicians, entertainers, and athletes who lent their talents to the service of the regime, these people—generally men—became a new elite. They had a vested interest in furthering a regime to which they owed everything. The old privileged class of noble landlords, already weakened at the time of the revolution, had ceased to exist. The industrial, commercial, and financial bourgeoisie, which was just coming into its own at the time of the revolution, was destroyed after 1928, despite the temporary reprieve it had experienced under NEP. Most of the old intelligentsia, who had favored a revolution, could not in the end accept Stalin's dictatorship, and many of them emigrated. Those who remained were expected to concentrate on technical advances and on new administrative devices for speeding the transformation of the country; that is, they were to be "social engineers," high-level bureaucrats, propagandists for the new society who did not question its basic tenets or its direction.

After 1928, therefore, the logic of Stalin's policies forced a systematic mobilization of thought that in time virtually became thought control. Marx had assumed that a radical change in human nature was possible by conditioning of the social environment. Lenin recognized, however, that the new socialist society presumed the existence of a "new man" and "new woman," who would have to be created as part of the revolution. Industrialization and the collectivizing of agriculture could work only if unproductive speculation gave way to applied thinking directed to the needs of the state; this was particularly so in economics, philosophy, and psychology, but history and literature must also be transformed. To transform them, they must be controlled.

The Soviet Union was noted for its economists, whose support was essential to give credibility to the NEP. Some economists felt that the potential scope of state planning was severely limited; others thought total planning possible; some were optimistic about how fast industrialization could proceed; others were pessimistic. Those whose arguments were contrary to the political needs of Stalin were accused of trying to undermine the first five-year plan. Though Stalin had attacked only the economists for their failure to keep pace with successes, the philosophers quickly understood his message and turned to the practical application of philosophy to social problems.

In psychology, researchers such as Ivan Pavlov (1849–1936) emphasized how human behavior could be explained in terms of biological reflexes. Psychology also influenced education, and in time educators would argue that four factors determined behavior: heredity, environment, training, and self-training. Schools ceased trying to provide an environment in which the personality might develop and became institutions geared to turning out productive and loyal citizens.

But it was in literature and history—and in their explicit censorship—that the need to mobilize thought was most apparent. Literature was important because it influenced people, not because it was a path to truth. Declaring that neutral art was impossible, the Central Committee of the party gave its full support to peasant writers. A series of industrial novels sought to energize the people to higher productivity and pride. Maxim Gorky (1868–1936) became editor of a magazine on socialism, and he and others launched a series of histories of factories to focus attention on the nation's industrial triumphs.

History was to take communist partisanship as its guiding principle. At first non-Marxist historians were allowed to continue their work, but with the organization of the Institute of Red Professors (1921) and the Society of Marxist Historians (1925), Soviet historiography became increasingly intolerant of those who did not see history as a science or who continued to write of Peter as "the Great" or of Catherine II as other than a "dissolute and criminal woman." Nonetheless, as Stalin realized that world revolution was increasingly unlikely, and as the need for patriotism to meet Hitler's challenge became more evident, historians were able to return to writing of past figures who would give the Russian people a sense of pride.

Finally, to make thought control effective and thus change the environment, restrictions and ultimately censorship were necessary. In 1922 a review agency, the Chief Administration for the Preservation of State Secrets in the Press (or *Glavlit*, its Russian abbreviation), was established to censor the press, manuscripts, photographs, radio broadcasts, lectures, and exhibitions. A subsection, begun in 1923, dealt with theater, music, and other arts. Glavlit

THE WRITTEN RECORD

The Dangers of Backwardness

The strength of Stalin's motives is revealed in a speech he made in 1931.

To slacken the pace means to lag behind, and those who lag behind are beaten. We do not want to be beaten. No we don't want to. . . . Old Russia . . . was ceaselessly beaten for her backwardness. She was beaten by the Mongol Khans, she was beaten by Turkish Beys, she was beaten by Swedish feudal lords, she was beaten by Polish-Lithuanian gentry, she was beaten by Anglo-French capitalists, she was beaten by Japanese barons; she was beaten by all—for her backwardness. For military backwardness, for cultural backwardness, for political backwardness, for industrial backwardness, for agricultural backwardness. She was beaten because to beat her was profitable and went unpunished. . . . We are fifty or a hundred years behind the advanced countries. We must make good this lag in ten years. Either we do it or they crush us.

Quoted in Isaac Deutscher, *Stalin* (New York: Mentor, 1950), p. 328.

---

placed an official in each publishing house, broadcasting studio, customshouse, and so forth, to monitor how the law was being obeyed. Some publications, such as the official newspaper of the Soviet, *Isvestiya*, were exempt from Glavlit, and the autonomous republics could establish their own Glavlits.

In an increasingly literate society of the kind Stalin intended, control over the press would prove to be even more important. The government encouraged the establishment of newspapers as a means of informing and educating the people to revolutionary socialism; by 1927 there were 1,105 newspapers and 1,645 periodicals in the Soviet Union; and by 1965 the number had grown to 6,595 and 3,833, respectively, in sixty-five languages. To control this vast outpouring, a decree of 1935 established the Telegraphic Agency of the Soviet Union (or *Tass*) as the central organ for information in the USSR. Until 1961 Tass held a monopoly over the distribution of all foreign information within the USSR and over all information that moved from one Soviet republic to another.

The Authoritarian State, 1931–1943

Stalin's program was not achieved without opposition. The crisis of 1931 and 1932, when industrial goals were not being met and starvation swept the countryside, created discontent inside the regime as well as outside. A few officials circulated memoranda advocating Stalin's removal as general secretary, an act that the party had the right to perform. Stalin jailed them for conspiracy, and one leading Bolshevik committed suicide. Stalin's second wife reproached him at this time for the ravages that the terror was working, and she, too, committed suicide in 1932. Then, in December 1934, Sergei Kirov (1888–1934), who was rumored to be heir to Stalin's position, was assassinated in Leningrad, probably on Stalin's orders. Using Kirov's death as an excuse, Stalin purged the party of his opponents, having hundreds of Soviets shot for alleged complicity in the killings and bringing his old colleagues Zinoviev and Kamenev to public trial in 1936. They and fourteen others either admitted involvement in Kirov's death or signed confessions fabricated for them; they were executed. In a second trial (1937), seventeen other leading Bolsheviks declared that they had knowledge of a conspiracy between Trotsky and the German and Japanese intelligence services by which Soviet territory was to be transferred to Germany and Japan. All were executed. Then in June 1937 came the secret liquidation of the top commanders in the Red Army, who were accused of conspiring with "an unfriendly foreign power" (Germany) with a view to sabotage. All were executed after an announcement that they had confessed. The last of the public trials took place in March 1938, as twenty-one leading Bolsheviks, including Bukharin, confessed to similar charges and were executed.

But these public trials and the secret trial of the generals provide only a faint idea of the extent of the purge that was now transformed into the period known as the Terror. Every member of Lenin's Politburo except Stalin and Trotsky either was killed or committed suicide to avoid execution. Two vice-commissars of foreign affairs and most of the ambassadors in the Soviet diplomatic corps, fifty of the seventy-one members of the Central Committee of the Communist party, almost all the military judges who had sat in judgment and had condemned the generals, two successive heads of the secret police, themselves the leaders in the previous purges, the prime ministers and chief officials of all the non-Russian Soviet republics—all were killed or vanished.

Not since the days of the witchcraft trials or of the Inquisition—and then not on so grand a scale—had the test of political and ideological loyalty been applied to so many people, and not since the days of the French Revolution had so many died for failing the test. Arrests multiplied tenfold in 1936 and 1937. Anything was used as an excuse for an arrest: dancing too long with a Japanese diplomat, buying groceries from a former kulak, not reporting an Armenian nationalist neighbor. People simply went out to work one day and did not return—killed or sent to one of many huge anonymous prisons, or banished to Siberia. Most academicians and writers took for granted periods of exile and prison as natural parts of the rhythm of life. By 1938 at least 1 million Soviets were in prisons, some 8.5 million people had been arrested and most sent to prison camps and colonies, and perhaps 700,000 had been executed.

Stalin apparently wanted to destroy utterly all possibility of future conspiracies. So he trumped up charges against anyone who could conceivably become a member of a regime that might replace his own. Yet despite the purges the state did not break down. New Stalin-trained officials filled all top-level positions, and terror was enthroned as a principle of government, keeping all officials in constant fear for their lives and their jobs. In the end the purgers, too, were purged, used as scapegoats by Stalin for the Terror they had carried out at his command. Even Trotsky was pursued and killed. In August 1940 an assassin tracked Trotsky down to his refuge in Mexico and killed him with an ax.

In the midst of the Terror in 1936 Stalin proclaimed a new constitution. By its provisions no one was disenfranchised, as priests and members of the former nobility and bourgeoisie had previously been. Civil liberties were extended on paper, though they could be modified in the "interest of the toilers." Because the USSR was a one-party state, elections were an expression of unanimity. The right to nominate candidates for the Supreme Soviet belonged to Communist party organizations, trade unions, cooperatives, youth groups, and cultural societies; but all were completely dominated by the party. The party picked the candidates, and no more than one for each post was presented to the voters. The party controlled the soviets, and the party hierarchy and government hierarchy overlapped and interlocked.

Every citizen could apply for membership in the party to a local branch, which voted on the application after a year of trial. Communist children's organizations fed the youth groups, which in turn fed the party. The party was organized both territorially and functionally in pyramid form, with organizations at the bottom level in factory, farm, and government office. These were grouped together by rural or urban local units, and these in turn by regional and territorial conferences and congresses. The party organizations elected the All-Union party congress, which selected the Central Committee of the party. The Central Committee selected the Politburo. At each level of the party pyramid there were organizations for agitation and propaganda (or "agitprop"), for organization and instruction, for military and political training. The party exercised nearly full control over the government.

The highest organ of the government was the Supreme Soviet, made up of two houses—a Soviet of the Union, based on population, and a Soviet of Nationalities, elected according to national administrative divisions. In theory the Supreme Soviet was elected for a term of four years. The Supreme Soviet itself did little; it appointed a presidium, which issued the decrees and carried on the work of the Supreme Soviet between sessions. It also appointed the Council of Ministers (long called the Council of People's Commissars). This cabinet, rather than the Supreme Soviet or its presidium, enacted most of the legislation and was thus both the legislative and the executive organ of the state. Stalin was chairman of the Council of People's Commissars and of the Politburo, and general secretary of the Communist party. He was also commissar of defense, chief of the State Defense Council, which ran the country during wartime, and supreme military commander.

With the new constitution in place and Stalin's enemies dead or intimidated, the late 1930s brought a softening of revolutionary fervor. Simultaneously with the purges and the new constitution, the bread ration was raised; individual farmers could own their homesteads; new medals and titles were awarded to leading workers in plants and to scientists, engineers, and military officers. In the Red Army, the traditional czarist distinctions between officers and men were restored, and marshals were named for the first time. The standard of living went up as the production of consumer goods was encouraged; and workers were invited to spend their earnings on small luxuries previously unavailable.

The early Bolsheviks had destroyed the old school system, abolished homework and examinations, and allowed children to administer the schools collectively with their teachers. Attendance fell off, the schools became revolutionary clubs of youngsters, and the training of teachers was neglected. The universities deteriorated, since anyone could enroll in them at age sixteen. Degrees were abolished, and technical training was stressed, to the exclusion of other subjects. Under NEP this chaotic situation was modified, and the basic problem of increasing literacy was tackled seriously. But the ordinary school curricula were replaced by heavy emphasis on labor problems and Marxist theory. The Communist party itself took over the universities, purged the faculties, and compelled the students to spend one week in three at work in factories.

But now this system again changed drastically. Training of teachers improved, their salaries were raised, and they were admitted to the civil service. The prerevolutionary system of admissions and degrees in the universities was restored, as was the prerevolutionary school curriculum. Emphasis on political education was reduced, and coeducation was abandoned. Tuition fees were restored for secondary schools making higher education difficult to obtain, except for children of the new elite or unusually talented students who won state scholarships. Literacy rose to about 90 percent.

Very reluctantly Stalin came last of all to modify the traditional communist position on religion. Militant atheism had been the policy of the early Bolsheviks. Behind their attitude lay more than the standard Marxist feeling that religion was the opiate of the masses; in Russia the Orthodox church had always been a pillar of czarism. Many years of attacks on religion, however, had failed to eradicate Orthodoxy from among the people. When in 1937 Hitler built a Russian church in Berlin and took every occasion to speak kindly of the Orthodox church,

Stalin had to respond. Declaring that Christianity had contributed to past Russian glory, the government abated its antireligious propaganda and permitted church attendance again. While the early revolutionaries had attacked the family as the backbone of the discredited social order, Stalin rehabilitated the sanctity of marriage and emphasized the family and its growth. The government lowered taxes on church property and appointed a new patriarch on whose subservience the regime could count.

Karl Marx, who had scorned and disliked Russia, would have been confounded had he lived to see that agricultural land, almost without a proletariat, produce the only major European communist revolution. Perhaps Marx was wrong, or perhaps what happened in Russia was not a Marxist revolution at all. It seems clear that Marx did not correctly estimate the revolutionary force latent in the Russian peasantry. Since Marx died in 1883, he could not foresee the ultimate inadequacy of the czarist regime, the start of effective Russian industrialization, the extent of the tensions created by World War I, or the feebleness of the provisional government of 1917. But it

also seems clear that, to bring the Bolsheviks to power, it took Lenin's recognition of the importance of the peasantry, his grasp of the immediate situation, his willingness to risk everything, and his good fortune at being in the right place at the right time with the right weapons.

On the other hand, the revolution was not wholly Marxist. Once the Bolsheviks were in power, it was natural that the real situations they faced would modify their Marxist-Leninist theories. When civil war and foreign intervention brought chaos, NEP provided a necessary respite. Stalin combined Marxism, Russian nationalism, and ruthless politics in ways no one could have foreseen. Although it fell short of its goal, Stalin's program created an industrial state able to resist the blows that Hitler was to deal it. Servants of the state though they were, collectivized by force, industrialized by force, purged, terrorized, and struggling by the millions to exist in forced labor camps or to leave the country, the Soviets in World War II nonetheless succeeded, with much help from the United States and other nations, in defeating Hitler and his allies.

Summary

The period from 1919 to 1939 was marked by the success of movements to the right. Although these movements were products of different societies, they had features in common: disillusionment with democracy for its failure to provide stability, aggressive nationalism, a sense of grievance, totalitarian government, and racism.

Fascism triumphed first in Italy after World War I. Mussolini, a socialist until the war, repudiated his old beliefs and shifted to militant nationalism. In a campaign of terror, Mussolini drove to power in the early 1920s. He established a fascist dictatorship, assuring his dominance by controlling the press and abolishing opposition parties.

Mussolini set up a corporative state in which the needs of labor and capital were subordinate to the interests of the state. Worker and producer syndicates had little real power or influence, which was held by the fascist bureaucracy. Mussolini pursued an aggressive foreign policy in the Mediterranean, Spain Ethiopia, and Albania.

After World War I, Germany experienced fifteen years of democratic government under the Weimar Republic. However, Weimar Germany went through three distinct phases: in the first, which lasted from 1918 to 1923, political threats arose from the left and right, and the nation was in economic chaos; in the second, which lasted from 1924 to 1929, Germany enjoyed political stability and relative economic prosperity; in the third, which lasted from 1929 to 1933, the right rose to power under Hitler, and economic depression cut the foundations from prosperity.

Hitler quickly established a dictatorship. He used the threat of a Bolshevik revolution to suspend constitutional

government and build a strongly centralized state. He dissolved opposition political parties and crushed opponents within his own party. Once in power, Hitler embarked on a policy of eliminating Jews, and racism became a state policy. In foreign affairs, Nazi racist policies were extended to claiming lands inhabited by Germans.

In Spain, turmoil caused by divisions between left and right increased after the death of King Alfonso in 1931. During the Spanish Civil War (1936–1939), General Franco, aided by Italian and German forces, won a victory over the leftists. Franco established an authoritarian regime supported by landowners, the army, and the church.

In Portugal, another dictator, Antonio Salazar, rose to power. In eastern Europe, the successor states to the Habsburg Empire lacked parliamentary traditions. In the interwar period, authoritarian regimes were established in these nations.

After Lenin's death in 1924, a desperate power struggle unfolded in the Soviet Union between Stalin and Trotsky. Stalin used his strong base of support in the party to force Trotsky out of power. Under Stalin, an authoritarian regime of the left was intensified.

By 1928 Communists had rejected Lenin's New Economic Policy, which had aimed at reconstruction after the civil war. Between 1928 and 1941, Stalin imposed massive changes on Soviet life: collectivization, industrialization, elimination of opponents, and a return to bourgeois standards in social and intellectual life.

By the late 1930s Stalin had mobilized writers and historians to use Russia's past to increase Russian nationalism. For by then, the Soviet Union faced a coalition of authoritarian fascist regimes pledged to exterminate communism.

CRITICAL THINKING

1. In earlier chapters in this book, often two centuries or more have been discussed in a single chapter. Is it legitimate to devote so much attention to a period of only twenty years? If so, why? What elements from these "interwar years" are still playing a major role in life today?

2. What were the differences between the fascist dictatorship in Italy and the dictatorship in Germany?

3. Why did the Weimar Republic ultimately fail? Did it have any chance of success?

4. Account for Hitler's rise to power in Germany.

5. How did authoritarian regimes in Spain and Portugal differ from those in Italy, Germany, and eastern Europe?

6. Much of Europe came under the control of authoritarian governments. How do you account for this? Which nations did not, and why? What benefits do you think residents of authoritarian nations felt they gained from such regimes?

7. What role did racism play in the creation of authoritarian regimes? Did religion or the concept of class warfare play a role, and if so, how?

8. Describe Stalin's rise to power in the Soviet Union.

9. How did the Soviet Union differ from Russia?

10. What role did the worldwide depression play in the rise of dictatorships?

The Democracies and the Non-Western World

IDEALISTS LIKE PRESIDENT WILSON HAD expected that the collapse of the Romanov, Habsburg, and Hohenzollern empires would automatically ensure an increase in the number of democratic states. But, instead, much of Europe came under regimes that were hostile to liberal democracy. In the 1920s and 1930s the core of democracy remained the great North Atlantic powers—Britain, France, and the United States; the smaller states of Scandinavia; the Low Countries; Switzerland; and the inheritors of the British tradition—Canada, Australia, and New Zealand. Certainly the totalitarian aggressors bore great responsibility for the unleashing of a second world war. Yet a major factor in the deterioration of the twenty years' truce was the failure of the democracies to present a unified front against those who threatened world peace.

In the early 1930s Britain, France, and the United States were preoccupied with domestic problems. But this was the very time when international problems demanded equally urgent attention. International trade was steadily shrinking in response to the depression and mounting tariff barriers; the prospects for peace were steadily fading in response to resurgent and authoritarian nationalism. Nor was this all. During the twenty years' truce, the democracies faced a third set of problems. This third set involved the relations between the democracies and the non-Western peoples, many of whom were still under colonial rule. Particularly in Asia and the Middle East, non-Western peoples were beginning to assert their nationalism and to demand the loosening of imperial ties.

Thus, the discrete histories of the non-Western peoples, always part of "world history," as we customarily call it, now became an integral part of the history of "Western civilization" as well. Problems that would have been viewed as quite distinct two or three centuries earlier took on global significance.

GREAT BRITAIN

Though on the winning side in World War I, Britain staggered from economic crisis to crisis. Immigration inward was steadily offset by emigration outward, especially to North America. Despite efforts to recover, the steam had left the British economy, which grew at half its prewar rate.

The Postwar Economic Crisis, to 1921

Besides tragic human losses from the war, Great Britain's economic losses were grave. The national debt after the war was ten times that of 1914. Many British investments abroad had been liquidated to purchase food and war materials. Forty percent of the great British merchant fleet had been destroyed by enemy action. The whole fabric of international trade on which Britain depended was torn in a thousand places in 1918 and could not be rapidly restored in the unsettled postwar world. To supplement British and French war production, the industrial plants of the United States, Canada, and India had been called on, and that stimulus made them more effective competitors of the British in peacetime. In addition, German industry, nourished in part by loans from America, once more took up the rivalry that had so alarmed the British before the war.

In short, the country that in Victorian days had been the "workshop of the world" could no longer provide full employment to its millions of workers. Those workers were in no mood to accept a lower standard of living, for they had fought the war and won it in the expectation of better things to come. They had been promised that the defeated enemy would pay the costs of the war and thereby give Britain a new start.

This hope was very early disappointed; no substantial reparations came through. The return to peace caused a sudden boom in production to meet the postwar demand for goods that had been denied to civilians in wartime. This was accompanied by a sharp rise in prices and quickly followed by the collapse of the boom, leaving Britain in a severe postwar depression. By the summer of 1921 there were more than 2 million people out of work, over one fifth of the labor force. Faced with the rising cost of living, the British government increased the very meager unemployment payments. However, large-scale unemployment continued, and some young workers never found jobs.

The British economic decline was not yet catastrophic, although some gravely depressed areas, like the coal-mining regions of South Wales, began to show signs of permanent decay. What happened generally was a relative decline, the slowing down of an economy geared to dynamic growth, with a working population conditioned psychologically to a gradually rising standard of living and a middle class similarly conditioned to traditional comforts. Moreover, the tabloid newspaper, the movie, and the radio made the British well aware that Americans and others enjoyed automobiles, radios, refrigerators, and telephones, while they did not.

Britain was suffering from those ills characteristic of postindustrial development, and it was the first nation to do so. There was still a lot of coal in Britain, for example, but much of it was costly to mine, since the most easily and cheaply worked seams were being exhausted. The industry was badly organized, with many small and inefficient mines running at a loss and with machinery and methods that were antiquated in comparison with the newer American and Continental mines. Productivity per work-hour was low. Worst of all, the 1920s saw the rapid rise of major competitors to coal—oil, and electricity based on water power—with a consequent decline of British coal exports. Since the British Isles had no petroleum and no very great potential in hydroelectric power, coal simply had to be mined. But the workers were unionized and in no mood to accept cuts in wages, while owners did not want to run their businesses at a loss. A strike in March 1921 focused national attention on this problem. The strike was settled in July by the government's consenting to pay subsidies to cover increased wages.

The Conservative and Labour Programs

Against the background of economic depression, British domestic politics during the twenty years' truce continued to display a fairly clear class basis. The Conservatives, still often called Tories, tended to get the support of aristocrats and of middle-class people, who generally wanted to attack new problems with traditional methods and with a minimum of government intervention. The Labour party tended to get the support of trade unionists and of intellectuals from all classes, who demanded that the government intervene more vigorously in the economy. In the struggle between Labour and Conservative, the old Liberal party was an early casualty. The Conservatives, who had won the lion's share of seats in 1918, decided in 1922 to withdraw their support from the coalition government headed by the immensely popular Liberal, David Lloyd George. In the ensuing elections the Conservatives won and the Liberals lost heavily.

Both Conservatives and Labour recognized the underlying difficulties of Britain's position. Both were fully aware that twentieth-century Britain had to sell enough goods and services abroad that income from them would buy food for its people and raw materials for its factories. But the parties could not agree on how to achieve this necessary task.

The state of world trade drove the Conservatives to advocate protective tariffs against competing foreign goods and to weld the Empire and Commonwealth, with their vast variety of resources, into a largely self-sufficient trade entity by "imperial preference" agreements. Such agreements would give raw materials from the colonies and dominions preferred treatment in the British market in return for preferred treatment of British manufactures in the colonial and dominion markets. In theory the scheme could have worked, for the Commonwealth and Empire of the 1920s had the requisite natural and labor resources and offered a potential market capable of supporting Britain in the style to which it was accustomed. In practice the great problem was the unwillingness of the individual parts of the Empire and Commonwealth to accept the subordinate role of producers of raw materials in exchange for British manufactured goods and services. The self-governing dominions, loyal though they had been during the war, were unwilling to assume a role essentially like that of colonies in the old mercantilistic days. They were looking toward independent nationhood, and they wanted their own industries.

The Labour solution was *nationalization*—that is, government purchase and operation of key industries with fair compensation to their private owners. The key industries were transportation, utilities, coal, steel, and perhaps even textiles, cutlery, pottery, and machine tools—all the industries that seemed to thrive best on large-scale organization. But even nationalized industries would still face the fundamental problem of selling enough goods abroad to keep the economy going. Labourites argued, therefore, that nationalization would also enable British industries to produce more cheaply and efficiently by doing away with wasteful competition and inefficiency.

Politics between the Wars, 1918–1936

Neither the Conservatives nor the Labourites were able to carry out their full platforms. The Conservatives were frustrated by the refusal of the Commonwealth countries to go any further than to accept certain limited imperial preferences. Labour came to power for two brief spans—for ten months in 1924 with Ramsay MacDonald (1866–1937), an intellectual and pacifist, as prime minister, and again from 1928 to 1931. In both instances, although Labour won more seats in the Commons than any other party, it did not have an absolute majority. These Labour governments, obliged to rely on the Liberals for parliamentary support, were still too shaky to introduce measures as controversial as the nationalization of any industry.

For a few weeks in 1926 some 2.5 million trade union members attempted a general strike to support coal miners, who were striking to protest a cut in their wages. The general strike failed, but its brief course revealed fundamental British attitudes. Thousands of people from the middle and upper classes volunteered to keep essential services operating when a state of emergency was declared. Both sides remained calm and moderate, with neither side seeking all-out victory in a class war. When the general strike was called off, the miners eventually had to return to the pits on the owners' terms. In 1927 a Trade Disputes and Trade Union Act made all sympathetic strikes or strikes against the government illegal.

Meanwhile, two more steps were taken toward the political democratization of Britain that had begun in 1832. In 1918, in preparation for the election, the government had put through a reform bill that eliminated all the old exceptions to universal male suffrage and gave the vote to all males over twenty-one. Culminating a long and spectacular campaign by suffragists who had gone to jail for women's rights, the bill also gave the vote to women. But it set the voting age for women at thirty years, thus ensuring that there would be more male than female voters. The distinction was too unsound to last, especially after experience demonstrated that women divided politically about the way men did. In 1928 a new bill gave women the vote at twenty-one.

Although signs of economic ill health persisted, Britain recovered somewhat in the late 1920s. But then came the Great Depression. Britain, already weakened, was one of the first nations to suffer; in eighteen months the number of unemployed jumped from slightly more than 1 million to 2.5 million. Faced by a serious government deficit and unwilling to meet it by cutting social services, the second Labour government of Ramsay MacDonald resigned in August 1931.

It gave way to a coalition of Conservatives, Liberals, and right-wing Labourites—headed by MacDonald. Many Labourites were dismayed by what seemed to them MacDonald's surrender to the forces of capitalism, and the deep split within the party crippled its effectiveness throughout the 1930s. The "national government," as the coalition cabinet was called, reduced social services. Late in 1931, it took the decisive step of going off the gold standard and letting the pound fall in value. In 1932 it made the first firm move away from free trade by enacting protective tariffs, and it also ceased to pay its war debts to the United States. These measures did little to help the unemployed or get at the roots of British economic troubles. Nevertheless, partly because of Labour's disarray, two general elections, in October 1931 and in June 1935, returned a majority supporting the national government.

The coalition government was dominated by Conservatives, and after the 1935 election the Conservative leader, Stanley Baldwin, became prime minister. Gradually the British economy pulled out of the worst of the depression, and Baldwin was able to balance the budget. In 1936, however, the great issue confronting Baldwin's cabinet was neither social nor economic but constitutional, as the cabinet forced the abdication of King Edward VIII (1894–1972) in the same year as his accession to the throne. Edward had fallen in love with an American divorcee and wanted to marry her. The royal family, the cabinet, and most of the British people opposed him, and he abdicated; he was succeeded by his brother, who became King George VI (r. 1936–1952).

The Irish Question, 1916–1949

The years between the wars were of great importance for Ireland. In 1916 the British put down the Easter rebellion with grim determination, creating nearly a hundred Irish political martyrs. The British government did not dare extend conscription to Ireland until April 1918, and that attempt led Irish nationalists to boycott the British Parliament. The crisis of 1914, postponed by the war, was again at hand.

But by 1919 home rule as decreed in 1914 was not enough for many Irish nationalists. The *Sinn Fein* party (Gaelic for "ourselves alone") wanted complete independence. The years 1919–1921 were filled with violence, ambushes, arson, and guerrilla warfare, as the Irish, who now had their own illegal parliament, the *Dáil Eireann*, moved into full revolution. The British were not prepared to use force effectively; the Irish were organized, fully aroused, and ready to fight.

The immediate result of the violent phase of the revolution was a compromise, for the Sinn Fein split in two. The moderate wing was willing to accept a compromise in which Protestant Ulster would remain under direct British rule and the Catholic counties would be given dominion status under an independent assembly. The moderates negotiated with the British, and in 1921 obtained for the twenty-six counties of southern Ireland dominion status under the name of the Irish Free State. The Free State had its own parliament, the Dáil, and was completely self-governing, with its own army and its own diplomatic services. It did, however, accept the British Crown as symbolic head. The six predominantly Protestant counties of Ulster maintained their old relationship with Britain, including the right to send members to the Parliament at Westminster, but they also acquired their own parliament at Belfast and considerable local autonomy. Henceforth, Britain was officially known as the United Kingdom of Great Britain and Northern Ireland.

The radical wing, led by Eamon De Valera (1882–1975), insisted that the whole island, Protestant and Catholic, achieve complete independence as a unified republic. For the radicals, the compromise negotiated by the moderates was unacceptable. The Irish revolution now became a civil war between partisans of the Free State and those of a single republic, with a return to burning, ambush, and murder. But when the moderate leader Michael Collins (1890–1922) was assassinated, public opinion began to turn away from the extremists. De Valera, after refusing to sit in the Dáil because he would have had to take an oath of loyalty to the British king, attacked the civil war and ultimately decided to bring his party, the *Fianna Fáil*, into the national parliament in 1927.

De Valera's party won a plurality in the Dáil in 1932 and a majority in 1933; thereupon it abolished the oath of loyalty to the Crown and cut the threads that still tied the Free State to the United Kingdom. In 1938 De Valera became prime minister, and in 1939 the Free State showed that it was free from British domination by maintaining neutrality throughout World War II. In 1949 the final step was taken when Britain recognized the fully independent republic of Eire (Gaelic for "Ireland").

The Commonwealth, 1931–1939

Constitutional recognition of the essential independence of the dominions seemed to make them more loyal. The new status acquired by the dominions with the Statute of Westminster in 1931 was symbolized by a change in terminology. They were no longer to be considered parts of the British Empire, but free members of the British Commonwealth of Nations. In this new relationship, Britain would have to negotiate with the Commonwealth countries about tariffs, trade conditions, or immigration as with foreign countries.

Although Britain was unable to build a self-sufficient economic unity out of its dominions, still in 1939 the dominions all ultimately came into the war on Britain's side. They made this decision independently, however, for they had the legal right to follow the example of Ireland and remain neutral. Transfer of power to the major dominions was complete.

France

In France both World War I and the postwar difficulties caused even more serious dislocation than they did in Britain. France had lost proportionately more in human lives and in material damage than had any other major belligerent. Two million Frenchmen in the prime of life were either killed or so seriously mutilated as to be incapable of normal living. In a land of only 39 million with an already low birth rate, this human loss affected all phases of activity. Three hundred thousand houses and twenty thousand factories or shops were destroyed. In a land of conservative economic organization where most work was done without large-scale machinery, this material setback would long be felt. Psychologically, victory did not compensate for the traumatic losses of the four years of struggle.

The Impact of the War, 1918–1928

France wanted revenge on Germany in every possible way. The French tried to extract reparations to the last possible sum, undeterred by the arguments of economists that Germany could not pay. But France insisted even more on keeping Germany isolated in international relations and without the physical means to wage war.

Meanwhile, France was experiencing an inflation that resulted in part from the cost of rebuilding the devastated areas—a cost that drained government finances and that was only partly covered by German payments. It resulted also from the high cost of maintaining armed forces (for the French dared not disarm), from the general disorder of international trade, and from the staggering debts piled up during the war by the French government, which, like the imperial German government, had preferred loans to taxes. By the mid-1920s the franc had slipped from its prewar value of twenty cents against the dollar to a dangerous low of about two cents. Premier Raymond Poincaré (1860–1934) initiated new taxes and stern economic measures which stemmed the decline of the franc. In 1928 it was officially revalued at 3.92 cents.

The French inflation, though mild compared with the German, nevertheless caused economic and social dislocation. Those French who had lent their government francs worth twenty cents were now repaid only one fifth of their loans. This very considerable loss fell with particular severity on the lower middle class, the *petite bourgeoisie*. The greatest sufferers were those living on their savings or on relatively fixed incomes. Inflation thus weakened a social class that had long been a mainstay of republicanism in France and added to the social tensions that formed the central theme of French domestic history between the two world wars.

Social and Political Tensions, 1928–1936

During World War I the French had temporarily put aside the great political and social conflict they had inherited from 1789. After the war the "sacred union" of political parties that had carried France through the struggle soon dissolved, and the traditional conflict was resumed. This is sometimes termed the conflict between the "two Frances"—the republican France of the left and the royalistic or authoritarian France of the right. The conflict was not a simple struggle between rich and poor. On the right the wealthier classes, many of them openly hostile to the existence of the parliamentary state, were reinforced by conservative peasants and by small business people and investors. Many of these petit bourgeois were not hostile to the Third Republic as such but were determined to resist any attempt to extend the social services of the welfare state.

On the left were the champions of the welfare state, the socialists and the communists, backed by the more radical workers, by many white-collar people, especially in the bureaucracy, and by some intellectuals. The postwar left was hampered by the split between the communists, who followed the Moscow line, and the socialists, who did not, and by a comparable schism within the major trade-union organization, the CGT (*Confédération Générale du Travail*, the General Confederation of Labor). Still nominally part of the left, but actually in the political middle and not anxious to extend the welfare state, was the Radical Socialist party, long the main party of the Third Republic. The Radicals were strong among the peasants of southern France and among white-collar and professional workers.

In the late 1920s, the Third Republic seemed to be getting the better of its internal difficulties. The world economic crisis that began in 1929 was late in striking France, and for a while it looked as though the French economy, less dependent on large-scale industry than that of the United States, Britain, or Germany, might weather the crisis much more easily. But France, too, depended on international trade, particularly on the export of luxuries. By 1932 the depression had struck, and the government was in serious economic and political difficulties.

The political crisis came to a head in February 1934 as a result of the Stavisky case, a financial scandal reminiscent of the Panama scandal of the 1890s. Serge Stavisky was a swindler with influential connections,

particularly in Radical Socialist circles. He was finally exposed in December 1933 and escaped to an Alpine hideout, where he committed suicide—or, as many believed, was killed by the police lest he implicate important politicians. France was rocked by the event and also by the mysterious death of a judge who had been investigating the case. On the extreme right, royalists had long been organized in a pressure group known as the *Action Française* and were gaining recruits among upper-class youth. The *Camelots du Roi* (King's Henchmen), strong-arm squads of the Action Française, went about beating up communists, who responded with violence. Less fascist in character yet also supporting the right was a veterans' organization, the *Croix de Feu* (Cross of Fire). During the agitation following the Stavisky case, the Camelots du Roi, the Croix de Feu, and other right-wing groups took part in demonstrations against the government. The left countered with a brief general strike. Fourteen demonstrators were killed, and many feared that France again faced revolution.

The Popular Front, 1936–1937

Once more, however, as in the time of Dreyfus, the republican forces rallied to meet the threat, and once more, after the crisis had been surmounted, France moved to the left. Edouard Daladier (1884–1970), Radical premier, resigned, and a coalition of all parties except the royalists, socialists, and communists formed a national government, including all living former premiers. But the franc was again falling in value. In 1935 a ministry in which the dominant figure was Pierre Laval (1883–1945), a former socialist turned conservative, attempted to cut back government expenditures by measures similar to those that had worked a decade earlier under Poincaré; this time, however, they did not work. The forces of the left responded by forming a Popular Front, which for the first time linked together the Radical Socialist, Socialist, and Communist parties. It also had the backing of CGT, which had temporarily healed the schism between communist and noncommunist unions. In the elections of 1936 the Popular Front won, with the socialists at the top. The premiership was accordingly offered to a socialist, the Jewish intellectual Léon Blum (1872–1950).

The Popular Front came to power with a mandate from voters who wanted the government to distribute wealth more equitably. In June 1936 the government introduced an ambitious program of reform. Labor gained a forty-hour workweek, higher wages, vacations with pay, and provision for compulsory arbitration of labor disputes. The Bank of France, the railroads, and the munitions industry were all partially nationalized. Quasi-fascistic groups like the Camelots du Roi and Croix de Feu were ordered to disband.

Impressive as this program was on paper, events conspired to block its successful implementation. The communists did not really cooperate, for they refused to participate in the Blum cabinet and sniped at it in parliament and in the press. Business took fright at the growth of the CGT and at the effectiveness of sit-down strikes of French industrial workers in June 1936—the first widespread use of this formidable economic weapon through which struck plants were occupied by the striking workers, preventing the owners from using their weapon, the lockout.

The nation was soon bitterly divided between partisans and enemies of the Popular Front. Business and farming classes were traditionally reluctant to pay income taxes, which would have to be raised to meet the costs of social services; the economy was not geared to labor-saving devices; there were competing demands on the nation's money. Capital, however, was rapidly leaving the country to be invested or deposited abroad, and the monied class would not subscribe to the huge defense loans that were essential if the French armed forces were to prepare for the war that seemed to be approaching. Faced by mounting opposition, Blum was obliged to step down as premier in favor of a Radical in 1937. The Popular Front disintegrated.

The morale of the French sagged badly after the collapse of the Popular Front. Under the mounting international tensions of 1938 and 1939, the Radical Socialist premier, Daladier, kept France on the side of Britain in unsteady opposition to the Rome-Berlin Axis. Various measures of retrenchment—including virtual abandonment of the forty-hour week—kept the French economy from collapse. But the workers resented the failure of the Popular Front, and as late as November 1938 almost achieved a general strike, which the government combated by putting the railway workers under military orders. The "have" classes, on the other hand, were outraged by Blum's measures. Many of them were convinced that their salvation lay in a French totalitarian state. The France that was confronted with war in 1939 was not only inadequately armed; it was also psychologically and spiritually divided, uncertain of what it was to fight for or against.

Many in France had relied on their great empire to restore the flagging morale and material capabilities of the nation. Colonial troops, particularly from Senegal and North Africa, had helped to replenish the diminished ranks of the army during World War I and might do so again. Enthusiasts spoke of France as a nation of 100 million, which included the populations of the colonial territories. But the colonial populations were beginning to desire home rule or independence, especially in Algeria, Senegal, and French Indochina. Although some leaders of the French left urged concessions to such desires, little was conceded. In 1936 the Popular Front government negotiated treaties with Syria and Lebanon, granting them independence with many reservations, so as to safeguard the primacy of French interests. But this compromise was too much for the Chamber of Deputies, which refused to approve the treaties. Perhaps no policy pursued in the interwar years could have averted the disintegration of the French Empire that occurred during and after World War II, but the unimaginative policy that prevailed did nothing to reconcile the nationalists among the French colonial peoples.

THE UNITED STATES

Neither the human nor the material losses of the United States in World War I were at all comparable with those of Britain and France. American casualties were 115,000 dead and 206,000 wounded; the comparable French figures were 1,385,000 dead and 3,044,000 wounded in a population one-third as large. Moreover, in purely material terms, the United States probably gained from the war. Yet in some ways the American postwar revulsion against the war was as marked as that in Britain, France, and defeated Germany. It helped to unseat the Democrats, who had controlled the federal government since 1913. The Republicans won the presidential elections of 1920 (in which women had the vote for the first time), 1924, and 1928.

Isolationism and Internationalism, 1920–1933

American revulsion against war also took the form of isolationism, the wish to withdraw from international politics outside the Western Hemisphere. The country was swept by a wave of desire to get back to "normalcy," as President Warren Harding phrased it. Many Americans felt that they had done all they needed to do in defeating the Germans, and that further participation in the complexities of European politics would simply involve American innocence and virtue even more disastrously in European sophistication and vice. As the months of negotiation went on in Europe with no final decisions, many Americans began to feel that withdrawal was the only effective action they could take. The Treaty of Versailles, containing the establishment of the League of Nations, was finally rejected in the Senate on March 19, 1920.

American isolationism was also expressed in concrete measures. Tariffs in 1922 and 1930 set successively higher duties on foreign goods and emphasized America's belief that its high wage scales needed to be protected from cheap foreign labor. The spirit of isolationism, as well as growing racist movements, also lay behind the immigration restrictions of the 1920s, which reversed the former policy of almost unlimited immigration. The reversal was hastened by widespread prejudice against the recent and largely Catholic and Jewish immigrations from southern and eastern Europe. The act of 1924 set an annual quota limit for each country of 2 percent of the number of nationals from that country resident in the United States in 1890. Since the heavy immigration from eastern and southern Europe had come after 1890, the choice of that date reduced the flow from these areas to a trickle. Northern countries like Britain, Germany, and the Scandinavian states, on the other hand, did not use up their quotas.

Isolationism did not apply to all matters, however. The United States continued all through the 1920s to

In 1920 women won the right to vote in the United States. Here suffragists ride down Pennsylvania Avenue from the Capitol toward the White House.

Library of Congress

insist that the debts owed to it by the Allied powers be repaid. Congress paid little heed to the argument, so convincing to most economists, that the European nations could not repay except with dollars gained by selling their goods in the American market, and that American tariffs continued to make such repayment impossible.

Yet the United States did not withdraw entirely from international politics. Rather, as an independent without formal alliances, it continued to pursue policies that seemed to most Americans traditional, but that in their totality gradually aligned them against the rising dictatorships. In 1928 the Republican secretary of state, Frank B. Kellogg (1856–1937), proposed that the major powers renounce war as an instrument of national policy. Incorporated with similar proposals by the French foreign minister, Aristide Briand (1862–1932), it was formally adopted that year as the Pact of Paris, commonly known as the Kellogg-Briand Pact, and was eventually signed by twenty-three nations. Although the pact proved ineffective, the fact that it arose in part from American initiative and that the United States was a signatory to it, was clear indication that even if Americans did not wish to enter into any formal alliances, they were still concerned with the problems of worldwide stability and peace.

During the 1920s the United States was hard at work laying the foundations for the position of world leadership it reached after World War II. American businesses

were everywhere; American loans were making possible the revival of German industry; American motors, refrigerators, typewriters, telephones, and other products were being sold the world over. In the Far East the United States led in negotiating the Nine-Power Treaty of 1922 that committed it and the other great powers, including Japan, to respect the sovereignty and integrity of China. When Democratic President Franklin D. Roosevelt resisted the Japanese attempt to absorb China and other Far Eastern territory, he was following a line laid down under his Republican predecessors.

Boom and Bust, 1923–1933

In domestic affairs, the 1920s were a time of frantic prosperity for the many who played the stock market. These were the years of Prohibition, of the speakeasy and the bootlegger, when the American media—newspapers, magazines, radio, and motion pictures—gave the impression that the entire nation was absorbed by short skirts, loosened sexual mores, new dances, and bathtub gin. Such activities occupied only a tiny minority of the people, of course, just as the "whipped cream" culture of turn-of-the-century Vienna had been unrepresentative of most Austrians. But by the 1920s there was a significant difference. Agricultural workers who had never recovered their sense of prosperity and people who still held to Victorian

THE WRITTEN RECORD

Why Women Shouldn't Be Allowed to Vote

At the height of the movement to gain the vote for women in the United States, Alice Duer Miller (1874–1942), an author and a feminist, compiled a list of all the reasons that were being given in newspaper editorials, by politicians, and in public debate, against allowing women to vote. Noting that the arguments were directly contradictory, she wrote the following set of paired statements to show how the contending arguments canceled each other out.

Our Own Twelve Anti-Suffragist Reasons

1. Because no woman will leave her domestic duties to vote.
2. Because no woman who may vote will attend to her domestic duties.
3. Because it will make dissension between husband and wife.
4. Because every women will vote as her husband tells her to.
5. Because bad women will corrupt politics.
6. Because bad politics will corrupt women.
7. Because women have no power of organization.

8. Because women will form a solid party and out-vote men.
9. Because men and women are so different that they must stick to different duties.
10. Because men and women are so much like that men, with one vote each, can represent their own views and ours too.
11. Because women cannot use force.
12. Because the militants did use force.

Alice Duer Miller, *Are Woman People? A Book of Rhymes for Suffrage Times* (New York: Dodd, Mead, 1924), in *Up from the Pedestal: Selected Writings in the History of American Feminisim,* ed. Aileen S. Kraditor (Chicago: Quadrangle Books, 1968), pp. 218–19.

standards of conduct would be led to believe that boundless riches, social vacuity, and sin were typical of the upper classes.

The era was also a time of marked industrial progress, of solid advancement of the national plant and productive capabilities, vindicating President Calvin Coolidge's contention that "the business of America is business." It was an era of the steady expansion of standards of living heretofore limited to the relatively few, standards of living that seemed to some intellectuals vulgar, but that were nevertheless a new thing in the world. Unknown in Europe and envied there, the new lifestyle, vulgar or not, was much desired by nearly everyone. The United States became, in this era, the first true consumer society.

The era ended with the onset of the Great Depression. In 1928 Wall Street had enjoyed an unprecedented boom. Speculators by the millions were playing the market, buying stocks in hopes of quick resale at huge profits. They paid only a fraction of the cost in cash, borrowing the balance from their brokers, and often borrowing the cash investment as well. Not only stocks but houses, furnishings, automobiles, and many other purchases were financed on borrowed money. Credit swelled until it was no longer on a sound basis in a largely unregulated economy. Eventually, shrewd investors began to sell their holdings in the belief that the bubble would soon burst. The result was a self-fulfilling prophecy: a disastrous drop in stock values, beginning in October 1929

and continuing almost without letup to 1933. Both the speculators and the lenders were ruined.

The immediate cause of the Great Depression, then, was the stock market crash. About the more deepseated causes there is no complete agreement. Yet this much seems certain: Prosperity was very unevenly distributed among the various sectors of the American economy and American society. Agriculture, notably, suffered a kind of permanent stagnation throughout the 1920s. In 1918 farmers had commanded very high prices for their produce and enjoyed an apparently insatiable market at home and abroad. They expanded their production and borrowed to finance the expansion, often at a reckless rate. Then, as "normalcy" returned in the early 1920s, the foreign market dried up, the home market shrank, farm prices fell rapidly, and the foreclosure of farm mortgages began. Wage-earning workers, though not as hard hit as the farmers, gained comparatively little increase in their purchasing power during the 1920s. Workers often did raise their standard of living by purchasing a house or a car, but they did it on credit, by assuming the burden of a heavy mortgage or by financing the purchase on long-term installments.

The Great Depression was very severe in many countries throughout the world, but nowhere was it worse over a sustained period than in the United States. Its effects may be measured by the figure of 16 million men unemployed at the low point in the early 1930s—something like one third of the national labor force. In terms

Even in America, a country that regarded itself as rich, many people were reduced during the Great Depression to the neighborhood soup kitchen, where they might receive a simple free meal.

AP/Wide World Photos

of gross national product (GNP), one widely accepted statistic for calculating the health of an economy, the figure in 1929 had been cut nearly in half by 1933.

Yet this grave crisis in the American economy produced almost no organized movements of revolt, no threat of revolution. Some intellectuals of the 1930s did indeed turn to "social consciousness," and Marxism made converts among writers and artists. But the bulk of the population did not abandon their fundamental belief that the solution lay in the legal means provided by existing American institutions. Even before the election of President Franklin D. Roosevelt (1882–1945) in 1932, local authorities and private charities did much to soften the worst sufferings of the unemployed. They were helped by the Reconstruction Finance Corporation (RFC), which advanced government credits to release the frozen assets of financial institutions severely affected by the wave of bankruptcies and bank failures. President Herbert Hoover was generally committed to the philosophy of laissez faire, however, and aside from the RFC, his administration did little to cushion the effects of the depression. People who wanted a more vigorous attack on economic problems voted for the Democrats in 1932; significantly, very few voted for the socialist or communist candidates. In the crisis of the Great Depression, the two-party system continued to meet the basic political needs of most Americans.

The New Deal, 1933–1941

Victory seemed to give the Democrats a clear mandate to marshal the resources of the federal government against the depression. Franklin Roosevelt took office on March 4, 1933, during a financial crisis that had closed banks all over the country. He at once summoned Congress to an emergency session and declared a bank holiday. Gradually the sound banks reopened, and the first phase of the New Deal began. In the early months of 1933 the mere fact that a national administration was trying to do something about the situation was a powerful boost to national morale. The nation emerged from the bank holiday with a new confidence, repeating the phrase from Roosevelt's inaugural address that there was nothing to fear but "fear itself."

The New Deal was a series of measures aimed in part at immediate difficulties and in part at permanent changes in the structure of American society. It was the application to the United States, under the special pressures of the Great Depression, of measures that were being tried in European countries, measures often leading to the welfare state.

By releasing the dollar from its tie with gold, the short-term measures of the New Deal aimed to lower the price of American goods in a world that was abandoning

THE WRITTEN RECORD

FDR's First Inaugural Address

The 1930s were a time of charismatic orators: Franklin Roosevelt, Churchill, Hitler, Mussolini. Roosevelt used his inaugural address on March 4, 1933, less to outline a program than to inspire the public to stand behind him in a series of sweeping reforms.

This is preeminently the time to speak the truth, the whole truth, frankly and boldly. Nor need we shrink from honestly facing conditions in our country today. This great nation will endure as it has endured, will revive and will prosper.

So first of all let me assert my firm belief that the only thing we have to fear is fear itself—nameless, unreasoning, unjustified terror which paralyzes needed efforts to convert retreat into advance.

In every dark hour of our national life a leadership of frankness and vigor has met with that understanding and support of the people themselves which is essential to victory. I am convinced that you will again give that support to leadership in these critical days. . . .

I favor as a practical policy the putting of first things first. I shall spare no effort to restore world trade by international economic readjustment, but the emergency at home cannot wait on that accomplishment.

The basic thought that guides these specific means of national recovery is not narrowly nationalistic.

It is the insistence, as a first consideration, upon the interdependence of the various elements in, and parts of, the United States—a recognition of the old and permanently important manifestation of the American spirit of the pioneer. . . .

I am prepared under my constitutional duty to recommend the measures that a stricken nation in the midst of a stricken world may require.

These measures, or such other measures as the Congress may build out of its experience and wisdom, I shall seek, within my constitutional authority, to bring to speedy adoption.

From *Documents of American History*, ed. Henry Steele Commager (New York: Crofts, 1934), pp. 417, 419. Though many editions of Commager's collection of documents have appeared since, it is interesting to note that only a year after Roosevelt had delivered his address, a professional historian already considered it to be one of the basic documents of American history.

---

the gold standard. They aimed to thaw out credit by extending the activities of the RFC and by creating such new governmental lending agencies as the Home Owners' Loan Corporation. They aimed to relieve unemployment by public works on a large scale, to safeguard bank deposits by the Federal Deposit Insurance Corporation, and to regulate speculation and other stock-market activities by the Securities and Exchange Commission. The National Recovery Act (NRA) of 1933 set up production codes in industry to regulate competition and to ensure labor's right to organize and carry on collective bargaining. The historical significance of many of these innovations rested in the fact that they were undertaken not by private business or by state or local authorities but by the federal government.

The long-term measures of the New Deal were, of course, more important. The Social Security Act of 1935 introduced to the United States on a national scale the unemployment insurance, old-age pensions, and other benefits of the kind that Lloyd George had brought to Britain. By extending and revising tax structures, including the income tax authorized by the Sixteenth Amendment to the Constitution in 1913, Congress in effect redistributed wealth to some degree. Congress also passed a series of acts on labor relations that strengthened and extended the role of organized labor. A series of acts on

agriculture regulated crops and prices and provided subsidies on a large scale. And a great regional planning board, the Tennessee Valley Authority, used government power to make over the economic life of a relatively backward area by checking the erosion of farmlands, instituting flood control, and providing cheap electric power generated at government-built dams.

The presidential election of 1936 gave Roosevelt an emphatic popular endorsement. Yet the New Deal never regained the momentum it had in his first term. In retrospect it seems evident that the measures taken by the Roosevelt administration, combined with the resilience of American institutions and culture, pulled the United States at least part way out of the depression. Full recovery, however, did not come until the boom set off by the outbreak of World War II.

The spring and summer of 1939 found Americans anxious to remain neutral if Europe should persist in going to war. Roosevelt and his Republican opponents had been for some time exchanging insults. Yet in the pinch of the international crisis of 1939 it became clear that, although the nation was not completely united, it was not deeply divided. As so often in American history, the violence of verbal politics—in which language is often used with more vehemence than in Europe—masked a basic unity.

FDR inspired confidence in people, and wherever he went crowds reached out to shake his hand. Here, as he waited for his wife, Eleanor, who had been addressing a meeting in December 1933, the president was surrounded by admirers. Friendly photographers almost always showed the president in a seated position and either behind a desk or in a car in order not to reveal that he was in a wheelchair.

UPI/Bettmann Newsphotos

When, on September 1, the war came, the United States had already made many efforts to enlist the support of the Latin American states, so that the New World might once again redress the grievances of the Old. In 1930, before the so-called Roosevelt Revolution in American diplomacy, President Hoover's State Department issued a memorandum specifically stating that the Monroe Doctrine did not concern itself with inter-American relations, but was directed against *outside* intervention in the affairs of the Western Hemisphere. The United States was no longer to land Marines in a Central American republic; rather, American policy was to try to strengthen hemispheric solidarity. On these foundations, President Roosevelt built his celebrated Good Neighbor policy toward the other American nations, withdrawing the United States from Cuba and beginning the liquidation of formal American empire.

THE EAST MEETS THE WEST: WESTERN HISTORY AND WORLD HISTORY

The interwar years were marked by a fundamental change in the relations between those nations associated with "Western civilization" and the nations and peoples of Asia and the Middle East, and to a lesser extent, of Africa. Though virtually the whole of the world had been brought into the European and American orbits during the age of imperialism, people in the West had not recognized that the societies of Asia and Africa had histories of their own. Even though the history of the West and that of other parts of the world had impinged upon each other through trade, cultural borrowing, the migration of peoples, and the setting up of empires, the histories of Japan or China, for instance, had not become significant as yet to an understanding of Western history. Now they would become so, and Western history and world history would be virtually indistinguishable.

Japan

Alone among non-Western peoples, the Japanese maintained full political independence during the golden age of imperialism. More than that, as the twentieth century opened, Japan was experiencing the industrial revolution and advancing to the status of a great power, a full (if unwelcome) participant in the struggle for imperial position. Since the Japanese made these impressive accomplishments without radically altering their traditional oligarchical and absolutist political structure, they remained fully "of the East," even as they became an integral part of Western history.

In the decade after World War I, it looked as though Japan might gradually liberalize its political institutions. The cabinets of the 1920s included many businessmen who favored vigorous expansion abroad but who also granted some measure of cautious liberalism at home. The suffrage was gradually extended, for example, and in 1925 all men received the right to vote; women were granted this right in 1949. For the first time, Western-style political parties began to develop, especially in the cities, and seemed likely to give new vitality to the Diet, the relatively weak Japanese parliament. Trade unions also began to win a following.

However, interwar Japan did not evolve into a parliamentary democracy. By the early 1930s political power was falling into the hands of army and navy officers, many of whom were descended from the feudal samurai class. This officer clique hated the prospect of liberal civilian government and envied and mistrusted the business class. It found a potent political weapon in the institution of the emperor, who was supposed to possess the kind of political infallibility that Westerners had associated with a divine-right monarch. Putting their own words into the emperor's mouth, the admirals and generals used his pronouncements to further their own ends.

The consequence was a military dictatorship in Japan during the 1930s. Although popular elections continued to be held, their results were disregarded; businessmen supported the new regime out of fear or in anticipation of the profits to be secured from its adventures abroad. A cult of emperor worship grew, focusing popular loyalties on the divine mission of the emperor and ensuring popular submission to the will of those who ruled in his name. A corps of ruthless agents, named "thought police," hounded people suspected of harboring "dangerous thoughts." In short, Japan now had a government that exploited many uniquely Japanese traditions but in its operations also bore a striking resemblance to the totalitarian governments of Europe.

Nowhere was the parallel with European totalitarianism more marked than in the foreign policy of Japan between the two world wars. Like Hitler's Germany or Mussolini's Italy, Japan claimed to be a "have-not" nation. The Japanese, too, pointed to their steadily growing population and did all they could to encourage its further growth. Having experienced 125 years of zero growth before 1853—during which time they had improved their standard of living, consolidated their natural resources, and begun to urbanize and accumulate capital—the Japanese were well into a sustained period of economic and population growth. Between 1850 and 1950 (despite the intervening wars) the population soared from 32 million to 84 million. The Japanese, too, harped on the overcrowding of the homeland, its inadequate resources, and its restricted markets.

Behind these arguments lay real economic problems of sustaining the Japanese economy in the face of the depression and the worldwide disruption of international trade, problems of providing food and work for the population, which in 1930 numbered 60 million. In seeking to solve these problems by imperial expansion, the militarists of the 1930s were following a pattern that had already been set by the West. And they were also following the path marked out by the Japanese officers and politicians who had secured Formosa in 1895 and annexed Korea in 1910. During World War I Japan had tried in vain to subjugate China; by World War II it had apparently almost succeeded in doing so.

Korea, once so isolated as to be called the Hermit Kingdom, had first been united in A.D. 668. At various times it was associated with the Chinese empire. Now, from 1910 until 1945, it would be governed by Japan, which changed its name to Chosun. Racism grew in Japan in the 1920s and 1930s, toward Koreans, Chinese, and Westerners, and during the destructive earthquake that swept across the Kanto plain in Japan in 1923, leveling Yokohama and two thirds of Tokyo and claiming 140,000 lives. Six thousand Koreans were killed by Japanese in frustration and rage.

China

China, meantime, was engaged in a great struggle to free itself from the hold of the Western colonial powers. The struggle was much more than a simple conflict between nationalists and imperialists. It was complicated by two additional elements in particular—the increasing threat to Chinese independence from an expansionist Japan and increasing communist intervention in Chinese politics. China faced the prospect of simply exchanging one set of imperial overlords for another.

By 1900 the Chinese Empire had lost much of its effective sovereignty through concessions of naval bases and economic and political privileges to the European powers and Japan. Following China's defeat by Japan in 1895, European imperialists had engaged in a hectic scramble for further concessions (see Chapter 22). A formidable reaction to this outburst of imperialist activity had erupted within China. The hard-pressed Manchu government had encouraged the formation of antiforeign nationalist secret societies, of which the most important was the Fists of Righteous Harmony. Missionaries called this group the *Boxers,* and when they revolted, the name was taken up by the Western press. The result of the Boxer Rebellion of 1900, in which more than two hundred foreigners were slain, was the use of troops by the foreign powers, including the United States, to protect their nationals and property against the Boxers. In 1901 they obliged the Manchu government to pay a large indemnity and to grant them rights that further impaired Chinese sovereignty.

The next Chinese rebellion, the revolution of 1911, was directed against the Manchu regime that had proved so incapable of resisting foreign imperialism. The movement was also directed against the West—against Westerners themselves or against local governors who seemed to be agents of the West. But it was a movement inspired at least in part by Western ideas and examples and often led by thoroughly "Westernized" Chinese.

From the start, two chief revolutionary groups displayed conflicting ideas about the nature of the new society that would replace the Manchus. One group formed the Nationalist party, the Kuomintang, led by Sun Yat-sen (1866–1925) and many young intellectuals who had studied and traveled in the West. Its leaders wanted a democratic parliamentary republic modeled on the Western political system, though preserving as far as possible the basic Chinese family and village structure, on to which Western industrial society was to be grafted. The other group, whose leader was Yüan Shih-k'ai (1859– 1916), wanted a strong central government basically authoritarian in structure, with authority not in the hands of an emperor and the traditional and highly conservative mandarin bureaucracy but in the hands of strong men capable of modernizing China from above.

A struggle for power broke out between the assembly elected after 1911 and Yüan Shih-k'ai. The party of Sun Yat-sen was defeated, and by 1914, after a purge of the Kuomintang members of the assembly, Yüan Shih-k'ai issued a constitutional declaration that put him in the presidential office for ten years. Sun Yat-sen and his followers had failed to turn China into a parliamentary democracy. Yüan, however, died in 1916, leaving the new republic facing the prospect of the dissolution of all but the shadow of central control and

The Western world first became fully aware of Generalissimo Chiang Kai-shek as a significant force in China by this press photo, sent out in December 1935, when he was chosen as chairman of the Executive Yuan, becoming virtual dictator of China.

AP/Wide World Photos

the assumption of real power by regional strongmen. A new era of provincial warlords had begun.

In the same years, China also faced the aggressive attempts of Japan to take over the Far Eastern imperial interests of European powers now at war among themselves. Early in 1915 the Japanese secretly presented to the Chinese government the Twenty-One Demands, which amounted to a demand for something close to a protectorate over China. The Chinese republic, now at the lowest point of its strength, countered by declaring war against the Central Powers, thus securing at least the nominal protection of Britain and France. Unable to defy Western objections, the Japanese contented themselves with taking over the German concessions. At the end of the war the victorious Allies, with the United States in the lead, checked the ambitions of their recent military partner. In 1922 Japan was forced to sign a Nine-Power Treaty guaranteeing the independence of China. This rebuff to Japan was one of the first in a long chain of events that intensified the hostility of Japan toward the United States and ended, two decades later, in war.

After World War I, then, the main elements in the Chinese political situation were the Kuomintang, the communists, and the Japanese invaders. After the death of Sun Yat-sen, the Kuomintang came under the leadership of his brother-in-law, Chiang Kai-shek (1887–1975), an army officer trained in Japan. The nationalists of the Kuomintang were engaged in a constant and unsuccessful struggle to set up an effective central government against the provincial warlords. The Chinese communist movement began in the early 1920s. At first it was inspired by direct contacts with the Comintern in Moscow, guided by Soviet agents, and encouraged by leaders of the Kuomintang itself. For a time the Chinese communists were little more than the left wing of the Kuomintang, but a breach soon occurred between them and the more conservative elements led by Chiang Kai-shek.

The communists did badly in this early struggle for power. In 1926 Chiang's forces began a campaign of persecution and assassination against them; in 1927 they were expelled from the Kuomintang. An important reason for this setback was the failure of the Chinese communists to get effective support from Moscow, for these were the years of the Trotsky-Stalin feud. The conflict between the two Soviet titans was intensified by their differences over the "correct" Chinese policy for the Soviet Union to follow. Stalin, who was rapidly gaining the ascendancy, believed that China was not ripe for a proletarian revolution; therefore, he did nothing to help his Chinese comrades.

Nationalists and communists fought in word and deed for the allegiance, or the passive acceptance, of nearly 500 million Chinese, for the most part illiterate peasants. To transform China into a nation in the Western sense required more than building railroads and factories or promoting the study of modern science instead of the Chinese classics. It required getting the Chinese peasants to regard themselves as Chinese citizens. This indispensable process was beginning in the 1920s and 1930s.

After heavy shelling, Japanese units advanced through the war zone around Shanghai in 1937. This dramatic news photo was rushed to the United States by the new trans-Pacific Clipper airmail service.

AP/Wide World Photos

The Japanese attack came in September 1931 in Manchuria, an outlying northern province of China that was a particularly tempting target for Japanese aggression. Manchuria had coal and iron; it adjoined Korea, already a Japanese possession; and it had never been fully integrated into China. Moreover, the Japanese regarded themselves as the natural successors of the Russians, whom they had driven from Manchuria in the Russo-Japanese war of 1904–1905. By 1932 the Japanese were strong enough to proclaim Manchuria the "independent" state of Manchukuo, under a puppet ruler, Henry Pu-yi (1905– 1967), who as a child had been the last emperor of old China. The Chinese responded by boycotting Japanese goods; the Japanese countered by carrying the war to the Chinese port of Shanghai. Given the weakness of the Kuomintang government, effective Chinese resistance would have required full support from strong outside forces. Neither the Western powers nor the League of Nations gave China more than verbal support; the Chinese had to give up their boycott, and the Japanese remained in Manchuria. Tensions between China and Japan persisted, and the Japanese soon decided to absorb most of the rest of China. The invasion came in July 1937 without a formal declaration of war.

Militarily, the Japanese did very well. By October, when the key southern Chinese city of Canton fell, they had taken the strategic points along the coastal area and the thickly populated river valleys. Chiang Kai-shek took

refuge in the interior province of Szechuan, where he set up his capital at Chungking on the upper Yangtze River. There, with Western aid, the nationalist government held out until the end of World War II and the collapse of Japanese imperialism.

Yet even at the height of their success, the Japanese had achieved no more than the stretching across China of a string of garrisons and the control of great cities like Shanghai and Peking. They held the railroads, subject to guerrilla attack, but away from the relatively sparse lines of modern communication they were helpless. Many Chinese villages in the area that were nominally Japanese never changed their ways during the occupation; nowhere did the Japanese win over the Chinese people.

The nationalists of the Kuomintang led the resistance to the Japanese from the beginning, but they, too, ultimately failed to win the full loyalty of the Chinese people. This was partly a military matter, for Chiang's armies were no match for the Japanese, who controlled the few industrial cities in China. During the long exile in Szechuan, moreover, the morale of the nationalists decayed. The ordeal, far from purifying and strengthening them, emphasized their alienation from the Chinese masses, their own corruption and intrigue, and their inability to live up to the early promise of Sun Yat-sen and the Kuomintang. It was the communists, not the nationalists, who succeeded in the end.

During the 1930s and the early 1940s the relative strength of communists and nationalists underwent a decisive shift. Both parties were in a sense totalitarian. Both were organized on the one-party pattern, which left no place for an opposition. The communists, pursued across much of China during the 1930s, ended up with a base in Yenan in the north; their strategic position somewhat resembled that of Chiang in Szechuan. But there was an important difference. In the long years of Japanese occupation, Chiang remained in Chungking with his army and his bureaucracy. The communists, on the other hand, managed to extend their network of organized armies and local councils in and around the Japanese in the north, and down to the sea and up through Manchuria. By 1945 the communists were ready for their successful conflict with the Kuomintang.

India

In India World War I had marked a crucial turning point. Indians, growing in numbers and educated in the Western tradition, responded to Allied propaganda in favor of the war to save the world for democracy. Monetary inflation and other war dislocations fostered growing agitation for self-government. Already during the war the British viceroy and his experts were planning reforms. These plans were conditioned by tensions between Hindus and Muslims. About a quarter of the total population of British India was Muslim. In the Indus Basin and part of the Punjab in the northwest and in part of Bengal in the east, the Muslims were a majority; elsewhere they lived scattered among the Hindus and other non-Muslims.

While they might mix socially and in the civil service or the British bureaucracy, Hindu and Muslim felt strong antipathy toward each other, in part on deeply held religious grounds. Muslims opposed idolatry in all forms and felt that Hindu worship of many gods was unacceptable, and that the depiction of those gods in a variety of human, and often explicitly sexual, forms was sacrilegious. To the Hindu, much in the world was divine; the Hindu might worship the cow or other animals, which the Muslim might slaughter. The Hindu regarded Muslim practices as unclean, while the Muslim saw Hindu practices as unholy. It was not surprising, therefore, that after serious attempts to bring Hindu and Muslim into a unified resistance movement against the British, two separate bodies arose in the twentieth century—the Indian National Congress and All-India Muslim League.

Despite these difficulties, the Indian drive for self-government and independence went on steadily after World War I. For the Hindus, the Congress party was held together effectively and given extraordinary influence over the masses by one of the great leaders of the twentieth century, Mohandas K. Gandhi (1869–1948). Gandhi was a member of the *bania*, or shopkeeping caste. Educated at Oxford and therefore familiar with the West, trained in practical politics as a young lawyer serving the Indian minority in South Africa, Gandhi was admirably equipped to deal with both British and Hindus. He devised the technique of insurrection called *Satyagraha*, or nonviolent noncooperation, which appealed to the fundamental Hindu belief that force is illusory and therefore ineffective. A characteristic measure sponsored by Gandhi was the organized Indian boycott of British goods. The Mahatma, as Gandhi was known, also defied Hindu prejudice, directing some of his hunger strikes not against the British but against the status of the untouchables as pariahs outside the caste system.

Other Congress leaders, especially at the local level, were willing to imitate Western methods of agitation, propaganda, and some violent "nonviolence." Concession after concession was wrung from the British, and as the Indians gained political experience in provincial self-government and in civil service, dominion status was thought to be just around the corner. This was the situation at the outbreak of World War II. By the time the war was over, however, the mutual antagonism of Hindus and Muslims seemed to require not a single unified India, but two separate states.

The Middle East

The European powers had a long history of attempts to secure an imperial stake in the Middle East. Before 1914 the region was still poverty stricken. But by 1914 the first discoveries of petroleum had been made; today the Middle East contains the richest nations in the world. The whole area was not to share in this new wealth. The major fields were found in southwestern Persia, in the river valleys of Iraq, and along the Persian Gulf. These newfound riches heightened the interest of the European powers, and in the 1930s, as American experts began to worry about the depletion of oil reserves in the Western Hemisphere, American business entered the area to compete with well-established French and British interests.

Although the Westerners tried to maintain sufficient control of the Middle East to ensure the orderly exploitation of oil, they also tried to avoid the cruder sort of political imperialism. After World War I the Arab territories of the old Ottoman Empire were administered as Western mandates, not annexed as Western colonies. The French had received the mandates for Syria and for Syria's half-Christian neighbor, Lebanon. The British, who already held a protectorate over Egypt, were given the mandates for Palestine and Iraq. The only major Arab state enjoying anything like full independence was Saudi Arabia. It was an essentially medieval state, the personal creation of a tribal chieftain, Ibn Saud (1880–1953). The postwar mandates, which brought so much of the Arab world under imperial control, frustrated the aspirations of Arab nationalists. In these nationalist movements the usual ingredients—Western education, hatred of Westerners, desire to emulate Western technology—were mixed with adherence to Islam and a feeling of a common Arab identity.

Arab nationalism was already focused on the special problem of Palestine, for by the Balfour Declaration of

Democracy at the Village Level

Mohandas Gandhi was in pursuit of *Swaraj* (independence), and he wrote of it often. In 1921 he sought to explain "the secret of *Swaraj*."

The householder has to revise his or her ideas of fashion and, at least for the time being, suspend the use of fine garments which are not always worn to cover the body. He should train himself to see art and beauty in the spotlessly white *Khaddar* and to appreciate its soft unevenness. The householder must learn to use cloth as a miser uses his hoard.

And even when the householders have revised their tastes about dress, somebody will have to spin yarn for the weavers. This can only be done by everyone spinning during spare hours either for love or for money.

Under the pre-British economy of India, spinning was an honourable and leisurely occupation for the women of India. It was an art confined to the women of India, because the latter had more leisure. And being graceful, musical, and as it did not involve any great exertion, it had become the monopoly of women. But it is certainly as graceful for either sex as is music, for instance. In handspinning is hidden the protection of women's virtue, the insurance against famine, and the cheapening of prices. In it is hidden the secret of *Swaraj*. . . . The revival of handspinning is the least penance we must do for the sin of our forefathers in having succumbed to the Satanic influences of the foreign manufacturer.

Do I want to put back the hand of the clock of progress? Do I want to replace the mills by hand-spinning and hand-weaving? Do I want to replace the railway by the country cart? Do I want to destroy machinery altogether? These questions have been asked by some journalists and public men. My answer is: I would not weep over the disappearance of machinery or consider it a calamity. But I have no design upon machinery as such. What I want to do at the present moment is to supplement the production of yarn and cloth through our mills, save the millions we send out of India, and distribute them in our cottages. . . .

Just as we cannot live without breathing and without eating, so is it impossible for us to attain economic independence and banish pauperism from this ancient land without reviving home-spinning. I hold the spinning wheel to be as much a necessity in every household as the hearth. No other scheme that can be devised will ever solve the problem of the deepening poverty of the people.

M. K. Gandhi, *The Village Reconstruction, by M. K. Gandhi*, ed. Anan T. Hingorani (Bombay: Bharatiya Vidya Bhavan, 1966), pp. 5–7.

1917 the British had promised to open this largely Arab-populated territory as a "national home for the Jewish people." The immigration of Jews into Palestine, especially after the Nazis took power in Germany, raised their proportion of the population from about 10 percent to about 30 percent and caused repeated clashes between Arabs and Jews. Caught between Jewish nationalism (or Zionism) and Arab nationalism, the British tried in vain to placate both sides. On the eve of World War II, the British restricted Jewish immigration into Palestine and Jewish purchases of Arab lands in the mandate. The seeds were thus sown for the acute Palestine problem of the postwar period.

The French made few concessions to Arab nationalism, infuriating the Syrians by bombarding their capital of Damascus while quelling an insurrection in 1925 and 1926. A decade later the expectations aroused by the Popular Front's willingness to grant at least some independence to Syria and Lebanon were nullified when the French parliament rejected the draft treaties, intensifying the Arab sense of betrayal. Soon nationalist leaders in Algeria and later in Tunisia were discussing with the Arabs of Syria and Lebanon how to make common cause against the French.

The British attempted a more conciliatory policy by granting some of their dependencies nominal independence. In Egypt nationalist agitation after World War I led Britain to proclaim that country an independent monarchy under King Fuad I (1868–1936). The British, however, still retained the right to station troops there. They also insisted that Westerners resident there be under the jurisdiction not of regular Egyptian courts but of mixed courts, on which Western judges outnumbered Eygptians. In 1936 an Anglo-Egyptian agreement provided for the eventual end of the mixed courts and the eventual withdrawal of British troops from the country, except along the Suez Canal. Meanwhile, Egypt continued to be closely allied with Britain.

Turkey, too, was undergoing a political renaissance. World War I reduced its territory to a cohesive national unit, the largely Turkish-populated Anatolia. To defend this core against further losses to the Greeks and to the victorious Allies, the Turks launched an ardent nationalist revival, dramatically extending the reforms begun by the Young Turks before 1914. The leader of this new political revolution was the gifted army officer Mustafa Kemal, who drove the Greeks from Anatolia and negotiated more

Naming and Nationalism

One aspect of both modernization and nationalism is to change names that have long been used in a way now regarded as derogatory, false, not properly indicative of the values of the new society, or simply out of date as new forms of transliteration replace old in the West. Instances abound throughout this chapter. The great capital city of China, long known as Peking (and so referred to here), is now Beijing (and will be so called in subsequent chapters) because of the modernization of methods for transliterating Chinese characters and their sounds into English. Persia is now officially Iran, though it is nonetheless still correct to refer to the citizens of Iran as Persians, for one is used as a noun and the other as an adjective.

Thus not only in changing place names, but in their pronunciation, in the creation of titles, in the translation of phrases, history shows its biases and is quickly dated. Even in so apparently simple a matter as the pronunciation of the former British East African colony of Kenya lurks the sound of historical transition, since before independence the colony was pronounced "keen-ya," while the independent nation was properly pronounced "ken-ya." Historians must observe these distinctions if they are to be true to the time they describe.

favorable terms with the Allies at Lausanne in 1923. Under his guidance, the republic of Turkey was proclaimed in 1922, with a constitution modeled on Western parliamentary lines, though with a one-party system.

Kemal also imposed rapid, wholesale, and sometimes ruthless measures of Westernization. Women received the vote, began to serve as deputies in the parliament, and were, at least in theory, emancipated from Muslim restraints, though even Kemal did not dare to sponsor legislation banning the wearing of the veil in public. He did, however, require men to wear Western garb. The sacred law of Islam was replaced by a European law code; polygamy was banned and civil marriage required; the Western calendar was introduced; and the building of new mosques and repair of old ones were discouraged. The Turkish language was reformed by the introduction of a Western alphabet—a measure of major importance, for only a fraction of the Turkish people had ever been able to master the old Ottoman Turkish, with its heavy content of Persian and Arabic words and its difficult Arabic script. All Turks were now required to take surnames in the Western manner, and Kemal himself took that of "Atatürk" (Father of the Turks). At his death in 1938 Atatürk had revolutionized his country. Moreover, he had established its independence of the West, as the neutrality of Turkey during World War II was soon to demonstrate.

The example of Turkey was followed by the other traditionally independent major state of the Middle East—Iran (Persia). The Iranian revolution began in 1905–1906 in response to imperialist encroachments by Britain and Russia. The political structure inherited from the Middle Ages was changed into a limited monarchy with an elected parliament. This revolution proved to be abortive, however. The country, with its powerful, wealthy

landlords, its peasants, and its tribes, did not adapt itself readily to modern Western political institutions. The shah was unwilling to give up his traditional powers, and the British and Russians were unwilling to give up their spheres of influence. During World War I, therefore, they both stationed troops in an ostensibly neutral Persia.

The Russian Revolution eased the czarist threat to Persian sovereignty, and at the end of the war Persian nationalists forced their government to reject a British attempt to negotiate a treaty that would have made the country a virtual British protectorate. The leader of the nationalists was Reza Khan (1878–1944), an able army officer of little education who deeply distrusted the Russians. He used his military successes to become, first, minister of war and then, in 1923, prime minister. Thereafter he tried to manipulate the *Majles*, or parliament, to his purposes, and he won the support of the army and the cabinet. After conferring with the clergy in the holy city of Qum, the forces of Islam also fell into line behind him. In 1925 the Majles deposed the Qajar dynasty and proclaimed Reza to be Reza Shah Pahlavi. Reza Shah lacked familiarity with the West, and his erratic attempts to modernize his isolated country often failed. He ruled in increasingly arbitrary fashion, also demonstrating mounting sympathy for the Nazis. In 1941, after Hitler's invasion of the Soviet Union, the British and Soviets sent troops into Iran and forced Reza Shah's abdication in order to secure the important trans-Iranian supply route to the Soviet Union.

The fate of Reza Shah was a reminder that some of the seemingly sovereign states of the non-Western world were not yet strong enough to maintain their independence against great powers. By World War II imperial ties had been loosened but by no means severed or dissolved; the full revolution against imperialism was yet to come.

SUMMARY

Great Britain was the first nation to suffer from the ills of postindustrial development. In the postwar period Conservatives wanted to preserve private industry and advocated protective tariffs against foreign competition. Labour called for nationalization of key industries.

Political democratization continued in Britain with all men over age twenty-one receiving the vote. Women over age twenty-one finally gained equal voting rights in 1928. A slight economic recovery in the later 1920s was followed by the Great Depression.

By 1919 Irish nationalists were demanding complete independence from Britain rather than home rule. In 1921 the twenty-six southern countries became the Irish Free State, while the six Ulster counties remained tied to Britain. Although Britain recognized the full independence of the Republic of Ireland in 1949, the problem of Northern Ireland remained.

France felt the impact of the war most heavily, both in terms of casualties and material damage. In the 1920s, as the rebuilding effort got under way, France suffered severe inflation as well as other economic and social dislocations. Political divisions inherited from the French Revolution resurfaced in postwar France.

Rocked by economic and political difficulties, French governments compromised with Hitler and Mussolini despite protests from the left. In 1939 France was poorly equipped militarily and psychologically to deal with the threat of war.

People in the French colonies of Algeria, Senegal, and Indochina demanded home rule or independence. The French mandates of Syria and Lebanon were given constitutions but not independence.

In the postwar period, the isolationist mood of the United States was reflected in its tariffs and in the policy of imposing quotas to limit immigration. Nevertheless, the United States was still involved in European and world affairs in the 1920s.

At home, the uneven prosperity of the Coolidge years and the unprecedented speculation on Wall Street ended with the stock market crash of 1929. The Great Depression was worse and lasted longer in the United States than elsewhere. Franklin D. Roosevelt introduced the New Deal to ameliorate conditions. Yet full recovery did not occur until the outbreak of World War II.

A liberalizing trend that occurred in Japan after World War I ended in the 1930s when the military acquired political power and imposed a military dictatorship. As in Italy and Germany, the Japanese regime embarked on an expansionist policy, claiming the need for living space, resources, and new markets.

In 1911 a revolution toppled the Manchu regime in China. China struggled to free itself from Western imperialist powers but was distracted by an internal conflict between nationalist and communist forces and by the threat of Japanese expansion. In 1931 Japan attacked Manchuria and in 1937 invaded China proper.

Indians agitated for self-government in the 1920s and 1930s, but irreconcilable differences between Hindus and Muslims prevented a united front. Gandhi, leader of the Congress party, advocated nonviolent noncooperation, which appealed to many Hindus.

In the Middle East, European powers were anxious to protect access to petroleum deposits. The mandate system that continued European control in the region frustrated the hopes of Arab nationalists. Although Egypt became independent, Britain had the right to keep troops there. In Turkey, Mustafa Kemal imposed wholesale Westernization. In Iran, Reza Shah's attempt to modernize rapidly met with only limited success.

CRITICAL THINKING

1. How did the programs of the Conservative and Labour parties in Britain differ?

2. What was "the Irish question," and what role did it play in British politics?

3. Was the Commonwealth of Nations simply a substitute for the old British Empire or was it a different form of political and economic grouping of nations?

4. Describe the impact of World War I on France.

5. How did Britain, France, and the United States deal with the postwar economic crisis?

6. What did American political leaders mean by a policy of "isolationism"? In what ways did the policy prove beneficial to Americans and in what ways did it prove harmful?

7. What were the main achievements of the New Deal in the United States?

8. There has always been "world history," and yet non-Western nations often are studied in the West only as they come to play roles in Western history, generally beginning in the eighteenth and early nineteenth centuries. Can this practice be defended? How? What are the major educational flaws that may arise from organizing knowledge in this way?

9. Which non-Western area—Japan, China, India, or the Middle East—played the most fundamental role in influencing Western policies in the years between the two world wars?

10. Which legacy from these roles is most evident today?

DATES	POLITICAL	THOUGHT AND ARTS	ECONOMY AND SOCIETY
1850 A.D.		1856–1939 Sigmund Freud 1861–1932 Frederick Jackson Turner 1864 George Perkins Marsh, *Man and Nature*	
1870	1869–1948 Mohandas K. Gandhi 1874–1965 Winston Churchill	1869–1959 Frank Lloyd Wright	
1900	1893–1976 Mao Zedong	1881–1973 Pablo Picasso 1888–1965 T. S. Eliot 1889–1976 Martin Hiedegger 1898–1986 Herny Moore 1901–1976 Werner Heisenberg 1901–1966 Walt Disney 1904–1989 Salvador Dali 1905–1980 Jean-Paul Sartre 1915– Frank Sinatra 1915–1980 Roland Barthes 1916 Albert Einstein publishes the general theory of reativity 1918 Oswald Sengler, *The Decline of the West*	20th century Rise of English as the international language 20th century Slow breakdown of traditional family and social order
1920	1919–1939 The Twenty Years' Truce 1919 Comintern founded 1921–1922 Washington Naval Conference 1922 Treaty of Rapallo 1925 Locarno Treaties	1920s The Dada Movement 1922 James Joyce, *Ulysses*	1920s Beginning of the modern environmental movement
1930	1931 Japan seizes Manchuria 1931 Mikhail Gorbachev 1932 World Disarmament Conference 1934–1936 The Long March 1935–1936 German rearmament begins 1935 Italy invades Ethiopia 1935 Franco-Soviet Alliance 1936 Germany remilitarizes the Rhineland 1936–1939 Spanish Civil War 1937 Japan invades China 1938 Germany invades Austria 1938 Munich Agreement	1934–1954 Arnold Toynbee, *Study of History*	
1940	1939 Germany occupies Czechoslovakia and Memel 1939 Hitler-Stalin Pact September 1, 1939 German invasion of Poland; start of World War II May 1940 German invasion of France, Churchill becomes prime minister 1941–1945 The Holocaust March 1941 Lend-Lease Act June 1941 Germany invades Soviet Union December 7, 1941 Japan attacks Pearl Harbor November 1942 Allies invade North Africa and Soviets defend Stalingrad June 6, 1944 D-Day February 1945 Yalta Conference May 1945 Soviets take Berlin and Germany surrenders 1945–1951 Attlee government August 1945 Atomic bombings lead to the surrender of Japan 1945 United Nations (UN) chartered 1946 Nuremberg trials 1947 Truman Doctrine 1947 Marshall Plan proposed 1947 India and Pakistan gain independence 1948 Berlin Airlift 1948 Youslav Rebellion 1949 Creation of East and West Germany 1949 Communists victorious in Chinese civil war 1949 North Atlantic Treaty Organization (NATO) founded 1949 First Soviet atomic bomb tested	1939 James Joyce, *Finnegan's Wake* 1939 The movie version of "Gone with the Wind" 1942 Albert Camus, *The Stranger* 1943–1944 Henry Moore, *Madonna and Child* 1944 T. S. Eliot, *Four Quartets* 1944 Jean-Paul Sartre, *No Exit* 1944 Aaron Copland, "Appalachian Spring" 1945 Benjamin Britten, "Peter Grimes" 1947 Discovery of the Dead Sea Scrolls 1948 Tennessee Williams, *A Streetcar Named Desire* 1949 George Orwell, *1984* 1949 Simone de Beauvoir, *The Second Sex* later 20th century Rise of the motion picture	1939 New York World's Fair 1940s–1980s Era of Decolonization 1940s Women enter the workforce in record numbers 1940 First successful helicopter flight 1942 Enrico Fermi splits the atom 1945 Women gain the right to vote in France 1947 Bell Laboratories invent the transistor 1947 GI Bill enables one million veterans to go to college 1947 Jet plane breaks the sound barrier late 1940s Rise of the suburb later 20th century Increasing concern for world opinion and human rights later 20th century Television becomes increasingly influential

DATES	POLITICAL	THOUGHT AND ARTS	ECONOMY AND SOCIETY
1950 A.D.	1950–1953 Korean War	1950s Rise of the conflict school of American historiography 1950–1951 Henri Matisse, murals for the Vence chapel 1950 Marc Chagall, King David	1950s–1960s The German and Italian Miracles early 1950s The McCarthy Era 1950s German and Italian economic miracles 1950s World wide migration of people begins 1950s Beginning of the civil rights movement in the U.S. 1950s Insecurities of Cold War lead to increase in racism
	1952 Egyptian revolution 1953 Death of Stalin 1953–1961 Administration of Dwight Eisenhower 1954 French defeated at Dien Bien Phu 1954 *Brown v. Board of Education of Topeka* 1956 Krushchev denounces Stalin 1956 Hungarian and Polish uprisings 1956 Suez crisis 1957 Treaty of Rome 1957 Ghana gains independence under Kwame Nkrumah late 1950s Chinese Great Leap Forward 1958 Charles de Gaulle returns to power 1959 Cuban Revolution	1952 "Revised Standard Version" of the Bible published 1952 Jackson Pollack, Number 12 1957 Leonard Bernstein, "West Side Story" 1958 Boris Pasternak, *Dr. Zhivago*	1951 Introduction of color television 1952 First contraceptive pill produced 1953 U.S.S.R. detonates the first hydrogen bomb 1954 Salk vaccine for polio 1956 "Rock and Roll" becomes the craze 1956 First transatlantic telephone service 1957 Soviet Union launches Sputnik 1959 Twenty-first Ecumenical Council (Vatican II)
1960	1960 Harold Macmillan makes "Winds of Change" speech 1960s–1970s Soviet agriculture declines and stagnets 1960 Sharpeville massacre 1961 Berlin Wall built 1962 Cuban Missile Crisis 1964 Coup ousts Khrushchev 1964 Federal Civil Rights Act mid–1960s Great Society programs 1965–1969 U.S. troops in Vietman increase from 12,000 to 625,000 1966–1977 Indira Gandhi governs India 1966–1969 Chinese Cultural Revolution 1967 Third Arab-Israeli War 1967 General Suharto takes power in Indonesia 1968 Soviet invasion of Czechoslovakia 1968 Martin Luther King, Jr. assassinated	1960s Pop art 1962–1965 Second Vatican Council later 1960s The Beatles 1967 Marshall McLuhan, *The Medium is the Message* 1967 Gabriel Garcia Marquez, *One Hundred Years of Solitude*	1960s Birth control pill becomes widely available 1960s Civil Rights movement in the U.S. 1961 First manned space flight 1965–1967 American race riots late 1960s Indian "green revolution" 1968–1969 Widespread student violence 1969 Neil Armstrong walks on the moon
1970	1970s–1980s Rise of terrorism as a political weapon 1970s Rise of the Parti Quebecois in Canada 1970–1981 Anwar el-Sadat governs Egypt 1970 Salvador Allende Gossens elected president of Chile 1972 Nixon normalizes American relations with China 1972–1974 The Watergate Affair 1973 Great Britain joins European Economic Community 1973 Roe V. Wade 1974 Arab oil embargo 1975 South Vietman falls 1976 Death of Mao later 1970s Decrease in cold war tension 1977–1978 Camp David accords 1979–1990 Thatcher Government 1979 Soviet Union invades Afghanistan 1979–1981 Iranian hostage crisis	1970s–1980s Growth of the modern feminist movement 1974 Alexander Solzhenisyn, *The Gulag Archipelago*	Late 1960s–1970s Anti-Vietnam War movement 1960s–1980s Increasing popularity of recreational drugs 1970s Movement for female equality grows 1973–1974 Energy Crisis in Europe and the U.S. c. 1975 Beginning of the Computer Age 1977 U.S. tests the neutron bomb 1978 First test-tube baby born, in Britain r. 1978– Pope John Paul II
1980	1980–1988 Iran-Iraq War 1981–1989 Administration of Ronald Reagan 1981 Suppression of the Polish Solidarity movement 1985 Gorbachev begins *perstroika* and *glasnost* 1986 Fall of the Marcos regime in the Philippines 1986 Iran-Contra scandal 1987 Gorbachev criticizes Stalin 1989 Communists defeated in free elections in Soviet Union 1989 Tiananmen Square massacre fall 1989 Communist regimes in Eastern Europe collapse 1990 Nelson Madela released from prison 1991 End of Communist rule in Soviet Union	1982 Sylvia Plath, *The Collected Poems* 1980s–1990s Islamic Fundamentalism 	1980s Beginning of the AIDS epidemic 1980s Rise of evangelical religions 1981 AIDS virus identified 1983 First CDs marketed 1984 Apple Macintosh retails the first micro-computers 1987 World population passes five billion late 1980s "Japan-bashing" grows in United States

The Second World War and Its Aftermath

WORLD WAR II WAS, IN many ways, a result of the flawed peace settlement at Versailles, though other causes, such as the Great Depression, also played a role. The cold war following World War II was in some ways a continuation in another form of the war of 1939–1945, though it was also in part a reversion to the Western fear of Bolshevism so prevalent in the 1920s. So troubled were international relations for the twenty years after 1919, and so closely in time did the second world war follow on the first, that the interval between the two is sometimes called the "twenty years' truce." It is likely that historians in the distant future will consider the two wars really one war, as they now consider the wars of the French Revolution and Napoleon essentially one war; but for the present, most historians continue to use the accepted terms: World War I (1914–1918) and World War II (1939–1945).

INTERNATIONAL POLITICS BETWEEN THE WARS

During the first part of the twenty years' truce, international leadership of the democratic world rested with Britain and France. Though supported in principle and at times in practice by the United States, they were increasingly unable to stem the rise of powers hostile to their preferred form of government—Italy, Germany, the Soviet Union, Japan. In the end, Germany once more waged aggressive warfare against the major Allies of 1918, though this time it was allied with two former enemies, Italy and Japan, each disappointed with its share of the spoils of 1918.

Nazi Germany maintained that the second war was the direct result of what its leaders called the "dictated peace" of Versailles. Supported by many sympathizers, the

Nazis claimed that Germany was humiliated by the "war-guilt" clause, stripped of territories and colonies, saddled with an unpayable reparations bill, and denied the normal rights of a sovereign state in armaments. The settlement of Versailles did saddle the new German republic with a heavy burden—a burden that was dictated in part by revenge and fear. With hindsight, a wiser Allied policy would perhaps have been to start the new government off without too great a burden. But hindsight is not history.

The West

What breaks down the argument that the iniquities of Versailles alone explain the Second World War is the so-called era of fulfillment. The landmark of this era was a series of treaties negotiated in 1925 at Locarno in Switzerland. Germany there agreed with France and Belgium on a mutual guarantee of their common frontiers; Britain and Italy agreed to act as guarantors—that is, to provide military aid against the aggressor if frontiers were violated. Germany affirmed its acceptance of the western frontier drawn at Versailles by the Rhineland Treaty. France affirmed the new moderate direction that its German policy had taken since the failure of the occupation of the Ruhr.

Ostensibly, the Locarno settlement endured for several years. It was nourished by the general prosperity of the French and the Germans and by the policies of their respective foreign ministers. In 1926 Germany was admitted to the League of Nations, an event that seemed to signify not only its restoration to international respectability but also its acceptance of the peaceful purposes of League membership. These hopeful impressions appeared to receive confirmation when Germany signed the Kellogg-Briand Peace Pact of 1928. In 1929 the French consented to withdraw the last of their occupation troops from the Rhineland by 1930, thus ending the Allied occupation of Germany at a date considerably in advance of the one stipulated in the Versailles Treaty.

Though not a member of the League, the United States took a leading part in furthering one of the League's chief objectives—disarmament. Meeting in Washington during the winter of 1921–1922, a naval conference of the major sea powers achieved an agreement establishing a ten-year "holiday" in the construction of capital ships (defined as battleships and heavy cruisers). A conference at London in 1930 had less success in limiting noncapital ships, including submarines. The partial failure of the London naval conference was a portent. Two years later, after long preparation, the League itself convoked a meeting to address the problem of limiting military armaments. Not only League members but also the United States and the Soviet Union sent representatives to Geneva. The World Disarmament Conference of 1932, however, accomplished nothing.

By 1932 the Locarno spirit was dead, and the era of fulfillment had ended. One obvious explanation was the worldwide depression that had begun in 1929. In Germany the depression was decisive in putting Hitler in power. In the democracies, too, it had serious consequences for the peace of the world, since the depression sapped their morale and made them less confident. In any case, even when the era of fulfillment was most successful, there had been clear warnings that appearances and reality did not fully coincide. The Germans had remained unwilling to accept a Locarno-style settlement of their eastern frontiers; the French had begun to seek out renewed alliances and to build a massive defensive line; and the Germans had begun a secret collaboration with the Soviets to bypass the Versailles restriction on armaments.

Another unsettling factor was Soviet Russia. The West regarded it as a revolutionary power that could not be fully integrated into the international state system. The Soviet Union was the center of a revolutionary faith hated by Western politicians. Westerners simply could not trust a government that was based on the Marxist belief that all Western capitalist democracies were destined to collapse and become communist after a violent class war.

Yet another factor that led to World War II was the continuing failure of the three major Western democracies—Britain, France, and the United States—to present a united front. Although each was a capitalist and a democratic state, the nature of their governments differed. The United States had widely diverse ethnic communities that traced their origins to Europe and took different positions on the problems emerging there. Britain and France were often at cross-purposes within the League of Nations, and the United States, not being a member, could exercise only modest influence in bringing them together.

France, exhausted and suffering a decline in population, was trying to play the part of a first-rate power with only second-rate resources, and it lived in growing fear of a revived Germany. The French sought not only to apply in full the economic and political measures of the Versailles Treaty that aimed at keeping Germany weak but also to make up for Russia's defection as its eastern ally against Germany. Beginning in 1921 France did this by making alliances with the smaller states to the east of Germany—Poland, Czechoslovakia, Romania, and Yugoslavia. All except Poland were informally linked together as the Little Entente. To British politicians who remembered the long story of Anglo-French conflicts from the Hundred Years' War to Napoleon, the France of the 1920s seemed once more to be aiming at European supremacy.

Some advocates of "splendid isolation" had survived the war and made the British unwilling to commit themselves to intervene with force in Continental Europe. Although Britain did accept Locarno and its commitment to punish any violator, in the previous year the dominions had played a large part in British rejection of the more sweeping Geneva protocol, which would have committed its signatories to compulsory arbitration of international disputes. Pacifist sentiment in Britain and the dominions further strengthened the German perception that Britain would not resist limited aggression on the Continent.

The difficulties of the Anglo-French partnership partly explain the weakness of the League of Nations. In addition, the League had no means to enforce its decisions, and it was top-heavy, since the fully representative Assembly counted for less than the smaller Council, which Britain and France dominated. When these two powers disagreed, the League scarcely operated at all. One example of how the grand purposes of the League suffered from Anglo-French friction was the rejection of the Geneva protocol; another was the Corfu incident of 1923, when Mussolini defied the League for a time. During the Corfu crisis the League was crippled by Anglo-French discord over the Ruhr policy of France. After 1935 Germany was engaged in what some historians have called a "unilateral armaments race," while two of the greatest nations in the world, the United States and the Soviet Union, were generally absent from the overall balance of power.

Soviet Foreign Policy

In 1919 Lenin founded the Third International, known thereafter as the Comintern. It summoned communists all over the world to unite against the "bourgeois cannibals" of capitalism. Gregory Zinoviev was put in charge, and his chief assistants were mainly Russians. Labor, socialist, and anarchist parties in Bulgaria, Norway, Italy, and Spain began to adhere to the new organization, although some idealists withdrew in disgust when it became clear that the Bolsheviks were establishing a dictatorship in Russia through their secret police and army. Yet the Comintern continued to operate side by side with the Soviet foreign office, and during the next few years often in apparent contradiction to it. This duality gave Soviet foreign policy a unique and at times unpredictable aspect.

Treaties were concluded between the Soviet Union and Poland, the Baltic states, Scandinavia, Germany, and Italy, exchanging trade for a promise not to interfere in the domestic affairs of these states. While binding on the Soviet foreign office, these agreements did not, in reality, affect the Comintern. In 1922 the Soviets were invited to an international economic conference at Genoa. The British and French assumed that NEP meant a return to capitalism, and they worked out a scheme for investment in Russia. Not only did the Soviets reject this plan, but they signed the Treaty of Rapallo (April 1922) with defeated Germany, which provided for the renunciation of all claims for reparations and implied a German willingness to recognize Bolshevik nationalizations of industry. The other powers, especially France, were unwilling to grant such recognition because of the large investments they had in Russia before the revolution.

In 1923 at Lausanne Russia lost a dispute with Britain over international regulation of the Straits, and further friction with Britain arose over Afghanistan. But Britain recognized the Soviet regime in 1924. Many members of the Labour party, while aware of the bloodshed in Russia, had great admiration for the rapidity with which Lenin was modernizing Russian society. Later in 1924 the so-called "Zinoviev letter" was published in England, which purported to instruct the British Communist party in the techniques of revolution. It was probably a forgery, but the Zinoviev letter influenced the British voters to turn MacDonald's Labour party out of office and elect Baldwin's Conservative government. In 1927 a raid on the offices of a Soviet firm doing business in London produced further evidence of communist agitation in England, and the British government broke relations with the Soviet Union altogether. The United States, meantime, had no diplomatic relations with the Soviet regime and did not recognize it until Roosevelt became president in 1933.

During 1918–1927 the Comintern compiled a record of failure. First, the Soviet Union failed to restrain the Italian left in 1921 and thus contributed to the success of Mussolini in the next year. Next, its failure in Bulgaria to collaborate with a liberal agrarian regime allowed a right-wing group to triumph in 1923. Most important, it failed in Germany, where a revolution actually threatened in 1923 as a result of French occupation of the Ruhr.

The Soviets also failed in Poland, where they helped Pilsudski gain dictatorial power in 1926, after which he turned against them. They failed in the Muslim and colonial world. But their greatest failure came in China, where in 1923 the Chinese nationalist revolutionary leader, Sun Yat-sen, agreed to take communist advice and received one of the Comintern's best men, Michael Borodin (1884–1953). Borodin helped Sun reorganize the Kuomintang and admit communists to it. In March 1926, Sun having died, Chiang Kai-shek led a coup against the government and began to arrest communists. Stalin now fell back on a theory that the Bolsheviks had not espoused since Lenin's return to Russia in April 1917—that a bourgeois revolution must precede a socialist revolution, and that all the communists could do in China was to help Chiang achieve this first revolution. The eventual result was the massacre of Chinese communists by Chiang and a loss of prestige for the Soviet Union.

Stalin had apparently never really believed in the effectiveness of the Comintern as an instrument of world revolution. When he came to power he could not abandon it, however, because of the criticism he would have aroused and because he sought to dilute and eventually to eradicate the Trotskyite sentiments of some communists in other countries. He therefore applied to the Comintern the same techniques he had used against the party at home, and used the Soviet delegation to establish full control over it. The Comintern was thus influenced to denounce the enemies of Stalin: Trotsky and the left in 1924, Bukharin and the right in 1928. Thereafter, there was no divergence between the Comintern and the foreign office.

Stalin then directed the Comintern into a new period of militant revolutionary activity. The Social Democrats of Western countries were now denounced as "social fascists" and the most dangerous enemies of communism. Yet Stalin's personal belief in the possibility of worldwide revolution seems always to have been slight. This lack of interest in the behavior of communists abroad led directly to the triumph of Hitler in Germany in 1933. The communists in Germany, who had been instructed by the Comintern that the Social Democrats and not the Nazis were their worst enemies, fought the

Nazis in the streets but allied themselves with them in the Reichstag. They believed that a Nazi triumph would very soon be followed by a communist revolution. Thus even after Hitler came to power, the Soviets renewed their nonaggression pact with Germany.

The shock of realization that Hitler had meant precisely what he said about liquidating communists and the fear that the Soviet Union itself might be in danger soon led Stalin to support collective security. After Hitler had refused to guarantee the Baltic states jointly with Stalin, the Soviet Union entered the League of Nations in September 1934. The Soviet delegate, Litvinov, became an eloquent defender of universal disarmament and of punishment for aggressors. Soon afterward, the Soviets began to negotiate for an "eastern Locarno" security pact to balance the agreement reached by the western European nations. Although no such structure could be created because of Polish and German hostility to the USSR, the Soviet Union did sign pacts with France and Czechoslovakia in 1935 providing for consultation under the terms of the League and for mutual aid in the event of aggression. However, Soviet aid to Czechoslovakia, if the Czechs became victims of aggression, was to be delivered only if the French, who were bound to the Czechs by an alliance, honored their obligations first.

With the shift in Soviet foreign policy, the Comintern also shifted its line. In 1935 the communists' recent enemies, the Social Democrats and bourgeois liberals of the West, were embraced as allies against the fascist menace. Communists were to join popular fronts against fascism and might welcome anyone, no matter how conservative, who would stand with them on this principle. Revolutionary propaganda and anticapitalist agitation were to be softened.

The Soviet Union and the western European bloc each assumed that the chief purpose of the other was to turn the full force of Hitler's forthcoming attack away from itself and in the opposite direction. That Hitler intended to attack, few doubted. On September 12, 1936, he specifically declared:

> If I had the Ural mountains with their incalculable store of treasures in raw materials, Siberia with its vast forests, and the Ukraine with its tremendous wheatfields, Germany under National Socialist leadership would swim in plenty.*

There was, then, much reason for the West to hope that the attack would be directed against the Soviets; this Stalin was determined to avert.

Soviet intervention in the Spanish Civil War demonstrated Stalin's real position. General Francisco Franco had obtained aid from Mussolini and Hitler. The Soviets, though reluctant to intervene in Spain because of their anxiety to prove their respectability to the Western powers, realized that a failure to help the Spanish republic would cost them support all over the world. But their aid was too little and too late. The Soviets hoped that the Western powers would also intervene, but Western neutrality

---

* Adolf Hitler, *My New Order*, ed. Raoul de Roussy de Sales (New York: Reynal and Hitchcock, 1941), p. 400.

in Spain helped convince Stalin that a Western alliance could not be counted on.

Still more important was the Western appeasement of Hitler, which reached its climax in the Munich agreement among Britain, France, Germany, and Italy in September 1938. From the Soviet point of view, Munich's grant of Czech lands to Hitler and the French failure to support Czechoslovakia and thus make operative the Russo-Czech alliance could have only one purpose—to drive Hitler east. Stalin was apparently ready to support the Czechs if the French did; when they did not, he apparently decided that he had better sound out Hitler for an understanding. Thus a truly effective alliance between Stalin and the West proved impossible between 1935 and 1939.

When the British and French realized that appeasement had failed to stop Hitler, they reluctantly sought a firmer alliance with the Soviets. From March to August 1939, Stalin kept open both his negotiations with the West and his slowly ripening negotiations with the Germans. The British and French mission, when it finally arrived in Moscow, was not composed of sufficiently high-ranking men to inspire Soviet confidence. Moreover, the Western powers would not agree to turn over to Stalin the territories that he wanted as a bulwark against Germany—Finland and the Baltic republics.

The growing eagerness of the Germans to secure a nonaggression pact gave Stalin his opportunity to divert war from the Soviet Union. In May 1939 Litvinov was dismissed as foreign minister because he was Jewish and therefore could not negotiate with the Germans; he was replaced by Vyacheslav Molotov (1890–1986). In the pact that Molotov eventually reached with Hitler on August 23, 1939, each power undertook to remain neutral toward the other in the event of war. A secret additional protocol provided for a division between Germany and the Soviet Union of Poland, which Hitler was about to attack; this put the Soviet Union's frontier farther west in the event of a subsequent German attack.

The publication of the Hitler-Stalin pact necessitated an abrupt shift in the world communist line. Now it was once more necessary for communists to denounce liberals and Social Democrats as enemies and to call the war that Hitler launched against Poland within a few days an "imperialist war," in which there was no difference between the two sides in which communists should not get involved. Thus Soviet foreign policy, especially under Stalin, was one major avenue in the road to the war that erupted in September 1939.

THE ROAD TO WAR, 1931–1939

By the mid-1930s, many commentators believed that a second world war was inevitable. A series of interconnected events, in China and Ethiopia, in Germany, Austria, and Spain, and sometimes faltering responses by Britain,

France, the United States, and other nations, brought full-scale war ever closer. Between 1931 and 1939, these events precipitated the world once again into war.

A First Step: Manchuria, 1931

The first decisive step along the road to World War II was the Japanese seizure of Manchuria in 1931. Henry L. Stimson (1867–1950), President Hoover's secretary of state, responded to the seizure by announcing that the United States would recognize no gains made by armed force. Stimson hoped that Britain and the other democracies might follow this American lead, but his hopes were largely disappointed. The League of Nations did send a commission headed by the earl of Lytton (1876–1947); the Lytton Report of 1932 condemned the Japanese act as aggression. Neither the United States nor the League, however, fortified its verbal protests by effective action. Japan, refusing to accept the report, withdrew from the League of Nations in March 1933.

A Second Step: German Rearmament, 1935–1936

The next breach in the League's structure was made by Germany. In October 1933 Hitler withdrew from the League. On March 16, 1935, he denounced the clauses of the Treaty of Versailles that limited German armaments and began openly rebuilding the German armed forces.

The response to this illegal act set the pattern for the next few years. On April 17, 1935, the League of Nations formally condemned Germany's repudiation of treaty obligations—and Germany continued to rearm. In May 1935 France and the Soviet Union concluded their treaty of alliance against German aggression—and Germany continued to rearm. In June 1935 the British signed a naval agreement with Germany limiting the German navy to one-third the size of the British and German submarines to 60 percent of those of Britain. Hitler's next act was the "reoccupation" of the Rhineland in March 1936—that is, the sending of German troops into the western German zone demilitarized by the Treaty of Versailles. Britain and France once more did nothing.

A Third Step: Ethiopia, 1935

Meanwhile, the Italians struck in Ethiopia, where an independent state had precariously maintained itself largely because its imperial neighbors—Britain, France, and Italy—would neither agree to divide it nor let any one of the three swallow it whole. In 1934 a frontier incident occurred at a desert post in Italian Somaliland—or in Ethiopia, for both sides claimed the site. France and Britain were ready to appease Italy, partly because they hoped to align Mussolini with them against Hitler. Over the protests of the Ethiopian emperor, Haile Selassie (1892–1975), they offered Mussolini generous economic concessions in Ethiopia. But since Ethiopia was a member of the League, the French and the British had to insist that its formal independence be observed. This Mussolini

would not accept, and in October 1935 his troops invaded Ethiopia. Early in 1936 the king of Italy acquired the coveted title of emperor of Ethiopia.

The League of Nations had already formally condemned the Japanese aggression in Manchuria and the German denunciation of the disarmament clauses of the Treaty of Versailles. In 1935 it promptly declared that, by invading Ethiopia, a League member, Italy had violated its obligations under the Covenant of the League. Now the League made the momentous decision to move from words to deeds. This decision was supported by most of its members and was urged on by the British, the French, and most movingly in a speech delivered to the League in Geneva by Haile Selassie, speaking in Amharic, the language of Ethiopia, while Italian fascists hissed and booed. On October 11, 1935, fifty-one member nations of the League voted to invoke Article 16 of the League Covenant, which provided for economic sanctions against a member resorting to war in disregard of its commitments.

But the sanctions against Italy failed. There were loop-holes; oil, for instance, was not included in the list of articles barred from commerce with Italy, which had only meager stockpiles of this vital war material. There was much recrimination among members of the League over what articles should be placed on the prohibited list and over the British and French failure to check Italian movements of troops and munitions through the Suez Canal, which Britain then controlled. Germany was no longer in the League and was wholly unaffected by its decisions. No major power applied sanctions rigorously, so that the effectiveness of economic sanctions was not really tested. The League was hardly a factor in the increasing tensions, and no one was surprised when Italy, like Japan and Germany, withdrew from the League in December 1937.

A Fourth Step: The Spanish Civil War, 1936–1939

The Spanish Civil War, which broke out in July 1936, was the emotional catalyst that aroused millions of men and women all over the Western world. The war pitted fascists, monarchists, and conservatives of the right against socialists, communists, anarchists, and a few liberals of the left. As in most great civil wars, there was really no center. It was a quasi-religious war, waged with the great violence that marks wars of principle. Almost from the very start it engaged the emotions of the West through individual foreign enlistments and the active though covert intervention of other nations.

The Spanish Civil War proved to be a rehearsal for the larger war that was approaching, as the fascist nations tested their weapons. One of the first deliberate aerial bombardments of a civilian population took place in April 1937, when low-flying planes, apparently German, devastated the Basque town of Guernica. Intervention by Italy and Germany was decisive and effective; it was less determined and effective by communist Russia; and it was feeblest of all by Britain and France. Early in 1939, with the fall of Barcelona, the civil war was over, and once more a fascist-leaning group had won.

A Fifth Step: The Marco Polo Bridge, 1937

The war between China and Japan had fallen into a lull when, on the night of July 7, 1937, a skirmish between troops of the two nations at the Marco Polo Bridge near Peking led to full-scale war once again. Later it would be claimed by both parties that the other had instigated the renewed conflict, though only the Japanese had reason to do so. A united anti-Japanese front had taken shape in China. An incident between Japanese and Russian forces on the Amur River the month before had made it clear that the Soviet Far Eastern army need not be feared, and a wave of nationalism in both China and Japan escalated mutual hatreds beyond the capacity of politicians to control them.

As first Peking and then Shanghai fell to the Japanese, the Chinese government appealed to the League of Nations. Sanctions would work only if the United States joined in them, but the American secretary of state suggested "parallel" rather than "joint" action with Britain, and President Roosevelt, though clearly opposed to Japanese advances in the Far East, called for a "quarantine" of aggressor states. But following a Japanese attack on the American gunboat *Panay* on the Yangtse River, the Americans appeared ready to discuss joint Anglo-American economic action. However, by then Britain wanted a political and military agreement that went further than the United States was prepared to go. This decision appears to have moved the Conservative British prime minister, Neville Chamberlain (1869–1940) to feel that, since the United States was "appeasing" Japan, he might do the same to Germany and Italy in Europe.

A Sixth Step: Anschluss, 1938

The immediate origins of World War II lay, however, in the mounting series of German aggressions. Hitler had begun openly rebuilding the German armed forces in 1935. Three years later he felt strong enough to make his first open effort at expansion. Ever since 1918 there had been a strong movement among Austrians for union (*Anschluss*) with Germany. This movement had been opposed by Italy and France, though the Rome-Berlin Axis lessened Mussolini's opposition to Anschluss. Early in 1938 Hitler began a violent propaganda campaign by press, radio, and platform against the alleged misdeeds of the Austrian government. In February 1938 he summoned Austrian chancellor Schuschnigg to Berchtesgaden, and in March he moved his troops into Austria, making Anschluss a fact.

A Seventh Step: Czechoslovakia Dismembered, 1938–1939

The Czechoslovak republic was the only state in central or eastern Europe where parliamentary democracy had succeeded after World War I. It had inherited some of the most highly developed industrial regions of the old Habsburg Empire; consequently, its economy was far better balanced between industry and agriculture than were those of the other states of eastern Europe. This healthy economy was mirrored in the social structure, where a working balance was maintained among peasants, middle classes, and industrial workers. But the Czech government could not keep the country from ultimately being destroyed by outside pressures working on its sensitive minorities. The Sudeten German minority of 3.25 million looked down on the Slavic Czechs and resisted the new republic. From 1933 on, Nazi agitation became increasingly serious in Czechoslovakia.

Early in 1938, having secured Austria, Hitler made demands on the Prague government for what amounted to complete Sudeten autonomy. On September 12 he made a violent speech at Nuremberg, insisting on self-determination for the Sudeten Germans. This was the signal for widespread disorders in Czechoslovakia, followed by the proclamation of martial law by the government of Eduard Beneš (1887–1948). Chamberlain made two preliminary visits to Hitler in Germany in an effort to moderate German demands. Finally, with the help of Mussolini, he persuaded Hitler to call a full conference of the four great Western powers. Hitler, Mussolini, Chamberlain, and Daladier of France met in Munich on September 29, 1938.

Munich was a sweeping victory for Hitler. Czechoslovakia was partially dismembered; its Sudeten borderlands were turned over to Germany; the Czechs were obliged to hand over Teschen and other areas to the Poles; their entire economy and transportation system were weakened; the defense of their frontiers was made impossible by the loss of the border mountains and their fortifications. Slovakia was given autonomy within a federal state, emphasized by the official change in spelling from Czechoslovakia to Czecho-Slovakia.

The Czech leaders had found it impossible to resist the Germans without French and British aid, and their people acquiesced bitterly in the settlement of Munich. The Germans had played skillfully on the differences between the more industrialized Czechs and the still largely agricultural Slovaks. But even had the country been strongly united, Munich would have ruined its morale. Hitler acted quickly. In March 1939 Hitler sent his army into Prague and took over the remaining Czech lands, meeting no real resistance. Hungary, anxious to reclaim some of its lost territory, occupied Ruthenia, the easternmost province of Czechoslovakia, with German consent.

The best defense that can be made for Munich and appeasement is that the West was either genuinely trying to avoid war or that it was buying time to prepare for a war that it knew to be inevitable but for which it was not yet ready. In September 1938 the democracies were in a stronger military position relative to that of Germany than they would be in September 1939. It also seems likely that Chamberlain and Daladier, as well as millions all over the world, hoped that the acquisition of the Sudeten Germans would satisfy Hitler. Some Westerners even hoped that Hitler might join with them against communist Russia,

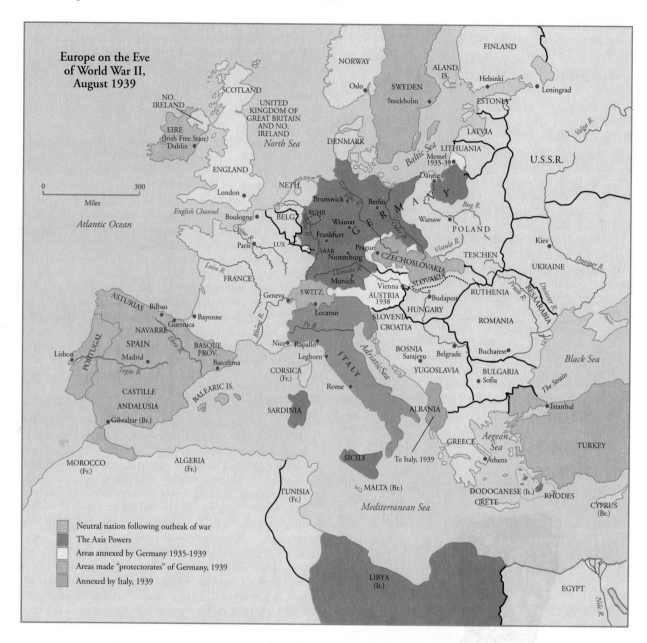

Europe on the Eve of World War II, August 1939

Neutral nation following outbeak of war
The Axis Powers
Areas annexed by Germany 1935-1939
Areas made "protectorates" of Germany, 1939
Annexed by Italy, 1939

or get himself so entangled in eastern Europe that he would bring on a Russo-German war. Hitler's words and deeds, however, had given no real basis for such hopes. As early as November 1937 he had announced to his close advisers his unalterable intention of destroying Czechoslovakia and moving on into Poland and the Ukraine.

The actual destruction of Czechoslovakia in March 1939 seems not to have surprised anyone. But the mixture of resignation, condemnation, and resolution with which this action was greeted in the West marks a turning point. The days of appeasement were over, as Britain and France made clear their intentions to guarantee the borders of Poland, and Britain started a peacetime draft. Nazi leaders made no secret of their feeling that the British and French were decadent, inefficient, and too cowardly to resist an inspired and rejuvenated Germany. Yet there is evidence that Hitler expected at least a local

war with Poland, and that he was quite prepared to confront the French and the British if need be. Hitler had strengthened his system on May 22 by concluding an offensive-defensive "Pact of Steel" with Mussolini, who only six weeks before had conquered Albania. Both nations obviously intended further aggression.

The Final Step: Poland, 1939

Poland was clearly going to be Hitler's next victim. The Germans regarded the Polish Corridor dividing East Prussia from the rest of Germany as an affront; so, too, was the separation from Germany of the free city of Danzig, German in language and tradition, on the edge of the Polish Corridor. On March 23, 1939, Hitler took the port town of Memel from Poland's northern neighbor, Lithuania. At the end of the month, the British and

French responded by assuring Poland of aid in the event of a German attack.

The critical issue in the tense half year that led up to the outbreak of war on September 1, 1939, was whether Poland would undergo the same fate as Czechoslovakia and receive no support from the Western democracies. The British government made it clear that it would back away no longer. The critical issue now was the attitude of the Soviet Union. Hitler had an understandable fear of a war against major powers on two fronts. But the Soviets deeply distrusted the British Tories under Chamberlain. This mistrust was not dispelled by a diplomatic mission that Britain and France sent to the Soviet Union in the summer of 1939. The Western powers proposed a mutual assistance pact, but the negotiations were inept and halfhearted and the British negotiators lacked high rank. Hitler, who was also negotiating with the Soviet Union, put Foreign Minister Ribbentrop himself on the job. The Anglo-French overture to Moscow came to nothing; the Soviet leaders had apparently concluded that if they did not come to terms with Hitler, he would attack them.

To the horror of the West, on August 23, 1939, Stalin signed a nonaggression pact with Hitler. On September 1 the German army marched into Poland. On September 3 Britain and France honored their obligations and declared war on Germany. The democracies had not been able to halt a dedicated, ruthless, organized state. Since the Great Depression the Western democracies had been committed to helping their citizens attain minimum standards of material comfort; normally they would produce butter before guns. Their totalitarian opponents, on the other hand, were able to convince or intimidate their people to agree that butter was to be attained in the future by making use of the guns if need be. They had persuaded their citizens to go without for the sake of military preparations; democratic states would find it difficult to get such sacrifices from their people until the war had actually begun.

WORLD WAR II, 1939–1942

Since military experts tend to prepare for the last war in planning for the next, both France and Germany in the 1930s built confronting lines of fortifications on their common frontier. The Maginot line on the French side and the Siegfried line on the German were far more formidable than were the trenches of 1914 to 1918. With the outbreak of hostilities, most people expected that the war would be decided primarily in the area between France and Germany, and that it would be a closely confined war, perhaps quite brief with at most only diversionary activity in other parts of the world.

But as Germany was joined by its Axis partners, Italy and Japan, and as the United States entered on the Allied side, World War II became much more fully a world war than World War I had been.

In 1939 Germany was ready for war, but neither France nor Britain was fully prepared. Moreover, Germany did not need to fight on two major fronts, since the pact with Stalin had neutralized the Soviet Union. However, France, which had held only one front in World War I, now had to maintain troops along the Spanish and Italian borders to guard against an attack by those nations. Still, German success was predicated on a quick victory;

Hitler reviews German troops in Vienna in April, 1938, following *Anschluss* in March.

UPI/Bettmann Newsphotos

The German motorized cavalry leads the German army into Poland. The sign indicates the invaders are near Bydgoscz, which was then about a hundred miles inside Poland. This photograph was taken by official photographers with the German army.

AP/Wide World Photos

otherwise, the United States might once again be drawn into the war, the British would gain time to supply their troops and resources from their dominions, and the obviously superior British navy would begin to close off German food supplies.

On land, the German forces were undoubtedly superior. They were better equipped than either the French or British. Still, the French army's reputation was excellent, and the German leaders saw the defeat of France as their essential first task. Because the French were known to be especially weak in tanks and antiaircraft defense, the Germans turned to the ideal combination—massive use of tanks in close cooperation with aircraft, especially the Stuka bomber, which could divebomb enemy positions.

German plans all focused on moving rapidly by means of the *blitzkrieg*, or "lightning war." This became even more true when Mussolini declared himself to be a "nonbelligerent." No one doubted that he stood behind Germany, but it was thought that he would not actively commit his troops to the war. For Britain and France, ultimate victory rested on delay, forestalling a quick German victory until their lack of preparation could be offset by control of the seas, superior industrial production, and the support of world opinion which, they felt, would be in their favor. The Soviet Union remained unpredictable and might be turned around. If Hitler did have to fight a real war on two fronts, the *Wehrmacht* (armed forces) might be bled deeply and long enough to weaken its western thrust. While this did not seem probable in 1939, this is what did, in fact, happen; as the Soviet, or eastern, front wore down Germany's forces, a successful invasion of occupied France became possible by 1944.

On all fronts aerial bombardment—toward the end of the war carried on by German pilotless aircraft and rocket missiles—brought the horrors of warfare to urban civilians. Military experts had been inclined to believe that civilians could not possibly stand aerial bombardment and that any country whose cities were subject to sustained bombardment would be obliged to sue for peace. Yet European and Asian civilian populations endured months of attack; German civilian deaths from air bombardment alone have been estimated at about 500,000. Organized systems of shelter and partial dispersal of populations enabled the people of heavily bombed cities like London, Berlin, and Tokyo to endure what were in effect front-line conditions.

At the very end of the war, a technical innovation was introduced that radically altered the character of war. This was the atom bomb, developed in secrecy by American, Canadian, and British experts, with scientific support from German and Italian refugees. It was first used by the United States on the Japanese city of Hiroshima on August 6, 1945; one single bomb destroyed something over half that city. Somewhat less damage was done by a second and different bomb dropped on Nagasaki three days later. More than 100,000 people were killed in the two cities by the two bombs.

Early Successes of the Axis

The first campaign of World War II reached its expected conclusion. No one had seriously expected isolated Poland to stand up for long against the German and Soviet armed forces or expected Britain and France to act rapidly enough to help their Polish ally decisively. Yet the speed

THE WRITTEN RECORD

Winston Churchill's Leadership

One skill of the highest value to leadership is the ability to inspire others with one's own example, and with one's oratory. Winston Churchill was a superb writer and public speaker. On May 13, 1940, he gave the House of Commons his fearsome prescription for victory.

I would say to the House, as I said to those who have joined this Government: "I have nothing to offer but blood, toil, tears and sweat." We have before us an ordeal of the most grievous kind. We have before us many, many long months of struggle and of suffering. You ask, what is our policy? I will say: It is to wage war, by sea, land and air, with all our might and with all the strength that God can give us; to make war against a monstrous tyranny, never surpassed in the dark, lamentable catalogue of human crime. That is our policy.

You ask, what is our aim? I can answer in one word: It is victory, victory at all costs, victory in spite of all terror, victory, however long and hard the road may be; for without victory there is no survival.

In Britain's darkest hour, when Hitler's troops had reached the English Channel and Britain's last continental ally, France, had collapsed, Churchill rallied the British people to a remarkable and united war effort.

We shall fight on the beaches, we shall fight on the landing grounds, we shall fight in the hills; we shall never surrender, and even if, which I do not for a moment believe, this island or a large part of it were subjugated and starving, then our Empire beyond the seas, armed and guarded by the British Fleet, would carry on the struggle, until, in God's good time, the New World, with all its power and might, steps forth to the rescue and liberation of the Old.

From Hansard, *British Parliamentary Debates,* House of Commons, June 4, May 13, 1940.

---

of the German conquest surprised almost everyone. The Luftwaffe (air force) soon gained absolute command of the air and used it to disrupt Polish communications and to spread terror with its dive bombers. Special fully motorized German task forces swept through the less mobile Poles.

Hitler's collaborator, Stalin, hastened to invade Poland from the east; he also occupied and then annexed the Baltic republics of Estonia, Latvia, and Lithuania. Fear of Germany and an imperialistic desire to expand also drove the Soviets into a war with neighboring Finland in November 1939. The Soviets, who had perhaps miscalculated the strength of the Finns, did rather badly at first. For a time the British and French considered massive aid to the Finns. By March 1940, however, Soviet forces had worn down the Finns; they secured bases and annexed Finnish lands that were close to Leningrad. This "winter war" with Finland helped push Hitler toward the fateful decision in 1941 to make war on the Soviet Union, for German military experts concluded from Soviet difficulties that an easy victory would be possible.

In April 1940 the Germans secured their northern flank. Without declaring war, they invaded neutral Denmark and Norway by sea and air. Denmark, totally unprepared, was occupied almost without resistance. Norway, also unprepared but favored by rugged terrain, put up determined opposition. Neither the British nor the French could help with more than token forces, and by the end of April Norwegian resistance had been broken. A puppet government was installed under the Norwegian fascist Vidkun Quisling (1887–1945), thus introducing into the English language a synonym for *traitor.* The Germans now had excellent bases for air and submarine action against the British.

The great blow was struck without warning on May 10, 1940. The German armies, invaded the Low Countries and thus bypassed the Maginot line. Both the Belgians and the Dutch had been anxious in the 1930s to avoid compromising themselves by planning for joint resistance with Britain and France against a possible German attack. They were now to suffer the full consequences.

Through the Ardennes hills on the Franco-Belgian border, the Germans poured their best motorized troops into France. In a blitzkrieg that once more capitalized on the lessons of 1914, the Germans resisted the temptation to drive at once for Paris, but instead pushed straight through northern France to the English Channel, where the port of Boulogne fell on May 26, a little more than two weeks after the start of the campaign. By this stroke the Germans separated the British, Belgian, and a large part of the French troops from the main French armies to the south.

Meanwhile, in Britain Chamberlain had resigned. He was succeeded as prime minister by Winston Churchill

(1874–1965). Chamberlain was neither a man of action nor an appealing or heroic figure; Churchill was to prove himself all this and more.

In despair, the British and French attempted to pinch off the German motorized thrust by a concerted attack from north and south. But the Belgians, badly disorganized, decided to surrender, and neither the French nor the British could rally themselves to carry out the movement. In the last days of May and the first days of June, the British withdrew some 215,000 British and 120,000 French soldiers by sea to England from the beaches around Dunkirk at the northern tip of France. With protection from the Royal Air Force, an extraordinary flotilla of all sorts of vessels, including private yachts and motorboats, got the men out, though most of their equipment had to be abandoned.

From documents captured after the final defeat of Germany, it appears (though the point is still controversial) that the "miracle of Dunkirk" was possible in part because Hitler himself decided not to press home the destruction of the British forces trapped on the coast, since he believed that Britain was no longer a real threat. At the last moment, he decided to push the attack on Paris at once. Here he was entirely and rapidly successful. The French could not rally, and the Germans marched southward almost unopposed. On June 13 the French declared Paris an open city and evacuated it without fighting.

The battle of France was thus decided by mid-June 1940. But the French might still have tried to defend the south or, failing that, used their navy and merchant marine to get as many troops as possible across the Mediterranean into French North Africa, where they might have continued the fight against the Germans with British aid. Some French leaders, of whom General Charles de Gaulle (1890–1970) was the most vocal, wished to do this. To persuade them to do so, Churchill made France the extraordinary offer of a complete governmental union of the two countries to continue the struggle. But his offer was not accepted.

On June 16 French premier Paul Reynaud (1878–1966) was supplanted by Marshal Henri Pétain (1856–1951). Pétain and his colleagues were determined on peace at any price, and on June 22, 1940, an armistice was signed at Compiègne. By this armistice the French withdrew from the war, handed over three fifths of France, including the whole Atlantic and Channel coasts, to German occupation, and retained only the central and Mediterranean regions under strict German supervision. "Unoccupied France" was ruled from the little resort city of Vichy, where Pétain set up an authoritarian, antidemocratic state of which he was chief. His government was known simply as Vichy France.

Some of Pétain's supporters were pro-German. But most of them were sure that Hitler had won the war and were coming to terms with what they regarded as the inevitable German total victory. They did not believe that Britain could successfully resist the German war machine that had defeated France. Their army was demobilized, and their navy either immobilized in France or scattered

among North African ports. The situation of Vichy France was extremely delicate and ambiguous, and the problem of who collaborated and who resisted the Germans would plague the French nation for years after the war was over.

Even in the dark days of June 1940, a few French patriots led by Charles de Gaulle refused to give up the fight. With British aid, de Gaulle, set up a French National Committee with headquarters in London. A nucleus of French soldiers taken off the beach at Dunkirk, plus a stream of refugees who left France in the next few years, made up the Free French, or Fighting French. Back in France, a secret Resistance movement gradually formed to prepare for eventual liberation. While North Africa, strongest of the French colonial areas, was controlled by Vichy, some of the colonies rallied to the Free French from the start. Although weak, the Fighting French were at least a rallying point. They set up an effective radio center in England from which they conducted a propaganda campaign against Vichy and the Germans, beamed across the Channel to the homeland.

On June 10, 1940, Mussolini brought the Italians into the war against France and Britain, too late to affect the outcome of the battle of France. This "stab in the back," as Franklin Roosevelt called it, further outraged American opinion. Italy was anxious to secure some kind of success that would offset the great gains of its German ally. The war, up to this time confined to northern and western Europe, would soon spread to the Mediterranean.

The Battle of Britain

The Germans had not really worked out a plan for dealing with Britain. Hitler seems to have believed that with France out of the war, Britain would make a separate, compromise peace in which Germany would dominate the Continent of Europe and Britain would retain its overseas empire. Mixed with his hatred for England was a misleading idea that Germany and England were natural allies. There were no natural allies available to him in Britain, however. Britain had interned all German subjects in the country (including Jewish refugees) and had locked up nearly eight hundred members of the British Union of Fascists, including their leader, Sir Oswald Mosley (1896–1981). For more than four centuries Britain had gone to war rather than accept one-power domination over western and central Europe or a hostile occupation of the Low Countries.

Hitler was counting heavily on the possibility that German submarines could eventually cut off British supplies of food and raw materials from overseas and thus starve it into submission. But this would take a long time, and Hitler was impatient. The obvious thing to do was to attempt a landing in England; however, the Germans had made no real preparation for amphibious warfare and had no specially designed landing craft. A hastily assembled flotilla of miscellaneous vessels was badly damaged by British aircraft, and early in August 1940 Hitler and Göring, his air marshal, made the fateful decision to try to do the job solely with air power.

Perhaps the most famous and effective wartime photograph of the battle of Britain was this International News Photo, taken late in 1940, of the massive dome of St. Paul's Cathedral rising above the burning city of London during a German incendiary bomb attack. Fire fighters stationed around the dome were able to save the cathedral, and when the photo ran in the influential American magazine, *Life* on January 27, 1941, it won thousands of reluctant Americans over to the British cause.

UPI/Bettmann Newsphotos

The battle of Britain that followed had two main phases. First, in August and September, the Luftwaffe attempted in daylight bombing attacks to wipe out merchant ship convoys, British airports, and fighter planes. The Royal Air Force, using the new radar technique to spot the attackers early, proved just barely strong enough to check the Germans, who began full-scale attacks with bomber fleets on August 13. In critical actions in September the level of German losses became too great to sustain, and on September 17 Hitler postponed any invasion. Germany still had enormous air-strike capacity, but it had failed to win air superiority. This was the "nation's finest hour," as described by Churchill, an exceptionally effective wartime leader and a master at stirring national pride. Though air attacks would continue against Britain until 1942, the aerial battle of Britain was over. Night bombings continued throughout 1940, but even in Coventry, where the cathedral was destroyed, the city's industrial capacity continued. Nor did civilian morale break. Rather, the night bombings strengthened the British will to resist.

Equally crucial during the battle of Britain was the battle of the Atlantic, since it was essential that convoys from North America bringing needed supplies get through to Britain. The British navy proved equal to the task, shepherding convoys across the ocean, sweeping harbors of mines floated in by the Germans, and seeking out the highly effective German submarines. Shipping losses for the British rose alarmingly through 1940 and into 1941. Unable to destroy the German submarines by aerial bombing, the British began to hunt them down at sea using radar. The German surface navy initially operated along the French coast and in the Indian Ocean, but it was beaten back from the Atlantic when the heavy battleship *Bismarck* was sunk in May 1941 by a com-

bined air and cruiser attack. Thereafter the British controlled the surface of the sea, while the Germans still prowled beneath the waters. Although Allied and neutral shipping losses ran to 23 million tons during the war, radar, sonar, escort carriers, and destroyer groups effectively neutralized the German submarine advantage.

The Mediterranean and Soviet Campaigns

Hitler now faced the possibility of a long stalemate. He turned at first to the strategy of getting at Britain through its Mediterranean lifeline to India and the East. His ally Mussolini invaded Greece from Albania in October 1940 without informing Hitler. The Greeks pushed the Italians back halfway across Albania, but the Germans rescued Mussolini.

Just how far Hitler himself wanted to invest in the Mediterranean is not clear. Certainly he toyed with the idea of a campaign against the British fortress of Gibraltar through Spain. But Franco wanted too high a price from the French for his consent to a German march through Spain, and Hitler was unwilling to risk driving Vichy France, which still controlled French North Africa, too far. The Germans had to be content with backing up Mussolini in Greece and attacking Egypt from the Italian colony of Libya. Their efforts to organize local action against the British and French in the Middle East were suppressed without grave difficulty by British and Free French troops in Syria.

The German commitment to help the Italians in Greece took valuable German divisions away from another task in the spring of 1941. Though Hitler forced on a

Winston Churchill proved to be a superb wartime leader for the British. His ability to rally them at their darkest hour—the battle of Britain—showed him at his finest moment. Here Churchill, leaving 10 Downing Street, gives the press his familiar "V" for Victory sign.
UPI/Bettmann Newsphotos

frightened Yugoslav government a treaty allowing German forces free passage across Yugoslavia to Greece, a Serbian uprising overthrew the Yugoslav regime, and thereafter the Germans had to combat guerrilla resistance and to dismember Yugoslavia. The British did their best to back up their Greek allies, but once more they were not strong enough. German air power crippled British naval power in the Mediterranean, and by May the Axis had conquered the Greek mainland. The British defeat appeared total, but in fact the Germans had invested far too much armament in the Balkan campaign.

The other task for which the German forces were needed in the spring of 1941 was the conquest of the Soviet Union. Hitler had firmly resolved not to engage in a war on two fronts. Yet by his invasion of the Soviet Union on June 22, 1941, he committed himself to just such a war. The Soviet Union was indeed a tempting goal. The Nazi plan had always looked to the fertile areas of Poland and southern Russia as the natural goal of German expansion. After the successful blitzkriegs in Poland, western Europe, and now Greece, Hitler and his military experts believed that they could beat the Soviets in a single campaign before winter set in, a view British and American military advisers privately shared. Once the Soviet Union was conquered, the Germans would have little trouble disposing of Britain.

Furthermore, Hitler had returned to his old suspicion of Bolshevism. He knew that Stalin had agreed to the pact with Germany for opportunistic reasons, and that the Soviet Union might well change sides in any event. The pact had destroyed Poland, the natural wall between the two enemies. And the Soviet Union had already been expanding in ways that reinforced Hitler's distrust. In June 1940 Stalin had demanded of Romania the province of Bessarabia, and also northern Bukovina. The Germans had expected the Soviet seizure of Bessarabia, but not of northern Bukovina; they permitted the seizure, however, telling the Romanians that they could expect no help from Hitler. But that was as far as Hitler's cooperation with Stalin in eastern Europe went. The reannexation of Bessarabia had given the Soviets the mouth of the Danube, controlling an important artery. The Soviets seemed to be moving into southeastern Europe, a region in which the Germans were not prepared to let them operate alone.

Only a few weeks after the Soviet seizure of Romanian territory, Hitler asserted his own southeastern interests by forcing the Romanians to cede territory to Hungary and then guaranteeing the new Romanian frontiers, a guarantee that could apply only against the Soviets. Soon afterward German troops appeared in Finland, "to reinforce the German armies in Norway," Hitler explained.

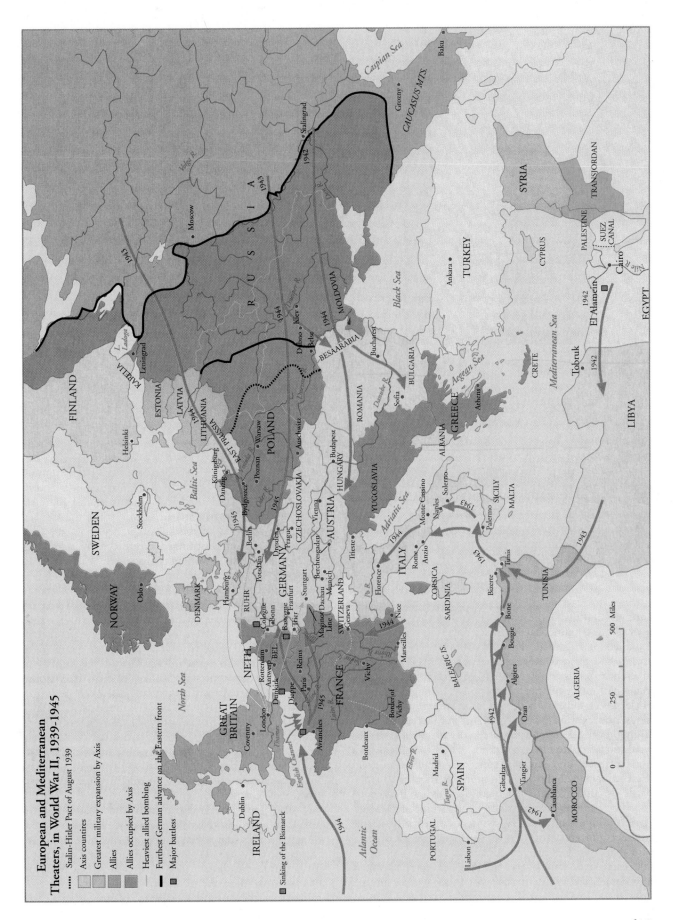

European and Mediterranean
Theaters, in World War II, 1939–1945

..... Stalin-Hitler Pact of August 1939
Axis countries
Greatest military expansion by Axis
Allies
Allies occupied by Axis
Heaviest allied bombing
Furthest German advance on the Eastern front
Major battles

☐ Sinking of the Bismarck

500 Miles
250
0

NORWAY
SWEDEN
FINLAND
KARELIA
Oslo
Stockholm
Helsinki
L. Ladoga
Leningrad
ESTONIA
LATVIA
LITHUANIA
EAST PRUSSIA
Königsberg
Danzig
Moscow
R U S S I A
Volga R.
Stalingrad
Grozny
CAUCASUS MTS.
Baku
Caspian Sea
Dnieper R.
Kiev
Dnepr
Pinsk
MOLDOVIA
BESSARABIA
Bucharest
Black Sea
ROMANIA
BULGARIA
Sofia
Danube R.
TURKEY
Ankara
CYPRUS
SYRIA
TRANSJORDAN
PALESTINE
SUEZ CANAL
Cairo
Nile R.
EGYPT
El Alamein
Tobruk
LIBYA
Mediterranean Sea
CRETE
GREECE
Athens
Aegean Sea
ALBANIA
YUGOSLAVIA
Adriatic Sea
Trieste
HUNGARY
Budapest
Vienna
AUSTRIA
CZECHOSLOVAKIA
Prague
Berchtesgaden
Munich
Dachau
POLAND
Warsaw
Poznan
Bydgoszcz
Auschwitz
Oder R.
GERMANY
Berlin
Dresden
Potsdam
Hamburg
Elbe
Stuttgart
Frankfurt
Bonn
Cologne
RUHR
Trier
Bastogne
Maginot Line
SWITZERLAND
Geneva
Po R.
ITALY
Florence
Rome
Anzio
Monte Cassino
Naples
Solerno
SICILY
Palermo
MALTA
SARDINIA
CORSICA
Nice
Marseilles
Rhône R.
Vichy
Border of Vichy
FRANCE
Paris
Reims
Loire R.
Avranches
Dieppe
Dunkirk
NETH.
BEL.
Rotterdam
Antwerp
English Channel
London
Coventry
Thames
GREAT BRITAIN
IRELAND
Dublin
North Sea
Baltic Sea
DENMARK
Atlantic Ocean
Bordeaux
SPAIN
Madrid
Tagus R.
Ebro R.
PORTUGAL
Lisbon
BALEARIC IS.
Gibraltar
Tangier
MOROCCO
Casablanca
ALGERIA
Oran
Algiers
Bougie
Bone
Bizerte
Tunis
TUNISIA
1942
1943
1944
1945

619

"Soviet Forces' parade in the Red Square, November 7, 1941," painted by the first chairman of the Union of Soviet Artists, Konstantin Yuon (1875—1958), in 1949.

Sovfoto

And in the autumn of 1940 German troops entered Romania proper "to guard the Romanian oilfields against British sabotage." These maneuvers on his new frontiers deeply disquieted Stalin. Then in October 1940 Italy attacked Greece, and the war spread to the Balkans; German troops moved into Bulgaria, which the Soviet Union regarded as essential to its own defense. With Germany established in Yugoslavia and victorious in Greece by May 1941, Stalin knew that an invasion of the Soviet Union was logically next.

The Soviet Union was not conquered, but Hitler's plan almost worked. There was a successful blitzkrieg; within two months the Germans were at the gates of Leningrad, and by the end of October they had conquered the Ukraine. Soviet losses rose into the millions of killed or captured. In sheer distance, the German armies had pushed more than twice as far as they had in France. Yet as the Russian winter closed in, the Germans had taken neither Moscow nor Leningrad. Much Soviet heavy industry had been transferred to the remote Urals, and existing plants there and in Siberia had been strengthened. The vast resources of the Soviet Union were still adequate for Soviet needs. The government had not collapsed, and national spirit was high. Moreover, the Germans had shown once more, as they had in the battle of Britain, that their planning was far from perfect. Their troops were not sufficiently equipped to withstand the rigors of a Russian winter. Confident that the summer and autumn would be sufficient to finish the campaign, the German planners had left the winter to take care of itself. In winter fighting between December 1941 and May 1942, the Soviets regained much useful ground.

The United States Enters the War

Although the United States had a strong isolationist element and some Nazi sympathizers, American opinion had, from the very beginning of the attack on Poland in 1939, been far more nearly unanimous against the Germans and Italians than it had been against the Central Powers in 1914. With the fall of France in 1940, anti-Axis sentiment grew stronger, reinforced by a growing belief that if Hitler won in Europe, the United States would be his next victim.

Between June 1940 and December 1941, the Roosevelt administration, with the consent of Congress and with the general backing of American public opinion, took a series of steps "short of war" to aid Britain and later the Soviet Union. The American government transferred fifty "overage" destroyers to the British in exchange for Atlantic naval bases in British colonies, supplied the British with arms, and used the American navy to help get these supplies across the Atlantic. Above all, in March 1941 by the Lend-Lease Act, the United States agreed to supply materials needed for defense, including food, to "any country whose defense the President deems vital to the defense of the United States." Supplies at once began flowing into Britain and later to other anti-Axis powers.

In 1936 Germany and Japan had concluded an Anti-Comintern Pact, agreeing to assist each other in case of aggression by the Soviet Union. In March 1939, as he prepared for European war, Hitler had pressed the Japanese emperor, Hirohito (1901–1989), to join a tripartite alliance with Germany and Italy, but the Japanese estimated that they would not be ready for a Pacific war before 1942. Hirohito agreed to a military alliance with Hitler, provided that Japan need not enter a general war until it felt strong enough to do so. Hitler rejected the latter provision. In September 1940 the two nations agreed that if the United States attacked Germany, Japan would come into the war. But the three-nation Axis would not be truly formed until Japan moved its timetable forward and struck at the United States in December 1941.

Meanwhile, the Japanese took advantage of the fall of France and the Netherlands and of the weakness of Britain. They penetrated into French Indochina (Vietnam) by agreement with Vichy France, even as they continued to press their campaign on the mainland of China. The American government continued to oppose what it considered Japanese aggression. The Japanese government fell increasingly into the hands of military leaders who felt that war with the United States was inevitable and who preferred to strike before the American democracy could fully prepare itself. Had the United States been willing to back away from its persistent opposition to Japanese expansion, the war in the Pacific could perhaps have been avoided, but the Americans remained adamant.

In the summer and autumn of 1941 the American government took steps to freeze Japanese credits in the United States, to halt Japanese access to raw materials, and to get the Japanese to withdraw from China and Indochina. Negotiations toward these ends were going on between the Japanese and Americans when on December 7, 1941, the Japanese struck the American naval base at Pearl Harbor in Hawaii. Grave damage was inflicted on ships and installations, but American power in the Pacific was by no means destroyed. Moreover, the "day of infamy" produced almost unanimous support in the United States for the immediate declaration of war against Japan. Germany and Italy honored their obligations to their Axis partner by declaring war against the United States on December 11. As 1942 began, the war was literally a world war.

Although the United States was far better prepared now than in 1917, it was still at a disadvantage. Against Germany, it could do no more than increase its aid to Britain and the Soviet Union and take part in the struggle against German submarines. Against Japan, the United States was almost as powerless. Its Pacific outposts of Guam, Wake Island, and the Philippines fell in rapid succession. Nor could the British and the exiled Dutch governments protect their colonies in Southeast Asia, which the Japanese had also attacked. By the spring of 1942, with the fall of Singapore, the Japanese had forced the largest surrender of a British army in history. They had acquired Indonesia from the Dutch, possessed the oil of Borneo, the rubber of the Malay States, and had virtual control of Siam (Thailand) and Burma.

The American Pacific Fleet rode at anchor at Pearl Harbor on December 7, 1941—eight battleships in a row, nine cruisers, twenty-nine destroyers, and five submarines. Three aircraft carriers were on detached duty. The Japanese attack came in two waves, forty-one minutes apart, and it took the Americans completely by surprise. Only four American airplanes got off the ground. The Americans lost five of their battleships and 2,400 men and women; the Japanese lost twenty-nine of their 360 planes.

National Archives

The Japanese attack on Pearl Harbor had been made possible only by close coordination of air and sea forces. They had attack bombers close to Australian shores, and they had dramatically demonstrated during their rapid conquest of the Malay peninsula that they dominated the seas at least to the mid-Pacific. Public opinion was particularly shaken when the only British capital ships east of Suez, the battleship *Prince of Wales* and the cruiser *Repulse*, were destroyed in the Gulf of Siam by Japanese air attack. The Americans, who understood that they were to carry the primary responsibility for the Pacific war, realized that they must turn the Japanese navy back if their own aerial strike forces were to be able to enter Far Eastern waters.

Victory for the United Nations

There were several turning points in the struggle thereafter. The earliest was a series of naval actions in which Japanese expansion was stopped. In these actions, carrier-based American airplanes played a decisive role. On May 7, 1942, in the battle of the Coral Sea in the southwest Pacific, Allied sea and air power halted a possible Japanese invasion of Australia and its protecting islands. In June American sea and air power dispersed a Japanese fleet that was seeking to conquer Midway Island. Although the Japanese landed on American territory at Attu and Kiska in the Aleutian Islands of Alaska, they never seriously threatened Hawaii or the mainland.

In Europe the Americans and the British were not yet able to respond to Soviet pressure for a second front on the Continent. But in November 1942 they did land in French North Africa and were rapidly established in force in Morocco and Algeria. The Libyan segment of the long North African coast had been held by the Germans and their Italian allies since the beginning of the war in the Mediterranean. At the time of the North African landings, the British, under General Sir Bernard Montgomery (1887–1976), were holding a defensive line inside the Egyptian frontier near El Alamein. But on October 23, 1942, the British started on a westward offensive, which was planned to coordinate with an eastward offensive by the American General Dwight D. Eisenhower (1890–1969), commander of the Allied forces in French North Africa. The vise closed slowly, but in May 1943 Free French, British, and American troops took the last Axis strongholds of Tunis and Bizerte and accepted the surrender of some 300,000 Axis troops.

The North African campaign had clearly been a turning point. The Allies had successfully made large-scale amphibious landings, and they had annihilated one of the most renowned of Axis forces, commanded by Erwin Rommel (1891–1944), "the Desert Fox." North Africa was by no means the main battleground, but it was nevertheless a major campaign in which the Allies gained confidence and prestige.

The great turning point on land was the successful Soviet defense of Stalingrad (now known as Volgograd). After their stalemate in the Soviet Union in the winter of 1941–1942, the Germans turned their summer offensive of 1942 away from Leningrad and Moscow and toward the oil-rich regions to the southeast. This push toward the Soviet oil fields carried the Germans deep inside the Soviet Union, but it fell just short of the rich oil fields of Grozny and Baku. Russian distance, weather, manpower, and ability to take punishment were too much for the overextended Germans. Their armies were thrown back at Stalingrad, and early in 1943 the Soviets started the long march westward that was to take them to Berlin two years later.

A much less spectacular turning point was the Allied victory in the battle of supply, yet this victory was of the greatest importance. Even for the Soviets, an important source of supplies was the United States. But the United States was separated from its allies by vast distances of water, and the precious supplies had to move across the seas. If the Germans could stop this movement or reduce it greatly, they might still win. They made important improvements in their submarines, but there were simply not enough of them, and the countermeasures of the Allies—radar, coordination of naval vessels and aircraft, the convoy system—slowly reduced the number of sinkings.

The Axis on the Defensive

In the last two years of the war the Axis powers were on the defensive. Both in Europe and in Asia the Allies attacked with land forces along definite lines of march—campaigns of the traditional kind. But the way for these armies was made easier by two new factors in warfare: air power and modern propaganda, or psychological warfare. Air bombardment, at least until the atom bomb at Hiroshima, was never the perfect weapon that the prophets of air power had predicted. But as the superior Allied air power grew and was used systematically to destroy enemy capabilities in critical materials like ball bearings, machine tools, locomotives, and oil—and as American airplanes dropped incendiary bombs on the relatively flimsy Japanese cities—air power did much to destroy the Axis will to resist. Intelligence achievements were also important: By 1943 the British were systematically reading most high-level German coded messages, and the Americans were breaking Japanese military and diplomatic ciphers.

The attack by land on Germany and Italy was pressed in three directions—by the Soviets from the east, and by the British, French, Americans, and other Allies from the south and west. In the south the Allies crossed from North Africa to Sicily in a successful amphibious operation (July 1943) within two months of their final victory in Tunisia. From Sicily they moved in another six weeks to the mainland of Italy at Salerno and Anzio. These landings were costly, and troops were pinned down for weeks. German forces kept the Italian campaign going for longer than the Allies anticipated, but the Allied victories of the summer of 1943 were sufficient to put Italy out of the war. Top officers of the Italian army and others

American troops wade ashore on the Normandy coast on D-Day, June 6, 1944.
The Bettmann Archive

close to the king, helped by dissident fascist leaders, engineered a coup in July that brought about the fall and imprisonment of Mussolini and resulted in some negotiations between the Allies and the new government headed by Marshal Pietro Badoglio (1871–1956).

But the Germans were unwilling to abandon their Italian defensive line. A detachment of German troops rescued Mussolini in September 1943 and set him up as the head of a "fascist republic" in the North—a post in which he continued until he was executed by partisans in April 1945. In June 1944 the Allies succeeded, after particularly severe fighting around Monte Cassino, in breaking through to Rome, which was declared an open city, and by August they were in Florence. They could not effectively move further north, however, until the final collapse of the Germans in their heartland early in 1945.

At a conference of Churchill, Roosevelt, and Stalin in Teheran in December 1943, the decision was made to open the long-delayed second front. The landings in France began on "D-Day," June 6, 1944. The Allies' choice of the Normandy coast surprised the German high command, who believed the landings would come farther north and east along the English Channel. In their four years of occupation the Germans had fortified the French coastline, but the Allies had also used those four years to study, invent, and plan. Allied landing craft, amphibious trucks, naval and air support, artificial harbors, and a well-organized supply system gained a beachhead for the allied land forces. From this beachhead, a little over a month after D-Day, they were able to break out at Avranches and sweep the Germans back across the Seine in a great flanking movement led by the American general George S. Patton (1885–1945).

A long-planned auxiliary landing on the French Mediterranean coast, to be followed by a march north up the Rhône-Saône valleys, was launched on August 15, 1944, and met very little opposition. Everywhere the French Resistance movement welcomed the liberating forces, some of whom were heirs of the Free French of 1940. Paris, a symbol as well as a place, was liberated toward the end of August.

The Germans were beaten back but not disorganized. In July 1944 conservative elements, both military and civilian, attempted to assassinate Hitler to pave the way for negotiations. But Hitler survived the bomb intended for him, executed the plotters, and retained a firm grip on the German state by killing five thousand people suspected of complicity. The Allies were encouraged by their rapid successes in July and August to try to destroy the German armies before winter or cut them off from their homeland; however, Patton's mechanized troops ran out of fuel. The new German pilotless planes and

THE WRITTEN RECORD

The Final Solution

During the International Military Tribunal, held at Nuremberg after the war to try German war criminals, a German engineer who was an eyewitness to a massacre of Jews in the Ukraine, where Ukrainian guards were used, dryly described what proved to be a relatively routine event.

On 5th October 1942, when I visited the building office at Dubno my foreman told me that in the vicinity of the site, Jews from Dubno had been shot in three large pits, each about 30 metres long and 3 metres deep. About 1,500 persons had been killed daily. All the 5,000 Jews who had still been living in Dubno before the pogrom were to be liquidated. As the shooting had taken place in his presence, he was still much upset.

Thereupon I drove to the site accompanied by my foreman and saw near it great mounds of earth, about 30 metres long and 2 metres high. Several trucks stood in front of the mounds. Armed Ukrainian militia drove the people off the trucks under the supervision of an S.S. man. The militiamen acted as guards on the trucks and drove them to and from the pit. All these people had the regulation yellow patches on the front and back of their clothes, and thus could be recognized as Jews.

My foreman and I went directly to the pits. Nobody bothered us. Now I heard rifle shots in quick succession from behind on one of the earth mounds. The people had got off the trucks—men, women and children of all ages—had to undress upon order of an S.S. man, who carried a riding or dog whip. They had to put down their clothes in fixed places, sorted according to shoes, to clothing, and underclothing. I saw a heap of shoes of about 800 or 1,000 pairs, great piles of underlinen and clothing.

Without screaming or weeping these people undressed, stood around in family groups, kissed each other, said farewells, and waited for a sign from another S.S. man, who stood near the pit, also with a whip in his hand. During the 15 minutes that I stood near I heard no complaint or plea for mercy. . . .

At that moment the S.S. man at the pit shouted something to his comrade. The latter counted off about 20 persons and instructed them to go behind the earth mound. . . . I walked around the mound and found myself confronted by a tremendous grave. People were closely wedged together and lying on top of each other so that only their heads were visible. Nearly all had blood running over their shoulders from their heads. Some of the people shot were still moving. Some were lifting their arms and turning their heads to show that they were still alive. The pit was already two-thirds full. I estimated that it already contained about 1,000 people. I looked for the man who did the shooting. He was an S.S. man, who sat at the edge of the narrow end of the pit, his feet dangling into the pit. He had a tommy-gun on his knees and was smoking a cigarette.

From Military Tribunal, *The Trial of German Major War Criminals* (London: Her Majesty's Stationery Office, 1952), XIX, p. 457.

rocket-propelled missiles limited Allied use of Antwerp as a port of supply, and by late autumn the Germans had retired in good order to their own Siegfried line.

Though falling back, the Germans hoped, as in World War I, to prevent an assault on Germany itself. They still had an army of 10 million in the field. Hitler was pressing the development of the jet plane, which he hoped could still save Germany. To buy another winter, in late September 1944 he called up the last reserves, ordering all able-bodied males between sixteen and sixty into the service. Not wishing to give Hitler the winter, Eisenhower ordered an airborne assault to leap over German defensive lines on the lower Rhine, but plans for a linked ground-air attack went badly, and the airborne army had to be rescued. The Allied offensive, having overreached its supplies, was now bogged down, and Hitler ordered a final counteroffensive sweep through the Ardennes forest on Antwerp, the Allies' supply port. A German armored attack on December 16, with the advantage of fog, snow, systematic infiltration, and complete surprise, threatened to throw the Allies

back in the Battle of the Bulge, just short of the German border, and completely surrounded an American airborne division at Bastogne. As the weather cleared, Allied air strikes and German fuel shortages stopped the German counteradvance.

Germany now had no more men or supplies to throw into the battle. German oil production had been given a deathblow, and tanks had to be hauled to the front by oxen. The catastrophic technique of firebombing was being used. The British put Dresden to the torch in a massive incendiary raid on February 13–14, 1945, with the loss of 135,000 lives, many of them refugees pouring in from the east, running from the Soviet advance.

The Soviets had been pushing on relentlessly ever since Stalingrad. In the campaign of 1943, while the Western Allies were busy in Italy, the Soviets won back most of their own territories that had been lost in 1941 and 1942. They kept up the pressure during the winter and started an early spring campaign in the south. By the autumn of 1944 the Soviets had been able to sweep across Romania and Bulgaria to a juncture with the

Yugoslav communist guerrillas under their leader Marshal Josip Broz, called Tito (1892–1980), and were ready for the attack on Hungary. In the center and north, they had recovered all their own territory and were ready to attack Germany across Poland from the east. Poland, caught between the advancing Soviets and the retreating Germans, was devastated. In August the provisional government of Poland in London ordered a mass uprising in Warsaw. The battle within Warsaw continued until October, when the Germans at last succeeded in crushing it, at the cost of more than 200,000 Polish casualties. The Soviets, on the outskirts of the city, did not intervene, waiting for the Polish Resistance to be destroyed so that they might create their own collaborators. This was the last German victory.

The rapid conclusion of the battle of Germany followed. The Soviets had not stopped for winter but had pressed on through Poland to menace Berlin early in March. The Western Allies broke through the Siegfried line in February, crossed the Rhine, and entered the heart of Germany. Early in February 1945, Stalin, Churchill, and Roosevelt held another summit conference, this time at Yalta in the Crimea, and confirmed final plans for the conquest of Germany. It was plain that the Germans could not hold out for long. The Allied planners wanted to settle peacefully which areas of Germany each of them would occupy and govern after the German defeat. The decision was reached to give the Soviets the honor of taking Berlin, a decision that, in effect, confirmed their hold on Poland as well. At the time this view seemed to

recognize the fact that during the two years of successful offensive against the Germans, the Soviets had pinned down many more German divisions than had the Western Allies. Stalin further demanded that Germany pay $20 billion in reparations, with half the sum to go to the war-torn Soviet Union. The Soviets fought their way into a Berlin already pulverized by the air power of the Western Allies. Hitler and his former mistress shot themselves in his bunker suite, and their bodies were covered with gasoline and burned.

The war Hitler had unleashed in Europe killed 17 million soldiers and 18 million civilians at the lowest extreme. No European war in history had been so destructive, so corrosive to the doctrine of progress and to the concept of human beings as rational. As fuller details of the war, suppressed by censors during the heat of battle, became known to the public, the sense of elation in victory was also seriously compromised by the awareness of how unpredictable and how devastating war had become.

The Allied advance into Germany had revealed for the first time the full horror of Nazi treatment of slave laborers from conquered lands, of political opponents, of homosexuals, and of peoples styled "inferior" by Nazi ideology, in particular Jews, Poles, and Gypsies. One after another the concentration camps were liberated in Germany, Austria, and Poland, and the names of Auschwitz, Belsen, Buchenwald, Dachau, Nordhausen, Mauthausen, and others, came to be associated with a savage war of genocide directed especially against the Jews. Hitler's "new world order" had brought with it

At Belsen the liberating troops discovered a mass grave, a scene they would encounter again at each of the German concentration camps.

UPI/Bettmann Newsphotos

The long, slow, island-hopping campaign in the Pacific was costly in lives on both sides. This photograph of the bodies of American soldiers on Buna Beach, New Guinea, was one of the first the American government permitted the press to use that showed American personnel killed in combat in World War II. It ran in *Life* magazine on September 20, 1943.

George Stock, Life Magazine. © 1943. Time, Inc.

the Holocaust, the systematic destruction of Jewish life in central Europe, as Heinrich Himmler, the head of the SS, applied modern technology to achieve "the Final Solution," the extinction of Jews in order to end "the Jewish problem." Near Auschwitz, in Poland, upwards of 2 million people were killed in gas chambers and crematoria in under three years, with twelve thousand executed in a single day. Others died in medical experiments, from starvation, and from firing squads armed with machine guns. By the end of the war between 6 and 7 million Jews had been slaughtered in the Holocaust. Jewish life and culture had, in large measure, ceased to exist in Austria, Germany, Poland, Romania, Lithuania, and the Ukraine.

The effects of the Holocaust were devastating. Efforts to cover up, account for, or explain away such monstrous behavior would corrode political and social life for generations. The nations that received Jewish immigrants—Britain, the United States, Canada, and others—benefited enormously. Displaced Jews, and Zionists who had long dreamed of a homeland in Palestine, would create a new Jewish state, Israel, leading to a state of almost constant undeclared war in the Near and Middle East. The diaspora of the Jews would enrich new

societies in ways the racist theories of Hitler could never have imagined.

After the war many people would ask why Germans who knew of the systematic killing of Jews had not protested it; why the Soviets, as they moved into Poland, had not stopped it; why the Western Allies had not made them early targets of liberation; why the pope had not spoken out; or why the Jews themselves had not organized more systematic resistance within the camps. There is little agreement on these questions, though little disagreement about the magnitude of the deaths and the importance of the questions those deaths give rise to.

On May 8, 1945, Churchill and Harry S Truman (1884–1972)—who had become the American president on Roosevelt's death that April—announced the end of German resistance, the day of victory in Europe, V-E Day. It was symbolic of difficulties to come that Stalin was offended because the Western Allies had accepted a formal surrender at Reims in France. He chose to announce separately, on the Soviet Union's part, the final victory over Germany, and not until the next day.

The War in the Pacific

V-J Day, the day of victory over Japan, was now the all-out goal of Allied effort. The Soviet Union had refrained from adding Japan to its formal enemies as long as Germany was still a threat. Britain and the United States, on the other hand, were anxious for the Soviets to enter the war against the Japanese. This desire was responsible for many of the concessions made to Stalin in the last months of the German war.

The attack on Japan had been pressed in three main directions. First, in a process that the American press soon called "island-hopping," the American navy drove straight toward Japan from the central Pacific. One after another, the small island bases that stood in the way were reduced by American naval forces, which used both air support and amphibious methods. Each island required an intense beach assault and pitched battle: Tarawa, Eniwetok, Kwajalein, Iwo Jima, Okinawa, Saipan, and Guam.

Second, the Americans and Australians, with help from other Commonwealth elements, worked their way up the southwest Pacific through the much larger islands of the Solomons, New Guinea, and the Philippines. The base for this campaign—which was under the command of the American general Douglas MacArthur (1880–1964)—was Australia and such outlying islands as New Caledonia and the New Hebrides. By October 1944 the sea forces had won the battle of the Philippine Sea and had made possible the successful landing of MacArthur's troops on Leyte and the reconquest of the Philippine Islands from the Japanese.

The third attack came from the south in the China-Burma-India theater. The main effort of the Allies was to get material support to Chiang Kai-shek and the Chinese Nationalists at Chungking and, if possible, to weaken the Japanese position in Burma, Thailand, and Indochina. After Pearl Harbor, when the Japanese seized and shut the "Burma Road," the only way for the Allies to communicate with

American marines raised the flag on Mount Suribachi, on Iwo Jima, in February 1945; in May of that year the Soviet banner of victory waved over a destroyed Berlin.

Defense Department, photo by Rosenthal; Sovfoto

Chiang's Nationalists was by air. Although the Western Allies did not invest an overwhelming proportion of their resources in the China-Burma-India theater, they did help keep the Chinese formally in the fight. And as the final campaign of 1945 drew on, the British, with Chinese and American aid, were holding down three Japanese field armies in this theater.

The end in Japan came with a suddenness that was hardly expected. From Pacific island bases, American airplanes had inflicted crippling damage on Japanese industry in the spring and summer of 1945. The Japanese fleet had been almost destroyed, submarine warfare had almost strangled the Japanese economy, and the morale of Japanese troops was declining. Nonetheless, American leaders were convinced that only the use of their recently invented atom bomb could avert the very heavy casualties expected from the proposed amphibious invasion of the Japanese home islands. Some commentators believe that racism also played a role in the decision to use the bomb on the Japanese rather than on any European people, though the bomb was not, in fact, ready for use in time to affect the European war. An additional motive

for its use was a desire to demonstrate to the Soviet Union, which many feared would turn upon the Allies at the end of the war, just how powerful America's new weapon was. The result was the dropping of the first atom bomb on Hiroshima on August 6, 1945.

On August 8 the Soviets, who had agreed to come into the war against Japan once Germany was beaten, invaded Manchuria in full force. Faced with what they felt was certain defeat after the dropping of a second atom bomb on Nagasaki, the Japanese government decided not to make a last-ditch stand in their own country. On September 2 the Japanese formally surrendered in Tokyo Bay. Japan gave up its conquests abroad and submitted to American military occupation. Purged of most of its militarists, the Japanese government continued to rule under nominal Allied (actually American) supervision.

The Allied Coalition

The Grand Alliance, as Churchill liked to call it, known in its last years as the United Nations, had mustered overpowering strength against Germany, Japan, Italy, and

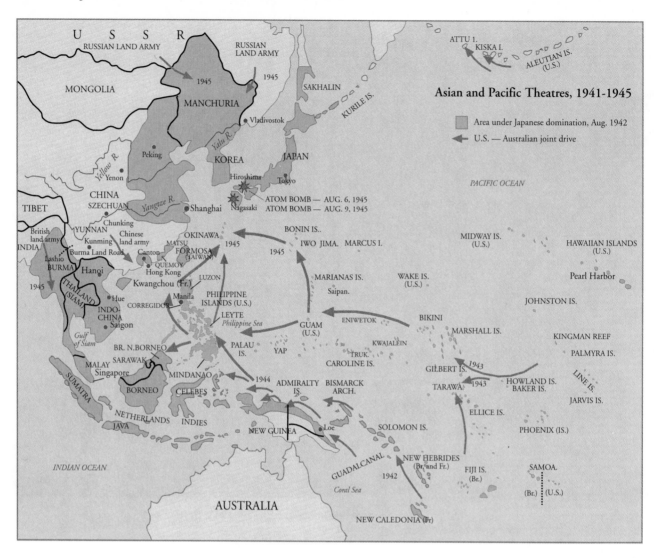

such collaborators as the Axis powers could secure in the Balkans, Southeast Asia, and western Europe. Britain and the Commonwealth, the Soviet Union, and the United States were the heart of the Allied coalition. Nationalist China, for all its inefficiencies, had tied down hundreds of thousands of Japanese soldiers, and the resources of the French Empire and the French Resistance movements at home and abroad had been valuable. The Allies had been able to count on the resources of many Latin American nations, and Brazil had been an active member of the alliance. In this truly global war, Brazilian troops had fought in Italy along with American (including Japanese-American), French imperial, British imperial, pro-Allied Italian, Polish, and other troops. At the very end of the European war, Argentina, too, declared war on Germany and Japan, even though its fascist leader, General Juan Perón (1895–1974) had hoped for a German victory.

The instruments of Allied union were the summit conferences of the Big Three—Roosevelt, Churchill, and Stalin—with the political and military advisers and experts, plus the more frequent Anglo-American conferences. Even before the United States entered the war, Roosevelt and

Churchill met off Newfoundland and issued the Atlantic Charter (August 14, 1941), in which they declared support for the freedom of the seas, equality of access to economic opportunity, abandonment of aggression, and the restoration of rights to conquered peoples. Formal conferences—between Roosevelt and Churchill at Casablanca (January 1943) and Quebec (August 1943), and among the Big Three at Teheran and Yalta—concluded agreements that had been steadily carried on at lower political and military levels. From July 17 to August 17, 1945, a final conference at Potsdam (near conquered Berlin) brought together the United States, Britain, and the Soviet Union. With two new figures attending, President Truman and Prime Minister Clement Attlee (1883–1967), they met to confirm the Yalta decisions.

But there were grave military and political matters to be ironed out. For the actual direction of operations in the field, the British and Americans had decided to set up a complete intermeshing of staffs. All down the line, an American in command always had a Briton as his second, and a Briton in command always had an American as his second. Even the intelligence-gathering apparatus of the two nations was meshed. At the highest level, the combined chiefs of staff, in close touch with top American and British government officials, did the overall planning. The Soviets could not be brought into such close military cooperation, and Soviet troops in the field always fought on their own.

During the war the Allies had agreed that the Axis powers were to be forced into "unconditional surrender." The Germans must be beaten unmistakably, and Allied troops must enter Berlin as conquerors. There must be no political negotiation at all, simply unconditional military surrender. In Britain and the United States there was some opposition to this policy during the war, partly on humanitarian grounds, but also because people feared that the prospect of unconditional surrender would stiffen the German will to resist and would unite the nation behind Hitler. In retrospect, it seems unlikely that Hitler would ever have negotiated with the Allies; and after the failure of the attempt to kill him in 1944, there was little chance that the Germans themselves would overthrow the Nazi government.

Another political problem created a much clearer rift between the British and the Americans. The underlying issue was just how far anti-German elements in France, Italy, and other occupied lands had to go to prove that they were democratic enough to secure the backing of the Western powers. Here the difference in the underlying tone of American and British policies was evident in the views of Roosevelt and Churchill. Roosevelt was convinced that if the Allies did not interfere to support conservatives and reactionaries in the occupied lands, but instead allowed these peoples to choose their form of government freely, they would choose democracy. Churchill was less idealistic. He was eager to use any elements that were hostile to the Germans, even if their hostility was quite recent. Furthermore, Roosevelt began to press Churchill for a commitment to decolonization, especially of India, at the end of the war, while Churchill responded that he would not preside over the dissolution of the British Empire.

In French politics the issue was further complicated by Roosevelt's suspicions of de Gaulle, the chosen leader of the French liberation movement. To Churchill, de Gaulle was a difficult but indispensable ally. As it turned out, the Gaullists, in collaboration with the organized French Resistance in the homeland, did take over the civilian administration of French territory as it was liberated, and France by free popular vote restored a democratic form of government. In 1946 the Italians also narrowly voted for a republic. What had threatened at one time to be a serious difficulty between American policy and British policy was resolved by the liberated people themselves.

But the political issue that bulked largest after World War II was the problem of potential Soviet domination in eastern and southeastern Europe. At Yalta the Western powers had allowed Stalin to push his armies westward and had relied on his promises to permit free elections in Poland, Hungary, Czechoslovakia, and the Balkans. Most of the smaller eastern European countries

had moved toward fascist totalitarianism before World War II, and a transition to communist totalitarianism would not be difficult. Churchill, who never trusted Stalin, did not dare risk losing Soviet manpower and material resources during the war. Appeasement of Stalin seemed absolutely essential. At the end of the war, the western European states, though victorious, were so near impoverishment that they could play no major role in the balance-of-power politics that would follow, so that the Soviets and Americans soon became the only superpowers. Contrary to its hopes and public expectations, the United States was drawn deeply into European and Asian matters.

When the war ended, there was no peace. The defeat of Germany and Japan was almost immediately followed by the rise of a new aggressor, the Soviet Union, which had already given clear warning of its intentions. The long shooting war was followed quickly by sharp antagonisms between the Soviet Union and its former allies, a degree of hostility so intense it was soon called the *cold war*.

THE COLD WAR BEGINS

The quarter century following World War II embraces the period conventionally identified as the cold war, even though in some respects a thaw had set in before 1970 and in others the hostilities of the cold war extended to the 1990s. A source of international insecurity, the cold war nonetheless marked a period longer than that between World Wars I and II without a renewed full-scale world war. However, the number of local and often intensely destructive and largely undeclared wars increased: wars of liberation in the European colonies, wars of nationalism in the Middle East, repeated wars between Israel and its Arab neighbors, a long war by the United Nations in Korea, a prolonged war in southeast Asia deeply involving the United States, insurgent wars in Cuba and Central America, and an intense conflict between Iraq and a UN coalition led by the United States. Taken together, this warfare claimed more lives than did World War I, so that the interval since 1945 has been referred to by some analysts as a period of perpetual war to assure perpetual peace.

The Postwar Settlement

The devastation wrought by the war, including the war in the Pacific, greatly exceeded that in World War I: at least 50 million dead, more than half of them civilians, and more than $2,000 billion in damage. Despite a sharply rising birth rate and vast programs of economic reconstruction, such losses could never be fully repaired. Moreover, new and terrifying problems faced the world. Atomic weapons, hydrogen bombs, and guided missiles made real the fear that a new general war might exterminate all life on this planet. The United States and the Soviet Union were at first the only powers able to initiate or pursue nuclear warfare. The postwar history of international politics thus became largely a history of Soviet-American rivalry: a cold war between superpowers.

Enemy attack and occupation had caused incalculable devastation inside the Soviet Union and left millions of survivors destitute; but the nation's capitalist ally, the United States, had remained unattacked in its heartland and had invented and used atomic weapons. It took Stalin four years (1945–1949) to catch up by making his own atomic bomb. Scientific information given the Soviets by agents and spies made some contribution to this achievement, but only the high level of Soviet science and technology and the Soviet capacity to concentrate government investments made it possible at all.

Though the Soviet Union and its former Western allies agreed on peace treaties with Italy, Hungary, Romania, and Bulgaria, no such treaty could be concluded with Germany or Japan. The Soviet Union also concluded a peace treaty with Finland in which it took a portion of Karelia. From Romania, the Soviet Union again took Bessarabia and northern Bukovina, and it annexed part of former East Prussia and the easternmost part of Czechoslovakia.

The chief surviving Nazi leaders were tried at Nuremberg in 1946, and twelve were sentenced to death for war crimes. Defeated Germany was divided into four occupied sections—American, British, French, and Soviet. The Soviet sector extended from eastern Germany to west of Berlin, which, as the former capital, was also divided into four occupation zones, one for each of the Allies. This arrangement was designed for temporary military occupation, but it continued because no treaty could be reached. The failure to reach any settlement over Germany left the most serious problem in Europe unresolved.

In 1949 the three Western powers promoted the union of their respective sectors as the Federal Republic of Germany—West Germany—with its capital at Bonn. The Soviets responded by creating the communist German Democratic Republic—East Germany—with its capital at Pankow outside Berlin. Many West Germans were eager for reunion with their fellow Germans in the Soviet zone. Yet a reunification of Germany under Western capitalist auspices was what the Soviets feared most, believing that it would mean a revival of aggression. An all-communist Germany was equally intolerable to the Western powers.

In Asia the most grievous problem remained that of China. The Chinese communists, who had challenged Chiang Kai-shek's ruling Kuomintang party for power, kept their forces active during the Japanese occupation. By 1949 the communists had defeated Chiang Kai-shek, who took refuge on the island of Formosa (Taiwan), where the communists could not follow because they had no fleet. In the last years of the struggle, Chiang had lost his hold over the Chinese people; the morale of his own forces was low, and an ever-mounting inflation ravaged the economy. By 1950 mainland China had gone communist and formed part of the Soviet bloc, while

Chiang's government in Taiwan remained part of the American bloc. American foreign policy had suffered a major defeat.

Elsewhere, the Soviet Union pursued its goal of world communism through the agencies of individual Communist parties. Communist parties existed in virtually every country, often varying in the degree of subservience to the Communist party of the Soviet Union (CPSU) and the Soviet government. The United States, by contrast, had no ideologically disciplined supporters in most of the world.

The two superpowers each became the leader of a great coalition whose members were attached by bonds of self-interest. The members of the loose American coalition in 1945 included the Western Hemisphere nations, Great Britain, the British Commonwealth, western Europe, Japan, and the Philippines. The Soviet coalition included the countries of eastern Europe and, by 1949, China. The border between the two coalitions in Europe—named the Iron Curtain by Winston Churchill in 1946—ran along a north-south line across central Europe. Turkey belonged to the Western coalition, and portions of the Middle East and of southeast Asia were linked to it by a network of pacts. The dividing line between North and South Korea—with the Soviet Union occupying the north and the United States the south—represented a kind of Asian extension of the long frontier between the two coalitions. Over this long frontier came aggressive Soviet probing operations that led to crises and in several cases to wars.

Repeatedly, the West made gestures toward easing relations between the two coalitions. In 1946 Stalin refused to join in a United Nations atomic energy commission. In 1947 the United States proposed an international plan of massive American economic aid to accelerate European recovery from the ruin of the war—the Marshall Plan, named for General George C. Marshall, American secretary of state (1880–1959). The Soviet Union refused to accept the aid for itself and would not let its satellites participate in the Marshall Plan. The former Western allies subsequently formed the nucleus of the North Atlantic Treaty Organization (NATO) in 1949. The Soviet coalition founded the Cominform (Communist Information Bureau) in 1947 as a successor to the former Comintern, and created the Warsaw Pact (1955), binding eastern Europe together, as a reply to NATO. The United States and Britain sought in the 1950s and 1960s to prevent the spread of atomic weapons. Their plan called for a joint multilateral (nuclear) force (MLF). Because the Germans would participate, the French rejected MLF and in 1966 withdrew their military forces from NATO and forced NATO headquarters to be moved out of France.

In the Middle East, the Baghdad Pact and its successor, the Central Treaty Organization (CENTO), proved to be no more than a series of unstable agreements among the United States, Britain, Turkey, Iran, and Pakistan. With the withdrawal of Iraq from the Baghdad Pact in 1959, no direct alliances linked the Arab world with the West. The neutral nations remained outside the coalitions. Some, like Switzerland or Sweden, were simply maintaining their traditional policies of not aligning themselves with any grouping of powers. But most were newly independent nations. Of these India was the most influential, taking much-needed economic assistance from both coalitions. As economic aid became an instrument in the cold war, neutral nations tried, often with success, to play one side off against the other.

Through the years of cold war, the United Nations—formed during World War II from among the opponents of the Axis and chartered in 1945 at San Francisco—served as an international organization where members of both coalitions and neutrals alike could confer. As the direct successor to the League of Nations, though with its headquarters in New York, it inherited the League's duty of keeping the peace; but, like the League, it lacked independent sovereignty or authority over its members. To deal with threats to the peace, its charter created a Security Council with eleven member states, five of which—the United States, the Soviet Union, Great Britain, France, and China—held permanent memberships. The other six were elected to rotating two-year terms by the General Assembly, to which all member states belonged. The secretary general, elected by the Security Council, could exert great personal influence in international affairs.

Each of the five permanent members of the Security Council could veto any substantive question. Both the Soviet Union and the United States insisted that decisions had to be unanimous before action could go forward. As a result, the Security Council often found itself unable to act because of a veto. Of the eighty vetoes cast in the first decade, the Soviets exercised seventy-seven.

In the mid-1950s new nations joined the UN: some pro-Western, some pro-Soviet, and some neutral. Japan joined in 1956. As the former colonies obtained their independence during the late 1950s and early 1960s, each joined the United Nations, where the Afro-Asian bloc came to command a majority in the General Assembly. The United States for twenty years successfully opposed the seating of the Chinese communists, which until 1971 left the permanent Chinese seat on the Security Council in the possession of Chiang Kai-shek's representative.

The League of Nations had never been able to put its own forces into the field, but the UN did so repeatedly: in Korea in 1950–1953; on the Arab-Israeli frontiers (1956–1967, and again in 1974 and 1982); in the former Belgian Congo; in Cyprus and elsewhere; and in 1991 in Iraq and Kuwait. Through its functional councils and special agencies—the Economic and Social Council, the Education, Scientific and Cultural Organization (UNESCO), the World Health Organization, the Food and Agricultural Organization, and the World Bank—the UN advanced loans to governments to initiate new development plans, controlled epidemics, and provided experts on modern farming techniques. But the UN was frequently unable to forestall war, and while it remained a valuable instrument of diplomacy, the high hopes originally entertained for it were not realized.

As the major nation least injured by World War II because virtually no fighting took place on its home soil, the United States was in the best position to respond immediately to Soviet pressures. Under President Truman a new balance of power began to emerge. As part of that balance, the United States first turned to a policy of containment designed to prevent the Soviet Union from extending its control beyond the limits it had consolidated in 1947. But by about 1952 the belief that inherent weaknesses in the Soviet system would cause it to disintegrate began to be seriously challenged. Containment was attacked by the left, which felt Truman was too hard on the Soviets; by the right, which wanted to roll the Soviets back to their original borders; and by the political middle, which argued that containment was only a defensive stance and that the United States must devise fresh initiatives to attract the newly independent nations of the so-called Third World.

For a brief time the United States supported the idea of liberation, or "rollback," but was disillusioned after the Hungarian uprising of 1956 in which Americans found they could do very little against Soviet domination. Since the first Soviet atom bomb test was detected in the West in September 1949, the United States had debated how best to deal with a growing tendency toward stalemate. If the Soviet bloc could be made to loosen its control of its satellites, some liberalization might take place within the Soviet bloc itself without direct Western intervention. Thus attitudes toward the nations of eastern Europe remained in flux, with the great powers trying to manipulate the balance.

The Soviet Union and the West, 1945–1970

The Soviet Union moved rapidly to consolidate its territorial position. Using the Red Army, the Soviets created "people's republics" in Poland, Romania, Hungary, and Bulgaria, which became Soviet satellites. Yugoslavia organized its own communist government, with Albania as its own satellite. Soviet troops occupied about a third of Germany, roughly between the Elbe and the Oder rivers, where the Soviets organized the communist-ruled satellite of East Germany. The part of Germany that lay east of the line formed by the Oder and Neisse rivers, except for the sections of East Prussia directly annexed to the USSR, was handed over by the Soviets to their Polish satellite; here a wholesale transfer of population replaced the Germans with Poles. Finland became a hostage to the Soviet security system but retained its prewar political institutions and a measure of neutrality. The four Allied powers detached Austria from Germany and divided it, like Germany, into four occupation zones. In 1948 the communists took over Czechoslovakia by a coup d'état and ousted the government of Eduard Benes. Within each satellite the communists aped Soviet policies, moving quickly to collectivize agriculture, impose forced industrialization, control cultural life, and govern by terror.

In other cases, the Soviet Union was rebuffed. In 1946 the Soviets at first refused to withdraw their forces from northwest Iran and yielded only to pressure from the United Nations. A more alarming probe came in

Greece, where a communist-dominated guerrilla movement during World War II had attempted to seize control and been thwarted by British troops. In 1946 the Greek communists tried again, backed this time by Albania, Yugoslavia, and Bulgaria. Simultaneously, Stalin pressured the Turks for concessions in the Straits area. In response, President Truman proclaimed that countries facing the threat of communist aggression could count on help from the United States. Under this Truman Doctrine he sent American military aid to Greece and Turkey. The threat to the Turks receded, and by 1949, after severe fighting, the Greeks put down the communist uprising with the help of American advisers.

The Soviets began one of the most bitter phases of the cold war in 1948 in Germany. By shutting off all major highways from the West to Berlin, they attempted to force the Western Allies to turn Berlin over to them. The Allies stood firm, however, and in the next six months airlifted more than 2.3 million tons of supplies to West Berlin. Though the Soviets then gave up and reopened the land routes, they remained determined to oust the Western powers from Berlin.

The Yugoslav Rebellion.

Also in 1948, the Soviets faced a rebellion from a country that had previously seemed the most pro-Soviet of all the new communist states of eastern Europe—Yugoslavia. Yugoslavia had overthrown a pro-German government in 1941 and throughout World War II remained a scene of intense guerrilla action against the Germans and Italians. There were two main groups of guerrillas: the Chetniks, representing the Serb royalist domination over the south-Slav kingdom; and the Partisans, led by Croatian-born, communist Tito. As the war continued, the communist-dominated Partisans gained ground against the Chetniks. The Soviets helped put Tito in control in 1944.

Once in power, Tito installed his own communist government, abolished the Yugoslav monarchy, and for three years adopted all the standard Soviet policies. Yet in June 1948 the Soviets expelled Tito's regime from the Cominform. The Soviet satellites broke their economic agreements with Yugoslavia, unloosed barrages of anti-Tito propaganda, and stirred up border incidents. Stalin believed that he could bully the Yugoslavs into submission. "I will shake my little finger," he said, "and there will be no more Tito."

But Tito remained in power, accepting the aid that was quickly offered him by the United States. Washington recognized that a communist regime hostile to Stalin was a new phenomenon that would deeply embarrass the Soviets. Gradually, Yugoslav communism evolved its own ideology, rejecting Stalin's politics and declaring that Tito and his followers were the only true Leninists. Tito decentralized the economy, beginning in the factories, where worker's committees began to participate actively in planning. From the economy, decentralization spread to the local government, then to the central government, and finally to the Yugoslav Communist party. Lest this new "national" communism spread to the other regimes, the Soviets directed a series of ferocious purges of "Titoists" in eastern Europe, terrorizing anyone who might hope to establish autonomy within the communist bloc.

The Korean War.

The Korean War, which broke out in June 1950, was in some measure a Soviet-sponsored operation, although the Soviets contributed only support and sympathy and allowed their Chinese ally to take the military lead. Korea had been a target of Soviet interest in the late nineteenth and early twentieth centuries, but the Japanese triumph over the Russians in 1905 had led instead to Japanese annexation of the country in 1910. In 1945 Soviet troops occupied the northern part of Korea and American troops the southern part. The country was divided in the middle by a line along the 38th parallel of latitude. A communist-inspired People's Democratic Republic of Korea was set up in the north and an American inspired Republic of Korea in the south. When all American forces except for a few specialists were withdrawn from South Korea, the North Koreans marched south to unite the nation under communist control.

The communists may have thought the operation would go unchallenged. But when the invasion began, the United Nations moved troops into Korea. Under General Douglas MacArthur, the largely American force halted the North Korean drive and pushed the enemy back almost to the frontier of China. At this point troops from the People's Republic of China (PRC) joined the North Koreans in pushing the Americans southward again. By 1951 the line of battle had been stabilized roughly along the old boundary between North and South Korea. After prolonged negotiations, an armistice was finally concluded in July 1953.

The Korean settlement did not end the tension between Communist China and the United States, and serious friction developed over Taiwan (Formosa) and smaller offshore islands in the hands of Chiang Kai-shek. Nor did the Korean settlement bring a closer understanding between the Soviet Union and the United States. It was at best a compromise. After all the fighting, the United States had managed to hold on to the devastated southern portion of the country, and the communists had been driven back to the north, which they governed undisturbed. Neither side could call it a victory.

By the time the Korean War ended, Stalin had been dead for more than three months. Stalin's heirs realized that any attack that threatened the vital interests of the United States might well touch off the ultimate disaster. To relax the tension would raise the danger that the Soviet Union would lose its position as leader of the world communist movement. In the end it proved to be impossible for the Soviet leadership to hold these threats in balance, and the choices they felt forced to make led to a major split in the communist world.

Eastern Europe.

In eastern Europe, the new first secretary to the Soviet Communist party, Nikita Khrushchev (1894–1971), sought to heal the breach with Tito. In May 1955 he went in person to Belgrade and publicly apologized for the quarrel. Relations between Tito and Moscow improved, although the Yugoslavs never abandoned their ties to the West. Khrushchev even went so far as to declare that many prominent victims of the Titoist purges had been executed wrongly. But in making these admissions Khrushchev opened the door to new troubles.

In 1956 Khrushchev denounced Stalin and admitted to many past injustices in the Soviet Union. This proved far too strong a brew for the European satellites. Anti-communist riots by workers in Poznan, Poland, in June 1956 were followed by severe upheavals elsewhere in Poland. The uprising was conducted by one wing of the Communist party, that led by Wladislaw Gomulka (1905–1982). Not even the presence in Warsaw of Khrushchev himself prevented Gomulka's rise to power, although at one moment the Soviets seem to have contemplated imposing their will by force. Yet because the new government in Poland was still communist, they allowed it to remain in power until 1970.

In Hungary, however, the upheaval went farther. Starting as an anti-Stalinist movement within the Communist party, the Hungarian disturbance at first brought Imre Nagy (1895–1958) into office as premier. But popular hatred for communism and for the Soviets got out of hand, and young men and women took up arms in Budapest in the hope of ousting the communists and taking Hungary out of the Soviet sphere. When Hungary denounced the Warsaw Pact, Khrushchev ordered full-fledged military action. In November 1956 Soviet tanks and troops swept back into Budapest and put down the revolution in blood and fire. A puppet government was installed and more than 150,000 Hungarian refugees fled to the West.

The Hungarian uprising demonstrated that Khrushchev was unwilling to permit much deviation from the Soviet line, and that he would use military power when that line was crossed. Perhaps most important, it demonstrated to other satellite states that they could not count on aid from the West in the face of Soviet resistance. The effect was to stabilize the Iron Curtain, putting an end to major probes across it by either side.

All the eastern European satellites had been bound together in the Council for Mutual Economic Aid (Comecon) established in 1949, which took measures to standardize machinery and coordinate economic policies and issued blasts against western European efforts at economic cooperation through the Common Market. Yugoslavia never joined Comecon, and after 1958 it was not invited to send observers. In 1958–1959 Comecon called for a specialization plan in which the more developed countries would concentrate on heavy industry, and Romania in particular on the production of raw materials (chiefly food and oil). The Romanian government protested, pointing to its already considerable achievement in heavy industry.

Thus the Romanians, like the Yugoslavs, assumed a more independent position within the communist bloc. They increased their trade with the noncommunist world and remained neutral in the growing Soviet-Chinese

quarrel. In 1963 the Soviets sanctioned Romania's continued efforts to build a steel industry. Soviet propaganda, however, called for integrating the lower Danube region—which would have meant taking territory from Romania—and denied that the Romanians had contributed to the Allied cause in World War II. The Romanians claimed full credit for their "liberation from fascism" and dared to demand the return of Bessarabia and northern Bukovina. Yugoslav-Romanian cooperation became an important part of Romanian policy. Largely owing to the balancing skill of the Romanian communist leaders, first Gheorghe Gheorghiu-Dej (party secretary 1952–1965) and then Nicolae Ceausescu (1918–1989), supported by the traditionally anti-Soviet sentiments of Romanians generally, the Romanians demonstrated a measure of independence in foreign and economic affairs.

Berlin.   In East Germany, there the Soviet Union had created its most industrially productive European satellite, fully integrated into Comecon. Strategically East Germany was of great importance to the USSR; control over East Germany enabled the Soviets to keep Poland surrounded and to keep communist troops within easy reach of West Germany. Every year thousands of East Germans had been escaping into West Berlin, and the East German population had declined by 2 million between 1949 and 1961. Because West Berlin provided an example of prosperity and free democratic government that was more effective than any propaganda, Khrushchev was determined to get the Western powers out of Berlin. He threatened to sign a peace treaty with the puppet government of East Germany, which was not yet recognized by the West, to turn over to it all communications to Berlin, and to support it in any effort it might make to force the Western powers out. Western refusal to abandon agreements concluded during World War II led to a prolonged diplomatic crisis in 1959.

The Western powers could not permit the Soviets to re-create the conditions that led to the airlift of 1948 or accept the suggestion that, once Western troops were removed, Berlin would become a "free city." Defenseless and surrounded by communist territory, Berlin and its 2 million citizens might soon be swallowed up. Moreover, the Soviet proposal for a confederation of East and West Germany aroused the gravest doubts. How could a state that was a full member of the Western coalition of NATO join with one that belonged to the Soviet coalition's Warsaw Pact? How could a state that stood for capitalist development federate with one completely communized? How could a parliamentary state governed by a multiparty system federate with a communist totalitarian state?

While the Berlin threat persisted, the new American president, Dwight D. Eisenhower, and Khrushchev agreed to exchange visits, and Khrushchev made a dramatic tour of the United States. But when the leaders of the two great powers met at the summit in Paris in May 1960, tensions were once again inflamed by a striking incident. A Soviet missile had brought down an American

In June 1961, Khrushchev and Kennedy met in Vienna, alternately at the American and (as shown in this picture) Soviet embassies.

Sovfoto

U-2, a lightweight, extremely fast plane that had been taking high-altitude photographs of Soviet territory from bases in Turkey and Pakistan. The Soviets had captured the pilot unharmed. After an initial denial, Eisenhower had to admit the truth of the charge; the incident ended both the summit meeting and the plans for his own visit to the Soviet Union.

When Eisenhower's successor, John F. Kennedy (1917–1963), met Khrushchev in Vienna (June 1961), Khrushchev insisted that his country would sign the treaty with East Germany before the end of the year. Tension mounted, and the number of refugees fleeing from East Berlin rose to a thousand a day. On August 13, East German forces cut all communications between East and West Berlin and began to build the infamous Berlin Wall to prevent further departures. Taken by surprise, the United States realized that it could not resort to arms to prevent the closing of East Germany's own border. The wall became the symbol of a government that had to imprison its own people to keep them from leaving. Escapes, recaptures, and shootings continued along the

wall for nearly three decades, but the immediate crisis proved to be over. Khrushchev had backed away from unilateral cancellation of the Berlin treaties.

Nuclear Tests: Cuba. Khrushchev now probed in another way, announcing in August 1961 that the Soviets would resume atomic testing in the atmosphere, a practice stopped by both powers in 1958. In the two months that followed, the Soviets exploded thirty bombs. President Kennedy decided that, unless Khrushchev would agree to a treaty banning all tests, the United States would have to conduct its own new tests. Khrushchev refused, and American testing began again in April 1962.

In the summer of 1962 Khrushchev moved to place Soviet missiles with nuclear warheads in Cuba. This former American dependency and economic satellite, which was of great strategic importance and which lay only ninety miles off the Florida coast, was now in the hands of a domestic Communist party led by Fidel Castro (1926–   ). Castro had overthrown Cuba's dictator, General Fulgencio Batista (1901–1973), in 1959. Castro's revolution, which had taken nearly six years, had at first seemed romantic and had been supported by many Americans. Once in power, Castro quickly entered into an alliance with the Soviets. Hoping to bring Castro down, anticommunist Cuban exiles in the United States had attempted a disastrous landing at the Bay of Pigs in 1961.

Castro quickly learned what it meant to be a Soviet satellite during the Cuban missile crisis. He may not have asked for the missiles, but he had accepted them, even though Soviet officers were to retain control over their use. Although their installation would effectively have doubled the Soviet capacity to strike directly at the United States, the chief threat was political. When known, the mere presence of these weapons ninety miles from Florida would shake the confidence of other nations in America's capacity to protect even its own shores, and would enable Khrushchev to blackmail America over Berlin. American military intelligence discovered the sites and photographed them from the air. Khrushchev announced that the Soviet purpose was simply to help the Cubans resist a new invasion from the United States.

But Kennedy could not allow the missiles to remain in Cuba. At first the only course of action seemed an air strike, which might well have touched off a new world war. Instead, Kennedy found a measure that would prevent the further delivery of missiles—a sea blockade ("quarantine") of the island—and he combined it with the demand that the missiles already in Cuba be removed. After several days of great tension, Khrushchev backed down and agreed to halt work on the missile sites in Cuba and to remove the offensive weapons there.

Kennedy now exploited the American victory to push for a further relaxation in tensions. In July 1963 the United States, the Soviet Union, and Great Britain signed a treaty banning nuclear weapons tests in the atmosphere, in outer space, or underwater. The treaty subsequently received the support of more than seventy nations, though

A CLOSER LOOK

Soviet-American Rivalry and the Cold War

In 1947, at the outset of the cold war, as the Soviet Union continued to expand its influence throughout Europe, a leading American policy analyst, George Kennan (1904–), published a highly influential article in the American journal *Foreign Affairs*. In it he discussed what the United States should do to offset Soviet influence. He wrote under the pseudonym "X," though he had, in March 1946, sent the text of his argument, called "The Sources of Soviet Conduct," as a cable directly to the U.S. Department of State. At the time Kennan was the second-highest ranking American diplomatic officer in Moscow. The Foreign Affairs article is reprinted here:

In actuality the possibilities for American policy are by no means limited to holding the line and hoping for the best. It is entirely possible for the United States to influence by its actions the internal developments, both within Russia and throughout the international Communist movement, by which Russian policy is largely determined. This is not only a question of the modest measure of informational activity which this government can conduct in the Soviet Union and elsewhere, although that, too, is important. It is rather a question of the degree to which the United States can create among the peoples of the world generally the impression of a country which knows what it wants, which is coping successfully with the problems of its internal life and with the responsibilities of a world power, and which has a spiritual vitality capable of holding its own among the major ideological currents of the time. To the extent that such an impression can be created and maintained, the aims of Russian Communism must appear sterile and quixotic, the hopes and enthusiasm of Moscow's supporters must wane, and added strain must be imposed on the Kremlin's foreign policies. For the palsied decrepitude of the capitalist world is the keystone of Communist philosophy. Even the failure of the United States to experience the early economic depression which the ravens of the Red Square have been predicting with such complacent confidence since hostilities ceased would have deep and important repercussions throughout the Communist world.

By the same token, exhibitions of indecision, disunity and internal disintegration within this country have an exhilarating effect on the whole Communist movement.

At each evidence of these tendencies, a thrill of hope and excitement goes through the Communist world; a new jauntiness can be noted in the Moscow tread; new groups of foreign supporters climb on to what they can only view as the bandwagon of international politics; and Russian pressure increases all along the line in international affairs.

It would be an exaggeration to say that American behavior unassisted and alone could exercise a power of life and death over the Communist movement and bring about the early fall of Soviet power in Russia. But the United States has it in its power to increase enormously the strains under which Soviet policy must operate, to force upon the Kremlin a far greater degree of moderation and circumspection than it has had to observe in recent years, and in this way to promote tendencies which must eventually find their outlet in either the breakup or the gradual mellowing of Soviet power. For no mystical, messianic movement—and particularly not that of the Kremlin—can face frustration indefinitely without eventually adjusting itself in one way or another to the logic of that state of affairs.

Thus the decision will really fall in large measure on this country itself. The issue of Soviet-American relations is in essence a test of the overall worth of the United States as a nation among nations. To avoid destruction the United States need only measure up to its own best traditions and prove itself worthy of preservation as a great nation.

George F. Kennan, "The Sources of Soviet Conduct," *Foreign Affairs*, XXV (July 1947), pp. 581–82.

France and the PRC—prospective nuclear powers—would not sign it. The installation of a "hot line" communications system between the White House and the Kremlin that enabled the leaders of the two superpowers to talk to each other directly, and the sale of surplus American wheat to the Soviets marked the final steps Kennedy was able to take to decrease tensions before he was assassinated on November 22, 1963.

Czechoslovakia. The settlement in 1968 on the terms of a nuclear nonproliferation treaty to prevent the spread of atomic arms beyond the nations that already possessed them seemed to represent another step forward, but

Soviet intervention in Czechoslovakia in the summer of 1968 delayed its ratification. Long the most Stalinist of the eastern European governments, the Czech regime was unpopular at home. Soviet exploitation and the rigidity of communist dogma had crippled the once flourishing Czech economy. Then in 1968 Alexander Dubcek (1921–1994), a Slovak communist trained in the Soviet Union, took over the Czech Communist party as first secretary and ousted his predecessor. The Dubcek government freed the press from censorship, and it appeared that the regime might even allow opposition political parties to exist. Some army officers apparently favored revision of the Warsaw Pact, which enabled the

Soviets to hold military exercises in the territory of any member state.

However, the Czechs could not put through such a radical liberalization without alarming the Soviets and the East German government. In the spring and summer of 1968 the Soviets moved from first denouncing the Dubcek regime to intimidating and bullying it, and finally to armed intervention. Soviet and satellite tank divisions, more than 500,000 strong, swept into the country and met no active resistance. There was little bloodshed, but there was great shock. Those who had been arguing that the Soviets had outgrown the Stalinist repression of earlier years found themselves proved wrong, and the French and Italian Communist parties joined the Yugoslav and Romanian parties in condemning the invasion.

The return of Stalinism to Czechoslovakia was inexorable. Dubcek was ousted, and a grim purge of Czech intellectuals followed. The Soviets had been so alarmed by the Czech cultural, economic, and political ferment and its military and diplomatic implications that they were willing, at least temporarily, to sacrifice much of the international goodwill that they had been able to accumulate. In 1969 and 1970 discussions between the United States and the Soviet Union over limitations of armaments (Strategic Arms Limitation Talks, or SALT) resumed. By then both powers had a compelling interest in reducing their huge expenditures on weapons and obtaining more resources to deal with major domestic problems.

Conflict in Asia, 1953–1970

Between Stalin's death in 1953 and Khrushchev's denunciation of Stalin in 1956, Chinese-Soviet relations were basically amicable, and PRC influence rose in the communist world. The Soviets returned Port Arthur and Dairen to China in 1955. But when Khrushchev attacked Stalin without consulting Mao Zedong (1893–1976), the Chinese communist leader, the Chinese denounced him for joining with Tito and the revisionists.

Mao had walked a long road to become head of the most populous nation on earth: He had organized the Red Army in 1928; had endured the six-thousand-mile Long March to a stronghold in northwest China in 1934–1936; had helped to repel the Japanese; had defeated Chiang Kai-shek; and had established the People's Republic of China in 1949. An undeviating Stalinist, Mao was convinced that the Soviet Union had deserted the true doctrine, and he was deeply offended at being ignored on so significant a matter as revealing to the world the extent of Stalin's purges and the nature of the Terror. To doctrinal matters Mao added practical grievances: He wanted far more economic aid than the Soviets had been able or willing to provide, especially aid in developing nuclear weapons. In 1956–1957 Mao experimented briefly with a liberated public opinion ("Let

one hundred flowers bloom") but soon resumed a thoroughly leftist militant course. At home he embarked on forced industrialization—the "great leap forward"—with backyard blast furnaces and mass collectivization of the "people's communes," ending in disastrous results to both industry and agriculture. Having been down this road themselves, the Soviets disapproved, and the latent disagreements between the two communist giants began to emerge.

The Soviet-Chinese Split

In 1959 Khrushchev told Beijing that the Soviet Union would not furnish the PRC with atomic weapons and tried unsuccessfully to unseat Mao. PRC bombardment of Quemoy and Matsu (1958), offshore islands claimed by Taiwan, plus a savage conquest of Tibet and an invasion of Indian territory in Ladakh were undertaken without consultation between the PRC and the Soviets. The Soviets publicly declared themselves to be neutral between the PRC and the Indians, and in 1960 Khrushchev withdrew all Soviet technicians from the PRC.

The PRC tried to influence other Communist parties against the Soviets and picked up a European satellite, Albania. The Albanian Communist party had thrown off Yugoslav domination after Tito's rebellion from Stalin in 1948. More than anything else, the Albanian communists feared renewed control by the Yugoslavs. When Khrushchev made his repeated efforts to conciliate Tito, the Albanians found an ally in the Communist Chinese.

In the midst of the 1962 crisis over Soviet missiles in Cuba, the PRC chose to attack India again. The PRC withdrew when it had what it wanted; but the Soviets, though ostensibly neutral, were clearly pro-Indian. India was of great importance in the eyes of both superpowers, and each preferred to see it nonaligned; thus both feared any possible Communist Chinese conquest there.

When the nuclear test ban treaty was signed, the PRC denounced the Soviets as traitors to the international communist movement. Khrushchev tried to arrange for a public excommunication of the Chinese by other Communist parties, but he was unable to win sufficient support. Mao called for Khrushchev's removal and accused the Soviets of illegally occupying eastern European and Japanese territory. By the time of Khrushchev's ouster in a bloodless coup in October 1964, the PRC had the support of the North Korean and North Vietnamese Communist parties and enjoyed a special position of strength in Indonesia and Algeria. In Africa, it had established a predominant influence in two former French colonies, and it took the lead in sponsoring a major rebellion in the former Belgian Congo. In South America, the PRC supported Castroites within the pro-Soviet Latin American parties in the hope of promoting more active revolutionary movements.

Power, Mao pointed out, came from the barrel of a gun, and he feared that the rising standard of living in the Soviet Union and elsewhere, together with doctrinal revisionism, had led the former world center of

The Chinese leader Mao Zedong in c. 1970.

UPI/Bettmann Newsphotos

international communism to go soft. Maoism had become the cutting edge of international revolutionary communism. But 1965 brought major setbacks to the PRC. A congress scheduled for Algiers, in which they had expected to condemn the Soviets, was canceled, in part because the Algerians overthrew their procommunist premier. An attempted communist coup in Indonesia failed after the assassination of numerous leading army officers. The Indonesian army took power and revenged itself with the help of the Muslim population upon the Chinese minority and upon the local communists, of whom perhaps 500,000 were killed. A PRC threat to renew the attack on India during the Indian-Pakistani conflict in 1965 evaporated when the United States and the Soviet Union tacitly cooperated in the United Nations to force a temporary cease-fire.

In part as the result of these successive setbacks abroad, and in part because of persistent failures to meet production goals at home, in 1966 the communist regime began to show signs of unbearable tensions. Denunciations and removals of important figures at the top of the government and party were accompanied by a new wave of adulation for Chairman Mao. Young people in their teens—the Red Guard—erupted into the streets, beating and killing older people whose loyalty they professed to suspect, destroying works of art and other memorials of China's precommunist past, and rioting against foreigners and foreign influences. In October 1966 the PRC successfully fired a guided missile with a nuclear warhead,

affirming that the political turmoil had not interfered with the development of military hardware. Yet the turmoil continued. The PRC's educational system was completely halted, and something like civil war raged in some provinces.

This artificially induced cultural revolution died down gradually in 1969, when the Ninth Chinese Communist Party Congress took place. In 1969 and 1970 the mystery that veiled mainland China from the West seemed to thicken. Since Western and even Soviet journalists, scholars, film makers, missionaries, and business people were not allowed in, foreign observers had to rely on guesswork. There is still no clear agreement on what happened during the cultural revolution or its immediate aftermath. Something like a fourth of the top party and government officials had been purged, leaving economic stagnation and ideological disillusionment behind. Though Soviet-PRC tension twice broke into open fighting on the frontiers, and though the hostile propaganda of both sides reached a shrill pitch, the two countries continued to negotiate.

Behind the series of incidents that revealed the mounting intercommunist quarrel to the world, there lay theoretical disagreements about the best way to bring communist control to the peoples of Asia, Africa, and Latin America. The PRC favored direct sponsorship of local communist revolutionary movements; the Soviets maintained that the communists could win the competition without world war by helping along local "wars of national liberation"—revolutions at least partly under communist control. The PRC refused to grant that nuclear weapons had changed the nature of war or imperialism, and they regarded world war as inevitable.

The PRC insisted that communists alone must take charge of all revolutionary movements from the beginning and claimed that aid to noncommunist countries was a delusion. They opposed disarmament. They wanted Khrushchev to freeze Soviet living standards at a low level and invest the savings to help the PRC catch up, but Khrushchev preferred to let his people enjoy some of the fruits of their labors. Race was also a factor. The Soviets disliked and feared the communist Chinese, the "yellow peril" on their borders. The huge Chinese masses frightened the Asian Soviets. Because the threat came from another race, the fear increased. Despite protestations to the contrary, the Soviets were race-conscious, and they reserved for the Chinese the deepest dislike of all. In turn, the PRC openly used race as a weapon in its efforts to win support among Asians, Africans, and Latin Americans, lumping the Soviet Union with the United States as symbols of the white intention to continue dominating the nonwhite world.

Vietnam

A special problem for the PRC, Soviets, and Americans arose in southeast Asia from the revolt of the Viet Minh (Revolutionary League for the Independence of Vietnam) against France that broke out in French Indochina after World War II. During the Korean War the United States, fearing that the Chinese communists would strike across

THE **WRITTEN RECORD**

America's Stake in Vietnam

In a speech in June 1956, then-Senator John F. Kennedy outlined what would later be known as "the domino theory": that if the democracies allow one nation to fall, all others in the vicinity will follow.

[Vietnam] represents the cornerstone of the Free World in Southeast Asia, the keystone to the arch, the finger in the dike. Burma, Thailand, India, Japan, the Philippines, and obviously Laos and Cambodia are among those whose security would be threatened if the red tide of Communism overflowed into Vietnam. . . .

Vietnam represents a proving ground for democracy in Asia. However we may choose to ignore or deprecate it, the rising prestige and influence of Communist China in Asia are unchallengeable facts. Vietnam represents the alternative to Communist dictatorship. If this democratic experience fails, if some one million refugees have fled the totalitarianism of the North only to find neither freedom nor security in the South, then weakness, not strength, will characterize the meaning of democracy in the minds of still more Asians. The United States is directly responsible for

this experiment—it is playing an important role in the laboratory where it is being conducted. We cannot afford to permit that experiment to fail. . . .

Vietnam represents a test of American responsibility and determination in Asia. If we are not the parents of little Vietnam, then surely we are the godparents. We presided at its birth, we gave assistance to its life, we have helped to shape its future. . . .

America's stake in Vietnam, in her strength and in her security, is a very selfish one—for it can be measured, in the last analysis, in terms of American lives and American dollars.

Quoted in American Friends of Vietnam, *America's Stake in Vietnam* (New York: Friends of Vietnam, 1956), pp. 10–11.

---

the border into northern Indochina, had given substantial assistance to the French. In 1954, when the French had been resoundingly defeated after the fall of their stronghold of Dien Bien Phu, a conference of powers at Geneva recognized the independence of the Indochinese provinces of Cambodia and Laos.

Vietnam, the third and largest portion of the former French colony, was divided roughly along the 17th parallel. The northern portion, with its capital at Hanoi, was governed by the communist Viet Minh party, whose leader was a veteran communist, Ho Chi Minh (1890–1969). The southern portion, with its capital at Saigon, was led by a Catholic nationalist leader, Ngo Dinh Diem (1901–1963). The Geneva agreements promised free elections in two years. Though the United States did not sign the agreements, it endorsed their intent, hoping that the area, in which it had already invested more than $4 billion, would not fall to the communists. Ho was receiving aid from Mao, with whom he shared a commitment to doctrine and the prestige of victory.

Between 1954 and 1959 Diem created the bureaucratic machinery for a new regime, provided for almost a million refugees from the communist North, and resettled in the countryside millions of peasants who had fled to the cities. After the departure of the French, the Americans assumed the responsibility for financial aid and technical advice. But Diem failed politically. He canceled the scheduled elections and together with his immediate family governed despotically. In 1958 and 1959 commu-

nist-led guerrilla activity broke out again. Now known as the Viet Cong (or VC), the guerrillas set up a national liberation front. In September 1960 Ho endorsed the Viet Cong movement, which he was already supplying with arms and training.

Neighboring Laos, strategically important, was less a nation than a collection of unwarlike Buddhist groups, where a small clique of families traditionally managed political affairs. In 1953 a communist-oriented political faction, calling itself the Pathet Lao and supported by Ho Chi Minh, seized the northeastern portion of the country. The United States tried with massive financial and military aid to build a national Laotian army and establish a firm regime, but instead succeeded largely in creating corruption and factionalism. The head of the government, Souvanna Phouma (1901–1984), who was the brother-in-law of the head of the Pathet Lao, agreed in 1957 to set up a coalition government. The United States objected, ousting Souvanna Phouma and introducing a right-wing government. By 1960 he was working with the Soviets, and a portion of the army was working with the Pathet Lao. Soviet airlifts of supplies to their side enhanced the possibility that the country would fall to the communists.

As president, Kennedy sought to neutralize Laos and to convince the Soviets that if his efforts failed, American military intervention would follow. Although the Soviets agreed to neutralization, fighting in Laos between Soviet-backed and American-backed forces continued

Brought vividly into every American home by news photographs and television, the war in Vietnam proved to be deeply divisive. Thousands of young Americans refused to serve in the military and fled to Canada, as Congress debated the legitimacy, morality, and strategy of the war. Two photographs above all deeply influenced American opinion against continuing the war. One, taken in 1968, showed the South Vietnamese national police chief executing a Viet Cong officer in Saigon; the other showed South Vietnamese children running from a napalm attack by their own government's aircraft.

AP/Wide World Photos and UPI/Bettmann Newsphotos

until mid-May 1961, when Khrushchev apparently realized that the United States was preparing to send in marines from Okinawa. Before an agreement was reached at Geneva in July 1962, Kennedy did send marines to Thailand to stop the Pathet Lao from continuing to violate the truce there. The Pathet Lao, now a strong force armed with Soviet weapons and still supported by Ho Chi Minh, kept control over its own portion of the country, which bordered on South Vietnam and included the Ho Chi Minh Trail, a supply route from Hanoi to the Viet Cong guerrillas.

In South Vietnam, American efforts to get Diem moving politically failed. All that emerged was the strategic-hamlet plan—a program to relocate peasants to fortified villages in the hope that this would provide protection against the guerrillas and thus make the communist campaigns first expensive and then impossible. Meanwhile, protests against Diem's rule increased, often led by Buddhist monks. In August 1963 Diem staged a mass arrest of Buddhists, and in November he and his brother were ousted and murdered in a coup led by dissident generals and permitted by the United States.

Thereafter, the South Vietnamese government changed hands many times, each time by military coup. The longest-lived regime, that of General Nguyen Cao Ky (1930–   ), successfully conducted elections in September 1966, with Ky emerging as vice-president under President Nguyen Van Thieu (1923–   ). But the hamlet program was a failure, and North Vietnamese troops appeared in South Vietnam in support of the guerrillas.

Between 1965 and 1967 the United States increased its troops from 12,000 to more than 500,000 and began bombing North Vietnamese installations. Massive American intervention prevented the Viet Cong from conquering the entire country and assured the United States of bases along the coast. Having increased the American commitment to such a level that none could doubt his intentions, President Johnson, in the hope of bringing Ho Chi Minh to the conference table, then assured the enemy that the United States had no long-range intention of remaining in the country and sought no military bases there. In 1966 Johnson suspended the bombings for a time, but the North Vietnamese insisted that there could be no negotiations until all American troops left the country. And the government in the South, nominally an ally of the United States, became increasingly dictatorial and corrupt. The communists' Tet offensive early in 1968 struck at Saigon and the provincial capitals and demonstrated the inability of the government to respond.

The Vietnam War was the first in history to be viewed on television in living rooms half a world away. The horror of the jungle fighting, the misery of the countless fleeing Vietnamese survivors, the corruption of the Saigon government were all brought home vividly to the American public. The war's mounting costs wrecked President Johnson's widely hailed Great Society program for domestic reform, and more and more voices called for American withdrawal. Mass protests, student strikes, demonstrations at military installations, and a

substantial number of refusals to register for the draft underscored the growing divisiveness of the war, as opposing public opinion urged that the war be intensified and won. Intensification of the war threatened a land war in Asia of unprecedented difficulty and unpredictable length; on the other hand, withdrawal meant abandoning the goals for which the United States had fought in Asia in World War II.

In 1968, as the time for American elections approached, Senator Eugene McCarthy (1916–   ), Democrat of Minnesota, challenged the Johnson administration by announcing his candidacy for the presidency on an antiwar platform. His impressive successes in early primary elections at the state level stimulated another opponent of the war, Senator Robert F. Kennedy (1925–1968), Democrat of New York, to enter the race on his own. The strength of the antiwar candidates brought about the withdrawal of President Johnson, who had been expected to run again. Ho Chi Minh, who had always thought that internal American politics would force the United States out of Vietnam, then consented to open peace talks, which began in Paris but dragged on inconclusively. Robert Kennedy was assassinated in Los Angeles, and the Democratic party, now led by Johnson's vice-presidential running mate, Hubert Humphrey (1911–1978), was turned out of office by the Republicans under Richard M. Nixon (1913–1994), who had served as Eisenhower's vice-president.

The Nixon administration inherited an increasingly unpopular war and the halting negotiations designed to end it. Nixon pledged the eventual withdrawal of all American forces and began substantially to reduce them. He hoped to "Vietnamize" the fighting by rapidly training and supplying South Vietnamese forces, who would replace the Americans in combat but continue to have American assistance, including massive air support, until a settlement could be reached with the North that did not involve the communization of the South. But even the death of Ho Chi Minh in 1969 did not weaken the North Vietnamese government. It seemed prepared to carry on with the war, obviously believing that the Americans had lost faith in the cause and that the communists would gain more by continuing the war than by ending it through negotiations.

The military picture was further clouded for the United States by the increasing Viet Cong domination of Laos, where the hard-won and tenuous settlement of the early 1960s was in jeopardy, and by the movement of Viet Cong forces into those portions of Cambodia nearest to South Vietnam. The head of Cambodia was a French-educated prince of an old ruling house, Norodom Sihanouk (1922–   ), who made some effort to maintain Cambodian neutrality despite his belief that in the end the PRC would dominate his part of the world and so must be appeased. These beliefs made him unpopular both in Washington and at home. In 1970 a coup d'état overthrew Sihanouk, who, from Beijing (formerly Peking), announced the formation of a government-in-exile.

Not long afterward American and South Vietnamese troops made an "incursion" into Cambodia. The invading forces failed to wipe out the Vietnamese forces believed to be the chief target of the expedition. Many of America's allies condemned the action, and anti-American demonstrations were widespread throughout western Europe and Canada. Despite the capture of many North Vietnamese supplies in Cambodia, the American forces failed to find a central enemy headquarters. Nixon withdrew the forces within the time promised, but there remained much doubt whether the Cambodian operation had been justifiable. During the Cambodian incursion the United States had resumed intensive bombing of North Vietnam, the most effective weapon left to the United States as its land forces in Vietnam were reduced.

Probably no war since the religious wars of the Middle Ages has been so complex, has posed so many moral problems, or has proved so unpopular with its participants. The United States could not, for political and military reasons, commit more troops to the war; without more troops, the Americans and South Vietnamese were slowly being pressed back by the invaders from the North. Withdrawal was advocated by those who condemned the regime in the South as corrupt and undemocratic, as well as by those who actively favored a communist victory on behalf of the peasants. Withdrawal was also advocated by the "realists" who, whatever the moral issues involved, felt the stakes had become too high and that the United States was wasting its resources over an area of less significance to it than Europe, the Middle East, or Latin America. Withdrawal was demanded by isolationists who felt the United States had no business trying to resolve what they saw as essentially a civil war in a remote land; withdrawal was called for by racists who thought American lives ought not to be spent on Asians; withdrawal was prayed for by pacifists, who felt that all war was evil. Few voices continued to advocate an all-out American commitment to Vietnam. American troops were pulled back, and a cease-fire was finally arranged in January 1973.

Persistent violations of the cease-fire on both sides accompanied the evacuation of South Vietnamese troops toward Saigon, an evacuation that advancing North Vietnamese turned first into a retreat and then a rout. The city of Saigon fell to the Viet Cong and North Vietnamese on April 30, 1975, as Americans were completing their own evacuation at the last moment by helicopter from their embassy roof. In this, America's longest and most expensive war, 58,000 American lives were lost. South Vietnam's military lost 220,000. North Vietnam

sustained an estimated 666,000 deaths, despite victory. In all, perhaps 1.5 million people died.

The war also unleashed the Cambodian Holocaust, in which an estimated 3 million Cambodians died at the hands of the Khmer Rouge, the army of the country's Communist party, after the withdrawal of U.S. forces. Mass relocation of city dwellers devastated Cambodian life and continued until the Vietnamese invaded and occupied the country in 1978–79. Sporadic warfare continued well into the 1980s, driving refugees into neighboring Thailand, and not until 1989 did the Vietnamese declare that they would withdraw their troops from Cambodia and seek to normalize relations.

The war in Vietnam changed the cold war and taught one superpower how difficult it was to wage unconventional warfare in a country that afforded ample opportunities for guerrilla tactics. The United States failed to achieve its objective of victory, or of a democratic and noncommunist Vietnam, for many reasons. Among them were its own waning will; the rising opposition to the war on the home front; the self-imposed limitations, largely for political reasons, with respect to the use of weapons and the rules of engagement; the growing unpopularity of the war with America's putative allies; the threat of Communist China entering the war; the nature of the terrain; and the fact that United Nations troops were fighting far from home against entrenched and skillful forces that were willing to sustain high rates of casualties, far exceeding the conventionally acceptable upper limit of attrition in democratic societies. In 1979 the Soviet Union would plunge into a similar war in Afghanistan, where as in Vietnam elements of a civil war made it difficult to be certain who the enemy was at all times, and it too would withdraw without achieving its intentions. Thus both superpowers learned that victory was illusive in an undeclared war.

To some extent there was a reduction of tensions in the cold war after 1975, marked by an increase once again in the early 1980s, and then, with the virtual collapse of the Soviet Union, an end to that war. During the cold war there was a flourishing of debate in universities and elsewhere about the nature and ethics of war, important changes in the world of art and literature, and above all in communications and information. While dissent was brutally stamped out in the Soviet Union, and at times intimidated even in the Western democracies, the period of the cold war, now conventionally dated from the Berlin blockade in 1948 to 1989, produced the intellectual climate in which we now live.

$\int$UMMARY

Some historians today consider the time between the two world wars as simply a twenty-year truce. Yet the 1920s had offered hope for peace, as shown by the Locarno spirit. This hope was dashed by the Great Depression that helped put Hitler in power.

Between 1918 and 1938 Soviet leaders shifted their view on the likelihood of a world communist revolution. Hitler's successful rise to power in Germany posed a threat to the Soviet Union. Stalin tried to counter this threat by negotiation. Both the West and the Soviet

Union sought to turn Hitler's aggression against the other.

The period from 1931 to 1939 was marked by various international crises, each of which moved the world closer to war. The major crises included: Japan's seizure of Manchuria (1931); German rearmament (1935–1936); Italian invasion of Ethiopia (1935); German and Italian intervention in the Spanish Civil War (1936–1939); Japanese invasion of China (1937); the Anschluss with Germany (1938); the dismemberment of Czechoslovakia (1938–1939); and the German invasion of Poland (1939)—the final crisis that forced Britain and France to abandon the policy of appeasement.

In September 1939 Germany was ready for war. Hitler had reached an accord with Stalin that gave Germany security from war on two fronts. In the opening stages of the war, the German blitzkreig resulted in a string of victories that gave the Axis powers control of much of western Europe. The use of aerial bombardment brought civilians into the front line of war.

Germany was drawn into the Balkans and the eastern Mediterranean in an effort to weaken Britain by cutting its route to India. In 1941 Hitler also attacked the Soviet Union. The Japanese attack on Pearl Harbor brought the United States into the war. By the spring of 1942 Japanese expansion in Asia and the Pacific had reached its height.

The turning point in the war came in 1942. In the Pacific, the battle of the Coral Sea prevented the Japanese invasion of Australia. The successful North African campaign (1942–1943), the Soviet defense of Stalingrad, and the Allied success in maintaining its supply lines forced the Axis powers on the defensive in 1943. The end of the war in Europe in 1945 revealed the full horrors of extermination camps and opened the controversy over how the Holocaust had been allowed to happen.

In the Pacific, American and Allied forces moved against Japan on several fronts. Finally, the Americans decided to use the newly developed atom bomb to prevent the heavy casualties that would be involved in an attack on the Japanese home islands.

When the war ended there was still no peace. Between 1945 and the 1970s a cold war raged between the Soviet Union and its former ally, the United States. Local wars of liberation were fought in European colonies; wars broke out in the Middle East, Southeast Asia, Cuba, and Central America. In China, the civil war ended in a communist victory.

Efforts to ease cold war tensions failed. The United Nations, successor to the League of Nations, tried to deal with threats to peace but had no authority over its members. The UN did, however, provide effective technical aid to new nations and offered a forum for debate on international issues.

During the cold war, the United States pursued a policy of containment. But when it perceived diversity in the communist world, it encouraged liberalizing trends in eastern Europe. After Stalin's death and Khrushchev's denunciation of Stalin, a split developed between the Soviet Union and China's communist leader, Mao Zedong. The Soviet Union and the PRC vied for influence over communist parties in Africa, Asia, and Latin America.

In Vietnam, Ho Chi Minh, leader of the communist North, received aid from the PRC. The South Vietnamese government was helped by the United States. The United States was increasingly drawn into the conflict between North and South Vietnam. In the 1960s the war spread to Laos and Cambodia. After antiwar protests intensified in the United States, a cease-fire was negotiated in early 1973. By 1975 Vietcong and North Vietnamese forces had defeated South Vietnam. With the end of the war in Vietnam came a marked, if temporary, decline in cold war tensions.

CRITICAL THINKING

1. Why did a second world war occur only twenty years after the First World War?

2. The text suggests that there were eight distinct steps toward war. This implies that at each step, except for the last, the movement toward war could have been turned back or, at the least, delayed. Do you agree? Which of the steps do you believe contributed most to the coming of war? Do you think it is useful to analyze events in terms of "steps," or is this subtly misleading? If so, how? What would you substitute?

3. Where would you place primary responsibility— often called "war guilt"—for the coming of World War I? Of World War II? Why? What counterarguments do you think the leaders of the societies you have named would offer to refute your arguments?

4. Why did the Axis powers achieve such overwhelming early success?

5. What was the "battle of Britain"? What was its short-range result? What was its long-range result?

6. Why did the United States enter World War II?

7. Distinguish between the European War and the Pacific War as to combatants, strategies, and results.

8. Why did the Allied nations win the war?

9. What is a "cold war"? When did the Cold War begin and why? Describe its development.

10. Describe the development of the Soviet-Chinese split. How did Vietnam become involved? How did the United States, in turn, become involved in Vietnam?

Twentieth-Century Thought and Letters

HISTORY IS CONSTANTLY CHANGING. So, too, is the way that we view history. Obviously, history extends forward in time, each day bringing new events that make a mockery of any attempt to survey the entire historical past of any one culture, much less of all cultures, or of all Western civilization. Even this last term has now lost much of its meaning, for in many ways there is now a world culture from which it is not possible to isolate any singular culture. Japanese prints influenced the French impressionist painters; postimpressionists such as Van Gogh and Gauguin sought inspiration in so-called primitive art; Picasso was influenced by African art and sculpture. Popular art forms in Africa, Latin America, and major portions of Asia were in turn deeply influenced by music, fashion, political thought, or economic policies that originated in the West. World War II and its aftermath involved non-Western societies fully as much as Western, making sharp distinctions between the West and non-West highly artificial. "Western civilization" could no longer be studied without reference to much of the entire world.

History also changes by virtue of the dynamics of its own discipline. New facts are found about old events, new documents discovered, new artifacts unearthed by archaeologists. Old facts are reinterpreted, their meaning changed, both by the simple passage of time, which permits more distance from and more objectivity toward an event, and by the discovery of new facts. Today the historian writes quite differently of ancient Greece and Rome than historians did only twenty years ago, in part because society now permits open discussion of subjects, such as the use of slaves in classical civilization, that were once reserved to the specialist. Today the historian writes quite differently of sixteenth-century England or eighteenth-century France than did historians twenty years ago, in part because new insights into social organization, population movements, the history of climate, disease, sexuality, or of the role of women and the family have forced a reassessment of what was truly significant about those centuries.

Today, nearly five decades removed from the first years of the cold war, the historian writes differently of those years, for recent events have changed judgments about the significance of intervening events and also quite simply because a new generation of historians who were not eyewitnesses to those events has arisen. And history is written differently today because the pervasive influence of the media has shaped a generation accustomed less to learning by reading than to learning by looking, while the steady advance of the computer and the word processor into education and learning is producing a generation rather more numerate and somewhat less literate.

THE MODERNITY OF HISTORY

Societies reveal much about themselves in what they choose to take pride in—what they consciously preserve from their past and from their environment. Societies also reveal much about themselves in what they exclude, as when history until recently passed over the underclasses in near-silence or neglected the role of women in national development. Indeed, this lack of balance led to the fall of "Western civilization" courses in many universities in the West and reflected a sense of doubt about Western values. The suspicion that such courses had been systematically neglecting much that was significant undermined the very notion that to know history was, in some measure, to know oneself. The renewed popularity of such courses, with their new balance between elite culture and popular culture—acknowledging those who prefer Tarzan to King Lear, comic books to opera, rock to Mozart, and are not necessarily the worse for it—is itself a historical development of the 1980s.

Three Americans—Walt Disney (1901–1966), Frank Sinatra (1915–   ), and Elvis Presley (1935–1977)—may have done as much to shape modern society as, for example, Sigmund Freud or Adolf Hitler. Yet because the significance of popular culture is less clear and the impact more diffuse and democratic, the historian

Family patterns of entertainment and education changed drastically and rapidly with the introduction of television into the average Western home. Potentially an enormous force for education, television was generally used as a tool for leisure and entertainment. Where once the kitchen had been the center of the household, the television room now became the family gathering place. Many commentators argue that television, by bringing graphic scenes of war and crime into the home, reduces the sense of community and increases the individual's tolerance for violence.

Larry Mulvehill/Photo Researchers, Inc.

cannot yet be sure. Leisure time spent watching a great worldwide professional sport such as soccer, or a more limited national sport such as baseball or cricket may shape history far more than leisure time spent listening to Beethoven and Bach, or attending the plays of Shaw and Ibsen, or examining the art of Rembrandt and da Vinci. Such matters cannot be measured. In a sense, their significance relative to each other cannot be known. Yet all are part of history, and to be uninformed about either elite or popular culture is to be isolated from the broad flow of historical reality.

Of all the major "modern" or industrial nations, the United States and Russia have been the most insulated against a comparative awareness of historical trends elsewhere. Yet the changes in both nations have been

In the 1980s women moved into a variety of jobs that had, in most Western societies, customarily been performed almost exclusively by men. Here women work as engineers and police officers.

Blair Seitz/Susan Kuklin, Photo Researchers, Inc.

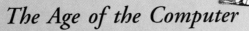

DOING HISTORY

The Age of the Computer

specious Drivel

We live today in an information society. Such a society is the result of a long evolution from the development of writing, to movable type, to the high-speed printing press, to the typewriter and carbon paper and the office duplicating machine. More than any other development, however, it has been the exceptionally rapid growth of computer technology—and the application of that technology to education, information retrieval, and word processing—that has changed the way we look at learning. The sociology of knowledge has changed.

Today much of humanity, especially in the West, is visually oriented. People learn from images—whether on television or a computer console—rather than from linear type. This new mode of learning has changed speech, promoted new skills, and made it possible to assemble, sort, and retrieve incredible amounts of data. It has also led some people to confuse *data* (items of information) and *creative thinking*. Thus, many observers of the new high-technology societies of the West and Japan feel that the period since about 1975 (when historians of the computer, such as those quoted below, say that society entered an "advanced third-generation computer age") has brought more rapid changes than any single generation has experienced before. These changes relate to unemployment created by technological changes and the threat of such unemployment; to vast transformations in the city as a communications center; to transportation, social relationships, finance, the arts, the use of leisure time; and to the nature of government and the challenge that pervasive government knowledge about its citizens poses to concepts of individuality and privacy.

Cooperation among individuals will become increasingly necessary and probably will be enforced by strong central—perhaps totalitarian—governments aided by computers acting as sources of information. Who shall this all-powerful and pervasive government be? Political scientists have suggested that some form of worldwide government is inevitable. Only time can prove the accuracy of these predictions. One thing, however, is certain—that government, whether a single global or a variety of national ones, will rely increasingly on the computer. The nature of any form of government requires that its citizens be kept track of. For, even in a feudal system, a knowledge of the subjects—their financial states and their major concerns—as well as a possession of some degree of their good will is mandatory. When the number of people being governed becomes as large as that with which future states shall have to contend, some extraordinary means of tabulation will be vitally necessary. The computer is that means.

Some people believe optimistically that not even a computerized spy ring would be able to control all possible movements of all people at all times. The past decade has witnessed the rise of an "underground" that is not really limited to newspapers and political movements. . . . Certainly, it is easy enough for an individual to lose himself among the masses of an urban area; this has been demonstrated more than once. All that need be done is to conform to certain surface expectations, such as dress and overt behavior. What you do in your own cubbyhole or in your own mind cannot be traced.

Individuality, despite governmental control of so many facets of life, thus might be maintained to some extent.

A more pessimistic approach suggests that no degree of individual freedom would be possible. The cashless society [of the credit card] would mean that no one could "hide." The government might find it expedient to create the illusion of freedom and even permit the existence of some rebellious groups, but these would be carefully controlled and manipulated. . . .

Quite possibly, there will be choice enough, perhaps too much, at least in most areas of life, simply because it would require too much effort, even using the most advanced technology, for a government to control every aspect of the existence of every individual under its power. Consequently, the majority of activities might be observed, but restrained only loosely. When given a choice of flying to the Bahamas, London, Tokyo, or Greece, of attending lecture or discussion sessions on several hundred different topics, of painting a picture or reading a book, of going to the gym, the museum, or to a circus all in one day, the average person might stay in bed and sleep, simply to avoid making the decision. However, once again the computer could come to the rescue. Having been programmed according to the individual's tastes, the home computer could simply set up a schedule of activities for the person to follow. Thus, computers could limit man's freedom, but only under his orders. . . .

Possibly the only limitation on the computer's usefulness is man's imagination. Dependence on the computer, whether developed with moderation or whether indulged to the fullest extent, places the responsibility for the course of society on the persons who program, coordinate, and oversee the workings of those computers. Thus, we are brought back full circle to the question: who shall the government be? The answer is that the government will be the person or persons who control society's major tool, the computer.

From Ralph J. Kochenburger and Carolyn J. Turcio, *Computers in Modern Society*. Copyright © 1974 John Wiley & Sons, Inc. Reprinted by permission of John Wiley & Sons, Inc.

Increasingly, English became the international language of speech and print, though French held its own as the language of diplomacy, and various forms of Chinese were spoken by huge numbers of people. An international language of signs and symbols developed, so that a traveler might recognize the command "No Parking," whether in Japanese or in English.

enormous in the last five decades, though they are more easily seen in the United States, the more open society. Syndication and wire services have turned once-parochial American newspapers into a national press; censorship and controlled news made Russian papers fully national rather than local, an equally significant role for the press.

In the United States, the old party system appeared to be in an advanced stage of dissolution by the 1980s, and few could predict what new coalitions would emerge, though it was most likely that they would appear under traditional labels. In Russia, historians lacked the information to judge even the immediate significance of most events. By the 1980s the United States was experiencing an industrial slump much like that of Great Britain in the 1950s, for its productive equipment was not being replaced or remodeled rapidly enough, and America's share of the world's gross national product had fallen from 40 percent to 20 percent. Religion in the United States—always stronger than virtually anywhere else in the modern West—was undergoing changes whose outcome was unpredictable, in which evangelical religion was acting as a safety valve for groups whose beliefs were threatened by vast upheavals in public opinion and in social mores and by a highly mobile population.

By the 1990s life was more uniform for much of human society, and the individual was subject to more laws than ever before. However, it seemed less certain that the world could be improved simply by finding out what was wrong with it and then taking steps to put it right, for there were deep disagreements over the ills as well as the remedies.

Each effort to achieve security seemed, to many commentators, to increase insecurity. The arms race, the ability of the United States and Russia to inflict untold damage on each other in a nuclear war, and the proliferation of conventional weapons around the world perhaps helped promote a sense of stalemate between the two great powers so that each was deeply reluctant to attack the other, but smaller states did not hesitate to resort to war. Deeply held religious beliefs, whether in a resurgent Islam or an evangelical Christianity, gave their adherents a sense of cohesion and a faith in the future but also

contributed to increased tensions between nations, ethnic groups, and sects.

Modern Thought About Human Nature

In the latter part of the nineteenth and early part of the twentieth century, a number of fields of inquiry became professionalized, and those who mastered these fields had a major impact on elite thought and indirectly on popular public opinion. Foremost among these fields were psychology, history, political science, sociology, and philosophy. All but the last subject had direct influence on the shaping of public policy.

Psychology

Taking its cue from psychology, the twentieth century has put its emphasis on the role of the unconscious in human thought and action, on the nonrationality of much human behavior. Foremost among the thinkers responsible for this emphasis was Sigmund Freud (1856–1939), a physician trained in Vienna in the rationalist medical tradition of the late nineteenth century. His interest was early drawn to mental illness, where he found cases in which patients exhibited symptoms of very real organic disturbances for which no obvious organic causes could be found. Under psychoanalysis, as Freud's therapy came to be called, the patient was urged to pour out what could be remembered about earliest childhood; after many such treatments, the analyst could make the patient aware of what was so disturbing.

From his clinical experience Freud worked out a system of psychology that has greatly influenced basic conceptions of human relations. Freud started with the concept of a set of drives with which each person is born. These drives, which arise in the unconscious, are expressions of the *id*. These drives try to find satisfaction and pleasure, to express themselves in action. Infants are uninhibited; that is, their drives well up into action from the id without restraint from the conscious mind. But as infants grow, as their minds are formed, they become conscious that some of what they want to do is objectionable to those closest to them—to parent or friend or brother or sister—on whom they are dependent. Therefore they begin to repress these drives.

With dawning consciousness of the world outside, the child develops another part of the psyche, which Freud at first called the censor and later divided into two phases, which he called the *ego* and the *superego*. The ego is a person's private censor, the awareness that in accordance with the "reality principle," certain drives from the id simply cannot succeed. The superego is conscience; it is a person's response as a member of a social system in which certain actions are considered proper and others are not. The drives of the id and most dictates of the

THE WRITTEN RECORD

Freud on Modern Civilization

Though not his most famous book, *Civilization and Its Discontents*, written in 1929–1930, is probably the most frequently read work by Sigmund Freud, for it appears to speak directly to the human condition.

It seems certain that we do not feel comfortable in our present-day civilization, but it is very difficult to form an opinion whether and in what degree men of an earlier age felt happier, and what part their cultural conditions played in the matter. We shall always tend to consider people's distress objectively—that is, to place ourselves, with our own wants and sensibilities, in *their* conditions, and then to examine what occasions we should find in them for experiencing happiness or unhappiness. This method of looking at things, which seems objective because it ignores the variations in subjective sensibility, is, of course, the most subjective possible, since it puts one's own mental states in the place of any others, unknown though they may be. Happiness, however, is something essentially subjective. No matter how much we may shrink with horror from certain situations—of a galley-slave in antiquity, or a peasant during the Thirty Years' War, of a victim of the Holy Inquisition, of a Jew awaiting a pogrom—it is nevertheless impossible for us to feel our way into such people. . . .

For a wide variety of reasons, it is very far from my intention to express an opinion upon the value of human civilization. I have endeavoured to guard myself against the enthusiastic prejudice which holds that our civilization is the most precious thing that we possess or could acquire and that its path will necessarily lead to heights of unimagined perfection. . . . One thing only do I know for certain, and that is that man's judgments of value follow directly his wishes for happiness—that, accordingly, they are an attempt to support his illusions with arguments. . . .

The fateful question for the human species seems to me to be whether and to what extent their cultural development will succeed in mastering the disturbance of their communal life by the human instinct of aggression and self-destruction. It may be that in this respect precisely the present time deserves a special interest. Men have gained control over the forces of nature to such an extent that with their help they would have no difficulty in exterminating one another to the last man. They know this, and hence comes a large part of their current unrest, their unhappiness and their mood of anxiety.

Sigmund Freud, *Civilization and Its Discontents*, from *The Standard Edition of the Complete Psychological Works of Sigmund Freud*, trans. James Strachey (New York: Norton, 1961), pp. 11, 36, 92. Reprinted by permission from the Sigmund Freud Copyrights Ltd., The Institute of Psycho-Analysis, The Hogarth Press, Ltd., and W. W. Norton & Co., Inc.

---

superego are a great reservoir of which a person is not normally aware—that is, the unconscious.

In a mentally healthy person, enough of the drives of the id succeed to provide a sense of contentment and security. But even the healthiest individuals repress many drives from their ids by a process Freud called *sublimation*, or substituting for a repressed drive a new and socially approved outlet of expression. Thus a drive toward forbidden sexual relations might be sublimated into poetry, music, war, or athletics. In the neurotic person, however, the drives are driven down into the unconscious without a suitable outlet and continue to fester in the id, trying to find some outlet. They display themselves in *neuroses* and *phobias*. Neurotic individuals are maladjusted; some are psychotic, living in an utterly unreal private world.

Freud's therapy rested on the long, slow process of psychoanalysis, in which the patient day after day reached back to memories of earliest childhood for concrete details, and the listening analyst picked from this "stream of consciousness" the significant details that pointed to the hidden repression that was expressing itself in neurotic behavior. Freud gave special importance to the patient's dreams, in which the unconscious wells up out of control or is only partly controlled by the ego. Once the patient became aware of what had gone wrong with a hitherto unconscious part of life, he or she might then adjust to society and lead a normal existence.

What was important in all this to political and cultural theory lay in the wider implications of Freud's work, particularly his concept of the role of unconscious drives. Ordinary reflective thinking was, for the Freudian, a very small part of existence. Much even of what is considered to be the exercise of reason was, according to the Freudian, *rationalization*—that is, thinking dictated not by an awareness of the reality principle but by the desires of the id. For the Freudian, truth cannot be distilled into a few simple rules of conduct that all people, being reasonable and good, can use as guides to individual and collective happiness. The Freudian is at bottom a pessimist who does not believe in human perfectibility.

The Austrian Alfred Adler (1870–1937) rejected Freud's emphasis on sex and coined the familiar phrase "inferiority complex" to explain human compensations for perceived inadequacies. The Swiss Carl Gustav Jung (1875–1961) attempted to expand the horizons of psychology by

The modern age has often been called the age of anxiety. Humanity's constant search for a sense of security is constantly being challenged by psychology, by art and music, by foreign affairs and war, by social policy. One artist who brooded on the themes of madness, death, and human alienation was the Norwegian Edvard Munch (1863–1944). Though well regarded in his lifetime, Munch's coruscating use of line and color seemed to speak most directly to the late 1970s and early 1980s, when major retrospective exhibits of his work made him even more widely known. Perhaps most representative of Munch's vision were the several different versions he prepared of the same theme, *The Cry*, first developed as a lithograph as long ago as 1895. The panic-stricken scream, the sexlessness of the sufferer, spoke of a primal terror that, as Munch later wrote, revealed "modern psychic life."

Courtesy The Museum of Fine Arts, Boston; William Francis Warden Fund

studying the evidence of the past in literature, mythology, and religious faith. His studies convinced him that there was a "collective unconscious," a reservoir of the entire human experience that is reflected symbolically in *archetypes* such as myths concerning the prophets and heroes that appear and reappear in art, literature, legend, and religion.

Such views of the nonrational origins of human action have deeply influenced daily life, from the relatively mundane, as in advertising, to the highly significant, as in the organization of political systems, the gratification of economic wants, and the satisfaction of human desires. The Freudian influence on imaginative writing has been especially great, as shown by stream-of-consciousness fiction. It has also deeply affected philosophy and the arts generally. Freud reinforced the intellectual reaction against scientific materialism and against nineteenth-century bourgeois optimism, and he strengthened the revival of intuition and sensibility in a kind of neoromantic and neo-Stoic protest against unbridled reason.

Freudian theories have no monopoly as explanation of human nature and behavior. The long debate of Plato and Aristotle, of the evolutionists and eugenicists of the nineteenth century, of social theorists in both democratic and totalitarian societies, continued: Did nature or nurture most influence the individual or groups of individuals? Intelligence testing, efforts to make prisons more comfortable, experiments with open classrooms, and a variety of theories in education all attested to the continued struggle between those who felt that humanity could be improved by reshaping the environment and those who felt that only through genetic engineering could humanity be made stronger or more intelligent—and thus perhaps more "moral."

Sociology and Political Science

In the social sciences, the twentieth century continued to question its inheritance of faith in the basic reasonableness and goodness of human nature. In fact, some social scientists found the term *human nature* to be so all-embracing as to make no sense. The specific programs and values of twentieth-century thinkers in this broad field were very varied. Yet most of them had a sense of the subtlety, the complexities, the delicacy—and the toughness and durability—of the forces that bind human beings together in society but also hold them apart. In the work of many different sociologists—the German Max Weber (1864–1920), the Frenchman Emile Durkheim (1858–1917), the Italian Vilfredo Pareto (1848–1923), and others—there was a common aim to study humanity in society "objectively" and still give full place to the role of the subjective and nonrational in human life, separating the rational from the nonrational in human actions. As is often the case with bodies of intellectual writing, there was a delay in impact, and the influence of these three thinkers, though clear in the years between the two world wars, was perhaps greatest during and after World War II.

What interested Pareto, for example, was the kind of action that is expressed in words, ritual, symbolism of some kind. For example, if wool socks for cold weather are bought deliberately to get the best socks at a price the buyer can afford, that is a rational action in accord with self-interest; it is the kind of action the economist can study statistically. If, however, they are bought because the buyer thinks wool is "natural" (as contrasted with synthetic fibers), or because the buyer finds snob value in imported English socks, or because the buyer wants to help bring sheep-raising back to Vermont, then the buyer has moved into a field less "rational" than that of price.

The practical economist will still study marketing and consumer demand, but will have to cope with many complex psychological variables. In such situations, behavior becomes the subject of study. In time *behavioralism* would dominate much of the study of politics (now called political science), as well as aspects of psychology, economics, and medicine.

Philosophy

A philosophy known as *existentialism* developed from such nineteenth-century sources as Nietzsche and the Danish theologian Søren Kierkegaard (1813–1855), who assailed the dehumanizing effects of the increasingly materialistic society of his day. In such works as *Fear and Trembling* (1843) and *Either/Or* (also 1843), he argued that Christian truth was not to be found in churches but in experiencing extreme human conditions through the act of existence.

The central theme of existentialism emerged after World War II in the work of the French philosopher Jean-Paul Sartre (1905–1980), who in 1946 argued that "existence is prior to essence." Sartre meant that subjectivity was essential to philosophy; that unchanging moral rules by which one may organize one's life without further thought do not exist; and that Christianity had long departed from its historical tenets to the point of lacking intellectual or metaphysical integrity. One chooses values, they are not given: Everything is done as a result of choice and thus there is absolute freedom. Such freedom is, of course, full of dread—and absolute freedom is virtually intolerable.

Existentialism provided a negative view of the human condition. Sartre and a second major figure in the development of this form of analysis, the German philosopher Martin Heidegger (1889–1976), showed how humankind escapes responsibility, hides the fact of having real choice, through shifts and evasions (called variously God, the church, the state, duty and so on) which provide order and thus make life tolerable. Heidegger did not see this view of life as unrelievedly gloomy, however, since life was possible through the honest and constant confrontation of death: Death was a creative force which lay at the center of Being.

The most original and most typical philosophic movement of the twentieth century is variously called logical analysis, logical positivism, linguistic philosophy, or, in some of its phases, symbolic logic. The movement accepted most of the new psychology and went ahead to insist that, although only a tiny bit of human experience could be defined as rational thought, that tiny bit should be protected and explored carefully. The movement's basic position held that when, applying the methods of scientific practice, a problem can be answered by an "operation" and the answer validated by logical and empirical tests or observations, knowledge can be achieved. But when no such "operation" is possible, as in such problems as whether democracy is the best form of government, whether a lie is ever justifiable, or whether a given poem is good or bad then the problem is "meaningless" for the logician. To be without meaning does not signify that the problem should be dismissed, however, as most of humanity must still discover "operable truths" by which to make decisions.

Logical positivists concluded that human beings are at present incapable of thorough, persistent, successful logical thinking. Rather, they are open to manipulation. This conclusion was chilling to those who believed in human progress or in an enlightened and educated electorate making well-informed and carefully calculated decisions at the polls. The succession of wars in the 1950s to the 1990s led some to abandon hope for democracy. While some followed the path of pessimism, concluding that

In the second half of the twentieth century, owning your own automobile became a symbol of success, maturity, and mobility throughout the Western world. Before the fuel shortages of the 1970s and 1980s, it was the prime status symbol in most societies. The average American, as depicted here in front of his 1961 Pontiac, assumed virtually as an economic right that the typical family would consist of two children, and that the family would own, first, its personal automobile and, second, its own home. This theme was captured in this painting by the artist Robert Bechtle (1932–   ).

Collection of Whitney Museum of American Art. Purchased with funds from the Richard and Dorothy Rodgers Fund. Acq. #70.16. Photo by Geoffrey Clements democratic thought was consistently being degraded through media manipulation, others concluded that it was possible for humankind to learn from the mistakes of the past, to change economic and social patterns to the benefit of the greater number and that, for all their faults, democracy and the free market offered the best hope for an optimistic future.

If formal philosophy seemed increasingly irrelevant to many, since it did not appear to grapple directly with daily concerns in a language that could be understood by the average person, so, too, by the 1980s had literature, especially at the formal and elite level, removed itself from general discussion. The impact of *structuralism*, a wide-ranging philosophical position centered in France, was especially great in literary criticism, anthropology, linguistics, and history. Its leading advocates, Roland Barthes (1915–1980) and Claude-Gustave Lévi-Strauss (1908–1994), were widely studied throughout the Western world. Barthes was a key creator of *semiology*, which viewed cultural phenomena as a series of signs with meanings that existed apart from their content. Systems, or structures, revealed such meaning as there was. Structuralism tended to be seen as in alignment with Marxism, since a practical application of its arguments would lead to concerns for systemic change rather than for the process of reform customary to most democracies.

Historicism

Probably the most widespread philosophical movement of the century developed on the margin of formal philosophy and the social sciences. This movement is called *historicism*—the attempt to find in history an answer to those ultimate questions of the structure of the universe and of human fate that the philosopher has always asked. Once Judaeo-Christian concepts of a single creation in time and of a God above nature were widely abandoned along with the rest of the traditional world view, people looking for answers to questions about these ultimates had to fall back on the historical record. Humans are not made by God but by nature, the historicists said, which amounts to saying that humanity makes itself in the course of history. Humanity gets its only clues about its capacities here on earth, from the record of the past.

But many of the thinkers who appealed to history found much more than the always tentative, never dogmatic or absolute "theories" the scientist produces. Many of these philosophers of history found in the course of history a substitute for the concepts of God or Providence. Of these historicisms, the most important was Marxism. For God, absolute and omnipotent, the Marxist substituted the absolutely determined course of dialectical materialism.

Another type of historicism was put forward by the German Oswald Spengler (1880–1936) in *The Decline of the West*, published at the end of World War I. Spengler argued from the historical record that societies or civilizations had an average life span, a thousand years or so for a civilization being the equivalent of seventy years or so for a human being. He traced three Western civilizations: a Hellenic from 1000 B.C. to about the birth of Christ; a

Levantine or Middle Eastern from then to about A.D. 1000; and a modern Western, which began (according to him) about A.D. 1000 and was, therefore, due to end about A.D. 2000. This type of history became highly popular between the two world wars, when many commentators spoke widely of the decline of the West, by which they often meant the collapse of all civilization.

Paralleling *The Decline of the West* but written by a trained historian was the enormously influential, multi-volume *Study of History* (1934–1954) by the Englishman Arnold Toynbee (1889–1975). Toynbee was a classicist with a Christian background and a strong family tradition of humanitarian social service. World War I aroused in Toynbee a hatred for war and a conviction that nationalism was evil. His work was an attempt to trace the causes of the rise and fall of dozens of societies in the past. Concluding his history at the height of the cold war, he argued that Western society was facing a very serious challenge, that in terms of the cyclical rise and fall of societies, it looked as if the West was stagnating. Societies grew, he said, when challenged and able to respond; if not challenged or incapable of a sufficient response, they declined. This dialectic of challenge and response proved attractive to western Europe and the United States, which felt challenged by the Soviet Union and improved by their competitive response.

More intriguing, perhaps, was the work of historians who asked questions not previously asked. French, British, and American historians in particular developed new fields of inquiry. Perhaps most representative was the enormous growth of interest in the history of slavery. In the United States the study of slavery had been seen as a branch of the history of the South. American scholars as a whole had favored the "consensus" view of certain progressive historians, especially Frederick Jackson Turner (1861–1932) and the relatively radical views of Charles A. Beard (1874–1948). Most maintained that American development was marked far more by cooperation than by conflict, and that slavery was peripheral to an understanding of the rise of American civilization. From the 1950s, however, many scholars challenged the consensus argument, pointing to the centrality of the problem of finding and retaining a predictable supply of labor in a rapidly growing agricultural and industrial nation, thus moving the issue of slavery into the center of American inquiry. In this and many other examples, historians in the West roundly condemned the conventional wisdom by which British or American history was viewed as a compilation of unalloyed success stories.

TWENTIETH-CENTURY SCIENCE

In the twentieth century each science, and each branch of each science, continued its ever more intense specialization. Cooperation among pure scientists, applied scientists, engineers, bankers, business people, and government officials produced exponential increases. The rate of travel is an example: In 1820 the fastest rate was still 12 to 15 miles an hour; railroads made it 100 miles or so by 1880; piston-engined airplanes made it 300 miles or so by 1940; jet planes broke the sound barrier in 1947, making speeds of close to 1,000 miles per hour possible; and starting in 1969 rockets propelled men to the moon at speeds exceeding 20,000 miles an hour.

Scientific respect for nature and natural laws, and scientific skepticism toward the supernatural, have added powerfully to the modern drive toward rationalism, positivism, materialism. Science continued to promote the world view that arose in early modern times and culminated in the Enlightenment of the eighteenth century. Thus the hopeful views once attributed to Voltaire or other philosophers or social scientists became increasingly, though not unfailingly, the preserve of science.

The Revolution in Physics

Perhaps the great scientific event of the twentieth century was the revolution in physics symbolized for the public by Albert Einstein (1879–1955). This revolution centered on radical revisions made in the Newtonian world-machine, the mechanistic model of the universe that had been accepted for more than two centuries. Many nineteenth-century scientists were convinced that light moved in waves and was transmitted through the ether, which supposedly filled outer space. In the 1880s, however, experiments demonstrated that there was no ether. If the ether did exist, then it would itself be moved by the motion of the earth, and a beam of light directed *against* its current would travel with a velocity less than that of a beam directed *with* its current. But experiments showed that light traveled at 186,284 miles per second, whether it was moving with or against the hypothetical current.

In 1905 Einstein, who was then twenty-six years old, published a paper asserting that since the speed of light is a constant unaffected by the earth's motion, it must also be unaffected by all the other bodies in the universe. This unvarying velocity of light is a law of nature, Einstein continued, and other laws of nature are the same for all uniformly moving systems. This was Einstein's special theory of relativity, which had many disconcerting corollaries. In particular, it undermined the idea of absolute space and absolute time, and made both space and time relative to the velocity of the system in which they were moving. Thus space and time are not absolutes but are relative to the observer.

Einstein maintained that space and time, therefore, are inseparably linked; time is a "fourth dimension." An air-traffic controller needs to know the position of an airplane not only in longitude, latitude, and altitude, but also in time, and the total flight path of a plane must be plotted on what Einstein called a *four-dimensional space-time continuum*—a term he also applied to the universe.

Einstein equated not only space and time but also mass and energy. His famous formula E = mc^2 means

that the energy in an object is equal to its mass, multiplied by the square of the velocity of light. It means also that a very small object may contain tremendous potential energy. Such an object, for example, can emit radiation for thousands of years or discharge it all in one explosion, as happened with the atom bomb in 1945, when a way was found to unlock the potential energy in uranium.

The problem of mass also involved Einstein in a review of the Newtonian concept of a universe held together by the force of gravity—the attraction of bodies to other bodies over vast distances. Einstein soon concluded that gravity—that is, the weight—of an object had nothing to do with its attraction to other objects. Galileo had demonstrated that both light and heavy bodies fell from the leaning tower in Pisa at the same speed. Einstein proposed that it would be more useful to extend the concept of the *magnetic field*, in which certain bodies behaved in a certain pattern, and speak of a *gravitational field*, in which bodies also behaved in a certain pattern. Einstein did not penetrate the mystery of what holds the universe together, but he did suggest a more convincing way of looking at it. This was the essence of his general theory of relativity (1916), which stated that the laws of nature are the same for all systems, regardless of their state of motion.

One of these laws of nature had been formulated in 1900 by Max Planck (1858–1947), a German physicist, who expressed mathematically the amount of energy emitted in the radiation of heat. He discovered that the amount of energy divided by the frequency of the radiation always yielded the same very tiny number, which scientists call Planck's constant. The implication of this discovery was that objects emit energy not in an unbroken flow, but in a series of separate minute units, each of which Planck called a *quantum*. Quantum physics suggested a basic discontinuity in the universe by assuming that a quantum could appear at two different locations without having traversed the intervening space. Other physicists soon made discoveries reinforcing the idea of continuity, with all physical phenomena behaving like waves. The old dilemma of whether light consisted of particles or of waves was therefore greatly extended.

During the 1920s it became evident that scientists might never be able to answer the ultimate questions about the universe. They could not fully understand the behavior of the electron, the basic component of the atom, because in the act of trying to observe the electron, they created effects that altered its behavior. Study of the electron led Werner Heisenberg (1901–1976), a German physicist, to propose the principle of indeterminacy or uncertainty, which concludes that the scientist will have to be content with probabilities rather than absolutes. Although the universe is no longer the world machine of Newton, its activity is by no means random, and it can still be expressed in the mathematical language of probabilities. Indeed, the new sciences of probability theory, molecular biology and biochemistry, and plasma physics, together with the discovery by Murray Gell-Mann (1929–   ) of the *quark*, which is any of three

In the 1980s, the use of computers created a new technology, new employment opportunities, new forms of education, new means of storing and retrieving information, and new challenges to humanity. The microchip, smaller than an ordinary paper clip, could store as much information as an entire library.

Ken Karp

types of elementary particles believed to form the basis for all matter in the universe, have nonetheless led scientists once again to feel that they may be on the verge of a unifying theory by which creation, matter, and even life may at last be explained.

The development of twentieth-century astronomy has been closely linked to that of physics. To the non-scientist, such astronomical concepts as the finite but expanding universe, curved space, and the almost inconceivable distances and quantities of light years and galaxies have made astronomy the most romantic science. A light year is the distance traversed by light in one year, or roughly 5,880,000,000,000 miles. The Milky Way galaxy, of which our universe is a part, has some 30,000 million stars and nebulae, in the form of a disk with a diameter of about 100,000 light years. To humanize these dimensions, and to make them comprehensible, Western writers produced works of science fiction and created television series and motion picture films that attempted to make sense at the level of popular culture of such abstract concepts as the light year. One such program, originally to be called *Wagon Train to the Stars*, became one of the most popular television programs of all time as *Star Trek*. It posed moral dilemmas in outer space to a generation of young people for whom the customary means of presenting moral issues, whether in church or through literature, seemed ineffective, and for whom the romance of outer space had replaced the romance of the old frontier. Politicians, too, were caught up in the popular fascination with space, referring to their policies as New Frontiers and using metaphors in their speeches derived from the new language of space travel and space conquest.

Science and the Quality of Life

Chemistry, which made possible plastics, synthetic fibers, and many other innovations, also greatly affected daily life by its impact on food, clothing, and most material objects. Chemistry assisted the very great gains made by the biological sciences and their application to medicine and public health. In the United States and elsewhere, infant mortality fell and many contagious diseases were conquered so successfully that the average expectancy of life at birth increased by more than twenty years since 1900. More children were being born and living longer worldwide, so that the problem of feeding an expanding population remained acute. Some relief resulted from the new technologies of irrigated farming, chemical fertilizers, and highly productive new hybrid strains of wheat and corn.

The advance of science created problems as well as solved them. Some of the problems were of the first magnitude, notably the prospect that modern military technology could destroy humanity. Pesticides, detergents, and plastics, which were originally thought to be purely beneficial to the quality of life, also threatened life by their harmful effects on ecology. Scientists and technicians came under attack as cold, inhuman, and unable to control the awesome gadgets they created.

Though every field of science grew exponentially in the years after World War II, the world's demand for practical applications of science to technology inevitably meant disproportionate growth in certain areas. At the same time, widely accepted scientific principles came under review, and physicists and geologists alike admitted that much of their most basic work was, at root, fundamentally philosophical. Indicative areas of growth and change included the technology of weaponry, medicine and the treatment of injury and disease, genetics, challenges to the theory of evolution, concern for population control, and matters of the environment, from worry about global warming to political responses to extensive and damaging oil spills.

Perhaps most immediately noticeable to the general public, and most open to democratic influence, was the rise of the environmental movement. The "father of ecology," the American George Perkins Marsh (1801–1882), published *Man and Nature*, with the cogent subtitle *Physical Geography as Modified by Human Action*, in 1864. Called "the Bible of the environmental movement," Marsh's work showed how each action in nature is followed by another. Noting that Greece, now dry and with sparse forest cover, was heavily forested until goats were introduced to the landscape, Marsh argued that every human act had a consequence in nature.

To this point, perhaps the culmination of such awareness is shown by the heated debate over global warming. Early in 1991 scientists reported that 1990 was the warmest year on the meteorological record. Historians and scientists had long been aware of climatic change across great periods of time, but growing concern over the "greenhouse effect," over how pollution in the upper atmosphere might well lead to a global warming so extensive and catastrophic that agriculturally productive areas would be turned into wastelands, that glaciers would melt and the seas rise, successfully dramatized the fact that the entire globe faced daunting problems in common.

Of course such problems are not simply scientific or managerial: They are political as well. No issue showed this so clearly in the 1980s and early 1990s as the intense struggle over population limitation, birth control, and—especially in the United States—abortion. By 1990 nearly ninety acres of tropical forests were being destroyed daily to create land for crops and cattle and to provide timber for fuel and construction. Every hour in 1990, 16,400 human beings were born around the globe. To many observers such statistics seemed inevitably linked. The industrial, or postindustrial societies, especially in western Europe, were virtually at a steady-state birth rate, with births and deaths canceling each other out, but in Africa, much of Asia, and Latin America the post–World War II population explosion remained essentially unabated. By 1990 the world's population stood at 5.3 billion. The population in less developed countries was doubling every 29 years. Science could provide contraceptive pills and medicine could make safe abortions possible, but such interference with life's processes was the focus of much moral anguish, political debate, and protest. While limiting family size came to be widely accepted in Japan, Singapore, the PRC, and much of Europe, the profound issue of whether abortion was murder rocked the New World democracies and many Roman Catholic countries.

Both weaponry and medical research benefited from World War II and the many wars of the last forty years. But war, and the upheavals of economic and social change, also opened the door to new ethnic tensions, to new diseases, and to a vast and growing international illegal drug trade. By 1989 the United States, Britain, and other Western democracies had announced a war on drugs; entire nations, most particularly Colombia, appeared to be at the mercy of drug barons, with hundreds of judges and politicians killed, their children held as hostages, entire police forces and armies corrupted. Drugs destabilized families and societies, adding yet one more force for change.

With rising taxes, inflation, and housing costs that made the dream of home ownership less and less realistic, more and more families had two parents who went off to work daily. Schools, already staggering from budget cuts, faced declining standards in most of the democracies at the same time they were being expected to provide substitutes for traditional family services. By 1991, only one child in four in the United States lived in the kind of household that was customary at the outbreak of World War II: with two married parents, both living at home, and only one at work. In such changes lay challenges and opportunities, as well as pressing problems, for the findings of scientists, economists, philosophers, and historians.

MODERN LITERATURE AND THE ARTS: ELITE AND POPULAR

As societies became more and more literate, reading matter changed, becoming both simpler and much cheaper and also more complex and symbolic in its more elite expressions. This was true of painting and the other arts as well. A wider gulf opened between those who read, or viewed, for entertainment and those who sought information, analyses, or complexity of emotional expressions.

Literature

Twentieth-century writers surprised the prophets of doom. Poetry remained, for the most part, what it had become in the late nineteenth century: difficult, cerebral, and addressed to a small audience. An occasional poet broke from the privacy of limited editions to wide popularity; representative was the attention given to T. S. Eliot (1888–1965). His difficult yet moving symbolic poem, "The Waste Land," or his invocation to "The Hollow Men," which closed with the lines

This is the way the world ends

Not with a bang but a whimper

captured for a whole generation its sense of quiet despair, its anguish hidden in boredom, and its expectation of a cleansing flame to purge society.

However, the novel remained the most important form of contemporary imaginative writing. Although no one could predict which novelists of our century would be read in the twenty-first century, the American William Faulkner (1897–1962), the German Thomas Mann (1875–1955), and the Frenchman Albert Camus (1913–1960) were already enshrined as classics. Mann, who began with a traditionally realistic novel of life in his birthplace, the old Hanseatic town of Lübeck, never really belonged to the avant-garde. He was typical of the sensitive, worried, class-conscious artist of the age of psychology. Camus, too, was sensitive and worried, but with an existentialist concern in his novels and plays over human isolation and the need to engage oneself in life.

A universal symbol of the American center of film production, Hollywood, and of cartoon films in particular, was Mickey Mouse, the creation of Walt Disney Studios. Mickey was recognized around the world.

AP/Wide World Photos

The most innovative novelist of the twentieth century surely was the Irishman James Joyce (1882–1941). Joyce began with a subtle, outspoken, but conventional series of sketches of life in the Dublin of his youth, *Dubliners* (1914), and an undisguised autobiography, *Portrait of the Artist as a Young Man* (1916). Then, in exile on the Continent, he wrote a classic experimental novel, *Ulysses* (1922), an account of twenty-four hours in the life of Leopold Bloom, a Dublin Jew. *Ulysses* is full of difficult allusions, parallels with Homer, puns, rapidly shifting scenes and episodes, and it is written without regard for the conventional notions of plot and orderly development. Above all, it makes full use of the recently developed psychology of the unconscious, as displayed in the stream of consciousness. The last chapter, printed entirely without punctuation marks, is the record of what went on in the mind of Bloom's wife, Molly, as she lay in bed waiting for him to come home. What went on in her mind was too shocking for most contemporaries, and *Ulysses*, published in Paris, had to be smuggled into English-speaking countries. The later widespread popularity of Joyce indicated the extent to which sexual mores and attitudes toward explicit language changed after World War II.

Postwar literature was explosive, diverse, and ever-growing. World War II released non-Western writers to publish widely in Europe and the Americas, so that figures previously known only in their own countries gained world renown. A growing permissiveness led to more and more realistic, as well as increasingly vulgar, forms of expression. The novel, and in particular novels consciously written to be best sellers, came to dominate the marketplace. Vastly increased literacy led to vastly increased sales, to the point that a popular writer like the English mystery novelist Agatha Christie (1890–1976) came to outsell all but the Bible and to be translated into eighty languages. Fictional heroes such as Sherlock Holmes, the creation of Sir Arthur Conan Doyle (1859–1930), came to be treated by millions as though they were real figures. The rise of a vast reading public that found writers like Eliot and Joyce too difficult, or simply not sufficiently entertaining, would have profound effects on education, literature, and society as a whole. Further, by the 1980s English had clearly replaced French as the language of diplomacy, German as the language of science, and all others as the major world language of commerce.

Painting

No painter could better serve as a representative of the endless variety and experimentation of twentieth-century painting than the versatile and immensely productive Pablo Picasso (1881–1973). A native Spaniard and adopted Frenchman, Picasso painted in many styles and periods. For example, the paintings of his "blue period" in the early 1900s, with their exhausted and defeated people, had a melancholy, lyrical quality that reflected the

On April 26, 1986, a Soviet nuclear reactor exploded, pouring a radioactive volcano over the city of Chernobyl. With ten times the fallout of Hiroshima, the cloud spread over Byelorussia, western Russia, and the Ukraine and then, taken into the atmosphere, into Poland and Scandinavia. Over thirteen thousand square miles were contaminated, and farmers as far away as Italy and Wales had to destroy their produce. Scientists estimate that over the next fifty years perhaps fifty thousand people will die of cancer as a result.

Sovfoto

Faulkner on Human Security

The objective conditions of human life have steadily improved over the centuries: the infant mortality rate has fallen, the longevity rate has risen, the caloric intake has increased, a wide range of diseases that once devastated humanity have been conquered, and labor-saving devices have taken the sweat from the brow of millions. At the same time, human ability to inflict grievous wounds has also increased: wars that once took thousands of lives can now take millions, and new forms of warfare can destroy all life on this planet. In this excerpt from his speech upon accepting the Nobel Prize for Literature in 1949, William Faulkner (1897–1962) discusses the long human search for security.

Our tragedy today is a general and universal physical fear so long sustained by now that we can even bear it. There are no longer problems of the spirit. There is only the question: When will I be blown up? Because of this, the young man or woman writing today has forgotten the problems of the human heart in conflict with itself which alone can make good writing because only that is worth writing about, worth the agony and the sweat.

He must learn them again. He must teach himself that the basest of all things is to be afraid; and, teaching himself that, forget it forever, leaving no room in his workshop for anything but the old verities and truths of the heart, the old universal truths, lacking which any story is ephemeral and doomed—love and honor and pity and pride and compassion and sacrifice. Until he does so, he labors under a curse. He writes not of love but of lust, of defeats in which nobody loses anything of value, of victories without hope and, worst of all, without pity or compassion. His griefs grieve on no universal bones, leaving no scars. He writes not of the heart but of the glands.

Until he relearns these things, he will write as though he stood alone and watched the end of man. I decline to accept the end of man. It is easy enough to say that man is immortal simply because he will endure; that when the last ding-dong of doom has clanged and faded from the last worthless rock hanging tideless in the last red and dying evening, that even there there will still be one more sound: that of his puny inexhaustible voice, still talking. I refuse to accept this. I believe that man will not merely endure: he will prevail. He is immortal, not because he alone among creatures has an inexhaustible voice but because he has a soul, a spirit capable of compassion and sacrifice and endurance.

William Faulkner, Nobel Prize address, in *William Faulkner: Three Decades of Criticism*, ed. Frederick J. Hoffman and Olga W. Vickery (East Lansing, Mich.: Michigan State University Press, 1969), pp. 347–48.

struggling young artist's own poverty. These pictures are said to have been influenced by the work of El Greco, the sixteenth-century Spanish master; certainly both artists conveyed a sense of concentrated emotion by exaggerating and distorting human proportions.

Around 1905–1906 Picasso turned to more daring innovations, much influenced by exhibitions of masks from black Africa and of large-eyed archaic sculptures newly discovered in the Mediterranean world. Picasso strove to capture in the two dimensions of a picture the three dimensions of the real world. Sometimes he used the techniques of abstractionism—the reduction of figures to a kind of plane geometry, all angles and lines; sometimes those of cubism—a kind of solid geometry, all cubes, spheres, and cones; and sometimes collage (paste-up), in which he glued onto a picture fragments of real objects.

Picasso often returned to more traditional representational painting, as in the almost classical portraits of his "white period" after World War I. Yet he also persisted in his more radical vein of showing the human or animal figure from two or more angles simultaneously; hence the misplaced eyes and other anatomical rearrange-

ments that he employed with such telling effect in *Guernica* (1937), which depicted the havoc wrought by an aerial attack upon a defenseless town during the Spanish Civil War. At his death Picasso was the most widely known artist in the world.

Art, like life, remained idiosyncratic, diverse, unwilling to be regimented. Some viewers denounced such art as decadent; this was Hitler's position. Others wished art to contribute in a direct way to the state; this was Stalin's position. Many found art simply irrelevant. The more it moved away from representing objective and visual reality, the less they could understand it. But many were fascinated by the new freedom, the new themes, and the new techniques. In varying ways this art sought to capture the courage and the anguish of modern humanity.

From early in the century, art had proven to be explosive, expressive, highly innovative, breaking away from the settled canons of earlier representational art. The *expressionists* declared that they must represent things not as they saw them but as they felt them, and such art took on a magical, poetic, even visionary quality. The *fauves,* artists who used pure color, and among whom Henri

Henry Moore's *Family Group,* completed between 1945 and 1949, emphasized the strength and continuity of the family at a time when it was under attack.

Collection, The Museum of Modern Art, New York

Matisse (1869–1954) was a central figure, worked with bold, flexible lines to convey an intensity of expression that went beyond the normal range of human emotions. *Surrealism* was linked to Freudianism, for it sought to express subconscious mental processes. The giant Picasso was the transition figure; Salvador Dali (1904–1989) and Yves Tanguy (1900–1955) enjoyed large financial success, in part because of the popularity of surrealist techniques.

For a brief time after World War I a protest movement in art known as *Dada* scandalized critics. This group protested the slaughter of millions in war, not only through their work but in their chosen name, for Dada sounded like a nonword representing the verbal nonsense that the artists felt the makers of war used in order to destroy sanity and security. Although it has been argued that Dadaist protest was more political and social than aesthetic, most of the artists associated with it made distinguished contributions to the arts. Jean Arp (1887–1966), who fled his native Alsace for Switzerland to avoid service in the German army, was a pioneer in abstractionist painting and sculpture. George Grosz (1893–1959) made bitter sketches satirizing the foibles of German society between the two world wars. Marcel Duchamp (1887– 1968) created a sensation at the New York Armory show of 1913, which introduced avant-garde art to the American public, by exhibiting his *Nude Descending a Staircase*, a cubist attempt to depict the human figure in a rapid motion.

Artists like Duchamp and Grosz eventually moved from Europe to the United States as part of the wave of artistic emigration that reached its peak in the late 1930s and early 1940s and ended the old dominance of Paris as the center of the avant-garde. In the 1940s and 1950s New York became the capital of *abstract expressionism*, which communicated ideas or moods by entirely nonrepresentational means through color, form, and a sense of movement or action. The American Jackson Pollock (1912–1956) dripped or hurled automobile enamel on huge canvases, which he laid out on his studio floor, creating an arresting effect of ordered chaos. In the 1960s the New York spotlight shifted to pop art, a neo-Dadaist reaction to mass-produced and mass-marketed commodities. Pop artists depicted boxes of Brillo, cans of Campbell's soup, road signs, soap operas, comic strips, and blurred pictures of movie stars from magazines or the television screen. Pop artists like Andy Warhol (1928–1987), together with the Americans Robert Motherwell (1915–1991) and Georgia O'Keeffe (1887–1986) and the British Francis Bacon (1909–1986), took up dominating positions.

The Other Arts

Pop sculpture featured plaster casts of real people surrounded by actual pieces of furniture in a three-dimensional comic strip of devitalized, defeated humanity. At the other extreme, sculpture in the grand manner experienced a rebirth, in good measure due to the work of two British artists. Barbara Hepworth (1903–1975) made classically fashioned standing abstract forms of great beauty. Henry Moore (1898–1986) came to be widely considered the ranking sculptor of the century. His powerful renditions of monumental human figures, simplified and reduced to essentials, created an effect like that of a cubist or expressionist painting. In sculpture as in painting, the variety and vitality of innovations were remarkable—from the highly polished rhythmic abstractions of the Romanian Constantin Brancusi (1876–1957), to the disturbing, emaciated figures of the Swiss Alberto Gia-

Alberto Giacometti, painter, sculptor, and poet, used simplified human forms to emphasize technology's growing control over human actions; the themes and methods of his abstractions were taken up by other artists twenty years later. In *Chariot* (1950), his diminished symbol of mankind is nonetheless monumental in the way in which it occupies space.

Collection, The Museum of Modern Art, New York

cometti (1901–1966), to the abstract or whimsical mobiles of the American Alexander Calder (1898–1976) and his larger, sometimes menacing, stabiles.

In architecture the twentieth century produced the first truly original style since the end of the eighteenth century. This functional style was no revival of the past, no living museum of eclecticism like many nineteenth-century buildings. It prided itself on honest use of modern materials and on adaptation to the site and to the demands of twentieth-century living, combined with avoidance of waste space and needless display. One of its pioneers was the American Frank Lloyd Wright (1869– 1959), who spent his apprenticeship with the designers of early Chicago skyscrapers and then developed the "prairie" style of house, emphasizing the planes and the uncluttered simplicity that Wright admired in Japanese houses. Toward the end of his life Wright made a radical experiment in the designing of the Solomon Guggenheim Museum in New York, which consisted mainly of one vast, open space through which visitors descend along a ramp that permits them to see the works displayed both close at hand and at several different removes of distance.

Modern music, like modern art, moved away from what the general public could comprehend into atonal and experimental music, often based on electronics. Popular music became a vast branch of the entertainment industry, represented by country and Western, modern jazz, and various forms of rock and roll. All had their innovators who sought to develop fresh ideas and sounds, and jazz in particular was often both intellectually and emotionally creative in ways that broke with the essentially derivative modes of much popular romantic music. Music for the millions reached them through radio and television and by traveling groups such as the Beatles.

The words and sounds of popular music came to dominate the sensory world of young western Europeans, Americans, and Japanese, representing an internationalization of tastes as pervasive as the Sony Walkman on which the music was played. All art distorts perspective in order to heighten concentration, and music, in distorting sounds, commanded intense attention. Distortion in art and music and hyperbole in literature, cinema, and consumer advertising were a response to the competition for public attention in a world of ever-increasing stimuli, with decibels, vulgarity, and "flash" adding adornments of a kind to the very real talent that popular culture displayed.

Dual Goals, Dual Models

Many observers feared that there had been a slow breakdown in what was once understood to be the social contract. Much of humanity was struggling with dual goals: to achieve freedom and to create equality, to protect the rights of the individual and to meet obligations to others. But must individual liberty be given up to guarantee equality? People more and more focused on devotion to self: A soaring divorce rate led to divided families; the desire for more and better possessions led to greater materialism; a sense of entitlement to the good things of life led to anger at those who took without being entitled or those who had been rewarded with an excess of good things. In the 1980s the delicately balanced pendulum that has moved back and forth across the face of Western history was beginning to emphasize duty in equal measure to rights, was beginning to place limits on the obligation of the state to the individual and of the individual to the state, in such a way as to create a sense of instability and uncertainty as to what values ought to be cherished.

One of the values under question was the study of history itself. History, it was agreed, attempted to demonstrate the relationship between cause and effect. Being itself about time, history attempted to show how people worked within the constraints of time to arrive at decisions. History sought to organize causes in some order of priorities, so that one could separate the important from the less important, the proximate from the remote, in a complex sequence of causation. But such efforts assumed that there were, in the end, *facts* that could be known, that there was a *rational* basis to decision making, that causes could be discovered and their effects could be charted, and that commonly held values could lead to agreement on priorities of action.

American popular music has become international in its appeal. Country and Western, once heard only regionally in the United States, is today heard everywhere, and rock music attracts large audiences throughout the Western world, in the Soviet Union, in parts of Africa, and in Japan. New cultural heroes who initially appealed to the young now attract all generations. Outstanding among the musical innovators over the years have been Frank Sinatra and the Beatles: John Lennon, Ringo Starr, Paul McCartney, and George Harrison, in 1965.

The New York Public Library Picture Collection and Gamma Liaison

In some ways, Western civilization in the late 1980s and 1990s appeared to constitute a unity. To the extent that this unity was defined by high industrial capacity or serious attention to new art forms (such as the motion picture, which many regarded as the most significant development in art as well as in entertainment in the previous fifty years), Japan was also a member of this Western world. These societies shared a concern for finding new sources of energy, especially oil, and for the environment. Perhaps most important symbolically was the

signing, by the twenty-two NATO and Warsaw Pact members, of a conventional arms treaty in November of 1990. However, by this time events had overtaken the Soviet Union and the nations of eastern Europe, and much of western Europe and the United States were on the brink of a war in the Persian Gulf.

Germany and Japan had experienced remarkable recoveries from World War II. Both had been highly organized states under totalitarian regimes before their defeat, and in the postwar years they could draw upon a

One of Frank Lloyd Wright's most famous structures was the private home he designed at Ohiopyle, in western Pennsylvania. Called "Falling Water," the house was incorporated directly into the landscape, as though it were ledges of stone jutting out above a waterfall.

M. E. Warren/Photo Researchers, Inc.

Motion pictures increasingly created the images by which the young, in particular, interpreted the world in the 1970s and 1980s. Science fiction was enormously popular, and the figure of Darth Vader—seen here from the film *The Empire Strikes Back*—was known to millions.

Movie Star News

heritage of strong public commitment to the idea of the central state. Both were, to a high degree, ethnically homogeneous, so that neither experienced the far-ranging and debilitating effects of race conflict and racism. Both were aided after the war by those who had defeated them, so that they entered into economic competition with new industrial plants as the older industrial nations were falling behind by failing to replace their obsolete equipment. Neither Germany nor Japan was faced with large defense budgets, since as a condition of the peace settlements they were prohibited from maintaining forces capable of aggressive action against another nation. Nations with high industrial capacity looked to them as models of social and industrial reorganization.

Other contending models often were authoritarian or repressive. Totalitarian dictatorships generally involve single-party government, control over most forms of communications, a weapons monopoly within the state, a terrorist police force, a centrally directed economy, and usually a single strong leader with an ideology attractive to a mass group. While most liberal democracies were firmly opposed to these contending models, even within the democracies groups appeared that wanted the greater stability that such methods could bring. The cost of

democracy was high, and it was under heavy and persistent challenge. The democracies had passed through periods of conflict over ideological commitment; the last such period had been in the late 1960s and early 1970s. By the mid-1990s such ideological passion appeared to be on the rise again.

To many observers, fragmentation of knowledge seemed to put the basic assumptions of Western civilization at risk. Many commentators expressed fear that two distinct cultures were developing in Western societies: one based on the assumptions of humanists, the other on the assumptions of scientists. The explosion in knowledge—in what a person needed to know to be considered educated, in how society viewed and used knowledge, and in the technical means by which knowledge was transmitted, acquired, stored, and retrieved—led to increased specialization, which hindered communication among intellectuals, political leaders, and all who needed to communicate across the barriers of class, race, nation, or specialization. A worldwide resurgence in religious conviction was observed. Perhaps most important, the long-defended orthodoxies of Marxism had been overthrown throughout eastern Europe and the former center of the communist faith, the Soviet Union, was in the throes of complex change and dissolution.

ᛋUMMARY

Views of history change constantly. As historians view the last forty years, they face the difficulty of evaluating recent historical trends, such as economic cycles or the world-wide impact of the arms race. Today Western civilization can no longer be seen as separate from world culture.

Whereas nineteenth-century thought emphasized the dynamics of change in time, the twentieth century

has focused on the role of the unconscious in human action and thought. The work of Sigmund Freud not only influenced the understanding of human relations but also had a vast impact on political and cultural theory. Sociologists sought to study society in the light of the subjective and nonrational elements in human life, as increasingly did historians and literary critics.

The three major philosophical movements of the twentieth century have been existentialism, influenced by such nineteenth-century thinkers as Nietzsche and Kierkegaard; logical analysis; and historicism, an attempt to find in history an answer to the ultimate philosophical questions. In the twentieth century historians have also asked new questions and opened up new fields of inquiry.

Intense specialization occurred in the sciences in the twentieth century. Einstein and others revolutionized physics by radically revising the Newtonian view of the world. Major developments in astronomy were closely linked to those in physics and contributed to popular fascination with space travel. Great gains were also made in chemical and biological sciences and resulted in, among other things, greatly expanded life expectancy and increased food production. Scientific findings were also politicized, especially where they touched upon the environment, population control, and issues of morality and the individual.

In literature, the novel remained the most important form of imaginative writing. The new psychology influenced novelists as they examined the individual's unconscious drives. James Joyce's experimental novel, *Ulysses*, made use of the new "stream of consciousness" style.

In the past 150 years artists have experimented with ways of expressing what lies beneath surface appearances. Impressionist painters of the 1870s and 1880s had experimented with the use of light and color, allowing the viewer to reassemble dabs of color into a recognizable scene. In the twentieth century a variety of artistic styles have held sway for a time, ranging from cubism, Dada, and surrealism to pop art, with Picasso certainly the most influential artist. In the 1940s and 1950s New York became the capital of abstract expressionism, nonrepresentational painting that emphasized color, form, and a sense of movement.

Twentieth-century architects used modern materials adapted to the demands of space and function. Frank Lloyd Wright was a leader in this movement, designing buildings that embodied uncluttered simplicity.

Modern musicians experimented with atonality while popular music grew into a vast entertainment industry dominated by well-known stars with global followings.

Liberal democracies were challenged by totalitarian and repressive states, as well as by their own fragmentation and intense specialization. The wide use of the computer, perhaps the most significant development in technology in the last two decades, promised to change the very organization of knowledge, and thus of life. Confusion about the present intermixed with dedication to the ideals of the past appeared to characterize most of the nations of the West as they approached the start of the twenty-first century. Eastern Europe and the Soviet Union had turned away from orthodox Marxism, the former to struggle with the problems of free enterprise, the latter with the prospect of dissolution in the face of rapid and perplexing liberalization, while resurgent nationalisms across the Soviet Union, in south Asia, and elsewhere projected the probability of significant changes on the political and social map of the world.

CRITICAL THINKING

1. This chapter implies that the whole of twentieth-century thought and letters must be seen as a continuum. Do you agree? If not, why not, and how would you organize our understanding of the subject?

2. In what way is history a "modern" subject, given that there have been historians writing since ancient Greece?

3. How did the social sciences change our view of human nature? Which aspects of this changing view do you believe most liberated people? Which aspects most destroyed social stability? How would you measure the relative value of freedom and stability to a people?

4. Though the revolution in physics was abstract and mathematically complex, it had very practical impacts on daily life. What were some of these?

5. What is meant by "the quality of life"? Do you believe the quality of life is better today than in ancient Rome? In the Middle Ages? In the Renaissance? In the eighteenth century? Why do you answer as you do?

6. Which aspect of "modern thought" do you find personally most compelling? Why?

7. Compare and contrast the idea of an "elite" literature or art with a "popular" literature or art, providing examples. To which do you relate most easily and why? How do particular writers or artists come to be called *elitist* or *popular*, and are these terms useful?

8. Choose one of the illustrations from this chapter, based on your positive response to it. Why have you chosen it? Do you consider your choice tells you more about yourself or more about the creator of the image concerned?

9. What is *environmentalism*? How do you think this term differs from *conservationism* or *preservationism*?

10. What do you see as the most fundamental intellectual trends of the last quarter century?

CHAPTER 28

Our Times:
Arriving at the Present

THOUGH DOMINATED BY THE COLD war, the history of the past five decades also speaks of many triumphs. Despite wars, political intimidation, and terror, both population and longevity have increased. Diseases that devastated populations in the Middle Ages have been virtually eradicated, and modern vaccines and medicines promise longer life and better health to millions. In all the Western democracies, concern for the rights of the individual has been heightened. Many societies have questioned their former values and conventional wisdoms, while reaffirming national pride and cohesion, just as others have begun to fragment into smaller units.

Inventions in one part of the globe are quickly known in another part, and technology continues to grow faster than humanity can comprehend: The microchip transforms storage of and access to knowledge; the jet plane shrinks time and distance; and new frontiers are discovered when humans walk in outer space and reach the moon. Also for the first time societies and governments systematically concern themselves with the conservation of resources, with the provision of a wide array of services for mind and body, and with the grim possibility of mutual and near-total destruction.

Against the very substantial gains—in health, productivity, and freedom—experienced by the majority of humankind must be set ever-deepening worries. The same technology that has created millions of new jobs, that has contributed to the recognition of equality between the races and between men and women, and that made possible a precarious peace based on the mutual ability of the major powers to destroy each other, also caused vast dislocations in populations, widespread damage to the environment, and the capacity through nuclear warfare to destroy vast portions of the globe. Greater longevity and better health in general terms must be set off against the rise, in the 1980s, of a deeply disturbing new disease, AIDS (Acquired Immune Deficiency Syndrome), which was sweeping across North America, Western Europe, and parts of Africa. In 1990 doctors estimated that perhaps 2 million Americans alone had the disease, and there was frightened talk of a new plague such as the world has not seen for decades if not centuries.

Without necessarily infringing upon political sovereignty, the world has become very small. All of humanity must be concerned with defining moral, ethical, and legal bases for life, though from different perspectives and out of different historical experiences. The long search for stability and security continues. New players on the stage join the nations of Western civilization in this search.

WESTERN EUROPE

After 1945 the nations of western Europe successfully preserved the forms of the sovereign state and the politics of nationalism, while also making real attempts to organize a "free Europe" on a level beyond the national state. In 1952, as a first step, France, West Germany, and Italy joined with Belgium, the Netherlands, and Luxembourg in setting up a European Coal and Steel Community. It created for their coal and iron industries a free market area of all six nations, in which a joint administrative body could make certain final and binding decisions without the participation of any government officials. Each nation had given up some part of its sovereignty, and the plan was a success.

By the Treaty of Rome in 1957, these same six countries established the European Economic Community (EEC), better known as the Common Market, with headquarters in Brussels. This was the beginning of closer economic union under a central administration of delegates from each partner nation. The treaty also provided for increasing powers over trade, production, immigration, currency, and the transport of goods for the Common Market, according to a carefully worked out schedule. Each nation moved toward *mixed economy*—free enterprise under government regulation. By the late 1970s the success of the Common Market had made western Europe competitive with the United States.

In 1973 Britain joined the Common Market; tariffs between member nations, now including Greece, Eire, Spain, Belgium, Luxembourg, the Netherlands, Italy, and Germany, were eliminated; labor migration among members grew. Visas were abolished, so that citizens of member countries could pass from one country to another with ease. Common policies on railway and highway construction, on the adoption of the metric system, and on the relative value of national currencies were adopted. Power relations shifted further in 1973 as the United States withdrew from Vietnam and the oil-producing nations joined together to affect oil prices and supplies. By the 1980s serious discussion of a common currency, the Eurodollar, made it clear that, despite disagreement and disappointments, the basic idea of the Common Market was sound.

Great Britain

In Britain a general election in July 1945—after the war had ended in Europe—ousted Churchill and the Conservative party and for the first time gave the Labour party an absolute majority in the House of Commons. The Liberal party was practically extinguished. The new prime minister was Clement Attlee (1883–1967), a middle-class lawyer of quiet intellect who was committed to major social reform at home and the decolonization of much of the British Empire abroad.

The new government—with a mandate for social change—proceeded to take over, with compensation to the owners, the coal industry, railroads, and parts of commercial road transportation, and began to nationalize the steel industry. Britain already had a well-developed system of social insurance; this was now capped by a system of socialized medical care for all who wished it. The educational system was partly reformed to make it more democratic and to lengthen the period of compulsory education.

When the Conservatives, with Churchill still at their head, were returned to power in 1951 and remained there for twelve years, they halted the nationalization of steel but otherwise kept intact the socialism of their opponents, including the national health plan. Thus a social revolution was achieved without bitter divisiveness between the parties.

In the postwar years the British were not able to keep up with the extraordinary pace of technological innovation. The British automobile industry, for example, which immediately after the war gained a large share of the world market, yielded the lead in the 1950s to the Germans, with their inexpensive, standardized light car, the Volkswagen. Furthermore, Britain was one of the last countries in Europe to develop a system of super highways, completing its first modern highway only in 1969. The British were falling behind because they had been the first to industrialize and now their plants were the first to become outdated and inefficient. While British management and labor remained bound to traditional ways, the West Germans, buoyed by vast sums of money provided for their economic recovery by their former enemies, and especially by the United States, embarked on new paths.

Even in apparent prosperity, Britain remained in economic trouble. Continued pressure on the pound in the 1960s repeatedly required help from Britain's allies to maintain its value. This weakness of the pound signaled an unfavorable balance of trade in which the British were buying more from the rest of the world than they could sell. In the 1950s and 1960s, in what came to be called the "brain drain," some of Britain's most distinguished scientists and engineers left home to find higher pay and more modern laboratories in the United States, Canada, or Australia.

Under Harold Wilson (1916–   ), a shrewd politician often criticized for opportunism, the Labour party came to power in 1964 and governed until 1970. In 1966 Wilson froze wages and prices in an effort to restore the

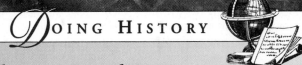

Is There a Grand Design in History?

Historians continue to debate their own purposes and their own methods. Some detect clear patterns and may even attempt to predict general trends for the future from their study of the past; others find history to be simply one event after another. Between these positions there are other, more moderate, defenses for the value of history. One finds it poetic, even beautiful, for it gives humanity a sense of itself, of what it is that makes it human. Another finds that while history may seem to lack any grand design, there is a form of design in this random appearance.

The following extracts, from two British historians of the twentieth century, present these views. The first is from G. M. Trevelyan (1876–1962); the second is from H. A. L. Fisher (1865–1940).

The appeal of History to us all is in the last analysis poetic. But the poetry of History does not consist of imagination roaming at large, but of imagination pursuing the fact and fastening upon it. That which compels the historian to "scorn delights and live laborious days" is the ardour of his own curiosity to know what really happened long ago in that land of mystery which we call the past. To peer into that magic mirror and see fresh figures there every day is burning desire that consumes and satisfies him all his life, that carries him each morning, eager as a lover, to the library and muniment room. It haunts him like a passion of almost terrible potency, because it is poetic. The dead were and are not. Their place knows them no more and is ours today. Yet they were once as real as we, and we shall tomorrow be shadows like them. In men's first astonishment over that unchanging mystery lay the origins of poetry, philosophy, and religion. From it, too, is derived in more modern times this peculiar call of the spirit, the type of intellectual curiosity that we name the historical sense. Unlike most forms of imaginative life it cannot be satisfied save by facts. . . . It is the fact about the past that is poetic; just because it really happened, it gathers round it all the inscrutable mystery of life and death and time. Let

the science and research of the historian find the fact, and let his imagination and art make clear its significance.*

One intellectual excitement has . . . been denied me. Men wiser and more learned than I have discovered in history a plot, a rhythm, a predetermined pattern. These harmonies are concealed from me. I can see only one emergency following upon another as wave follows upon wave, only one great fact with respect to which, since it is unique, there can be no generalizations, only one safe rule for the historian: that he should recognize in the development of human destinies the play of the contingent and the unforeseen. This is not a doctrine of cynicism and despair. The fact of progress is written plain and large on the page of history; but progress is not a law of nature. The ground gained by one generation may be lost by the next. The thoughts of men may flow into the channels which lead to disaster and barbarism.**

---

*G. M. Trevelyan, *The Present Position of History*, and **H. A. L. Fisher, *A History of Europe*, in *The Practical Cogitator: The Thinker's Anthology*, ed. Charles P. Curtis, Jr., and Ferris Greenslet (New York: Houghton Mifflin, 1983), pp. 123–24, 147–48.

---

balance between what the British spent and what they produced. In his own party, such measures were deeply unpopular and were regarded as exploiting the poor to support the rich. Wilson had to devalue the pound after heavy foreign pressure against it. Despite the unpopularity of his policies, by 1969 the deficits had disappeared and general prosperity continued, along with high taxes and rapid inflation. Prices were rising so fast that the gains from rising wages were largely illusory. The national health plan and education for working-class mothers had freed more women for an increasingly technical work force. But a spiral continued with only momentary breaks, regardless of the party in office, and except for a period of prosperity and relative confidence in the late 1960s and early 1970s, Britain's decline in relation to its competitors continued. By the 1980s, when the Conservative Margaret Thatcher (1925–   ) was prime minister, British inflation had been lessened but still remained dangerously high,

unemployment stood at depression levels, and the British standard of living had been surpassed by most nations in western Europe.

Even so, conditions of life improved for most people. The Labour government had imposed heavy income taxes on the well-to-do and burdensome death duties on the rich, using the income thus obtained to redistribute goods and services to the poor. An increasing number of new universities offered young people of all classes educational opportunities that had previously been available only to the upper and upper-middle classes.

In the postwar years race became serious issue in Britain for the first time. Indians, Pakistanis, West Indians, and Africans—Commonwealth subjects with British passports—left poor conditions at home and migrated freely to Britain in large numbers to take jobs in factories, public transportation, and hospitals. Despite its liberal and antiracist protestations, the Wilson government was forced to curtail immigration sharply. Some Conservative politicians predicted bloody race riots (which, in fact, occurred in 1981) unless black immigration was halted, and some extremists proposed that nonwhites already in Britain be deported.

Closely related to the race issue at home was the question of official British relations with southern Africa, to which the Labour government refused to sell arms because of the *apartheid* policies of the South African regime from the late 1940s. Brought gradually into place from 1948 to the late 1960s, apartheid laws (the term means "apartness") led to separate tracks of development for whites, blacks, coloureds, and Asians: a complex and highly expensive system of segregation by race. Relations deteriorated quickly after South African police fired upon a mass demonstration at Sharpeville in 1960, killing many black Africans. In 1961, under pressure from the prime ministers of Canada and India and with Britain's approval, the rigidly racist government of South Africa withdrew from the Commonwealth.

To this strain was added a major challenge to British authority when the white-dominated government in Southern Rhodesia, unwilling to accept a constitution that provided for full black participation in legislation, unilaterally declared Rhodesia independent of Great Britain, citing the American colonies in 1776 as a precedent. This move led to the imposition of sanctions by the United Nations and years of delicate negotiations punctuated by civil war, until a cease-fire, a constitution, and elections were ultimately accepted by all parties, and the Thatcher government declared Rhodesia independent, as Zimbabwe, in 1980.

Perhaps most persistently debilitating to British security, however, was the Irish problem, long quiescent, which arose again in the late 1960s. In Ulster (the northern counties that were still part of the United Kingdom), the Catholics generally formed a depressed class and were the first to lose their jobs in bad times. They were inflamed by the insistence of Protestant extremists (the Orangemen) on publicly celebrating the anniversaries of victories of William III in the 1690s that had ensured English domination over the region. Marching provocatively through Catholic districts, the Orangemen in the summer of 1969 precipitated disorders that began in Londonderry and spread to Belfast and other areas. The regular police were accused by Catholics of being mere tools of the Protestant oppressor and had to be disarmed. The British army then intervened to keep order.

The government of Eire suggested that the United Nations be given responsibility for the problem, a suggestion unacceptable to both the Northern Irish and British governments. Extremists of the south, the Irish Republican Army (IRA), who had always claimed the northern counties as part of a united Ireland, now revived their terroristic activities. But the IRA itself was split between a relatively moderate wing and the Provisionals (Provos), anarchists dedicated to nearly indiscriminate bombing. The level of fighting steadily escalated in Northern Ireland. In 1972 the British suspended the Northern Irish parliament and governed the province directly. In 1981 a group of prisoners, insisting that they not be treated as common criminals but as political prisoners, resorted to hunger strikes; although ten prisoners died, the British government continued to refuse political status to people they viewed as terrorists. In early 1995 there at last appeared the prospect of an enduring cease-fire.

Yet Britain was by no means wholly gloomy or depressed. Many British products continued to set the world's standards, especially for the upper classes. Beginning with the enormous popularity and stylistic innovations of the Beatles in the early 1960s, England for a time set the style for young people in other countries. Long hair for men, the unisex phenomenon in dress, the popularity of theatrical and eccentric clothes, the whole "mod" fashion syndrome that spread across the Atlantic and across the Channel started in England. Carnaby Street, Mick Jagger (1943–), and the Rolling Stones all had their imitators elsewhere, but the originals were English. Thus Britain continued to play a major role in fashion, music, social attitudes, and in tourism, through a tourist boom that brought millions of visitors to Britain, making it the front-ranking tourist nation in the world.

Most evident was the gradual erosion of rigid class distinctions in England, traditional bastion of political freedom and social inequality. The Beatles were all working-class in origin; lower class, too, were most leading English pacesetters of the new styles in song, dress, and behavior. These styles spread not only abroad, but among the middle and upper classes of the young in Britain as well, who were increasingly impatient to have done with the class sentiment that had so long pervaded English thought. By the 1990s even the monarchy, once revered, came under increasing criticism.

This impatience reflected the growing fragmentation of British social and economic life. The Labour party suffered from chronic disunity. In 1980 some of its members founded the Social Democratic party, hoping to take up the middle ground politically through an alliance with the remnant of the Liberals, but by the end of the decade this effort was dead. In 1982 a successful war with Argentina, occasioned by that country's attempt to occupy the Falkland Islands, buoyed national spirits, but Prime Minister Thatcher's popularity fell as unemployment continued to rise, even though she won her third election victory in 1987. On October 19, Black Friday, the stock market came down with a bump, and thereafter her popularity waned. An unpopular poll tax imposed in 1990 led to street riots. In November she resigned, having been in office for eleven and a half years.

France

Defeat by the Germans, brutal German occupation and economic exploitation, the spectacle of French collaboration with the enemy—all this was followed by a liberation that, despite the part played in it by the Fighting French and the French Resistance movement, was clearly the work of American, British, and Soviet arms. Nor had France since the early nineteenth century kept pace with the leading industrial nations in production, finance, or population growth. Only a rising birth rate gave cause for optimism. Hundreds of thousands of French men and women decided to have children—a clear sign of the recovery that lay ahead. The arrival of nearly a million refugees from the colonial war in Algeria in 1962–1963 and the influx of almost 4 million foreign workers made France, already a cosmopolitan nation, even more so, and assured the nation a labor supply on which to base its rapid industrial expansion.

The French government-in-exile, led by General de Gaulle, had easily reestablished in liberated France the old republican forms of government, called the Fourth Republic. But after de Gaulle temporarily retired from politics in 1946, the Fourth Republic began to look like the Third. Cabinets lasted on an average only a few months; to the old splinter parties was added a Communist party of renewed strength, openly dedicated to revolutionary change. After nine years of war, Indochina was lost in 1954; in the same year an active rebellion against the French in Algeria; Morocco and Tunisia were both lost in 1956, and the crisis deepened.

In 1958 de Gaulle took power again. A plebiscite confirmed a new constitution. The constitution of the new Fifth Republic provided for a president to be elected for a seven-year term by direct popular vote. An absolute majority was required, and, if not achieved in a first election, was to be obtained in a runoff between the two candidates with the most votes. Elected outright in 1958, de Gaulle was reelected to a second term in 1965 in such a runoff. Under the new constitution the French president appointed the premier, who could dissolve the legislature and order new elections at any time after the first year. Thus the new constitution gave the executive more power, the legislature much less.

De Gaulle's enemies soon called him a dictator, the personification of French haughtiness and superiority. He was obstinate, opinionated, and authoritarian; yet he was also consistent, clear, capable, and utterly committed to creating a stable and progressive French state. He intended that France be taken seriously in world affairs. To this end he fought to keep Britain out of the Common Market, worked to prevent American dominance in Europe, and sought to establish a creditable French military presence. He did not want to see France bled by further colonial wars, and though he believed strongly in the unity of all French-speaking peoples (seeking even to establish a separate cultural mission to the French-speaking people of Quebec), he nonetheless worked out a settlement making Algeria independent in 1962.

Starting with Marshall Plan aid in 1947, great economic and social changes began in France. A full-scale reorientation of the economy was undertaken in accordance with the practices of modern industry. Helped by foreign investment, especially American, France began to experience a real boom. Prosperity meant that for the first time the French, by the hundreds of thousands, bought cars, television sets, and record players; that they traveled in ever growing numbers; that they experienced fearful traffic jams; and that those who found the new ways unsettling blamed all the changes on the Americans.

Those who feared that France would adopt the new British-American culture emphasized the continuity, unity, complexity, and alleged purity of the French language, and looked for their own cultural influences to offset Americanization and "Coca-Colanization."

De Gaulle retained a strong personal dislike of *les Anglo-Saxons*. The thought of such supranational bodies as the Common Market and NATO that could rob France of sovereignty even to a small degree was uncomfortable, and talk of a United States of Europe was totally unacceptable. He spoke instead of *Europe des patries*, a "Europe of fatherlands," in which France would take the lead. But to do this France must have its own atomic weapons. Therefore de Gaulle refused to join the United States, Great Britain, and the Soviet Union in a treaty barring atomic tests, and France continued to test nuclear weapons in the atmosphere, exploding its first hydrogen bomb in 1968. Vigorously opposed to communism at home, de Gaulle nonetheless came to terms with the Soviet Union; the Soviets, he argued, no longer represented the threat to the general peace that they had represented in the 1950s. In balancing the scales against the industrial and military power of the United States and Britain, France needed friends. To South America, to Canada, to Poland, and to Romania, de Gaulle carried his message that France would be the leader of Europe.

In the spring of 1968, however, while de Gaulle was in Romania, Paris erupted. The French universities had been ignored by the regime in a period when the young throughout western Europe were bursting with resentment against "the machine civilization" of the cold war society. Students in Paris occupied university buildings, fought the police, and eventually drew a reluctant Communist party into the battle in order that it not lose the support of the French workers, who had already begun to strike in sympathy with the students.

De Gaulle returned to Paris, assured himself of army support, proposed a referendum, which he was obliged to abandon in favor of new elections, and then won a great victory at the polls, obtaining larger majority in the legislature than before. His new minister of education, acknowledging the legitimacy of many of the grievances of the students, pushed through the legislature a reform bill decentralizing the educational system. De Gaulle now staked his political future on the issue of regional reform in a public referendum—and lost. As he had done before, he withdrew into private life. In the 1969 elections the Gaullists were returned to office with a substantial majority, and Georges Pompidou (1911–1974) became president of France.

France now entered more readily into competition rather than confrontation with its former allies. To make the French more competitive, the franc was devalued. The veto against Britain's entry into the Common Market was abandoned, and, without rejoining NATO, France began more formal cooperation with it. An economic recession began in 1973, however, and public confidence wavered. France returned to governments that could administer programs only with the help of complex coalitions, as the aristocratic Valéry Giscard d' Estaing (1926–) became president. Fearful of the left, and ultimately beset by political scandal, Giscard did not press the social reform his platform had promised. From 1972 to 1977 the Socialist and Communist parties formed a common front to oppose the right and center parties, but the communists withdrew in 1977.

In 1981 an able Socialist party regular who had worked to broaden the socialist base by weakening the communists, their traditional enemies, won the presidential election. This man, François Mitterrand (1916–), brought four communists into his cabinet and announced plans to nationalize certain sectors of industry. At the same time, Mitterrand took a strongly anti-Soviet stance over the Soviet Union's invasion of Afghanistan, which had begun in December 1979. He declared himself committed to a mixed-enterprise economy and to cooperation with the Americans in their efforts to renew disarmament talks while seeking to base a nuclear missile force within Europe. In 1986 France began a graduated process of industrial privatization, achieved by 1993, and in 1995, Mitterand retired.

France was one of the first countries to face the problem of large-scale immigration from former colonies, followed by substantial new immigration from politically unstable, repressive, or poverty-stricken states. At first France accepted Muslim immigrants from North Africa and French-speaking blacks from sub-Saharan Africa, but by the 1990s public opinion was turning against the influx of immigrants, many of whom were in fact refugees. In 1993 France restricted entry and passed laws making it possible to expel foreigners more easily. In the meantime the same problem—that of international "boat people"—became serious in the United States, to which thousands of Cubans and Haitians were fleeing. Germany, attractive to workers from the Balkans and Turkey, experienced anti-immigrant rioting. Britain had long since closed its doors to much Commonwealth immigration, especially South Asian and West Indian. France thus joined other Western nations in turning to more restrictive policies in the face of a worldwide problem that no one nation could solve and that calls for action from the United Nations barely seemed to touch.

The Two Germanies

The West German postwar recovery was the most remarkable of all. The wartime destruction of much of Germany's industrial plant had paradoxically proved beneficial; the new plant was built with the latest technological equipment. The Allied High Commission gradually abolished controls over German industry, save for atomic energy and certain military restrictions. It provided economic aid and scaled down prewar German debts. By the early 1950s West Germany had a favorable balance of trade and a rate of industrial growth as high as 10 percent a year.

The West German gross national product rose from $23 billion in 1950 to $103 billion in 1964, with no serious monetary inflation. This prosperity was spread through all classes of society. The working class in West Germany had begun to enjoy affluence; new buildings rose everywhere, while superhighways grew overcrowded and had to be widened and extended. The economic miracle attracted population into West Germany from southern Europe and drew other Germans out of East Germany into the Federal Republic. East Germany thus had a net loss in population as West Germany boomed. By the late 1960s the German birth rate had fallen, however, and in the 1980s the population had stabilized at 62 million. This made for a highly industrialized, close-knit, urban nation.

The independent West German state had a constitution that provided for a legislature whose lower house represented the people directly and whose upper house represented the states (*Länder*). The president, elected by a special assembly for a five-year term, was largely a ceremonial figure. Real executive leadership was vested in the chancellor, a prime minister dependent on a parliamentary majority. Under the firm leadership of Konrad Adenauer (1876–1967), the Christian Democrats held power until 1961. A Rhineland Catholic, former mayor of Cologne, conservative, pro-French, and democratic, Adenauer was forced to retire only because of age and continued to wield enough influence to weaken his successor, Ludwig Erhard (1897–1977), a Protestant and professional economist, who remained in office for five more years.

Germany had been rather successfully "deNazified"—a requirement stipulated by the Allied High Commission. As a result of the Nuremburg trials in 1946, seventy-four major Nazi leaders were convicted of war crimes. In general, lower-level Nazis were required only to demonstrate that they fully accepted the new democratic government; to have dismissed all civil servants who had held posts under the Nazi regime would have utterly crippled any administrative recovery. Some Nazis who had escaped to other parts of the world, notably South America, continued to be hunted out, and if captured, were tried for war crimes.

The major political question remained that of an eventual reunion with communist-dominated East Germany. Neither Germany recognized the other diplomatically. After years during which the East Germans, attracted by better living conditions in West Germany, crossed the border by the tens of thousands, the East German government in August 1961 began building a wall between the two parts of Berlin. Though on special holidays families in West Berlin were allowed to cross into East Berlin briefly to visit relatives and friends, the wall stood as the visible symbol of a divided Germany.

As a consequence of the cold war, the Americans, British, and French permitted the West Germans to rearm early in the 1950s and to join NATO. Military conscription was introduced in 1955, and by 1970 West Germany had developed a sizable modern military. Access to the atom bomb was not included in this rearmament. Even so, and despite low-key political leadership, the spectacle of a rearmed Germany caused much concern—in the Soviet bloc, in Britain, and among Jewish voters in all nations.

French president Charles de Gaulle met with West German chancellor Konrad Adenauer (left) at the Elysée Palace in July 1962 to discuss the political union of Europe and the formation of the Common Market.
UPI/Bettmann Newsphotos

Chancellor Erhard's government fell in 1966, when a small disciplined party, the Free Democrats, in coalition with which the Christian Democrats were ruling, refused to support his proposals for higher taxes. The Christian Democrats now proposed a "grand coalition" with their chief opponents, the Social Democrats. The very popular mayor of West Berlin, Willy Brandt (1913–   ), became vice-chancellor and foreign minister. This grand coalition commanded popular support, and it lasted until the elections of 1969.

In these elections Brandt, a Social Democrat, became chancellor and formed a coalition in his turn with the Free Democrats. Brandt moved slowly and cautiously to open discussions with the East Germans. The chief stumbling block was Soviet fear of West Germany. It gradually became apparent that a treaty between West Germany and the Soviet Union in which both renounced the use of force would be one of the necessary preliminaries. In the summer of 1970 Brandt reached agreement with the Soviets on the text of such a treaty. It recognized all existing European frontiers, which Germans and Soviets agreed never to try to alter by force, leaving open future negotiations. The second step was an agreement with Poland, which Brandt concluded during 1970. Brandt's *Ostpolitik*, or Eastern policy, culminated in a treaty with Czechoslovakia and in the entry of both Germanies into the United Nations in 1973. A form of detente with the Soviet bloc was nearly

achieved, when in 1974 Brandt resigned upon the discovery that one of his closest assistants had been an East German spy, a discovery that renewed German fears of the designs of the Soviet bloc.

The 1970s also dimmed the West German economic miracle. While the German inflation rate, roughly 6 percent in 1975, was mild compared to the rest of Europe, and the growth rate continued at over 5 percent, unemployment began to climb. German social services were not among the best in the world, and German per capita income had surpassed that of the nations that had defeated Germany in Europe in World Word II, but a deep-seated memory of the inflation that had destroyed the democratic hopes of Weimar made the Germans cautious and insecure. Waves of terrorism further disconcerted the German leadership. Only Brandt, and after 1974 Helmut Schmidt (1918–   ), had seemed to provide the vigorous leadership the Germans had enjoyed under Adenauer. Together with other nations in the West, Germany often appeared to lack able new leaders with dramatic solutions to the nation's problems. Although the electorate recognized that the range of dramatic new solutions was severely limited by the constraints of superpower confrontation and an eroding economy, they nonetheless hoped for a renewal of vigor at the top. Politics in the Federal Republic became fragmented when the grand coalition broke up, with powerful leaders emerging on the

West Berlin citizens continue their vigil atop the Berlin Wall in front of the Brandenburg Gate, November 10, 1989. The opening of the Berlin Wall symbolized the collapse of the communist governments in eastern Europe.

Reuters/David Brauchli/The Bettmann Archive

basis of strong local support. In 1982 the Christian Democrats, led by Helmut Kohl (1930–   ), won a landslide victory.

West Germany's economic growth, though slowed, remained prodigious, and chancellor Kohl felt emboldened to pursue a more independent course in international affairs. While he kept West Germany in NATO, he forced the removal of nuclear missiles that were deployed on German soil and intended for Soviet targets, and he called for negotiations with the Soviet Union on reducing short-range missiles, causing a rift with both Britain and the United States. Faced with protests at home, with soaring social costs, and signs of a resurgence from the political right, Kohl moved to take advantage of the unexpected and overwhelming changes in eastern Europe and the Soviet Union. Soon the unthinkable was being thought on both sides of the rapidly crumbling Iron Curtain, and with communist leadership abandoned in East Germany, reunification appeared possible.

While much of western Europe worried about a reunited Germany, which with 80 million people and controlling 40 percent of Europe's industrial production could well dominate the European Community, Kohl moved quickly, and one of the richest capitalist nations absorbed one of the richest formerly communist countries to create a united Germany in October 1990. In December the first parliament for all of Germany since the end of World War II was elected. The new nation took the title Federal Republic of Germany, and East Germany acceded to the jurisdiction of West German Basic Law. The newly united nation set about the incredibly complex problem of integrating two economies, two industrial forces with vastly different experiences, two research establishments for science and technology, two armies, two trade policies, and even two Olympic teams. The problem proved daunting, for East Germans were not prepared for a free market economy, and economic problems soon gave rise to neo-Nazi groups and attacks on minorities.

Italy

Unlike Germany, Italy was in turmoil for much of its postwar period. In 1946 a plebiscite showed 54 percent of the voters in favor of a republic, which was therefore established. Some monarchists and fascists remained, but neither group influenced parliamentary politics to any great extent. A strong Christian Democratic party (a Catholic party with a relatively liberal program) held power under a succession of leaders, with support from other groups. The government broke up large landed estates in the south to redistribute the land. A very strong Communist party, with which the larger faction of the Socialists was allied, offered a persistent challenge. In the early 1960s a series of complicated negotiations began a process called the *apertura a sinistra* the "opening to the left," in which the Christian Democrats won over some Socialist support.

Italy's economic growth between 1953 and 1966 was so remarkable that the Italians, too, spoke of an economic miracle. As In France, this growth was achieved with some government ownership and with much government regulation and planning. Membership in the Common Market gave Italian enterprise opportunities that it had never had before. The grave problems of southern Italy, Sardinia, and Sicily were attacked by programs of investments, by providing jobs in the north or in Germany or Switzerland for the surplus workers of the south, and by old-age pensions. In the Italian balance of payments, an income of about $1 billion annually from tourists proved enormously important. Italian fashions became popular throughout the world, further bolstering both the economy and the national sense of well-being. The Italian motion picture industry began to rival that of France and ultimately overtook the immediate postwar leader, Britain.

By the late 1960s Italian political stability began to crumble, in part due to severe internal political strains within the Christian Democratic party, and in part due to the uncertainty of the party's relationship with its supposed partners, the Socialists. In part it was also due to the inflation that Italy was perhaps less able to bear than were the advanced industrial nations. Strikes occurred sporadically and unpredictably, and 1969 was marked by mass strikes.

The Italian bureaucracy was marked by no-show jobs, scandal, corruption, and pettiness. Economic mismanagement became evident in the 1970s. The Italian inflation rate soared; nearly 2 million Italians were unemployed. By 1974 Italy had a huge trade deficit and had to turn to the International Monetary Fund and to West Germany for credit. The government was unable to restrain demands for wage increases, which ran at 30 percent annually, spurring further inflation in prices and overburdening the middle class. The Mafia, a centuries-old alliance of secret criminal societies organized along feudal lines and particularly powerful in Sicily, began to show itself overtly in southern Italy. Terrorists openly attacked judges, teachers, journalists, and police officers in the streets. In 1978 one group, the Red Brigade, kidnapped former premier Aldo Moro (1916–1978) and murdered him after the Italian government refused to negotiate his release. The universities were in chaos; students throughout the nation went on frequent and prolonged strikes, so that the ablest sought their education in other countries. Of all the nations of western Europe, Italy's experiment with liberal democracy seemed most clearly on trial.

During this time the large Italian Communist party increased in size and organizing skills. In 1976 the communists polled 35 percent of the popular vote for the Chamber of Deputies. Led by Enrico Berlinguer (1922–1984), the Communists declared their desire to enter into a coalition government with their former enemies and promised to abide by the constitution and to keep Italy in NATO. The United States doubted the sincerity of these promises and supported those Italian leaders best able to block Berlinguer's move toward power. But by entering into what it called a "historic compromise," the Communist party won a new middle-class following. In 1978 the Communist party was granted equality with other parties in shaping government policies when it promised to support a national unity government. Ministries continued to change hands with bewildering rapidity in Italy, the entire cabinet resigning in 1981 when it was revealed that many officials were members of an illegal and secret Masonic lodge. Scandals in banking and politics, the kidnapping of public officials, instability in leadership, and recurrent social unrest continued to plague Italy throughout the 1980s and 1990s.

The Vatican

In the eye of the hurricane, one force for continuity seemed clear. The pope, based in the Vatican City, in the heart of Rome, began to assert bold new initiatives in the political sphere, while holding to traditional positions on doctrinal church affairs. The feeling that Pope Pius XII (r. 1939–1958) had not done enough forestall World War II or to assist beleaguered Jews within the Nazi-controlled nations persisted, and after the war he and his successors sought to take clear positions on world affairs.

These positions were defined in the context of substantial changes within the church itself. The most extensive changes were initiated by Pope John XXIII (r. 1958–1963), who in 1959 called the twenty-first Ecumenical Council of the church, in a tradition begun by Constantine the Great in the fourth century. Known as Vatican II, this council continued to meet under his successor, Pope Paul VI (r. 1963–1978). The council made many changes in the liturgy, encouraged celebration of Mass in vernacular languages, and opened up relations with many other denominations.

While the church continued to be identified in many parts of the world with the forces of conservatism—especially in its opposition to women clergy, in its emphasis on the child-bearing responsibilities of women, and in its support of Catholic dictators in South America—elsewhere the church was increasingly associated with the forces of reform. Radical priests in Central America, innovative church leaders in North America, and activist bishops in the non-Western world were urging the church to face the statistical fact that most Catholics apparently practiced some form of birth control, argued that the church should be a force for land reforms that would benefit the peasants, and held that the nature of the church service needed to be changed even further if the younger generation were to be retained.

These trends, marked by a concern for public affairs, continued under a dynamic new pope, John Paul II, elected in 1978 as the youngest pope since 1846 and the first non-Italian pope since the sixteenth century. A Pole, Karol Wojtyla (1920–   ), former archbishop of Kracow, worked to expand the role of the church in the non-Western world. He made extensive overseas visits, including to the United States, where church doctrine was frequently questioned by younger priests, and took strong positions against military aggression, political terrorism, and abortion. Of particular concern to this pope was the government suppression of the Polish Solidarity movement in 1981–1982. John Paul was seriously injured in an assassination attempt in Rome in 1981, but he recovered and was able to pay an official visit to his native Poland in 1983 and thereafter to many other nations, including a triumphant trip to the Philippines in 1995.

Other Western European Countries

The Low Countries shared the general European prosperity and the common problems. In Belgium, which enjoyed great material well-being, the chronic difficulties between the minority of French-speaking Walloons and the majority of Dutch-speaking Flemings continued to worsen and to threaten stability. The Netherlands at first enjoyed prosperity and stability, though there, too, student unrest, terrorist outbreaks, and serious environmental pollution created persistent problems. Mass emigration from Indonesia and Suriname, which became independent in 1975, revealed racial prejudices for the first time within

Women as heads of state: Gro Harlem Brundtland of Norway in 1990; Kim Campbell of Canada in 1993; Mary Eugenia Charles of Dominica in 1980; Mary Robinson of Ireland in 1990; Chandrika Bandaranaike Kumaratongo of Sri Lanka in 1994; Corazon Aquino of the Philippines in 1986; Violeta Barrios de Chamorro of Nicaragua in 1990; Tansü Ciller of Turkey in 1994; Vigdis Finnbogadottir of Iceland in 1980; Benazir Bhutto of Pakistan in 1988; and Edith Cresson of France and Khaleda Zia of Bangladesh, both elected prime ministers in 1991.

AP/Wide World Photos; UPI/Bettmann Newsphotos; Department of Foreign Affairs, Dublin; Hoda Bakhshandaji/Black Star; Cindy Karp/Black Star; Charles Crowell/Black Star

the Netherlands. A political scandal over the business activities of Queen Juliana (r. 1948–1980), which contributed to her abdication in favor of her daughter Beatrix (1938–   ), challenged even the monarchy.

Spain under Franco had taken major steps toward modernization and a few mild measures to relax political tyranny. Low wages and bitter government opposition to the Basques prevented full economic or political stability. Five languages were accorded formal recognition: Spanish, Catalan, Basque, Galician (a Portuguese dialect), and Valencian (a Spanish dialect). Franco arranged that after his death the monarchy would be restored under Prince Juan Carlos (1938–   ), grandson of Alfonso XIII, and in 1975 Juan Carlos became king. The actual government remained in the hands of political parties,

since Juan Carlos was a constitutional monarch. Still, it was Juan Carlos who presided over the dissolution of many of Franco's institutions.

The first free elections since the Spanish Civil War took place in 1976, returning moderates and democratic socialists to office. As Spain turned from agriculture to industry, and as tourism grew larger in its balance to payments, the need for stability became paramount. To this end Spain attempted in 1982 to come to a peaceful settlement with Britain over a longstanding dispute concerning ownership of Gibraltar, and the Spanish government granted substantial home rule to Catalonia and the Basque lands in 1980.

Elsewhere in the Mediterranean democracy was also restored. In 1968 the Portuguese dictator Salazar, too ill to continue, passed the government to a successor. In 1974 a military coup by radical Portuguese army officers brought down the dictatorship. For a time the army junta worked in alliance with Portuguese communists, who were supported by the trade unions, the peasants of southern Portugal, and much of the press. However, in the elections of 1975 the Socialists won the largest following. Portugal was faced with formidable problems: a continuing colonial war that was feeding the highest rate (34 percent) of inflation in Europe, unproductive agricultural practices, and the absence of a solid industrial base. As the war in Africa went badly, unemployment in Portugal was forced upward by an influx of refugees from the colonies. Portugal became dependent on foreign loans, and the Socialists had to incorporate the center and some right-of-center elements into a coalition government to remain in office. In the 1980s, with the colonial war over and the former colonies now independent states, the inflation rate began to moderate, but political stability continued to elude the Portuguese people.

Greece, too, had been ruled by a military junta. The 1950s and early 1960s had been prosperous years. By 1965 industrialization had become more important than agriculture, tourism was producing a large income, and the Greek merchant fleet prospered. Aid under the Truman Doctrine had stabilized both Greece and Turkey, and the Americans continued to support Greece, regardless of the government in power, as an important bulwark against the Iron Curtain countries. With the end of the Greek Civil War in 1955, a succession of ministries had struggled for authority until April 1967, when several army officers (later called "the colonels") staged a coup and established a right-wing military dictatorship. The king went into exile, the colonels suspended civil liberties, and the government became increasingly brutal.

World opinion was turning against the colonels when they decided in 1974 on a gamble intended to win nationalist support. They tried to overthrow Archbishop Makarios III (1913–1977), the president of Cyprus, who, the colonels felt, was not sufficiently aggressive against the Turkish minority on that island. This led to a full-scale Turkish invasion of Cyprus and its occupation by Turkish forces, subjecting the large Greek majority (75 percent of the population) to military rule. The Greek regime was humiliated. It had lost its war, lost the Greek Cypriots, driven a wedge deep into NATO (since both Greece and Turkey were members), and angered the United States. Elections late in 1974 brought back civilian government under Konstantin Karamanlis (1907–   ). The monarchy was abolished, the galloping inflation rate was brought under reasonable control, and the Western nations attempted to mediate the hostility between Greece and Turkey. However, they were unsuccessful, and the Greek coalition governments of the late 1970s to mid-1980s continued to be marked by political instability.

The general exception to this instability was Scandinavia. The three constitutional monarchies of Denmark, Norway, and Sweden were progressive, democratic, and highly prosperous. The Scandinavians went further and more rapidly in providing full equality to women than had any other countries in the world. Standards of living soared, to become among the highest in the world. To varying degrees the Scandinavian countries embarked on substantial social-welfare programs. Denmark and Sweden in particular committed themselves to the international marketplace, requiring all schoolchildren to learn English, the new international language of trade. Denmark set the pace in design, especially of furniture, kitchenwares, and fabrics. By the 1980s the Danish per capita income was well above that of the United States, once the richest nation in the world.

Sweden, which had enjoyed industrial growth as a neutral during World War II, experienced similar prosperity. Its steel, automobile, shipbuilding, and machine industries were modernized and progressive, as were its labor policies. Heralded as representing "the middle way," Sweden became a democratic and socialist state with a per capita income third only to Denmark and Belgium.

For forty years the Social Democratic party ruled in Sweden, but by 1976 inflation had begun to soar, and grave doubts about social policy at home and foreign policy abroad introduced a period of modest political instability. By the 1980s the troubles the Swedes had seemed to have avoided were upon them: Soviet submarines were found spying in Swedish waters; the domestic crime rate was rising dramatically; and in 1980 a massive series of strikes almost brought the country to an industrial standstill. The assassination in Stockholm of its internationally minded and popular socialist premier Olaf Palme (1927–1986) marked a growing sense of doubt about the Swedish political future. While still maintaining one of the world's highest per capita gross national products, Sweden found it was not immune to the problems that plagued other democracies.

NORTH AMERICA

Nor could the largest and most populous of the Western democracies avoid instability even though it was to provide the leadership for the Western alliance and was clearly a superpower in trade and military terms. Though racked by social tensions at times, the United States was markedly prosperous and politically stable for much of this period. Nonetheless, significant new elements were introduced to the American sense.

The United States

Rather than reverting to isolation, the United States took the lead in 1945 in organizing both the United Nations and a network of alliances. It put through vigorous programs of economic aid to other countries, first through the Marshall Plan, then by direct assistance to the newly independent former colonies, and also by massive assistance through internationally organized financial institutions, such as the International Monetary Fund and the World

Bank. Both political parties generally endorsed these programs; not until the American government began to suffer deep economic strains in its domestic programs under the impact of the escalating cost of the war in Vietnam did the sums appropriated or foreign aid begin to be cut.

Agreement between the Republican and Democratic parties on foreign policy was generally shared on domestic issues as well. Broadly, the Democrats, except for their southern wing, were somewhat more committed to interventionist positions in the economy, to social-welfare programs, and to expanding civil liberties. The Republicans were relatively more committed to laissez-faire positions on the economy and government, to somewhat more cautious programs for social welfare, and to the need to more closely match a sense of duty with a sense of rights in civil liberties. However, the majority of the Republican party either did not wish, or did not consider it politically possible, to undo the major programs associated with Roosevelt's New Deal.

During his eight years as president (1953–1961) Dwight D. Eisenhower not only did not repeal the New Deal enactments but even expanded the system of Social Security. Nor did the Republicans shift the bases of foreign policy. Eisenhower's secretary of state, John Foster Dulles (1888–1959), spoke of "rolling the Russians back" and "liberating" their satellites in eastern Europe, but when he was challenged by Soviet military intervention in Hungary in 1956, he was unable to do anything, and the Democrats had no alternative policy to offer.

The early 1950s brought an episode in which a single senator, Joseph McCarthy (1908–1957) of Wisconsin, attacked American civil servants and others, whom he called communists. A frightened people, not used to defeat, was persuaded that communists in high places had "lost" China or "sold" eastern Europe to the international communist movement. McCarthy's attacks fed upon these unproved fears, as he attacked and demoralized the diplomatic service, the movie industry, and university faculties. McCarthy's tactics were similar to the Salem witch trials of the seventeenth century, being based on fear and rumor, thus posing a challenge to the constitution's insistence on strict canons of evidence. In 1954 McCarthy was condemned by his fellow senators for abuse of his powers.

The United States was generally prosperous and productive during the decades following World War II. So remarkable was the steady growth of the gross national product that it appeared that the Americans had learned how to avoid depression altogether. The general affluence did not, however, by any means filter down satisfactorily to the society's poorest members. President Lyndon Johnson's series of programs to assist the poor had to be abandoned because of the heavy expense of the war in Vietnam. The strains imposed by the war, accompanied by increasing domestic unrest, inflation, and rising unemployment, continued to mount, though unevenly.

That so many of the poor in the United States were black worsened what was already the gravest American social problem. Though individual blacks had won recognition in the arts, in sports, in entertainment, and often in business and the professions, blacks in general were handicapped by the failure of American society to provide them with equal opportunities for education and for jobs. This was true not only in the South but also in the cities of the North, where during the war hundreds of thousands of blacks had flocked to work.

In 1954 in *Brown* v. *Board of Education of Topeka*, the Supreme Court unanimously declared that the existence of separate compulsory public schools for blacks was unconstitutional. The years that followed saw varying degrees of compliance with the new requirement. Most parts of the South were determined to disobey the Court by one means or another, or if they obeyed, to admit only token numbers of black students to white schools. The many efforts to speed compliance met with some success, and by 1970 in some southern cities, such as Atlanta, desegregation was well advanced.

But the existence of black ghettos in the northern cities and the prevalence of neighborhood schools everywhere meant that public education in New York or Boston was often as segregated as in Mississippi. Northern whites often opposed busing children to schools out of their home neighborhoods as a method of balancing the numbers of black and white children. Southern white support for the Republican, Richard M. Nixon, in the election of 1968 left him with a political debt to southern politicians, and many observers felt that the diminished efforts of the federal government to enforce desegregation during his administration reflected an effort to repay this debt. The problem of equal education for all, including the rapidly increasing number of predominantly Spanish-speaking students, remained a serious one into the 1990s.

The drive to improve conditions for African-Americans extended far beyond education, however. In the late 1950s and early 1960s activist whites and blacks worked to increase the registration of black voters in the South and to liberalize real estate practices in the North. Both drives made considerable headway, though some whites responded with intimidation and terror, others by quietly refusing to be involved. Some blacks, feeling that justice would never be gained by gradual means, turned away from organizations such as the National Association for the Advancement of Colored People (NAACP), which had traditionally preferred to work by persuasion, toward more militant groups. The Reverend Martin Luther King, Jr. (1926–1968)—a nonviolent black minister from the South who in 1955 had sponsored a successful black boycott of segregated buses in Montgomery, Alabama, and in 1957 had founded the Southern Christian Leadership Conference to press for nonviolent change throughout the South—lost some of his large following to other groups advocating Black Power.

During the summers of 1965 through 1967 severe rioting broke out in Los Angeles, Newark, Detroit, and other northern cities. Blacks burned their own neighborhoods, looted shops, and fought with the police. The passage of a federal Civil Rights Act in 1968 and the outlawing of discrimination in real estate transactions did not calm the stormy situation. Black violence aroused bitter protest, even among white moderates who favored the

THE WRITTEN RECORD

I Have a Dream

In 1963, on the occasion of a massive civil rights rally held in the U.S. capital, Martin Luther King gave his most famous speech.

Fivescore years ago, a great American signed the Emancipation Proclamation. This momentous decree came as a great beacon light of hope to millions of Negro slaves who had been seared in the flames of withering injustice. It came as a joyous daybreak to end the long night of their captivity.

But one hundred years later, the Negro still is not free; one hundred years later, the life of the Negro is still sadly crippled by the manacles of segregation and the chains of discrimination; one hundred years later, the Negro lives on a lonely island of poverty in the midst of a vast ocean of material prosperity; one hundred years later, the Negro is still languishing in the corners of American society and finds himself in exile in his own land.

So we've come here today to dramatize a shameful condition. In a sense we've come to our nation's capital to cash a check. When the architects of our republic wrote the magnificent words of the Constitution and the Declaration of Independence, they were signing a promissory note to which every American was to fall heir. This note was the promise that all men, yes, black men as well as white men, would be guaranteed the inalienable rights of life, liberty, and the pursuit of happiness.

It is obvious today that America has defaulted on this promissory note in so far as her citizens of color are concerned. Instead of honoring this sacred obligation, America has given the Negro people a bad check; a check which has come back marked "insufficient funds." We refuse to believe that there are insufficient funds in the great vaults of opportunity of this nation. And so we've come to cash this check, a check that will give us upon demand the riches of freedom and the security of justice. . . .

There are those who are asking the devotees of Civil Rights, "When will you be satisfied?" We can never be satisfied as long as the Negro is the victim of the unspeakable horrors of police brutality; we can never be satisfied as long as our bodies, heavy with the fatigue of travel, cannot gain lodging in the motels of the highways and the hotels of the cities; we cannot be satisfied as long as the Negro's basic mobility is from a smaller ghetto to a larger one; we can never be satisfied as long as our children are stripped of their selfhood and robbed of their dignity by signs stating "For Whites Only"; we cannot be satisfied as long as the Negro in Mississippi cannot vote and a Negro in New York believes he has nothing for which to vote. No! no, we are not satisfied, and we will not be satisfied until "justice rolls down like waters and righteousness like a mighty stream." . . .

I say to you today, my friends, so even though we face the difficulties of today and tomorrow, I still have a dream. It is a dream deeply rooted in the American dream. I have a dream that one day this nation will rise up and live out the true meaning of its creed, "We hold these truths to be self-evident, that all men are created equal." I have a dream that one day on the red hills of Georgia, sons of former slaves and the sons of former slave owners will be able to sit down together at the table of brotherhood. I have a dream that one day even the state of Mississippi, a state sweltering with the heat of injustice, sweltering with the heat of oppression, will be transformed into an oasis of freedom and justice. I have a dream that my four little children will one day live in a nation where they will not be judged by the color of their skin, but by the content of their character.

I have a dream today!

Flip Schulke, ed., *Martin Luther King, Jr.: A Documentary, Montgomery to Memphis* (New York: Norton, n.d.), p. 218.

---

black advance but were growing more and more anxious about public order.

The new wave of violence in American life derived not only from the race question. Democrat John F. Kennedy, the first Roman Catholic to be elected president, succeeding Eisenhower and defeating vice-president Nixon (1960), was a young man of intelligence, personal elegance, and charm. To the young he seemed to offer a new start and charismatic leadership, and abroad he was widely respected. His New Frontier envisioned federally sponsored medical care for the aged, tax reform, civil rights, and antipoverty measures. But Kennedy had deeply angered the far right and was hated for his efforts to fight organized crime and to press forward with civil rights. He was assassinated in 1963 by Lee Harvey Oswald (1939–1963) while riding through Dallas in a motorcade. Televised details of the crime came into every American home, as did the subsequent murder of the assassin.

The failure of the nation to protect its president, of the Dallas police to protect the accused assassin, and of subsequent investigations to come to a definite conclusion about the assassination added to the national sense of suspicion and fear. The murder of Martin Luther King, Jr. in 1968, and the murder of President Kennedy's brother, Senator Robert F. Kennedy of New York, while he was campaigning to secure the Democratic nomination for the presidency in 1968, all combined to produce a major public revulsion. Though many black civil rights leaders continued to advocate nonviolent tactics to achieve their goals, King's murder in particular gave new strength to those leaders who argued that full equality could be achieved for blacks in the United States only through the use of force.

Crime continued to present a severe and growing problem, and easy access to guns continued to set the United States apart from all other nations. Some saw the failure to enact strong anti-gun laws as a sign that the United States did not realize it was no longer a frontier society; others felt that the constitution guaranteed the right to bear arms, and they argued that infringements on this right were an attack on a basic civil liberty. These three assassinations, as well as subsequent attempts on other presidents and public figures, would stir a debate that clearly posed the democratic dilemma of how best to define the public good.

After the assassination of John Kennedy, Vice-President Lyndon B. Johnson assumed office and, in an intensive legislative drive, successfully put through much of the social program that Kennedy had not been able to achieve. His goal, he said, was to create the Great Society. But the gains were outweighed in the public mind by the cost in life and money of the war in Vietnam and by the rising discontent with a society that could not fairly distribute its own affluence.

Children of the well-to-do were "opting out" of society in large numbers. Some took drugs—the increasingly fashionable marijuana, heroin, cocaine, or LSD. Many dropped out of school and left home: the "hippies" of the late 1960s. Behind their veneer of long hair and strange clothing they revealed much about which a thoughtful segment of society worried: that the structure of society was alienating many young people; that the cost of drugs was leading to ever higher crime rates; that a gap was opening between generations; that the family as a unit for promoting stability was being threatened.

Other young people rebelled actively against the institutions of their immediate world—the university and the draft board. Student violence in 1968 and 1969 sometimes took the form of sit-ins or building seizures, accompanied by the disruption of classes, the theft of documents from files, and the attempted intimidation of classmates, professors, or administrators. When university authorities summoned police or the National Guard to quell the violence, the effect often was to turn moderate students into radicals. The universities were thus faced with a painful dilemma: either to submit to intimidation and violence, usually from the left, or to fight, thus vastly increasing the numbers of the disenchanted. When the National Guard fired into a student demonstration at Kent State University in Ohio in 1970, killing four white students, and a few days later police in Jackson, Mississippi, killed two more who were black, there was a cry of outrage and guilt on university campuses and in homes throughout the nation.

The radical protests, the campus violence, and the long battle in the media and in Congress between "hawks" (who favored pursuing the war in Vietnam with vigor) and "doves" (who considered the war immoral, impractical, or lost) had injected a high level of apprehension and confusion into the lives of most Americans. By 1967 the total number of casualties in Vietnam had exceeded 100,000. That fall 70,000 demonstrators picketed the Department of Defense. Though de-escalation of the war began before he took office in 1969, Nixon inherited the domestic chaos of the preceding years.

As we have seen, Nixon moved quickly to effect basic changes in foreign policy, while narrowing the range of newly acquired civil liberties at home. Under the guidance of his national security adviser and eventual secretary of state, Henry Kissinger, Nixon took several bold initiatives. He sped up the de-escalation of American involvement in Vietnam, accepting Kissinger's argument that the conflict there was essentially a civil war from which the United States must slowly extricate itself. Once unencumbered in southeast Asia, the United States could maintain an equilibrium of power among itself, the Soviet Union, an increasingly assertive China, the growing industrial might of Japan, and the new unity of Europe. To this end, Nixon initiated Strategic Arms Limitation Talks (SALT) with the Soviet Union; declared that there must in future be "Asian solutions to Asian problems"; and most dramatically, sent Kissinger on a secret mission to the People's Republic of China in July 1971, and then visited the country himself early in 1972, to "normalize relations" between the two nations. A politician who had based his early reputation on intense anticommunism, Nixon was now ready to recognize the need to do business with those regimes. Nixon thus brought about a diplomatic revolution in which, by the mid-1970s, Communist China appeared to be cautiously aligned with the United States against the Soviet Union. This, in turn, created renewed strains with both the Soviet Union and Japan.

Nixon had reasoned that an easing of world tensions and an end to the bloodshed in Vietnam would also ease tensions at home. He was correct. Student protests slackened, an uneasy racial peace was achieved, and the early 1970s were marked by relative tranquility. Perhaps as a result, Nixon was returned to office in a landslide election in 1972, capturing every state save one. But a new instability soon plagued the nation, for early in his second administration it became known that a group of President Nixon's supporters had not only burglarized the headquarters of the Democratic party in the Watergate complex in Washington but that Nixon's closest aides appeared to have had knowledge of the burglary. Soon hearings in the Senate and intense investigative reporting by journalists revealed that the president had tape-recorded conversations in his Oval Office and that the Federal Bureau of Investigation and the Central Intelligence Agency (the latter barred by law from domestic surveillance activities) had been pressed into service to obtain information that would help the Nixon reelection and to cover up the initial revelations about Watergate.

Facing almost certain impeachment for misconduct in office, President Nixon finally resigned on August 9, 1974. He was succeeded by Gerald R. Ford (1913–   ), a respected Michigan Republican who had served in the

THE WRITTEN RECORD

Let the Word Go Forth

In his inaugural address, newly elected President John F. Kennedy demonstrated charismatic powers of oratory. He did more, however, for he also issued a challenge to his fellow Americans that was more dramatic, more sweeping, a tinge more arrogant, and perhaps more idealistic than they had heard, or would hear, for some time.

Let the word go forth from this time and place, to friend and foe alike, that the torch has been passed to a new generation of Americans, born in this century, tempered by war, disciplined by a hard and bitter peace, proud of our ancient heritage, and unwilling to witness or permit the slow undoing of those human rights to which this nation has always been committed. . . .

Let every nation know, whether it wishes us well or ill, that we shall pay any price, bear any burden, meet any hardship, support any friend, oppose any foe to assure the survival and the success of liberty. . . .

Finally, to those nations who would make themselves our adversary, we offer not a pledge but a request: that both sides begin anew the quest for peace, before the dark powers of destruction unleashed by science engulf all humanity in planned or accidental self-destruction.

We dare not tempt them with weakness. For only when our arms are sufficient beyond doubt can we be certain beyond doubt that they will never be employed.

But neither can two great and powerful groups of nations take comfort from our present course—both sides overburdened by the cost of modern weapons, both rightly alarmed by the steady spread of the deadly atom, yet both racing to alter that uncertain balance of terror that stays the hand of mankind's final war.

So let us begin anew, remembering on both sides that civility is not a sign of weakness, and sincerity is always subject to proof. Let us never negotiate out of fear, but let us never fear to negotiate. . . .

Let both sides seek to invoke the wonders of science instead of its terrors. Together let us explore the stars, conquer the deserts, eradicate disease, tap the ocean depths and encourage the arts and commerce. . . .

All this will not be finished in the first one hundred days. Nor will it be finished in the first one thousand days, nor in the life of this Administration, nor even perhaps in our lifetime on this planet. But let us begin. . . .

In the long history of the world, only a few generations have been granted the role of defending freedom in its hour of maximum danger. I do not shrink from this responsibility; I welcome it. I do not believe that any of us would exchange places with any other people or any other generation. The energy, the faith, the devotion which we bring to this endeavor will light our country and all who serve it, and the glow from that fire can truly light the world.

And so, my fellow Americans, ask not what your country can do for you; ask what you can do for your country.

My fellow citizens of the world, ask not what America will do for you, but what together we can do for the freedom of man.

Quoted in Theodore C. Sorensen, *Kennedy* (New York: Bantam Books, 1966), pp. 275–78. This edition also provides examples of the drafts through which the speech passed.

House of Representatives for a quarter of a century and had been appointed vice-president to replace Spiro Agnew, who had resigned in 1973.

The Watergate affair had proved deeply divisive, and President Ford set out to bind up the nation's wounds. He pardoned Nixon to avoid the extended rancor of a trial, although Nixon's assistants were convicted and sentenced to jail. He then turned to the problem of inflation, which mounted in 1974 in the face of higher oil prices, and public attention turned to energy policy.

Despite peace in Vietnam and a rise in the stock market, Ford was unable to win a widespread following. Though low by European standards, the American inflation rate stood at 7.6 percent and unemployment at 8 million. An oil embargo against the West by Arab states had revealed that the United States was vulnerable in its consumption of energy. And the right wing of the Republican party was up in arms against what it regarded as a

weak American policy in the Middle East, in Latin America, and even in Israel, which was thought to have precipitated the energy crisis by its war against the Arab states in 1973–1974.

Thus a political unknown who had captured the Democratic nomination, James Earl Carter, (1924–   ), known even formally as Jimmy Carter, attained the presidency by a narrow margin. Voters were prepared to try a new approach; above all, they wanted to return to a sense of security about the economy. In this and much else, the Carter presidency disappointed many.

Carter achieved some gains, most notably in environmental legislation, urban redevelopment, and deregulation of some sectors of the economy. Although he brought the Israeli and Egyptian leaders together to sign an accord that appeared to end the longstanding hostility between their nations, Carter's presidency was crippled by an event in Iran. There the United States had long

In 1979 the shah of Iran was forced into exile by a fundamentalist revolution. Huge crowds of demonstrators filled the streets of Iranian cities in support of the ayatollah Ruhollah Khomeini. In this news photograph Iranian women are seen marching through the streets of Teheran carrying a picture of Khomeini.

UPI/Bettmann Newsphotos

supported the powerful shah, Mohammed Reza Pahlavi (1919–1980), son of Reza Shah, who had abdicated in 1941. Iran under the Pahlavis was a test case of modernization; to go too fast would alienate the traditional Islamic clergy and the peasantry; to go too slowly would lose the middle class and the Westernized Iranians. Although the shah had instituted a White Revolution—agricultural reforms that gave Iran a steadily rising standard of living—he was seen as corrupt, despotic, enriching himself and his family at the expense of the peasantry.

The United States failed to see revolution in Iran coming and, when it came, appeared to deal with it falteringly. Iran, a Shi'ite Muslim nation but not an Arab land, was ill understood in the United States, where the study of the Middle East generally, and of Islam in particular, was little developed. Violence was followed by martial law in 1978. From France the exiled Shi'ite religious leader, the ayatollah Ruhollah Khomeini (1902–1989), orchestrated a rebellion that drove the shah into exile in January 1979. The ayatollah returned to Iran the next month, and soon his power was virtually absolute.

In the meantime, the shah had been admitted to the United States for treatment of cancer. On November 4, 1979, militant students stormed the American embassy in Teheran and seized ninety hostages, including sixty-five Americans, whom they refused to release unless the shah

was returned to Iran to stand trial for crimes against the people. The Iranians remained in control of the embassy for 444 days, despite international condemnation, an abortive rescue mission by American forces, and intense diplomatic pressure from the United States. For fifteen months Americans were faced nightly on their television sets with the dramatic (and inflated) spectacle of "America held hostage."

While Carter was faulted for not having taken precautions to protect the American embassy, there was little that he could do thereafter. And it was this very sense of national helplessness that turned the electorate against him. To underscore how they could help manipulate American elections, the Iranians released the hostages on January 20, 1981, jut minutes after a new president of the United States, Republican Ronald Reagan (1911–   ), was sworn into office. The turmoil continued in Iran as the revolution passed through phases of vengeance and countervengeance, much like the French Revolution. Waves of executions eliminated Marxists, those who had collaborated with Americans, those who had worked for the shah, and those who opposed the new Islamic Republic's constitution, which had been shaped by the clergy. Members of the ecumenical, international Bahai faith, which had a following in the United States, were also systematically killed, while the United States stood helplessly by.

Ronald Reagan had been elected on a wave of public frustration. He was a right-wing conservative who offered voters a clear alternative to previous administrations. Once in office, however, he proved to be less conservative than the right wing had hoped, and he soon tempered some of his stands. Reagan appealed to Americans who felt that government had become too big, too interfering, and too central to their lives. He promised deregulation, decentralization, and a restoration of public and private morality. Working against these goals were the risks inherent in an arms race with the Soviet Union, a resurgence of the environmentalist movement, and apparently intractable inflation and unemployment.

In the 1980s the United States was undergoing unprecedented change. A nation once thought to be committed to isolation was now involved with events virtually everywhere. A nation that once had the highest standard of living in the world had sadly discovered the poor in its midst and was acutely aware of its dependence on other nations for resources such as oil. By 1989 the United States had fallen to fifth place in per capita income among Western nations (omitting the oil-rich Arab states), and stood twelfth in its health rate. Its illiteracy and infant mortality rates were climbing. The United States was still the dominant nation in the world, but on the indicators most significant in time of peace, it had been marginally—and to Americans, quite unexpectedly—overtaken by several nations.*

---

*Economists use many different indicators for measuring standard of living, and per capita income and health rate are only two of them. In many other indicators, the United States was first or second in the world. For these statistics, see the figures under each nation in any current edition of *The World Almanac and Book of Facts* (New York: Funk & Wagnalls).

Once shaped by an economy of abundance, so that each succeeding generation, as well as arriving immigrants, could anticipate a better future, the United States now faced shortages in areas crucial to the economy, rising demands from the less privileged part of the population, and an agonizing awareness of the magnitude of the problems. Once shaped by an illusion of "free security"—security from foreign invasion, virtually free of cost, since neither land neighbor, Canada or Mexico, posed a military threat and other nations were thousands of miles across the seas—the United States feared for its security in the atomic era and could maintain such security as it had only at great cost. Many Americans turned toward their past, nostalgically hoping that these old, formative influences might still work for American society. But by the 1980s many other people were on the path to the future, determined to find an American-style solution to American problems, to maintain civil liberties and democratic government, to achieve security and stability.

Canada and Mexico

One of the nations that briefly surpassed the United States in per capita income was its immediate neighbor, Canada. Exploiting its vast hydroelectric resources and oil and mineral wealth, Canada had become a major industrial nation. Between 1954 and 1959 the United States and Canada built an extensive new seaway to join the Great Lakes with the St. Lawrence River, so that Canadian and midwestern goods could flow to world markets more readily. Yet Canada increasingly asserted an independent foreign policy—independent of both Britain and the United States. Its foreign minister played a major role in mediating the Suez crisis; Canada recognized and traded with Communist Cuba and China; and in the 1970s Canadian nationalist leaders were seeking to achieve greater economic independence from the United States.

But in Canada political instability threatened. French-speaking Canadians continued to lag behind English-speaking Canadians in their standard of living. Because the hundreds of thousands of immigrants were assimilating predominantly into English rather than into French Canada, French Canada felt that its language and culture were under attack. When an Official Languages Act, which made French equal to English in all federal matters, did not satisfy French expectations and was often ignored in the English-speaking provinces of western Canada, terrorist groups kidnapped a British diplomat and killed a Quebec government official. The French-Canadian prime minister, Pierre-Elliott Trudeau (1919–   ), applied emergency powers with such vigor that he further alienated the population of the province of Quebec, where a separatist movement grew in strength over the next decade. The *Parti Québécois*, committed to greater autonomy for Quebec, won much support within the province and was soundly reelected in 1981. Meanwhile, despite changes in the federal government, Trudeau continued to dominate the national political scene, and in 1980 he embarked on the delicate task of constitutional reform. Opposed by eight of the ten

Canadian provinces, Trudeau found himself presiding over a nation deeply divided on fundamental issues relating to civil rights, the use of natural resources, the distribution of wealth, and the legitimacy of biculturalism, and in 1984 he resigned, to be followed by the Conservative party leader, Brian Mulroney (1939–   ). Though he remained in office until 1993, Mulroney fared little better with respect to inflation, the problem of Québécois separatism, or giving Canada a clear voice in international affairs outside the North American arena. In June 1993 he succeeded in gaining Canadian ratification of the North American Free Trade Agreement with the United States and Mexico and support for the creation of a self-governing homeland in the Northwest Territories for the indigenous Inuit.

Mexico, in the meantime, was also posing a challenge to the United States. Larger and more populous than any country in Europe and point of origin for thousands of immigrants to the United States, Mexico had remained in relative poverty while experiencing political stability. The Institutional Revolutionary party had dominated since 1929; despite its title, it had consistently used strong measures to put down radical opposition. But by the 1970s Mexico's foreign policy was tending to the left. A reversal of reforms in land redistribution after 1976 left a substantial part of the population angry, while the great significance of oil as a bargaining chip in international affairs was giving Mexico far more authority in the world's marketplaces. A period of unprecedented prosperity was abruptly ended by a severe currency devaluation in 1982. Unemployment rose to nearly half the work force, 4 million peasants remained without land, and a tense controversy broke out with the United States over the treatment of illegal Mexican entrants into the American Southwest. Always a leader in Latin America, Mexico appeared poised for significant change. With an estimated population of 92 million in 1994, and 38 percent of that population under age fourteen, Mexico was growing twice as fast as the United States; it had one of the highest rates of natural increase of any nation in the world, and the flow of illegal immigrants to the United States was steadily mounting. By 1995 Mexico was in a state of near crisis caused by a precipitous decline in the value of its peso, an ongoing rebellion in the state of Chiapis in southern Mexico, and a series of political assassinations.

Eastern Europe and the Soviet Union

The Soviet Union and the countries of eastern Europe were not exempt from the cycle of prosperity, growth, economic stagnation, and social and political unrest, even though they could prevent the unrest from getting out of hand or from being made known outside their borders. Problems for the Soviet leadership proved to be fully as difficult as those faced by the Western democracies, but

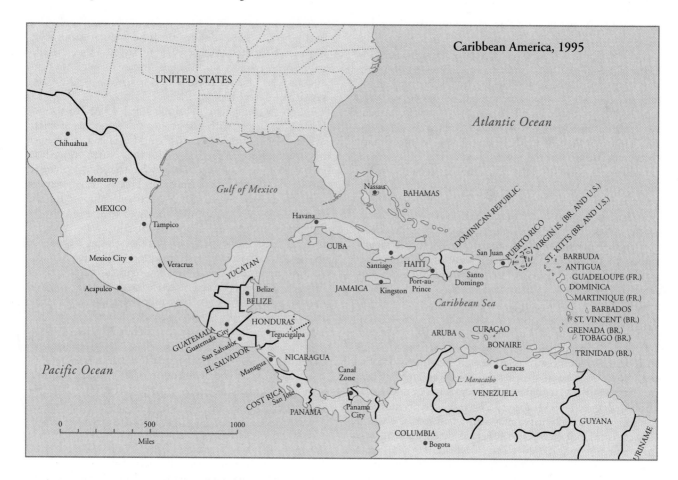

Caribbean America, 1995

totalitarian states did not have to engage in divisive public debate over how to allocate resources. Thus the Soviet Union was free to concentrate on postwar industrial recovery and parity in the arms race.

Zapatista National Liberation Army parades in ceremonies marking the seventy-fifth anniversary of the assassination of Emilio Zapata and first 100 days of revolt in Chiapis, Mexico, April 11, 1995.

Reuter/Gerardo Alberto/The Bettmann Archive

The Decline of Marxist Ideology

When Stalin died, the stage seemed set for a full-scale anti-Semitic drive. But fear of the West and hatred of Zionism alone did not explain Soviet anti-Semitism. Despite long years of preaching cultural autonomy for nationalities, many Soviet leaders were personally anti-Semitic and perhaps recognized the latent anti-Semitism of the population at large. Official Soviet anti-Semitism would continue into the 1980s, and the door would be periodically opened, then closed, to emigration to the West or to Israel. The Soviet Union viewed Israel as a client state of the United States, and therefore Soviet foreign policy was generally pro-Arab.

In March 1953 Georgi Malenkov (1902–1993), personally close to Stalin, succeeded him as premier but surrendered the party secretaryship to Nikita Khrushchev. It was thus made clear that no one person would immediately inherit all of Stalin's power. Soon the regime began to denounce the "cult of personality" (Stalin's despotic one-man rule) and proclaimed a "collegial" system (government by committee). The dreaded chief of the secret police, Presidium member Lavrenty Beria (1899–1953), was executed for treason. At a party congress early in 1956 Khrushchev denounced Stalin, emotionally detailing the acts of personal cruelty to which the psychopathic nature of the late dictator had given rise. As the details of the speech leaked out to the Soviet public, there was some distress at the smashing of the idol they had worshiped for so long, but the widespread disorder that some observers were predicting failed to materialize. Abroad, however, the speech produced turmoil in the Soviet satellites in Europe and so gave Khrushchev's opponents at home an opportunity to unite against his policies. Within the Presidium they had a majority, but Khrushchev was able to rally to his support the Central Committee of the Communist party. Khrushchev emerged from this test in 1957 with his powers immeasurably enhanced.

Already in his sixties, Khrushchev could hardly hope for a quarter-century of dictatorship such as Stalin had known. Moreover, in making himself supreme he had deprived himself of some of the instruments available to Stalin. After 1953 he had released millions of captives from prisons and slave-labor camps. Almost everyone in the Soviet Union had a relative or friend now freed. Within a year or two Soviet society at every level except at the very top of the bureaucracy had absorbed these sufferers from tyranny. The secret police no longer enjoyed independent power in the state, a power that might challenge the party or the army; Khrushchev himself had emotionally denounced police terror. It was still possible to prosecute people by terroristic means, but Stalin's mass terror as a system of government had disappeared.

In October 1964 Khrushchev was removed from power and succeeded by two members of the Presidium. Leonid Brezhnev (1906–1982) replaced him as first secretary of the Central Committee of the Communist party, and Alexis Kosygin (1904–1980) as premier. Both were "Khrushchev men." The two, but especially Brezhnev, would provide the Soviet government with stability until Brezhnev became increasingly ill and, in the early 1980s, virtually a figurehead. Khrushchev was denounced for his failures in agricultural policy, for departures from conventional wisdom on foreign affairs, and for "commandism"—rule by fiat. He was not, however, executed, and no large-scale purge followed his removal.

Most spectacular during these years were the successes achieved in rocketry and space. The Soviet successfully launched the first earth satellite (Sputnik, 1957) and first reached the moon with a rocket (1959). The first manned orbital flight by Yuri Gagarin (1934–1968), in April 1961, was followed in less than a month by the first American flight, by Alan B. Shepard, Jr. (1923–   ), and in February 1962 by the first American orbit, by John H. Glenn, Jr. (1921–   ). By the mid-1960s the United States had caught up in most aspects of space technology, and American landings of manned space vehicles on the moon beginning in 1969 overshadowed Soviet accomplishments in space.

The exciting race in outer space commanded the world's imagination, though for both the Soviet Union and the United States it diverted millions of dollars from domestic programs. In the 1970s both nations cut back on their space programs, placing greater emphasis on satellites for monitoring the activities of other nations. The Soviets set a new space endurance record of 175 days in 1979, while the two countries engaged in a joint flight, including a link-up between their respective crews in space, in 1975. In the mid-1980s both nations had decreased their space programs substantially in the face of economic pressures.

But it was agriculture that presented the Soviet planners with apparently insoluble problems. In 1953 Khrushchev had embarked on a crash program to plow under more than 100 million acres of prairie in the Urals region, Kazakhstan, and Siberia. Drought and poor planning and performance led to a clear failure by 1963. By the following year, the number of collective farms was down to about 40,000 from an original 250,000 and the average size of the new units was far larger. Soviet economic performance continued to fail to meet its goals. The Soviet standard of living remained low by Western measurements, and by the mid-1970s general stagnation set in, followed by crop failures and the need to purchase grain from the United States.

De-Stalinization extended to arts and letters the same partial relaxation that occurred in other fields. Two outstanding Soviet composers with followings in the West, Aram Khachaturian (1903–1978) and Dmitri Shostakovich (1906–1975), spoke out for boldness, and in mid-1954 Ilia Ehrenburg (1890–1967), veteran propagandist for the regime, hailed the relaxation of coercive measures over artists in *The Thaw*, which gave a name to the entire period. Boris Pasternak (1890–1960) took advantage of the "thaw" to offer for publication *Dr. Zhivago*, his novel about a doctor who, through all the agonies of World War I and the Russian Revolution, affirmed the freedom of the human soul. Accepted for publication in the Soviet Union, the novel was also sent to Italy to be published. Then the Soviet censors changed their minds and also forced Pasternak to ask that the manuscript in Italy be returned to him. The Italian publisher refused, and versions in Russian, Italian, English, and other languages appeared abroad, arousing great admiration. In 1958 the Nobel Prize Committee offered Pasternak the prize for literature and he accepted. But Pasternak's follow writers reviled him as a traitor, and the government threatened him with exile if he accepted the prize. As a patriotic Soviet, he then declined it. Pasternak's Jewish origins, his intellectualism, his proclamation of individualism had offended Khrushchev, making it impossible to publish *Dr. Zhivago* in the land in which it was written.

But the spirit of individualism found more vigorous expression among the younger poets and novelists who had grown up since the World War II. A young Ukrainian poet, Evgeny Yevtushenko (1933–   ), denounced Soviet anti-Semitism in his *Babi Yar* (the name of the ravine near Kiev in which the Nazis, with the help of the Soviets, had massacred thousands of Jews). When Yevtushenko recited his verses, the halls were crowded with eager, excited, contentious young people.

The Pasternak affair had shown the limits of the new freedom; the case of Alexander Solzhenitsyn (1918–   ) would be even more instructive to the new readership. A former army officer, Solzhenitsyn had been interned for eight years in a forced labor camp.

When he published his autobiographical novel *One Day in the Life of Ivan Denisovich* in 1963, he described for the first time in print the camps of which all Soviets knew but did not speak. Solzhenitsyn was immediately attacked for being concerned with "marginal aspects" of Soviet life, and the censor refused to pass his next important novel, *The First Circle*. After his expulsion from the Soviet Union in 1974, his best-known work, *The Gulag Archipelago*, revealed extensive knowledge of the Terror and the great camps of Siberia. In 1970, to the embarrassment of Soviet leaders, Solzhenitsyn was awarded the Nobel Prize for Literature.

In 1968 the repression of young writers fed a dissident movement that continued to grow thereafter. Soviet citizens accused their own government of violating the human rights provisions of the Helsinki accords of 1975. A Nobel Prize physicist, Andrei Sakharov (1921–1989), joined the dissidents, and in the late 1970s and early 1980s the Soviet leadership attacked those who sought to criticize cultural policy, or to emigrate to Israel, or to speak favorably of the outcast Solzhenitsyn, who had settled in the United States.

Despite the reversion to repression in literature, film, and art, the communist bloc was no longer monolithic, for the Soviet leaders were unable to prevent a drift toward *polycentrism* (the existence of independent centers of power in the satellites). Warsaw Pact members remained more uniformly aligned than those in NATO, but nonetheless cracks began to appear in the Iron Curtain. So long as the satellite countries pursued a foreign policy in common with the Soviet Union, they gained some freedom to make their own economic decisions. Hungary and Romania struck out on paths of their own—Hungary toward a consumer economy, and both countries toward heavier industry, tourism, and trade with the West. Though the Soviet Union crushed liberalization in Czechoslovakia in 1968, it had to accept a declaration by Communist parties in 1976 that there could be several separate paths to the socialist state. This loosening of the Soviet hold was only marginal, however, as events in Poland made clear. The Polish Solidarity movement, an independent labor-led movement under the leadership of Lech Walesa (1943–   ), led the challenge against both the Polish Communist party and the hegemony of the Soviet Union. Under pressure from Moscow, the Polish army suspended Solidarity and took control of Poland in 1981. Nonetheless the movement survived underground, and in 1989 Poland was permitted its first free election in forty years.

With the death of Brezhnev late in 1982 and the selection of Yuri Andropov (1914–1985) as his successor, the Soviet Union appeared poised for renewed confrontation and repression. Andropov had presided over the crushing of Hungary in 1956; he had been head of the Committee for State Security (KGB) from 1967 to 1982 and demonstrated a willingness to silence dissent. But Andropov's death appeared to set the Soviet Union on another course as a younger man, Mikhail S. Gorbachev (1931–   ), took over leadership of the party. Tough, resolute, and Westernized, Gorbachev embarked in 1985 on a dangerous, highly delicate modernization of the Soviet state, and though he challenged neither the party nor the military directly, it was clear that he favored a more open society. He allowed dissidents who had been exiled to Siberia and elsewhere to return home, he called for extensive industrial and agricultural reforms, and he moved to extricate the nation from the costly war in which it was mired in Afghanistan. Severely criticized in the West for not quickly disclosing the nature and extent of a disastrous nuclear accident at Chernobyl in April 1986, the Soviet Union appeared to have decided upon the course of openness, with most newspaper, radio, and television censorship abolished, protesters permitted to gather freely in Soviet cities, and Marxism largely expunged from school curriculums.

Observers debated whether Mikhail Gorbachev was leading the Soviet Union into liberalization or simply riding the back of a tiger unleashed by a declining Soviet economy. Decades of failed production schedules, declining harvests, and inefficient management had made Russia and most of the socialist republics ripe for change. Gorbachev's sense of urgency, his frequent trips to the West, and his relative youthfulness made him especially attractive from abroad.

In April 1985, Gorbachev announced a series of reforms intended to reshape the economy and to reduce the rigidity of the Soviet system, calling the process *perestroika*. He admitted his nation's need for Western expertise, and his policy of *glasnost*, or "openness," brought thousands of Westerners into the Soviet Union to promote trade, display industrial skills, exchange educational programs and artists, and reshape administrations. In 1987 voters were given a choice of candidates in local elections, and in the first free elections since 1917, held in March 1989, party officials were roundly defeated and the new national legislature, the Congress of People's Deputies, was filled with new faces.

Gorbachev faced opposition from both the left and the right. Those who advocated even swifter change rallied behind Boris N. Yeltsin (1931–   ), an engineer who was first secretary of the Moscow city party committee. Yeltsin emerged victorious in the 1989 elections, winning massive popular support for sweeping changes within the Russian Soviet Federated Socialist Republic. Throughout this period of rapid change, the Soviet army remained resolutely on the sidelines, despite widespread fears that it would come to the support of the conservatives, and for the time even the hated KGB appeared to have maintained neutrality.

But Gorbachev, despite enormous popularity in the West and genuinely major concessions with respect to issues of arms control (in part recognized by the award of the Nobel Peace Prize in 1990), was walking a tightrope. In July 1989, with conservatives openly concerned that the Communist party would lose control, Gorbachev called from sweeping reforms and purged the party ranks; then, in November, in an attempt to retain moderate conservative support, he published a manifesto declaring that Marxism would be revived under his leadership, to show a "humane socialist" face. In December Lithuania broke

Latvian people in the streets express their support for the Latvian Supreme Soviet independence decision, May 5, 1990.

AP/Wide World Photos

with Moscow and declared its intention to reestablish separate nationhood for the first time since 1940. In 1991 Russia recognized the independence of Lithuania, Latvia, and Estonia.

In 1990 Gorbachev was able to persuade the Communist party's Central Committee to end the party's constitutionally guaranteed monopoly on power, and the right turned increasingly from him. In March, elections in the Russian, Ukrainian, and Byelorussian republics placed them out in front of Gorbachev in their demands for democracy, while local government in several cities, including Moscow and Leningrad, was in the hands of even more insistent reformers. Under Yeltsin the Russian Republic declared its sovereignty, and twelve other republics followed suit; Yeltsin then announced a "five-hundred-day" program for transition to open markets, and Gorbachev was forced to accept it. Still Gorbachev held on, moving first to conciliate those who wished to break up the Soviet Union, promising to consider readjustments in the distribution of powers between Moscow and the republics, then tilting toward the hard-liners, putting soldiers onto the streets of Soviet cities allegedly to patrol against a rising crime rate, and reinstituting forms of censorship. These events were, in part, the result of the disintegration of communism in eastern Europe, a disintegration set in motion by Gorbachev's own reforms.

Disintegrating Communism in Eastern Europe

The collapse of repressive regimes was unexpected and sudden. In April 1989 an accord between factions in Poland had promised free elections, and in August the first noncommunist head of an Eastern bloc nation was elected prime minister. In Hungary, *glasnost* was warmly embraced, and its parliament passed legislation to legalize freedom of assembly, speech, and association. In October 1989 the Communist party formally dissolved. In Czechoslovakia police initially crushed the largest antigovernment protests since 1968, but protests continued, taking to the streets in Prague to demand free elections. On November 24, 1989, the entire Communist party leadership resigned, and in December the first cabinet in more than forty years without a communist majority took power, choosing the playwright and human rights campaigner Vaclav Havel (1936–), a man who had spent nearly a decade in communist prisons, as president. Even isolated Albania, not part of the former Soviet bloc, moved tentatively toward greater freedom, allowing many of its citizens to travel abroad and in 1990 restoring the right to practice religion. In 1992 Albania elected a noncommunist president.

The transition from communist dictatorship went less smoothly in Romania and East Germany. Nicolae Ceausescu, who had shown much independence from the Soviet Union as Romania's president since 1967, had become increasingly repressive. All industry had been put under state ownership, state farms owned nearly all of the arable land, and conservative Marxist economic policies had crushed individual initiative. Pollution was widespread and health problems severe. Inspired by protesters elsewhere, a large group assembled in the city of Timisoara, and on December 16, 1989, at Ceausescu's command, his hated security forces opened fire on the demonstrators and buried hundreds in mass graves. Protests spread rapidly, and the Romanian army joined in the rebellion rather than cooperate with the security forces. On December 22 a group calling itself the Council of National Salvation overthrew the government, and the next day, following a trial for genocide, Ceausescu and his wife were condemned to death.

Chaos also marked the transition in East Germany. In October 1989, Erich Honecker (1912–1994), longtime East German party leader, faced with mounting demonstrations, a faltering economy, charges of widespread party corruption, and the proposed withdrawal of Soviet troops, resigned under pressure. East Germany opened its border with Czechoslovakia, and thousands of East Germans sought to leave. On November 9 the government agreed to issue exit visas, and the last of the infamous Berlin Wall came down in the midst of wild celebration. Parliament revoked a constitutional clause assuring the Communist party a leading role in the nation, and the new premier promised free elections and a multiparty system. The chancellor of Western Germany, Helmut Kohl, called for a confederation of the two Germanys and in March 1990, a slate that supported Kohl won the elections. A non-

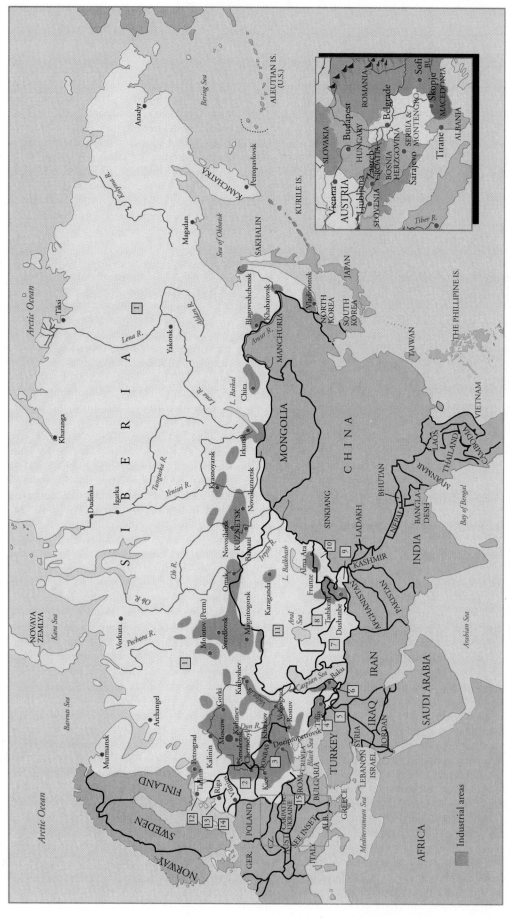

The Russian Federation, Commonwealth of States, 1995

1. Russian Soviet Federated
   Socialist Republic
2. Belarus
3. Ukraine
4. Georgia

5. Armenia
6. Azerbaidjan
7. Turkmenistan
8. Uzbekistan

9. Tadjikistan
10. Kyrgystan
11. Kazakhstan
12. Estonia

13. Larvia
14. Lithuania
15. Moldova, Croatia, Serbia, Bosnia,
    Slovenia, Montenegro, Macedonia

Industrial areas

Sarajevan woman wounded by shell fragment gets help at Kosevo Hospital in Sarajevo, Bosnia, 1994.
Rikard Larma/AP/Wide World Photos

communist government was installed in April, and at a meeting with Gorbachev in July the Soviet Union gave its blessing, in exchange for $10 billion in economic aid, while the two Germanys and the four original Allied occupying powers jointly guaranteed Poland's postwar border with a united Germany. The last obstacles to the reunification of Germany were removed, and on October 3, 1990, the two Germanys declared themselves one. All foreign troops were withdrawn in 1994.

The final collapse of communism in the Soviet Union came rapidly and dramatically. On August 19, 1991, communist hard-lines attempted a coup, seizing control of the press and television, declaring that Gorbachev was ill, and replacing him with the vice-president. The Russian republic's president, Yeltsin, denounced the coup, called for a general strike, and rallied the Russian people, who barricaded the Russian Parliament. Massive protests in Moscow and Leningrad, world-wide denunciation of the coup leaders, and declarations of noncompliance in several of the Soviet republics brought the coup toppling down, and on August 21 Gorbachev returned to Moscow. By then Yeltsin had demonstrated his popularity and courage to the world and had emerged as the dominated political leader. Three days later Gorbachev resigned as head of the Soviet Communist Party, disbanded its leadership, and in effect ended communism's seventy-four year reign.

Reform had begun first in the Soviet Union. Gorbachev's denunciation of Stalin had freed the satellite states to criticize communist rule, and all of eastern Europe had moved out ahead of the Soviet Union in dismantling communism, largely in the space of eighteen months. This collapse of a monolithic communist bloc placed further pressures upon the Soviet Union to change.

The West was now to some extent reunited, with no Western bloc or Eastern bloc. Into the 1990s formerly communist nations struggled to realize their ambitions of free market economies despite little experience and virtually no infrastructure.

Still, grave problems remained. People in eastern Europe and the former Soviet Union had little experience with free market economies, and inflation soared. With the removal of authoritarian restrictions there was a flowering in countercultures, the arts, and free enterprise; there also was a rapid increase in crime and corruption. Former communists often won reelection under other party names. Ethnic conflict broke into the open: Slovakia separated from the Czech state in 1993, and Russia found itself faced with breakaway movements in numerous areas. The bloodiest dissolution was in Yugoslavia, however.

The Yugoslav disintegration was particularly rapid. Early in 1990 the Communist party renounced its constitutionally guaranteed place in society and asked Parliament to move to a multiparty system. On June 25, 1991, Croatia and Slovenia declared their independence, and fighting between Croats and ethnic Serbs broke out in Croatia. Serbia sent arms to the Croatian Serbs. In 1992 Serbia and Montenegro declared themselves the Federal Republic of Yugoslavia. War broke out between ethnic Serbs and others in Bosnia, which had a large Muslim population. In southern Serbia Albanians in Kosovo declared their independence as well. Bosnian Serbs, supplied by Serbia, shelled Bosnian cities, especially Sarajevo. In an effort to end the bloodshed, the United Nations imposed sanctions on Serbia and Montenegro. After Bosnia and Herzegovina declared their independence, Serb forces turned to "ethnic cleansing"—the systematic massacre or removal of Muslims and other non-Serbs. Despite an accord signed in 1994 to create a Muslim-Croat confederation in Bosnia, the fighting continued, with the Bosnian Serbs taking control of two thirds of the country. There seemed little prospect for a lasting peace in 1995.

THE NON-WESTERN WORLD IN INTERNATIONAL AFFAIRS

During World War II the Japanese had seized Western possessions in the Far East and had initially defeated Western armies, ending the myth of Western supremacy. Even though Japan was defeated in the end, Western prestige did not recover. Everyone knew that the French and Dutch had not really won, that British power had been seriously weakened. The only real victors in the war were the United States and the Soviet Union, each in its way anticolonial.

The causes of anticolonialism lay in the record of Western expansion and in the Western tradition itself. Westerners brought with them the Bible, the American Declaration of Independence, the French Declaration of the Rights of Man, *The Communist Manifesto*. It was hardly possible to keep on insisting that "all men are created equal" meant "white men are created superior." Western imperialism carried within itself the seeds of self-determination for all peoples.

Even if stimulated by the West, independence movements in Asia and Africa were nonetheless authentic movements from within. Nationalism had been implanted in some lands, unleashed in others. At first modernization tended to take the form of imitation of the West, but such imitation was quickly combined with a desire to preserve traditional culture.

Educated non-Westerners wanted independence. Many were revolutionaries; some admired the Bolshevik revolution, and a few were trained in Moscow. A great many Westerners made the mistake of assuming that these people did not represent the local populations and that the great colonial masses were indifferent as to who governed them. Instead, the urban masses and then, more gradually, the peasant masses began to demand that the foreigner go. Often this demand was sharpened by the rapid increases in population made possible by the dramatically lower death rates resulting from the sanitary engineering, medical facilities, and law and order imposed by the imperialist powers. Thus, within two decades of the end of World War II, the British, French, Dutch, Belgian, and American empires were virtually dismantled, and by the late 1980s only the Soviet empire remained.

Through the Commonwealth of Nations, Britain continued to exert considerable influence in parts of its former empire, though some former colonies either declined to join the Commonwealth or resigned from it. The French retained substantial influence in French-speaking West Africa, and the Americans in the Philippines and Panama. But many former colonial dependencies formed a determined neutralist block. Some looked to the Soviet Union, others to Communist china for technical assistance. Increasingly those parts of the former empires that were primarily Islamic began to unite in a common policy of opposition to Israel, which led them to take positions that were basically anti-Western. Of the great non-Western nations, only one aligned itself unequivocally and consistently with the West: Japan.

Japan

The occupation of Japan was wholly American. Despite some strong opposition from American opinion, the emperor was left on this throne, deprived of his divine status, and subjected to the close control of the forces of occupation. When the American occupation ended in 1952, the Japanese had made a promising start on a democracy of the Western type. Their economy grew so rapidly that it overtook France and West Germany, to rank third in the world after the Untied States and the Soviet Union. Industrious, efficient, loyal to their employers, and well-educated, the Japanese work force had by the 1970s displaced both West Germany and the United States in many critical areas of the new high technology. Leadership in automobile production also passed to the Japanese, the Datsun overtaking the Volkswagen even in the American market. By 1980 Japanese per capita income was only slightly behind that of the United States.

Signs of change and of affluence multiplied. Programs of birth-control education were successful, and the birth rate dropped, to become one of the lowest in the world. Peasants migrated to the cities, especially to Tokyo, which surpassed London and New York as the world's largest city until Mexico City moved past it by 1980. Weekend traffic jams resulted from the rush of Tokyo residents to the beaches in the summer and to the ski slopes in winter. Western styles of dress became customary in urban centers. Japanese tourists became known as the most avid and wealthy in the world as the yen soared in value.

Politically, democratic parliamentary institutions flourished under successive cabinets of the conservative Liberal Democratic party. The left-wing opposition, including both socialists and communist, objected to the mutual security pact binding Japan and the United States after the official restoration of full Japanese sovereignty in 1952, but otherwise it lacked widespread appeal.

The greatest strain between Japan and the United States arose over Nixon's trip to China in 1972. In going to China, Nixon was shaking the foundations of the special American relationship with Japan. And by failing to let the Japanese know about his plan before the public announcement in 1971 Nixon offended them seriously, leading them to ask whether the Americans were preparing to abandon them. The enormous economic success of the Japanese had stimulated the Chinese fear that Japan would rearm, and Chinese propaganda constantly stressed "renewed Japanese imperialism." To allay this fear, Nixon concealed his plans from the Japanese, hoping that he could later repair the damage.

But the United States followed the same tactics in proclaiming a series of surprising new economic measures. The president freed the dollar from gold, allowing it to float, and imposed a new customs surcharge on foreign goods. Both these measures were damaging to the Japanese, who were forced to revalue their undervalued currency and whose enormous sales of manufactured goods in the United States would no longer be so profitable. The Japanese continued to feel betrayed despite all efforts to reassure them. Premier Eisaku Sato (1901–1975), who had presided over Japan's growth as a world power, now resigned, beginning a period of relative political instability for the island nation. After meeting with Nixon, the new Japanese premier went to Beijing in September 1972, and regular Chinese-Japanese diplomatic relations were established. This meant that Japan would no longer recognize the Taiwan government. Upon its formal diplomatic recognition of the People's Republic of China in 1978, the United States also severed relations with Taiwan, leaving this island of 18 million people isolated and fearful. Thus a complex relationship among Japan, mainland China, and the Untied States brought a diplomatic revolution and relative stability to East Asia for the first time since World War II.

Japan's economic power, combined with a lack of a substantial military force, since the postwar settlement had limited it to self-defense, had proved unique. Protected by the United States, not having to put any substantial part of its national income into arms, prohibited from developing the nuclear capacity for war, Japan had been able to catch up rapidly with its protector. Now the tension between wishing to continue the economic advantages of such protection and apprehension that such protection was suspect led the Japanese to explore new initiatives. Yet these initiatives were largely limited to new diplomatic and commercial ventures. The Japanese vigorously developed close trade relations with Australia, becoming that nation's major trading partner, and sent whaling and fishing fleets throughout the Pacific. In 1978 a Japanese-Chinese friendship treaty completed the regularization of relations with the old enemy on the mainland.

By 1990 serious strains had opened up between Japan and the West, and in particular the United States. Recurrent political scandals suggested that the lessons of democracy had not been so well learned after all. Clashes over fishing rights and environmental issues complicated the relationship between the two nations. At the end of the Reagan administration and early in the presidency of his successor, George Bush, "Japan-bashing" became popular in the United States, with Japanese trade practices, its often closed markets, its paternalistic industrial customs, and its culture of hard work and achievement being blamed for America's relative industrial decline, especially in the automobile, electronics, camera, and computer industries.

By 1994 Japanese political instability was accompanied by signs of economic weakness. Early in 1995 a catastrophic earthquake devastated Kobe, at the center of Japan's second largest metropolitan complex, taking over four thousand lives and leaving perhaps two hundred thousand homeless, a staggering blow both economically and socially. Slow and often inefficient rescue and aid operations by the government led Japanese citizens to question the capacity of their bureaucracy more than at any time since World War II, giving rise to the likelihood of greater political turmoil.

People's Republic of China

The People's Republic of China, the most populous country in the world (in 1994, with an estimated population of 1,190,431,000, the only nation with more than a billion people), remained important in Western economic and political calculations and also relatively isolated. After years of upheaval, with massive purges during the cultural revolution in 1965, the nation's leadership appeared to realize that it had done untold damage to China's educational system, to its industrial capacity, and even to the revolutionary principles it espoused. Starting in 1968, purged officials were permitted to return to office, and factional fighting decreased. With the decline of Mao's authority and the rise of the more pragmatic Zhou Enlai (1898–1976) and Deng Xiaoping (1904–   , relations with the West appeared to improve. However, with the death of both Zhou and Mao in 1976, Deng was purged for a time, together with Mao's widow and other leftists.

With the opening to the West initiated by President Nixon, sweeping changes in the central government in 1982, and a series of substantive economic reforms, China appeared to be on the verge of normalizing relations with the West. However, on May 4, 1989, some 100,000 students and workers marched in the nation's capital, demanding far more sweeping democratic reforms. Believing that the demands called for too much change too quickly, Deng called for martial law, purged the Communist party of those who would not support him, and brought back some of the survivors of the Long March generation to help combat "bourgeois liberalism."

When protests spread to twenty other cities, and the capital city was filled with more than a million demonstrators, Deng called upon the Chinese army. On June 3–4, 1989, tanks and armored personnel carriers attacked the assembled protesters—largely students and workers—in Beijing's Tiananmen Square. An estimated five thousand protesters died, perhaps another ten thousand were injured, and hundreds were arrested. Most Western nations condemned the Chinese leadership, and the PRC appeared to have moved back into a repressive stance. Badly in need of additional Western technology to continue its own rapid industrialization and well aware of its increasingly isolated position in a crumbling world of communism, the PRC was obviously cautiously

The world was riveted by this photograph of a single Chinese protester standing in front of advancing tanks in Beijing on June 5, 1989. Though the tanks did not slow their advance, they did turn around the protester.

Reuters/Bettmann Newsphotos

considering its options for the 1990s, as Deng formally stepped down and Li Peng (1928–   ), also a conservative, emerged at least for the moment as China's primary leader.

The Koreas

South Korea had also attempted constitutional government in the Western manner but ran into serious difficulties. After the disruptive Korean War of the early 1950s, the government of Syngman Rhee (1875–1965), South Korean president since 1948, came under mounting criticism for corruption and arbitrary actions. In 1960 massive protests by students forced Rhee out of office and inaugurated a tumultuous period marked, first, by the political intervention of the army and, then, by another attempt at constitutional rule. While the economy boomed during the 1960s, political instability continued, and in 1979 the chief of the Korean intelligence division assassinated the head of state. South Korea again became a police state under martial law.

There were signs of hope in the lessening of tensions with North Korea, which though also strongly authoritarian, agreed in 1972 to seek the common goal of reunification of the two states by peaceful means. But there had been little real movement toward this goal by 1990. South Korea nonetheless boomed industrially and achieved some measure of world regard by successfully staging the Summer Olympic Games in 1988. By 1990 democratization had moved forward in the south.

There was no such democratization in North Korea, however, and in 1993 North Korea became the first state formally to withdraw from the Nuclear Nonproliferation Treaty, an international pact aimed at limiting the spread of nuclear weapons. The following year North Korea's leader Kim Il Sung (1912–1994), who had

ruled over the nation for forty years, died, ushering in a period of uncertainty.

Southeast Asia

Once the Japanese occupation ended in southeast Asia, the major Western colonial powers found that they could not revert to the prewar status quo. The United States had granted the Philippines independence in 1946. In 1949 the Dutch had to recognize the independence of the Netherlands East Indies as the republic of Indonesia, with a population of 100 million people. Britain gave Burma independence outside the Commonwealth (1948) and the Federation of Malaya independence within the Commonwealth (1957). The island of Singapore at the tip of Malaya, with a largely Chinese population, became fully independent in 1965, after a period of union with the former Malaya, now called Malaysia after the addition of certain Borneo territories in 1963. Singapore, the fourth greatest port in the world, soon experienced its own economic miracle, attaining the second highest standard of living in Asia, remarkable productivity and stability, and high standards of health, education, and housing under its brilliant long-term prime minister, Lee Kwan Yew (1923–   ), who held office from 1959 until 1990. In marked contrast, Burma, originally led by a vigorous advocate of democracy, U Nu (1908–1995), became increasingly isolated, economically bereft, and authoritarian following a military coup in 1962, after which Burma was renamed Myanmar.

The Dutch in Indonesia had not prepared the people for independence by education. Nevertheless, the Indonesians at first attempted to run their government as a parliamentary democracy. Almost everything went wrong; the economy was crippled by inflation, by shortages, by administrative corruption and the black market, and by the expulsion of experienced Dutch business leaders. The Muslims, who made up the bulk of the population, proved unable to form stable political parties. The outlying islands of the archipelago, resentful of domination by the island of Java—which contained the capital, Jakarta (the former Batavia), and two-thirds of the population—rebelled against the central government. As the high expectations raised by the achievement of independence were disappointed, President Sukarno (1901–1970), the hero of the Indonesian struggle for independence, urged a "guided democracy" based upon indigenous rather than borrowed political institutions.

Sukarno suspended the ineffectual parliamentary regime in 1956 and 1960 and vested authority in himself and in the army and an appointive council. But "guided democracy" created still more turmoil. Inflation ran wild, necessities vanished from the market, pretentious new government buildings were left unfinished for lack of funds, and all foreign enterprises were confiscated. In external policy, Sukarno initiated an alternating hot and cold war with the new federation of Malaysia for control of the island of Borneo, where both states had territory. He annexed former Dutch New Guinea (called West Irian by the Indonesians). When the United Nations supported Malaysia early in 1965, Sukarno withdrew Indonesia from membership; he also rejected United States offers of aid and moved closer to Communist China.

A coup planned by Indonesian communists misfired at the last moment in the autumn of 1965; 300,000 local communists were then slaughtered. Anticommunist forces came to power under military leaders, among whom General Suharto (1921–   ) took the lead, becoming head of state in 1967, reaching a settlement with Malaysia and rejoining the United Nations. Inflation was brought under control, a five-year plan was launched, and parliamentary elections were held in which Suharto was elected from 1973 through 1993. In 1976 Suharto took advantage of civil war in Portuguese Timor to annex that colonial remnant, and a continuing war marked by massacres festered on the island. In the 1980s the military, together with a growing navy, remained the principal source of power in Indonesia, which, in part on the basis of its oil reserves, was again experiencing growth. This vast nation, stretching along the Indian and Pacific oceans on 13,000 islands, with 200 million people—exceeded only by China, India, and the United States—held the promise of stability or chaos for southeast Asia.

Equally critical to regional stability was the Philippines. A vast island nation, substantially Westernized—English was recognized as an official language, and there was a considerable overlay of both Spanish and American culture—the Philippines faced chronic economic and social problems, complicated by persistent urban and rural violence in part instigated by Communist-led Huk guerrillas and later by Muslim secessionists. A liberal and reforming administration under President Ferdinand Marcos (1917–1989) grew increasingly authoritarian, first through martial law, then through a new constitution by which Marcos had himself proclaimed president, and through the grant of powers to Marcos's wife Ismelda.

The assassination of a respected opposition leader in 1983 touched off widespread demonstrations. In the election of February 1986, Marcos was declared the victor over the widow of the assassinated leader, Corazon Aquino (1932–   ); in the midst of allegations of fraud against the Marcos machine, Mrs. Aquino declared herself the lawful president. Under pressure from the United States Marcos resigned and Mrs. Aquino abrogated the constitution, dismissed the National Assembly, and instituted rule by decree, until holding full elections in May of 1987. A failed military coup late in 1989 underscored President Aquino's problems, however, as the economy remained weak and the army unpredictable. In 1992 she stepped down.

South Asia

The Labour victory in Britain in 1945 made the emancipation of India a certainty. But the deep-seated tensions between Muslims and Hindus had assumed critical importance. When the Hindu Congress party and the All-India Muslim League faced the need to draw up a working constitution for the new India, they found themselves in complete disagreement. The Muslims had long been working for separate Hindu and Muslim states, which were in the end reluctantly accepted by the Hindus. In 1947 Hindu India and Muslim Pakistan were set up as separate self-governing dominions within the Commonwealth.

Pakistan was a state divided into two parts, widely separated by Indian territory—the larger, arid West Pakistan in the northwest, and the smaller, more fertile, and far more densely populated East Pakistan in former East Bengal. The rest of the British Indian Empire and four fifths of its inhabitants became the republic of India. Pakistan, with its smaller population and its relatively poorly developed industry, was weaker than India and at first kept closer political ties with the British.

Violence accompanied partition. It was not possible to draw a boundary that would leave all Hindus in one state and all Muslims in another. Bitter Hindu-Muslim fighting cost hundreds of thousands of lives, as Hindus moved from Pakistani territory into India and Muslims moved from Indian territory into Pakistan. A particular source of trouble was the mountainous province of Kashmir. Though mainly Muslim in population, it was at the time of partition ruled by a Hindu prince, who turned it over to India. India continued to occupy most of Kashmir, to the economic disadvantage of Pakistan. The United Nations vainly sought to arrange a plebiscite.

In domestic politics the two states went through sharply contrasting experiences. The chief architect of Pakistani independence, Mohammed Ali Jinnah (1876–1948), head of the Muslim League, died shortly after independence. Thereafter Pakistan floundered in its attempts to make parliamentary government work and to solve its pressing economic difficulties. In 1958 the army commander, the British-educated Mohammed Ayub Khan (1907–1974), took full power, attacked administrative corruption and the black market, and instituted a program of "basic democracies" to train the population in self-government at the local level and then gradually upward through a pyramid of advisory councils. A new constitution in 1962 provided for a national assembly and also for a strengthened presidency, an office that Ayub continued to fill. But as Ayub grew older, charges of corruption were made against his family and his officials, and the depressed peoples of East Bengal protested loudly against policies that discriminated in favor of West Pakistan. Disorder spread, and in 1969 a new military government ousted Ayub.

The tension between West Pakistan, whose Punjabis had a disproportionately large role in the central government, and the underrepresented and miserably poor Bengalis of East Pakistan erupted in civil war in 1971. The East, assisted by India, declared itself independent. As fighting continued, 10 million East Pakistanis fled into India, straining to the limit that nation's resources. War between India and Pakistan followed, ending in a pact in 1972. East Pakistan became independent as Bangladesh; West Pakistan, shorn of its eastern portion, turned increasingly toward Islamic nationalism. In 1979 the leader of Pakistan's People's party was executed by military rulers who had taken over in a coup, and the American embassy in the capital of Islamabad was stormed and burned. Even though the nation became more reactionary, the United States concluded a new agreement to provide Pakistan with economic and military aid. Benazir Bhutto (1943–   ), the daughter of the executed leader, became the first woman head of state in a Muslim nation by election in 1988, and though defeated two years later, she returned to power in 1993.

Newly independent India had suffered a grievous loss when Gandhi was assassinated by an anti-Muslim Hindu in 1948. But Jawaharlal Nehru (1889–1964), a seasoned politician, at once assumed leadership. India successfully inaugurated a parliamentary democracy of the Western type. Nehru's daughter, Indira Gandhi (1917–1984), who became prime minister in 1966, successfully carried India through the war with Pakistan. Feeling that the United States was anti-Indian in the conflict, Mrs. Gandhi signed a twenty-year friendship pact with the Soviet Union in 1971. As the old Congress party split into two camps, Mrs. Gandhi's New Congress party became less democratic; in 1975 she used the emergency provisions of the Indian constitution to arrest thousands of her opponents and to impose press censorship. However, she did not turn to dictatorship, and in 1977 she was defeated in federal and state elections, in part because of a highly unpopular attempt to institute birth-control measures that were repugnant to most Hindus. She was returned to office in 1980 and assassinated by Sikh extremists in 1984. Her son Rajiv Gandhi (1944–1991) succeeded her until 1989, when he, too, was assassinated.

India faced acute overpopulation; by 1975 it had more than 600 million people, with a projection of 1 billion for the year 2000. The threat of famine was always present. In 1950 the government launched the first in a series of five-year plans for economic development, per-mitting the expansion of private industry but stressing government projects: irrigation and flood control, transport and communications, and especially agricultural education. In the late 1960s a new strain of high-yielding wheat was planted experimentally; the initial results were promising. But the very success of the new foods (the "green revolution") threatened a new form of crisis, as farmers displaced from the countryside by new agricultural techniques flooded into the cities of India, where there was no employment for them.

Political controversy also arose over the question of language. There were thirteen major regions in India, each with its own distinctive tongue. Believing that a common language was essential to national identity, the government supported Hindi as the national language, to which it gave official status in 1965. It also recognized English as an associate language. The elevation of Hindi to official status aroused especially strong opposition among the speakers of Tamil in the south. The government met the problem by making some concessions but without abandoning its aim.

The debate over the relative weight to be given to industry and agriculture also continued. In 1970 India dedicated a nuclear power plant near Bombay, built with American assistance. Canada helped build two nuclear reactors, and in May 1974 India exploded an underground nuclear device. India was determined to pursue a path between the West and the Soviet Union, ably playing one against the other, hoping to be dependent on neither.

Nonetheless, India remained the most populous democracy in the world, with a largely unintimidated legal system, continued if declining use of the world's international language, English, and an apparent commitment to economic reforms. These hopeful signs were somewhat offset by a wave of communal violence in 1993 and a continuing low-level war between Indian troops and pro-independence demonstrators in Kashmir. Political instability and persistent corruption challenged the democracy at every turn, but it remained intact and hopeful.

The Middle East

In Saudi Arabia, in the small states along the Persian Gulf, and in Iraq and Iran, the Middle East possessed the greatest oil reserves in the world. Developed by European and American companies that paid royalties to the local governments, these oil resources influenced the policies of all the powers. Many of the oil-producing states had banded together in 1960 to form the Organization of Petroleum Exporting Countries (OPEC), and they quickly discovered a powerful new weapon in international diplomacy. They used the mechanism of oil pricing and threatened increases both to frighten Western industrial nations dependent on a continued flow of oil and to manipulate Western foreign policies toward Israel.

When the British withdrew their forces from Palestine in 1948, the Jews proclaimed the state of Israel and secured its recognition by the United Nations. The Arab nations declared the proclamation illegal and invaded the new state from all directions. Outnumbered but faced

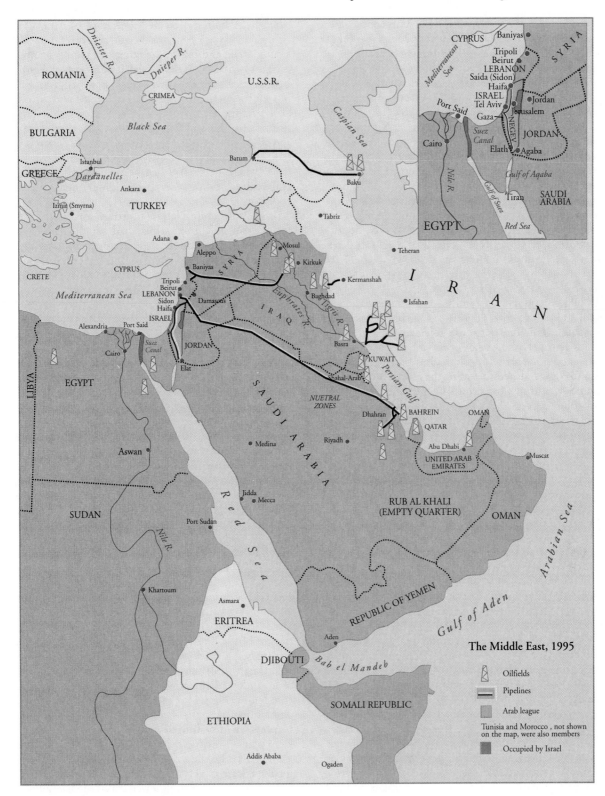

The Middle East, 1995

Oilfields
Pipelines
Arab league
Tunisia and Morocco, not shown on the map, were also members
Occupied by Israel

by an inefficient enemy, the Israelis won the war. A truce that was not a formal peace was patched together under the auspices of the United Nations in 1949. Israel secured more of Palestine than the UN had proposed, taking over the western part of Jerusalem, a city the UN had proposed to neutralize. However, the eastern part, or "old city" of Jerusalem together with eastern Palestine, remained in the hands of the Arab state of Jordan.

During the 1948 war almost a million Palestinian Arabs fled from Israel to the surrounding Arab states. The United Nations organized a special agency that built camps and gave relief to the refugees and tried to arrange for their permanent resettlement. The Arab states, however, did not wish to absorb them, and many refugees regarded resettlement as an abandonment of their belief that the Israelis would soon "be pushed into the sea," and that they themselves would then return to their old homes. This problem made the truce of 1949 very delicate.

The new state of Israel continued to admit as many Jewish immigrants as possible, from Europe, North Africa, Yemen, and later the Soviet Union. The welding of these human elements into a single nationality was a formidable task. Much of Israel was mountainous, and some of it was desert. The Israelis applied talents and training derived from the West to make the best use of their limited resources, and they depended on outside aid, especially from their many supporters in the United States.

In 1952, less than four years after the Arab defeat in Palestine, revolution broke out in Egypt, where the corrupt monarchy was overthrown by a group of army officers led by Gamal Abdel Nasser (1918–1970). They established a republic, encouraged the emancipation of women, and pared down the role of the conservative religious courts. Only one party was tolerated, and elections were closely supervised. As an enemy of the West, which he associated not only with colonialism but with support for Israel, Nasser turned for aid to the Soviets. Czechoslovak and Soviet arms flowed into Egypt, and Soviet technicians followed.

Nasser's chief showpiece of revolutionary planning was to be a new high dam on the Nile at Aswan. He had expected the United States to contribute largely to its construction, but in mid-1956 the United States changed its mind. In retaliation, Nasser nationalized the Suez Canal, previously operated by a Franco-British company, and announced that he would use the revenues thus obtained to build the dam. For several months, contrary to expectations, the new Egyptian management kept canal traffic moving smoothly. The French and British governments, however, secretly allied themselves with Israel.

In the fall of 1956 Israeli forces invaded Egyptian territory, and French and British troops landed at Suez. The Soviet Union threatened to send "volunteers" to defend Egypt. Nor did the United States, angry at its British and French allies for concealing their plans, give its support to them. With the United States and the Soviet Union on the same side of an issue for once, the United Nations condemned the British-French-Israeli attack, and eventually a United Nations force was moved into the Egyptian-Israeli frontier areas, while the canal, blocked by the Egyptians, was reopened and finally bought by Nasser.

After the Suez crisis, Nasser's economic policy was governed by the grim struggle to support a fast-growing population. He undertook programs to reclaim land from the desert by exploiting underground water, and to limit the size of landholdings so that landless peasantry might hope to acquire land. To provide more jobs and to bolster national pride, he also accelerated the pace of industrialization. Most foreign enterprises in Egypt were nationalized.

In 1967 Nasser demanded that the United Nations troops that had kept the Egyptians and Israelis separated since 1956 be removed. UN Secretary General U Thant complied. The Egyptians began a propaganda barrage against Israel and closed the Strait of Tiran, the only water access to the newly developed Israeli port of Elath. The Israelis then struck the first blow in a new war, destroying the Egyptian air force on the ground and also hitting at the air forces of the other Arab states. In six days they overran the Sinai peninsula, all of Palestine west of the Jordan, including the Jordanian portion of Jerusalem, and the Golan heights on their northern frontier with Syria, from which the Syrians had been launching raids for several years. This third Arab-Israeli war in nineteen years ended in an all-out Israeli victory.

It was a humiliation not only for Nasser but also for the Soviet Union, which had supplied much of the equipment that had been abandoned as the Egyptian army retreated. The Soviets moved vigorously to support the Arab position, arguing their case in the United Nations, denouncing Israel, and rearming Egypt. Israeli armies remained in control of all the territory they had occupied. Had negotiations begun soon after the war, much of this territory could perhaps have been recovered, but as time passed the Israeli attitude hardened, and it became difficult for any Israeli government to give up any part of Jerusalem or the Golan heights, whose possession ensured Israeli territory against Syrian attack. Sinai, the Gaza strip, and perhaps the West Bank of the Jordan might be negotiable.

But the Arabs, led by Nasser, refused to negotiate directly with the Israelis or to take any step that would recognize the existence of the state of Israel. Rearmed and retrained partly by the Soviets, the Egyptians repeatedly proclaimed their intention of renewing the war. Israel existed as an armed camp, its men and women serving equally in the military forces, ever prepared for an attack.

In 1969 and 1970 tension again mounted dangerously in the Middle East. Arab Palestinians organized guerrilla attacks on Israel or on Israeli-occupied territory from Jordan, Syria, and Lebanon. The Lebanese government—precariously balanced between Christians and Muslims—was threatened by the Palestinian guerrillas and forced to concede Lebanese territory nearest the Israeli frontier. In various airports—Zurich, Athens, Tel Aviv—terrorists attacked planes carrying Israelis. At times the Palestinian Arab terrorist movement took on the aspects of an independent power, negotiating with the Chinese, compelling Nasser to modify his pronouncements, and demanding that its leaders be heard in the United Nations. In the autumn of 1970 terrorists hijacked four large planes—Swiss, British, German, and American—in a single day, holding the passengers as hostages in Jordan for the release of certain captives of their own. During the tense negotiations that followed, full-scale hostilities broke out between the Arab guerrillas and the Jordanian government. The Syrians intervened on the side of the guerrillas, and the threat of American intervention on the side of Jordan's King Hussein (1935–   ) and of a Soviet response was suddenly very real. Jordanian successes, Syrian withdrawal, and American and Soviet restraint helped the critical moment pass.

Just as grave was the continual Arab-Israeli confrontation in Egypt. Here Egyptian raids across the Suez Canal into Israeli-occupied territory in the Sinai were followed by Israeli commando raids into Egyptian territory on the west side of the canal and by Israeli air raids deep into Egypt. During 1970 the installation of Soviet missile sites near the canal forced the suspension of the Israeli attacks. But the Soviet involvement in Egyptian defense also threatened open confrontation between the Soviet Union and the United States. To avoid this danger, the United States, Britain, and France held four-power discussions with the Soviets on the Arab-Israeli conflict. With the Soviets totally committed to the Arab side and the French increasingly pro-Arab, with Britain balancing between the two sides, and with the United States trying to help Israel but determined to avoid another entanglement like Vietnam, the Israelis regarded with skepticism the possibility of any favorable solution emerging from the big powers' discussions. They insisted that only direct talks between themselves and the Arabs could lead to a satisfactory settlement. Arab insistence that a return of all occupied territory must precede any discussions rendered such meetings impossible. In the summer of 1970, however, the Egyptians and Israelis agreed to a cease-fire. But as hopes were renewed that discussions might at least begin, President Nasser died suddenly, to be replaced by Mohammed Anwar el-Sadat (1918–1981), who pledged himself to regain all occupied territories.

Sadat became suspicious of the Soviets' intentions, and in 1972 he expelled them from Egypt. Determined to regain Egypt's lost lands, he attacked Israeli-held territory, in concert with Syrian forces, on the Jewish holy day of Yom Kippur in October 1973. For the first time the Israelis were caught by surprise, and the Egyptians inflicted heavy losses. An Israeli counterattack turned the

Egyptians back, however, and in November a truce was signed in the Sinai by Israel's prime minister, Golda Meir (1898–1978). Oil diplomacy now demonstrated its force. At the outbreak of the war, the Arab oil-producing states cut off the flow of oil to Europe and the United States to force the West to bring pressure on Israel. While Americans had alternative sources of supply, many European nations had none, and the Arabs' policy had the desired response of pressure on Israel.

Sadat, however, was convinced that his people needed relief from constant conflict. In 1977 he committed himself to achieving Egyptian-Israeli peace. Flying to Israel, he addressed the parliament and met with the new Israeli prime minister, Menachim Begin (1913–   ). Begin had taken a particularly hard line on all issues relating to the Arab states, including the question of a homeland for the Palestinians. Though immediately condemned by most Arab states, Sadat persevered, and both he and Begin later accepted an invitation to meet with the American president, Jimmy Carter, at Camp David outside Washington. There a series of accords was worked out in September 1978 as the basis for future negotiations on a wide range of Middle Eastern questions.

But the "spirit of Camp David" did not last. The Arab states refused to join Egypt in negotiations. The Palestine Liberation Organization (PLO), as the principal voice for the Palestinian refugees, mounted an increased terrorist campaign. PLO leader Yasir Arafat (1929–   ), helped by growing Western disenchantment with Begin's tough bargaining positions, began to make inroads into Western support for Israel. Then three blows disrupted the delicate peace once again. In October 1981 Sadat was assassinated in Cairo by Muslim extremists. Two months later the Israeli parliament annexed the Golan heights.

A devastating by-product of the Gulf War was the great flood of Kurdish refugees seeking to escape from Iraq into Turkey and Iran. By April 1991, millions had fled and the world faced the need to feed starving victims of war in makeshift camps.

Reuters/Bettmann Newsphotos

Charges of bad faith drove a wedge between the new Reagan administration and Israel. Then in 1982 the long-explosive situation in Lebanon was ignited.

Determined to drive the Palestinians out of south Lebanon, the Israeli army had previously staged a massive invasion in 1978 and had withdrawn in favor of a United Nations peacekeeping force. However, Israel continued to aid Christian forces in Lebanon. A second Israeli occupation of southern Lebanon occurred in 1980 in retaliation for a raid on a *kibbutz* (Israeli collectivist agricultural settlement). Israel next declared Jerusalem to be its capital. In response to an Israeli attack on Syrian helicopters, Syria moved Soviet-built surface-to-air-missiles into Lebanon. In June 1981 an Israeli air strike on an Iraqi atomic reactor near Baghdad was widely condemned even by Israel's friends.

Even though the new Egyptian leader, Hosni Mubarak (1929–   ), stood by the spirit of Camp David, the Arab-Israeli conflict continued to make the Middle East the world's most unstable region. Begin, narrowly reelected in 1981, was determined not to appease the Palestinians. In the fall of 1982 he and his military advisers decided that they must at last clear the Palestinians out of all of Lebanon; They mounted a massively destructive attack on the city of Beirut. Shortly thereafter a Lebanese Christian Phalangist militia was allowed—probably with Israeli knowledge and clearly without sufficient Israeli supervision—to move into two large Palestinian refugee camps and massacre men, women, and children.

Even as Israel moved to institute a full inquiry into the killings at the Lebanese camp, tensions ran high in Israel and throughout the world. The investigating commission found several top Israeli military and government officials "indirectly responsible," which led to their demotion or dismissal. Weary and in poor health, Begin resigned in October 1983, and Israeli politics fell into a period of instability.

Iraq, at first closely aligned with the British after World War II, had ousted its monarchy and proclaimed a leftist, pan-Arab republic in 1958. Extremists of the left and right thereafter subjected the country to a series of coups and abortive coups. In 1968 the *Ba'ath* (Renaissance) party took control, and within three years one of its activists, Saddam Hussein (1937–   ), had emerged as leader. The party ruled by decree; in 1972 it signed an aid pact with the Soviet Union and began to receive heavy armaments in great quantities, and it supported Syria against Israel. Between 1969 and 1978 Iraq developed the most terror-ridden regime of the Arab states. Iraq and Syria—also in the hands of a Ba'ath party—soon became enemies.

Saddam Hussein had sought to conciliate Iraq's largest minority, the Kurds, who had been in sporadic rebellion for decades in quest of the autonomy promised to them by the Treaty of Sèvres in 1920, a promise broken by the Treaty of Lausanne three years later. The Kurdish leader, Mustafa al-Barzani (1901–1979), led a revolt in Iraq from 1960 to 1970 and, convinced that he could not trust Saddam, renewed the rebellion in 1974, continuing until his death. Iran had supported the Kurds until 1975, and the continued revolt led to Iraqi bombing of Kurdish villages in neighboring Iran.

In September 1980 Iraq and Iran entered into open warfare with air strikes and heavy ground fighting. The war expanded into the Persian Gulf in 1984, with attacks on oil fields and oil tankers. This fierce war ended in August 1988, when Iraq accepted a United Nations resolution for a cease-fire. Saddam then turned his forces against the Kurds once again, thoroughly crushing all opposition. He also continued to acquire the instruments of war from a variety of sources until, by 1990, he had one of the largest and best equipped armies in the world. The Western nations, particularly the United States, had thus far been content to see Iraq engage Iran, which had turned against the West and decreed the United States to be "the Great Satan."

Saddam Hussein declared in July 1990 that some Persian Gulf states, inspired by America, had conspired to keep oil prices down through overproduction and that Iraq's oil-rich and small neighbor Kuwait was part of an "imperialist-Zionist plan" to deny just free market prices to Iraq for its oil. At the end of the month the OPEC ministers agreed to a rise in oil prices, though not sufficiently high to satisfy Saddam. Iraq had claimed sovereignty over Kuwait since 1961, insisting that it was the artificial creation of the Saudi monarchy supported by the West, and before dawn on August 2 Saddam sent Iraqi tanks and infantry into Kuwait, occupying and looting the state. Later that day the United States denounced Iraq's aggression, the United Nations condemned the invasion and demanded the withdrawal of Iraqi troops from Kuwait, and the Soviet Union suspended arms sales to Saddam's army. Fourteen of the Arab League's twenty-one members also voted against Iraq's aggression, and the United Nations called for a boycott of Iraq.

The West, as well as Saudi Arabia, hoped that economic and moral pressure would force Iraq to withdraw. The United States President, George Bush, wanted a firm deadline to be given to Saddam, and the UN named January 15, 1991. Fearful that Iraq might launch an attack on Saudi Arabia, the Western nations began a massive troop movement to take up positions along the Iraqi and Kuwaiti borders. With financial aid from Saudi Arabia, West Germany, and Japan, and troop contingents from several Western nations, the United States took the lead in putting pressure on Saddam to withdraw.

When Saddam had not done so by the announced deadline, the United States led a concerted air attack against Iraq on January 16. Iraq replied by sending missiles against Saudi and Israeli targets, by the latter hoping to draw a response from Israel that would fracture the anti-Iraq coalition and lead to the withdrawal of some of its Arab members. Jordan, caught between the contending forces, turned from its formerly pro-Western stance to show increasing sympathy for Iraq.

In just two months, the coalition had thoroughly defeated the Iraqi armies, and Saddam Hussein had agreed to accept UN observers, to destroy Iraq's nuclear stores, and to rescind his annexation of Kuwait. In the

President Clinton with Israeli Minister Yitzhak Rabin and PLO Chairman Yasir Arafat after the signing of the Israeli–PLO peace accord, September 13, 1993.

Reuters/Gary Hershorn/The Bettmann Archive

United States, President George Bush's (1924–) popularity soared, and the sense of disenchantment with the military, pervasive since the war in Vietnam, was replaced with widespread patriotism and enthusiasm for the victorious American generals, in particular the Chief of Staff, Colin Powell (1937–) and the commanding officer in Kuwait and Iraq, General Norman Schwartzkopf (1934–). There were unforeseen results of the war as well: As the Iraqis retreated from Kuwait, they set fire to virtually all of that nation's oil wells, sending into the Persian Gulf unprecedented airborne pollution that would take years to correct; and millions of Kurds fled from Iraq into Iran and Turkey. The United Nations coalition failed to achieve one of its goals in the Gulf War: bringing down Saddam Hussein, who remained firmly in power. He employed chemical weapons in his ongoing war against the Kurds, attempted to defy the teams sent by the UN to verify that Iraq had dismantled its nuclear capacity, and in 1994 declared himself to be prime minister as well as president. The Middle East remained a powder keg, though there was hopeful movement on the Arab-Israeli conflict. When the Labor party of Yitzhak Rabin (1922–) was elected in 1992, Rabin called for reconciliation with Israel's neighbors, and despite repeated incidents of terrorism, Rabin and Arafat met to conclude an agreement in September 1993 by which the PLO recognized Israel's right to exist and Israel recognized the PLO as the representative of the Palestinians. Self-rule was extended to the Gaza strip and in the West Bank, and on July 25, 1994, Israel and Jordan signed a declaration ending their state of war forty-six years after it had begun.

Africa

The rebellion against imperialism reached Africa in the 1950s. Ethiopia was taken from its Italian conquerors after World War II and restored to Emperor Haile Selassie, who had been ousted in 1936. In 1952 he annexed the former Italian colony of Eritrea. Selassie embarked on various programs of internal modernization though not liberalization, and he worked hard to assist in the development of the Organization of African Unity. However, he misjudged both the speed and the nature of his reforms. An army mutiny, strikes in Ethiopia's cities, and massive student demonstrations in the capital, Addis Ababa, led to his imprisonment in 1974. The military junta then turned to local Marxists and the Soviet Union for support. In 1978 Soviet advisers and twenty thousand Cuban troops helped rout a Somalian independence force; in the same year a famine took an estimated million lives. Governed by a provisional military administrative council, Ethiopia was clearly far worse off in the 1980s than it had been under Selassie. Widespread famine and bloody civil war destroyed the nation's fragile economy, and in May 1991 its communist dictator fled the country in the face of an impending rebel victory. In 1993 Eritrea declared itself independent once again.

Particularly unpredictable was the unstable nature of Somalia, a nation on the Horn of East Africa formed from Italian and British colonial holdings in 1960. A bloodless coup in 1969, led by a Supreme Revolutionary Council, began a chaotic series of changes. Somalia claimed the Ogaden from Ethiopia on the ground that it was populated largely by ethnic Somalis, and Ethiopia turned to Soviet arms and Cuban troops to drive out the Somalian troops in a war that lasted until 1988 and brought 1,500,000 refugees into the already impoverished Somalian republic. One-man rule ended in 1991, but civil war, drought, and growing lawlessness took 40,000 lives in the next two years and the refugees faced starvation. In July 1992 the UN took the unusual action of declaring Somalia to be a nation without a government; the United States offered to send troops to safeguard food deliveries to the starving. In the face of casualties and further chaos, the United States withdrew its troops in March 1994, though some UN forces stayed to protect the distribution of relief aid. Violence continued, and Somalia remained without a viable government.

Among the Muslim and Arabic-speaking states bordering the Mediterranean, the former Italian colony of Libya achieved independence in 1951, and the French-dominated areas of Morocco and Tunisia in 1956. Morocco became an autocratic monarchy and Tunisia a republic under the moderate presidency of Habib Bourguiba (1903–   ). Algeria followed, but only after a severe and debilitating war of independence against the French. Its first ruler after independence, Ahmed Ben Bella (1918–   ), was allied with the Chinese communists. Colonel Houari Boumédienne (1925–1981), who ousted Ben Bella in 1965, in large part because of the slumping economy, favored the Soviets. Algeria and Libya strongly supported the Arab cause against Israel; Morocco and Tunisia did so hardly at all, though Tunis did become the headquarters for the Arab League in 1979.

In 1987 Bourguiba was deposed, and his successors systematically repressed Islamic fundamentalism. Algeria was less successful in doing so, and an ambitious intention to establish a multiparty system was abandoned when, in 1992, the government canceled national elections in the face of a likely Islamic fundamentalist victory. The president was assassinated, and over the following years security forces, foreigners, high-ranking officials, and intellectuals were killed by the fundamentalists while, in turn, the state took thousands of lives in its drive to end the insurgency. By 1995 the assassinations were being carried into France, which supported the government's hard line, while other Western powers urged conciliation, leading to a rift that the fundamentalists clearly hoped to capitalize upon.

In Libya a coup d'état in 1969 brought to power a group of army officers. In 1970 they confiscated Italian- and Jewish-owned property. American evacuation of a huge air base in Libya and Libyan purchases of French and Soviet arms added to the general apprehension in North Africa. A temporary "union" of Egypt, Libya, and the Sudan in 1970 had little political importance, but it marked the emergence of Colonel Muammar el-Qaddafi (1942–   ), the Libyan political boss and prime minister, as the most fanatic Muslim fundamentalist and most dictatorial ruler in the Arab world. He was also one of the richest, and he used his oil riches to instigate rebellion and political assassination throughout the Arab world. After 1975 he purchased billions of dollars worth of modern Soviet arms and became the supplier to terrorist groups in much of the world. Mercurial and unpredictable, Qaddafi waged border wars against Egypt in 1977 and in Chad from 1977. In 1980 he conscripted civil servants into his army, casting the economy into chaos and paralyzing administration. Even so, he continued to command a widespread loyal following, perhaps in part because of American air and sea attacks on Libya in 1986. In 1992 the UN imposed sanctions on Libya for its failure to surrender men believed to be linked to the bombing in 1988 of an American commercial aircraft over Lockerbie, Scotland, but Qaddafi remained in power.

South of the Muslim tier of nations lay the former colonies of the French, British, and Belgians. The West African climate had discouraged large-scale white settlement, except in portions of the Belgian Congo; but in East Africa—in Kenya and Uganda especially—many Europeans had settled in the fertile highlands, farmed the land, and regarded the country as their own, as did the large white population of the Union of South Africa. Here, too, were substantial Indian populations, usually small merchants, who carried on trade across the Indian Ocean.

In the areas with little white settlement, independence came quickly. The Gold Coast, with a relatively well-educated population and valuable economic resources, became the nation of Ghana in 1957. Its leader, the American-educated Kwame Nkrumah (1909–1972), made a hopeful start on economic planning within a political democracy. But he grew increasingly dictatorial, jailing his political enemies and sponsoring grandiose projects that personally enriched him and his followers. A promising democracy became a dictatorship in the 1960s, while the economy was in serious disarray. Rising foreign debt and Nkrumah's inability to persuade the rich and populous Asante people to submerge themselves in a greater Ghanaian nationalism, led to his overthrow by a military coup early in 1966. Many coups later, however, Ghana remained economically stagnant and overpopulated.

The French colonies all achieved independence in 1960, except for Guinea, which broke away in 1958 under the leadership of a pro-Soviet, Ahmed Sékou Touré (1922–1984). After independence, most of the colonies retained close economic ties with France as members of the French Community. Guinea did not; the French left in 1958, and the country developed a socialist economy with some success. The neighboring states of Mali (formerly French Sudan) and Mauritania also pursued a generally pro-Soviet line.

Of the newly independent former French colonies, two proved especially important. Senegal grew under the twenty-year leadership of Léopold Senghor (1906–   ), a noted poet who spoke of the beauties of negritude, helping give rise to the slogan "black is beautiful" around the world. The Ivory Coast, whose leader Félix Houphouët-Boigny (1905–1993) had long parliamentary experience as a deputy in Paris, also proved to be stable and prosperous. The Ivory Coast led a pro-Western bloc within the Organization of African Unity, while Senegal often played the role of intermediary between factions, developing a multiparty system and full democratic elections at home.

In 1960 Nigeria, most important of the British colonies, achieved independence. With 60 million people and varied economic resources, it represented a great hope for the future. The British had trained many thousands of Nigerians in England and in schools and universities in Nigeria itself. The country was divided into four regions, each semiautonomous, to ease tribal tensions, of which perhaps the most severe was that between the Muslim Hausa of the northern region and the Christian Ibo of the eastern region. In the Hausa areas, the well-educated, aggressive, and efficient Ibos ran the railroads, power stations, and other modern facilities, and formed an important element in the cities. When army plotters led by an Ibo officer murdered the Muslim prime minister of Nigeria and seized power in 1966, the Hausas rose and massacred the Ibos living in the north, killing many thousands.

By 1967 the Ibo east had seceded and called itself the Republic of Biafra, and the Nigerian central government embarked on full-scale war to force the Ibos and other eastern groups to return to Nigerian rule. Misery and famine accompanied the operations, and the war dragged on until 1970, with both Britain and the Soviet Union helping the Nigerian government. The Biafrans got much sympathy but no real help. When the war finally ended, the mass slaughter that had been feared did not materialize and the nation devoted its energies to reconciliation and recovery. Nigeria was able to use its growing oil revenues for economic development. In 1979 it returned to civilian government after thirteen years of military rule, but in 1983 a coup ended democratic government.

In east Africa, the British settlers in Kenya struggled for eight years (1952–1960) against a secret terrorist society formed within the Kikuyu tribe, the Mau Mau, whose aim was to drive all whites out of the country. Though the British imprisoned one of its founders, Jomo Kenyatta (1893–1978), and eventually suppressed the Mau Mau, Kenya became independent in 1963. Kenyatta became its first chief of state and steered Kenya into prosperity and a generally pro-Western stance. However, Kenya moved increasingly toward authoritarian government under Kenyatta's successor, Daniel Arap Moi (1924–   ). In 1961, under the leadership of Julius Nyerere (1922–   ), Tanganyika became independent. A violent pro-Chinese communist coup d'état on the island of Zanzibar was followed in 1964 by its merger with Tanganyika as the new country of Tanzania. Nyerere solicited assistance from Communist China to build the Tanzam railroad from Dar es Salaam, the Tanzanian capital, to Zambia, to help that new nation achieve greater economic independence from South Africa. Nyerere also nationalized the banks, established vast new cooperative villages to stimulate more productive agriculture, and sought to play a major role in holding African nations to a neutralist course. Still, all efforts to create an East African federation failed, as Kenyatta pursued a generally capitalist path, Nyerere a socialist one, and Uganda an intensely nationalist and isolationist policy.

In contrast to the British, who had tried to prepare the way for African independence by providing education and administrative experience for Africans, the Belgians, who had since the late nineteenth century governed the huge central African area known as the Congo, had made no such effort. When the Belgian rulers suddenly pulled out in 1960, it was not long before regional rivalries among local leaders broke out. A popular leftist leader, Patrice Lumumba (1925–1961), was assassinated; the province of Katanga, site of rich copper mines and with many European residents, seceded under its local leader, who was strongly pro-Belgian; other areas revolted. The United Nations sent troops to restore order and force

the end of the Katangese secession, while the Chinese supported certain rebel factions and the South Africans and Belgians others. By 1968 the military regime of General Joseph Mobutu (1930–   ) was firmly in control. Soon after, Mobutu renamed the cities and people of his country to erase all traces of the colonial past: the Congo became Zaire, and he changed his own name to its African form, Mobutu Sese Seko.

Two small Belgian enclaves, originally under German control from 1899 and administered by the Belgians as a League of Nations mandate from 1916 and a UN trusteeship after World War II, also experienced civil war. Originally Ruanda-Urundi, the two areas became Rwanda and Burundi in 1962. The Hutu people were in a substantial majority in both states, though they were ruled by the Tutsi, who took the best positions in government and the military. An unsuccessful Hutu rebellion in Burundi in 1972–1973 left 150,000 Hutu dead and propelled 100,000 refugees into Zaire and Tanzania. The first democratic election in Burundi, in 1993, was followed by the assassination of the elected Hutu leader, resulting in waves of ethnic violence. In April 1994 the presidents of both Burundi and Rwanda were killed in an unexplained plane crash, and systematic massacres followed, especially in Rwanda. Hutu militias killed over 200,000 Tutsi, and 2 million refugees fled to miserable camps in Zaire and elsewhere, where cholera decimated the starving populations. French troops, acting for the UN, moved in to establish a "safe zone," but the inter-ethnic strife, and the fact that many Roman Catholic clergy had been killed in the predominantly Christian country, left deep wounds and simmering suspicion even as the French gave way to an African peacekeeping force later in the year.

In Portuguese Angola a local rebellion forced Portuguese military intervention. Angola, which provided Portugal with much of its oil, together with Mozambique on the east coast and the tiny enclave of Portuguese Guinea on the west, remained under Lisbon's control despite guerrilla uprisings. The Portuguese regarded these countries as overseas extensions of metropolitan Portugal. But the guerrilla war proved expensive and unpopular at home, and in the mid-1970s Portugal abandoned Africa. Thereafter Angola became a center for African liberation groups aimed at South Africa. The Angolan government invited in many thousands of Cuban troops, to the dismay of the United States, and the remained until 1991.

Most stubborn of all African problems was the continuation and extension of the policy of apartheid in South Africa, where whites were a minority of about one in five of the population. The nonwhites included blacks, *coloureds* (as those of mixed European and African ancestry were called), and Asians, mostly Indians.

The Afrikaners, who had tried unsuccessfully to keep South Africa from fighting on Britain's side in World War II, had emerged after the war as a political majority. Imbued with an extremely narrow form of Calvinist religion that taught that God had ordained the inferiority of blacks, the ruling group moved steadily to impose policies of rigid segregation: separate townships to live in, separate facilities, no political equality or inter-

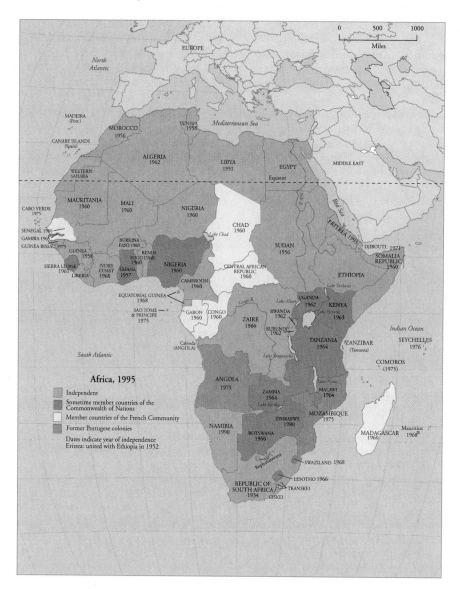

marriage, little opportunity for higher education or advancement into the professions, and frequent banning of black leaders. The Afrikaners also introduced emergency laws making it possible to arrest people on suspicion, hold them incommunicado, and punish them without trial. Severe censorship prevailed, and dissent was curbed. In 1949, in defiance of the United Nations, South Africa annexed the former German colony and League mandate of Southwest Africa, where the policy of apartheid also prevailed. The International Court of Justice in 1971 ruled that South Africa was holding the area illegally.

One possible solution to the Afrikaner problem—how to maintain segregation, prevent rebellion by the black majority, assure South Africa of a continuing labor force, and satisfy world opinion—seemed to be a combination of modest liberalization of the apartheid laws and the establishment of partially self-governing territories, known as Homelands, to which black Africans would

be sent. Begun in 1959 as *Bantustans,* or "Bantu nations," the plan called for pressing most blacks onto 13 percent of the country's land area. Virtually no African nation would support such a plan, and much of the West was also opposed. The United States equivocated. It saw South Africa as a strategically important potential ally in case of war with the Soviet Union and appreciated its staunch anticommunist position on world affairs, but it also realized that any unqualified support to the South African regime would cost the United States nearly the whole of black Africa and would also be opposed by many at home. Thus when South Africa finally created its first allegedly independent Homelands—the Transkei in 1976, Bophuthatswana and Ciskei in 1977, and Venda in 1979—not one nation, including the United States, gave them diplomatic recognition.

Despite South Africa's most efficient and well-equipped military force, and the very competent Bureau for State Security (mockingly called BOSS), the appar-

Nelson Mandela is inaugurated as the president of South Africa in 1994.

Reuters/Peter Andrews

ently secure, white-dominated government was repeatedly challenged by black youth, a rising labor movement, and the African National Congress which, in 1983, turned to terrorism. International condemnation of South Africa did not appear to shake the determination of the government of P. W Botha (1916–   ) to maintain white supremacy.

In 1989 Botha stepped down and was succeeded by F. W. de Klerk (1936–   ), who had committed himself to phasing out white domination, though without permitting black majority rule. De Klerk surprised the world by doing as he had promised, and at the cost of the withdrawal of several members of his Nationalist party, he ended many of the segregated practices and, early in 1991, declared before parliament that full racial equality was his goal. The many nations that had applied economic sanctions against South Africa to force change now felt vindicated, as apartheid appeared to be near an end.

Two black African leaders who had opposed each other also appeared to have made their peace early in 1991. Nelson Mandela (1918–   ), in particular, became a worldwide symbol of hope for racial harmony in southern Africa. Until the Sharpeville massacre of 1960 he had been an advocate of nonviolence and a vice-president of the African National Congress (ANC), but when he turned to sabotage he was imprisoned for life in 1964. From prison he became the rallying point for the South African freedom movement. Botha offered Mandela his freedom subject to a promise not to use violence to achieve change, and Mandela refused; in February 1990, de Klerk released him unconditionally. After a triumphant trip to the United States and elsewhere, Mandela returned to South Africa to attempt to create a unity movement.

The leader of the most prominent tribe, the Zulu, was Gatsha Buthelezi (1928–   ), who favored negotiation with the white government and was believed to be angling for Zulu dominance in any multiracial administration that might result. At times Buthelezi had openly opposed the ANC, and the Inkatha Movement, which he led, fomented street fighting in black communities throughout the 1980s. However, with Mandela's release and de Klerk's denunciation of apartheid, Buthelezi agreed to work with Mandela and the ANC.

Despite repeated outbreaks of local violence, the transition to full democracy was far smoother than virtually any observers had predicted. In 1993 the ANC and the National Party agreed on the outline of a new constitution, and in April 1994 South Africa held its first election in which people of all races could vote. Mandela became president, the ANC taking over 62 percent of the vote. The last legal vestiges of racial separation were cast down.

Latin America

Although most of the Latin American republics had by 1945 enjoyed political independence for more than a century, they had much in common economically and socially with the emerging nations of Asia and Africa. Like the Asians and Africans, the Latin Americans had been suppliers of foods and raw materials to the rest of the world. Bananas, coffee, sugar, beef, oil, nitrates, and copper fluctuated widely in price on the world market; before the Latin Americans could raise their standards of living, they would have to build on a more stable and diversified economic base. Most of Latin America had a racially mixed population: some native-born whites or immigrants from Europe (like the Italians in Argentina), some descendants of the indigenous peoples, and some blacks (chiefly in Brazil and Haiti). Nominally governed under a democratic system of elected officials and parliaments, they had all too often lived under military dictatorships that shifted whenever a new army officer felt strong enough to challenge the one in power.

Latin Americans traditionally felt a mixture of envy, dislike, and suspicion toward the United States. Upper-class Latin Americans educated in Europe believed that North Americans lacked true culture; North Americans generally seemed to know little about Latin America. Whenever the United States ceased to be indifferent and devoted some attention to Latin America, it did so by intervening in their affairs. Upper-class Latin Americans were well aware of the miserable poverty in which most of their people lived, but they hoped that social revolution would not disturb the system. Thus, when President Carter applied his test of "human rights" to the authoritarian regimes of South America, they were deeply resentful.

Some earlier attempts—the Pan-American Union in 1910 and President Franklin Roosevelt's Good Neighbor policy after 1933—were primarily cultural in emphasis. After World War II the Pan-American Union became the Organization of American States (OAS). Somewhat looser than an alliance, the OAS provided a means for consultation among all the American nations on all important matters of mutual concern. The Alliance for Progress—launched under President Kennedy and designed to enable the United States to help the Latin Americans to help themselves—proved a disappointment, in part because it was difficult to allay Latin American suspicions of American intentions, in part because of the deeply entrenched ruling families that dominated most Latin American countries.

Not every Latin American country was invariably a dictatorship. Uruguay, for example, a small country with a population largely European in origin, had created a welfare state so advanced that by 1970 the Uruguayan economy collapsed, largely because of the payment of state funds to individual citizens for the many types of benefits available. However, the eroding economy gave the terrorist Tupamaros an opportunity to win some support, and in 1974 the military succeeded in defeating the Tupamaros at the cost of imposing a virtual military dictatorship on Uruguay.

Venezuela, with rapidly developing oil resources, in 1959 ousted the last of a long line of military dictators and made the transition to moderate democratic rule. As a member of OPEC, Venezuela moved in the 1970s into an era of prosperity and stability. Meanwhile Colombia underwent a lengthy terrorist campaign in the country-side—virtually a civil war—in which many thousands were killed, and even when this ended was still experiencing extremes of wealth, poverty, and crime. Brazil, the enormous Portuguese-speaking land larger than any other Latin American country, suffered from recurrent economic crises and military coups. Its poverty-stricken northeast, where many thousands lived in virtual serfdom on big plantations, contrasted sharply with the luxurious apartment-house and beach life of the big cities; but these, too, had their festering slums. Brazilian government was, until 1990, a military dictatorship that stood accused of torturing its political prisoners.

Chile, too, was plagued by military intervention. In 1970 Chileans elected a Marxist, Salvador Allende Gossens (1908–1973), as president. Though Allende was a minority president, having won less than 40 percent of the votes, he took office in relative calm and moved gradually to expropriate foreign properties. But some of his supporters felt he was not nationalizing rapidly enough, and the United States feared that he would not provide just compensation for the properties he expropriated. In a still controversial series of events in which the American CIA and possibly the International Telephone and Telegraph Corporation were involved, the Allende administration was toppled by a military coup in September 1973. By then the economy was in chaos. The military junta declared that it would exterminate Marxism, and it resorted to mass arrests and kidnappings. The economy did not improve, and in 1990 an elected civilian government succeeded the military.

Argentina—peopled almost entirely by European immigrants and their descendants—continued to have a social system that gave power to a small landlord class. The beginnings of industrialization deepened popular dissatisfaction with the regime. Brought to power in the national election of 1946, Colonel Juan Perón (1895–1974) became a dictator on the model of Mussolini, Hitler, and Franco. In 1955 he was removed by a military coup. He had begun to appeal to the poorer masses, the *descamisados* (shirtless ones), and thus lost much of

his following among the conservative upper classes. Moreover, he had quarreled with the Roman Catholic church and put through anticlerical measures that cost him further support. Nor could he solve the grave economic and financial problems arising out of his country's essentially colonial position; indeed, his uncontrolled spending on public works and welfare projects, and the extravagant lifestyle of his wife, Eva Duarte (1919–1952), virtually bankrupted Argentina.

During the years that followed, many Argentines continued to support Perón, who lived in exile in Spain. Twice a weak elected government was overthrown by a military coup. The army regime installed in 1966 promised to purge Argentina of corruption but aroused much opposition by its repression of academic freedom. The old problems remained unsolved, indeed almost untackled. Perón returned to Argentina in 1973 and was again elected president, but he died before he could initiate new policies. He was succeeded by his second wife, Isabel (1931–   ). She, too, was removed by a military coup in 1976 and placed under house arrest. The military government turned to widespread repression, killing perhaps five thousand Argentines, suppressing civil liberties, using torture to extract confessions, and becoming increasingly anti-Semitic. Inflation ran out of control, unemployment reached the highest levels since the depression, and the peso was devalued. To distract attention from the economy, the Argentine military attempted an invasion of the Falkland (or Malvinas) Islands and suffered a humiliating defeat at the hands of the British in 1982. By 1987, however, Argentina seemed on the road to democracy. Political unrest continued, however, in the Caribbean states and in Central America. The United States was deeply stung by the failure to anticipate Castro's successful revolution in Cuba and was determined not to recognize his regime and to force Cuban submission by prohibiting American trade. The Cuban situation proved divisive at home, bringing as it did thousands of anti-Castro Cuban exiles and poverty-stricken refugees into Florida. While the United States boycotted Cuban goods, hoping to destroy the Cuban tobacco and sugar economy, other nations filled the trade gap. Castro, who had come to power in 1959, remained firmly in control.

In 1965 the United States concluded that a revolution in the Dominican Republic, a neighbor of Cuba, was inspired by Castro. Between 1930 and 1961 the Dominican Republic had been ruled by a ruthless and corrupt dictator. After his assassination, the first freely elected government in a generation took office, but increasing tension between the army and the new reformers led to military coups and finally to a civil war in 1965. Fearing that communists might take over, President Johnson sent in American troops, and then tried to internationalize the intervention by appealing to the Organization of American States. By a narrow margin, the OAS responded, and five of its member states sent troops to join the Americans. The Dominican Republic was pacified sufficiently for constitutional elections to be held in 1966. A political moderate, Joaquin Balaguer (1907–   ), became president and retained his office

Haitian President Jean-Bertrand Aristide waves as he arrives at the National Palace, Port-au-Prince, Haiti, October 15, 1994.

Reuters/Jim Borg/The Bettman Archive

when elections were held in the 1970s and 1980s, and again in 1994.

It would have been political suicide in 1965 for any president of the United States to allow another Caribbean country to fall into pro-Soviet hands. But the Dominican episode aroused much opposition among Americans; and in Latin America the reappearance of an American occupation force served to heighten the suspicion that the United States was still determined to intervene when its interests appeared threatened. Although the United States did not intervene directly in Trinidad, Jamaica, or Guyana, it did provide "advisers" to any mainland Central American nation that considered itself threatened by Cuban communists. In 1975 a guerrilla war in Guatemala was launched against the military government there; by 1981 the dictatorial Somoza family in Nicaragua had been overthrown by the Marxist Sandinista guerrillas, who established a five-member junta to shape a socialist state. In 1979 a military coup in El Salvador was followed by a protracted guerrilla war, political assassinations, and the prospect of deepening American involvement. By the 1980s Central America was in ferment.

Four small nations in particular were the focus of explosive events. Grenada, the smallest independent nation

in the Western Hemisphere, appeared to the United States to have fallen under Soviet or Cuban influence. When, in 1983, the Grenadan prime minister was overthrown by a coup and executed, the United States invaded and until mid-1985 occupied the island state. The detested Duvalier regime ended twenty-six years of dictatorship in Haiti in 1986, and after a period of repression and instability, in 1990 the Haitians were permitted a free election in which a radical Roman Catholic priest, Jean-Bertrand Aristide (1953–   ) emerged as president. However, a coup led by the Duvalier family's private militia, the Tonton Macoutes, tried to depose him, and the resulting rioting and rise of the power of the military led to Aristide's arrest and exile in September 1991. Military suppression spurred thousands of Haitian refugees toward the United States, and in June 1993 the UN imposed a worldwide embargo on the Haitian regime. In September 1994 the military leaders agreed to step down; thousands of American troops were sent to Haiti, and in October Aristide resumed office.

In Nicaragua civil war broke out in 1979, with Marxist Sandinista guerrillas the victors. Thereafter the United States backed *contra* (anti-Marxist) rebels in the hope of bringing down the Sandinistas, and despite an adverse ruling by the International Court of Justice, the American government continued to supply aid to the rebel leaders. Late in 1986 the discovery that money intended for the purchase of arms for Iranian use—in a complex attempt to secure the release of American hostages held by Islamic fundamentalists in Lebanon—had been diverted illegally by officials of the United States government to supply the contras, contrary to the express vote of the Congress, threatened the Reagan administration with its most severe political crisis. Reagan's intense personal popularity helped him to weather the storm, however, and in 1990, in a peaceful election, the Sandinista government was defeated in Nicaragua.

In December 1989, United States forces invaded Panama, joining up with American forces already stationed there. The immediate cause was concern for the security of the Panama Canal, which by treaty in 1979 was in process of being nationalized into Panamanian hands. The deeper cause for American intervention was fear that a former client, Manuel Noriega (1938–   ), head of the Panamanian armed forces and dictator of Panama from 1982, was engaged in the international drug trade, had maintained himself in power by nullifying an election, and was threatening both American civilian and military facilities in Panama. In four days of fighting, American forces defeated the Panamanian army. Widespread destruction in the capital city left fourteen thousand Panamanians homeless. Though most Panamanians appeared to welcome the Americans as liberators, substantial resentment against the United States grew when it failed to supply the anticipated massive aid to rebuild the damaged area and to improve the foundering Panamanian economy.

Guerrilla warfare and widespread terrorism had by the mid-1980s become common tactics of both the political right and the political left. The United States had returned to its old practice of military intervention in the Caribbean area. Wars were no longer declared, they simply broke out when, usually without warning, the troops of one nation moved onto the territory of another. Casualties ran high, for technology had provided vastly more destructive weaponry. The United States had suffered more casualties in World War II than in all its previous foreign wars combined, and yet American casualties in the localized Korean and Vietnam wars, combined with a variety of military actions elsewhere, were nearly 40 percent the World War II figure. Conventional strategic and tactical approaches to war would not work, and the high-technology nations were slow to adjust to the new methods of warfare.

The nature of diplomacy, and the ability of the most powerful nations to exert pressure on weaker states, changed drastically as terrorism became a disruptively fearsome weapon. The Olympic Games of 1972, held in Munich, were shattered by the murder of several members of the Israeli Olympic team by terrorists. The hijacking of aircraft and cruise ships intimidated thousands of potential travelers. As powerful a nation as the United States had to admit that it could no longer protect its citizens abroad. The murder of ambassadors on their way to work or even in their offices, the unpredictable bombings of shopping malls and military outposts in dozens of countries, forced upon normally open democracies extraordinary security measures. Most nations, however, refused to give in to terrorism and resolutely sought to conduct their affairs with as much semblance of normalcy as possible.

If the cold war between the Soviet Union and the United States was over, then its legacy continued, for in the Middle East, in Central America, and potentially in Africa prolonged instability and the prospect of involvement by one or more of the major powers remained a daily threat to the world. Our times were, in standard of living, the best of times; our times were, in terms of stability, peace, and safety, not the worst of times but they nonetheless seemed so to millions. Western civilization had arrived at the present with little prospect that the immediate future would differ greatly from the immediate past.

ROSPECTS

Historians do not deal with the future. Yet one justification for the writing and reading of history is that it helps us better to understand the present and to interpret more intelligently the future as it rushes in upon us. In 1846 the young French poet Charles Baudelaire (1821–1867) defined modernity as that phase of experience in which life is lived in fragments, in which the pace of change and an inability to separate the important from the unimportant create a sense of confusion, of one's life being out of control or in the control of others. The rapidity of observed change in one's own time would lead to the illusion that life in the past was both more coher-

ent and understandable and, somehow, actually slower. Such a view of history produces hope: A fixed past that one might study and comprehend, could be contrasted with a future that lacked confining definition and to which no walls had yet been set. But the historian also knows that the past helps to define the future.

What changes of "our times" would be most important in shaping the next times? What might history conclude before the fragmentation of life as experienced takes over? Certainly technology will continue to transform daily life, massive population growth will induce vast social change, and the world will become ever more interconnected. But what beyond this?

One obvious trend of the recent decades was a worldwide movement of peoples, of emigrations and immigrations, so that once ethnically or racially homogeneous peoples were dramatically less so and the cultures of once-distant peoples became parts of other cultures. Perhaps no impact of World War II and the period of decolonization and localized postcolonial wars has been more obvious than the movement of great numbers of Asians, Africans, West Indians, and others into countries once overwhelmingly European in their cultures. Such movements of people have changed clothing styles and eating habits, enriched European languages, and utterly altered communication, education, and medical knowledge.

By the 1990s the concept of human rights was thoroughly embedded in Western societies and increasingly throughout the world, and even where given only lip service, concern for "world opinion" often shaped diplomacy, military strategy, and business tactics. The range of agreed-upon rights had been greatly widened to include the concept of the right to privacy, the right not to incriminate oneself, and the right of access to education, health care, and public safety. Many claimed a right to an unpolluted environment as well. By no means did everyone enjoy such rights, even in the most stable of democracies, but they represented agreed-upon aspirations for all societies. Before our times there was little agreement on what constituted basic human rights at the international level and little concept of "world opinion."

The last thirty years have brought the most remarkable social progress and increase in standard of living in history. In the Western democracies, purchasing power for the average employed person increased by nearly half, overseas travel increased twentyfold, and two-family incomes became commonplace. Thirty years ago most of the world lacked personal computers, microwave ovens, audiocassettes, videos, television, FM radio, electronic toys, and credit cards or automatic bank tellers. There were no CAT scans, lens implants, or artificial joints; there was no microsurgery, magnetic imaging, or in-vitro fertilization. There was no genetic engineering as the term is understood today. The divorce rate was one fifth of its present level, and in most of the Western world "crime in the streets" was not a political issue. Life expectancy in the industrial world rose to nearly eighty, creating an aging population.

The past three decades have also brought, in much of the Western world, the emancipation of women. The contraceptive pill, which became widely available in the

1960s, made family planning possible where social custom or religion did not prevent it. The movement in the 1970s to award equal pay for equal work, followed by equal opportunity and affirmative action programs, opened up a vast new labor market, with millions of new earners. Families were smaller, income was larger, and thus real income rose for the great majority. Yet, single parent families rose rapidly, with half of the children in such families living below the poverty line as defined by Western societies. In many nations gay and lesbian individuals were also assured of the full exercise of their rights.

Two major changes influenced the way history was studied, giving rise to the question, Who owns history? "Women's history" was increasingly replaced by gender history. The former had tended to mean simply adding women to the basic historical story, being certain that the achievements of women were recorded. This "add-on" approach also meant that sections of texts, courses, and curriculae included women more systematically and in far greater depth than before. But gender history meant far more. First, it weakened class as a primary category of analysis, making it no more than simply equal to gender ethnicity, and sexuality. This meant that labor history, for example, which had tended to be heavily male in its orientation, had to be reexamined, for more was required than simply placing women at the scene, in work places and strikes or on revolutionary barricades. Gender does not equate with women, just as race relations are not "about" nonwhites; gender is part of an inquiry even if women are not. As men had felt threatened by the feminization of work, which assailed their class positions,they also felt threatened by the idea that masculinity was a feminist issue. Thus genderized history insisted on a reconstruction of categories so that women would not be required to fit into units of study that had been developed largely to explain the actions of men. Kinship, family, sexuality, and production were seen to be aspects of the dispersal and use of power.

The second change was a challenge to the idea that there was a coherent story of Western civilization that could be outlined between the pages of a book. That books were written on, and students studied, Western societies as opposed to other world societies was argued to be a form of racism or, at least, cultural blindness in the eyes of some. At first schools and universities simply turned to the "add-on" solution, adding courses on Africa, Asia, or Latin America, or on a variety of ethnic histories, especially in the United States. The sense that university education was organized around dominant masculine and Western values was attacked by those who were convinced that society must be freed of organizing principles that seemed to "empower" one group or another. However, demands for revised curriculae often resulted in an irony, in which members of ethnic communities preferred to study only themselves and with individuals of the same background, precisely the organizing principles of which they often had complained when knowledge was said to be dominated by white, middle-class, or Protestant values. For the most part the discipline of history was less caught up in this debate than most subjects of study in the social

sciences and humanities, however, since historians could hardly abandon the principal organizing force of historical narrative, which is sequence. To argue that the great African author Wole Soyinka (1934   ), who won the Nobel Prize for Literature in 1986, was a writer of equal stature to Shakespeare was one thing, while to argue that Shakespeare was irrelevant and Soyinka relevant to history was quite another, simply because one preceded the other: Shakespeare influenced Soyinka, while the Nigerian writer did not influence Shakespeare. Where pure matters of chronology were involved, there was little debate; where aesthetic judgments about relative merit or, even more dramatically, about relevance to understanding the present time were at issue, there was frequent discussion. Such discussions also led to the question, Who owns history?, something not often asked in the previous century.

Typically Western governments responded to unemployment, soaring interest rates, falling educational levels, and rising crime, poverty, and illness by creating social welfare programs. Some, as with medical care in Great Britain following World War II, or sweeping programs concerning sexual mores in Scandinavia, or housing loan insurance in Australia, became long-term changes within the society, while others were mere palliatives, tried and abandoned, attempted largely for their political effect. By the end of the 1980s the United States, for example, had 200 separate welfare programs operated by the federal government. Taxes rose throughout the Western nations, in many countries to half the income of the middle class, and while substantially less in North America, nonetheless to the point by 1991 that taxes were the single largest item in the budget of a typical citizen. The state, the government, had in all societies become a player in the life of the individual to a greater extent than ever before. By 1995 nearly everywhere citizens appeared to want less government. Still, in most of the West less than five years from the twenty-first century there continued to be a basic faith in democracy rather than some allegedly more efficient form of government, in the value of one's labor, hope for one's fellow beings, respect for the environment, and love of country.

There was, by the 1980s and 1990s, much talk about the decline of the West. Certainly there was a decline, if a monopoly on technology or the ability to force the world into a Western mold by trade, industrial efficiency, or military expertise were the criteria. Yet looking beyond nation to culture, the historian could easily note the continuing global ascendency of the English language and of popular Western mass culture, especially in its American variant, if not of elite culture. American ideas continued to absorb the ideas of others, to cross borders, to change; attempts to stave off this global culture, most notably in Muslim lands, posed vast transnational problems in terms of respecting other societies, and the future was by no means certain. But the cultures customarily described as "Western civilization" remained vigorous, demonstrably attractive to the rest of the world, and relatively coherent. A historian could guess that in the twenty-first century the body of ideas embraced by that collective term would remain interesting, significant, and usefully true.

By the early 1990s the western world faced enormous problems: homeless people in the United States alone had, by some estimates, reached 100,000; illegal drugs, especially "crack," had devastated families and led to a soaring murder rate in the cities; racism and outrage led to continued violence; political leaders often were held in low regard; abuse of the elderly, and of children, had become more obvious, while Alzheimers, AIDS, and other diseases took a sweeping toll; migrant labor poured across the U.S. border from Mexico, often to face discrimination and low wages; and pollution was only gradually being brought under control, as scientists and government figures continued to discuss acid rain and global warming.

AP/Wide World Photos; Lisa Quinones/Black Star; Rob Nelson/Black Star; Andrew Holbrooke/Black Star; C. Blankenhorn/Black Star

SUMMARY

After World War II the nations of western Europe maintained their sovereignty and nationalist outlook but formed an economic union, the Common Market. In Britain a social revolution was accomplished with the nationalization of some industries and the extension of social programs. In the 1980s, however, Britain still faced economic difficulties and the unresolved problem of Northern Ireland.

In France, General de Gaulle reestablished republican government after liberation. Although he left office in 1946, he returned in 1968 to preside over the birth of the Fifth Republic.

In the postwar period the West German economy benefited from the building of new, modern, industrial facilities. Democratic government was established but reunion with East Germany was not accomplished until 1990.

Italy experienced turmoil in the postwar years although it enjoyed economic growth. The Italian

Communist party increased in size but declared its willingness to enter into a coalition government. The Catholic church took bold initiatives in politics, especially during the pontificate of Pope John XXIII.

Dictatorships in Spain and Portugal were replaced by constitutional governments. The Scandinavian and Low countries enjoyed prosperity and stability in the postwar period.

The United States experienced unprecedented changes after World War II. Instead of isolation, it organized worldwide alliances and became involved throughout the globe. It was forced to deal with the existence of the poor within its own borders and recognize that the traditional notion of an economy of abundance had its limitations. It was challenged by the Soviet Union in foreign affairs. The assassinations of three political leaders, the radical youth movements of the 1960s and 1970s, antiwar and antiabortion protests, and demands for social

change reflected serious tensions. Three successful Republican party presidential victories brought a high degree of stability, though by the 1990s economic problems had become acute.

Canada experienced growth but faced the demands of French-speaking Canadians. In Mexico, serious economic troubles threatened the nation.

As elsewhere, the Soviet Union and the nations of eastern Europe experienced cycles of prosperity, growth, and economic stagnation, as well as social and political unrest. In 1956 Khrushchev denounced Stalin and ended the policy of mass terror. Soviet leaders emphasized production, but agricultural production remained below desired levels. After Mikhail Gorbachev became the Soviet leader, instituting many reforms, the Soviet Union was substantially democratized, free enterprise was permitted, the Eastern bloc satellites all denounced old-style

communism, and the cold war appeared to be at an end. Ethnic nationalism broke Yugoslavian unity and threatened to do so in Russia.

In the non-Western world, educated people as well as urban and rural populations wanted independence. Britain, France, the Netherlands, Belgium, and eventually Portugal were forced to dismantle their empires.

In Asia, Japan established a democratic government during the American occupation. Its economy was rebuilt, resulting in spectacular growth. Tensions between the United States and Japan developed in the 1970s as a result of the American decision to recognize China and of economic measures that hurt Japanese trade with the United States. South Korea suffered through political instability and dictatorship in a time of economic growth.

In southeast Asia, new nations emerged, although some, such as Indonesia, were poorly prepared for independence and faced political turmoil. In 1947 South Asia was partitioned between India and Pakistan. The divided nation of Pakistan was torn by civil war in 1971 when East Pakistan became the independent nation of Bangladesh, and India emerged as a regional power.

Oil and tensions between Arab nations and Israel caused frequent international crises in the Middle East during the postwar period. Oil was used as a weapon in international diplomacy. Despite Egypt's recognition of Israel, conflict between other Arab nations and Israel continued to make the region unstable. In 1991 war broke out between an American-led United Nations coalition and the government of Iraq over the latter's sudden annexation of oil-rich Kuwait. Nonetheless, Israel and the PLO reached an agreement in 1994.

African nations achieved independence but faced the problem of political instability. In South Africa, the white-controlled government imposed a rigid separation of races known as apartheid in 1948, not abandoning it until 1991.

As in Africa and Asia, the nations of Latin America had traditionally been exporters of raw materials and food crops. Independence and industrialization caused economic strains and political unrest that threatened many nations of the region and resulted in military coups, even in countries such as Chile and Uruguay that had democratic traditions.

Though the historian does not deal with the future, there were clear trends from the past that would continue to shape at least the near term. "Our times" had brought vast movements of people, great changes in technology, enormous population growth in many societies (and "no growth" policies to others). The definition of human rights had been broadened and "world opinion" was now a legitimate concern. The nature of the family had changed, and for each social improvement, there seemed to be a counterweighing social ill. Racial discrimination was, at the least, far less overt; in much of the West, the emancipation of women had been achieved; forms of the welfare state were nearly universal. Western civilization, especially in its mass cultural expressions and in forms originating in North America, continued to have a vital and deep impact on all other societies.

CRITICAL THINKING

1. Earlier this book suggested that life may be more easily studied by thinking in terms of four areas of human activity: political, economic, social, and intellectual/religious. Do you now believe these areas are sufficient? Which, if any, do you consider most important for understanding human history?

2. Describe developments in the Western democracies in the last twenty-five years.

3. What have been the most fundamental changes in North America during this time?

4. How do you account for the decline of Marxist ideology and the disintegration of communist states?

5. At what point would you judge the cold war to have ended?

6. Describe post–World War II Japan and compare its development to events and policies in the People's Republic of China.

7. All areas of the world now have a daily impact on the Western world. Which non-Western areas do you regard as most vital in this respect?

8. Describe the essential postwar changes in Africa, from decolonization to the end of *apartheid*.

9. Discuss the worldwide movement of peoples in relation to both Western national policies and the policies of the societies from which people are moving.

10. Often it is said that the contemporary world is filled with problems. Others reply that for every problem there is an opportunity. What do you regard as the most serious problem? What is the most significant opportunity? If problem and opportunity coincide, why; if not, why not?

ʃUGGESTED READINGS

Lists of supplementary or additional readings are usually intended to offer the student guidance into fuller, more specialized or more advanced historical literature. These lists also include sources—that is, primary documentary materials—for students who want to enter into the spirit of the period under study by reading of that period in the words of contemporaries. The following list is not intended to serve as a formal bibliography of books used in preparing the text. No titles are included that author Robin Winks has not read, but titles are not supplied to support all potentially controversial statements made in the text. Rather, the purpose of these lists, which are broken down by chapter and general subject matter, is to provide the student with a way to learn more about the major subjects.

Information listed refers to the latest edition available at the time this text went to press. Obviously there are dozens, even hundreds, of books on any of the subjects discussed in the text. The criteria for selection, therefore, have had to be clear: books, preferably short, written in a manner likely to be of interest to students of history, and when possible, books that are in print and in paperback editions. Clarity, accuracy, and availability were the primary tests. The most recent book on a subject is not always the best, though many recent titles have been included if they met the criteria. The authors believe that this list of suggested readings is therefore both up-to-date and useful, and books that have been included should be available in any good college library.

ʃHE VALUE OF HISTORY

Our first controversy was to define *civilization*, and this was done in the introductory chapter. Readers wishing to pursue this thorny problem further might best begin with Robert Redfield, *The Primitive World and Its Transformations* (Ithaca, N.Y.: Cornell University Press, 1953); move on to Lloyd Warner, *A Black Civilization*, rev. ed. (New York: Harper and Row, 1958); A. L. Kroeber, *The Nature of Culture* (Chicago: University of Chicago Press, 1952); and Arnold Toynbee, *Civilization on Trial* (Oxford: Oxford University Press, 1953), of which Kroeber was critical. Then explore Glyn Daniel, *The First Civilizations: The Archaeology of Their Origins* (New York: T. Y. Crowell, 1968) and *The Idea of Prehistory* (Cleveland: World Publishing Co., 1962).

CHAPTER 15 ʃHE PROBLEM OF DIVINE-RIGHT MONARCHY

Europe in General

Maurice P. Ashley, *The Golden Century* (New York: Praeger, 1969). A valuable introduction to seventeenth-century Europe.

Richard S. Dunn, *The Age of Religious Wars, 1559–1717*, 2d ed. (New York: Norton, 1979). Crisp, comprehensive survey.

Carl Joachim Friedrich, *The Age of the Baroque, 1610–1660* (New York: Harper and Row, 1952); Frederick L. Nussbaum, *The Triumph of Science and Reason*, 1660–1685 (New York: Harper and Row, 1953); John B. Wolf, *The Emergence of the Great Powers, 1685–1715* (New York: Harper and Row, 1951). Detailed, scholarly volumes with very full bibliographies; in the Rise of Modern Europe series (Harper and Row Torchbooks).

Eli Heckscher, *Mercantilism*, 2d ed. (New York: Macmillan, 1962). A famous and controversial work.

Henry Kamen, *European Society 1500–1700* (London: Hutchinson, 1984). Fine survey.

Frederick L. Nussbaum, *A History of Economic Institutions in Modern Europe* (New York: Kelley, 1967). An abridgment of Sombart's *Modern Capitalism*, which argues that war is economically creative. The arguments are attacked by John U. Neff, *War and Human Progress* (New York: Norton, 1968).

Nikolaus Pevsner, *An Outline of European Architecture* (London: Penguin, 1953). Clear, opinionated romp through the whole of western Europe.

France

Davis Bitten, *The French Nobility in Crisis, 1560–1640* (Palo Alto, Calif.: Stanford University Press, 1969). Sound study of their declining role.

Carl J. Burckhardt, *Richelieu: His Rise to Power and Assertion of Power and Cold War* (London: Allen and Unwin, 1940). Scholarly two-volume study of the great cardinal.

Charles W. Cole, *Colbert and a Century of French Mercantilism* (Hamden, Conn.: Archon, 1964). A solid, detailed study.

Albert Guerard, *France in the Classical Age: The Life and Death of an Ideal*, rev. ed. (New York: Brazillier, 1956). Stimulating interpretation of early modern France.

Ragnhild H. Hatton, *Europe in the Age of Louis XIV* (New York: Norton, 1979). Instructive study of the links among economic, social, and cultural developments.

James E. King, *Science and Rationalism in the Government of Louis XIV* (Baltimore: Johns Hopkins University Press, 1978). Monograph showing the relations between intellectual and political history.

W. H. Lewis, *The Splendid Century* (New York: Morrow, 1954). Stresses the nature of society in France under Louis XIV.

Andrew Lossky, *Louis XIV and the French Monarchy* (New Brunswick, N.J.: Rutgers University Press, 1994). A fresh interpretation.

John D. Lough, *An Introduction to Seventeenth Century France* (New York: Longmans, Green, 1955). Designed for the student of literature.

Orest A. Ranum, *Richelieu and the Councillors of Louis XIII* (Westport, Conn.: Greenwood, 1976). An important monograph on administration.

Warren C. Scoville, *The Persecution of the Huguenots and French Economic Development, 1680–1720* (Berkeley: University of California Press, 1960). Enlightening evaluation.

W. J. Stankiewicz, *Politics and Religion in Seventeenth Century France* (Westport, Conn.: Greenwood, 1976). Illuminating study of their interrelations.

G. R. R. Treasure, *Seventeenth Century France* (London: John Murray, 1981). Full and lucid survey.

England

Maurice Ashley, *England in the Seventeenth Century* (Totowa, N.J.: B and N Imports); and Christopher Hill, *The Century of Revolution, 1603–1714* (New York: Norton, 1982). Two sound surveys by experts.

Robert Ashton, *Counter-Revolution: The Second Civil War and Its Origins, 1646–1648* (New Haven; Yale University Press, 1995). A breakthrough account.

Stephen B. Baxter, *William III and the Defense of European Liberty* (Westport, Conn.: Greenwood, 1976). Clear and sympathetic.

D. C. Coleman, *The Economy of England, 1450–1750* (Oxford: Oxford University Press, 1978). Short, clear look that combines the perspectives of historian and economist.

Hans Baron, *The Crisis of the Early Italian Renaissance* (Princeton, N.J.: Princeton University Press, 1966). Monograph incorporating recent scholarship and affording many insights into Renaissance politics.

Geoffrey Barraclough, *The Origins of Modern Germany* (Oxford: Blackwell, 1957). The best general treatment of late medieval Germany in English.

Marvin B. Becker, *Florence in Transition*, 2 vols. (Baltimore: Johns Hopkins University Press, 1967–1968). Up-to-date study of Florence in the fourteenth century. Consult also *Medieval Italy* (Bloomington: Indiana University Press, 1981), a study of the relationship between religious and secular thought.

Gene A. Brucker, *Renaissance Florence* (Melbourne, Fla.: Krieger, 1975). A sound introduction.

Jacob Burckhardt, *The Civilization of the Renaissance in Italy*, 2 vols. (New York: Harper and Row, 1958). Famous interpretation now more than a century old; its contention that the modern state originated in Renaissance Italy is no longer generally accepted.

F. L. Carsten, *Princes and Parliaments in Germany from the Fifteenth to the Eighteenth Century* (Oxford: Clarendon Press, 1959). Scholarly study of Württemberg, Saxony, Bavaria, and other states.

Federico Chabod, *Machiavelli and the Renaissance* (Cambridge, Mass.: Harvard University Press, 1960). Pithy, sympathetic evaluation, which may be contrasted with the more critical Herbert Butterfield, *The Statecraft of Machiavelli* (New York: Collier, 1962).

John R. Hale, *Machiavelli and Renaissance Italy* (New York: Harper and Row, n.d.). Good brief account.

J. G. A. Pocock, *The Machiavellian Moment: Florentine Political Thought and the Atlantic Republican Tradition* (Princeton, N.J.: Princeton University Press, 1975). A fine, original interpretation.

Sources

Jean Froissart, *Chronicles of England, France, Spain, Etc.* (Baltimore: Penguin, 1978). A great narrative source of late medieval history.

Sam Kinser and Isabelle Cazeaux, *The Memoirs of Phillippe de Commynes* (Columbia: University of South Carolina Press, 1969). Well-edited translation. Another recent translation is by M. Jones: *Commynes. Memoirs* (Baltimore: Penguin, 1972).

Niccolò Machiavelli, *The Chief Works and Others*, 3 vols., trans. Allan Gilbert (Durham, N.C.: Duke University Press, 1965). A scholarly translation. Older translations of *The Prince* and *The Discourses* are available in many paperback editions.

Arthur J. Slavin, *The "New Monarchies" and Representative Assemblies: Medieval Constitutionalism or Modern Absolutism?* (Lexington, Mass.: D. C. Heath, n.d.). Illuminating exploration of the pros and cons about the degree of newness in the new monarchies.

CHAPTER 11   *T*HE RENAISSANCE

General Accounts

Susan G. Bell, ed., *Women from the Greeks to the French Revolution* (Belmont, Calif.: Wadsworth, 1973). A seminal collection.

Jacob Burckhardt, *The Civilization of the Renaissance in Italy*, 2 vols. (New York: Harper and Row, 1958). The classic statement of the view that the Renaissance was unique and revolutionary.

Peter Burke, *Culture and Society in Renaissance Italy, 1420–1540* (New York: Scribner's, 1972). Major look at how "taste" developed in Renaissance terms; by a leading inquirer into the methods of popular culture studies.

Karl H. Dannenfeldt, ed., *The Renaissance: Medieval or Modern?* (Lexington, Mass.: D. C. Heath, 1973). A collection of essays directed to the question.

Elizabeth L. Eisenstein, *The Printing Press as an Agent of Change* (Cambridge: Cambridge University Press, 1979). Fundamental, brilliant examination of how print revolutionized the world.

Lucien Febvre, *Life in Renaissance France*, trans. Marian Rothstein (Cambridge, Mass.: Harvard University Press, 1979). Short, provocative "silhouette of a civilization."

Lucien Febvre and Henri-Jean Martin, *The Coming of the Book: The Impact of Printing, 1450–1800*, trans. David Gerard (New York: Schocken, 1976). Develops a basis for seeing the Renaissance in two major phases; looks at the introduction of paper and at the book as a commodity.

Wallace K. Ferguson, *The Renaissance in Historical Thought: Five Centuries of Interpretation* (New York: AMS Press, 1977). Valuable and stimulating monograph.

J. R. Hale, *Renaissance Europe: Individual and Society, 1480–1520* (Berkeley: University of California Press, 1978). Exceptional history that shows us how the individual viewed the world.

J. R. Hale, ed., *A Concise Encyclopaedia of the Italian Renaissance* (Oxford: Oxford University Press, 1981). Thorough, well-organized coverage by topics and persons.

Denys Hay, *The Italian Renaissance in Its Historical Background* (Cambridge: Cambridge University Press, 1977). Valuable treatment of the historiography of the topic.

Denys Hay, ed., *The Renaissance Debate* (Melbourne, Fla.: Krieger, 1976). Excerpts illustrating contrasting points of view.

Robert S. Lopez, *The Three Ages of the Italian Renaissance* (Charlottesville: University Press of Virginia, 1970). Fine lectures that argue for three stages of Renaissance development.

Garrett Mattingly et al., *Renaissance Profiles* (New York: Harper and Row, n.d.). Lively sketches of nine representative Italians, including Petrarch, Machiavelli, Leonardo, and Michelangelo.

The New Cambridge Modern History, Vol. I: *The Renaissance* (Cambridge: Cambridge University Press, 1957). Chapters by experts in many fields; uneven but useful for reference.

J. H. Plumb, *The Italian Renaissance* (New York: Harper and Row, 1965). Concise historical and cultural survey.

Eugene F. Rice, Jr., *The Foundations of Early Modern Europe, 1460–1559* (New York: Norton, 1970). Good general introduction.

Lucette Valensi, *The Birth of the Despot: Venice and the Sublime Porte* (Ithaca: Cornell University Press, 1993). Crisply clear.

The Economy

Fernand Braudel, *Capitalism and Material Life, 1400–1800*, trans. Mariam Kochan (New York: Harper and Row, 1974). A rich look at the detail of fashion, housing, food, and drink.

The Cambridge Economic History of Europe, Vol. II: *Trade and Industry in the Middle Ages*; Vol III: *Economic Organization and Policies in the Middle Ages* (Cambridge: Cambridge University Press, 1954, 1965). Advanced scholarly work and a mine of information.

Richard Ehrenberg, *Capital and Finance in the Renaissance: A Study of the Fuggers and Their Connections* (New York: Kelley, 1963). Another instructive case history.

Richard W. Unger, *The Ship in the Medieval Economy, 600–1600* (London: Croom Helm, 1980). Brings together the most recent reinterpretations on the significance of medieval shipping.

Literature and Thought

R. R. Bolgar, *The Classical Heritage and Its Beneficiaries from the Carolingian Age to the End of the Renaissance* (Cambridge: Cambridge University Press, 1977). On the question of continuity.

Natalie Zemon Davis, *Society and Culture in Early Modern France* (Palo Alto, Calif.: Stanford University Press, 1975). Especially good on attitudes toward women.

Eugenio Garin, *Italian Humanism* (Westport, Conn.: Greenwood, 1976). Good scholarly survey.

Economics and Society

Carlo M. Cipolla, *Guns, Sails, and Empires* (New York: Minerva Press, 1965). Short, original inquiry into how specific technological innovations gave specific European nations dominance in the early phases of the great wars for empire.

Phyllis Deane, *The First Industrial Revolution* (Cambridge: Cambridge University Press, 1980). Study of the British economy from 1750 to 1850.

Roderick Floud and Donald McCloskey, eds., *The Economic History of Britain since 1700* (2nd ed., New York: Cambridge University Press, 1994). Excellent summaries of up-to-date views.

Albert Goodwin, ed., *The European Nobility in the Eighteenth Century* (London: Black, 1953). Very helpful essays arranged country by country.

H. J. Habakkuk and Michael Postan, eds., *The Cambridge Economic History of Europe*, Vol. VI, Parts 1 and 2 (Cambridge: Cambridge University Press, 1965). Scholarly essays by many writers on the economic revolutions.

Paul Mantoux, *The Industrial Revolution in the Eighteenth Century* (New York: Harper and Row, 1961). Classic study of the factory system in England.

David Ogg, *Europe of the Ancien Régime* (New York: Harper and Row, 1966). A social study, focused on Britain.

The Established Powers

J. V. Beckett, *The Aristocracy in England, 1660–1914* (Oxford: Blackwell, 1986). A solid summary of the present scholarship.

Catherine B. A. Behrens, *The Ancien Régime* (London: Thames and Hudson, 1967). Readable and generously illustrated study which stresses French society.

Reed Browning, *The War of the Austrian Succession* (New York: St. Martin's, 1995). The first comprehensive history of the war.

Alfred Cobban, *A History of Modern France*, Vol. I: *1715–1799* (London: Penguin, 1966). Good general survey.

William Doyle, *The Old European Order, 1660–1800* (2nd ed., New York: Oxford University Press, 1993. A short, modern history.

Franklin L. Ford, *Robe and Sword* (Cambridge, Mass.: Harvard University Press, 1953). An instructive study of the French aristocracy during the generation following the death of Louis XIV.

Olwen H. Hufton, *The Poor of Eighteenth-Century France, 1750–1789* (Oxford: Clarendon Press, 1974). Superb answer to the question, "Who were the poor?"

Henry Kamen, *The War of Succession in Spain, 1700–1715* (Bloomington: Indiana University Press, 1969). Detailed study of the initial Bourbon impact upon Spain.

Louis Kronenberger, *Kings and Desperate Men* (New York: Knopf, 1942). Lively essays on eighteenth-century English society and personalities.

John Lough, *An Introduction to Eighteenth Century France* (London: Longmans, Green, 1978). Clear and enlightening discussion of the Old Regime.

Lewis B. Namier, *The Structure of Politics at the Accession of George III*, 2d ed. (New York: St. Martin's, 1957), and *England in the Age of the American Revolution* (New York: St. Martin's, n.d.). Detailed studies that revise the older concepts of eighteenth-century English political institutions. Much less influential today.

David Spadafora, *The Idea of Progress in Eighteenth-Century Britain* (New Haven: Yale University Press, 1990). A fresh look at the power of ideas.

William B. Wilcox, *The Age of Aristocracy* (Lexington, Mass.: D.C. Heath, 1976). Fine, short history of England from 1688 to 1830.

Basil Williams, *The Whig Supremacy, 1714–1760*, 2d ed., rev. (Oxford: Oxford University Press, 1962). A competent modern survey.

Arthur M. Wilson, *French Foreign Policy during the Administration of Cardinal Fleury* (Cambridge, Mass.: Harvard University Press, 1936). A sound monograph; one of the relatively few good books in English on the France of Louis XV.

The Newcomers

Francis L. Carsten, *The Origins of Prussia* (Westport, Conn.: Greenwood, 1982). Excellent monograph that carries the story through the reign of the Great Elector.

Gordon A. Craig, *The Politics of the Prussian Army, 1640–1945* (Oxford: Oxford University Press, 1964). Excellent scholarly study.

Christopher Duffy, *Russia's Military Way to the West* (London: Routledge and Kegan Paul, 1982). A careful examination of the emergence of Russia as a great European power in the eighteenth century.

Robert R. Ergang, *The Potsdam Fuhrer* (New York: Octagon, 1973). A splendid study of Frederick William I of Prussia.

Sidney B. Fay, *The Rise of Brandenburg-Prussia to 1786* (Melbourne, Fla.: Krieger, 1981). A lucid little volume packed with information.

V. D. Klyuchevsky, *Peter the Great* (New York: Vintage, 1961). Stirring account by a Russian scholar.

Marc Raeff, ed., *Peter the Great Changes Russia* (Lexington, Mass.: D. C. Heath, 1972). Good cross-section of judgments on the controversial czar.

Hans Rosenberg, *Bureaucracy, Aristocracy, Autocracy* (Boston: Beacon, 1966). A controversial analysis of Prussian history from 1660 to 1815.

Ferdinand Schevill, *The Great Elector* (Hamden, Conn.: Archon, 1965). A helpful study of the founder of the Hohenzollern despotism.

Benedict H. Sumner, *Peter the Great and the Emergence of Russia* (London: English Universities Press, 1950). A very good introductory account.

The International Balance

Christopher T. Atkinson, *A History of Germany, 1715–1815* (Westport, Conn.: Greenwood, 1970). An older account, particularly full on war and diplomacy.

Jeremy Black, *The Rise of the European Powers, 1679–1793* (London: Edward Arnold, 1990). Combines narrative with analysis very well.

Ludwig Dehio, *The Precarious Balance* (New York: Knopf, 1962). Reflections on the balance of power by a German scholar.

John F. C. Fuller, *A Military History of the Western World* (New York: Funk and Wagnalls, 1954–1956). The second volume of this stimulating survey covers the seventeenth and eighteenth centuries.

Lawrence H. Gipson, *The Great War for the Empire: The Culmination, 1760–1763* (New York: Knopf, 1954). Magisterial history of the war; Volume VIII of a detailed, sustained analysis.

K. M. Panikkar, *Asia and Western Dominance* (London: Allen and Unwin, 1965). Strong survey; emphasis on India.

Albert Sorel, *Europe under the Old Regime* (New York: Harper and Row, 1964). A famous little essay by a French expert on the eighteenth-century balance.

Benedict H. Sumner, *Peter the Great and the Ottoman Empire* (Hamden, Conn.: Shoe String, 1965). A short and meaty monograph.

Leslie C. Tihany, *A History of Middle Europe* (New Brunswick, N.J.: Rutgers University Press, 1976). Straightforward survey.

Sources

Norbert Elias, *The History of Manners*, Vol. I: *The Civilizing Process*, trans. Edmund Jephcott (New York: Pantheon, 1982). Fascinating inquiry into changing forms of courtesy in daily life.

Robert Forster and Elborg Forster, *European Society in the Eighteenth Century* (New York: Walker, 1969). Excellent anthology.

George P. Gooch, *Courts and Cabinets* (New York: Arno, 1972). A graceful introduction to the memoirs of some of the great personages of the era.

Carlile A. Macartney, ed., *The Hapsburg and Hohenzollern Dynasties in the Seventeenth and Eighteenth Centuries* (New York: Harper and Row, 1970). Helpful collection of documentary materials on Austrian and Prussian history.

Lady Mary W. Montagu, *Letters* (Oxford: Clarendon Press, 1965). By perhaps the best of the century's excellent letter writers; particularly valuable on the Habsburg and Ottoman empires.

Arthur Young, *Tours in England and Wales* (London: Penguin, 1981). Reports of a prolific and perceptive agricultural expert.

CHAPTER 17 *The* ENLIGHTENMENT

General

Catherine B. A. Behrens, *Society, Government, and the Enlightenment: The Experiences of Eighteenth-Century France and Prussia* (New York: Harper and Row, 1986). Fine comparative study.

Walter L. Dorn, *Competition for Empire, 1740–1763*; and Leo Gershoy, *From Despotism to Revolution, 1763–1789* (New York: Harper and Row, 1944). These two informative volumes in the Rise of Modern Europe series have very full bibliographies.

Leonard Krieger, *Kings and Philosophers, 1689–1789* (New York: Norton, 1970). Comprehensive survey; includes a succinct, up-to-date bibliography.

Robert R. Palmer, *The Age of Democratic Revolution* (Princeton, N.J.: Princeton University Press, 1964). A thoughtful survey of political ideas and unrest in Europe and America at the close of the Old Regime.

The Ideas of the Enlightenment

Robert Anchor, *The Enlightenment Tradition* (Berkeley: University of California Press, 1979). A stimulating interpretation.

Carl Becker, *The Heavenly City of the Eighteenth-Century Philosophers* (New Haven: Yale University Press, 1932). A still-delightful essay, now much criticized. Its ideas are reassessed in Raymond O. Rockwood, ed., *Carl Becker's Heavenly City Revisited* (Hamden, Conn.: Shoe String, 1968).

Dino Carpanetto and Giuseppe Ricuperati, *Italy in the Age of Reason, 1685–1789* (London: Longmans, 1987). Covers all fields, including demography.

Ernst Cassirer, *The Philosophy of the Enlightenment* (Princeton, N.J.: Princeton University Press, 1951). An important and lucid study of the great principles of eighteenth-century thought.

Lester G. Crocker, *An Age of Crisis*, and *Nature and Culture* (both Baltimore: Johns Hopkins University Press, 1959, 1963). Penetrating criticisms of the implications of the Enlightenment.

Peter Gay, *The Enlightenment* (New York: Simon and Schuster, 1974). Comprehensive survey by a leading expert in the field; contains extensive bibliographies.

Norman Hampson, *The Enlightenment* (London: Penguin, 1977). Concerned chiefly with ideas and their background.

George R. Havens, *The Age of Ideas: From Reaction to Revolution in Eighteenth-Century France* (New York: Irvington, 1955). Most useful biographical sketches of the philosophes.

Sylvia H. Myers, *The Bluestocking Circle: Women, Friendship, and the Life of the Mind in 18th-century England* (Oxford: Clarendon Press, 1990). Provocative study.

Sidney Pollard, *The Idea of Progress* (London: Pelican, 1971). Stimulating look at why philosophers thought progress was inevitable.

Some Individual Thinkers

Alfred Cobban, *Rousseau and the Modern State*, 2d ed. (Hamden, Conn.: Archon, 1964). A good introduction to the implications of Rousseau's thought. For a highly critical appraisal, see J. L. Talmon, *The Origins of Totalitarian Democracy* (New York: Norton, 1970).

Jean Guéhenno, *Jean Jacques Rousseau* (New York: Columbia University Press, 1966). A full-dress study.

Mark Hulliung, *The Autocritique of Enlightenment: Rousseau and the Philosophes* (Cambridge, Mass.: Harvard University Press, 1994). Fine new study.

Frank E. Manuel, *The Prophets of Paris* (New York: Harper and Row, 1965). Turgot and Condorcet are among those considered.

Norman L. Torrey, *The Spirit of Voltaire* (New York: Russell, 1968); and Peter Gay, *Voltaire's Politics* (New York: Vintage, n.d.). Thoughtful studies.

Arthur M. Wilson, *Diderot* (Oxford: Oxford University Press, 1972). The best scholarly biography.

The Enlightened Despots

Paul P. Bernard, *Joseph II* (Boston: Twayne, 1968). Succinct appraisal by a scholar who has written more detailed works on Joseph's reign.

T. C. W. Blanning, *Joseph II and Enlightened Despotism* (London: Longmans, Green, 1970). Good brief introduction.

Walter H. Bruford, *Germany in the Eighteenth Century* (Cambridge: Cambridge University Press, 1935). Stresses social and intellectual developments.

Edward Crankshaw, *Maria Theresa* (New York: Viking, 1969). A capable biographical study.

John G. Gagliardo, *Enlightened Despotism* (Arlington Heights, Ill.: Harlan Davidson, 1967). Informative and brief.

Richard Herr, *The Eighteenth-Century Revolution in Spain* (Princeton, N.J.: Princeton University Press, 1969). Important reappraisal of the Enlightenment's effect upon Spain.

Carlile A. Macartney, *Maria Theresa and the House of Austria* (London: English Universities Press, 1969). Brief scholarly appraisal.

Gerhard Ritter, *Frederick the Great* (Berkeley: University of California Press, 1968). Well-balanced lectures by a German scholar.

Rober Wines, ed., *Enlightened Despotism: Reform or Reaction?* (Lexington, Mass.: D. C. Heath, 1967). All sides of the question examined by various authorities.

Catherine the Great

John T. Alexander, *Catherine the Great* (New York: Oxford University Press, 1988). Fine narrative history.

Jerome Blum, *The End of the Old Order in Rural Europe* (Princeton, N.J.: Princeton University Press, 1978). Fine broad history of the relationship between seignors and peasants.

Paul Dukes, *Catherine the Great and the Russian Nobility* (Cambridge: Cambridge University Press, 1968). Study of a most significant aspect of her policy.

Lawrence J. Oliva, *Catherine the Great* (Englewood Cliffs, N.J.: Prentice-Hall, 1971); and Marc Raeff, ed., *Catherine the Great: A Profile* (New York: Hill and Wang, 1972). Instructive appraisals of the Russian empress.

Marc Raeff, *Imperial Russia, 1682–1825* (New York: Knopf, 1971). Survey from Peter the Great through Alexander I.

Benedict H. Sumner, *Peter the Great and the Emergence of Russia* (London: English Universities Press, 1950). An able, quite short prelude to Catherine.

Gladys Scott Thomson, *Catherine the Great and the Expansion of Russia* (London: English Universities Press, 1961). A sound, short introduction.

Piotr S. Wandycz, *The Lands of Partitioned Poland, 1795–1918* (Seattle: University of Washington Press, 1974). Careful, full account of the aftermath of partition and the efforts to reconstruct a Polish state.

England

Roy Porter and Lesley Hall. *The Facts of Life: The Creation of Sexual Knowledge in Britain, 1650–1950* (New Haven: Yale University Press, 1995). A history of ideas.

George Rudé, *Wilkes and Liberty* (Oxford: Oxford University Press, 1962). Analysis of the unrest in Britain during the early years of George III's reign.

J. Steven Watson, *The Reign of George III, 1760–1815* (Oxford: Oxford University Press, 1960). Enlightening general account in the Oxford History of England.

American Independence

Bernard Bailyn, *Ideological Origins of the American Revolution* (Cambridge, Mass.: Harvard University Press, 1967); and John C. Miller, *Origins of the American Revolution* (Palo Alto, Calif.: Stanford University Press, 1959). Illuminating studies of the background.

I. A. Christie, *Crisis of Empire* (London: Arnold, 1966). Very short analysis from the perspective of British concerns.

Robert Middlekauff, *The Glorious Cause* (New York: Oxford University Press, 1982). Fresh, full, well-written history of the Revolution.

Edmund S. Morgan, *The Birth of the Republic, 1763–1789* (Chicago: University of Chicago Press, 1977); Lawrence H. Gipson, *The Coming of the Revolution, 1763–1775* (New York: Harper and Row, 1954); and John R. Alden, *The American Revolution, 1775–1783* (New York: Harper and Row, 1954). Standard scholarly accounts.

Esmond Wright, *Franklin of Philadelphia* (Cambridge, Mass.: Harvard University Press, 1986). The best biography of the "first American."

The Arts

Frederick Antal, *Hogarth and His Place in European Art* (London: Routledge and Kegan Paul, 1962). Ingenious study which stresses parallels with earlier and later artists.

Germain Bazin, *Baroque and Rococo Art* (Oxford: Oxford University Press, 1964); and A. Charles Sewter, *Baroque and Rococo* (London: Thames and Hudson, 1972). Concise introductions.

Manfred F. Bukofzer, *Music in the Baroque Era* (New York: Norton, 1971). Survey through 1750.

Stephanie Faniel, ed., *French Art of the Eighteenth Century* (New York: Simon and Schuster, 1957). Valuable for its coverage of the minor arts.

Eva Marie Grew and Sidney Grew, *Bach* (Totowa, N.J.: Littlefield, 1979); Alfred Einstein, *Gluck* (New York: McGraw-Hill, n.d.), and *Mozart* (Oxford: Oxford University Press, 1965). Enlightening works on individual composers.

Julius Held and Donald Posner, *17th and 18th Century Art* (Englewood Cliffs, N.J.: Prentice-Hall, 1972). A comprehensive survey that discusses rococo.

James M. Morris, ed., *On Mozart* (New York: Cambridge University Press, 1994).

Tervio Pignatti, *The Age of Rococo* (London: Paul Hamlyn, 1969). Brief, but valuable for its stress on the Italian contribution and its unusual illustrations.

Charles Rosen, *The Classical Style* (New York: Norton, 1971). Perceptive study of Mozart, Haydn, and Beethoven.

Arno Schonberger and Halldor Soehner, *The Age of Rococo* (London: Thames and Hudson, 1960). Handsomely illustrated survey.

Jacques Thuillier and Albert Châtelet, *French Painting from Le Nain to Fragonard* (Geneva: Skira, 1964). Handsomely illustrated survey; covers from the midseventeenth to the late eighteenth century.

Ellis Waterhouse, *Reynolds* (New York: Phaidon, 1973). Sympathetic assessment of Sir Joshua.

Sources

Max Beloff, ed., *The Debate on the American Revolution, 1761–1783* (London: Kaye, 1949). Handy compilation of British speeches and writings for and against the rebels.

Crane Brinton, ed., *The Portable Age of Reason Reader* (New York: Viking, 1956); and Isaiah Berlin, ed., *The Age of Enlightenment: The Eighteenth-Century Philosophers* (Salem, N.H.: Arno Press, 1956). Two valuable anthologies.

Lester G. Crocker, ed., *The Age of Enlightenment* (New York: Walker, 1969); and Carlile A. Macartney, ed., *The Hapsburg and Hohenzollern Dynasties in the Seventeenth and Eighteenth Centuries* (New York: Walker, 1970). Volumes in the Documentary History of Western Civilization.

Robert Forster and Elburg Forster, eds., *European Society in the Eighteenth Century* (New York: Walker, 1969). Well-selected anthology.

Ben R. Redman, ed., *The Portable Voltaire* (London: Penguin, 1977). A well-edited selection.

CHAPTER 18 *The* FRENCH REVOLUTION AND NAPOLEON

General Survey Texts

Peter Amann, ed., *The Eighteenth-Century Revolution: French or Western?* (Lexington, Mass.: D. C. Heath, 1963). Selections both hostile and sympathetic to the Palmer thesis.

Crane Brinton, *A Decade of Revolution, 1789–1799* (New York: Harper and Row, 1934); and Geoffrey Bruun, *Europe and the French Imperium, 1799–1814* (New York: Harper and Row, 1938). Comprehensive volumes in the Rise of Modern Europe series; contain full bibliographies.

Jacques Godechot, *France and the Atlantic Revolution of the Eighteenth Century, 1770–1799*, trans. Herbert R. Rowen (New York: Free Press, 1965). A ranking French scholar comes to conclusions similar to Palmer's. Godechot's views on Napoleon may be sampled in Jacques Godechot, B. Hyslop, and David Dowd, *The Napoleonic Era in Europe* (New York: Holt, Rinehart, 1971).

Norman Hampson, *The First European Revolution, 1776–1815* (New York: Norton, 1979); and George Rudé, *Revolutionary Europe, 1783–1815* (New York: Harper and Row, n.d.). Two good general surveys.

Georges Lefebvre, *The Coming of the French Revolution*, trans. Robert Palmer (Princeton, N.J.: Princeton University Press, 1976), and *Napoleon* (New York: Columbia University Press, 1969). Comprehensive accounts by an eminent French scholar with a modified Marxian point of view.

Robert R. Palmer, *The Age of the Democratic Revolution* (Princeton, N.J.: Princeton University Press, 1959–1964). Defends the thesis that the French Revolution was part of a general democratic revolution in the West; particularly useful for detailed material on smaller European states.

Histories of the Revolution in France

William Doyle, *The Oxford History of the French Revolution* (Oxford: Oxford University Press, 1988). Short, clear analysis of the range of issues, with an exceptionally fine survey of the historiography since 1939.

Ralph W. Greenlaw, ed., *The Social Origins of the French Revolution: The Debate on the Role of the Middle Classes* (Lexington, Mass.: D. C. Heath, 1975). Covers the range of views on whether the Revolution was essentially middle class in origin.

Norman Hampson, *A Social History of the French Revolution* (Toronto: University of Toronto Press, 1963). Excellent synthesis of recent scholarship.

Olwen H. Hufton, *The Poor of Eighteenth Century France, 1750–1789* (Oxford: Clarendon Press, 1979). Close inquiry into the meaning of poverty and crime.

Ernest John Knapton, *Revolutionary and Imperial France, 1750–1815* (New York: Scribner's, 1972). Short, balanced survey.

Gaetano Salvemini, *The French Revolution, 1788–1792* (New York: Norton, 1962). Colorful narrative.

William H. Sewell, *Work and Revolution in France: The Language of Labor from the Old Regime to 1848* (Cambridge: Cambridge University Press, 1980). Superb, complex examination of the social history of labor.

More Specialized Studies of the Revolution

Crane Brinton, *The Jacobins* (New York: Russell, 1961); and M. J. Sydenham, *The Girondins* (Westport, Conn.: Greenwood, 1973). Careful studies which greatly revise popular notions about the nature of revolutionary factions.

William F. Church, ed., *The Influence of the Enlightenment on the French Revolution*, 2d ed. (Lexington, Mass.: D. C. Heath, 1972); and J. H. Shennan, *The Parlement of Paris* (Ithaca, N.Y.: Cornell University Press, 1968). Appraisals of two significant factors in the background.

Richard C. Cobb, *The Police and the People* (Oxford: Oxford University Press, 1970). Important study of French popular protest from 1789 to 1820.

Alfred Cobban, *Aspects of the French Revolution* (New York: Brazillier, 1968), and *The Social Interpretation of the French Revolution* (Cambridge: Cambridge University Press, 1964). Lively critiques of the Marxian interpretation.

Paul Farmer, *France Reviews Its Revolutionary Origins* (New York: Octagon, 1963). A history of writings about the Revolution by French scholars.

Jacques Godechot, *The Taking of the Bastille* (New York: Scribner's, 1970). Definitive monograph on July 14, 1789.

Jacques Godechot, *The Counter-Revolution: Doctrine and Action, 1789–1804*, trans. Salvator Attanasio (Princeton, N.J.: Princeton University Press, 1981). An important study of the opposition to the Revolution.

P. M. Jones, *The Peasantry in the French Revolution* (New York: Cambridge University Press, 1988). A fresh and balanced study.

Linda Kelly, *Women of the French Revolution* (London: Penguin, 1989). A series of minibiographies.

Emmet Kennedy, *A Cultural History of the French Revolution* (New Haven: Yale University Press, 1989). A study in the *longue durée*.

John McManners, *The French Revolution and the Church* (London: S.P.C.K., 1969). Superb brief study.

Robert R. Palmer, *Twelve Who Ruled: The Year of the Terror in the French Revolution* (Princeton, N.J.: Princeton University Press, 1978). Highly readable collective biography of the Committee of Public Safety.

George Rudé, *The Crowd in the French Revolution* (Oxford: Oxford University Press, 1959). Study of the participants in the great revolutionary "days" and of their motives.

Albert Soboul, *The Sans-Culottes and the French Revolution* (Princeton, N.J.: Princeton University Press, 1980). Detailed French monograph. Based on police records, it examines the role of the Parisian sans-culottes in 1793 and 1794 from a Marxist perspective.

J. M. Thompson, *Leaders of the French Revolution* (Oxford: Blackwell, 1968), and *Robespierre and the French Revolution* (London: English Universities Press, 1960); Geoffrey Bruun, *Saint-Just: Apostle of the Terror* (Hamden, Conn.: Shoe String, 1966); and Louis Gottschalk, *Jean-Paul Marat* (New York: Gordon, n.d.). Biographies of major revolutionary figures.

Charles Tilly, *The Vendee* (Cambridge, Mass.: Harvard University Press, 1976). Revisionist study showing that much more was involved in the Vendean revolt than peasant devotion to throne and altar.

Alec R. Vidler, *The Church in an Age of Revolution* (London: Penguin, 1980). Survey from 1789 to the 1960s; especially good on the Gallican church.

Napoleon

David G. Chandler, *The Campaigns of Napoleon* (New York: Macmillan, 1973). Thorough scholarly account.

Owen Connelly, *Napoleon's Satellite Kingdoms* (New York: Free Press, 1970). Informative studies of Spain, Holland, Westphalia, Italy, and Naples.

Peter Geyl, *Napoleon, For and Against* (New Haven: Yale University Press, 1949). Survey of judgments passed on Bonaparte by historians.

Eli Heckscher, *The Continental System* (Boston: Peter Smith, 1964). Old, still-important monograph by an economic historian.

Robert B. Holtman, *The Napoleonic Revolution* (Baton Rouge: Louisiana State University Press, 1979). Emphasizing institutional changes under Bonaparte.

Felix Markham, *Napoleon and the Awakening of Europe* (Mystic, Conn.: Verry, 1972). Brief survey; argues that European nationalisms were as yet underdeveloped.

David H. Pinkney, ed., *Napoleon: Historical Enigma* (Princeton, N.J.: Princeton University Press, 1972). A brief introduction to the contrasting interpretations of the man.

Edith Saunders, *The Hundred Days* (New York: Norton, 1964). On the next-to-last act of the Napoleonic drama.

Sources

Edmund Burke, *Reflections on the Revolution in France* (several eds.). A celebrated indictment of the destructive character of the Revolution.

Armand de Caulaincourt, *With Napoleon in Russia* (Westport, Conn.: Greenwood, 1976), and its sequel, *No Peace with Napoleon* (Westport, Conn.: Greenwood, 1976). Vivid and revealing memoirs by one of Bonaparte's chief aides.

J. Christopher Herold, ed., *The Mind of Napoleon* (New York: Columbia University Press, 1955). Another fine collection; arranged topically.

Maurice Hutt, *Napoleon* (Englewood Cliffs, N.J.: Prentice-Hall, n.d.). A capsule biography; contains selections from his own words and a sampler of other views on his career.

Frank A. Kafker and James M. Laux, *The French Revolution: Conflicting Interpretations* (New York: Random House, 1968). Balanced selections of primary and secondary materials.

Jeffry Kaplow, *New Perspectives on the French Revolution: Readings in Historical Sociology* (New York: Wiley, 1965). A series of valuable case studies.

John H. Stewart, *A Documentary Survey of the French Revolution* (New York: Macmillan, 1951). Excellent collection of constitutional texts and other official documents.

J. M. Thompson, ed., *Napoleon's Letters* (New York: Dutton, 1954). A fascinating collection, arranged chronologically.

Arthur Young, *Travels in France*, (Cambridge: Cambridge University Press, 1929). Lively diary by an English farm expert who journeyed throughout France from 1787 to 1789.

CHAPTER 19   *R*OMANTICISM, REACTION, AND REVOLUTION

General Accounts

Frederick B. Artz, *Reaction and Revolution, 1814–1832* (New York: Harper and Row, 1969); and William L. Langer, *Political and Social Upheaval, 1832–1852* (New York: Harper and Row, 1969). Comprehensive volumes in the Rise of Modern Europe series; both have still-useful bibliographies.

Jacques Droz, *Europe between Revolutions, 1815–1848* (Ithaca, N.Y.: Cornell University Press, 1980). A survey that stresses the workings of economic and social forces and their political consequences.

Eric J. Hobsbawm, *The Age of Revolution, 1789–1848* (New York: New American Library, 1962). Provocative survey stressing economic and political developments.

The New Cambridge Modern History, Vols. IX and X (Cambridge: Cambridge University Press, 1957–1970). Chapters by many scholars; uneven in quality, but provides information on topics and areas often neglected in general surveys.

George Rudé, *Debate on Europe* (New York: Torchbooks, 1972). Fine summary of conflicting and developing views on events from 1815 to 1850.

The Romantic Protest

The full texts of almost all the landmarks in romantic literature mentioned in this chapter are available in paperbound editions.

Crane Brinton, *Political Ideas of the English Romanticists* (Oxford: Oxford University Press, 1926). A perceptive analysis.

Kenneth Clark, *The Gothic Revival* (New York: Harper and Row, 1974). Entertaining essay; focuses on architecture in Britain.

David L. Dowd, *Pageant-Master of the Republic* (Salem, N.H.: Arno Press, 1972). David's role as propagandist of the Revolution.

Walter Friedlaender, *David to Delacroix* (Cambridge, Mass.: Harvard University Press, 1952). Good study of neoclassical and romantic painting in France.

Lilian R. Furst, *Romanticism in Perspective*, 2d ed. (Atlantic Highlands, N.J.: Humanities Press, 1979). Helpful interpretation; contains chapters on the historical perspective and on individualism, imagination, and feeling.

K. B. Klaus, *The Romantic Period in Music* (London: Allyn and Bacon, 1970). A useful introduction; goes well beyond the chronological limits of this chapter.

Thomas Prideaux, *The World of Delacroix* (New York: Time-Life Books, 1966). Relates the painter to the larger social scene.

M. Reynal, *The Nineteenth Century* (Geneva: Skira, 1951). Handsomely illustrated survey of painting.

Charles Rosen, *The Classical Style* (New York: Norton, 1972). Treats Beethoven in addition to Mozart and Haydn.

The Reconstruction of Europe

Guillaume de Sauvigny, *Metternich and His Times* (Atlantic Highlands, N.J.: Humanities Press, 1962). By a French expert on conservatism.

Henry A. Kissinger, *A World Restored* (Boston: Peter Smith, 1973). Focuses on efforts of conservative forces to restore the European balance of power from 1812 to 1822.

Arthur J. May, *The Age of Metternich*, rev. ed. (New York: Holt, Rinehart, 1967). Brief appraisal of Habsburg history.

Harold Nicolson, *The Congress of Vienna* (New York: Harcourt Brace Jovanovich, 1970); Guglielmo Ferrero, *The Reconstruction of Europe* (New York: Norton, 1963). Detailed studies of the settlement of 1814–1815.

H. F. Schwarz, ed., *Metternich, the Coachman of Europe: Statesman or Evil Genius?* (Lexington, Mass.: D. C. Heath, n.d.). Instructive selection of contradictory interpretations.

Isser Woloch, *The New Regime: Transformations of the French Civic Order, 1789–1820s* (New York: Norton, 1993). Remarkable synthesis.

Works on Individual States

Janis Bergman-Carton. *The Woman of Ideas in French Art, 1830–1848* (New Haven: Yale University Press, 1995). From salon to motherhood.

Raymond Carr, *Spain, 1808–1939* (Oxford: Oxford University Press, 1982). Scholarly account.

Douglas Dakin, *The Greek Struggle for Independence, 1821–1833* (Berkeley: University of California Press, 1973). Definitive scholarly study.

Guillaume de Sauvigny, *The Restoration* (Philadelphia: University of Pennsylvania Press, 1966). Sympathetic, detailed interpretation of France under Louis XVIII and Charles X.

Theodore S. Hamerow, *Restoration, Revolution, Reaction* (Princeton, N.J.: Princeton University Press, 1958). Scholarly reevaluation of German economics and politics from 1815 to 1871.

W. O. Henderson, *The Zollverein*, 2d ed. (Totowa, N.J.: Biblio, 1968). A standard work on the subject.

Marshall G. S. Hodgson, *The Venture of Islam: The Gunpowder Empires and Modern Times* (Chicago: University of Chicago Press, 1974). Good coverage on the decline of the Ottoman Empire.

T. E. B. Howarth, *Citizen-King* (London: Eyre and Spottiswoode, 1961). Biography of Louis Philippe.

Charles Jelavich and Barbara Jelavich, *The Establishment of the Balkan National States, 1804–1920* (Seattle: University of Washington Press, 1977). Survey of Balkan nationalisms.

Douglas W. J. Johnson, *Guizot: Aspects of French History, 1787–1874* (London: Routledge and Kegan Paul, 1963). Illuminating biography of the French conservative liberal.

R. F. Leslie, *Polish Politics and the Revolution of 1830* (London: Athlone Press, 1956). Detailed analysis of the stresses and antagonisms that doomed the Polish movement.

Mary D. R. Leys, *Between Two Empires* (London: Longmans, Green, 1955). Brief survey of French social and political history from 1814 to 1848.

Carlile A. Macartney, *The Habsburg Empire, 1790–1818* (New York: Macmillan, 1969). By a ranking expert in the field.

Ted W. Margadant, *French Peasants in Revolt: The Insurrection of 1851* (Princeton, N.J.: Princeton University Press, 1979). Trenchant analysis of the radicalization of the French peasant.

A. G. Mazour, *The First Russian Revolution* (Palo Alto, Calif.: Stanford University Press, 1937); and Marc Raeff, *The Decembrist Movement* (Englewood Cliffs, N.J.: Prentice-Hall, 1966). Valuable studies of the abortive coup of 1825 and its background.

David H. Pinkney, *The French Revolution of 1830* (Princeton, N.J.: Princeton University Press, 1972). Important scholarly study that revises many older ideas about the nature of the July Revolution.

Peter Sahlins, *Forest Rites: The War of the Demoiselles in Nineteenth-Century France* (Cambridge, Mass. Harvard University Press, 1994). On an uprising of male peasants dressed in women's clothes in 1829 to 1832.

Gaetano Salvemini, *Mazzini* (Palo Alto, Calif.: Stanford University Press, 1957). Sympathetic analysis.

A. J. P. Taylor, *The Course of German History* (London: Hamilton, 1945). Clear and debatable.

A. J. P. Taylor, *The Habsburg Monarchy, 1809–1918* (Chicago: University of Chicago Press, 1976). Spirited, brief treatment.

R. Hinton Thomas, *Liberalism, Nationalism, and the German Intellectuals* (Westport, Conn.: Greenwood, 1975). Good study of the period from 1822 to 1847.

Arthur J. Whyte, *The Evolution of Modern Italy* (New York: Norton, 1965). Sound introduction.

The Revolutions of 1848

Melvin Kranzberg, ed., *1848: A Turning Point?* (Lexington, Mass.: D. C. Heath, 1959). Diverse evaluations as to whether Europe failed to turn.

Arno J. Mayer, *The Persistence of the Old Regime* (New York: Pantheon, 1981). Brilliant explanation of why, despite revolutions, the Old Regime survived until the Great War.

Lewis B. Namier, *1848: The Revolution of the Intellectuals* (New York: Anchor, 1964). Trenchant essay castigating liberals, especially in Germany, for their illiberal attitudes.

P. H. Noyes, *Organization and Revolution* (Princeton, N.J.: Princeton University Press, 1966). Enlightening study of working-class disunity in Germany.

Raymond Postgate, *Story of a Year: 1848* (Westport, Conn.: Greenwood, 1975). A lively and well-illustrated chronicle.

Reuben J. Rath, *The Viennese Revolution of 1848* (Westport, Conn.: Greenwood, 1977). Solid, clear monograph.

Priscilla Robertson, *Revolutions of 1848* (Princeton, N.J.: Princeton University Press, 1952). Uneven social history; valuable for stressing the role taken by women and by students.

George Rudé, *The Crowd in History, 1730–1884* (Atlantic Highlands, N.J.: Humanities Press, 1981). Includes a chapter on the socioeconomic background of the Parisian demonstrators of 1848.

William H. Sewell, *Work and Revolution in France* (Cambridge: Cambridge University Press, 1980). Especially good in describing the emergence of a class consciousness by 1848.

Jean Sigmann, *1848: The Romantic and Democratic Revolutions in Europe* (New York: Harper and Row, 1973). Revisionist study focused particularly on the economic, social, and political difficulties during 1846 and 1847.

Sources

Irene Collins, *Government and Society in France, 1814–1848* (New York: St. Martin's, 1971). Very useful collection of documents.

John B. Halsted, ed., *Romanticism: Problems of Definition, Explanation, Evaluation* (Lexington, Mass.: D. C. Heath, 1965). Informative samplings of many different points of view. Halsted has also edited a good anthology of romantic writing, *Romanticism* (New York: Harper and Row, 1969), a volume in the Documentary History of Western Civilization series.

Howard Hugo, ed., *The Romantic Reader* (New York: Viking, 1975). Imaginatively arranged anthology with an enlightening introduction.

James G. Legge, ed., *Rhyme and Revolution in Germany* (New York: AMS Press, 1972). Lively anthology of German history and literature from 1813 to 1850.

Ignazio Silone, ed., *The Living Thoughts of Mazzini* (Norwood, Penn.: Telegraph, 1982). Selections from his writings.

Denis Mack Smith, ed., *The Making of Italy, 1796–1870* (New York: Harper and Row, 1968). Excellent volume in the Documentary History of Western Civilization series.

Mack Walker, ed., *Metternich's Europe* (New York: Harper and Row, n.d.). Useful collection of sources; a volume in the Documentary History of Western Civilization series.

CHAPTER 20   THE INDUSTRIAL SOCIETY

The Industrial Revolution

Asa Briggs, *The Age of Improvement, 1783–1867* (New York: McKay, 1962). Fine summary of Victorian Britain.

Carlo M. Cipolla, ed., *The Industrial Revolution* (London: Penguin, 1973), and *The Emergence of Industrial Societies* (London: Penguin, 1973) and *Before the Industrial Revolution* (3rd ed., New York: Norton, 1994). Perhaps the best short summaries of the current scholarly position. Also *The Economic History of World Population*, 6th ed. (London: Penguin, 1975). Brief look at sources of energy.

D. C. Coleman, *Myth, History and the Industrial Revolution* (London: Hambledon Press, 1992). Difficult and important corrective essays.

François Crouzet, ed., *Capital Formation in the Industrial Revolution* (London: Methuen, 1972). Excellent essays on how the Industrial Revolution was financed.

François Crouzet, W. H. Chaloner, and W. M. Stern, eds., *Essays in European Economic History, 1789–1914* (London: Arnold, 1969). Fascinating essays on the cotton trade, the railway age, and "how revolutions are born."

P. M. Deane, *The First Industrial Revolution* (Cambridge: Cambridge University Press, 1980); Paul Mantoux, *The Industrial Revolution in the Eighteenth Century* (New York: Harper and Row, 1961); Thomas S. Ashton, *The Industrial Revolution, 1760–1830* (Oxford: Oxford University Press, 1948); R. M. Hartwell, ed., *The Causes of the Industrial Revolution in England* (New York: Methuen, 1967). Four useful, short works on the early history of modern industrialism.

Alexander Gerschenkron, *Economic Backwardness in Historical Perspective* (Cambridge, Mass.: Harvard University Press, 1962). Famous essay on why eastern Europe was slow to industrialize.

H. J. Habakkuk and Michael Postan, eds., *The Cambridge Economic History of Europe*, Vol. VI, parts 1 and 2 (Cambridge: Cambridge University Press, 1965). Essays on the industrial revolution by ranking scholars. The contribution by David Landes has been amplified and issued separately: *The Unbound Prometheus: Technological Change and Industrial Development in Western Europe from 1750 to the Present* (Cambridge: Cambridge University Press, 1969).

W. O. Henderson, *The Industrialization of Europe, 1780–1914* (London: Thames and Hudson, 1969); and Tom Kemp, *Industrialization in Nineteenth-Century Europe* (Atlantic Highlands, N.J.: Humanities Press, 1969). Valuable for developments on the Continent.

Eric J. Hobsbawm, *The Pelican Economic History of Britain*, Volume III: *Industry and Empire* (London: Penguin, 1970). By the author of the provocative *Age of Revolution, 1789–1848* (New York: Praeger, 1969), and *The Age of Capital, 1848–1875* (London: Weidenfeld and Nicolson, 1975).

Paul Hohenberg, *A Primer on the Economic History of Europe* (New York: Random House, 1968). Short and clear.

Peter Mathias, *First Industrial Nation* (London: Methuen, 1983). A pioneering study.

Neil McKendrick, John Brewer, and J. H. Plumb, *The Birth of a Consumer Society: The Commercialisation of Eighteenth-Century England* (London: Europa, 1982). Provocative.

Thomas McKeown, *The Modern Rise of Population* (New York: Academic Press, 1976). Striking synthesis of the present state of knowledge on demographic trends and disease.

Alan S. Milward and S. B. Saul, *The Development of the Economies of Continental Europe, 1850–1914* (Cambridge, Mass.: Harvard University Press, 1977). Excellent on France and Germany.

Sidney Pollard, *Peaceful Conquest: The Industrialization of Europe, 1760–1970* (Oxford: Oxford University Press, 1981). A careful examination of the phases through which the industrial revolution passed.

E. P. Thompson, *The Making of the English Working Class* (New York: Random House, 1966). Detailed, influential account of the impact of the French Revolution and the early industrial revolution on the shaping of class consciousness.

Lorna Weatherill, *Consumer Behavior and Material Culture in Britain, 1660–1760* (London: Routledge, 1988). Fascinating look at middle-class life on the verge of the industrial revolution.

The Responses of Liberalism

Ester Boserup, *The Conditions of Agricultural Growth* (Chicago: Aldine, 1965). Significantly challenges Malthusian assumptions, arguing that historically, sustained population growth has been more likely to stimulate economic development than declining populations will.

Louis Chevalier, *Laboring Classes and Dangerous Classes,* (New York: Fertig, 1973). How society came to define crime in urban conditions in the first half of the nineteenth century.

Elie Halévy, *The Growth of Philosophic Radicalism* (New York: Faber, 1972). Celebrated older study of Bentham and his Utilitarian followers.

Robert Heilbroner, *The Worldly Philosophers*, 5th ed. (New York: Touchstone, 1980). A lively, clear introduction to the philosophy of laissez faire.

William L. Langer, *Political and Social Upheaval, 1832–1852* (New York: Harper and Row, 1969). Succinct look at "the social question."

Mary Mack, *Jeremy Bentham* (London: Heinemann, 1962). A good biography.

Michael S. Packe, *The Life of John Stuart Mill* (New York: Macmillan, 1954). Sound biography. For a psychohistory of the father and son, consult Bruce Mazlish, *James and John Stuart Mill* (New York: Basic Books, 1975).

Donald Winch, *Classical Political Economy and Colonies* (London: Bell, 1965). Clear examination of the classical liberal economists.

The Socialist Responses

Shlomo Avineri, *The Social and Political Thought of Karl Marx* (Cambridge: Cambridge University Press, 1971); and George Lichtheim, *Marxism: An Historical and Critical Study* (New York: Columbia University Press, 1982). Thoughtful recent evaluations.

Isaiah Berlin, *Karl Marx: His Life and Environment*, 4th ed. (Oxford: Oxford University Press, 1978). Brilliant study.

Julius Braunthal, *History of the International* (Boulder, Colo.: Westview, 1980). Sound, scholarly study.

John Foster, *Class Struggle and the Industrial Revolution* (New York: St. Martin's, 1974). An original look at early industrial capitalism in English towns.

John F. C. Harrison, *Quest for the New Moral World: Robert Owen and the Owenites in Britain and America* (London: Routledge and Kegan Paul, 1969). The standard study of the radical British businessman and of his impact.

Harry W. Laidler, *A History of Socialism* (New York: Thomas Y. Crowell, 1968). Updated version of an older standard account.

George Lichtheim, *Origins of Socialism* (New York: Praeger, 1969) and *A Short History of Socialism* (New York: Praeger, 1970). Highly useful introductions.

David McLellan, *Karl Marx* (London: Penguin, 1976). A very short study of the kernel of Marx's changing thought.

Nicholas V. Riasanovsky, *The Teaching of Charles Fourier* (Berkeley: University of California Press, 1969). The standard work on the French Utopian.

Joan Wallach Scott, *The Glassworkers of Carmaux* (Cambridge, Mass.: Harvard University Press, 1974). Study of an elite craft and its eventual radicalization.

Edmund Wilson, *To the Finland Station* (New York: Farrar Straus & Giroux, 1972). A sympathetic and balanced history of socialism.

Apostles of Violence—and Nonviolence

Michel Foucault, *Madness and Civilization*, trans. Richard Howard (New York: Vintage, 1973). Imaginative—perhaps too imaginative—analysis of how society coped with the idea of madness by instituting asylums.

James Joll, *The Anarchists* (Cambridge, Mass.: Harvard University Press, 1980). Helpful introduction.

Lilian Lewis Shiman, *Women and Leadership in Nineteenth-Century England* (Basingstoke, Eng.: Macmillan, 1992). Wide-ranging analysis.

A. B. Spitzer, *The Revolutionary Theories of Louis-Auguste Blanqui* (New York: AMS Press, 1957). Good study of the French agitator.

General Accounts of Intellectual Trends

R. C. Binkley, *Realism and Nationalism, 1852–1871* (New York: Harper and Row, 1941); Carlton J. Hayes, *A Generation of Materialism, 1871–1900* (New York: Harper and Row, 1941); Oron J. Hale, *The Great Illusion, 1900–1914* (New York: Harper and Row, 1971). Volumes in the Rise of Modern Europe series.

W. H. Coates and H. V. White, *The Ordeal of Liberal Humanism* (New York: McGraw-Hill, 1969). A compact and useful survey of intellectual history since 1789.

David Sorkin, *The Transformation of German Jewry, 1780–1840* (New York: Oxford University Press, 1987). An imaginative portrait.

Roland N. Stromberg, *European Intellectual History since 1789* (Englewood Cliffs, N.J.: Prentice-Hall, 1975). A helpful textbook.

Science and Darwinism

Jacques Barzun, *Darwin, Marx and Wagner*, 2d ed. (Chicago: University of Chicago Press, 1981). Suggestive study stressing the common denominators among three contemporaneous innovators once cataloged as very different from one another.

Charles C. Gillispie, *The Edge of Objectivity* (Princeton, N.J.: Princeton University Press, 1960). Darwin and other nineteenth-century scientific innovators appraised. Gillispie has also written *Genesis and Geology* (Cambridge, Mass.: Harvard University Press, 1951). A study of the tension between science and religion prior to Darwin.

John C. Greene, *The Death of Adam* (Ames: Iowa State University Press, 1959). Assessment of the impact of evolution on Western thought.

Gertrude Himmelfarb, *Darwin and the Darwinian Revolution* (New York: Norton, 1968). Excellent critical introduction. For a rather different assessment consult Michael T. Ghiselin, *The Triumph of the Darwinian Method* (Berkeley: University of California Press, 1969).

Richard Hofstadter, *Social Darwinism in American Thought* (Boston: Beacon, 1955). An admirable study.

William Irvine, *Apes, Angels and Victorians* (New York: McGraw-Hill, 1955). A lively study of the social ramifications of Darwinism.

Nancy Stepan, *The Idea of Race in Science* (London: Macmillan, 1982). Fine examination of how science, and especially eugenics, fostered racism.

Frank Miller Turner, *Between Science and Religion* (New Haven: Yale University Press, 1974). Sensitive treatment of six figures who sought the middle ground.

W. P. D. Wightman, *The Growth of Scientific Ideas* (New Haven: Yale University Press, 1951). A most enlightening interpretation.

Literature and the Arts

Carlo M. Cipolla, *Literacy and Development in the West* (London: Penguin, 1969). On the expansion of the reading public.

Pierre Courthion, *Impressionism* (New York: Abrams, 1977). Well-illustrated introduction to the painters of light and color.

George H. Hamilton, *19th and 20th Century Art* (Englewood Cliffs, N.J.: Prentice-Hall, 1972). Encyclopedic, copiously illustrated survey.

Humphrey House, *The Dickens World*, 2d ed. (Oxford: Oxford University Press, 1960). Excellent, brief introduction.

K. B. Klaus, *The Romantic Period in Music* (London: Allyn and Bacon, 1970). Organized by topic (melody, harmony, counterpoint, chamber music, vocal music); covers through the early 1900s.

Harry Levin, *The Gates of Horn: A Study of Five French Realists* (Oxford: Oxford University Press, 1965). Scholarly assessments of Stendhal, Balzac, Flaubert, Zola, and Proust.

Jean Leymarie, *French Painting: The Nineteenth Century* (Geneva: Skira, 1962). Well-illustrated survey through the mid-1880s.

J. Hillis Miller, *The Disappearance of God* (Cambridge, Mass.: Harvard University Press, 1976). A study of five nineteenth-century writers.

Fritz Novotny, *Painting and Sculpture in Europe, 1780–1880* (London: Penguin, 1973); and H. R. Hitchcock, *Architecture: The Nineteenth and Twentieth Centuries* (London: Penguin, 1958). Detailed and informative volumes in the Pelican History of Art.

Joseph C. Sloane, *French Painting between Past and Present* (Princeton, N.J.: Princeton University Press, 1973). Stresses the years from 1818 to 1870, which marked "the birth of modern painting."

Francis Steegmuller, *Flaubert and Madame Bovary* (Chicago: University of Chicago Press, 1977). Illuminating portraits of the great French realist and his famous heroine.

G. M. Young, *Victorian England: Portrait of an Age* (New York: Oxford University Press, 1957); and Walter E. Houghton, *The Victorian Frame of Mind, 1830–1870* (New Haven: Yale University Press, 1963). Informative introductions to the English scene.

Philosophy and Political Thought

William L. Burn, *The Age of Equipoise* (New York: Norton, 1964). Stimulating study of the mid-Victorian intellectual climate.

Donald G. Charlton, *Secular Religions in France, 1815–1870* (Oxford: Oxford University Press, 1963). Scholarly survey of surrogate religions.

Mark Francis and John Morrow, *A History of English Political Thought in the Nineteenth Century* (New York: St. Martin's, 1995). Arnold, Bentham, Mill, and Spenser.

F. C. Green, *A Comparative View of French and British Civilization* (London: Dent, 1965). A look at morals and conventions through representative thinkers of the time from 1850 to 1870.

Walter Kaufmann, *Nietzsche: Philosopher, Psychologist, Antichrist*, 3d ed. (Princeton, N.J.: Princeton University Press, 1968). A fine book on the controversial German.

Karl Löwith, *From Hegel to Nietzsche* (Garden City, N.Y.: Doubleday, 1962). Analysis of the revolution in nineteenth-century thought, especially in Germany.

Frank E. Manuel, *The Prophets of Paris* (Cambridge, Mass.: Harvard University Press, 1962). Comte is the last of the five figures treated in this informative study.

Gerhard Masur, *Prophets of Yesterday: Studies in European Culture, 1890–1914* (New York: Macmillan, 1966); and H. Stuart Hughes, *Consciousness and Society: The Reorientation of European Social Thought, 1890–1930* (New York: Vintage, 1961). Two very suggestive studies of the twilight of the nineteenth century.

Walter M. Simon, *European Positivism in the Nineteenth Century* (Ithaca, N.Y.: Cornell University Press, 1963). Scholarly assessment of Comte and his disciples.

Sources

Henry D. Aiken, ed., *The Age of Ideology* (Salem, N.H.: Arno, 1977). Selections from nineteenth-century philosophers, with helpful introductory comments.

Edward Bellamy, *Looking Backward, 2000–1887* (several eds.); H. G. Wells, *A Modern Utopia* (Lincoln: University of Nebraska Press, 1967); and William Morris, *News from Nowhere* (London: Routledge and Kegan Paul, 1970). Three contrasting visions of utopia in the light of science and industrialism.

Charles Darwin, *Autobiography* (New York: Norton, 1969); *Voyage of the Beagle* (New York: Dalton, 1979); *On the Origin of Species* (several eds.). Three key works for understanding the development of Darwin's ideas. His writings may be sampled in *The Darwin Reader*, ed. Marsten Bates and Philip S. Humphrey (New York: Scribner's, 1956).

Robert Forster and Orest Ranum, eds., *Food and Drink in History* (Baltimore: Johns Hopkins University Press, 1979). Fascinating collection of essays from the *Annales* school of historians in France; examines (among several subjects) the rise of café culture, the use of leftover food in Paris, and the role of the potato in the diet.

Albert Fried and Ronald Sanders, *Socialist Thought: A Documentary History* (New York: Anchor, 1964). Informative collection of source materials.

V. A. C. Gatrell, *Robert Owen's A New View of Society and Report to the County of Lanark* (London: Penguin, 1969). Includes a fine introduction.

F. A. Hayek, *John Stuart Mill and Harriet Taylor* (Chicago: University of Chicago Press, 1951). Revealing correspondence on their friendship and marriage.

Vincent J. Knapp, *Europe in the Era of Social Transformation: 1700–Present* (Englewood Cliffs, N.J.: Prentice-Hall, 1976). Especially good on the idea of "mass society."

P. A. Kropotkin, *Selected Readings on Anarchism and Revolution* (Cambridge, Mass.: MIT Press, 1970). Useful introduction to his ideas.

Thomas R. Malthus, *Population: The First Essay* (Ann Arbor: University of Michigan, 1959). The original essay of 1798; states Malthusianism in its most undiluted form.

Frank E. Manuel, ed., *Utopias and Utopian Thought* (Cambridge, Mass.: Harvard University Press, 1979). A useful documentary collection.

Karl Marx and Fredrich Engels, *Basic Writings on Politics and Philosophy*, ed. L. S. Feuer (Boston: Peter Smith, 1975). Good selection.

David McLellan, ed. and trans., *The Grundrisse* (New York: Harper and Row, Torchbooks, 1972). A selection from Marx's unpublished manuscript.

John Stuart Mill, *Autobiography* (several eds.); *Principles of Political Economy* (London: Penguin, 1962); *On Liberty* (New York: Norton, 1975); *On the Subjection of Women* (Cambridge, Mass.: MIT Press, 1970); *Utilitarianism* (Indianapolis: Hackett, 1978). Major writings of the great Victorian liberal.

Henri de Saint-Simon, *Social Organization, The Science of Man, and Other Writings*, ed. Felix Markham (New York: Harper and Row, 1964). Well-edited anthology.

Georges Sorel, *Reflections on Violence* (New York: AMS Press, 1970). The famous defense of direct revolutionary action and the general strike.

Herbert Spencer, *Man versus the State* (Indianapolis: Liberty Fund, 1982). Representative work by an English Social Darwinist.

Emile Zola, *Germinal* (London: Penguin, 1954). Famous French novel about a strike in a coal mine.

CHAPTER 21   *THE* MODERNIZATION OF NATIONS

General Accounts

Liah Greenfeld, *Nationalism: Five Roads to Modernity* (Cambridge, Mass.: Harvard University Press, 1992). Provocative and controversial, almost encylopedic analysis.

William L. Langer, *Political and Social Upheaval, 1832–1852* (New York: Harper and Row, 1969). Sensitive, synthetic treatment of a most difficult period.

Michael Mason, *The Making of Victorian Sexual Attitudes* (New York: Oxford University Press, 1995). Excellent survey on the development of modernity.

George L. Mosse, *Toward the Final Solution: A History of European Racism* (New York: Fertig, 1978). Clear examination of racist thought, especially anti-Semitism.

W. E. Mosse, *The Rise and Fall of the Crimean System, 1855–1871* (London: Macmillan, 1963). Careful treatment of the diplomatic revolution associated with the war.

The New Cambridge Modern History, 14 vols. (Cambridge: Cambridge University Press, 1957–1970). Volumes X, XI, and XII of this collaborative work are a handy source of information.

A. J. P. Taylor, *The Struggle for Mastery in Europe, 1848–1919* (Oxford: Clarendon, 1954). Crisp and provocative; a volume in the Oxford History of Modern Europe series. Informative sociological analysis.

Charles Tilly, Louise Tilly, and Richard Tilly, *The Rebellious Century, 1830–1930* (Cambridge, Mass.: Harvard University Press, 1980). Complex, original combination of history and sociology.

C. Vann Woodward, ed., *The Comparative Approach to American History* (New York: Basic Books, 1968). Enlightening essays comparing American with European developments.

France

Denis W. Brogan, *The French Nation from Napoleon to Petain* (New York: Harper and Row, 1957). Brilliant essay of interpretation. Brogan has also written a detailed and perceptive study of the Third Republic, *France under the Republic* (New York: Harper & Row, 1940).

Guy Chapman, *The Dreyfus Case: A Re-assessment* (Westport, Conn.: Greenwood, 1979); and D. Johnson, *France and the Dreyfus Affair* (New York: Walker, 1967). Scholarly appraisals.

Albert Guérard, *France: A Modern History*, rev. ed. (Ann Arbor: University of Michigan Press, 1969). By an American scholar of French background who also wrote sympathetic studies of Louis Napoleon: *Napoleon III* (Westport, Conn.: Greenwood, 1979), and a biogra-

phy with the same title for the series Great Lives in Brief (New York: Knopf, 1955).

John H. Jackson, *Clemenceau and the Third Republic* (Westport, Conn.: Hyperion, 1979); and Geoffrey Bruun, *Clemenceau* (Hamden, Conn.: Shoe String, 1968). Succinct studies of a formidable politician.

John Rothney, *Bonapartism after Sedan* (Ithaca, N.Y.: Cornell University Press, 1969). Clear view of the complex political events of 1871 to 1879.

Frederick H. Seager, *The Boulanger Affair* (Ithaca, N.Y.: Cornell University Press, 1969). A revisionist refutation of myth.

Roger H. Soltau, *French Political Thought in the Nineteenth Century*, new ed. (New York: Russell, 1959). An older and still useful work.

J. M. Thompson, *Louis Napoleon and the Second Empire* (New York: Norton, n.d.). A standard scholarly synthesis. Other useful up-to-date works on the Second Empire are Theodore Zeldin, *The Political System of Napoleon III* (New York: Norton, 1971); and *Emile Ollivier and the Liberal Empire of Napoleon III* (Oxford: Clarendon Press, 1963); Roger L. Williams, *The World of Napoleon III*, rev. ed. (New York: Free Press, n.d.); and Benedict D. Gooch, *The Reign of Napoleon III* (Chicago: Rand McNally, 1969).

David Thomson, *Democracy in France since 1870*, 5th ed. (Oxford: Oxford University Press, 1969). Brilliant essay of interpretation; particularly good on the period from 1870 to 1914.

Eugen Weber, *Peasants into Frenchmen: The Modernization of Rural France, 1870–1914* (Palo Alto, Calif.: Stanford University Press, 1976). A complex, rich, and very significant achievement.

Eugen Weber, *France, Fin de Siècle* (Cambridge, Mass.: Harvard University Press, 1986). A most impressive general history.

Roger L. Williams, *The French Revolution of 1870–1871* (New York: Norton, 1969). Study of the highly controversial period climaxed by the Commune.

Gordon Wright, *France in Modern Times*, 5th ed. (New York: Norton, 1994); Alfred Cobban, *History of Modern France*, rev. ed., Vol. II (1799–1871), and Vol. III (1871–1962) (London: Penguin, 1962–1966). Enlightening surveys.

Theodore Zeldin, *France, 1848–1945* (Oxford: Clarendon Press, 1979). Richly detailed social and intellectual history.

Italy

Derek Beales, *The Risorgimento and the Unification of Italy* (London: Longman, Green, 1982). Useful, clear appraisal.

Benedetto Croce, *A History of Italy, 1871–1915* (Oxford: Clarendon Press, 1929). A classic analysis by a famous philosopher-historian.

Clara M. Lovett, *The Democratic Movement in Italy, 1830–1876* (Cambridge, Mass.: Harvard University Press, 1982). A full, sophisticated examination.

A. W. Salomone, ed., *Italy from the Risorgimento to Fascism* (Garden City, N.Y.: Anchor, 1970). An informative survey of the background of totalitarianism.

Christopher Seton-Watson, *Italy from Liberalism to Fascism, 1870–1925* (New York: Methuen, 1967). Detailed scholarly study.

Denis Mack Smith, *Italy: A Modern History* (Ann Arbor: University of Michigan Press, 1959). Standard account by a ranking expert. He has also written other illuminating studies, including *Cavour and Garibaldi, 1860: A Study in Political Conflict* (Cambridge: Cambridge University Press, 1954), and *Garibaldi* (New York: Knopf, 1956).

Germany

Ann Taylor Allen, *Feminism and Motherhood in Germany, 1800–1914* (New Brunswick, N.J.: Rutgers University Press, 1991). Excellent exploration of motherhood in German thought.

Gordon A. Craig, *Germany, 1866–1945* (New York: Oxford University Press, 1978). A fine, thorough, well-balanced survey.

Erich Eyck, *Bismarck and the German Empire* (New York: Norton, 1964). Translation and condensation of a large, standard work in German.

L. L. Farrar, Jr., *Arrogance and Anxiety: The Ambivalence of German Power, 1848–1914* (Iowa City: University of Iowa Press, 1981). Close look at the years immediately preceding World War I.

Eckart Kehr, *Economic Interest, Militarism, and Foreign Policy*, trans. Grete Heinz (Berkeley: University of California Press, 1977). Often complex, careful essays on the nature of bureaucracy in Germany.

Gerhard Masur, *Imperial Berlin* (London: Routledge and Kegan Paul, 1974). Lively social history.

W. N. Medlicott, *Bismarck and Modern Germany* (London: Hodder and Stroughton, 1974). A short biography.

Friedrich Meinecke, *The German Catastrophe* (Boston: Beacon, 1963). A useful antidote to Taylor by a German historian.

Alan Palmer, *Bismarck* (London: Weidenfeld and Nicolson, 1976). A balanced, lively portrait.

Otto Pflanze, *Bismarck and the Development of Germany* (Princeton, N.J.: Princeton University Press, 1963). Only covers up to 1871; a brilliant study that sets the man in his time and digests the vast controversial literature about him.

James J. Sheehan, *German Liberalism in the Nineteenth Century* (Chicago: University of Chicago Press, 1978). Difficult, careful unraveling of the failure of German liberalism.

Walter M. Simon, *Germany: A Brief History* (New York: Random House, 1969). Clear, short, straightforward survey.

Fritz Stern, *Gold and Iron: Bismarck, Bleichroder, and the Building of the German Empire* (New York: Vintage, 1979). Superb, full examination of Bismarck and banking.

Michael Stürmer, *Regierung und Reichstag in Bismarck-staat, 1871–1880* (Düsseldorf: Droste, 1974). For those who read German, a fine interpretation of Bismarck's "Cäsarismus."

A.J.P. Taylor, *Bismarck: The Man and the Statesman* (New York: Random House, 1967). A provocative and often hostile reevaluation.

A.J.P. Taylor, *The Course of German History* (New York: Coward-McCann, 1946). A lively essay on the period since 1815, with strong anti-German overtones.

Hans-Ulrich Wehler, *Das Deutsche Kaiserreich, 1871–1918* (Göttingen: Vandenhoeck and Ruprecht, 1973). Complex, exciting reinterpretation.

The Habsburg Monarchy

Robert A. Kann, *The Multinational Empire* (New York: Octagon, 1964). A monograph, arranged nationality by nationality; discusses national sentiments and the government's efforts to deal with them.

Claudio Magris, *Der habsburgische Mythos in der österreichischen Literatur* (Salzburg: Otto Müller, 1966). Imaginative look at Franz Grillparzer (1791–1872), an Austrian dramatist, and the implications of the Beidermeier style in decoration.

A. J. May, *The Hapsburg Monarchy, 1867–1914* (Cambridge, Mass.: Harvard University Press, 1951). Concise general account.

Robin Okey, *Eastern Europe, 1740–1980: Feudalism to Communism* (Minneapolis: University of Minnesota Press, 1982). Clear, short history for the beginner.

Steven T. Rosenthal, *The Politics of Dependency: Urban Reform in Istanbul* (Westport, Conn.: Greenwood, 1980). On the influence of the Tanzimat.

Carl E. Schorske, *Fin-de-Siècle Vienna: Politics and Culture* (New York: Vintage, 1981). Brilliant essays on the relationship between culture as politics and Vienna as power center.

A. J. P. Taylor, *The Hapsburg Monarchy, 1809–1918* (Chicago: University of Chicago Press, 1948). A spirited, brief treatment.

Russia

James H. Billington, *The Icon and the Axe* (New York: Vintage, 1970). Markedly rich, controversial interpretation of Russian culture.

Peter Brock, *The Slovak National Awakening* (Toronto: University of Toronto Press, 1976). Short essay on the intellectual history of cultural nationalism.

Ronald Hingley, *A Concise History of Russia* (New York: Viking, 1972). Very short illustrated survey.

Charles Jelavich and Barbara Jelavich, *The Establishment of the Balkan National States, 1804–1920* (Seattle: University of Washington Press, 1977). Balanced, full account.

James Joll, *The Anarchists* (Cambridge, Mass.: Harvard University Press, 1980). Excellent chapters on Bakunin and Peter Kropotkin; a fine study of the movement.

Martin Malia, *Alexander Herzen and the Birth of Russian Socialism* (New York: Grosset and Dunlap, Universal Library, 1965). Excellent monograph on Herzen's life and thought.

Sidney Monas, *The Third Section: Police and Society in Russia under Nicholas I* (Cambridge, Mass.: Harvard University Press, 1961). Pioneering study of the repressive machinery.

Nicholas V. Riasanovsky, *A History of Russia*, 4th ed. (New York: Oxford University Press, 1984). Full text.

Nicholas V. Riasanovsky, *Russia and the West in the Teaching of the Slavophiles* (Boston: Peter Smith, 1980), and *Nicholas I and Official Nationality in Russia, 1825–1855* (Berkeley: University of California, n.d.). Useful studies.

Gerold T. Robinson, *Rural Russia under the Old Regime* (Berkeley: University of California Press, 1967). A splendid monograph on the peasant question.

CHAPTER 22 *M*ODERN EMPIRES AND IMPERIALISM

Great Britain

C. J. Bartlett, ed., *Britain Pre-eminent: Studies in British World Influence in the Nineteenth Century* (London: Macmillan, 1969). A concise summary of the factors that made Britain the dominant power in the nineteenth century.

G. F. A. Best, *Mid-Victorian Britain, 1851–1875* (London: Weidenfeld and Nicolson, 1971). Solid account of a quarter-century of reform and resistance to it.

David Cannadine, *Aspects of Aristocracy: Grandeur and Decline in Modern Britain* (New Haven: Yale University Press, 1994). A sweeping examination of the decline of aristocracy.

Richard Koebner and Helmut Dan Schmidt, *Imperialism: The Story and Significance of a Political Word* (Cambridge: Cambridge University Press, 1964). An enlightening monograph.

William L. Langer, *The Diplomacy of Imperialism, 1890–1902*, 2d ed. (New York: Knopf, 1951). Detailed case histories from a particularly complex period.

Kenneth S. Latourette, *A History of the Expansion of Christianity* (New York: Harper and Row, 1975). Volumes V and VI treat its expansion into the non-European world.

Octave Mannoni, *Prospero and Caliban* (New York: Methuen, 1964). Analysis of the psychology of colonization.

Philip Mason, *Patterns of Dominance* (Oxford: Oxford University Press, 1970). Examples of the varieties of colonial rule.

Wolfgang J. Mommsen, *Theories of Imperialism*, trans. P. S. Falla (Chicago: University of Chicago Press, 1982). Concise, short discussion of the range of theories—Marxist, anti-Marxist, and non-Marxist—on the causes of imperialism.

Ronald Robinson, John Gallagher, and Alice Denny, *Africa and the Victorians* (New York: St. Martin's, 1961). The classic formulation of the "collaborator thesis," which offers a non-Marxist, as opposed to pro- or anti-Marxist, analysis of the causes of expansion after 1870.

A. P. Thornton, *Doctrines of Imperialism* (New York: Wiley, 1965); and Tom Kemp, *Theories of Imperialism* (London: Dobson, 1968). Useful analyses of the ideological background.

Africa

Michael Crowder, *West Africa under Colonial Rule* (Evanston, Ill.: Northwestern University Press, 1968). Fine survey.

James Duffy, *Portugal in Africa* (London: Penguin, n.d.). The best study of an important and often-neglected colonial enterprise.

Peter Duignan and L. H. Gann, *Colonialism in Africa*. Vol. I: *The History and Politics of Colonialism* (Cambridge: Cambridge University Press, 1969). A comprehensive survey. The same authors have also published *Burden of Empire* (Stanford, Calif.: Hoover Institution, n.d.), a defense of the contribution of the colonial powers to the development of sub-Saharan Africa.

Robert B. Edgerton, *The Fall of the Asante Empire: The Hundred-Year War for Africa's Gold Coast* (New York: Free Press, 1995). A well-written account of the four Asante wars.

John Flint, *Cecil Rhodes* (Boston: Little, Brown, 1974). Fine, short biography.

Prosser Gifford and Wm. Roger Lewis, eds., *France and Britain in Africa* (New Haven: Yale University Press, 1971); *Britain and Germany in Africa* (New Haven: Yale University Press, 1967). Materials on their rivalry and their respective institutions of colonial rule.

John D. Hargreaves, *Prelude to the Partition of West Africa* (London: Macmillan, 1963). Best analysis of the idea of partition as it relates to the argument that the nature of imperialism changed after 1870.

A. G. Hopkins, *An Economic History of West Africa* (New York: Columbia University Press, 1973). Highly original reinterpretation of the economic impact of imperialism.

Lord Kinross (Patrick Balfour), *Between Two Seas* (London: Murray, 1969). Lively account of the creation of the Suez Canal.

David S. Landes, *Bankers and Pashas* (Cambridge, Mass.: Harvard University Press, 1980). Illuminating account of French economic imperialism in Egypt during the midnineteenth century.

Roland Oliver and G. N. Sanderson, eds., *The Cambridge History of Africa*, especially Vol. VI: *From 1870 to 1905* (Cambridge: Cambridge University Press, 1985). A full European view.

John Sender and Sheila Smith, *The Development of Capitalism in Africa* (London: Methuen, 1987). Succinct, readable study of a complex subject.

Ruth Slade, *King Leopold's Congo* (Westport, Conn.: Greenwood, 1974); and Roger Anstey, *King Leopold's Legacy* (London: Oxford University Press, 1966). These two critical volumes examine Belgian rule in the Congo from 1884 to 1960.

R. L. Tignor, *Modernization and British Colonial Rule in Egypt, 1882–1914* (Princeton, N.J.: Princeton University Press, 1966). Full and balanced appraisal of the British record.

Monica Wilson and Leonard Thompson, eds., *The Oxford History of South Africa* (New York: Oxford University Press, 1969 and 1971). Authoritative history; Volume I ends at 1870; Volume II comes to 1966.

Asia

J. F. Cady, *The Roots of French Imperialism in Eastern Asia*, rev. ed. (Ithaca, N.Y.: Cornell University Press, 1967). Lucid scholarly study.

Michael Edwardes, *The West in Asia, 1815–1914* (New York: Putnam's, n.d.). Good introduction to the increasing involvement of the imperialist powers.

John K. Fairbank, *The United States and China*, 4th ed. (Cambridge, Mass.: Harvard University Press, 1979). With greater stress on Chinese history and culture than the title suggests.

John W. Hall, *Japan: From Pre-History to Modern Times* (New York: Delacorte, 1970). Fine survey.

Kenneth S. Latourette, *China* (Englewood Cliffs, N.J.: Prentice-Hall, n.d.). Concise introduction.

J. T. Pratt, *The Expansion of Europe into the Far East* (New York: Sylvan Press, 1947). Excellent introductory account.

E. O. Reischauer, *Japan Past and Present*, 4th ed. (New York: Knopf, n.d.). Admirable introduction.

B. H. Sumner, *Tsardom and Imperialism in the Far East and Middle East, 1880–1914* (Hamden, Conn.: Shoe String, 1968). Good short account.

The Middle East

R. H. Davison, *Turkey* (Englewood Cliffs, N.J.: Prentice-Hall, n.d.). Clear and concise introduction.

Albert Hourani, *Arabic Thought in the Liberal Age, 1798–1939* (Oxford: Oxford University Press, n.d.). Informative study; considerable stress on Western influences.

Marian Kent, *Oil and Empire* (London: Macmillan, 1976). Close look at oil imperialism to 1920.

Bernard Lewis, *The Emergence of Modern Turkey*, 2d ed. (Oxford: Oxford University Press, 1968). A good study of the Ottoman Empire in the nineteenth century.

The British Empire and Commonwealth

George D. Bearce, *British Attitudes toward India* (Westport, Conn.: Greenwood, 1982). Perceptive survey of the period from 1784 to 1858.

Max Beloff, *Imperial Sunset*. Vol. I: *Britain's Liberal Empire, 1897–1921* (New York: Knopf, 1970). Useful, ironic account.

The Cambridge History of the British Empire (London: Macmillan, 1929–1940). With separate volumes on India, Canada, and Australia and New Zealand together.

Charles E. Carrington, *The British Overseas: Exploits of a Nation of Shopkeepers*, 2d ed. (Cambridge: Cambridge University Press, 1968). Detailed study.

Gerald M. Craig, *The United States and Canada* (Cambridge, Mass.: Harvard University Press, 1968). Sound scholarly study with much stress on Canadian developments.

Lance Davis and Robert Huttenback, *Mammon and the Pursuit of Empire: The Political Economy of British Imperialism* (Cambridge: Cambridge University Press, 1987). An attempt to answer the question, Did the Empire pay?

Christopher Hibbert, *The Great Mutiny: India 1857* (London: Penguin, 1980). Lively short history.

Francis G. Hutchins, *The Illusion of Permanence* (Princeton, N.J.: Princeton University Press, 1967). Describes how the British could imagine they would remain in India for all time.

Donald F. Lach, *India in the Eyes of Europe* (Chicago: Chicago University Press, 1968). Shows how sixteenth-century attitudes were shaped and carried over to subsequent times.

D. A. Low, *Lion Rampant* (London: Cass, 1973). Exceptionally fruitful essays on the impact of "social engineering" within the British Empire.

R. J. Moore, *Liberalism and Indian Politics, 1872–1922* (London: Arnold, 1966). Discusses India in British politics.

Cormac O Gráda, *Ireland: A New Economic History* (New York: Oxford University Press, 1944). Excellent on Ireland's economic struggles.

Other Empires

W. E. Beasley, *Japanese Imperialism, 1894–1945* (Oxford: Clarendon Press, 1987). Fine survey.

Raymond F. Betts, *Assimilation and Association in French Colonial Theory* (New York: Columbia University Press, 1961). Best analysis in English of the policy of assimilation.

Henri Brunschwig, *French Colonialism: Myths and Realities, 1871–1914* (New York: Praeger, 1966). Perceptive study by a French scholar.

Ernest R. May, *Imperial Democracy* (New York: Harper and Row, 1973), and *American Imperialism: A Speculative Essay* (New York: Atheneum, 1968). By a scholarly expert; deals with America's emergence as a world power.

J. W. Pratt, *America's Colonial Experiment* (Englewood Cliffs, N.J.: Prentice-Hall, 1950). Good survey.

S. H. Roberts, *History of French Colonial Policy* (Hamden, Conn.: Archon, 1963). A valuable, detailed, older work.

Woodruff D. Smith, *The German Colonial Empire* (Chapel Hill: University of North Carolina Press, 1978). Clear, basic survey.

Barbara L. Solow, *Slavery and the Rise of the Atlantic System* (New York: Cambridge University Press, 1992). Relates slavery to trade.

M. E. Townsend, *The Rise and Fall of Germany's Colonial Empire, 1884–1918* (New York: Macmillan, 1930). A standard account. May be supplemented by W. O. Henderson, *Studies in German Colonial History* (New York: Quadrangle, 1963).

Sources

Reginald Coupland, ed., *The Durham Report* (Oxford: Clarendon, 1946). The document that in a sense marks the beginning of the development of the British Commonwealth.

E. M. Forster, *A Passage to India* (several eds.). Classic novel on the gap between East and West.

H. Rider Haggard, *King Solomon's Mines* (several eds.). A splendid example of the rousing novel of imperialist adventure.

Louis Hémon, *Maria Chapdelaine* (New York: Macmillan, 1940). The best-known classic novel about rural French Canada.

John A. Hobson, *Imperialism: A Study* (Ann Arbor: University of Michigan Press, 1965). A celebrated hostile critique.

Benjamin Kidd, *The Control of the Tropics* (New York: Macmillan, 1898). A characteristic defense of imperialism.

Rudyard Kipling, *Kim* (several eds.), and *Soldiers Three* (several eds.). Famous works by the even more famous champion of imperialism.

V. I. Lenin, *Imperialism: The Highest Stage of Capitalism* (New York: International, n.d.). The classic communist critique.

Wm. Roger Louis, ed., *Imperialism: The Robinson and Gallagher Controversy* (New York: Franklin Watts, 1976). Presents all sides to the Robinson and Gallagher thesis.

C. J. Lowe, *The Reluctant Imperialists* (London: Routledge, 1967). One volume analyzing British policy and a second containing documents.

Frederick J. Lugard, *The Dual Mandate in British Tropical Africa* (New York: Biblio, 1965). Significant detailed account of British policy in Nigeria.

Robin W. Winks, ed., *The Age of Imperialism* (Englewood Cliffs, N.J.: Prentice-Hall, 1969). A short volume in the Sources of Civilization in the West series, edited by Crane Brinton and Robert Lee Wolff.

CHAPTER 23   *G*REAT WAR, GREAT REVOLUTION

The Background

J. J. Becker, *The Great War and the French People* (Leamington: Berg, 1986). A perceptive exploration of the French home front.

V. R. Berghahn, *Germany and the Approach of War in 1914* (2nd ed. New York: St. Martin's, 1994). Careful look at the war from the German perspective.

Oron J. Hale, *The Great Illusion, 1900–1914* (New York: Harper and Row, 1971). Stressing the economic and cultural background; includes full bibliographies.

James Joll, *The Origins of the First World War* (London: Longmans, 1984). A multifaceted approach.

Paul M. Kennedy, *The Rise and Fall of British Naval Mastery* (London: Allen Lane, 1976). Fine review of a subject central to the war.

Lawrence Lafore, *The Long Fuse* (New York: Harper and Row, 1971); and Joachim Remak, *Origins of World War I* (New York: Holt, Rinehart, 1967). Illuminating studies incorporating recent scholarship.

William L. Langer, *European Alliances and Alignments, 1871–1890* (Westport, Conn.: Greenwood, 1977), and *The Diplomacy of Imperialism, 1890–1902*, 2d ed. (New York: Knopf, 1951). Detailed scholarly analyses; include valuable bibliographies.

Walter Laqueur, *Russia and Germany: A Century of Conflict* (Boston: Little, Brown, 1965). Yet another factor in the background scrutinized.

George Monger, *The End of Isolation* (Westport, Conn.: Greenwood, 1976). British foreign policy reviewed. For Anglo-American relations, it may be supplemented by Bradford Perkins, *The Great Rapprochement* (New York: Atheneum, 1968).

Karen A. Rasler and William R. Thompson, *The Great Powers and Global Struggle, 1490–1990* (Lexington: University of Kentucky Press, 1995). Places all modern wars in historical perspective.

Gerhard Ritter, *The Sword and the Scepter: The Problem of Militarism in Germany*, 2 vols. (Miami, Fla.: University of Miami Press, 1970). Volume II deals with the European powers and William II's Germany from 1890 to 1914.

Raymond J. Sontag, *Germany and England: Background of Conflict, 1848–1894* (New York: Norton, 1969). Excellent study of Anglo-German tension.

A. J. P. Taylor, *The Struggle for Mastery in Europe, 1848–1918* (Oxford: Oxford University Press, 1971). A crisp and suggestive survey.

Barbara Tuchman, *The Proud Tower* (New York: Macmillan, 1966). Instructive and readable account of the European societies that produced the Great War.

Samuel R. Williamson, *The Politics of Grand Strategy* (Cambridge, Mass.: Harvard University Press, 1969). An assessment of the Anglo-French rapprochement before 1914.

The War

Frank P. Chambers, *The War behind the War* (New York: Arno, 1972). On the "home front."

Richard Collier, *The Plague of the Spanish Lady* (New York: Atheneum, 1974). The drama of the influenza pandemic that swept the world in 1918 to 1919.

Fritz Fischer, *Germany's Aims in the First World War* (New York: Norton, 1968). A revisionist estimate of German policy that has caused considerable debate.

Paul Fussell, *The Great War and Modern Memory* (New York: Oxford University Press, 1977). Powerful study of how World War I was shaped in modern memory by major literary figures.

Martin Gilbert, *The First World War: A Complete History* (New York: Henry Holt, 1995). A clear account, overbalanced with British detail.

Ernest R. May, *World War and American Isolation, 1914–1917* (Cambridge, Mass.: Harvard University Press, 1959), and *The Coming of War, 1917* (Chicago: Rand McNally, 1963). The most reliable and balanced treatment of the events that made the United States a belligerent.

Elizabeth Monroe, *Britain's Moment in the Middle East, 1914–1956*, rev. ed. (Baltimore: Johns Hopkins University Press, 1981). Persuasive explanation of the contradictions in Britain's policy toward Arabs and Jews, particularly during World War I and the ensuing peace negotiations.

Alan Moorehead, *Gallipoli* (Annapolis: Nautical, 1982); and Alistair Horne, *The Price of Glory: Verdun, 1916* (London: Penguin, 1979). Excellent accounts of particular campaigns.

Gerhard Ritter, *The Schlieffen Plan: Critique of a Myth* (Westport, Conn.: Greenwood, 1979). Scholarly reassessment.

A. J. P. Taylor, *The First World War* (London: Penguin, 1978); B. H. Liddell Hart, *The Real War* (Boston: Little, Brown, 1964). Lively, opinionated surveys.

Barbara Tuchman, *The Guns of August* (New York: Macmillan, 1962). Well-written narrative of the first critical month of the war and the crisis preceding it.

Richard M. Watt, *Dare Call It Treason* (New York: Simon and Schuster, 1963). The story of the most concerted French attempt to break the deadlock of trench warfare and of the mutiny that resulted in 1917.

J. M. Winter, *The Experience of World War I* (New York: Oxford University Press, 1989). Profusely illustrated, covers both military and civilian life.

Zloynek Zeman, *The Gentlemen Negotiators* (New York: Macmillan, 1971). Study of diplomacy during the war.

The Peace

Paul Birdsall, *Versailles Twenty Years After* (New York: Reynal and Hitchcock, 1941). Excellent appraisal by an American scholar.

John M. Keynes, *The Economic Consequences of the Peace* (several eds.), and Etienne Mantoux, *The Carthaginian Peace; or, the Economic Consequences of Mr. Keynes* (New York: Arno, 1979). Respectively, the most famous attack on the Versailles settlement and a thoughtful study of the results of that attack.

Arno J. Mayer, *The Political Origins of the New Diplomacy, 1917–1918* (New York: Random House, 1970), and *The Politics and Diplomacy of Peacemaking* (New York: Knopf, 1967). Two studies that stress the role played by the fear of Bolshevism. For another interpretation, see J. M. Thompson, *Russia, Bolshevism and the Versailles Peace* (Princeton, N.J.: Princeton University Press, 1966).

Harold Nicolson, *Peacemaking 1919* (Boston: Peter Smith, n.d.). Informative study by a British expert on diplomacy.

Robert Skidelsky, *John Maynard Keynes: The Economist as Saviour, 1920–1937* (New York: Penguin, 1994). The 2nd volume in a 3-volume biography.

The Russian Revolution: General

Robert V. Daniels, *The Nature of Communism* (New York: Random House, 1962). A valuable study of totalitarianism.

R. N. Carew Hunt, *The Theory and Practice of Communism* (New York: Macmillan, 1951). An excellent introduction to the subject.

Barrington Moore, Jr., *Soviet Politics: The Dilemma of Power* (Armonk, N.Y.: Sharpe, 1977). An illuminating analysis of the relationship between the Communist ideology and Soviet practice.

Richard Pipes, *The Russian Revolution* (New York: Knopf, 1991). The fullest and best account.

CHAPTER 24   𝐵ETWEEN THE WARS: A TWENTY-YEAR CRISIS

Russia: General Accounts

Edward H. Carr, *A History of Soviet Russia* (New York: Macmillan, 1951–1964). The only attempt at a complete history of the Soviet Union from original sources.

Merle Fainsod, *How Russia Is Ruled* (Cambridge, Mass.: Harvard University Press, 1963). An analysis of the Soviet system, firmly rooted in the historical background.

Barrington Moore, Jr., *Soviet Politics: The Dilemma of Power* (New York: Sharpe, 1977). An illuminating analysis of the relationship between communist ideology and Soviet practice.

The Russian Revolution: Special Studies

Crane Brinton, *The Anatomy of Revolution* (New York: Random House, 1965). Comparison of the Russian Revolution with the French Revolution of 1789 and the English seventeenth-century Revolution.

Isaac Deutscher, *The Prophet Armed, The Prophet Unarmed, The Prophet Outcast* (Oxford: Oxford University Press, 1980). Biography of Trotsky in three volumes.

Merle Fainsod, *Smolensk under Soviet Rule* (Cambridge, Mass.: Harvard University Press, 1958). A unique study, based on a collection of captured documents, of the actual workings of the Communist system in Smolensk in the 1930s.

Marc Ferro, *The Russian Revolution of February 1917*, trans. J. L. Richards (Englewood Cliffs, N.J.: Prentice-Hall, 1972). Close study of the fall of czarism and the defeat of the February revolution. Marc Ferro, *October 1917: A Social History of the Russian Revolution*, trans. Norman Stone (London: Routledge and Kegan Paul, 1980). Fine social history.

Alan Moorehead, *The Russian Revolution* (New York: Harper, 1958). A lively, generally sound survey.

M. C. Morgan, *Lenin* (London: Edward Arnold, 1971), Clear, short biography.

Richard Pipes, *The Formation of the Soviet Union* (New York: Atheneum, 1968). Excellent monograph on the question of national minorities in Russia from 1917 to 1923.

David Shub, *Lenin* (London: Penguin, 1977). A good biography of Lenin.

Nicholas Timasheff, *The Great Retreat* (Salem, N.H.: Arno, 1972). An account of the "Russian Thermidor."

Donald W. Treadgold, *Lenin and His Rivals: The Struggle for Russia's Future, 1898–1906* (Westport, Conn.: Greenwood, 1976). Examines the alternatives to Lenin.

Adam B. Ulam, *The Bolsheviks: The Intellectual and Political History of the Triumph of Communism in Russia* (New York: Macmillan, 1968), and *Stalin: The Man and His Era* (New York: Viking, 1973). Excellent detailed accounts.

Adam B. Ulam, *Expansion and Coexistence: The History of Soviet Foreign Policy, 1917–1967*, 2d ed. (New York: Holt, Rinehart, 1974). The first six chapters of this excellent analytical work deal with the period to 1941.

Theodore H. Von Laue, *Why Lenin? Why Stalin? A Reappraisal of the Russian Revolution, 1900–1930* (Philadelphia: Lippincott, 1964). Thoughtful analysis of the causes of the communist victory in Russia.

Bertram D. Wolfe, *Three Who Made a Revolution* (New York: Dell, 1978). Triple study of the careers of Lenin, Trotsky, and Stalin down to 1914.

Sources

Henri Barbusse, *Under Fire* (Totowa, N.J.: Biblio, 1975), and E. M. Remarque, *All Quiet on the Western Front* (New York: Fawcett, 1929). Two famous novels—by a Frenchman and a German, respectively—reflect the horror aroused in intellectuals by trench warfare.

James Bunyan and H. H. Fisher, eds., *The Bolshevik Revolution, 1917–1918* (Palo Alto, Calif.: Stanford University Press, 1961). Substantial collection of documents and other materials.

Robert V. Daniels, ed., *The Russian Revolution* (Englewood Cliffs, N.J.: Prentice-Hall, 1972). A well-chosen and well-discussed selection of sources.

Leon Trotsky, *The History of the Russian Revolution* (New York: Pluto, 1980). A brilliant but biased study by one of the leading participants.

Donald W. Treadgold, *Twentieth Century Russia* (Boston: Houghton Mifflin, 1981). Good basic survey.

The Roots of Fascism

Edward Hallett Carr, *The Twenty Years' Crisis, 1919–1939* (New York: Harper and Row, 1964). Clear exposition of the relationship between fascism and foreign policy.

Alfred Cobban, *Dictatorship: Its History and Theory* (New York: Haskell, 1970). Highly suggestive survey reaching well back into history.

George Mosse, *The Crisis of German Ideology: Intellectual Origins of the Third Reich* (New York: Fertig, 1981); and Fritz Stern, *The Politics of Cultural Despair* (Berkeley: University of California Press, 1974). Contrasting, solid studies of Hitler's forerunners.

Hans Rogger and Eugen Weber, eds., *The European Right: A Historical Profile* (Berkeley: University of California Press, 1965). A learned and stimulating collection of essays on right-wing movements in the various countries of Europe; includes good bibliographies.

Raymond Sontag, *A Broken World, 1919–1939* (New York: Harper and Row, 1971). A fine survey.

Henry A. Turner, Jr., ed., *Reappraisals of Fascism* (New York: Franklin Watts, 1975). Review of interpretations of fascism, with emphasis on the arguments of the German scholar Ernest Nolte.

Russia

William L. Blackwell, *The Industrialization of Russia* (Arlington Heights, Ill.: Harlan Davidson, 1982). Full survey.

Robert Conquest, ed., *The Politics of Ideas in the U.S.S.R.* (Westport, Conn.: Greenwood, 1976). Intriguing study of the mobilization of thought.

Robert Conquest, *The Great Terror: A Reassessment* (New York: Oxford University Press, 1990). An examination of how the Terror came about and of the heritage it left.

Loren R. Graham, *The Ghost of the Executed Engineer: Technology and the Fall of the Soviet Union* (Cambridge, Mass.: Harvard University Press, 1993). The sub-title tells all.

Naum Jasny, *Soviet Economists of the Twenties* (Cambridge: Cambridge University Press, 1972), on the NEP and post-NEP economic thought, and *The Socialized Agriculture of the USSR* (Palo Alto, Calif.: Stanford University Press, 1949), especially good on the *kolkhoz*.

Moshe Lewin, *Russian Peasants and Soviet Power: A Study of Collectivization*, trans. Irene Nove (London: Allen and Unwin, 1968). Good study of the drive to collectivize.

Christopher Reed, *Culture and Power in Revolutionary Russia* (London: Macmillan, 1990). Focuses on the intelligentsia.

Adam B, Ulam, *Stalin: The Man and His Era* (New York; Viking, 1973). Excellent detailed accounts.

Italy

Herman Finer, *Mussolini's Italy* (Hamden, Conn.: Archon, 1964); and H. A. Steiner, *Government in Fascist Italy* (New York: McGraw-Hill, 1938). Two solid studies by political scientists.

Gaetano Salvemini, *Under the Axe of Fascism* (New York: Fertig, 1970). Lively work by an important antifascist Italian.

Denis Mack Smith, *Mussolini* (New York: Viking, 1982), and *Mussolini's Roman Empire* (New York: Viking, 1976). Recent appraisals that, despite much new literature on Italian fascism, remain essentially hostile to Mussolini.

Elizabeth Wiskemann, *Fascism in Italy: Its Development and Influence* (London: Macmillan, 1970). Very brief, clear analysis.

Germany

William Sheridan Allen, *The Nazi Seizure of Power* (New York: Franklin Watts, 1973). A close examination of how Nazism took over at the local level.

Karl D. Bracher, *The German Dictatorship* (New York: Holt, Rinehart, 1972). Excellent comprehensive study by a German scholar.

Alan C. Bullock, *Hitler: A Study in Tyranny* (New York: Harper and Row, 1964). A fine biography.

Erich Eyck, *A History of the Weimar Republic* (New York: Atheneum, 1970). A superb, full examination.

Joachim C. Fest, *Hitler*, trans. Richard and Clara Winston (New York: Harcourt Brace Jovanovich, 1974); and Norman Stone, *Hitler* (New York: Knopf, 1982). Two excellent, well-researched, and fresh appraisals.

Ruth Fischer, *Stalin and German Communism* (New Brunswick, N.J.: Transaction, 1982). A study of the role played by the communist movement in the history of Germany between the wars.

Samuel W. Halperin, *Germany Tried Democracy* (New York: Crowell, 1946). A reliable history of the Weimar Republic from 1918 to 1933.

Franz L. Neumann, *Behemoth: The Structure and Practice of National Socialism* (New York: Octagon, 1963). A good analytical description.

Henry A. Turner, Jr., *Gustav Stresemann and the Politics of Weimar* (Westport, Conn.: Greenwood, 1979). A fine inquiry into a failed leader.

Robert G. Waite, *Vanguard of Nazism* (Cambridge, Mass.: Harvard University Press, 1952). A study of the Free Corps movement.

J. W. Wheeler-Bennett, *Wooden Titan* (New York: Morrow, 1936), and *Nemesis of Power* (New York: St. Martin's, 1954). Two first-rate studies, the first dealing with Hindenburg, the second with the role of the German army in politics from 1918 to 1945.

Elizabeth Wiskemann, *The Rome-Berlin Axis* (New York: Oxford University Press, 1949). A study of the formation and history of the Hitler-Mussolini partnership.

Other Countries

Gerald Brenan, *The Spanish Labyrinth*, 2d ed. (Cambridge: Cambridge University Press, 1960). A useful study of the Spanish Civil War against its historical and economic background.

Raymond Carr, *Spain, 1808–1939* (New York: Oxford University Press, 1982). Includes a careful examination of Franco in the light of earlier history.

Nicholas M. Nagy-Talavera, *The Green Shirts and the Others: A History of Fascism in Hungary and Rumania* (Stanford: Hoover Institution, 1970). Full examination.

Stanley G. Payne, *Falange* (Palo Alto, Calif.: Stanford University Press, 1961). Good study of the Falangist movement.

Frederick B. Pike, *Hispanismo* (Notre Dame: University of Notre Dame Press, 1971). A look at corporativism in Spain.

Paul Preston, *Franco: A Biography* (New York: Basic Books, 1994). A shrewd, balanced narrative.

Mary Louise Roberts, *Civilization Without Sexes: Reconstructing Gender in Postwar France, 1917–1927* (Chicago: University of Chicago Press, 1993). A stunning work of feminist theory.

Hugh Seton-Watson, *Eastern Europe between the Wars, 1918–1941*, 3d ed. (Hamden, Conn.: Archon, 1962). A useful account dealing with all the eastern European countries except Greece and Albania.

James Hinton, *Labour and Socialism: A History of the British Labour Movement, 1867–1974* (Brighton: Harvester, 1983). The best introductory text.

Hugh Thomas, *The Spanish Civil War*, rev. ed. (New York: Harper and Row, 1977). The best single work on the subject.

Sources

Adolf Hitler, *Mein Kampf* (several eds.). A complete English translation of the Nazi bible, the basic work to read for an understanding of the movement.

Adolf Hitler, *My New Order*, ed. R. de Sales (New York: Octagon, 1973). Speeches after the Fuhrer's coming to power.

Robert Payne, ed., *The Civil War in Spain* (Greenwich, Conn.: Fawcett, 1962). Original documents on the war.

Albert Speer, *Inside the Third Reich: Memoirs*, trans. Richard and Clara Winston (New York: Macmillan, 1970). Memoirs of Hitler's own city planner and architect; an invaluable picture of life among the Nazis.

Franz von Papen, *Memoirs* (New York: AMS Press, 1978). An apologetic autobiography by the right-wing politician.

Eugen Weber, ed., *Varieties of Fascism* (Melbourne, Fla.: Krieger, 1982). A short history with a selection of sources.

CHAPTER 25 THE DEMOCRACIES AND THE NON-WESTERN WORLD

The Political and Economic Climate

Alan Bullock, *Hitler and Stalin: Parallel Lives* (New York: Harper Collins, 1991). Stimulating comparative study.

Eric Fischer, *The Passing of the European Age* (Cambridge, Mass.: Harvard University Press, 1943); and Felix Gilbert, *The End of the European Era, 1890 to the Present* (New York: Norton, 1979). Reasoned defenses of the thesis that World War I cost Europe its old hegemony.

John Kenneth Galbraith, *The Great Crash* (New York: Avon, 1980). Wall Street, 1929, revisited by an articulate economist.

H. Stuart Hughes, *Contemporary Europe* (Englewood Cliffs, N.J.: Prentice-Hall, 1981); and A.J.P. Taylor, *From Sarajevo to Potsdam* (New York: Harcourt, n.d.). Surveys stressing intellectual and military-diplomatic history, respectively.

Great Britain

George Dangerfield, *The Damnable Question: A Study in Anglo-Irish Relations* (Boston: Little, Brown, 1976). A balanced account of the Irish Question in British politics.

Robert Graves and Alan Hodge, *The Long Weekend* (New York: Norton, 1963). Lively social history of interwar Britain.

Robert Rhodes James, *The British Revolution, 1880–1939* (New York: Knopf, 1977). A fine exploration of how Britain changed in fundamental ways.

Keith Middlemas and John Barnes, *Baldwin* (New York: Macmillan, 1970). A sound biography.

Charles L. Mowat, *Britain between the Wars, 1918–1940* (Chicago: University of Chicago Press, 1955); Arthur Marwick, *Britain in the Century of Total War, 1900–1967* (Boston: Little, Brown, 1968); W. N. Medicott, *Contemporary England, 1914–1964* (New York: McKay, 1967); David Thomson, *England in the Twentieth Century* (London: Penguin, 1965); A.J.P. Taylor, *English History, 1919–1945* (Oxford: Oxford University Press, 1965). Good general surveys.

Henry Pelling, *Winston Churchill* (London: Macmillan, 1974). Balanced, full biography.

Stephen Roskill, *Naval Policy between the Wars*, 2 vols. (New York: Walker, 1968). The first volume is especially good on the period of Anglo-American antagonism, from 1919 to 1929.

Martin J. Wiener, *English Culture and the Decline of the Industrial Spirit, 1850–1980* (London: Cambridge University Press, 1985). Strong survey.

France

René Albrecht-Carrie, *France, Europe, and the Two World Wars* (Westport, Conn.: Greenwood, 1975). Illuminating study of French difficulties against their international background.

D. W. Brogan, *France under the Republic* (Westport, Conn.: Greenwood, 1974). Stimulating survey.

Nathaniel Greene, *From Versailles to Vichy* (Arlington Heights, Ill.: Harlan Davidson, 1970). Lucid survey of interwar France.

Stanley Hoffmann et al., *In Search of France* (Cambridge, Mass.: Harvard University Press, 1963); James Joll, ed., *The Decline of the Third Republic* (London: Chatto and Windus, 1959). Insightful essays.

The United States

Frederick Allen, *Only Yesterday* and *Since Yesterday* (New York: Harper and Row, 1972). Evocative social histories of the 1920s and 1930s, respectively.

James M. Burns, *Roosevelt: The Lion and the Fox* (New York: Harcourt Brace Jovanovich, 1970). Analysis of FDR as a politician.

William E. Leuchtenburg, *Perils of Prosperity, 1914–1932* (Chicago: University of Chicago Press, n.d.), and *Franklin D. Roosevelt and the New Deal, 1932–1940* (New York: Harper and Row, 1963). Well-balanced studies.

Arthur M. Schlesinger, Jr., *The Age of Roosevelt* (Boston: Houghton Mifflin, 1957). Detailed study by a sympathetic though not uncritical historian.

The Non-Western World

George Antonius, *The Arab Awakening* (New York: Capricorn, 1965). The classic sympathetic account; stresses the rapid growth of Arab nationalism in the years during and immediately after World War I.

Erik Erikson, *Gandhi's Truth* (New York: Norton, 1969). Appraisal by a distinguished psychohistorian. May be supplemented by Robert Duncan, *Gandhi: Selected Writings* (New York: Colophon, n.d.).

John K. Fairbank, *The United States and China*, 4th ed. (Cambridge, Mass.: Harvard University Press, 1979); Edwin O. Reishauer, *The United States and Japan*, 2d ed. (Cambridge, Mass.: Harvard University Press, 1965); W. Norman Brown, *The United States and India, Pakistan, Bangladesh*, 3d ed. (Cambridge, Mass.: Harvard University Press, 1972); W. R. Polk, *The United States and the Arab World*, rev. ed. (Cambridge, Mass.: Harvard University Press, 1969); J. F. Gallagher, *The United States and North Africa* (Cambridge, Mass.: Harvard University Press, 1963). These volumes in the American Foreign Policy Library furnish scholarly appraisals of the recent history of the countries indicated.

Firuz Kazemzadeh, *Russia and Britain in Persia, 1864–1914* (New Haven: Yale University Press, 1968). Excellent background for understanding the persistence of Iranian fears of Russia and the West.

Jean Lacouture and S. Lacouture, *Egypt in Transition* (New York: Methuen, 1958); Stephen H. Longrigg, *Syria and Lebanon under French Mandate* (New York: Octagon, 1972); and Joseph M. Upton, *The History of Modern Iran: An Interpretation* (Cambridge, Mass.: Harvard University Press, 1960). Perceptive studies of individual Middle Eastern states.

Gordon Lewis, *Turkey*, 3d ed. (New York: Praeger, 1965); and Lord Kinross (Patrick Balfour), *Ataturk* (London: Weidenfeld and Nicolson, 1964). Respectively, a lively survey of the Turkish revolution and a clear biography of its chief architect.

Sources

F. Scott Fitzgerald, *The Great Gatsby* (New York: Scribner's, 1982). The famous novel about the jazz age.

Frank Freidel, ed., *The New Deal and the American People* (Englewood Cliffs, N.J.: Prentice-Hall, 1964). Sampling of different views.

André Gide, *The Counterfeiters* (New York: Random House, 1973). French middle-class values put under the microscope by a talented novelist.

Ernest Hemingway, *The Sun Also Rises* (New York: Scribner's, 1982). Widely considered the classic novel about the "lost generation" of disillusioned American idealists after World War I.

Aldous Huxley, *Point Counterpoint* and *Brave New World* (several eds.). Mordant novels written in the 1920s appraising contemporary mores in England and forecasting their future, respectively.

André Malraux, *Man's Fate* (New York: Random House, 1969). Excellent novel about Chinese communists in the 1920s.

Frances Perkins, *The Roosevelt I Knew* (New York: Viking, 1946). Perceptive appraisal by the secretary of labor in the Roosevelt years.

Howard Spring, *Fame Is the Spur* (New York: Viking, 1940). The career of the fictional hero, who is corrupted by political ambition, has many parallels with that of Ramsay MacDonald.

John Steinbeck, *The Grapes of Wrath* (several eds.). "Okies" journeying from Oklahoma to California in the wake of drought and depression.

Evelyn Waugh, *Decline and Fall* and *A Handful of Dust* (Boston: Little, Brown, 1977). Two corrosive short novels, published in one volume, on English society in the interwar years.

CHAPTER 26   *𝒯HE* SECOND WORLD WAR AND ITS AFTERMATH

General Accounts

P. M. H. Bell, *The Origins of the Second World War in Europe* (London: Longmans, 1986). A fine, short inquiry.

Maurice Cowling, *The Impact of Hitler* (Chicago: University of Chicago Press, 1977). An original look at British policies from 1933 to 1940.

Eric Hobsbawm, *The Age of Extremes: A History of the World, 1914–1991* (New York: Pantheon, 1995). A sweeping history that knits togther much of the 20th century.

Akira Iriye, *The Origins of the Second World War in Asia and the Pacific* (London: Longmans, 1987). The author sets the war into the context of world history.

Donald Kagan, *On the Origins of War and the Preservation of Peace* (New York: Doubleday, 1965). A fine analysis from ancient to present time.

Jon Livingston, Joe Moore, and Felicia Oldfather, eds., *Imperial Japan, 1800–1945* (New York: Pantheon, 1973). Draws upon Japanese scholars to give their point of view.

Henri Michel, *The Second World War*, trans. Douglas Parmee (London: Andre Deutsch, 1975); and Peter Calvocoressi and Guy Wint, *Total War: Causes and Courses of the Second World War* (London: Allen Lane, 1972). Two superb, massive histories.

Samuel Eliot Morison, *History of United States Naval Operations in World War II*, 15 vols, (Boston: Little, Brown, 1947–1962). Official but detached and professional history; pays full attention to political and diplomatic problems.

R. A. C. Parker, *Struggle for Survival* (Oxford: Oxford University Press, 1989). Superb on economic, diplomatic, and military history.

Gordon W. Prange, *At Dawn We Slept* (New York: Penguin, 1983). The most nearly definitive account of the entry of the United States into the war.

Albert Seaton, *The Battle for Moscow, 1941–1942* (London: Hart-Davis, 1971). A model study of a crucial battle.

Nikolai Sivachyor and Eugenic Yazkov, *History of the USA since World War I*, trans, A. B. Eklof (Moscow: Progress, 1976). The War from the Soviet point of view.

Christopher Thorne, *The Approach of War, 1938–1939* (New York: Macmillan, 1969). Good short examination of the critical months that led up to war.

D. W. Urwin, *Western Europe since 1945* (New York: Longmans, 1985). A crisp introduction.

Gerhard L. Weinberg, *A World at Arms: A Global History of World War II* (New York: Cambridge University Press, 1993). A balanced, sweeping history.

Gordon Wright, *The Ordeal of Total War* (New York: Harper and Row, 1968). A good survey.

Special Studies

Edward Bishop, *Their Finest Hour* (New York: Ballantine, 1968). A succinct illustrated history of the battle of Britain in 1940.

Larry Collins and Dominique LaPierre, *Is Paris Burning?* (New York: Simon and Schuster, 1965). Deservedly popular account of the liberation of Paris.

Herbert Feis, *Churchill, Roosevelt, Stalin* (Princeton, N.J.: Princeton University Press, 1967). A fascinating and fair-minded account of their wartime relationship.

Otto Friedrich, *The End of the World: A History* (New York: Coward, McCann and Geoghegan, 1982). Through a close examination of Auschwitz, places the Holocaust into perspective.

Felix Gilbert and G. A. Craig, eds., *The Diplomats 1919–1939* (Princeton, N.J.: Princeton University Press, 1953). A helpful symposium.

David L. Gordon and Royden Dangerfield, *The Hidden Weapon: The Story of Economic Warfare* (New York: Harper, 1947). A good popular account.

William L. Langer and S. Everett Gleason, *The Challenge to Isolation, 1937–1940* (Boston: Peter Smith, 1978), and *The Undeclared War, 1940–1941* (Boston: Peter Smith, 1976). Solid studies of America's role.

Charles L. Mowat, ed., *The Shifting Balance of World Forces, 1898–1945* (Cambridge: Cambridge University Press, 1968). A massive, synoptic history; Vol. XII of the *New Cambridge Modern History*.

Williamson Murray. *Luftwaffe* (London: Allen and Unwin, 1985). The best book on the German air force in World War II.

Alfred L. Rowse, *Appeasement: A Study in Political Decline, 1933–1939* (New York: Norton, 1963); and Neville Thompson, *The Anti-Appeasers* (Oxford: Clarendon, 1971). Controversial, lively arguments concerning the issue of appeasement.

S. R. Smith, *The Manchurian Crisis, 1931–1932* (New York: Columbia University Press, 1948). On the watershed between the postwar and prewar periods.

Charles C. Tansill, *Back Door to War: The Roosevelt Foreign Policy* (Westport, Conn.: Greenwood, 1975). Alleging that Roosevelt pushed America into war.

Barton Whaley, *Codeword Barbarossa* (Cambridge, Mass.: MIT Press, 1973). Discusses why Stalin did not believe Hitler would attack; a study in psychological warfare and military and political intelligence.

John W. Wheeler-Bennett, *Munich: Prologue to Tragedy* (London: Macmillan, 1948); and Lewis B. Namier, *Diplomatic Prelude, 1938–1939* (London: Macmillan, 1948). Good studies of the last international crises before World War II.

Roberta Wohlstetter, *Pearl Harbor: Warning and Decision* (Palo Alto, Calif.: Stanford University Press, 1962). First-rate monograph.

Leni Yahil, *The Holocaust: The Fate of European Jewry, 1932–1945* (New York: Oxford University Press, 1990). Unique in its scope and detail.

Sources

Hamilton F. Armstrong, *Chronology of Failure* (New York: Macmillan, 1940); "Pertinax" (André Géraud), *The Gravediggers of France* (Garden City, N.Y.: Doubleday, 1944); Marc Bloch, *Strange Defeat* (Darby, Penn.: Darby Books, 1981). Three perceptive studies of the French defeat in 1940.

Winston S. Churchill, *The Second World War*, 6 vols. (Boston: Houghton Mifflin, 1948–1953). Magisterial account by a chief architect of Allied victory.

Charles de Gaulle, *The Complete War Memoirs* (New York: Simon and Schuster, 1940–1961). Beautifully written firsthand account of de Gaulle's own experiences.

Desmond Flower and James Reeves, eds., *The Taste of Courage: The War, 1939–1945* (New York: Harper and Row, 1960). A good anthology of "war pieces."

Paul Fussell, *Wartime* (New York: Oxford University Press, 1990). A narrative, but replete with quotations and extracts from sources.

Robert Gelletely, *The Gestapo and German Society* (New York: Oxford University Press, 1990). On racial policy.

A. J. Liebling, ed., *The Republic of Silence* (New York: Harcourt, Brace, 1947). Excellent collection of materials pertaining to the French resistance movement.

Esmonde M. Robertson, ed., *The Origins of the Second World War* (London: Macmillan, 1971). Documents and secondary extracts on the thesis of A.J.P. Taylor that Hitler was rational in his policy and that he was driven into war.

There are many memoirs of actors in this great war. The following make a good beginning: Dwight D. Eisenhower, *Crusade in Europe* (New York: Da Capo, 1977); Harry Truman, *Memoirs*, 2 vols. (Garden City, N.Y.: Doubleday, 1958); Bernard Montgomery, *Memoirs* (New York: Da Capo, 1982).

CHAPTER 27 *T*WENTIETH-CENTURY THOUGHT AND LETTERS

Unlike suggested reading lists for the other chapters, the list for Chapter 27 is intended only to provide titles that will illuminate generalizations made in the chapter itself, since no list of readings for contemporary intellectual trends can be more than superficial and indicative of themes worthy of further exploration. For a good survey consult Carter V. Findley and John A. M. Rothney, *Twentieth-Century World*, 2d ed. (Boston: Houghton Mifflin, 1990).

Psychology

Ernest Jones, *The Life and Work of Freud* (New York: Basic Books, 1961). Detailed study; also available in an abridged version.

John Rickman, ed., *A General Selection from the Works of Sigmund Freud* (New York: Liveright, 1957). A well-chosen anthology.

R. L. Schoenwald, *Freud: The Man and His Culture* (New York: Knopf, 1956); and Philip Rieff, *Freud: The Mind of the Moralist* (Chicago: University of Chicago Press, 1979). Two good studies stressing Freud's place in contemporary culture.

Sociopolitical Thought

Franklin Ford, *Political Murder: From Tyrannicide to Terrorism* (Cambridge, Mass.: Harvard University Press, 1985). A sweeping study of how terrorism is defined and defended.

John Kenneth Galbraith, *The Affluent Society*, 3d ed. (New York: Mentor, 1978). Lively assessment of consumerism by an economist.

H. Stuart Hughes, *Consciousness and Society* (New York: Octagon, 1976). Excellent study treating not only social thought but also other facets of intellectual history from 1870 to 1930.

Walter Lippmann, *A Preface to Politics* (New York: Macmillan, 1933). Another pioneering study.

Vilfredo Pareto, *The Mind and Society* (New York: Harcourt Brace Jovanovich, 1978). A major work in general sociology.

Talcott Parsons, *The Structure of Social Action*, 2d ed. (New York: Free Press, 1949). A landmark in American sociological thinking.

Graham Wallas, *Human Nature in Politics* (New Brunswick, N.J.: Transaction, 1981), and *The Great Society* (Boston: Peter Smith, n.d.). Pioneering studies of the psychology of politics.

Philosophy

M. F. Ashley-Montagu, *Toynbee and History* (Boston: Porter Sargeant, 1956); and Isaiah Berlin, *Historical Inevitability* (Oxford: Oxford University Press, 1954). Criticism of Toynbee in particular and historicism in general, respectively.

Olive Banks, *Faces of Feminism: A Study of Feminism as a Social Movement* (New York: St. Martin's, 1982). Good comparison of British and American feminist movements.

Albert Camus, *The Stranger* (New York: Vintage, 1946), and *The Plague* (New York: Random House, 1972). Existentialist novels by a gifted writer.

Ralph Harper, *Existentialism: A Theory of Man* (Cambridge, Mass.: Harvard University Press, 1949). A sympathetic introduction.

Walter Kaufmann, ed., *Existentialism from Dostoevsky to Sartre* (New York: New American Library, 1956). Instructive selections from existentialist writings; includes helpful editorial comments.

Arne Naess, *Modern Philosophers* (Chicago: University of Chicago Press, 1968). Carnap, Wittgenstein, and Sartre are among those discussed.

Morton G. White, ed., *The Age of Analysis: Twentieth-Century Philosophers* (New York: Mentor, n.d.). Excerpts and comments, very well chosen.

Science and Technology

Isaac Asimov, *The Intelligent Man's Guide to the Physical Sciences* (New York: Pocket Books, n.d.), and *The Intelligent Man's Guide to the Biological Sciences* (New York: Pocket Books, n.d.). Informative surveys by a prolific popularizer of difficult material.

Peter J. Bowler, *The Non-Darwinian Revolution: Reinterpreting a Historical Myth* (Baltimore: Johns Hopkins University Press, 1988). Survey of evolutionary thought.

Robert V. Bruce, *The Launching of Modern American Science* (New York: Knopf, 1987). Fine study of the nineteenth-century roots of American scientific dominance.

C. T. Chase, *The Evolution of Modern Physics* (New York: Van Nostrand, 1947); and Lincoln Barnett, *The Universe and Dr. Einstein*, rev. ed. (New York: Bantam, n.d.). Helpful popular accounts of key developments in twentieth-century science.

Stephen S. Hall, *Ivisible Frontiers* (New York: Atlantic Monthly Press, 1987). On gene mapping.

Richard Rhodes, *The Making of the Atom Bomb* (New York: Simon and Schuster, 1986). Superb, detailed account.

David J. Rothman, Steven Marcus, and Stephanie A. Kiceluk, eds., *Medicine and Western Civilization* (New Brunswick, N.J.: Rutgers University Press, 1995). A comprehensive anthology from ancient times to the present.

René Taton, ed., *Science in the Twentieth Century* (New York: Basic Books, 1966). Translation of a comprehensive French survey.

Literature and the Arts

H. H. Arnason, *History of Modern Art* (New York: Abrams, 1969). Encyclopedic introduction to twentieth-century painting, sculpture, and architecture.

John Cage, *Silence: Lectures and Writings* (Cambridge, Mass.: Harvard University Press, 1961). By an experimenter in extending musical frontiers.

Joseph Campbell and Henry M. Robinson, *A Skeleton Key to Finnegans Wake* (London: Penguin, 1977); and William P. Jones, *James Joyce and the Common Reader* (Norman: University of Oklahoma Press, 1970). Two guides to a baffling writer.

George H. Hamilton, *19th and 20th Century Art* (New York: Abrams, 1972). A lucid and less-detailed survey.

Henry-Russell Hitchcock, *Architecture: 19th and 20th Centuries* (London: Penguin, 1977). A meaty volume in the Pelican History of Art series.

Frederick J. Hoffman, *Freudianism and the Literary Mind* (Westport, Conn.: Greenwood, 1977). A suggestive exploration.

Claude Mauriac, *The New Literature* (New York: Brazillier, 1959). Essays translated from the French; treats mainly French writers.

Hans Richter, *Dada: Art and Anti-Art* (Oxford: Oxford University Press, 1978); Patrick Waldberg, *Surrealism* (Oxford: Oxford University Press, 1978); J. Russell and S. Gablik, *Pop Art Redefined* (New York: Praeger, 1969). Useful introductions to particular movements.

Harry Slochower, *Literature and Philosophy between Two World Wars* (New York: Octagon, 1973) (originally titled *No Voice Is Wholly Lost*). An informative study of the relations between intellectual and literary history.

Lael Wertenbaker, *The World of Picasso* (New York: Time-Life Books, 1967); and C. Tomkins, *The World of Marcel Duchamp* (New York: Time-Life Books, 1966). Informative attempts to relate two artistic pioneers to the cultural world of the twentieth century.

Edmund Wilson, *Axel's Castle* (New York: Scribner's, 1947). A study in imaginative literature from 1870 to 1930; extends to Joyce and Gerttrude Stein.

CHAPTER 28 *O*UR TIMES: ARRIVING AT THE PRESENT

General Accounts

C. E. Black, *Dynamics of Modernization* (Boston: Peter Smith, n.d.). Illuminating study.

Peter Calvocoressi, *World Politics since 1945*, 4th ed. (London: Longmans, 1982). Factual study.

Desmond Donnelly, *Struggle for the World* (New York: St. Martin's, 1965). A history of the cold war, which traces it back to 1917.

Norman A. Graebner, ed., *The Cold War: Ideological Conflict or Power Struggle?* 2d ed. (Lexington, Mass.: D. C. Heath, 1976). Divergent interpretations.

Louis L. Snyder, *The New Nationalism* (Ithaca, N.Y.: Cornell University Press, 1968). Wide-ranging and provocative survey.

The West

Francis Boyd, *British Politics in Transition, 1945–1963* (New York: Praeger, 1964). Solid account.

Colin Cross, *The Fall of the British Empire, 1918–1968* (London: Hodder and Stoughton, 1968). Analysis of a central aspect of Britain's altered position.

Marion Dönhoff, *Foe into Friend: The Makers of the New Germany from Konrad Adenauer to Helmut Schmidt* (London: Weidenfeld and Nicolson, 1982). Useful journalistic study.

Paul Ginsborg, *A History of Contemporary Italy: Society and Politics, 1943–1988* (London: Penguin, 1990). Especially strong on politics and the state.

Alfred Grosser, *The Federal Republic of Germany* (New York: Praeger, 1964). Concise history.

H. Stuart Hughes, *The United States and Italy*, 3d ed. (Cambridge, Mass.: Harvard University Press, 1979). Guide to postwar Italian politics and society.

Arthur Marwick, *Britain in the Century of Total War* (Boston: Little, Brown, 1968). Assessment of the impact of war on society.

Michael M. Postan, *An Economic History of Western Europe, 1945–1964* (New York: Barnes and Noble, n.d.). Comprehensive review.

K. P. Tauber, *Beyond Eagle and Swastika* (Middletown, Conn.: Wesleyan University Press, 1967). Study of German nationalism since World War II.

Theodore H. White, *Fire in the Ashes* (New York: Sloane, 1953). Postwar economic recovery and the role of the Marshall Plan.

Philip Williams, *Crisis and Compromise*, 3d ed. (Hamden, Conn.: Archon, 1964). Analyzing the failures of the Fourth Republic.

The Communist Bloc

C. E. Black, *The Eastern World since 1945* (New York: Ginn, n.d.). Instructive scholarly survey.

William Echikson, *Lighting the Night* (New York: Morrow, 1990). On the revolution in eastern Europe.

Graeme Gill, *The Collapse of a Single Party System: The Disintegration of the Communist Party of the Soviet Union* (New York: Cambridge University Press, 1994). Covers 1985 to 1991.

Leszek Kolakowski, *Main Currents of Marxism*, Vol. III: *The Breakdown* (New York: Oxford University Press, 1978). Rigorous analysis by a philosopher of post–World War II problems in Marxist thought.

Joseph Rothschild, *Return to Diversity: A Political History of East Central Europe since World War II*, 2nd ed. (New York: Oxford University Press, 1993). A balanced narrative intended for students.

Leonard Schapiro, *The Government and Politics of the Soviet Union*, rev. ed. (New York: Random House, 1978). Short authoritative treatment.

Vladimir Tismaneanu, *Reinventing Politics: Eastern Europe from Stalin to Havel* (New York: Free Press, 1993). Crisp survey.

Adam Ulam, *Expansion and Coexistence: The History of Soviet Foreign Policy, 1917–1967* (New York: Praeger, 1968). Lucid, brief account.

The Emerging Nations

G. M. Carter, ed., *Politics in Africa: Seven Cases* (New York: Harcourt Brace Jovanovich, 1977). Informative.

Laing G. Cowan, *The Dilemmas of African Independence* (New York: Walker, 1964). A mine of information.

Charles C. Cumberland, *Mexico: The Struggle for Modernity* (Oxford: Oxford University Press, 1968).

Stewart C. Easton, *The Rise and Fall of Modern Colonialism* (New York: Praeger, 1962). Sweeping survey.

John K. Fairbank, *The United States and China*, rev. ed. (New York: Compass, n.d.); Edwin O. Reischauer, *The United States and Japan*, 2d ed. (Cambridge, Mass.: Harvard University Press, 1965). Authoritative surveys.

Herman Giliomee and Richard Elphick, eds., *The Shaping of South African Society* (Capetown: Longmans, 1979). Excellent collection of original essays.

John Hatch, *A History of Postwar Africa* (New York: Praeger, n.d.). Clear and helpful guide.

Franklin W. Houn, *A Short History of Chinese Communism* (Englewood Cliffs, N.J.: Prentice-Hall, 1973). Useful recent introduction.

Paul M. Kennedy, *African Capitalism: The Struggle for Ascendency* (New York: Cambridge University Press, 1988). A study of the capitalist state.

Misagh Parsa, *Social Origins of the Iranian Revolution* (New Brunswick, N.J.: Rutgers University Press, 1990). Especially good on social groups in Iran.

W. R. Polk, *The United States and the Arab World*, rev. ed. (Cambridge, Mass.: Harvard University Press, 1969); H. B. Sharabi, *Nationalism and Revolution in the Arab World* (New York: Van Nostrand, 1966). Introductions to the Middle East.

Hugh Thomas, *The Cuban Revolution* (London: Weidenfeld and Nicolson, 1986). Shortened form of the fullest general history.

The Cold War and Aftermath

Dean Acheson, *Present at the Creation* (New York: Norton, 1969). Beautifully written memoirs of the 1950s.

Curtis Cate, *The Ides of August: The Berlin Wall Crisis, 1961* (New York: Evans, 1979). A close look at the mechanics of a specific Soviet-American confrontation.

John Lewis Gaddis, *Strategies of Containment* (New York: Oxford University Press, 1983). Superb and restrained examination of postwar American national-security policy.

Louis J. Halle, *The Cold War as History* (New York: Harper and Row, 1971). An early attempt to take an historical perspective on the cold war.

Marion Kaplan, *Focus Africa* (New York: Doubleday, 1982). A journalist's account of issues in Africa in the 1980s which packs in good historical background.

Paul M. Kennedy, *The Realities behind Diplomacy* (London: Allen and Unwin, 1981). Thoughtful look at how a nation shapes its external policy; focuses on Britain.

Walter Laqueur, *The Rebirth of Europe* (New York: Holt, Rinehart, 1970). Good, hard-headed history, reprinted with a new chapter as *Europe since Hitler* (London: Penguin, 1982). Laqueur's *A Continent Astray: Europe 1970–1978* (New York: Oxford University Press, 1979), helps bring the account up to date.

Guenter Lewy, *America in Vietnam* (New York: Oxford University Press, 1978). While excessively defensive with respect to the American position, and illustrative of the perils of writing recent history, this provides a good chronological examination of the issues.

Evan Luard, *A History of the United Nations* (London: Macmillan, 1982). Covers "the years of Western domination," 1955, with another volume yet to come.

John Lukacs, *A History of the Cold War* (New York: Anchor, 1962). Beautifully written survey; fully supportive of Western views on the origins of the cold war.

Norman Luxenburg, *Europe since World War II: The Big Change*, rev. ed. (Carbondale: Southern Illinois University Press, 1973). Good general history.

Charles S. Maier, *The Origins of the Cold War and Contemporary Europe* (New York: Franklin Watts, 1978). Good collection of essays; some emphasis on views hostile to the American position.

Nelson Mandela, *Long Walk to Freedom: The Autobiography of Nelson Mandela* (Boston: Little, Brown, 1994). A moving recollection.

Keith Middlemas, *Politics in Industrial Society* (London: Deutsch, 1979). Uses Britain as a case study for "postindustrial" political changes.

George Donelson Moss, *Vietnam: An American Ordeal* (Englewood Cliffs, N.J.: Prentice-Hall, 1990). A sound basic history with emphasis on the U.S.

Theodore Zeldin, *An Intimate History of Humanity* (New York: Harper/Collins, 1994). This remarkable book ranges over all aspects of contemporary personal life from the sexual revolution to cooking.

INDEX

Note: Pages in boldface locate substantial discussions of entries; pages followed by *m* locate maps

Chopin, Frédéric [fray-day-REEK shoh-PAN], 408

Chotek, Sophie (wife of Francis Ferdinand), 528

Christian Democrats (Italy), **445-46**, 668; fascist terror campaign against, 558-59

Christian Democrats (West Germany), 666, 667

Christianity, existentialism and, 649; *See also* Catholics and Catholicism; *entries under Church*

Christian Socialists, **445-46**; in Austria, **477**, **574-75**

Christie, Agatha, 654

Chronometer, 340

Chungking, 626

Church, Anglican: Charles I and, 318; Irish home rule issue and, 505; James I and, 317; Parliament and, 317; Root and Branch Bill (1641), 319; *See also* Christian Socialists

Church, Gallican, 311; divine right and, 310

Church, Roman Catholic: birth control and, 669; Bismarck's attack on (*Kulturkampf*), **469**; Bourbon dynasty and, 311-12; Concordat (1801) and, 393; concordat with Austria (1855), 473; condemnation of *Encyclopédie*, 359; Dreyfus affair and, 463; French National Assembly's confiscation of land belonging to, 383; Gallicanism and, 311-12; in Hungary, 477; Italian unification and, 465-66; Josephism and, 365; Perón and, 698; Peter the Great and, 351; reform movements, during French Revolution, **384-85**; Reign of Terror and, 389; Spanish constitution of 1931 and, 573; after World War II, 669; *See also* Christian Democrats (Italy); Christian Democrats (West Germany); Papacy

Church, Scottish Presbyterian, 318

Church and state: Napoleonic France and, 393; separation in Soviet Union, 552; *See also* Divine-right monarchy

Churchill, John, 315

Churchill, Winston, 532, 618, 623, 626, 662; aid to Tito, 632; Dardanelles campaign and (1915), 537; on democratic leanings of Europeans, 629; leadership of, **615**; meetings with Roosevelt, 628; succession to prime minister, 615-16; at Teheran conference (1943), 623, 628; at Yalta conference (1945), 625, 628

Ciller, Tansü, 670

Cisalpine Republic, 392

Ciskei, 696

City(ies), 426; aerial bombardment of, 614; prosperity and, 674; in Third French Republic, 463

Civil Constitution of the Clergy (1790), 384-85

"Civil death," Russian concept of, 350

Civilization, corrupting influence of, 362-63

Civilization and Its Discontents (Freud), 647

Civil liberties, under Napoleon, 393

Civil Rights Act (1965), 672

Civil war(s): American (1861-1865), **488-90**, 513; English (1642-1649), **319-20**; Russian (1918-1921), **553-55**; Spanish

(1936-1939), 573-74; *See also* English Civil War (1642-1649)

Clarissa Harlove (Richardson), 374

Class, social: in 18th C., 343; grievances and aspirations during Industrial Revolution, **435-37**; Lenin and, 548; racial intermixture and, 524; *See also* Bourgeoisie [boorzh-wah-ZEE]; Middle class; Peasantry; Working class

Class consciousness, development of, 425-26

Class distinctions, erosion in England of, 663

Class struggle, 442; June Days of 1848 revolution and, 419; nationalism and, 443; nonviolent forms of, **445-46**; violent forms of, 444-45

Clemenceau, Georges [zhorzh klay-mahn-SOH], 541, 543; Saar Basin and, 544

Clement XIV, Pope, 362

Clergy: Austrian society (1867-1914) and, 477; French Revolution and, **379-80**; philosophes attack on, **362**; *See also* Religion; *entries under Church*

Clermont (steamship), 429

Cleveland, Grover, 521

Cleves, estates authority in, 347

Climate, changes in, 363

Clinton, Bill, 693

Clive, Robert, 353

Clover, 341

Coal industry, English, **427-28**, 587

Coalition party system, 500

Coal mining, transformation into big business, 342

Code Napoléon, **393**, 400

Coffeehouses, 338

Coinage. *See* Money

Coitus interruptus, 459

Coke [cook], Sir Edward, 317

Colbert, Jean [zhahn kohl-BAYR], **312-13**

Cold war, **629-36**; changed complexion of, 641; Vietnam War and, 641; West German rearmament and, 666; *See also* Soviet Union (post-World War II); United States (post-World War II)

Cole, G.D.H., 504

Coleridge, Samuel Taylor, **405**, 408

Collaborator model of imperialism, **509**

Collaborators, **524**

Collective unconscious, 648

Collectivization, 579, **580**

College, Russian (political division), 351

Collins, Michael, 589

Colombia, 698

Colonial empires: English, 342; French, 343-44; mercantilistic approach to, 313; in North America, 342, 343-44; Seven Years' War and, 353-55; *See also* American Revolution; *specific colonies*

Colonialism, 426, **506**; capital investments in, 508-9; capitalism and, 506; mercantilism and, 506; strategic motivations for, 506; *See also* Empires, modern

Colonial Society (Germany), 471

Colonies: economic feasibility of, 508-9; immigration from former, 666; indirect rule of, 516; Japanese attack on, 621; local rulers and, **509**; revolution against Ferdinand VII, 412; transient European population in, 509; World War I in, **537-38**

Colons, 519

Combination Acts, 436

Combinats, 581

Comecon. *See* Council for Mutual Economic Aid (Comecon)

Cominform (Communist Information Bureau), 630

Comintern, 573, **608**; Soviet foreign policy and, 608

Commerce: 18th C. revolution in (1713-1745), **338-41**; supreme power of, 355; *See also* Mercantilism; Money; Trade

Commoners (third estate), French Revolution and, **380-81**; *See also* Serfdom; *entries under Peasantry*

Common Market, 633, **662**; British attempts to join, 662

Common sense, systematized, 449

Communications, improvement in, 429

Communism: Chinese, 598-600; collapse of, 668, 680-81; defined, 440; fascism compared to, **559**; in Greece, 577; inevitability of, 442; in interwar France, 590; Kuomintang and, 598-600; Marx and, **442-44**; socialism vs., 440; Stalin-Hitler nonaggression pact and, 613; war, **552-53**, 577; *See also* People's Republic of China; *entries under Soviet Union; other communist countries*

Communist, The (newspaper), 552

Communist League, 443

Communist Manifesto, The (Marx & Engels), 423, **443**

Communist parties, 630; Albanian, 636; German, inflation in Weimar Republic and, 564; Italian, 669; Soviet, 577, 582; Spanish, 573

Compagnie des Indes [kohn'-PAY-nyee days AHND] (Mississippi Company), 340

Competition, 457; industrial society and, 426; Social Darwinism and, 448

Compradors, 511

Computers, **645**, 652

Comte [kohnt], Auguste, 440, **449**

Conan Doyle, Sir Arthur, 654

Concentration camps, World War II, 625-26

Concord, battle of (1775), 371

Concordat (1801), 393, 463

Condition of the Working Class in England, The (Engels), 443

Condorcet [kon-dohr-SAY], marquis de, 358, 387

Confédération Générale du Travail (CGT), 590

"Confession of Faith" (Rhodes), 515

Congo, **695**; revolution of 1965, 636; *See also* Belgian Congo

Congo Free State, 520

Congregationalists (Independents), 320

Congress of Soviets, 550

Congress of Vienna (1814), 404

Congress Party (India), 688

Congreve [KON-greve], William, 328

Conscription during peacetime, 530

Conservation of resources, 661

Conservatism, counterrevolutionary, 410

Conservative party (England), **500**, 662; electoral following, 500; interwar program of, **587-88**; repeal of Corn Laws and, 501

Conspiracy of the Equals (1796-1797), 390

Constable, John, 408

economics and, 359-60; Mill's theory of, 440; size of state and, 362

Goya, Francisco de, 366, 398, 408

Grand Alliance, 315, **627-29**; Anglo-American collaboration, **627-29**; Soviet intentions and, 629; unconditional surrender policy of, **629**; See also World War II

Grande Armée, French, 401

Grande nation, la, 306

Grand Remonstrance (1641), 319

Grand siècle [grahnd see-EK-luh] (17th-18th C France), 306

Grant, Ulysses S., 490

Gravitational field, 651

Gravity, 651

Great Depression (1929-1933), **566-68,** 606; causes, 593; in England, 588, 607; in France, 589-90; Hitler's rise and, 607; New Deal and, **594-96**; in United States, **593-94**; Weimar Republic and, **566-68**; world peace and, 607

Greater Colombia, 412

Great Fear, 382-83

Great Northern War (1700-1721), 345, 348, **349-50**; British intervention in, 353; international balance of power and, 352

Great Protestation, 317

Great Society program, 640, 674

Great Trek (1835-1837), 513

Great War. See World War I

Greco, El [el GREK-oh], 655

Greece, modern, 671; acquisition of Thrace, 544; authoritarian government in interwar period, **577**; Balkan Wars (1912-1913), 532; in Common Market, 662; communism in, 577, 631-32; conflict with Turkey (1974), 671; Greco-Turkish War (1921-1922), 544; Italian invasion of (1940), 617, 620; post-World War I instability in, 542; revolution against Ottoman Turks (1804), **413-14**; Smyrna and, 544; territorial gains from Versailles treaty, 544; in World War I, 537

Greek War (late 1820s), Nicholas I's intervention, 479

Greenhouse effect, 653

Greenwich mean time, 340

Gregory, Lady Augusta, 505

Grenada, 699

Grey, Earl Charles, 497-98

Grey, Sir Edward, 533

Grimm, Jacob, 396

Grimm, Wilhelm, 396

Grosz [grohs], George, 656

Grozny, 622

Guadalupe Hidalgo, Treaty of (1848), 488

Guam, 626; American acquisition of, 521; Japanese capture of, 621

Guatemala [gwah-tuh-MAH-luh], guerrilla war (1975), 699

Guernica, air raid on (1937), 610

Guernica [gair-NEE-kah] (Picasso), 575, 655

Guerrilla warfare, 699-700

Guggenheim Museum, 657

Guiana [ghee-AH-nah] (S. America), 517

Guilds, restrictive influence on business, 340

Guillotine, 388

Guinea [GHIN-ee], **694**

Guizot, François [frahn-SWAH ghee-ZOH], 415, 418

Gulag Archipelago, The (Solzhenitsyn), 680

Gulliver's Travels (Swift), 374

Gumbinnen [goom-BIN-en], battle of (1941), 536

Gunboat diplomacy, 509

Gustavus III, king of Sweden, as enlightened despot, **367**

Guyana [ghee-AHN-uh], 699

Guyon, Mme. Jeanne Marie [zhahn mah-REE gur-ee-YOHN], 312

Gymnasium educational system, 471

Habsburg [HABZ-burg] Empire, 392, **473-79**; Austria under, 346-47; Bach system and, 473; concordat with Catholic church (1855), 473; Congress of Vienna and, 411; Constitution of 1867, 474; Crimean War and, 473; dismemberment by Versailles treaty, 544; dual monarchy (*Ausgleich*), **474**; emancipation of peasantry, 423; expansionism of, 352; French-Piedmontese war against (1859), 459, 464, 473; liberalism in, 421; modernization of, 473; modern political parties in, 487; nationalism in, 421; nationalities under, 421; nationalities under, dissatisfaction of (mid-1800s), 473; nobles' acceptance of Crown's strength, 311; October Diploma (1860), 474; Polish kingship and, 352; Pragmatic Sanction and, 346-47; revolutions of 1848 and, 420, **421-23**; War of the Spanish Succession (1701-1714) and, 315; See also Austria (19th C. to World War I); Austria-Hungary; Holy Roman Empire; *entries under Germany*; *entries under Spain*; *successor states of empire*; See also Holy Roman Empire; *entries under Germany*; *entries under Spain*; *successor states of empire*

Haig, Sir Douglas, 539

Haiti [HAY-tee], 699; as American protectorate, 523; revolt againt Napoleon, 395

Haitian refugees, 699

Haldane, Viscount. See Burdon, Richard, Viscount Haldane [HALL-dun] of Cloan

Hals, Frans [frahns hahls], 329-30

Hampden [HAM-duhn], John, 318

Handel, George Frederick, **375**

Hannibal, 406

Hanoi, French colonization of, 519

Hanover, house of, Seven Years' War and, 354

Hardie, Kier, 501-2

Harding, Warren, 591

Hard Times (Dickens), 422

Hardy, Thomas, 451-52

Hargreaves, James, 342

Harmsworth, Alfred, 529

Hausa people, 517, 694-95

Haushofer, Karl, 570

Haussmann, Georges-Eugène [zhorzh ur-ZHEN ohs-MANN], 458

Havel, Vaclav, 681

Hawaii, 493, 520-21

"Hawk"-"dove" conflict, 674

Hay, John, 521

Hay-Bunau-Varilla Treaty (1903), 523

Haydn [HIGH-d'n], Franz Joseph, 376

Hearst, William Randolph, 529-30

Hegel [HAY-gul], G.W.F., **408-9**, 442

Heidegger, Martin, 649

Heimwehr [HIGHM-vair] (home guard), 574

Heisenberg, Werner, 651

Helsinki accords (1975), 680

Helvetian Republic, 392

Henrietta Maria (sister of Louis XIII), 317

Henry IV, German emperor, 469

Henry IV, king of France, 307, 329

Henry of Navarre. See Henry IV, king of France

Hepworth, Barbara, 656

Herder, Johann Gottfried von, 406

Heredity, 447

Heredity-environment debate, Locke on, 357-58

Hernani (Hugo), 406

Herzegovina, 683-84

Herzen [HAIR-tsin], Alexander, 440

Herzl, Theodor, 477

Hess, Rudolf, 565

Hijacking, plane, 690, 700

Himmler, Heinrich, 567, 626

Hindenburg, Field Marshal Paul von, 536, 562-63; election of, 566; reelection of, 566; under Schleicher's influence, 567

Hindi language, 688

Hindu Congress party, 687

Hippies, 674

Hirohito, emperor of Japan, 620-21

Hiroshima, 614, 627

Historical analysis, literature and, 422

Historical determinism, 449

Historicism, **650**

History: changing nature of, 643-44; critique of, 657; genderized, 701; modernity of, **644-46**; "ownership" of, 701; Russian mobilization of thought and, 581; value of, 657, 663

History of the Decline and Fall of the Roman Empire (Gibbon), 374

Hitler, Adolf, 562, **568-72,** 573, 608-9; alliance with Mussolini, 562; Anschluss and, 611; anti-Semitism of, 565, 569-70; artistic views, 571, 655; assassination attempt on, 623; Austria invasion, 575; beer hall putsch (November 1923) of, 565; chancellorship for, 568; collaborators of, 565; concordat with Vatican, 571-72; consolidation of power, 568-69; decision to attack Russia (1941), 615, 618; "folk" justice under, 570; formation of Rome-Berlin Axis, 611; formation of SS, 567; German Communist party and, 567, 568; German treatment at Versailles and, 543; in German Workers' party, 565; Great Depression and rise of, 607; Hungarian revisionism and, 575; National Socialism of, 572; Nuremberg laws of, 569; "Pact of Steel" with Mussolini, 612; Poland invasion (1939), **612-13**; Romania and, 576; Russian church in Berlin constructed by, 584; Stalin's disinterest in international communism and, 608-9; suicide, 625; suspicion of Bolshevism,

Parlement (France), Bourbon monarchy and, 312

Parliament, English: Act of Settlement (1701), 325; Anglicanism and, 316; Bill of Rights (1689), 324-25; Charles I and, 317-18; checks and balances in, 362; Civil War (1642-1649) and, **319-20**; George III and, 370; Glorious Revolution and, **324-25**, 343; Grand Remonstrance (1641), 319; growth of representative government and, 316; James I and, 317; Long Parliament (1640), 316, 321; loss of power, 662; as model for representative government, 497; New Model Army of, 320; Nineteen Propositions (1642), 319; Petition of Right (1628), 317-18; reforms in early 19th C., **498-500**; representation, 497-98; Root and Branch bill (1641), 319; Rump Parliament, 320-21; Short Parliament (1640), 318; Stuart monarchy and, 306; taxation of American colonies by, 371; Triennial Act (1640), 319; Waltham Black Act (1723), 341; *See also* Conservative party (England); Labour party (England); House of Commons; House of Lords; Liberal party (England); Tories, English; Whigs, English

Parliament Act (1911), 503, 505

Parliamentary representation, Italian fascist syndicalism and, 561

Parnell, Charles, 505

Parthenopean Republic, 392

Parti Québécois [kay-bay-KWAH], 677

Partisans (Yugoslavia), 632

Parts, standardized and interchangeable, 427

Party, political, proletarian revolution and, 444

Pascal, Blaise [blays puhs-KUHL], 312, **327**

Passarowitz [pah-sah-ROH-vits], Treaty of (1718), 352

Passchendaele [PAHS-endall-uh], battle of (1917), 539

Passion According to St. Matthew, The (Bach), 408

Pasternak, Boris, 679

Pasteur, Louis, 446

Pathet Lao, **638-40**

Patton, George S., 623

Paul I (Pavel Petrovich), czar of Russia, **368**, 392; Baltic League of Armed Neutrality and, 394

Paul VI, Pope, 669

Pavlov, Ivan, 581

Pearl Harbor, 521, 621

Peasant revolts: French, 332; at Morea (1821), 414; Russian, 332, 351

Peasantry: Andalusian, anarchism among, 572; emancipation of, in Habsburg Empire, 423; Japanese, 523; kulak extermination of, 580; modernization of, 458; revolutions of 1848 and, 423

Peasantry, French: French Revolution and, **380-81**, 399; under Napoleon, 394; revolts of, 332; taxation of, 380-81

Peasantry, Russian: bank for, 484; populist movement and, 483; requisitioning of, 552; revolutionaries and, 479; Russian civil war and, 554; Russian provisional government and, **547**; Stolypin's "wager on the strong and sober" program, 486

Peel, Sir Robert, 497, 501

Peers, House of (Japan), 523

Peking, 602; Treaty of (1860), 482

Peninsular War (1808-1813), **396**

Pennsylvania Dutch, 374

Pensées [pahn-SAYS] (Pascal), 327

"People's Budget" (1909), 503

People's Charter, **498**

People's Commissars, Council of. *See* Ministers, Council of (USSR)

People's Democratic Republic of Korea. *See* North Korea

People's party (Pakistan), 688

People's party (Weimar Republic), 563, 568

People's Republic of China: agenda for spreading communism, 637; Albania annexation, 636; Canadian trade with, 677; cultural revolution (1966-1969), 637; defeat of Chiang Kai-shek, 630; establishment of, 636; Japanese relations with, 684-85; Khrushchev and, 637; Kissinger mission to, 674; Korean War and, 632; North Korean support of, 636; North Vietnam's support of, 637; on nuclear test-ban treaty, 636; Soviet ideological differences with, 633; Soviet racist attitudes toward, 637; Soviet split with, **636-37**; Taiwan and, 632; use of racist sentiments among Asians, 637

People's Will, 483

Perak, 509

Perestroika, 680

Perón, Colonel Juan, 628, 698

Perón, Isabel, 698

Perry, Matthew C., 511, 520

Persia, oil discoveries in (20th C.), 600; *See also* Iran

Persian Gulf, 600

Persian Gulf War (1991), 691, **692-93**

Pessimism: *fin de siècle*, 454-55; 17th C., **325-27**

Pesticides, 652

Pétain, Henri [ahn-REE pay-TENH], 616

Peter I (the Great), czar of Russia, **348-51**; attack on manners, 349, 351; childhood, 348; church and, 351; Great Northern War with Sweden (1700-1721), 349-50; military under, 350; nobility under, 350; secret police of, 351; *streltsi* revolt (1698) and, 348-49; taxation under, 350-51; trip to West, 348; Turks and, 348

Peter III (Pëtr Feodorovich), czar of Russia, 354, 368

Peterloo massacre (1819), 497

Petite bourgeoisie, inflation in interwar period and, 590

Petition of Right (1628), 317

Petrovic, Karadjordji [pet-RO-vik kar-a-JAW-gee], 413-14

Phalanges, Fourier's concept of, **441**

Phanariot Greeks, 414

Phenomenal realm, Kantian concept of, 373

Philadelphia convention (1787), 488

Philhellenic movement, 414

Philip V (Philip of Anjou), king of Spain, 315, 345

Philippe II, duc d'Orléans, 344

Philippe de Champaigne, 309

Philippine Islands, 684, **687**; Japanese capture of, 621; MacArthur's return to, 626; U.S. annexation of, 493, 521

Philosophers: political, 449-50; Russian, 581

Philosophes [feel-oh-SOHFS], **357-64**, 427; attack on religion, **362**; deist outlook of, **362**; French leadership, **358-59**; on justice and education, **360-62**; Newtonian world-machine concept of, 358, 373; philosophical challenges to, **373-74**; political thinking of, **362-64**; unpredictability of human nature and, 373; *See also* Enlightenment

Philosophical Letter (Chaadaev), 482

Philosophic Radicals, 438, **500-503**

Philosophy, **649-50**; dialectical, 408-9; idealism, 449-50; positivism, **449**; realism, 449-50; Romanticism and, **408-9**

Phobias, 647

Photography, 452; newspaper, 529

Phouma, Souvanna, 638

Physics: in Enlightenment, 358; revolution in, **651-52**

Physiocrats, **359-60**, 373; *See also* Enlightened despotism

Piano, 408

Piazza Obliqua, 332

Picasso, Pablo, 643, **654-55**

Picquart, Col. Georges [zhorzh pee-KAR], 462

Piedmont, 419; in Crimean War, 464; liberal constitution (1848), 435; Napoleon III and, 464-65; nationalist movement in, 420; war with Austria (1859), 459, 464, 473; *See also entries under Italy*

Piedmont-Sardinia, kingdom of, 411

Piedmont-Savoy (Sardinia), 346

Pietists and Pietism, **373-74**, 408

Pilsudski, Marshal Józef, 553-54, 576, 608

Pitt, William, 355, 370; accession to prime minister, 355

Pitt, William (the Younger), 373

Pius VII, Pope, 393

Pius IX, Pope, 419-20, 445-46

Pius XI, Pope, 466, 562

Pius XII, Pope, 669

Plague(s), 363; of 1600s, 332

Plain (Marsh), the, 385-86

Planck, Max, 651

Planck's constant, 651

Plane hijacking, 690, 700

Plastics, 652

Play, problem, 452

Plekhanov [plyeh-KAH-noff], George, 484

PLO, 691, 693

Poetry: Enlightenment and, 405-6; romantic, **405-6**; twentieth century, 653

Poincaré [pwahn-kah-RAY], Raymond, 589-90

Poison gas, 539

Poland (16th - 18th C.): Alexander I of Russia and, 368; Diet, 351-53; first partition of (1772), 351, 369, 371*m*; government, 351-52; Great Northern War (1700-1721), 349-50; Polish question, **352**; Polish Succession, War of the (1733-1735), **352**, 369; Russian expansion and, 352; second partition (1793), 369, 371*m*, 391; third partition (1795), 369-70, 371*m*, 391

Poland (19th C. - World War I): acquisition of Upper Silesia, 564; Alexander I of

Viet Minh, 638
Vietnam, **637-41**
Vietnamese, French conflict with (1883), 519
Vietnam war, 640; de-escalation of American involvement in, 674; Great Society program and, 674; protests against, 674; U.S. economy and, 672
Vigée-Lebrun, Elisabeth, 379
Villeneuve [veel-NURV], Adm. Pierre de, 395
Vimy Ridge, battle of (1917), 539
Virginia, University of, 408
Virgin Islands, 523
V-J Day, 627
Vladimirov, I.A., 485
Vladivostok [vlad-ih-vah-STOK], 482, 553
Volgograd (formerly Stalingrad), 622
Volksgeist, 406
Volkswagen, 662, 684
Voltaire, 357, 358, 359, **362**, 364; Catherine the Great and, 367; on Peter the Great, 349

Wages, 437; Iron Law of, 438, 442
Wagner, Richard [RIK-art VAHG-nur], **454**, 565
Wagram [VAH-grom], battle of (1809), 398
Wake Island, 621
Wales, economic depression in, 587
Walesa, Lech, 680
Walloons [wah-LOONZ], 416, 669
Walpole, Robert, 341, 343, 353
Waltham Black Act (1723), 341
War and Peace (Tolstoy), 483
War(s) and warfare: guerrilla, 699-700; undeclared, 630; *See also specific wars*
War communism, **552-53**, 577
War debts to United States, 588, 591-92
War of the League of Augsburg (1688-1697), 314, 315
War of the Spanish Succession (1701-1714), 315
Warsaw, duchy of, 398
Warsaw Pact (1955), 630, 633, 635-36, 680
Warsaw uprising (1944), 625
Washington, George, 341, 353
Washington naval conference (1921-1922), 607
"Waste Land, The" (Eliot), 653
Watergate scandal, 674-75
Waterloo, battle of (1815), 399
Watt, James, 342
Wealth, Physiocratic concept of natural, 361
Webb, Beatrice, 504
Webb, Sidney, 504
Weber [VAY-bur], Carl Maria von, 408
Weber, Max, 472, 648
Weights and measures, 18th C. business and nonstandardized, 340
Weimar Republic, **562-68**; constitution of, 563; Dawes Plan and, 566; economic recovery of (1923-1929), **566**; Enabling Act (1933) suspending constitution of, 568; formation of, 562; "fulfillment" policy toward Allies, 563-64; inflation in, 564; left- and right-wing threats to, 563-64; political organization of, 563; *putsch* of March 1920, **563**; "rationalization" of industry in, 566; reappearance of parties of imperial Germany, 563; vertical trusts and

cartels in, 566; world depression and (1929-1933), **566-68**; years of instability (1918-1923), **563-65**; Young Plan for reparations and, 566, 567
Welfare programs, **701**; English, 503; New Deal and, 595; New Poor Law (1834), 501; utilitarianism and, 438-39
Wellesley, Sir Arthur (duke of Wellington), 399
Wells, H.G., 504
Wentworth, Thomas, 318
Wesley, Charles, 507
Wesley, John, 374, 507
West Africa, 684, 694
West Germany, **666-68**; Allied assistance to, 666; constitution, 666; Czechoslovakia treaty, 667; economic recovery, 658-59, 662, 666; under Kohl, 668; rearmament and entry into NATO, 666; reunification with East Germany, 668, **681-82**; Soviet Union treaty, 667; terrorism in, 667
West Indies, 431, 517
West Pakistan, 687-88
Westphalia, kingdom of, 396
Westphalia, Peace of (1648), 306, 346
Whigs, English, 324; control of House of Commons, 343; parliamentary reforms and, 497-98; social composition of, 343; *See also* Parliament, English
Whistler, James McNeill, 453
White Revolution (Iran), 676
Whites (anti-Bolshevik groups): defeat of, 553-54; resistance to November Revolution, 551
Whitman, Walt, 452
Whitney, Eli, 427, 430
Wilkes, John, 370
Will: general, **363**; Victorian preoccupation with, 450
William I, king of Holland, 416
William I, king of Prussia, 464, 467; proclamation as emperor, 469; secret treaty with Italy, 468; Spanish royal succession (1868) and, 469
William II, king of Germany, **470-71**, 530; abdication, 539; ceremonial visit to Tangier, 531; dismissal of Bismarck, 531; naval and colonial policies, 471
William III (William of Orange), king of England: ascension to throne, 324; Louis XIV's attack of Holland and, 314; as Protestant champion, 315; War of the League of Augsburg and, 314-15
William IV, king of England, 497
William the Silent, 314
Will to Believe (James), 450
Will to Power (Nietzsche), 450
Wilson, Harold, 662-63
Wilson, Woodrow, 491-92, 507, 586; campaign platform (1916), 534; Fourteen Points, 539, **542**; German submarine warfare and, 534; U.S. refusal to ratify Versailles Treaty and, 546; at Versailles, 543-44
"Winter war" (1939), 615
Witches, search for (16th C.), 332-33
Witte, Count Sergei [syir-GYAY-ee VIT-uh], 484, 485, 486
Wojtyla, Karol. *See* John Paul II, Pope
Wolfe, James, 355
Wollstonecraft, Mary, 376
"Woman Question," 496

Women: during American Civil War, 491; in Bismarck's Germany, 471; emancipation of, 700-701; English Revolution and, 322-24; factory work during World War I, 541; as heads of state, 670; in industrial revolution, 435; inheritance of land in 17th C. and, 333; in Kemal's Turkey, 602; property ownership in England, 500; religious rights of Quaker, 322-24; Scandinavian reforms favoring, 671; suffrage for American, 592, 593; unemployment after World War I, 541; voting rights in England, 500; in working class Third French Republic, 463; as writers during enlightenment, 376
Women Regents of the Haarlem Hospital, The (Hals), 330
Women's Christian Temperance Union, 491
Women's history, 701
Women's movement: in the French revolution, 384; in pre-World War I Britain, 496
Women's suffrage societies, 496
Word processor, 644
Wordsworth, William, **405-6**
Workers: grievances and aspirations during Industrial Revolution, **435-37**; urban population growth and influence of, 432; *See also* Labor; Unions, labor
Workers' and Peasants' Inspectorate, 578
Work ethic, Protestant, 427
Working class: Austrian, 477; Bismarck's policies on, **470**; British Labour party and, 504; factory, 427; of Hungary, 479; inflation in Weimar Republic and, 564; July Monarchy and, 418; laissez-faire doctrine and, 438; revolutions of 1848 and, 423; in Second Empire, 458; in West Germany, 666; women in, 463
Workshops, national (France), 419
World Bank, 631, 671-72
World Court, German-Austrian tariff plan and, 567
World Disarmament Conference (1932), 607
World Health Organization (WHO), 631
World-machine, Newtonian, 358, 373, 409, 651
World War I, **528-46**; air warfare in, 538-39; Allied victory, **538-39**; Anglo-German commercial rivalry and, 530; armistice, 539; assassination of archduke Ferdinand and Sophie Chotek, 528; Austrian annexation of Bosnia-Herzegovina and, 531; Austrian declaration of war on Serbia, 528; Balkan campaign, **537**; Balkan Wars (1912-1913) and, 532; causes of, **528-35**; colonies and, **537-38**; course of, **535-39**; Dardanelles campaign, **537**; debate over responsibility for, 528; demographic changes resulting from, 541; eastern front, **535-36**; English entry into, 533; entry of other powers into, **533-34**; French entry into, 533; German declaration of war against Russia, 533; Greece in, 537; home fronts, **540-41**; Italian front, **536-37**; Japan's entry into, 533; military campaigns (1914-1918), **535-38**; Mussolini's positions on, 558; nationalism and, **534-35**; national